The Law of Finance

Edition

The Law of Finance

Second Edition

By

Alastair Hudson LL.B, LL.M, Ph.D (Lond), FRSA, FHEA
Professor of Equity and Finance Law, University of Southampton
Barrister, Lincoln's Inn
National Teaching Fellow

SWEET & MAXWELL

THOMSON REUTERS

First Edition   2009
Second Edition 2013

Published in 2013 by Sweet & Maxwell, 100 Avenue Road, London NW3 3PF part of
Thomson Reuters (Professional) UK Limited (Registered in England & Wales, Company No
1679046.
Registered Office and address for service: Aldgate House, 33 Aldgate High Street, London
EC3N 1DL)

For further information on our products and services, visit *www.sweetandmaxwell.co.uk*

Typeset by Letterpart Limited, Caterham on the Hill, Surrey CR3 5XL

Printed and bound by CPI Group (UK) Ltd, Croydon, CR0 4YY.

No natural forests were destroyed to make this product; only farmed timber was used and
re-planted.

A CIP catalogue record of this book is available for the British Library.

Disclaimer: This book is not intended to and does not give any advice in relation to any
transaction whatsoever in any circumstances whatsoever.

ISBN: 978-0-414-02764-0

© 2013 Alastair Hudson

Preface

Creating the law of finance

The aim of this book is to create a comprehensive account of the law of finance which marries an analysis of the principles of the substantive law of England and Wales with the principles of financial regulation in the UK (further to the Financial Services and Markets Act 2000 and EU law). This book provides a comprehensive analysis of the law of finance which can be taught and understood as a discrete legal field, as opposed simply to presenting a description of documentation practices or an economist's account of regulatory principles. The book is divided in half between the "General Principles" of the law of finance and the "Specific Financial Techniques" which apply those general principles to particular kinds of market activity. The effect is a combined analysis of fundamental legal concepts, financial regulation and financial market practice. Since the first edition of this book was published there has been a stream of revelations about the practices of financial institutions, ranging from criminal activity (such as money laundering, sanctions-busting, and the fraudulent fixing of market rates) through to rank incompetence (such as misreporting millions of transactions to the regulatory authorities and mis-selling financial products to ordinary customers).

The reputation of the banking community could not possibly be lower among their customer bases nor among policymakers than it is now. And yet the responses to the financial crisis of 2007–09 and to the more recent revelations of malpractice have generally been mild. Nevertheless, the UK regulatory structure has been superficially reorganised with talk of a change in attitude, a large swathe of litigation against banks for fraud, negligence and breach of fiduciary duties in various contexts is underway, and financial markets have tried to get themselves back to the position they were in before the crisis began. The European Union has seen both a permanent crisis in the eurozone and the beginnings of a change in its regulatory culture for finance, which will come to affect the UK ever more in time. Consequently, the development of a distinct law of finance, which was the focus of the first edition of this book, has come on apace in the last four years and will clearly continue to do so. The United Kingdom needs a coherent law of finance which combines both substantive law and financial regulation so as to protect its people and its businesses from the worst excesses of the finance industry, as has become evident over the last two or three years even to those who would not previously have believed it. There is much in the old case law which is instructive for our modern law; and much that needs to be done to embed a jurisprudence into the constantly changing detail of financial regulation.

This book is the product of my work in the law of finance in a variety of contexts: in particular three books for finance law practitioners and scholars on *The Law of Financial Derivatives, The Law on Investment Entities*, and *Securities Law*; treatises on general areas of English law including *The Law of Trusts* and *Equity & Trusts*; a variety of essays and conference papers, culminating in publications such as *Credit Derivatives, Modern Financial Techniques, Derivatives and Law*, and *New Perspectives on Property Law, Obligations and Restitution*; and contributions over many years to *Palmer's Company Law*.

The image on the cover of this book is a painting by Jean-Léon Gérôme called *L'Éminence Grise* (1873), which depicts the power behind the French throne, François Leclerc du Tremblay. It seemed appropriate because it illustrates a concept called "soft power". The unarmed, oblivious grey friar is carrying a mere book and yet everyone on the staircase bows to him anyway. He clearly has enormous power which causes these courtiers, soldiers, aristocrats and other clergymen to bow instinctively. Financiers have similar power in the world today because they hold the access to the all-important money which, in the modern world, is needed by businesses, citizens and even governments just to function normally. It is the power of these financiers, and the way in which law and regulation deals with them, which is examined in this book.

Conceptualising the law of finance

One of the great concerns among people—practitioners, publishers, scholars—to whom I have spoken over the years about writing books in the finance law field has been the perceived difficulty of describing a "moving target", in that financial innovation and financial markets are constantly in flux and consequently that these markets are thought by some to be impossible to describe. I have never agreed. It is of course true that the products used in financial practice have changed rapidly in recent years—particularly with the development of financial derivatives and securitisation—and that financial theory has consequently undergone many changes too. However, the fundamental principles of the substantive law have not changed. When a lawyer is analysing a financial transaction, her tools have remained much the same: contract, tort, property, criminal law and so forth have remained within predictable boundaries, even if the practice of financial markets has not. Indeed the financial crisis of 2007–09 can be understood in part as a failure to understand the underpinnings of financial products as being built on simple foundations which do not change. Assuming that finance is too complex to describe means that we are more likely to overlook simple errors: such as lending money to people who cannot pay it back. That crisis is discussed in Chapter 45.

Most of the developments in finance law in recent years have been caused by legislative change—particularly in relation to EC financial services legislation, the Banking Act 2009, and the reform of the Financial Services and Markets Act 2000 and its subordinate legislation—as well as by the concomitant development of financial regulation at the national and at the international levels. Consequently, the principal intellectual goal of this book is to present an understanding of how the context of financial regulation and substantive legal concepts combine to constitute a comprehensive "law of finance".

Importantly, this book is also a result of my own experience working in financial institutions both as banker and legal counsel something which is lacking from many other commentators in this field. The financial crisis of 2007–09 was inevitable to anyone who had actually worked in banks if they had stood back and considered how many compliance blind-spots there were and how deeply embedded was the ideology that financial markets would never fail. Too many commentators in this area predicate their work on a superficial understanding of modern economics, all of which is in turn based on a discredited free market ideology. The law of finance is a legal field in itself, and not just a technical subset of economics or finance theory. Therefore, this book makes no apology for analysing the law which is important to financial market practice, as well as financial regulation and standard market contracts. A synthesis of all three is necessary for a proper understanding of the practice of finance law.

Companion website: podcasts, supplementary text, teaching materials, updates and case notes

This book functions in a very different way from any other book in publication at this time (except for my own *Equity & Trusts*). The book is supported by a free-to-view website—*http://www.alastairhudson.com*—which supports all of my books with podcasts, updates on cases and legislative developments, interactive online links, detailed research essays and also essays on introductory material.

In relation to this book specifically, it contains *podcasts* and *vidcasts* covering the core elements of a finance law course and discussing keys issues in finance law, and recordings of my lectures on the law of finance at various institutions. On that website are a series of "Author's Cuts" of my books which extend beyond the material which it was possible to include in this book. The law of finance is a potentially enormous subject and therefore this book cannot contain every item of detail relating to it. So, my website will supplement this core text with a large amount of further material and text. In the "finance law" area of my website are *course documents* and supporting podcasts for law of finance courses as I would suggest teaching them both to undergraduates and to postgraduates: that material is intended to encourage the teaching, discussion and dissemination of this subject to a broader audience than has been possible up to now. The podcasts comprise a series of brief explanations of finance law terminology and short, *summary lectures* covering the whole of a university finance law course. The underlying aims of this book are to facilitate the teaching of the law of finance at university and to help to educate any other professional who wants an explanation or a refresher in the law of finance. The finance area of my website also includes *links* to other useful websites, and links directly to regulatory material. The website will grow over time and will cater for new developments and for material which it was not possible to consider in this book in detail. Consequently, this book is more than just a book.

The structure and methodology of this book

I have written this book both as a book which can be read from beginning to end as a single, coherent text, and also as a reference work which can be dipped in and out of as the reader requires. If you are studying the law of finance, I suggest you approach reading it in the following way. Each chapter begins with a summary of the core principles which are contained in that chapter, and then the chapter demonstrates how those principles arise in detail in the law of finance; use those core principles as a map through the detail, together with the online podcasts. The text combines clear definitions of the legal concepts and of the financial products with easy-to-understand examples of those legal principles being put to work.

I have divided this book in half: *Section One: General Principles* sets out the principles on which financial regulation and finance law operates in the UK, and *Section Two: Specific Financial Techniques* puts those general principles to work in relation to particular financial markets. So, instead of repeating the same basic information in relation to different products, such as the structure of master agreements or the most effective means of taking security in financial transactions, *Section One* centralises the discussions of the core legal and regulatory concepts before *Section Two* puts them to work in context. For most students, and nearly all practitioners, the core legal principles will be familiar (issues of contract, tort, property and criminal law), but their application to finance and the principles of financial regulation may not be. Nevertheless, familiarity with those core legal concepts should make the study of finance law less forbidding than otherwise it might be. My aim is to consider finance law from a lawyer's perspective, using language and concepts which are familiar to lawyers, and not to begin with the mysteries and idiosyncrasies of finance theory.

Beginning with a statement of principle, laying out the core concepts and then demonstrating how those concepts apply in context, is a teaching technique which I have always employed and which I dub "cognitive reinforcement". By starting with familiar legal concepts and fusing them together with financial regulatory concepts, the reader can understand the basis of finance law more easily. Undoubtedly the integrity of our economies and of our financial systems will benefit from a clearer understanding among lawyers, students and teachers of how the law of finance functions. So each chapter begins with a simple statement of the concepts and then moves into the detail: *Section One* of this book sets out the core material before *Section Two* applies those concepts to the detail of particular financial techniques and products. To help the student reader (and possibly the practitioner too), I have included a number of podcasts explaining the key principles from each chapter on my website.

Due to the extent of the regulatory changes in 2012 and 2013, it has been necessary to put some material online instead of including it in the hard-copy version of the book. Think of them as being like the "extras" on a DVD.

The extensive reforms to financial regulation in the EU and in the UK since the last edition, and the financial crisis itself, have caused this book to grow. In consequence, many points of detail have been removed from this edition and chapters on communal investment, collective investment schemes, foreign exchange, stock-lending, repos and so forth have been removed. A considerably lengthier, practitioner-orientated treatise, *The Law and Regulation of Finance* (Sweet & Maxwell, 2013) deals with these markets and with standard market documentation in other markets.

Studying the law of finance

The suggested method for reading this book and for studying this subject is as follows. First, think of the themes set out in Parts I and II of this book as setting the scene and explaining the role which the law and regulation play in financial markets. Second, see the principles of financial regulation discussed in Part III, and the principles of the substantive law and legal practice discussed in Parts IV through VIII, as forming the bedrock of concepts on which the law of finance is built. Third, see the analysis of the various different forms of financial services, the specific legal issues which they raise, the regulation which covers them specifically, and the way in which they are documented as constituting the various contexts in which those bedrock principles are applied. Come to know the law and the detail of the regulation before seeing how it applies to particular markets.

REF statement

This second edition, along with the first edition of this book (Sweet & Maxwell, 2009), were both published in the current REF period. They are both the product of primary research which I set out to conduct into financial markets when I was employed by Citibank and by Goldman Sachs in the 1990s, which became my doctoral research, and also therefore the product of the series of books and articles which I set out to publish in the area of finance law on leaving employment in that sector, beginning with *The Law on Financial Derivatives* in 1996. This entire book is an attempt to explain, organise and rationalise a complete law of finance for the first time in this jurisdiction. It is therefore a scholarly work, with many references to social theory and world literature as well as to standard market documents, court judgments and regulations, which synthesises many different areas of law into a whole. It is a genuinely inter-disciplinary work in that it draws on finance theory (in that I was enrolled on a formal Citibank MBA-style programme, created and taught by business school academics, when employed there) and financial market practice, as well as law and legal theory. It is a genuinely scholarly work in that it discusses considerably more of the general law than other books dealing with disparate aspects of finance law. It is a determined attempt to *construct* something new in the legal canon so that finance law can be demystified for practitioner, academic and student alike.

Glossary

At its end, this book contains a short glossary of useful market expressions and terminology as they are used in this book. The glossary in this book defines and explains the main products and jargon terms which the newcomer will encounter—of course, where those terms arise in the text they are discussed in detail. There is nothing in here which is unknowable or incomprehensible to a lawyer or a law student.

The writing of this book

This book took a number of years to gestate in my mind: the first edition was written in 2008 as the financial crisis was reaching its peak, and this second edition was written primarily in 2012 with extensive additions being made in early 2013. It builds on work from my earlier books—*The Law on Financial Derivatives; Securities Law; Equity & Trusts; Company Law; The Law on Investment Entities; Swaps, Restitution and Trusts*; and numerous essays and articles. The law and regulation analysed in this book is, as it seemed to me from the materials available to me during that period, with the incorporation of the impact of the Financial Services Act 2012 (which received the Royal Assent on December 19, 2012) and of my work for the Parliamentary Commission on Banking Standards and other committees in early 2013.

Every effort has been made at the proof stage to ensure that references to regulations are to the new FInancial Conduct Authority and Prudential Regulation Authority rulebooks, which came into effect on April 1, 2013, where appropriate.

I would like to thank my family and the team at Sweet & Maxwell for their support during the writing of this book (especially Nicola Thurlow, Constance Sutherland, and Mat Beal); and in particular I would like to thank my colleague of many years, Dr Helena Howe, whose comradeship during the writing of this book has been quite literally invaluable.

The role of the law of finance

The law of finance is in its infancy. This book attempts to describe it, to lay bare its core principles and to map it out. As lawyers creating the law of finance we must understand and know the bedrock of the law before we consider how it informs the river of financial activity which washes over it every minute of every day. Our business at the start of the 21st century is to create the law of finance and to understand how it fits together before allowing ourselves to be buffeted by the exigencies and demands of financial practice. The depth of the crisis that engulfed the world's financial system in the autumn of 2008, and the aftermath which the citizens of many countries are still suffering, demonstrate that the law of finance must be a code of legal principle first and a tool for financiers second. The law and financial regulation must control the excesses of financial practice and it must provide safety nets for banks, customers and the broader economy alike. Consequently, when describing the law of finance we must do so using established legal concepts and legal models instead of using financier's fluctuating models to create models into which we attempt to shoe-horn legal concepts. Even though financial market innovation appears to be creating new structures time and time again, in fact much of the innovation is the adaptation of well-known ideas for a new purpose: for example, in legal terms, securitisations are effectively the same as old-fashioned debt factoring, equity options are at root the same legal concepts as old-fashioned options to buy land, and so on. The established legal concepts of contract, property, equity, tort, criminal law and so forth are able to meet the challenge of describing financial markets. Financial innovation is not something impossible for lawyers to understand: any suggestion to the contrary is either hubris or cowardice.

For any lawyer, the law is the bedrock; financial practice washes over it. Of course, each influences and shapes the other. The river's course is shaped by the rock, and in turn the shape of that rock is moulded and smoothed by torrent that flows past it. But the bedrock remains.

Alastair Hudson
LL.B LL.M Ph.D NTFS FRSA FHEA
Professor of Equity & Finance Law
University of Southampton
National Teaching Fellow
Of Lincoln's Inn, Barrister
Valentine's Day, 2013

Acknowledgments

Grateful acknowledgment is made to the following authors and publishers for permission to quote from their work:

Brindle, M. and Cox, R., *Law of Bank Payments,* 3rd edn (London: Sweet & Maxwell, 2004)

Falcon Chambers, *Fisher and Lightwood's Law of Mortgage*, 11th edn (London: Lexis Nexis, 2002)

Hudson, A.S., *Equity & Trusts,* 7th edn (Oxford: Routledge, 2012)

Hudson, A.S., *Securities Law*, 2nd edn (London: Sweet & Maxwell, 2013)

Hudson, A.S., *The Law on Financial Derivatives*, 5th edn (London: Sweet & Maxwell, 2012)

Hudson, A.S., *The Law on Investment Entities*, 6th edn (London: Sweet & Maxwell, 2000)

Hudson, A.S., *Swaps, Restitution and Trusts* (London: Sweet & Maxwell, 1999)

Hudson, A.S. (ed.), *Modern Financial Techniques, Derivatives and Law* (Kluwer, 1999)

Hudson, A.S. (ed.), *Credit Derivatives: law, regulation and accounting issues* (London: Sweet & Maxwell, 1999)

Hudson, A.S., "Capital Issues" in *Palmer's Company Law,* G. Morse (ed.) (London: Sweet & Maxwell, 2007)

Hudson, A.S., "Open-ended Investment Companies" in *Palmer's Company Law,* G. Morse (ed.) (London: Sweet & Maxwell, 2007)

Palley, T., "Financialization: What It Is and Why It Matters" (The Levy Economics Institute, 2007) accessed at: *http://www.levy.org/pubs/wp_525.pdf*

Thomas, G.W. and Hudson, A.S., *The Law of Trusts,* 2nd edn (Oxford University Press, 2010)

Whilst every care has been taken to establish and acknowledge copyright and contact the copyright owners, the publishers tender their apologies for any accidental infringement. They would be pleased to come to a suitable arrangement with the rightful owners in each case.

Abbreviations

Equity & Trusts	Alastair Hudson, *Equity & Trusts*, 7th edn (Oxford: Routledge, 2012)
Securities Law	Alastair Hudson, *Securities Law*, 2nd edn (London: Sweet & Maxwell, 2013)
Financial Derivatives	Alastair Hudson, *The Law on Financial Derivatives*, 5th edn (London: Sweet & Maxwell, 2012)
Investment Entities	Alastair Hudson, *The Law on Investment Entities* (London: Sweet & Maxwell, 2000)
Swaps, Restitution and Trusts	Alastair Hudson, *Swaps, Restitution and Trusts* (London: Sweet & Maxwell, 1999)
Modern Financial Techniques	Alastair Hudson (ed.), *Modern Financial Techniques*, Derivatives and Law (Kluwer, 1999)
Credit Derivatives	Alastair Hudson (ed.), Credit Derivatives: law, regulation and accounting issues (London: Sweet & Maxwell, 1999)
Law of Trusts	Geraint Thomas and Alastair Hudson, *The Law of Trusts*, 2nd edn (OUP, 2010)
Capital Issues	Alastair Hudson, "Capital Issues" in G. Morse (ed), *Palmer's Company Law* (London: Sweet & Maxwell)
Open-ended Investment Companies	Alastair Hudson, "Open-ended Investment Companies" in G. Morse (ed), *Palmer's Company Law* (London: Sweet & Maxwell)
Understanding Company Law	Alastair Hudson, *Understanding Company Law* (Oxford: Routledge, 2012)

Introduction

At The Roots

The purpose of this *Introduction* is to provide a map through the law of finance as it is presented in this book. It is much easier to understand how the law of finance functions if we first have some overarching understanding of how its principles operate and how they knit together. In particular it is important to understand the many different sources of the law of finance so that it is possible to understand how they will interact. The principal sources of the law of finance are financial regulation (drawn ultimately from European Union law), English case law (from common law and equity), and UK statute. The law of finance is a synthesis of these sources, and understanding the practice of the law of finance requires us to consider the standard market contracts used in many financial markets (such as derivatives) and the specific market rules (often produced by trade associations rather than by statute or by the courts) which apply in other markets.

Consequently, the study of the law of finance requires us to understand how different sources are synthesised. It is part of what makes this field fascinating, dynamic and unique. These syntheses of the substantive law, financial regulation (both domestic and international) and market practice are common in many areas of the law of finance. The criminal law interacts with financial regulation in many contexts, for example to prevent market abuse,[1] money laundering[2] and insider dealing,[3] where one involves formal legal prosecution and the other involves merely civil penalties being imposed by a regulator.[4] Similarly, private law may impose liabilities to pay damages,[5] or may recognise rights in property,[6] or may enforce the performance of contractual obligations:[7] all of which are dependent upon formal litigation and the use of centuries-old legal principles. By contrast, statute also provides rights to compensation which operate sometimes in parallel to private law and sometimes in place of private law.[8] There is also the very important international dimension to financial law whereby regulators in other jurisdictions and other systems of law may be important in resolving disputes.[9] For example, EU legislation has been particularly important in the development

---

[1] See para.12–01.
[2] See para.15–01.
[3] See para.14–01.
[4] See para.9–01.
[5] See para.20–01.
[6] See para.21–01.
[7] See para.20–01.
[8] e.g. Financial Services and Markets Act 2000, s.90 and s.90A respectively.
[9] See para.6–01.

of UK finance law, and the Bank for International Settlements policy programmes have set the framework for banking regulation around the world. Beyond the substantive law, there is also the very important role played by financial regulation in the operation of financial markets.[10] From this very brief overview, we can see that there is a complex web of legal, non-legal, and quasi-legal rules at play. The early chapters of this book analyse these various sources of law; this introduction presents them to you briefly so as to give you an understanding of the lie of the land from the outset.

Sources of the Law of Finance

The components of the law of finance

The law of finance is a combination of fundamental legal concepts taken from the general law which when combined with statutory principles and regulatory principles synthesise into a single system of law which is referred to in this book as "the law of finance". The components of the law of finance are discussed in more detail in Chapter 1: what follows here is an introductory outline of them.

The substantive legal concepts considered in this book are drawn principally from the law of contract, the law of torts, the criminal law, the law of property, equity, and private international law. These principles are referred to in this book as "*substantive law*" and are drawn, for the purposes of this book, from the laws of England and Wales, unless otherwise stated.

The statutory principles considered in this book are drawn either from EC directives and other European Union legislation (which has been implemented into the law of finance in the UK by means of principal or subordinate legislation enacted by the UK Parliament), or else by ordinary legislation enacted by the UK Parliament which is not predicated on EU legislation. The principal Act in this context in this jurisdiction is the Financial Services and Markets Act 2000 ("FSMA 2000").

The regulatory principles considered in this book are the principles created by the regulatory authorities, as discussed in Part III of this book. The Financial Services Authority ceased to exist on April Fool's Day 2013, and was renamed the Financial Conduct Authority ("FCA").[11] The bulk of the former authority's responsibilities passed to the FCA; except for prudential regulatory matters which passed to the new Prudential Regulatory Authority ("PRA"): the second of these entities is a subsidiary of the Bank of England.[12] These regulatory authorities draw their powers from FSMA 2000, which in turn implements in this context a number of principles contained in EC directives.

We shall refer to "the UK" as the relevant jurisdiction for statutory and for regulatory purposes because, further to European Union ("EU") law, it is the United Kingdom ("the UK") which is a Member State of the EU, and in turn the UK which is required to implement the principles of EU law relating to financial

---

[10] See para.3–01.

[11] Financial Services Act 2012, s.6.

[12] Some other matters are the responsibility of the Office for Fair Trading ("OFT"). This regulatory architecture is set out in Ch.8.

services generally, and to securities and other markets in particular. Therefore, the principles which are implemented by the UK further to EU law apply to the whole of the UK as a single jurisdiction for the purposes of finance law. This is true of company law under the Companies Act 2006, and is also true of tax law. However, for the purposes of substantive law, the relevant jurisdiction remains for most other purposes "England and Wales" and it is to the decisions of the courts of England and Wales that we shall have reference primarily in this book, except where international comparisons are fruitful.

Concepts and contexts

The aim of this book is to create a comprehensive account of the law of finance which marries a discussion of the most significant, substantive law principles in England and Wales with the regulation of financial services activity in the UK by the Treasury and by the Bank of England. There are books which seek to explain a narrow range of legal issues which are thought to face finance lawyers in practice, there is a series of books which seeks to describe the principal documentation and regulatory issues facing finance practitioners, and there are a lot of "handbooks" and collections of essays which ruminate about the challenges facing practitioners in easy-to-follow bullet-pointed lists. The first type of book, however, does not seek to present an understanding of how all of the fundamental concepts in the existing law should be understood in the context of finance; the second tends to avoid referring to any or to many substantive legal authorities for its propositions, and certainly avoids a close analysis of any of them; and the third contains no discussion of any law at all, as though financial practice was an entirely closed area containing only those few issues which a consensus of practitioners deem worthy of discussion.

One of the great problems with writing a book about the law of finance is always said to be that one is describing a "moving target" because the pace of innovation means that financial markets are constantly in flux and consequently some people think those markets are impossible to describe. I have never agreed with that point of view. It is of course true that the products[13] used in financial practice have changed rapidly in recent years—particularly with the development of financial derivatives and securitisation—and that financial theory has consequently undergone many changes too. However, the fundamental principles of the substantive law have not changed, and the core principles on which most of these financial products are based have not changed from a lawyer's perspective so much as all that. When a lawyer is analysing a financial transaction, her tools have remained much the same: contract, tort, property, criminal law and so forth have remained within predictable boundaries, even if finance theory has not. The principal area of development for the legal practitioner has been in legislative change—particularly in relation to EC financial services directives, and the FSMA 2000 and its subordinate legislation—and in the concomitant development

---

[13] Bankers like to use the term "product" to describe the financial instruments which they create. I would suggest that they like to use this word because it creates a reassuring image of a factory or a foundry creating solid, useful goods in the traditional manner of heavy industry, as opposed to the intangible manipulation of mathematical and accounting concepts.

of financial regulation at the national and at the international levels. Consequently, the principal intellectual goal of this book is to present an understanding of how the context of financial regulation and substantive legal concepts combine to constitute a comprehensive "law of finance".

There are concepts at play in finance law which are not simply legal concepts. There are also concepts of financial theory—such as the repackaging of payment obligations by means of interest rate swaps, to take an example from derivatives theory—which alter the understanding of financial markets and the value of financial products. There are concepts of risk and of credit measurement which are very important in the transaction of financial products. Both of these concepts are fundamental to financial practitioners but they may be of only peripheral relevance to a legal analysis of a financial product: after all, a binding contractual obligation to deliver gold is a contractual obligation to deliver gold no matter how it is dressed up in financial pricing models and so forth; unless there is something about the transaction—such as undue influence by one party over the other bound up with the complexity of that financial model or a misrepresentation by one party to the other as to the effect of that financial model—in which case the legal analysis of the transaction may change. Therefore, there is a territory in which non-legal and legal concepts and contexts may overlap in the law of finance.

The Structure of This Book

This book divides between two sections of about 700 pages each. The first half, *Section One: General Principles*, synthesizes principles of financial regulation with principles of substantive law so as to generate the fundamental principles of the law of finance. The second half, *Section Two: Specific Financial Products*, analyses the principal forms of product in finance practice and shows how the fundamental principles of the law of finance will apply to them, which issues arise in particular in documenting or structuring particular products, and so forth. This book presents a close, scholarly analysis of the substantive law as well as descriptions of the financial products at issue: in that sense it goes beyond the typical thematic descriptions of financial markets which make up so much of the literature at present.

Section One: General Principles considers the context in which the law of finance operates under the Financial Services and Markets Act 2000. In particular it covers the powers and responsibilities of the FCA and the PRA under that Act and the key principles of UK financial regulation—covering authorisation to deal in financial services, conduct of business, financial promotion, and market abuse. *Section One* also considers the fundamental concepts of substantive English law which are significant in the law of finance: principally contract law, tort law, property law, criminal law and equity. Within the scope of contract law are issues as to the formation of contracts, the validity of contracts, the key terms in complex financial contracts inter alia permitting termination of such a contract (whether a loan agreement or a master agreement or otherwise). Within tort law are issues relating to negligence, breach of statutory duty and fraud in the creation of contracts and the conduct of financial transactions. Within equity are a range of issues relating to the liabilities of fiduciaries beyond ordinary contractual liability, and the operation of trusts, charges and some liens. Within criminal law are insider dealing, market manipulation, fraud and specific offences under the FSMA 2000. Within property law is a discussion of the various legal means of taking security in financial transactions and actions to recover property. This *Section One* therefore covers both the underpinning principles of the general law and also considers how those principles apply specifically to the law of finance. *Section One* is therefore both a reference work on aspects of the general law which are vital to the law of finance, and also a scholarly treatise on the manner in which the law of finance develops a distinct legal field in that context out of the concepts of the general law, by reference to key themes such as financial, legal and social risk, and the nature of regulation itself. *Section One* also includes a number of predictions as to the future development of the substantive law in reaction to the global financial crisis of 2007–09 in relation to banks' fiduciary liability, liability for fraud and liability for negligent misstatement.

Section Two: Specific Financial Products considers all of the various financial products set out in the second half of this book. The purpose of those discussions is to demonstrate how the central financial regulatory and general, substantive law principles apply to particular types of financial product. The lay-out of these different products and the reason why they are grouped together in the way they are is set out in Chapter 1.[14] The first tranche of financial activity is traditional banking, beginning with the nature of its regulation in the UK, the banker-customer relationship, the law governing bank payments, and an account of the global banking crisis of 2007–09 and its effect on bank regulation. Thereafter, *Section Two* moves through lending (ordinary lending, syndicated lending, bonds and foreign exchange), securities law (prospectuses, transparency obligations, listing securities, and general law liabilities for securities issues), financial derivatives (documentation, collateralisation, termination of agreements, and securitisation), proprietary finance (mortgages, stock lending, and repos), collective investment entities (unit trusts, oeics, friendly societies, co-operatives and credit unions), pension funds, and insurance business. In each chapter there is a discussion of the nature of the products, the key legal issues in contracting for those products, any regulation relating specifically to those products, and of the ways in which security may be taken in each context.

Each chapter begins with a summary of the principles which are discussed in that chapter which is intended to enable a student reader to read each chapter with greater confidence and to enable the general reader to focus rapidly on the issue which she wants to consider.

The Methodology of Financial Regulation in a Nutshell

The regulation of financial markets is in fact concerned primarily with the regulation of information. Financial markets are "markets" in that the participants in those markets are required to make their own choices about their investments; no regulator promises to protect them from their own stupidity nor from their own bad luck. Clearly in all financial markets there are some participants who

---

[14] para.1–30.

have more expertise, better information and a stronger bargaining position than others. So, in effect, financial regulation seeks to produce a level playing-field in financial markets by equalising the amount of access which each type of participant has to certain types of information. For example, conduct of business regulation (discussed in Chapter 10) requires that when an expert deals with an inexpert customer that the expert must deal with that inexpert investor appropriately by providing her with suitable information, by making the terms of their contract entirely clear, by acting in that customer's "best interests", and by explaining all of the risks which a person of her level of expertise would need to understand. Financial regulation does not promise that the inexpert investor will be protected from loss. All that is promised is that the inexpert investor will be given the information necessary to make her own informed choices by ensuring that she has access to appropriate forms of information and by ensuring that she is not nakedly taken advantage of by an expert financial services provider. So, prospectus regulation specifies the level and type of information which must be made public by a person issuing securities; conduct of business regulation specifies how sellers must treat different categories of customer (ranging from the expert to the inexpert); transparency regulation specifies the types of information which issuers of securities must make available to the market; financial promotion regulation prevents inappropriate marketing information being circulated in unsuitable ways; and market abuse regulation prevents "inside information" from being used to make unfair gains for some at the expense of others. We must remember though that financial markets are markets in the truest sense of the word because there will be some people who gain and some who lose in a place where everyone is trying to sell their wares and to make a profit. All that finance law will do is to specify a minimum level of fair dealing that is required of all regulated market participants.

The Role of the Lawyer

RISK MANAGER

A lawyer plays a number of different roles in the financial arena. Much of the financial practice which involves a lawyer's intervention either involves the documentation of frequently-used products or, more significantly, it may involve the transacting of a financial product with novel features. In the latter context, the lawyer's role is to give counsel in a situation in which it may not be possible to give definitive advice. All the lawyer can do in such circumstances is to give an educated "best guess" as to the validity of a transaction and its legal ramifications. In some circumstances it will of course be possible to give definitive advice. However, in new markets or in relation to new products it will be difficult to be definitive. This risk was demonstrated in the local authority swaps cases (such as *Westdeutsche Landesbank v Islington* [15] and *Kleinwort Benson v Lincoln CC*[16]) in which all the financial community had to work on was a consensus among the City of London law firms that local authorities had the

---

[15] [1996] A.C. 669.
[16] [1998] 4 All E.R. 513.

legal capacity necessary to create valid interest rate swaps: in the event it transpired that local authorities did not have the necessary capacity after a decision of the House of Lords.[17] The two hundred writs which followed that decision should be a valuable lesson to us all that lawyers are taking risks when they advise their clients that the law in relation to a novel circumstance or to a novel financial product is *x*, because the law may actually turn out to be *y*. The lawyer is therefore advising her clients on taking risks, even when giving legal advice.

A good finance lawyer is a risk manager: that is, someone whose role is to identify future risks and then to identify ways of minimising or controlling those risks as well as possible. When a lawyer acts as a risk manager, she identifies risks and structures products so as to minimize those risks while maximizing her client's profitability. The concept of "risk" is considered in greater detail in Chapter 1.[18]

TRANSLATOR

Much of what the lawyer is seeking to do when discussing financial transactions is translating into legal concepts what is done on the trading floor, in high street banks and in corporate finance departments. Finance is conducted in the language of finance theory and is based on the mathematics which banks and actuaries use to predict future market trends, to calculate risk, and to structure their products. For a lawyer, these same concepts are understood as being obligations to make payment, rights to property, conditions precedent to the enforceability of a transaction and so forth. A good transactional lawyer must be able to operate bi-lingually in the language of the markets and in the many, many legal fields which inform the law of finance (the full range of which are set out in *Section One* of this book).

STRUCTURING PRODUCTS

What the lawyer is usually doing is advising on how to *structure* financial products. While many financial transactions involve simple speculative agreements (such as spot trades on the foreign exchange markets) the transactions in which there is the most lawyering done (financial derivatives, securitisations, securities issues, and so on) involve more than simply rendering the parties' intentions into written form. What a lawyer is doing is *structuring* the transaction by deploying appropriate legal concepts and models to facilitate the parties' purposes. A good transactional lawyer is not simply a recorder of other people's intentions but instead participates in the formulation of those intentions with practical devices to achieve commercially useful goals. So, taking a large number of mortgages off a bank's balance sheet and acquiring a large capital sum from them (a commercial objective known as "securitisation") is achieved by lawyers using a hybrid of trusts, holding companies, contracts to pay money, the transfer of title in property, conflict of laws, and so on. Achieving banks' intentions under

---

[17] *Hazell v Hammersmith & Fulham LBC* [1991] A.C. 1.
[18] See para.1–46.

these transactions required lawyers to sculpt existing legal techniques to achieve those particular goals. In complex financial transactions, lawyers are involved in manipulating legal concepts to make these transactions commercially viable, tax efficient and secure. Therefore, in this book we shall frequently consider how law assists market participants to *structure* their goals.

The financial crisis 2007–09

Naturally, extensive reference is made to the North Atlantic financial crisis which began as a "credit crunch" in 2007 as banks stopped lending money to one another in the ordinary way (such that the liquidity in the global financial system began to dry up) and which became a solvency crisis in 2008–09 as financial institutions failed, requiring either their insolvency (as with Lehman Brothers) or their acquisition by other institutions (too numerable to mention here) or their nationalisation by government (as with Northern Rock). The economic ramifications for countries in the North Atlantic (particularly the USA, the UK and Europe) have been profound. Countries like Greece, Ireland, Portugal have been pushed close to insolvency, and even Spain and Italy have been put under enormous pressure. The result has been the replacement of democratic government by technocratic oversight (Italy) or its equivalent as democratic government has had to subject itself to the diktat of supra-national bodies like the EU and the IMF in return for bail-outs (Greece, Ireland, Portugal). Indeed, all democratic government has had to operate at the whim of the bond markets as they persist with deficit financing of their spending plans (USA) and austerity cuts in public spending (UK) on everything except sporting tournaments. The global economy in general terms has suffered a concomitant slowdown just as much of the balance of economic power was beginning to pass to China, India, Brazil, Russia and other countries. The events and the aftermath of that crisis are considered in detail in Chapter 45.

What also emerged in the wake of the crisis—just as Warren Buffett warned us that what would happen when the tide of a financial boom drew out was that we would see who had been swimming naked—was that a number of banks (in particular UK banks) had been involved in criminality and incompetence of previously unimaginable proportions. UK banks had been involved in mis-selling payment protection insurance ("PPI") to ordinary customers in staggering amounts, in fraudulently setting the Libor interest rate for their own advantage, in money laundering to assist drug cartels and in sanctions-busting to help agencies of foreign governments, and so on. Among the rank incompetence was the mispricing of the assets which caused the financial crisis and the misreporting by Barclays of 57.5 million transactions to the Financial Services Authority. Indeed, the sheaves of "Final Notices" which the Financial Services Authority began to issue in 2011 (finding serious breaches of the regulations by banks and others, and imposing enormous fines) indicated that when the regulators began to lift the rocks in the financial system then there were enormous numbers of unpleasant revelations about abusive and illegal practices slithering there in the dark. No longer could it be argued that banks were always acting in the best interests of the financial system in all circumstances. The extent of their wrongdoing and the inability of their own management to contain this wrongdoing was undeniable.

A history of the financial crisis 2007–09 is set out in Chapter 45. So as to avoid cluttering up the analysis of the law of finance with a lengthy, continuous survey of that crisis, all of that discussion has been concentrated in one place. However, necessarily the discussion of the substantive law and of financial regulation in the book before then requires discussion of the crisis: therefore, individual chapters contain case studies from relevant aspects of the crisis and cross-references to the appropriate sections of Chapter 45. In the confusion caused by the crisis there is a need for practitioners and for students of this subject to be able to understand the new legal order without too much journalistic coverage of the crisis itself. Consequently, those two elements have been separated out.

The effect on the law of finance and on financial regulation in particular has not been as profound as one is entitled to expect. Rather, in public policy terms, the principal goal has been to try to return the financial sector to its condition before the boom years began at the turn of the millennium. The changed regulatory attitude and structure in the EU is considered in Chapter 7. Notably, there has been little detailed change in the content of existing regulation, although the regulation of derivatives and hedge funds has been introduced for the first time (albeit in a limited form), and there is now an impetus to create a single regulatory rulebook for the entire EU (albeit that many aspects of financial regulation will remain outside that net).

The changed regulatory structure in the UK is considered in Chapter 8 and the detailed regulatory fundamentals are set out in Chapter 9, with chapters 10 through 12 considering conduct of business, financial promotion and market abuse in detail respectively. In essence, all regulatory responsibility has been subsumed within the Bank of England and the Treasury with, as yet, very little change to the contents of the regulatory rulebooks and a number of the survivors from the financial crisis still in post in spite of earlier regulatory failures. The various regulatory authorities—principally the Financial Conduct Authority ("FCA") and the Prudential Regulatory Authority ("PRA")—will develop their own rulebooks from the old Financial Services Authority Handbook after assuming control of their respective areas from April Fool's Day 2013.

The Financial Services (Banking Reform) Bill was published in early 2013, putting into effect the recommendations of the Vickers Commission on the separation between investment banking and retail banking activities in UK banks. The reform of ordinary banking regulation (as imposed to investment regulation) at the international level through Basel III and at the UK level through the Banking Reform Bill is considered in detail in Chapter 28. Of particular significance in Chapter 28 is the Banking Act 2009 which provided for bank insolvency and for the sale of failed banks: it is this Act which is the principal response to the financial crisis 2007–09 in that it gave legal powers to the regulatory authorities to intervene when banks fail. The problems which had been caused to banking regulation by that financial crisis are considered in Chapter 45.

The Parliamentary Commission on Banking Standards, to some of whose commissioners I gave detailed advice and assistance, was convened in the autumn of 2012 in a blaze of publicity. Its remit was to look into banking standards, albeit that its work focused primarily on the technical question of "ring-fencing" investment banking off from retail banking. During that Commission's activities, a slew of new revelations about fraud, incompetence and downright wickedness emerged from the financial sector. The undoubtedly disappointing and unimaginative report of that Commission had not been published at the time of completing the manuscript for this book.

The Regulations Referred to in this Book

The regulatory landscape is in flux at the time of writing. Therefore, this section explains which regulations are in force at the time of writing, which regulations are the subject of the footnoted references in the text in this book, and the rolling development of the regulatory rulebooks which is expected in the UK from April 2013 onwards.

The financial regulations in the UK were contained in the Financial Services Authority rulebooks—referred to collectively as the "*FSA Handbook*", which contained all of the rules and guidance notes issued by the Financial Services Authority before April 2013. As was outlined above, further to the Financial Services Act 2012, operational responsibility for conduct of business and related matters remained with the "renamed" authority in its new guise as the Financial Conduct Authority ("FCA") and operational responsibility for prudential matters passed to the new Prudential Regulatory Authority ("PRA"). The *FSA Handbook* was divided between a new *FCA Handbook* and a new *PRA Handbook* on April Fool's Day 2013. Those two new regulatory handbooks will come into effect from April Fool's Day 2013 because that is when the FCA and the PRA took control of regulatory matters from the Financial Services Authority. A large number of those regulations implement EU legislation and therefore will not change significantly or at all as a result of the changes. The other regulations are expected to develop over time in the customary way by consultation with the marketplace as the new regulatory bodies settle into their roles. There will be a transfer process as the Financial Services Authority ceases to exist and the FCA and the PRA come into full force and effect.

Therefore, references in this book are to the FCA and PRA rulebooks, and also to the EU legislative sources for those regulations where appropriate. The author's website *http://www.alastairhudson.com*, in the finance law area, will maintain a survey of the regulatory changes as they are introduced prior to a new edition of this book being produced thereafter.

Definitions of financial products

In the *Glossary* to this book I attempt to define the key terms used in financial and legal practice. This short section is important for the whole underpinning of this book. It relates to the descriptions I will give of different forms of financial product in this book. Three significant points arise. First, my goal is to summarise how these products function and not to consider in detail all the possible financial and mathematical models which are used to price or to structure them. Second, different financial institutions in different markets at different times for different clients or contexts use different versions of similar products. There is not always one single form of a product: instead innovation, like a jazz musician improvising on a musical phrase, is the heart and soul of finance. Therefore, I shall try to give references for the particular model which I am using, but it is perfectly possible that that model is not the one used in all circumstances in all markets. My goal in describing these products is to facilitate a legal analysis of them. In any given situation, the good lawyer will need to be able to think in a lawyer's frame of reference and so to anticipate the legal issues which are known to arise in that context and which may arise in the future in that context. Where appropriate, I will consider standard form contracts as an aid to analysing those products. The aim of this book, however, is not simply to give comprehensive accounts of standard market contracts or regulations.[19] Third, it is important that as lawyers we develop a lawyer's understanding of how these products function and do not seek simply to lash ourselves to one financial model or another. It is important that we understand what contractual obligations, what proprietary rights, what fiduciary obligations and so on, are created by these products, as opposed to focusing solely on financial models.

---

[19] I have attempted this exercise in relation to derivatives in my book *The Law on Financial Derivatives* and in relation to securities in my book *Securities Law*, but this book could not contain such an undertaking across the whole of finance and is not intended to do so.

Overview of Contents

Section 1: Principles of the Law of Finance

Part I: An Ordering of the Law of Finance

1. The Components of the Law of Finance
2. The Legal Nature of Money and Financial Instruments
3. The Relationship Between Substantive Law and Financial Regulation

Part II: Substantive Legal Concepts in the Law of Finance

4. Fundamental Legal Concepts: Contract, Property and Wrongs
5. Fiduciary Duties
6. Conflict of Laws

Part III: Financial Services Regulation

7. EU Financial Regulation
8. The UK Regulatory Structure
9. Fundamental Principles of UK Financial Regulation
10. Conduct of Business
11. Financial Promotion
12. Market Abuse

Part IV: Criminal Law

13. Criminal Offences in the Law of Finance
14. Insider Dealing
15. Money Laundering
16. Fraud in the Criminal Law

Part V: Contract

17. Formation of Contract
18. Validity and Performance of Contracts
19. Master Agreements and Common Contractual Terms and Conditions
20. Termination of Contracts

Part XII: Crisis, Regulation and Finance Law

TABLE OF CONTENTS

                                                                    PARA

SECTION 1
PRINCIPLES OF THE LAW OF FINANCE

PART I
An Ordering of the Law of Finance

1. THE COMPONENTS OF THE LAW OF FINANCE

CORE PRINCIPLES

2. THE LEGAL NATURE OF MONEY AND FINANCIAL INSTRUMENTS

CORE PRINCIPLES

3. THE RELATIONSHIP BETWEEN SUBSTANTIVE LAW AND FINANCIAL REGULATION

CORE PRINCIPLES

PART II
Substantive Legal Concepts in the Law of Finance

4. FUNDAMENTAL LEGAL CONCEPTS: CONTRACT, PROPERTY AND WRONGS

6.   CONFLICT OF LAWS

CORE PRINCIPLES

PART III
Financial Services Regulation

7. EU FINANCIAL REGULATION

CORE PRINCIPLES
The system for developing legislation
Core regulatory principles
Securities regulation
Banking regulation

8. THE UK REGULATORY STRUCTURE

CORE PRINCIPLES
   The Bank of England
   The Financial Conduct Authority
   The interaction of the regulatory bodies

9. FUNDAMENTAL PRINCIPLES OF UK FINANCIAL REGULATION

CORE PRINCIPLES

10. CONDUCT OF BUSINESS

11. FINANCIAL PROMOTION

12. MARKET ABUSE

PART IV
Criminal Law

13. CRIMINAL OFFENCES IN THE LAW OF FINANCE

CORE PRINCIPLES

14. INSIDER DEALING

15. MONEY LAUNDERING

CORE PRINCIPLES

16. FRAUD IN THE CRIMINAL LAW

CORE PRINCIPLES

PART V
Contract

17. FORMATION OF CONTRACTS

18. VALIDITY AND PERFORMANCE OF CONTRACTS

CORE PRINCIPLES

19. MASTER AGREEMENTS AND COMMON CONTRACTUAL TERMS AND CONDITIONS

PART VI
Property

21. TRUSTS

CORE PRINCIPLES

22. TAKING SECURITY AND INSOLVENCY

CORE PRINCIPLES
   Taking security
   Insolvency

23. TRACING AND PROPRIETARY CLAIMS

CORE PRINCIPLES

PART VII
Wrongs

24. FRAUD AND UNDUE INFLUENCE

Core principles

25. NEGLIGENCE AND OTHER LIABILITY IN TORT

26. BREACH OF TRUST

CORE PRINCIPLES

SECTION 2
SPECIFIC FINANCIAL TECHNIQUES

PART VIII
Banking

27. FUNDAMENTALS OF BANKING LAW

CORE PRINCIPLES

28. BANKING REGULATION

29. THE BANKER AND CUSTOMER RELATIONSHIP

CORE PRINCIPLES

30. PAYMENT METHODS

31. RETAIL BANKING AND CONDUCT OF BUSINESS REGULATION

CORE PRINCIPLES

PART IX
Lending

32. ORDINARY LENDING

CORE PRINCIPLES

33. SYNDICATED LENDING

CORE PRINCIPLES

34. BONDS

CORE PRINCIPLES

PART X
Stakeholding

35. THE FUNDAMENTALS OF UK SECURITIES LAW

CORE PRINCIPLES
Sources of UK securities law
The policies underpinning the EC directives
Prospectus regulation
Transparency obligations
Listed securities
Private companies may not offer securities to the public

36. PROSPECTUSES AND TRANSPARENCY OBLIGATIONS

39. LIABILITY FOR SECURITIES ISSUES

CORE PRINCIPLES

PART XI
Financial Derivatives & Refinancing

40. FINANCIAL DERIVATIVES PRODUCTS AND REGULATION

CORE PRINCIPLES
    Derivatives Products
    Regulation of derivatives

42. COLLATERALISATION

43. TERMINATION OF FINANCIAL DERIVATIVES

CORE PRINCIPLES

44. SECURITISATION

CORE PRINCIPLES

PART XII
Crisis, Regulation and Finance Law

45. THE FINANCIAL CRISIS AND ITS AFTERMATH

CORE PRINCIPLES

46. REFORM PROPOSALS

Core principles

TABLE OF CASES

TABLE OF FINANCIAL CONDUCT AUTHORITY RULES

TABLE OF STATUTES

TABLE OF STATUTORY INSTRUMENTS

SECTION 1

PRINCIPLES OF THE LAW OF FINANCE

PART I

AN ORDERING OF THE LAW OF FINANCE

CHAPTER 1

THE COMPONENTS OF THE LAW OF FINANCE

CORE PRINCIPLES

The law of finance in England and Wales derives from a number of sources: EU directives, Acts of the UK Parliament, and the general, substantive law of England and Wales as applied to the law of finance. In this book, "finance" is to be understood as being "the wherewithal to act". It is significant that the subject matter of financial transactions is intangible (i.e. it cannot be touched or held) and therefore this poses a number of challenges to traditional legal concepts. Furthermore, the financial system depends on the confidence of its largest participants to continue in existence precisely because its subject matter has no tangible existence. This facet of the financial system was illustrated most starkly by the global financial crisis of 2007–09, as discussed in Chapter 45.

[5]

There are seven different aspects to finance as it should be understood from a lawyer's perspective. That is, in spite of the way in which financiers might have understood their activities, it is important that the law of finance understands those markets and those transactions in terms of its own legal categories. Thus, *Section Two* of this book is divided between traditional banking; lending; stakeholding (including shareholding); speculation; refinancing; proprietary finance; and communal investment. Each category involves different core legal *concepts* being applied in particular *contexts*: whether in the form of contract law, property law, tort law, equity, public law or criminal law.

Finance must be understood as being predicated on *risk*. The lawyer advising parties to financial transactions is acting primarily as a risk manager. There are six aspects of risk highlighted in this chapter. First, the manner in which all financial instruments are based and priced on a calculation of the risks contained in them, primarily by means of theoretical models being applied to the circumstances. Secondly, an application of the risk/return calculation to identify the amount of profit which is acceptable for the level of risk that is taken. Thirdly, a panoply of risks which inform legal practice: systemic risk, market risk, counterparty risk, collateral and credit support risk, insolvency risk, payment risk, documentation risk, personnel risk, regulatory risk, tax risk, cross default risk, and so on. Most significant of these during the financial crisis of 2007-09 was systemic risk: that is, the risk that the failure of one particularly significant market participant or marketplace could cause the entire financial system to fail. The lessons which will flow from that systemic risk almost coming to pass in 2008 will (it has to be hoped) haunt the law of finance for the remainder of the 21st century. Fourthly, sociological understandings of risk as being something which the financial system imposes on ordinary citizens. Fifthly, the risks caused by "financialisation": that is, the effect on the economy of huge amounts of capital being funnelled into the financial system, and the reliance on financial models and techniques to manage much economic activity. Sixthly, the law itself as a risk: whether in the form of changes in the common law or changes to regulatory practice or statute.

1. THE AMBIT OF THE LAW OF FINANCE

A. The definition of "finance"

1–01 The first item of business is to identify what we mean by the term "finance". The term "finance" is used deliberately in this book rather than "banking" or "corporate finance" because we are concerned with the effect of financial activity on society generally and not only on the sorts of financial activity which take place in the boardrooms of major companies or on the trading floors of large financial institutions. In this book among the things we shall consider are the legal dimensions to the services which banks and investment firms (collectively, "financial institutions") provide to corporate and private customers in the form of contracts of loan, securities and other instruments traded on exchanges, derivatives traded off-exchange, security taken for performance in financial transactions, and collective investment entities such as unit trusts and occupational pension funds. However, this merely serves as a general description of the sorts of things which will be discussed under the rubric of "finance"; but it does not give us a definition of what the term "finance" means. So, let us begin by defining what we mean by "finance" for the purposes of this book. We will do that by considering the etymology of that word.

The English word finance comes originally from the Latin "finis" meaning an "end"; and latterly the modern sense of the word[1] comes from the French verb "finer" meaning "to end or settle", and the French noun "fin" meaning "an end".[2] The pecuniary connotations of the word "finance" derive from its later sense of the activity of "settling a debt". So, when a debt was settled, it was "finished".[3] By 1494 the word "finance" was used more particularly to refer to a person who was required "to pay a ransom". So, a kidnapping would be "finished" when the ransom was paid. In raising ransoms, for example, the ransom needed to release Richard I from imprisonment in Austria in the 12th century, required the levying of taxes and borrowing or taking money from a number of places: in that sense, the ransom itself had to be financed.[4] By 1555, the term "finance" was used to refer to the "fineness" of gold—at that time the most important measure of money. The worth of gold was linked to its quality, or its "fineness". By 1866 a more familiar meaning (to modern ears) of the word "finance" had developed: that is, "to furnish with finances and to find capital for" an activity.[5] So in discussing finance we are concerned with using finance so as to achieve a goal: that is, the wherewithal to act so as to make a goal possible. As in the Latin meaning of "finis", the role of "finance" is to finish or complete an objective by providing the monetary wherewithal to do it. This idea is considered in the next section.

1–02

B.   Finance as the wherewithal to act

How different forms of finance provide the wherewithal to act

The modern understanding of "finance", as it is discussed in this book, is concerned with providing a person with the wherewithal to act by means of providing her with sufficient money (or its equivalent) so that she can achieve her goals. Finance is not limited to cash money. It may relate to a bank account facility, or a credit card, or a loan, or an investment portfolio, or one of a number of corporate finance mechanisms for advancing money's worth to a company or for re-calibrating a person's financial assets and obligations. In each sense, the recipient of this financing is able to act. This is also at the heart of economic theory: the ability to borrow money or to access capital markets is considered to

1–03

---

[1] As explained in the *Oxford Shorter English Dictionary*.
[2] *Oxford Shorter English Dictionary* and *Encarta World Dictionary*.
[3] This is the sense in which the etymology is explained in the Encarta World Dictionary.
[4] *Oxford Shorter English Dictionary*. Perhaps this idea of using finance to pay off a ransom will resonate most clearly with people who have mortgages and with businesses which are struggling against the economic current.
[5] *Oxford Shorter English Dictionary*.

be essential for economic activity and for economic growth.[6] Each of the financing models considered in this book is linked by this ability which it grants to the parties.

1–04   The simplest means of providing the wherewithal to act for an individual is by means of earning money, paying it into a bank account and then spending it in cash as necessary. If that person does not have sufficient income to pay for a large capital project in one go, then she may borrow money by way of a loan from her bank. That loan may be secured by way of a mortgage over her house: that is, if she fails to repay the loan then the bank can sell her house to pay off her mortgage debt. If the person were a company then the company could also borrow money by means of issuing a bond in the form of a promise to pay interest to a large group of investors if they each lend her small amounts of money. Instead, a large company could borrow money from one bank or could borrow a very large amount of money from a syndicate of banks necessary to put together enough capital. Alternatively, a company could issue shares to the investing public whereby, in exchange for giving money to the company, the company grants those investors shares which contain rights to vote in decisions over the company's activities, and grants those investors the right to receive a share of the company's distributable profits (if there are any) in the form of a dividend, and also grants those investors an ability to sell their shares to other investors to make a capital profit on their investment. Clearly, all of these means of acquiring finance are concerned with the ability of a person (whether an individual or a company) to acquire money so as to pursue personal or commercial goals which investors or lenders consider to be worthwhile supporting. The investors or lenders may consider those activities to be "worthwhile" in the sense that they support them in an ethical sense, or far more likely because they consider that the person who acquires the finance will act appropriately and so generate a profit for herself and for her investors.

Increasing financial sophistication

1–05   All of the techniques for raising finance which we have been mentioned so far, and which are considered in far greater detail throughout this book, are very well-established. Modern financial markets have developed more sophisticated techniques both for raising finance and for generating profits. Borrowing is now possible for companies in a number of different jurisdictions simultaneously in very large amounts because a number of lenders from different jurisdictions will group together in syndicates to make up the entire loan amount. Borrowers can access money in different currencies through financial institutions which have offices in hundreds of countries worldwide or which transact with financial institutions in other jurisdictions by borrowing on the money markets and the foreign exchange markets. This money could be used as spending money on a foreign holiday at one end of the scale, or it could be used to pay for the construction of a new factory in another country at the other end.

---

[6] See, the policies underpinning the various EC directives in Ch.7.

Aside from the achievement of specific goals, financial markets are also used **1–06**
simply to make profit. Clearly a bank which enters into a loan contract is doing so
because it wants to earn a profit, principally by means of acquiring a flow of
interest payments from the borrower before the capital is repaid. However,
financial institutions and increasing numbers of private individuals invest in
financial markets in the hope of earning profit. Therefore, we might buy shares
simply in the hope that they will be worth more tomorrow than they are today.
Financial markets have developed sophisticated instruments called derivatives to
allow investors to speculate on the future market value of financial instruments
(whether shares, bonds, or whatever) without even needing to buy that particular
financial instrument. So, if I have a hunch that technology shares in Thailand will
increase in value over the next month, but I do not have the means to actually go
to Thailand and buy those shares, then I can enter into what is known as a
"cash-settled equity call option" (in return for the payment of a fee) so that I can
be paid the profit (if any) which I would have received as if I had actually bought
those Thai shares myself, but without my actually having to buy those Thai
shares. Increasing sophistication has thus made previously unimaginable ranges
of investments open to many people. In each circumstance, finance provides a
wherewithal to act.

Finance is intangible but it has real effects

What is important about derivatives of this sort is that they underline one very **1–07**
important fact about finance: finance is intangible but it has very real effects. The
call option we have just considered in relation to the Thai shares enabled me to
speculate on the performance of technology companies in Thailand without me
needing to interact with anyone in Thailand. The financial institution which sold
me that option may have been physically resident in an office block in London
just a few miles from me: but I became entitled to receive a payment from that
financial institution if my speculation was successful. Similarly, there may have
been an effect on technology companies in Thailand if it became known that
investors in London were speculating on the future profitability of such
companies. Thai technology companies may have been able to acquire finance
more easily and more cheaply simply because the perception in the global
financial markets was that they were likely to become more profitable in the
future, even if no trades relating to their shares were done on a stock exchange in
Thailand. Or, contrariwise, if speculators had expected the value of those
companies to fall, then their ability to access finance would have shrunk.

Thus the universe of finance operates on the basis of rumour and opinion. If you **1–08**
read a financial newspaper on any given day, you will see reports of a consensus
in international and national markets on the previous day that such-and-such was
a good or a bad investment, and you will also see reports of the perceived value
of those investments increasing or decreasing as a result. During the financial
crisis of 2008, for example, there were huge falls (of up to 60 per cent in a few
days) in the share prices of banks like HBOS and Citigroup based on market
perception of the risks associated with their business prospects. This has two
effects for our purposes. First, it means that a person whose credit worth is

perceived to be low will have trouble acquiring the wherewithal to act by means of finance because investors and lenders will be reluctant to deal with them simply because of the market's perception of them and their area of activity; and by contrast someone whose perceived credit worth has increased will find it easier to acquire finance more cheaply than before because investors and lenders will want to deal with them, again due to market sentiment. Thus, the intangibility of financial markets can have a real effect on someone seeking finance. Secondly, we see that financial markets are both involved in providing the wherewithal to act and also with speculating so as to make profits which give the speculator greater wherewithal to act (often to make further speculation and thus make further profits).

C. The intangible nature of most financial markets

1–09   Language has been a particularly significant part of human evolution: it has effectively created modern humanity. Language also has the ability to call into existence phenomena which have no tangible, physical existence. A joke can make you happy: the words that constitute the joke when spoken by a human being can alter the level of happiness of human beings who hear it. Bad news will make you sad. And so on. This is true of finance. Finance has no tangible existence—being a wherewithal to act, just as strength is a wherewithal to exert force—but its effects are so real in the physical world that it is tempting to assume that finance and also money have a tangible existence. In a short story entitled "Tlon, Uqbar, Orbis Tertius", Jorge Luis Borges[7] tells of an imaginary planet which is created by a shadowy secret society simply by means of writing an encyclopaedia which set out the cultural, psychological and philosophical make-up of that imaginary planet's inhabitants. The conceit underpinning that story was that simply by writing about the detail of a non-existent world as though that world did actually exist would cause that imaginary world to be brought into existence. So, in the story, the world of Tlon does come to exist simply because it was talked about in such a way that it came to be real.

1–10   In a similar way, we might think of finance as being another example of something coming into existence because people talked about it in a way which made it become real. Let us take an example to show how mere words have real effects in finance. Suppose that Profit Bank hears from GoTech Plc that GoTech is going to manufacture an excellent computer games system and the two corporations agree that Profit Bank will lend money to GoTech to do this. What Profit Bank is doing is putting GoTech's ambitions into effect by giving it the wherewithal to act. What Profit Bank is also doing is saying to GoTech "you can spend money because we have credited your bank account with enough money to do so". The money does not exist in cash in the form of physical notes and coins. Rather Profit Bank registers an increase in the value of GoTech's bank accounts by the amount of the loan. Consequently, GoTech can write cheques to its suppliers and employees, or it can make electronic funds transfers into their bank accounts, which in turn will cause the suppliers' banks and the employees' banks

---

[7] *Fictions* (1944).

to treat those suppliers and employees as though they too have more money, even though all that has happened is that the value of their bank accounts is agreed by everyone to have increased in value.

If we go further back down the chain, we should ask where Profit Bank got its money from. Remarkably, Profit Bank will not have held an amount of cash in a vault somewhere equal to its loan to GoTech. Instead Profit Bank itself will be treated by other banks as having a value which is sufficiently large to assume that it would be able to provide enough cash to GoTech if it were needed. So, what other banks do is to accept that Profit Bank has a sufficiently high credit rating to meet its obligations. Profit Bank, therefore, does not own very much money in the form of notes and coins, instead Profit Bank has a perceived value among other banks. That value will be based on Profit Bank's success in wringing profits from the loans it makes or from the speculative investments it makes. If the perception among other banks was that Profit Bank was too unprofitable ever to be able to meet its obligations, then it would literally go "bankrupt".[8] Thus, Profit Bank's ability to trade as a bank is built on what is said about it, on its reputation. The bank will be required by its regulator to hold assets in ring-fenced accounts equal to a given percentage of its total obligations to guard against the risk of its insolvency, but otherwise there will be no other obligation to show it actually has the money—those ring-fenced accounts are ordinarily just electronic records that it has assets of a given value and not physical piles of gold.

1–11

We should not fixate on Profit Bank too much because every other bank in the world is similarly reliant on perceptions of their worth and on their ability to trade. Banks borrow money from other banks—on what are known as "the money markets"—because no bank has very much cash stored on deposit. Therefore, banks give each other credit lines. For a bank to have money stored on deposit is a waste. At the end of every business day, or rather during business days in the modern age, every bank's treasurer monitors how much money the bank has and tries to make sure that every penny, cent and rupee is invested in something. Money sitting idly in a bank account is money that is not being invested and so it is money which is not earning a profit.

1–12

Therefore, banks do not have money or assets of money's worth which are equal to all of their obligations. That is the way that our financial markets work. Computers store records of how much each of us is worth. We measure that worth in cash terms in different currencies. If our currency becomes less valuable, then we become worth less too. Consider Germany in the 1930s as the Deutschemark became worth less on financial markets to people outside Germany. It became difficult for Germany to import goods from overseas unless they spent massive amounts of Deutschemarks to do so. As a result, inflation in Germany surged. Eventually, going to do ordinary food shopping required Germans to carry huge quantities of banknotes around in suitcases to have enough Deutschemarks to pay for even the basics. At present, the currency in Zimbabwe is subject to astonishing levels of inflation which make the currency almost worthless.

1–13

---

[8] As is explained in Ch.28, the "bank" comes from the Italian "banco" for bench, being a reference to the benches and tables at which early Florentine bankers used to sit and conduct business. When a banker went into insolvency his bench was broken—it was "ruptured". Hence the term "bankrupt".

1–14   The global financial crisis (or, "credit crunch") of 2007/08 was caused by banks dealing in mortgages made to customers who were unable to make repayment.[9] The effect was that banks became reluctant to lend money to one another because they did not know which other banks had large exposures to this market. Therefore, because banks do not hold all of their assets in cash, they need to be able to borrow from other banks: thus when banks stop lending to one another there is a seizure in the banking sector generally. This is known as a "drying up of liquidity". If banks cannot borrow money then they do not have any money to lend to ordinary customers, and so the economy dries up too. Therefore, these virtual movements of virtual money have very tangible effects in the "real economy". In the summer of 2008 a truly remarkable number of very old banks either went into insolvency (such as Lehman Brothers), or had to be bought up by other banks so as to avoid bankruptcy (such as Bear Stearns, HBOS, Washington Mutual, Wachovia, Merrill Lynch), or had to be nationalised by their governments to prevent them going into bankruptcy (such as Northern Rock, Citigroup, and Fortis). If I had suggested the idea in 2006 that the US and UK governments would ever have to nationalise banks, I would have been laughed at. Such was the change in global banking culture during 2008. The effect of the 2007–09 financial crisis is considered in Chapter 45.

1–15   What we have done with our financial markets then is to describe them in such a way that we have brought them into existence: just like Borges's story about the planet of Tlon which was referred to above. But does that observation have any impact on our discussion of the law of finance? I would suggest that it does. If we are dealing as lawyers with intangible markets then we need to think in that way about the financial instruments involved. What if someone refuses to make payment under a financial contract? How do we take security, for example, over contracts to transfer intangible amounts of money in exchange for intangible securities? The nature of intangible financial products poses subtle challenges for lawyers to ensure that their clients will be paid what they are owed, and also to ensure that those financial markets can continue to function properly. It also impacts on securities markets: for example, whereas once upon a time shares and bonds were bought and sold in the form of physical certificates, a little like banknotes, they are no longer represented by certificates because financial people realised that it was cheaper, more convenient and more secure to have the owners of securities registered on a computer database (rather than run the risk of those physical certificates being lost or damaged or stolen). Whereas once the owner of a bond used to collect her payment of interest by presenting herself at the offices of the bond issuer and by tearing the appropriate coupon off her bond certificate, now those payments of interest are made electronically.[10] To use the financial markets' jargon expression, the financial world has become "dematerialised": that is, fewer and fewer of these financial instruments exist in tangible, physical form anymore. Instead they are registered and traded electronically.

---

[9] See para.31–01.

[10] Interest on bonds is still known as "coupon" as a result.

D. From domestic banking to cross-border transactions

Now that we have removed financial instruments from existing tangibly in space **1–16** in the form of certificates and so forth, it is also important to remember that financial markets reach across national boundaries. As will be discussed below, this means that a number of different legal systems may compete to have the right to decide disputes which arise between people acting through a number of different jurisdictions. What this also means is that financial markets do not need to cease trading because when night-time arrives in Tokyo, people are arriving at work in London; and when night-time arrives in London, people are arriving at work in New York; and when night-time arrives in New York, people are arriving at work in Tokyo.[11] Consequently, we could say that financial markets have conquered time because trading is always occurring somewhere in the world (except for certain parts of the weekend and certain bank holidays). And yet at night-time and over weekends there are still plenty of people at work in the offices of the banks, the law firms and the accountancy firms around the world to keep this vast machine working.

Finance has therefore conquered time and space. And all because human beings **1–17** have dreamed it into existence, just like the planet Tlon. Our goal now is to consider how the law deals with these phenomena.

2. CONSTRUCTING THE LAW OF FINANCE

A. The distinction between the substantive law and financial regulation

It is important to distinguish between substantive law and financial regulation. **1–18** The substantive law includes private law (contract, property, tort, and so on), criminal law, and judicial review in public law. It is the substantive law specifically of England and Wales which is discussed in this book. Financial regulation is based on the EC financial services directives as implemented into UK finance law principally by the rule-making powers given originally to the Financial Services Authority ("FSA") by the Financial Services and Markets Act 2000 ("FSMA 2000"), but which have now passed to the Financial Conduct Authority ("FCA") and the Prudential Regulatory Authority ("PRA") (as explained in Chapter 8).[12] Substantive law is that system of rules and principles

---

[11] While those are the principal financial market centres, we should not forget that as the Earth revolves before the sun, there are people across the world going to work, leaving work and trading in financial instruments. Financial activity never ceases. Once you go to bed at night, any money you paid into your bank account that day will be being invested by your bank around the world, and then re-invested by whoever received your original money, and so on and so on. If you have seen the film *The Matrix*, it may help to think of all of this investment capital being invested and reinvested constantly in different financial centres around the world as being a little like "The Matrix" that exists and lives in a parallel, electronic universe.

[12] The Financial Services Authority, which had borne the regulatory responsibility in this context previously, was renamed the Financial Conduct Authority ("FCA") as a result of the enactment of the Financial Services Act 2012, s.6. The bulk of the former authority's responsibilities passed to the

drawn from case law and statute which is implemented by the courts in accordance with the doctrine of precedent. By contrast, financial regulation is not subject to a formal doctrine of precedent; instead the rules of financial regulation are created further to powers granted to the regulatory authorities by statute, but those rules are not enforced directly in court. Rather, financial regulations are implemented by the FCA and the PRA and are subject to appeal only to a tribunal ("the Markets Tribunal", created by the FSMA 2000) which has no formal doctrine of precedent. As such, financial regulation is not "law", as strictly defined.

1–19   The regulator is, in effect, a participant in financial markets in the sense that it consults on the rules which it creates, and its rulebooks are subject not only to occasional, systematic overhaul but are also subject to regular, low-level tinkering: it is not a court. Efficient regulation of the securities markets and other financial services activity has, however, required that the FCA and the PRA are given a range of powers which mimic the substantive law. So, the "civil offence" of market abuse[13] has given the FCA the power to impose penalties in relation to the abuse of inside information in a way which parallels the criminal jurisdiction under Part V of the Criminal Justice Act 1993 on insider dealing[14]; and the regulatory authorities have been given powers to investigate allegations of market abuse. The former function is a regulatory function which leverages off the FCA's powers of investigation, which is less complex and unwieldy than the criminal law function of the latter.

1–20   Another significant, if trite, point is that substantive case law—for example, in contract law, tort law and in equity—is not created with financial transactions specifically in mind, unless the facts of any individual case happen to relate to a financial transaction. Consequently, principles of substantive law need to be interpreted and adapted so as to fit the finance law context. That is not to say that the principles of the substantive law can be overlooked when they are inconvenient. Rather, it is to require that the operation of those principles of the substantive law must be applied to the finance law context or interpreted so as to decide how they should apply in the finance law context.

1–21   There is a distinction here between the central concepts of the general law (such as criminal law, public law, contract law, tort law, property law and equity) as they are applied in different contexts so as to generate different areas of law (such as company law, family law, and securities law) which meld central legal concepts with statutes and regulations which were created for those specific contexts.[15] This point is developed in the next section. Within finance law there is then a distinction between this hybrid form of substantive law adapting substantive law concepts to the particular context, and specific financial regulations created in relation to financial markets.

FCA; except for prudential regulatory matters which passed to the Prudential Regulatory Authority ("PRA") and other matters to the Office for Fair Trading ("OFT"), as is explored in Ch.8.

[13] Financial Services and Markets Act 2000 s.397.

[14] See Ch.26 "Insider Dealing and Market Abuse" generally.

[15] See, A.S. Hudson, "Rapporteur: Differentiation in property and obligations", in A. Hudson (ed.) *New Perspectives on Property Law, Human Rights and the Home*, (London: Cavendish, 2004), p.319.

As a result, in this book the substantive law will be referred to as the "*general law*"; whereas Bank of England, FCA and PRA regulation of financial services will be referred to as "*financial regulation*".

B. Creating the substantive law of finance out of private law *concepts* applied in a particular *context*

The law of finance does not yet exist as a complete, discrete field. This book is an attempt to describe how it could exist and how we could understand its existence now. My aim in writing this book is to make it easier to teach finance law and to practise in finance law. To do that it is important that we understand how the subject is put together, and what should be considered to be a part of the subject. As considered in detail below, the law of finance should be understood as being comprised primarily of a combination of private law concepts of contract, tort and property, together with financial services regulation and the legislation which is drafted specifically for this purpose so as to put those concepts into context. This theme is considered in more detail in Chapter 4.

1–22

C. The sources of the law of finance

The three sources of the law of finance

There are three principal sources of the law of finance. First, those fundamental concepts of English private law which are significant in the context of finance. Secondly, the legislation dealing specifically with finance: principally the Financial Services and Markets Act 2000 ("FSMA 2000"), its attendant statutory instruments, and the Company Law Act 2006 ("CA 2006"), which are in turn built on a combination of European Union ("EU") Directives and consolidations of pre-existing domestic statutes. Thirdly, the regulations created by the regulatory authorities (FCA and PRA) further to powers granted to them by the FSMA 2000 and often implementing EU financial services legislation.

1–23

A combination of English private law and EU legislation

Therefore, we have two principal sources of finance law at root: first, English case law and statute (not all of which relates specifically to finance) much of it created originally centuries ago, naturally in isolation from modern financial practice; and, secondly, EU legislation which has been implemented and often adapted by UK legislation and regulation. The detailed EU processes for generating that legislation are considered in detail below. What is important about this legislation is both that it obliges the UK Parliament to give effect to certain legislative and regulatory principles, and also that it demonstrates how important the international dimension of finance can be in creating the law of finance. Policy at the European level has been created through the "Lamfalussy process" (discussed in detail in Chapter 7) whereby over-arching policy principles are created first—and given effect to as "high-level principles" in the EU

1–24

Directives—before the EU Commission then produces very detailed "technical regulations" which guide the creation of financial regulation in the UK and (it is hoped) near-identical regulation across the rest of the EU by the financial regulators of each state. In the wake of the financial crisis 2007–09, the "de Larosière Report" (discussed in detail in Chs 7 and 45) identified the causes and regulatory failures associated with the crisis and suggested a number of changes to EU financial services policy, including: a restructuring of the EU regulatory institutions, the use of Regulations to impose a single regulatory rulebook across the EU,[16] and a change in the attitude of regulators.

Global financial marketplaces

1–25   The principal marketplaces for the most complex financial products are international, which means that large companies, other large entities and very rich individuals move across national boundaries and use different financial products in different jurisdictions and between different jurisdictions.[17] It is much less likely that ordinary individuals will use financial products in different jurisdictions in this way, except possibly when they are on holiday or when their work requires them to travel abroad. These ordinary individuals may well participate in large pension funds or other collective investment entities which in turn invest either in different jurisdictions or in products which derive their value from different jurisdictions. While retail banking for ordinary customers is frequently contained within a particular jurisdiction, the significance of the core deposits of ordinary customers cannot be forgotten; similarly, the possibility for investment banking and ordinary banking to impact disastrously on one another was demonstrated by the financial crisis 2007–09. Thus, markets in one jurisdiction can have unlikely impacts on different markets in other jurisdictions. Consequently, in legal terms it is important to understand how the laws of different jurisdictions interact to deal with cross-border investments. In this book we shall focus on English substantive law, and on English private international law rules which govern issues relating to financial transactions concerning parties, actions or offices in different jurisdictions.

1–26   The law in this book is predicated in large part on the law of the EU as well as English law. However, beyond the EU there is a vast financial marketplace, or a series of distinct marketplaces, which also overreach national boundaries. Whereas legal systems are generally locked into national boundaries, financial practice carries on across those boundaries constantly. Financial institutions frequently have many offices in many jurisdictions. The hunger for mergers between financial institutions to create ever larger financial institutions is built in part on a desire to maximise the strengths of different institutions in different

---

[16] At present, Member States of the EU are able to implement EC Directives in whatever form they consider appropriate, as opposed to a single rulebook based on Regulations which would give the Member States no option but to implement the EU legislation in its original form.

[17] One must be careful with this idea, of course. The financial crisis of 2007–09 began in retail markets involving ordinary individual customers and was then amplified across the world by derivatives markets. Moreover, the core deposits which are made by ordinary customers are central to the capitalisation of the largest universal banks like Citigroup and Barclays. Therefore, this book does not overlook the significance and importance of retail banking markets, as is considered in Ch.32.

countries or regions. Otherwise, financial institutions may merge so as to maximise the position which they may have separately in different market sectors. Therefore, it should come as no surprise that there are a number of international initiatives to cope with cross-border commercial activity.

First, there are formal organisations such as the World Trade Organization which itself seeks to create legislation and to convene a court to govern trade on a global basis. The EU is unique in its ability to create legal rules binding on citizens and corporations in a large number of sovereign territories in Europe. Secondly, there are formal and informal groupings of central bankers, think-tanks and market participants which produce intermittent reports on the conduct of particular markets and the risks and challenges which face them. While this type of organisation may have neither legal force nor legal authority, their reports may help to shape the thought processes, attitudes and practices of regulators and legislators in key jurisdictions. Thirdly, there are quasi-formal organisations, such as the Bank for International Settlements ("BIS"), which create over-arching principles for specific regulatory functions. These international organisations are considered in more detail in Chapter 28. At this stage it is important to observe that there is a difficulty for the law of finance in relying solely on national laws to deal with international financial activity, and therefore that international organisations will have an important part to play.

Private international law

A very important dimension of municipal law is private international law (also known as "conflict of laws"). This topic receives its own discussion in Chapter 6. Given that this is an English law book, we will consider private international law from the perspective of English law.[18] An example of this area of law would be as follows: what if a dispute arose in relation to a contract which was created between a French company and a Thai company for payment in US Dollars in a bank account in London relating to the sale of gold held physically in Bangkok? Which system of law would govern this contractual dispute: French, Thai, US or English law? In which courts in which country would the parties sue: English, French, Thai or American? This is the problem of conflict of laws as it applies to the substantive law governing disputes between private parties, which is completely separate from any questions as to financial regulation and so forth. It is a question of English law—for the purposes of this book—which system of law and which jurisdiction will apply. English private international law will not always select English law and the English courts: indeed EU regulation may prevent the courts from doing that.

1–27

1–28

---

[18] Private international law, or "conflict of laws", as considered in Ch.6 is in truth a branch of English law despite its name. That system of rules explains how the courts of England and Wales deal with issues involving different jurisdictions. Those English law principles are now informed by EU legislation in this area.

The jurisdictions appropriate to this book: UK financial services law and the English general law

1–29   For the purposes of the law of finance, the appropriate jurisdictions which are covered by this book are the substantive law of England and Wales and the financial services statutes which now apply to the entire UK (including the jurisdictions of Scotland and of Northern Ireland which otherwise operate on the basis of different general law). Ordinarily, a book of this sort (that is, a treatise written by an English lawyer) would only be concerned with English law. However, the role of the Bank of England regulatory authorities overseeing the whole of the UK within the context of the EU directives, and the reach of the Companies Act 2006 across the entire UK, means that we have a corpus of legislation which covers the entire UK albeit that that legislation falls to be interpreted in England and Wales in accordance with English (and Welsh) general law.

3.   THE SEVEN CATEGORIES OF FINANCE

A.   The purpose of the division

1–30   One of the first steps towards creating a law of finance is to divide up the business conducted by finance professionals into categories which make conceptual sense to a lawyer. The division I have made in this section is between traditional banking; lending transactions in which the lender acquires merely a contractual right to repayment of capital and interest; transactions in which the investor acquires some stakeholder right of ownership in the entity providing the investment by virtue of that investment; speculation whereby an investor acquires a purely contractual right to receive some future return; refinancing, whereby some existing financial obligation is altered so that that obligation is either renewed or overlaid by a new obligation; proprietary finance in which some right to some asset is acquired by means of lease or trust or otherwise; and collective investment whereby many investors' capital is pooled for a common investment purpose on a number of different models. Each category is explained in greater detail below, and then each specific activity receives its own detailed consideration in a later part of this book.

1–31   As will emerge from the discussions to follow, each of these types of transaction constitutes a very different form of activity from a lawyer's perspective precisely because the parties' acquire different qualities of right: whether rights to property, purely contractual rights, voting rights to control an entity, and so forth. These distinctions are not as significant for a financier whose principal concern will be the profitability of the underlying transaction. Consequently, it is important when establishing a law of finance to differentiate as a lawyer should between the various forms of financial activity. The purpose of this section is to present a lawyer's understanding of how the contents of this book operate.

B.   Banking

The law of finance is about more than banking law, although a large part of the   **1–32**
subject matter of the law of finance is comprised of things that banks do.
Traditional English banking law is concerned with such topics as the
establishment of the Bank of England and successor regulators of deposit taking
business; the legal nature of the relationship between bank and client; the law
governing bank accounts, cheques and negotiable instruments; and latterly the
operation of electronic payment systems. This book is consciously about
"finance": that is, a range of transactions beyond merely the operation of bank
accounts, the clearance of cheques and so forth. All of those traditional topics are
covered in this book, they do remain significant in their own ways, and they are
governed for the most part by long-standing legislation which has been adapted
for that purpose in the modern context. There are other phenomena which have
intruded on the canon of banking law since Paget first wrote his treatise on
Banking Law in 1904, such as the provision of credit and debit card services by
banks and others; the rise of electronic banking and payment systems; and so
forth. Each such facet of ordinary banking activity is considered in turn in Part
VIII of this book. That section of the book is therefore concerned with the
services which banks ordinarily provide to their customers which are covered by
long-standing legal principles and which do not overlap with the other six
categories. The cornerstone of banking law is the law of contract, between banker
and client (whether a corporate or individual client), as adapted by banking
legislation.

C.   Lending

Lending is a long-standing activity of banks and other moneylenders, discussed   **1–33**
in Part IX of this book. What is particular to lending as an activity is its focus on
the contract between lender and borrower, without necessarily any of the
paraphernalia of bank accounts, cheque books and so on which are a central focus
of ordinary client banking. It may be that in relation to bank accounts there are
loans made by way of overdrafts, but the root of the overdraft remains in the
contractual nexus between banker and client as to repayment of the capital of the
loan facility plus interest. Otherwise ordinary lending is comprised of that single
executory contract between lender and borrower whereby the lender transfers
money outright to the borrower at the commencement of the loan transaction
subject to obligations in the borrower to repay that capital as some future date and
also to pay periodical amounts of interest. The lender has only a personal,
contractual claim against the borrower in this context and so, if the borrower
defaults in repayment or goes into insolvency, the lender will be required either to
recognise the fragility of his contractual remedies or to have recourse to
proprietary financing. Contractual remedies are fragile in the banking context
because rights to receive money will only be remediable by means of damages or
by specific performance of the obligation to pay (in limited circumstances): if the
borrower has no means of making payment then the lender will not receive
payment. The lender's risk is therefore on the borrower's ability to pay. If the

lender is able to construct some proprietary mechanism whereby she can have recourse to some identified property to satisfy her right to receive payment, then that may offer her protection against insolvency or the borrower's simple unwillingness to pay. The various forms of taking security are considered in Chapter 22, and range from trusts, mortgages, charges, liens, and pledges to purely contractual guarantees.

1–34   In loan contracts there will also be a range of covenants entitling the lender to terminate the contract if the borrower breaches one of those covenants. Breach of covenant will, in a well-drafted contract, trigger one of a number of mechanisms for taking security. These covenants are frequently in the form of a number of trapdoors or escape hatches which will open automatically to allow the lender to escape from an undesirable contract if the borrower, for example, defaults under another loan contract (cross-default) or if the borrower's credit worth deteriorates.

1–35   Lending may also take place in two other important forms. First, lending to large corporate entities may require the borrowing of a huge sum of money which requires a large syndicate of lenders to put up a part of the loan each. This is known as "syndicated lending" and is attractive to bankers because it spreads out the risk of a borrower defaulting on a loan, as discussed in Chapter 33. Secondly, a borrower may issue a bond which means that the amount of money which the borrower requires is acquired from a number of investors in the bond market by means of those investors buying up as many individual bonds as they consider to be a good investment. The borrower who issues this global bond is therefore actually issuing a large number of small units of equal denomination which comprise the total bond issue. The purchase money for each bond is paid to the borrower. In turn the borrower promises to repay those capital purchase moneys at the expiry of the bond and, in the meantime, to make periodic payments of interest (known as "coupon" payments) to the investors. The further attraction of bonds for their investors is that the investors are able to trade the bonds and so speculate on the comparative attractiveness of the borrowers rate of interest when compared to ordinary market interest rates or the rates of interest being paid by other bond issuers. In both of these examples—syndicated lending and bond issues—the borrower and lender (or lenders) are entering into purely contractual arrangements which provide no protective proprietary rights in themselves (except that the bond investor acquires the bonds which he may be able to sell at a profit).

D.   Stakeholding

1–36   Stakeholding is a form of financial activity, discussed in Part X of this book, which involves the investor taking a stake in the investment entity, for example, in the form of a share. Whereas a borrower has only a personal, contractual interaction with a lender, and a client has only a contractual relationship with a bank, the stakeholder has some direct inter-relationship with the investment entity. As opposed to an ordinary contractual relationship, an ordinary shareholder (for example) owns rights to vote in the affairs of the company and has a right to participate in the property of the company in the event of a winding up: in that complex collection of senses, the shareholder has a stake in the company. The company acquires finance from the shareholders' acquisition of shares; the shareholder frequently hopes in turn to acquire finance through the appreciation in value of those shares, or else hopes to acquire some other benefit from owning those shares such as dividend income. (Other securities dealt with in Part X include bonds, and so forth, which do not grant stakeholding rights, but which are governed by the same regulations, and are therefore dealt with in the same discussion.) Shareholding is a particular form of legal relationship which is distinct from contractual rights, even though there will be a contractual relationship between the company issuing the share and the subscribers for that share at the outset.

E. Speculation

In one sense, speculation does not connote any particular type of legal relationship. Speculation is the activity of making an investment or entering into a transaction with the sole aim of generating as much profit as possible. The investor does not seek any other service, such as the availability of a credit card or bank account, nor does the investor necessarily have any other commercial purpose, such as taking security or acquiring voting rights in the investment vehicle. Therefore, all that speculation connotes is a contractual nexus whereby the investor and the counterparty agree that, in consideration for the transfer or money or other assets, the investor shall be entitled to receive a cash flow calculated by reference to the success of the investment. Simply by reference to speculation, the investor acquires no other rights beyond a contractual right to receive money. As is considered in the next section, instruments such as derivatives (considered in Chapter 40) may be used either for purely speculative purposes, or for the purposes of reducing the risks associated with an existing financial instrument, or for some combination of the two.

1–37

There are limited contexts in which speculation may have a legal effect beyond its contractual context. For example, there are certain types of entity which are only permitted to invest in derivatives if the investment is for the sole purpose of off-setting some other obligation which that entity already bears. To use derivatives for purely speculative purposes for such entities will be unlawful. When we come to consider unconscionable transactions in Chapter 18 we shall see that if the defendant sought to earn an unconscionably large speculative profit from a transaction at the other party's expense, then that transaction may be unenforceable. Charles Dickens presented the following, mordant description of speculation in *Nicholas Nickleby* (published in 1839):

1–38

> "Speculation is a round game: the players see little or nothing of their cards at first starting; gains *may* be great—and so may losses. The run of luck went against Mr Nickleby; a mania prevailed, a bubble burst, four stock brokers took villa residences at Florence, four hundred nobodies were ruined, and among them Mr Nickleby."

This is the oldest story in financial markets: some make enormous profits and others are ruined. The effect of speculative activity during the global financial crisis is discussed in Chapter 45.

F.   Refinancing

1–39   There are a number of financial instruments which are concerned with altering the effect or profitability of existing financial instruments. Suppose that Ace Ltd has entered into a loan contract with a floating rate of interest shortly before interest rates began to rise. Ace Ltd would want to move from a floating rate of interest into a fixed rate of interest so that its interest rate cost on its loan could be capped at a maximum level. By using an interest rate swap, a form of derivative considered in Chapter 40, Ace Ltd would be able to do exactly that. The interest rate swap would pay Ace Ltd the difference between the fixed rate of interest it wanted to pay and the floating rate of interest which it was obliged to pay under its loan contract. This has the effect, it is suggested, of refinancing the original loan contract by changing its economic effect for Ace Ltd. The complex web of payment obligations and other legal issues raised by financial derivatives are considered in detail in Part XI of this book.

1–40   Refinancing involves taking an existing financial product and either pricing a second product on the basis of that first instrument (such as an option to buy shares[19]) or as a re-organisation of the effect of that first instrument (such as an interest rate swap[20] which can alter the effective interest rate payable on a loan by a borrower[21]) or as a re-packaging of financial instruments so as to create a new instrument which has its own market and its own risk profile (such as a securitisation,[22] or a future[23]). The common link between these products is that the refinancing alters the commercial effect of a financial instrument. So, a securitisation takes a number of near-identical underlying products—such as mortgages—and transforms them into a security which can then be sold off to the market as something different from the original mortgage (as discussed in Chapter 44). From a lawyer's perspective the new product—derivative or securitisation product—carries different risks which need to be expressed in the documentation, they are regulated differently, and so constitute a different category of instrument from the underlying instrument itself (even though that underlying instrument continues in existence).

1–41   This refinancing needs some further explanation. Let us take the example of a refinancing transaction which would be in the form of a simple asset securitisation. Suppose a building society sold 10,000 fixed-rate, 25-year

---

[19] See para.40–17.

[20] See para.40–26.

[21] The borrower, in essence, is committed to the interest rate payable on its loan but can find a swaps dealer who will provide the interest rate the borrower owes in return for a different rate of interest payable by the borrower to the swaps dealer. Both parties take a speculative view on the future movements of interest rates and on their own ability to acquire cheap funding for this transaction. The pricing of the transaction also provides a fee, in effect, for the swaps dealer.

[22] See para.44–01.

[23] See para.40–24.

mortgages of a particular kind in July 2006 and suppose further that each mortgage requires an average payment each month of £2,000 from the borrower. Each of those mortgages will therefore generate £2,000 per month for 25 years. The building society may wish to realise a lump sum today rather than to wait for 25 years to receive all of those monthly payments. Consequently, rather than wait for those 10,000 cash flows to dribble in, the building society may "securitise" these cash flows by selling to investors the right to receive those 10,000 cash flows over 25 years in exchange for the payment of a lump sum to the building society in an amount to be agreed between the parties, just like buying a share or a bond. This has the economic effect of refinancing the economic effect of the 10,000 mortgage transactions for the building society.

These sorts of complex financial transactions are becoming a very powerful means of maximising people's assets and other rights in the modern marketplace. What will be complicated from circumstance to circumstance will be identifying the extent to which the refinancing transaction has the effect only of altering the economic effect of the transaction and the extent to which it also alters the legal relations between the original contracting parties. These issues are considered in Part XI of this book.

1–42

G.   Proprietary finance

Proprietary finance is concerned with situations in which finance is acquired by means of acquiring property rights or manipulating property rights in assets. These techniques considered in Part XII of this book. The foregoing types of finance were concerned with property rights only in the limited sense that a security or a contract constitutes a chose in action between the contracting parties and can therefore be transferred as an item of property in itself; but that contract does not grant the contracting parties proprietary rights, only contractual rights between one another. Proprietary finance in this book includes mortgages, asset-leasing and stock-lending. The financing techniques discussed under this head use proprietary rights to secure and to generate income. From a lawyer's perspective, then, the organisation, manipulation and documentation of those proprietary rights are different from types of financing which are concerned solely with contractual rights.

1–43

H.   Communal investment

Communal investment covers speculative financial investment and also social investment. Collective investment schemes—unit trusts and open-ended investment companies—pool investment capital drawn from ordinary investors and invest it under the management of a financial professional in specified types of investment. The investors acquire proprietary rights in the investment scheme in the manner set out by the legislation.[24] The social investment models—friendly societies, credit unions, co-operatives, and so on—provide financial services for

1–44

---

[24] This topic is beyond the scope of this book, but is analysed in detail in Alastair Hudson, *The Law and Regulation of Finance* (Sweet & Maxwell, 2013), Ch.52.

their members, and those members are thus making an investment in their communal interests (known as "social capital") while also taking different forms of financial service depending on the nature of the investment entity.[25] Similarly, occupational pension funds provide financial services in the form of pension rights to the individuals who invest in the fund as well as providing them with the rights of beneficiaries in that trust in accordance with the terms of the scheme instrument.

I.   The usefulness of the division

1–45   Dividing between the various forms of finance in this fashion takes this subject out of the categories used by financiers and instead organises them in accordance with the way in which lawyers understand the differences between lending, owning property, and so forth. It is important that if the law of finance is to identify itself as a distinct discipline that it becomes a legal field and is not simply an issue-by-issue account of "the things financial institutions do". It is also important to understand the law of finance as being a distinct legal field within the UK like company law or revenue law, and not simply as a technical branch of economics and finance theory as too many commentators do.

4.   RISK IN THE INTERNATIONAL LAW OF FINANCE

A.   Introduction

1–46   This section sets out a discussion of some key themes in the law of finance which will be pursued elsewhere in this book. We begin with a lengthy consideration of risk, which is key to all financial activity. Then we consider globalisation, dematerialisation and the privatisation of dispute resolution.

B.   The concept of risk

1–47   To discuss the concept of risk fully would require a book in itself. Nevertheless, because risk is such an important concept both in finance and in the social sciences, it receives an initial discussion here. We begin with financial concepts of risk, before moving through types of risk which are addressed in financial contracts and then into a consideration of risk in social theory.

Financial risk management

1–48   "All investment involves risk": so said Lord Nicholls.[26] Indeed, all banking involves risk. When an ordinary customer deposits her salary with a high street bank, she is taking the risk that the bank will remain solvent long enough to allow her to withdraw an equivalent money in the future, and that the bank's officers

---

[25] See, A.S. Hudson, *The Law on Investment Entities* (London: Sweet & Maxwell, 2000).
[26] *Royal Brunei Airlines v Tan* [1995] A.C. 378.

will be sufficiently honest not to steal her money. When a bank makes a loan to an ordinary human being or to a company it is taking the risk that the client will not repay the loan, or that market interest rates will move so that the client's interest payments will turn out to be much less than the lender could otherwise have earned on its money. When an investor of whatever sort makes an investment there is a risk that that investment will lose money, or make less profit than a feasible alternative investment could have made. Importantly though there would not be much profit for professional investors unless there was some risk. Risk creates volatility in markets, so that a clever investor can acquire investments when they are cheap and sell them when their price rises. If markets were always flat and always predictable, there would be little opportunity for large profits other than the comparatively small profits which can be made from charging fees to ordinary banking clients. A financial institution which does not take deposits from the public is reliant entirely on the amount of money which it can borrow from lending banks, or which it can raise from its shareholders or other investors, and which it can then generate from its investment profits. Thus, for financiers "risk" is both hazard and opportunity: the risk of loss is always present, but without that risk there would be no possibility of making the level of profit required by a bank's shareholders. So, without the volatility of financial markets there would be little hope of the profits which the banks and investment institutions expect to generate. Profitability and wealth are thus dependent on a game of speculative hazard.

There are risks perceived by regulators too in even the most mundane banking transactions. Such a banking model might see a bank take deposits from its customers and then invest those deposits for itself: a bank's profitability on this model would be the difference between the interest it is required to pay out to its customers and the amount of profit it is able to make on its investments. The Glass-Steagall Act in the US, repealed in recent times, was enacted so as to insist on a division between banks' speculative investment activities (investment banking) and its activities for its clients (commercial and retail banking). This sort of division has been recommended for UK banks by the Vickers Committee report, considered in Ch.29.[27] This recognises that banking activity of different types contained different types of risk which could infect one another: such as the investment and loss of clients' ordinary deposits on risky speculation. The Great Crash of 1929 in the USA had shown that investment by banks on their own behalf could cause enormous losses for ordinary banking customers as well as for serious investors[28]; the financial crisis of 2007–09 has double-underlined this risk. If a bank were to take all of the core deposits from its ordinary customers and invest them in risky markets, then that bank might lose all of that money and be unable to pay those deposits back to its customers. This is effectively what Northern Rock did in the UK. Thus, risk in investment markets could infect ordinary bank deposit markets if those businesses are not kept separate or if regulators do not ensure that banks maintain enough capital to cover those potential losses. Risks in one part of the financial markets can thus cause stress

1–49

---

[27] See para.28–01.
[28] See para.10–01.

and loss in other markets. Banking regulators[29] thus require (amongst other things) that banks calculate their exposures to various markets and that they put aside a suitable amount of capital in the event that there may be loss; and there is a scheme effectively to insure ordinary bank deposits up to £85,000.[30] Regulations and the practices of regulators in giving effect to those regulations are therefore very important in seeking to manage those risks across a market.

1–50   Risk management is a very important part of banking activities, and will become even more important in the wake of the financial crisis of 2007–09, as is discussed in Chapter 45.[31] Indeed finance theory gives a centrally important place to risk and to volatility in pricing complex financial instruments and in creating investment strategies. Take, by way of example, the mathematical concepts involved in calculating the beta co-efficient in bond yields, the volatility priced into the Black-Scholes option pricing model, the arbitrage possibilities offered by the comparative performance of different currencies. In pricing an interest rate swap, for example, one of the components which a financier will take into account is the risks associated with movements in the underlying price. Risk in the form of hazard (that is, losing as well as winning) is necessarily a part of financial activity in global financial markets. Risk is one of the factors which financiers attempt to anticipate by use of mathematical models. Risk is therefore built into the price of financial instruments.

1–51   Therefore, it is clear that the financial industry operates on risk and manipulates risk. The investment policies of financial institutions are dependent on strategies based on expectations of volatility, price movement and risk. For example, those who manage pension funds (and the future security of every pensioner) are concerned with the exploitation of risk in that they balance high-risk/high-yield investments with lower risk investments to construct a balanced portfolio: hence there is risk borne by any pensioner who buys into a pension plan. The finance industry has created a sub-industry which offers management of the risks created by banks' main speculative activities. Ironically, these risk management strategies can create greater risks than the hazards which they were created to control: the best examples being financial derivatives and securitisations.[32] The financial derivative (whether future, option or swap) offers both the possibility of risk management and of speculation: all in the same tablet.[33] As is explained in Part XI, derivatives seek to "hedge" financial risks by creating financial instruments which have the opposite characteristics and sensitivities to the original risks. For the cynical, the legacy of financial derivatives has been the collapse of financial institutions like Barings and the generation of exceptionally complex litigation to decide how to unpack derivatives transactions once they go wrong[34]; the legacy

---

[29] See para.28–01.

[30] See para.45–01.

[31] See para.31–01.

[32] Both of which are discussed in detail later in this book.

[33] This discussion cannot encompass the detail of derivatives products: the reader is referred to Part XI of this book and A.S. Hudson, *The Law on Financial Derivatives*, 5th edn (London: Sweet & Maxwell, 2012).

[34] On which see the local authority swaps cases considered exhaustively by the authors in Birks and Rose, (eds), *Lessons from the Swaps Litigation* (Mansfield Press, 2000).

of securitisation was the collapse of Northern Rock, Bear Stearns, Lehman Brothers, and so on, in 2008. There are a number of specifically financial conceptions of risk which are considered next; thereafter, we have a discussion of the fact that, in truth, the whole of society is now predicated on risk, not just the financial system.

Financial conceptions of risk

In finance theory, there are two key senses in which risk is important. First, the risks associated with any particular financial product will be priced into that product when assessing how much is required from the buyer of that product. That type of risk is considered in the sections to follow. Secondly, risk management is a key function within modern financial institutions: principally, risk management identifies the risks associated with the institution's business generally, with its exposure to particular markets, and with its exposure to particular customers and counterparties. Risk management is a mathematical methodology for modelling and confronting risks and also a strategy for identifying risk both within and without financial markets. That process underpins the categories of risk to be considered next.

1–52

The "Risk-Return" calculation

Key to any discussion of risk in financial markets is the measurement of risk against return. Given that all investment and all banking business involves a greater or a lesser level of risk, a financial institution has to decide what level of profit (or, "return") it requires for that business to be worthwhile. All institutions will have a view as to the return which it requires on any type of business. Within any market, though, dealing with a counterparty that is a poor credit risk will only be worthwhile if the return is sufficiently high to make that worthwhile; whereas dealing with a counterparty that is a good credit risk will require a lower profit to make that business worthwhile. Furthermore, a good credit risk will find it easy to acquire financial services and therefore there is another reason why financial institutions need to offer a good price (and so earn a lower profit) when dealing with such a person because a good credit risk will need to be encouraged to transact with a bank.[35] For example, the so-called Capital Asset Pricing Model developed in the 1960s,[36] which measures the perceived risk of an investment against its expected return (or, profit), has long been a feature of financial activity by measuring the expected profit to be earned on a transaction against the level of risk which is associated with dealing with a given client in a given market: the level of profit will need to be acceptable for a client of that type. This model is simply a pricing of market value to risk and volatility: in the following sections

1–53

---

[35] See, Brealey, Myers and Allen, *Corporate Finance* (McGraw-Hill, 2006), p.188 et seq.
[36] Brealey, Corporate Finance, p.188. See, W. Sharpe, "Capital Asset Prices: A Theory of Market Equilibrium under Conditions of Risk", (1964) Journal of Finance Col.19, p.425; J. Lintner, "The Valuation of Risk Assets and the Selection of Risky Investments in Stock Portfolios and Capital Budgets" (1965) *Review of Economics and Statistics*, vol.47, p.13.

we will consider specific forms of risk which are of particular importance to lawyers when dealing with financial transactions.

C.   Species of risk

(1)   Systemic risk

1–54   Systemic risk is the risk that if one sufficiently large market participant, or a few market participants, were to go into insolvency then that would have the effect of putting sufficient pressure on other market participants to whom the insolvent party owed money that those other market participants would similarly go into insolvency, with a further effect on yet more market participants with whom that second tier of insolvent entities had dealings. Systemic risk, then, is a fear of a domino effect whereby one or two people's insolvency leads to the insolvency of others with the result that the entire market ceases to function. The term "systemic risk" is defined in the Financial Services and Markets Act 2000 to mean "a risk to the stability of the UK financial system as a whole or of a significant part of that system".[37] This focus on the entire financial system is a result of the financial crisis: before then, the existence such a risk was simply not taken sufficiently seriously to merit its inclusion in the statutory framework for financial regulation.[38] During the global banking crisis of 2008 there was a concern that the collapse of large institutions like Bear Stearns and Lehman Bros in the USA, and the near collapse of many others, would have caused so many defaults on so many transactions with so many other institutions, that the pressure of (for example) Lehman Brothers' inability to meet its obligations would have driven other institutions into default and then into insolvency. Like ripples on a pond, the fear was that one pebble dropped into the pond would cause more and more turbulence. In the event, in relation to Bear Stearns, the US government oversaw a buy-out of Bear Stearns by JP Morgan for a rock-bottom price, and latterly buy-outs of Merrill Lynch, Washington Mutual, Wachovia and other large banks. The bankruptcy of Lehman Bros would have caused systemic failure but for a series of extraordinary weekend meetings of that bank's counterparties in New York to set off the outstanding transactions owed between them and Lehman Bros on their derivatives and other businesses, to auction off a number of the outstanding assets of that bank, and (lest we forget) unprecedented levels of government support around the world for failing banks running into trillions of dollars, pounds and euros.

1–55   In the USA, the administration of President George W Bush (under the leadership of Treasury Secretary Hank Paulson) introduced legislation which permitted it to spend nearly US$ 1 trillion by way of the Troubled Asset Relief Program ("TARP") so as to make loans to financial institutions and to buy up "toxic assets" from financial institutions so that those institutions could rebuild their balance sheets and thus stave off the collapse of the entire financial system. The

---

[37] Financial Services and Markets Act 2000, s.9C(5).
[38] See para.8–34 on the new Financial Policy Committee within the Bank of England which is tasked with the analysis of systemic threats to financial stability.

mismanagement of the manner in which those funds were distributed has been the subject of a startling book by Neil Barofsky, who was appointed as the "Special Investigator General in Charge of Oversight of TARP".[39] In the meantime, the UK government committed many billions of pounds by means of quantitative easing and recapitalising its banks.[40] This also led to the enactment of the Banking Act 2009 to create a mechanism for failing banks to be nationalised or sold off to private sector purchasers in the future. The direct impact on the global economy was severe: as is discussed in detail in Chapter 45.

Systemic risk was previously considered by some people to be a form of "bogey man" used to frighten financiers but which did not really exist. The financial crisis of 2008 proved that the risk of systemic collapse was real. Of course, we had always known that if we had looked back to 1720 in London, 1895 in New York, 1929 in New York, 1987 in New York, 1991 in Japan and in Sweden, in the 1990's with the "dot.com" crash, in 1998 in Russia (with effects elsewhere in the world) and in the USA with the failure of Long-Term Capital Markets, and so on. One of the key features of financial markets is their inability to remember crashes from previous generations. The memory of markets which seek to make short-term profits is necessarily always short. The two creatures with the shortest memories in our world are goldfish and banks' traders. The spectre of systemic risk is always with us because a market with a short-term perspective on earning profit is resistant either to external regulation or to effective self-regulation which could prevent a repetition of those market failures.

1–56

Systemic risk is the greatest risk which financial markets face. It is the risk that the entire financial system might cease to function. It was systemic risk which caused a number of different trade associations and financial market associations to create the standard form contracts (described in Chapter 19) which govern most business in financial derivatives, foreign exchange, repo, stock lending and the other markets which are considered in *Section Two: Specific Financial Techniques* of this book. It is fear of systemic risk which ought to inform the practice of financial regulation, as well as the process of creating rules to cater for financial regulation. When the next boom comes, we must not forget the crash of 2008. That crisis is discussed in Chapter 31 of this book. For in the run-up to that crash of 2008, the majority view of the investing herd was that a crash would not come and that markets would continue to rise forever.

1–57

(2) Market risk

Market risk is the risk that a market will fail, or that the market will move so significantly that a seemingly profitable transaction will be switched into a loss-bearing transaction. Market risk, as is discussed in Chapter 41, may simply constitute a short-term disruption which is sufficiently serious, and which takes place on a single day on which payment is to be made according to the disrupted market price, so that the price quoted no longer reflects the parties' original contractual intentions. Alternatively, the market disruption may be a continuing,

1–58

---

[39] N. Barofsky, *Bailout* (New York: Free Press, 2012).
[40] *Financial Times*, October 7, 2008.

serious cessation of normal trading on a market. Contracts will need to identify what would constitute a market disruption event so that the disrupted price can be adjusted or ignored, as appropriate; or else the parties will have to rely on the general law concept of frustration so as to set the contract aside.[41] There were frequent market disruptions during 2007–09: often many in one day on some markets.

(3)   Counterparty credit risk

1–59   The risk that the other party to a transaction will fail to perform is one of the key risks in financial transactions. Counterparty risk can take a number of forms. First, it could be the risk that the counterparty goes into insolvency, meaning that it is generally unable to pay its debts as they become due. Secondly, it could be the risk that the counterparty is solvent but nevertheless refuses to pay. Thirdly, it could be that the counterparty is unable to perform because its powers to act do not permit it to enter into the transaction into which it has purported to enter. Thus, when dealing with any party, these risks have to be measured—and so the credit departments of any financial institution will have to reach a decision on the credit risk that is associated with each counterparty, and thus will decide the price that is required to make that business worthwhile, as was discussed above in relation to the risk-return equation. Failure of counterparties was a feature of the financial crisis of 2007–09 with the bankruptcy, nationalisation and enforced takeover of a number of very large financial institutions.

(4)   Collateral and credit support risk

1–60   When deciding on the necessary return to be earned from dealing with a particular counterparty, the credit department of a bank will need to decide what form of credit support is required—whether a guarantee or whatever—before that transaction is put in place. Taking security in this context is discussed in detail in Chapter 22. One of the key means of taking security in relation to complex financial products like derivatives is collateralisation—a process which itself bears a risk that the property posted as security will decrease in value or that the agreement to pay under a collateral agreement is not performed. Therefore, using financial structures like collateral or even hedging transactions to take security against other financial instruments creates new risk while seeking to provide protection against risk.[42]

(5)   Insolvency risk

1–61   The most acute form of counterparty risk is insolvency risk. The legal risks are that the insolvent person will not be able to account for any of its obligations once the insolvency is worked through. In particular, for counterparties which have many, many transactions with that insolvent person, the risk is that it will have to make payment to the insolvent person and yet that it will receive nothing in

---

[41] See para.19–76.
[42] See para.42–01 for an outline of these techniques.

return, not even the right to set off payables against receivables when calculating what is owed. This issue is discussed in detail in Chapter 22.[43] Insolvency law differs from jurisdiction to jurisdiction, which creates a further tier of risk as to the system of rules which will govern the insolvency, and whether or not any credit support agreement will be valid under that system of law.

(6)   Payment risk

Payment risk is the risk that payment will not be made. In relation to complex derivatives transactions where each party owes payments one to another (one at a fixed rate and the other at a floating rate), it is usual to provide that such payments will be set off against one another.

1–62

(7)   Documentation risk

Documentation refers to the risk either that the documentation is ineffective, or that no documentation has been put in place. Documentation may be ineffective if it does not cover a risk which latterly transpires, or if it is ambiguous about such a problem, or if the transaction is void under contract law in any of the ways discussed in Chs 18 and 20. The lack of documentation has been a very real problem in the over-the-counter derivatives markets, particularly in high volume business between large financial institutions or in transactions involving unregulated entities, either because the transactions have expired before documentation could be put in place or because the parties cannot agree to a set of terms which will govern their ongoing transactions.

1–63

(8)   Personnel risk

Personnel risk refers to the risk of malfeasance by a single employee (or a group of employees) or to some error by a single employee of a participant in financial transactions. There has been a particular problem in some high profile bank failures with "rogue traders" creating deals which they had no authority to create, such as Nick Leeson at Barings in 1994, Jerome Kerviel at Societe Generale in 2007, and Kweku Adoboli at UBS in 2012. The need to ensure the authority of the people who are transacting (so as to bind their employers) is as significant at the capacity of the entity which they purport to represent.

1–64

(9)   Regulatory risk

Regulatory risk is considered in detail in Part III of this book. It refers to the risk that a regulator may take an approach which the parties consider unfortunate to their transaction. It would also refer to the situation in which regulatory rules change. The generation of high-level regulatory principles should mean that regulated entities have an understanding in the longer term of their general obligations, than in the days when regulatory rules were made up almost

1–65

---

[43] See para.22- 91.

exclusively of detailed rules which were subject to complete re-writing periodically. Another form of regulatory risk, which appeared in relation to Northern Rock, is that the regulator may fail to regulate either the market or troubled market participants properly with the effect that systemic risks are created.

(10)　Tax risk

1–66　Complex financial derivatives as well as simple transactions are only profitable if they are taxed in ways which the parties anticipate. A change in the tax treatment of any structure—whether by a change in a statute, or in case law, or even in the practices of HM Revenue and Customs—can therefore have a great impact on the profitability or viability of financial transactions.

(11)　Cross-default risk

1–67　The contracts between institutions and their clients, or between institutions and other institutions, create a very tangled web of obligations. If you imagine each individual contract between two banks as being a single thread in a web, then the nexus which constitutes all of the contracts for all of the thousands and thousands of contracts between them create remarkably dense webs. If there is a breach under one contract, there is a risk that there will be a default under some or all of those thousands of transactions. So, in putting documentation in place, the parties are well advised to ensure that if one strand in the web snaps—that is, if there is one default under one contract—that should trigger a termination of all of the other contracts in the web if the counterparty has become a bad credit risk as a result of that first breach. This is known as "cross default": breach under one contract triggers the right in the non-defaulting party to terminate all of the other transactions between those parties. It is also possible to have a contract between X and Y triggered by a cross default under a contract which X has with Z. Cross-default is therefore a means of anticipating a future problem which X may have, and to allow the non-defaulting party to untangle itself from its web with X.

D.　Risk in legal theory

Social risk

1–68　The meaning that is applied to "risk" in the newer sociology is often positive.[44] It is said that risk is bound up with choice: wherever there is risk, there is also a decision to be made which may lead to positive or negative outcomes.[45] We have more life choices than ever before: people are living longer, the average health and education of the population at the start of the 21st century is better than at the start of the 20th, and many members of society (principally women) have greater

---

[44] U. Beck, "The Cosmopolitan Society" in *Democracy without enemies* (Polity, 1995).
[45] U. Beck, "The reinvention of politics" in Beck, Giddens and Lash (eds), *Reflexive Modernization* (Polity, 1994), p.1.

opportunity to select their own life patterns than before. Thus opportunity and choice are in greater abundance than before. The bulk of our most significant life choices are built on investment: pensions, the home, education, healthcare. All involve more investment than ever before by individuals, financial service providers or government. This new "risk society"[46] is said by other people to have negative side effects in that the increase in choice reduces the level of security and predictability for our citizens and that a focus on individual choice reduces social cohesion by promoting an atomisation of social relations.[47]

On this model, risk is omnipresent in modern life. With the enhanced focus on financial services, on efficiency, and on value for money in the modern age, the pressure to organise one's financial affairs is greater than ever. We are conscious of the money which we have and which we do not have. A more widely-travelled population with access to television, newspaper and the internet can know much more about the lives and life chances of others than was possible for previous generations. Expectations are therefore higher; and potential for feelings of inadequacy are also more acute. With the expansion of choice and existential dilemma comes the shrinking of the welfare state.[48] The structures which once would have sheltered the citizen against the hazards of life are receding. Instead, we must all take responsibility for our old age, for the risk of redundancy, and for those same risks awaiting our children. The language transmutes from hazard (tidal waves, epidemic illness, external dangers[49]) into risk—something which is bound up now with need for us to make choices between a variety of options rather than simply to shelter ourselves against acts of god. Risk is something which arises in this form as "manufactured risk"[50] because we are responsible for the choices we make: we take the risk that their outcomes are not as desirable as other potential outcomes, that our chosen pension fails to perform, that we have not insured against the loss we have suffered. The harm caused to the world economy by the financial crisis of 2008 is the ultimate form of manufactured risk: without the financial system in its current form, there would not have been the harm caused to the real economies of the world that were otherwise created.

1–69

The new risk society

Investment is singularly important in the public life of the UK and in the private lives of ordinary citizens. The welfare state is rolling back and being replaced by reliance on investment to provide personal welfare services, infrastructural public investment and general economic growth. All of this social change necessarily carries with it greater manufactured risk than hitherto. It is in this context that risk becomes an important element of all forms of shared, communal investment. Risk

1–70

---

[46] U. Beck, *The Risk Society* (Sage, 1992) who views it positively; except, see, U. Beck and E. Beck-Gernsheim, *Individualization* (Sage, 2002).

[47] Z. Bauman, *Liquid modernity* (Polity, 2001). See, also Z. Bauman, *Community* (Polity, 2000); Z. Bauman, *Does ethics have a chance in a world of consumers?* (Harvard University Press, 2008). On which, see, A.S. Hudson, "The unbearable lightness of property" in A.S. Hudson (ed.), *New Perspectives on Restitution, Obligations and Property Law* (Cavendish, 2004), p.1.

[48] A. Giddens, *Modernity and Self-Identity* (Polity Press, 1991).

[49] Or "external risk" as Giddens calls it: A. Giddens, "Risk and Responsibility" [1999] 62 M.L.R. 1.

[50] A. Giddens, "Risk and Responsibility" [1999] 62 M.L.R. 1.

is expressed differently but is present in this discussion at every level. There is risk not only in financial-speculative investment but also in the ordinary decisions of citizens in their everyday lives in their pensions, in their homes and in providing for their families' futures—whether through mainstream financial services or through self-help groups. Risk-taking and speculation is required of ordinary citizens seeking to protect themselves against their old age every bit as much as in the financial derivatives markets. The erosion of the protective role of the welfare state makes speculative investors of us all because we are all required to take out private pensions which invest in speculative markets, and because the activities of speculative markets feed into the "real economy" of food prices, mortgage interest rates and so on. The construction of hospitals and other types of public sector infrastructure are predicated more and more on Private Finance Initiatives and on Public-Private Partnerships.[51] Thus public sector construction projects are built on commercial financing more than was ever the case in the past when governments simply borrowed money or raised taxes. This is an indication of the financialisation of our social and public life, as is considered in the next section.

Financialisation and risk

1–71   There is a different aspect to financial conceptions of risk from the financial risks which are accommodated in contracts and the social risk considered above: that is the creeping process of financialisation. Modern society is drifting into the use of financial instruments more than ever it did before. This means that a large amount of capital which might previously have been devoted to investment in manufacturing and so on, is now invested in financial markets seeking quick financial profit. Concomitantly, it is said, that capital and income are being drained from the "real economy"—manufacturing activity, individuals' income, and so on—and instead are being ploughed into the financial sector. So, in the words of Thomas Palley:

> "'Financialisation' is the process whereby financial markets, financial institutions, and financial elites gain greater influence over economic policy and economic outcomes. Financialisation transforms the functioning of economic systems at both the macro and micro levels. Its principal impacts are to (1) elevate the significance of the financial sector relative to the real sector, (2) transfer income from the real sector to the financial sector, and (3) increase income inequality and contribute to wage stagnation. Additionally, there are reasons to believe that financialisation may put the economy at risk of debt deflation and prolonged recession. Financialisation operates through three different conduits: changes in the structure and operation of financial markets, changes in the behaviour of non-financial corporations, and changes in economic policy."[52]

At the time of writing, the risks posed by failure in the financial sector are self-evident: a drying up of liquidity, rising interest rates leading to increased numbers of house repossessions and so on. What is also evident is the persistence of economic recessions in the Western economies caused by the drying up of

---

[51] On which, see, A.S. Hudson, *The Law on Investment Entities*, p.320 et seq.
[52] T. Palley, "Financialisation: what it is and why it matters", *The Levy Economics Institute for Democratic and Open Societies*.

liquidity (which means there is less capital available to fuel growth) and the rising price of commodities such as oil, which increases costs. It seems that financial speculation is adding to the pressure in commodities and other markets which are having real effects in the "real economy" by causing economic growth to slow. It is also having the effect that to prevent inflation in the economy generally, rising commodity prices and interest costs have to be balanced out by controlling wage rises (particularly in the public sector). The dictates of the financial sector are thus driving economic policy. The question to be considered in this book is how growing financialisation should affect the law of finance: that is, should the substantive law increase its control of commercial, financial transactions—perhaps by increasing contract law's control of unfair contract terms and the breadth of "unconscionable" transactions—and to what extent there should be a change in financial regulation. But let us consider how financialisation might be said to include the use of the financial instruments which are considered in this book.

Once upon a time, seeking to protect oneself against the world might have involved building a castle, or buying a baseball bat to keep behind the bedroom door, or taking out insurance. Today it is more common for large corporations to use financial instruments to protect themselves. Thus, financial derivatives (discussed in Part XI of this book) are used to "hedge" risks. Hedging involves identifying the risk that you face—for example, a cost if interest rates rise—and then acquiring a derivative contract which is expected to make a profit if interest rates do rise, so that the gain on the derivative instrument will offset the loss on interest rate movements. The trouble with the use of financial instruments to absorb spare capital in the economy and with the use of financial instruments to manage risks, is that those financial instruments themselves create brand new risks. If the hedging instrument is in a market which moves unexpectedly, this may itself cause the investor a large loss which could be even worse than the original risk which the investor was seeking to avoid by using the hedge.   **1–72**

This was one of the lessons from the financial crisis of 2007–09.[53] Financial instruments such as asset securitisations and credit default swaps were intended to generate short-term capital for their originators (in the case of securitisations[54]) or to provide protection against default on bonds (in the case of credit default swaps[55]). In truth they created enormous problems for the entire, global financial system. Securitisations which were based on loans made to bad credit risks turned into enormous losses; and credit default swaps which obliged banks to make huge payments on the reduction in the credit worth of the issuers of commercial paper to speculators who had bet on such a deterioration. These financial instruments which were intended to introduce more liquidity to the financial system and to provide protection against pressures in that same system, in fact caused illiquidity and the effective insolvency of some long-established financial institutions in the UK, in the US, and beyond.[56]   **1–73**

---

[53] See, the discussion in Ch.12 of the credit crunch and its impact on debates about financial regulation.

[54] See para.44–01.

[55] See para.40–49.

[56] See para.31–01 for a discussion of the effects of the credit crunch.

1-74   The principal lesson to take from the process of financialisation is that the financial system has become even more powerful than it was before because it has become so much larger than it was before and because its techniques are fulfilling more functions than ever before. The result is that any risks contained in the financial system have become amplified as the reach of the financial system has increased. In relation to the credit crunch, what began as some misguided policies in mortgage lending in the US, which were in turn based on a view in high-powered trading rooms that securitisations were an activity which could only make profit, reached out in the "real economy" such that trading companies and ordinary people could not find any money to borrow to expand their businesses or to buy homes. The key lesson for any finance lawyer is that any new financial solution to risk management problems will create new risks. Finance is built on risk. The risks that are realised are simple enough: if you lend to people who cannot pay, you will lose money in the long run; if your contracts do not provide an exit strategy in the event that the worst case scenario comes to pass (e.g. that there is no liquidity in the financial system, or a doubling in the price of oil, or war, or terrorism) then that worst case scenario will eventually come to pass and you will suffer enormous losses. When markets are in profit, no-one wants to listen to the voices of doom like this. But the role of the transactional lawyer is, in part at least, to make sure that if the worst does happen, then her clients are insulated against it as far as possible. Some might say that the role of the lawyer is to act as the adult in the excitable play of financial markets.

Risk allocation in law

1-75   There is a large literature on risk allocation in commercial law. The basic principle is based on the idea that when a contract is created, both parties undertake risks in relation to one another. Each takes the risk that the other will not perform its obligations properly. Thus, in a contract for the sale of a car, the buyer takes a risk as to the quality of the car and as to its proper delivery, whereas the seller takes a risk as to the buyer's ability to pay. Therefore, this contract can be thought of as a series of allocations of risk between seller and buyer as to when and how payment will be made, as to who takes the risk of the car being of insufficient quality, and so forth.[57]

Law as a risk in itself

1-76   When lawyers give advice in financial transactions, I would suggest, they are acting as risk managers. A good legal advisor recognises that in relation to many novel financial transactions there will be legal issues raised about which it is not possible to opine with complete certainty: therefore, there is necessarily a risk that that legal issue will cause loss or hardship for the client. This book is a compilation of some of the key legal issues in the key financial products, ranging from the risk of unenforceability of transactions to potential criminal liability to

---

[57] Dr Benjamin conceives of financial law as being primarily concerned with the allocation of risk between contracting parties: J. Benjamin, *Financial Law* (OUP, 2007). That is not how the law of finance will be presented in this book, fascinating as Dr Benjamin's model undoubtedly is.

fiduciary liability, and so on. For example, when interest rate swaps were first sold by banks to local authorities in the UK in the late 1980s and early 1990s, it was not known whether or not those contracts were within the powers of local authorities. The banks' legal advisors took the view, on an interpretation of the appropriate legislation, that those contracts should be considered to be within the powers of local authorities. The House of Lords, when asked whether or not interest rate swaps were within the powers of local authorities, took the view that interest rate swaps entered into with local authorities in the UK were void *ab initio* because they were beyond the authorities' powers. Thus, the banks' legal advisors were acting as risk managers: the risk was that the courts would interpret the appropriate law in a way that was contrary to their clients' interests. That risk ultimately worked against the banks and their lawyers. Consequently, the law itself was a risk.

In common law legal systems there is a risk that the courts will change the direction or interpretation of common law rules. In all legal systems there is a risk that the courts will take unexpected interpretations of statutes. However, in common law systems the majority of the law is established by case law and therefore it is susceptible to change either by the courts changing those laws in line with the doctrine of precedent or alternatively by virtue of an old rule simply failing to be enforced. It is difficult for busy practitioners to know when these laws have been altered. It is also difficult to know how those laws will apply to financial instruments, either because no decision has been made specifically relating to financial instruments or because the law in another factual context has changed or taken a new direction (which in turn may either be difficult to apply to the finance context or which may escape the notice of busy transactional lawyers). The purpose of this book is to attempt to bridge that knowledge gap.   1–77

What is important to note, however, is that common law systems are capable of more subtle change than changes taking effect by statute or by well-advertised change to regulatory principles. This should not be taken to mean that common law systems are in any way more dangerous; rather, they are capable of dealing more flexibly with novel contexts than civil code systems. Advisors in a common law system have as part of their knowledge base an understanding as to how those rules may adapt and how to find the latest sources. They need a cultural understanding as to how those rules should be interpreted and adapted. Increasingly, the community of legal advisors is becoming more adept at preparing the judicial, practitioner and academic community for the need for change in the application of legal principle.   1–78

Specific commercial activities like insurance business and sale of goods necessarily involve risk but the law has not developed any particular theory of risk itself in that context.[58] It is only in the context of financial regulation that notions of risk have been considered in detail—for example, in prospectus regulation for issues of securities, and in capital adequacy regulation in relation to banking business, a set of risks have been identified and a legislative and   1–79

---

[58] See, for example Sale of Goods Act 1979 ss.20, 32, 33; Goode, *Commercial Law*, 2nd edn (Harmondsworth: Penguin, 1995), p.248 et seq.

regulatory framework identified to cater for them.[59] Thus the Financial Services and Markets Act 2000 focuses on the need for the regulatory authorities to take account of particular forms of financial risk.

---

[59] See para.38–01 et seq.

CHAPTER 2

THE LEGAL NATURE OF MONEY AND FINANCIAL INSTRUMENTS

CORE PRINCIPLES

Money has transformed from being only notes and coins into being an amount of value ascribed to an intangible form of bank account held in banks' electronic records and payment systems. The uses of money have transformed over the centuries, although they still revolve around the three principal uses which were identified in Aristotle's *Politics*: namely, as a means of exchange (i.e. to pay for things), as a measure of value (i.e. to provide a price and a market value for things), and as a store of value (i.e. as a means of saving and building capital).

There have of course been many changes in the nature of money since Aristotle's time. The uses of money in the modern financial system revolve around the use of money as a means of exchange and foreign exchange; money as a thing in itself which can be transferred in property law, but in a complex way in its electronic form; money less as a store of value in modern markets given the predilection for turning money to account as opposed to hoarding it in financial transactions; and money as legal tender in the English legal system.

Money as a measure of value should be understood in different ways in its modern sense. Money is a measure of value through its use as expressing value in bank records; through marking-to-market models for valuing financial instruments; through measurement of loss so as to establish entitlement to remedies; and through fluctuations in foreign exchange. Money is also a source of status in modern society by which citizens perceive wealth as constituting existential worth, in the manner understood by Simmel and Bauman.

[39]

1. INTRODUCTION

2–01   This chapter is concerned with the legal nature of money, outlining the historical development of money and finance, and of financial instruments generally. This is a book about finance and not a book solely about money; but to understand the roots of the law of finance it is important to understand the history of the use of money and to understand how money is used now. As well as notes and coins, the modern use of money conceives of money in the form of the value held in electronic bank accounts or of the value exchanged through electronic payment systems. This latter sort of money is now dematerialised, in that it generally has no physical form. This is true of financial instruments, bank accounts and most of uses of "money" by ordinary citizens. Even notes and coins are now a very stylised physical form of money. Nevertheless, a lot of the cases and the legislation dealing with money have tended to conceive of it as being tangible. It is a very powerful metaphor in the language of finance to talk of "money passing", money being "held", and "money had and received". With this understanding of the development of money and finance we can establish the foundations on which we can build an understanding of how modern banking law operates, and how litigation relating to the recovery of money or the enforcement of money judgments conceives of this money. So, we shall come to the law in time. As with the general approach of this book, we are concerned to establish the core principles of law and the core principles of financial practice first.[1]

2. WHAT IS MONEY?

A. The classical economists' categories of money

2–02   Aristotle had three principal understandings of money, which remain a useful starting point today[2]: on this model, money can be either a means of exchange; a measure of value; or a store of value. That money is a means of exchange accepts that money has replaced barter and thus operates as a means of making payment for goods and services. If I want to buy bread, I can exchange an appropriate amount of money for an appropriate amount of bread: I do not need to barter a chicken in place of that bread. The money is exchanged for the bread. That money is a measure of value means that money is a means of expressing the value of objects. If I want to express the market value of my house or of shares in X Plc, then I will express the value of that property in terms of the amount of money which would be needed to buy it. That money is a store of value means that money itself can be saved and so can constitute a hoard of value in itself. If I want to store value for the future I could hoard tinned food, or gold, or I could "save" money by storing it in cash under my mattress or in electronic form in a bank

---

[1] The most celebrated book on the legal nature of money is that by F.A. Mann, *The Legal Aspect of Money*, 5th edn (OUP, 1992), which has been published in a new edition by C. Proctor, *Mann on the Legal Aspect of Money*, 6th edn (OUP, 2005).

[2] These three categories emerge from the discussion in Aristotle, *Politics*, Book 1, Ch.9.

account. This core distinction between the basic types of money remains useful even today, and still forms the starting-point for most economic theories of money.

Karl Marx, in the first volume of his excellent handbook on capitalism, *Das Kapital* ("*Capital*"),[3] considered money to be an independent form of capital, with the result that capitalist society became concerned with the accumulation of money, instead of seeing money solely in Aristotle's terms. The opening sections of Capital deal with the exchange value of money and later with its use to hoard money into capital. In the *Grundrisse*[4] this theory of money was understood as being a theory of domination and of exploitation whereby the bourgeoisie and the moneyed classes were able to exert control over the proletariat by locking the proletariat into a perpetual quest for money by means of the employment contract.[5] Marx referred to this as being "the magic of money". As a result of it, he wrote that "men are henceforth related to one another in their social process of production in a purely atomistic way" and that:

> "Since money does not reveal what has been transformed into it, everything, commodity or not, is convertible into money. Everything becomes saleable and purchasable. Circulation becomes the great social retort into which everything is thrown, to come out again as money crystal. Nothing is immune from this alchemy..."[6]

2–03

Money therefore acquires a special role and purpose in capitalist societies. Whereas skilled labour had once had its own value which was linked to the quality of the goods that were produced, the effect of capitalism (and the employment laws which it created) was to dismantle the link between the artisan's skill and the profit from his production, and instead replaced it with a right to a wage but nothing more.[7] Money comes to replace all the previous complex relationships. It is not simply a means of measurement and exchange, but it is the engine of social and political relations.

Similarly, George Simmel in his *Philosophy of Money*[8] focused on the psychological process by which an entire society comes to see money as its main expression of value and of success, as opposed to being merely a means to acquire goods and services with its exchange value. The acquisition of money has itself become a key objective in our society.[9] This is similar to the notion of financialisation which we considered in Chapter 1[10]: in that a large amount of the

2–04

---

[3] K. Marx, *Capital* (Vol.1, 1867).

[4] K. Marx, *Grundrisse* (1858).

[5] The employment contract relationship has this effect, it is said, because workers become subjugated to their masters' money and their rights are controlled by employment law in a situation in which they have little bargaining power; whereas in an earlier age, skilled workers had been able to control the application of their labour and were directly related to the effects of their work. See, S. Clarke, "Money" in W. Outhwaite and T. Bottomore (eds), *Twentieth Century Social Thought* (Blackwell, 1993).

[6] K. Marx, *Capital* (Vol.1, 1867).

[7] Anyone who doubts the effect on a person's commitment to their work if they have no connection to the quality of their output should read Scott Adams's "Dilbert" cartoons, or ring a UK call centre.

[8] G. Simmel, *The Philosophy of Money* (1907).

[9] Z. Bauman, *Liquid Modernity* (2002).

[10] See para.1–71.

capital in society is being diverted into financial instruments and away from the "real" economy, and financial instruments are being used more and more as a means of dealing with risk. The consequence of this process of financialisation is that the financial system is becoming ever more powerful, much in the way that Simmel considered ordinary cash money to do at the beginning of the 20th century.

The novelist Charles Dickens had a clear idea of the moral and social place of money in society even in the 19th century. In *Dombey and Son* the very young Paul Dombey has the following conversation with his aloof, successful and very rich father Mr Dombey some time after the unhappy death of his mother:

> "'Papa! what's money?'
>
> 'What is money, Paul,' he answered. 'Money?'
>
> Mr Dombey was in a difficulty. He would have liked to give him some explanation involving the terms circulating-medium, currency, depreciation of the currency, paper, bullion, rates of exchange, value of precious metals in the market, and so forth; but looking down at the little chair [where his son was sitting], and seeing what a long way down it was, he answered: 'Gold, and silver, and copper. Guineas, shillings, half-pence. You know what they are?'
>
> 'Oh yes, I know what they are,' said Paul. 'I don't mean that, Papa. I mean, what's money after all.'
>
> 'What is money after all!' said Mr Dombey, backing his chair a little, that he might the better gaze in sheer amazement at the presumptuous atom that propounded such an inquiry.
>
> 'I mean, Papa, what can it do?' returned Paul, folding his arms (they were hardly long enough to fold), and looking at the fire, and up at him, and at the fire, and up at him again.
>
> 'Money, Paul, can do anything.'
>
> 'Anything, Papa?'
>
> 'Yes. Anything—almost,' said Mr Dombey.
>
> 'Why didn't money save me my mama?' returned the child. 'It isn't cruel, is it?'
>
> 'Cruel!' said Mr Dombey, settling his neckcloth, and seeming to resent the idea. 'No. A good thing can't be cruel.'
>
> 'If it's a good thing, and can do anything,' said the little fellow, thoughtfully, as he looked back at the fire, 'I wonder why it didn't save me my mama.'"

The capitalist economies exist in a universe which worships and reveres money. The acquisition of money is the entire purpose of some people's lives, the need to earn money takes up most people's lives. It is a measurement of happiness and of security, as well as a measure of value, a store of value and a mere means of exchange. But money, as young Paul Dombey noticed, is not all-powerful. It may be a means to an end, but it cannot be an end in itself. It is instead a wherewithal to act.

2–05 The world that Simmel described was very different from that which Aristotle described: in Aristotle's *Politics* he considered that a man might be both wealthy and yet unable to acquire food. Aristotle was concerned with "household management" and commerce,[11] and saw money as emerging from these processes. Aristotle did not see money becoming an end in itself as Simmel and our modern societies have come to understand money as being the means of acquiring everything from goods and services to a path to earthly paradise.

---

[11] Where "natural wealth" would involve growing and providing food; whereas "commerce" is concerned with the production of goods for the express purpose of selling them for money: Aristotle, *Politics*, Book 1, Ch.9.

J.M. Keynes, in his *Treatise on Money*,[12] stressed the importance of "money-of-account" over money being used solely as a means of exchange. In relation specifically to the theory of money in the 1920's and 1930's Keynes came to acknowledge that it was the banking system which controlled the availability of money in the system. This control of liquidity by banks was self-evident in 2008 during the global financial crisis discussed in Chapter 31. The Keynesian model of money sees the role of the central bank as being to equalise investment with savings by control of the money supply. However, the State or the central bank cannot on this model seek to control the money supply alone because the participation of banks in making that money available to the broader economy is pivotal, unless the State was to intervene as a lender directly into the economy rather than simply to banks through sales of government bonds. In the ordinary case of affairs, therefore, it is the lending policies of banks which stabilise the real economy. "Money", however, is in the form of credit and not simply in the form of notes and coins. This theory of money is another important plank in the modern understanding of money. The following sections move into ways in which money is used in modern financial practice.

2–06

B. Other conceptions of money

I would add some categories to Aristotle's analysis, partly by amendment of the existing categories and by adding some new ones. The reason for adding these categories is to make plain some of the ways in which we shall need to think about money for the purposes of this book: to think of money as lawyers do.

2–07

A means of exchange

Control of the supply of money in the economy is generally believed to restrict inflation because if money is the means for acquiring goods and if there is little money in the system, then prices cannot rise far. As a means of exchange, money replaced the need to barter precious metals for spices, and instead created a capitalist system in which all goods and services had a market value which could be satisfied by payment of money. As a means of controlling the key indicators in the economy by means of the money supply, money has acquired a significance which its mere function as a shorthand for the bartering process could never have foreseen.

2–08

A thing in itself—an item of property

Money is in itself property, in whatever form it may take: either as a chattel or in the form of a chose in action expressed by a bank account. That money can be owned, transferred or otherwise turned to account is a very important facet of its nature for lawyers. The nature of money as property is considered in Chapter 21.

2–09

---

[12] J.M. Keynes, *A Treatise on Money* (London, 1930).

A measure of value: records in an account

2–10   When financial transactions are created, they are typically priced in terms of a cash value, the parties have to make cash payments to one another on the happening of contractually specified events, and so on. The parties do not expect that notes and coins will be transferred between them, but rather that the payer's bank accounts will diminish in value by the amount of the payment and that the payee's bank accounts will increase in value by the same amount. We tend to use the shorthand expression that "money has passed between them", but more usually what has actually happened is an alteration in the value of these two bank accounts which are held as electronic "book entries". As is discussed in Chapter 29, bank accounts are debts owed by banks to their customers, and thus in transfers between bank accounts it could be said that "money" is moving between accounts or it could be said that the value attached to those accounts is altering: the payer's account decreases in value by the amount of the transfer and that the payee's account increases in value by the same amount. It is important for a lawyer to come to terms with this truth and with the metaphorical force of "money moving between accounts" because in property law it is usual to think of money as being a tangible item of property even when it is merely held in an electronic account: this issue is considered in Chapter 21.[13] These bank accounts are simply choses in action: that is, debts held by the bank to express the amount which is owed to customer (when the account is in credit) or to express a loan which is to be repaid by the customer (when the account is in debit, or "overdrawn"). Yet we tend to talk of them as being money. The law is caught up in this metaphor from a time when the courts were dealing solely with notes and coins. The parties to a transfer expect that there is "money" moving between accounts: that is, the parties' expectation is that property will be moving between them because that money, even though electronic in form, translates to the wherewithal to buy goods and services, and therefore it has tangible effects in their worlds.

A measure of value: transactions in-the-money; marking-to-market

2–11   Even the most complex financial transactions use this notion of money passing between accounts, even though what is happening in truth is merely an alteration in the value of those accounts. Money is used as a means of valuing the expected, future profitability of complex transactions. For example, in Chapter 40 we consider financial derivatives in detail and in that discussion we consider cash-settled share options in which the buyer is entitled to receive a cash payment if the market value of a share rises above the price set out in the option contract. If the market value of the share does rise in this way, the option is said to be "in-the-money". All of these valuations and payments use the idea of money as a means of valuation. The market value of the share is expressed in terms of money; the strike price which is identified in the option contract is expressed in

---

[13] See para.21–07.

terms of money; and the amount which is to be paid between the parties is expressed in an amount of money and actually paid by a transfer between bank accounts.

Similarly, when banks measure their own exposures (i.e. their expected profits and losses) across financial markets they do so by taking a monetary value of their obligations and entitlements, and then reaching a net figure: or more likely a series of net figures expressed in each of the currencies in which they have conducted their business. This process is known as "marking-to-market" in that the financial institution identifies the monetary value of its transactions by identifying the value of those transactions on the open market from time-to-time, even if the transaction has not yet terminated. What this enables that institution to do is to know how profitable its transactions are from time-to-time. This is a process which only works, of course, when there is a functioning market which makes the identification of a price possible.

A measure of value: measurement of loss and of remedy

As a means of measurement, of course, money plays a centrally important part in the lawyer's practice of identifying and calculating losses and remedies due under the general law and under some statutory provisions, as outlined particularly in Chapter 4. Therefore, money acts as a measuring stick even in relation to private law claims.

A measure of value: foreign exchange transactions

It should be observed that money in the form of sterling is only the unit of account in the United Kingdom. If one crosses the Channel to France, then sterling is a foreign currency. Thus, sterling is no longer a steady measurement of account in the form of an unmoving standard; rather, sterling becomes more or less valuable as its value moves in comparison with other currencies in other jurisdictions. Sterling is therefore a means of valuing property which is itself a moving indicator. Moreover, each currency has an interest rate attached to it. On the money markets each currency is valued according to the interest rate which attaches to it. So, the value of sterling itself is not only its "spot" price as against other currencies but also includes a recognition of the interest rate value which attaches to it, as is discussed in Chapter 36.[14] So, if an asset is worth £3 on Monday and still worth £3 on Tuesday, then that asset will actually be less valuable if the value of sterling fell by half first thing on Monday morning against the US dollar because that asset would only realise half the number of dollars on Tuesday that it would have done on Monday. Therefore, sterling as a means of value is both a measuring stick and also a measuring stick which itself has a fluctuating market value. This process of measuring value and risk exposure with a variable measure is an important part of collateralisation and taking security in financial markets, as discussed in Chapter 42.

2–12

2–13

2–14

---

[14] J.M. Keynes, *The General Theory of Employment, Interest, and Money* (1936), Ch.17.

A store of value: money as capital—an outmoded idea?

2–15   As Marx recognised, money is not just a means of creating a store so that you can buy food in the depths of winter; it is also a means of accruing power by means of accumulating large amounts of money so that it can be used as investment capital. It is less common for money to be used as capital exactly in the same fashion today: rather, if one has access to a large amount of money it is more usual to invest that money in an investment which will generate an income, and so what might have been "capital" in Marx's day actually becomes a cash flow in modern financial transactions. Instead of relying on having large amounts of cash on deposit, it is more common for ordinary people today to use credit cards or bank debt to make purchases, and large companies are more likely to invest their cash and instead use share or bond issues to raise cash when they need it. Consequently, "money" in the modern context of capital actually means book entries as opposed to cash stuffed in the mattress. And so a person may well express the total value of her assets as being worth an amount of money in the form of a balance sheet. However, those assets among the rich will typically not be held in the form of cash or even ordinary bank deposits: instead they will be held in the form of investment in securities, in land, and so on.

Money as status

2–16   It is clear that money operates as a symbol of status and of power in modern society, whether that is cash money in hand or access to finance (mainly credit card or hire purchase debt) which is used to acquire goods. The rich can acquire power, status, high quality services, expert advice, and protection from the thousand natural shocks that flesh is heir to. Therefore, while the economists tend to focus on the rational use of money for a variety of purposes, there is also a large range of irrational uses of money: we have all heard of people indulging in a little "retail therapy", by which they mean spending money (or increasing their credit card debts) for no better reason than to make themselves feel happy in the short-term. Indeed, advertising depends upon encouraging us to spend money on things which we had never previously thought we wanted, and many high street shops tempt us with cheaper and cheaper goods that we may never even use. Money therefore has a much more emotional role in our social life, as Simmel observed.

Electronic funds transfers: "electronic money"

2–17   Money "ain't what it used to be". Quite literally, money is not what it used to be. Where once "money" meant the coins made of precious metals in a man's purse, now money more usually means the amount that is recognised as being held in bank accounts on that bank's computer systems and which may be manipulated by the use of automated teller machines ("ATMs", or "cashpoints" in the UK), credit cards, debit cards, cheques, internet banking and so on. Money also means notes and coins, which are no longer intrinsically worth their face value. So, we have to be careful that when we talk of "money" sometimes we mean notes and coins, sometimes electronic money, sometimes a market value expressed in terms of money, and so on.

3. THE LEGAL NATURE OF MONEY

A. Introduction

It is always tempting to think that the way things are now is the way that they have always been. This has never been less true than in the case of cash money. The past is a different country: they do things differently there. It is fair to think of our financial system, with its electronic payment systems and internet bank accounts, as constituting a radical development in the practice of financial transactions. The electronic age has undoubtedly generated rapid and fundamental change to financial markets. However, much of what is done today in financial markets has its roots in the way that things have always been done, and much else that is done in today's financial markets is a radical change from previous centuries. Nowhere is this more true than in relation to money. This section of this chapter will do two things: first, it will consider the history of financial practice and where some of our legends about money have come from; and, secondly, it will consider the legal nature of money as a result.

2–18

B. Defining "money" in legal terms

The definition of "money" set out by Dr Mann in *The Legal Aspect of Money*[15] was in the following form:

2–19

> "... the quality of money is to be attributed to all chattels which, issued by the authority of the law and denominated with reference to a unit of account, are meant to serve as universal means of exchange in the State of issue."[16]

Interestingly, money is understood here as being a chattel and not as a means of exchange held in electronic accounts. Dr Mann's analysis[17] begins with the observation that chattels attract the quality of money by virtue of being accepted as legal currency by their state of issue, and such as being a "chattel personal". This conception of money as being a tangible chattel is peculiar (and is dubbed in this section "tangible money theory"). Its roots are necessarily historical and therefore it is an idea which has soaked into law almost unseen. At one level the English attitude towards money has been culled from an understanding of notes and coins[18] as part of a system of barter in which one item of property (the note

---

[15] Mann, 5th edn (Oxford: Clarendon Press, 1992), Ch.1 generally.
[16] Mann, *Legal Aspect of Money*, p.8.
[17] This analysis is continued by Mr Proctor in the 6th edition of this work: C. Proctor, *Mann on the Legal Aspect of Money*.
[18] With reference to coins, this is a form of property where once the coin contained an amount of metal of an intrinsic value equal to the face value of the coin. In that sense the early coins were another form of barter in which precious metal was being exchanged for other property.

or coin) is exchanged for other property. That is not unusual. The requirement for consideration in contract is built on similar notions of barter and reciprocal promise. As a fragment of legal historical trivia, that is acceptable; as a foundation of the modern law of finance, it is not.

2–20   In *Moses v Hancock*[19] money was defined as being:

> "... that which passes freely from hand to hand throughout the community in final discharge of debts and full payment for commodities, being accepted equally without reference to the character or credit of the person who offers it and without the intention of the person who receives it to consume it or apply it to any other use than in turn to tender it to others in discharge of debts or payment for commodities".

Money, clearly, needs to be accepted as payment by all in society for it to function as money. Thus it is a unit of exchange, as well as an expression of value. In *Suffel v Bank of England* it was held, however, that money "is not an ordinary commercial contract to pay" but rather it serves a far more essential function than that: "it is part of the currency of the country",[20] and thus a thing without which the economy could not operate. These common law definitions do not tell us anything startling about money: they simply tell us that it is required to operate as a means of exchange within this jurisdiction.

C. Notes and coins

2–21   The most obvious form of money is currency: that is, notes and coins in general circulation. It is this form of money which seems most akin to tangible property. However, notes and coins are really nothing more than evidence of personal claims of a value equal to their face value. For example, the £10 note sitting on the desk beside me bears the legend "I promise to pay the bearer on demand the sum of ten pounds",[21] under the words "Bank of England" and alongside a visual representation of the Queen in profile. The signature of the Chief Cashier of the Bank of England is also reproduced on the note. Literally, it is merely a promise to pay £10, and not actually £10. A bank note is therefore a promissory note within the meaning of s.83 of the Bills of Exchange Act 1882, as considered in Chapter 29. It is a commonplace of our modern economies that money in England and Wales is produced in this form and that those notes and coins are taken to have the same intrinsic value as is represented on their face. Notes and coins are treated differently from other forms of personal property when passed between people in that the transferor of money is not ordinarily entitled to recovery of the specific notes and coins which she passed because it is thought that money should be free to pass from hand-to-hand and so to circulate, with the result that one is simply entitled to recover "an amount of money equal to what one is owed"

---

[19] [1899] 2 Q.B. 111, 116.

[20] (1882) 9 Q.B.D. 555, 563; and also *The Guardians of the Poor of the Lichfield Union v Greene* (1857) 26 L.J. Ex. 140.

[21] cf. *Banco de Portugal v Waterlow* [1932] A.C. 452, where even though the banknotes in question had been fraudulently made from the official printing plates by criminals, it was held that the central bank in question had lost money in the amount of the face value of the "fake" bank notes.

rather than to recover any particular notes and coins.[22] It is suggested, however, that if Susan passed notes and coins which were held in a particular velvet purse to Zena for Zena to hold on trust for Susan, then if Zena retained that purse unopened with the same notes and coins within it, then there is no reason why Susan should not have back both the very notes and coins which she passed to Zena as trustee and the purse in which they were contained; albeit that the law on money does not ordinarily require the return of the specific coins.[23]

D. Legal tender

Banknotes

At one level, money could be said to be anything which is accepted as being money. For our purposes, however, the meaning of "cash money" will be taken to be official notes and coins issued by the Bank of England in this jurisdiction. The jargon expression to define those "official notes and coins" is "legal tender". If a thing is legal tender then it constitutes good payment for goods or services of a value identified by statute. A person is not obliged to accept payment by any means which is not legal tender[24] (unless she has contractually agreed to do so[25]): payment by legal tender of sterling amounts is sufficient.

2–22

Bank of England notes are legal tender for amounts above £5 (in that that is the smallest denomination banknote) in this jurisdiction as a result of s.1 of the Currency and Bank Notes Act 1954.[26] Therefore, it is suggested, that sterling banknotes have a different place from any other form of money as the currency of this jurisdiction. Strictly speaking banknotes are choses in action in the form of promises to pay which are theoretically payable at the Bank of England.[27] Alternatively, the holder of a banknote may receive banknotes of lower denominations from the Bank of England.[28]

Coins

The Coinage Act 1971 defines the coins which are legal tender in the UK.[29] Gold coins (that is, coins made of gold) are legal tender.[30] Ordinarily coins are manufactured out of cupro-nickel, or silver, or bronze, but are not intrinsically

2–23

---

[22] *Wookey v Pole* (1820) 4 B. & Ald. 1, 6, per Best J.; *Banque Belge pour l'Etranger v Hambrouk* [1921] 1 K.B. 321, 329, per Scrutton L.J.

[23] It would be different if there was something special about the particular coin—for example, if it had been unearthed at an archaeological dig and thus had some historical significance. Ordinarily, coins in current circulation can be replaced by any other coin of like value.

[24] *Gordon v Strange* (1847) 1 Exch. 477.

[25] See, e.g. *The Brimnes* [1975] 1 Q.B. 929; *Mardorff Peach & Co Ltd v Attica Sea Carriers Corp of Liberia* [1977] A.C. 850.

[26] Currency and Bank Notes Act 1954 s.1(1) and (2).

[27] Currency and Bank Notes Act 1954 s.1(3).

[28] Currency and Bank Notes Act 1954 s.1(4).

[29] The Coinage Act 1971 was introduced when sterling was devalued and the denomination of sterling coins changed. It was done to alleviate economic problems faced by the UK at the time.

[30] Coinage Act 1971 s.2(1).

worth the amount which they are stated on their face to be worth: i.e. their "face value" is what counts. So, coins made of cupro-nickel or silver in denominations of more than 10p are legal tender for payment of any amount which does not exceed £10. Coins made of cupro-nickel or silver in denominations of not more than 10 pence are legal tender for payment of any amount which does not exceed £5. Coins made of bronze are legal tender for any amount which does not exceed 20 pence.

E. Dematerialisation

2–24   Money has dematerialised to a large extent, becoming electronic payment flows, debit and credit card payments, and so on.[31] It has certainly dematerialised beyond any comparison with a system of barter or tangible, reciprocal exchange.[32] It is only in relation to notes and coins that there can be any claim to a continued physical context in which money could be said to operate. Therefore, the more complex question in relation to financial products in global markets is as to the proprietary nature of money held in electronic bank accounts (or, "electronically-held units of value"). Electronically-held units of value are generally treated by the law as constituting tangible chattels, in the same way as other money, despite the intangible nature of the property involved.[33] A good example of this tendency to see money in a bank account as a tangible chattel is *Clayton's Case*,[34] which dealt with tracing through current bank accounts and which held that the first money paid into the account is deemed to be the first money to be paid out of the account for the purposes of tracing property passed into a mixed bank account. This treatment of "money" passed into a current bank account is reminiscent of a stock control system used for perishable goods in warehouses (in which the older stock is typically dispatched first while newer stock is placed at the rear of the warehouse), or is reminiscent of double-entry book-keeping in which payments-in and payments-out are treated as transfer of physical stock. Money is thus conceived of as a chattel at a literal level as well as at an analytical level. This idea is pursued in Chapter 21.

---

[31] On dematerialisation of money and securities generally, see, Benjamin, "Dematerialisation of Securities" in Hudson (ed.), *Modern financial techniques, derivatives and law* (Kluwer International, 2000), p.61.

[32] A further discussion of dematerialisation is taken in Ch.6 in relation to bonds issued under a global note together with a system of registering the rights of bondholders, and not by means of bearer bonds.

[33] As suggested in *Bishopsgate v Homan* [1995] 1 W.L.R. 31; *MacJordan Construction Ltd v Brookmount Erostin Ltd* [1992] B.C.L.C. 350; *Westdeutsche Landesbank Girozentrale v Islington L.B.C.* [1994] 4 All E.R. 890, Hobhouse J., CA; and reversed on appeal [1996] A.C. 669, HL. The manner in which this tangible money theory is expressed on these cases is considered in more detail below.

[34] (1816) 1 Mer. 572. See, generally Hudson, *Principles of Equity and the Law of Trusts* (London: Cavendish, 1999), Ch.13.

F. Foreign exchange

As was discussed above, the value of money is not a rigid standard but rather **2–25** represents a merely fluctuating measurement of value in that sterling has a fluctuating value on foreign currency markets and therefore the very thing— sterling money—which is being used to value goods and services is itself changing in value. Currencies appear to maintain their value within the jurisdiction of their issue, except for the operation of inflation and interest rates over time (that is, fewer or more goods can be purchased with the same amount of cash-money). The value of currency within the jurisdiction therefore changes against the value of goods and services which can be acquired with that currency. However, the value of those currencies changes constantly against the value of currencies issued in other jurisdictions. Therefore, there is always a means of valuing these currencies externally by considering their value on the foreign exchange markets. Each currency also attracts an interest rate, which offers another means of their valuation.

The status of foreign exchange as property is equivocal. Within England and **2–26** Wales, the US dollar, for example, would be conceived of by the law as a commodity and not as "money" because the US dollar is not "legal tender" in the UK.[35] However, the decision of the Court of Appeal in *Camdex International Ltd v Bank of Zambia*[36] accepted that foreign currencies should not be thought of as being merely commodities, but that rather they should be thought of as being a means of exchange.[37] Nevertheless, it is suggested that the value of that other currency will not remain constant, instead it will have its value fluctuate against sterling. The US dollar becomes "other" to the English law concept of sterling as the currency in this jurisdiction. The US dollar is not a form of "money" in this sense, although it is clearly another form of exchange, just as parties agreeing to pay each other in coloured beads would render those beads something similar to money in one sense. This accords more closely with the view of Dr Mann.[38] A foreign currency has value in the sense that land has value on the open market, or that a second hand car has a market value, or that an ordinary share in a company has a market value. It is not intrinsically "money" in same way that sterling is "money as legal tender" in England and Wales.[39] It is important to recognise though that the weight of authority in English law is to see all currencies as being media of exchange, and therefore "money": at this point, the notion of money has become of little use to us in analysing "the law of finance" because in the law of finance we are concerned with any means of acquiring the "wherewithal to act"[40] and if there is no special weight to be given to sterling in that sense, then "money" has indeed shattered as a concept into the many senses which have been posited for it in this chapter. Not least of these is the phenomenon of electronic money, as is considered next.

---

[35] *Miliangos v George Frank (Textiles) Ltd* [1976] A.C. 443.
[36] [1997] C.L.C. 714.
[37] See, C. Proctor, *Mann on the Legal Aspect of Money*, p.45 et seq.
[38] Gleeson, *Personal Property* (London: FT Law and Tax, 1997), p.146.
[39] See para.2–22 above.
[40] See para.1–03.

G. Electronic money

2–27   Electronic means of payment and of holding bank accounts are considered in detail in Part VIII of this book. Clearly, they constitute an entirely different conception of money from that which has gone before. Just as it was said above that anything which is accepted as payment can thus be conceived of as being "money", it has come to pass that the sterling-denominated electronic payment systems which are now used are in effect "money" even though they are neither note nor coin issued by the Bank of England.[41] This indicates, I would suggest, the endless conceptual fluidity of financial concepts and of the law of finance.

4. The Nature of Financial Instruments and Transactions

2–28   Describing the nature of financial instruments and financial transactions will take much of the rest of this book. What can be said at a general level is that financial transactions are contracts between the contracting parties which create personal rights and duties between those parties, and which may create proprietary rights if the terms of the contract provide that such rights are to be created. A financial instrument, strictly so-called, is a bundle of rights expressed in the form of a written document, which may be a contract or alternatively it may be a series of promises by a person (such as a share) which is not strictly a contract. A financial transaction or a financial instrument will also be a chose in action which is capable of transfer and which is therefore a piece of property in itself. Such a transaction or instrument may well also contain a right to cash flows which can themselves be treated as property.[42] These property law elements of financial instruments are considered in Chapter 21. The discussion of financial instruments and of financial transactions will be begun in Pts V, VI and VII of this book in relation to the principles of the general law of England and Wales, and then in *Section Two: Specific Financial Techniques* of this book as to particular instruments and transactions.

2–29   In Chapter 32 there are two interesting ideas: first, that there is no such thing as identity theft because the money that is held in bank accounts is neither tangible money nor is it the property of the accountholder (because the accountholder has merely a debt claim against their bank), and, secondly, that theft from a bank account does not involve the taking of any money but rather simply the increase in value of one account and the diminution in the value of another account (with the result that this is a fraud offence and not a theft offence).[43] These issues are both very significant for financial market practice and they cut to the very heart of the legal nature of money.

---

[41] The Electronic Money Directive 2000/46/EC.
[42] See para.21–18.
[43] See para.31–49 et seq.

CHAPTER 3

THE RELATIONSHIP BETWEEN SUBSTANTIVE LAW AND FINANCIAL REGULATION

CORE PRINCIPLES

This chapter considers how financial regulation and substantive law operate differently and the circumstances in which they pursue complimentary goals. Financial regulation in the UK is conducted by the Financial Conduct Authority ("FCA") and the Prudential Regulatory Authority ("PRA") further to powers which were granted to them by the Financial Services and Markets Act 2000 ("FSMA 2000").

The objectives of the regulatory authorities are set out in FSMA 2000. The regulatory authorities' general objectives are to promote public awareness of the financial system, to promote the protection of consumers (requiring an understanding of risk, different degrees of experience and expertise among consumers), to carry out their roles in a proportionate way, and to procure the reduction of financial crime. The regulatory authorities have an explicitly economic role, with the result that their regulations and practices have been shaped with a view to maximising the effectiveness of the financial sector in the UK. A second objective is to maintain the integrity of the financial system, inter alia, by preventing insider dealing, by ensuring the provision of suitable information to investors in securities markets, and so on. A third objective is to protect investors

[53]

through the provision of information and education. The regulatory authorities provide for the appropriate conduct of business between investment firms and clients, and for the suitability of the products which are sold to those clients. The regulatory authorities, most significantly, conduct a responsive dialogue with market participants when formulating their regulatory principles.

By contrast, the objectives of the substantive law in relation to financial markets can be understood as being threefold. First, to ensure the enforcement of valid contracts through specific performance, liability for damages, and so on. Secondly, to protect property rights for parties who have taken security as part of their transactions (for example, for protection against the insolvency of a counterparty); and to protect all participants in financial markets from harms suffered as a result of civil wrongs. Thirdly, to punish criminal offences and civil wrongs under FSMA 2000. The substantive law operates in a positivist sense by requiring obedience to that law, as opposed to seeking to consult with the marketplace before exercising its powers or negotiating for the extent of any person's compliance with those rules. Courts give judgments which bind the parties without entering into negotiation. The substantive law is both formulated in the abstract to cover all cases, without necessarily thinking about its theoretical impact on financial markets in particular, and yet in so doing it is also focused on resolving the dispute between the particular litigants before it. In this sense, even though some judges may from time-to-time acknowledge the effect of their judgments on financial markets, the substantive law is not market-orientated in the way that financial regulation is market-orientated.

There is a common objective of the substantive law and financial regulation in that both are concerned with the allocation of risk between various parties. There is also a growing overlap between the two sources of finance law in that an increasing number of cases have relied on financial regulation as establishing the objective principles against which liability under a range of substantive law claims should be measured. The high-level principles of financial regulation should also be interpreted in the same way that substantive doctrines like equity operate by reference to high-level principles.

1. INTRODUCTION

3–01   The purpose of this chapter is to consider some fundamental questions about the nature of the law of finance: principally, the overlap between financial regulation and the substantive law as it applies to finance. The detail of the financial regulatory code in the UK is considered in Part III of this book, and the main principles of the substantive law are considered in Pts IV through VII. This chapter is intended to introduce some of the key thematic differences between them, but also some of the important senses in which they mesh together to form a complete law of finance. The principles which are developed as a result of this synergy of regulation and law are then applied to different financial market sectors in Section Two of this book.

2. WHAT ARE THE DIFFERENT OBJECTIVES OF LAW AND OF REGULATION?

There is a distinction between law and regulation both in theory and in practice, although there is a growing synergy between these two sources of law.[1] It is usual within financial institutions and the legal community to divide between those who specialise in issues dealing with regulation (or, "compliance") on the one hand, and those who consider substantive law on the other. As a starting point it is useful to bear in mind that law and regulation typically operate in their own distinct areas of competence: the law is concerned with the establishment of liability and the award of compensation, whereas the financial regulator has a more general remit to foster a smoothly functioning financial system in which investors and bank customers can have confidence and through which issuers can gain access to capital. The purpose of this section is to model the different goals and approaches of financial regulation and of the substantive law.

3–02

A. The objectives of financial regulation

What it means to be a financial regulator

This section considers what it means to be a regulator of financial markets, and identifies the fact that a financial regulator in fact has a number of goals which mean that it is not simply a part of the mainstream legal system. The detail of the regulatory powers and obligations of the regulatory authorities (the Financial Conduct Authority ("FCA") and the Prudential Regulatory Authority ("PRA"),[2] as the UK's principal financial regulators[3]) are considered in detail in Part III of this book (in Chs 7 through 12). This section will consider the differing natures of those regulators' many duties and powers in conceptual terms, before later sections will contrast them with the nature of the general law as it relates to financial activity.

3–03

It might be thought in the abstract that financial regulation would be similar to the sort of regulation which the criminal justice system performs: that is, making the FCA into a sort of policeman of the financial sector, patrolling trading floors and rooting out misfeasance. This we might describe as being a "coercive-regulatory" activity, in that the regulator is a controller and a policeman. In that sense,

3–04

---

[1] See para.3–25; and see A. Hudson, "The liabilities of trusts service providers in international trusts law", in Glasson and Thomas (eds), *The International Trust* 2nd edn, (Jordans, 2006), p.638, and "Trusts and Finance Law" in Hayton (ed), *The International Trust* 3rd edn, (Jordans, 2011), p.635.

[2] The Financial Services Authority ceased to exist on April Fool's Day 2013, and was renamed the Financial Conduct Authority ("FCA") by the Financial Services Act 2012, s.6. The bulk of the former authority's responsibilities passed to the FCA; except for prudential regulatory matters which passed to the Prudential Regulatory Authority ("PRA") and other matters to the Office for Fair Trading ("OFT"). This regulatory architecture is set out in Ch.8.

[3] Exceptions at the time of writing relate to the regulation of pensions and to certain other matters, such as pawnbroking, which fall within the remit of the Office of Fair Trading.

financial regulation would appear to be like many positivist systems[4] of the mainstream, general law in which the law is considered to be a "sovereign" which gives "commands" to all citizens and organisations within a society under the rule of law. There are elements of the activities of the regulatory authorities which do bear some resemblance to this sort of activity: such as the criminalisation of regulated financial activity not carried on with the authorisation of the FCA or the PRA,[5] and the regulators' specific powers of investigation and punishment.[6] The regulatory powers of the PRA, within the Bank of England, do have a clear role in investor protection which is achieved by means of maintaining the integrity of the marketplace (for example, through its powers in relation to market abuse[7]), and the FCA is important in setting out the principles governing the way in which financial institutions must conduct business with customers,[8] and so on. These regulatory powers are part of a coercive-regulatory role in that the FCA—under a range of statutory powers and duties—is directing how regulated people must behave and what they are not permitted to do. As is considered in Chapter 45, there have been many examples of banks acting in a way which shows a breathtaking disregard for their regulatory obligations (including Lehman Brothers knowingly breaching its regulatory obligations to segregate client money; JP Morgan knowingly misreporting credit derivatives positions to its regulators; and Barclays misreporting 57.5 million transactions in one year) which suggests that regulatory compliance is not a matter of positivist law for them, but rather simply a cost of doing business: if compliance is inconvenient or will impact on profitability, then the cost of a fine and the small reputational harm that results is simply one of the costs of doing that business.

3–05   However, that is not all that the FCA does. (In truth the financial crisis of 2008 suggests that the old Financial Services Authority did not even do this particularly well, if at all.) There are at least three other dimensions to the activities which the FCA and the PRA carry on beyond this coercive-regulatory dimension: an economic dimension, an educational dimension and an ethical dimension. To understand how these other dimensions come into existence it is necessary first to consider the statutory duties which are imposed on the FCA and the PRA, a task which is carried out in the next section.

The objectives of the regulatory authorities under the Financial Services and Markets Act 2000

3–06   The objectives of the FCA and the PRA are set out in detail in the Financial Services and Markets Act 2000 ("FSMA 2000", as was the case with the old Financial Services Authority) and are discussed at length in Chapter 8.[9] Both regulatory authorities are subject to the overriding remit of the new Financial

---

[4] Such as those associated with Hart, *The Concept of Law* and Austin, *The Province of Jurisprudence Explained.*
[5] Financial Services and Markets Act 2000, s.19.
[6] See para.9–44.
[7] See para.12–01.
[8] See para.10–01.
[9] See para.8–08.

Policy Committee ("FPC") of the Bank of England. The functions of the FPC are to monitor "the stability of the UK financial system with a view to identifying and assessing systemic risks", giving directions and making recommendations in that regard (as considered below), and preparing financial stability reports as required by statute.[10] This is fundamental to one of the Bank of England's statutory objectives which is to ensure financial stability in the UK.[11] Another of the Bank of England's statutory objectives through the Monetary Policy Committee is to develop monetary (including interest rate) policy as part of the general economic management of the UK. Thus the regulatory activities of the Bank of England are ultimately subject to its policy functions. As with the old Financial Services Authority, there is a dangerous mixture of responsibility for the health of the general economy and responsibility for controlling the excesses of the financial system. Before a boom turns into a crash, there is usually a time at which economic policy wants continued expansion (i.e. the application of the accelerator) while prudent financial regulatory practice requires that excesses are reined in (i.e. the application of the brake). Therefore, within the one organisation is control both of accelerator and brake, which means that either one or the other will be applied. It is suggested that in practice this will mean that booms will be perpetuated without an independent voice being able to counsel caution contrary to mainstream economic policy.

The FCA is charged with regulating the conduct of business in financial markets, whereas the PRA is charged with regulating to solvency and soundness of the larger financial institutions which it oversees. The FCA has a number of different goals, as set out by the FSMA 2000. The FCA's "strategic objective" is "ensuring that the relevant markets function well".[12] The FCA's "operational objectives" are identified as being its "consumer protection objective", aimed at "securing an appropriate degree of protection for consumers";[13] its "integrity objective", aimed at "protecting and enhancing the integrity of the UK financial system";[14] and its "competition objective",[15] which involves "promoting effective competition in the interests of consumers and the markets" for both regulated financial services and services provided by a recognised investment exchange.[16] The PRA similarly has statutory objectives: principally "promoting the safety and soundness" of the financial institutions which it is bound to oversee, by means of "seeking to ensure that the business of PRA-authorised persons is carried on in a way which avoids any adverse effect on the stability of the UK financial system"[17] and by "seeking to minimise the adverse effects that the failure of a PRA-authorised person could be expected to have on the stability of UK financial system".[18] The PRA is therefore focused on the potential effect on the economy of each individual financial institution. All of these regulatory objectives have

3–07

---

[10] Financial Services and Markets Act 2000, s.9G.
[11] Financial Services and Markets Act 2000, s.2A.
[12] Financial Services and Markets Act 2000, s.1B(2).
[13] Financial Services and Markets Act 2000, s.1C(1).
[14] Financial Services and Markets Act 2000, s.1C(1).
[15] In the Bill, the third objective had been the "efficiency and choice" objective.
[16] Financial Services and Markets Act 2000, s.1E(1).
[17] Financial Services and Markets Act 2000, s.2B(3)(a).
[18] Financial Services and Markets Act 2000, s.2B(3)(b).

been formulated in the wake of the financial crisis 2007–09 during which the failure of Lehman Brothers, the US investment bank, caused such a shock to the financial system that the concept of systemic risk was finally taken seriously by policymakers: that is, the failure of one strategically placed institution could cause the entire financial system to collapse. It was only the intervention of the US government with the Troubled Asset Relief Program and its injection of nearly US$1 trillion that steadied the financial system. Similar stimulus programmes were commenced by other governments around the world. The change from the ancien regime in UK regulation—which established the Financial Services Authority—is instructive. The old regime focused on the economic success of the UK financial sector, whereas the new regime has emphasised guarding against the risk of future systemic problems. The old regime is outlined in the next section: it demonstrates an approach to public policy which did not believe that systemic failure was likely.

The economic role of the old Financial Services Authority

3–08   The old Financial Services Authority had a more conflicted range of statutory objectives before the Financial Services Act 2012 came into force, including ensuring "market confidence, public awareness, the protection of consumers, and the reduction of financial crime".[19] It also had to work to ensure the integrity of the financial system and the protection of investors, but those straightforward objectives were muddied somewhat by the economic objective of protecting the competitive position of the UK economy and financial sector in relation to other jurisdictions. The economic, statutory objective of looking to the "international character of financial services and markets and the desirability of maintaining the competitive position of the United Kingdom" made the old Authority an economic actor in itself.[20] This conflicted with its coercive regulatory role. The old authority had a statutory responsibility beyond being simply concerned with the coercion, oversight or control of regulated people because it had a responsibility to maintain the health of the UK economy as a provider of financial services to global markets. Consequently, its control of the financial sector was not limited to a coercive regulatory role, but rather required the Authority to frame its rules and conduct its practices in a way that will actively "maintain" the place of the UK in relation to other, competing jurisdictions. For the UK—by which we really mean London in this context—to maintain its reputation as a global financial centre there is a perception that regulation must not be too heavy: not just in the sense that the rules must not be too demanding but also in the sense that the regulatory authorities must not be too overbearing in the administration of those roles. The old Financial Services Authority therefore had a minor role as a cheerleader for the British economy, alongside its coercive regulatory role. Moreover, the Financial Services Authority was required both to avoid "adverse effects on competition" and not to interfere with "the desirability of facilitating innovation in connection with regulated activities" in financial markets.[21]

---

[19] Financial Services and Markets Act 2000, s.2(2).
[20] Financial Services and Markets Act 2000, s.2(3)(e).
[21] Financial Services and Markets Act 2000, s.2(3)(d).

Ironically, it was innovation in the form of credit default swaps and collateralised debt obligations which caused the financial crisis of 2007–09.

Maintenance of the integrity of the system

A common thread through the old and the new regulatory systems is an obligation to ensure the "integrity" of the system. The maintenance of the integrity of the financial system relates to the financial markets but is not limited, as one might expect, simply to the control or oversight of financial institutions. In general terms, the good health of the financial sector relates to the facilitation of innovation and maintaining the confidence of the marketplace, and not simply to the use of powers of compulsion and discipline as though the FCA were a branch of the criminal justice system. As was outlined above the role of the old Financial Services Authority was at times coercive but it was also economic: the Financial Services Authority was required to maintain the integrity of the system not simply for its own sake but also to add to the economic health and standing of the UK. It is unclear whether the FCA, as well as the Bank of England which is also responsible for the good health of the economy (through the PRA, the Monetary Policy Committee and the Financial Policy Committee), will in time come to prioritise an expansionist, light-touch approach to regulation so as to encourage economic growth instead of controlling activity in the financial sector so as to encourage slower, more sustainable performance. However, there is also an ethical dimension to this notion of the integrity of the system. Just as the insider dealing legislation is addressed at integrity of the markets—by ensuring no one party can take unfair advantage of another through possession of inside information—so the FCA is concerned to protect the reputation of the UK financial system as being free from corruption. The core principle in the Principles for Businesses, at the heart of the FCA Handbook, is that regulated persons must act with "integrity". Indeed the first principle in the Principles for Businesses rulebook provides precisely that "[a] firm must conduct its business with integrity".[22] Consequently, the FCA has an ethical goal in common with its coercive-regulatory goal and its economic goals. Therefore, the role of the regulator is as a guardian of the conscience of the financial system too. However, the word "integrity" is being used in two senses here: first, we are concerned with the ethical integrity of the financial institutions which are conducting regulated activities and, second, we are concerned with the integrity and soundness of the financial system in the much the same way that one might be concerned about the integrity of a ship's hull. These two senses of the term integrity appear in different parts of the regulation without any real thought being given to what they are supposed to mean in practice. So, for example, in the PRIN rulebook (considered in Chapter 9) we are concerned with ethical integrity in the first principle; whereas in the statutory objectives of the Financial Policy Committee, for example, we are concerned with the soundness and resilience of the entire financial system (and not simply with its morals).

3–09

---

[22] This ethical idea of "integrity" is considered in detail in Ch.9.

Protection of the investor through information and education

3–10   As the old saying goes: "give a man a fish, and he'll eat for a day; teach him how to fish and he'll eat forever".[23] The attitude which the FSMA 2000, and consequently the FCA, takes to investor protection is in part to erect regulatory requirements to govern the activities of financial institutions, but also to try to provide investors with all of the tools that they will need to make good decisions for themselves. In effect, the FCA (like the Financial Services Authority before it) is seeking to teach investors how to fish and to give them the equipment they need, so that the investing community generally can operate as far as possible on free market principles in a context of conducting business with integrity. Thus, one of the FCA's tasks under the FSMA 2000 is to educate the population as far as possible in financial matters. One of the key tenets of its detailed regulation is the provision of information by financial institutions to their clients (through the conduct of business rules considered next) and the provisions of extensive amounts of information, for example, by companies whose securities are offered to the public. The goal of these sorts of regulation—as considered in Part III of this book—is to enable the investors to know what risks are involved in particular kinds of investment, to require investment firms to treat their clients appropriately, and to give the investors all the information necessary for them to make informed decisions about their financial activities.[24] The FCA will not make decisions for ordinary investors. Rather one of its goals as regulator is to help the investment community to learn how to fish. The result is hoped to be mass participation in financial services across the UK and from investors outside the UK so as to generate a vibrant financial sector in commercial and retail sectors, and thus deep pools of capital and financial expertise in the UK.

Conduct of business and suitability in the treatment of clients

3–11   A key part of regulating investment and financial services business is to place the onus on the selling financial institution to ensure both that the manner in which its customers are being treated is suitable for each customer, and also that the types of financial product which are being sold to each customer are suitable for that customer. This is done by the "conduct of business" regulation,[25] as is discussed in Chapter 10. This type of regulation has the moniker "know your client" regulation in that it requires the financial institution to assess the level of expertise of each customer and the real needs of each customer for financial services: treatment and product should therefore be targeted at the nature and needs of the customer. This is hoped to prevent misselling complex products to inexperienced customers who did not appreciate the risks involved, and so on. Expert customers can be treated in a more hands-off manner. This regulation in effect introduces an ethic which displaces the "caveat emptor" approach of much contract law, which meant under contract law that a seller of goods could simply

---

[23] There is another version of this saying which runs: "give a man a fish and he'll eat for a day; teach him how to fish and you've wasted a whole day teaching a man how to fish".

[24] See, for example, para.36–01.

[25] See para.10–01.

leave it to the buyer to assess the risks provided that there had been no fraud or other unconscionable behaviour on her part. The latest incarnation of this type of regulation reflects the Markets in Financial Instruments Directive ("MiFID") which sought not only to ensure the appropriate treatment of customers but also to promote competition between service providers across the EU.[26]

Significantly, this sort of financial regulation creates positive obligations for regulated persons. That means regulated persons are required to take action, suffer expense, reorganise their operations and so on, so as to comply with these obligations. The general law (as opposed to financial regulation) is usually very reluctant to impose positive obligations on people who have not contractually nor otherwise agreed to bear those obligations. Because of the context of financial services in an arena where expert financiers could easily fleece the inexpert or overly enthusiastic, financial regulation does impose such obligations to ensure compliance with the overarching need for integrity in the system. Conduct of business is therefore at the very heart of financial regulation and is a key distinction between financial regulation and the general law. This is a theme which is picked up again towards the end of this chapter.

3–12

Connection to the markets: a responsive dialogue

One of the key features of financial regulation in practice is that the regulatory rules are not created in a vacuum by the regulator. Rather, those rules are created after long consultation periods between the regulators and the banking community: indeed, the FCA is obliged to consult with the marketplace.[27] In tandem with the its regulatory objectives under statute, the Bank of England works very closely with leading financial institutions. Market practice is a great driver of regulation and of changes in the substantive law. An example of market practice changing regulation came with the Listing Rules which were rewritten in 2005 to replace a version only finalised in 2002 to reflect a movement away from different types of companies seeking to have their securities listed, and instead to recognise the importance of securitised derivatives and securitisations with a reduced emphasis on the types of entity which may seek to have their securities listed.[28] In the substantive law, the importance of collateralisation in financial markets led to the promulgation of the EC Collateral Directive.[29] It is true that in other fields like company law there is generally consultation before change is made to legislation, but once that law is made it is effectively passed over to the courts to develop it in the ordinary way for a common law jurisdiction. In the financial field, however, rules once made are subject to implementation by the regulator in ways that do not stifle innovation in the marketplace and are subject to review as part of an ongoing dialogue between the regulator and the regulated. The day-to-day business of regulating entities is actually a process of exchanges of information between the regulated and the regulator. Consequently, the tone in which financial regulation is carried on is one of partnership which is, it is

3–13

---

[26] See para.7–22.
[27] Financial Services and Markets Act 2000, s.8.
[28] See para.37–01.
[29] See para.42–15.

suggested below, really quite different from the way in which substantive law functions through the courts system (especially in relation to the criminal law).

B.   The objectives of the substantive law

3–14   The goals of the substantive law are different, or certainly differently stated, from the goals of financial regulation as identified immediately above. The present substantive law has been in existence—growing, spreading, transforming—for centuries in England and Wales since at least the first courts of Kings Bench in the reign of Henry II.[30] Therefore it is not surprising that the intellectual foundations of these legal principles are not responsive to the needs of financial markets specifically but rather are concerned with the needs of society generally and are expressed in terms of their own internal logic and concepts.

Enforcement of contracts

3–15   The enforcement of contracts is a key part of English law. Once consideration has passed between the parties, then the common law and equity will enforce the bargain. There are numerous contexts in which agreements can be vitiated because the context suggests that it would be unfair to enforce them. For example, where the contract has been created under duress or undue influence or otherwise such that it was not created with the informed consent of all the parties, or where there are straightforwardly unfair contract terms. Contract law is pivotal in the law of finance. The core principles of contract law are considered in Part V of this book.

Protection of property rights and protection from wrongs

3–16   Another key goal of the substantive law is the protection of citizens from the effect of "force and fraud". This has long been important in England since at least the work of the philosophers Hobbes and Locke in the 17th century. The protection of rights in property has been one of the key tenets of English common law for centuries.[31] The contexts in which property rights will and will not be awarded or recognised by the courts are subject to their own complex logic, as discussed in Part VI of this book. Finance law has to work within these structures to take good title in property. Interestingly, and a key part of this book, private law also throws up techniques for manipulating phenomena like property rights—as discussed in Chapter 22 in detail—so that it is not simply about giving instructions, but also about identifying those circumstances in which it will

---

[30] Some academics suggest that the common law is built on something immutable and more ancient than that: see R. Cotterrell, *The Politics of Jurisprudence*, 2nd edn (Butterworths, 2005). The idea of equity rests on foundations laid by Aristotle (see A.S. Hudson, *Equity & Trusts* (Routledge, 2012), s.1.1) and has been traced by some judges to the judgments of individual judges (see *Re Hallett's Estate* (1880) 13 Ch. D. 696).

[31] See H.R. Howe, 'Copyright limitations and the stewardship model of property' [2011] *Intellectual Property Quarterly*, 183-214; and HR Howe (ed), *Concepts of Property in Intellectual Property Law* (Cambridge University Press, 2013).

enforce the rights of parties such that the well-advised need to ensure that their affairs are organised in one way rather than another. There is a complex jurisprudence on the many forms of wrongs which are punished (through the criminal law) and compensated (through the common law and equity). The categories of legally remediable wrongs are the product of this complex jurisprudence too. The case law, considered first in Part VII of this book, is founded on centuries-old principles which must be understood in the context of finance, because they will not be rewritten root-and-branch simply to appease the concerns of bankers. The well-advised banker, through the interpretative skills of her lawyers, comes to know the sensitivities which will make the courts find one way or another in such cases, and thus how business is to be organised to minimise or avoid any legal liability. Recent history has demonstrated that the tenets of financial regulation will change far more frequently and far more profoundly than will the tenets of English law, no matter how much money is at stake.

Punishment in respect of civil wrongs and criminal offences

There is an expansive role for the criminal law in relation to financial activity. The offences which have been crafted specifically for financial activity (and which do not therefore form part of the general criminal law) are discussed in Part IV of this book, and the issues which surround the criminalisation of some financial activity are set out in Chapter 13. There are criminal offences in relation to market abuse (insider dealing and market manipulation), money laundering (in truth, the acquisition of property as a result of criminal activity), and a range of specific offences in FSMA 2000 which are used to coerce regulated persons into obedience to particular requirements of that Act. The criminal law is different from financial regulation in that it can imprison people. That is the stark difference. A criminal offence leads to a criminal record and a reduced likelihood of the human beings involved working in positions of responsibility in the financial industry again. Simply put, as with all other criminal offences, there is therefore hoped to be a deterrent element in criminalising some areas of activity and also a punishment element once guilt has been proved. The criminalisation of some aspects of financial activity is concerned with macro-political areas of policy such as dealing with the profits of the drugs trade and cutting off the financial lifeblood of terrorists (through money laundering legislation); levelling the playing field between parties contracting to deal in securities and maintaining the integrity of the securities market (through insider dealing legislation); and ramping up the authority of the FCA by criminalising breaches of certain key provisions of FSMA 2000. By comparison, other infractions of financial regulation are dealt with by means of censure and removal of authorisation in general terms: which is a different quality of punishment from imprisonment or a fine under the criminal law.

3–17

It is in relation to the criminal law that there are the greatest differences between the substantive law and financial regulation—even though it might be thought, as

3–18

was said above[32] at the beginning of this section, that the practices of a regulator would have much in common with a system of criminal law. Indeed, the problem which criminal law has faced in the financial context, especially in relation to insider dealing, is that so few prosecutions have been brought in relation to an activity which is thought by finance journalists to be rife.[33] Thus, the detection and prosecution of insider crime was considered to be so problematic that powers to investigate and prosecute claims of "market abuse" (including insider dealing types of activity) have been bestowed on the FCA: with the consequence that the FCA bears the Janus-faced[34] burden of both seeking to promote activities in financial markets and to prosecute abuses in those markets. We might therefore think of the FCA as being a kindly Victorian headmaster who twinkled encouragement at his pupils on the one hand and yet was not afraid to use his cane with the other.[35]

Obedience to the law on the positivist model

3–19   Law demands obedience. In terms of the criminal law, for example, the law issues commands in the sense that it punishes certain actions. As a result it produces a negative ethics. It is a "negative ethics" in that its delineation of what is not permitted leaves us knowing that all else is permitted. In terms of private law—contract law, property law and so forth—the law approves of certain models and will not give its support to other models. Therefore, private law generally creates a "positive ethics" by supporting appropriate behaviour. Thus, for example, a contract is only valid if it is contained in a deed or if consideration has moved between the parties together with an offer and an acceptance[36]; no other models than those stipulated by the law will have the support of law. Thus no other form of contract will receive enforcement under the law nor remedies for breach. The availability of remedies is thus the other significant element in private law: the law will command performance, or payment of compensation, or the transfer of property, or whatever, if the circumstances are such as to fall within the law's understanding of what shall and shall not be provided. In either aspect of the law, the law commands obedience.

3–20   The positivist jurisprudential models of law all share the characteristic that at their heart they consider that the law acts as a sovereign and commands obedience from us all. This is not the same with a regulator like the FCA who does have powers to compel information, documents, and so forth, but who also consults with the community of regulated institutions, shapes rules to appeal to those who might become regulated if they enter the markets, and so on. In most financial institutions there is a "compliance department". The word "comply" has a root meaning of working with someone, as opposed simply to obeying them.

---

[32] See para.3–03.
[33] See para.14–70.
[34] Janus was the god of doorways who therefore had two faces so that he could look both ways from the doorway.
[35] I know that metaphor is horribly twisted (the metaphorical hand and the real, anatomical hand), but I rather like it nevertheless.
[36] See para.17–14.

There is a sense of an uneasy partnership and cooperation between the FCA (as expressed in its FSMA 2000 objectives) and not simply one of obedience to the other's pronouncements.

Law is not market-orientated

The substantive law as operated through the courts is not market orientated in anything like the way in which the Bank of England is orientated to the market both through its statutory obligations to encourage innovation and so forth, and also through the requirement that it consult widely before producing draft regulations for public comment.[37] No High Court judge will seek the approval of any visitors to her website for a judgment in draft, in the way that the regulator publishes draft regulations. The attitude of the law to its litigants is therefore very different. First, a judge is primarily concerned with dealing only with the litigants before her; albeit that she is likely to have an eye to the broader effect her judgment will have if it relates to a particularly sensitive market or sensitive area of the law. Secondly, a judge is creating or interpreting or applying law which we are all obliged to obey. There is no hope of dialogue with a judge after judgment is handed down in the manner that a warning notice before regulatory action entitles a regulated person typically to make representations to the regulator and so negotiate a conclusion.

3–21

There are, of course, judges who do take great care to assist commercial practice wherever they can. It was after all the House of Lords in *Saloman v A Saloman & Co Ltd*[38] which created the company with separate personality, which is central to modern company law. In the very important case on interest rate swaps in the House of Lords in *Westdeutsche Landesbank v Islington*[39] Lord Woolf lamented the decision which the majority were planning on taking (to the effect that compound interest was not to be made available to a bank) on the basis that it would harm the reputation of English law among commercial people, and possibly also harm the place of London as a financial centre among commercial people more generally, if the courts were seen not to make an award to a bank which bankers had expected.[40] This pronouncement is so remarkable that it effectively throws the paucity of judicial comment of this sort into relief: and we should be glad of it. The law is something which should operate on its own principles of right and wrong, conscionable and unconscionable, reasonable and unreasonable, and so forth. It is not at all appropriate for judges to hear a case and to realise that one of the parties is a bank and consequently to make an order which they consider the banking community would want to receive. The law must remain above the concerns of the marketplace.

3–22

The law must remain a mandatory body of rules and techniques, to which bankers must show the same obedience as everyone else. It is not as though private law, as in cases like *Westdeutsche Landesbank v Islington*, is part of the criminal law.

3–23

---

[37] Financial Services and Markets Act 2000, s.8.
[38] [1897] A.C. 22.
[39] [1996] A.C. 669.
[40] See A.S. Hudson, *Swaps, Restitution and Trusts* (London: Sweet & Maxwell, 1999).

Rather, that part of the legal community which was advising banks about their interest rate swap business at the time simply got their analysis wrong, the courts thus invalidated their contracts, and perfectly predictable results as to the availability of proprietary remedies flowed from that decision. That is no reason for judges to feel compelled to decide in banks' favour all the time. Nor does it mean that judges should avoid the opportunity to generate commercially appropriate rules when it arises. It means that the substantive law has its own logic and principle: that logic should be maintained, except where valid reasons within that logic arise.

Common objectives of regulation and law in the allocation of risk

3–24   Among the commonalities between regulation and law are their effects on allocating risks between contracting parties. The regulation of the conduct of business between parties is significant because it redresses the ordinary common law position that in a contract of sale it is ordinarily the buyer who must beware. Because the financial institution selling the financial product is required to identify the level of expertise of its customer and to conduct business in the manner required by those regulations, the buyer is shielded from its own lack of expertise which might otherwise cause it to make unfortunate decisions. The customer may still make unfortunate decisions but not because it had not been informed of the risks associated with the product, and so on. Contracts allocate risks between the parties, but in the sense that the terms of the contract decide who is entitled to what and in what circumstances: in that sense, contracts are concerned with dealing with risks and leaving other risks open. In Chapter 4 and in Chapter 19, we consider in detail some of the most common terms in financial contracts and in Chapter 41 we consider many of them as they are put to work in relation to financial derivatives contracts.

3.   THE GROWING OVERLAP BETWEEN REGULATION AND THE SUBSTANTIVE LAW

A.   Circumstances in which regulatory principles have been used to inform private law

The general elision of substantive law and regulatory principle

3–25   There are contexts in which the courts are already beginning to use regulatory principles to decide whether or not case law tests are satisfied on any given set of facts.[41] The point is a simple one. Suppose you are a judge, you are deciding a case involving a complex financial instrument and it relates to a question of the substantive law: perhaps the defendant is alleged to have dishonestly assisted in a breach of fiduciary duty (a common claim in recent years). You are required to

---

[41] See, for example: *Investors Compensation Scheme v West Bromwich Building Society* (1999) Lloyd's Rep. PN 496; *Loosemore v Financial Concepts* (2001) 1 Lloyd's Rep. 235; *Seymour v Christine Ockwell* (2005) P.N.L.R. 39.

decide whether or not the defendant has been dishonest.[42] The applicable test is whether or not the defendant has failed to act as an honest person would have acted in the same circumstances. Suppose the defendant is a stockbroker regulated by the FCA. FCA regulation stipulates clearly the manner in which business was to be conducted between the seller of the instrument and its customer. Therefore, the judge is likely to consult the terms of those regulations to decide what would constitute proper behaviour for a stockbroker and in turn what an honest person should have done in those circumstances.

The case of *Bankers Trust v Dharmala*[43] is a good indication of how a judge may use financial regulation to develop principles of substantive law. In that case Bankers Trust sold two interest rate swaps to Dharmala. Dharmala was an Indonesian financial institution but not one which dealt in swaps. The swaps generated large losses for Dharmala. Dharmala claimed, inter alia, that it had not understood the risks posed by potential movements in US interest rates and that Bankers Trust should have explained the risks to it. By measuring the level of expertise of Dharmala against the applicable code of financial regulation, Mance J. was able to decide that Dharmala was not an inexpert client and so Bankers Trust was not required to have treated Dharmala as such. If Dharmala had been inexpert then Bankers Trust would have been obliged to explain all of the risks associated with the swaps to its traders, and failure to do so would thus have made it liable to Dharmala in damages. Thus, the decision on the substantive law flowed directly from the application of the financial regulations.

3–26

An example of the elision of principles of substantive law and regulation

The clearest example of this development, it is suggested, is in relation to the law on dishonest assistance and on unconscionable receipt in which the claimant has to demonstrate that the defendant was dishonest or had knowledge of a breach of trust respectively. This issue is discussed in detail in Chapter 26[44] but some of the key points can be identified here.

3–27

In *Cowan de Groot Properties Ltd v Eagle Trust Plc*[45] Knox J. held that the defendant would be held to have acted dishonestly if he had been guilty of "commercially unacceptable conduct in the particular context". The court is thus inviting us to identify what will be acceptable conduct in the commercial market at issue and then to ask whether or not the defendant complied with such standards for the purpose of imposing liability under the general law. The standards for commercially acceptable conduct in financial markets are made clear in FCA regulation. Thus, a person who treats a customer in a way which would be, for example, contrary to conduct of business regulation as required by the FCA, would prima facie be acting unacceptably and so be at risk of being found to have acted dishonestly or unconscionably, as appropriate. This approach in *Cowan de Groot v Eagle Trust* has been approved in a number of other cases.

3–28

---

[42] The law in this area is considered in detail in Ch.27.
[43] [1996] C.L.C. 252.
[44] See para.26–22.
[45] [1992] 4 All E.R. 700, 761, per Knox J.

3–29   In *Heinl v Jyske Bank (Gibraltar) Ltd*[46] it was considered, inter alia, that contravention of the norms of financial regulation would satisfy the test of knowledge (at that time applicable both to knowing receipt and to knowing assistance) in that the defendant would be deemed to have knowledge of anything which he ought to have known about if he had complied with the applicable regulation. Similarly, in the complex litigation in *Sphere Drake Insurance Ltd v Euro International Underwriting Ltd*[47] there had been trading in the reinsurance market in the losses generated by the US workers' compensation insurance system. The claimant contended that the nature of this market and the arbitrage involved between a small group of traders dealing the same products in a circle was dishonestly represented to him. It was held that this was not a market in which a rational and honest person would have become involved had he understood the nature of the market. The source of the defendants' liabilities was the finding that no honest underwriter in the reinsurance market would have acted in this way in selling these products to these clients (who acted in ignorance of the true nature of the market). Thus, a perception of proper market behaviour will guide a court in its decision as to the liability of trustees and investment advisors: it does not even require the embodiment of such perceptions in formal regulation. Equally, it is suggested, formal regulatory principles should govern a court's perception of what would have constituted proper behaviour in financial markets even by non-regulated persons. In fact in *Manolakaki v Constantinides*[48] Smith J. held that such an indication of honest behaviour need not be in formal regulatory principles but rather could be divined from guidance notes circulated by a regulator: in that case the Law Society. The decision in *Investors Compensation Scheme Ltd v West Bromwich BS*[49] referred to the regulatory standards in considering the liabilities of an investment bank in relation to investment advice given to its customers. The courts may interpret the parties' contract as expressly excluding the inclusion of regulatory standards,[50] although the parties may not exclude a number of regulatory obligations (if they are regulated persons) such as the obligations imposed on them under conduct of business regulation.[51] More recent cases, such as *Titan Steel Wheels v Royal Bank of Scotland*[52] and *JP Morgan v Springwell*[53] (affirmed by the Court of Appeal),[54] have tended to overlook the regulatory obligations incumbent on banks which were sued by their clients for selling them unnecessarily complex and risky financial instruments. Had the courts considered the obligations which the banks owed to their

---

[46] [1999] Lloyd's Rep Bank 511, 535, per Colman J.

[47] [2003] EWHC 1636 (Comm). The bank's principal concern was as to its obligations to assist the police in relation to the contents of a bank account which it had reason to believe had been obtained by fraud, its obligations under criminal law not to "tip off" its client, and its potential civil law liabilities to its client if it froze the account.

[48] [2004] EWHC 749.

[49] [1999] Lloyd's Rep. PN 496.

[50] *Clarion Ltd v National Provident Institution* [2000] 1 W.L.R. 1888, Rimer J.

[51] .COBS, 2.12R: on which see para.10–18.

[52] [2010] EWHC 211 (Comm).

[53] [2008] EWHC 1186 (Comm).

[54] [2010] EWCA Civ 1221. Reliance was also placed on *Trident Turboprop (Dublin) Ltd v First Flight Couriers Ltd* [2008] EWHC 1686, relying ultimately on *Henderson v Merrett* [1995] 2 AC 145, [1994] 3 All ER 506, [1994] 3 WLR 761.

customers to treat them suitably, then the banks would have been liable for selling unnecessarily complex instruments to those inexpert customers. Many complex banking law cases, such as *Cassa di Risparmio della Repubblica di San Marino SpA v Barclays Bank Ltd*,[55] have shown how the High Court will often become so focused on the detailed facts of the cases in front of them that they not only ignore the detail of the bank's regulatory obligations but also the detail of the common law claim which the claimant has brought.

Looking to regulatory principles when establishing a common law duty of care

In relation to the establishment of any duty of care at common law, there have been cases in which the courts have examined the regulatory obligations of regulated firms when deciding whether or not that firm should be treated as owing its client a duty at common law.[56] In the FCA Principles for Businesses, considered in Chapter 9, all regulated firms are required to conduct their businesses with due skill, care and diligence, and to obey conduct of business regulation in their treatment of their customers. In cases such as *Beary v Pall Mall Investments*[57] it has been suggested that the common law should continue to apply its traditional principles and not simply to rely slavishly on regulatory principles. But, it is suggested, that where those principles call, for example, for "reasonableness" or for the finding of a duty of care then the courts should look to regulatory standards when deciding what is reasonable or whether there should be a duty of care or not. So, in cases like *Seymour v Christine Ockwell*[58] it was held that the regulatory principles could inform the finding of a common law duty—in that they "afford strong evidence as to what is expected of a competent advisor in most situations"—although they would not necessarily be dispositive of the matter in themselves because they are merely "evidence" of what is required. It is suggested that common law courts do not need to be so coy. Given that statutory powers have imposed positive obligations on a regulated person to act in a particular way, then that should be sufficient to establish that that regulated person does bear the appropriate duty. In *Loosemore v Financial Concepts*[59] the court considered the appropriate conduct of business regulation in formulating the terms of the common law duty. A different slant on this issue arose in *Gorham v British Telecommunications Plc*[60] in which a pensions provider argued that its duty of care to its client, when selling pensions advice negligently, should be limited to extent of its regulatory duties: the Court of Appeal held that the obligations would not be limited in this fashion when the

3–30

---

[55] *Cassa di Risparmio della Repubblica di San Marino SpA v Barclays Bank Ltd* [2011] EWHC 484 (Comm).
[56] See for example: *Investors Compensation Scheme v West Bromwich Building Society* (1999) Lloyd's Rep. PN 496; *Loosemore v Financial Concepts* (2001) 1 Lloyd's Rep. 235; *Seymour v Christine Ockwell* (2005) P.N.L.R. 39.
[57] (2005) EWCA Civ 415.
[58] (2005) P.N.L.R. 39, at [77]; citing with approval *Lloyd Cheyham & Co Ltd v Eversheds* (1985) 2 PN 154.
[59] (2001) 1 Lloyd's Rep. 235.
[60] (2000) 1 W.L.R. 2129.

common law duty of care extended further. Therefore, the position would appear to be that the courts will consider the extent of a defendant's common law duties by reference to the defendant's regulatory obligations, although the defendant will not be able to limit its obligations by relying on a narrow set of obligations in the appropriate context if the common law imposes a higher requirement.

The precise point here: osmosis not takeover

3–31   This debate is distinct, it is suggested, from those academic discussions about the overlap between "private law" and "regulatory law" which relate specifically to the question whether or not regulations which are created under statutory powers may override the common law.[61] The question here is not a question of one code replacing another code, rather the issue considered here is whether or not one code—that of financial regulation—may seep into the very marrow of the other—the general law—and thus mould its norms. What is suggested is that the norms of regulation and the general law are actually melding together so as to form the concepts of the law of finance and that it is desirable that they continue to do so.

B.   The nature of high-level principles in financial regulation

3–32   The principles of financial regulation are coming closer to principles of private law all the time. We have just considered how private law is likely to take principles of financial regulation as the best guide to the appropriate test to apply in many private law circumstances. The different point considered here is as to the methodology by which financial regulation which is organised around a combination of high-level principles and detailed rules will operate, and how financial regulation would do well to learn from private law in so doing. As is considered in Chapter 7, EU securities law is organised around the high-level principles contained in the EC securities directives and the very detailed, technical rules contained in the Commission's technical regulations. Therefore, at the European level there is a combination of high-level principle and detailed rules. The FCA Handbook is intended to follow this format more closely with more of the Handbook being presented in the form of high-level principles. The Principles for Businesses constitute the starting-point for the FCA Handbook with their requirement that all regulated persons act with "integrity".[62] Observance of the detailed rules elsewhere in the Handbook is only satisfied if these overarching principles are also complied with. It is a little like the "spirit" of the Handbook being contained in the over-arching principles and the "letter" of the Handbook being contained in the more detailed rules.

3–33   To an English lawyer this combination of high-level principle and detailed rules should be familiar. To some people the notion of regulated persons acting with "integrity" may seem to be a vague notion. What might "integrity" mean? How

---

[61] See J. Black, "Law and Regulation: The Case of Finance" in C. Parker, et al. (eds), *Regulating Law* (Hart Publishing, 2004), 33, at p.47.
[62] See para.9–01.

could one know from context to context what it meant? The same could be said, and occasionally is said, of the notion of "conscience" which is the heart of equity in English private law.[63] And yet, the law of trusts, which is a part of equity, is a marriage of the general notion of "conscience" with detailed rules as to the creation, management and remedy for the breach of trusts. For trusts lawyers, the notion of conscience is not a vague notion but rather a concept which operates in a nuanced way as established by numerous decided cases. In a similar vein, the notion of "integrity" and the other Principles for Businesses in finance law will therefore have to be understood as applying in subtly different ways in different contexts too, but always based on the same fundamental principle.[64] The technique of applying high-level principles to individual cases, and also the technique of developing the application of those high-level principles in subtly different ways in different contexts, are well-known to the common law. They are also the mainstay of EU treaties and now of EC securities directives after the Lamfalussy methodology was introduced. This way of thinking, it is suggested, is also typical of civil code systems' private law: general principles are applied to individual cases by the courts, like the Market Tribunal, without any necessary development of a stream of binding precedent. (There is a different issue, considered in Chapter 12, as to whether or not this high-level principle approach had the effect of making the Financial Services Authority too "hands-off" and lazy in regulating high-risk institutions, like Northern Rock, before the financial crisis 2007–09.) The weakness of high-level principles is, however, said to be that it goes hand-in-hand with regulators exercising a "light touch", which means that those regulators are deliberately avoiding regulating financial institutions too closely. So, the principles of MiFID, considered in Chapter 7, encourage regulated firms to decide how best they should organise their businesses so as to comply with the high-level principles in that directive.

The consequence is the development of culturally-specific legal norms of two types—the core principles and the manner in which they are applied in identified contexts—which is typical, for example, of English trusts law. It is not simply a question of the notion of "integrity" being too vague for its purpose or not too vague for its purpose. Rather, the manner in which the Bank of England will put that principle into effect will need to become understood by market professionals and to become a part of the financial markets' culture. A jurisprudence needs to emerge. A jurisprudence based on fundamental principles applied coherently and consistently to subtly different situations.

3–34

---

[63] See A.S. Hudson, *Equity & Trusts*, s.1.1 and 32.2; *Earl of Oxford's Case* (1615) 1 Ch. Rep. 1; *Westdeutsche Landesbank v Islington* [1996] 1 A.C. 669.

[64] See para.9–01 et seq.

PART II

SUBSTANTIVE LEGAL CONCEPTS IN THE LAW OF FINANCE

Part II sets out the fundamental concepts of the substantive law on which the law of finance is built. Chapter 4 outlines the way in which contract law, property law, equity and tort law interact in practical circumstances, before those various legal fields are considered in greater detail in Parts IV through VI. Chapter 5 then considers fiduciary law, which is of particular significance when financial institutions are advising clients or managing their financial affairs. Fiduciary law imposes more stringent obligations on financial institutions than the ordinary substantive law and therefore financial institutions are ordinarily keen to avoid them wherever possible. Chapter 6 considers the principles of private international law which are particularly important in cross-border financial transactions. These legal issues underpin the remaining discussion in *Section One: General Principles* in this book. These discussions are intended to facilitate the teaching of finance law by setting out core principles at the outset; they are intended to assist practitioners by collecting core principles in one place and so to facilitate ease of reference. This foundation is then built on in Pts IV through VI.

CHAPTER 4

FUNDAMENTAL LEGAL CONCEPTS: CONTRACT, PROPERTY AND WRONGS

CORE PRINCIPLES

Private law is formed by legal *concepts* being applied in particular *contexts*. The private law context of the law of finance is formed by a synthesis of contract law, property law and the law dealing with wrongs (whether tort, breach of contract, or breach of trust). The private law context is then synthesised with financial regulation, as considered in outline in the previous chapter.

A large amount of financial law practice is built on the creation of contracts, many of which come in a standardised form and which are adapted by the parties for their particular transaction. There are a number of contractual provisions which arise frequently in different forms of financial contract: those common forms of agreement are considered in detail in Chapter 19.

To help explain the background to much litigation in the financial arena, this chapter divides litigation between two broad types: cases involving the mis-selling of a financial product and cases seeking restitution. The mis-selling cases generally involve a claim that a service provider has breached some norm of private law or of financial regulation when selling a product to one of its clients. Mis-selling may be predicated on a misrepresentation; on undue influence; on a breach of a fiduciary obligation; or on a failure to observe an obligation under conduct of business regulation resulting in an inappropriate treatment of a client or the selling of an unsuitable product. The restitution cases concern circumstances in which the claimant is seeking either to recover property from the defendant or to trace into property in the defendant's hands; or is seeking a personal remedy against the defendant in the form of money had and received, or to impose some personal liability to account for dishonest assistance or unconscionable receipt; or to impose a constructive trust or a *Quistclose* trust.

One important facet of financial services provision is the management of investments as part of a "portfolio". This means that the risks associated with any investment strategy are spread among different types of investment in different markets so that loss in relation to one investment can be balanced out by the other investments in unrelated markets. A good investment portfolio will be suitable for the particular client and will be sufficiently well diversified so as to spread the client's risks effectively. The weakness of portfolio investment strategies is that they work by buying lots of different investments of variable quality instead of selecting a few investments which are likely to generate a sustainable and high return over the long term.

This chapter ends with an overview of the principles of company law and partnership law as they relate to an understanding of the law of finance.

1. INTRODUCTION

4–01 Part II of this book sets out the fundamental concepts on which the law of finance will be built: in effect a marriage between equity, contract, property, and tort and other wrongs. Of particular significance is the discussion of "fiduciary fund management" which will cover the liabilities fund managers generally, portfolio investment strategies, and other activities by intermediaries. The law relating to fiduciaries—including the general law on trustees' and agents' obligations—is particularly significant in this context. Finally, the core principles of private international law, as they relate to global financial markets, are set out. This foundation is then built on in Pts IV through VI.

4–02 The purpose of this chapter is to think out the structure of English general law and then to set out the way in which the law of finance can be built on those foundations. The first task is to divide English law between its core concepts and the various contexts in which those concepts are applied as part of the natural evolution of a legal system. So this chapter explains how these combinations of private law claims combine in practice both in litigation and in structuring financial instruments, before later chapters analyse the specific rules in greater detail.

2. THE EVOLUTION OF PRIVATE LAW—CONCEPTS AND CONTEXTS

It is important to recognise that the law of finance is a combination of financial regulation created further to the Financial Services and Markets Act 2000 ("FSMA 2000") and its attendant instruments, and the substantive law of England and Wales.[1] The law of finance has begun to emerge as a distinct legal field both through the standardisation of its own commercial practices and the increased formalisation of its statutory base with the enactment of FSMA 2000 and the statutory architecture that came with it. This book explores how the law of finance sits as a part of English private law. This section tries to explain how we should think of English private law as being organised. **4–03**

Think of private law[2] as being like a castle. A classic castle has a central "keep", which is the highly-fortified heart of the castle containing all of the castle's most important people, property and offices. Outside the central keep is usually a ring of open ground between the keep and the outside castle wall. Along this outer castle wall, with the ramparts on which you will have seen the archers stand in any films set in the medieval period, are towers located in the corners and at strategic points in between. The idea is that the outer wall constitutes the main defence against attack, but if the outer wall is breached then the defenders can retreat into the even better defended central keep. All castles have a central gate letting the outside world in and allowing the castle's defenders out. They often have lots of other smaller gates too. The towers are all linked by the ramparts along the outer wall. It is possible to move between the towers and the gates to the central keep. The result is that people can move between the towers and the central keep. **4–04**

Now imagine that the central keep represents the central concepts of private law: contract, property, tort, and equity. It is no surprise that these core elements are also the core private law elements of any undergraduate law degree in England and Wales. These core principles in different combinations are used as the foundations for the various other contexts in which private law operates, such as: company law, family law, and finance law. Each of these different legal contexts arises when there is a social need for it. All of these contextual legal fields mature from being a collection of disparate rules into being something cohesive and socially relevant; usually they have a network of statutes, statutory instruments or statute-based regulations which define the context as being a field distinct from other legal rules. The example of the development of company law is considered below.[3] Briefly put, the earliest forms of companies were hybrid forms of **4–05**

---

[1] The sources of financial regulation in the UK are discussed in Ch.8. This chapter focuses on the substantive law, as opposed to financial regulation.

[2] "Private law" means all non-criminal law that relates to private situations, as opposed to public law.

[3] See para.4–33.

contract and property—combining partnerships (based on contract law) and trusts (based in property law and equity)—but when companies acquired separate legal personality, there very quickly arose a statutory architecture to describe how companies should operate, what obligations the company's officers bore in terms of document filing, and so on. Thus company law is a combination of its roots in legal concepts, taken from that central keep, which were combined with a number of statutes culminating in the Companies Act 2006 which have consequently built another tower in the castle of private law.

4–06   There is then interplay between the central concept and the differentiated contexts, just as people can move between the central keep of the castle and the towers on the outer wall: the concepts are the central keep in this analogy, and each different legal context is represented by a separate tower in the outer castle wall. To complete the analogy, ideas from non-legal sources are able to penetrate the private law citadel just as people can pass in and out of the gates on the outer castle wall. So, economic ideas can influence company law; philosophical ideas of right and wrong can interact with equity's notion of good conscience; developments in standard market practice can influence the idea of reasonable behaviour or integrity in finance law.[4] The law of finance is predicated on contract law, property law, tort law and equity (principally fiduciary law and trusts), as qualified by and combined with finance statute and financial regulation. The study of finance law, as well as its practice, at this stage in time will create the law of finance of the future. What emerges will be a set of contextual principles through which to analyse and regulate the most dynamic aspect of human activity.

3.   THE PRIVATE LAW TRIPTYCH: CONTRACT, PROPERTY AND WRONGS

A.   Contract

4–07   Contracts are at the heart of financial transactions. That much is evident. The French sociologist Emile Durkheim suggested that contracts were socially positive because they enabled people to come together and to organise their common interactions. In terms of the collective investment entities which are discussed in Part XIII of this book, it is the use of contract which enables people to form co-operative ventures for their communities or to pool investment capital solely to earn investment income. Contracts underpin every form of financial instrument and financial transaction in the rest of Section Two of this book. They allocate the parties' rights and obligations as between one another; they specify the means by which profit and loss will be calculated, who has what rights to which property, what amount is to be paid by whom on what date and in which currency. In Chapter 1 we considered the nature of risk[5] and identified its importance in financial transactions. It is in contracts that parties typically

---

[4] This model of a castle is a little like the model used by biologists like Maturana to explain how cells ingest and excrete material through semi-permeable membranes. Social theorists like Niklas Luhmann have used this model to explain how social systems like law inter-act with other systems (like finance) by receiving inputs and making outputs in stylised ways.

[5] See para.1–47.

allocate the risks of a transaction between themselves: if the contract is well-drafted they will certainly do so. At the end of this chapter we consider some of the most common contractual provisions in complex financial transactions and we can observe that each of them is concerned to protect the parties from risk or to identify which of the parties bears a risk in any particular circumstance.[6] In this book our discussion of contract divides between the creation of contracts, circumstances in which the validity of contracts may be doubted in the financial context, the performance of contract, and the rules governing the termination of contracts (including reasons for termination and the remedies which attend termination).

B. Property

The rules of property law are very significant in financial transactions primarily as a means of taking security against the failure of another party to a transaction, as discussed in Chapter 22. Property law also provides techniques like the trust, leases, mortgages and charges which are used to structure financial transactions—from pension funds, collective investment schemes, title finance, and so on—outside the area of taking security. In many transactions, the narrow commercial line between taking absolute title in property, taking only an equitable interest in property, or retaining title, becomes an enormous conceptual gulf to a lawyer. The distinction between having merely a contractual right to be paid an amount of money (a "personal" right, or a right in personam) is distinct from a proprietary right to identified property (a "proprietary" right, or a right in rem). The significance of appropriately structured proprietary rights is that they will survive the insolvency of a counterparty to a transaction. Insolvency remains the most significant event which could happen in a financial transaction because it means that the insolvent party will not be able to meet any of its contractual obligations. Yet, if the insolvent person is, for example, a trustee of property for the benefit of its counterparty, then the trust property continues to be held on trust even after the insolvency and so is not distributed among the insolvent person's unsecured creditors in the insolvency proceedings.[7]

4–08

C. Wrongs

The commission of wrongs is a significant aspect of the law of finance. The criminal law punishes identified offences—as is considered in Part IV of this book. The law of tort and equity provide damages, compensation and other remedies in the event of civil wrongs being committed: ranging from fraud, through negligence, misrepresentation, unconscionable activity, breach of trust, breach of contract and so forth, as is considered in Part VII of this book.[8] The Financial Services and Markets Act 2000 ("FSMA 2000") also provides a range

4–09

---

[6] See para.4–10.
[7] See para.21–13.
[8] Note that liability may arise concurrently in contract and in tort in relation for example to solicitors: *Midland Bank Trust Co Ltd v Hett, Stubbs & Kemp* [1979] Ch. 384, Oliver J.

of entitlements to compensation and provides the FCA with the power to deal with "civil offences" which are in effect criminal offences relating to market abuse which have been enlarged so as to make their regulation more efficient.[9]

4.   COMMON CONTRACTUAL PROVISIONS AND ISSUES

4–10   In Chapter 19 of this book, Performance of Contracts, there is a discussion of some of the most common contractual issues and provisions in finance contracts.[10] That discussion draws together some of the key legal concepts which face lawyers who are concerned with the coal-face of finance law: expressing the commercial intentions of the parties in a contract. That discussion supplies us with a lot of the fundamental jargon which is necessary for an understanding of the transactional issues which arise in relation to the financial products which are considered in Section Two of this book, as well as acting as a preface to the discussion of contract law in Part V of this book.

5.   COMMON ISSUES IN LITIGATION CONCERNING FINANCIAL INSTRUMENTS

A.   A summary of the key issues in complex financial litigation

4–11   This section acts as a summary of some of the complex litigation which surrounds financial instruments under English law. The specific legal principles themselves are necessarily discussed in different Parts of this book because they are drawn from different parts of English law. Therefore, it seemed useful to collect the key transactional issues together in this introductory chapter. These issues divide into two general types: first, litigation brought by disgruntled customers against banks whom they contend have mis-sold them financial instruments; and, secondly, litigation which is brought to achieve restitution (whether through recovery of property or compensation or otherwise) as a result of the failure of a party to a contract to perform its obligations. As is evident from the discussion in Section One of this book, generally, there have been many other forms of litigation in finance law. However, these two species of litigation require some introduction here precisely because they cross established divisions between areas of law. That is, they raise issues from contract law, tort law, property law, and so on, and are not limited to any one field of law. Without a central discussion of this sort, it would be too easy to overlook the way in which different legal concepts may be drawn together in litigation.

4–12   What might be most apparent from this discussion is the way in which a claimant in litigation of these types will tend to hurl every possible legal claim at the defendant, in the hope that she will recover what she is owed by one means or another. This may be because a number of different legal avenues may be equally successful; or because the claimant's counsel cannot be sure whether or not the

---

[9] See para.12–01.

[10] See para.19–02 et seq.

documents or the witnesses will come up to proof on any given claim at trial; or because the claimant's counsel wish to intimidate the defendant with the breadth and depth of the claim itself and also with the likely cost of defending so many different claims simultaneously. This discussion will merely outline the claims that are brought here because each of them is discussed in much more detail in later chapters: particularly in Chs 20, 23, 25, and 26.

B.   Litigation concerning the mis-selling of financial instruments

When a buyer of a financial instrument suffers a loss as a result of the performance of that financial instrument, it is common for the buyer to seek to argue that it was either sold an unsuitable product or that it was sold the product in an unsuitable way. If it is contended that the product was unsuitable, the buyer may allege that the product was badly described by way of a fraudulent misrepresentation[11] or a negligent misrepresentation[12]; or that the product was negligently constructed so that it exposed the buyer to loss[13]; or the buyer may allege that the seller sold a product which was simply excessive for the buyer's needs or too expensive for the buyer's needs or too risky for a customer of the buyer's type, and so that the seller failed to comply with the terms of applicable "conduct of business" regulation.[14] If it is contended that the product was sold in an unsuitable way, the buyer may allege that the seller failed to comply with the terms of applicable conduct of business regulation and so treated the buyer inappropriately, for example, by failing to explain the risks properly[15]; that the seller committed a fraudulent or negligent misrepresentation in describing the product[16]; that the seller unduly influenced the buyer into buying the product[17]; or that the seller breached its fiduciary obligations in the way in which that product was sold.[18]

4–13

Five cases, which are discussed in numerous places in this book, illustrate the way in which banking business should be and should not be conducted. At the simplest level it may be that the bank exerts some form of duress over an inexperienced and unsuspecting customer, just as Lloyds Bank was found by Lord Denning to have done to an elderly man ("old Herbert Bundy") in *Lloyds Bank v Bundy*.[19] Alternatively, the bank may not necessarily be found to have acted wrongly, but the allegation may be made that, under the applicable banking regulations, the bank treated the customer inappropriately. In Chapter 10 we discuss "conduct of business regulation" by which the Financial Conduct Authority imposes positive obligations on regulated institutions to assess the level of expertise of their clients and also their needs, and to deal with them

4–14

---

[11]   para.24–01 et seq.
[12]   para.25–01 et seq.
[13]   para.25–01 et seq.
[14]   para.9–01 et seq.
[15]   para.9–01 et seq.
[16]   para.24–01 et seq. and para.26–01 et seq.
[17]   para.24–01 et seq.
[18]   para.5–01 et seq.
[19]   [1975] Q.B. 326.

appropriately. So, in *Bankers Trust v Dharmala*[20] Mance J. relied in part on the regulations in force at that time to decide that when an expert financial institution sold complex interest rate swaps to a comparatively inexpert financial institution, the expert institution was entitled to rely on the fact that its customer was a financial institution and so that that customer should have been able to assess the risks of the proposed transaction for itself. Importantly, on those facts the customer also contended that it had been the victim of the fraud of one of the defendant's directors and the victim of undue influence in the selling of the swaps, and negligence in the structuring of those swaps. Mance J. dismissed the claims of fraud and undue influence as not having been proved on the facts; and was not prepared to find that one financial institution owed a duty of care to explain all of the risks of a transaction to another financial institution. Here we see that it is, obviously, important to be able to prove one's allegations with documents, or taped telephone conversations between traders, or by way of correspondence. We can also see how the financial regulations discussed in Part III of this book may also inform the decision of private law claims.

4–15   An example of a case in which documentary evidence and the evidence of witnesses was important was *Peekay International v ANZ*[21] in which a corporate client of ANZ was sold investments in the Russian banking market just before those investments were declared, in effect, to be worthless by the government of the Russian Federation. In the long negotiation of the transaction between different employees from different departments of ANZ and the individual who acted on behalf of Peekay, the nature of the transaction changed significantly in form so that its later form contained greater risks and exposure to a different currency. Some of the officers of ANZ had not themselves appreciated the change that had been made by their fellow employees. The different documents that had been generated demonstrated the change and the witnesses both from within ANZ and from Peekay demonstrated how there had been great confusion between the parties. In the event it was found at first instance that the product had been missold to Peekay and the contract was therefore unenforceable against it. However, this decision was reversed on appeal because the Court of Appeal took the view that it was the client's duty to read the documentation closely and therefore that it was client's fault that its manager had not appreciated the difference in the financial products sold to it.[22]

4 16   The practices of banks in selling complex products to customers was evident from *Bankers Trust v Dharmala*, and similar issues in relation to the creation of investment portfolios (explained in the next section) are illustrated by *JP Morgan Chase v Springwell*.[23] In this latter case individuals acted on behalf of a family investment company which accepted investment advice from Chase, a large financial institution. Some passing reference was made to the applicable conduct of business regulation by Gloster J. in finding that the individuals who made the decisions for the family company had sufficient commercial knowledge and acumen to appreciate the risks of the investments which were being proposed to

---

[20] [1996] C.L.C.
[21] [2005] EWHC 830 (Comm).
[22] See para.17-26 et seq.
[23] [2008] EWHC 1186.

the family company, even though they had no financial qualifications or employment experience themselves. Rather, their high-risk approach to investment in foreign exchange markets generally contributed to a sense that they should be treated as being sufficiently knowledgeable to rebut any suggestion that they had been influenced into a course of dealing against their will or contrary to Chase's obligations to treat them suitably. It was held therefore that no duty of care was owed by Chase to this client company.[24] This is an odd finding because it was based in part on a finding by Gloster J. after listening to 12 days of evidence that the individuals would not have acted any differently even if they had had the extensive documentation for the transaction explained to them: however, how could one know that if the individuals making the company's decisions had had the risks explained to them then they would not have acted differently on the basis of that knowledge?

Importantly for our purposes, the claimant company in *JP Morgan Chase v Springwell* contended that in advising investment in risky Russian government bonds (just as in *Peekay v ANZ*) there had been negligent misselling in tort, negligence in tort in general terms, breach of fiduciary duty, and breach of the contract between the parties. The claimant assembled all of the possible arguments which could found a right to compensation to recover the loss it suffered on those Russian bonds, and argued them at once. The court will not allow double recovery for one loss, but this litigator's tactic of arguing everything at once is standard practice because the litigator cannot know in advance which claim will eventually come up to proof at trial. The legal principles underpinning these issues are discussed in detail in Chs 5, 20, 25 and 26 in relation to fiduciary duties, breach of contract, fraud, and negligence respectively.   **4–17**

In *Morgan Stanley UK Group v Puglisi Cosentino*,[25] the claimant bank sold a complex derivative known as a "principal exchange rate linked security" (a "PERL") to the defendant, P. The bank was held to have been in breach of TSA r.980.01, the conduct of business regulation then in force, in advising P to enter into the transaction as a private customer. The documentation which was faxed to the customer identified him as an "expert customer" despite the fact that he was a private individual acting in that capacity, despite the fact that Morgan Stanley had not dealt with him before and despite the fact that he had not dealt in the precise forms of complex derivatives and repo products recommended by Morgan Stanley before.[26] Morgan Stanley sought to enforce the PERL against P when it generated large losses for him. It was held that P was not required to pay up under this transaction because it was found that P would not have entered into the transaction if P had received proper advice from Morgan Stanley under the regulations, including an appropriate risk warning. There was, however, no evidence of undue pressure having been put on P. This case is important because   **4–18**

---

[24] This approach was upheld by the Court of Appeal: [2010] EWCA Civ 1221. Reliance was also placed on *Trident Turboprop (Dublin) Ltd v First Flight Couriers Ltd* [2008] EWHC 1686, relying ultimately on *Henderson v Merrett* [1995] 2 A.C. 145, [1994] 3 All E.R. 506, [1994] 3 W.L.R. 761.

[25] [1998] C.L.C. 481.

[26] There were also questions about his ability to speak English, even though the seller did on occasions provide Italian speakers with whom he could communicate, let alone his ability to understand the products themselves in whatever language.

it underlines the obligations of the seller properly to allocate the expertise of the customer before commencing any business dealings, and then of treating that customer suitably. Further, it identifies that the procedure by which documentation is provided to the customer and signed by the customer is important. On these facts it appears that the wrong documentation was sent—or that insufficient consideration was given to this issue—and that there were documents as to the seller's standard terms which were not sent to the customer at all before he signed the conduct of business letter. The word "suitability" crops up in the typically elegant judgment of Longmore J. It is suggested that the most significant issue here is the double-barrelled concept of suitability: first, the means by which the product is sold must be suitable and, secondly, the substance of the product which is sold must itself be suitable.

C. Litigation concerning restitution for failure to perform obligations

4–19   Let us suppose that two parties have entered into a contract and that one party will, for one reason or another, not perform its contractual obligations. This failure to perform may be intentional, or it may be inadvertently the result of some other legal or commercial factor (as is discussed below). This failure to perform raises issues as to how the claimant may achieve restitution. The word "restitution" is being used here in its classic, general legal sense of achieving "recovery" either in equity or at common law by means of a personal claim for compensation or for unjust enrichment or by means of a proprietary claim.

4–20   First, let us consider the facts of *Westdeutsche Landesbank v Islington*[27] as a good example of the way in which a number of legal claims may arise at once in this context. In that case a bank entered into an interest rate swap agreement with a local authority which it transpired was beyond the powers of the local authority: the contract was therefore held to have been void ab initio, as though it had never been created, and the bank had the problem of how to recover the money which it had already transferred to the local authority. These claims divide between personal claims and proprietary claims. Let us take the personal claims first.

4–21   A personal claim is a claim only to an amount of money which does not grant any rights to any particular property. The bank could rely on there having been a mistake, because it thought the contract was void when the money was paid; or the bank could rely on there having been failure of consideration in its transaction with the local authority, because the contract (and thus its consideration) failed when the contract was held to be void: either mistake or failure of consideration would entitle the bank to claim that the local authority had been unjustly enriched by the receipt of the moneys under the void contract. The remedy which would flow from such a claim would be a claim for "money had and received", which means that the bank would be entitled to an amount equal to the amount of money which was paid to the local authority. Because this claim is a purely personal claim, it will be ineffective if the local authority has gone into insolvency. Some

---

[27] [1996] A.C. 669.

commentators prefer to call "money had and received" a "personal claim in restitution".[28] This claim is considered in Chapter 20. The bank is also entitled to interest on its claim. This amount of interest may be compound interest if the court considers it just and reasonable to award compound interest on the facts of the case[29]; alternatively merely simple interest will be awarded.

If the local authority had gone into insolvency, or if the transaction had involved the transfer of property which was intrinsically valuable, then the bank would prefer to have a proprietary claim over some identified property owned by the local authority so that it could stand as a secured creditor of the authority and so take an advantage in any insolvency or other proceedings. If the counterparty was a company which has its principal business and place of incorporation in another jurisdiction, then the bank may wish to have property in England and Wales to which it can have easy and enforceable recourse in the event of a failure by that counterparty to perform its contractual obligations. If any one of the means of taking security in Chapter 22 were in existence—express trust, charge, mortgage, pledge, lien, guarantee, etc.—then the bank could rely on its rights, as discussed Chapter 22.

4–22

However, if there was no such mechanism for taking security in place, the claimant would have to rely on the general law. This will be the situation if that security device was contained in the contract which has been found to be void. In such a circumstance the bank will seek to argue that the property was held on constructive trust for it if, at the time that the authority received the property or at any time before that property was transferred away, the authority had knowledge of any factor which affected its conscience: such as knowledge that the contract was void or that the payment had been made under a mistake. Alternatively, if the money had been advanced to be used solely for a specified purpose, then a *Quistclose* trust would be implied.[30] If any such equitable proprietary interest under a trust or an equitable charge could be demonstrated, then the claimant bank would be entitled to trace into any bank account into which that money was transferred and mixed with other money. This would entitle the bank to enforce a proprietary remedy—usually a constructive trust, charge or lien—over the mixture to the value of the money it is owed. Tracing is considered in Chapter 23. If there was no pre-existing equitable interest in the property, the bank would have to rely on tracing at common law which would not permit tracing into a mixture of property.

4–23

If in the contract between the bank and the local authority, the transaction had been valid and the local authority was simply refusing to pay because it was short of funds or alternatively was refusing to pay simply out of sheer badness, then the bank's claims would be for specific performance (to require performance of the authority's contractual obligations) or for damages for breach of contract. If the contract simply provided for payment of money it is likely that damages will be awarded instead of specific performance.[31] In any event, the claim would be a

4–24

---

[28] For example, Lord Goff in *Westdeutsche Landesbank v Islington* [1996] A.C. 669.
[29] *Sempra Metals v IRC* [2007] UKHL 34.
[30] See para.22–24.
[31] See para.19–86.

claim in contract law. Alternatively, the contract may provide for a series of events which will constitute events of default: the contract may provide for the mechanism for achieving restitution in those contexts, or else the contract may be rescinded under the general law and/or damages may be payable for any attendant breach of contract, as considered in Chapter 19.

6.   PORTFOLIO MANAGEMENT AND ATTENDANT LEGAL ISSUES

A.   The nature of portfolio investment strategies

4–25   This section considers the way in which portfolio investment is carried on and the legal liabilities which it creates. There are two basic philosophies in any business strategy: either one can limit oneself to a small range of activities in which one is expert, or one can attempt to operate in a number of different activities. There was a very important change in investment theory by the end of the 1980's to the effect that one should not limit oneself to one strand of investment activity: instead, one should diversify one's investments so as to construct a portfolio. Limiting oneself to investments of a limited kind in a world of volatile global markets is to take the risk that that particular kind of investment will fail; whereas, diversifying one's investments across a portfolio facilitates a spreading of risk.

4–26   Ideally, the portfolio will be invested in different types of investment in different markets in different jurisdictions, with different sensitivities to different types of market conditions. In effect a selection of the types of investment considered in Section Two of this book. The extent of the diversification will be governed by the amount of money which the investor has to invest: the more money there is, the greater the level of investment diversification that is possible. The types of investment that are made will depend on the "risk appetite" of the investor: an investor who is prepared to take a large amount of risk will be prepared to invest in more complex investments which will typically carry with them the greater possibility of profit to balance out their inherent riskiness.

4–27   Whether or not a financial institution will be prepared to advise that any given investor should take the risks associated with particular investments will depend upon the level of the investor's expertise: this is considered in Chapter 9 in relation to the conduct of business regulations, whereby regulated institutions are required to assess the level of expertise of their clients and to sell them only appropriate investments or other financial products. An example of the sort of assessment which banks perform was illustrated in *JP Morgan Chase v Springwell*[32]: in that case Gloster J. took the view that the investors, even though they were private individuals with no formal experience of financial matters, had sufficient commercial experience to understand the risks associated with the investments they wanted from the defendant financial institution. In the Court of Appeal in *Socimer International Bank Ltd v Standard Bank London Ltd*[33] it was considered significant in effecting termination provisions in a financial

---

[32] [2008] EWHC 1186.
[33] [2008] EWCA Civ 116; [2008] Bus. L.R. 1304.

instrument that both parties were sophisticated parties who understood the nature of the agreement between them and that they could therefore be held to the terms of their agreement.

The governing adjective which qualifies the care which must be exercised by an investment professional is significant: whether it requires that a person be "prudent" or "reasonable". The old case law, for example, on the investment of trusts stressed the importance of "prudence". If a person is required to be "prudent" then that person is required to be careful and to avoid risk.[34] Investment on behalf of private individuals in relation to their life savings would require prudence, unless that person was very rich and prepared to take large risks with some of her savings so as to generate larger profits. If the professional is required to be "reasonable" then that would raise the question, "'reasonable' from whose perspective?". Reasonableness from the perspective of other investment professionals would recognise that more risk can be taken as part of a portfolio of investments so as to generate profit for the investor. If an investment professional is allowed to act "reasonably" then she can make investments which take a level of risk which is appropriate for the particular investor in question, in line with the conduct of business approach considered in Chapter 10. After all, all investment involves some risk[35]: as the 2008 financial crisis underlined, even depositing money with a high street bank (once thought to be the safest form of investment) might prove to be risky if the bank went into insolvency.

4–28

The standard required of the investment manager may be set by the law generally in certain circumstances—such as with trusts[36]—or more usually it will be set in the contract governing the investment services between the parties. As is discussed in Chapter 9, the obligations imposed on a regulated investment firm by the FCA's conduct of business rules may not be excluded by contract,[37]even though the general law of contract permits exclusion of liability by any provision which is not an unfair contract term.[38] If the requirement was for absolute caution then if the trustee took any hazardous risk at all she would be liable for breach of trust if a loss resulted; however, if a trustee is permitted to act "reasonably" then she may be excused liability for breach of trust if the risk she took was reasonable in the circumstances. For example, if a billionaire acquired investments with the express purpose of the investment firm investing a large sum of money so as to make as much profit as possible, then it would be reasonable for the investment firm to invest in complex and risky investments because they would be expected to generate the highest levels of profit. It would not be reasonable to take such risks if the trustees were investing only a few thousand pounds in relation to a bare trust the only beneficiary of which was an elderly widow with no other source of income and whose trustees would therefore need to be more careful not to lose the trust fund.

4–29

---

[34] para.21–24.

[35] A point accepted explicitly by Lord Nicholls in *Royal Brunei Airlines v Tan* [1995] 2 A.C. 378.

[36] para.21–01.

[37] para.10–18.

[38] para.18–39.

4–30 The term "suitability" requires that, in general terms, investment managers are required to consider whether or not the risk associated with a given investment is appropriate for the client proposing to make that investment. In consequence, the investment manager could not sell, for example, complex financial derivatives products to inexpert members of the general public who could not understand the precise nature of the risks associated with such a transaction. The FCA Conduct of Business regulations might give us some guidance as to what suitable behaviour would involve. Having categorised each client in this manner, the service provider is then required to treat them in a manner which is commensurate with their expertise and also to ensure that the investments sold to them are suitable for their purposes. This issue is considered in greater detail in Chapter 10.

B. The argument against portfolio investment strategies

4–31 The well-known private investor and billionaire, Warren Buffett, has long expressed himself as being antipathetic to portfolio investment strategies. Buffett's very successful strategy, beginning with his acquisition of Berkshire Hathaway and continuing for decades thereafter, has been to identify solid businesses with good long-term prospects and sound management, and then to invest in them expecting an investment return only over the long-term; instead of acquiring a large number of small investments which are to be held in a short-term portfolio with the expectation that some of those investments will fail but that in the aggregate the gains from the portfolio should outweigh the losses. Thought of in this way, portfolio investment strategies seem more like throwing a handful of stones at a wall and hoping that some of them will hit, and that even if a few miss then the hits should outnumber the misses.[39] A slower strategy is to identify a sound investment for the long-term and to invest all of the investment capital which one is prepared to invest in a sound investment: that does not involve throwing pebbles at a wall, but rather selecting a smaller number of investments which are likely to generate a good return over time. What is particularly problematic is that in modern financial practice, investment strategies are not formulated by teams of analysts looking at investments carefully with an eye to the long term, but rather are constructed on the basis of computer models of anticipated future market movements so that those computers are programmed automatically to buy or sell securities when the market values of those securities cross thresholds identified in the computer model.[40]

---

[39] See, for example, Cunningham, *The Essays of Warren Buffet* (Wiley, 2002), p.8.

[40] See B. Malkiel, *A Random Walk Down Wall Street* (1973) which demonstrated that a random selection of investments was at least as profitable as portfolio investment strategies.

7.   THE BASIC PRINCIPLES OF COMPANY LAW

A.   The purpose of this section

This is not a book on company law but nevertheless there are a few core features   **4–32**
of company law which are important to understand some of the issues and
structures which are considered in this book. This short section acts as a short
general statement of those principles.[41]

B.   The distinct legal personality of companies

A company under English law is a distinct legal person separate from all the   **4–33**
human beings who may work for it, or hold shares in it, or whatever.[42] Therefore,
companies can enter into contracts in their own name and can hold property in
their own name. Consequently, if one wanted to have property held in another
person's name then one could transfer that property to a company so that the
company would then be the owner of that property. No human being would be a
beneficiary of that property holding because companies do not ordinarily hold
property as trustees (unless that is the specific arrangement which is intended):
rather companies are simply the absolute owners of their own property. So, a
company can hold assets and human beings who own a controlling majority of
the shares in that company can thus direct how the property is to be used without
the need for a trust. Companies are frequently organised into "groups of
companies" whereby the main company in the group will act as "holding
company" in that it owns all of the shares (or a majority of the shares) in each of
the other companies in the group (where each company is known as a
"subsidiary"). Different subsidiary companies may be located in different
countries if that is where those subsidiaries have been incorporated.

C.   The rights of shareholders

When shares are issued in the first place, the original subscribers for shares pay   **4–34**
capital amounts to the company for the number of shares they acquire. A
shareholder who owns "ordinary shares" in a company has very little right to
anything. A shareholder does not own the company's property because the
company is the absolute owner of its own property. A shareholder will have rights
to vote at company meetings. Each share carries one vote normally, and so if one
owns enough shares one will have a majority and so be able to control the
company's business. The shareholders have the power to dismiss the board of
directors. A shareholder in a public company will find it easy to sell her shares on
the stock exchange to other investors and so attempt to make a profit on the sale
price of that share versus the original purchase price. There is no such market for
private companies (because their shares may not be offered to the public) and so
selling shares in such companies is more difficult. A shareholder will be entitled

---

[41] See more generally A.S. Hudson, *Understanding Company Law* (Routledge, 2012).
[42] *Salomon v A Salomon & Co* [1897] A.C.

to a dividend, if one is declared: that is, each year (usually) the directors will consider how much profit the company has and how much profit can be spared so as to pay a dividend to each shareholder. Each shareholder will receive the same dividend per share she owns. The shareholder has no right to receive any dividend until one has been declared. While the directors may prefer to withhold profits in the business either to increase their own wages or to improve the business, the directors also need to keep the shareholders satisfied so that the shareholders do not vote to dismiss them in a general meeting and so that the company will be able to encourage more people to become shareholders in the future when the company needs more capital. Shareholders who acquire "preference shares" in a company are entitled to a fixed dividend every year but are not usually allowed to vote, as a quid pro quo for having a fixed dividend. The securities law issues surrounding shares are considered in Part X of this book.[43]

D.   The duties of directors

4–35   For the purposes of this book it is enough to know that directors owe fiduciary duties to the company, as described in Chapter 5. There are a number of equitable duties imposed on directors by the case law and by the Companies Act 2006 not to permit conflicts of interest, to act in the best interests of the company, and so forth. The directors have the power to manage the company under the company's constitution, but may be dismissed by the shareholders acting in general meeting.

8.   THE BASIC PRINCIPLES OF PARTNERSHIP LAW

4–36   This is not a book on partnership law, but nevertheless there are a few core features of partnership law which it would be useful to understand to make clearer some of the issues and structures which are considered in this book. This short section acts as a short general statement of those principles.[44] A "partnership" in English law is a business partnership in which the partners agree to share both profits and losses in the management of their business in common, in which the interaction between the partners is governed by contract law, in which the partners owe one another fiduciary duties, and in which the partnership as such has no separate legal personality, but instead must act through its partners. Significantly, the liability of the partners for any losses caused by the partnership and for any liabilities of the partnership are owed jointly and severally by the partners individually. So, if the partnership's business was to owe money to a third party, then that third party could proceed against all of the partners personally or against any of the partners individually.

4–37   The core element of the partnership is set out in Partnership Act 1890 s.1:—

> "Partnership is the relation which subsists between persons carrying on a business in common with a view of profit."

---

[43] See generally A.S. Hudson, *Understanding Company Law* (Routledge, 2012).
[44] G. Morse, *Partnership Law* 6th edn (2006).

The term "business" is one which is susceptible to a broad definition and it may depend on whether or not the activity at issue is generally accepted as being a business.[45] Section 45 of the Partnership Act 1890 defines the term "business" so as to include: "every trade, occupation or profession". In *Smith v Anderson*, James L.J. held that a society acquiring shares for common benefit did not constitute a business,[46] unless the purpose of the society was to speculate on shares under direction of the society's managers with a view to generating profit.[47] The profit motive marks the partnership out from the forms of collective, benevolent communal undertakings considered in Part XII of this book. In general terms, an agreement to share losses as well as profit will also indicate that the participants in the business are acting as partners and not merely as a form of mutual investment fund which intends to make a profit but intends no shared liability for losses among those participants. For the purposes of this discussion, the partnership constitutes a contract between commercial people to carry on a business activity. The extent of their rights and liabilities inter se will be governed by the contract formed between them. The anticipated return realised by each partner will be delineated by that contract, as will proprietary rights between those partners in any property provided for the business's activities. As such the partnerships encapsulates a rudimentary form of investment structure. It is only the Limited Liability Partnership ("LLP"), created by the Limited Liability Partnership Act 2000, which will have distinct legal personality and whose partners will have only limited liability in the same way as shareholders in companies.

---

[45] *Re Padstow Total Loss and Collision Assurance Association* (1882) 20 Ch.D. 137, CA; *Jennings v Hamond* (1882) 9 Q.B.D. 225; *Re Thomas, Ex p. Poppleton* (1884) 14 Q.B.D. 379.
[46] (1880) 15 Ch.D. 247, 276.
[47] (1880) 15 Ch.D. per Cotton L.J. at 281.

CHAPTER 5

FIDUCIARY DUTIES

CORE PRINCIPLES

The status of being a fiduciary imposes onerous obligations of good faith on a person; for the beneficiary of a fiduciary relationship there are therefore great concomitant benefits. Fiduciary obligations are imposed on trustees, directors of companies, business partners, and agents in relation to their principals. The category of fiduciary relationships is however an elastic one and so fiduciary obligations are imposed on other types of person in other circumstances as well. Fiduciary obligations may be imposed in novel situations where the courts consider it appropriate, typically where a duty of trust and confidence arises or where one person is acting in the affairs of another.

No two fiduciary relationships are identical. Each will depend upon its own terms. There are, however, minimum levels of responsibility which will apply to all fiduciaries in all circumstances: particularly the obligation to avoid conflicts of interests and the obligation to act in the best interests of the beneficiary of the relationship.

The significance of being subject to fiduciary obligations in the financial services context is that it will impose more stringent obligations on a financial services provider who is a fiduciary than ordinary contract law would, unless the fiduciary's obligations are limited in the terms of her appointment. Whereas a seller of financial services ordinarily seeks to earn fees from an ordinary client and generally seeks to earn a speculative profit at the expense of professional counterparties, a finding that that seller owes fiduciary obligations to a client means that it cannot earn profits at the expense of that client (unless it has a specific dispensation to do so in the terms of its fiduciary obligations). Financial institutions would therefore wish to avoid acting as a fiduciary, or else to have their fiduciary obligations clearly limited in the instrument which creates them: an express limitation of fiduciary obligations in an instrument is generally supported by the authorities in the absence of any dishonesty by the fiduciary.

Express fiduciary obligations arise most obviously in circumstances in which a person is acting as a trustee or as a company director or whenever she is administering a special purpose vehicle as part of a complex structure like a securitisation. However, fiduciary obligations may also be inferred from the circumstances if, for example, a service provider is found to have exerted undue influence over a client or to have acted unconscionably so as to render itself a constructive trustee. This chapter considers the circumstances in which fiduciary obligations will be found in financial transactions, and in particular whether regulatory obligations to act in the best interests of the client should be understood as giving rise to fiduciary obligations. Those obligations are then discussed in detail in later chapters.

1.   INTRODUCTION—THE SIGNIFICANCE AND ROLE OF FIDUCIARY LAW

5–01   In any system of commercial or financial law there are two types of private law: there are the obligations which the parties choose to impose on one another in the form of a contract, and there are the obligations which the law imposes in a mandatory fashion on the parties regardless of their wishes. In line with this second category of mandatory rules are the law of tort (which provides compensation for wrongs), the criminal law (which seeks both to deter and to punish specified types of activity), financial regulation (which seeks to maintain the integrity of the financial system), and fiduciary law. The former context may include fiduciary responsibilities where the parties expressly create those obligations in their contract, such as in an agency contract. Fiduciary law identifies particular categories of person who are subjected to duties of especial rigour to their beneficiaries,[1] both in the form of specific categories (such as trustees, agents, partners, and company directors) and in the form of a general category of fiduciary duties which are implied from case-to-case. What is particularly significant about fiduciary liability is that it both imposes a much larger range of obligations on fiduciaries than arise at common law and that those obligations are not dependent on common law notions of proximity, causation and so forth. As is considered in this chapter, fiduciaries are precluded from earning profits from their fiduciary offices and obliged to hold any such profits on constructive trust for their beneficiaries, they owe duties of good faith to their beneficiaries, and so on.

For financiers there is no doubt that the imposition of fiduciary obligations is something to be avoided or to be limited by means of express provision in the instrument which creates those obligations. Fiduciary obligations are more extensive and more onerous than common law duties under contract. The advantage of contract law for financial people is that the obligations which they bear under contract law are limited by the terms of the contract itself. Fiduciary law, in the financial context, constitutes a category of mandatory obligations which exist outside ordinary contract law. However, significantly, many of these obligations may be capable of exclusion or limitation by express contractual provision, except where financial regulation specifically prohibits this (as considered in para.5–40). Ordinarily within the context of financial activity, financial institutions will not want to bear fiduciary obligations either at all or else not without contractual limitation on the extent of those obligations. A number of financial structures necessarily include fiduciary obligations: particularly pension funds, unit trusts and potentially any situation in which a financial institution acts on behalf of a client. This chapter considers the ambit of fiduciary law, the effect of the "best execution" principle on fiduciary law, the relationship of bank and customer as being potentially a fiduciary concept, and the limitation of fiduciary liability. Fiduciary obligations are an expression of the mandatory reach of private law regardless of the parties' wishes, and in that sense are different from financial regulation in that financial regulation is typically created after consultation with the marketplace.

5–02

This chapter is primarily concerned with identifying the situations in which fiduciary liability will arise both in general terms and specifically in financial transactions, and the significance of a finding that there is a fiduciary relationship between parties. The remedies and equitable doctrines available to the

5–03

---

[1] The term "beneficiaries" is used in this chapter for ease of reference to refer to all of the persons who take a benefit from fiduciary obligations being imposed on another person, whether as trustee, director, agent, partner, or otherwise.

beneficiaries of fiduciary relationships are considered in various places in this book—principally in Chapters 20 (equitable remedies in the termination of contracts), 21 (constructive trusts for breach of fiduciary office), 23 (proprietary remedies consequent to tracing actions) and 26 (breach of trust and equitable compensation). Consequently, this chapter considers four things. First, the nature of a fiduciary relationship. Secondly, a discussion of the traditional categories of fiduciary obligation and then a longer discussion of the sorts of financial activity which should be taken to impose fiduciary obligations on one or other of the parties. Thirdly, a general discussion of the liabilities faced by fiduciaries in general terms. Fourthly, the possibility of limiting the terms of fiduciary obligations by exclusion of liability clauses in the parties' conduct of business agreement.

2. THE NATURE OF A FIDUCIARY RELATIONSHIP

A. The definition of a fiduciary relationship

5–04   The first question is to define what is meant by a fiduciary obligation. Lord Browne-Wilkinson described a fiduciary relationship as coming into existence by reference to the following, simple principle:

> "The paradigm of the circumstances in which equity will find a fiduciary relationship is where one party, A, has assumed to act in relation to the property or affairs of another, B".[2]

From these dicta we can identify, at its broadest, that a fiduciary obligation will arise when one person has agreed to act in the affairs of another person. In the financial context, then, this would apply when a financial institution acts in the financial affairs of a customer or with the property of a customer. This would seem on the face of it to apply to all dealings between a bank and its customers: although as will emerge below, ordinary banking activity does not impose fiduciary obligations on the bank without there being something more in the transaction. All investment management activity, similarly, would appear to impose fiduciary obligations on the investment manager because prima facie that manager is investing the client's property and clearly acting in the client's affairs. In relation specifically to people providing financial advice is has been held by Evans-Lombe J. that:

> "Where an adviser undertakes, whether pursuant to a contract and for consideration or otherwise, to advise another as to its financial affairs it is commonplace for the courts to find that the adviser has placed himself under fiduciary obligations to that other."[3]

These dicta indicate that the apparent breadth of Lord Browne-Wilkinson's dicta when applied to financial services contracts. That is, financial services providers will be taken to be fiduciaries when advising other people about their financial affairs. The apparent breadth of these fiduciary duties will then have to be limited

---

[2] *White v Jones* [1995] 2 A.C. 207 at 271.
[3] *Investors Compensation Scheme Ltd v West Bromwich Building Society* [1999] Lloyds Rep. PN 496, 509; citing with approval *Woods v Martins Bank* [1959] 1 Q.B. 55, 72, per Salmon J.

by exclusion of liability clauses as considered at the end of this chapter. Exclusion of liability clauses are more likely to limit fiduciary liabilities than a hope that English courts will not find fiduciary obligations because, as is evident from the judicial dicta quoted so far, English judges are likely to find the existence of a fiduciary relationship where any person advises another person as to her financial affairs. What emerges from the discussion of exclusion of liability clauses is that there are a number of significant forms of liability for financial service providers which may not be excluded by contract.[4] Nevertheless, the early portions of this chapter are concerned with identifying those circumstances in which fiduciary obligations will and will not apply.

On the one hand, Lord Browne-Wilkinson's definition of a fiduciary relationship (as set out above) does have the benefit of being concise; but on the other hand it is perhaps too elliptical to be comprehensive. What it does indicate is that when a financial institution is acting with the property or in the affairs of another person then that financial institution may become a fiduciary. In financial transactions, a financial institution or an individual financial advisor (whether working for an institution or as a sole trader) is ordinarily acting in the affairs of other people: namely its retail customers, its market counterparties and all others in-between. In many of these contexts, a finance professional will seek to limit his liability for any losses occasioned in the course of those dealings and he will also seek to exclude various forms of liability, such as fiduciary liability, at the same time. This section considers the nature of fiduciary liability, the effects of a finding of fiduciary liability, and the extent to which it is possible to exclude that liability.[5]

5–05

Those sentiments have been expressed by Millett L.J. in the following terms:

5–06

> "A fiduciary is someone who has undertaken to act for or on behalf of another in a particular matter in circumstances which give rise to a relationship of trust and confidence. The distinguishing obligation of a fiduciary is the obligation of loyalty. The principal is entitled to the single-minded loyalty of his fiduciary. The core liability has several facets. A fiduciary must act in good faith; he must not make a profit out of his trust; he must not place himself in a position where his duty and his interest may conflict; he may not act for his own benefit or the benefit of a third person without the informed consent of his principal. This is not intended to be an exhaustive list, but it is sufficient to indicate the nature of fiduciary obligations. They are the defining characteristics of the fiduciary."[6]

What emerges further from this discussion is that the obligations of a fiduciary, while being subject to general rules, are nevertheless sensitive to context and capable of arising in entirely novel situations.[7] What is also made clear is the "one-way" nature of fiduciary obligations: that is, the fiduciary owes duties of good faith, from which the beneficiary takes the entire benefit.

A further definition of being a "fiduciary" was suggested in *Reading v R*[8] by Asquith L.J. in the following terms:

5–07

---

[4] See para.5–37 et seq.
[5] See G.W. Thomas and A.S. Hudson, *The Law of Trusts*, para.25–15 et seq.
[6] *Bristol and West Building Society v Mothew* [1998] Ch. 1, 18, per Millett L.J.
[7] *Collings v Lee* [2001] 2 All E.R. 332. See also *Sphere Drake Insurance Ltd v Euro International Underwriting Ltd* [2003] EWHC 1636.
[8] [1949] 2 K.B. 232 at 236.

"A consideration of the authorities suggests that for the present purpose a 'fiduciary relation' exists (a) whenever the plaintiff entrusts to the defendant property, including intangible property as, for instance, confidential information, and relies on the defendant to deal with such property for the benefit of the plaintiff or for purposes authorised by him, and not otherwise . . . and (b) whenever the plaintiff entrusts to the defendant a job to be performed, for instance, the negotiation of a contract on his behalf or for his benefit, and relies on the defendant to procure for the plaintiff the best terms available . . ."

In this definition are qualities such as "trust", "confidence" and acting on behalf of another person in their (for present purposes) financial affairs. There are four well-established categories of fiduciary relationship: trustee and beneficiary, company directors, partners inter se (within the terms of the Partnership Act 1890), and principal and agent. Nevertheless, the range of potential fiduciary offices are infinite[9] and may extend from an errand boy obliged to return change to the person who sent him on the errand, through to the situation in which one person reposes all of his most confidential and intimate affairs and property into the hands of another.[10] Furthermore, liability as a fiduciary can be imposed in entirely novel circumstances: there is no need to demonstrate a close analogy with any existing category of fiduciary relationship.[11] Furthermore, the liability imposed on a trustee is not necessarily linked to any pre-existing relationship but may arise in relation to some subsequent act and relate only to that act.[12] The existence of a fiduciary duty raises in the court a heightened suspicion of anything which may conceivably benefit the fiduciary without sufficient authorisation under cover of an abstract standard of good faith and loyalty.[13]

5–08 From an understanding that the number of fiduciary offices is potentially infinite, and that the category of fiduciary relationships is therefore an elastic one, it should be recognised that the obligations befitting a fiduciary will differ from circumstance to circumstance. As Lord Browne-Wilkinson has held:

". . . the phrase 'fiduciary duties' is a dangerous one, giving rise to a mistaken assumption that all fiduciaries owe the same duties in all circumstances. That is not the case. Although so far as

---

[9] Or are certainly not closed: *English v Dedham Vale Properties Ltd* [1978] 1 W.L.R. 93, 110, per Slade J. Latterly see *Collings v Lee* (2001) 82 P. & C.R. 3.

[10] *Re Coomber* [1911] 1 Ch. 723 at 728, per Fletcher Moulton L.J.

[11] *Attorney General for Hong Kong v Reid* [1994] 1 A.C. 324; [1993] 3 W.L.R. 1143. We should consider the instructive example of *Attorney General for Hong Kong v Reid*, in which a public official was required to hold property on constructive trust for an unestablished category of beneficiaries in circumstances in which that property had never belonged to any person who could possibly have been considered to be a claimant. The money used to bribe the Director of Public Prosecutions had only ever belonged to those whom the DPP had refused to prosecute. In some general sense the bribes were held on trust for the people or the government of Hong Kong. The niceties of trusts—that is, the need for title in property and for identified beneficiaries—were overlooked in the court's enthusiasm to find a justification for taking the proceeds of the bribes from the defendant. See also *Reading v AG* [1951] 1 All E.R. 617.

[12] cf. *Attorney General v Blake* [2000] 4 All E.R. 385.

[13] See, for example, *Keech v Sandford* (1726) Sel. Cas. Ch. 61 in which the court imposed a constructive trust on a trustee who renewed a lease in circumstances in which the infant beneficiary for whom the lease had previously been held could not have done so, whilst expressly providing that it was not necessary for the imposition of the trust that the trustee have behaved wrongly but rather that it was the policy of the court to remove even the possibility that a trustee might be able to benefit from his fiduciary office on an unauthorised basis.

I am aware, every fiduciary is under a duty not to make a profit from his position (unless such profit is authorised), the fiduciary duties owed, for example, by an express trustee are not the same as those owed by an agent."[14]

So it is with the precise obligations borne by any commercial agent or trustee acting on behalf of another person: that person's precise obligations of the trustee will fall to be defined from context to context.

One important point to recognise is that the office of fiduciary can be imposed in addition to other legal obligations. So, for example, commercial partners have contractual obligations between them as set out in their partnership agreement. Similarly, agents also stand in a contractual relationship to their principals. Both partners and agents bear fiduciary obligations above and beyond their contractual duties. A professional trustee will only agree to act if sufficient limitations on her potential liability for breach of duty are included in the contract.[15] In consequence, the professional trustee will be authorised to take a commission from the management of the fund and the trustee's general obligations to achieve the best possible return for the fund will be circumscribed by a contractual variation on the usual legend "this investment may go down as well as up". In all of the situations there will also be another kind of obligation owed beyond that of contract.

5–09

B. That fiduciary obligations in financial contexts may arise *a priori* or they may arise as a result of the bank's unsuitable behaviour

There are two ways in which a fiduciary relationship may be said to come into existence. That relationship could be one which a priori is considered to be a fiduciary relationship, in relation to trustees, directors, agents and business partners. Alternatively, we must consider whether or not a bank's misbehaviour might cause the relationship to be categorised as being a fiduciary relationship even if there would not otherwise have been such a relationship, because the courts may therefore imply a fiduciary relationship in appropriate circumstances. In the abstract, we ought to be careful not to hang the finding of fiduciary liability on the question whether or not the bank has misbehaved. After all, if a bank is negligent, its negligent acts will give rise to liability in tort for damages, but not necessarily to fiduciary liabilities. Rather, the question ought to be whether or not the circumstances warrant the finding of a fiduciary office. However, as will emerge from this section, there are cases in which the courts have imposed fiduciary obligations on banks based on their breach of standards of proper behaviour.

5–10

The primary question in this context is whether or not the relationship between the parties is one in which the financial institution is in a position of power and influence over the client such that it should be treated as being a fiduciary.

5–11

---

[14] *Henderson v Merrett Syndicates* [1995] 2 A.C. 145 at 206.
[15] For the court's willingness to accept the efficacy of such provisions see *Armitage v Nurse* [1998] Ch. 241.

Answering the question whether or not such a fiduciary relationship exists can be approached in two ways. First, the relationship itself may be one in which the bank is (for example) holding property on trust for its client, and so should be treated as being a fiduciary. These classes of traditional fiduciary obligation are considered below.

5–12   Secondly, in the alternative, it may be that an ordinary transaction is being carried on in such a manner that it falls to be treated as a fiduciary relationship. So, the ordinary sale of an interest rate swap to a corporate client might involve the sale of such a complex product which introduces risks and possible benefits which the client would not have wanted if it had been properly advised, then that might transform an ordinary sales relationship into a fiduciary relationship. In deciding whether or not a relationship has crossed such a boundary, it would be appropriate to consider what financial regulation would ordinarily have required of that institution in those circumstances. Thus in *Bankers Trust v Dharmala* it was held by Mance J. that because the bank had acted in accordance with the Bank of England London Code (which was the system of rules then in force) that it had not committed any breach of duty. Similarly, in *Lloyds Bank v Bundy*[16] an ordinary banking relationship became a fiduciary relationship when the bank cajoled an elderly customer into buying unsuitable products: thus the bank's inappropriate behaviour in the context created the fiduciary obligations, even though the ordinary banking relationship would not have imposed fiduciary obligations otherwise.

5–13   There are situations in which the finding of a fiduciary obligation appears to have been based solely on the unconscionable actions of the defendant. An obvious example of this phenomenon is a constructive trust: a constructive trust imposes fiduciary duties on a defendant if that defendant has knowingly acted unconscionably in relation to the claimant's property[17] regardless of whether or not there was a pre-existing fiduciary relationship between the parties. So, for example, in *Attorney General for Hong Kong v Reid*[18] the Director of Public Prosecutions ("DPP") in Hong Kong received bribes from criminals not to prosecute them. The role of a DPP is not ordinarily a fiduciary office, whereas being a trustee is. Nevertheless, a fiduciary office was found because of the DPP's unconscionable activities in accepting bribes. Thus, fiduciary obligations may be imposed by the courts in the ways considered in Chapters 21 and 23 in relation to trusts and to tracing.

C.   The nature of fiduciary obligations

5–14   The beneficiary in a fiduciary relationship acquires a range of equitable claims against the fiduciary in equity. There are five principal obligations: first, the fiduciary may not permit any conflict between its personal capacity and its fiduciary obligations; secondly, the fiduciary may not take any unauthorised

---

[16] [1975] Q.B. 326.
[17] *Westdeutsche Landesbank v Islington* [1996] A.C. 669. A bank will not ordinarily be a trustee, unless there is something particular about the situation, see para.29–04.
[18] [1994] 1 A.C. 324.

profit from its fiduciary obligations; thirdly, the fiduciary must maintain the confidentiality of its beneficiaries' affairs; fourthly, the fiduciary must act entirely in good faith in the interests of its beneficiaries; and, fifthly that the fiduciary must act with care and skill. This last obligation is a significant one in relation to financial institutions acting on behalf of their customers. Lord Browne-Wilkinson held in *Henderson v Merrett Syndicates Ltd* that[19]:

> "The liability of a fiduciary for the negligent transaction of his duties is a not a separate head of liability but the paradigm of the general duty to act with care imposed by law on those who take it upon themselves to act for or to advise others.... It is the fact that they have all assumed responsibility for the property or affairs of another which renders them liable for the careless performance of what they have undertaken to do, not the description of the trade or position which they hold."

The liability for negligence at common law is considered in Chapter 25; this chapter focuses specifically on the basis of liability for breaches of fiduciary duty, and transmits the reader on to later discussions of many of those remedies elsewhere in this book. So, beyond the liability to account for failures of care and skill, a fiduciary will hold any property received in breach of its duties (including any profit acquired without authorisation) on constructive trust for the beneficiary.[20] Furthermore, accepting that the fiduciary is required to refrain from any conflict between her personal interest and that of the beneficiaries, the fiduciary is required to act even-handedly and disinterestedly between all beneficiaries, and the fiduciary is obliged to refrain from any dealing with any property held for the beneficiaries on her own account unless it is authorised by the terms of her office. The beneficiary is also entitled to be compensated for any loss made by the fiduciary in dealing with property which was held on a constructive trust for the beneficiary as a result of some breach of duty.[21] A fiduciary may be prevented from acting in conflict of its fiduciary obligations by means of an injunction.[22] The beneficiary can acquire compound interest on any judgment received against the fiduciary for breach of duty.[23]

The responsibilities of the fiduciary are based on a standard of utmost good faith in general terms. The older case law took the straightforward attitude that if there were any loss suffered by a beneficiary, then the fiduciary would be strictly liable for that loss.[24] This attitude has been perpetuated by the decisions in *Regal v Gulliver*[25] (concerning directors of a company) and *Boardman v Phipps*[26] (concerning a solicitor advising trustees) which imposed strict liability for all

5–15

---

[19] [1995] 2 A.C. 145, 205.
[20] As considered above in relation to *Attorney General for Hong Kong v Reid* [1994] 1 A.C. 324 and *Boardman v Phipps* [1967] 2 A.C. 46.
[21] *Boardman v Phipps* [1967] 2 A.C. 46.
[22] *Koch Shipping Inc v Richards Butler* [2002] EWCA Civ 1280.
[23] *Westdeutsche Landesbank v Islington* [1996] A.C. 669.
[24] *Keech v Sandford* (1726) Sel. Cas. Ch. 61.
[25] [1942] 1 All E.R. 378; [1967] 2 A.C. 134n. The company directors in *Regal v Gulliver* were prevented from making a profit from a business opportunity which it was felt by the court ought to have been exploited on behalf of the company rather than on behalf of the directors personally.
[26] [1967] 2 A.C. 46. The solicitor invested his own money in tandem with the trust but was found to have taken an unauthorised personal profit which could not be permitted because there was a possible conflict of interest between his personal and his fiduciary positions.

unauthorised gains made by the fiduciaries deriving, however obliquely it would seem, from their fiduciary duty. The requirement of good faith required by a court of equity is therefore a strict requirement.[27] These equitable principles are considered in greater detail in Chapter 21.

3. THE CIRCUMSTANCES IN WHICH THERE WILL BE A FIDUCIARY RELATIONSHIP

A. Established categories of fiduciary liability under the general law

5–16 Where a financial institution is acting as a trustee for a client, or as an agent of that client, or as a partner of that client, or as a director of a company for that client, then it will be in an express fiduciary relationship in connection with that client. That much is trite law. In consequence the trustee will be liable to account to the client for any loss which is connected to any breach of any fiduciary duty (for ease of reference, referred to as a "breach of trust" in this chapter) which the fiduciary commits.[28] This section aims to set out the parameters of fiduciary liability in the financial context. The general principles underpinning fiduciary liability were set out at the beginning of this chapter.

B. Decided case law on fiduciary obligations in the banker-client relationship

5–17 As is discussed in Chapter 29, the relationship of banker and customer—in relation to taking deposits and operating accounts—does not ordinarily create a fiduciary relationship.[29] So, if a bank is not explicitly required to advise a customer on a particular matter, and there is nothing in the terms of the contract between the parties to the contrary effect, a banker will not owe fiduciary obligations to that customer.[30] However, there are a number of situations in which fiduciary relationships have been held to arise: where the bank induces a financial transaction by agreeing to become financial advisor[31]; where the bank advises a customer to enter into a transaction put in place by it, particularly where the customer is an inexpert customer tending to place complete reliance on the bank's expertise and where the bank exercises some undue influence over her[32]; where a bank has discretionary control of a customer's assets (but only to the extent of that discretionary control[33]); and where the bank advises a person to enter into a transaction which is to their financial disadvantage without ensuring that they

---

[27] [1994] 1 A.C. 324.

[28] *Target Holdings v Redferns* [1996] 1 A.C. 421; [1995] 3 W.L.R. 352; [1995] 3 All E.R. 785.

[29] *Kelly v Cooper* [1993] A.C. 205.

[30] *Kelly v Cooper* [1993] A.C. 205 (PC); *Clark Boyce v Mouat* [1994] 1 A.C. 428 (PC).

[31] *Woods v Martins Bank Ltd* [1959] 1 Q.B. 55; *Standard Investments Ltd v Canadian Imperial Bank of Commerce* (1985) 22 D.L.R. (4th) 410.

[32] *Lloyds Bank v Bundy* [1975] Q.B. 326; *Royal Bank of Canada v Hinds* (1978) 88 D.L.R. (3rd) 428.

[33] *Ata v American Express Bank* Unreported October 7, 1996 (Rix J.), June 17, 1998 (Court of Appeal).

have taken independent advice.[34] These cases are concerned with a finding of fiduciary office. The duties and the remedies which flow from the finding of such an office are considered below: typically, they revolve around the need to avoid conflicts of interest and the proper treatment of the customer's confidential affairs and property.

It has been held by the Federal Court of Australia that "a fiduciary relationship arises between a financial adviser and its client where the adviser holds itself out as an expert on financial matters and undertakes to perform a financial advisory role for the client".[35] A conceptualisation of the extent of a fiduciary office between an investment firm or bank and its client of this breadth will capture all situations in which the firm offers advice to its customer and will not be limited to situations in which the firm has some discretion over the management of its customer's assets.

First, we need to consider what it is about a particular type of role which may lead to it being defined as being a fiduciary role. In doing this we shall consider some axiomatic examples of fiduciary office in financial transactions.

C.   Portfolio management and the fiduciary

In the previous section we established that in ordinary terms, a bank will not be   **5–18**
acting in a fiduciary capacity in relation to its customers unless there is something about the transaction which suggests that the imposition of fiduciary obligations would be appropriate. The general principle that there will not be a fiduciary relationship applies in relation to the ordinary taking of deposits, the management of accounts and so forth: what is referred to in this book as "ordinary banking business". However, many financial institutions offer very different services which stretch far beyond mere deposit-taking and so forth. When financial institutions are managing portfolios of assets on behalf of their clients, it is suggested that those institutions will, however, generally be acting as fiduciaries. Portfolio investment is common in client investment arrangements.[36] The most obvious example is the unit trust in which investments are taken from the public by a scheme manager who makes investments on behalf of the unit trust in accordance with the terms of the scheme's documentation. In that situation the scheme property is held on trust for the investors, and the scheme manager and the scheme's trustee will act as fiduciaries in relation to the investors. Even beyond unit trusts, whenever a financial institution holds money and invests it on behalf of a customer, that institution will be acting as a fiduciary. The institution will either be acting as agent or as trustee in relation to those investments. The extent and nature of those fiduciary relationships, however, will be governed by the terms which are inserted into the parties' agreement. Thus, as Millett L.J. has

---

[34] *National Westminster Bank Plc v Morgan* [1985] A.C. 686; *Barclay's Bank v O'Brien* [1993] 3 W.L.R. 786; *CIBC v Pitt* [1993] 3 W.L.R. 786. cf. *Royal Bank of Scotland v Etridge (No.2)* [2002] A.C. 773 in relation to domestic mortgages.
[35] *Securities and Investment Commission v Citigroup Global Markets Australia Pty Ltd* [2007] F.C.A. 963.
[36] See para.4–25 et seq. for a discussion of portfolio investment.

held,[37] the terms of fiduciary relationships are not identical but rather depend on the precise terms in which they are cast. Therefore, those liabilities may be limited by terms to that effect inserted into the investment contract. In the following sections we shall consider some of the traditional fiduciary arrangements and other contexts in which fiduciary obligations may be found in the future.

D. Circumstances in which there will always be fiduciary obligations

5–19   Among the classes of person who always occupy a fiduciary office in financial transactions, because their offices are explicitly fiduciary in nature, are trustees of pension funds; scheme managers and trustees in unit trusts,[38] and the Authorised Corporate Director and the depositary in open-ended investment companies[39]; a person acting as trustee under an express trust over another person's property; anyone who acts as agent for a principal in relation to that principal's affairs; and any person who is declared to be a trustee of property under constructive trust or resulting trust principles. The precise duties and incidents of these fiduciary offices are different in nature. For example, the extent to which the scheme manager of a unit trust ought to be considered to be specifically a trustee (as opposed generally to being considered to be a fiduciary) has been debated[40]: although those debates surrounded the nature of these schemes before the enactment of FSMA 2000. What is of particular importance at this stage is identifying not only the self-evident categories of fiduciary obligation, but rather considering the more marginal examples in the next section.

E. Marginal cases and the analytical distinctions in imposing fiduciary liability

5–20   This section considers some categories of person who may be considered to bear fiduciary obligations even though they are not among the classical categories of fiduciary. This is not intended to be an exhaustive list of financial actors, but rather a collection of examples. Deciding whether or not these relationships will be fiduciary relationships will require close analysis of the particular circumstances.

5–21   The first category is that of financial intermediaries. A "financial intermediary" is a person who stands impartially (usually) between two contracting parties, owing obligations to each of them, so as to put a transaction in place for them. Thus in a

---

[37] *Bristol and West Building Society v Mothew* [1998] Ch. 1.

[38] Financial Services and Markets Act 2000 s.237. See also A. Hudson, *Investment Entities*, p.206 and G. Thomas and A. Hudson, *Law of Trusts*, p.1580.

[39] See also A. Hudson, *Investment Entities*, p.218; and A. Hudson, "Open-ended investment companies" in *Palmer's Company Law*, Pt 5A generally.

[40] See, e.g. Sin, *The Legal Nature of the Unit Trust*, (Clarendon Press, 1997), pp.170, and 220. For the contrary view, now undoubtedly constituting English law after the Financial Services and Markets Act 2000 but also, it is suggested, undoubtedly the law before that time, see Hudson, *Investment Entities*, p.206 and G. Thomas and A. Hudson, *Law of Trusts*, p.1580 et seq.

number of the decided cases on interest rate swaps, a financial institution acted as an intermediary between an ordinary lending bank and a local authority in circumstances in which the local authority wanted to acquire an interest rate swap and the intermediary located a bank with the capital available for the transaction.[41] It is suggested that financial intermediaries who act on behalf of both counterparties to a transaction may owe both parties fiduciary obligations because the intermediary merely takes a fee and otherwise owes obligations to both parties to ensure that each receives the best possible deal in the circumstances.

Secondly, when the employees of financial institutions advise their employers' clients as to their investments, subject to the contents of the documentation between the parties, there may well be a fiduciary obligation. It is suggested that any individual acting as a trader for a financial institution which advises a customer on its investment activities will, absent other considerations, be interposing herself in the financial affairs of that person and so fall within Lord Browne-Wilkinson's conception of a fiduciary, as set out above.[42] It is suggested that the individual employee may be personally liable as a fiduciary in circumstances in which she goes beyond the terms of her authority from her employer in giving advice to a customer. Clearly, if the trader was acting intentionally in a fraudulent manner, for example to foist unprofitable investments which that trader has already bought onto unsuspecting customers so as to get those investments off her own books, then this would suggest a context in which the trader has overstepped her authority and thus assumed personal fiduciary liability. It is suggested that at the other end of the spectrum, the financial institution is acting as a fiduciary in the ordinary course of events whenever it or its employees are acting in the affairs of its customers, in the terms suggested by Lord Browne-Wilkinson[43] quoted at the start of this chapter—except that financial institutions will always include in their conduct of business documentation exclusions of this sort of liability. It is suggested, therefore, that the efficacy of such an exclusion would depend upon whether or not it accorded with the financial institution's obligations under FCA regulation, as is considered in Chapter 9. Thus, it is suggested that the exclusion of a fiduciary liability by means of a contractual exclusion clause is unlikely to be considered appropriate either when the customer is not treated appropriately under conduct of business regulation or when the trader advises that the customer take a risk which is unsuitable under applicable conduct of business regulation.[44]

5–22

There are circumstances, it is suggested, in which conduct of business regulation may also create fiduciary obligations, as well as negative their avoidance. Thus, as considered below,[45] the obligation under conduct of business regulation that investment firms acquire the best available price for the transaction (the "best

5–23

---

[41] e.g. *Morgan Grenfell v Welwyn Hatfield DC* [1995] 1 All E.R. 1; *Kleinwort Benson v South Tyneside MBC* [1994] 4 All E.R. 972.

[42] See para.5–04.

[43] See para.5–04.

[44] See the discussion of dishonest assistance at para.26–08.

[45] See para.5–32.

execution" requirement) tallies exactly with the dicta of Asquith L.J. that such an obligation constitutes a fiduciary obligation.[46]

5–24 It is conceivable that a financial advisor might overstep the ordinary bounds of giving advice to a customer and, as opposed merely to giving advice, assumes control of a customer's property. A financial advisor who assumes de facto control of a customer's investments will become a trustee de son tort by dint of that assumption of control.[47] This will impose a fiduciary obligation on the advisor, with the ramifications considered below.

5–25 Any financial advisor dealing with the confidential affairs of a customer will owe that customer fiduciary obligations in relation to that confidential material.[48] Owing fiduciary obligations in relation to confidential information means that the fiduciary will be prevented from earning unauthorised profits from the misuse of that confidential information and will also be required to compensate the customer for any loss caused by a breach of confidentiality. On the other hand, there are circumstances under statute—as considered in Chapter 15 in relation to money-laundering—in which banks will be obliged to pass information about suspicious transactions to the relevant authorities, thus breaching the prima facie duties to maintain a customer's confidence. A banker dealing with the confidential affairs of another person will owe fiduciary duties in the form of a constructive trust if she earns unauthorised profits from the misuse of that confidential information.

F. General types of activity which may give rise to fiduciary obligations

Fiduciary obligations arising in finance law

5–26 Fiduciary relationships do not arise in all ordinary banking relationships.[49] Rather their existence will depend upon the circumstances of the case. The terms of each fiduciary office will be dependent on their own circumstances, and that the categories of fiduciary office are open-ended so that new categories may always be added to the list with the result that the precise nature of those obligations will differ from case to case.[50] The general context of finance law, however, extends beyond ordinary banking transactions, as was considered in Chapter 1. Consequently, the range of circumstances in which fiduciary obligations may arise in financial transactions are all the broader. The following sections consider the general circumstances in which fiduciary obligations are found to exist, beyond the examples already considered in the previous section. This section is concerned with more thematic questions as to fiduciary liability.

---

[46] *Reading v Att Gen* [1949] 2 K.B. 232.
[47] *Mara v Browne* [1896] 1 Ch. 199.
[48] See para.21 37.
[49] *Kelly v Cooper* [1993] A.C. 205. See para.29–04; banks are not ordinarily trustees for their customers: *Foley v Hill* (1948) 9 E.R. 1002.
[50] *Henderson v Merrett Syndicates Ltd* [1995] 2 A.C. 145, 205, per Lord Browne-Wilkinson; *Bristol and West Building Society v Mothew* [1998] Ch. 1, 16.

Circumstances in which financial institutions interfere in their customer's affairs or assume control of those affairs

There may be other situations in which a financial institution may intermeddle   **5–27**
with a pre-existing fiduciary relationship to such an extent that it would be
deemed to be a fiduciary itself. The likelihood of such a finding is increased
where the financial institution is making all of the investment decisions for that
trust. However, it has been held that a trustee, and therefore by extension it is
suggested a constructive trustee, may limit its liabilities for negligent dealings
with the trust fund by means of contract in the form of a conduct of business
letter.[51] In circumstances in which a solicitor interfered with the running of a trust
to the extent where he was making its investment decisions, that solicitor has
been held to be a constructive trustee in relation to that trust.[52] Where a person
who has not been officially appointed as a trustee of an express trust interferes
with or involves himself in the business of the trust so as to appear to be acting as
a trustee, then that person shall be deemed to be a trustee. Smith L.J. stated the
nature of this form of constructive trust in the following way[53]:

> "... if one, not being a trustee and not having authority from a trustee, takes upon himself to
> intermeddle with trust matters or to do acts characteristic of the office of trustee, he may
> therefore make himself what is called in law trustee of his own wrong—i.e. a trustee de son
> tort, or, as it is also termed, a constructive trustee."

Therefore, a trustee de son tort is a person who intermeddles with trust business
or with some similar fiduciary relationship. Thus, one general context in which
fiduciary obligations are likely to arise is that in which the financial advisor takes
over responsibility for the customer's affairs in a manner which was not
anticipated in the parties' conduct of business agreement.

The context of the "house bank" and undue influence

One context in which a banker may become a fiduciary is in a situation in which   **5–28**
the bank operates as the customer's *"house bank"* in circumstances in which the
customer has no expertise in the instrument at issue and in which the customer is
intended by both parties to rely upon the expertise of the banker. The expression
"house bank" is one used to denote a bank which is the sole or principal banker
for a particular client: for banks dealing with large companies, to become such a
customer's house bank is the primary goal of its account management activities.
A house bank will seek to be the only person giving banking and financial advice
to the client. This will necessarily tend to make the client reliant on the bank's
advice if the client does agree that the bank should be the sole advisor. What has
happened in cases such as *Bankers Trust v Dharmala*[54] (which was discussed in
detail in Chapter 3) is that the bank has used this position of influence to
encourage the client into buying complex financial products which were both

---

[51] *Armitage v Nurse* [1998] Ch. 241.
[52] *Boardman v Phipps* [1967] 2 A.C. 67.
[53] *Mara v Browne* [1896] 1 Ch. 199, 209.
[54] [1996] C.L.C. 252.

more complex than was needed in the circumstances and which were more complex than the client's expertise could cope with. It is this use, or misuse, of the position of confidence which will open the bank up to fiduciary liabilities.

5–29   Thus, where there is such a relationship of trust and confidence it is more likely that the bank will be found to be a fiduciary because it is all the more likely that the customer would be taken to be entirely at the mercy of the bank's advice. When this relationship is considered in the light of the dicta of Millett L.J. then it will be all the more likely to lead a fiduciary obligation: those dicta were to the effect that: "[a] fiduciary is someone who has undertaken to act for or on behalf of another in a particular matter in circumstances which give rise to a relationship of trust and confidence."[55] It is suggested that this is a matter of context. The question is whether or not a customer of the type of the customer at issue would reasonably be entirely dependent on the advice of the bank in making the decision whether or not to acquire a financial instrument of the type that is at issue. Thus, an elderly customer who was nervous and unsure of how to act[56] would require more and better advice and explanation as to the risks involved in relation to a comparatively straightforward financial product, than a person with expertise in financial matters. If the bank failed to explain the risks to that elderly customer and then cajoled that customer into investing all of her life savings into a risky investment, then Lord Denning has held that that would constitute the bank a fiduciary.[57] Similarly, a corporate client may be in need of extensive advice and assistance in relation to a complex financial product, like an interest rate swap, where that client's level of expertise in relation to that particular product is such that it requires that advice.

5–30   A further result of the finding of a fiduciary liability in this context is that the bank is more likely to be found to be liable for undue influence due to that same relationship of trust and confidence which may lead a customer to consent to disadvantageous transactions.[58] Thus, if a bank cajoles a customer into buying an unsuitable product, then that will enable the contract to be set aside on the grounds of the undue influence. The following test for the application of the doctrine of undue influence was derived from *Bank of Credit and Commerce International SA v Aboody*[59] and is that applied in the House of Lords in *Barclays Bank v O'Brien*:

> "Class 1: actual undue influence,. Class 2: presumed undue influence ... the complainant only has to show, in the first instance, that there was a relationship of trust and confidence between the complainant and the wrongdoer of such a nature that it is fair to presume that the wrongdoer abused that relationship ..."

Therefore, the doctrine of undue influence divides into two: first, situations in which there has been de facto undue influence, and, second, circumstances in which undue influence is presumed. Typically it is required that there is a suitable

---

[55] *Bristol and West Building Society v Mothew* [1998] Ch. 1, 18, per Millett L.J.
[56] Not to assume that that is true of all elderly customers—rather this example asks us to imagine a person who is both elderly and also nervous and unsure.
[57] *Lloyds Bank v Bundy* [1975] Q.B. 326.
[58] See para.24–39; and A. Hudson, *Equity & Trusts*, Ch.29.
[59] [1992] 4 All E.R. 955.

degree of trust and confidence between the parties such that it could be presumed that one party would tend to rely on the other. It is not sufficient to demonstrate that one party is in a fiduciary relationship with the other.[60] This is because fiduciary relationships arise in a variety of situations, some of which would not necessarily include the possibility of undue influence.

Thus, in the case of *Lloyds Bank v Bundy*,[61] Lord Denning held that an elderly **5–31** bank customer who was cajoled into charging his only capital asset, his house, to the bank on the advice of the bank manager was entitled to rely on a presumption of undue influence between banker and a customer in the position of that particular customer. Lord Denning was concerned to protect the interests of a person who was vulnerable and who was in a situation in which he would tend to rely on the advice given to him by the bank. However, Lord Denning's formulation of the appropriate principles has been much criticised, as will emerge below; nevertheless the categories identified by Lord Denning are considered in Chapter 24. Instead, the tighter formulation of the *Barclays Bank v O'Brien* principle has been favoured over Lord Denning's concern to achieve the right result first and then to explain the intellectual means of getting there second. Lord Hoffmann in the Privy Council held that[62]:

> "Certain relationships—parent and child, trustee and beneficiary, etc—give rise to a presumption that one party had influence over the other.... if the transaction is one which cannot reasonably be explained by the relationship, that will be prima facie evidence of undue influence. Even if the relationship does not fall into one of the established categories, the evidence may show that one party did in fact have influence over the other."

The question then revolves around whether or not there is a relationship of trust and confidence such that one party has influence over the other. In relation to financial instruments which are sold in an unsuitable fashion or which are intrinsically unsuitable, it is suggested that the possibility of undue influence being found is all the greater and that the possibility of a fiduciary obligation being found is also all the greater.

Best execution and fiduciary liability

The categories of fiduciary liability are open-ended, as was outlined above. One **5–32** of the key tenets of this book is that a part of the future for finance law will be in the convergence between principles of private law and principles of financial regulation. Financial regulation, as is discussed in Chapter 7, functions ever more on the basis of high-level principles as opposed solely to detailed regulatory rules. Consequently, new fiduciary and quasi-fiduciary relationships may emerge from that regulation, in particular when positive obligations are imposed on regulated firms which require them to act in a particular way when dealing with their clients. An example of this drift emerges from the conduct of business obligations created by the Markets in Financial Instruments Directive ("MiFID"). In particular there is an obligation to obtain the best price available for a customer

[60] *Re Coomber* [1911] 1 Ch. 723; *Goldsworthy v Brickell* [1987] Ch. 378.
[61] [1975] Q.B. 326.
[62] *R. v Attorney General* Unreported March 17, 2003 (Privy Council appeal 61 of 2002), para.21ff.

in any transaction conducted for that customer: this is known as the "best execution" principle.[63] In *Reading v R*[64] Asquith L.J. proposed the following summary of those circumstances in which a fiduciary relationship can be said to exist:

> "A consideration of the authorities suggests that for the present purpose a 'fiduciary relation' exists ... whenever the plaintiff entrusts to the defendant a job to be performed, for instance, the negotiation of a contract on his behalf or for his benefit, and relies on the defendant to procure for the plaintiff the best terms available ..."

The reference to acquiring "the best terms available" could be said to encompass the requirement in MiFID that investment firms provide best execution for clients.[65] Thus if an investment firm is obliged to seek the best method and price for completing a transaction for a customer, then it would be acting in a fiduciary capacity in so doing. As such the earlier discussion of fiduciary liability in the banker-client relationship would need to be amended in relation to circumstances in which an investment firm is obliged to seek "best execution" for a client because that is a fiduciary activity. Thus if the investment firm acquired a price for the customer from which the firm stood to earn some personal profit and which was not the best price which could possibly have been obtained, to the extent envisaged in the FCA COBS regulations, then either that profit or the excess portion over the best price available would be held on constructive trust for the client. The nature of the constructive trust is considered in Chapter 21.[66]

G. Banker's fiduciary liability in the global financial crisis 2007-09

The lack of fiduciary liability in a banker-customer relationship

5–33   As is discussed in Chapter 29, a bank will not ordinarily owe fiduciary duties to its customers unless there is something special about the relationship. So, if the bank was acting as trustee in any event, then it will owe fiduciary duties to its customers as a trustee. What is more complicated is whether or not the court will infer the existence of a fiduciary duty (such as a constructive trust) when a bank has acted inappropriately during the financial crisis of 2008. The likely fall-out from the crisis will be a large amount of litigation relating to allegations of fraud, negligence and breach of contract brought by customers against financial institutions in different jurisdictions around the world. Those issues are considered in Chapters 24 and 25. This section considers whether or not there might be fiduciary duties imposed too.

---

[63] See para.10–15.
[64] [1949] 2 K.B. 232 at 236.
[65] See para.10–15.
[66] See para.21–35.

When do bankers acquire fiduciary liability due to their misfeasance, and when necessarily due to their status?

As was discussed above, there is an interesting question as to whether fiduciary liability is always based solely on the nature of the relationship between a firm and its customer, or whether there are occasions in which fiduciary liability is imposed because of the unconscionable actions of the defendant. It is suggested that if the banker has acted fraudulently (as considered in Chapter 24) then that banker will have acted unconscionably and therefore any profits earned from fraud will be held on constructive trust. This point is not without complications. It has been held that in cases of fraudulent misrepresentation there will be no constructive trust imposed on the bank.[67] However, the core of trusts law, identifiable for example in *Westdeutsche Landesbank v Islington*,[68] provides that "when property is obtained by fraud, equity places a constructive trust on the fraudulent recipient". It is suggested that in any circumstance in which a bank had discretionary management powers over a customer's assets or in which a bank exerted undue influence over a customer, then there will be a fiduciary duty imposed over any profits taken from that transaction. Fiduciary liability is not just a structure, it is also the conscience of English private law—it exists primarily to prevent benefits being taken from fraud.

5–34

4. LIABILITIES UNDER FIDUCIARY LAW IN GENERAL TERMS

A. Fiduciary liabilities in essence

Thus far we have concentrated on identifying those circumstances which will give rise to fiduciary obligations. This section considers the liabilities which will arise in general terms if those obligations are broken. The principal liabilities of fiduciaries arise under constructive trust principles—which are considered in detail in Chapter 21 and in Chapter 26. In essence, whenever a fiduciary takes an unauthorised profit from her fiduciary office, then that profit will be held on constructive trust for the beneficiaries of the fiduciary relationship.[69] The purpose of this principle is to prevent the possibility of conflicts of interest between a fiduciary's personal interests and her fiduciary obligations.[70] Thus, when a fiduciary acquires property held under the fiduciary obligation, further to the dicta of Megarry V.C. in *Tito v Waddell (No.2)*[71] the beneficiaries of that relationship are entitled to have the sale set aside. Any unconscionably earned profits will be held on constructive trust. This principle also applies to fiduciary

5–35

---

[67] *Daly v Sydney Stock Exchange Ltd* (1986) 160 C.L.R. 371, 387; *Lonrho v Al Fayed (No.2)* [1992] 1 W.L.R. 1. cf. *Collings v Lee* (2001) 82 P. & C.R. 3. Although the opposite was accepted, without close analysis, in *Daraydan Holdings Ltd v Solland International Ltd* [2004] EWHC 622, at [88], per Lawrence Collins J.

[68] [1996] A.C. 669.

[69] *Boardman v Phipps* [1967] A.C. 67.

[70] [1967] A.C. 67.

[71] [1977] Ch. 106. cf. *Prince Jefri Bolkiah v KPMG* [1999] 1 All E.R. 517—with reference to "Chinese walls".

relationships such as acquisitions by agents of the interests of their principals,[72] and to purchases by directors from their companies[73] although most articles of association in English companies expressly permit such transactions.

B.   Not all breaches by fiduciaries will result in fiduciary liability

5–36   It is important to understand that just because a person who happens to be a fiduciary commits a breach of some other duty, that does not necessarily hold her open to liability under fiduciary law. Thus, if, for example, a banker were to commit an act of negligence, then that banker's liability will lie only in the tort of negligence. As Millett L.J. put the matter: "not every breach of duty by a fiduciary is a breach of fiduciary duty".[74] However, if the same banker committed a breach of a specifically fiduciary duty—such as preserving the customer's confidence, from which she earned an unauthorised profit—then that would constitute a breach of a fiduciary duty and would thus attract liability under fiduciary law. Similarly, a financial intermediary acting for both sides of a transaction will owe fiduciary obligations as the agent of both parties not to permit conflicts between her own interests and his fiduciary duty, and also not to permit conflicts between the interests of both parties to the transaction. Again, causing loss through negligence as an agent will not be a fiduciary matter; although if that intermediary was acting as trustee of property for both parties and caused both parties loss through some breach of trust then her liability would be liability either to recover the property or for equitable compensation for breach of trust.[75] Therefore, it is not possible simply to read from a list of fiduciary categories so as to whether or not fiduciary liability applies. And even deciding that someone is a fiduciary does not mean that that person will always bear fiduciary liability for all of their actions.

5.   EXCLUSION AND LIMITATION OF LIABILITY

A.   Exclusion of liability in general terms

5–37   The principal means of avoiding liability as a fiduciary would be for the financial institution to seek to acquire authorisation or indemnity or exclusion of liability in the conduct of business letter between the parties for any act or omission which would otherwise constitute a breach of fiduciary duty. For example, in relation to fiduciaries' responsibilities for profits made from their fiduciary office, a constructive trust will only take effect over *unauthorised* profits and therefore if those profits are authorised in the terms of any conduct of business agreement, then they would not be *unauthorised*. There are types of fiduciary who are not able to limit or exclude their liabilities: for example managers of unit trusts[76] and

---

[72] *Edwards v Meyrick* [1842] 2 Hare 60.
[73] *Aberdeen Railway Co v Blaikie Brothers* (1854) 1 Macq. 461.
[74] *Bristol and West Building Society v Mothew* [1998] Ch. 1, at p.16.
[75] *Target Holdings v Redferns* [1996] A.C. 421.
[76] See para.52–01.

trustees of pension funds.[77] It is suggested that positive obligations considered in relation to the *FCA Handbook*—as considered in Part III and Part X of this book—constitute mandatory obligations which may not be excluded by an instrument setting out a fiduciary's obligations. It is suggested that this must be at the heart of a finance law analysis of exclusion of liability clauses. If the Financial Services and Markets Act 2000 ("FSMA 2000") or financial regulation does not permit an exclusion of liability, then that provision cannot take effect. Otherwise, the purported exclusion of liability will take effect in accordance with the decided case law. The decided cases on the liabilities of trustees are considered in the next section.

B.   Exclusion of trustees' liability

On the exemption of trustees' liabilities specifically, the decision of the Court of Appeal in *Armitage v Nurse*[78] will permit exclusion of liability to include liability for gross negligence but not for dishonesty.[79] Millett L.J. held that it was permissible for a trustee to exclude her liability for all defaults including gross negligence, except that a trustee could not exclude her own liability for breach of trust if that breach of trust was caused by her own fraud or dishonesty. Earlier authorities which had suggested that gross negligence could not be excused were not followed.[80] On the *Armitage v Nurse* approach to this area of law, a trustee exemption clause will be effective in relation to the matters for which it seeks to exclude the trustee's liability for breach of trust, in the words of Millett L.J.,[81] "no matter how indolent, imprudent, lacking in diligence, negligent or wilful he may have been, so long as he had not acted dishonestly". The court's role when faced with an exclusion clause is that the court 'must construe the words of the exemption clause in light of the conduct complained of and decide whether liability has been excluded by the terms of the clause. This approach has been followed in numerous cases: *Bogg v Raper*[82]; *Barraclough v Mell*[83]; and *Baker v JE Clark & Co (Transport) UK Ltd.*[84]

5–38

In explaining the limit of the trustee's obligations, Millett L.J. had the following to say:

5–39

> "[T]here is an irreducible core of obligations owed by the trustees to the beneficiaries and enforceable by them which is fundamental to the concept of a trust. If the beneficiaries have no rights enforceable against the trustees there are no trusts. But I do not accept the further submission that there core obligations include the duties of skill and care, prudence and diligence. The duty of trustees to perform the trusts honestly and in good faith for the benefit of the beneficiaries is the minimum necessary to give substance to the trusts, but in my opinion

---

[77] See para.55–01.
[78] [1998] Ch. 241.
[79] *Armitage v Nurse* [1998] Ch. 241; *Walker v Stones* [2001] Q.B. 902.
[80] See *Pass v Dundas* (1880) 43 L.T. 665, as held by Millett L.J. at [1998] Ch. 241, 256.
[81] Followed in *Barraclough v Mell* [2005] EWHC 3387 (Ch.), [2006] W.T.L.R. 203, [90].
[82] (1998/99) 1 I.T.E.L.R. 267.
[83] [2005] EWHC 3387 (Ch.), [2006] W.T.L.R. 203.
[84] [2006] EWCA Civ 464.

it is sufficient . . . a trustee who relied on the presence of a trustee exemption clause to justify what he proposed to do would thereby lose its protection: he would be acting recklessly in the proper sense of the term."

Thus, while it is accepted that one does not have an arrangement which can properly be defined as being a trust if the obligations imposed on the fiduciary are too slight, almost all of the liabilities ordinarily associated with being a trustee can be excluded. The issue could be considered in the following manner. The trustee would argue that she only agreed to act as a trustee on the basis that her liability was limited to the extent of the exclusion of liability clause. Therefore, the trustee would not be acting in bad conscience by insisting that she should not be liable for any default beyond that specified in the exclusion of liability clause because she did not agree to be bound by anything else. Alternatively, it might be said that if someone agrees to act as a trustee then she must be taken to accept the general obligations of good conscience and good management required of a trustee and therefore that to allow extensive exclusion clauses to be effective subverts the necessary stringency of the office of trustee. There is, it is suggested, no middle course which will satisfy both of these policies. In the context of the law of finance, it is suggested, matters are different when financial regulation imposes positive obligations on the fiduciary as a regulated person to perform particular acts—such as the classification of a client's expertise or such as acquiring "best execution" of a transaction—because the regulated person cannot claim that her liabilities have been excluded when financial regulation compels action. It is also important to note that the liability of fiduciaries in relation to unit trusts cannot be excluded,[85] and the same is true of trustees in occupational pension schemes.[86] These two categories of trust are separately regulated and the obligations of their fiduciaries, of the sort considered above, may not be excluded.

5–40   A different approach to exclusion of liability by fiduciaries was advanced by two dissenting judgments in the Privy Council in *Spread Trustee Company Ltd v Hutcheson*.[87] Lady Hale noted that the Supreme Court has yet to have the opportunity to consider the judgment of Millett L.J. in *Armitage v Nurse* and also doubted that the law in England and Wales had always been clear about the treatment of grossly negligent breaches of trust. Her ladyship made the point that cases on which Millett L.J. has relied (such as *Re City Fire and Equitable Insurance*[88] and *Re Trusts of Leeds City Brewery Debenture*[89]) did not in fact consider the point whether or not trustees were entitled to exclude their liabilities.[90] Of particular interest were the remarks of Lord Kerr who doubted the very notion of fiduciary's being allowed to limit their liabilities under the general law:[91]

---

[85] Financial Services and Markets Act 2000 s.253.
[86] Pensions Act 1995 s.35.
[87] [2011] UKPC 13, [2012] 1 All E.R. 251. See generally Matthews, 1989, which is referred to extensively by the Privy Council.
[88] [1925] Ch 407.
[89] [1925] Ch 532n.
[90] [2011] UKPC 13, [2012] 1 All E.R. 251, at [136].
[91] [2011] UKPC 13, [2012] 1 All E.R. 251, at [180].

"If, as I suggested at the beginning of this judgment, the placing of reliance on a responsible person to manage property so as to promote the interests of the beneficiaries of a trust is central to the concept of trusteeship, denying trustees the opportunity to avoid liability for their gross negligence seems to be entirely in keeping with that essential aim."

Properly-speaking, a fiduciary like a trustee ought not to be able to exclude liability for gross negligence. A trustee is a fiduciary who is required to act selflessly in the interests of her beneficiaries, or to take proper advice where that is not otherwise possible. It is not too high a standard to set for that person to avoid grossly negligent performances of those duties. The decision in *Armitage v Nurse* does appear to be capable of operating as an opiate on the assiduity of professional trustees.

C.   Exclusion of investment firms' liability by agreement letter, Conduct of Business regulation, and the Unfair Contract Terms Act

It was held by the Federal Court of Australia in *Securities and Investment Commission v Citigroup Global Markets Australia Pty Ltd*[92] that a bank's fiduciary obligations may be limited by means of a "terms of agreement" letter which established the basis on which the bank and its customer would do business. What is different about the Australian context of fiduciary law and the UK context of finance law is that conduct of business regulation in the UK prohibits regulated firms from excluding their obligations under conduct of business regulation: therefore, under English law a financial institution may exclude its fiduciary obligations by agreement (provided that the institution is not acting dishonestly) but it may not exclude any fiduciary obligations which are required by conduct of business regulation, including the regulatory obligations to act in the best interests of the customer, to avoid conflicts of interest[93] and to achieve best execution of transactions for its customers.[94] Furthermore, an investment firm will not be able to exclude its liability by means of a provision which breaches the Unfair Contract Terms Act.[95]

5–41

---

[92] [2007] F.C.A. 963.
[93] COBS, para.2.1.2. C. Band and K. Anderson, "Conflicts of Interest in Financial Services and Markets: the Regulatory Aspect" (2007) *Journal of International Banking Law and Regulation*, pp.2, 99.
[94] See para.10–01 et seq.
[95] See para.18–53.

CONFLICT OF LAWS

CORE PRINCIPLES

Much of the law of finance is concerned with transactions which are created across borders and therefore issues will arise as to the manner in which international disputes are to be resolved. It may well be that one country's laws will offer a beneficial outcome to one party whereas another country's laws or procedural rules would offer a beneficial outcome to the other party. Furthermore, a litigant resident in one country would not wish to incur the expense and uncertainty of litigating in another country.

Private international law (also known as "conflict of laws") is the means by which English law decides which system of rules and also which jurisdiction should resolve any dispute which arises across borders. There is an important distinction between two issues. First, identifying the system of rules which should be used to decide the dispute (e.g. whether French law, English law, German law, or whatever): this is known as identifying the "governing law". Secondly, identifying which jurisdiction's courts should have the competence to hear the case: this is known as "choice of jurisdiction".

In relation to contractual disputes within the EU, the governing law is identified by reference to the Rome Convention; otherwise disputes arising outside the EU are decided by the traditional common law principles. Where there is an express choice of a governing law in a contract, that will be the governing law of the contract. However, where there is no such choice of governing law (if the contract omits to mention it or if the contract was made orally) then the governing law will ordinarily be the system of law with which the transaction has the closest connection.

In relation to tortious disputes, the identification of the governing law will be resolved by identifying in which legal jurisdiction the most significant elements of the tort were committed: such that the system of law connected to that jurisdiction will be the system of rules which will resolve the dispute.

Ordinarily a well-drafted contract will contain a choice of jurisdiction clause: such an express choice of jurisdiction will be binding between the parties.

1. INTRODUCTION

6–01   Financial markets operate across borders, particularly in the corporate context. Indeed the purpose of the EC securities directives is to promote pan-European financial markets between Member States. Law functions primarily in terms of distinct jurisdictions. Therefore, issues may arise as to which system of law should decide an issue which arises in relation to cross-border financial transactions, and which jurisdiction's courts should hear any dispute. These issues are referred to as "the conflict of laws", in that different systems of law may have different rules which will then come into conflict. This area is also known as "private international law", although it is important to note that private international law is primarily a field of English law (except to the extent that European Union law now dictates some of its key concepts) under which English law decides how those issues should be resolved.[1] This chapter considers the principal rules of private international law as they relate to cross-border financial transactions.

6–02   There are two key questions in the private international law context: in which jurisdiction and subject to which system of rules will any such cross-border dispute be decided? It is important to distinguish between two types of private international law question. The first is a question as to which rules will decide any question. This is a question as to the appropriate "system of law". The second question is as to which courts will hear the case and decide on the question. This is a question as to the appropriate jurisdiction to hear the case. Suppose the following example. A bank from Ruritania enters into a contract with a company from Suntopia, but the contract is entered into between branches which both parties maintain in Utopia with the intention that the contract is performed in Utopia and in Utopian dollars. A dispute arises in contract law as to whether or not damages are payable. It is likely that the bank would want the dispute to be decided in accordance with Ruritanian law and heard in the courts of Ruritania because that would make the litigation cheaper for it and because it is more likely to be familiar with the laws of that jurisdiction; whereas the company is likely to prefer that the matter is heard in accordance with the law and by the courts of Suntopia for the same reasons.[2] The system of law issues relates to whether it is the contract law of Ruritania or Suntopia or Utopia which should decide whether or not damages are payable. It is likely, as considered below, that on these facts

---

[1] It should be noted that within the UK there are three common law jurisdictions which may raise conflicts of law issues between them: England and Wales, Scotland and Northern Ireland.

[2] This would be true unless for some reason there was something particular about the law of one of the other jurisdictions which the parties would think was more likely to make them successful.

the contract would be considered to have the closest connection with Utopia. There is then a distinct question as to which courts should hear the claim. It is possible that the claim should be heard in Utopia because that is the jurisdiction which has the closest connection to the performance of the transaction. As will emerge below, English private international law is governed by EU law if the dispute relates to the Member States of the EU, or else by the old common law if there is no connection between that dispute and the EU. The following sections consider, in turn, choice of law in contract disputes, choice of law in tort disputes, and choice of jurisdiction.

2.   CONTRACT—CHOICE OF LAW

A.   The sources of law on contract in conflicts of law

This section considers the principles of private international law which deal with contract disputes between different jurisdictions. It is possible for contracting parties from different jurisdictions to choose which system of law—known as the "governing law"—they want to govern their contract. That system of law may be the jurisdiction in which the parties are doing business, it may be one of the jurisdictions in which the parties are doing a part of their business, it may be a neutral system of law (often English law or New York law in financial practice) which the parties consider is appropriate to deal with their transaction, or it may be the system of law of one or other of the parties' home jurisdictions with which they are familiar.[3] In the context of complex financial transactions the use of foreign currency, the use of subsidiaries in different jurisdictions, and the use of multiple branches and transactions across borders are the mainstay of market activity. Therefore, the English approach to conflicts of laws is of great importance when dealing with contracts executed in such circumstances.

Disputes between countries in the UK

6–04

6–03

Traditional English private international law rules apply to disputes between legal jurisdictions within the United Kingdom, and in particular the Contracts (Applicable Law) Act 1990. The Rome Convention will not apply in relation to conflict of laws disputes within the United Kingdom. The approach in English private international law to the selection of the system of rules which would govern a contract was known as the identification of "the proper law of contract",[4] as set out by Lord Wright in the following terms:[5]

> "English law ... has refused to treat as conclusive, rigid or arbitrary criteria ... and has treated the matter is depending on the intention of the parties to be ascertained in each case on a consideration of the terms of the contract, the situation of the parties, and generally on all the surrounding facts. It may be that the parties have in terms in their agreement expressed what

---

[3] The assumption being that if one is a citizen of Utopia and ones knows the laws and courts of Utopia well, then one is likely to prefer the laws and jurisdiction Utopia to govern one's contracts.
[4] *Mount Albert BC v Australasian Temperance and General Assurance Society* [1938] A.C. 224, 240; *Bonython v Commonwealth of Australia* [1951] A.C. 201, 209, Lord Simonds.
[5] *Mount Albert BC v Australasian Temperance and General Assurance Society* [1938] A.C. 224, 240.

law they intend to govern, and in that case prima facie their intention will be effectuated by the court. But in most cases they do not do so the parties may not have thought of the matter at all. Then the court has to impute an intention, or to determine for the parties what is the proper law which, as just and reasonable persons, they ought [to] or would have intended if they had thought about the question when they made the contract."

Thus the English courts would consider all of the circumstances and decide with which of the possible systems of law the contract and the parties' transaction had the closest connection.[6] In general terms, the courts would give effect to an express choice of law clause in a contract.[7]

Introduction: conflict of law issues outwith the UK

6–05 Contracts created before December 17, 2009 are governed by the Rome Convention, as considered in this section of this chapter; whereas contracts created after December 17, 2009 are governed by the Rome I Regulation, as considered in the following section of this chapter. The change has been signalled by the introduction of the Rome I Regulation by the European Union which has updated the Rome Convention which had been in place previously. The development of EU law in this area is part of the movement towards harmonisation of private international law rules within the EU.

Contracts created on or before December 17, 2009

Introduction

6–06 This section relates to the choice of a governing law in a contract created on or before December 17, 2009. The Rome Convention deals with questions as to choice of the system of law which will govern a contract created within that time period. The underlying philosophy of the regulation is that "the autonomy of the parties to a contract . . . must be respected with the result that express choices of jurisdiction in a contract will be respected by the courts. The broader policy goal of the Convention was the "sound operation of the internal market".[8] Competence ultimately to decide issues as to the interpretation of the Convention lies with the European Court of Justice ("ECJ"). Municipal courts are, however, only required to refer questions to the ECJ in circumstances in which they consider that there is a point of law at issue on which they require the ruling of the ECJ. However, in reaching their own decisions, municipal courts are required to act "in accordance with the principles laid down by, and any relevant decision of [the ECJ]".[9] There is similarly an obligation to effect a uniform application of the Convention across the EU rather than simply applying the old English common law rules.[10]

---

[6] See, for example, *The Assunzione* [1954] P 150; and *Re United Railways of the Havana Regla Warehouses Ltd* [1960] Ch 52, 91 where it was held that: "many matters have to be taken into consideration. All these the principle of a place of contracting, the place of performance, the places of residence or business of the parties respectively, and the nature and subject matter of the contract."
[7] See, however, *Vita Food Products Inc v Unus Shipping Co* [1939] A.C. 277.
[8] Council Regulation No.44/2001, para.(1).
[9] s.3(1) of the 1990 Act.
[10] Art.18, Rome Convention.

The scope of the Rome Convention

Article 1(1) of the Rome Convention provides that "The rules of this Convention **6–07** shall apply to contractual obligations in any situation involving a choice between the laws of different countries".[11] Therefore, the first issue is to demonstrate that the dispute is contractual in nature.[12] There must be a choice of law problem for the provisions of the Rome Convention to apply. The requirement that there must be "a choice between the laws of different countries" does not apply to purely procedural or evidential matters between the parties.[13] The reference is specifically to "country" and not to "system of law" means that the laws of, for example, individual US states would not fall within the Convention as not relating to distinct countries[14] but only to regions within a country. Article 2 provides that: "Any law specified by this Convention shall be applied whether or not it is the law of a Contracting State." Therefore, the Convention is to have universal application and is not restricted to the application of the legal systems of member states. For example, the parties would be free to choose the law of New York, and are thus not restricted to choosing European systems of law.

Express choice of law

Where the parties make an express choice of law, Art.3 of the Rome Convention **6–08** provides that "a contract shall be governed by the law chosen by the parties".[15] Thus the contracting parties are at liberty to select any system of law they wish.[16] It is no objection to such a choice of law that the system of law chosen has no other connection with the subject matter of the contract.[17] An express choice of law is made where the parties use words such "this contract is governed by" or "this contract is to be construed in accordance with" or "this contract is subject to" whichever system of law is intended.[18] The parties are also entitled to alter their choice of law at any time during the course of the agreement.[19]

Where the parties have no contract in writing, or where there is only an inferred governing law provision

A choice of governing law provision may be valid even if that choice is merely **6–09** "demonstrated with reasonable certainty by the terms of the contract or the

---

[11] The issue raised must not be tortious or restitutionary for the Convention to apply.

[12] See for example *Kleinwort Benson v Glasgow CC* [1997] 4 All E.R. 641, HL.

[13] Art.1(2)(h), Rome Convention.

[14] However, Cheshire and North take the view that the Convention may be applicable in such situations, *op cit.* 469.

[15] Art.3(1), Rome Convention. At common law see *Whitworth Street Estates (Manchester) Ltd v James Miller and Partners Ltd* [1970] A.C. 583, 603, *per* Lord Reid.

[16] For an account of the development of this principle, see *Dicey and Morris on the Conflict of Laws* 13th edn (Sweet & Maxwell, 2000), pp.1216 et seq.

[17] *Vita Foods Products Inc v Unus Shipping Co Ltd* [1939] A.C. 290.

[18] *Helbert Wagg & Co Ltd, Re* [1956] Ch. 323, 340.

[19] Art.3(2), Rome Convention.

circumstances of the case".[20] Thus a contract effected between English counterparties in London and denominated in sterling for delivery in London would have an English governing law with reasonable certainty.[21] A choice of arbitration clause will often suggest that the governing law is intended to be the same as the system identified for the arbitration.[22] However, in cross-border transactions it will not necessarily be reasonably certain which system of law is intended without an express contractual choice of law provision. For example, if a transaction is contracted between the London branch of a German bank and the Parisian branch of a Spanish bank, denominated in US dollars for delivery in Panama, then it is suggested that there will not be "reasonable certainty" as to the intended governing law of that contract simply based on those factors because each factor suggests a different system of law. Equally, if the parties conduct their business solely by means of conversation between their traders then there will probably be a verbal contract of some sort between them but that contract will not usually include a choice of governing law provision. The "circumstances of the case" in this context may include, in the case of transactions where there is incomplete documentation, taped telephone conversations between traders which indicate the intention to use one system of law rather than another. A previous course of dealing between the parties would be evidence tending towards the conclusion that a particular system of law had been selected.[23]

Governing law applying to a part only of the contract

6–10 It is also possible for the parties to choose to have any given governing law apply only to a part of their contract, in that the Convention provides that: "By their choice the parties can select the law applicable to the whole or a part only of the contract".[24] The only reservation with this sort of structure would be that it is awkward for there to be different systems of law governing different parts of the contract if disputes arise which in turn raise problems simultaneously as to different systems of law.

Mandatory rules

6–11 The only restriction on freedom of choice is where the parties' choice would offend against the "mandatory rules"[25] of a jurisdiction.[26] That is, where "all the other elements" of the contract "are connected with one country only", then the parties may not select as their governing law the law of another country so as to "prejudice the application of rules of the law of that country which cannot be

---

[20] Art.3(1), Rome Convention.
[21] See *Amin Rasheed Shipping Corp v Kuwait Insurance Co* [1984] A.C. 50, as well as Art.3(1) of the Convention.
[22] *Egon Oldendorff v Libera Corp (No.2)* [1996] 1 Lloyd's Rep 380, 389.
[23] See the Giuliano and Lagarde Report, p.17, OJ C282 of October 31, 1980.
[24] Art.3(1), Rome Convention. This is known as "depecage".
[25] Art.3(3), Rome Convention.
[26] In English law this would appear to encompass provisions such as the Unfair Contract Terms Act 1977.

derogated from by contract",[27] which are referred to as the "mandatory rules" of that jurisdiction. For example, a choice of law by two German parties with a view to eluding some provision of German criminal law unlawfully would be ineffective under the terms of the Convention. Furthermore, it is open to the courts to apply the mandatory rules of another country "with which the situation has a close connection".[28] Both of these principles ensure that there is no illegality effected as part of a commercial transaction.

No express choice of law

Where there has not been any choice of law made expressly by the parties, as considered immediately above, Art.4(1) provides: **6–12**

> "To the extent that the law applicable to the contract has not been chosen in accordance with Article 3, the contract shall be governed by the law of the country with which it is most closely connected."

This provision may also apply where there has been an ineffective choice of law, as a result, for example, of choosing conflicting laws to govern the contract. It has been held[29] that where a German party and a Japanese party to a contract failed to specify a choice of law, because they used a standard form contract it was held that they should be taken to have chosen English law because that was the system of law most commonly used in relation to that standard form contract and because it contained an English choice of arbitration clause.

Contracts created after December 17, 2009

Introduction

This section relates to the choice of a governing law in a contract created after December 17, 2009, to which the Rome I Regulation ("the Regulation") applies.[30] The Rome I Regulation is very similar to the Rome Convention, so this section will focus on the key differences between the Convention and the Regulation. The principles of the Regulation apply "in situations involving a conflict of laws, to contractual obligations in civil and commercial matters".[31]   **6–13**

Choice of law under the Regulation

The most significant provision in the Regulation is article 3. The central principle remains party autonomy: that is, the parties can choose their own governing law rather than have one imposed by operation of law. Article 3(1) provides that a contract is governed by the system of law chosen by the parties: **6–14**

---

[27] Art.3(3), Rome Convention.
[28] Art.7(1), Rome Convention.
[29] *Egon Oldendorff v Libera Corp (No.2)* [1996] 1 Lloyd's Rep 380.
[30] Regulation 593/2008.
[31] Regulation, art.1(1).

"A contract shall be governed by the law chosen by the parties. The choice shall be made expressly or clearly demonstrated by the terms of the contract or the circumstances of the case. By their choice the parties can select the law applicable to the whole or to part only of the contract."

Consequently, under the Regulation the choice of law must either be "expressly" chosen or "clearly demonstrated" in the parties' agreement. Further to article 2, any system of law can be chosen whether belonging to a Member State of the EU or not.

Failure to make a choice of law

6–15 The Regulation provides for a list of rules in circumstances in which the parties have not made an express choice of law. When the parties have not selected a choice of law expressly, then Article 4(1) provides as follows:

"To the extent that the law applicable to the contract has not been chosen in accordance with Article 3 and without prejudice to Articles 5 to 8, the law governing the contract shall be determined as follows:
(a)   a contract for the sale of goods shall be governed by the law of the country where the seller has his habitual residence;
(b)   a contract for the provision of services shall be governed by the law of the country where the service provider has his habitual residence …
(e)   a franchise contract shall be governed by the law of the country where the franchisee has his habitual residence;
(f)   a distribution contract shall be governed by the law of the country where the distributor has his habitual residence; …
(h)   a contract concluded within a multilateral system which brings together or facilitates the bringing together of multiple third-party buying and selling interests in financial instruments, as defined by Article 4(1), point (17) of Directive 2004/39/EC, in accordance with non-discretionary rules and governed by a single law, shall be governed by that law."

The reference to multilateral systems would cover the multilateral trading platforms and similar trading environments facilitated by the Markets in Financial Instruments Directive which is discussed in Chapter 7.

Where a contract falls outwith the provisions of Article 4(1), then Article 4(2) provides that:

"Where the contract is not covered by paragraph 1 or where the elements of the contract would be covered by more than one of points (a) to (h) of paragraph 1, the contract shall be governed by the law of the country where the party required to effect the characteristic performance of the contract has his habitual residence."

6–16 The issue then is in identifying which party is required to effect the "characteristic performance" of the contract. This will be difficult to identify in relation to contracts for differences and interest rate swaps, for example, where more than one party is required to perform equally significant obligations under the contract. In relation to physically-settled options, for example, it would easier to identify the party which is required to make delivery of the underlying assets. However, in such circumstances it would still be difficult to know whether the performing party acts through its head office or the branch through which the particular transaction was contracted. In such situations it is suggested that the test in Article 4(3) or (4) should govern the choice of law question.

Article 4(3) and (4) provide general exceptions to the two previous provisions in circumstances in which there is another country with which the contract is "more closely connected", in which case it is the system of law of that country which shall govern the contract. Article 4(3) provides that:

> "Where it is clear from all the circumstances of the case that the contract is manifestly more closely connected with a country other than that indicated in paragraphs 1 or 2, the law of that other country shall apply."

And article 4(4) provides, where (1) and (2) do not address the case, for a test in which the governing law is allocated to the system of law of the country with which the transaction has the closest connection:

> "Where the law applicable cannot be determined pursuant to paragraphs 1 or 2, the contract shall be governed by the law of the country with which it is most closely connected."

This, it is suggested, returns the law to the sorts of considerations which used to be the meat and drink of the traditional English approach to conflict of law questions, as considered above.[32]

Mandatory rules

The Regulation is clearer than the Rome Convention about rules of municipal law which may not be excluded by the parties' contract. The mandatory rules of a system of law are not excluded by a choice of law. As is provided by Article 9(1), mandatory rules are defined as follows:

6–17

> "Overriding mandatory provisions are provisions the respect for which is regarded as crucial by a country for safeguarding its public interests, such as its political, social or economic organisation, to such an extent that they are applicable to any situation falling within their scope, irrespective of the law otherwise applicable to the contract under this Regulation."

Again, it is the mandatory rules of a system of law, such as its criminal law and its insolvency law, which are excluded. In relation to mandatory rules Article 9(3) provides that:

> "Effect may be given to the overriding mandatory provisions of the law of the country where the obligations arising out of the contract have to be or have been performed, in so far as those overriding mandatory provisions render the performance of the contract unlawful. In considering whether to give effect to those provisions, regard shall be had to their nature and purpose and to the consequences of their application or non-application."

So, where the performance of the contract would be unlawful, the mandatory laws of that jurisdiction will override the parties' contractual provisions.

---

[32] Para 10-11.

3. TORT—CHOICE OF LAW

6–18   It is possible that torts can be committed across borders, as with as negligence or defamation. The internet and email, of course, are mechanisms which make it possible for an act to be committed in a number of jurisdictions simultaneously. Therefore, there will be questions as to which system of tort law will deal with the dispute. The choice of law rules for tort claims are governed by Pt III of the Private International Law (Miscellaneous Provisions) Act 1995: that is in relation to claims which are "actionable in tort".[33] The general rule is that the applicable law to govern a claim in tort is the law of the country in which the events which constituted the tort occurred.[34] Therefore, in relation to torts concerning financial transactions or issues of securities, the law of the country in which the most significant elements of the tort took place.[35]

6–19   This raises questions in relation to financial transactions when it is not clear in which country a tort took place, for example, in relation to a prospectus used to market shares that is prepared by the issuer in London but relied on by someone in Paris. The court would be required to identify in which jurisdiction the preponderance of the constituent elements of the tort took place. Thus in relation to the negligent misrepresentation of some matter in a prospectus prepared in London in relation to a company incorporated in London and trading mainly in the UK, which is seeking admission to trading on the regulated markets in London and Paris, the preponderance of the elements of the tort have been committed in London in relation to an issuer which conducts most of its activities in London. This would suggest the use of English law. However, if the prospectus was read in Paris and relied on by French investors who acquired securities on a regulated market in Paris, then there would be reason to suggest that that particular tort had taken place in Paris and so should be subject to French law.[36] There is also a question as to a tort which takes place in more than one country, such as a defamatory email being sent to recipients in two different countries. In this situation the court will consider whether it would be more appropriate to apply the rules of another country than that which would be suggested by the general rule.[37] The principles in this context are necessarily less certain than those in relation to contractual disputes because there is no prior agreement on which to base a decision as to the choice of law. This may encourage litigants to seek to rely on claims for misrepresentation under contract law rather than claims for misrepresentation under tort law because the resolution of choice of law issues is more certain.

---

[33] Private International Law (Miscellaneous Provisions) Act 1995 s.9.

[34] Private International Law (Miscellaneous Provisions) Act 1995 s.11(1).

[35] Private International Law (Miscellaneous Provisions) Act 1995 s.11(2)(c).

[36] See generally *Dicey and Morris on the Conflict of Laws*, para.35–085: referring to the common law cases considering these issues, such as *Distillers Co Ltd v Thompson* [1971] A.C. 458.

[37] Private International Law (Miscellaneous Provisions) Act 1995, s.11(2).

4. CHOICE OF JURISDICTION

A. Choice of jurisdiction

The question as to which jurisdiction is entitled to hear any particular case is different from the question as to which system of rules (or, governing law) will be used to decide that question. As considered below, it is perfectly possible that, while the preceding discussion might decide that it is the applicable principles of English law which are to be used to decide an issue, it may nevertheless be the French courts which will be considered the more appropriate forum to hear the case, albeit that those French courts would use English legal rules to decide the dispute. Therefore, the parties to a financial contract also need to specify the jurisdiction which they wish to have exclusive jurisdiction over their disputes, as well as the system of rules which they would like that jurisdiction to use.

6–20

General principle—domicile

Under Council Regulation 44/2001[38] ("the Brussels I Regulation") the general principle is that "persons domiciled in a Member State shall, whatever their nationality, be sued in the courts of that Member State".[39] It replaces, although in very similar terms, the Brussels Convention which was originally created in 1968 and modified at various times after. The Brussels I Regulation now applies in every member state of the European Union.[40] The interpretation of the Brussels I Regulation is subject ultimately to the decisions of the European Court of Justice. Where the defendant is not domiciled in a Member State, then the jurisdiction of the courts in any Member State is to be determined by the law of that Member State.[41] The key expression beyond is therefore one of "domicile". A company or other legal person is domiciled in its place, incorporation, where it has its central administration, or where it has its principal place of business.[42] In relation to individuals, the question of domicile is decided by the internal law of the Member State seised of the question.[43]

6–21

General principle—place of performance

The jurisdiction regulation provides that "in matters relating to contract" a person domiciled in a Member State may be sued "in the courts for the place of performance of the obligation in question".[44] There is a difficulty with knowing the place in which, for example, a derivatives contract would be performed. The regulation provides merely that the place of performance will be the place where

6–22

---

[38] EC No.44/2001. This regulation is referred to by some commentators as "the Judgments Regulation", by others as the "Brussels I Regulation", and by others as the "Brussels Regulation".
[39] EC No.44/2001, art.2(1).
[40] Civil Jurisdiction Order 2001 applies to conflict of laws disputes within the United Kingdom in very similar terms to the Brussels Convention.
[41] EC No.44/2001, art.4(1).
[42] EC No.44/2001, art.60(1).
[43] EC No.44/2001, art.59(1).
[44] EC No.44/2001, art.5(1)(a).

"the services were provided or should have been provided".[45] Similarly, in relation to claims for tort, the jurisdiction is "the courts for the place where the harmful event occurred or may occur".[46] In relation to questions of trust, the jurisdiction is the place where the trust is domiciled.[47]

Express choice of jurisdiction

6–23　Under the Brussels I Regulation[48] the autonomy of the parties to a contract is to be respected; therefore, an express choice of jurisdiction in a contract will be enforced by the court. As provided for in the regulation:

> "[i]f the parties, one or more of whom is domiciled in a Member State, have agreed that a court or the courts of a Member State are to have jurisdiction to settle any disputes which have arisen or which may arise in connection with a particular legal relationship, that court or those courts shall have jurisdiction".[49]

Under the Brussels I Regulation the general principle is that "persons domiciled in a Member State shall, whatever their nationality, be sued in the courts of that Member State".[50] The agreement conferring such a choice of jurisdiction is required to be in writing or in another form which the parties have agreed between themselves or in a form which is "widely known" to any given international trading or commercial area.[51] It is sufficient that the natural interpretation of a contractual provision suggests that a jurisdiction has been selected for that choice of jurisdiction to be enforceable under the Regulation.[52] There may be dispute, however, as to whether or not an express choice of jurisdiction clause constituted a consensus between the contracting parties. This will be rare if a contract has been properly created, and has tended to arise in the cases where an agent has purportedly exceeded her authority in creating such an agreement. In such cases the court will consider the circumstances surrounding the creation of the contract.[53] A valid choice of jurisdiction clause will, however, ordinarily be enforceable. Importantly, further to art.5(5), in relation to a person acting through a branch or an agent:

> "A person domiciled in a Member State may, in another Member State, be sued as regards disputes arising out of the operations of a branch, agency or other establishment, in the courts for the place where the branch, agency or other establishment is situated."

---

[45] EC No.44/2001, art.5(1)(b).
[46] EC No.44/2001, art.5(3).
[47] EC No.44/2001, art.5(6).
[48] EC No.44/2001.
[49] EC No.44/2001, art.23(1).
[50] EC No.44/2001, art.2(1).
[51] EC No.44/2001, art.23(1).
[52] *7E Communications Ltd v Vertex Antennentechnik GmbH* [2007] 1 W.L.R. 2175. See also *WPP Holdings Italy Srl v Benatti* [2007] 1 W.L.R. 2316.
[53] *Bols Distilleries v Superior Yacht Services Ltd* [2006] UKPC 45; [2007] 1 W.L.R. 12; *Fiona Trust v Privalov* [2007] UKHL 40; [2007] Bus. L.R. 1719; *Deutsche Bank AG v Asia Pacific Broadband Wireless Communications Inc* [2008] EWHC 918; [2008] 2 Lloyd's Rep. 177.

Therefore, in relation to financial institutions operating through multiple branches, or through agents or intermediaries, the jurisdiction may be decided by reference to the place where that branch is situated.

One effective exception to the principle that an express choice of jurisdiction clause will be binding arose in *AWB (Geneva) SA v North America Steamships Ltd*[54] where the defendant, which was organised under Canadian law, had gone into insolvency. It was held that Canadian law governed the defendant's insolvency and could not be excluded by a choice of jurisdiction provision to the contrary. Moreover, an express choice of jurisdiction clause will only bind the parties to that agreement and not other group companies which were not parties to that agreement, as had been argued unsuccessfully in *Morgan Stanley & Co International Plc v China Haisheng Juice Holdings Co Ltd*.[55]

6–24

No express choice of jurisdiction

Where there is no express choice of jurisdiction, the place of performance is the place where the court considers that the issues should be heard. Where there is more than one defendant in different jurisdictions, the approach is that the issues shall be heard in the place where any one of them is domiciled.[56] However, this general rule is qualified by a requirement that the claims are "so closely connected that it is expedient to hear and determine them together to avoid the risk of irreconcilable judgments resulting from the same proceedings".[57]

6–25

Contradictory choices of jurisdiction

One of the most important aspects of legal practice in financial transactions is to ensure that there are no mismatches between the terms of different documents governing a single transaction. There have been a number of cases in which the parties' selections of jurisdiction in various documents have contained different terms as to the choice of jurisdiction. So, in *UBS AG v HSH Nordbank AG*[58] a complex collateralised debt obligation ("CDO") was put in place. Some of these documents relating to the notes identified New York as the jurisdiction in which disputes would be heard and New York law as the governing law; whereas other documents identified England and Wales and English law as the jurisdiction and as the governing law respectively. The claimant sought relief for numerous actions against the defendant in New York broadly relating to mis-selling of the product and mismanagement of the pool of investments. Lord Collins expressed the view that the English proceedings were commenced simply with a view to pre-empting proceedings which had already been begun in New York, and

6–26

---

[54] [2007] EWCA Civ 739; [2007] B.P.I.R. 1023. cf. *Antony Gibbs & Sons v La Société. Industrielle et Commerciale des Métaux* (1890) 25 QBD 399 in which it was held that a party was not excused from its contractual obligations under English law by insolvency under French law. See Fletcher, *Insolvency in Private International Law*, 2nd edn (OUP, 2007), at para.2.85.
[55] [2009] EWHC 2409 (Comm); [2011] 2 B.C.L.C. 287.
[56] EC No.44/2001, art.6(1).
[57] EC No.44/2001, art.6(1).
[58] [2009] EWCA Civ 585; [2010] 1 All E.R. (Comm) 727; on appeal from the decision of Walker J. in *UBS AG v HSH Nordbank AG* [2008] EWHC 1529 (Comm), [2008] 2 Lloyd's Rep. 500.

therefore held that the jurisdiction agreement must be construed in the light of the whole agreement and as such "sensible business people" would not have intended a dispute such as this to be heard in two different jurisdictions. On balance, then, it was held that New York was the better jurisdiction for this claim. Similarly, in *Deutsche Bank AG v Sebastian Holdings Inc (No.2)*[59] there had been several agreements put in place between the parties with choice of jurisdiction clauses which identified different jurisdictions for different transactions. It was held that even though it might have made more sense in the abstract to have all issues heard in one jurisdiction, the parties' express choice of jurisdiction provisions would be effective in relation to the various transactions being litigated in different jurisdictions.

Recognition of judgments

6–27 Significantly, any judgment given in one Member State shall be recognised in any other Member State without the need for further action.[60] The only circumstances in which judgments are not to be recognised is: where it would be "manifestly contrary to public policy"; where it was given in default of the respondent's appearance in court where no copies of proceedings were delivered to the respondent; where it is irreconcilable with existing judgments; or where it is irreconcilable with a dispute between those same parties which is already in train.[61] However, the regulation contains a general principle that "under no circumstances may a foreign judgment be reviewed as to its substance".[62]

B. Allocation of jurisdiction under a contract void ab initio

6–28 The decision of the House of Lords in *Kleinwort Benson Ltd v Glasgow City Council*[63] ("*Glasgow*") considered the proper classification of interest rate swap contracts so that it was possible to identify their appropriate forum to deal with the question of remedies and restitution. *Glasgow* was an appeal which arose in the wake of the decision in *Hazell v Hammersmith & Fulham*[64] that local authorities were not capable of entering into interest rate swaps. The local authority had contracted seven interest rate swaps with the bank, under which the bank had made net payments to the authority. The bank commenced proceedings to recover amounts paid to the local authority on the grounds of unjust enrichment. The proceedings were commenced before the English High Court. The authority contended that the Scots courts had sole jurisdiction.[65]

---

[59] [2010] EWCA Civ 998, [2011] 2 All E.R. (Comm) 245; on appeal from Burton J. in *Deutsche Bank AG v Sebastian Holdings Inc (No.2)* [2010] 1 All E.R. (Comm) 808. And note also the decision of Walker J. in *Deutsche Bank AG v Sebastian Holdings Inc* [2009] EWHC 2132 (Comm), [2009] All E.R. (D) 133 (Aug).

[60] EC No.44/2001, art.33(1).

[61] EC No.44/2001, art.34.

[62] EC No.44/2001, art.36.

[63] [1997] 4 All E.R. 641, HL.

[64] [1992] 2 A.C. 1.

[65] The eagerness to proceed in England was predicated on the favourable limitation period available to the bank: see Lord Goff, [1997] 4 All E.R., 644.

The local authority contended that, further to art.2 of the Brussels Convention on Jurisdiction and the Enforcement of Judgements in Civil and Commercial Matters 1968 ("the Brussels Convention", then in force) that it was entitled as a person "domiciled in a part of the United Kingdom ... [to be] sued in that part". The bank argued that, further to art.5 of the Brussels Convention, it was entitled to proceed in England because its claim concerned "matters relating to a contract" and that England contained "the courts for the place of performance of the obligation in question".[66]

6–29

The House of Lords[67] held by a majority that the decision in *Hazell*[68] meant that the contract had been void ab initio and had therefore never existed. A contract void ab initio is analysed as something which never came into being. Therefore, it was held that this case could not be considered to be one which fell within art.5 of the Brussels Convention as raising matters concerning a contract because no contract had ever existed.[69] By reference to decided authority of the European Court,[70] Lord Goff demonstrated that art.5(1) requires that there be a "contractual obligation forming the basis of the legal proceedings".[71]

6–30

The second decision is considered in the next section.

6–31

C. Express choice of jurisdiction in an arbitration clause

In *Bankers Trust Co v PT Jakarta International Hotels and Development*,[72] two companies in the Bankers Trust group of companies entered into several cross-currency swaps with the respondent, an Indonesian company. These transactions were governed by an ISDA Master Agreement, with an express choice of English law as its proper law. In the event of any dispute, the master agreement provided that all disputes arising out of the contract or being connected to that contract were to be decided by arbitration in London. The respondent failed to make payment under those derivative transactions and latterly commenced proceedings against the Bankers Trust companies in Indonesia. The Bankers Trust companies commenced arbitration proceedings in London and they also applied for an injunction to stay the Indonesian action on the basis that it was in breach of the arbitration clause in the master agreement. It was held by Cresswell J. that an applicant for such an injunction seeking restraint of foreign proceedings had to demonstrate with a high degree of probability that its case was right, that its application had been brought forward promptly and before the foreign proceedings had become too far advanced. On these facts, it was found that the Bankers Trust companies had brought their application in good time and that the arbitration clause covered all of the disputes between the parties with the result that there was no good reason to refuse to grant the

6–32

[66] art.5(1) of the Brussels Convention.
[67] Lord Goff, Lord Clyde, and Lord Hutton.
[68] [1991] 1 A.C. 1.
[69] [1997] 4 All E.R. 641, 649, per Lord Goff.
[70] *Ets A de Bloos SPRL v Societe en commandite par actions Bouyer* Case 14/76 [1976] E.C.R. 1497, 1508 (para.11); *Shenavai v Kreischer* [1987] E.C.R. 239; cf. *Ivenel v Schwab* [1982] E.C.R. 1891.
[71] [1997] 4 All E.R. 641, 651, per Lord Goff.
[72] [1999] 1 All E.R. (Comm) 785.

injunction.[73] Among the powerful reasons which his Lordship identified in favour of the grant of an injunction was the need to give effect to the arbitration clause so as to avoid undermining the worldwide market in swaps and derivatives which the court considered at that time to be in its infancy.

5. ILLEGAL CONTRACTS

6–33   A contract will not be enforced under the Convention where it is illegal under its applicable law.[74] In the constantly changing world of financial markets, new products as well as established products are at risk of being held to be illegal or otherwise unenforceable by reference to one or other system of law. The more difficult issue is where the contract is illegal in the place of its performance if the applicable governing law is English law. In *Ralli Bros v Cia Naviera Sota y Aznar*,[75] in a case of supervening illegality,[76] the Court of Appeal held that it is an implied term of a contract that it shall not be illegal by the law of the state where that contract is to be performed.[77] Therefore, English law requires that the contract be valid by the law of the place of its performance, as well as that it accord with English law. The issue which perhaps remains at large is the approach which the English courts must take if the contract is illegal by reference to a different system of law which such an English court is required to give effect to under the Convention. The preferable approach would be for the English court to give effect to any rules of illegality contained in that system of law.[78]

6–34   The issue of illegality in the place of performance and the context of judicial comity in the enforcement of awards arose in *Westacre Investments Inc v Jugoimport-SDPR Holding Co Ltd*,[79] where a preliminary issue arose as to the enforceability of a Swiss arbitral award from the International Chamber of Commerce. The award related to an agreement for the supply of arms from Yugoslavia to Kuwait under which it was alleged that bribes were to be made to Kuwaiti officials to secure the sales. It was therefore alleged that the agreement would have been contrary to Kuwaiti law and contrary to public policy in Kuwait. The issue therefore arose whether the Swiss arbitration clause in the agreement was itself enforceable. It was held that where an underlying contract is void on grounds of illegality, and hence void ab initio, it would remain possible for an arbitration clause to be enforced nevertheless.[80] It was further held that the court deciding on the enforcement issue would have to consider whether the policy of

---

[73] *Bankers Trust Co v PT Mayora Indah* (January 20, 1999, unreported) applied. See also *Aggeliki Charis Cia Maritima SA v Pagnan SpA, The Angelic Grace* [1995] 1 Lloyd's Rep. 87; *Toepfer International GmBH v Societe Cargill France* [1997] 2 Lloyd's Rep. 379; *Shell International Petroleum Co Ltd v Coral Oil Co Ltd* [1999] 1 Lloyd's Rep. 72.

[74] art.8 of the Rome Convention.

[75] [1920] 2 K.B. 287.

[76] That is, that the contract was not unlawful at the time of its creation but became unlawful only later.

[77] Per Scrutton L.J., 304.

[78] *Nuova Safim SpA v The Sakura Bank Ltd* [1999] C.L.C. 1830; [1999] 2 All E.R. (Comm) 526.

[79] [1998] C.L.C. 409.

[80] Following *Heyman v Darwins* [1942] A.C. 356, *Bremer Vulkan v South India Shipping Corp Ltd* [1981] A.C. 909; and *Harbour Assurance Ltd v Kansa Ltd* [1993] Q.B. 701.

not enforcing illegal judgements or the policy of encouraging finality in judgements. On those facts it was found that the policy of encouraging the enforcement of international arbitral awards should outweigh the policy of discouraging international corruption.[81] However, the applicant would not be entitled to re-open issues of fact already decided upon by the arbitrators under s.5(3) of the Arbitration Act 1975. This decision perhaps highlights some of the problems of seeking judgement in foreign jurisdictions, or in respect of products performed in other jurisdictions, and also the difficulty of conducting the sort of arbitration preferred by financial institutions in such circumstances.

---

[81] Following *Henderson v Henderson* (1843) 3 Hare 100; *E D and F Man (Sugar) Ltd v Yani Haryanto (No.2)* [1991] 1 Lloyd's Rep. 429; and *Kok Hoong v Leong Cheong Kweng Mines* [1964] A.C. 993. cf. the approach of the courts in the local authority swaps cases in holding the entire master agreement void when the local authority was held to have been acting beyond its capacity.

PART III

FINANCIAL SERVICES REGULATION

This Part III considers the underlying principles of financial regulation from its roots in the Lamfalussy process for creating legislation at the European Union level, through the implementing measures in the UK, and the Financial Services and Markets Act 2000. In the wake of the financial crisis 2007–09, EU policy in relation to financial regulation changed, further to the Larosière Report, and the new species of financial regulations are now beginning to emerge, for example in relation to financial derivatives.

Of particular significance to the regulation of financial markets and the financial system in the UK are the powers of the regulatory authorities: the Financial Conduct Authority ("FCA"), the Prudential Regulatory Authority ("PRA"), and the Bank of England's policy bodies the Monetary Policy Committee and the Financial Policy Committee. The Financial Services Act 2012 restructured the financial regulatory system in the UK, albeit some time after the financial crisis 2007-09.

This Part III introduces the core provisions of the Financial Services and Markets Act 2000, the *FCA Handbook* and the *PRA Handbook* which contain the regulations governing financial services in the UK, which are considered in Chapters 8 through 12. Later chapters apply those regulatory principles to specific market sectors, particularly in the second half (*Section Two: Specific Financial Techniques*) of this book.

CHAPTER 7

EU FINANCIAL REGULATION

CORE PRINCIPLES

A large amount of financial regulation in the UK is predicated on European Union law. Much of the regulation created by the UK Financial Conduct Authority and the Prudential Authority implements EU financial services legislation; albeit that there are regulations which have their origins entirely within the UK. This chapter considers the basic principles of EU law which inform the creation of EU financial services legislation, and then it analyses the core principles of EU securities regulation, investment business, banking regulation and financial services regulation generally, together with regulations governing the structure of the financial system, which are then pursued in greater detail in later chapters. Later chapters consider the regulation of market abuse, conduct of business between bank and customer, and advertisement and promotion of financial services in particular.

The system for developing legislation

The EU developed a system (known as the "Lamfalussy process") by which EU financial services law was to be created before the financial crisis 2007–09 (discussed in Chapter 45). It had been realised that the previous methodology was too cumbersome to react to the rapid pace of development of financial markets. The Lamfalussy process began originally in the securities markets but was then rolled out across the sector. The core idea was that "high-level principles" would be established in Directives, such that the general principles governing financial regulation would be established at that level, and then implemented into the municipal law of Member States; the detail of the regulatory rulebooks was provided by the Commission in "technical regulations" which supplement the Directives. Financial regulations in the UK now generally reproduce the Commission's technical regulations in full. However, after the financial crisis, the Larosière Report criticised the several inadequacies of EU legislation and the Lamfalussy process, with the result that the EU is slowly embarking on a process of producing a "single regulatory rulebook" which will apply directly across the EU. To achieve this, Directives are being replaced with Regulations. Whereas

Regulations set out legislation which is binding across the entire EU, Directives merely set out legislative goals which Member States must implement in ways appropriate to them in their own jurisdictions. The latter approach permitted too much divergence in the detail and format of the national implementation of EU standards for there to be a single regulatory rulebook.

Core regulatory principles

The EC Treaty provides for the creation of a single market for financial services and for the free movement of capital within the EU. This has led to the policy of "passporting" approvals within the EU. This means that once an investment firm or a securities issue has been authorised in one Member State of the EU, then that authorisation is deemed to be sufficient to grant the firm or the securities in question admission to the markets of any Member State. This is sometimes also known as the "single licence" approach. The underlying intention of EU policy in relation to financial services—whether banking or investment or whatever—is to provide as far as possible for a single regulatory approach so that barriers between Member States (in the form of different regulatory standards and so forth) are eliminated and a single market for financial services created across the EU. EU financial services regulation then divides between investment activity, securities markets and banking. The Markets in Financial Instruments Directive ("MiFID") provides for the core principles dealing with the authorisation of investment firms to sell financial services, the required organisation of investment firms, and the principles governing the conduct of business between firms and their clients. Of particular significance in relation to the conduct of client business is the obligation on the firm to act in the best interests of the client and to ensure "best execution" of transactions. One of the key developments introduced by MiFID was a levelling of the regulatory oversight imposed over different forms of market providers: whether formal exchanges, "multilateral trading platforms" or firms making bid and offer quotes to their customers. MiFID in turn is to be the subject of further reform so as to enhance consumer protection.

Securities regulation

Securities regulation focuses on the circumstances in which offers of securities are made to the public, as opposed to exempt or private offers of securities. Securities regulation is found in the Consolidated Admissions and Reporting Directive, the Prospectus Directive, the Transparency Obligations Directive, the Market Abuse Directive and the International Accounting Standards Directive, as well as the structure of securities dealing being organised in accordance with MiFID. The collective purpose of these directives is to stimulate securities markets in the EU so as to provide deep pools of liquid capital for European undertakings seeking investment. These directives are also directed at the provision of adequate amounts of information to the investing public through prospectuses, transparency compliance statements, financial information and so forth. Securities regulation is then discussed in detail in Part X of this book.

[139]

Banking regulation

Banking regulation is based primarily on the Second Consolidated Banking Directive 2006, the Capital Adequacy Directive 2006 and the Deposit Guarantee Directive. Banking regulation is based on the maintenance of minimum amounts of capital by banks to cover their liabilities and so to protect their deposit-holders. In the financial crisis of 2007–09, this regulatory approach was demonstrated to be inadequate for purpose, as is discussed in detail in Chapter 45.

1. INTRODUCTION

7–01   Financial services regulation in the UK can only be understood by reference to its roots in European Union law. Much, but not quite all, of financial regulation in the UK is predicated on the implementation of European Union ("EU") financial services legislation. The law of the EU has among its key tenets freedom of movement of capital and the creation of a single market in financial services, as is considered below. Therefore, the EC financial services directives currently in force, which are considered in this chapter, create the bedrock principles for the regulation of financial services across the EU. Those directives are then implemented in the UK by means of principal legislation or subordinate legislation, as appropriate. Importantly, the methodology for creating these legal principles has meant that each Member State has been permitted to implement those Directives into their municipal law in a manner that was appropriate to them, provided that they achieved the ultimate legislative objective set out in the Directive. This meant, for example, that Member States could make their municipal law more stringent than the Directive, which has had benefits in terms of encouraging investors to believe that those jurisdictions had more dependable regulatory procedures in place. Legislation was created in accordance with the "Lamfalussy process", discussed below, which created high-level principles by way of Directives, with the detail being supplied by Commission technical regulation. However, in the wake of the financial crisis 2007–09, the Larosière Report identified several inadequacies in the EU legislation and in the Lamfalussy process, with the result that the EU is slowly embarking on a process of producing a "single regulatory rulebook" which will apply directly across the EU. To achieve this, Directives are being replaced with Regulations. All of these initiatives are considered in detail in this chapter. What this overview is intended to illustrate is the interaction of EU law and financial regulation in the UK, and that the underlying EU law is in the process of development.

7–02   The distinction between the *general law* of England and Wales, and *financial regulation* was discussed in Chapter 1.[1] This Part of this book is concerned solely with financial regulation; this particular chapter is concerned with financial regulation created at the EU level and then implemented into UK finance law, which in turn is administered by the Financial Conduct Authority ("FCA") and the Prudential Regulatory Authority ("PRA") as the competent authorities for the

---

[1] As set out in the *Introduction* to this book.

UK in different regulatory contexts.[2] In this chapter we will outline the architecture of the EU regulation of financial services, but it is in the following chapters of this Part III that we will analyse them in detail, in particular considering the manner in which they have been implemented in the UK.

This discussion begins by outlining the key principles of EU law as they apply to financial services. There then follows a discussion of the development of financial services regulation in the EU, which led up to the completion of the internal market in 2005, and the seemingly continuous reform of financial services regulation thereafter. Then we shall consider in turn the key EU legislation which deals with investment services, securities, and banking. These provisions are considered only in outline at this stage: each area of EU legislation is then considered in detail in the appropriate, later chapters of this book.

7–03

2. THE CENTRAL TENETS OF EU LAW

A. Introduction and terminology

The scope of this section

This section considers some of the underlying principles of EU law and the way in which they apply specifically in the financial services context. Of particular importance are the treaty provisions which established the single market and free movement of capital, as well as other principles as to the effectiveness of different types of EU legislation. What is also significant is the way in which those EU legislative principles apply in the laws of individual Member States. Our principal focus will be on the interaction between the EU legal principles and finance law in the UK.

7–04

In the UK, day-to-day compliance with regulations created in the UK is carried out by the FCA (in relation to the protection of investors) and PRA (in relation to the prudential oversight of financial institutions). The old Financial Services Authority, which was "renamed" the FCA from April Fool's Day 2013 onwards,[3] had been the single regulatory authority in the UK which had been responsible for the implementation of EU financial regulation in the UK through the *FSA Handbook*: that work is now done by the FCA and the PRA through their own *Handbooks*, which contain all of the regulations which are effective in the UK. Typically, legislation can take two years to pass through the EU legislative machinery, before it then has a period of between two years and six months (depending on the legislation) to become fully effective in the law of all Member States. As is discussed below, there is a difference in EU jurisprudence between legislation being effected by means of a Regulation and a Directive. In either case, this time period between legislation being passed at the EU and it becoming fully effective in the municipal law of each Member State allows the regulatory authorities and the financial markets in those individual states to prepare

7–05

---

[2] The fundamentals of UK financial regulation are considered in Chs 8 and 9.
[3] Financial Services Act 2012, s.6.

themselves for the changes that the new regulations will make to their businesses, the processes needed to ensure regulatory compliance and so forth.

The creation of EU financial services legislation

7–06   The mechanics of passing legislation in the EU are beyond the scope of this book: it should be observed that they operate at the level of legal principles and, as with all parliamentary processes, at the level of raw politics. Nowhere is this more true than in relation to financial services legislation. There have been situations in which intense lobbying from the financial sector has resulted in legislation taking much longer to come into effect than was outlined above. For example, the Directive which imposed regulation on hedge funds and similar investment funds was first introduced as a formal proposal in 2008 but did not become law until July 2012, its implementing regulations did not come into effect until December 2012, and at the time of writing it has still not been implemented into UK law.[4] This particular delay was the result of a lobbying effort by national politicians (particularly from the UK) as well as financiers, even though the regulation of such investment funds for the first time in the EU was considered to be a core part of the EU's response to the financial crisis of 2007–09. Therefore, the creation of legislation at the EU level in relation to financial services is a very political process in which interest groups (especially financial industry groups) work very hard indeed to limit the effect of regulatory changes on their industry. This backdrop to EU legislation should never be overlooked. It is a feature of financial regulation, as was discussed in Chapter 3, that it is created in consultation with the finance industry and not simply imposed on it by legislators.

The interaction of EU law and English law

7–07   There is also a question of the interaction of EU financial regulation and the private law of Member States, such as contract law, tort law, property law and so forth. At one level, EU financial regulation should have no effect on the question whether or not a contract or a trust has been validly created in England: those are questions for English law. However, there may be situations in which financial institutions are required by financial regulation to deal with clients' assets in a particular way, or to explain the risks of a financial instrument to a customer before entering into a contract with that customer. The argument was raised in Chapter 3 that these regulatory principles should influence the finding in private law as to whether or not a valid trust or a valid contract has been created. While liabilities under English substantive law need not raise questions of EU law, the interpretation of UK financial services regulation may require an analysis which goes back to fundamental principles of EU law. EU law and UK finance law become intertwined at this point. For example, the Supreme Court began its analysis of a private law question as to whether or not there was a trust over

---

[4] That Directive—the Alternative Investment Fund Managers Directive ("AIFM")—is discussed at the very end of this chapter.

assets held by Lehman Brothers, at the time of its insolvency,[5] by considering the terms of the UK Client Asset Sourcebook regulations, which implemented a part of the EU Markets in Financial Instruments Directive, by analysing that EC Directive.[6] Consequently, understanding the genesis of much UK financial regulation requires a close understanding of the EU law which gave birth to it; and its interaction even with private law is only beginning to emerge.

B. The core provisions of the EC treaty impacting on financial services

The core economic objectives of the EC treaty

The Treaty Establishing the European Community (the "EC Treaty") provides the following objectives for the "European Community" in art.2[7]:

> "The Community shall have as its task, by establishing a common market and an economic and monetary union and by implementing common policies or activities referred to in Articles 3 and 4, to promote throughout the Community a harmonious, balanced and sustainable development of economic activities... sustainable and non-inflationary growth... and economic and social cohesion and solidarity among Member States."

7–08

The Treaty's aim is therefore to provide for sustainable economic development across the EU in a way that is harmonious and balanced. The underlying objective is then to provide a single market for capital—whether securities, debt, or other financial services—across the EU.[8] The EU seeks to create a single, internal market applies across a range of activities including the provision of finance. To this extent, art.3 of the EC Treaty provides, inter alia, that the Community's activities shall include:

> "(c) an internal market characterised by the abolition, as between Member States, of obstacles to the free movement of goods, persons, services and capital;...(h) the approximation of the laws of Member States to the extent required for the functioning of the common market..."

One of the principal obstacles to a truly successful single market for financial services in the EU is considered to be the need in previous years, if one wanted to deal across borders, to seek regulatory approval in each Member State in which one wanted to deal in accordance with the different regulatory principles of each Member State. These different requirements were said to constitute obstacles to the free movement of capital and to the creation of a single market for financial services because there was cost and delay involved in meeting the different

---

[5] The Lehman Brothers insolvency and its aftermath are considered in Ch.57.
[6] *Re Lehman Brothers International (Europe) (in administration) v CRC Credit Fund Ltd* [2012] UKSC 6, [2012] Bus LR 667.
[7] As it is referred to in Treaty of Rome art.1.
[8] Under the Lamfalussy Process, EU regulatory principles were to be predicated on "framework principles" established by EU law. These "framework principles" are the high-level principles on which the appropriate Directives are now based, as supplemented by more detailed "technical regulations". Now, the policy (as considered below in this chapter) is to enact EU law by means of Regulations.

regulatory requirements of different jurisdictions, and because some financial activity may be refused authorisation in one jurisdiction, but granted authorisation in another. The solution to this problem, as considered below, has been twofold. The first solution has been to provide for minimum regulation in the form of the financial services directives, discussed below. The second solution, in addition to the first, has been to "passport" approvals such that an approval given by one regulator in one Member State is deemed to be sufficient approval for that activity to be carried on in any other Member State. Thus, the removal of obstacles to free movement of capital includes the establishment of a pan-European securities market and other capital markets in which regulatory authorisations can be "passported" around the EU to prevent the friction and inertia caused by a requirement to meet different regulatory requirements in each jurisdiction in which securities are to be marketed.

Free movement of capital

7–09   Under art.56 of the Treaty, there is specific provision for the free movement of capital:

> "(1)   . . . all restrictions on the movement of capital between Member States and between Member States and third countries shall be prohibited."

Thus, more than working towards harmony, the EC Treaty prohibits obstacles on the free movement of capital. And it is capital which securities markets seek to generate. Offers of securities to the investing public not just in any single Member State but across the Union, therefore, present a huge potential market for issuers. The EC Treaty permits the adoption of measures on free movement of capital relating specifically to "the provision of financial services or the admission of securities to capital markets" by qualified majority on a proposal from the Commission.[9] However, any enactment under art.56 is without prejudice to the rights of Member States "to take all requisite measures to prevent infringements of national law and regulations, in particular in the field of tax law and the prudential supervision of financial institutions . . . or to take measures which are justified on grounds of public policy or public security".[10] Prudent supervision in the form of, for example, financial regulation or for the management of national monetary policy outside the euro and monetary union systems, is thus retained in the EC Treaty—although its literal effect may be thought to be circumscribed by the very presence of the EC securities directives. The provisions relating to free movement of goods in the Treaty of Rome do not apply to the means of making payment for goods.

C.   The applicability of the principle of subsidiarity

7–10   Article 5 of the EC Treaty provides that:

---

[9] Treaty of Rome art.57(2).
[10] Treaty of Rome art.58(1)(b).

> "In areas which do not fall within its exclusive competence, the Community shall take action, in accordance with the principle of subsidiarity, only if and insofar as the objectives of the proposed action cannot be sufficiently achieved by the Member States and can therefore, by reason of the scale or effects of the proposed action, be better achieved by the Community. Any action by the Community shall not go beyond what is necessary to achieve the objectives of this Treaty."

The purpose of the subsidiarity principle is to allocate responsibility for regulation appropriately between action by Member States and action by the Community; it is based on a principle in the Catholic Church of making decisions at an appropriate level. The issue then arises as to the extent to which the Community is competent to impose detailed financial services regulation so as to remove all discretion from the national regulators. The EC securities directives permit national regulators to impose higher standards than those contained in the directives, provided that they are applied evenly to all participants. What, it is suggested, the Community would not be competent to do would be to provide detailed provisions as to the remedies appropriate during litigation under the municipal laws of any member state, for example for rescission or damages or whatever, as discussed in Parts V and VII of this book. The EC securities directives only go so far as to require that municipal laws make judicial review available from the decision of a regulator and for the availability (but not the precise form) of a remedy.

D. The efficacy of EC legislation

Introduction

This section identifies the principles governing the different tiers of legislation in the EU. Different pieces of financial services legislation have been effected by means of Directives or by means of Regulations, with different legal effects. As is identified in the next section of this chapter, EU policy in this regard has shifted from the use of Directives to the use of Regulations so as to create a single, uniformly effective code for financial services law across the EU.

7–11

The general principles governing direct effect in EU law

A question arises as to the overlap between EU law and the municipal law of Member States. Put briefly, is EU legislation directly effective in the municipal law of Member States once it has been enacted by the appropriate organs of the EU? Treaty obligations are directly effective.[11] It was felt that for the purposes of EU law to be effected then Treaty obligations must be directly effective in the municipal law of Member States. Regulations are directly effective by virtue of express provision to that effect in art.249 of the EC Treaty. However, before 2009, the bulk of EC legislation relating to financial services was effected by way of Directives and therefore a question arises as to the direct effect of directives.

7–12

---

[11] *Van Gend en Loos* [1963] E.C.R. 1.

The direct applicability of Regulations

7–13   Regulations are directly effective by virtue of express provision to that effect in art.249 of the EC Treaty which reads that a regulation "shall be binding in its entirety and directly applicable in all Member States". Consequently, it has been held that regulations will be part of municipal law and therefore that they will be actionable in the UK. So, in *Commission v Italy*[12] it was held that all of the provisions of a regulation would come into effect "solely by virtue of their publication in the *Official Journal*". However, municipal law (such as an implementing measure passed by the UK Financial Conduct Authority or the UK Parliament) is entitled to implement a regulation without itself being ineffective provided that it does not "alter, obstruct or obscure"[13] the underlying intention of the EU regulation. The keynote is that no national measure must "obstruct the direct effect inherent in regulations".[14]

7–14   The Larosière Report, considered below, has signalled a shift for the future into the use of Regulations as the principal method for creating EU financial services legislation with a view to creating a single rulebook which will be effective across the EU. This is a change from the previous system which relied on the use of Directives, considered next, to establish high-level principles (which were supplemented by Commission technical regulations) so that legislation could be created rapidly enough to respond to changes in the financial markets, something which the EU had not been able to do previously due to its slow legislative processes.

The direct effect of Directives

7–15   The position relating to the direct effect of Directives is more complicated. Article 249 of the EC Treaty states that:

> "A directive shall be binding, as to the result to be achieved, upon each Member State to which it is addressed, but shall leave to the national authorities the choice of form and methods."

Significantly, then, it is only the objective (or, "result") sought to be achieved by a directive which is "binding" on a Member State. The precise detail of the municipal legislation or regulation which puts that objective into effect is, however, a matter for each Member State. The most appropriate method of implementation may differ from Member State to Member State in accordance with the natures of their respective legal systems. Thus the UK can decide in which form to give effect to the terms of any directive.[15] Consequently, financial services directives have been put into effect variously by means of domestic financial regulation and by means of principal legislation and subordinated legislation.[16] The powers of the FCA and the PRA to make regulations are

---

[12] [1973] E.C.R. 101.
[13] Craig and De Burca, *EU Law*, 3rd edn (OUP, 2003), p.191.
[14] *Amsterdam Bulb BV v Produktschap voor Siergewassen* [1977] E.C.R. 137.
[15] *Commission v Italy* [1983] E.C.R. 3273.
[16] See para.2–16.

derived in turn from the Financial Services and Markets Act 2000 ("FSMA 2000").[17] The terms of the implementing legislation or regulation do not need to be exactly the same as the terms of the directive,[18] although it has been noticeable that recent implementing measures in the UK have tended to adopt the precise language of the directive more and more instead of paraphrasing it. What is important is that the precise terms of people's obligations are made clear in the implementing legislation.[19]

The possible synthetic direct effect of EC directives

The central principle as to the direct effect of EC legislation, then, is based on the proposition that directives are qualitatively different from Treaty obligations and regulations, and that directives in general terms are not directly effective. However, there are four contexts in which a stylised form of direct effect may be observable even in relation to directives: this could be thought of as a type of "synthetic" direct effect applying to directives. Before any form of direct effect, as considered in the following paragraphs, may be applicable, two requirements must be satisfied.[20] First, the terms of the directive must be sufficiently precise so that the directive could be interpreted as intending direct effect. The applicable provisions of the directive must be set out in "unequivocal terms".[21] Second, the terms of the directive must be unconditional, meaning that there must not be any discretion as to the manner in which, or the extent to which, the terms of that directive may be put into effect.[22] It has been held that technical regulations effected by the Commission are sufficiently detailed and unconditional to constitute legislative material which may have direct effect.[23] In practice this has been of little importance in UK finance law because the regulatory authorities have taken to copying the terms of the EC legislation verbatim into most of its regulations.

7–16

First, then, directives may be "vertically directly effective" in that Member States may not fail in their obligations to implement Directives. It was held in the case of *Van Duyn v Home Office*[24] that if the directive imposes an obligation on a Member State to follow a particular course of action then "the useful effect of such an act would be weakened if individuals were prevented from relying on it before their national courts"[25] and if those national courts in turn were prevented

7–17

---

[17] Financial Services and Markets Act 2000 s.73A.
[18] *Commission v Belgium* [1987] E.C.R. 3029.
[19] *Commission v Greece* [1996] E.C.R. I–4459.
[20] *Foster v British Gas Plc* [1990] E.C.R. I–3313, [18].
[21] *Comitato di Coordinamento per la Difesa della Cava v Regione Lombardia* [1994] E.C.R. I–483, [10].
[22] *Comitato di Coordinamento per la Difesa della Cava v Regione Lombardia* [1994] E.C.R. I–483, [9].
[23] *CIA Security International SA v Signalson SA* [1996] E.C.R. I–2201, [44]; *Unilever Italia SpA v Central Food SpA* [2000] E.C.R. I–7535.
[24] [1974] E.C.R. 1337.
[25] [1974] E.C.R. 1337, [12].

from relying on the terms of that directive. However, this does not necessarily mean that all directives will be directly effective in this way. Rather, as was held further in *Van Duyn v Home Office*,

> "... [i]t is necessary to examine, in every case, whether the nature, general scheme and wording of the provision in question are capable of having direct effects on the relations between Member States and individuals".[26]

A statutory regulator and the state itself may not seek to rely on their failure to give effect to the terms of a Directive. What a claimant would have to demonstrate[27] is that the terms of the directive should be interpreted as imposing a clear obligation on that regulator or on the state more generally.

7–18   Secondly, we must consider whether or not directives may be "horizontally directly effective": that is, whether or not directives may create obligations between private individuals or legal persons, as opposed to between private persons and public bodies. The general principle is that directives do not impose horizontally directly effective obligations.[28] However, a form of "administrative direct effect" can be observed from the decided cases. Administrative direct effect relates to the obligations of public bodies, as well as the Member State itself, to give effect to directives. Thus a health authority may be obliged to put directives into effect.[29] Thus it has been held that if the public body must obey the terms of the directive in carrying out its functions then an individual may be able to rely on the directive to force the public body to carry out those functions in accordance with the terms of the directive.[30] As before, the terms of the directive would have been sufficiently clear and direct so as to permit such an obligation to be divined from them.

7–19   Thirdly, it has been argued that directives may have something akin to direct effect arises in relation to the interpretation of municipal law.[31] National courts are required to interpret national law "in the light of" the terms of any directive[32]: this is referred to by the commentators as the principle of "harmonious interpretation".[33] The purpose underlying this principle is to ensure that directives have some effect even if the Member State has failed to implement them properly. Thus the European Court of Justice ("ECJ") in the *Van Colson* case held that:

---

[26] [1974] E.C.R. 1337, [12].

[27] *Van Duyn v Home Office* [1974] E.C.R. 1337, as above.

[28] *Marshall v Southampton and South-West Hampshire AHA* [1986] E.C.R. 723; [1986] 1 C.M.L.R. 688.

[29] *Marshall v Southampton and South-West Hampshire AHA* [1986] E.C.R. 723; [1986] 1 C.M.L.R. 688.

[30] *Fratelli Costanzo SpA v Comune di Milano* [1989] E.C.R. 1839.

[31] See for example Arnull, et al. *Wyatt and Dashwood's European Union Law*, 4th edn (London: Sweet & Maxwell, 2000), p.102.

[32] *Van Colson v Land Nordrhein-Westfalen* [1984] E.C.R. 1891.

[33] See, e.g. Craig and De Burca, *EU Law*, 3rd edn (OUP, 2003), p.211.

"... [i]t is for the national court to interpret and apply the legislation adopted for the implementation of the directive in conformity with the requirements of Community law, in so far as it is given discretion to do so under national law".[34]

The technical rationale for extending the principle of direct effect to the courts' interpretation of national law is an understanding that the courts of a member state constitute a part of the state and thereby fall within the direct effect principle. It has been held in the *Marleasing* case[35] by the ECJ that:

"... in applying national law, whether the provisions in question were adopted before or after the directive, the national court called upon to interpret it is required to do so, as far as possible, in the light of the wording and the purpose of the directive in order to achieve the result pursued by the latter and thereby comply with [art 189(3) EC]".[36]

Thus decisions of national courts must take into account the wording and objectives of directives, granting them a form of, if you will pardon the expression, "indirect direct effect".

However, it may be thought that the preparedness of an English court to use regulatory principles to shape private law liabilities could incorporate this principle in the directive into English substantive law.[37] It has been held that as a matter of English law that the (now-repealed) 1977 Banking Directive did not create directly enforceable rights for depositors in a bank to sue the Bank of England directly for alleged failures by the Bank to regulate the entity holding their deposits appropriately.[38] Therefore, these regulations operate only at a level between the legislator and the regulator, not horizontally between consumers and the regulator.

7–20

Fourthly, there are cases in which private persons have sought to rely on unimplemented directives as creating rights and obligations between them. In particular an issue has arisen as to whether or not a technical regulation (equivalent to the Commission technical regulations implemented in relation to financial services directives) may be relied upon in litigation between private persons. This issue was considered in *Unilever Italia SpA v Central Food SpA*[39] where it was held that a technical regulation may be interpreted as being inapplicable if it is in some way in breach of the terms or the objectives of the directive which gave it birth in the first place. However, the future use of Regulations will make the EU legislative process more concrete and, significantly, it will eradicate much of the enormous difference in detail between the financial services regulations of different states.

7–21

---

[34] *Van Colson v Land Nordrhein-Westfalen* [1984] E.C.R. 1891, [28].
[35] *Marleasing SA v La Comercial Internacionale de Alimentacion SA* [1990] E.C.R. I–4135; *Coote v Granada Hospital* [1998] E.C.R. I–5199; *Oceano Grupo Editorial v Rocio Murciano Quintero* [2000] E.C.R. I–4491, [32].
[36] *Marleasing SA v La Comercial Internacionale de Alimentacion SA* [1990] E.C.R. I–4135, at [8].
[37] See para.3–25 et seq.
[38] *Three Rivers District Council v Bank of England* [2001] UKHL 16; [2003] 2 A.C. 1.
[39] *Unilever Italia SpA v Central Food SpA* [2000] E.C.R. I–7535, at [50].

E. The applicability of the principle of proportionality

7–22   The principle of "proportionality" requires that a measure taken is suitable to achieve its objective, that a measure taken was necessary to achieve its objective, and that the measure imposed a burden on the individual that was not excessive in relation to its objective.[40] This is a court-based principle in EU law against which the lawfulness of EC legislation may be measured. Its significance for present purposes is that the FCA, as a public body created by statute, is required to conduct itself so that an exercise of its powers is proportionate to its objectives and proportionate to the harm that would otherwise be done, whether in the exercise of its powers to create regulations or in the exercise of its regulatory powers. This requirement as encapsulated in the *FCA Handbook* and the *PRA Handbook* is considered in Chapter 8.

F. The structure of EU financial services regulation

7–23   Financial services regulation divides between three different types of activity: investment services, securities markets, and banking. Each is considered in turn, after a discussion of the evolution of the main principles which now underpin all three areas. What we shall see is a convergence of regulatory principles such that a single, internal market within the EU can develop across all areas of financial services activity.

3. THE DEVELOPMENTS IN POLICY UNDERPINNING THE EU LEGISLATIVE PROCESS

A. Introduction

The transition from Lamfalussy to Larosière

7–24   One of the principal developments in EU financial services law was the development of the Lamfalussy Process, which streamlined the process for creating financial services regulation in the EU, but which will give way in the future to a more rigid process which will use Regulations to create a single regulatory rulebook across the EU as a result of the recommendations of the Larosière Report which examined the lessons of the financial crisis 2007–09 for the EU legislative process. At the end of this section, we consider the current structure of regulation within the EU bureaucracy. Those developments are considered in this section, beginning with the situation before the implementation of the Lamfalussy Process.

---

[40] This statement of the principle is adapted from Craig and De Burca, *EU Law*, p.372.

B. The development of EU financial services policy

The 1957 Treaty of Rome created the principle of free movement of capital   **7–25**
within the European Economic Community, such that capital should be able to
move between Member States of the EU. The original approach to financial
services in the European Economic Community was predicated solely on the idea
of free movement of capital; however, that principle was not in itself sufficient to
spark the creation of an effective single market in financial services because each
Member State retained its own law on financial services, securities regulation and
so on. In 1966, the Segré Report[41] highlighted the many shortcomings in the
regulation of financial services markets across the Community. These shortcomings included enormous differences in the regulatory regimes of the different
Member States and different regulation of banking and the provision of
investment services between Member States. The Segré Report suggested that
there should be harmonisation of national laws dealing with financial services.
Nevertheless, no noticeable progress was made to that end in the following ten
years. In relation to securities markets, in 1977 the Commission recommended a
European Code of Conduct relating to Transferable Securities[42] but this also
failed to jump-start the development of a viable, pan-European securities market;
although it did provide a central reference point for regulators in considering the
manner in which securities were issued in their jurisdictions. The problem
remained that financial markets were regulated differently in different Member
States.

The well-known *Cassis de Dijon* decision[43] had established a principle that,   **7–26**
mutatis mutandis, if an instrument were acceptable in one Member State then it
ought to be considered to be acceptable in another member state. The *Cassis de
Dijon* decision created this principle for situations involving goods originally; it
was expanded to the service field by the decision in the *Citodel* case.[44] The EC
Commission issued a White Paper in 1985 titled "Completing the Internal
Market"[45] which began the movement towards the harmonisation of minimum
standards, the principle of regulation by the "home State", and of passporting
regulatory approvals across the Community. However, while the central policy
was directed at the harmonisation of regulation across the Community, the
various systems of substantive law in each jurisdiction would have made it
impossible to have finance law made *identical* in each Member State in any
event. For example, the substantive English law of contract is fundamentally
different from the French law of contract within the French civil code, that there
could not be *equalisation* of finance law in those two states (let alone the

---

[41] Report by a Group of Experts Appointed by the EEC Commission, *The Development of a European Capital Market* (1966).
[42] Recommendation 77/534/EEC [1977] OJ L212/37.
[43] Case 120/78 *Rewe-Zentral AG v Bundesmonopolverwaltung fur Branntwien (Cassis de Dijon)* [1979] E.C.R. 649.
[44] C–262/81. *Citodel v Cine-Vog Films* [1982] E.C.R. 3381.
[45] COM(85) 310, June 14, 1985.

remainder of the community) but rather only some *approximation* of the financial regulations across the community. This has led to the "passporting" policy set out below.

7–27   The beginnings of a serious legislative movement towards the modernisation of securities regulations in the Community can be identified in the Investment Services Directive of 1993[46] ("ISD", which has since been superseded by MiFID as from 2007). Nevertheless, it required the Financial Services Action Plan ("FSAP") of 1999[47] to refocus the EU. The principal concern was that the lethargy in the production of adequate, harmonised securities regulation across the EC was due in the part to the slowness with which directives were produced compared to the pace of change in the securities markets themselves. Market practice since the passage of the ISD in 1993 has seen four important changes: an explosion in the electronic trading of securities, great developments in trading platforms operated outside formal exchanges, the growth of over-the-counter derivatives and securitisation products, and a large number of securities-related corporate governance scandals. Consequently, the markets changed rapidly very soon after the implementation of the ISD.[48] This was when it became clear that the original legislative processes in the EU were simply too slow to keep pace with market change. The ISD was out of date before it even came into force in Member States, principally because of the seismic change which derivatives markets brought to the EU financial services environment in the early 1990's. Derivatives in particular had been in existence (in their modern form) since the late 1980's, but it was in the early 1990's that they really began to have an impact on many areas of financial life and the size of these new markets began to boom at a disquieting pace. (Derivatives are analysed in Chapter 40). It was clear that the EU moved so slowly in introducing legislation that it would be unable to keep pace with the financial markets and therefore something needed to be done. Consequently, the FSAP sought to refocus attention on the harmonisation of securities markets and the Lamfalussy report on the legislative process, of which more below.

C.   The general principles underpinning EU financial service regulation

The creation of the single, internal market

7–28   The movement towards a single market in all financial services has been a key tenet of EU policy. There has been a difference in the way in which banking regulation and securities regulation policies have functioned, until the Lamfalussy methodology was developed, as considered below.

---

[46] Directive 93/22/EEC [1993] OJ L141/27.
[47] COM(1999) 232.
[48] This directive has now been displaced by MiFID, as implemented in 2007.

"Passporting"

Rather than attempting to create a genuinely single market in which Member States disappear and there is only the EU left, it was decided that there should be a mechanism whereby an authorisation to issue securities in one jurisdiction would apply in all jurisdictions within the EU. This is referred to by some commentators as being the "single licence" approach. It is referred to by other commentators, slightly more memorably, as being a form of "passport" for issues of securities.[49] In effect, once the competent authority in one jurisdiction has authorised an issue of securities or any other matter, then the issue of securities is deemed to have acquired a passport which permits it to travel throughout the entire EU and which in turn enables those securities to be offered to the public in any member state in the EU. Thus that entity or instrument acquires a "passport" from the first Member State which permits it to be marketed in all Member States. Passporting remains an important part of the policy established by the Market in Financial Instruments Directive ("MiFID") in relation to regulatory approvals, such that approval in one Member State is applicable in all other Member States, as considered below.[50]

7–29

D.   A brave new world in EU financial regulation

When President Nicolas Sarkozy of France announced in a speech in the immediate aftermath of the financial crisis that *"le laissez faire: c'est fini"*[51] this signalled an end to the previous policy in the EU of light-touch regulation of financial markets and of suffering the presence of dark pools of finance within a shadow banking system that was beyond formal regulation. This section begins with an analysis of the core EU legal principles which are significant in this area and the Lamfalussy methodology which has emerged for the creation of legislation in the financial services field, before turning to the new EU institutions which have been created for financial markets, and the proposals for the regulation of derivatives. It then considers in detail the very significant de Larosière Report which was published in February 2009 and which contained both an analysis of the crisis of the autumn of 2008 and a detailed series of proposals for the regulation of financial services (especially derivatives) in the wake of that crisis. The result of that report has been the promulgation of three particularly significant proposed regulations inter alia for the regulation of derivatives, as considered in Chapter 40. In part those regulations are significant because they mark a development from the Lamfalussy methodology into a new world in which a single, directly effective rulebook for financial regulation is being developed by the EU.

7–30

---

[49] Hudson, *Securities Law*, 2-09.
[50] See para.7–22.
[51] Speaking in Toulon on September 25, 2008. See for example: *http://www.liberation.fr/politiques/010133587–le-laisser-faire-c-est-fini*.

E.   The Lamfalussy Process

Introduction

7–31   Large commercial entities and public authorities in the UK and in the USA have always raised capital far more commonly by means of securities issues than is the case in continental Europe, and concomitantly there has also been a greater use of those markets by financial institutions for speculation than in the rest of Europe. It was more common in continental Europe to use ordinary bank lending to fund large scale economic and commercial activity, whereas the UK/US model more typically used a wider range of complex financial instruments (such as derivatives and securities issues) alongside traditional capital raising methods. It was decided at the EU level to try to replicate the seeming success of the UK/US model in an effort to raise capital to fund economic growth across the EU. Rather than pass legislation which might create a single capital market, the policymakers tended instead to hope that bureaucratic policy based on the EC Treaty would lead automatically to a single market.[52] One of the principal issues was that the European legislative process was simply too slow, whereas financial markets have become ever more nimble over the decades. Therefore, as outlined above, by the time legislation was enacted, financial practices had typically rendered it obsolete. Consequently, it needed the Lamfalussy Report to revolutionise the approach to financial services legislation.

The Lamfalussy Report

7–32   The Lamfalussy Report, published on February 15, 2001,[53] changed the direction of financial services legislation across the EU and moved the EU a step closer towards some sort of harmonisation of the various finance law and regulatory codes of its Member States.[54] The Report was the product of a Committee which inquired into the state of financial regulation and legislation in the EU. The Lamfalussy Committee was chaired by the Baron Lamfalussy, a central banker. Somewhat vaingloriously, the committee which prepared this report was known as "the Committee of Wise Men". This became the foundation for EU financial services regulation, until 2009. The report divided between setting out the reasons for changing the method of introducing legislation and the committee's recommendations for regulatory reform.

7–33   The Lamfalussy Report identified the fact that there had been some integration in some financial markets in the EU but that many securities markets lagged behind. The effect of having different securities markets across the EU means that there are lots of barriers to free trade, differences in regulatory systems making it more

---

[52] Hudson, *The Law of Finance*, 37–12 et seq; Hudson, *Securities Law*, 2-01 – 2-15.
[53] *http://ec.europa.eu/internal_market/securities/docs/lamfalussy/wisemen/final-report-wise-men_en.pdf*
[54] Hudson, *The Law of Finance*, 37–13–37–19; Hudson, *Securities Law*, 2-01-2-15.

difficult and expensive to issue securities or to invest in securities in different member states, and a large number of other transactional and clearing costs between different jurisdictions.[55]

The report identified two requirements. First, a need to speed up the legislative process. As the report points out, the Takeover Directive had taken 12 years in the legislative pipeline and had still not been enacted by the time the report was prepared. Clearly, the legislative process was unwieldy and too slow; while at the same time the pace of market change was accelerating. Secondly, to introduce a system which would promote a single market for securities. This required not only a new legislative mechanism but also a means for regulators to share information between one another to ensure the proper oversight of financial markets across the EU. The three regulatory issues which are identified in the report are: a need for convergence of regulatory and supervisory structures; a need for more efficient clearing and settlement processes across the EU; and the need to manage the regulatory and prudential implications of widening securities markets. The ways in which the report suggested dealing with these issues are considered in the next section. The committee made recommendations for reforming regulation: the principal suggestion was for the introduction of a four level process for creating and overseeing securities regulation, which is considered next.[56]

7–34

The four-tier Lamfalussy Process

The Lamfalussy process, in a nutshell, created a new process for creating financial services legislation which operated at four levels: the creation of framework principles in Directives; the provision of detailed regulations in Commission technical regulations; the provision of guidance from the Committee of European Securities Regulators ("CESR"); and an enforcement mechanism effected by the Commission. These structures have since been overreached in the wake of the Larosière Report, but the concepts remain significant to EU financial services regulation and many of the Directives created under this structure are still in force.

7–35

Framework principles are described in the report is being the "core political principles". It is interesting that they are described as being "political" principles and not simply regulatory or economic principles. The framework principles are high-level principles which set out the general objectives which the organs of the EU wanted to achieve by means of this legislation. Any implementing measures taken by member states would necessarily have to comply with these framework principles. What these framework principles do not do is to set out the detailed technical regulations which take so much time to create. Nevertheless, it is those detailed technical regulations which are important in practice. The directives to contain all of the essential elements of the legislation in that they set out all of the

7–36

---

[55] It is important to note that there are also great differences (and those differences remain) between the insolvency laws of different jurisdictions, the contract law of different jurisdictions, the legal procedures in different jurisdictions, and so on.
[56] Hudson, *The Law of Finance*, 37–13–37–19; Hudson, *Securities Law*, 2-01–2-15.

key principles which the legislation is intended to achieve. By only needing to negotiate on these framework principles, it was expected that the legislative process could speed up enormously because there would be less information to be negotiated between the various organs of the EU. The initial proposal for legislation would come from the Commission. It was also envisaged by the committee that there would be a greater use of fast track procedures to get this legislation through.[57]

The harmonisation agenda

7–37   The EU dream was to create a genuine, single market which would cover the whole of the EU without any borders. There were so many failures to create a single market in financial services that in effect this goal was downgraded from an objective of making every jurisdiction's securities regulations exactly the same, to a process of either "harmonising" or merely "approximating" or "coordinating" their regulations.[58] Typically, each jurisdiction is entitled to make its regulations more stringent than the European minimum set out in any given Directive in any event: a process known as "gold-plating". However, as is considered below in the wake of the de Larosière Report, which suggested how the EU should respond to the financial crisis 2007–09, the policy has changed towards a need for there to be a "single rulebook" for financial legislation across the EU. This means a change away from using Directives towards using directly applicable Regulations which do not allow the Member States to have the option of how exactly the high-level principles in Directives are to be implemented into their national law.

7–38   It is this shift in the wake of the Larosière Report which will finally signal a genuine beginning to the process of harmonisation. Before then, even though the EU legal theorists used to talk of harmonisation, in truth each Member State was able to implement Directives however they saw fit, provided that they achieved the underlying legislative goal of each Directive, with the result that the precise regulations in each Member State were very different from one another. It has been a notable feature just in the EU's common law jurisdictions that Directives were implemented very differently in Ireland (which has used the traditional format of a principal Act and supporting statutory instruments) and in the UK (which has used a format of granting powers to the regulator in a principal Act to implement EU Directives by means of its own regulations, which have typically simply reproduced the EU Directive and technical regulations in parallel with UK-specific regulations, although on occasions statutory instruments have been used to implement some provisions). This means that the detail of Irish and UK financial services law on specific questions such as the classification of statements made in offering documents as being either a mere invitation to treat

---

[57] An issue which runs through all discussions in financial law is the following: while we can discuss the content of the law time and time over, what is often more important than anything is the assiduity with which regulators use the powers which are available to them. One of the lessons of global financial crisis 2007–11 has been the importance of regulators taking action with appropriate vigour and expecting the worst from the markets they regulate.

[58] Hudson, *Securities Law*, 2-07–2-08.

or a binding contractual offer are answered differently in the two jurisdictions, where Ireland has explicit statutory provisions addressing that question but England does not. In consequence, the use of Directives achieved only to loosest form of harmonisation of laws at the level of framework principles in many circumstances; whereas the detail of finance law in each Member State could be very different indeed.

F.   Responding to the financial crisis 2007–09

The financial crisis 2007–09 is considered in detail in Chapter 45. European Union policy towards financial services in the wake of the global financial crisis is set out in an attractive booklet titled "Towards more responsibility and competitiveness in the European financial sector" which was published by the European Commission in 2010.[59] This booklet summarised EU policy relating primarily to private sector speculation in financial markets, but did not deal with the sovereign debt crisis which began in Greece and which has spread latterly around the eurozone.[60] Its underlying attitude is that the crisis had an impact on the real economy of each Member State (i.e. employment, productivity and so on) and was not limited to the financial sector, and that it "triggered a deep and widespread recession". The Commission expresses its determination not to allow financial markets to remain the same and instead aims to tackle four principal causes of the financial crisis, namely:

7–39

> "an unstable and inadequately supervised financial system; opaque financial operations and products; irresponsibility in some financial institutions, who pursued short term profits, neglected risk management and paid unjustifiable bonuses, and a financial system that overlooks the fact that it was supposed to serve the real economy and society as a whole, contributed to the creation of bubbles, and often disregarded consumer interests."

This document set out, in populist terms, the approach of the EU to the financial crisis. However, the key document in the EU's response to the global financial crisis was the so-called de Larosière Report which is considered next.

G.   The de Larosière Report

Fundamental policy assumptions in the report

The de Larosière Report ("the Larosière Report") was commissioned in November 2008 by the President of the European Union and published in February 2009.[61] The group which prepared the report was given a remit of

7–40

---

[59] *http://ec.europa.eu/internal_market/finances/docs/leaflet/financial_services_en.pdf*
[60] At the time of writing in late 2012, the eurozone currency crisis seems to have abated temporarily, even though the deep economic problems in many countries in the eurozone remain.
[61] http://ec.europa.eu/internal_market/finances/docs/de_larosiere_report_en.pdf. The financial crisis began in the summer of 2007 with the failure of Northern Rock in the UK and the failure of two funds operated by the French institution, BNP. It intensified in March 2008 with the failure of Bear Stearns and reached its nadir with the failure of Lehman Brothers in September 2008. Consequently, the entire means of regulating and operating the financial system required re-examination.

making proposals "on how to organise the supervision of financial institutions and markets in the EU; to strengthen European cooperation on financial stability oversight; and to enable EU supervisors to co-operate globally". It is a passionate and engaged document which makes many far-reaching proposals for the reform of financial regulation both inside and beyond the EU. The impact of the Larosière Report on financial services policy in the EU cannot be over-emphasised. In that sense, the report was very much a creature of its time in that the mood in which the financial crisis was discussed in 2008 and 2009 was febrile. This is not a criticism of the report; instead it identifies its genesis as a crisis management document in many senses. One of its key goals through its recommendations at the EU level and beyond is to prevent "systemic and interconnected vulnerabilities... which have carried such contagious effects" both during and in the aftermath of the crisis.[62]

7–41   The principal shortcomings which are identified by the Larosière Report, in summary, are as follows. First, there was too much opacity in complex financial markets, whereby it was impossible for regulatory authorities to gather sufficient information about the condition of the derivatives and other markets in which financial institutions had stockpiled risks. Equally it was unclear whether or not financial institutions would be able to set off their mutual obligations amongst themselves (because the nature, volume and value of their transactions were unknown) or whether there would be further bank collapses like Lehman Brothers. This was not unjustified panic: several banks across the EU required government bail-outs to keep them solvent. Second, mispriced risk, whereby financial institutions had valued their assets and obligations incorrectly, and when the markets fell they were obliged to write down their assets massively. Third, incorrect ratings by credit rating agencies, whereby ratings agencies were paid by the entities for which they were producing the ratings and those ratings had replaced a large amount of due diligence which should have been conducted by the parties to transactions.[63] Fourth, corporate governance failures, whereby the senior management of financial institutions had simply failed to control the activities of trading desks, or even to be aware that their institutions had such large exposures to some markets.[64] For example, as considered in Chapter 45, Citigroup's senior management had been unaware of the CDO and CDS exposures of their institution. Fifth, "regulatory, supervisory and crisis manage-ment failures", whereby regulated entities (such as traditional banking institu-tions) had nevertheless caused the crisis, and there had been a complete failure among regulators to anticipate that such a crisis could take place with the result that they had failed to plan for it.[65]

7–42   The Report also argued that it was a US regulatory failure to control mortgage lending practices and securitisation issues which spread across to the EU, as though the EU had caught a disease from the USA:[66] in that sense, it was argued that it was the business model used by "US-type investment banks" which bred

---

[62]   Larosière Report, para.4.
[63]   Larosière Report, para.19.
[64]   Larosière Report, para.23.
[65]   Larosière Report, para.28.
[66]   Larosière Report, para.28.

the "contagion" which in turn infected the global economy.[67] (The metaphor of a disease is used throughout the Larosière Report.) The problem was identified as being at root a US problem.[68] A detailed commentary on the issues identified in the Report is set out in Chapter 45: at this stage we are concerned with the principles which have fed into a change in the legislative processes in the EU.[69] However, it is important to take a sample of the political rhetoric which underpinned the Report and the changed EU agenda. It cannot be overstated that, while the EU had previously been in thrall to the pounding growth which the Anglo-American derivatives and capital market models had promised for the EU up to 2007, the policy agenda changed directly sharply from 2009 and onwards with a far more restrictive approach to the regulation of financial markets.

In this vein, while the Report identified the genesis of the crisis as having been in **7-43** the US domestic housing market and in a build-up of cheap cash in the financial system, nevertheless the policy response focuses primarily on the "parallel banking system" —relating to derivatives markets, hedge funds, short-selling,[70] and credit ratings agencies in particular. The spreading of the contagion from the US housing market around the world was identified as having been the fault of those markets and those funds. Indeed, hedge funds are described as being a "carrier" of these risks: a metaphor which also suggests a disease. The source of the Larosière Report's approach to regulatory policy is the following passage in a communiqué issued by the G30 which is contained in the following extract from the Report itself:

> "A robust and competitive financial system should facilitate intermediation between those with financial resources and those with investment needs. This process relies on confidence in the integrity of institutions and the continuity of markets. "This confidence taken for granted in well functioning financial systems, has been lost in the present crisis in substantial part due to its recent complexity and opacity, . . . weak credit standards, misjudged maturity mismatches, wildly excessive use of leveraged on and off-balance sheet, gaps in regulatory oversight, accounting and risk management practices that exaggerated cycles, a flawed system of credit ratings and weakness of governance.[71]"

Even though this passage is clearly critical of the practices of investment banks before the crisis, nevertheless the Report is still committed to the traditional ideologies of free markets. For example, it is argued in the Report that over-regulation would be negative, whereas innovation in financial markets is positive.[72] The macroeconomic thesis underpinning the Report is that the crisis was predicated on "excessive liquidity fuelled by too loose monetary policy".[73]

---

[67] Larosière Report, para.28.

[68] Mixed in with this analysis may be a recognition that for the previous decade financial services policy in the EU had been focused on developing a capital markets environment which mimicked the US model rather than traditional continental European approaches to the provision of banking services both to private citizens and to businesses.

[69] See para.45–04.

[70] Short-selling is the process by which speculators take positions which expect that the market price of a security will fall in the future by betting on future lower prices. That people take these positions means that they become a self-fulfilling prophecy because they cause the market value to fall.

[71] Larosière Report, para.40; G30 report, Washington, January 2009.

[72] Larosière Report, para.42.

[73] Larosière Report, para.46.

The report identifies a need to focus more supervisory attention on liquidity risk management in the future: indeed, the report in general terms seeks to focus more on macro-prudential issues (like systemic liquidity) than merely micro-prudential issues.[74]

7–44 The Report stresses the need for greater supervisory cooperation, in particular so that large, multinational entities like the American insurance giant AIG cannot become central to a significant part of the financial system without that being noticed.[75] In one important passage, the Larosière Report attacks the lack of genuine sanctions available to supervisory authorities and identifies a general failure of regulators to impose them in advance of the crisis. The report considered that sanctioning regimes in the EU were "in general weak and heterogeneous".[76]

7–45 Significantly, as outlined above, the Report identifies the need for there to be a single rulebook for financial regulation in the EU.[77] This is a significant change from the Lamfalussy approach which had accepted that individual Member States should be free to gold-plate their regulations and to implement them into their national law in whatever way seemed appropriate. The Larosière Report considered that such differences in national implementation of EU standards should be replaced by a system of directly effective Regulations which would have the effect of generating a single rulebook for financial regulation across the EU.

Measurement issues

7–46 A key factor in the gestation of the financial crisis was the practice of some financial institutions of identifying a market value for their assets which was greatly in excess of the value which other financial institutions gave to similar products. This had the effect of distorting the size of the balance sheets of different financial institutions and, when the steady collapse of financial markets began, the lowering of asset values meant that many financial institutions saw their balance sheets contract sharply with result that other financial institutions were reluctant to deal with them on any basis. The clearest examples of this process of complacent over-valuation were Lehman Brothers and Citigroup, as considered in Chapter 45.[78] A key problem then was the process of marking to market which was done on different business models in different financial institutions. Clearly, given that financial markets depend so much on the free flow of accurate information, it is essential that there is greater standardisation and honesty in the process of marking to market. The Larosière Report suggests that

---

[74] There is a separate question as to whether or not regulators have sufficient, explicit powers to deal with these sorts of matters on an ongoing basis or whether they simply have a lead role in crisis management in practice.

[75] Larosière Report, para.81

[76] Larosière Report, para.83 and 84.

[77] At the time of writing, the German and French governments are proposing rewrites of the European Union treaties which would, inter alia, introduce compulsory financial regulation around the EU, in place of the mere approximation of regulations as at present.

[78] see the discussion of the Lehman Bros reports in Ch.18 of this book.

the International Accounting Standards Board ("IASB") needs to do more work on this issue and to open itself up to discussions with regulatory and other bodies.

"Closing the gap in regulation"

The Larosière Report conducted a close scrutiny of two aspects of investment banking which were considered to be particularly blameworthy in relation to the global financial crisis: the "parallel banking system" (sometimes referred to as the "shadow banking" system) and the derivatives markets. The parallel banking system —by which is meant the activities of unregulated entities like hedge funds and unlicensed mortgage brokers, financial instruments which are held off-balance sheet, activities which are conducted through offshore subsidiaries and so forth —is criticised on a number of grounds.[79] Principally, it is criticised for being hidden and non-transparent so that regulators can neither control it nor understand the size and nature of its activities. This is particularly dangerous because in difficult times it is this parallel banking system which is particularly vulnerable when liquidity evaporates: so, a number of hedge funds went into insolvency after the collapse of Lehman Brothers when they could no longer access funding. Furthermore, and significantly for EU regulatory policy, it is considered that hedge funds had a "transmission" function in spreading the contagion of the US housing crisis into the world's financial markets more generally, for example by short-selling shares in the institutions involved thus driving their share prices down and thus reducing their access to liquidity. Hedge funds, however, are not considered to have been one of the causes of the financial crisis in the report. Nevertheless, Recommendation 7 in the report identifies the need to regulate hedge funds. This recommendation gives rise to the AIFM directive (which is discussed at the end of this chapter).[80]

7–47

Recommendation 8 of the Larosière Report is the source of the draft regulations for the treatment of derivatives ("EMIR" and "MiFIR" which are discussed in detail in Chapter 40). In essence, the report recommends the creation of a clearing-house for credit default swaps as soon as possible; the simplification and standardisation of derivatives products; and the need, in relation to securitisation products, for the issuer of such products to keep the bonds issued as part of the securitisation on its balance sheet for the life of the transaction rather than shifting them off their balance sheet into a special purpose vehicle (and, in essence, selling on sub-standard products to investors at arm's length).[81]

7–48

The collapse of the Madoff empire[82] is used to illustrate the need to "control" funds better than at present.[83] In consequence, Recommendation 9 advocates a more systematic legal treatment of funds. Across the EU there are many different

7–49

---

[79] Larosière Report, para.85.
[80] Hudson, *The Law of Finance*, para.7–50 et seq.
[81] Larosière Report, para.93 to 95.
[82] Bernard Madoff had operated a criminal Ponzi scheme in New York for several decades (which took deposits but made no real investments such that its operators simply lived off the capital it raised) which was worth between US$15 and 60 billion. Madoff is serving several prison sentences of 150 years in the aggregate.
[83] Larosière Report, para.96.

types of entity which can conduct investment activities on behalf of their clients. Their different legal models, different powers and obligations, mean that their treatment in the EU generally is haphazard at best. They are creatures of their own national legal systems. The report advocates that there is some rationalisation of their definition and regulation.

"Equipping Europe with a consistent set of rules"

7–50   As was considered earlier in this chapter, one of the great policy objectives of the EU has been the creation of a single market for financial services, which in turn has required the creation of standardised regulations: however, the EU has singularly failed to produce such standardised regulations. Instead, all that has been achieved in the security field has been an approximation or coordination of minimum standards. What the Larosière Report advocates instead is a single rule book which will be obligatory in all member states of the EU. This will also impact on the corporate governance of financial institutions and will impact directly on the levels of remuneration which financial institutions may pay to their traders and other employees.[84] Interestingly, the report pays more attention to "shareholder interests" and the obligations of shareholders in the control of financial institutions than to talk of macroeconomic questions like systemic integrity. It is not a typically American nor British approach to the role of a shareholder to understand them as having obligations to govern their investments in the public interest; whereas the UK-US model of shareholder ownership emphasises their rights to share in the profits of the entity without further responsibility in their capacity as shareholders. Therefore, it is suggested in the report that investors must also have duties.[85]

7–51   One of the further innovations suggested by the report is a re-emphasis on the importance of internal risk management within financial institutions.[86] It is proposed that the individual ultimately responsible for internal risk management should be identified as a separate executive and be a member of the senior management team. In this sense risk management would become a more significant function within the entity as a whole.

"EU supervisory repair"

7–52   The Report argues that, hitherto, the focus of regulators had been focused too much on "micro-prudential" regulation: that is, the regulation of individual firms. As a result, there had been insufficient focus on systemic, or "macro-prudential" regulatory questions.[87] (As is explored in Chapter 8, the new UK regulatory structure includes a Financial Policy Committee in the Bank of England and a Prudential Regulatory Authority which aim to address this shortcoming.) In the wake of the financial crisis what was needed was systemic financial stability. From the perspective of the EU there was a need for an EU body which would be

---

[84] Larosière Report, para.117.
[85] Larosière Report, para.124.
[86] Larosière Report, para.122.
[87] Larosière Report, para.153.

responsible for macro-prudential regulation. There were several features of the shortcomings of the regulatory and supervisory authorities in the EU area before the crisis: ineffective early warning mechanisms to warn about the upcoming crisis;[88] supervisory failures such as in relation to Northern Rock, IKB and Fortis in which regulators had failed to anticipate the failure of those institutions;[89] failure to challenge cross-border supervisory failures, such as a failure to challenge the decision of the home regulator in relation to worries about particular institutions.[90] This last concern is troubling because it illustrates a shortcoming in the key EU regulatory policy: that of "passporting". The idea behind the passporting (or, "single licence") concept is that once the home regulator authorises an action then that authorisation is valid across the EU. However, if there were concerns about the decisions of home regulators which were not taken seriously then that would produce disequilibria in the EU because some jurisdictions would become places through which inappropriate activity could be approved by the less diligent regulatory authorities and conducted by unscrupulous financial institutions. This problem was compounded by the possibility for each member state to gold-plate and implement the EC directives as they considered appropriate into their domestic jurisprudence under the Lamfalussy process. There were two other shortcomings identified: a lack of frankness and co-operation between national regulators,[91] and no means for supervisors to make common decisions.[92] Again, these shortcomings are significant in relation to the perceived failure of the EU to establish cross-border regulation within the EU area.

The upshot of these observations was the recommendation for an entirely new regulatory structure within the EU. That new structure is considered below. **7–53**

H.   The new regulatory structure

The elements of the new regulatory structure

The Larosière Report took the view that the European Central Bank ("ECB") should not have the regulation of the financial system added to its remit on the basis that this would obfuscate its principal, existing role of ensuring monetary stability within the EU.[93] It was accepted that it could participate in the macro-prudential oversight in tandem with its role in relation to monetary stability. To meet the need for reinforced systemic regulation, the Report advocated the creation of the European Systemic Risk Council ("ESRC"—which in time became the "ESRB", a "board" rather than a "council").[94] To draw the **7–54**

---

[88] Larosière Report, para.154.
[89] Larosière Report, para.155. In large part those failures to anticipate bank insolvency were ideological in that it simply had not occurred to regulators who had become used to the boom years that a bank could possibly go into insolvency.
[90] Larosière Report, para.156.
[91] Larosière Report, para.159.
[92] Larosière Report, para.162.
[93] Larosière Report, para.167.
[94] Larosière Report, para.177.

national regulators together, a functional differentiation was created between the securities regulators, the insurance regulators, and the banking regulators: these colleges of regulators would deal with micro-prudential regulation.[95] It is a principle of micro-prudential regulation that government must be kept out of this sort of supervision so that political priorities do not interfere with the objective business of overseeing individual firms.

7-55   The new EU regulatory structure is divided up in two ways. The first division is *functional*: that is, regulation is divided among the various regulatory functions. Therefore, there are regulators to deal with macro-prudential regulation, micro-prudential regulation, and specific conduct of business regulation. Macro-prudential regulation is concerned with the regulation of the entire financial system and with protecting that system against *systemic risk*, as discussed in Chapter 1.[96] Micro-prudential regulation is then concerned with the solvency and condition of individual financial institutions (whether banks, investment houses, insurance companies, pension funds and so forth). This form of regulation considers each financial institution separately but is not necessarily concerned with over-arching macro-prudential questions. The third tier of regulation relates to the way in which financial institutions deal with their customers ("conduct of business" regulation, discussed below and in Chapter 10), and market products to their customers, and behave in the market generally (i.e. avoiding criminal activity such as market abuse (Chapter 12), insider dealing (Chapter 14), and money-laundering (Chapter 15). The new EU regulatory architecture looks like this, in four tiers:

ESRB
European Systemic Risk Board—responsible for *macro*-prudential regulation, i.e. the protection of the entire EU financial system from systemic risks.

ESFS
European System of Financial Supervisors—responsible for *micro*-prudential regulation, i.e. the solvency and condition of individual, regulated financial institutions (such as banks and investment houses) across the EU. The ESFS in turn draws together the following sectoral bodies (i.e. bodies which are responsible for specific financial markets):

EBA—European Banking Authority;[97]

EIOPA—European Insurance and Occupational Pensions Authority;

ESMA—European Securities and Markets Authority[98]

---

[95] Larosière Report, para.183.
[96] para 1-47.
[97] There is also the European System of Central Banks.
[98] 1095/2010.

National supervisory authorities

The competent regulatory authorities of individual Member States mirroring the EU bodies, such as the Bank of England's subsidiary entities in the UK: the Financial Policy Committee (macro-prudential); the Prudential Regulatory Authority (micro-prudential); and HM Treasury's body the Financial Conduct Authority (conduct of business, etc.). The UK entities are discussed in Chapter 8 in detail.

Thus macro-prudential oversight is maintained at the top of this diagram by the ESRB looking across the entire financial system and not being caught up in the minutiae of individual firms. However, many financial crises are, of course, precipitated by the failure of sensitively placed individual firms. Nevertheless, micro-prudential regulation is collected into the ESFS which draws together the three sectoral regulators—which are responsible for the significant financial market sectors of banking, insurance and pensions, and securities and related markets generally—which in turn draw together the national supervisory authorities which are the competent authorities in each Member State of the EU for each of these functions (macro-prudential, micro-prudential and other regulation) and each of these market sectors. Of course, the national supervisory authorities will often be involved both in the micro-prudential regulation of individual institutions within their jurisdictions and in the macro-prudential regulation of financial markets in their jurisdictions. For example, as considered in Chapter 17, it is planned that the Bank of England will have both micro- and macro-prudential powers exercised through its various subsidiaries.

A hypothetical example of the new EU regulatory structure in operation

To illustrate how this regulatory hierarchy is supposed to work, let us imagine a hypothetical situation. Suppose that Universal Bank (a bank which offers banking services across the EU in every sector from retail bank accounts on the high street, through insurance and pensions, to investment banking in securities and derivatives trading) has been found to have mis-sold hundreds of thousands of complex financial instruments to small businesses and to moderately wealthy private individuals. Those instruments promised high investment returns and to protect customers against movements in interest rates: however, as the market developed all of those instruments showed a large loss. It would be a question for private law (principally contract law, tort law and equity) to identify what obligations Universal Bank had to compensate its customers on an individual basis. Conduct of business regulation (regulated in the UK by the Financial Conduct Authority and by ESMA at the EU level) would be responsible for dictating how Universal Bank should have treated its customers (identifying their level of expertise, explaining risks to them, and so forth). However, the size of the claims being brought against Universal Bank might cause concerns about its solvency if it is both required to pay out billions of pounds in damages and reparations at the same time as the markets generally have hurt its profitability. Therefore, the Prudential Regulatory Authority in the UK and the ESFS at the EU

7–56

level would be responsible for the micro-prudential regulation of Universal Bank as an individual entity. This regulation would have required that Universal Bank held an amount of capital in reserve as a buffer against this sort of eventuality, and the regulator should have been conducting regular analyses of Universal Bank's ability to withstand different types of market circumstances.

However, if there was a genuine concern about Universal Bank going into insolvency (as Lehman Brothers did in September 2008) then that might threaten the stability of the entire financial system because of the size of Universal Bank's transactions with other investment banks across the entirety of the financial system in the EU (and beyond). That is where the macro-prudential regulatory reach of the ESRB across the EU (and the Financial Policy Committee with its financial stability remit in the UK) would apply. The ESRB would be concerned to look to the stability of the entire financial system across the EU. In the event that Universal Bank went into insolvency, then the practical reality would be a financial crisis (more commonly known as a panic) in which regulators, bankers, professional advisors, public relations teams, politicians and others would seek to find means of controlling the crisis and finding a way of working through the problem. In a perfect world, the regulatory structure would have identified and dealt with the increasing risks as they escalated through the system.

7–57   What law achieves in these situations, it is suggested, is a means of providing powers to the various regulators to compel or prevent action in different situations so that crises can be controlled and disaster averted. Importantly, the law does not often tell the regulators what they must do in this context. Instead, the role of the law is to provide the regulators with a range of powers so that they can select the appropriate response in any given set of circumstances. Crisis management is about knowing what has worked in the past and, importantly, being able to identify the right response for the circumstances. In the market jargon, this is commonly referred to as identifying the right tool for the job. Policy papers in the wake of the financial crisis 2007–09 tended to talk of "the regulatory toolkit", by which was meant the range of legal powers which regulators had so as to deal with different types of problem or crisis. Before the financial crisis 2007–09 it became clear that regulators (and government) had not had the necessary legal powers to deal with the situation in that they could only use political pressure to compel banks how to act (often by offering or refusing government help or bail-out money in that circumstance) instead of having legal powers to compel action, or to take banks into public ownership and so forth.

7–58   This is a very important jurisprudential phenomenon for lawyers. All law schools begin by teaching the rule of law to students: that is, all lawyers begin their careers with a study of the constitution and acquire a belief that law is the supreme voice in a democratic society. However, in relation to financial crises, the sole role of the law is to empower politicians and regulators to do whatever they deem necessary to solve any given crisis. Of course, the law is supreme in that banks, their shareholders and others are required to obey the lawful commands of the person who holds those legal powers, but the law itself does not compel the power-holder to act in any given way. Instead, politics and economics tend to take over when crises occur, and law is simply the backdrop against which regulators and politicians decide how to act in the circumstances. Therefore, the

UK Banking Act 2009 (discussed in Chapter 28 in detail) is really just a play-book which presents the Bank of England with a series of options for crisis management, ensuring that the law will compel others to obey its lawful commands in practice.

"Global repair"

The Larosière Report identifies a need for global co-operation between regulators primarily because the development of "financial conglomerates" presents a new regulatory challenge. In essence, the growth of large, cross-border investment banks through a period of mergers and takeovers in the sector has led to the massification of banks[99] and in turn the increased internationalisation of financial markets in consequence. A good example is Citigroup which emerged from a merger of Citicorp with Travelers to create the largest financial institution in the world which in turn generated the largest write-downs and losses during the financial crisis—US$60.8 billion by October 2008—and had to be taken effectively into public ownership to prevent its insolvency. Such huge entities which were identified during the crisis as being "too large to fail"—or more accurately "too large to be allowed to fail"—and in consequence made demands on the public exchequer which were an affront to the Friedmanite logic of free markets that failing entities must be allowed to fail. These enormous entities acting across borders were simply too large for regulators to contain them. As a result, the Report considered that national regulators acting alone were unable either to control such institutions or to gather information about their activities.[100] Consequently, there is a call in the Report for supra-national bodies to shoulder much of the burden, not least the OECD and the Financial Action Task Force ("FATF") in relation to unco-operative jurisdictions which offer harbours for the parallel banking system.

7–59

I. EU Policy after the de Larosière Report

The majority of the policy proposals made in the de Larosière Report have been adopted by the Commission. Beyond the scope of that report, the Commission is moving to tighten up the rules on banking capital so as to create larger buffers by requiring banks to hold larger reserves in the event of future failure. The focus in the de Larosière Report on international co-operation, macro-prudential oversight and supervision of systemic stability and liquidity have been woven into the EU

7–60

---

[99] The problem of universal banks (offering all financial services in one place) and investment banks being "too big to fail" became clear during the financial crisis: those institutions were so massive that they could not be allowed to go into insolvency without wrecking the entire financial system and national economies. However, the effect of the crisis was to see even more banks merge than had been the case before. The 1990's and the 2000's had already seen numerous bank mergers. The few remaining banks on this scale – such as Citigroup, JPMorgan, Bank of America, Barclays, RBS, and even investment houses like Morgan Stanley and Goldman Sachs – are now so massively and so structurally important to the global economy that it is difficult to foresee how they could be allowed to fail, which in turn (it is said) will affect the way in which they control the risks that they take because they can be confident that they will be bailed out.

[100] Larosière Report, para 233.

policy. The Commission has also identified problems with crisis management in that in the USA, in the UK and across the EU area it was found that regulators had very few explicit powers to deal with bank failures. In the UK, as is considered in the next chapter, the Banking Act 2009 dealt with this gap; the EU Commission is committed to producing legislation to deal with this issue. Credit rating agencies and investment funds in general terms are to be regulated. There is a focus on stricter supervision by the competent authorities of member states as well as the creation of a new regulatory architecture within the EU. It is hoped that the "new supervisory architecture will contribute to a safer, sounder, more transparent and responsible financial system, working for the economy and society as a whole".[101]

4. EU REGULATION OF INVESTMENT SERVICES UNDER "MiFID"

A. The core objectives of MiFID

7–61   The Markets in Financial Instruments Directive ("MiFID")[102] is a far-reaching and controversial piece of legislation at the European Union level which aims to equalise the regulatory burden borne by different types of financial services provider. It is expected to usher in a revolution in the way in which dealings in financial instruments are conducted in the EU. The activity in financial institutions prior to its enactment was intense and concerns about the effect of its implementation were febrile.[103] There are three principal objectives underpinning MiFID.

7–62   First, MiFID has far-reaching effects on the composition of securities markets by encouraging competition with long-established stock exchanges in the EU for the business of providing markets on which securities are traded. Thus, rather than regulation focusing solely on established exchanges, regulation will now not only cover traditional exchanges (such as the London Stock Exchange), but will also cover on-line exchanges, multi-lateral trading platforms ("MTFs"), and the activities of investment firms which quote prices to clients (known as "systematic internalisers"). The objective is that all of these mechanisms for trading in securities will be subject to the same regulations so there that will be no competitive advantage to businesses which offer services through one mechanism rather than any other. The underlying policies of this directive are to increase competition and to encourage more investors to participate in European securities markets through an increased range of service providers.

7–63   Secondly, MiFID will also change the nature of financial services regulation by moving away from densely-drafted rulebooks full of detailed rules and signal a move towards *principles-based regulation*.[104] Regulation based on high-level

---

[101] EU Commission, "Towards more responsibility and competitiveness in the European financial sector", European Union, 2010, 13.
[102] The Markets in Financial Instruments Directive ("MiFID"), 2004/39/EC.
[103] For an excellent account of the concerns and views of market participants see generally C. Skinner (ed.), *The Future of Investing in Europe's Markets after MiFID* (Wiley Finance, 2007).
[104] See para.3–32.

principles is concerned with the establishment of framework principles which leave it to individual firms to decide how to conduct their activities in compliance with those general principles rather than simply setting out all of their obligations in detailed, micro-managing rules. This form of regulation will require investment firms to produce business practices which comply with the general principles set out in the regulations, as opposed to simply requiring rigid compliance with a series of detailed rules. There are two possible ways in which principles-based regulation can operate. The practice in the UK under the Financial Services Authority involved a "light touch" approach such that regulated firms had to show they were complying with these general principles (especially in relation to prudential regulation as to their solvency) but without too much onerous or invasive oversight. The global financial crisis of 2007–09 has been blamed in part on too light a regulatory touch for banks which have had inappropriate business models, as is considered in Chapter 42. The alternative use of principles-based regulation is as a tool which requires regulated firms to identify how they can comply with those general principles most effectively, such that the firms feel obliged to overreach the limits which they might otherwise have faced so as to ensure compliance with the regulations. The downside remains, however, that firms are effectively identifying their own regulatory norms. "Principles based" regulation was considered in Chapter 3.[105]

Thirdly, MiFID will also enhance the regime for passporting regulatory approvals around the EU, such that approval in one jurisdiction can be relied upon in another jurisdiction. This development will have the result that Member States may not rely on further regulatory hurdles unique to their own jurisdiction to impede issuers and others who have regulatory approval in another Member State. MiFID replaced the earlier Investment Services Directive 1993.[106] MiFID has been supplemented by the MiFID Implementing Directive ("MID")[107] and a Commission Regulation.[108] MiFID was implemented by the Financial Services and Markets Act 2000 (Markets in Financial Instruments) Regulations 2007[109] as from November 1, 2007. There are three areas of regulation considered in this section on MiFID: first, the authorisation and organisation of investment firms; secondly, the organisation and transparency of securities markets; and, thirdly, regulation of the conduct of business between investment firms and their customers. Each of these regulatory developments is considered in turn in the discussion to follow.

7–64

---

[105] See para.3–32.
[106] 93/22/EEC.
[107] 2006/73/EC.
[108] 1287/2006/EC.
[109] Financial Services and Markets Act 2000 (Markets in Financial Instruments) Regulations 2007 (SI 2007/126).

B. The benefits which are expected to flow from MiFID

7–65   It was anticipated that MiFID would lead to six principal benefits.[110] First, increased competition between market service providers and within securities markets generally. Secondly, enhanced investor protection through new conduct of business rules which require both appropriate provision of services and suitable provision of services, as considered below.[111] Thirdly, increased transparency for customers as to the practices of service providers, the costs of services, and reassurance that service providers are obliged to take all reasonable steps to procure the best form of execution for the customer. Fourthly, increased transparency as to the available investment markets in relation to pre-transaction information,[112] such as requirements that prices are quoted and publicly available, and in relation to post-transaction information as to completed transactions.[113] As outlined above, the markets in question are not only stock exchanges but also regulated markets, multilateral trading platforms ("MTFs") and "systematic internalisers" when dealing in "liquid shares", so that there is no concentration of market activity in non-transparent transactions away from regulated markets. Each of these benefits, as they arise from the provisions of MiFID, are considered in the discussion to follow. Fifthly, more effective and more approximate regulation between Member States across the EU. Sixthly, principles-based regulation which will make the core principles of financial regulation more evident. In this sense, MiFID is developing the work begun by the Lamfalussy process in that it is using high-level principles to modernise financial regulation and to make it more reactive to market conditions.[114]

C. The categories of activity regulated by MiFID

7–66   The regulation of financial services by MiFID divides between the authorisation of people to conduct investment business, the regulation of the markets on which investments are bought and sold, and the regulation of the conduct of business. Each is considered in turn.

D. Authorisation and organisation of investment firms

Introduction

7–67   MiFID has two general fields of regulation in relation to investment firms: their authorisation to provide financial services and as to their internal organisation.

---

[110] See White, "The benefits, opportunities and challenges of MiFID", in C. Skinner (ed.), *The Future of Investing in Europe's Markets after MiFID*, p.3.
[111] See para.7–33.
[112] MiFID, art.29 for MTFs.
[113] MiFID, art.28 for investment firms; MiFID, art.30 for MTF's.
[114] See Ryan, "An Overview of MiFID", in Skinner (ed.), *The Future of Investing in Europe's Markets after MiFID*, p.13.

Authorisation of investment firms

Investment service providers are to be authorised by their home Member State.[115] In the UK, authorisation may not be given to a firm by the FCA (or the PRA) unless the applicant has satisfied Chapter 1 of Title 2 of MiFID (that is, arts 5 through 15) and any directly applicable regulation.[116] Banks (known as "credit institutions" in EU parlance), which do not provide investment services do not require authorisation under MiFID[117] because they are already regulated under the Credit Institutions Directive, as considered in Chapter 28.[118]

7–68

MiFID requires that investment firms, being any person whose "regular occupation or business is the provision of... investment services to third parties",[119] acquire authorisation before conducting their businesses.[120] Those authorisations are subject to ongoing review by the competent authorities of Member States.[121] The organisational requirements imposed on investment firms by art.13 in this context are considered next.

7–69

Organisation of investment firms

Article 13 of MiFID sets out the organisational requirements which investment firms must satisfy before authorisation may be granted.[122] Those requirements are that an investment firm shall (following the numbering in the article):

7–70

2. establish adequate policies and procedures sufficient to ensure compliance of the firm including its managers, employees and tied agents with its obligations under the provisions of this Directive as well as appropriate rules governing personal transactions by such persons.
3. maintain and operate effective organisational and administrative arrangements with a view to taking all reasonable steps designed to prevent conflicts of interest as defined in art.18 from adversely affecting the interests of its clients.
4. take reasonable steps to ensure continuity and regularity in the performance of investment services and activities. To this end the investment firm shall employ appropriate and proportionate systems, resources and procedures.
5. ensure, when relying on a third party for the performance of operational functions which are critical for the provision of continuous and satisfactory service to clients and the performance of investment activities on a continuous and satisfactory basis, that it takes reasonable steps to avoid undue additional operational risk. Outsourcing of important operational functions may not be undertaken in such a way as to impair materially the

---

[115] MiFID, Preamble (17).
[116] Financial Services and Markets Act 2000 (Markets in Financial Instruments) Regulations 2007 (SI 2007/126) reg.4(1).
[117] MiFID, Preamble (18).
[118] 2000/12/EC, a directive relating to the taking up and pursuit of the business of credit institutions.
[119] MiFID, art.4(1).
[120] MiFID, art.5.
[121] MiFID, art.16.
[122] MiFID, art.13(2)–(8).

quality of its internal control and the ability of the supervisor to monitor the firm's compliance with all obligations.

An investment firm shall have sound administrative and accounting procedures, internal control mechanisms, effective procedures for risk assessment, and effective control and safeguard arrangements for information processing systems.

6. arrange for records to be kept of all services and transactions undertaken by it which shall be sufficient to enable the competent authority to monitor compliance with the requirements under this Directive, and in particular to ascertain that the investment firm has complied with all obligations with respect to clients or potential clients.

7. when holding financial instruments belonging to clients, make adequate arrangements so as to safeguard clients' ownership rights, especially in the event of the investment firm's insolvency, and to prevent the use of a client's instruments on own account except with the client's express consent.

8. when holding funds belonging to clients, make adequate arrangements to safeguard the clients' rights and, except in the case of credit institutions, prevent the use of client funds for its own account. These organisational obligations deal generally with internal compliance procedures, systems to prevent conflicts of interest, appropriate systems to ensure continuity in service provision, supervision of third party agents to control operational risk, maintenance of sound administrative and accounting procedures, maintenance of records to facilitate regulatory oversight, and procedures as to the holding of clients' money and other property. MID, the implementing directive, adds to this list of organisational requirements, in art.5, the need for investment firms to ensure that they have suitable internal procedures and that their staff are suitably trained and knowledgeable about the responsibilities which they will be required to discharge. Thus art.5 of MID is primarily concerned with the control of operational and of personnel risk in investment firms.[123] Commission technical regulation then deals with the proper performance of these obligations in the context of various different activities.[124]

Passporting

7–71 The policy of passporting of authorisations to act as an investment firm is set out very clearly in the recitals to MiFID such that[125]:

> "An investment firm authorised in its home Member State should be entitled to provide investment services or perform investment activities throughout the Community without the need to seek a separate authorisation from the competent authority in the Member State in which it wishes to provide such services or perform such activities."

---

[123] MID, art.5.
[124] MiFID, art.13(10), further to MiFID, art.64(2).
[125] MiFID, Preamble (23).

The principal derogation from this principle relates to activities conducted through a branch of an investment firm in a different Member State from its home Member State (a "host Member State") whereby that host Member State may assume regulatory control for that particular activity if it is the closest regulator to the conduct of that activity.[126]

E.   Conduct of business obligations in MiFID

One of the most significant aspects of investor and client protection in financial regulation arises under so-called "*conduct of business*" regulation. In essence, conduct of business regulation requires investment firms to assess the expertise of their clients so that they can both only sell those clients suitable financial products and also so that it conducts business with them in a suitable way (for example, explaining the risks associated with those products to the extent that that client is not considered sufficiently expert to understand the risks). MiFID recast the detail of conduct of business regulation radically. The discussion of conduct of business regulation is set out in Chapter 10.

7–72

F.   Best execution

Perhaps the most difficult requirement from the perspective of implementation by investment firms is the requirement in art.21 of MiFID that:

7–73

> "...investment firms take all reasonable steps to obtain, when executing orders, the best possible result for their clients taking into account price, costs, speed, likelihood of execution and settlement, size, nature or any other consideration relevant to the execution of the order."

This is referred to in the preamble to the directive as the "best execution" requirement. It imposes a difficult obligation on investment firms to seek out the best price for their clients, executed in the cheapest and most efficient manner, and concurrent with the client's general objectives. This requirement is considered in detail in Chapter 10 with the remaining principles relating to conduct of business.[127]

G.   Securities markets and market transparency in MiFID

The market coverage in MiFID in the abstract

MiFID recognises that there are many more investors in the marketplace than was the case when its forerunner (the Investment Services Directive) was enacted in 1993, and that those investors are of many different types (not only more retail customers, but also hedge funds and other types of financial institution).[128]

7–74

---

[126] MiFID, Preamble (32).
[127] See para.10–01.
[128] MiFID, Preamble (2).

MiFID aims to improve the execution of customer transactions[129] and to recognise that in many MTF and regulated market transactions the investment firm is not standing as a "riskless counterparty" but may have a position of its own in relation to the investments in question.[130] This market coverage also extends to investment professionals who, while they do not operate MTF's or a regulated market, do sell securities as market makers on the basis of internal systems for pricing those securities:[131] these professionals are to be regulated by MiFID so that there is no imbalance between the regulatory coverage of such "systematic internalisers" and other markets.

Regulated markets

7–75   The competent authority of each Member State is required to maintain a list of regulated markets.[132] Authorisation of a regulated market must be granted by a competent authority in accordance with the provisions of Title III of MiFID[133] when the authority is satisfied by the competence of the market operator and are also satisfied that the systems of that regulated market are suitable.[134] The management of the market operator must be of "sufficiently good repute and sufficiently experienced as to ensure the sound and prudent management and operation of the regulated market".[135] Similarly any persons able to exercise "influence" over the management of that regulated market must be "suitable".[136] The regulated market must also be organised in accordance with art.39 of MiFID as to systems for the management of conflicts of interest, appropriate risk management systems, arrangements for the sound management of the technical operation of the regulated market's systems, establishment of transparent and non-discretionary rules and procedures to provide for fair and orderly trading, effective arrangements for the finalisation and execution of transactions, and sufficient financial resources to ensure the orderly operation of the regulated market. The regulated market must create clear and transparent rules by reference to which securities can be admitted to trading on that market, in compliance inter alia with s.85 of the FSMA 2000 as to the issue of securities.[137]

Market transparency and integrity

7–76   The FCA is obliged by art.25(1) of MiFID to "ensure that appropriate measures are in place to enable the competent authority to monitor the activities of investment firms to ensure that they act honestly, fairly and professionally and in a manner which promotes the integrity of the market".[138] For their part,

---

[129] MiFID, Preamble (5).
[130] MiFID, Preamble (6).
[131] MiFID, Preamble (8).
[132] MiFID, art.47.
[133] MiFID, art.36(1).
[134] MiFID, art.36(1).
[135] MiFID, art.37(1).
[136] MiFID, art.38(1).
[137] MiFID, art.40(1).
[138] MiFID, art.25(1).

investment firms are required to maintain records of transactions for at least five years to facilitate regulatory oversight.[139] Investment firms and the operators of MTFs are required to maintain effective arrangements and procedures to facilitate the regular monitoring of compliance with FCA regulation.[140] Any disorderly market conditions which may indicate market abuse are to be reported by investment firms and the operators of MTFs to the FCA.[141]

Systematic internalisers are required to publish a firm quote in relation to shares which are admitted to trading on a regulated market for which they are systematic internalisers and for which there is a liquid market.[142] Those firm quotes are to be made public on a regular and continuous basis during normal trading hours.[143] Publication is achieved by any method which is "easily accessible to other market participants on a reasonable commercial basis".[144] However, systematic internalisers may (without undue discrimination) decide to which clients they will make their quotes available,[145] and they may limit the number of transactions undertaken with any one customer (again without undue discrimination) to avoid exposure to that one client in relation to multiple transactions.[146] The systematic internaliser is then required to execute that transaction at the published price at the time of the receipt of the order[147]; except in relation to professional counterparties where execution at a better price would be acceptable conduct under market conditions. This is not the case in relation to retail customers.[148]

7–77

H.   The proposed Markets in Financial Instruments Regulation ("MiFIR")

Introduction

A proposed regulation on Markets in Financial Instruments Regulation ("MiFIR")[149] was published by the Commission in October 2011.[150] The principal aim of this regulation is to ensure that all trading is conducted on exchanges, on multi-lateral trading platforms (MTF's), or through organised trading facilities (OTF's), as opposed to being conducted purely over-the-counter. This should be understood in common with the Regulation requiring clearing of derivatives transactions ("EMIR") which is analysed in Chapter 40.

7–78

---

[139] MiFID, art.25(2).
[140] MiFID, art.26(1).
[141] MiFID, art.26(2).
[142] MiFID, art.27(1).
[143] MiFID, art.27(3).
[144] MiFID, art.27(3).
[145] MiFID, art.27(5).
[146] MiFID, art.27(6).
[147] MiFID, art.27(3).
[148] MiFID, art.27(3).
[149] 2011/0296 (COD).
[150] *http://ec.europa.eu/internal_market/securities/docs/isd/mifid/COM_2011_652_en.pdf*

The delivery of services

7–79   The Explanatory Memorandum from the Commission which accompanies the proposal for MiFIR identifies a difference between exchanges and MTF's on the one hand, and OTF's on the other, on the basis that the operators of OTF's have discretion about the manner in which transactions are executed, and in consequence different investor protection rules are required which encompass conduct of business and best execution requirements.[151] Their operators are required to publish bid and offer prices so as to provide transparency as to market prices;[152] except in relation to especially large transactions for which prices need not be published, provided that a waiver has been acquired from the appropriate competent regulatory authority.[153] This also requires prices and other information to be made public after transactions have been created, again unless a waiver has been obtained from the competent authority.[154]

7–80   Systematic internalisers ("SIs") settle transactions against their own capital, so that ultimately the investor takes a risk on that SI. However, because such an SI does not bring buyers and sellers together like exchanges, MTFs or OTFs, then it is not treated as being a trading venue by the regulation. Consequently, SIs need to have different transparency requirements imposed on them to recognise this difference in their practices,[155] however the regulation applies only to SIs if they deal in sizes less than the standard average size. Such SIs have the power to "decide the size or sizes which they will quote".[156] SI's must "make public their quotes on a regular and continuous basis during normal trading hours", although those quotes may be withdrawn in "exceptional market conditions".[157] SIs are also given more flexibility as to their quotations on the basis of their size.[158] Moreover, SIs "shall be allowed to decide, on the basis of their commercial policy and in an objective non-discriminatory way, the investors to whom they give access to their quotes" and to limit the number of transactions done with a particular client,[159] unlike other providers who are required to deal in a non-discriminatory way in the ordinary course of events. They must provide firm quotes in relation to bonds and structured products which were subject to a

---

[151] Another approach would have been to provide for rigid rules which would govern the activities of OTF's instead of allowing them to continue to operate in a different manner. The underlying ideology of these regulations is to permit parties to proceed on the basis of freedom rather than prohibiting or controlling tightly particular types of activity. In the abstract, there is no reason why the operator of an OTF as opposed to an MTF should be permitted to function on a different basis when ultimately the principal concern is with the provision of equal levels of treatment to investors from whichever trading mechanism in terms of price, execution and so forth.

[152] MiFIR, art.3.

[153] MiFIR, art.4.

[154] MiFIR, art.5 and art.9 in relation to different types of derivative product.

[155] MiFIR, art.13.

[156] MiFIR, art.13(3).

[157] MiFIR, art.14(1).

[158] MiFIR, art.14(4).

[159] MiFIR, art.16.

prospectus.[160] In turn, ESMA is required to monitor these transactions and the market for these products in this format.[161]

I. MiFID II

Introduction

In September 2011, the Commission published a proposal[162] for a new Directive (known colloquially as "MiFID II") which would recast MiFID so as to deal with some problems which had arisen in the operation of the original directive. The directive would still apply only to investment firms and to regulated market delivery systems,[163] and so would not apply to all participants in markets except as outlined below in relation to powers to intervene in overly-large derivatives positions. The principal focus of the changes to the Directive is directed at the multilateral trading platforms and other mechanisms for delivering financial services to investors, in particular the need to maintain an equal playing field for investors and service providers and the need to accommodate technological developments in the delivery of financial services (including circuit breaking, the resilience of electronic systems to high volumes of trading, and so forth).[164]

7–81

Conduct of business reform

Concerns have also arisen as to investor protection and the use of light-touch regulation in relation to derivatives and other products negotiated between professional counterparties in the wake of the crisis. One particular area of concern, which was considered in Chapter 6 in relation to interlocutory proceedings raising questions of jurisdiction, is the use of complex derivatives by public authorities around the EU which led to large losses in the wake of the Lehman Brothers collapse in September 2008. Two principal results flow from this. First, it is thought that the current regime for client classification fails to accommodate counterparties like these public authorities. Second, the obligations to act in the client's best interest and to ensure that communications are fair, clear and not misleading must apply to all non-retail clients and cannot be diluted to taste in relation to different types of counterparty, although it is recognised that many of the detailed investor protection norms would be inappropriate for each item of high-volume business conducted, for example, between two swaps dealers which are necessarily experienced financial institutions. The proposed directive emphasises these changes.[165]

7–82

---

[160] MiFIR, art.17.

[161] MiFIR, art.18.

[162] *http://ec.europa.eu/internal_market/securities/docs/isd/mifid/COM_2011_656_en.pdf*

[163] MiFID II, art.1.

[164] However, as with the US Dodd-Frank Act, it is for the trading venues themselves – whether exchanges, multi-lateral trading platforms or others – to identify clear rules for trading on their platforms.

[165] MiFID II, art.30.

The power to intervene and to demand information in relation to derivative positions

7–83   The global financial crisis demonstrated that national regulators had insufficient powers to act in the teeth of the crisis and that they had too little information to know how to act. Consequently, MiFID II bestows those regulators with powers to demand information about derivatives trading positions.[166] More significantly, however, supervisory authorities are to be granted powers to intervene in relation to derivatives positions which are considered to be too large. An example of what might be meant by such an overly large position has arisen in the USA in relation to the failure of MF Global (run by Jon Corzine, once a US Senator, Governor of New Jersey and chief executive at Goldman Sachs) with the unexplained loss of US$1.2 billion from its funds,[167] which became a feature of Congressional inquiry in December 2011. MF Global had taken a position in relation to European sovereign risk of about US$6.3 billion which has been blamed for sinking the firm.[168] This enormous position concerned regulators as well as investors. The power under MiFID would permit a supervisory authority to intervene in relation to derivative positions of such a scale so as to demand that those positions are reduced. This is a particularly significant regulatory power to intervene in market behaviour and to interfere directly in the commercial decisions of market participants.

5.   EU SECURITIES REGULATION

A.   The nature of EC securities regulation

7–84   Securities regulation deals with the those markets in which securities are issued to the public or where securities are admitted to trading on a regulated market.[169] Securities regulation across the EU is driven by the *EC securities directives*—namely, the Consolidated Admissions and Reporting Directive, the Prospectus Directive, and the Transparency Obligations Directive—and the Commission's technical regulations which supplement them. Securities regulation, including the terms of the EC securities directives, is considered in detail in Part X of this book. This section intends only to be an outline of those directives the better to understand the composition of EU financial services regulation more generally. The regulation of the securities markets is a key part of EU financial services policy.

7–85   The policy underpinning EC securities regulation is the upshot of the development of a single market for securities across the EU so that companies and other issuers will be able to access a much wider and deeper market for

---

[166] MiFID II, art. 61, 72, 83.

[167] This is all the more surprising in the context of the Sarbanes-Oxley legislation which imposes obligations on the chief executive to know about the financial and accounting position of the firm. It is all the more ironic in that Mr Corzine was instrumental in drafting that legislation.

[168] See, for example, "Corzine's American dream that turned sour", *The Financial Times*, December 9, 2011.

[169] A.S. Hudson, *Securities Law*, (London: Sweet & Maxwell, 2008).

capital than is possible in ordinary debt markets.[170] The policy underlying the European Union's approach to securities market regulation is based on two assumptions. First, a perception that the securities markets in the EU are too fragmented. Secondly, a determination embodied in the Financial Services Action Plan that the different regulatory norms previously in use in each Member State of the EU required some harmonisation. As a result the directives governing the offers of securities to the public and to the admission of securities to trading on regulated markets or to listing on stock exchanges within the EU were introduced. In turn the securities directives have the following principal policy objectives. First, the creation of efficient markets so that companies are able to access "deep pools of liquid capital" by means of issuing securities to a large investment population. Secondly, to ensure investor protection in these securities markets: an area of regulation which has recently been revamped by the implementation of MiFID.[171] These policies are considered next.

B. The principal policy objectives of EC securities regulation

The principal goal of the EU's securities regulations, in its somewhat lyrical phrase, is to create "deep, liquid pools of capital".[172] Deep pools of capital are thought to be made available through stronger securities markets because securities markets enable investors and issuers of securities to act innovatively and without the limiting effect of too much institutional control. In continental Europe the tradition has been for raising capital through ordinary bank lending. In a nutshell, the policy presumption is that raising capital through securities markets is better than simply relying on bank lending because it increases the sources of potential funding. The ironic consequence of the *credit crunch* of 2008 is that innovative use of securities—such as securitisation and derivatives such as credit default swaps—may create greater systemic risks than the traditional, conservative banking model which was used more generally in continental Europe. This was considered above by reference to the Larosière Report.

7–86

The policy goals for the EU are consequently threefold. First, to make securities markets more accessible to investors and to issuers across the EU. By removing obstacles which effectively restrain or deter issues of securities in other Member States, such as more stringent regulatory requirements in some states, there is a broader marketplace available both to issuers and to investors. Secondly, to enhance investor protection across the Community by enacting prudential legislation which will ensure market integrity. This is expected to instil confidence in investors and so make the capital markets more liquid. Thirdly, to prevent the misuse of inside information—whether in the form of insider dealing, market abuse more generally, or market manipulation—all with the ultimate objective of enhancing investor confidence in the integrity of regulated securities

7–87

---

[170] There are two lengthy analyses of the European Union perspective on the creation of a single market for securities and investment services more generally: N Moloney, *EC Securities Regulation* (OUP, 2002) and E. Ferran, *Building an EU Securities Market* (Cambridge University Press, 2004).
[171] See para.10–01.
[172] If you repeat that phrase to yourself over and over again you will find that it has a very pleasant lulling quality.

markets. Fourthly, following on from the other three, to harmonise securities regulations so that issuers will face equivalent obligations in each member state and so that investors will receive equivalent protections.

C. The six EC securities directives

7–88   There are six EC Directives which are of relevance to issues of securities and, in some cases, limited to the listing of securities. First, the Consolidated Admission and Reporting Directive of 2001[173] which consolidates the principles relating to the admission of securities to official listing in earlier directives. Secondly, the Prospectus Directive[174] which was implemented by means of amendment to FSMA 2000 and by the new listing rule arrangements effected by the FSA as of July 1, 2005. Thirdly, the Transparency Obligations Directive[175] which was implemented in the UK in 2007 by Pt 43 of the Companies Act 2006. The two other directives relate to financial matters more generally but they have great bearing on securities markets. Fourthly, then, is the Market Abuse Directive, dealing with the disclosure of price sensitive information and insider dealing, implemented in 2005 and, fifthly, the International Accounting Standards Directive, implemented in 2005 relating to the form of accounting information provided by companies. Finally, MiFID, as discussed above,[176] governs the whole of financial services activity. The principal focus of these directives is on securities which are to be offered to the public and on securities which are to be admitted to trading on a regulated market, as to the procedures necessary for their authorisation, the documentation which must be approved and published before any offer is made, and on the information which must be made available after the securities have been issued. These policies of these directives are considered in detail in Chapter 35 of this book, and the detailed regulations which are culled from them are considered in Part X of this book generally.

6.   EU BANKING REGULATION

A.   The current regulatory structure for banking

7–89   In this context, the concept of "banking" relates to traditional banking services such as operating bank accounts, clearing cheques, making loans and so forth, as opposed to investment services, insurance and so on. The EU term for a "bank" in this context is a "credit institution". Banking is considered in detail in Part VIII of this book, and banking regulation in particular is considered in Chapter 28 in detail. What emerges from Chapter 28 is that banking regulation policy begins at the international level with the Bank for International Settlements ("BIS") in Basel which has generated framework principles for banking regulation and the detailed Basel II and Basel III accords which set out the detail in particular of the

---

[173] 2001/34/EC.
[174] 2003/71/EC [2003] OJ L345.
[175] 2004/109/EC [2004] OJ L390.
[176] See para.7–22 et seq.

prudential regulation of banks (that is, the ways in which banks are required to act and to hold capital so as to protect themselves against insolvency).[177] Therefore, EU banking regulation policy is drawn similarly from those international roots. This section considers the principal EU directives which deal with banking regulation at present, although the EU Commission has published proposals in September 2012 for the reform of banking regulation, as outlined below.

The regulation of banking at the EU level falls into line with the general **7–90** principles identified above in relation to investment activities. The development of banking regulation followed a slightly different path from that for investment services, but one which has always been broadly in parallel to it.[178] The keynote of the regulation of "credit institutions" was free movement of capital at the outset, although latterly the keynote of banking regulation policy was the drive towards completion of the EU single market in 2005. The passporting policy referred to above was adopted for the regulation of banking so that once a bank was authorised to act as such in its home Member State, then it would be able to establish branches to provide banking services in other Members States of the EU. The principal EU legislation dealing with banking regulation is now the Second Consolidated Banking Directive 2006 ("CBD 2006"),[179] which recast and replaced the Consolidated Banking Directive of 2000.[180] The CBD 2006 restates the principles of the 2000 Directive which in turn consolidated the provisions of the Second Banking Co-ordination Directive.[181]

The CBD 2006 is "the essential instrument for the achievement of the internal **7–91** market" in relation both to credit institutions' freedom to establish themselves across the EU and their freedom to provide financial services.[182] The aim of the directive is to harmonise banking laws across the EU and to provide a "single licence" for banks to be passported from their home State across the EU. Furthermore the directive is concerned to ensure competition between banks and to safeguard depositors.[183] Responsibility for "supervising the financial soundness of a credit institution, and in particular its solvency" lies with the home Member State.[184] At the regulatory level, the directive calls for increased regulatory co-operation at the national level.[185]

The Capital Adequacy Directive 2006 ("CAD 2006")[186] is the fourth directive **7–92** dealing with capital adequacy. Capital adequacy regulation, as is considered in Chapter 28, is a key part of banking regulation, governing as it does the level of

---

[177] See Ch.29.
[178] See generally J. Usher, *The Law of Money and Financial Services in the European Community*, 2nd edn (OUP, 1999), which is now a good bit out of date; G. Walker, *European Banking Law* (BIICL, 2007).
[179] 2006/48/EC (June 14, 2006).
[180] 2000/12/EC.
[181] 89/646/EEC.
[182] 2006/48/EC, Recital (3).
[183] Directive 2006/48/EC, Recital (9).
[184] Directive 2006/48/EC, Recital (21).
[185] Directive 2006/48/EC, Recital (22).
[186] 2006/49/EC.

capital which a bank is required to maintain to cover its business activities. The theory is that a minimum amount of capital held in this way, will enable a bank to rise out of difficulties in the event of its failure. The content of EU regulation in this context has been greatly influenced by the proceedings of the Basel Committee on Banking Supervision, and in particular by "Basel II", as it is known, which has altered the direction of banking regulation in the 21st century.[187] "Basel II" is discussed in detail in Chapter 28. Briefly put, it creates three "pillars" for regulatory supervision: regulatory capital, supervisory review, and market discipline. The Basel Committee established in 1975 by the central banks of the G-10 leading economies in an attempt to co-ordinate the financial sectors of those economies in the hope ultimately of preventing a systemic banking collapse. The Basel Committee has no legal standing nor any authority to create law. However, its influence is great and thus the products of the Committee, such as "Basel II", are influential "soft law".[188] The proof of that statement is evident in that the CAD 2006 implemented the Basel II structure. The Basel II regime, however, did not prevent the systemic shocks suffered in the global financial crisis of 2007–09, and is to be replaced in time by the Basel III regime which takes a similar approach albeit with the different market risks sliced into smaller segments. These various standards are considered in Chapter 28. At present in the EU, at the time of writing, an interim measure between Basel II and Basel III dubbed "Basel 2.5" in the press has been introduced to require banks to set aside more capital against the risk of loss.

7–93   The Deposit Guarantee Directive[189] requires Member States to create a scheme whereby 90 per cent of deposits up to £20,000 can be recovered. The Investor Compensation Scheme Directive[190] requires a similar scheme be put in place for investment services activity. The Electronic Money Directive 2000[191] deals with payments by means of electronic payment systems, as is discussed in Chapter 28.

B.   The reform of EU banking regulation

7–94   The EU Commission announced in September 2012 that it intended to introduce reforms to banking regulation in the EU to set up a single supervisory mechanism ("SSM") that contains, in the Commission's own words.

> "•   a legislative proposal for a Council Regulation to give specific tasks related to financial stability and banking supervision to the European Central Bank (ECB);
> •   a legislative proposal for a Regulation of the European Parliament and of the Council designed to align the existing Regulation 1093/2010 on the establishment of the European Banking Authority (EBA) to the modified framework for banking supervision; and
> •   a communication outlining the Commission's overall vision for the banking union, covering the single rulebook and the single supervisory mechanism, as well as the next

---

[187] See *http://www.bis.org*.
[188] "Soft law" is a term given to principles created by influential persons which are obeyed or observed by people regardless of them being legally unenforceable in a strict sense.
[189] 94/19/EEC.
[190] 97/9/EEC.
[191] 2000/46/EC.

steps involving a single bank resolution mechanism. The proposal for the future regulatory structure is set out in the following terms:[192]

'The ECB would be exclusively responsible for key tasks concerning the prudential supervision of credit institutions. In particular, it would:

- authorise and withdraw the authorisation of all credit institutions in the euro area;
- assess acquisition and disposal of holdings in banks;
- ensure compliance with all prudential requirements laid down in EU banking rules and set, where necessary, higher prudential requirements for banks, for example for macro-prudential reasons to protect financial stability under the conditions provided by EU law;
- carry out supervisory stress tests to support the supervisory review, and carry out supervision on a consolidated basis – such stress tests are a supervisory tool also used by national authorities to assess the stability of individual banks; they will not replace the stress tests carried out by the EBA with a view to assessing the soundness of the banking sector in the Single Market as a whole;
- impose capital buffers and exercise other macro-prudential powers;
- carry out supplementary supervision over credit institutions in a financial conglomerate;
- apply requirements for credit institutions to have in place robust governance arrangements, processes and mechanisms and effective internal capital adequacy assessment processes
- carry out supervisory tasks in relation to early intervention when risks to the viability of a bank exist, in coordination with the relevant resolution authorities;
- carry out, in co-ordination with the Commission, assessments for possible public recapitalisations;
- co-ordinate a common position of representatives from competent authorities of the participating Member States in the Board of Supervisors and the Management Board of the EBA, for topics relating to the abovementioned tasks. National authorities would assist the ECB. They would prepare and implement the ECB acts under the oversight of the ECB, including day-to-day supervision activities.' "

At the time of writing, those detailed proposals are not yet available. In essence, the policy seeks to place the ECB at the heart of supervising monetary policy in the EU so as to cope with the shocks which they eurozone currency area suffered between 2009 and 2012 in particular. The Commission has suggested that the "ECB will ensure a truly European supervision mechanism that is not prone to the protection of national interests and which will weaken the link between banks and national sovereigns". The solution to the eurozone crisis is therefore understood to be an increasing Europeanization of banking regulation: that is, more Europe, not less.

7.   THE REGULATION OF FINANCIAL DERIVATIVES

Over-the-counter derivatives are to be regulated, for the first time, by means of the European Markets Infrastructure Directive ("EMIR") and the Markets in Financial Instruments Regulation ("MiFIR"). Both of these Regulations are analysed in detail in Chapter 40. This discussion draws parallels with the ongoing reform of EU financial services regulation in the wake of the Larosière Report.

7–95

---

[192] *http://europa.eu/rapid/press-release_MEMO-12-662_en.htm* [Accessed January 30, 2013.]

7–96   The underlying purpose of EMIR is to require that all derivatives are required to be cleared through a central counterparty ("CCP"), which operates as though it was a clearing house structure: that is, each financial institution which sells prescribed types of derivative is required to set off amounts it owes and amounts it is owed on its derivatives business through a clearing house in the form of a CCP. Thus, the amounts owed in the market are reduced to net amounts. Moreover, market participants are required to report their transactions to trade repositories so that regulators will be able to amass information about the condition of the marketplace. Interestingly, the CCP's and the trade repositories are both private sector bodies which will be authorised and regulated by regulatory authorities. A different approach would have been for a regulatory body to perform those functions, rather than giving it over to the private sector.

7–97   The underlying purpose of MiFIR is to require that financial derivatives of specified types will be performed on public forums: exchanges, MTF's and OTF's. Through these media, prices will be obtainable easily and transparently. This will also aid the commoditisation and the clearing of derivatives.

7–98   The introduction of systematic regulation for financial derivatives was about 20 years overdue. The development of derivatives regulation is discussed in Alastair Hudson, *The Law on Financial Derivatives*, Chapter 15. In essence, it was a free market ideology which maintained that derivatives markets needed to be free from regulation so that they could be innovative. While derivatives appeared to reduce financial risk and to maximise profits in the first decade of the 21st century, it appeared possible to maintain that derivatives should not be regulated. The effect of the financial crisis, with the involvement of credit derivatives in causing a cataclysmic crash, was a change in that approach to the regulation of financial derivatives.

8.   THE MARKET ABUSE DIRECTIVE

7–99   The development of dependable financial markets across the EU requires a large amount of investor confidence and thus the rooting out of abusive practices, insider dealing, market manipulation and so on. The Market Abuse Directive 2003 ("MAD")[193] is directed at the prevention of the misuse of inside information and at the prevention of market manipulation. Market abuse is discussed in detail in Chapter 11.

9.   THE TAKEOVER DIRECTIVE

7–100   There have been a large number of mergers and acquisitions across borders within the EU in recent years. Indeed, in times of economic expansion there is often merger and acquisition to enable growth, and in hard times there are sometimes corporate restructurings aimed at consolidation. The context within which acquisitions and mergers are conducted is governed by EU legislation as well as, in the UK, provision by the Companies Act 2006 and the City Code on

---

[193] 2003/6/EC.

Mergers and Takeovers. In this regard, the Takeover Directive[194] is discussed in Chapter 42 of *The Law and Regulation of Finance* in relation to *Acquisitions*.

10. The Regulation of Hedge Funds and Private Equity

A. The background to the draft AIFM Directive

Hedge funds, private equity managers and other alternative investment funds are to be regulated in the EU for the first time when the Alternative Investment Fund Managers Directive ("AIFM")[195] and the Delegated Regulation on Alternative Investment Fund Managers come into effect in July 2013. The urge to introduce such a directive was prompted by the global financial crisis of 2007–09, and in particular the systemic risks posed by hedge funds (in particular to asset prices); risks to market integrity and efficiency; the effect on risk management; the dangers connected with the highly leveraged nature of such funds; and the need for greater transparency in investment markets.

7–101

While the roots of the financial crisis were in bad banking and mortgage lending practices in the USA, the contagion of bank failure was transmitted and exacerbated by financial speculation in credit markets (on credit default swaps) and by the activities of "short sellers". During the financial crisis 2007–09 several hedge funds went into insolvency as the markets moved sharply, and others earned large profits when their speculative bets turned out to have been correct.

7–102

In a somewhat clumsy phrase, the Explanatory Memorandum accompanying the first draft of the AIFM Directive explained that it sought "to extend appropriate regulation and oversight to all actors and activities that embed significant risks" and that it "aims at providing a harmonised and stringent regulatory and supervisory framework" for the activities of these types of funds.[196] The regulatory focus is really on acquiring sufficient information to enable the various financial regulators within the EU to co-ordinate their responses to the effect of speculative activity on financial markets.

7–103

B. The scope of the directive

The meaning of "hedge fund" and so forth in this sense is a reference to "all funds" which are not regulated under the UCITS Directive (which governs collective investment schemes). The directive is also aimed at those private equity firms which are currently outwith the regulatory net: those funds are considered in Chapter 42. The directive refers to hedge funds as "alternative investment funds" ("AIFM") which encompasses hedge funds, private equity firms and other funds not falling within UCITS. It is estimated that about €2 trillion is currently under management by such funds in Europe.

7–104

---

[194] 2004/25/EC.
[195] 2011/61/EU.
[196] AIFM, Recital 7.

C. Requirements of authorisation and for the provision of information to competent authorities

The scope of the regulations

7–105   The underlying purpose of AIFM is to provide regulation at two levels: first, authorisation for an AIFM to act in the EU from the competent authority in their home Member State, and, secondly, ongoing regulatory oversight of their activities after authorisation is granted. An AIFM is required to seek authorisation to trade from the competent authority of its home member state.[197] Among the issues about which the competent authority would need to be satisfied before granting authorisation would be a statement of the fund's investment objectives, and also information as to internal controls, governance and management of the AIFM. All AIFM's are then required to "act honestly, with due skill, care and diligence and fairly in conducting their activities".[198]

Organisational requirements

7–106   The organisational requirements of an AIFM are then set out in Section 2 of the directive. The general principles are that the AIFM "shall at all times, use adequate and appropriate resources that are necessary for the proper performance of their management activities".[199] Furthermore, such funds "shall have updated systems, documented internal procedures and regular internal controls of their conduct of business, in order to mitigate and manage the risks associated with their activity".[200] Among the organisational requirements which implement these general principles are the following. In relation to valuation of its assets, a valuer must be appointed to conduct at least an annual valuation of assets, shares and units held by the fund.[201] The fund must have a depositary – akin to the fiduciary required for collective investment schemes – to ensure the sake-keeping of the fund's financial instruments, to receive payments made by investors, and to verify acquisition of title in the fund's investments.[202] The AIFM itself shall not act as a depositary.

The provision of accounting information and information to facilitate monitoring of the market

7–107   The second main branch of the directive is the requirement that information be given by the AIFM to the competent authority so that each competent authority and the competent authorities of more than one member state acting in concert can monitor financial markets. The AIFM is required to "make available" an

---

[197] AIFM, art.6.
[198] AIFM, art.12.
[199] AIFM, art.18.
[200] AIFM, art.18.
[201] AIFM, art.19.
[202] AIFM, art.21.

annual report for each financial year.[203] Notably, the financial reporting requirement in art.22 is much less demanding than that imposed, for example, on companies who have offered their securities to public under the Transparency Obligations Directive (see Chapter 36) who must provide interim financial statements half-yearly as well as audited accounts. The AIFM is required only to make available to investors and the competent authority a balance sheet (or a statement of assets and liabilities), an income and expenditure account, and a "report on the activities of the financial year".[204] These statements must be audited. One of the key aspects of macro-prudential regulation which relates to AIFM's under the proposed scheme is a requirement for AIFM's to provide information about the principal markets in which they are dealing and the instruments in which they are dealing.[205]

Providing information about leverage

A key issue is the highly leveraged way in which hedge funds and private equity firms operate. The capital base of such funds is small compared to the amount of investment which they are able to make because their investments are funded out of debt. In the event of failure such funds would be unable to meet their obligations if they could not borrow more money. Consequently, the directive requires that hedge funds and private equity firms report the levels of capital which they hold against their obligations, or in the event that their capital coverage exceeds given thresholds then that information must be passed on to the competent authority regulating their activities. The purpose of the directive in this regard is that competent authorities will co-operate, even though the directive stopped short of placing positive obligations on competent authorities to take particular forms of action.[206] There are therefore requirements that disclosure is made to investors "on a systematic basis" about the level of leverage taken to capitalise each fund.[207] The competent authority must also be informed about leverage.[208] Significantly, the Commission is then empowered to set limits on the amount of leverage which may be employed by funds.[209] This power can be exercised only to "ensure the stability and integrity of the financial system".[210]

7–108

The requirement for the maintenance of capital

The capital requirements in the directive are that an AIFM shall have own funds of €125,000 or that an internally managed AIF (the fund itself) has capital of €300,000.[211] Once the value of funds under management crosses a threshold of

7–109

---

[203] AIFM, art.22.
[204] AIFM, art.22(2).
[205] AIFM, art.24.
[206] AIFM, Recital 63 et seq.
[207] AIFM, art.15; and art.23 requires notification of leverage to investors.
[208] AIFM, art.24.
[209] AIFM, art.25(3).
[210] AIFM, art.25(3).
[211] AIFM, art.9.

€250 million, then the AIFM is required to provide an additional amount of own funds equal to 0.02 per cent of the amount by which those funds under management exceed €250 million.

Information to be provided to investors

7–110   An AIFM can have only professional investors. Article 23 of the directive requires that certain information be provided to investors. The AIFM is required to "describe" the investment strategy and objectives of the fund, the procedures by which that strategy and those objectives may be changed, the governing law of investment contracts, the terms on which any delegation of investment management will take place, the fund's valuation procedures, the fund's liquidity risk, all fees and commissions charged by the fund and its operators.

CHAPTER 8

THE UK REGULATORY STRUCTURE

This chapter considers the regulatory structure in the UK for financial services and banking in general; whereas the next chapter, Chapter 9, considers the fundamental principles which underpin those regulations. The structure of financial regulation in the UK changed significantly in 2013 in response to the financial crisis of 2007–09 (which is discussed in detail in Chapter 45) by means of the Banking Act 2009 and the Financial Services Act 2012. Those two Acts amended the Financial Services and Markets Act 2000, which remains the principal Act in this context. However, it remains to be seen what the impact of that new regulatory structure will be and whether it will have a real effect on banking standards in the UK in the future. More important than the structure of the regulatory regime will be the attitude of the new regulatory bodies in practice.

The reorganisation of the financial regulatory system in the UK took effect on April Fool's Day 2013. The Financial Services Authority was renamed the "Financial Conduct Authority" (referred to here as the "FCA") and is responsible for the authorisation of financial institutions and for the regulation of business. The prudential regulation of financial institutions was brought under the umbrella of the Bank of England for the first time in 2013. Significantly, the Bank of England also has responsibility for two significant aspects of economic policy: monetary policy and financial stability. Therefore, this chapter considers the nature and structure of the Bank of England, and of its several sub-committees and subsidiary regulatory entities, as well as the FCA. The Financial Services Act 2012 provided for a complex web of powers, obligations and protocols to govern the interaction and operation of those agencies: all of which are considered in this chapter.

The Bank of England

The Bank of England acts through a number of different subsidiary entities which have responsibility for different aspects of regulation, and through a number of different policy committees. Bank of England publications stress the independence of these bodies, but nevertheless they are all responsible ultimately to the Court of Directors of the Bank of England, under the chairmanship of the Governor of the Bank of England. The Bank of England has three principal zones of responsibility.

First, economic policy and policy in relation to the financial system. The Monetary Policy Committee of the Bank of England is responsible for monetary policy in relation to the general economy.

Second, the Financial Policy Committee ("FPC") is responsible for the integrity of the entire financial system, as opposed to individual institutions; and as such the role of the FPC relates to "macro-prudential" regulation. Notably then, the Bank of England has responsibility for policy (and thus the success of those aspects of the British economy) as well as for regulation of financial markets. There is clearly a tension here between the Bank of England's responsibility both for economic success and for the oversight and control of economic activity.

Third, the regulation of traditional banking. The Prudential Regulatory Authority ("PRA"), which is part of the Bank of England, is responsible for the regulation of the solvency and condition of individual financial institutions: this is known as "micro-prudential" regulation because it focuses on individual institutions. Under the Banking Act 2009, the Bank of England has responsibility for the regulation of traditional banking activity (including the operation of bank accounts, loans, and the operation of the payments system). That Act also creates the mechanisms for dealing with failing banks and with bank insolvency which was designed in the wake of the financial crisis 2007–09.

The Financial Conduct Authority

The Financial Conduct Authority ("FCA") has responsibility for the regulation of the conduct of business between financial institutions and their customers, and for the authorisation of financial institutions. In essence, this role is concerned with consumer protection, albeit that the core principle is to ensure that customers are provided with the necessary information in a suitable format for them to make their own decisions as to whether or not to invest. The FCA is answerable to HM Treasury.

The independent Office of Fair Trading also has regulatory responsibility in for the regulation of money lending.

The interaction of the regulatory bodies

Each of these regulatory bodies is given detailed statutory objectives which they are obliged to pursue (as laid out in the text to follow). The FSMA 2000 also provides in detail for the manner in which these bodies interact with one another. This regulatory structure is the primary focus of this chapter.

The obligations of the Bank of England and the FCA as regulators are more extensive than simply oversight or supervision of financial markets. Among the regulators' other obligations are duties as to the condition of the UK economy and the education of the public in financial matters. These obligations appear to create a conflict between ensuring the integrity of the system and ensuring compliance with prudential regulatory requirements on the one hand, and encouraging the economic competitiveness and success of that same system on the other. In Chapter 4 we considered the idea of a financial regulator in the UK as having a coercive-regulatory role, an economic role and an educational role as a result of the powers granted to it by the FSMA 2000. This chapter considers the obligations and objectives of the various regulatory bodies in the UK.

1.   FUNDAMENTALS OF FINANCIAL SERVICES REGULATION IN THE UK

A.   The scope and purpose of this chapter

The sources of financial regulation in the UK

8–01   This chapter explains the structure of the regulation of financial services in the UK principally by means of powers granted to the Bank of England and to HM Treasury by the Financial Services and Markets Act 2000 ("FSMA 2000"), as amended by the Banking Act 2009 and the Financial Services Act 2012.[1] The aim of this chapter is to explain the regulatory structure through which that regulation is administered. Each regulatory agency has been furnished with general statutory objectives which it must pursue in the performance of its duties. Those objectives are considered below, together with the policies which underpinned the reform of UK financial regulation in 2013. The next chapter considers the overarching regulatory principles which apply to all financial markets: in particular the core "principles for businesses" (especially the principle of "integrity"), the requirement for regulatory authorisation to sell financial services, and so forth. Later chapters in this Part III deal in greater detail with specific aspects of regulation such as the conduct of business between investment firms and their clients,[2] financial promotion,[3] market abuse,[4] and the regulation of banking services.[5] So, in this chapter we are concerned with the big picture relating to the structure of the regulatory system and the policies which created it; whereas, it is in later chapters that we turn our attention to more detailed matters. It should be recalled from Chapter 3 that in this book there is a division made between "financial regulation" (which refers to the regulation of financial markets specifically in the UK further the FSMA 2000) and "the general law" (which

---

[1] The following texts deal with the overarching context of financial regulation. In relation specifically to the securities markets, there is A.S. Hudson, *Securities Law* 2nd edn (London: Sweet & Maxwell, 2013); and in relation to derivatives markets, there is A.S. Hudson, *The Law on Financial Derivatives* 5th edn (London: Sweet & Maxwell, 2012). The following texts are of interest but are now out-of-date: M. Blair and G. Walker (eds), *Financial Markets and Exchanges Law* (OUP, 2007); M. Blair and G. Walker (eds), *Financial Services Law* (OUP, 2006); and R. Cranston, *Principles of Banking Law* 2nd edn (OUP, 2002). A full analysis of the company law and securities law issues in this context is set out in A.S. Hudson, "Capital Issues" in G. Morse (ed), *Palmer's Company Law* (London: Sweet & Maxwell, loose leaf), para.5–001 et seq., and in S. Girvin, A. Hudson and S. Frisby, *Charlesworth's Company Law*, 18th edn (Sweet & Maxwell, 2010). Encyclopaedic reference to financial regulation is made E. Lomnicka and J. Powell, *Encyclopedia of Financial Services Law* (London: Sweet & Maxwell, looseleaf) and P. Creswell et al., *Encyclopaedia of Banking Law* (LexisNexis, looseleaf).

[2] See para.10–01.

[3] See para.11–01.

[4] See para.12–01.

[5] See para.28–01.

refers to the ordinary statute and case law of England and Wales as it applies in the context of financial markets). In this chapter we are concerned specifically with financial regulation.

The regulations in force at the time of writing

Until April Fool's Day 2013, the principal financial regulations in the UK were contained in the old Financial Services Authority rulebooks, referred to collectively as the *"FSA Handbook"*, which comprised all of the rules and guidance notes issued by the Financial Services Authority. Further to the Financial Services Act 2012, operational responsibility for conduct of business and related matters remained with the "renamed" authority in its new guise as the "Financial Conduct Authority" ("FCA"), while operational responsibility for micro-prudential matters[6] passed to the new Prudential Regulatory Authority ("PRA"). As is considered below, the FCA is responsible, in effect, to HM Treasury; whereas the PRA is part of the Bank of England. The two new regulatory bodies assumed control of their various spheres of financial regulation from April Fool's Day 2013. The *FCA Handbook* is effectively the same as the old FSA Handbook, which is appropriate given that the FCA is simply a renamed version of the Financial Services Authority. The *FCA Handbook* and the *PRA Handbook* have almost identical "contents pages" and they are governed by the same high-level "principles for businesses", but the *PRA Handbook* does not contain all of the regulatory rules which apply to the *FCA Handbook* because the PRA is only concerned with micro-prudential regulation and therefore does not require regulations relating, for example, to conduct of business. Therefore, where the regulations are contained online, the web-pages which set out the contents of each of the handbooks appear to be identical; however, on closer inspection the *PRA Handbook* lacks many of the provisions of the *FCA Handbook* because they are not appropriate to its work. It is expected that the two rulebooks will evolve over time in the usual way and, aside from the *PRA Handbook* being shorter due to the smaller number of regulations within it from the outset, they will therefore develop further differences. Ordinarily, regulatory handbooks develop gradually over time by way of consultation with the marketplace, and in reaction to EU and UK legislative developments.

8–02

B. How to understand the operation of financial services regulation in the UK

There is a simple principle at the heart of UK financial regulation: it is a criminal offence under s.19 of FSMA 2000 to conduct any of the activities identified in the FSMA 2000 or the Regulated Activities Order 2001 without formal authorisation to do so either from the FCA or the PRA (as appropriate), or from the competent

8–03

---

[6] The detail of these regulations is considered below. The expression "micro-prudential" regulation refers to the solvency and good health of individual financial institutions, as opposed to the "macro-prudential" regulation of the financial system as a whole (which is to be overseen by the Financial Policy Committee of the Bank of England).

authority of another Member State of the European Union.[7] Therefore, to be able to conduct financial business of the types identified in the statute in the UK, one must have regulatory authorisation to do so. From this central principle grows the idea that almost all of the financial services activities discussed in *Section Two: Specific Financial Techniques* of this book are governed by the FSMA 2000 financial regulatory code in the UK. A number of other statutory principles extend outwards from this central principle, including the criminalisation of making any advertisement or "financial promotion" to any person of any regulated financial services activity, further to s.21 of FSMA 2000. The underlying objective of this structure is both to ensure that users of those services will be protected from abuse by financial institutions, and to ensure that the UK's financial markets have sufficient integrity to maintain investor confidence and to support the UK economy.

8–04   Having identified the fact that it is a criminal offence not to have regulatory authorisation to deal in financial services, it is important to identify the principles on which the regulators will act. The *FCA Handbook* is the publication containing all of the rules which the FCA is empowered to make by the FSMA 2000, including rules and guidance notes.[8] That handbook is organised around central principles contained in the *Principles for Businesses* rulebook. Those central principles govern the interpretation of all other regulations, primarily requiring regulated persons to act with "integrity", as considered below. Different market sectors are then regulated in accordance with detailed rulebooks contained in the *Handbook*. The regulations which are specific to each market sector as discussed in the appropriate chapter in Section Two of this book, whereas this chapter and Chapter 9 consider the foundational regulatory principles which apply in the UK. The *FCA Handbook* and the *PRA Handbook* incorporate material contained in UK statute, EC directives and Commission technical regulations, as was considered in Chapter 1. The PRA Handbook deals with "micro-prudential" regulations governing the health and solvency of regulated financial institutions which, as mentioned above, are structurally the same as the FCA Handbook at the time of writing.

8–05   This Part III of this book considers the UK financial regulatory architecture: while this architecture appears to be complex and somewhat gothic at first glance, it is easily comprehensible if it is understood as being based on these core principles. This Chapter 8 considers the role, powers and duties of HM Treasury and the Bank of England's regulatory bodies; whereas Chapter 9 considers the regulatory rules which are based on the foundational principles in s.19 of FSMA 2000 and in the *Principles for Businesses* rulebook. While there may appear at first to be a lot of technical jargon in this chapter, each of the terms is defined and explained as the chapter progresses.

---

[7] It is a feature of EU financial services law, as discussed in the previous chapter, that an authorisation from the appropriate regulator of one Member State constitutes a "passport" to conduct the authorised forms of business across the EU.

[8] The *FCA Handbook* can be accessed through *http://www.fca.gov.uk.*

C. The limited role of law in the oversight of the financial system

This chapter considers how the Bank of England and the Treasury have control of the regulation of the financial system in the UK, and it explains the statutory powers and obligations which were bestowed on each of the regulatory agencies by Parliament in the wake of the financial crisis, before later chapters consider how the detail of those regulations impact on different financial markets. However, it is very important to understand the limited role which law actually plays in the oversight of the financial system. The most significant aspect of financial regulation in practice is finance theory, which is in itself a hybrid of economics and mathematics. Complex mathematics underpin all of the risks which the banks take—ranging from decisions whether or not to lend on domestic mortgages right through to the most complex derivatives transactions. In each circumstance, financial institutions have a complex mathematical understanding of their assets and liabilities across all of their activities, and those mathematical models control their behaviour. Similarly, regulators use mathematical models to assess the condition of each financial institution and to assess the risks associated with different financial markets under its purview. In essence, the regulators stand on the touchline of financial markets, assessing the flow of information which comes to them from the people playing in those financial markets, and then they make managerial decisions as a result. The manner in which the regulatory regime is constructed and the manner in which the regulators use their powers (whether strictly or leniently) is based on political decisions which are dominated by economic theory as to whether or not too much regulation is beneficial or harmful to the success of those financial institutions and the vibrancy of those markets.

8–06

Law plays only a subsidiary role here, as is discussed in Chapter 45. The failure of the high street bank Northern Rock in August 2007, as its ordinary customers began a "run" on the bank (with pictures on the television news of lines of nervous depositors queuing down the street so that they could remove their money), demonstrated that the regulatory authorities (at that time the Treasury, the Bank of England and the old Financial Services Authority) did not have sufficient legal powers to deal with the crisis. They could not compel Northern Rock to do anything because no legislator had previously thought it necessary to create a statute for that purpose because bank failures were thought to be so unlikely. (That is, in spite of the failures of Johnson Matthey, Barings Bank and BCCI in the UK in living memory.) Therefore, the Banking (Special Provisions) Act 2008 was hurried through Parliament so that those three regulatory authorities would have powers to compel a sale of a failing bank, or a break-up of a failing bank so that it could be sold in pieces, or the nationalisation of a failing bank. This Act expired after one year and one replaced by the Banking Act 2009. The Banking Act 2009 is a play-book of the process which Chancellor of the Exchequer Alistair Darling faced at the time that Northern Rock failed: he sought a private sector purchaser to no avail, then he sought to break the bank up to no avail, before finally nationalising the bank and waiting for matters to improve. Importantly, the role of the 2009 Act was *not* to dictate what any of the regulators must do in any given situation; rather its role was to grant those regulators the

8–07

necessary powers to do any of the things which Alistair Darling had been forced to contemplate but which he had previously never had power to do under UK banking law. So, in future the regulators and the politicians have the power to compel actions by financial institutions, their management and shareholders by choosing from a statutory menu of options. The position had been the same in the USA: none of their regulators had had the necessary legal powers to deal with the failures of Lehman Brothers, Washington Mutual, Citigroup and so on. Therefore new laws had to be passed to grant them the necessary powers.

8–08   Therefore, the role of law in relation to financial regulation generally, and in relation to banking crises in particular, is to grant the powers to identified bodies to act in whichever ways they consider to be pragmatic and appropriate from a list of statutory alternatives. The law is not positivist in the sense that it compels that any particular thing must be done. Rather, the holders of the power can choose their preferred course of action from within the statute and then compel other people to comply with their choice. Law plays a simple enabling function here. However, the real decisions as to which course of action is to be followed, and whether regulatory policy will favour stringent or weak applications of the rules, is something which is governed by finance theory and politics. In consequence, the structure of the various policymaking and regulatory bodies in the UK is simply the arena within which those various bodies (and their human actors) will put their ideas into effect and play out their disagreements.[9] That is why so much of the legislation which is considered in this chapter is focused on identifying the processes which each body must follow in relation to any question which appears to overlap between their various competencies. It is not law in the sense of a code of rules in this chapter, but rather it is law in the sense of a series of powers being granted to public bodies to act as they think fit.

2.   THE BANK OF ENGLAND

A.   The Bank of England emerging from the financial crisis 2007–09

8–09   In many senses, the principal beneficiary of the financial crisis 2007–09 was the Bank of England. The Labour government which passed the FSMA 2000 created the Financial Services Authority to be the principal regulator of financial services in the UK, akin to huge US regulatory bodies like the Securities and Exchange

---

[9] This process reminds me of the board game *Risk*. As with any board game there is a rulebook and a board with a design on it which control the moves which the players are allowed to make. Just as *Risk* sets out different regions in the world with players attempting to build up control in different parts of the world through rolls of the dice and clever manoeuvres, the FSA 2012 set out the various bodies within the Bank of England and HM Treasury with their different statutory powers and duties. However, the way in which those bodies and their employees choose to act is governed by their own decisions as to best way to win a game of *Risk* and their own preferred moves. Law is simply the board on which this particular game is played: it sets out the rules, it sets out the lay-out of the board, but it is up to the players to decide what happens thereafter. And the financial system is, after all, entirely about using clever manoeuvres to manipulate risk to your advantage.

Commission ("SEC").[10] This replaced the previous system in which the Bank of England had acted as the central bank in the UK (as the controller of the currency and the lender of last resort), but in which financial regulation had otherwise been controlled by self-regulatory organisations which had been incapable of dealing effectively with financial markets. However, as with the US system, there were still too many regulatory bodies with significant areas of overlap in their responsibilities, with the result that there was no single line of regulatory policy and consequently insufficient practical action. So, in the UK, the Financial Services Authority, the Bank of England and HM Treasury (the UK's ministry of finance) together constituted the "tri-partite authority" with responsibility for regulatory oversight of the largest banks in the UK. Their interaction was purportedly governed by a "memorandum of understanding" between them: that is, an extra-statutory document setting out the way in which they proposed to interact with one another. However, when the financial crisis of 2007–09 hit (as is described in detail in Chapter 45), it was the Financial Services Authority which attracted most of the blame due to its ineffective "light-touch" regulation of financial markets and its inability to anticipate the oncoming financial crisis.[11] The Financial Services Authority has long been lampooned by the satirical magazine *Private Eye* as being the "Fundamentally Supine Authority" given its craven indulgence of the banks it was supposed to regulate. However, the other members of the tri-partite authority avoided their share of the blame for failures of banks which fell within their joint regulatory remit. The Bank of England waged an effective enough public relations campaign to recover regulatory powers for the micro-prudential regulation of banks by the Conservative-led Coalition Government in 2012, in spite of its own evident failings.[12] However, the Bank of England had been in existence for centuries before then, and its complex inner workings are the result of the antiquity of that institution. Consequently, it is as well to begin with a short history of that institution and to trace its development into the principal regulator and central bank in the UK today.

B. A brief history of the Bank of England

The Bank of England was formed by the Bank of England Act 1694 so as to fund **8–10** the war with France and to rebuild the economy. After William and Mary acceded to the throne in 1688, the national debt was enormous. The Bank of England was formed by amassing a loan of £1.2 million and incorporating the Bank of England by Royal Charter for the benefit of the people who subscribed that loan capital.[13]

---

[10] For the detail of the creation of the old Financial Services Authority and its powers, see the first edition of this book *The Law of Finance* (Sweet & Maxwell, 2009), para.8–01 et seq.

[11] See para.45–01 et seq.

[12] The Bank of England had singularly failed to prevent the failures of Johnson Matthey, Barings Bank and the Bank for Credit and Commercial International before the financial crisis of 2007. Indeed, its own chequered history and the overly "clubby" feel to the City of London had been part of the impulse for creating the Financial Services Authority.

[13] It was provided by s.19 of the Bank of England Act 1694 that King William and Queen Mary could "incorporate all and every such Subscribers and Contributors, their ... Successors, or Assigns, to be one Body Corporate and Politick, by the name of The Governor and Company of the Bank of

The Bank of England's own history describes itself as having been "banker and debt-manager" for the government from that time.[14] However, it is worth noting that the Bank of England had only a limited official status then (predicated on that initial debt) which was very different from its role today. Indeed during the lead-up to the "South Sea Bubble" crisis in 1720, the Bank of England seemed to have been overshadowed by the Sword Blade Bank in dealing with the national debt.[15] The Sword Blade Bank funded the exchange of bonds against the government for shares in the South Sea Company: that was, until the Sword Blade Bank's demise along with the fraudulent South Sea Company scheme in that same year. This illustrated how, at various times in its history, the Bank of England was simply one bank among many. Even though it was linked with government and with government borrowing, it remained an independent entity. Nevertheless, over time, signs of its role as part of the establishment emerged. So, when the Bank of England's charter was renewed in 1781 it was described as being "the public exchequer". It was not until the Bank Charter Act 1844, when its right to issue banknotes was tied to its gold reserves, that it acquired sole competence for the issuance of banknotes in London, although even after that time other private banks were able to issue their own banknotes outside London.[16]

8–11   It was not until the 19th century that the Bank of England really took on the role of a central bank. The Bank of England became the "lender of last resort" for the banking system, which means that if the banking system could not find money from elsewhere, then it would borrow (in theory) from the Bank of England. In this way, a central bank operates as a sort of long-stop against the banking system collapsing. A lender of last resort is the central bank which will ultimately provide funds to commercial banks when they have no other access to funds. Nevertheless, the Bank of England remained an independent entity until the end of the Second World War. It was not until 1946 that the Bank of England was nationalised and as a consequence began to take on the mantle of the public body which we recognise today.

8–12   As is explored below, the Bank of England assumed very different responsibilities under the Labour Government which passed the Bank of England Act 1998. Of particular significance was the granting of powers to the Bank of England to control monetary policy (principally the setting of the base interest rate) so as to achieve the government's inflation target. To that end, the Monetary Policy Committee was created in 1998. Latterly, the Bank of England has been given a

England". Thus, the people who lent money to the government through this scheme became part of this body corporate known as the Bank of England, and in consequence acquired rights to be repaid.
[14]   *http://www.bankofengland.co.uk/about/Pages/history/default.aspx#1.*
[15]   M. Balen, *A Very English Deceit* (4th Estate, 2002). A similar scheme had been hatched in France through the Mississippi Company in 1719. The attraction of the new companies was that they took investments from the public which offered a stake in newly discovered lands in the "South Seas" (and the promise of enormous profits). People who were owed bonds by the government were encouraged to dispose of their bonds (thus reducing the national debt) in exchange for stock in the new company. Many people (including royalty and cabinet ministers) were ruined when the companies collapsed.
[16]   At that time, Scottish and Irish banks could issue their own banknotes, but in England and Wales it was only the Bank of England that could issue banknotes in London (with some provincial banks continuing to issue their own banknotes until the 1930s).

further objective related to the maintenance of financial stability by the Banking Act 2009. These various legal responsibilities are considered in turn below.

C.   The role of the Bank of England as a central bank

The economic roles of a central bank in outline

A central bank has several key roles. While an analysis of the economic purpose of each of them is beyond the scope of this book, a short outline will suffice for present purposes. A central bank may potentially have a number of different roles. Clearly, the precise powers and responsibilities of any given central bank will depend upon the policies of the jurisdiction in which it acts. The first function of a central bank is "monetary". The principal mechanism for controlling monetary policy is the setting of base interest rates[17] whereby low interest rates are generally understood to increase economic activity by making it cheaper to borrow money (so as to achieve economic growth, but at the risk of inflation) and high interest rates are generally understood to decrease economic activity by making it expensive to borrow money (so as to slow excessive economic growth, but at the risk of a contraction in the economy). A central bank can also control "money supply" through the sale or purchase of government bonds,[18] as well as potentially having control of interest rates within its monetary role, usually in co-operation with a ministry of finance (in the UK, that is Her Majesty's Treasury).[19] A second function, in which the Bank of England plays no real role,

8–13

---

[17] Simply put, the base interest rate is ordinarily the lowest rate in that jurisdiction in which the central bank will deal with those financial institutions which are permitted to deal directly with it. By moving those base rights higher or lower, commercial interest rates which are offered to businesses and private individuals by banks will ordinarily tend to move higher or lower as a result. In essence, then, base rates act as a sort of foundational benchmark for ordinary interest rates in the marketplace.

[18] Monetary theory operates broadly as follows. If a government wants to borrow money then it can issue bonds to investors: in return, the investors receive a rate of interest and the repayment of their loan capital at the end of the life of the bond. These investors are usually the largest banks and financial institutions. This also has the effect of soaking up excess money which those investors would otherwise lend into the economy: the more money that is in the economy, the more growth there will be (which is usually positive) but also the more inflation there can be (which is usually negative). Equally, when there is too little money in the economy, the government can buy back its bonds from those investors with the result that public money is released into the economy through those investors. The result is expected to be more money which is available to fund economic growth. This theory requires that those investors lend that money on to other people, and not that they hoard it for themselves.

[19] By means of control of the money supply, a central bank can make interest rates lower and money "cheaper" by simply allowing more money to be released into the system. A central bank will therefore typically be responsible for the issuance and integrity of the currency. This can be done by buying up UK government bonds from the marketplace and thus giving the market cash; or it can restrict the supply of money by issuing government bonds at an attractive rate and thus mopping up excess money that it is in the system (this might be done for example to control inflation). The issue of government bonds is also the way in which much government borrowing is conducted in the modern era—with the result that bond traders have assumed immense power over economic policy in Europe, since the financial crisis in particular. The control of central interest "base rates" by the Bank of England has an effect (it is hoped, while the markets are functioning normally) on the level of interest rates which the commercial and retail banks charge their customers: making interest rates lower makes borrowing money cheaper and so encourages an expansion of economic activity using

is the "fiscal" function—this relates to tax rates and tax policy, where high taxes are expected to reduce economic activity and low taxes to encourage it. The third function relates to the integrity of the financial system: in short, financial regulation and regulatory policy. A central bank may play a role in this context in regulating the activity of deposit-taking banks, and also whichever financial institutions beyond deposit-taking banks are considered appropriate for it to regulate. To be a central bank does not require control of financial regulation. However, in the wake of the financial crisis 2007–09, there has been a closer link between regulation of financial institutions, central banking and general economic policy because the impact of a failure in the financial system was shown to be potentially catastrophic for all of those other vital economic activities.

The legal and regulatory roles of the UK central bank in outline

8–14   The legal powers and responsibilities which come with each of the central bank's functions in the UK are set out and analysed below. There are five principal roles for a central bank which impact on its legal structure and its legal powers and responsibilities. First, acting as lender of last resort to the banking system, as outlined above. Second, overseeing monetary stability: that is, setting interest rates so as to achieve the government's stated inflation target. Third, overseeing financial stability: that is, regulating the macro-prudential condition of the entire financial system so as to prevent a repeat of the credit crunch and the resulting economic crash which began in the summer of 2007.[20] Fourth, taking responsibility for the printing of banknotes (as discussed in Chapter 2) and for the maintenance of the government's foreign exchange and gold reserves. The Bank of England also assumes responsibility under the new regime for regulating "systematically important infrastructure" under the new Part 18 of the FSMA 2000, which includes regulated clearing houses, recognised information providers and payment systems. Fifth, acting as banker to the government.[21]

3.   THE POWERS AND RESPONSIBILITIES OF THE BANK OF ENGLAND AND HM TREASURY

A. Introduction

8–15   Control of financial regulation and of financial activity in the UK is divided between the Bank of England and HM Treasury: where the Bank of England acts as the central bank for the UK as well as overseeing traditional banking activity, whereas the Treasury is the UK's ministry of finance and the body to which the FCA is ultimately accountable. All of these terms and activities are defined

---

that cheap money. Contrariwise, raising base interest rates can reduce inflation by lowering the amount of economic activity because money becomes more expensive to borrow.
[20] This is discussed in Ch.45.
[21] The complex management of government finances in the modern era involves borrowing money from the markets by means of issuing government bonds (such that the government pays interest on those bonds and repays the capital at the end of the life of the loan, as discussed in Ch.34).

through this chapter. The Bank of England was granted significant powers by the Banking Act 2009 and by the Financial Services Act 2012 with the result that it has extraordinary powers in three different contexts.[22] First, the monetary context in which the Bank of England's Monetary Policy Committee ("MPC") has control over the setting of interest rates. This committee was created in 1997 by the incoming Labour government in an effort to hand control of interest rate (and thus monetary) policy to an independent body so as to take it out of political hands.[23] Second, in relation to the stability of the financial system as a whole, the Bank of England had imposed on it a "Financial Stability Objective" by the Banking Act 2009.[24] A Financial Stability Committee within the Bank was created at the same time to strategise for the pursuit of this objective.[25] Third, the PRA is responsible for the regulation of the solvency and condition of individual financial institutions (known as "micro-prudential regulation"), further to Pt 2 of the Financial Services Act 2012. The FCA is responsible for the regulation of the conduct of business between financial institutions and their customers, as well as for the authorisation of financial institutions. The FCA is governed ultimately by HM Treasury. It retains the regulatory responsibilities formerly held by the Financial Services Authority. These regulatory responsibilities and divisions are considered in detail through this chapter.[26] First, however, we consider the principal division in financial regulation in the UK: that between banking business and investment business.

B. The distinction between traditional banking and investment business

The role of the Bank of England in relation to the regulation of traditional banking activity is examined in detail in Chapter 28. There had always been a distinction between traditional banking on the one hand (including the operation of bank accounts, loans and overdrafts, and the payment systems), and investment business on the other hand (including securities, derivatives and so forth). These different activities were regulated separately by different regulators. The micro-prudential regulation of banks (that is, their condition and solvency) has been passed to the Bank of England through the PRA; whereas investment business regulation rests with the FCA.[27] In this section we shall consider the different objectives of the Bank of England in outline terms, according to the

8–16

---

[22] Both of those statutes create those powers by making amendments to the principal Act: the Financial Services and Markets Act 2000.

[23] The dual purpose behind that change was to ensure that interest rates were created for the long-term benefit of the economy and not for short-term political purposes, and secondly to mimic the purported success of the Federal Reserve in New York in setting US interest rates. It emerged with the financial crisis and the boom-and-bust cycle in the US property market that at the beginning of the 21st century that the Federal Reserve, under the leadership of Alan Greenspan, had been significantly less successful in steering the US economy into calm waters than had at first appeared.

[24] Financial Services and Markets Act 2000, s.2A, inserted by the Banking Act 2009, s.238, and amended by the Financial Services Act 2012, s.2.

[25] Financial Services and Markets Act 2000, s.2B, inserted by the Banking Act 2009, s.238.

[26] See especially para 8–28 et seq. below.

[27] For a definition of these terms see para 8–28 *et seq.*

powers granted to the Bank by the FSMA 2000, before the powers of each of the regulatory bodies are considered in greater detail in the appropriate chapters later in this book.

C. The monetary policy role of the Bank of England

8–17   The first function of the Bank of England is "monetary". The Bank of England's Monetary Policy Committee acquired independent control over the setting of base interest rates (and thus of a key lever of monetary policy) under the Bank of England Act 1998. Section 11 of the Bank of England Act 1998 provides that:

> "In relation to monetary policy, the objectives of the Bank of England shall be—
> (a)   to maintain price stability, and
> (b)   subject to that, to support the economic policy of Her Majesty's Government, including its objectives for growth and employment."

Therefore, the Bank of England plays a significant role in the achievement of government economic policy. The Bank is required in particular to pursue the government's goal for inflation in its attitude to monetary policy. The Governor of the Bank of England is obliged to write a letter to the Chancellor of the Exchequer in the event that it misses the government's inflation target by more than one per cent in any given period of measurement. Two things emerge: the Governor is responsible for the success of economic policy (which can therefore be expected to influence his approach to all of the Bank's other activities and responsibilities) and policy is as much a part of the Bank's thinking as the detail of financial regulation.

D. The financial stability objective of the Bank of England

8–18   The second key function of the Bank of England was introduced by the Banking Act 2009 relating to the stability of the financial systems in the UK. Part 7 of the Banking Act 2009 amended the structure and functions of the Bank of England in this sense. Section 238 of the 2009 Act introduced a new s.2A to the Bank of England Act 1998, such that:

> "(1)   An objective of the Bank shall be to contribute to protecting and enhancing the stability of the financial systems of the United Kingdom (the "Financial Stability Objective").
> (2)   In pursuing the Financial Stability Objective the Bank shall aim to work with other relevant bodies (including the Treasury …).
> (3)   The court of directors shall, consulting the Treasury, determine and review the Bank's strategy in relation to the Financial Stability Objective."

Therefore, the Bank is central to a further aspect of economic policy (as opposed to regulatory practice): the stability of the financial systems in the UK. Importantly, the UK economy is very reliant on its financial sector for growth, jobs and a significant fraction of the total tax take. Consequently, there is a great overlap between economic policy and regulatory policy. Economic growth in the UK has come from the financial sector more than most other sectors of the economy in recent decades, and therefore anything which dampens growth in the financial sector (whether to enhance stability or to rein in abusive practices) will have an effect on general economic growth as the British economy is currently organised. The Bank is also required to interact with HM Treasury and other agencies in relation to the exercise of this power.

A Financial Stability Committee was created within the Bank of England by s.238 of the Banking Act 2009 which in turn created a new s.2B of the Bank of England Act 1998, whereby:

8–19

> "(2)   The Committee shall have the following functions –
>
> (a)   to make recommendations to the court of directors, which they shall consider, about the nature and implementation of the Bank's strategy in relation to the Financial Stability Objective,
>
> (b)   to give advice about whether and how the Bank should act in respect of an institution, where the issue appears to the Committee to be relevant to the Financial Stability Objective,
>
> (c)   in particular, to give advice about whether and how the Bank should use stabilisation powers under Part 1 of the Banking Act 2009 in particular cases [which are considered at the end of this chapter],
>
> (d)   to monitor the Bank's use of the stabilisation powers,
>
> (e)   to monitor the Bank's exercise of its functions under Part 5 of the Banking Act 2009 (inter-bank payment systems), and
>
> (f)   any other functions delegated to the Committee by the court of directors for the purpose of pursuing the Financial Stability Objective."

The Bank of England thus received an enhanced role in relation to the maintenance of the stability of the financial system. A central bank may play a role in this context in regulating the activity of deposit-taking banks specifically or financial activity more generally. The purpose of the Banking Act 2009 is to furnish the regulatory authorities in the UK with the powers necessary to confront a future banking crisis or the failure or insolvency of a particular bank. In any event, one of the principal objectives of that legislation is to preserve the integrity of the financial system: consequently that has been written into the objectives of the Bank of England.

E.   The regulatory powers of the Bank of England

The regulatory powers of the Bank of England, as distributed between the three new subsidiary entities of the Bank created by the Financial Services Act 2012, are considered in detail in the following sections of this chapter. The public pronouncements of the Bank of England continue to suggest that those regulatory authorities are independent but, as explained in the next subsection of this chapter, they are locked into the constitutional structure of the Bank of England.

8–20

F.   The structure of the Bank of England

8–21   The Bank of England is a labyrinth of committees and subsidiary entities. Seen from the outside, even its offices resemble Mervyn Peake's fictional city state "Gormenghast",[28] not least given the very complexity of its building on Threadneedle Street in London.[29] Indeed, the Bank of England's architecture—whether the original building on that site designed by Sir John Soanes, or Sir Herbert Baker's considerably less interesting 20th century replacement[30]—have always tended to the labyrinthine and the mock-classical. The intricate legislative web of committees and regulatory bodies, and the knot of principles which are intended to implement overlaps between the responsibilities of those bodies, all suggest a half-hidden, powerful organisation. It is "half-hidden" in the sense that while all of the organs and structures are set out in statute, the ways in which they will actually operate in practice and the precise disagreements which will naturally arise between their human actors are all concealed within its day-to-day practices. That all of these deliberations happen within the Bank of England means that they will not become public. Consequently, much of the detail of financial regulatory practice and monetary and financial policy will be shielded from public scrutiny. The opportunity for a new brand of "groupthink" to emerge within the Bank of England, under the direction of its Governor, is enormous. It remains to be seen whether the new subsidiary entities of the Bank will be able to fight their own corners in policy terms so as to replicate a system in which the different agencies responsible for different aspects of financial regulation and for financial policy are genuinely at arm's length, and which can therefore genuinely debate their ideas and assumptions in public.

8–22   At the heart of the Bank of England is the "Court of Directors". That somewhat antiquated nomenclature refers to the governing body of the Bank of England, which is broadly akin to a board of directors in an ordinary company. Those directors are bound by the statutes governing the Bank. The chair of the court of directors is the Governor of the Bank of England. The FSA 2012 created the positions of Deputy Governors to head the PRA and the FPC. This is intended to give those agencies some independence. However, each of those agencies reports to the Governor. Moreover, it is the Governor of the Bank of England who serves as the chair of most of the significant committees within the Bank, with the result that he is a particularly powerful individual. Indeed, given the broad powers

---

[28] See, for example, M. Peake, *The Gormenghast Trilogy* (Vintage, 1999); the first volume of which is *Titus Groan*, published originally by Eyre and Spottiswoode in 1946.

[29] Even the very name "Threadneedle" Street suggests the medieval past of that area of London being populated by seamstresses and so on, even before the banking institutions began to take hold of the area. The *Gormenghast* novels make great play of the superstitious manner in which its inhabitants cling to a culture in which they occupy rooms which have antiquated names for the performance of nonsensical rituals. The plan of the Bank of England building consciously harks back to the ancient, classical age. It is all very much at odds with the pace of modern finance. This is something which would be positive, if there were not the lurking sense that it embodied the home of a secret, ancient order moving slowly through its own rituals while cloistered away from the world outside.

[30] The architectural historian Nikolaus Pevsner famously described the demolition of Sir John Soanes's masterpiece to make way for Baker's modern version as "the greatest architectural crime, in the City of London, of the twentieth century".

givcn to the Bank of England in relation to monetary policy, policy governing the stability of the financial system, and the regulation of financial services generally, the Governor of the Bank of England is the second most powerful, unelected individual in the United Kingdom, second only to the Queen herself. It is ironic then that the first Governor of the Bank to have these powers is a man with the name Mervyn King.

An "Oversight Committee" was created by the Financial Services Act 2012[31] to "keep under review" the Bank of England's "performance" in relation to its various statutory objectives. The Oversight Committee is in point of fact a sub-committee of the court of directors of the Bank of England. That is, the committee which is intended to oversee the Bank is actually contained *within* the Bank itself, as opposed to being distinct from it. It is a matter of some concern that the Oversight Committee is a committee that is contained within the Bank of England and is not a committee that is open to public scrutiny or to members drawn from beyond the closed group which provides the directors and non-executive directors of the Bank.

8–23

The principal concern about the Bank of England must be the democratic deficit between its powers and the extent to which it can be held publicly to account. When disputes are ventilated or crises are confronted, all of that will take place within the Bank of England. The arguments will be fought out between different departments within that organisation. There is little which compels publication of *the detail* of these issues, aside from the need for superficial reports (considered in the text above); occasional, statutorily-mandated meetings between the Governor of the Bank and the Chancellor of the Exchequer; and occasional, formalised jousting sessions between the Governor, the Deputy Governors and the Treasury Select Committee in Parliament. In essence the British response to the financial crisis of 2007–09 has been to wall nearly all of the policymaking and regulatory activities within an institution created in the 17th century and hide them away from democratic oversight. This is the ideal scenario for the creation of a new groupthink in relation to financial policy when those parts of the Bank of England (including the Governor) which are responsible for economic growth seek to pressure those parts of the Bank which are responsible for restraining over-exuberance in the financial sector to relax their controls so that the City of London can once again innovate the real economy into the sort of peril which faced it in the autumn of 2008. Because that body is responsible for economic growth, there will always be internal pressure to relax its regulatory authorities. This is exactly the sort of situation that is likely to create another boom and bust in the future.

8–24

---

[31] Financial Services and Markets Act 2000, s.3A, inserted by the Financial Services Act 2012, s.3.

4.   The Regulatory Structure for Investment Business in the UK from April Fool's Day 2013

A.   Introduction

8–25   The structure of the regulation of finance in the UK underwent a very significant change in 2013 with the implementation of the Financial Services Act 2012 ("FSA 2012").[32] In essence, the FSA 2012 amends the principal Act—the Financial Services and Markets Act 2000 ("FSMA 2000")—by shifting responsibility for financial regulation (which had previously lain with the Financial Services Authority) to various subsidiary entities of the Bank of England and to the Financial Conduct Authority ("FCA") . From April Fool's Day 2013, the Financial Conduct Authority ("FCA") assumed the powers of the old Financial Services Authority. However, responsibility for micro-prudential regulation of banking passed to the Bank of England's subsidiary entity, the Prudential Regulatory Authority ("PRA"); together with the policy remit of the new Financial Policy Committee ("FPC") of the Bank of England. Technically, as it is expressed by the FSA 2012, the Financial Services Authority is "renamed" as the FCA, albeit that some of its former responsibilities have shifted to the PRA. Therefore, the old Financial Services Authority continues to exist under another name.

8–26   This legislation constituted, in effect, the UK government's response to the financial crisis 2007–09,[33] a crisis which continued to bite in the real economy in the UK at the time that this Act received the Royal Assent on December 19, 2012. Given that the functions formerly performed by the Financial Services Authority are to be subsumed within the FCA and the Bank of England, it does appear at first blush that all that has happened at the legislative level is that the labels on the existing regulatory authorities have been changed. For the most part, the same human beings continue to hold office and the same regulatory principles continue in effect. If there is a significant change to come in relation to financial regulation then it will be in the form of a changed regulatory attitude: the regulators will have to take a different attitude to the implementation of their powers.[34] It is important to note that the reform process is not yet complete. After the FSA 2012 had begun its passage through Parliament, a number of banking scandals came to light which necessitated the creation of the Parliamentary Commission on Banking Standards, which together with the Vickers Commission report into banking, has led to the Financial Services (Banking Reform) Bill 2013 and will lead to further reform proposals (as considered at the end of this chapter). Now, we shall turn in detail to regulatory structure which was created by the FSA 2012.

---

[32]   The Financial Services Act 2012 received the Royal Assent on December 19, 2012. The provisions relating to the regulation of financial services considered in the text are scheduled, at the time of writing, to come into effect on April 1, 2013.

[33]   The financial crisis is considered in detail in Ch.57.

[34]   In Ch.45, the FSA's Supervisory Enhancement Programme ("SEP") is considered, in particular its attempt to overhaul the manner in which and the philosophy by which the Authority conducted itself as a regulator, as discussed in the Turner Review, p.86: see para.45–99.

B.   THE FINANCIAL SERVICES ACT 2012 MODEL OF FINANCIAL REGULATION

Introduction

The purpose of Part 2 of the FSA 2012 is to create and establish the FCA, as an independent body answerable to HM Treasury, and the PRA and the FPC as subsidiary entities of the Bank of England, to set out their powers and obligations when conducting different aspects of financial regulation, and to explain the several ways in which they may interact when their regulatory responsibilities intersect. The manner of this interaction is complex. Part 2 of the statute is, in effect, comprised of a lattice of powers for the various entities to make "recommendations" or to give "directions" to one another, as well as granting them powers to create regulatory rules and to enforce those rules. As outlined above, the statute does not require the entities to act in a particular way, but rather it grants powers to those entities so that they are able to act in any way which they consider appropriate (within the scope of those powers) as circumstances require. The purpose of the FSA 2012 (as with the Banking Act 2009) is to ensure that the regulators have the powers they need to act in whatever way they feel they ought to act in the event of a future crisis (or even just for the ordinary operation of the regulatory process). In Chapter 3, we considered how primary legislation in this area is concerned simply with empowering regulators so that they can act as they deem fit; as opposed to setting out in detail how they should act in any given circumstances. The lesson from the financial crisis was that the regulators (including the government) had no statutory powers to act and to compel other people to obey, with the result that initially they were relying on straightforward political influence when trying to deal with failing banks and the potential failure of the financial system. Therefore, the role of the law in this context is to grant a wide range of powers to the regulators and to government to act in future, but so that those agencies can use whichever powers are considered to be appropriate in the circumstances of any future crisis. What follows in this discussion is an explanation of the powers which are granted to each of those regulatory entities, the obligations which are imposed on them, and the manner in which each of them interacts one with the other and with the Treasury.[35]

8–27

The reason for the threefold division between regulatory responsibilities in FSA 2012

Regulatory structures are usually a product of their history. It is common for the political environment in any jurisdiction to lead to the particular form of regulation which that jurisdiction creates. So, after the experience of the financial

8–28

---

[35] The Treasury ("Her Majesty's Treasury" or "HM Treasury") is the government department which is responsible for financial, economic and fiscal matters in the UK, and it is headed by the Chancellor of the Exchequer.

crisis in 2007–09 in the UK, it is considered that there are three different zones in which regulation is required, and there is now a different regulatory body with responsibility for each of them.

8–29 First, there is a need to protect customers when they make investments or buy banking services. This is done by regulating the way in which financial institutions conduct business with their customers and, crucially, specifies the sorts of information which must be provided to those customers and what sorts of risk need to be explained to them. Under this system, customers are not necessarily preserved entirely from the risk of loss[36]: instead, the policy is to provide customers with all of the necessary information which is appropriate both for the type of product involved and for a person with their personal level of expertise in finance. Once the customer has that requisite information provided suitably to them, then it is up to the customer to decide whether or not they want to take the risk of making that investment or buying that banking service. If they have been treated suitably by the seller, then the risk of suffering loss is theirs alone, in regulatory terms.[37] This regulation of the conduct of business is the responsibility of the Financial Conduct Authority ("FCA"). (Conduct of business regulation is discussed in detail in Chapter 10.)

8–30 Second, there is a need to regulate individual financial institutions to try to ensure that they are themselves solvent, protected against potential future shocks, properly managed and so forth. This is known as "prudential" regulation. The term "prudence" was a favourite of former Labour Chancellor of the Exchequer Gordon Brown: its modern definition denotes being careful, erring on the side of caution, and assessing risks carefully so as to avoid unnecessary risk; however, its older definition also denoted "wisdom" in business matters and earning a profit.[38] Because this particular regulatory activity is concerned with individual financial institutions (as opposed to the entire marketplace) it is known as "*micro-prudential*" regulation. The sorts of things which regulated institutions are required to do include setting aside an amount of capital equal to an identified proportion of their liabilities at any given time. The idea is that there should be enough capital set aside to meet any likely problems which that institution might encounter in the future. Again, there is no guarantee that everything will be well; instead, the regulators identify the amount of risk which is likely to be realised and assess how that could be offset from within that institution's own resources. Responsibility for these micro-prudential issues lies with the Prudential Regulatory Authority ("PRA"), a subsidiary entity of the Bank of England.

8–31 Third, there is a need to consider risks which affect the entirety of the financial system: that includes the general economy in the UK and the world economy

---

[36] That is, except in relation to ordinary bank accounts up to a value of £85,000 under the Financial Services Compensation Scheme considered in the next chapter.

[37] That is, there may be liability under the substantive law to compensate the customer (as discussed in Pts V and VII of this book).

[38] The *Oxford Shorter English Dictionary* defines "prudent" as meaning: "1. Characterized by or proceeding from care in following the most politic and profitable course; having or showing sound judgement in practical affairs; circumspect, sensible. 2. Wise, discerning, sapient ..." There is therefore a combination of wisdom and profitability, as well as the more modern sense of circumspection and caution.

more generally, the condition of all financial markets (from retail banking through to complex financial instruments like derivatives) and the risks which they pose to the economy and to the UK financial system, and any other risks which might impact on the financial system. The effect of the financial crisis was that systemic risk—that is, the prospect of the failure of the entirety of the financial system[39]—had to be taken seriously. It was also made clear that all financial markets are potentially connected, whether they are in different countries or in seemingly unrelated market sectors. So, the US sub-prime housing market caused waves in the global credit default swap markets (an example of a regulated, basic market in one country coming to infect a more sophisticated, unregulated market traded worldwide) and a crash in the core inter-bank market for lending money (another largely unregulated global market),[40] with the result that governments and regulatory authorities in different countries had to work very hard together to identify a solution to the risks of calamity for the global financial system. Again, the watchword is for "prudential" regulation, although in the context of protecting the entire financial system this is referred to as "*macro*-prudential" regulation. The responsibility for these "macro-prudential" questions lies with the Financial Policy Committee ("FPC") which is also a subsidiary entity of the Bank of England.

The new regulatory bodies and their core functions

As outlined above, the FSA 2012 created three new regulatory bodies by making amendments to the FSMA 2000.[41] Responsibility for conduct of business and related regulation passes to the new Financial Conduct Authority ("FCA") with powers and responsibilities created by a new Part 1A of the FSMA 2000.[42] At the macro-prudential level there is the Financial Policy Committee, the establishment of which is set out in s.9B of the FSMA 2000;[43] and at the micro-prudential level, the new Prudential Regulatory Authority ("PRA") is created by a new in the new Part 2A of the FSMA 2000.[44] Because the activities of this various bodies overlap at the edges, there are also overlaps in some of their statutory powers and responsibilities. In the sections to follow we shall consider the specific objectives of each of these regulatory authorities in turn, but there are some common

8–32

---

[39] See para.1–54 et seq.

[40] The inter-bank money markets are the core of the global financial system: no bank has much liquid cash because all cash is necessarily invested or loaned out, and therefore banks constantly need to borrow money from other banks (or from government quantitative easing programmes since 2009) to maintain their activities. Once those money markets dry up, then the system begins to grind to a halt.

[41] Financial Services Act 2012, s.6.

[42] Financial Services and Markets Act 2000, s.1A.

[43] As inserted by the Financial Services Act 2012, s.4.

[44] It is a difficult question to know which body to take in which order in this discussion, because the amendments to the FSMA 2000 place the FCA first, followed by the PRA and then the FPC. However, the FSA 2012 deals with the FPC first (perhaps because that was the most important development in the mind of the legislators at that time), followed by the FCA and then the PRA last. The FCA assumes the bulk of the responsibilities of the old Financial Services Authority and therefore appears to be more significant than the PRA; and the Bank of England has treated the new PRA as a body which will have to define itself as time goes on. Therefore, we shall consider the new bodies in the order in which they are laid out in the FSA 2012.

regulatory principles which apply both to the FCA and the PRA which shall be considered first. These two bodies—the FCA and the PRA—are identified as being "the regulators" in FSMA 2000;[45] a term which does not include the FPC even though the FPC does have the power to issue recommendations to the FCA and the PRA as considered below, such that a non-regulator can therefore give directions to the regulators in matters which affect macro-prudential regulation. The regulatory principles which govern both the FCA and the PRA are set out in s.3B(1) of the FSMA 2000 in the following terms:

"(a)   the need to use the resources of each regulator in the most efficient and economic way;

(b)   the principle that a burden or restriction which is imposed on a person, or on the carrying on of an activity, should be proportionate to the benefits, considered in general terms, which are expected to result from the imposition of that burden or restriction;

(c)   the desirability of sustainable growth in the economy of the United Kingdom in the medium or long term;

(d)   the general principle that consumers should take responsibility for their decisions;

(e)   the responsibilities of the senior management of persons subject to requirements imposed by or under this Act, including those affecting consumers, in relation to compliance with those requirements;

(f)   the desirability where appropriate of each regulator exercising its functions in a way that recognises differences in the nature of, and objectives of, businesses carried on by different persons subject to requirements imposed by or under this Act;

(g)   the desirability in appropriate cases of each regulator publishing information relating to persons on whom requirements are imposed by or under this Act, or requiring such persons to publish information, as a means of contributing to the advancement by each regulator of its objectives;

(h)   the principle that the regulator should exercise the functions as transparently as possible."

Many of these principles are repeated in the separate obligations which are imposed on each regulatory authority individually: for example, the notion that consumers should take responsibility for their decisions. They are similar to the obligations which were imposed on the old Financial Services Authority previously. Significantly, the idea that the senior management of regulated financial institutions should bear "responsibilities" in relation to the obligations of that institution is interesting: the question arises whether or not it should be deemed to be sufficient to impose personal obligations under the substantive law on senior management in tort or in equity in relation to any breaches of duty under private law by the financial institution as a whole.[46] The requirement of regulatory transparency speaks for itself, and mirrors suggestions elsewhere that a regulator's power must be applied evenly, fairly and equally to all persons. Moreover, the regulators are obliged to follow principles of good governance, although these principles are not defined.[47] The reference to "sustainable growth" in the economy in paragraph (c) was added to the Bill during debate and sensibly imposes a requirement for the regulators to look to the long-term needs of the economy as opposed to the short-term profit which financial markets ordinarily seek (particularly on a year-to-year basis when traders' bonuses are calculated). It

---

[45] Financial Services and Markets Act 2000, s.3A.

[46] The idea that senior management should bear personal responsibilities in private law is considered in detail in Ch.45.

[47] Financial Services and Markets Act 2000, s.3C.

had long been a complaint that financial markets were interested only in short-term gain, careless of the longer term impact of their activities: this complaint was demonstrated most clearly with the short-sightedness even as to their own interests which the banks had exhibited in the run-up to the financial crisis. Therefore, this provision looks to the sustainability of any growth in the economy, as opposed to a short-term in financial markets of the sort seen before the financial crisis.

How conflicts between regulatory bodies are treated in the FSA 2012

As considered above, the intention behind the FCA 2012 was that the three key zones for financial regulation in the UK should be divided between FCA, PRA and FPC: that is, between conduct of business, micro-prudential and macro-prudential regulation respectively. That three-fold division was the result of the regulators' experience of the financial crisis in the UK. Clearly, however, there will be situations in which some issues cross the boundaries between these three entities and their particular responsibilities. For example, a micro-prudential problem with a specific bank facing the risk of insolvency might present the risk of the entire financial system in the UK facing collapse (as when Lehman Brothers failed in September 2008). This would create conflict between the PRA and the FPC as to whether the problem should be treated as a micro-prudential problem relating solely to that bank for the PRA to solve, or whether the problem should be treated as a macro-prudential one affecting the entire system for the FPC to solve. Equally, if that bank had been mis-selling derivatives to its customers (thus breaching conduct of business regulations), such that the risk of those contracts being found to be void threatened to affect the entire marketplace, then there would be a jurisdictional dispute between FCA and FPC as to how this issue should be handled. The FCA might want to sanction the bank. The customers of the bank might want to cancel their contracts further to ordinary litigation, which would in turn raise the issue whether it is better for those contracts to be enforced so that the market can be controlled, or whether those contracts should be set aside so that the bank will have to pay huge damages to its customers and thus risk insolvency.[48] Consequently, the FSA 2012 creates a number of (perhaps overly-complex and over-hopeful) mechanisms for overseeing how the three regulatory bodies are to inter-act with one another. The mechanisms for the resolution of conflicts of that sort are considered below, after an analysis of the individual objectives of each of the new regulatory bodies, beginning at the macro-prudential level with the FPC.

8–33

---

[48] Broadly, this was the issue in the Lehman Brothers litigation discussed in Ch.21 at para.21–19 et seq.

C. The Financial Policy Committee

The core principles of the FPC

8–34   The Bank of England has a Financial Stability Objective, as considered above,[49] enshrined in s.2A of the Banking of England Act 1998. To deal with the macro-prudential dimension of pursuing that financial stability objective by means of "protecting and enhancing" financial stability in the UK, the FSA 2012 created a new macro-prudential regulatory authority in the form of the Financial Policy Committee ("FPC"). The business of the FPC is concerned with "the analysis of threats to financial stability".[50] In practice, the FPC was established within the Bank of England in 2011 as an ad hoc committee so that it could begin its work even before the legislation was formally introduced to Parliament. The FPC is "a sub-committee of the court of directors of the Bank [of England]".[51] It is chaired by the Governor of the Bank of England. The FPC "is to exercise its functions" so as to contribute to the Bank's Financial Stability Objective by dealing with "systemic risks".[52] The term "systemic risk" is defined in the statute to mean "a risk to the stability of the UK financial system as a whole or of a significant part of that system".[53] This focus on the entire financial system is a result of the financial crisis: before then, the existence such a risk was simply not taken sufficiently seriously to merit its inclusion in the statutory framework for financial regulation. It is concerned with macro-prudential oversight of the financial system as a whole: in consequence its concern is with systemic and similar scale risks. A part of its work is the preparation, together with the Treasury, of the financial stability strategy which the Bank of England will use to pursue its statutory Financial Stability Objective. The powers of the FPC in this regard are to make "recommendations" to the court of directors of the Bank of England.[54]

The functions of the FPC

8–35   The functions of the FPC are to monitor "the stability of the UK financial system with a view to identifying and assessing systemic risks", giving directions and making recommendations in that regard (as considered below), and preparing financial stability reports as required by statute.[55] The statute also explains how the FPC is required to conduct its meetings.

---

[49] See para.8–18.
[50] Financial Services and Markets Act 2000, s.9B(?)
[51] Financial Services and Markets Act 2000, s.9B(1).
[52] Financial Services and Markets Act 2000, s.9C(1)(a) and (2).
[53] Financial Services and Markets Act 2000, s.9C(5).
[54] Financial Services and Markets Act 2000, s.9A(3).
[55] Financial Services and Markets Act 2000, s.9G.

The inter-action of the FPC with other regulatory bodies

The difficulty with having a number of regulatory bodies is that there will be overlaps between the competences of those different bodies. The FPC is empowered to give a direction to the Financial Conduct Authority (considered next) and the Prudential Regulatory Authority (considered below) in relation to a "macro-prudential measure"[56] with which they are required to comply or to explain why they are not complying as to the exercise of their "functions".[57] In essence, then, the macro-prudential regulator can give directions to the micro-prudential and the conduct of business regulators. That makes sense if it is assumed that the systemic risks are more significant than the risks specific to particular firms; but it also means that the FCA and the PRA do not have complete, operational independence in the operation of their rulebooks. Furthermore, the FPC "may make recommendations within the Bank [of England]",[58] for example as to the provision of financial assistance to a financial institution in financial difficulties or as to the exercise by the Bank of England of its powers in relation to payment and settlement systems.[59] The FPC can also make recommendations to the Treasury.[60] The Treasury is empowered to make recommendations to the FPC as to matters which it might regard as relevant to its deliberations, and so forth.[61]

8–36

The conduct of meetings and reaching decisions

The FPC is to have four meetings per year with a quorum of only seven people being required. Significantly, the chair of a meeting of the FPC[62] must seek to secure that decisions of the committee are reached by consensus wherever possible,[63] with a vote being taken if a consensus cannot be reached.[64] This presumption that there should be consensus only adds to the impression that by containing all of the policy and regulatory activities within subsidiaries of the Bank of England any hope of dissent or open debate will be swallowed up within that institution. That decisions are to be reached by consensus will mean either that dissentient voices are silenced, or that there are no dissentient voices in the first place, or that the decisions of the FPC are mealy-mouthed compromises between competing positions. One of the key lessons that was learned from the global financial crisis (although it was plain for all to see before then) is that there is an important role in policy-making and in prudential regulation for maverick voices and doomsayers among the pro-cyclical boom enthusiasts who always

8–37

---

[56] Treasury regulation will identify what a macro-prudential measure is.
[57] Financial Services and Markets Act 2000, s.9H.
[58] The idea of this recommendation being "within" the Bank of England does perhaps give the lie to the idea that the various regulatory bodies will be operationally independent.
[59] Financial Services and Markets Act 2000, s.9O.
[60] Financial Services and Markets Act 2000, s.9P.
[61] Financial Services and Markets Act 2000, s.9E.
[62] Ordinarily this will be the Governor of the Bank of England although there is provision for one of the Deputy Governors to sit in for the Governor where appropriate.
[63] Financial Services Act 2012, Sch.1, para.11(4).
[64] Financial Services Act 2012, Sch.1, para.11(5).

emerge at such times. There is as much need for Eeyore as there is for Piglet in macro-prudential regulation.[65] The new Bank of England regulatory architecture does not ensure a hearing for such alternative voices as it is currently organised. For a financial system which has operated for so long on the basis of a disastrous groupthink, this is a poor structure for the future.

Publication of information about FPC deliberations

8–38   There are statutory requirements on the Bank of England to make certain types of information about the deliberations of the FPC public but there remains a significant democratic deficit in that a large amount of information can be withheld at the Bank's discretion with the result that it will not always be possible for the FPC to be held publicly accountable. There are two particular contexts in which information must be published. First, the Bank of England must prepare a record of each meeting of the FPC, however it is only obliged to minute the decisions and a summary of the discussion at those meetings.[66] Consequently, again, maverick voices need not loom large in the public records of these meetings. Moreover, it is possible to exclude material from those public records when the FPC considers that it would be contrary to the public interest to publish information.[67] Of course, it will be in times of brewing crisis that the views of the FPC are more likely to affect financial markets and so be contrary to the public interest. What is unsatisfactory about this structure is that it is left to the Bank of England to decide ultimately what is published about its policy decisions in relation to systemic questions. Secondly, the FPC is also required to prepare and publish reports as to the financial stability of markets in the UK.[68] Those reports must include a statement as to "the stability of the UK financial system", its "strengths and weaknesses", the risks to its stability, and the future outlook.[69] The form of the report is such as the Bank of England "thinks fit".[70] As before, the contents of that report may exclude anything which the FPC considers to be contrary to the public interest.[71] Copies of the reports must be "laid before Parliament" by the Treasury.[72] The Governor and the Chancellor of the Exchequer are required to meet to discuss these FPC reports.[73] This, in essence, becomes a part of the democratic accountability of the FPC: tea with the Chancellor.

---

[65] In the *Winnie the Pooh* books, Eeyore was ever the miserable pessimist while Piglet was generally bright and optimistic.
[66] Financial Services and Markets Act 2000, s.9U.
[67] Financial Services and Markets Act 2000, s.9U(8).
[68] Financial Services and Markets Act 2000, s.9W.
[69] Financial Services and Markets Act 2000, s.9W(3).
[70] Financial Services and Markets Act 2000, s.9W(11).
[71] Financial Services and Markets Act 2000, s.9W(8).
[72] Financial Services and Markets Act 2000, s.9W(10).
[73] Financial Services and Markets Act 2000, s.9X.

D. The Financial Conduct Authority

The objectives of the FCA

The Financial Conduct Authority ("FCA") is the reincarnation of the old Financial Services Authority in that it is simply the Financial Services Authority "renamed", as provided for in s.1A(1) of the FSMA 2000.[74] In truth, the FCA is the new body with responsibility for conduct of business regulation and for matters relating to the authorisation of financial institutions to conduct financial services business of the types which are discussed in Chapter 9.[75] The FCA was described in the White Paper which prepared the ground for the FSA 2012 as being the "consumer champion"[76] in that its principal regulatory role is in relation to the conduct of business between financial institutions and their customers, ensuring that those institutions treat their customers suitably,[77] that they market their wares suitably,[78] that there is no market abuse,[79] and so forth. The FCA also bears duties both to regulate financial institutions and to promote competition: that is, a prudential role and a role which is aimed at economic growth simultaneously. Section 1B of the FSMA 2000 sets out the FCA's general duties in the following terms:

8–39

> "(1)   in discharging its general functions, the FCA must, so far as is reasonably possible, act in a way which—
> (a)   is compatible with its strategic objective, and
> (b)   advances one or more of its operational objectives."

The FCA's strategic objective when the Bill was first published was "protecting and enhancing confidence in the UK financial system"; although the strategic objective in the Act is rendered as: "ensuring that the relevant markets (see s.1F) function well".[80] This is a particularly vague objective, with the value judgment that is bound up in the idea that the markets must function "well" being particularly problematic: well for whom, for banks, for the economy or for consumers? The concept of "well" is to be judged by reference to which criteria? Therefore, the central strategic objective of the FCA (that the "markets function well") is qualified by operational objectives. The FCA's operational objectives are threefold: its "consumer protection objective", its "integrity objective", and its "competition objective",[81] each of which is considered in turn below.[82] Importantly, there is some tension between these three operational objectives

---

[74] Financial Services and Markets Act 2000, s.6.

[75] It is important to note that there are also financial institutions regulated by the PRA as their economic condition, as considered below, so the transposition from the old Financial Services Authority to the FCA is not exact; furthermore the Bank of England generally has acquired some other functions from the old Financial Services Authority.

[76] HM Treasury, White Paper "A new approach to financial regulation: the blueprint for reform" (Cmnd 8083), p.28.

[77] As considered in detail in Ch.10.

[78] As considered in detail in Ch.11.

[79] As considered in detail in Ch.12.

[80] Financial Services and Markets Act 2000, s.1B(2).

[81] In the Bill, the third objective had been the "efficiency and choice" objective.

[82] Financial Services and Markets Act 2000, s.1B(3).

which means that the overall success of the FCA in achieving its central strategic objective may still be difficult to isolate.

The consumer protection objective of the FCA

8–40   The consumer protection objective is described as being an objective aimed at "securing an appropriate degree of protection for consumers".[83] when deciding the level of protection which is appropriate for consumers in a given context, the FCA is required to have regard to the following:

(a)   the differing degrees of risk involved in different kinds of investment or other transaction;

(b)   the differing degrees of experience and expertise that different consumers may have;

(c)   the needs that consumers may have for the timely provision of information and advice that is accurate and fit for purpose;

(d)   the general principle that consumers should take responsibility for their decisions;

(e)   the general principle that those providing regulated financial services should be expected to provide consumers with a level of care that is appropriate having regard to the degree of risk involved in relation to the investment or other transaction and the capabilities of the consumers in question;

(f)   the differing expectations that consumers may have in relation to different kinds of investment and other transaction;

(g)   any information which the consumer financial education body has provided to the FCA in the exercise of the consumer financial education function;

(h)   any information which the scheme operator of the ombudsman scheme has provided to the FCA pursuant to s.232A.

The heart of the FCA's activities is to ensure that regulated firms observe the regulations as to the treatment of their customers. However, this does not mean that customers are always to be protected against the possibility of loss. Rather, the FCA is obliged simply to observe the contract law philosophy that all parties to a contract have the freedom to create whatever bargain they wish, provided that one party is not taking unconscionable advantage of the other. Ultimately then, this comes down to a case of caveat emptor in that all consumers are ultimately responsible for their own decisions, purchases and so forth under para.(d). Significantly, paras (e) and (f) were added during the passage of the Bill: they reflect the terms of the Conduct of Business Sourcebook ("COBS"), which is the heart of conduct of business regulation in the UK, and which implements the provisions of the important Markets in Financial Instruments Directive ("MiFID") which was considered in the previous chapter. Importantly, in the wake of the several mis-selling scandals in the UK, there is a clear statutory onus placed on the seller of financial instruments to deal with customers in a way that exhibits a suitable level of care concomitant with the risk which is being assumed

---

[83] Financial Services and Markets Act 2000, s.1C(1).

as part of that transaction. (What this provision omits is a recognition of the fact that the seller of those financial services must also classify the expertise of the customer such that only suitable products are sold to the customer, as required by COBS.[84]) This differentiation between different levels of risk and experience among the buyers of financial services could be understood as operating in parallel to the conduct of business standards. Given that COBS is orientated around the measurement of risk and expertise on the part of consumers, that it would make these various regulatory standards and objectives more coherent if they were read together in this way.[85]

The integrity objective

The integrity objective is described in s.1D(1) of the FSMA 2000 as being an objective of "protecting and enhancing the integrity of the UK financial system".[86] While the term "integrity" is used in the PRIN rulebook as being the fundamental objective of regulated entities, it has a particular definition in this context in the following terms:[87]

    8–41

> "The "integrity of the UK financial system includes—
> (b)   its not being used for a purpose connected with financial crime,
> (c)   its not being affected by behaviour that amounts to market abuse,
> (e)   the orderly operation of the financial markets, and
> (f)   the transparency of the price formation process in those markets.""

Consequently, there are two general senses underpinning this idea of integrity. First, integrity in this context relates to the reputation of the UK financial system as much as anything else, in the sense that it must be free from financial crime, market abuse and so forth. Second, integrity relates to the ability of the financial system to withstand market shocks and to operate in an orderly fashion. Interestingly, there are two meanings of the word "integrity" in its ordinary, colloquial usage. Integrity can refer to a moral soundness of principle, which is the sense in which that term is being used in relation to the activities of individual financial institutions in the PRIN rulebook, as considered in the next chapter. The other meaning of the word "integrity" relates to the physical soundness of something like the hull of a ship. It is this second sense of the word "integrity" which is meant here: it relates to the ability of the UK financial system to withstand outside shocks and so continue to function soundly, just as the hull of a ship will continue to be watertight so long as it has integrity. Interestingly also, the references here are to the integrity of the UK financial system and not to the integrity of the global financial system nor the financial system across the EU. Therefore, the FCA would be acting in accordance with its statutory objective if it allowed harm to come to the financial systems of other nations, provided that it

---

[84] MiFID, art.19(7).

[85] See A.S. Hudson, "The synthesis of public and private in finance law", in K. Barker (ed), *The Public-Private Divide* (Cambridge University Press, 2013).

[86] Among the powers of the FCA in this context (as explained by the Explanatory Notes to the Bill, para.76) are bans on short-selling of securities or deals which involve money laundering or creating disclosure rules under the Listing Rules in Pt 6 of the FSMA 2000.

[87] Financial Services and Markets Act 2000, s.1D(2).

was ensuring the soundness and so forth of the UK financial system. With the number of universal banks (that is, integrated retail banks, investment banks, and so forth in one corporate group) centred in the UK, this may require a particular treatment of those entities which prioritises the needs of UK consumers and markets which are organised in the UK.

The competition objective

8–42   The competition objective is defined as being "promoting effective competition in the interests of consumers and the markets" for both regulated financial services and services provided by a recognised investment exchange.[88] This objective was added to the Bill during its passage through Parliament. The need for greater competition was identified through the wash-out from the financial crisis given that one of the principal problems (identified in Chapter 3) with the financial markets is a concentration of market share in a very few financial institutions, particularly in the cross-border markets.[89] Therefore, there is an irony in establishing the promotion of competition as a statutory goal for the regulator when the number of large high street banks has shrunk markedly with the mergers that took place in 2009.[90] The statute does, however, refer to consumers who have trouble accessing financial services due to being resident in areas characterised by "social or economic deprivation".[91] This suggests that the competition which might be important would be the use of credit unions, friendly societies, and so forth, which typically provide financial services to those who cannot access mainstream banking services, as outlined in Chapter 32.

The general functions of the FCA

8–43   The FCA has the power to create regulations further to s.137A of the FSMA 2000: this is particularly significant because it empowers the FCA to create the *FCA Handbook* which contains all of its regulations and guidance notes, and which will instrumental in implementing many of the EU's regulatory requirements into UK finance law. The FCA's general functions are as set out in s.1B(8) of the FSMA 2000 in the following terms:

> "(a)   its function of making rules . . .
> (b)   its function of preparing and issuing codes . . .
> (c)   its functions in relation to giving a general guidance . . .
> (d)   its function of determining the general policy and principles by reference to which it performs particular functions."

---

[88] Financial Services and Markets Act 2000, s.1E(1).

[89] The counter-argument is that countries with limited competition between banks fared better in the financial crisis: such as Australia and Canada. The argument is that banking and financial services provision is such a significant activity in a modern economy that it is better to have a narrow range of producers which are tightly regulated and which offer a narrow range of conservative financial products to their customers which consequently have a low risk of causing loss or harm.

[90] Lloyds TSB and HBOS merged; Bradford and Bingley and the Alliance and Leicester ceased to exist separately as they were absorbed into Santander; RBS had already merged with NatWest; and so forth.

[91] Financial Services and Markets Act 2000, s.1E(2).

The FCA is obliged to prepare and issue guidance about the way in which it intends to pursue its objectives.[92] The FCA is in turn subject to some regulatory oversight beyond the Bank of England. To this end, the Treasury may appoint an independent person to evaluate the "economy, efficiency and effectiveness with which the FCA has used its resources in discharging its functions".[93] However, noticeably, the FCA is only regulated in relation to its efficient use of its resources (such as not wasting money), and not the overall effectiveness of its activities in maintaining markets which "function well".

Shortcomings in the FCA's duties and role

It is a clear criticism of the FCA's duties that they are all too generic. What would **8–44** be more useful would be for those duties to be more sector specific: that is, for there to be clearer, different regulations in relation to different market sectors. Having generic obligations which are supposed to cover everything from domestic mortgages to investment by rich individuals in derivatives products is unhelpful. Conduct of business regulation in particular needs to give clearer guidance to financial institutions on how to deal differently with different types of customer in relation to different types of product. This has been demonstrated by the proposals for MiFID II considered in the previous chapter.[94] Financial institutions have simply not differentiated with sufficient subtlety between different types of products being sold to a larger range of different customers than hitherto. The example highlighted in the MiFID II proposals cited the inappropriate treatment of public authorities as though they were expert counterparties; just as the English case law has demonstrated the insensitive treatment by investment firms of high net worth individuals as though they were professional investors and not simply retail investors.[95] In these situations, it is suggested that the justification for selling a derivative to a private individual needs to be much greater than the justification for selling an ordinary deposit account: one is much riskier than the other. Furthermore, there may be risks of a bank concealing its fees or the uncompetitive nature of its interest rate on a deposit bank account which should be disclosed to a customer, even though the deposit account is not otherwise a risky investment (unless the bank goes into insolvency). The risks in relation to the derivative product are not only greater but, importantly, they are very different from the risks associated with the deposit account. The risks associated with the derivative relate to movements in market rates, the minutiae of the formula used to calculate payments under that derivative, the valuation of collateral, and so forth. Therefore, simply to have one set of standards in relation to the activities of the regulator does not really help to identify how the FCA should be treating different markets and different products differently. Similarly, those standards give no indication as to what would constitute failure.

---

[92] Financial Services and Markets Act 2000, s.1G.
[93] Financial Services and Markets Act 2000, s.1S.
[94] See para.7–80.
[95] See the discussion in Chs 25 and 26 in relation, for example, to *JP Morgan v Springwell* [2008] EWHC 1186 (Comm).

The duty to consult

8–45   The FCA also bears a general duty to consult with market practitioners:[96] something which led to great criticism of the old Financial Services Authority because it was considered by many commentators to be too close to market practitioners and thus insufficiently objective in the use of its powers. There is, however, also a duty to consult with consumers for the first time. More specifically, the duty to consult is a duty to "make and maintain effective arrangements for consulting practitioners and consumers on the extent to which its general policies and practices are consistent with its general duties". To this end, four expert panels are to be created: first, a panel of practitioners (the Practitioner Panel) representing regulated entities and recognised investment exchanges;[97] second, a Smaller Business Practitioner Panel to represent the position of "eligible practitioners";[98] third, a Markets Practitioner Panel to represent regulated entities, issues of financial instruments, sponsors of securities issues, recognised investment exchanges, information providers and others as the FCA considers appropriate;[99] and, fourth, a Consumer Panel comprising such consumers as it considers appropriate.[100] It is an important reverse in the earlier policy that there is to be a Consumer Panel which is to be created to represent the position of consumers.[101] After the many misselling scandals of recent years, the position of consumers needs to be considered much more than hitherto: up to now, the only voice which was considered important was the collective voice of the banks themselves. Consumers in this sense are people who are not authorised persons (that is, not market professionals) under the financial services legislation.

The competent authority for official listing

8–46   Importantly, for the purposes of securities regulation, the FCA is to replace the old Financial Services Authority as the "competent authority" for the official listing of securities under Part 6 of the FSMA 2000.

E. The Prudential Regulatory Authority

Introduction

8–47   The purpose of the Prudential Regulation Authority ("PRA") is to oversee micro-prudential regulation. That is, regulation of the condition and financial soundness of financial institutions. Therefore, those financial institutions require authorisation from the PRA to be able to conduct financial services business in the UK. In essence, then, the role of the PRA is to oversee the solvency and financial condition of those institutions, which involves not simply looking at the

---

[96] Financial Services and Markets Act 2000, s.1M.
[97] Financial Services and Markets Act 2000, s.1N.
[98] Financial Services and Markets Act 2000, s.1O.
[99] Financial Services and Markets Act 2000, s.1P.
[100] Financial Services and Markets Act 2000, s.1Q.
[101] Financial Services and Markets Act 2000, s.1L.

historic accounts of those institutions but rather measuring the likely future performance of those institutions in the light of future market movements and conditions. The process which is used by regulators to assess the likely ability of individual financial institutions to cope with adverse, future market conditions is known as "stress-testing". Prior to the financial crisis 2007–09, stress-testing of financial institutions did not seem to anticipate sufficiently calamitous market conditions to prepare the institutions themselves nor regulators nor government for the effects of that crisis. Therefore, stress-testing has tended to become a more rigorous process in which the regulators imagine and play-out hypothetical market scenarios and the ability of individual institutions to cope with them. This obligation to look to so-called prudential regulation was borne by the old Financial Services Authority previously through its prudential rulebooks. However, in practice those regulations were insufficient and the practices of the Financial Services Authority were also insufficient for that purpose. The prudential regulation of each market sector (banking, insurance, and so forth) in the new regulatory environment after the creation of the PRA is considered in the appropriate chapters on those specific markets. In this section, we shall consider the statutory objectives which have been imposed on the PRA itself.

The general objective of the PRA

The PRA was created by the FSA 2012 and is established by s.2A of the FSMA **8–48** 2000. The PRA is concerned with the macro-prudential regulation of financial markets in the UK. The PRA has the power to create regulations further to s.137E of the FSMA 2000. The general objective of PRA is set out in s.2B(2) of the FSMA 2000 in the following terms:

> "The PRA's general objective is: promoting the safety and soundness of the PRA-authorised persons."

The reference to "safety" in this objective is interesting because it could refer either to the safety of the remainder of the economy and the financial system from any failure of a PRA-authorised person, or it could refer to the safety of that PRA-authorised person from events in the financial markets. The "soundness" of PRA-authorised persons would appear to refer prima facie to their financial condition, and in particular their solvency. However, the concept of "soundness" could refer in theory to the soundness of the management and internal systems of a regulated firm to manage their business. After all, the solvency of a business may depend as much on the ability of senior management to operate a risk management system which is nimble enough to identify future hazards and to operate a legal culture which ensures that the institution's security mechanisms in various markets will be effective in the event that security needs to be realised. Given that any regulated person operates on a tightrope between the maximum use of all of its assets to earn a return, and the loss of those assets in adverse market conditions, then the skill of its employees and management to control its risks will be important in maintaining the soundness of that institution in practice. In consequence, the PRA will have to develop a culture of overseeing the micro-prudential condition of individual institutions appropriately so as to protect the economy from those institutions, and to protect those institutions from themselves and from each other. The PRA itself is required to act in a way which advances its general objective "so far as is reasonably possible".[102] The "primary"[103] ways in which this general objective is to be met by means of "seeking to ensure that the business of PRA-authorised persons is carried on in a way which avoids any adverse effect on the stability of the UK financial system"[104] and by "seeking to minimise the adverse effects that the failure of a PRA-authorised person could be expected to have on the stability of UK financial system".[105] The only definition of what would constitute an "adverse effect" in the legislation is a reference to "the disruption of the continuity of financial services".[106] The "financial system" in this context includes "financial markets and exchanges", "regulated activities", and any connected activities.[107] Within the remit of the PRA will fall insurance firms as well as financial services firms, and so there is an "insurance objective" relating to the regulation of those particular institutions.

8–49   The PRA has a general duty to consult with authorised persons and is empowered to establish any panels which it considers fit for this purpose.[108] The PRA is also duty bound to consider any representations made to it in relation to such panels.[109] Interestingly, Bank of England publications before the PRA came legally into existence clearly anticipated that the PRA would have to find its own way in the world after its creation. The FSMA 2000 provided that the Treasury may appoint an independent person to conduct a review of the "economy, efficiency and effectiveness with which the PRA has used its resources in discharging its functions";[110] and that independent person shall have a right to access documents and information that any reasonable time for the purposes of conducting such a review.

The prudential powers of the PRA and of the FCA

8–50   Section 22A of the FSMA 2000 grants a power to the Treasury to create regulations to specify the activities which are to be undertaken by the PRA. Further objectives can be added to the remit of the PRA further to that provision.[111] Section 55A and 55F of the FSMA 2000, and the sections following that, identify principles which govern applications for permission to conduct regulated financial services activities. This includes threshold conditions as to the nature and size of the business involved.[112] Section 55E identifies powers for the FCA to grant permission to act. The interaction of these two regulatory bodies is

---

[102] Financial Services and Markets Act 2000, s.2B(1).
[103] Financial Services and Markets Act 2000, s.2B(3).
[104] Financial Services and Markets Act 2000, s.2B(3)(a).
[105] Financial Services and Markets Act 2000, s.2B(3)(b).
[106] Financial Services and Markets Act 2000, s.2B(4).
[107] Financial Services and Markets Act 2000, s.2B(6).
[108] Financial Services and Markets Act 2000, s.2L.
[109] Financial Services and Markets Act 2000, s.2M.
[110] Financial Services and Markets Act 2000, s.2N.
[111] Financial Services and Markets Act 2000, s.2D.
[112] The threshold conditions are in Sch.6 of the FSMA 2000, further to s.55B.

considered in the next section. Both regulatory bodies also have powers to impose requirements company in any authorisations. The detail of these issues will be expanded on by regulation over time.

The interaction of the PRA and the FCA

Simply from the discussion in the foregoing section, there is clearly a potential for overlap between the functions of the FCA and the functions of the PRA. Section 22A of the FSMA 2000 grants a power to the Treasury to create regulations to specify the activities which are to be undertaken by the PRA. After all, the PRA is the new regulatory entity here, whereas the FCA is simply the "renamed" Financial Services Authority. Section 3D of the FSMA 2000 imposes a duty on both bodies to ensure a coordinated exercise of their respective functions. They are required to consult one another where the exercise of any other appropriate functions would have a "material adverse effect on the advancement by the other regulator of any of its objectives".[113] The regulators are also required to obtain information and advice from one another.[114]

8–51

One particular problem which arises is as to which regulatory body should take the lead when an issue arises which straddles their regulatory competences. In a somewhat vague provision, the Act provides that both regulators must comply with their respective duties.[115] This lack of specificity, particularly in an overly-complex regulatory scheme like that in the FSMA 2000, is fraught with the possibility of mishap.[116] Instead, it is with a sinking heart that one realises that in s.3E of the FSMA 2000 that this potential boundary dispute is to be decided by the use of a "memorandum of understanding": that was exactly the mechanism which was used in relation to the tri-partite authorities which failed so visibly to prevent a market collapse after the failure of Northern Rock. A memorandum of understanding is a formal agreement between regulatory bodies as to the manner in which they anticipate using their regulatory powers in the event of any significant event which crosses their regulatory competences. When Northern Rock failed in August 2007, it was clear that the tri-partite authorities could not co-ordinate their activities. Alternatively, under the statute, the Treasury is *also* empowered to specify which matters will fall within the remit of the FCA and which matters fall within the remit of the PRA. Again, this seems to be using yet another mechanism to address exactly the same problem as before.[117]

8–52

However, the complexity does not end there. The PRA is empowered to require the FCA to refrain from identified forms of action further to s.3I of the FSMA

8–53

---

[113] Financial Services and Markets Act 2000, s.3D(1)(a).

[114] Financial Services and Markets Act 2000, s.3D(1)(b).

[115] Financial Services and Markets Act 2000, s.3D(1)(c).

[116] If there are differences between the different regulatory bodies, it is not clear how those differences will emerge into the public arena where they could usefully be ventilated; instead they will be resolved within the committee structure of the Bank of England and within the Treasury. While this scheme really rests in part on the idea that debate in the Court of the Bank of England will in itself constitute a ventilation of such issues, it is unlikely that the detail of any such debates will penetrate the public consciousness.

[117] Financial Services and Markets Act 2000, s.3G.

2000. This can only be done if the FCA is proposing to exercise its powers in relation to a person which is regulated by the PRA; and also if the PRA believes that such an act by the FCA would either threaten the stability of the UK financial system or would result in the failure of that regulated person; and provided that the PRA considers that the giving of such a direction is necessary to avoid "the possible consequence" of the failure of that regulated person.[118] So, through this mechanism, the powers of the PRA trump the powers of the FCA. What is unclear is what would happen if either the Treasury regulations or the memorandum of understanding suggest that the FCA would have the power to act in a particular circumstance. It is suggested that the better answer would be that the failure of a regulated person or a threat to the stability of UK financial system should be avoided, and therefore that the PRA should always have priority.

8–54   Yet a further layer of co-operation is required, however. There is the question of the interaction of these two regulatory bodies with the overall financial stability objective of the Bank of England under the FSMA 2000. Each entity has its own statutory powers and objectives. It is provided by s.3Q of the FSMA 2000 that each of these two regulatory bodies "must take such steps as it considers appropriate to co-operate with the Bank of England in the pursuit by the Bank of its Financial Stability Objective". Again, in practice, questions relating to the ambit of the PRA will be settled by internal discussions within the Bank of England between the various departments or they will be settled in the Court of the Bank of England, beyond outside view.

The rule-making powers of the PRA and FCA

8–55   The new Part 9A of the FSMA 2000 sets out the rule-making power of the PRA and FCA in relation to the remuneration of employees, bank recovery plans in relation to the Special Resolution Regime in the Banking Act 2009 relating to failed banks. Section 22 of the FSA 2012 sets out the powers of those bodies to create short-selling rules (so as to prevent investors speculating against the price of securities inappropriately).

F.   Failure of a regulated entity: collaboration between the Treasury and the Bank of England, FCA or PRA

8–56   Beyond the discussion immediately above, provision is made in the FSA 2012 to provide for those situations in which there must be collaboration between the various regulatory bodies: that is, the Treasury, the Bank of England, the FCA and the PRA.[119] There are four "cases" in which there is an obligation on these

---

[118] Financial Services and Markets Act 2000, s.3I(2),(3) and (4).

[119] Again, the very existence of these provisions highlights the irony behind the government's policy of reducing the number of bodies so as to simplify decision-making in times of crisis, although at least attempts are being made to anticipate overlaps in function on this occasion.

regulatory bodies to collaborate. The general case is that in which the FCA and the PRA are obliged to co-operate with the Bank of England in the pursuit of its financial stability objective.[120]

The first case arises in situations in which "the Treasury or the Secretary of State might reasonably be expected to regard it as appropriate to provide financial assistance in respect of a financial institution".[121] This is a difficult provision not least because it will always be considered to be an exceptional, or even an extraordinary, event for such financial assistance to be provided; therefore, to identify in advance whether or not it would be "reasonable" is not a straightforward matter.

8–57

The second case arises when the regulatory authorities might consider it appropriate to exercise any of the powers under Pts 1 to 3 of the Banking Act 2009, as discussed above.[122] This relates to bank failure or insolvency in the powers of the regulatory authorities to intervene in such situations, as would be the case in relation to their bank failure similar to that which engulfed Northern Rock in the summer of 2007. The provisions of the Banking Act are considered in detail in Chapter 28.

8–58

The third case arises when "the scheme manager of the financial services compensation scheme might reasonably be expected to request" either financial assistance from the Treasury or a loan from the National Loans Fund.[123]

8–59

The Bank of England and the PRA are required to prepare and maintain a memorandum "describing how they intend to coordinate the discharge of their respective relevant functions" in the event of any of these cases are rising. That memorandum is required to identify the following: what will constitute a material risk in these circumstances; what the respective roles of the regulatory authorities would be both as to the assessment of threats and the taking of steps in response to threats to the stability of the UK financial system; the manner in which the regulatory authorities will share information between themselves; and a requirement that the regulatory authorities will co-operate with one another. It is suggested that it will be difficult for any memorandum to identify in advance the precise nature, timing and emergence of such a crisis. Consequently, while the preparation of that memorandum would undoubtedly constitute a useful fire drill for the regulatory authorities involved, it would not necessarily have them prepared to meet the particular exigencies of any given set of circumstances which might cause a regulated entity to fail. A copy of this memorandum is required to be laid before Parliament.

8–60

---

[120] Financial Services and Markets Act 2000, s.3Q.
[121] Financial Services and Markets Act 2000, s.58(3), 60(5)(a).
[122] Financial Services and Markets Act 2000, s.60(5)(b).
[123] Financial Services and Markets Act 2000, s.60(5)(c).

5.   BANKING REGULATION

8–61   Banking regulation is considered in detail in Chapters 28 and 31. The nature of banking regulation in the EU is in flux at the time of writing. The European Central Bank and the European Banking Authority (as discussed in Chapter 7) are continuing to generate legislation to deal with traditional deposit-taking banks (referred to as "credit institutions" in EU parlance). This is complicated by the current shift towards creating one set of rules for Member States within the "eurozone" (which comprises those states which are members of the euro currency zone, which excludes the UK), and another set of rules for the EU as a whole which encompasses all Member States whether they are part of the eurozone or not (which therefore includes the UK). At the time of writing, that legislation is still progressing tortuously through the legislative process. Debate rages about the extent to which there should be a single regulator for credit institutions across the EU, as opposed to having powers resting with regulators within Member States, and the extent to which those regulations should control the remuneration of bank employees and so forth in the wake of the financial crisis. As outlined in Chapter 7, the regulatory environment is therefore in flux at present.

8–62   However, in the UK the regulatory structure is as set out above. The Bank of England subsidiaries are responsible for the regulation and authorisation of deposit-taking banks in the UK. The FCA is responsible for the authorisation of institutions to conduct regulated business and it is also responsible for conduct of business regulation which governs the way in which those institutions treat their customers (in particular through the Conduct of Business Sourcebook[124] and the Banking Conduct of Business Sourcebook[125]). The PRA is responsible for the authorisation and regulation of the micro-prudential risks associated with each individual institution, while the FPC oversees the condition of the entire banking system. These regulations are considered in detail in Part VIII of this book "Banking": Chapter 28 considers the micro-prudential context of banking regulation in general terms, and in particular the terms of the Banking Act 2009 in relation to failing banks and so forth; whereas Chapter 31 concentrates on conduct of business regulation in banking, in particular the treatment of bank customers in the light of the Banking Conduct of Business Sourcebook which was introduced with a view to protecting those customers better than the voluntary codes of practice had done beforehand.

8–63   The principal reform of the UK banking sector is intended to be the proposal for bank "ringfencing" which was proposed by the report of the Vickers Committee and which is contained in the first version of the Financial Services (Banking Reform) Bill 2013. The precise meaning of the term "ringfencing" is not defined by the Bill, and public pronouncements by Chancellor of the Exchequer Osborne suggest that those details will be supplied by statutory instrument and that the Bill is intended to become law in 2014. This proposal is considered in detail in Chapter 28. For present purposes, the idea can be summarised as an intention that

---

[124] Discussed in Ch.10.
[125] Discussed in Ch.32.

the speculative, so-called "casino banking" activities of UK banks will be "ringfenced" from the ordinary retail banking activities of those same banks. It is unclear, however, what is meant by ringfencing at the time of writing. In essence, the underlying intention of these proposals is to protect retail banking activities (including the operation of ordinary bank accounts, deposit-taking, and so forth for ordinary customers) from the sort of speculative, investment banking activities (especially derivatives markets) which were involved in the cause of the financial crisis of 2007–09.[126]

6.   INSURANCE REGULATION

The regulation of insurance business is conducted structurally in the same way as investment business: that is, the conduct of insurance business is overseen by the FCA and the prudential regulation of insurance providers is governed by the PRA. Insurance regulation is conducted in accordance with EU legislation, as considered in Chapter 7. These threads are drawn together with the detail of the rulebooks specific to insurance business in the FCA Handbook and the PRA Handbook in the analysis in Chapter 56 of the practitioner edition of this book, *The Law and Regulation of Finance*.

8–64

7.   THE POLICY CONTEXT BEHIND THE REGULATORY REFORMS OF 2013

A.   Introduction

This section considers the policies which underpinned the reforms to the regulatory system in 2013. The financial crisis which gave rise to these changes is analysed in detail in Chapter 45.

8–65

B.   The Treasury White Paper of 2011

The policy priorities

The policy foundations for the Financial Services Act 2012 were laid out in the Treasury White Paper "*A new approach to financial regulation: the blueprint for reform*"[127] which was published in June 2011, and which focused on the reform of prudential regulation of financial services and banking in the UK.[128] That White Paper identified the underlying problem in the UK financial system as being a "lack of systemic oversight and effective tools" for financial regulators.[129] It was argued that the previous regulatory approach had involved too much micro-prudential regulation (focusing on individual firms, and then not effectively as in the case of Northern Rock) and insufficient focus on risks to the

8–66

---

[126]   The financial crisis is discussed in Ch.45.
[127]   HM Treasury, White Paper "A new approach to financial regulation: the blueprint for reform" (Cmnd 8083), hereafter "the White Paper".
[128]   *http://www.hm-treasury.gov.uk/d/consult_finreg__new_approach_blueprint.pdf*
[129]   White Paper, p.15.

entire system; and furthermore that banking law created too few powers for regulators to deal with bank failures (in the way that the Banking Act 2009 sought to remedy). The creation of the FPC was intended to fill this gap in systemic regulation, in part by means of the publication of three-year strategies by the Court of the Bank of England.[130] That the FPC is empowered to make recommendations and give directions to the other regulatory bodies suggests that systemic considerations will trump micro-prudential considerations.

8–67   It was said in the White Paper that "[w]eaknesses in the banking system remain a headwind on growth". This short burst of purple prose is something of an understatement as the systemic weaknesses in the British economy have been exposed by the imposition of austerity economics on a country attempting to recover from one of the worst recessions in living memory.

8–68   This is a very different approach to that adopted in the EU or in the USA where a creative tension has been created between the many bodies which exist there with responsibility for different areas of financial markets and for different aspects of economic policy. It is only in the UK that all of these different functions have been collected into the Bank of England and the Treasury: two intertwined public bodies. This structure is predicated on two facts. First, that the British experience of the crisis is understood as having been made more difficult by the failure of the "tri-partite" regulatory authorities under the ancien regime (the Treasury, the old Financial Services Authority and the Bank of England) to fix upon a single course of action during the Northern Rock collapse and thereafter. Therefore, British policy is focused on bringing responsibility into one place, even if centring control of that policy on a small group of individuals within two organisations is the opposite of every corporate governance and regulatory advance made elsewhere in the world. Second, the Conservative-led Coalition Government in the UK wished to dismantle the old Financial Services Authority which had been closely associated with the Labour administrations that had created it originally, and which had of course singularly failed to supervise financial institutions in the lead-up to the financial crisis.

8–69   In essence, the White Paper replaces the Financial Services Authority with a variety of bodies which will operate as subsidiaries of the Bank of England, and the FCA under the oversight of the Treasury. In spite of the Bank of England's successive failures in the oversight of a series of failed banks in the modern era beginning with Johnson Matthey and ranging through higher-profile failures like BCCI, Barings, Northern Rock, HBOS, RBS, Alliance and Leicester, and Bradford and Bingley, it has nevertheless been given a remit which spreads across the banking and financial services regulatory arenas, as well as having control over monetary policy. The Bank of England thus occupies a dangerous position in which it is both responsible for economic growth (through monetary policy) and for the prudential regulation of banks and financial services firms. In essence, it is responsible both for the accelerator and the brake.

8–70   The proposals which are made in the White Paper are heavy with jargon. Not least the irritating euphemism "toolkit" to describe the range of powers, duties

---

[130] Financial Services and Markets Act 2000, s.9C.

and obligations which are incumbent on the various regulatory bodies. If the White Paper talked more seriously about rights and obligations instead of "tools" then it might be easier to understand the precise nature of the proposals which are being made. Whereas much of the complaints about the manner in which the old Financial Services Authority had conducted itself prior to the global financial crisis centred on its being too close to the financial institutions which it regulated, the White Paper still provides for overmuch consultation on individual uses of regulatory powers. Moreover, the White Paper continues to assume that financial institutions will be so concerned with their reputations that that will present misfeasance. It is as though the integrity of the financial system is still supposed to take a secondary place to the profitability of the financial services sector.

In the White Paper, paras 2.41 and 2.42 consider that in spite of the spaghetti of inter-locking powers and obligations of the various regulatory bodies which are assembled inside the Bank of England and the Treasury, "[t]he fundamental responsibilities of the authorities in a crisis are clear".[131] With respect and looking in from the outside, this does not appear to be the case. What seems likely, at some point in the future, on the basis of this structure is that the Bank of England over time will develop a corporate view of the macroeconomic position of the British economy which will be disseminated from the Governor through the MPC and the FPC, and which will cascade down into the other regulatory bodies, which will become wedded to economic growth through the powerful financial sector and which will therefore seek to tread lightly on the brakes offered up by prudential regulation of financial institutions. The groupthink which will develop within the Bank of England will harden into a corporate resistance to outside criticism of these various subsidiary entities, and in consequence the United Kingdom will suffer from the next market crash which will be described as another "perfect storm" that no-one could have predicted. No-one, that is, caught inside the bubble of the Bank of England. The new memorandum of understanding to be established between the Bank of England's regulatory bodies, the FSA and the Treasury, was exactly the "tool" which failed so miserably before the financial crisis of 2007–09.

8–71

As mentioned above, the Governor of the Bank of England is now the second most powerful unelected person in the UK (after the Queen) with power over economic policy, monetary policy, financial policy, prudential financial regulation, and conduct of business financial regulation. This concentration of power in one person is deeply troubling in a democratic society. Moreover, the Governor has responsibility at the same time for the success of the economy and for controlling financial institutions: which means that the Governor will both want to advance policies which encourage growth while also being expected to prevent growth from overheating. The Governor is therefore responsible simultaneously for applying the accelerator and the brake. During a time of weak growth and rising inflation, the Governor will be caught in a difficult position between needing to follow potentially inflationary policies to deliver growth while also needing to look prudently to the future to prevent either a boom-and-bust cycle or rising inflation (which can only be prevented by slowing growth).

8–72

---

[131] White Paper, p.22.

C. The reform of banking regulation

8–73   Key proposals for the reform of the regulation of banking were made by the Independent Commission on Banking, chaired by Sir John Vickers, broadly to the effect that retail banking should be "ring-fenced" off from investment banking. The report did not specify exactly how the ring-fencing would work. The first version of the Financial Services (Banking Reform) Bill 2013, which was supposed to implement these recommendations, did not even define the term "ringfence". Therefore, the basis on which this key element of banking law reform is supposed to function is entirely unclear. The work of that commission in considered in Chapter 28.

D. The Parliamentary Commission on Banking Standards

8–74   That the FSA 2012 reforms were considered inadequate before they were even enacted is indicated by the creation of the Parliamentary Commission on Banking Standards in the autumn of 2012[132] and the promulgation of the Financial Services (Banking Reform) Bill 2013 to introduce further reforms to banking law and regulation in the UK. The creation of the Parliamentary Commission was a result of the exposure of a number of banking scandals (discussed in detail in Chapter 45) but principally the "Libor rate-fixing" scandal in which traders in a number of banks (although Barclays was the first bank to be identified) conspired to fix the published level of the London Inter-Bank Offered Rate, which is the principal rate of interest paid between banks which is used to calculate the amounts payable on a huge number of financial instruments from the most complex interest rate swaps to ordinary home mortgages. It became clear that there was a lot more that was wrong with the financial system than its inability to anticipate or to avoid a systemic crash. Moreover, the Financial Services (Banking Reform) Bill 2013 proposes a re-organisation of banks in the UK to separate retail banking activities off from investment banking activities. The work of the Commission is considered in Chapter 45.[133]

E. The key to financial regulation: the implementation of regulatory powers

8–75   The key point about financial regulation is that it is not just the content of the rulebook which matters. What matters is the level of persistent aggression, precision, and suspicious, questioning mind with which the regulators use their powers. The ideal financial regulator is one part terrier, one part safecracker, and one part Sherlock Holmes. What emerges from the discussion in Chapter 45 is that there are often errors and occasionally criminality hidden in every financial institution ranging from the huge universal banks to the small hedge funds, which requires the terrier's dogged spirit to find and worry over. It needs the precise

---

[132] The impetus to create this Parliamentary Commission was the "Libor rate fixing" scandal, discussed in Ch.57.
[133] At para.45–108.

patience of the safecracker to take apart regulatory filings from banks to ensure they are factually correct and to investigate what they may conceal under their surface. For example, the risks which Citigroup had hidden under the surface were unknown to senior management and equally unknown to the regulators who were permanently on-site at Citigroup's offices in New York.[134] If regulators are not sufficiently inquisitive or intrusive then an enormous book of rules will not in itself control banks. Regulators need to be suspicious in the sense of refusing to accept any explanation which is given to them by senior management in banks because senior management necessarily seeks to spin every piece of news into being positive or, at worst, neutral. Their public statements or explanations are necessarily made with an eye to enhancing the firm's reputation in the eyes of financial markets. Every financial instrument or market circumstance which eventually causes a loss can always be explained away at the time, but that does not mean that the banker has considered all of the potential risks appropriately: just as the investment banks had failed to consider the potential future risks of a failure of the US housing market or of the CDO and CDS markets in 2005. The role of the regulator is to look beneath the surface and to anticipate the worst.

---

[134] See the report of the Financial Crisis Inquiry Commission on this point, as considered in Ch.45 generally.

CHAPTER 9

FUNDAMENTAL PRINCIPLES OF UK FINANCIAL REGULATION

CORE PRINCIPLES

This chapter considers the fundamental principles which underpin financial regulation. There are six tiers of regulatory principles in the UK. Those six levels are: high level principles; generally applicable regulatory standards; supervisory rules; prudential rules; specific market regulation; and complaints and compensatory mechanisms. The high-level principles are considered below in this chapter, together with the supervisory, prudential, complaints and compensatory rule-books. Consequently, financial regulation in the UK operates on the basis of high-level principles which govern the interpretation of the detailed regulations which apply to specific market sectors, to specific forms of financial institution, and to particular types of financial instrument. In this way, the *FCA Handbook* and the *PRA Handbook* divide between over-arching regulations which apply to all forms of business, and different types of financial activity which have their own regulatory codes. The overarching regulatory principles governing the regulation of conduct of business, financial promotion, and market abuse are considered in detail in turn in the chapters to follow in Part III of this book. The more-detailed regulations governing specific types of financial instrument are considered in *Section Two: Specific Financial Techniques* of this book. The core prohibition under s.19 FSMA 2000 is a prohibition on conducting forms of financial business which require regulatory authorisation without actually having such authorisation:

breach of s.19 is a criminal offence. The types of business which fall to be regulated are set out in the Regulated Activities Order 2001. As discussed in the previous chapter, the Financial Conduct Authority ("FCA") and the Prudential Regulatory Authority ("PRA") assumed responsibility for the regulation of financial services in the UK from April Fool's Day 2013, further to amendments made to the Financial Services and Markets Act 2000 ("FSMA 2000") by the Financial Services Act 2012.

1. INTRODUCTION

A. The scope and purpose of this chapter

This chapter considers the detail of the foundational principles which underpin financial services regulation in the UK, as administered by the Financial Conduct Authority ("FCA") and the Prudential Regulatory Authority ("PRA") further to the powers granted to them by the Financial Services and Markets Act 2000 ("FSMA 2000"),[1] as it was amended by the Financial Services Act 2012. The aim of this chapter is to introduce the general, "framework" principles which underpin that regulation, before later chapters will deal more specifically with particular aspects of regulation such as market abuse,[2] financial promotion,[3] the conduct of business between investment "firms"[4] and their clients,[5] and the regulation of banking.[6] So, here we are concerned with the big picture; it is in later chapters that we turn our attention to more detailed matters. It should be recalled from Chapter 3 that in this book there is a division made between "financial regulation" (which refers to the regulation of financial markets by the FCA and the PRA specifically in the UK further the FSMA 2000) and "the general law" (which refers to the ordinary substantive statute and case law of England and Wales as it applies in the context of financial markets). In this chapter we are concerned specifically with financial regulation.

9–01

---

[1] The following texts deal with the overarching context of financial regulation. In relation specifically to the securities markets, there is A.S. Hudson, *Securities Law*, 2nd edn (London: Sweet & Maxwell, 2013); and in relation to derivatives markets, there is A.S. Hudson, *The Law on Financial Derivatives*, 5th edn (London: Sweet & Maxwell, 2012). The following texts are of interest but are now out of date: M. Blair and G. Walker (eds), *Financial Markets and Exchanges Law* (Oxford University Press, 2007); M. Blair and G. Walker (eds), *Financial Services Law* (Oxford University Press, 2006); and R. Cranston, *Principles of Banking Law* (OUP, 2002). In relation specifically to the securities markets, there is A.S. Hudson, *Securities Law, op cit*. Encyclopaedic reference to financial regulation is made E. Lomnicka and J. Powell, *Encyclopedia of Financial Services Law* (London: Sweet & Maxwell, looseleaf) and P. Creswell et al. *Encyclopaedia of Banking Law* (London: LexisNexis, looseleaf).

[2] See para.12–01.

[3] See para.11–01.

[4] The *FCA Handbook* refers to all regulated organisations—whether companies, partnerships, associations, trusts, bodies corporate, and so on—as being "firms". To an English lawyer the word "firm" would ordinarily relate to a "partnership" specifically. However, in this book we shall use the word "firm" in the sense it is used in UK financial regulation to refer to all regulated organisations (as opposed to regulated individual human beings).

[5] See para.10–01.

[6] See para.29–01.

B. The central principle in this chapter

9–02 The principles considered in this chapter are based on the following simple rule: it is a criminal offence under s.19 of FSMA 2000 to conduct any of the activities which are identified as being regulated activities by either the FSMA 2000 or the Regulated Activities Order 2001 without having authorisation from the FCA or the PRA to do so. The *FCA Handbook*[7] and the *PRA Handbook*[8] then set out the manner in which authorisation is obtained from each body respectively, and the *FCA Handbook* provides for the manner in which business must then be conducted with customers. When interpreting those regulatory rulebooks, the foundational principles which are considered in this chapter apply such that the detailed regulatory rules are to be understood as operating by reference to those high-level, foundational principles: for example, the requirement that all regulated entities must act with "integrity". From these central principles grows the idea that almost all of the financial services activities discussed in *Section Two: Specific Financial Techniques* of this book are governed by FCA financial regulation in the UK,[9] while the condition of the institutions which sell financial instruments is regulated by the PRA.

C. Fundamental distinctions made in this chapter

The distinction between banking, investment and insurance regulation

9–03 There is a threefold distinction to be made in regulatory terms between traditional banking activity, investment business, and insurance. It should be recalled from Chapter 7 that that is the division which is made between the various regulatory bodies within the EU regulatory architecture and in EU financial services legislation. First, *traditional banking activity* relates to the taking of deposits from customers, the operation of bank accounts, lending, the operation of payment systems, and so forth.[10] Given the central role which banks (especially the leading "clearing banks" in the UK[11]) play in the economy, they were always regulated by a combination of authorities including the Bank of England, the old Financial Services Authority[12] and the Treasury.[13] The effect of the Financial Services Act 2012 was to pass responsibility for different aspects of this area of

---

[7] Accessible through *http://www.fca.org.uk* from April Fool's Day 2013. It is a website which looks like it is trying to sell you shoes, as opposed to setting out financial regulation.

[8] Accessible through *http://www.bankofengland.co.uk/pra* from April Fool's Day 2013.

[9] Some aspects of foreign exchange and of securitisation business, for example, are effectively outside FCA regulation; this chapter will focus on regulated business, as set out below.

[10] Traditional banking activity is considered in Part VIII, and lending is considered in Part IX, of this book (Chs 27–34).

[11] The "clearing banks", as discussed in para.29–36, are the largest "high street", retail banks which operate the system for clearing cheques in the UK.

[12] As considered in the previous chapter, the old Financial Services Authority was renamed the "Financial Conduct Authority" by the Financial Services Act 2012, s.6, as from April 1, 2013. However, some of its powers were passed to the Prudential Regulatory Authority by the same means at the same time.

[13] Her Majesty's Treasury ("HM Treasury") is the government department which acts as the UK's equivalent of a ministry of finance. Its chief minister is the Chancellor of the Exchequer.

regulation to different subsidiary entities of the Bank of England and to the FCA, as was discussed in the previous chapter. The bulk of the regulation which is considered in this chapter relates to investment business. Second, *investment business* includes: securities markets (including trading in shares and bonds),[14] investment through collective investment schemes (including unit trusts and other mutual funds), and derivatives markets.[15] The activities which fall within this heading are considered below. The regulation of investment business encompasses financial institutions receiving authorisation to sell financial products, investor protection in general terms, conduct of business rules,[16] and regulatory recourse in the event of a breach of the regulations. Importantly, for the purposes of this chapter, those detailed regulations are subject to high-level regulations which govern the way in which they are to be interpreted. Third, *insurance* regulation was added to the old Financial Services Authority's portfolio of responsibilities in 2005.[17] It fits within the same general principles as investment business but it has its own prudential and conduct of business regulation.

The distinction between conduct of business and prudential regulation

There is also a distinction to be made in regulatory terms between conduct of business regulation and prudential regulation. Conduct of business regulation is overseen by the FCA. It relates to the manner in which regulated financial institutions must conduct their dealings with their customers. This is the heart of investor protection regulation. It overlaps with the private law rules relating to fiduciary duties, contract law, the availability of damages for wrongs, and so forth, in that both are concerned to protect customers from inappropriate treatment by financial institutions.[18] Conduct of business regulation controls the manner in which financial institutions must communicate with their customers, how they can promote their products to customers, and so forth.[19] It establishes a number of core principles (including the requirement that financial institutions act with integrity, that they act in the best interests of the customer, and so forth) as well as very detailed rules as to the types of information which must be made available to customers and so forth. By contrast, prudential regulation is overseen by the PRA and by the Financial Policy Committee ("FPC") of the Bank of England. Prudential regulation is concerned with the solvency and condition of individual financial institutions, and with the condition of the entire financial system. Regulation of the condition of individual financial institutions is referred to as "micro-prudential" regulation and falls within the remit of the PRA; whereas regulation of the entire financial system is referred to as "macro-prudential" regulation and falls within the remit of the FPC. (This regulatory

9–04

---

[14] Securities regulation is considered in Part X of this book (Chs 35–39).

[15] Derivatives markets are considered in Part XI of this book (Chs 40–44).

[16] Conduct of business regulation is considered in Ch.10.

[17] Insurance regulation does not form part of mainstream finance law in the sense that that term was defined in Chapter 1 (para.1–03) as relating to a "wherewithal to act" (because it does not finance an activity, but rather it seeks to protect against loss), and therefore does not receive detailed consideration.

[18] Those private law principles are considered in Pts V through VII of this book.

[19] Conduct of business regulation specifically is analysed in Ch.10 of this book.

structure was considered in the previous chapter.) One of the lessons which was drawn from the financial crisis 2007–09 was that there needed to be a division between conduct of business regulation and prudential regulation because it was felt that the regulatory authorities had lost sight of the prudential risks both to the entire financial system and to the solvency and robustness of individual financial institutions. Therefore, by separating prudential regulation out from conduct of business regulation it would be possible to lavish a necessary amount of attention on it.

2.   THE SIX TIERS OF REGULATION IN THE UK

9–05   This section provides an overview map of UK financial regulation to help the reader to negotiate through the various types of regulatory material. While much discussion of financial regulation among economists and policymakers deals with it as though it is a binary system of permitting or denying permission to act (i.e. as though financial regulation is like a switch which means that there is either total regulation or no regulation), the regulatory rulebooks are in fact lengthy and complex. It is useful to think of there as being six tiers of financial regulation in the UK: high-level principles; generally applicable regulatory standards; supervisory rules; prudential rules; specific market regulation; and complaints and compensatory mechanisms. Each is described in turn.

9–06   The first tier of regulation—*the high-level principles*—is exemplified by the *Principles for Businesses* rulebook ("PRIN") which creates high-level principles in accordance with which the rest of the regulatory architecture is to be interpreted. The central principles of PRIN are considered in detail below. The aim of these principles-based rulebooks is to impose general obligations on regulated persons—such as the duty to act with "integrity" at all times—both as a means of controlling the interpretation of all of the other rulebooks and also as constituting a ground for finding a breach of the regulations in themselves. This form of regulation is said by some finance practitioners to be overly vague because it does not tell a regulated person exactly what to do, for example, so as to be acting with integrity. However, the underlying purposes of this sort of regulation are to provide an aid to interpretation, to provide for flexible regulatory principles which can be adapted to changing circumstances, and to impose an obligation on regulated firms to reflect on the manner in which they ought to treat their customers and organise their businesses practices. This last purpose of high-level regulation supplies an ethical core to the regulations both in the sense that it establishes "integrity" and similar obligations as being at the heart of the regulatory code, and in the sense that it places the onus on regulated firms to ensure compliance with this standard as opposed simply to satisfying these regulations formulaically by ticking a series of boxes. (These characteristics of high-level regulatory principles were considered in Chapter 3.[20]) It is the financial institutions which are more concerned about standards being vague than anyone else: those institutions would often prefer to know exactly what their obligations are, instead of being given a general standard with which they must

---

[20]   At para.3–32 et seq.

comply (because they cannot know for sure whether or not they have complied with it). It is the rest of society watching the aftermath of the credit crunch which wishes that "principles-led" regulation had not actually meant "light touch" regulation in practice because insufficient regulatory oversight in the USA and in the UK allowed poor lending practices and opaque credit markets to build up, thus causing enormous financial and economic turmoil. There is, however, no reason why high-level principles need to mean light-touch regulatory practice. The Principles for Business rulebook is considered in detail below.

The second level of regulation is comprised of *generally applicable regulatory standards* which inform all market sectors. Of particular importance are the regulations governing the "conduct of business" between seller and buyer of financial services; the marketing of financial products by way of "financial promotion" regulation; and the regulation of "market abuse". Each of these topics has a specific chapter in this Part III of this book. These general principles apply to all forms of market activity. They are not simply high-level regulations, however, because the appropriate rulebooks reach into much greater detail than the does the *Principles for Businesses* and similar sourcebooks. **9–07**

Thirdly, *supervisory rules* are the mechanisms by which the FCA and the PRA carry out their supervision of regulatory "firms"[21] and individuals. The Supervision Manual ("SUP") provides for the detail of the supervision process. It was reviewed by the old Financial Services Authority in the wake of the financial crisis with a view to bolstering the rigour with which the Authority enforced its rules. **9–08**

Fourthly, *prudential rules* focus on the obligations on regulated firms to maintain sufficient capital to guard against the risk of loss, and thus the various prudential rulebooks set out the risk-measurement methodology used by the Bank of England in calculating the size of those firms' exposures to loss on financial markets and other risks. There are a number of sourcebooks for this type of regulation, some aimed at specific market sectors and others aimed at more general principles, such as the general sourcebook "GENPRU". This type of rulebook provides for regulations which relate to the "financial soundness of regulated firms".[22] The financial soundness of firms refers to their solvency: that is, their ability to pay their debts as they become due. Prudential regulation of investment firms and banks therefore requires the maintenance of capital, the maintenance of their liquidity, and controls to prevent over-concentration of exposure to particular markets. The PRA's approach to micro-prudential requirements generally is based on a series of risk models by reference to which the PRA attempts to establish to which of four levels of risk (from lowest to highest) an entity belongs. **9–09**

---

[21] The *FCA Handbook* refers to all regulated organisations—whether companies, partnerships, associations, trusts, bodies corporate, and so on—as being "firms". To an English lawyer the word "firm" would ordinarily relate to a "partnership" specifically. However, in this book we shall use the word "firm" in the sense it is used in UK financial regulation to refer to all regulated organisations (as opposed to regulated individual human beings).

[22] Sharma, "The Integrated Prudential Sourcebook", in Blair & Walker (eds), *Financial Services Law*, p.369.

9–10   The fifth tier of regulation is comprised of *specific market regulations*[23] which are the detailed operating regulations that apply to particular market sectors. This is by far the largest type of regulation in the *FCA Handbook*. It is in the second half of this book (*Section Two: Specific Financial Techniques*) that the detail of these regulations is considered. While some commentators have suggested that principles-based regulation has replaced detailed regulation, this is simply untrue. Rather, while the principles-based regulations and the prudential sourcebooks set out tiers of general principles, there are still vast swathes of more detailed regulations relating to particular markets. In this sense, *specific market regulations* govern the way in which business is conducted in detail in different types of financial market, and are the sort of regulations which are set out in the Commission's technical regulations at the EU level, as considered in Chapter 7. They are predicated on the high-level principles set out above, but are far more focused. Examples of such detailed operating regulations include the detailed "building blocks" in the FCA Prospectus Rules[24] which specify in detail the required contents of prospectuses for each kind of security that may be offered to the public. The *FCA Handbook* contains many hundreds of pages of such regulations covering much of the minutiae of securities markets, banking, insurance and so on.

9–11   The *specific market regulations* are of two types. The first type is paired with a particular prudential sourcebook so as to provide detailed regulation in tandem with prudential regulation. This is why it was so important in the previous chapter to consider how the FCA and the PRA will interact when their different regulatory fields overlap in practice. So, in the banking context there are regulations covering banks' operations as well as prudential regulations. In the mortgage context, there is a conduct of business sourcebook covering operations in the mortgage market beyond the prudential requirements placed on mortgage firms. And so on. The second type of detailed operating regulations govern more general markets like the securities markets, in that context in the form of listing rules, prospectus rules, and disclosure and transparency rules.

9–12   The sixth tier of regulation comprises the *complaints and compensatory mechanisms* which are the means by which the clients of regulated firms can seek redress for any alleged misfeasance under FSMA 2000 and the *FCA/PRA Handbook* by a regulated firm. The principal means of seeking redress is through the Financial Services Ombudsman; whereas compensation can be sought through the Financial Services Compensation Scheme or through one of the specific rights to compensation which are set out in the FSMA 2000 (or under private law generally), as considered at the end of this Chapter.

---

[23] This is not a jargon term used by the FCA, but rather it is my own.
[24] See para.36–01.

THE GENERAL PROHIBITIONS ON UNAUTHORISED ACTIVITIES AND THE DEFINITION OF REGULATED ACTIVITIES

A. Introduction

This first half of this section identifies the core prohibitions in the FSMA 2000 which criminalise dealing in regulated activities without authorisation. The second half of this section then identifies which activities are "regulated activities" for this purpose.

9–13

B. Authorisation is necessary to conduct a regulated activity

The general prohibition on unauthorised regulated activity

The kernel of the UK regulatory regime is the requirement that no-one may carry on regulated activities without authorisation from the FCA. The scope of the regulated activities which are caught by the *FCA Handbook* and by the *PRA Handbook* is discussed below[25]: it is spelled out in Sch.2 of the FSMA 2000 and in the Regulated Activities Order 2001 ("RAO").[26] The outline of the relevant statutory provisions dealing with the definition of activities caught under the FSMA 2000 is as follows. Section 19(1) of the FSMA 2000 contains "the general prohibition"[27] to the effect that:

9–14

> "No person may carry on a regulated activity in the United Kingdom, or purport to do so, unless he is—
> (a)   an authorised person; or
> (b)   an exempt person."

Thus, by implication, s.19 requires that only authorised persons may carry on a regulated activity, or that a person must fall within one of the statutory exemptions. The centrality of this short provision to the whole architecture of FCA and PRA regulation cannot be over-emphasised. Section 22 of the FSMA 2000 then defines the term "regulated activity" so as to encompass any activity identified in Sch.2 to the FSMA 2000. In turn, Sch.2 to the FSMA 2000 then provides seven categories of regulated activity and fourteen categories of "investment"; before the Regulated Activities Order then defines the various categories of investment in detail. Between them, those provisions then also identify the exempt categories of activity. Acting without the necessary authorisation is deemed to be a contravention of a requirement imposed on a person by the FCA.[28] Breach of s.19 has a series of criminal law and private law consequences, as considered in the following sections.

---

[25] See para.9–10.
[26] The Financial Services and Markets Act 2000 (Carrying on Regulated Activities by Way of Business) Order 2001. *R. v Napoli* [2012] EWCA Crim 1129.
[27] As referred to in Financial Services and Markets Act 2000, s.19(2).
[28] Financial Services and Markets Act 2000 s.20(1). That does not in itself constitute a criminal offence nor a ground for an action in tort for breach of statutory duty; rather, it founds a series of potential liabilities under the Act: *ibid*.

The criminal penalty for unauthorised persons who breach the general prohibition

9–15 A person who contravenes the general prohibition in s.19 is guilty of a criminal offence under s.23 of the FSMA 2000.[29] Therefore, it is an offence[30] to carry on a regulated activity in the UK without authorisation from the FCA or the PRA (as appropriate) so to do. It is a defence for the defendant to demonstrate that she took "all reasonable precautions and exercised all due diligence to avoid committing the offence".[31]

The effect of authorised persons acting outside their authorisation

9–16 If an authorised person carries on a regulated activity in the United Kingdom in a way that exceeds or contravenes any permission they have been given by the FCA then they are taken to have committed a contravention of a requirement imposed on them by the FCA, further to s.20 of the FSMA 2000.[32] This is not a criminal offence, but rather a contravention of the terms of that permission given by the FCA.[33] Any agreement entered into in breach of this permission is not automatically void and unenforceable,[34] nor does it necessarily give rise to an action in tort for breach of statutory duty.[35] Thus, a contract is not necessarily void if the financial institution has some limited authorisation that it is breaching by entering into this contract. However, where identified as such in the Act or in the *FCA Handbook*, a person who suffers loss as a result of this contravention may bring an action against the authorised person.[36] The private law context is considered in the next section. A person receives authorisation further to s.40 of the FSMA 2000 by making an application under that section to the FCA or PRA, as appropriate. The relevant authority may then grant permission further to s.42, including threshold conditions as to nature of the applicant, and the authority may impose requirements on the applicant to act or to refrain from acting, further to s.43 of the FSMA 2000, and limitations on the activities which the applicant may pursue under its authorisation. The terms of that authorisation may be varied on the request of the authorised person under s.44; or on the authority's own initiative under s.45 if it considers that the regulated person may breach the threshold conditions imposed on it. Importantly, if an authorised person is acquired by someone else (or if a third person acquires "control" over an authorised person) then, under s.46, the authority may vary the authorised person's permission to perform regulated activities. Under s.33 of the FSMA

---

[29] Financial Services and Markets Act 2000 s.23(1). This is referred to as an "authorisation offence": Financial Services and Markets Act 2000 s.23(2).

[30] The expression "it is an offence" in this context refers to the commission of a criminal offence. As considered in Ch.13, what the FSMA 2000 is doing in this context is to reinforce the authority of the regulatory authorities by providing that breach of the legislation or their regulations (as appropriate) will have consequences under the criminal law.

[31] Financial Services and Markets Act 2000, s.23(3).

[32] Financial Services and Markets Act 2000, s.20(1).

[33] Financial Services and Markets Act 2000, s.20(2)(a).

[34] Financial Services and Markets Act 2000, s.20(2)(b).

[35] Financial Services and Markets Act 2000, s.20(2)(c).

[36] Financial Services and Markets Act 2000, s.20(3).

2000, in an elliptically drafted provision, the relevant authority is given a power to withdraw a "person's status as an authorised person" – thus effectively removing their authorisation, although s.33 itself does not specify the grounds for such a withdrawal.

The private law unenforceability of agreements entered into in breach of s.19

Further to s.26 of the FSMA 2000, any agreement entered into by a person in contravention of the general prohibition in s.19 of the FSMA 2000 (of carrying on a regulated activity without authorisation or without being an exempt person) will be "unenforceable against the other party".[37] As s.26(1) provides: **9–17**

> "An agreement made by a person in the course of carrying on a regulated activity in contravention of the general prohibition is unenforceable against the other party."

Therefore, to make the same point more simply, if a contract relating to a regulated activity is made by a person who is not authorised to conduct that sort of business, then that contract is unenforceable. Thus, a contract is unenforceable where the "person" has no authorisation to conduct financial business. That agreement must have been made after the Act came into force.[38] Section 26 further provides that the counterparty is entitled to recover any money or other property transferred under the agreement and also to recover compensation for any loss sustained in connection with having "parted with" that money or other property.[39] Therefore, the measure of compensation under the Act would, on a literal reading of the statute, include any cost of funding associated with entering into the unenforceable agreement but possibly not any loss otherwise recoverable at law or in equity which is not connected strictly to having "parted with" the money or other property under the agreement; however, the pursuit of those common law or equitable claims is not precluded by the Act. Under the terms of the statute itself, the amount of compensation may be an amount agreed between the parties[40] or an amount determined by the court[41]; although it is suggested that the statute remains opaque as to those items which the court or the parties are required to take into account or to ignore in relation to the calculation of such compensation thus throwing the parties back onto the general law.

Section 27 provides slightly differently, as follows: **9–18**

> "(1) An agreement made by an authorised person ("the provider")—
>   (a) in the course of carrying on a regulated activity (not in contravention of the general prohibition), but

---

[37] Financial Services and Markets Act 2000, s.26(1); except in relation to the acceptance of deposits, s.26(4). See generally *CR China Trading Ltd v China National Sugar* [2003] 1 Lloyd's Rep. 279.
[38] Financial Services and Markets Act 2000 s.26(3).
[39] Financial Services and Markets Act 2000, s.26(2).
[40] Financial Services and Markets Act 2000, s.28(2)(a).
[41] Financial Services and Markets Act 2000, s.28(2)(b).

> (b)   in consequence of something said or done by another person ("the third party")
> in the course of a regulated activity carried on by the third party in
> contravention of the general prohibition,
>
> is unenforceable against the other party."

Any agreement entered into by a person who is an authorised person is nevertheless unenforceable if a third party either says or does anything which is a contravention of the general prohibition in s.19 of the FSMA 2000.[42] Therefore, if a financial intermediary acting as an agent for an authorised person made a representation to a customer which was in breach of the *FCA Handbook* (for example, the conduct of business regulations) then that would have the effect of invalidating the contract even though the seller was authorised to enter into that type of transaction.

9–19   In the event that a contract is unenforceable on the basis of either s.26 or s.27, s.28(2) of the FSMA 2000 provides as follows:

> "The amount of compensation recoverable as a result of [either s.26 or 27] is—
> (a)   the amount agreed by the parties; or
> (b)   on the application of either party, the amount determined by the court."

Therefore, if the contract identified an amount of compensation to be paid, then that would be the amount payable. However, if the contract is unenforceable, this requires the enforcement of a provision which identifies the amount of compensation payable, which in turn means that a part of the contract is therefore being enforced. Under private law, if the contract were void then any provision which purported to identify an amount payable under that contract would also be void and thus unenforceable.[43]

9–20   There is a power for the FCA to enforce the agreement in spite of the provisions of s.26 or s.27, in the following terms as provided by s.28(3):

> "If the court is satisfied that it is just and equitable in the circumstances of the case, it may allow—
> (a)   the agreement to be enforced; or
> (b)   money and property paid or transferred under the agreement to be retained."

Therefore, the court must be satisfied that it is "just and equitable" either to allow the agreement to be enforced, or else to allow money or property already transferred under the agreement to be kept by its recipient. So, in *Helden v Strathmore Ltd*[44] Newey J. held that a mortgage loan contract could be enforced on the just and equitable ground where none of the parties had realised there was a need for authorisation, where there was no question of the defendant having taken advantage of the claimant, and where the claimant had taken a significant profit from the transaction (which had involved the acquisition of a flat in Chelsea which had increased greatly in value).[45] Importantly, s.150 of the FSMA

---

[42] Financial Services and Markets Act 2000, s.27(1).
[43] *Westdeutsche Landesbank v Islington LBC*[1996] A.C. 669. See para 20-27.
[44] [2010] EWHC 2012 (Ch), [2011] Bus LR 59.
[45] Upheld by the Court of Appeal.

2000 provides that any breach of a rule in a regulatory Handbook which causes loss to a private person will found an action in tort for breach of a statutory duty, as considered in Chapter 25.[46]

C.   The regulation of "regulated activities" under FSMA 2000

The definition of "regulated activity"

As considered immediately above, a person must be authorised by the FCA if that person is to carry on a regulated activity. It is important, therefore, to define the meaning of the term "regulated activity". The statutory definition of a "regulated activity" given in s.22 of the FSMA 2000 is as follows[47]:

9–21

> "(1)   An activity is a regulated activity for the purposes of [FSMA 2000] if it is an activity of a specified kind which is carried on by way of business and—
>   (a)   relates to an investment of a specified kind; or
>   (b)   in the case of an activity of a kind which is also specified for the purposes of this paragraph, is carried on in relation to property of any kind.(2) Schedule 2 makes provision supplementing this section.(3) Nothing in Schedule 2 limits the powers conferred by subsection (1).(4) "Investment" includes any asset, right or interest.(5) "Specified" means specified in an order may by the Treasury."

Therefore, there are two key elements to this definition: the activity must be carried on by way of business and it must relate to a specified form of investment. Each of these elements is considered in turn below.

The regulated activities identified in Sch.2 to the FSMA 2000 are the activities which are within the scope of financial services regulation. The seven categories of regulated activity which are identified in Pt I of Sch.2 to the FSMA 2000 are[48]: dealing in investments (whether by buying, selling, underwriting, offering or agreeing to do any of those things as principal or agent); arranging deals in investments (for example as an intermediary or broker or otherwise); accepting deposits (just as a bank accepts deposits); safeguarding or administering assets in the form of investments (such as custodian or trustee services whereby any investment asset is held by the professional); managing investments; giving or offering investment advice; establishing collective investment schemes[49]; and using computer-based systems for giving investment instructions.

9–22

The categories of "investment" identified in Pt II of Sch.2 are[50]: securities, instruments creating or acknowledging indebtedness, government and public securities, instruments giving entitlement to investments, certificates representing securities, units in collective investment schemes, options, futures, contracts for differences, contracts of insurance, participation in Lloyd's syndicates, deposits, loans secured on land, and rights in investments. The definition of what

9–23

---

[46]   See para.25-74 et seq.
[47]   Financial Services and Markets Act 2000, s.22(1).
[48]   Financial Services and Markets Act 2000, Sch.2, paras 2 through 9.
[49]   *Financial Services Authority v Fradley* [2005] 1 B.C.L.C. 479.
[50]   Financial Services and Markets Act 2000 Sch.2, paras 10–24.

constitutes "securities" includes any "shares or stock in the share capital of a company" where the term "company" includes any body corporate or any unincorporated body constituted under the law of a country or territory outside the United Kingdom other than an oeic.[51] Under the heading "instruments creating or acknowledging indebtedness" come debentures, debenture stock, loan stock, bonds, certificates of deposit and any other instruments creating or acknowledging a present or future indebtedness. Under the heading "government and public securities" come loan stock, bonds and other instruments creating or acknowledging indebtedness and issued on behalf of a government, local authority or public authority. Under the heading "instruments giving entitlement to investments" comes warrants or other instruments entitling the holder to subscribe for any investment, whether or not that investment is in existence or is identifiable. Under the heading "certificates representing securities" come certificates or other instruments which confer contractual or property rights in respect of any investment by someone other than the person on whom the rights are conferred and the transfer of which may be effected without requiring the consent of that person. Under the heading "options" comes options to acquire or dispose of property.

9–24   The definition of the various forms of regulated financial activity are qualified in the Financial Services and Markets Act 2000 (Regulated Activities) Order 2001 (referred to hereafter as the "RAO"). This statutory instrument serves as the source for definitions of financial products generally and of securities in particular in a number of contexts.[52]

The significance of identifying a regulated activity

9–25   It is important to know whether or not an activity is a regulated activity within the RAO because any person conducting a business in relation to any of those activities will require authorisation to do so from the FCA, as set out above. So, organising a horse betting organisation whereby members of the public were sent unsolicited invitations to participate in a collective scheme to use non-public information to bet on horses for their mutual profit, constituted a collective investment scheme; and therefore there was a breach of s.19 by dint of that arrangement not having authorisation from the appropriate authority.[53] Conducting a regulated activity as a business without authorisation constitutes a criminal offence,[54] unless one has taken all reasonable precautions and exercised all due diligence to avoid the commission of that offence.[55] It is also an offence to claim to be an authorised person or to hold oneself out as being an authorised person if one is not so authorised,[56] unless one has taken all reasonable precautions and

---

[51] Where an "oeic" is an open-ended investment company.
[52] On which see also A.S. Hudson, *Financial Derivatives*, para.14–16 et seq.
[53] *Financial Services Authority v Fradley* [2005] 1 B.C.L.C. 479. See also *Financial Services Authority v Woodward* [2005] 1 B.C.L.C. 479 (i.e. *Fradley* at first instance) which held (oddly) that the promotion of the scheme was not a breach of the s.21 FSMA 2000 prohibition on financial promotions.
[54] Financial Services and Markets Act 2000, s.23(1).
[55] Financial Services and Markets Act 2000, s.23(3).
[56] Financial Services and Markets Act 2000, s.24(1).

exercised all due diligence to avoid the commission of this offence.[57] It is also an offence to advertise any investment business by means of "an invitation or inducement to engage in investment activity"[58] as set out under the "financial promotion" code, considered below.[59]

The meaning of "business"

As outlined above, the specified investments must be carried on by way of business to constitute a regulated activity. The definition of the term "business" in the law of finance is something which must be divined from those few cases which have considered this term. The meaning of "activities carried on by way of business" is defined by Treasury regulation, further to s.419 of the FSMA 2000. However, the appropriate regulation is very vague about the content of "business" for these purposes.[60] In *Morgan Grenfell & Co v Welwyn Hatfield DC*[61] Hobhouse J. suggested that there was no reason to impose a narrow meaning on the term "business" in the context of the Financial Services Act 1986 (now repealed) and that that term "should not be given a technical construction but rather one which conformed to what in ordinary parlance would be described as a business transaction as opposed to something personal or casual".[62] A similar approach has been taken in all of the case law in this context.[63]

9–26

The frequency of the investment activity might be a guide to, but not conclusive of, the question whether or not a business of investment is being carried on.[64] While many of the decided cases on the meaning of the term "business" have emphasised the frequency with which the activity must be carried on to constitute a business,[65] there are two other factors which must be of importance. First, the volume of the business and the amount of profit involved. The term "volume" in this context refers both to the quantity of investment transactions entered into and also the size of those transactions. Where, for example, a financial institution conducted many hundreds of investment transactions in a single day, there would be no doubt that the volume of trades constituted a business even if they were for comparatively small amounts. Indeed, where there is an intention to carry on a large number of transactions in the future, then the fact that a person has only conducted a few transactions would not prevent that activity from being considered to be a business.[66] Secondly, the quantity and sophistication of the investment choices made: thus putting in place complex securities transactions as opposed to selling ordinary shares would indicate that the seller is conducting a

9–27

---

[57] Financial Services and Markets Act 2000, s.24(2).
[58] Financial Services and Markets Act 2000, s.25(1).
[59] Financial Services and Markets Act 2000, s.25(1).
[60] The Financial Services and Markets Act 2000 (Carrying on Regulated Activities by Way of Business) Order 2001, para.3.
[61] [1995] 1 All E.R. 1.
[62] [1995] 1 All E.R. 1.
[63] *American Leaf Blending Co Sdn Bhd v Director General of Inland Revenue* [1979] A.C. 676.
[64] *Morgan Grenfell & Co v Welwyn Hatfield DC* [1995] 1 All E.R. 1.
[65] *Re Debtor, Ex p. Debtor (No.490 pf 1935)* [1936] Ch. 237.
[66] *Re Griffin, Ex p. Board of Trade* (1890) 60 L.J. Q.B. 235; *CIR v Marine Steam Turbine Co Ltd* [1920] 1 K.B. 193.

business.[67] In spite of the formulaic principles considered in this discussion, it is suggested that it is the question of the quality of the investment activities which will be decisive of whether or not she is acting in the course of a business.[68] As such "business" would generally connote "the fundamental notion of the exercise of an activity in an organised and coherent way and one which is directed to an end result".[69] It is suggested, therefore, that there are four general badges of business in this context: time, volume, profit and quality,[70] where the activity would need to be conducted with appropriate regularity, in sufficiently large amounts, with a view to profit and in a manner which suggests the establishment of a commercial venture.[71]

9–28   There have been cases considering the ambit of the meaning of "business" in this and other contexts under the FSMA 2000. In so doing, those more recent cases have tended to do so by reference to the specific statutory principles governing them, instead of by reference to the financial services case law. So, in *Helden v Strathmore Ltd*[72] issues arose as to whether or not the last in a series of mortgage loans made by a company which was not authorised under the FSMA 2000 constituted "business" for the purposes of s.22 of that Act. The human beings involved were well-known to one another and the corporate entities through which they conducted their businesses were commonly involved in property speculation in high-value residential properties in central London. The claimant borrowed money from the defendant company to acquire a property in Chelsea. There had been several loans of different amounts for different purposes (relating to different properties) between the various connected persons involved between 2002 and the commencement of the litigation. The particular issue was whether or not the loans were being "carried on by way of business" within the statute, which required some sort of repeated, regular activity of that sort. It was held by Newey J. that because there had been several loans over a long period of time that that constituted carrying on the activity of lending by way of business.

9–29   There was, however, a further question under s.28(3) of the FSMA 2000 in *Helden v Strathmore Ltd* as to whether or not the loan contract could nevertheless be enforceable. It was argued on the just and equitable ground that the loan

---

[67] *Re Brauch* [1978] 1 Ch. 316, in which case it was accepted that for a business to be being conducted the defendant would need to be acting on behalf of other people. cf. *R. v Wilson* [1997] 1 All E.R. 119, in which to be carrying on an insurance business one had to be acting for one's own benefit and not for the benefit of others.

[68] *Morgan Grenfell & Co v Welwyn Hatfield DC* [1995] 1 All E.R. 1.

[69] *Calkin v IRC* [1984] 1 N.Z.L.R. 1.

[70] e.g. *Calkin v IRC* [1984] 1 N.Z.L.R. 1: in which the New Zealand Court of Appeal considered that the term "business" concerned "the nature of the activities carried on including the period over which they are engaged in. the scale of operation and he volume of transactions, the commitment of time, money and effort, the pattern of activity and the financial results".

[71] Where the regulations encompass "arrangements" to participate in a form of regulated activity, it has been held that such "arrangements" included any acts connected to that activity which need not necessarily involve nor facilitate the execution of a regulated activity: *In Re The Inertia Partnership LLP* [2007] EWHC 502 (Ch.); [2007] Bus.L.R. 879. So, performing acts which are preparatory to the performance of a regulated activity will themselves constitute a regulated activity which requires authorisation from the appropriate authority, where the RAO encompasses such "arrangements" within the activities requiring authorisation.

[72] [2011] Bus LR 59, Newey J.

contract ought nevertheless to be enforceable. That the defendant's controlling mind had been unaware of the need to be authorised under FSMA 2000 in relation to an activity which he had not realised might constitute regulated financial services business militated in favour of the loan contract being enforceable. Newey J. found several factors which supported a finding that it was just and equitable to enforce the contract under s.28(3) in spite of the failure to acquire authorisation from the Financial Services Authority (as was required at the time). Among the factors were the defendant's ignorance of the regulatory context of their activities,[73] the fact that the claimant had not been taken advantage of by the defendant (given the claimant's experience of financial matters), that the claimant had earned a large profit from the increase in the market value of the Chelsea flat, that the claimant had had the use of the Chelsea flat as a result of the claimant's loan to him, and that it would have made no difference to the claimant if the defendant had been properly authorised under the FSMA 2000.[74]

His lordship raised the question whether or not it would have been open to the court to enforce the contract in part (for example at a lower interest rate) further to s.28. However, because neither counsel had raised the question, his lordship left it unanswered. At first blush, it must be said that there is something unattractive in principle about the court re-writing the parties' agreement so as to enforce it in a different manner from the agreement which they had effected between them. The FSMA 2000 contains no explicit power to alter the terms of the agreement and therefore it is suggested that the court should decide whether it is just and equitable to enforce the agreement in its entirety or not at all. The decision of Newey J. was upheld by the Court of Appeal: their lordships concluded that Newey J. had come to an entirely appropriate conclusion based on the facts before him.[75] **9–30**

For the most part, the courts rely on common sense and treat activities as crossing a line into being "business" when they are carried on with sufficient regularity and so forth, as considered above in relation to the four badges of finance business. So, in *Re Whiteley Insurance Consultants*[76] it was held that a partnership was conducting insurance business within the meaning of the Act **9–31**

---

[73] None of the parties were financial institutions, nor did they realise that their activities in relation to domestic accommodation (buying and selling expensive London residences) fell within the ambit of financial regulation.

[74] The other context in which a "just and equitable" ground arises is in relation to winding up companies further to s.122(1)(g) of the Insolvency Act 1986. As Lord Wilberforce held in *Ebrahimi v Westbourne Galleries* [1973] AC 360 "The foundation of it all lies in the words 'just and equitable' and, if there is any respect in which some of the cases may be open to criticism, it is that the courts may sometimes have been too timorous in giving them full force. ... [The requirement of a "just and equitable" finding] does, as equity always does, enable the court to subject the exercise of legal rights to equitable considerations; considerations, that is, of a personal character arising between one individual and another, which may make it unjust, or inequitable, to insist on legal rights, or to exercise them in a particular way." See, generally, Alastair Hudson, *Understanding Company Law* (Routledge, 2012), Ch.8.

[75] [2011] Bus. L.R. 1592.

[76] [2008] EWHC 1782 (Ch), [2009] Bus. L.R. 418.

when it was acting as principal, accepting liability to policyholders as principal, and accepting premiums from policyholders as principal.

9–32 Two cases indicate the extent to which an intermediary[77] will be engaging in financial business within the FSMA 2000. In *Inertia Partnership LLP*[78] a partnership, which had traded as a management consultancy, introduced three companies seeking investors to investors who were known to the partnership. Because all that the partnership was doing was making introductions between third parties, as opposed for example to constructing the financial transactions effected between the parties, it was held that it was not conducting finance business within the FSMA 2000. By contrast, in *Watersheds Ltd v Da Costa*[79] the issue arose whether or not the claimants were "making arrangements" within the meaning of the 2000 Act in introducing borrowers and lenders to one another and organising meetings. The defendants were seeking to resist a claim requiring them to pay the claimants what was owed under their contract for that work, inter alia, on the basis that the claimants were not authorised further to the FSMA 2000 and that they were performing regulated activities. Having distinguished *Inertia Partnership*, Holroyde J. found that the claimant was doing more than merely making introductions when they helped to arrange funding for the defendants. To constitute regulated activities, a person would have to be doing more than merely making introductions between parties and convening meetings. His lordship expressed himself to be unsure whether or not bringing the defendants together with lenders and taking a fee constituted regulated activities. In essence, he was reluctant to find that their activities were regulated activities on the basis that this might have relieved the defendants from a requirement to pay under their otherwise enforceable contract. However, his lordship did hold that, even if those activities had been regulated, he would have relied on the just and equitable ground under s.28(3) to enforce the contract nevertheless simply because he was not convinced that the defendants were entitled to avoid making payment under an otherwise valid contract.

4. THE CORE REGULATORY PRINCIPLES IN THE *FCA* AND *PRA HANDBOOKS*

A. The role of the *Principles for Businesses* rulebook

The core principles

9–33 The FCA *Principles for Businesses* rulebook ("PRIN") contains general, foundational principles which underpin the remainder of the *FCA* and *PRA Handbooks*. Guidance notes in PRIN make it clear that "breaching a Principle

---

[77] An intermediary is a financial institution which brings other parties together—such as an independent financial advisor which advises a client to use products sold by a bank: that intermediary will stand between the client and the bank, and typically will take a fee.
[78] [2007] EWHC 539 (Ch), [2007] Bus.L.R. 879.
[79] [2009] EWHC 1299 (QB), [2010] Bus.L.R. 1.

makes a firm liable to disciplinary sanctions".[80] The FCA or PRA is required to demonstrate "fault" before imposing such a sanction on a regulated firm.[81] Whether there has been fault and the extent of the breach will depend upon which Principle has been breached and the context of the particular client and market in question. The Principles are as follows[82]:

"1. *Integrity.* A firm must conduct its business with integrity.
2. *Skill, care and diligence.* A firm must conduct its business with due skill, care and diligence.
3. *Management and control.* A firm must take reasonable care to organise and control its affairs responsibly and effectively, with adequate risk management systems.
4. *Financial prudence.* A firm must maintain adequate financial resources.
5. *Market conduct.* A firm must observe proper standards of market conduct.
6. *Customers' interests.* A firm must pay due regard to the interests of its customers and treat them fairly.
7. *Communications with clients.* A firm must pay due regard to the information needs of its clients, and communicate information to them in a way which is clear, fair and not misleading.
8. *Conflicts of interest.* A firm must manage conflicts of interest fairly, both between itself and its customers and between a customer and another client.
9. *Customers: relationships of trust.* A firm must take reasonable care to ensure the suitability of its advice and discretionary decisions for any customer who is entitled to rely upon its judgment.
10. *Clients' assets.* A firm must arrange adequate protection for clients' assets when it is responsible for them.
11. *Relations with regulators.* A firm must deal with its regulators in an open and cooperative way, and must disclose to the [authority] appropriately anything relating to the firm of which the [authority] would reasonably expect notice."

These eleven principles thus underpin the interpretation of the regulatory *Handbooks* and the behaviour of regulated firms generally. It has been held that these provisions constitute the outcomes which regulated firms are required to achieve in observing their financial regulatory obligations generally, and that they can be used to augment more detailed regulations because they are the well-spring from which those detailed regulations are drawn.[83] Many examples of breaches of these principles are considered in Chapter 45 in relation to the regulatory aftermath of the financial crisis of 2007–09. Each of these principles is considered in turn in the discussion to follow. References here to the FCA should also be read as references to the PRA, in this section.

---

[80] PRIN,1.1.7G.
[81] PRIN,1.1.7G.
[82] PRIN,2.1.
[83] *R. (British Bankers Association) v Financial Services Authority* [2011] EWHC 999 (Admin), [2011] Bus. L.R. 1531.

B. The core principle of business integrity

The meaning of "integrity"

9–34   The first principle in the "Principles for Businesses" rulebook is that:

> "[A] firm must conduct its business with integrity".[84]

The term "integrity" is not defined, in keeping with the status of FCA regulation as being expressed in non-formal, non-legal language accompanied by guidance notes. The word "integrity" in the *Shorter Oxford English Dictionary* has the following definition[85]:

> "Freedom from moral corruption; innocence, sinlessness. Soundness of moral principle; the character of uncorrupted virtue; uprightness, honesty, sincerity."

Thus the term integrity in this context relates to ethics in the conduct of business practice. It will be very important to know whether or not integrity in this context is to be interpreted in a subjective or in an objective manner.[86] However, the word "integrity", when used in relation to something like the hull of a ship, relates to its physical soundness. This second sense of "integrity" is used in relation to the systemic "integrity" of the financial system, which refers to its ability to withstand shocks and to operate normally. In PRIN, however, the principal sense is that of moral probity.

Subjective and objective integrity

9–35   There may be two significantly different senses to this dictionary definition of "integrity": one subjective and the other objective. That a person be "free from moral corruption" contains a sense of subjective (but possibly passive) avoidance of moral turpitude: this would, it is suggested, encompass a person who knowingly shut her eyes to the obvious so that she would not actually learn of anything which would have prevented her from actually knowing that she was acting immorally, and who might therefore claim to have been acting in a subjectively honest manner. The second sense, relating to "soundness of moral principle", would encompass objective dishonesty more comfortably: objective dishonesty would mean that it is not sufficient for a person to shut her eyes to the obvious and claim innocence, but rather her behaviour would have to be judged against the standard of behaviour of an objectively honest and reasonable

---

[84] Dubbed the "PRIN" rulebook in regulatory jargon.

[85] There are, in the interests of full disclosure, two other senses of the word integrity, which it is suggested are of no interest in this context, relating to "completeness" and not being married or violated.

[86] As Albert Camus put it: "I have seen people behave badly with great morality and I note every day that integrity has no need of rules": *The Absurd Man*. For Camus, integrity is something ingrained. In relation to financial regulation, however, integrity certainly has need of rules.

person.[87] That is: what would an honest and reasonable person have done in those circumstances, and did the defendant behave in that manner? If the defendant did not behave in that manner then she would not have acted with objective integrity.[88] This second sense of integrity—that a person must have acted as an objectively honest person would have acted in the circumstances—is, it is suggested, closer to the policy underpinning the *FCA Handbook* which is seeking to establish objective principles of good business conduct in financial markets. The purpose of establishing a rulebook containing rules and statements of principle is, it is suggested, precisely to identify such objective standards of appropriate and inappropriate business conduct.[89]

By way of example, in English private law the issue of subjective and objective propriety has been considered in detail comparatively recently in two House of Lords and two Privy Council (and many High Court) decisions relating to the liability of company directors and others for dishonest assistance in a breach of fiduciary duty.[90] The weight of judicial opinion in that private law context supports an objective test predicated on identifying what an honest person would have done in the circumstances and considering whether or not the defendant acted in that way.[91] There, the courts have held (by reference on occasion specifically to investment transactions[92]) that a person may not escape liability by claiming that she had not had actual knowledge of factors which would have made her behaviour unethical or "dishonest", or that her own moral code meant that she did not consider such behaviour to be unethical or "dishonest": instead, the courts have held (in the majority) that the honesty or integrity of a person's behaviour must be judged from the perspective of an objectively honest person acting in their circumstances.[93] This, it is suggested, is the more appropriate approach in relation to the regulation of the securities and other markets. The alternative, subjective approach is closer to that found in criminal law to the effect that it is not sufficient to show what an honest person would have done in the circumstances, but rather it must also be shown that the defendant knew that her behaviour did not correspond to the behaviour of an honest person.[94]

9–36

---

[87] See the detailed discussion of subjective and objective honesty and behaviour in good conscience in A. Hudson, *Equity & Trusts*, 7th edn (Routledge, 2012), s.20.2.

[88] That it is a standard of "business integrity" means that the objective and reasonable person would have to be taken in a business context, with an understanding that profit is not in itself a bad thing and so forth, and could not, for example, be taken necessarily from the perspective of a person with strong religious opinions against making profit or earning interest.

[89] See further A.S. Hudson, "Trusts and Finance Law" in Hayton (ed) *The International Trust*, 3rd edn (Jordans, 2011), 638, at p.675 et seq.

[90] See G.W. Thomas and A.S. Hudson, *The Law of Trusts* (OUP, 2004), p.973 et seq.

[91] *Royal Brunei Airlines v Tan* [1995] 2 A. C. 378; *Dubai Aluminium v Salaam* [2002] 3 W.L.R. 1913.

[92] An idea considered in detail in A.S. Hudson, "Trusts and Finance Law", in Hayton (ed) *The International Trust*, 3rd edn (Jordans, 2011), 638, at p.675 et seq.

[93] As in *Barlow Clowes v Eurotrust* [2005] UKPC 37, [2006] 1 All E.R. 333: on which see A.S. Hudson, *Equity & Trusts*, s.20.2.

[94] *Twinsectra v Yardley* [2002] 2 All E.R. 377, 387, per Lord Hutton.

C. The remaining business principles in PRIN

Skill, care and diligence

9–37   A firm must conduct its business with due skill, care and diligence. In private law terms this would be thought of as imposing a duty of care on the regulated person. As is discussed in Chapter 10, the courts are tending to look at a regulated firm's regulatory obligations when deciding on the limit of that firm's duties under common law and in equity.[95]

Management and control

9–38   PRIN provides that "a firm must take reasonable care to organise and control its affairs responsibly and effectively, with adequate risk management systems". The presence of risk management systems is a reference to internal measurement systems which calculate the risk profile of financial institutions and management systems which can respond effectively to all those categories of risk identified in Chapter 1.

Financial prudence

9–39   Prudence in the context of financial regulation (as considered later in this chapter) relates to the maintenance of capital to off-set against any loss suffered in any given financial market. Prudential regulation therefore incorporates the calculation of the level of risk exposure faced by a firm, and the evaluation of the risk profile of that type of financial business and therefore the amount and type of capital which must be set aside to meet that exposure. The presence of security for any such transaction, including financial collateral of the type discussed in Chapter 42, will typically be taken into account in calculating the level of risk exposure. Thus PRIN provides that "a firm must maintain adequate financial resources".

Market conduct

9–40   PRIN provides that "a firm must observe proper standards of market conduct". In many markets, it is impossible to say in the abstract what any "rules" of market conduct would be because few such rules have been formulated outside the *FCA Handbook*, except possibly for the rules of any exchange which might be in issue or alternatively the rules of a trade body. So, it is suggested, this principle does not refer to "rules" but rather simply to "standards" (as the precise wording suggests) which are not prescribed in advance but rather which are standards a reasonable market participant or regulator might consider to have been broken by any inappropriate action of a regulated firm. This principle only makes sense in relation to markets without formal standards of behaviour if it is read along with

---

[95] See for example: *Investors Compensation Scheme v West Bromwich Building Society* (1999) Lloyd's Rep. PN 496; *Loosemore v Financial Concepts* (2001) 1 Lloyd's Rep. 235; *Seymour v Christine Ockwell* (2005) P.N.L.R. 39.

the requirement of "integrity". Other markets, such as those which trade on exchanges, will have formal rules and standards. It is suggested that the Conduct of Business sourcebook ("COBS") is the clearest identification of market standards in relation to the issues on which COBS makes provision: such as client classification, notification of fee levels, and so forth.

Customers' interests

PRIN provides that "a firm must pay due regard to the interests of its customers and treat them fairly". It is suggested that COBS, in applying MiFID, provides a body of rules which expand on the notion of treating customers suitably. For example, the "best execution" principle (requiring best price and performance) and the "best interests" principle which requires a regulated firm to act in the best interests of its customers. These principles, among others, are considered in Chapter 10. Indeed, COBS seems to require more than simply treating a customer "fairly": rather it requires that the regulated firm act in the best interests of the customer, which is a positive obligation and not simply a request to regulated firms not to act unfairly.

9–41

Communications with clients

The COBS principles, referred to above, also deal with the manner in which communications are made with customers, as considered in Chapter 10. PRIN provides that "a firm must pay due regard to the information needs of its clients, and communicate information to them in a way which is clear, fair and not misleading". The principle that communications be "clear, fair and not misleading" is rehearsed in various places in the regulatory rulebooks.

9–42

Conflicts of interest

A key part of the law relating to fiduciary duties is the need to avoid conflicts of interest. This principle was explored in Chapter 5.[96] However, in most circumstances a regulated firm will not be acting as a fiduciary; that is, unless there is something specific about the relationship between the parties to call a fiduciary relationship into existence, such as an agency or trust relationship. However, PRIN provides that "a firm must manage conflicts of interest fairly, both between itself and its customers and between a customer and another client". Thus, a regulated firm bears duties under PRIN to "manage" conflicts of interest whether or not it is acting as a fiduciary. Notably, the duty under PRIN is to "manage" conflict of interest, and not to avoid them as under fiduciary law. Managing a conflict of interest would permit a conflict of interest to exist but would require that conflict of interest not to influence the regulated firm's action inappropriately. Nevertheless, the conflict of interest can continue. This is unfortunate in contexts where, for example, a regulated firm is giving investment advice to a customer which involves the firm selling securities which it already owns to the customer: there is a conflict between the firm's desire to sell its own

9–43

---

[96] See para.5–14.

stock and the customer's need for impartial, professional advice. If the firm were a fiduciary, then any profit earned from that transaction (which was not permitted by the terms of the firm's fiduciary duties) would be held on constructive trust for the customer[97]; but no such obligation would apply under the PRIN provision if a fiduciary duty did not exist. It is suggested that the duty to "manage conflicts of interest" should be read in the light of the duty to act with "integrity". Acting with integrity, it is suggested would preclude regulated firms from selling securities to customers simply because they owned them if that firm did not also consider them to be securities which advanced the best interests of the customer under COBS. Again, it is suggested, that within the *FCA Handbook* it is the COBS principles which set the bar highest for regulated firms, and that it is when PRIN is interpreted in the light of those principles (assuming fiduciary law generally does not apply) that it is most demanding of a regulated firm. The context of firms providing advice is considered further in relation to the next principle.

Customers: relationships of trust

9–44   PRIN provides that "a firm must take reasonable care to ensure the suitability of its advice and discretionary decisions for any customer who is entitled to rely upon its judgment". The previous principle required "management of conflicts of interest"; this principle is related in that it imposes an obligation of "reasonable care" for the "suitability of its advice" in general and its "discretionary decisions" (such as managing its customer's funds) in relation to customers (such as inexpert customers or customers who have made it plain that they are relying entirely on the firm's advice) who are entitled to rely on that advice. That there is a duty of reasonable care imposed on regulated firms may influence the ambit of that regulated firm's liabilities under the tort of negligence as has been held in some decided cases which are discussed in Chapter 25.[98]

Clients' assets

9–45   The *FCA Handbook* contains the "Clients Assets" sourcebook ("CASS") which is considered in detail below. In essence, CASS obliges regulated financial institutions to segregate client money from other money and to hold those assets on trust. In practice, it has emerged that many financial institutions have been breaching these obligations and pooling client assets with the bank's own money.

Relations with regulators

9–46   PRIN provides that "a firm must deal with its regulators in an open and cooperative way, and must disclose to the FCA appropriately anything relating to the firm of which the FCA would reasonably expect notice". Clearly, compliance with financial regulation requires compliance with the regulator when the regulator is acting within its powers. What is lacking from the FCA regulatory

---

[97] *Boardman v Phipps* [1967] 2 A.C. 46.
[98] See para.25–19 and generally in that chapter. See for example: *Seymour v Christine Ockwell* (2005) P.N.L.R. 39.

scheme as a whole is a single provision which makes breach of a regulatory requirement or instruction by the FCA an offence or something similar. The effect of breach of FCA rules is considered below. The purposive role of the high-level principles in PRIN was accepted in *R. (British Bankers Association) v Financial Services Authority*.[99] The FSA had published Policy Statement 10/12 which made amendments to the *FSA Handbook*, including the manner in which PPI mis-selling claims would be treated as breaches of fundamental provisions of PRIN. It was argued on behalf of the Financial Services Authority that the purpose of the high-level principles in PRIN was to establish "what" regulated firms were required to do, as opposed to "how" they were supposed to do it (which was for the firms to identify for themselves). Consequently, those principles had always been intended to impose regulatory obligations on the firms. Ousley J. held that the purpose of PRIN was to establish overarching principles from which the more detailed provisions of the FSA Handbook were drawn. Therefore, those principles could augment specific, detailed rules in the Handbook.

D. The organisation of regulated firms, internal systems and personnel

The organisation of the firm under MiFID

The Markets in Financial Instruments Directive ("MiFID") sets out the requirements for the organisation of regulated firms, as is discussed in Chapter 7.[100] Those provisions create obligations such that an investment firm is required to establish adequate policies and procedures to ensure compliance of the firm (including its managers, employees and tied agents) with its regulatory obligations; to maintain effective organisational, accounting and administrative arrangements; to perform its obligations to its clients suitably; to ensure that any agents also act suitably; to keep appropriate records; to ensure that client's property rights are adequately protected; and to prevent client funds being used for its own account. These last two obligations correlate closely with the fiduciary obligations considered in Chapter 5.

9–47

Internal systems under the SYSC rulebook

Regulated firms are required to have appropriate internal systems and controls in place. If one considers the traditional approach of UK company law to questions of personnel liability, it is commonly the case that the company as an abstract entity takes on all of the business's liabilities; contrariwise, the company is only liable for the defaults of its employees if they are part of the directing mind and will of the company or if tortious vicarious liability applies. In relation to the largest universal banks in particular, this would make it very unlikely that the

9–48

---

[99] *R. (British Bankers Association) v Financial Services Authority* [2011] EWHC 999 (Admin), [2011] Bus LR 1531.
[100] MiFID art.13.

bank would ever be liable for the defaults of individual traders because there are so many traders and other employees employed by those banks that none of them is likely to constitute the directing mind and will of the company; and even if that concept is widened to include being the directing mind and will of the company in relation to a particularly significant transaction, there would still be many transactions which might be considered to be so small in the total scheme of the bank's operations as to be too small to be worthy of notice.[101] Therefore, it is imperative that financial regulation recognises that regulated financial institutions must be fixed with liability for the activities of all of their employees and agents by imposing obligations on senior management to put in place suitable internal controls and procedures to oversee their own personnel across all of their activities. In this way, there is no possibility of the firm arguing that it is not responsible for the acts or omissions of its traders.

9–49   This area of regulation is particularly significant given the protestations by many senior bank executives when giving evidence in the autumn of 2012 to the UK Treasury Select Committee that those parts of the businesses which had caused losses or which were involved in scandals had been outside the executives' personal control. The SYSC regulations, however, require that a regulated financial institution is subject to internal systems and controls which ensure that it is properly managed. Nevertheless, the problems are stark. For example, Citigroup CEO, Chuck Prince, gave evidence to the Financial Crisis Inquiry Commission in the USA that the department which caused that bank such catastrophic losses (involving losses of US$60 billion in 2008) was not on his radar and that even in hindsight he would have made the same management choices because the CDO products in which that department was investing were rated AAA by the credit ratings agencies and therefore were considered to be low risk.[102] The principal claim that is made by many critics of the universal banks in the current environment is that they are simply "too big to manage" because they employ so many people in so many different jurisdictions, and even comparatively unremarkable businesses in obscure branch offices can now incur losses which can ruin the entire bank: such was the case with Nick Leeson dealing in derivatives in Singapore so disastrously that Barings Bank went into insolvency. Even JP Morgan suffered a multi-billion dollar loss from the actions of one trader in its London office, as did UBS, and so on. In 2007, Citigroup had US$ 2 trillion on its balance sheet and US$1.2 trillion held off-balance sheet across more than 2,000 subsidiary entities.[103] That institution is clearly too large for one individual to manage from the top. (These factual scenarios are considered in Chapter 45 in detail.) What emerges from this quick overview is

---

[101] See for example *Tesco Stores Ltd v Nattrass* [1972] AC 153; *El Ajou v Dollar Land Holdings* [1994] 2 All E.R. 685; *Meridian Global Funds v Securities Commission* [1995] 3 All E.R. 918; *Crown Dilmun v Sutton* [2004] EWHC 52 (Ch); *Lebon v Aqua Salt Co Ltd* [2009] UKPC 2, [2009] 1 B.C.L.C. 549.

[102] The condition of Citigroup during this period is considered in Ch.45. See the report of the US Financial Crisis Inquiry Commission (New York: Public Affairs, 2011), p.260 et seq.

[103] As found in the report of the US Financial Crisis Inquiry Commission, (New York: Public Affairs, 2011), at p.260.

how important it is that such enormous, powerful and potentially dangerous[104] organisations have "robust" internal procedures and controls in place.

The FCA's "Threshold Conditions" sourcebook (known as "COND") provides the minimum standards with which the organisation and composition of a regulated firm are required to comply.[105] Those conditions relate to the legal status of the firm; the location of the firm's offices; the appointment of a claims representative where appropriate; the firm's close links; the adequacy of the firm's resources; and the suitability of the firm and of its personnel.

9–50

The personnel and internal systems of regulated firms

The personnel of regulated firms are clearly very important when overseeing the proper behaviour of those firms. The unimaginatively titled FCA "Senior Management Arrangements, Systems and Controls" sourcebook ("SYSC") sets out principles relating to the way in which firms must be organised, internal systems created suitable for the conduct of financial services business, senior staff sufficiently well trained, and suitable controls in place over its employees. The guidance notes which begin the SYSC rulebook are somewhat mealy-mouthed: their goal is to "encourage the firms' directors and senior managers to take appropriate practical responsibility for their firms' arrangements",[106] but not apparently to *require* anything. Moreover, a breach of the provisions of SYSC does not ground any right in damages.[107]

9–51

The internal organisation of a regulated firm must make it clear which members of the board of directors and of senior management have responsibility for which issues, and to ensure that the firm's activities can be "adequately monitored and controlled by the directors".[108] Identified people must be granted the responsibility for creating such systems. As considered below, it is generally protested by boards of directors of universal banks that they cannot be expected to control every nook and cranny of the business. Nevertheless, they bear this regulatory responsibility. Significantly, the Chief Executive of a regulated firm is ultimately responsible for the creation of the firm's systems and controls.[109] It is then provided that:

9–52

---

[104] Potentially dangerous, that is, on the basis that when entities the size of Lehman Brothers and Washington Mutual fail they cause enormous damage to the real economy as well as to the global financial system.

[105] The Threshold Conditions in Sch.6 to the FSMA 2000, as they relate to the present context, are as follows. If the person involved is carrying on a regulated banking activity then it must be a body corporate or a partnership. Its head office must be in the UK if it is a body corporate constituted under the law of any part of the United Kingdom. If the person has close links with another person, then the authority must be satisfied that those links are not likely to prevent the authority's effective supervision of that person. The resources of the person concerned must, in the opinion of the authority, be adequate in relation to the regulated activities that are being carried on. That includes a survey of the assets of any group of companies to which the person belongs. The person concerned must satisfy the regulatory authority that it is a fit and proper person, including that it conducts its affairs soundly and prudently.

[106] SYSC,1.2.1G.

[107] SYSC,1.4.2R.

[108] SYSC,2.1.1R.

[109] SYSC,2.1.4R.

"A firm must take reasonable care to establish and maintain such systems and controls as are appropriate to its business."[110]

However, this does not identify the underlying objective of this regulation: is it to remove risk entirely, to reduce risk, to ensure customers suffer no harm, to preserve the micro-prudential health of the firm, or to contribute to the larger soundness of the financial system of which that firm (depending on its size and strategic significance) forms a part? Each of the Bank of England regulatory authorities (whether dealing with conduct of business, micro-prudential regulation or macro-prudential regulation) will have different views of the risks associated with any given institution in their light of their different regulatory responsibilities.

9–53   Of particular importance to the SYSC schemata is the establishment of systems and controls which control financial crime and money laundering.[111] There must be an employee identified as being responsible for money-laundering reporting.[112] The regulations clearly identify that the firm must install systems which prevent the firm from being used as a conduit for criminal activities by other people, and not simply that its own employees refrain from criminal actions. By way of example of the sort of thing which can happen, in 2012 HSBC was found to have allowed Mexican subsidiaries to be used for laundering drug money, and Standard Chartered was found to have allowed Iranian entities to use it to access the New York payment system in breach of US sanctions legislation. Neither of these actions were the deliberate policies of the management of the bank but rather the fault of dishonest bank employees in far-flung subsidiaries. More worryingly, however, was evidence that senior management had been warned about the risks of exactly these sorts of activities.

9–54   Among the firm's systems to comply with SYSC must be appropriate systems for dealing with operational risk. The FCA "SYSC" rulebook requires that board directors and "senior managers" take "appropriate practical responsibility for their firms' arrangements" in relation to FCA regulation. The CEO is specifically identified as being responsible for these structures. Under SYSC, "A firm must take reasonable care to establish and maintain such systems and controls as are appropriate to its business". SYSC also provides[113]:

"A firm must have robust arrangements, which include a clear organisational structure with well defined, transparent and consistent lines of responsibility, effective processes to identify, manage, monitor and report the risks it is or might be exposed to, and internal control mechanisms, including sound administrative and accounting procedures and effective control and safeguard arrangements for information processing systems".

The "senior personnel" must ensure that the firm "complies with its obligations under the regulatory system" and those personnel must "assess and periodically review the effectiveness of those policies". So, regulated firms are required to have "robust governance arrangements, which include a clear organisational

---

[110] SYSC,3.1.1R.
[111] SYSC,3.2.6R.
[112] SYSC,3.2.6IR.
[113] SYSC,4.1.1R.

structure with well defined, transparent and consistent lines of responsibility, effective processes to identify, manage, monitor and report the risks it is or might be exposed to". These vague and optimistic expressions, of course, had no impact on firms like Barclays which failed to prevent the Libor misquoting scandal or the systematic mis-selling of payment protection insurance to ordinary retail customers. For example, in evidence to the Treasury Select Committee, former CEO Bob Diamond said that he had been unfamiliar with that part of the bank which had been responsible for the Libor misquotation in spite of his personal responsibilities as CEO under SYSC to ensure the bank had appropriate systems in place and to ensure that the bank had a proper monitoring and control mechanism. In general terms, "senior personnel" are responsible for ensuring that the firm complies with its regulatory obligations.[114] That executives like Diamond are not held to task publicly for failing to comply with these precise regulations is troubling; that executives like Diamond seem to be oblivious to the fact that they were subject to those regulations is deeply worrying.

Among the firm's systems must be appropriate systems for facilitating whistle-blowing on inappropriate activity by managers to be made by other employees of the firm further to the Public Interest Disclosure Act 1998. Protection for whistleblowers is particularly important in the wake of the several banking scandals which have revealed that traders in several banks have been conspiring to alter artificially the level of Libor (the interest rate which banks charge one another in London, and which is used as the benchmark for many financial instruments when calculating the level of profit or loss). It is important that these sorts of concerns can be brought forward to management and to regulators without the whistleblowers being at risk of losing their jobs or of being unfairly treated as a result of identifying wrongdoing at their firms. As has become clear with some rogue trader scandals (as considered in Chapter 45) it is often the case that the rogue trader is able to bully or pressure other employees around him into maintaining silence about their trading patterns.

9–55

The standards which are expected of "approved persons" within regulated firms are set out in the FCA "Statements of Principle and Code of Practice for Approved Persons" ("APER"). Approved persons are personnel who are empowered to carry out "controlled functions" on behalf of a regulated firm under FCA regulation. The seven principles set out in APER are similar to the PRIN principles for businesses. Under those seven principles, when carrying out her controlled functions, an approved person is required: to act with integrity; to act with "due skill, care and diligence"; to "observe proper standards of market conduct"; to deal with the FCA in an "open and cooperative way"; and if that person carries on a "significant influence" function, then: to ensure that the firm's business is organised so that it can be controlled effectively (for example, in ensuring that traders and other employees can have their activities suitably overseen); to exercise due skill, care and diligence in managing the firm's business; and to take reasonable steps to ensure that the firm's business is conducted in a manner which complies with regulatory and market standards.

9–56

---

[114] SYSC,4.3.1R.

9–57   MiFID requires that regulated firms employ only "personnel with the knowledge, skills and expertise necessary for the discharge of the responsibilities allocated to them" by FCA regulation.[115] The "Fit and Proper Test" rulebook ("FIT") identifies the criteria which are used by the FCA when assessing the fitness and propriety of a candidate for a "controlled function", which is a function identified by s.59 of the FSMA 2000 and by the Supervision rulebook ("SUP") as requiring particular qualifications. Such a candidate must be a "fit and proper person". This is an example of the information which may be required further to s.60 of the FSMA 2000 when authorisation to deal in financial services is sought from the FCA. In assessing whether or not a person is fit and proper, the FCA will consider three things: that person's "honesty integrity and reputation"; that person's "competence and capability"; and that person's "financial soundness".[116]

9–58   If the FCA considers that an individual is not a fit and proper person then it may make an order prohibiting that individual from carrying on either specified activities or regulated activities generally.[117] Breach of a prohibition order, or an agreement to breach such an order, constitutes an offence.[118]

9–59   A regulated firm must take "reasonable care to ensure that no person performs a controlled function" under s.59 of the FSMA 2000 unless the FCA "approves the performance" of that act by that person.[119] What is difficult about this provision is that it does not actually provide that authorisation must be formally sought but rather than the Authority must in some way "approve". An application for authorisation "may be made by the authorised person concerned" under s.60(1), but that provision does not require that an application must be made.[120] It is suggested that the requirement for authorisation is implied by s.59 but the drafting of that provision is somewhat opaque.

E.   Permission to undertake regulated activities

9–60   Permission to undertake regulated activities is granted further to s.40 of the FSMA 2000. In deciding whether or not to grant authorisation, the FCA must consider whether or not the applicant will continue to satisfy the Threshold Conditions considered above,[121] and the FCA will also consider any other persons with whom the applicant is connected.[122] The FCA can demand information from the applicant to help it decide on the granting of permission.[123] The FCA is then required to decide on each application within six months.[124] An aggrieved applicant may refer any complaint to the Markets Tribunal.[125] The

---

[115] FIT,1.2.4A.
[116] FIT,1.3.1G.
[117] Financial Services and Markets Act 2000, s.56(2).
[118] Financial Services and Markets Act 2000, s.56(4).
[119] Financial Services and Markets Act 2000, s.59(2).
[120] Financial Services and Markets Act 2000, s.60(1).
[121] Financial Services and Markets Act 2000, s.41(2).
[122] Financial Services and Markets Act 2000, s.49.
[123] Financial Services and Markets Act 2000, s.51.
[124] Financial Services and Markets Act 2000, s.52.
[125] Financial Services and Markets Act 2000, s.53.

overriding objective for the FCA here is the protection of consumers.[126] If permission is granted, the FCA will grant permission specifying the extent of the permission,[127] and "requirements" may be imposed on the applicant either to take or to refrain from taking identified actions.[128] The permission is capable of being varied at the applicant's request inter alia by removing activities from the scope of the permission or cancelling the permission,[129] or that variation may be made on the FCA's own initiative.[130]

5. PRINCIPLES-BASED REGULATION

A. The nature of principles-based regulation

The benefits of principles-based regulation

There has been much discussion of the likely effect of "high-level" regulatory principles in the financial press at the time when MiFID was introduced in 2007 with its use of such high-level principles as the "best interests" and the "best execution" requirements which demanded that a financial institution do the best possible for its customers in any given context. The onus was thus placed on the institution to assess the appropriate form of behaviour. It is generally assumed that market participants prefer detailed regulation to high-level principles because detailed regulation carries with it greater certainty that a regulated person will have complied with its regulatory obligations if each regulation has been followed closely: "if I am told to tick Box A, then I know when I have ticked Box A". By contrast, it was generally considered in the financial press that high-level regulations are too vague and consequently that they tend to put the onus on regulated persons and their advisors to create systems and procedures which will be compliant with those regulations even though they cannot be entirely sure that that is the case without specific approval by the regulators. MiFID in particular, as discussed in Chapter 7,[131] has generated a movement towards abstract, high-level principles which, in many circumstances, require investment firms and the operators of markets to develop their own regulatory-compliant systems. This is something of a reversal of the previous concerns of market participants that the rulebooks were too large and too demanding of them. The introduction of high-level principles will at least make the rulebooks shorter.

9–61

High-level regulatory principles are, in truth, very similar to the rulemaking with which all lawyers are very familiar under the substantive law of any jurisdiction. Law always, as Aristotle observed, provides for the general case:[132] that is, rules are always universal in that they create general principles which are to be

9–62

---

[126] Financial Services and Markets Act 2000, s.41(3).
[127] Financial Services and Markets Act 2000, s.42.
[128] Financial Services and Markets Act 2000, s.43.
[129] Financial Services and Markets Act 2000, s.44.
[130] Financial Services and Markets Act 2000, s.45.
[131] See para.7–22.
[132] See A.S. Hudson, *Equity & Trusts*, s.1.1.6, quoting Aristotle's *Ethics*, (Penguin, 1955), p.198, para.1137a17,x.

followed and obeyed, but they do not necessarily cater fairly for all individual sets of circumstances. The task of the judge is then to apply those principles to individual cases. This always involves, even in Civil Code jurisdictions, taking a general principle and considering how best to apply it to the facts in front of the judge at first instance. In England, of course, being a common law system means that most of the law is judge-made. Therefore, the law is generally comprised of previous judicial statements of principle which have been applied to particular cases. Lawyers are therefore trained to identify both the principles in play and also to understand culturally in what sorts of circumstances those principles will be applied in what sorts of fashion by what sorts of judge. Thus family courts deal with legislation differently from commercial courts, and so forth. One exception to this observation that most English law is judge-made is the law of finance where the law is a combination of financial regulation (often derived from EU legislation), statute (often implementing EU legislation) and case law: there is much more statute and regulation in finance law than in most areas of English law. Nevertheless, lawyers are well-used to the application of general principles to individual cases. There ought to be no difficulty in applying principles-based regulation in financial markets as a result. The difficulty in the early twenty-first century is that these regulations are new and therefore there is no cultural context in which those regulations have been applied in the past, there is no cultural sense of how the regulators will apply those rules in the majority of cases. Unlike the common law, significantly, there is no jurisprudence in the form of a doctrine of precedent which can give lawyers a reliable guide as to the likely future approach of the FCA or the Markets Tribunal to individual cases. The development of such a jurisprudence for financial regulation would be a huge leap forward. At present, nervousness in the marketplace is the understandable fear of the new.

9–63   The high-level, regulatory principles are not simply vague statements: rather they are islands in a sea of detailed regulation in the FCA rulebooks. The high-level principles are best thought of as aids to the interpretation and to the application of the detailed rules, as well as being rules themselves capable of direct application (for example, in relation to the censure of a regulated person who has failed to act with integrity under the *Principles for Businesses*). The Lamfalussy process (considered in Chapter 35) embraced the use of high-level principles with two beneficial results. First, it is easier to understand the shape of the law if its central principles are clear, instead of needing to dig through inches of regulatory rulebooks before trying to assemble the bigger picture for oneself. Familiarity with these high-level principles promotes transparency and confidence in the shape of securities regulation. Secondly, and more importantly perhaps, the use of high-level principles means that the detailed regulation of financial markets is not susceptible to regular overhaul and re-writing when market practice changes beneath the feet of old regulations. Thus the Investment Services Directive of 1993 was rapidly overtaken by the growth of derivatives markets, securitisation markets, and electronic trading with the result that it became outdated very quickly. Higher level principles mean that the core tenets of the legislation can be maintained over time, or adjusted visibly when necessary, and only the appropriate detailed regulations require updating. Thus regulatory rule-making can respond much more nimbly to substantial changes in market practice. This, it is suggested, will promote greater certainty across the markets in time as to the central tenets of regulation because rulebooks will not require root-and-branch rewriting, but instead can continue to float on a raft of familiar central principles.

A deontological methodology

The methodology which is suggested by the PRIN rulebook is deontological: that **9–64** is, the rulebooks establish a central ethical principle and any disputes or complaints are then to be resolved by reference to that principle. This supposes that the meaning of that central principle is well-understood and that any problem can be resolved by applying that central principle to it. The alternative ethical methodology would be a consequentialist approach which would mean that individual disputes or complaints would be resolved pragmatically on a case-by-case basis, without reference to a central ethical principle. However, given that there is no doctrine of precedent in the application of the PRIN principles, there is an argument that in practice those principles are really being applied on a consequentialist, case-by-case basis by the FCA. In a common law system, the development of precedent is arguably effected by means of deducing the nature of the central ethical principle in the deontological method from an observation of the cases: the central principle is thus taken to mean whatever those cases have suggested that it means. It is a weakness of the UK regulatory system that the FCA is able to reach findings of a breach of the regulations without express reference to its previous decisions and without the development of a clear jurisprudence as to its decision-making. Instead the guidance notes in the FCA Handbook must stand as the only attempt to rationalise the meaning of those regulations.

Does it matter which regulatory methodology is used?

At one level, it might be wondered whether or not the regulatory philosophy **9–65** which is employed really matters. Briefly put, the point appears to be this. It may not matter precisely how the UK's regulatory architecture is organised quite as much as it matters how assiduously the regulator polices those regulatory principles. Clearly, the methodology used by the regulator in framing regulations and the precise wording of the regulations matter both to ensure compliance with EU legislation and because (as all lawyers know) the precise construction of an obligation can be all-important; but what is suggested here is that that is merely window-dressing if the regulator is not in practice using its supervisory, enforcement and disciplinary powers effectively. The lesson from the global financial crisis of 2007 and 2008—which arguably began in earnest in the UK with the old Financial Services Authority's failure to supervise the business models of organisations like Northern Rock effectively—is that it matters most how assiduous regulators are in putting their powers into effect, now matter how all-encompassing the Basel II accord or the EU financial services framework may otherwise have appeared to be at that time. These issues are considered in greater detail in Chapter 45.

B. The focus on investor protection

9–66   The second principal issue in relation to FCA regulation, beyond the introduction of principles-led regulation, is the enhancement of investor protection through requirements of the giving of suitable information to investors both by the issuers of securities, and also by the service providers who are selling investments and other services to a customer. Thus, conduct of business regulation (considered in Chapter 10) requires transparency from service providers as to their charges and fees, and also requires (after the introduction of the Markets in Financial Instruments Directive ("MiFID")[133]) those service providers to acquire "best execution" for customers so that the service provider must act in the best interests of the customer.[134] This is a positive obligation: which means that it requires the person bearing the obligation to carry out a positive action, perhaps involving the expenditure of money, as opposed merely to refraining from action.

9–67   In relation to securities markets specifically, the principal focus of FCA regulation is on ensuring that potential investors have sufficient information placed at their disposal in the form of prospectuses before securities are issued[135] and in the form of transparency requirements to maintain the flow of information after the initial issue has been completed.[136] Together with those sets of regulations are regulations as to the conduct of business,[137] to prevent market abuse[138] and insider dealing,[139] and as to the proper advertisement of financial services.[140] Taken together, they constitute a significant machine for the protection of investors. Notably, there are also different regimes dealing with different market activities: such as offers of securities to the public, insurance business, mortgage business, collective investment schemes business, and so on: these various types of business are considered in *Section Two: Specific Financial Techniques* of this book. In common with the principle of protecting investors is a principle that investors must make their own investment decisions once they have been provided with sufficient information for a person of their level of expertise. By creating a separate code for transactions with expert counterparties, the market can facilitate a light regulatory touch for dealings between such experts. It is time, after this long, thematic overture, to consider some of the detail of the FSMA 2000 regime itself.

Financial regulation as a distinct discipline in practice

9–68   Financial regulation is a technical discipline in its own right. Regulatory questions generally fall into two kinds in practice: first, questions as to compliance with "high-level" regulatory requirements of best practice; and,

---

[133] 2004/39/EC.
[134] See para.10–16.
[135] See para.36–01.
[136] See para.36–57.
[137] See para.10–01.
[138] See para.12–01.
[139] See para.14–01.
[140] See para.11–01.

secondly, detailed requirements to comply with regulatory standards in relation to specific activities. Therefore, a regulatory specialist must be able to move freely between the open-textured application of high-level regulatory principles and guidance notes, and the application of detailed regulatory rules to particular transactions and to particular issuers.[141]

6. THE SUPERVISION PROCESS

A. The obligation to supervise regulated firms

The FCA conducts the supervision of regulated firms by reference to its Supervision manual ("SUP") in the *FCA Handbook*. SUP discharges the FCA's obligation under the FSMA 2000 to "maintain arrangements designed to enable it to determine whether persons on whom requirements are imposed by or under [FSMA 2000], or by any directly applicable Community regulation made under MiFID, are complying with them".[142] The provisions of SUP are designed to ensure that the FCA has carried out its regulatory objectives set out in FSMA 2000.[143] Importantly, in the wake of the financial crisis, the old Financial Services Authority initiated a review of its (remarkably lax) approach to the supervision of regulated entities: this was known as the Supervision Enhancement Programme ("SEP"). The result of this review – the equivalent, it is supposed, of a stern half-time team-talk from an irate coach – has been a very different attitude to the enforcement of regulatory powers, especially in relation to insider dealing. Rather than place its faith in light-touch regulation and in the self-correcting powers of the marketplace, the regulator came to realise that it needed to regulate the financial institutions that fell under its remit. We shall consider the SUP methodology developed by the Financial Services Authority in the wake of the financial crisis and passed to the FCA.

9–69

B. The SUP methodology

Under s.1.3 of SUP, the FCA identifies its methodology for supervising regulated persons as being a "risk based approach". What this means is that the FCA uses an "impact and probability" risk assessment approach to measuring the risks faced by each regulated firm. This process is described as being a "standard risk assessment process applied consistently across all of its activities" which more specifically assesses "the risk posed by [each regulated] firm against a number of impact and probability factors, both initially and on a continuing basis".[144] Therefore, what the FCA does is to use mathematical models to predict the likely risks and sensitivities of a regulated firm's business activities and that firm's business practices, and then considers the extent to which that firm's business is likely to interfere with one of the core regulatory objectives. The sorts of matter

9–70

---

[141] See para.7–22 et seq. (in relation to policy issues created by MiFID).
[142] Financial Services and Markets Act 2000 Sch.1, para.6(1); SUP, 1.1.2G.
[143] SUP,1.1.3G.
[144] SUP,1.3.2G.

which are to be taken into account are the firm's strategy; the level of the firm's business risk; the financial soundness of the firm; the nature of the firm's customers, products and services; the culture of the firm's internal systems and compliance systems; and the organisation of the firm and its management.[145]

9–71 This risk modelling approach is similar to one of those computer games in which the player attempts to create and govern an imaginary society. In truth, those games are based on the sort of mathematical models which are used to predict the future of firms' business models. One takes that firm's financial information and feeds it into a computer model. On the basis of the firm's business strategy, one imagines a range of different economic futures (involving different interest rates, different economic conditions, different market behaviour, and so on and so forth). As a result one can understand the likely performance of that firm in the event of a number of different market conditions: that is to identify the sensitivities which will drive that firm's future performance. The FCA is then able to predict the likely financial prognosis for each regulated firm when measured against its own assumptions about the future and about the sorts of risks against which a firm should be forearmed. The important factors in this sort of modelling are both the assumptions which are fed into the mathematical model and the sorts of reactions which the mathematical model is programmed to produce; and of equal significance is the willingness of the FCA simply to accept the information which is given to it by regulated firms as to their understanding of their own market and the risks which that business model faces. In the wake of the Northern Rock failure, the old Financial Services Authority accepted that it had not "stress tested" Northern Rock's business model stringently enough so as to anticipate the effect of changes in Northern Rock's business model which exposed that bank to securitisation and sub-prime mortgage markets instead of simply relying on investing reliable customer deposits as it had done previously. A tendency towards light-touch regulation meant that the old Financial Services Authority tended to rely on the information fed to it by regulated firms, instead of questioning or doubting the assumptions as to the future on which those firms were operating.

C.   The result of generating a risk profile of the firm

9–72 Once the FCA has identified the firm's risk profile, the FCA allocates that firm to one of a number of categories ranging from high risk to low risk. The level of supervision which is lavished on high risk firms is different from low risk firms. The FCA is not limited, of course, to measuring the risk only of individual firms. Necessarily, this involves consideration of the risks associated with particular market sectors and the identification of particular types of risk. A firm with exposure to a market which is deemed to be high risk in itself will mean that that firm will be exposed to a higher level of risk too, even if its fundamentals as an investment firm are sound. There are four types of response once these risks have been measured: diagnostic; monitoring; preventative; and remedial.[146] Diagnostic

---

[145] SUP.1.3.
[146] SUP.1.4.2G.

tools are those considered thus far: namely, tools used to identify, assess and measure risks. The monitoring process is concerned to identify risks as they emerge, and to monitor their development and likely effect on regulated firms. Preventative activity serves to try to stop those risks from "crystallising or increasing".[147] Remedial activity is then taken to manage the fall-out of risks which have hit home. In a light-touch regulatory scheme this means that too little will be done too late. Unless one's model anticipates events like the financial crash of 2008, then that model will always be surprised by anything that occurs outwith the common assumptions about the future which are shared by all market participants.

D. The way in which supervision is actually conducted

The FCA conducts its work in a number of different ways. Some review work is done entirely sitting behind a desk, other work is done by liaising with other regulators or agencies; other work is conducted on a face-to-face basis meeting with the employees of regulated firms, sometimes by on-site visits. Yet other work is conducted on the basis of published financial information, auditor's reports and so forth. What matters is the culture in which this work is done. If meetings are entirely convivial and do not ask genuinely searching questions, then nothing important is likely to be discovered. If the regulator gives many months' notice of its intention to conduct an on-site inspection then it is likely to find nothing of importance because anything of note it would have needed to discover will have been tidied away. Therefore, while a rulebook can appear either far-reaching or timid, what will really make a difference will be the manner in which that regulator actually performs its role. The FCA has significant investigative powers set out below, so the powers are there; what is needed is the will to wield them.

9–73

What can be said about the old Financial Services Authority's approach to the supervision, for example, of banking was that it was not fit for purpose. The Financial Services Authority's admitted failures in relation to the failure of Northern Rock in 2007 demonstrated that its approach to modelling and classifying the risks of banks were too often predicated on an insufficiently interventionist means of investigating their business models and the risks that were genuinely associated with their business practices. It is to be hoped that the FCA in the future takes it upon itself to discharge its obligations in a considerably more effective manner.

9–74

---

[147] SUP,1.4.3G.

7.   POWERS TO CONDUCT INVESTIGATIONS

A.   The power to conduct investigations

9–75   As a financial regulator, information about breaches of regulatory rules will reach the FCA as a rumour, possibly one passed around the market first. It is difficult for a regulator to establish fact in the abstract: breaches of regulations are rarely accompanied by a voluntary admission of fault. Therefore, the regulator requires the power to find out the facts for itself. To this end, the FCA has numerous powers to find facts. Thus, under Pt 11 of the FSMA 2000, the FCA has broad powers to gather information and to conduct investigations. The FCA has powers to require that information is provided to it by "authorised persons" or anyone connected to an authorised person.[148] The FCA then has a power to require reports from "skilled persons", such as professional accountants or other experts, as to information gathered further to those powers under s.165 of FSMA 2000. Significantly, under s.167 of FSMA 2000, professionals can be appointed to conduct the investigation, such that:

> "... [i]f it appears to the [FSA] or the Secretary of State ('the investigating authority') that there is good reason for doing so, the investigating authority may appoint one or more competent persons to conduct an investigation".

Those investigations may be investigations into "the nature, conduct or state of the business of [a recognised investment exchange or] an authorised person or of an appointed representative", or any particular aspect of that business; or "the ownership or control of [a recognised investment exchange or] an authorised person".[149] This "business" need not be limited to regulated activities under the FSMA 2000.[150] Investigations may then be broadened out into the affairs of any group to which the target of the investigation has belonged or any partnership to which that target has belonged.[151]

9–76   The FCA may appoint investigators to act on its behalf in a number of circumstances.[152] First,[153] if there are "circumstances suggesting" that there has been a commission of any one of a range of offences whether under s.177 of FSMA 2000 (relating to the FCA's powers to conduct investigations[154]); or under s.191 of FSMA 2000 (relating to the FCA's powers to effect control over authorised persons); or under s.346 of FSMA 2000 (relating to the provision of false information to an auditor or an actuary); or under s.398(1) of FSMA 2000 (relating to misleading the FCA); or under Sch.4 of FSMA 2000 (relating to EU Treaty rights); or where there has been a breach of a regulation made under s.142 of FSMA 2000 (the FCA's powers to regulate insurance business). Secondly, if

---

[148] Financial Services and Markets Act 2000, s.165.

[149] Financial Services and Markets Act, s.167(1).

[150] Financial Services and Markets Act, s.167(5).

[151] Financial Services and Markets Act, s.167(2).

[152] Financial Services and Markets Act, s.168(3).

[153] Financial Services and Markets Act, s.168(1).

[154] Refusal to attend further to s.177 is a criminal offence punishable by imprisonment as a contempt of court: *Financial Services Authority v Westcott*, Unreported October 9, 2003.

there has been a breach of the insider dealing and market manipulation offences[155]; or if there has been a breach of the general prohibition on dealing in financial services without authorisation under s.19 of the FSMA 2000[156] or of making financial promotion similarly under s.21 of the FSMA 2000[157]; or where market abuse may have taken place.[158] There is also a power under s.97 of the FSMA 2000 for the FCA to appoint people to investigate any of the obligations discussed in Part X of this book to do with issues of securities.

Under s.348 of the FSMA 2000 the FCA may not disclose confidential information to another person, unless it is necessary for the performance of a "public function" by the FCA or is otherwise permitted by Treasury regulation.[159] Confidential information in this context includes information as to its business,[160] provided that information has not already been made public.[161] However, the information which the investigators find may be used in other legal proceedings, for example in relation to the disqualification of a company director, on the basis that the judge would have to exclude from consideration any inappropriate or admissible material among those findings.[162]   **9–77**

B.   The right to present a petition for winding up

The FCA may present a petition to the court for the winding up of an authorised person (whether a company or a partnership or some other "body") under s.367 of the FSMA 2000[163]. So, in *Real Estate Opportunities Ltd v Aberdeen Asset Managers Jersey Ltd*,[164] an investigation into three companies which had advised the claimant negligently and in breach of contract led the FCA to seek the winding up of those companies. An issue arose, further to s.348 of the FSMA 2000, as to whether this would involve the FCA breaching its obligation not to disclose confidential information to another person. However, on the facts it was held that the information was already held by other people (including the person complained of by the claimant).   **9–78**

8.   THE PRUDENTIAL SOURCEBOOKS

While the *PRA Handbook* (and also the *FCA Handbook*) contains a number of "prudential sourcebooks" which relate to specific market sectors, these distinct sourcebooks are being collected slowly into a single prudential sourcebook covering all markets. The General Prudential Rulebook ("GENPRU") was   **9–79**

---

[155] See para.14–71.
[156] See para.9–06.
[157] See para.11–01.
[158] Financial Services and Markets Act 2000, s.168(2).
[159] Financial Services and Markets Act, s.349.
[160] Financial Services and Markets Act, s.348(2).
[161] Financial Services and Markets Act, s.348(3).
[162] *Secretary of State for Business Enterprise and Regulatory Reform v Aaron* [2008] EWCA Civ 1146; [2009] Bus L.R. 809.
[163] Financial Services and Markets Act 2000 s.367.
[164] [2007] EWCA Civ.197; [2007] Bus.L.R.971.

introduced in October 2006 to take effect from January 1, 2007 dealing with the core principles relating to the prudential regulation of all financial services coming under the purview of the old Financial Services Authority. The purpose of prudential regulation of this sort is to provide for the level of capital which regulated firms are required to hold in relation to particular market activities to provide for protection against those market sectors failing or causing risk, and to ensure that regulated firms have suitable internal controls to cope with the management of prudential risks.[165] Among the risks which the FCA is required to consider are: credit risk; market risk; liquidity risk; operational risk; insurance risk, concentration risk, business risk; and interest rate risk: which were considered in Chapter 1. Regulated firms are required to allocate sufficient financial resources, capital resources and internal capital as required by the regulations for that particular type of business.[166] Each market sector has its own prudential rulebook, or a specific sector in the general prudential rulebook, which specifies the applicable levels for a firm dealing in that market sector. A good example of prudential regulation in detail is set out in Chapter 28 in relation to the prudential regulation of banks. All credit institutions (or, "banks") and all investment firms are required to maintain sound, effective and coherent strategies to manage risk, and to conduct stress tests and scenario analysis of the risks which confront their businesses. The aim of the GENPRU regulation is therefore to identify the level of risk facing each regulated entity and thus to identify how much capital is required to cover the likelihood that that business will suffer adverse trading conditions or fail.

9.   THE OMBUDSMAN AND COMPENSATION POWERS IN THE FSMA 2000

A.   The Financial Ombudsman Service

9–80   The Financial Ombudsman Service ("FOS") was created further to the requirement in s.225 et seq. of the FSMA 2000 to carry on the function of an ombudsman for complaints made by consumers in relation to action in the financial services sector. The FOS is a person who is intended to provide "a scheme under which certain disputes may be resolved quickly and with minimum formality by an independent person".[167] The aim of having an ombudsman is to save ordinary customers of financial services the complexity, delay and expense of ordinary litigation to resolve disputes by providing a comparatively cheap, quick and informal means of having disputes resolved. The use of an ombudsman also redresses the imbalance in expertise between a service provider on the one hand and a retail customer on the other. The FOS was created to provide a single ombudsman service for all forms of financial services and so replace the many different ombudspeople which had existed previously for different market sectors. The FOS operates informally, identifying what is fair and reasonable in

---

[165] GENPRU,1.2.12G.
[166] GENPRU,1.2.53R.
[167] Financial Services and Markets Act 2000, s.225(1).

the circumstances, but it also operates as a tribunal.[168] It is susceptible to judicial review in spite of its ability to act otherwise comparatively informally.[169]

A complaint can be made by an "eligible complainant" in any of three **9–81** circumstances, that is on the basis that it falls within: the "compulsory jurisdiction" specified by the FCA[170]; or on the basis of the consumer credit rules[171]; or within the "voluntary jurisdiction" identified by the FCA.[172] These principles are set out in the FCA's "DISP" rulebook. Complaints can be made on the basis of any relationship between service provider and customer which relates to any regulated financial services activity. Eligible complainants are consumers, individuals, and small businesses, but not customers classified as being market counterparties with sufficient expertise to look after themselves. These categorisations of customer are considered in Chapter 10 of this book. The FOS is empowered as a "party to a complaint" to demand the production of information and documents which are necessary to determine the complaint.[173] Failure to comply would constitute a contempt of court.[174] The FOS must reach whatever decision it considers in its own opinion to be "fair and reasonable in all the circumstances".[175] The FOS is required to reach that decision based on its own subjective opinion of what is fair and reasonable, but may not limit itself to a view of what the common law would permit and not permit[176]: in that sense, it could be said that FOS cannot purport to fetter its own decision making. However, s.228 required the creation of a statutory scheme which was compliant with human rights law and with the law generally.[177] It is a matter for the FOS as to whether or not an oral hearing is necessary or whether the matter can be disposed of purely by reference to documents.[178] Any purported failure by the FOS is considered to be remediable by judicial review;[179] although it is suggested that the very purpose of ombudsman schemes is to avoid the complexity, delay and expense involved with judicial review and similar legal proceedings. The decision of the FOS must be given in writing.[180] The FOS's decision is binding on both the complainant and the firm if the complainant notifies the FOS that it is content with that state of affairs.[181] The FOS may make an award of compensation in an amount it considers to be "fair",[182] whether to compensate the complainant for financial loss or to compensate the complainant for any other

---

[168] *Andrews v SBJ Benefit Consultants Ltd* [2010] EWHC 2875, [2011] Bus LR 1608
[169] *R (Heather Moor & Edgecomb Ltd) v Financial Ombudsman Service* [2008] Bus LR 1486, CA.
[170] Financial Services and Markets Act 2000 s.226.
[171] Financial Services and Markets Act, s.226A.
[172] Financial Services and Markets Act, s.227.
[173] Financial Services and Markets Act, s.231.
[174] Financial Services and Markets Act, s.232.
[175] Financial Services and Markets Act, s.228(2).
[176] *R. Heather Moor & Edgecombe Ltd v FOS* [2008] Bus.L.R. 1486.
[177] *R. Heather Moor & Edgecombe Ltd v FOS* [2008] Bus.L.R. 1486.
[178] *R. Heather Moor & Edgecombe Ltd v FOS* [2008] Bus.L.R. 1486.
[179] *R. Heather Moor & Edgecombe Ltd v FOS* [2008] Bus.L.R. 1486. See also *Andrews v SBJ Benefit Consultants Ltd* [2010] EWHC 2875, [2011] Bus. L.R. 1608.
[180] Financial Services and Markets Act 2000, s.228(3).
[181] Financial Services and Markets Act 2000, s.228(5).
[182] Financial Services and Markets Act 2000, s.229(2).

form of loss or damage;[183] or may require the regulated firm to "take such steps in relation to the complainant as the ombudsman considers just and appropriate".[184] These steps may include an order that the financial institution set up an annuity for the customer or that the financial institution simply pay an amount of money to its customer to compensate her.[185]

9–82   The manner in which FOS is required to proceed is very different from the law on negligence. As was explained in *R (Heather Moor & Edgecomb Ltd) v Financial Ombudsman Service*,[186] and approved in *R (British Bankers Association) v Financial Services Authority*,[187] the FOS is entitled to take into account a wide range of materials, and the FOS is entitled to reach decisions which depart from the common law on negligence and from the materials which are submitted to it provided that that is necessary to reach a fair conclusion. However, the FOS must be able to explain their decisions.

B.   The Financial Services Compensation Scheme

9–83   The Financial Services Compensation Scheme ("FSCS") was created in discharge of the FCA's obligation under s.212 of the FSMA 2000 to create a compensation scheme. The statutory compensation scheme is intended to supplement the FCA's objective of ensuring market confidence among investors and other users of financial services in the UK. This scheme gives effect to the UK's obligations under EU law: namely, the Deposit Guarantee Directive[188] relating to bank deposits, and the Investor Compensation Scheme Directive,[189] as well as entitlements to compensation under insurance law.[190] The process of seeking compensation is set out in the FCA "COMP" rulebook.[191] The scheme is intended to protect customers against the risk of its service provider going into insolvency or being otherwise unable to meet its obligations as they become due. Such a failure to perform obligations would constitute a default.[192] The scheme manager will seek to enforce a right to fair compensation in the circumstances of the case. In 2008, the level of compensation allowable for each customer in relation to each bank account held with an authorised firm was raised to £50,000. The Banking Bill 2008 will make amendments to the FSCS, as discussed in Chapter 28. In relation to bank accounts, that amount has been raised again to £85,000.

9–84   Litigation has arisen on the basis of the FCA's ability to make regulations within the FSCS to provide for the assignment of claims to third parties. It has been held

---

[183] Financial Services and Markets Act 2000, s.229(3).
[184] Financial Services and Markets Act 2000, s.229(2).
[185] See, e.g. *Bunney v Burns Anderson Plc* [2008] Bus.L.R. 22.
[186] [2008] Bus.L.R. 1486.
[187] [2011] Bus.L.R. 1531.
[188] 94/19/EEC.
[189] 97/9/EEC.
[190] *R. v Investors Compensation Scheme, Ex p. Bowden* [1995] 3 All E.R. 605.
[191] Financial Services and Markets Act 2000, s.214.
[192] COMP/3.2.1R.

that the authority was empowered to make such regulations[193] on the basis that by analogy with the previous legislation such powers were upheld by the courts.[194]

10.   THE TREATMENT OF CLIENT ASSETS

A.   Introduction

The Client Asset Sourcebook ("CASS") in the FCA Handbook deals with the important matter of the treatment of assets which regulated financial institutions hold on behalf of their customers. Principle 10 of PRIN provides that "a firm must arrange adequate protection for clients' assets when it is responsible for them".

9–85

B.   The CASS rulebook

The CASS rulebook has emerged (from the case law considered in the next section) to be among the worst drafted regulations in the entire UK financial services scheme, and (from the number of Final Notices served on regulated institutions for its breach) to be among the least well observed. The CASS rulebook implements the policy in MiFID that firms holding client money must segregate that client money from all other money and thus protect it against loss. However, that admirably simple goal is lost in the over-complexity of the drafting of the CASS rulebook. CASS imposes a statutory trust over all client money once it has been received by a regulated firm—that is the analysis which is put on provision 7.7.2R by the majority of the Supreme Court.[195] However, importantly, those regulations did not countenance the possibility that any regulated firm would fail actually to segregate those client moneys, and therefore had no explanation as to the legal treatment of amounts which should have been segregated but which in fact were not. As Lord Walker observed in the Supreme Court, a mixture of client money and the bank's own money should have been treated as a fund into which the client was entitled to trace on the basis that the bank had spent its own money out of that mixture before using client moneys. Instead, the majority of the Supreme Court took the view that *all* client money should be treated as being held on trust even if there had not in fact been any segregation, and that all of the clients with entitlements to such moneys should rank *pari passu* in relation to whatever moneys were left representing that trust in the hands of the bank.

9–86

---

[193] *Financial Services Compensation Scheme Ltd v Abbey National Treasury Services Plc* [2008] EWHC 1897.

[194] *Investors Compensation Scheme v West Bromwich Building Society (No.1)* [1998] 1 B.C.L.C. 493, and *Investors Compensation Scheme v Cheltenham & Gloucester Building Society* [1996] 2 B.C.L.C. 165. See also *Financial Services Compensation Scheme Ltd v Abbey National Treasury Services Plc* [2008] EWHC 1897 (Ch), [2009] Bus. L.R. 465 which held that the Financial Services Authority had the power to assign rights to sue to, or from, third parties.

[195] *Re Lehman Brothers International (Europe) (in administration) v CRC Credit Fund Ltd* [2012] UKSC 6, [2012] Bus. L.R. 667.

9–87   The central principle is based on the provision in principle 10 of PRIN that "a firm must arrange adequate protection for clients' assets when it is responsible for them". This suggests two different duties. First, the firm will acquire fiduciary duties in relation to those assets to ensure their safekeeping while in the firm's custody. Secondly, the firm is required as a matter of practicality to ensure that its customer's assets are held appropriately (commodities should not be allowed to spoil, and so forth). The requirement in COBS that the firm ensure "best execution" would require that the firm acquire the highest reasonably available rate for money held on deposit for the customer, and so forth; but it is suggested that most firms will seek to discharge their obligations to their client's assets subject to contractual obligations limiting their obligations to ensure a maximum return as opposed to best return which can be reasonably obtained in the circumstances. This tension between regulatory requirements and any purported contractual limitation of those requirements will remain a feature of financial practice in the future: obligations under COBS, as is considered in Chapter 10, may not be limited by contract.[196]

C.   The proper interpretation and application of CASS in the case law

Introduction

9–88   There have been several decisions relating to the ownership of assets held by insolvent financial institutions which should have been segregated to the account of their customers under the CASS principles. It was important for the claimant customers to show that there was a trust over assets in their favour so that they would have the status of secured creditors in those financial institutions' insolvencies.

The traditional approach

9–89   The traditional approach to questions of certainty of the subject matter of a trust emerged from the decision of Park J. in *Re Global Trader Europe Ltd (in liquidation)*.[197] As considered in Chapter 21,[198] the traditional approach is that if there is no segregated fund of property which is held on the terms of the trust, then the trust is void. The *Global Trader* case related to derivatives transactions ("contracts for differences" and spread-betting) conducted with a financial institution, Global Trader, which went into insolvency. Global Trader, in essence, held money in accounts for the benefit of its many different customers: some of those accounts were segregated and others were not. It was held that those customers who did not actually have property held separately to their account could not show a trust in their favour; whereas those customers who actually had property held separately to the account could show a trust in their favour. It was

---

[196] See para.10–18.
[197] *Re Global Trader Europe Ltd (in liquidation); Milner and another (liquidators of Global Trader Europe Ltd) v Crawford-Brunt and others* [2009] EWHC 602 (Ch), [2009] 2 B.C.L.C. 18.
[198] para.21–22.

argued on behalf of those customers unfortunate enough not to have had property held separately for them as a matter of fact that the CASS regulations required that property should have been held on trust for them in segregated accounts and therefore that a trust should nevertheless be found: but it was held that because no assets had actually been segregated then there would not be a trust.

The issues following the insolvency of Lehman Brothers

As Lord Walker pointedly observed in the Supreme Court in *Re Lehman Brothers International (Europe) (in administration) v CRC Credit Fund Ltd*,[199] the CASS regulations had been drafted without catering for the possibility that they would be broken: that is, the regulations assume that assets will be segregated in practice and therefore make no provision for a financial institution which fails to segregate client money. So, in *Re Lehman Brothers International (Europe) (in administration)*[200] Briggs J. upheld the traditional principle in the same way as Park J. in *Re Global Trader* to the effect that if, as a matter of fact, assets have not been segregated to the customer's account then there cannot be a trust because a trust must have a trust fund segregated from all other property. In *Re Lehman Brothers International (Europe) (in administration)* Briggs J. was very clear about the principle to be applied in relation to segregation. In that case, Lehman Brothers International Europe ("LBIE") was in the practice of dealing with securities on behalf of itself and affiliated entities through a "hub" entity. In essence, LBIE was in straightforward breach of its regulatory obligations under CASS. This problem was known to the management of Lehman Brothers: "[these problems] were perceived to be of sufficient gravity, either immediately or in the near future, to give rise to the setting up of a small project group of persons within LBIE known as the Regulation and Administration of Safe Custody and Global Settlement working party, or "Rascals" for short, tasked with devising a solution to them. That catchy acronym became the label used for the identification of the processes adopted to address those three perceived problems and, in due course, as the name for this litigation."[201] The "Rascals" project was commenced in 1993 but it had failed to reach an answer by the time the bank fell into insolvency 15 years later.

9–90

The decision in the Supreme Court

The higher courts, however, have taken more purposive approaches to the Lehman Brothers litigation, as is considered in Chapter 21. In essence, the courts were required to consider a situation in which LBIE had failed to segregate client money from other money with the result that there was simply a huge pool of money—containing "house assets" in the form of LBIE's own money, money from LBIE affiliates, and third party clients' money – from which Lehman Brothers generally completed its obligations. On the basis that there was no

9–91

---

[199] [2012] UKSC 6, [2012] Bus. L.R. 667.
[200] [2010] EWHC 2914 (Ch).
[201] [2010] EWHC 2914 (Ch).at [9]. The term "rascals" might be better rendered as "lawbreakers" so as to sound less coy.

segregation of assets, traditional trusts law would have held that there was no valid trust with the result that none of the customers would have been entitled to any secured rights against that fund. Therefore, the Court of Appeal in *Re Lehman Brothers International (Europe) (in administration)*[202] held that there was a single trust over this huge pool of money. In a different Court of Appeal decision in *Re Lehman Brothers International (Europe) (in administration) v CRC Credit Fund Ltd*[203] it was held similarly that on a proper interpretation of the CASS regulations there was a trust imposed over all of the assets held by LBIE and therefore that those assets did not fall to be distributed in the general Lehman Brothers insolvency but rather as assets held for all of the clients whose money was traceable into that central pool.

9–92   The Supreme Court in *Re Lehman Brothers International (Europe) (in administration) v CRC Credit Fund Ltd*[204] held, by a majority, that on the proper interpretation of the CASS regulations (in CASS 7 particularly) there was a statutory trust created over the clients' money from the moment of its receipt by the bank because that is what CASS 7.7.2R suggests literally on its face. The alternative analysis, in accordance with general trusts law, was said (in argument) to be that the trust only arose once the bank segregated the clients' money from other property; however, this analysis was inconvenient because it would mean that no clients would have property rights if the bank simply failed to segregate client money as required by CASS. However, it was held that the statutory trust was to take effect on receipt of the money as suggested by the wording of the statute. Lord Dyson argued, because CASS was implemented to effect the requirements of MiFID in relation to client money, that the intention of CASS should be interpreted to be to safeguard client assets as MiFID required in its recitals. Lord Dyson held that *all* client money is deemed to be held on trust and therefore that all client money is to be protected by the statutory scheme in relation to a distribution of assets on the event of the bank's insolvency. In essence, then, once all client money is deemed to be subject to the trust then all of that money is deemed to be held aside from the general assets of the bank in its insolvency and instead to be distributed according to the CASS rules. Importantly, though, all clients with assets held by the bank under CASS are entitled to share in such a distribution, on a close textual analysis of the provisions of CASS. Moreover, Lord Dyson also advanced a purposive argument on the basis that it was the purpose of MiFID and CASS to protect *all* clients and not simply those who were fortunate enough to have assets set aside for them in fact. As Lord Collins pointed out, a statutory trust can be a very different creature from a trust arising under the general law. Lord Walker, dissenting, felt that this did great harm to the concept of a trust because it allowed a trust to take effect without any trust fund being identified.

---

[202] [2011] EWCA Civ 1544.
[203] [2010] EWCA Civ 917.
[204] [2012] UKSC 6, [2012] Bus. L.R. 667.

D. The general failure of banks to obey and perform their CASS obligations

The failure by Lehman Brothers to perform its regulatory obligations was **9–93** described by Lord Dyson as being a "shocking underperformance" and by Lord Walker (and Briggs J) as being "startling". In truth, there is the usual combination of the arrogance and the concomitant incompetence of the largest banking institutions. As any lawyer who has worked inside banks will attest, there is always an assumption that the banks' profitability and internal perception of its own efficiency will override all other considerations. Before the financial crisis in the era of light-touch regulation there was an assumption that this overrode a bank's regulatory obligations. Other investment banks have failed to obey their obligations under CASS. By means of a Final Notice,[205] Barclays Capital Securities Ltd was found to have breached principle 10 of PRIN (relating to the treatment of client money) and the principles of CASS by failing to segregate client money in the form of money market day deposits, something which had remained undetected for eight years: it was fined £1.12 million. JP Morgan was treated similarly[206] for failing to place client money in a segregated trust account, so that those customers would have been unsecured creditors in any insolvency: the amount of client money at issue over a period of about seven years varied between US\$ 2 billion and US\$ 23 billion. The fine was in excess of £33 million. There have been several other fines levied on smaller firms for breaches of CASS. Notably, all of these actions have taken place since the financial crisis hit (and regulatory practices became sharper) even though many of them stretched back over periods of time before the beginning of the crisis. All of these institutions were knowingly in breach of their fiduciary duties to their customers. A bank is trusted to take proper care of its clients' affairs and deposits. What the CASS breaches reveal is that banks cannot be trusted even to operate accounts on this basis in accordance with the law. This is not about profitability: rather it is about basic competence in the operation of accounts and basic ethics in obeying banks' statutory trust to their customers.

11. THE EFFECT OF A BREACH OF REGULATORY RULES

Breach of the FCA rules does not in general terms constitute a criminal **9–94** offence.[207] That is, the breach of any FCA regulation will not necessarily constitute an offence simply because it is a breach of FCA rules. There are, however, some principles in the FSMA 2000 which, if breached, will constitute an offence: such as the prohibition on selling financial services without authorisation under s.19 of the FSMA 2000 or the prohibition on offering securities to the public without first publishing an approved prospectus under s.85 of the FSMA 2000, and so on. The general context of criminal offences under the FSMA 2000 is considered in Chapter 13.

---

[205] FSA Final Notice, January 24, 2011.
[206] FSA Final Notice, May 25, 2010.
[207] Financial Services and Markets Act 2000, s.151(1). It is suggested that this is something which ought to be revisited: see para.58-01 et seq.

9–95 Section 150 of the FSMA 2000 provides that if a regulated person breaches a regulatory rule under the FSMA 2000 scheme and if that breach causes loss to a private person, then that person has an action at common law in the form of the tort for breach of statutory duty. However, that a provision of the *FCA Handbook* has been breached does not in itself render a transaction void and unenforceable under private law.[208] In part, this saving provision means that a party to a transaction which lost it money cannot simply argue that that transaction is void because it breaches a provision of the *FCA Handbook*. The terms of any agreement between the parties may nevertheless provide for the invalidity of the transaction under ordinary principles of contract law.

9–96 The FCA has powers to seek injunctions and to freeze a person's assets where there has been a breach of a relevant rule. Section 380 of the FSMA 2000 provides that if, on the application of the FCA or the Secretary of State, the court is satisfied that there is "a reasonable likelihood that any person will contravene a relevant requirement" or that any person "has contravened a relevant requirement and that there is a reasonable likelihood that the contravention will continue or be repeated", then "the court may make an order restraining ... the contravention".[209] That person may be ordered to take action to remedy that breach by the FCA over and above the power to seek an injunction.[210] In circumstances in which the FCA has overreached this power, it has been held that the court may supplement its power by awarding an injunction further to s.37 of the Supreme Court Act 1981 to freeze assets held in an investor's bank accounts.[211] The court also has a general power to award injunctions if it is satisfied that that "there is a reasonable likelihood that any person will engage in market abuse" or that "any person is or has engaged in market abuse and that there is a reasonable likelihood that the market abuse will continue or be repeated".[212]

9–97 The court also has the power to make restitution orders. Under s.382 of the FSMA 2000 the court can make a restitution order on the basis of an application from the FCA or the Secretary of State, provided that the court is satisfied that "a person has contravened a relevant requirement" (where a relevant requirement is any rule made further to the FSMA 2000 or an EC directive) or that a person has been "knowingly concerned in the contravention of such a requirement", and furthermore that "profits have accrued to him as a result of the contravention" or "that one or more persons have suffered loss or been otherwise adversely affected as a result of the contravention".[213]

---

[208] Financial Services and Markets Act 2000, s.151(2).

[209] Financial Services and Markets Act 2000, s.380(1).

[210] Financial Services and Markets Act 2000, s.380(2). See *Financial Services Authority v Martin* [2005] EWCA Civ 1422; [2006] 2 B.C.L.C. 193; [2006] P.N.L.R. 11.

[211] *Financial Services Authority v Fitt* [2004] EWHC 1669, Lewison J. See also *Financial Services Authority v John Martin & Co* [2004] EWHC 3255 and *Financial Services Authority v Matthews* [2004] EWHC 2966 (where a failure to comply with s.380 was challengeable only by judicial review). See also *R. (Ex p. Brinsons) v Financial Ombudsman Service Ltd* [2007] EWHC 2534 and *R. (Ex p. IFG Financial Services Ltd) v Financial Ombudsman Service Ltd* [2005] EWHC 1153, where judicial review would not be permitted where the regulator had stuck to its statutory powers and procedures.

[212] Financial Services and Markets Act 2000, s.381(1).

[213] Financial Services and Markets Act 2000, s.382(1).

12. The Powers of the Regulatory Authorities

A. Disciplinary powers

Following on from the preceding section of this chapter, it is clear that the regulatory authorities do not have particularly wide-ranging powers in the event of a breach of a regulatory rule. The regulatory authorities can conduct investigations and freeze assets, but the disciplinary measures which can be imposed are comparatively limited. The absence of a general criminal offence for any breach of a regulatory rule in either the FCA Handbook or the PRA Handbook is perhaps surprising – even if the prosecution of such a breach should be taken out of the hands of the regulatory authorities themselves.

9–98

The regulatory authorities can issue a public censure in relation to any regulated person who contravenes a "requirement" which has either been imposed on that person by the FSMA 2000 or by the regulatory authorities.[214] Such a public censure takes the form of a statement which the authority publishes.

9–99

Similarly, if a regulatory authority considers that a regulated person has breached a "requirement" imposed on them by a regulatory authority or by the FSMA 2000, then the authority may impose a penalty of any amount it considers appropriate on them.[215] However, the authority may not both impose a financial penalty on such a person and also withdraw their authorisation to act under the FSMA 2000 in relation to regulated financial services business.

9–100

The procedure for publishing censure or imposing a penalty is that the authority must first issue a warning notice to the regulated person involved, and only after that may it give the person involved a decision notice.

9–101

B. Removal of securities from trading

The regulatory authorities have the power, further to s.313A of the FSMA 2000, to "require an institution to suspend or remove a financial instrument from trading" wherever that is considered to be appropriate "for the purpose of protecting" either "the interests of investors" or "the orderly functioning of the financial markets".[216] The term "trading" here relates to over-the-counter trading, which is trading not conducted on a regulated market nor on a multilateral trading facility.[217] Any decision to exercise this power can be appealed to the Tribunal.[218] The requirement to remove an instrument from trading takes effect as soon as the notice is "given" or at any other date identified in that notice.[219] Written notice must be given both to the institution in question and to the issuer of the instrument.[220] The notice must give the authority's reasons[221] and inform the

9–102

---

[214] Financial Services and Markets Act 2000, s.205.
[215] Financial Services and Markets Act 2000, s.206.
[216] Financial Services and Markets Act 2000, s.313A(1).
[217] Financial Services and Markets Act 2000, s.313A(3).
[218] Financial Services and Markets Act 2000, s.313A(2).
[219] Financial Services and Markets Act 2000, s.313B(1).
[220] Financial Services and Markets Act 2000, s.313B(2).

recipient that they may make representations to the authority.[222] The authority must also publish its decision in any manner which it deems appropriate, and it must inform the competent authorities of other Member States in the EU.[223] These provisions implement provisions of MiFID.

C. Injunctions and restitution orders

9–103   The authority or the Secretary of State may seek an injunction, further to s.380 of the FSMA 2000, if it believes, and the court is satisfied, that there is "a reasonable likelihood that any person will contravene a relevant requirement".[224] A "relevant requirement" is defined as being any requirement imposed by the FSMA 2000 or by any directly applicable provision of EU law.[225] Alternatively, an injunction may be sought if the authority, and the court, is satisfied that "any person has contravened a relevant requirement and that there is a reasonable likelihood that the contravention will continue or be repeated".[226]

9–104   There is further power to seek an injunction from the court in relation to market abuse. There are two bases on which an injunction may be sought in those circumstances by the FCA. First, where there is considered to be "a reasonable likelihood that any person will engage in market abuse",[227] as the term "market abuse" is defined in Chapter 12 and in s.118 of the FSMA 2000. Second, where "any person is or has engaged in market abuse and that there is a reasonable likelihood that the market abuse will continue or be repeated".[228] The injunction may be one "restraining the market abuse".[229]

9–105   The court may make a restitution order further to s.382 of the FSMA 2000 in circumstances in which there has been a breach of a relevant requirement of the FSMA 2000 or any directly applicable terms of EU law. The court is empowered to make that restitution order obliging the defendant to make a payment of money in circumstances in which "it appears to the court to be just" in the light of any profits that have accrued, or any loss that has been suffered.[230] Restitution orders may be made similarly in situations in which market abuse has taken place or the defendant has encouraged others to commit market abuse.[231] Alternatively, a restitution order may be made in circumstances which the authority considers it appropriate to make a payment of money. The private law analogues for these actions, however, remain opaque. It is unclear whether or not they are intended to map onto English law (or Scots law) actions either at common law, or in equity, or whether they should be limited to "restitution of unjust enrichment" as

[221] Financial Services and Markets Act 2000, s.313B(3)(b).
[222] Financial Services and Markets Act 2000, s.313B(3)(c).
[223] Financial Services and Markets Act 2000, s.313C(1).
[224] Financial Services and Markets Act 2000, s.380(1)(a).
[225] Financial Services and Markets Act 2000, s.380(6).
[226] Financial Services and Markets Act 2000, s.380(1)(b).
[227] Financial Services and Markets Act 2000, s.381(1)(a).
[228] Financial Services and Markets Act 2000, s.381(1)(b).
[229] Financial Services and Markets Act 2000, s.381(1).
[230] Financial Services and Markets Act 2000, s.382.
[231] Financial Services and Markets Act 2000, s.383.

narrowly defined. There is nothing in the statute to suggest a narrow interpretation would be appropriate. The absence of a definition, and the absence of a requirement of an unjust factor, simply requires that the court thinks it appropriate to make restitution in general terms. The requirement is that there must have been a breach of the regulations which have caused a loss to the claimant, or a gain to the defendant, and that a payment of money can then be ordered. There is nothing in the statute which limits the treatment of the gain to being the subtraction of an amount which has been made at the claimant's expense further to an unjust factor, as required by the narrow form of unjust enrichment under English law. The powers of the FCA and the PRA are very broad indeed. It is possible, subject to appeal, for the regulatory authorities to act as investigator, prosecutor, judge and jury in many cases. A good example of this possibility arises in relation to restitution orders where the open nature of the statutory language grants them very broad powers indeed.

13.   THE FSA MARKET TRIBUNAL

The FSMA 2000 creates an enforcement mechanism in the form of the Market Tribunal ("the Tribunal") which was established by s.132 of the FSMA 2000.[232] The Tribunal's rules are created in part under the Financial Services and Markets Tribunal Rules 2001. The Tribunal may have an oral hearing or it may give its decision without a hearing, it may call witnesses, and the applicants and respondents have the opportunity as described in the rules to make representations. Various provisions of the FSMA 2000 permit a reference to be made to the Tribunal by way of appeal from a decision of the FCA. As is considered through Part IV of this book in particular, the FCA will frequently make decisions as to dealings in securities, as well as exercising its general powers under the FSMA 2000 as considered in this chapter.

9–106

14.   JUDICIAL REVIEW

A.   Introduction

Judicial review relates to the actions or culpable inactions of public bodies, in particular the improper exercise of their powers. The FCA is a public body exercising powers given to it under statute, as is the PRA. Therefore, in the exercise of its rule-making powers, its discretions and its powers to penalise regulate persons, the FCA is subject to judicial review. The applicability of principles of judicial review in this context are considered briefly in this section.[233]

9–107

---

[232] SI 2001/1775.
[233] See generally P. Craig, *Administrative Law*, 5th edn (London: Sweet & Maxwell, 2003).

B. Improper exercise of powers by a public body

9–108   The famous formulation of the principle governing improper exercise of its powers by a public body by Lord Greene in *Associated Provincial Picture Houses Ltd v Wednesbury Corporation*[234] was that a court can only interfere with the decision of a public body in exercising its powers if that decision "is so unreasonable that no reasonable authority could ever come to it". This precise formulation has been doubted in later cases but no clear expression of the principle has yet replaced it, with terms such as "irrationality" being used on occasion (but nevertheless failing to convince all commentators completely).[235] The sorts of issue which are covered by judicial review include bad faith, dishonesty, bias, failing to take into account relevant considerations, taking into account irrelevant considerations, disregard of public policy, failure to apply appropriate common law or statutory rules as to the exercise of powers, and failure to follow the appropriate procedures in an appropriate fashion. Hence use of the general heading for this section "improper exercise of powers by a public body". If a public body, such as the FCA, were to commit any of these improper exercises of its powers, then it would be open to proceedings for judicial review and the types of remedy considered below. However, it has been held that it is not an abuse of process for the FCA to exercise its statutory powers to make prohibition orders under s.56 of the FSMA 2000,[236] or where it has followed the procedure set out in its regulations creating further to the FSMA 2000.[237]

C. Procedural impropriety

9–109   When the FCA is exercising its powers to admit securities to listing, to approve a prospectus, and so forth, it must exercise those powers appropriately and in accordance with its own rules and procedures as contained in the *FCA Handbook*. The case law on judicial review has developed principles of natural justice[238] and "fairness"[239] in relation to the implementation of such procedures. Thus, a regulated person who is subject to such a decision by the FCA is entitled to have the procedures in the *FCA Handbook* adhered to and, for example, to have information given to her about the nature of the complaint which has been made against her.[240] There are some cases which suggest a distinction between applications for rights (such as applications to the FCA for approvals) and the forfeiture of rights which have already been granted (such as the discontinuance of a listing of securities) or which were expected to be granted.[241] However, this

---

[234] [1948] 1 K.B. 223.

[235] See, e.g. De Smith, Woolf and Jowell, *Principles of Judicial Review* (Sweet & Maxwell, 1999), p.447.

[236] *R. (Ex p. Davis) v Financial Services Authority* [2003] 1 W.L.R. 1284, affirmed [2004] 1 W.L.R. 185.

[237] *R. (Ex p. Griggs) v Financial Services Authority* [2008] EWHC 2587.

[238] *Ridge v Baldwin* [1964] A.C. 40.

[239] *Re HK* [1967] 2 Q.B. 617, 630, per Lord Parker C.J.

[240] e.g. in *Ridge v Baldwin* [1964] A.C. 40 a chief constable subject to disciplinary proceedings was entitled to know the detail of the complaint made against him.

[241] *McInnes v Onslow Fane* [1978] 1 W.L.R. 1520.

distinction would seem irrational because it would deny, in the securities context, applicants for admission to listing a fair hearing.[242] It is suggested that the presence of the Market Tribunal is significant in providing a forum for fair hearings: the question will be whether or not the hearings which are provided are fair in practice.

D. Legitimate expectations

The principal context in which a person may form legitimate expectations would be in relation to the exercise of decision-making powers by the FCA where the FCA had given that person to believe that the power would be exercised in a given way when in fact it was not so exercised.[243] The representation made to the applicant must have been clear and unambiguous, or its inference must have resulted from some consistent behaviour over a lengthy period of time sufficient to create such an expectation in the applicant's mind.[244] The former type of representation would be formed by an express communication from the FCA, which may include a circular or statement of regulatory guidance which is addressed to the market generally and not necessarily to the applicant specifically.[245] By contrast, the latter might be created by a consistent approach of the FCA to a particular form of behaviour by the applicant which was suddenly subjected to a harsher regulatory treatment which had not previously been the case (unless, it is suggested, there had been an intervening change in the substance of financial regulation or legislation[246]). It is suggested that the guidance notes in the *FCA Handbook* (particularly those which suggest clear examples of the sorts of activity which will attract a particular regulatory treatment) are the clearest statements which will raise expectations in the minds of regulated persons or issuers of securities seeking approvals and so forth from the FCA.

9–110

E. Remedies

Generally, judicial review proceedings seek to require the public body to make its decision again and to give relief to the successful applicant, but the court will not seek to make the public body's decision for it. An applicant may seek an interim injunction before trial seeking to postpone to effect of the decision which is being challenged. After trial, the principal remedies would be an order of mandamus to compel the proper performance of the public body's powers where the public body has made a jurisdictional error in deciding not to exercise a power which could be exercised in respect of a person such as the applicant; an order of certiorari to quash the decision and thus to require that the decision be taken again; an injunction on equitable grounds, for example preventing the public

9–111

---

[242] See De Smith et al, *Principles of Judicial Review*, 277.

[243] *Ex p. Coughlan* [2001] Q.B. 213.

[244] *Ex p. Unilever* [1996] S.T.C. 681.

[245] *Ex p. Hamble* [1995] 2 All E.R. 714.

[246] e.g. *Ex p. Kingsley* [1996] C.O.D. 241, cited in P. Craig, *Administrative Law*, p.651.

body from committing some sort of wrong or to prevent an unlawful decision; or a declaration, pronouncing on the "legal state of affairs"[247] in relation to the applicant.

15. THE REGULATION OF PARTICULAR MARKET SECTORS AND THEIR DISCUSSION IN THIS BOOK

A. In general

9–112 A number of the key heads of regulation imposed by the FCA and the PRA are discussed in the remaining chapter of this Part III of this book. This section introduces the principles underpinning those rules and cross-refers the reader to the appropriate discussions.

B. Conduct of business

The purpose of conduct of business regulation

9–113 One of the key regulatory codes in the *FCA Handbook* relates to conduct of business. These rules are effected further to the provisions of the EU Markets in Financial Instruments Directive ("MiFID")[248] and are discussed in detail in the next chapter. In essence, conduct of business regulation requires regulated entities to classify the expertise of their clients and so to ensure that they are selling only suitable products to those clients in a suitable manner. Regulated entities are also required to be transparent about their fees and charges and any other terms and conditions on which business is conducted.

The impact of MiFID on conduct of business regulation

9–114 MiFID was implemented by the Conduct of Business Sourcebook ("COBS") as from November 1, 2007.[249] Broadly speaking there are three areas of regulation covered by MiFID: first, the authorisation and required organisation of investment firms; secondly, the organisation and transparency of securities markets; and, thirdly, regulation of the conduct of business between investment firms and their customers. MiFID has required the re-drawing and intensification of conduct of business regulation. Conduct of business is considered in Chapter 10.

---

[247] See De Smith et al. *Principles of Judicial Review*, p.597.
[248] 2004/39/EC.
[249] Financial Services and Markets Act 2000 (Markets in Financial Instruments) Regulations 2007 (SI 2007/126).

C.   Financial promotion

The financial promotion rules control the manner in which advertisements and   **9–115**
promotion of financial products are made by regulated entities. The principal rule
is that such promotions may not be made by people who are not authorised,
unless they fall within the detailed exceptions to the legislation. The financial
promotion code—in what is termed the "financial promotion restriction"—
provides that no person shall "in the course of business, communicate an
invitation or inducement to engage in investment activity".[250] Contravening this
provisions constitutes a criminal offence.[251] Financial promotion is discussed in
Chapter 11.

D.   The criminal law and regulatory offences

The principal discussion of criminal law relating to financial market activity is set   **9–116**
out in Part IV of this book. In particular, Chapter 13 considers the basis of the law
on financial crime. The following are the principal criminal offences which apply
in relation to finance law.

Market abuse

The abuse of inside information about an entity's securities or the manipulation   **9–117**
of a market are both forms of market abuse. Market abuse is regulated by the
FCA, as is discussed in Chapter 12. Insider dealing and market manipulation are
both criminal offences, as is discussed in Chapter 14.

Insider dealing

The offences relating to insider dealing are set out in Pt V of the Criminal Justice   **9–11**
Act 1993 ("CJA 1993").[252] Part V was passed to enforce the provisions of the EC
insider dealing directive,[253] the preamble to which set out the purpose of the
legislation to be to provide an "assurance afforded to investors that they are
placed on an equal footing and that they will be protected against the improper
use of inside information". There are three offences relating to insider dealing.
The principal offence in s.52(1) of the CJA 1993 is on individuals who deal in
"price-affected" securities using information which they gleaned as an insider.
The second offence relates to encouraging others to deal in price-affected
securities. The third offence relates to disclosing inside information to others.
There are then a range of defences to these offences.

---

[250] Financial Services and Markets Act 2000, s.21(1).
[251] Financial Services and Markets Act 2000, s.23(1).
[252] See para.14–01.
[253] 89/592/EC [1989] OJ L334/30.

Market abuse under FSMA 2000

9–119   The creation of the "civil offences" of market abuse under s.118 et seq. of the
FSMA 2000 which have empowered the regulatory authorities to impose
penalties outside the mainstream criminal law.[254] Any criminal offences are still
prosecuted under the criminal law in the ordinary way, but the FCA has limited
competence under market abuse regulation to impose penalties by means of the
Market Tribunal[255] for a limited range of acts as provided in FSMA 2000. Section
119 of the FSMA 2000 requires the FCA to create a Code on Market Conduct to
specify with greater exactitude what sorts of behaviour would and would not
constitute market abuse.[256] That Code is referred to as "MAR 1" within the *FCA
Handbook* and is considered in detail in Chapter 12.

9–120   Among the criminal offences is the offence of making misleading statements is
contained in s.397 of the FSMA 2000.[257] That offence is committed when a
person makes a statement, promise or forecast which "he knows to be misleading,
false or deceptive in a material particular";[258] or, secondly, where a person
"dishonestly conceals any material facts" in relation to a statement, promise or
forecast[259]; or, thirdly, where a person "recklessly makes (dishonestly or
otherwise) a statement, promise or forecast which is misleading, false or
deceptive in a material particular".[260] There is a further offence provided for in
s.397(3) of the FSMA 2000 if a person performs any act which creates a "false or
misleading impression as to the market in or the price or value of any relevant
investments", provided that that act was done "for the purpose of creating that
impression and of thereby inducing another person", broadly, to deal in any given
way with those securities.

E.   Money laundering

9–121   Money laundering is regulated as part of the code of regulation concerned with
property which is derived from a criminal lifestyle. This code is discussed in
Chapter 15, in common with its related criminal offences. Money laundering,
properly so-called, relates to the use of the financial system to procure and to
conceal money for organised crime. The public policy behind this area of law has
tended to relate to money acquired from drug trafficking and money used in
terrorist activities, although the legislation as contained in the Proceeds of Crime
Act 2002 extends further than that.

---

[254] It is, of course, a nice jurisprudential question to consider the line between the ordinary criminal
law, whereby guilt and sentence are established by the courts, and the situation in which a statutory
public body (the FSA) is empowered to imposed financial and other penalties on market participants.
[255] See para.9–61.
[256] Financial Services and Markets Act 2000, s.119.
[257] cf. *R. v De Berenger* (1814) 3 M. & S. 66.
[258] Financial Services and Markets Act 2000, s.397(1)(a).
[259] Financial Services and Markets Act 2000, s.397(1)(b).
[260] Financial Services and Markets Act 2000, s.397(1)(c).

F. The Financial Conduct Authority's power to make regulatory rules for the protection of consumers

The FCA is empowered to "make such rules", that is its general rules[261] applying to authorised persons and regulated activities, "as appear to it to be necessary or expedient for the purpose of protecting the interests of consumers".[262] The reference to consumers in this context is telling because it displaces the possible claims to pre-eminence of any other of the regulatory duties such as the integrity of the market for financial services or the economic interests of the UK. "Consumers" are defined as anyone who uses or may simply be contemplating using the services of an authorised financial services provider and, significantly, also refers to people whose rights may be derived from the users of such services.[263]

9–122

G. Liability for losses arising from an investment

Section 150(1) of the FSMA 2000, breach of a statutory rule is actionable by any private person who has suffered loss as a consequence to recover damages. Any regulation may, however, exclude the operation of s.150(1) if it does so expressly.[264] Breach of statutory duty is discussed in Chapter 25.[265] Otherwise, the FCA is authorised to create a range of types of rules relating to price stabilisation,[266] financial promotion by way of cold-calling or advertisement,[267] money laundering,[268] and control of information.[269] Those rules may exclude explicitly any penalty otherwise provided for under FSMA 2000[270] but otherwise a claimant would be entitled to recover damages for loss in general terms under the Act subject to "the defences and incidents" of, what is termed, "breach of statutory duty".[271]

9–123

---

[261] Financial Services and Markets Act 2000, s.138(2).
[262] Financial Services and Markets Act 2000, 138(1).
[263] Financial Services and Markets Act 2000, s.138(7).
[264] Financial Services and Markets Act 2000, s.150(2).
[265] See para.26–53.
[266] Financial Services and Markets Act 2000, s.144.
[267] Financial Services and Markets Act 2000, s.145.
[268] Financial Services and Markets Act 2000, s.146.
[269] Financial Services and Markets Act 2000, s.147.
[270] Financial Services and Markets Act 2000, s.149(1).
[271] Financial Services and Markets Act 2000, s.150(1).

CHAPTER 10

CONDUCT OF BUSINESS

CORE PRINCIPLES

Conduct of business regulation is concerned with the proper treatment of customers by regulated firms. In effect, firms are required to sell only suitable financial products to their clients and they must do so in a suitable manner. To ensure that this is done, the firm must classify each customer's level of expertise and treat them accordingly.

The source of conduct of business regulation is in the EC Markets in Financial Instruments Directive ("MiFID"). This directive is based on the establishment of general principles with which regulated firms must comply. This marks a change from earlier regulatory styles in which the regulations tended to specify in detail the requirements with which the firm should comply, so that the firm did not need to consider in any greater detail how their business was conducted beyond simply obeying the rules. Now firms are required to consider how to organise their businesses so as to comply with much more general principles.

All regulated persons must act "honestly, fairly and professionally". Regulated persons are required to communicate with their customers in a way which is "clear, fair and not misleading". The firm is required to warn the client if she is proposing to participate in investments which are beyond her expertise, but bears no obligation to prevent the client from so doing once that warning has been given. The firm is more generally required to act in the client's best interests and must ensure that the price at which any investment is acquired is the best available price (the "best execution" requirement). The regulations provide in detail for the manner in which information must be provided to clients. None of these obligations may be excluded by contract.

Clients must be classified between professional clients, "eligible counterparties", and inexpert retail clients. It is possible for clients to move between categorisations so as to be treated differently in general terms or in relation to specific transactions.

One particularly interesting possibility for conduct of business principles is as a means of supplying the objective standards of "reasonableness", "honest behaviour" and so forth which are required to make out a number of private law claims. Put briefly, if a judge needs to know what would have constituted, for example, reasonable behaviour for a regulated financial institution then the conduct of business regulations provide a statement of exactly how that person should have behaved.

1. INTRODUCTION

10–01   At its roots, financial regulation is concerned to protect investors from the worst excesses of the open market. The Financial Conduct Authority ("FCA") is the agency charged in the UK with responsibility for overseeing investor protection. One of the most significant means in the *FCA Handbook* of ensuring that investors are protected is the Conduct of Business Sourcebook ("COBS") which was introduced in its amended form on November 1, 2007 by way of the implementation of the Markets in Financial Instruments Directive ("MiFID").[1] COBS is also the most significant means of ensuring that there is one way of conducting financial business between expert counterparties and another way of conducting business when an expert firm is dealing with inexperienced investors, so that the fabled "widows and orphans" (that is, inexpert investors in need of advice) receive a more benign treatment than professional investors. It is important to recall that financial regulation is not intended to prevent investors from suffering losses, as was discussed in Chapter 3. Instead, the purpose of financial regulation is to ensure that investors are provided with enough information to make informed decisions when buying financial products (and thus to take the risk of either making a profit or suffering a loss) and that those investors are treated suitably by regulated financial firms during the contractual process. One way of thinking of the principles considered in this chapter is as a compilation of regulations which supplement the ordinary rules of contract law by imposing positive obligations on regulated firms. More straightforwardly, the regulations considered in this chapter impose obligations on regulated firms when acting with different types of customer.

---

[1] The Financial Services Authority was renamed the Financial Conduct Authority ("FCA") by the Financial Services Act 2012, s.6. The FCA assumed its powers and responsibilities from April 1, 2013.

The old Financial Services Authority has been "renamed" as the "Financial Conduct Authority" ("FCA"). As explained in Chapter 8, the *FCA Handbook* came into effect on April 1, 2013, and replaced the FSA Handbook in nearly identical terms.

2. CONDUCT OF BUSINESS OBLIGATIONS IN MiFID

A. The purpose of conduct of business regulation

The cultural change ushered in by MiFID

The purpose of conduct of business regulation is to place the onus of ensuring proper behaviour on regulated institutions ("authorised firms" in the jargon) in accordance with principles set down in the regulations. It is not a system whereby the regulator watches the conduct of business in each transaction. Rather, the authorised firm is required to develop appropriate procedures of its own to ensure that it complies with the general, framework principles contained in the legislation and in the regulations. So, in an effort to give authorised firms enough leeway to develop their own ways of conducting business, there are few "hard-and-fast", black-letter rules which require simple obedience. The method of conducting regulation by means of so-called "black letter" rules was criticised in the old days for encouraging a "box ticking headset"—meaning that authorised firms did not give any real thought to whether or not they were treating their customers properly, because they were instead going through the motions of obeying the detailed regulations by simply "ticking boxes" and carrying out the precise tasks required of them by the regulations without thinking any more deeply about whether or not they were providing the best service to their customers. This "box-ticking" approach could be thought of as obeying the letter of the regulations, but not really complying with their spirit.

10–02

The whole culture of regulation changed with MiFID: instead of generating only strict rules, authorised firms were given a range of principles with which they were required to comply and compliance in turn required that the authorised firms devise their own mechanisms for doing business appropriately. This new culture is a form of "light touch" regulation in that the authorised firms are being left to create their own compliance mechanisms. Within authorised firms this caused tremendous disquiet in the lead-up to the implementation of MiFID. Those firms were very concerned that their structures and systems might not pass muster with the old Financial Services Authority. Because there were no hard-and-fast rules, they could not know with certainty what approach the Authority would have taken to the practical implementation of the regulations' general principles. The benefit of framework principles of this sort is that they ought to allow authorised firms to innovate and to develop systems in a way that suits their organisation and business best, instead of having to comply with a "one size fits all" regulatory model. The downside for regulated firms is that they cannot always be sure that their systems will be considered satisfactory by the regulator: in some ways, people employed in the compliance departments of

10–03

financial institutions prefer a list of tasks they are required to do because once all the boxes are ticked they know that they have done all that is required of them. However, it is a changed world now. In the wake of the financial crisis 2007–09, in the wake of the many banking mis-selling scandals such as the PPI and interest rate swap mis-selling revelations in relation to ordinary bank customers and small businesses, and in the wake of the "Libor fixing" scandal (all of which are discussed in Chapter 45) it is unlikely that the newly-minted FCA will be quite so relaxed in its regulatory approach about the way in which banks treat their clients in any context. Therefore, the era of "light touch" regulation is, hopefully, gone. However, the principles-based approach to regulation which requires financial institutions to act in "the best interest of their client" still presents a pro-active and ethical component in the regulatory armoury. By requiring financial institutions to reflect actively on the ways in which they can best serve their customers and achieve "best execution" for them (as considered below) it is impossible for them to rest on their laurels or to overlook their duties to their customers.

"Know your client"

10–04　The keynote of conduct of business regulation is establishing a "suitable" way of doing business with each customer. This is sometimes referred to as "know your client" regulation because it requires that the financial institution find out about its clients: the level of their expertise in financial matters, the purposes for which the financial product in question is being sought, whether or not the client understands the risks associated with the strategy that is being proposed, and so on. There are other obligations imposed on authorised firms by the regulations which generally aim for transparency in the way that the firms conduct their business: making fees plain, and so forth.

High-level principles

10–05　Conduct of business regulation must be understood in the light of the high-level principles which are set out in the *Principles for Businesses* rulebook. Thus, authorised firms must act with "integrity".[2] Furthermore, MiFID requires that authorised firms act "honestly, fairly and professionally in accordance with the best interests of its clients".[3] This underlines the nature of the regulation in this area: firms' compliance with the conduct of business regulations will be interpreted in the light of these principles of integrity and proper behaviour. These principles are considered in greater detail below.

10–06　As outlined above MiFID has signalled a change in regulatory style as well as content. That regulation is now organised by reference to high-level principles, as was discussed in Chapter 9, requires investment firms to think about how they will organise their businesses to be compliant with financial regulation, instead of simply obeying a series of simple regulatory rules unthinkingly. Conduct of

---

[2] See para.8–29.
[3] MiFID, art.19(1).

business regulation has undergone a cultural shift, for example, by requiring investment firms to seek the "best execution" of transactions in the customer's interests: something which requires a three-dimensional understanding of each customer's objectives, status and requirements, as opposed simply to a "box-ticking" regulatory style which would not require such a close analysis of the appropriateness and suitability of investment products for each customer.

The imposition of positive obligations

One of the key distinctions between private law and conduct of business regulation is that conduct of business regulation imposes "positive obligations" on authorised firms. That means authorised firms are required to take action to discharge their obligations, as opposed to "negative obligations" which require simply that one refrain from doing something. Private law is generally reluctant to impose positive obligations on parties; unless they have agreed to assume those obligations, for example by way of contract. As discussed in Chapter 26, Scott L.J.[4] and Millett J.[5] both took the view, in relation to claims that the defendant banks ought to have known that money had passed through their hands in breach of trust, that "account officers are not detectives" and therefore that neither bank bore any positive obligations to investigate the source of payments which were made through their accounts.[6] The courts are concerned not to create obligations which the parties have not voluntarily assumed. This is the exact opposite of financial regulation. The purpose of financial regulation is to impose regulations on authorised firms to ensure the proper functioning of financial markets. So, in Chapter 15 *Money Laundering* we shall see that banks do bear positive obligations to notify the authorities about any suspicious payments which pass through its accounts; in this chapter we shall see that authorised firms bear positive obligations in relation to the conduct of business with their customers. In this chapter in examining conduct of business regulation we shall consider positive obligations in the proper treatment of customers. This form of regulation is, in many ways, at the heart of the regulation of transactional finance.

10–07

B.   The scope of MiFID

The Markets in Financial Instruments Directive ("MiFID")[7] replaced the Investment Services Directive[8] of 1993 in relation to the regulation of markets in financial instruments. Its implementation in the UK has been effected by the introduction of a Conduct of Business Sourcebook ("COBS"), which replaced a previous version, from November 1, 2007, and also by secondary legislation.[9]

10–08

---

[4] *Polly Peck v Nadir (No.2)* [1992] 4 All E.R. 769.
[5] *Macmillan v Bishopsgate (No.3)* [1996] 1 W.L.R. 387.
[6] By "its accounts" in this contexts is meant accounts which are managed by the bank for its customers.
[7] 2004/39/EC.
[8] 93/22/EEC.
[9] Financial Services and Markets Act 2000 (Markets in Financial Instruments) Regulations 2007 (SI 2007/126). See *Financial Services Authority v Fox Hayes* [2009] EWCA Civ 76 for an example of

MiFID has been supplemented by the MiFID Implementing Directive ("MID")[10] and a Commission Regulation.[11] Broadly speaking there are three areas of regulation covered by MiFID: first, the authorisation and required organisation of investment firms; secondly, the organisation and transparency of securities markets; and, thirdly, regulation of the conduct of business between investment firms and their customers. It is this last purpose which concerns us here. For the future, as considered in Chapter 7, there is a proposal to replace MiFID with a Regulation (dubbed "MiFIR") which would create a single rulebook for client treatment across the EU with a stiffened approach to client care:[12] these policy questions are considered in the text to follow.

C. The general obligations of proper behaviour

Acting "honestly, fairly and professionally"

10–09   MiFID imposes a number of obligations of what could be termed broadly "proper behaviour": these are general principles by reference to which the behaviour of an authorised firm will be analysed. Investment firms are required to act "honestly, fairly and professionally in accordance with the best interests of their clients"[13] and to comply with the conduct of business obligations set out in the directive.

Article 19 of MiFID: that communications be "fair, clear and not misleading"

10–10   A number of high-level obligations are imposed on investment firms by art.19 of MiFID. The principal obligation imposed on an investment firm is an obligation of acting with integrity in relation to information provided to clients, such that all information addressed to clients or potential clients "shall be fair, clear and not misleading".[14] The second obligation relates to the provision of information about the investment firm itself to its clients and also about the proposed investment[15] such that information should be provided in a comprehensible form, whether relating to the investment firm itself, or to the financial instruments and proposed investment strategies which are being suggested to the client; or to the level of guidance as to the risks associated with investments in those instruments, or to the costs involved. The investment firm is required to avoid conflicts between its own interests and the interests of its customers.

---

communications which did not satisfy this standard, where a firm of solicitors forwarded information from overseas companies (in return for a secret commission) about investment opportunities to potential investors.

[10] 2006/73/EC.
[11] 1287/2006/EC.
[12] See para.7–61 et seq.
[13] MiFID art.19(1).
[14] MiFID art.19(2).
[15] MiFID art.19(3).

The assumption of risk by the customer

The keynote is always that the proposed investment or instrument be suitable for the client's purposes. EC legislation, just like the FSMA 2000, functions not by requiring the seller of an instrument to remove all possible risks but rather by requiring the seller to provide the buyer with sufficient, suitable information for a buyer of that level of expertise to form an informed view of the appropriateness of the risks involved. To do this the investment firm is obliged to take active steps to identify the client's level of expertise, in the form of that client's "knowledge and experience in the investment field relevant to the specific type of product or service", as well as his personal circumstances.[16] It is then required that member states—through the FCA in the UK—ensure that investment firms undertake this scrutiny of their clients.[17]

10–11

However, the extent of the investment firm's obligations stop at warning the client: the client may nevertheless decide to continue with the investment or financial strategy: in this regard the investment firm would be required to demonstrate that it had acted suitably in bringing all of the risks to the client's attention.[18] The investment firm is required to keep documentation of each stage of the transaction: documentation risk being a major part of the risk in many complex financial markets.[19] Finally, there is an obligation imposed on investment firms in the form of a kind of transparency requirement, such that the client "must receive from the investment firm adequate reports on the service provided to its clients", including information about costs and services undertaken on his behalf.[20]

10–12

Client classification

The heart of conduct of business regulation is identifying the needs and level of expertise of each customer. There is a division generally between different categories of client: retail clients, that is ordinary individuals or companies without expertise in financial matters; professional clients, being people with some expertise in financial matters; and market counterparties who are other financial institutions with expertise in the appropriate financial markets.[21] The technical division between these categories are considered in greater detail below. In essence, the regulations require that investment firms assess the knowledge and expertise of each client according to those broad categorisations, and that those investment firms then deal with each client appropriately taking into account that client's objectives and the suitability of any investment product for that client as a result. The detail of the client classification rules contained in the "COBS" rulebook, based on MiFID, are considered in detail below.

10–13

---

[16] MiFID art.19(4).
[17] See A.S. Hudson, *Securities Law*, para.3–68.
[18] MiFID, art.19(6).
[19] MiFID, art.19(7).
[20] MiFID, art.19(8).
[21] MiFID, Preamble (31).

10–14   The conduct of business rules prioritise the need for the sellers of financial products—that is, those who are authorised under the FSMA 2000 to sell financial services and financial instruments—to categorise their customers according to the level of each customer's knowledge and expertise, and as to the suitability of the investments in question for the customer's purposes. The regulatory aim is to ensure that authorised financial service providers then deal with their customers in an appropriate manner: taking care to explain risks and documentation to inexpert, "retail" customers, in a way that is not considered necessary in relation to expert, "market counterparty" customers because the latter type of customer has knowledge and expertise with which to enable it to assess the risks associated with the activities in which it is involved which the former does not. Consequently, the manner in which business is done and the type of business which can be done with inexpert customers differs from that which can be done with more expert customers; and also the manner in which business is done with inexpert customers differs from the manner in which it can be done with expert customers. In effect, the seller of financial products is required to maintain the suitability of both the means by which the product is sold and the nature of the product itself.

Procuring "best execution" for the customer

10–15   One of the most significant developments made by MiFID over previous practice was the requirement that any authorised firm must ensure that when conducting business for its clients that it procures the "best execution" of that business. This requirement is expressed art.21 of MiFID to the effect that:

> "investment firms take all reasonable steps to obtain, when executing orders, the best possible result for their clients taking into account price, costs, speed, likelihood of execution and settlement, size, nature or any other consideration relevant to the execution of the order."

This is referred to in the preamble to the directive as the "best execution" requirement. It imposes a difficult obligation on investment firms to seek out the best price, executed in the cheapest and most efficient manner, and concurrent with the client's general objectives. This requirement is considered in detail later in this chapter with the remaining principles relating to conduct of business.[22]

3.   THE REGULATION OF CONDUCT OF BUSINESS

A.   The core principle: looking to "the client's best interests"

The requirement of looking to the client's best interests

10–16   Each investment firm is required to act "honestly, fairly and professionally in accordance with the best interests of its client".[23] This rule is referred to in COBS as the "client's best interests rule". As is referred to below in relation to the "best

---

[22] See para.10–41.
[23] MiFID art.19(1); COBS, 2.1.1R.

execution principle",[24] the conduct of business principles are important because they impose positive obligations on investment firms to look to the best interests of their clients. This is more, it is suggested, than simply avoiding conflicts of interest under FCA regulation or under the general law of fiduciary obligations: those obligations are, in effect, a negative obligation not to allow conflicts of interest. By contrast, conduct of business regulation imposes positive obligations on investment firms to act in their clients' best interests, which in turn requires that investment firms assess their clients' objectives so that their clients' best interests can be ascertained and achieved. Otherwise, the requirement to act honestly may be satisfied by acting in compliance with regulation and otherwise than dishonestly, and the requirement of acting fairly might be satisfied by avoiding acting unfairly. However, the qualification that the firm must act in accordance with the client's best interests imposes an important positive gloss on that obligation. Private law does not ordinarily impose positive obligations to act unless a person has voluntarily accepted them; whereas conduct of business regulation does impose positive obligations to act in the client's best interests, as well as to act honestly and fairly in general terms. Moreover, a firm will not be considered to be acting in accordance with the client's best interests rule if they receive any fee or commission beyond that payable for the services provided to the client as an inducement and so forth.[25] Any such commissions must be disclosed.[26] The investment firm is also obliged to comply with the conduct of business obligations set out in the directive.

Whether looking to the client's best interests is a fiduciary requirement

An issue of private law arises here too: there is a question as to whether or not an obligation to act in the client's best interests imposes a fiduciary duty on the investment firm when handling that client's affairs. Millett L.J. described as fiduciary as being "someone who has undertaken to act for or on behalf of another in a particular matter in circumstances which give rise to a relationship of trust and confidence".[27] Lord Browne-Wilkinson held that a fiduciary is characterised by the circumstance in which "one party, A, has assumed to act in relation to the property or affairs of another, B".[28] It is questionable whether on Lord Browne-Wilkinson's definition the investment firm has "assumed to act" in the client's affairs: it could be said that the investment firm may simply have agreed to advise the client, not to manage her affairs. If the investment firm assumed responsibility for the investment decisions in the client's portfolio—such as a trustee or the scheme manager in a unit trust—then the firm would be acting as a fiduciary. By contrast, the conception of Millett L.J. that there must be a "relationship of trust and confidence" chimes in far more closely with the entire purpose of conduct of business regulation which is that an investment firm is an organisation which must act in the best interests of its client and on whose advice

10–17

---

[24] See para.10–41.
[25] MID, art.26; COBS, 2.3.1(1)R.
[26] COBS, 2.3.1(2)R and COBS, 2.3.2R.
[27] *Bristol and West Building Society v Mothew* [1998] Ch. 1, 18, per Millett L.J.
[28] *White v Jones* [1995] 2 A.C. 207 at 271.

the client is entitled to place reliance: that is a relationship of trust and confidence, which would therefore appear to be fiduciary in nature. As considered next, the investment firm may not exclude its liabilities under the directive. However, the firm may point to the fact that the detail of its obligation is to provide advice to the client and so leave the final decision as to the making of the investment to the client: which means that the fiduciary responsibility could be said to extend only to the giving of advice and not as to the decision which the client ultimately chooses to make. This issue is considered below in relation to "best execution" and was considered in Chapter 5.[29]

B. No exclusion of liability

10–18 An important part of the limitation of positive obligations under the general law is the use of exclusion of liability clauses in contracts and in trust deeds and so forth. Ordinarily, unless there is some unconscionable quality to the creation of such a contract or trust, the courts will enforce those exclusion of liability provisions. However, this is not the case with financial regulation. Financial regulation should be thought of instead as being a code of mandatory legal principles: that is, principles which cannot be excluded by agreement of the parties. COBS provides explicitly that:

> "A firm must not, in any communication[30] relating to designated investment business seek to:
> (1)   exclude or restrict; or
> (2)   rely on any exclusion or restriction of
> any duty or liability it may have to a client under the regulatory system.[31]"

Thus the obligations created, inter alia, by COBS and the rest of the regulatory rulebook may not be excluded by the firm in communications with its clients. The Unfair Contract Terms Regulations and the rest of the general law (except, it is suggested the law on exclusion of liability, or else this provision would be rendered otiose) are explicitly prayed in aid to the extent that they prevent a firm from seeking to restrict or exclude any duty or liability owed to a consumer.[32] Best practice under the client's best interest rule is not to seek to exclude one's liability as a firm.[33]

---

[29] See para.5–32.

[30] It is not clear whether "any communication" is intended to cover the initial conduct of business agreement between the parties as well as later communications, or not. It is suggested that if it were not covered then this provision would be of no practical effect because it would be circumvented by an ordinary exclusion of liability clause.

[31] COBS, 2.1.2R.

[32] COBS, 2.1.3(2)G.

[33] COBS, 2.1.3(1)G.

C.   The obligations relating to provision of information

Communications to be fair, clear and not misleading

As was considered in outline above, the second obligation in art.19 of MiFID relates to the provision of information, in the following terms:

10–19

> "(2)   All information, including marketing communications, addressed by the investment firm to clients or potential clients shall be fair, clear and not misleading.[34]"

The overriding principle is therefore an obligation of acting with integrity in relation to information provided to clients. Fairness in communications, it is suggested, should include a notion that the information be suitable for the particular client. For example, the information should not seek to cajole an inexpert client into purchasing an overly complex and overly risky product for the client's purposes by emphasising some information and suppressing other information. Fairness would also require that it present a balanced view of the information at issue and not over-emphasise, for example, investments in relation to which the investment firm is acting as a market maker or as a systematic internaliser and in relation to which it stands to make some personal profit. Fairness should also require that the investment firm observe its fiduciary obligations: the breach of such an obligation could not constitute fair or conscionable behaviour by an investment firm.[35] Clarity in communications should be appropriate, it is suggested, for the level of expertise of the intended type of recipient and, inter alia, their ability to understand market jargon and complex financial information. That the information should not be misleading speaks for itself, and reflects on the discussion of misrepresentation and the doctrine in *Hedley Byrne v Heller* in Chapter 25.[36]

The obligation to provide appropriate information

The regulation of financial services is predicated primarily on giving customers all of the information necessary for them to make informed decisions as to their use of financial instruments. Thus, the third obligation in art.19 of MiFID relates to the provision of information about the investment firm itself to its clients and also about the proposed investment[37]:

10–20

> "(3)   Appropriate information shall be provided in a comprehensible form to clients or potential clients about:
> the investment firm and its services,
> financial instruments and proposed investment strategies; this should include appropriate guidance on and warnings of the risks associated with investments in those instruments or in respect of particular investment strategies,
> execution venues, and
> costs and associated charges

---

[34] MiFID art.19(2).
[35] See para.5–01 et seq.
[36] See para.25–26 et seq.
[37] MiFID art.19(3); COBS 2.2.1R.

so that they are reasonably able to understand the nature and risks of the investment service and of the specific type of financial instrument that is being offered and, consequently, to take investment decisions on an informed basis. This information may be provided in a standardised format."

An essential part of conduct of business regulation is that the proposed investment or instrument be suitable for the client's purposes. All of the responsibility for ensuring that the instrument is suitable is not imposed on the investment firm which is selling it. Rather the provision of appropriate information is in part concerned with enabling the customer to make an informed decision. In this sense the requirement is that the seller provided information giving "appropriate guidance on and warnings of the risks associated with investments in" the proposed "instruments or in respect of particular investment strategies": that is, the seller must warn the client and explain the context of the proposed strategy. Also of great significance is the provision of information as to all costs and charges which may arise in relation to the parties' business.

Standard of communication with customers and a comparison with case law

10–21 As considered above, COBS provides a general requirement that when the seller communicates information to a customer, it must do so in a way which is "clear, fair and not misleading".[38] This principle is an advance over the pre-FSMA 2000 (and therefore now defunct) Bank of England London Code, particularly as it affected the decision of the High Court in *Bankers Trust v Dharmala*.[39] In that case it was held by Mance J., partly in reliance on best practice established by the Bank of England London code, that the seller was not obliged to disclose all of the risks associated with a product to the buyer and also, importantly, that the seller's officers were entitled to recognise that it would make a large profit from the transaction at its client's expense without being liable for regulatory breach or for misrepresentation or fraud. Under this expanded principle of "clear, fair and not misleading" communications in COBS it is suggested that the seller would need to ensure that its marketing material and also any statements made at meetings were not capable of being misconstrued, that they were clear as to their effect, and that they were entirely "fair" with regard to the customer's own position. In this regard, the regulations provide that the seller must have regard to the level of knowledge which the buyer has of the transaction at issue when making written or oral communications.[40] Further, the seller must ensure that its officers do not take any inducements or "soft commissions" in effecting transactions.[41]

10–22 A retail client, or an inexpert professional client (who was either recognised as being inexpert by the seller or who asked to be treated as being inexpert (as permitted under s.3.7 of COBS, considered above)) would be in a better position now in relation to common law or equitable claims of the sort brought in *Bankers*

---

[38] COBS, 4.2.1R.
[39] [1996] C.L.C. 481.
[40] COBS, 4.8.1R et seq.
[41] COBS, 2.3.1R.

Trust v Dharmala because the investment firm would not be able to hide behind either the less exacting London Code nor behind a judge's finding that as a professional firm Dharmala ought to have been able to form its own assessment of the risks associated with the products in question. Rather, it is suggested, the investment firm's knowledge that their clients were inexpert, and therefore that profits could be made comparatively easily from transacting with them due to the investment firm's greater knowledge and expertise, in itself would constitute a breach of the requirement that an investment firm must act with integrity, and use its power to identify a professional client as having insufficient expertise so that that client should be re-categorised under COBS 3.7.3R, even though in COBS 3.7.2G it is the responsibility of a professional client to ask for the higher protections offered under COBS.

D.   Client classification under MiFID

Investment advice: client classification under MiFID and the obligations to take active steps to assess the client's level of expertise, and personal objectives

A key part of conduct of business regulation is the so-called "know your client" process whereby an investment firm must evaluate the nature of its clients and the suitability of any investment product which is intended to be sold to a client. The fourth and fifth obligations in art.19 of MiFID relate to the investment firm's duties to take active steps to identify the client's level of expertise, in the following terms[42]:

10–23

> "(4)   When providing investment advice or portfolio management the investment firm shall obtain the necessary information regarding the client's or potential client's knowledge and experience in the investment field relevant to the specific type of product or service, his financial situation and his investment objectives so as to enable the firm to recommend to the client or potential client the investment services and financial instruments that are suitable for him."

Suitability requirements are at the heart of conduct of business regulation. The investor is required to make her own decisions but only on the basis that she has been provided with sufficient information in an appropriate form to make informed decisions. To identify the appropriateness of the proposed investments, the investment firm selling the security is required to evaluate the client's level of expertise in the appropriate form of instrument, her financial circumstances, and her personal objectives.

This fourth principle requires that the financial institution consider the client's situation. This principle applies when the institution is either providing "investment advice"—which it is suggested would not include banking or mortgage lending, but would include the acquisition of securities—or "portfolio management", which relates to a range of investments which is intended to minimise the risk of loss across the portfolio. Therefore, the considerations here

10–24

---

[42]   MiFID art.19(4).

are as to the client's ability to understand the risks associated with any given investment strategy and her investment objectives. For example, in an investment portfolio one might seek to maximise profit, which requires an increase in risk. An expert investor might therefore wish not only to acquire shares in blue chip companies but also bonds of a low credit worth (because they tend to generate the highest returns in the bond market) and derivatives. An inexpert investor with an intention of earning steady profits over the long-term would probably require a portfolio with blue chip shares and perhaps government or high credit worth bonds, intending to earn income profit over time. These are the sorts of considerations which the financial institution would be required to consider, and having done so to refrain from selling complex derivative investments to inexpert clients, and so on. The language of this principle is also interesting: the institution should "recommend" investments to the client, and not "instruct" nor "take charge" of the investment portfolio.

The obligation on the financial institution if the investment is unsuitable for the client

10–25   The previous discussion related to advice as to investment advice and portfolio investment strategies under the fourth principle. The fifth principle identifies what is to happen in the event that the financial institution forms the view that the financial instruments under discussion are not suitable for that client. MiFID's fifth principle provides as follows[43]:

> "(5)   Member States shall ensure that investment firms, when providing investment services other than those referred to in paragraph 4 [set out immediately above], ask the client or potential client to provide information regarding his knowledge and experience in the investment field relevant to the specific type of product or service offered or demanded so as to enable the investment firm to assess whether the investment service or product envisaged is appropriate for the client.
>
> In cases the investment firm considers, on the basis of the information referred to under the first subparagraph, that the product or service is not appropriate to the client or potential client, the investment firm shall warn the client or potential client. This warning may be provided in a standardised format.
>
> In cases where the client or potential client elects not to provide the information referred to under the first subparagraph, or where he provides insufficient information regarding his knowledge and experience, the investment firm shall warn the client or potential client that such a decision will not allow the firm to determine whether the service or product envisaged is appropriate for him. This warning may be provided in a standardised format."

The investment firm is required to obtain information from the client as to her levels of knowledge and experience. The obligation on the investment firm is then to "warn" the client if the investment is not appropriate. Significantly, the investment firm is not obliged to resile from a transaction which it believes might be inappropriate for the client at issue. Instead, its obligation is to warn the client either that the instrument may be inappropriate or that the client has failed to provide sufficient information for such an assessment to be conducted by the

---

[43] MiFID art.19(5).

investment firm. Under COBS, an investment firm must ensure that the buyer understands the risks associated with the product[44] and give an appropriate risk warning, as considered above.

There are contexts in which investment firms do not have to follow the fifth **10–26** MiFID principles. So, investment firms will not be obliged to perform this assessment in (5) above in the following circumstances[45]:

> "(6)   Member States shall allow investment firms when providing investment services that only consist of execution and/or the reception and transmission of client orders ... to provide those investment services to their clients without the need to obtain the information or make the determination provided for in paragraph 5 ..."

So, if the firm is not giving advice, and in that sense is not structuring investment structures or portfolios for the client, but rather is merely taking orders from the client, then the firm is not required to inquire whether or not the investment is suitable for the client. An analogy for this distinction might be as follows: if you hire a caterer to cater for your wedding celebration then you might rely on the caterer to help you construct an appropriate menu, in which case the caterer would owe obligations to ensure that the menu is appropriate for the customer's needs; whereas if you are simply ordering takeaway food from the counter at a "fish 'n' chip" shop, then there is no obligation on the chip shop owner to ask whether the meal is intended for a wedding breakfast and whether it is therefore appropriate. So, if a financial institution is advising a client on the structure of its portfolio, then it is required to consider the suitability of the product for the client; whereas if the client merely contacts the institution to make a single order, then there is no such obligation.

What might be problematic is the situation in which the institution gives advice to **10–27** the client on Day 1, and then some time later the client delivers an order to the institution without taking any further advice. If this arrangement has been procured by the investment firm to avoid liability under the COBS principles— that is, organising that advice is given in one transaction, and that the client is required to make the order separately on its own cognisance—then it is suggested that that would not be sufficient for the institution to act with integrity because it is artificially organising the arrangement without looking to the client's best interests nor its expertise so as effectively to exclude its own liability. However, if a year had passed since the advice was given originally, and if the client had decided that she did not want to transact with the investment firm at that time, but later changed her mind and contacted the firm to acquire simple investments such as a parcel of shares in a publicly quoted company, then it is suggested that the investment firm would simply be receiving an order and so might not bear obligations to inquire into the suitability of those investments in the context. If the client in this second example had contacted the investment firm to acquire a complex investment like an interest rate swap, then it is suggested that the firm's obligations would have been revived due to the inherent complexity of that financial instrument.

---

[44]   COBS, 10.3.1R, and see also COBS, s.9.6 generally.
[45]   MiFID art.19(6).

E.   Client classification under COBS

The categories of client under COBS

10–28   Chapter 3 of COBS, titled "client categorisation", sets out the FCA regulation on how investment firms are required to approach the categorisation of clients. There are four categories of client in Chapter 3: clients, retail clients, professional clients, and eligible counterparties. The first question is to identify who will be a "client" in the first place. Any person for whom a firm carries on regulated business under the Regulated Activities Order or any ancillary activity is a client of that firm.[46] A client includes any potential client of such a firm.[47] Any person to whom a financial promotion is communicated or "is likely to be communicated" is a client of that firm.[48] These rules do not include corporate finance contracts nor venture capital contracts.[49]

10–29   Then we come to the business of classification. There are three types of client: professional clients, eligible counterparties and retail clients. A "retail client" is defined as being a person who is neither a professional client nor an eligible counterparty.[50] Therefore, we need to define those two latter provisions first. We shall consider professional clients and then eligible counterparties.

Professional clients

10–30   A "professional client" is a client, as defined above, and who is either a "per se professional client" or an "elective professional client".[51] A "per se professional client" will include (unless classified differently under a later classification[52]) a credit institution (that is, a bank), an investment firm, an insurance company, a collective investment scheme, a pension fund or its management, a commodity or commodity derivatives dealer, "a local", or any other institutional investor.[53] In relation to MiFID or third-country business, a "per se professional client" would be either an institution which satisfies two of the following standards in that it has: a balance sheet total of £20 million, net turnover of £40 million, or own funds of £2 million; or is a large body corporate or limited liability partnership with called up share capital of £10 million or a large undertaking which satisfies two of the following standards in that it has: a balance sheet total of £12.5 million, net turnover of £25 million, or an average number of employees during the year of 250.[54]

10–31   A person may elect to be treated as a professional counterparty so that investment business may be done in a different fashion. Such "elective professional clients"

---

[46] COBS, 3.2.1(1)R.
[47] COBS, 3.2.1(2)R.
[48] COBS, 3.2.1(3)R.
[49] COBS, 3.2.2G.
[50] COBS, 3.4.1R.
[51] COBS, 3.5.1R; MiFID art.4(1)(11).
[52] COBS, 3.5.2(1)R.
[53] COBS, 3.5.2(1)R.
[54] COBS, 3.5.2R generally.

may be treated as such if the firm has undertaken "an adequate assessment of the expertise, experience and knowledge of the client that gives reasonable assurance, in light of the nature of the transactions or services envisaged, that the client is capable of making his own investment decisions and understanding the risks involved".[55] It is also required that the client must ask in writing to be treated as an elective professional client, and that the client has been given a written warning by the firm of the rights and protections which the client may thus lose, and the client must state in writing in another document that it is aware of the consequences of losing those rights and protections.[56] In relation to MiFID or third-country business, it is required that two of the following three requirements are satisfied: the client must have carried out at least ten transactions of sufficient size per quarter over the previous four quarters; that the client's instrument portfolio exceeds 500,000; or that the client has worked in the financial sector for at least one year in a professional position which required knowledge of the transactions which he envisages entering into.[57] However, an elective professional client is not to be assumed to possess the knowledge and experience of a "per se professional client".[58]

Eligible counterparties

The categories of eligible counterparties divide between "per se" clients and "elective" clients, as with professional clients above. A "per se eligible counterparty" will include (unless classified differently under a later classification[59]) a credit institution, an investment firm, an insurance company, a collective investment scheme, a pension fund or its management, any other EC or EEA approved financial institution in the securities or banking or insurance sectors, an exempted dealer under MiFID, a national government, a central bank, or "a supranational organisation".[60]   **10–32**

A client may be an elective eligible counterparty if it is a "per se professional client" or if the client requests such a categorisation in respect of transactions in relation to which it could be treated as a professional client.[61] A counterparty's confirmation that it wishes to be treated in this fashion may be obtained under a general agreement covering all future transactions or on a transaction-by-transaction basis.[62]   **10–33**

While clients may request to "trade up" to a higher, elective category, a firm is obliged to allow a professional client or an eligible counterparty to be re-categorised as a form of client with a higher degree of protection.[63] Alternatively, a firm may "on its own initiative" treat clients as retail clients or   **10–34**

[55] COBS, 3.5.3(1)R.
[56] COBS, 3.5.3(3)R.
[57] COBS, 3.5.3(2)R.
[58] COBS, 3.5.7G.
[59] COBS, 3.6.2(1)R.
[60] COBS, 3.6.2(1)R. cf. MiFID art. 24(2).
[61] COBS, 3.6.4R.
[62] COBS, 3.6.6R.
[63] COBS, 3.7.1R.

otherwise under a more beneficial regime from the perspective of client protection.[64] Re-categorisation may take place on a trade-by-trade basis or in relation to classes of transaction or in relation to all transactions.[65] The client must be informed of such a re-categorisation.[66]

Re-classification under COBS

10–35   An important issue arises in relation to the possibility of the re-classification of a client under the COBS categories, in particular in relation to an investment firm realising on its own initiative that a client should be re-classified under COBS. Significantly it was the old Financial Services Authority's view that it is the responsibility of a professional client to ask for the higher protections offered under COBS[67] if that client has been classified as being overly expert, and therefore the onus is not on the investment firm to re-categorise a client it considers to be less expert than the client considers. It is a thorny question, however, whether or not an investment firm could be said to be acting with integrity if it failed to re-categorise a client when its officers realised that that client did not possess the knowledge and expertise that the parties have previously considered the client had. After all, if I do not have sufficient knowledge or expertise to judge a transaction, then how can I be said to have had the knowledge or expertise to attest that I had sufficient knowledge or expertise to understand and thus accept the risks associated with a particular categorisation? A firm acting with integrity, it is suggested, should refuse to treat a client in accordance with the categorisation which the client desires if there is good reason to believe, either before or after the original categorisation, that that client does not have the appropriate level of expertise or knowledge. To do otherwise would be severely to diminish the effect of both parts of the "know your client" regulatory project, which are: first, the client's evidence as to its own expertise and, secondly, the investment firm's genuine investigation and ongoing sense of whether or not that evidence gives as meaningful assessment of that client's knowledge and expertise. Investor protection regulation, such as that in COBS, requires that firms protect clients from their own naivety at this stage, even if it does not go anything like as far as requiring a firm to refrain from making a profit from a client with greater self-confidence than skill. The purpose of this regulation is to expose investors to appropriate levels of risk and that must require that the classification process is carried out in good faith. Once the client has been properly classified, then the appropriate level of risk and the appropriate form of product can be identified; but if the client is knowingly misclassified, then the purpose of the regulation is subverted. Consequently, it is appropriate for the firm to be liable if the client is knowingly misclassified either from the outset or at some later stage.

---

[64] COBS, 3.7.3R.
[65] COBS, 3.7.7G.
[66] COBS, 3.7.6G.
[67] COBS 3.7.2G.

When mixed business involving MiFID and third country business is conducted **10–36** with a client, then that client must be categorised in a way which is appropriate for MiFID business.[68]

Procedures relating to communications

Firms are required to document their classification decisions.[69] The firm's **10–37** internal policies and procedures for the categorisation of clients must be put in writing.[70] Communications with clients must be conducted in accordance with the financial promotions rules in Chapter 4 of COBS. These communications must comply with art.19(2) of MiFID considered above[71] in that those communications must be fair, clear and not misleading.[72] In so doing the firm must take into account the information which is to be conveyed and the purposes for which it is being conveyed.[73] Financial promotions in this regard must explain any risk to a client's capital, must give a balanced impression of the short and long term prospects for an investment's yield, must give sufficient information in relation to complex charging structures for a product from which the firm earns some commission or benefit, must name the FCA as regulator, and must give an appropriate impression of packaged or stakeholder products.[74] Provided that an investment firm has taken reasonable steps to ensure that its communications comply with the requirement for fair, clear and not misleading communications, then this constitutes a defence to an action for damages under s.150 of the FSMA 2000.

The following principles relate to communications to retail customers. When **10–38** communicating with retail clients, information must include the firm's name, must not emphasise the benefits of relevant investments without also giving a "fair and prominent indication of any relevant risks", must be sufficient to be understood by a member of the group at whom it was directed and must be presented in a way so as to be similarly understood.[75] Any comparisons made with other products or other firms must be meaningful and presented in a fair and balanced way.[76]

The principles relating to financial promotion in general are considered in Chapter 11.

---

[68] COBS, 3.1.4R.
[69] COBS, 3.8.2R.
[70] COBS, 3.8.1R.
[71] See para.10–10 above.
[72] COBS, 4.2.1R.
[73] COBS, 4.2.2G.
[74] COBS, 4.2.4G.
[75] COBS, 4.5.2R.
[76] COBS, 4.5.6(1)R.

F.   The need to document transactions appropriately

10–39   One vexed issue in relation to transactions between professional counterparties is that of failure to document transactions, and a further problem which arises all too frequently is that of mistakes made in negotiations between parties or misapprehensions being formed in the minds of inexpert clients. Thus, the obligation in the seventh paragraph of art.19 of MiFID provides that[77]:

> "(7)   The investment firm shall establish a record that includes the document or documents agreed between the firm and the client that set out the rights and obligations of the parties, and the other terms on which the firm will provide services to the client. The rights and duties of the parties to the contract may be incorporated by reference to other documents or legal texts."

The investment firm is required to keep a record of the various rights and obligations between the parties. There are two problems with this provision as drafted. First, there is no obligation here to provide a copy of that record to the client. Secondly, it is not always the case that contracts between parties to financial transactions will be effected in writing and therefore there will not necessarily be "documents agreed between" the parties.

G.   The obligation to provide adequate reports

10–40   The further obligation to provide adequate reports is a form of transparency requirement, in the following terms[78]:

> "(8)   The client must receive from the investment firm adequate reports on the service provided to its clients. These reports shall include, where applicable, the costs associated with the transactions and services undertaken on behalf of the client."

The foregoing conduct of business obligations do not apply if the investment service is already regulated by another provision of Community legislation.[79]

H.   Best execution under MiFID

The "best execution" requirement

10–41   The most difficult requirement from the perspective of implementation by investment firms is the requirement in art.21 of MiFID that:

> "investment firms take all reasonable steps to obtain, when executing orders, the best possible result for their clients taking into account price, costs, speed, likelihood of execution and settlement, size, nature or any other consideration relevant to the execution of the order."

---

[77] MiFID art.19(7).
[78] MiFID art.19(8).
[79] MiFID art.19(9).

This is referred to in the preamble to the directive as the "best execution" requirement. This requirement is set out in Ch.11 of COBS.[80] It imposes a difficult obligation on investment firms to seek out the best price, executed in the cheapest and most efficient manner, and concurrent with the client's general objectives. Compliance with this requirement is dependent on the following factors.

To comply with this objective, the investment firm is required, in the words of the directive,[81] to achieve the best possible result for the client. The firm must develop execution policies to achieve that result in respect of "each class of instruments".[82] Those policies must consider different venues for the execution of such transactions and the factors affecting the choice of execution venue.[83] Investment firms are then required to provide information about these policies to clients, including whether or not execution may involve execution outside a regulated market or MTF.[84] Clients are then entitled to receive information from the firm to demonstrate that execution was carried out in compliance with those policies. Investment firms are then required to monitor the effectiveness of their execution policies with a view to correcting any deficiencies in those policies.[85] Commission regulations in this regard are then required to ensure the "fair and orderly functioning of markets".[86]

10–42

The best execution requirement in art.21 of MiFID, it is suggested, adds a new dimension to the obligations imposed on investment firms. Whereas the common law would look only at the terms of the contract between the parties and enforce them—unless there was some unconscionable factor, such as duress or undue influence, bound up in its creation—financial regulation takes a different approach. Financial regulation imposes positive obligations on investment firms regardless of the terms of their contracts with their customers. The requirement of best execution is an example of such an obligation; the requirement that an investment firm act with integrity under the *Principles for Businesses* rulebook is another. A requirement to procure "best execution" is a requirement, in the words of the Directive,[87] to achieve "the best possible result" for the client in any given transaction. So, high transaction costs and so forth cannot simply be passed on to retail customers without the investment firm first conducting a form of due diligence as to the most appropriate structure and execution package from the client's perspective. Instead, the investment firm bears a positive obligation to seek the best overall deal for the client which is in accordance with that client's general objectives.

10–43

---

[80] COBS, 11.2.1R, et seq.
[81] MiFID art.21(2).
[82] MiFID art.21(2).
[83] MiFID art.21(3).
[84] MiFID art.21(3).
[85] MiFID art.21(4).
[86] MiFID art.21(6).
[87] MiFID art.21(2).

Whether the "best execution" requirement imposes fiduciary obligations on a regulated firm

10–44 There are circumstances, it is suggested, in which conduct of business regulation may also create fiduciary obligations, as well as negative their avoidance. The definition of what constitutes a person a "fiduciary" advanced by Asquith L.J. in *Reading v R*[88] was that

> "'fiduciary relation' exists . . . whenever the plaintiff entrusts to the defendant a job to be performed, for instance, the negotiation of a contract on his behalf or for his benefit, and relies on the defendant to procure for the plaintiff the best terms available . . ."

This reference to procuring the "best terms" correlates closely with the requirements of best execution in that investment firms acquire the best available price for the transaction (the "best execution" requirement) tallies exactly with the dicta of Asquith L.J. that such an obligation constitutes a fiduciary obligation.[89] It is suggested that when going through the process of seeking to acquire the best terms for the client, the financial institution is obliged to act selflessly in the client's interests and therefore should be interpreted as being a fiduciary in that context. This issue was considered in Chapter 5.[90]

I. Client order handling

10–45 Investment firms are required to ensure that orders executed on behalf of clients are conducted by reference to "procedures and arrangements" which "provide for the prompt, fair and expeditious execution of client orders".[91] In deciding what will constitute prompt, fair and expeditious execution of client orders reference should be had to their performance "relative to other client orders or the trading interests of the investment firm".[92]

J. Suitability

Suitability in the conduct of business: suitability of method of sale and suitability of the product in itself

10–46 It is important not only that the product is suitable for its purpose, but also that the product is appropriate for the particular client[93] and also that its advice to buy a particular product is given in a suitable way.[94] As COBS provides,[95]

---

[88] [1949] 2 K.B. 232 at 236.
[89] *Reading v Att Gen* [1951] 1 All E.R. 617.
[90] See para.5–32.
[91] MiFID art.22(1).
[92] MiFID art.22(1).
[93] COBS, 10.2.1R.
[94] COBS, 9.2.1R. Practice in conduct of business regulation has been that, in relation to retail clients, the seller is required to keep its treatment of such customers under regular review. The polarisation rules require that the seller be giving independent advice wherever possible and that in circumstances in which it is acting otherwise than entirely in the clients interests—for example, if it is a market

"A firm must take reasonable steps to ensure that a personal recommendation, or a decision to trade, is suitable for its client".

Therefore, the test adopted throughout MiFID and COBS, as considered above, is that the seller must have taken "reasonable steps"—an expression which is also adopted in the case law for example in relation to the enforcement of domestic mortgages against co-habitees of the mortgagor[96]—in relation to its treatment of that client. The type of reasonable steps which will be suitable are not susceptible of general definition but rather will vary greatly, depending on the needs and priorities of the private customer, the type of investment or service being offered, and the nature of the relationship between the firm and the private customer and, in particular, whether the firm is giving a personal recommendation or acting as a discretionary investment manager. In so doing the firm is required to ensure that the product is the most suitable of that type of product for the purpose,[97] and bear in mind that further to MiFID in terms of best execution another product may be more suitable if it would be available at a lower price and would achieve the client's objectives.[98] To achieve that objective, COBS provides further that:

"A firm must obtain from the client such information as is necessary for the firm to understand the essential facts about him and have a reasonable basis for believing, giving due consideration to the nature and extent of the service provided, that the specific transaction to be recommended, or entered into in the course of managing:
(a)   meets his investment objectives;
(b)   is such that he is able financially to bear any related investment risks consistent with his investment objectives; and
(c)   is such that he had the necessary experience and knowledge in order to understand the risks involved in the transaction or in the management of his portfolio."

Therefore, the firm is required to inquire closely into the client, the client's own level of experience and expertise, and that person's risk appetite in effect. The firm must also consider whether or not the client is likely to be able to meet the cost of that transaction. Therefore, a regulated firm may not simply rely on the common law concept of caveat emptor (i.e. let the buyer beware) and simply sell the client anything it wishes to sell in the expectation that the client will protect itself. Instead, conduct of business regulation imposes a significant limitation on the freedom of regulated firms to contract in private. For a firm to be acting with integrity (under Principle 1 of the PRIN rulebook) then that firm must observe these regulations relating to the treatment of its clients, even if the common law (of contract and tort) might otherwise have treated the situation differently.[99] What a firm must do, in consequence, is to prepare a questionnaire

---

maker or acting as a discretionary fiduciary of some sort—then that status must be communicated adequately to the client in the context of the buyer's level of expertise.
[95]   COBS 9.2.1R.
[96]   *Barclays Bank v O'Brien* [1994] A.C. 180.
[97]   COBS, 9.2.1R et seq.
[98]   COBS, 11.2.1R et seq.
[99]   As is considered in Chs 25 and 26, the law set down by *Hedley Byrne v Heller* [1963] 2 All E.R. 575, [1964] A.C. 465 is much more sensitive to context than traditional common law principles; although the law of contract, as considered in Ch.17, for example, is still wedded to traditional concepts of caveat emptor in the creation of contracts, as the Court of Appeal held in *Peekay v ANZ* [2006] EWCA Civ 386, see para.17–34.

on which the client will provide all of these sorts of information. The firm is then entitled to rely on the information given to it by its customer, unless it is aware that that information is manifestly out of date, inaccurate or incomplete.[100] As will emerge, some of the cases considered in relation to fraud (Chapter 24[101]) and negligence (Chapter 25[102]) like *JP Morgan v Springwell*, have tended to overlook the inquiries which a regulated firm is required to make and which a regulated firm will have made into its client when deciding what sorts of product to sell to that client and the manner in which it will deal with that client. However, other cases, such as *Camerata Property Inc v Credit Suisse Securities (Europe) Ltd*,[103] have paid them more attention. This issue of the overlap between financial regulation and the substantive law was considered in Chapter 3.[104]

The obligation to give warnings as to risks

10–47   Under COBS and under art.19(5) of MiFID, an investment firm must ensure that the buyer understands the risks associated with the product[105] and give an appropriate risk warning, as considered above. This notion of sufficient risk warning was significant in *Bankers Trust v Dharmala*[106] in deciding whether or not the buyer could be taken to have understood fully all of the risks associated with the *interest rate swaps* involved.[107] Another interesting example of this development of a notion of suitability in the case law is *Morgan Stanley v Puglisi*[108] in which the Italian-speaking Mr Puglisi, contracting on his personal account, was classified by Morgan Stanley as an "expert customer" by virtue of an expert's version of the bank's terms of business letter being sent to him. Morgan Stanley sold Puglisi a principal exchange-rate-linked security which lost Mr Puglisi a large amount of money when the Italian lira and the Spanish peseta were devalued in 1992. The principal issue in that case was whether or not the product at issue constituted a contract for differences and whether the customer was entitled to rescission on the basis that the effects of and the risks associated with the transactions into which he was induced to enter had been misrepresented to him. In this context, the question related to the means by which the seller misallocated the customer's status—by treating an inexpert customer as an expert—whilst also trying to repackage the failed derivative contract as a repo to achieve rollover of the transaction. It was held that as a private customer, even one who had some experience of entering into smaller but complex transactions with other sellers, he ought not to have been sold the complex contracts for differences by Morgan Stanley. In consequence this constituted a breach of the applicable regulatory principles. However, Longmore J. would not imply further terms into their contract as to the seller's obligations to provide information

---

[100] COBS 9.2.5R.
[101] See para.24–24 et seq, 24–29, and 24–36 et seq.
[102] See para.25–16 et seq.
[103] [2011] EWHC 479 (Comm); [2011] 2 B.C.L.C. 54.
[104] para.3–25.
[105] COBS, 10.3.1R, and see also COBS, s.9.6 generally.
[106] [1996] C.L.C. 481.
[107] See A. Hudson, *Financial Derivatives*, para.7–01 et seq. See also para.40–26 of this book.
[108] [1998] C.L.C. 481.

outwith the principles of the relevant financial regulations. The obligations imposed by COBS, however, it is suggested, provide a more extensive set of positive obligations on the investment firm in any event, as considered immediately above in relation to *Banker Trust v Dharmala*.

CHAPTER 11

FINANCIAL PROMOTION

CORE PRINCIPLES

One of the key components of financial regulation is control over the manner in which investment products are marketed to the general public. It is an offence under s.21 of FSMA 2000 to market regulated products to any person without authorisation from the Financial Conduct Authority ("FCA"). There are a number of statutory exceptions to this offence. Of particular concern are the activities of "boiler rooms" which pressure members of the public into investing in (often) inappropriate products. Financial promotion regulation is thus aimed at investor protection.

1 INTRODUCTION

11–01   The Financial Services and Markets Act 2000 ("FSMA 2000") contains a code on "financial promotion" which provides that no person may "in the course of business, communicate an invitation or inducement to engage in investment activity", unless they are already authorised to promote that particular financial product or unless their liability is excluded.[1] So, the general prohibition is hedged in with exceptions where the communication is made by an authorised person or is an authorised communication. It is important to regulate the manner in which financial institutions of all types sell and market their products to every type of customer. The preceding chapter considered the regulations on the classification of clients so that they are sold products which are suitable for them in a suitable way. Regulating the manner in which financial promotion is conducted—whether that is through telephone marketing, advertisements, information on websites or otherwise—is one of the key ways in which the regulators can ensure that financial products are sold to customers in a suitable way. Financial products can be dangerous because they involve risks which the inexperienced customer may not understand. Private customers stand to lose their homes, their savings and their livelihoods if they acquire the wrong product, or they stand to be unprotected against other risks which they might otherwise have avoided. Therefore everything from oleaginous salesmanship in high street banks to high-pressure sales techniques from criminal enterprises need to be controlled, and the customer protected.

11–02   When regulating financial activity, one of the key phenomena which requires regulation is the way in which financial products are sold and to whom they are sold. Perhaps the most egregious types of mis-selling in modern financial markets are the methods used by the so-called "boiler rooms". A boiler room is a group of people who are brought together by an unregulated, unauthorised and therefore illegal organisation to sell worthless or non-existent investments to unsuspecting private individuals. Many of these boiler rooms selling into the UK, and targeting ordinary UK citizens (usually in their homes or sometimes at their workplaces), are physically located in other countries (often coastal resorts) where English-speaking travellers seeking temporary work can be found easily and where office space is cheap. A boiler room was defined in *In re Inertia Partnership LLP*[2] in the following terms:

> "These are generally off-shore entities which are not authorised or exempt for the purposes of the 2000 Act. They cold-call private individuals in the UK … and try to encourage them to buy shares in unlisted companies.[3] The shares tend to be significantly overpriced. The sales

---

[1] Financial Services and Markets Act 2000, s.21(1).

[2] [2007] EWHC 502 (Ch), [2007] Bus. L.R. 879, at [5], *per* Jonathan Crow QC.

[3] That is, smaller companies which are not entered on the Official List and thus not compliant with the regulatory code governing those shares, as considered in Chs 39 and 40.

techniques of boiler rooms are typically persistent, often high pressure. They may also make misrepresentations, usually concerning the imminent flotation of the company on an investment exchange, and/or the likely resale value of the shares currently on offer. Their activities are pernicious."

A boiler room is probably so-called because they are high pressure selling environments in small rooms in which the sellers are encouraged to use high pressure telephone sales techniques to sell these unattractive investments to unsuspecting and unsophisticated members of the public. As will emerge from this chapter, selling, promoting or advertising financial products, securities or investments without authorisation is a criminal offence,[4] whether that is done from inside the UK or from another jurisdiction selling into the UK.

A good example of one sort of activity that is carried on by boiler rooms can be seen in the film *Boiler Room*.[5] This film has become a hit with young traders. An unscrupulous young man called Michael Brantley establishes a stockbroking firm called JT Marlin (deliberately so-named to make it sound like Wall Street's JP Morgan) in a small office block far from New York City on the Long Island Expressway.[6] He filled the trading floor with unqualified but aggressive young men[7] who sell worthless companies that Michael is promoting illegally. These young men are all promised that they will become millionaires within three years. He offers unlawfully high commissions (called "rips") to his traders so that they will do whatever it takes to sell their worthless stock to "whales"—inexperienced but moderately wealthy private individuals whom they cold-call on the phone. The scene in which Vin Diesel's character (Chris Varick) manipulates a doctor over the phone into buying worthless shares, in front of a hushed and awed trading floor, is one of the high points of the film, and a favourite among real-life traders.[8] Unsuspecting customers are induced by these clever criminals into investing all of their savings in worthless companies, while Michael Brantley already has a plan to move his operation at a moment's notice to another office block if the authorities find him. Before the payment protection insurance ("PPI") scandal hit UK banks with fines and awards of damages worth billions of pounds in 2012, it would have been thought that sly, unscrupulous sales tactics were the preserve of criminal, unregulated organisations like the fictional JT Marlin. But what the PPI scandal showed, as discussed in Chapter 45, was that all of the major high street banks in the UK were actively involved in mis-selling insurance

11–03

---

[4] Financial Services and Markets Act 2000, s.19.

[5] *Boiler Room*, 1999, in which a trading floor (on a more lavish scale than most boiler rooms) is established in New Jersey to sell worthless securities under high pressure by testosterone-fuelled young men to middle-class professionals who are beguiled by the salesmen and their promises of quick profits.

[6] We are told that the offices are located near "Exit 53 on the Long Island Expressway".

[7] We first meet these traders at a cocaine-fuelled celebration in an out-of-town hotel, where prostitutes wait for them in hotel rooms. It would be reassuring if all of this were fictional: but see Seth Freedman, *Binge Trading: The real inside story of cash, cocaine and corruption in the City* (Penguin, 2009). The final scene in the film is the denouement of the FBI and the SEC arriving at the firm's offices to make arrests.

[8] The film is reputedly based on interviews with real-life traders in the USA. Ironically the traders in the film also hero-worship Michael Douglas's unscrupulous character Gordon Gecko in the film *Wall Street* and his best known speeches: "lunch is for wimps", "greed is good", and so forth. These traders even know the precise moments when Michael Douglas coughs while delivering his lines.

to customers who simply did not need it. It also shows that financial promotion regulation has much further to go both in terms of regulating the sales practices of everything from fly-by-night boiler rooms to well-established clearing banks in the UK.

2. THE RESTRICTION ON FINANCIAL PROMOTION

A. The general restriction on financial promotion

11–04 The general code on financial promotion, set out in s.21 of the FSMA 2000, provides that no one may either invite or induce another person to engage in investment activity[9] in the course of a business.[10] This is the heart of the code: unauthorised (and therefore unregulated) people may not sell financial services and investments of the types discussed in Chapter 9. The financial promotion restriction does not apply to authorised firms, as a result of s.21(2) of the FSMA 2000.[11] Therefore, a firm which is regulated by the Financial Conduct Authority ("FCA") is not bound by this general prohibition to the extent that it is authorised to act; rather, the conduct of business rulebook governs the manner in which such a firm conducts its business (as discussed in the previous chapter. The general prohibition is also circumscribed by further exceptions. All of these issues are discussed later in this chapter.

11–05 The principal restriction on financial promotion is thus contained in s.21 of the FSMA 2000 in the following terms:

> "(1)   A person ('A') must not, in the course of business, communicate an invitation or inducement to engage in investment activity."

Breach of this central prohibition on financial promotion constitutes an offence[12]; although it is a defence to that offence for the accused to show that he took "all reasonable precautions and exercised all due diligence to avoid committing the offence".[13] There are four key terms to be explored in this restriction in s.21(1): "business"; "communication"; "invite or induce"; and "engagement in investment activity". Each of these terms is considered in the discussion to follow, once we have considered the policy underpinning this restriction and its principal exceptions. An unenforceable agreement resulting from an unlawful communication under s.21 of the FSMA 2000 may, however, be enforced by a court or a court may order that money or property transferred under the agreement to be retained[14] provided that the court is satisfied that it would be "just and equitable"

---

[9] Financial Services and Markets Act 2000, s.21(1).

[10] This provision came into effect on February 25, 2001 for the purposes of making orders or regulations; it came into effect on December 1, 2001 otherwise.

[11] See para.11–06.

[12] Financial Services and Markets Act 2000, s.23(1).

[13] Financial Services and Markets Act 2000, s.23(3). That contravention of such provisions is an offence is in itself a departure from the repealed Financial Services Act 1986.

[14] cf. *Westdeutsche Landesbank v Islington LBC* [1996] A.C. 669, below, where a transfer of property under a contract void ab initio was nevertheless held to have been a good transfer of title in spite of

to do so.[15] The court is obliged to consider[16] whether or not the offeror realised the communication was unlawful[17] and whether or not the offeror knew that the agreement was being entered into as a result of that unlawful communication.[18]

B.   The purpose of the prohibition on financial promotion

The general prohibition on financial promotion under s.21 has been established above. The purpose of the restriction is to prevent unsolicited calls being made to potential investors or uncontrolled advertisements for investment services being made. By controlling and regulating the people who can undertake such promotional activity and by regulating the manner in which those promotional activities are undertaken with different types of investor, the aim is to enhance investor protection by limiting the possibilities for ordinary investors being gulled into unsuitable investments.

11–06

C.   The consequence of the exclusion of the prohibition on financial promotion

Given the policy of preventing calls, advertisements or promotions being made by unauthorised persons, s.21(2) of the FSMA 2000 excludes the restriction on financial promotion where the promoter is authorised to act or if the content of the promotion has already been approved: that subsection provides as follows:—

11–07

> "... subsection (1) does not apply if—
> (a)   A is an authorised person; or
> (b)   the content of the communication is approved for the purposes of this section by an authorised person."

This is a particularly significant limitation on the financial promotion code. If the communicator is an authorised person and making an authorised communication (i.e. a communication made in accordance with the scope of its authorisation from the FCA) then the financial promotion restriction does not apply. Instead, such a person is governed by the conduct of business regulations as to the suitability of the products it sells to its customers and the suitability of the manner in which it sells products to its customers. The FCA conduct of business regulations (as effected further to MiFID) were considered in detail in Chapter 10. A summary of those principles is given below to the extent that they relate specifically to the promotion of financial services.[19]

---

the void nature of that contract, thus requiring the claimant to seek restitution either at common law or in equity: A. Hudson, *Swaps, Restitution and Trusts* (London: Sweet & Maxwell, 1999) generally.

[15]   Financial Services and Markets Act 2000, s.30(4).
[16]   Financial Services and Markets Act 2000, s.30(5).
[17]   Financial Services and Markets Act 2000, s.30(6).
[18]   Financial Services and Markets Act 2000, s.30(7).
[19]   See para.11–32.

11–08   The next few sections of this chapter therefore focus specifically on financial activities undertaken by non-authorised persons. The exception is the discussion relating to authorised persons and the conduct of business regulatory code that was introduced by MiFID.[20]

D.   The component parts of the restriction on financial promotion

What constitutes "business"?

11–09   The concept of what constitutes a business activity in regulatory terms was considered in detail in Chapter 9.[21] In relation to financial promotion and the concept of business, s.21(4) of the FSMA 2000 provides the Treasury with a power to create regulations for the purposes of deciding when a person is acting in the course of business or not acting in the course of business as discussed in Chapter 10.

What constitutes a "communication"?

11–10   There is a requirement that a communication of an appropriate type be made. For the purposes of the financial promotion code the term "communicate" includes "causing a communication to be made".[22]

What constitutes "investment"

11–11   For the restriction on financial promotion to apply, it must be investment activity which is being conducted. Therefore, it is important to know what will constitute an investment for this purpose. An "investment" for the purposes of the financial promotion code includes "any asset, right or interest".[23]

The definition of "engagement in investment activity"

11–12   The concept of engaging in an investment activity is defined by s.21(8) of the FSMA 2000 in the following terms:

> "'Engaging in investment activity' means—
> (a)   entering or offering to enter into an agreement the making or performance of which by either party constitutes a controlled activity; or
> (b)   exercising any rights conferred by a controlled investment to acquire, dispose of, underwrite or convert a controlled investment."

Schedule 2 to the FSMA 2000 qualifies these definitions of "controlled activity" and "controlled investment".[24] Although nothing in that Schedule is intended to

---

[20] See para.7–22.
[21] See para.9–15.
[22] Financial Services and Markets Act 2000, s.21(13).
[23] Financial Services and Markets Act 2000, s.21(14).
[24] Financial Services and Markets Act 2000, s.21(11).

limit the scope of the definitions of those two terms.[25] Further to s.21(9) of the FSMA 2000, an activity is a "controlled activity" if:

(a)   it is an activity of a specified kind or one which falls within a specified class of activity; and

(b)   it relates to an investment of a specified kind, or to one which falls within a specified class of investment.

In relation to the meaning of a "controlled investment", under s.21(10) of the FSMA 2000 the term "investment" includes "any asset, right or interest":[26]

"An investment is a controlled investment if it is an investment of a specified kind or one which falls within a specified class of investment."

The term "specified", in relation to the specified classes of investment in these provisions, means as specified in an order made by the Treasury.[27]

3.   COMMUNICATIONS FROM OUTSIDE THE UNITED KINGDOM

One of the most straightforward problems for a code restricting financial promotion is what is to be done about communications which are made from outside the UK either by telephone or by email communication or by means of the internet. The territorial effect of the financial promotion restriction is explained by s.21(3) of the FSMA 2000 in the following terms:

11–13

"In the case of a communication originating outside the United Kingdom, subsection (1) applies only if the communication is capable of having an effect in the United Kingdom."[28]

Therefore the regulation takes effect only over communications which have "an effect" in the UK. The financial promotion restriction does not apply to communications which take effect outside the UK.[29] However, with the growth of internet communication it is perfectly possible for an advertisement for financial services to be made on a website situated on a server outside the UK but which can be viewed by potential investors in the UK. It is only if the communication is directed only at persons outside the UK, and makes that clear on its face, that it could be said to fall within this exemption from the financial promotion code.[30] This would be made clear on the communication's face if it stated that it was directed only at investors outside the UK and if it also contained a warning that it must not be acted on by people within the UK.[31] It is suggested that it would be a question of fact whether any given communication of this sort was genuinely intended to be denied to UK residents, or whether a statement to that effect on the

---

[25] Financial Services and Markets Act 2000, s.21(12).

[26] Financial Services and Markets Act 2000, s.21(14).

[27] Financial Services and Markets Act 2000, s.21(14).

[28] The Treasury may by order repeal this subsection (3): Financial Services and Markets Act 2000, s.21(7).

[29] Financial Services and Markets Act 2000 (Financial Promotion) Order 2005, art.12(1).

[30] Financial Services and Markets Act 2000 (Financial Promotion) Order 2005, art.12(1)(b).

[31] Financial Services and Markets Act 2000 (Financial Promotion) Order 2005, art.12(4)(a) and (b).

website was in fact a sham seeking to conceal the fact that the website's operators were intending to lure in clients from within the UK. One indication of a sham might be a large number of orders taken from UK resident clients in contravention of the purported disclaimer on the website. If the operators did not want UK customers then presumably they would not take orders from UK customers. It is suggested that if the website accrued customers from within the UK, then it must have "an effect" in the UK. The financial institution involved would need to have systems in place to exclude UK resident investors from sales to demonstrate that this was not a sham,[32] and those systems must genuinely be put into operation. The discussion of exemptions from liability in the next section consider this issue in greater detail.

4.   EXEMPTIONS FROM THE FINANCIAL PROMOTION CODE

A.   Introduction

11–14   The scope of the financial promotion code is defined in large part by means of the exemptions from the otherwise broad restriction contained in s.21(1) of the FSMA 2000. Those exemptions are to be found in powers exercised under s.21(5) and (6) of the FSMA 2000, and thus in the Financial Promotion Order 2005.[33] The relevant provisions of each are considered in turn.

B.   The power to create exemptions: the Financial Promotion Order 2005

11–15   Exemptions to the financial promotion code are created further to s.21(5) of the FSMA 2000. Regulations exempting liability under the financial promotion code are provided further to s.21(6) of the FSMA 2000. Those regulations take the form of the Financial Services and Markets Act 2000 (Financial Promotion) Order 2005 (hereafter "the Financial Promotion Order"). These regulations set out the exempt communications.

Communication initiated by customer

11–16   The Financial Promotion Order 2005 explicitly excludes from the restriction those communications which are made by clients to a financial institution seeking information about controlled investments.[34] However, it is suggested, such an exclusion cannot be relied upon if the financial institution puts an invitation to treat on its website to encourage UK resident customers to contact that institution so as to learn more detail about investments which are already described in some

---

[32] Financial Services and Markets Act 2000 (Financial Promotion) Order 2005, art.12(4)(d).

[33] Financial Services and Markets Act 2000 (Financial Promotion) Order 2005 (SI 2005/1529), as amended by Financial Services and Markets Act 2000 (Financial Promotion) (Amendment) Order 2005 (SI 2005/3392), which in turn had repealed and amended Financial Services and Markets Act 2000 (Financial Promotion) Order 2001 (SI 2001/1335).

[34] Financial Services and Markets Act 2000 (Financial Promotion) Order 2005, art.13(1).

detail on the website. Thus, it is suggested, wording to the effect "you the customer will be seeking information and communicating with us" cannot be taken to displace the financial promotion restriction if that wording is merely a sham seeking to dress up what is in substance a clear offer of investments by the financial institution on its website.

Follow-up communications

In circumstances in which an exempt communication has been made, follow-up communications will also fall outside the code if they are not real-time communications and if they are genuinely made by or on behalf of the person who made the first communication.[35] The communication must take place within 12 months of the first communication and relate to the same investment opportunity.[36] The purpose here is to prevent customers being lured into contacting the financial institution and then being subjected to pressured cold-calling about other investments.

11–17

Generic communications

Given what was said in the immediately preceding section, remarkably, also exempted are generic communications which do not identify the person making the communication.[37] The intention here is to exempt communications which advertise no particular service provider because they are, supposedly, equivalent to unbiased newspaper articles.[38] There is provision in the wording of this exemption to prevent sufficient information being given in that generic communication so as to steer the potential customer towards one service provider: for example, "fantastic opportunities to invest in x... the clear leaders in this field are y", such that potential clients are likely to contact y as the only person whom they know from that communication specialises in that type of business. However, that does not seem to exclude, it is suggested, a communication which lists a table of service providers (like a consumer affairs magazine giving points for certain aspects of service provision) and which indicates one service provider as being strong in certain aspects of service provision or as being stronger than all of the other providers mentioned. This is, it is suggested, a case in which one should look to the substance of the communication as opposed merely to its form. Otherwise a financial services provider could simply set up a market research company which in fact operated as a means of raising the profile of its brands with the public through the facade of asking potential customers about their knowledge of that firm's services by means of cold-calling, market research questionnaires.

11–18

---

[35] Financial Services and Markets Act 2000 (Financial Promotion) Order 2005, art.14(2).
[36] Financial Services and Markets Act 2000 (Financial Promotion) Order 2005, art.14(2).
[37] Financial Services and Markets Act 2000 (Financial Promotion) Order 2005, art.16.
[38] There is an exemption also for communications by journalists in qualifying publications: Financial Services and Markets Act 2000 (Financial Promotion) Order 2005, art.20.

5. CRIMINAL OFFENCES FOR CONTRAVENTION OF THE FINANCIAL PROMOTION RESTRICTION

11–19   Section 25 of the FSMA 2000[39] provides that contravention of the financial promotion restriction in s.21 of the FSMA 2000 will constitute a criminal offence. That offence is subject to two defences. The first defence is that the defendant "believed on reasonable grounds that the content of the communication was prepared, or approved for the purposes of section 21, by an authorised person".[40] This defence could be made out if the promotion was carried on in the name of a subsidiary which was not formally authorised to carry on that type of business. The second defence requires that the defendant "took all reasonable precautions and exercised all due diligence to avoid committing the offence". In the first defence genuine error may make out the defence; whereas in this second defence a simple mistake would not demonstrate that one had exercised "all due diligence" or that one had taken "reasonable precautions". Suppose the defendant relied on being told verbally in passing in a meeting the day before that a communication would be authorised: is that diligent if there was no follow-up to verify the existence of that permission? A requirement of "all due diligence" would seem to require that a system was in place to ensure the proper transmission of information and that that system was followed up; or in the absence of such a system that the defendant took active steps to ensure that the communication would be an authorised communication.

6. PRIVATE LAW CONSEQUENCES OF A BREACH OF THE FINANCIAL PROMOTION RESTRICTION

A.   The principle in s.30 FSMA 2000

11–20   An unenforceable agreement resulting from an unlawful communication[41] under s.21 of the FSMA 2000 may be enforced by a court or a court may order that money or property transferred under the agreement be retained,[42] provided that the court is satisfied that it would be "just and equitable" to do so.[43] The court is obliged to consider[44] whether or not the offeror realised the communication was unlawful[45] and whether or not the offeror knew that the agreement was being entered into as a result of that unlawful communication.[46]

---

[39] This provision came into effect on December 1, 2001.
[40] Financial Services and Markets Act 2000, s.25(2)(a).
[41] Financial Services and Markets Act 2000, s.30(9) any reference to "making a communication" includes "causing a communication to be made".
[42] cf. *Westdeutsche Landesbank v Islington LBC* [1996] A.C. 669, see below, where a transfer of property under a contract void ab initio was nevertheless held to have been a good transfer of title in spite of the void nature of that contract, thus requiring the claimant to seek restitution at common law or in equity.
[43] Financial Services and Markets Act 2000, s.30(4).
[44] Financial Services and Markets Act 2000, s.30(5).
[45] Financial Services and Markets Act 2000, s.30(6).
[46] Financial Services and Markets Act 2000, s.30(7).

It is provided in s.30(2) of the FSMA 2000 that a bargain which was struck in contravention of the s.21 prohibition is unenforceable for the defaulting party and that there are proprietary and personal remedies for the non-defaulting party, in the following terms:

11–21

> "(2) If in consequence of an unlawful communication a person enters as a customer into a controlled agreement, it is unenforceable against him and he is entitled to recover—
> (a) any money or other property paid or transferred by him under the agreement; and
> (b) compensation for any loss sustained by him as a result of having parted with it."

An "unlawful communication" is defined in s.30(1) to mean a communication in relation to which there has been an contravention of s.21(1). An agreement entered into in that context will be ordinarily unenforceable (subject to s.30(4)) against the non-defaulting party[47]: thus the person making the communication will not be able to rely on her illegal act so as to enforce the agreement. The non-defaulting party is then entitled to recovery. The form of recovery is interesting. Section 30(2)(a) provides that the non-defaulting party's entitlement is "to recover—any money or other property paid or transferred by him under the agreement": that is, on its face, a right to recover *the very money* or *the very property*, such that the non-defaulting party has a proprietary right in that money or property justifying a tracing claim if that property has been dissipated.

Yet s.30(13) provides that:

11–22

> "[i]f any property required to be returned under this section has passed to a third party, references to that property are to be read as references to its value at the time of its receipt by the person required to return it".

This elliptical provision could be read in one of two ways. The first reading would be to preclude a tracing action to pursue the property into the hands of that third party, as permitted in general terms by the general law of tracing,[48] and instead to replace that property claim with a personal claim to the value of that property in money or money's worth against the defendant. Alternatively, and it is suggested a more attractive reading in the context of the general law of property, the person obliged to return the property (which under the law of equitable or common law tracing may be the third party recipient, as well as the defaulting party) may be required to account in the form of the identifiable property passed under the contract or alternatively simply to the traceable value of that property by way of charge or lien.[49] Paragraph (b) then also provides for a personal claim for compensation for any consequential loss resulting from the breach of s.21(1), including it is suggested the cost of unwinding a hedge, costs associated with exiting from the transaction, and any foreseeable loss of bargain which the non-defaulting party intended to enter into but for this transaction being illegally communicated by the defendant.

---

[47] That is, the person who received the communication.
[48] See para.23–01.
[49] See para.22–01.

11–23 The bargain is ordinarily unenforceable (subject to s.30(4)) against a non-defaulting party also in the following circumstance, under s.30(3):

> "(3) If in consequence of an unlawful communication a person exercises any rights conferred by a controlled investment, no obligation to which he is subject as a result of exercising them is enforceable against him and he is entitled to recover—
> (a) any money or other property paid or transferred by him under the obligation; and
> (b) compensation for any loss sustained by him as a result of having parted with it."

The remedies for the non-defaulting party are in exactly the same format as those considered in relation to s.30(2) immediately above. The term "controlled investment" has the same meaning as in s.21[50]: that is, any investment listed in Sch.2 to the FSMA 2000 which is a regulated activity.[51]

11–24 The expectation under s.30(10) of the FSMA 2000 is that amount of compensation due under subs.(2) or (3) will be an amount agreed between the parties, but that it may be determined by the court on the application of either party to the court.

B. A power in the court to enforce an agreement against a non-defaulting party where just and equitable to do so

11–25 Despite the foregoing provisions in s.30(2) and (3), s.30(4) permits the court to allow:

> "(a) the agreement or obligation to be enforced, or
> (b) money or property paid or transferred under the agreement or obligation to be retained,
> if it is satisfied that it is just and equitable in the circumstances of the case."

In considering whether to allow the agreement or obligation to be enforced, or the money or property paid or transferred under the agreement to be retained, on the just and equitable ground in s.30(4), the court is required to have regard to the considerations in s.30(6) and (7).[52] Those considerations are:

> "(6) If the applicant made the unlawful communication, the issue is whether he reasonably believed that he was not making such a communication.
> (7) If the applicant did not make the unlawful communication, the issue is whether he knew that the agreement was entered into in consequence of such a communication."

The term "applicant" here means the person seeking to enforce the agreement or to retain the money or property paid or transferred.[53] It is suggested that subs.(6) is unsatisfactory: the person who made an unlawful communication will be thus entitled to rely on her own lack of diligence in failing to obey the financial promotion restriction so as to renege on an agreement or to enforce an

---

[50] Financial Services and Markets Act 2000, s.30(1).
[51] Financial Services and Markets Act 2000, s.21(10).
[52] Financial Services and Markets Act 2000, s.30(5).
[53] Financial Services and Markets Act 2000, s.30(8).

agreement (as appropriate). This does not promote obedience to financial services regulation. It is suggested, however, that a regulated investment firm could not reasonably believe that a communication was lawful if it was made erroneously through a subsidiary, unless there had been genuine clerical error. For non-authorised firms to make such communications is simply in contravention of the financial promotion restriction. The non-defaulting party at the very least ought to be entitled to recover its losses and costs where they are caused by the other parties' fault or failure to ascertain the regulatory position. In relation to subs.(7) it will be difficult to prove what the defendant "knew": and therefore the test for knowledge in this context should be an objective test of what the defendant ought to have known in the circumstances, particular by reference to the level of expertise which ought reasonably to have been expected of the defendant in that context.

C.   Consequential matters relating to the enforceability of agreements

There are, however, limits placed on the extent to which the parties may seek to rely or renege on agreements under s.30. Either party to such an agreement may elect not to perform that agreement or any obligation under it which (by virtue of subs.(2) or (3)) is unenforceable against him, but if so he must repay any money and return any other property received by him under the agreement.[54] Furthermore, s.30(12) provides that: "[i]f (by virtue of subsection (2) or (3)) a person recovers money paid or property transferred under an agreement or obligation" then "he must repay any money and return any other property received by him as a result of exercising the rights in question".

11–26

7.   CONDUCT OF BUSINESS REGULATION IN RELATION TO PROMOTION BY AUTHORISED PERSONS

A.   Introduction

This section considers conduct of business regulation which governs the promotion of securities and other investments by authorised persons. As considered above, authorised persons do not fall within the financial promotion restriction.[55] Conduct of business regulation was considered in detail in Chapter 10.

11–27

---

[54] Financial Services and Markets Act 2000, s.30(11).
[55] Financial Services and Markets Act 2000, s.21(2).

B.   The MiFID conduct of business principles in relation to communications

11–28   The conduct of business principles set out in MiFID relate to all dealings between an authorised person and its customers. What follows is a summary of those principles as they apply to financial promotion undertaken by authorised persons who fall outside the financial promotion code by virtue of s.21(2) FSMA 2000. When making communications, investment firms are required to act "honestly, fairly and professionally in accordance with the best interests of its clients".[56] The first obligation relates to the provision of information and requires that:

> "All information, including marketing communications, addressed by the investment firm to clients or potential clients shall be fair, clear and not misleading."[57]

Therefore, the key requirement is that any communication be "fair, clear and not misleading". This principle, in itself, does not require that clients are wrapped in cotton wool in relation to financial transactions; rather, the client must be given all the necessary information in a manner which enables her to form an informed judgment as to the desirability of any given investment opportunity. This chimes in with the second obligation which requires, inter alia, that an investment firm must provide appropriate information in a comprehensible form about its services.[58]

11–29   An investment firm must provide each client with information giving "appropriate guidance on and warnings of the risks associated with investments in" the proposed "instruments or in respect of particular investment strategies".[59] The means by which one acquaints clients with the risks associated with their proposed investments is, first, by deciding what level of expertise that client has. Thus, the third principle requires that "[w]hen providing investment advice or portfolio management the investment firm shall obtain the necessary information regarding the client's or potential client's knowledge and experience in the investment field relevant to the specific type of product or service, his financial situation and his investment objectives" so that that investment firm is able to provide suitable advice about suitable products.[60] Consequently, MiFID requires that national regulations require investment firms to identify this sort of information "so as to enable the investment firm to assess whether the investment service or product envisaged is appropriate for the client".[61]

---

[56] MiFID art.19(1).
[57] MiFID art.19(2).
[58] MiFID art.19(3).
[59] Also of great significance is the provision of information as to all costs and charges which may arise in relation to the parties' business.
[60] MiFID art.19(4).
[61] MiFID art.19(5).

C. FCA Financial Promotion Rules

The FCA financial promotion rules are a subset of the Conduct of Business sourcebook. Therefore, a discussion of financial promotion in this context is a discussion of conduct of business. The preceding discussion of MiFID forms the basis for the FCA rules which implement that directive.

11–30

The FCA rules divide between real-time communications on the one hand—which include telephone calls, face-to-face meetings and any other real-time interaction (perhaps such as communication in a chat-room environment online); and on the other hand non-real-time communications which take place otherwise—this would include correspondence by letter and possibly correspondence by email if it did not include such a rapid exchange of correspondence so as to become in fact a real-time conversation online.[62] The heart of the FCA rules can be summarised in the following key principles. An authorised firm must be able to demonstrate that any real-time communication is fair, clear and not misleading. By contrast a non-real-time communication must contain a fair and adequate description of the proposed investment, including an appropriate explanation of the risks involved. Where an authorised firm makes a non-real-time communication then it must certify that that communication complies with the financial promotion rules within the conduct of business sourcebook.

11–31

D. FCA Conduct of Business principles

Conduct of business regulation by the FCA is discussed in detail in Chapter 10. Those principles are set out in the Conduct of Business Sourcebook ("COBS"). COBS applies to authorised investment firms. This section therefore considers financial promotion by such firms.

11–32

Communications with clients generally under COBS

Communications with clients must be conducted in accordance with the financial promotions rules in Chapter 4 of COBS. These communications must comply with art.19(2) of the MiFID in that those communications must be "fair, clear and not misleading".[63] In so doing the firm must take into account the information which is to be conveyed and the purposes for which it is being conveyed.[64] Financial promotions in this regard must explain any risk to a client's capital, must give a balanced impression of the short and long term prospects for an investment's yield, must give sufficient information in relation to complex charging structures for a product from which the firm earns some commission or benefit, must name the FCA as regulator, and must give an appropriate impression of packaged or stakeholder products.[65]

11–33

---

[62] COBS art.7.
[63] COBS,4.2.1R.
[64] COBS,4.2.2G.
[65] COBS,4.2.4G.

11–34 Statements as to past, simulated past, and future performance are dealt with in s.4.6 of COBS. Information as to past performance of relevant investments must include information going back five years, it must give the source and reference period of the information, it must state clearly that past performance is no promise of future performance, it must state clearly the currency involved, and if gross figures are used then the effect of any fees, commissions or other charges must be disclosed.[66] The communication must be made in a proportionate and appropriate manner given the purpose of the communication.[67] Information about simulated past performance must relate to an investment or financial index, it must be based on the actual past performance of one or more investment or financial indices which are the same as the investment concerned in the communication, it must contain a prominent warning that figures based on simulated past performance are no reliable indication of future performance.[68]

11–35 A firm must not make cold calls.[69] The exceptions to this restriction are threefold.[70] First, where the recipient of the cold call and the firm have an established existing client relationship which envisages the receipt of cold calls. Secondly, where the cold call relates to a generally marketable package product which is not a higher volatility product nor a life policy. Thirdly, the cold call relates to a controlled activity to be carried on by an authorised person. Cold calls and any non-written communication must make clear the purpose of the communication, the firm making the communication and it must be made at an appropriate time of day.[71]

Communications specifically with retail customers

11–36 When communicating with retail clients, information must include the firm's name, must not emphasise the benefits of relevant investments without also giving a "fair and prominent indication of any relevant risks", must be sufficient to be understood by a member of the group at whom it was directed, and must be presented in a way so as to be similarly understood.[72] Any comparisons made with other products or other firms must be meaningful and presented in a fair and balanced way.[73]

---

[66] COBS,4.6.2R.
[67] COBS,4.6.3G.
[68] COBS,4.6.6R.
[69] COBS,4.8.2R.
[70] COBS,4.8.2R.
[71] COBS,4.8.3R.
[72] COBS,4.5.2R.
[73] COBS,4.5.6(1)R.

MARKET ABUSE

CORE PRINCIPLES

Further to the EC Market Abuse Directive, the FCA regulates "insider dealing and market manipulation" so as to preserve "market integrity". Insider dealing involves the misuse of "inside information" when investing in securities. Market manipulation involves giving a false impression as to the supply or price of instruments, for example seeking to create a false market for shares by making them appear to be more valuable than in fact they are. The FCA has the power to impose "civil penalties" for market abuse under FSMA 2000. The FCA has also acquired powers to prosecute criminal offences of insider dealing.

The market abuse code under FSMA 2000 is concerned with misuse of "inside information", which is defined in s.118 as falling into seven categories: insider dealing; improper disclosure of information; misuse of information; causing a false or misleading impression about securities; employing fictitious devices or contrivances; disseminating information so as to give a false or misleading information about investments; and failure to observe the standard of behaviour reasonably expected of a person in that market.

The *FCA Handbook* contains a rulebook ("MAR 1") which is concerned with the prevention of market abuse. There is also a "Model Code" in the UKLA Listing Rules relating to the prevention of misuse of inside information in relation to listed companies.

1. INTRODUCTION

12–01   The Financial Conduct Authority ("FCA") regulation of market abuse is concerned with the imposition of civil penalties, as opposed to criminal offences. The principles considered in this chapter are drawn from the EC Market Abuse Directive as implemented by Part 8 of the Financial Services and Markets Act 2000 ("FSMA 2000"), and the FCA Market Abuse Rulebook ("MAR") focusing particularly on the Code on Market Conduct (referred to as "MAR 1") which is found in Chapter 1 of MAR. The principal focus of this chapter is on the market abuse principles of the FSMA 2000 as supplemented by MAR 1. The topic of market abuse is also considered in Chapter 14 in relation to the criminal offences of insider dealing and market manipulation. This chapter, however, is limited to a discussion of the regulation of market abuse by the FCA and does not consider criminal offences.[1] However, the FCA has the power to prosecute any allegations of insider dealing.[2] Thus, the day-to-day regulator of the securities markets is given an inquisitorial and prosecutorial power in relation to insider dealing, which operates in tandem (it is suggested) with its powers to regulate market abuse more generally. There is also the Model Code in the UKLA Listing Rules, considered in Chapter 38, which deals with the use of inside information in relation to public companies whose shares are admitted to the Official List.

12–02   The regulation of market abuse is concerned to maintain the integrity of the securities markets. Without a perception of market integrity among the potential investor base for the securities markets there may not be sufficient capital available to fuel economic growth in the EU. The particular mischief at which FCA market abuse regulation is aimed is the misuse of "inside information" in relation to companies whose securities are in issue. Access to inside information gives its holder an unfair advantage in the securities markets. In the criminal law context this is a concern with insider dealing, but insider dealing prosecutions have been few and far between such that it was considered necessary to empower

---

[1] Parts of this chapter are based on elements of A. Hudson, *Securities Law* (London: Sweet & Maxwell, 2008), Ch.26.
[2] Financial Services and Markets Act 2000, s.402.

national regulators to oversee market abuse too. The principles on which this regulation is based are set out in the Market Abuse Directive. So, it is with that directive that we shall begin.

2.   THE MARKET ABUSE DIRECTIVE

A.   The Market Abuse Directive

The Market Abuse Directive ("MAD")[3] deals with "insider dealing and market manipulation" and is concerned with the preservation of "market integrity". It is important to understand the policy which underpins this drive for market integrity. The opening to the preamble to the directive considers that market integrity is necessary for an "integrated and efficient financial market" which in turn is considered to be necessary for "economic growth and job creation" in the EU.[4] The recitals to the directive further provide that "market abuse harms the integrity of financial markets and public confidence in securities and derivatives".[5] The economic objective underpinning the directive is the need to develop a pan-European securities market to provide a pool of liquid investment capital. To develop a pool of liquid capital, however, requires the confidence of a concomitant pool of investors. Maintaining investor confidence requires, inter alia, market integrity and therefore requires control of market abuse. There is therefore an ethical dimension to the preservation of market integrity which is subordinate, in the terms of the directive, to its economic goals: whatever harms market integrity in turn harms the productivity of the European capital markets, which in turn harms the real economy.

12–03

This policy is different from that which underpinned the criminal code on insider dealing in Part V of the Criminal Justice Act 1993: that legislation was concerned to prevent one party to a transaction from having unfair access to information which the other party does not have. This is an explicitly ethical element which is less apparent in the MAD. On one view this might be said to come to the same thing: preventing manipulation of the market has a macroeconomic effect when applied to all transactions on the securities markets and it also has a microeconomic effect from transaction to transaction by preventing one party to a transaction from taking advantage of the other party. Some commentators consider that this concern with market integrity is overblown: this debate is considered in Chapter 14 in relation to the criminal offence of insider dealing.[6] The directive is nevertheless concerned with insider dealing and with market manipulation. Moreover, the directive is concerned with levelling the differences in the protection of market integrity between jurisdictions.

12–04

---

[3] 2003/6/EC.
[4] Market Abuse Directive, 2003/6/EC, ("MAD"), Recital, (1).
[5] MAD, Recital, (2).
[6] See para.14–64 et seq.

B. The concepts of market abuse and market manipulation in MAD

12–05   This short section introduces the concepts of market abuse, insider dealing and market manipulation as they are defined in MAD. There then follows a more detailed analysis of the statutory and regulatory provisions relating to each of these concepts in Pt 8 of the FSMA 2000[7] and in the FCA's MAR rulebook which implement the provisions of MAD and associated legislation.[8] Under MAD, "market abuse" encompasses both insider dealing and market manipulation outside the criminal law.[9]

The regulation of the misuse of "inside information" in MAD

12–06   MAD requires that member states prohibit insiders from misusing inside information, whether directly or indirectly, to deal in financial instruments so as to earn personal profits or for other personal ends.[10] The policy underpinning this requirement is a perception that insider dealing and market abuse "prevent full and proper market transparency, which is a prerequisite for trading for all economic actors in integrated financial markets".[11] The categories of insider for this purpose are members of the issuer's administrative, management or supervisory bodies; or shareholders or people otherwise holding capital in the issuer; or people having access to the information through the exercise of an employment, profession or other duties; or by virtue of criminal activities.[12] The reference in MAD to "inside information" is a reference to:

> "information of a precise nature which has not been made public, relating, directly or indirectly, to one or more issuers of financial instruments or to one or more financial instruments and which, if it were made public, would be likely to have a significant effect on the prices of those financial instruments or on the price of related derivative financial instruments".[13]

There are other matters which member states are required to prohibit: the disclosure of inside information to another person[14]; recommending that a person deal in securities on the basis of the inside information[15]; inducing a person to deal in securities on the basis of the inside information[16]; and making sure that all

---

[7] See also the following statutory instruments implementing MAD: Financial Services and Markets Act 2000 (Market Abuse) Regulations 2005 (SI 2005/381) and Investment Recommendation (Media) Regulations 2005 (SI 2005/382).

[8] Market Abuse Commission Directive 2004/72/EC.

[9] MAD recital (12).

[10] The coverage of financial instruments in the directive is to units in collective investment schemes, money-market instruments, forward rate agreements, futures, swaps, cash-settled and physically-settled options, and any other instruments admitted to trading on a regulated market: MAD art.1(3).

[11] MAD recital (15).

[12] MAD art.2(1). These definitions include any human being who takes part in a decision taken by a corporate entity which constitutes that entity one of the categories of insider.

[13] MAD art.1(1).

[14] MAD art.3(1).

[15] MAD art.3(2).

[16] MAD art.3(2).

of the foregoing prohibitions apply to any person in possession of the inside information who should have been aware that it was inside information.[17] These concepts are considered in detail in the discussion to follow.

C. The regulation of "market manipulation"

Market manipulation is a process by which a person, or a group of people, try to inflate or to depress the market value of securities by dealing in them in concert and possibly while circulating rumours as to the prospects for those securities. Member states are required to prohibit "any person from engaging in market manipulation".[18] The reference in the directive to "market manipulation" is a reference to[19]:

12–07

> "(a)   transactions or orders to trade:
> —   which give, or are likely to give, false or misleading signals as to the supply of, demand for or price of financial instruments; or
> —   which secure, by a person, or persons acting in collaboration, the price of one or several financial instruments at an abnormal or artificial level, unless the person who entered into the transactions or issued the order to trade establishes that his reasons for so doing are legitimate and that these transactions or order to trade conform to accepted market practices on the regulated market concerned;
> (b)   transactions or orders to trade which employ fictitious devices or any other form of deception or contrivance;
> (c)   dissemination of information through the media, including the Internet, or by any other means, which gives, or is likely to give, false or misleading signals as to financial instruments, including the dissemination of rumours and false or misleading news, where the person who made the dissemination knew, or ought to have known, that the information was false or misleading. In respect of journalists when they act in the professional capacity such dissemination of information is to be assessed [. . .] taking into account the rules governing their profession, unless those persons derive, directly or indirectly, an advantage or profits from the dissemination of the information in question."

The concern here is with distorting a market in several ways. The simplest means of manipulation would arise by giving out incorrect or misleading information, in effect, so as to encourage investors to deal in a way in which, or at a price at which, they would not otherwise have dealt had they known the true position. Another means of manipulating a market would be to enter into a number of transactions so as to make it appear that there is a market for a security at a price at which there would not have been such a market but for those transactions. Yet another means of manipulating the market is to disseminate rumours or misleading stories which would affect the value of securities.[20] The reference to "accepted market practices" is defined in the directive to mean "practices that are reasonably expected in one or more financial markets and are accepted by the

---

[17] MAD art.4.
[18] MAD art.5.
[19] MAD art.1(2).
[20] For example, Citigroup was fined £13.9 million by the FSA for breaching PRIN 2 and 3 in buying up and then dumping huge numbers of European government bonds in the space of an hour on August 2, 2004.

competent authority in accordance with guidelines adopted by the Commission in accordance with the procedure laid down in art.17(2)".[21]

3.   CIVIL PENALTIES FOR MARKET ABUSE IN THE FSMA 2000

A.   The nature of the civil market abuse code

12–08   The market abuse provisions in Pt 8 of FSMA 2000 (ss.118 through 131A, hereafter referred to as "the market abuse code") creates a code of rules which empowers the FCA to impose penalties on people who deal on the basis of inside information in the manner described in s.118 et seq. of the FSMA 2000. Strictly speaking these rules are not part of the criminal law but rather grant powers to the FCA to impose penalties, as considered immediately below. The market abuse regime relates to "qualifying investments" traded on the London Stock Exchange and other prescribed markets[22] where the behaviour falls into one of the seven categories of behaviour set out in s.118(1) of the FSMA 2000, as considered below.

B.   The nature of the FCA's powers under the market abuse code

12–09   The market abuse code is not a code which creates criminal offences, although the proper jurisprudential categorisation of the right of a public body to impose penalties is an interesting question, in that giving a public body like the FCA the power to impose penalties does seem to create a quasi-criminal jurisdiction for that public body. The aim of the market abuse regime is to expand the powers of the FCA to deal with those market participants—whether authorised or unauthorised under the legislation—who act inappropriately but nevertheless outside the ambit of the ordinary criminal law for misfeasance in financial dealings. The importance of this regime is that it carries punitive penalties but that it does not replicate all of the protections and rights which are characteristic of the criminal law; this in itself may cause difficulties in relation to art.6 of the European Convention of Human Rights and its guarantees of a right to a fair trial. If the FCA were to exercise its powers inappropriately in public law terms, then an action for judicial review of its decision would be available to the object of the penalty, as discussed in Chapter 9.[23] Its legislative purpose was therefore to make successful prosecutions for market abuse easier to obtain than had been the case under the pre-existing criminal law.

---

[21]   MAD art.1(5).
[22]   Financial Services and Markets Act 2000 s.118(1).
[23]   See para.9–62.

4. MARKET ABUSE AND MISUSE OF INSIDE INFORMATION

A. The scope of the market abuse provisions

The provisions of the Market Abuse Directive and the FSMA 2000 market abuse **12–10**
code are concerned with abuses of inside information and are also concerned with
preventing an insider from allowing themselves to be put in a situation in which
there could be a suspicion that they have misused "inside information".[24] The use
of inside information will constitute market abuse for the purposes of the FSMA
2000. Section 118 of the FSMA 2000, as amended to give effect to MAD,
provides that:

> "(1) For the purposes of this Act, market abuse is behaviour (whether by one person alone
> or by two or more persons jointly or in concert) which—
> (a) occurs in relation to—
> (i) qualifying investments admitted to trading on a prescribed market,
> (ii) qualifying investments in respect of which a request for admission to
> trading on such a market has been made, or
> (iii) in the case of subsection (2) or (3) behaviour, investments which are
> related investments in relation to such qualifying investments, and
> (b) falls within any one or more of the types of behaviour set out in subsection (2)
> to (8)."

There are therefore seven types of behaviour which will constitute market abuse.
Market abuse can be committed by an individual or by a legal person or by more
than one person acting "jointly or in concert". The reference to "joint action"
would encompass any action performed by two people together or in a way which
made them joint tenants or tenants in common of property. Acting "in concert"
would not require that they acted together in this manner but rather would require
simply that they had undertaken some co-ordinated plan of action or otherwise
acted in a manner which constituted a form of conspiracy between them. The
term "qualifying investment" is not defined in Pt 8 of the FSMA 2000, although
the term "investment" is defined by reference to s.22 of FSMA 2000 and Sch.2 to
that Act, which define the financial instruments which constitute regulated
activities for the purposes of the Act. The various forms of behaviour are
considered in turn below.

B. The types of behaviour constituting market abuse

*The types of market abuse as divined from FSMA 2000 and the Market
Abuse Rulebook, MAR 1*

As provided in s.118(1)(b) of the FSMA 2000, behaviour constituting market **12–11**
abuse is any one or more of the seven following forms of behaviour. In relation to
the various forms of behaviour, the term "behaviour" itself constitutes either
action or inaction.[25] Thus a person may commit market abuse either by acting or

---

[24] Listing Rules, Ch.9, Annex 1R.
[25] Financial Services and Markets Act 2000, s.130A(3)

by omitting to act. The term "inside information" is considered below,[26] as is the term "insider".[27] The FCA then sets out its Code on Market Conduct in Chapter 1 of the Market Abuse Rulebook (known as "MAR 1") which fleshes out the various types of market abuse. The following parts of this section of this chapter knit together the types of market abuse provided for in s.118 of the FSMA 2000 with the provisions of MAR 1 so as to generate a comprehensive picture of what will constitute market abuse in regulatory terms in the UK.

(1)   Dealing in a qualifying investment: "insider dealing"

12–12   The first type of behaviour is akin to insider dealing, as s.118(2) of the FSMA 2000 sets out in the following terms:

> "The first type of behaviour is where an insider deals, or attempts to deal, in a qualifying investment or related investment on the basis of inside information relating to the investment in question."

The principal distinction from the criminal offence of insider dealing in s.52(1) of the CJA 1993 is that the investments in question here do not need to be "price-affected securities" in relation to the information. This behaviour constitutes market abuse when there is a dealing in securities or an attempt to deal in securities, thus if the counterparty refuses to perform the transaction due to a suspicion about the information involved or if the transaction is otherwise not completed then behaviour constituting market abuse will still have been committed. The information at issue must be inside information as defined for these purposes below.[28]

12–13   The FCA gives examples of behaviour which it considers would fall within this head of behaviour in "MAR 1". Quite simply, in the first place, "dealing on the basis of inside information which is not trading information" constitutes market abuse.[29] In this sense, "trading information" should be taken to be information akin to market rumour which is not inside information because it is not restricted to insiders and which is not inside information because it is not the sort of analytical information on which all competent, reasonable traders could be expected to act in any event.

12–14   There are three further examples of market abuse given in the regulations. First, "front-running" whereby a person deals in securities in advance of the publication of the information by taking advantage of the "anticipated impact" of the order on the market price.[30] Secondly, in relation to takeovers, an offeror or potential offeror takes a position which provides "a merely economic exposure to movements in the price of the target company's shares", such as taking a spread bet on that share price or acquiring a cash-settled put option on those shares.[31]

---

[26]   See para.12–37
[27]   See para.12–36.
[28]   See para.12–37.
[29]   MAR, 1.3.2(1)E.
[30]   MAR, 1.3.2(2)E.
[31]   MAR,1.3.2(3)E.

Thirdly, in relation to takeovers, a person acting for the offeror or a potential offeror deals on his own account in relation to the target company's shares.[32] Generally speaking, the FCA will not consider a deal to be market abuse if the deal took place before the dealer had the information, or if the dealer was satisfying some pre-existing legal obligation (such as a contractual obligation to supply those shares to a client under a physically-settled option), or in relation to a corporate dealer if the particular employees involved did not know the information at the time of dealing.[33] There are other examples of insider dealing given in MAR in relation to the use of information in relation to commodities transactions.[34]

The acid test, it is suggested, based on FCA guidance, is that if the inside **12–15** information is either the reason for the dealing in securities or is a material influence on that dealing, then it will be presumed to be a dealing made on the basis of inside information, and so market abuse.[35] By contrast, if the information had been retained behind an effective and properly constructed Chinese wall[36] then that would suggest that the dealing was not on the basis of that inside information (always assuming, it is suggested, that the dealer was not on the side of the Chinese wall which had access to the information).[37]

The sorts of activity which will not constitute market abuse in the ordinary course **12–16** of events include the legitimate business of market makers, assuming that the dealings can be demonstrated (it is suggested) to be demonstrably in accordance with the ordinary course of such business[38]; the execution of client orders (assuming, it is suggested, that those client orders are in the ordinary course of business and are not predicated on that inside information)[39]; the proper conduct of a takeover or merger including preparations for such a takeover or merger,[40] although the information that an offer is to be made is itself inside information.[41] In 2012, there were several findings of market abuse by the Financial Services Authority. For example, the high-profile head of Greenlight Capital, David Einhorn, was found to have sold 11.6 million shares in Punch Taverns immediately after hearing confidential information about the company, and so was fined £7.2 million in January 2012.[42] The facts set out in a Financial Services Authority press release,[43] explaining their reasons for imposing this fine, disclosed a clear case of market abuse. That press release related that Einhorn had been told (by Punch's former financial advisor at Merrill Lynch on a telephone call) of Punch Taverns' need to raise capital, and its embryonic plans to do so, at

---

[32] MAR,1.3.2(4)E.
[33] MAR,1.3.3E.
[34] MAR,1.3.20G through 1.3.23.
[35] MAR,1.3.4E.
[36] A.S. Hudson, *Equity & Trusts*, s.12.5.6.
[37] MAR,1.3.5E.
[38] MAR,1.3.7C; MAD, recital 18.
[39] MAR,1.3.12C; MAD, recital 12.
[40] MAR,1.3.17C; MAD, recital 29.
[41] MAR,1.3.18G.
[42] The FSA Decision Notice is set out at *http://www.fsa.gov.uk/static/pubs/decisions/dn-einhorn-greenlight.pdf*.
[43] *http://www.fsa.gov.uk/library/communication/pr/2012/005.shtml* [Accessed January 18, 2013].

a time when that information had not been publicly disclosed. This information suggested that Punch Taverns was in difficulties. Greenlight held 13.3 per cent of Punch Taverns' total share equity. It was found that Greenlight's programme of selling Punch Taverns shares began only minutes after the telephone call. Einhorn claimed not to have understood that this would constitute market abuse.[44]

(2) Disclosure of inside information: "improper disclosure"

12–17 The second form of behaviour constituting market abuse is set out in s.118(3) of the FSMA 2000 in the following terms:

> "The second is where an insider discloses inside information to another person otherwise than in the proper course of the exercise of his employment, profession or duties."

The second form of market abuse behaviour is therefore committed where an insider discloses information to another person. This could be done by letter, by email, or verbally to a single person or, it is suggested, to a number of people (each of whom would constitute "another person") whether to a particular individual or to any agent of a legal person. The recipient of the information could be someone who is intended to disseminate that information or who intends to profit from it personally or who intends to do nothing at all: the subsection does not require any particular motive or reaction on the part of the recipient of that disclosure. The exemption from liability here is where the disclosure is made by a person in "the proper course of the exercise of his employment, profession or duties". Thus an officer of a company sending information to a RIS would be acting properly in the course of his employment; a solicitor transmitting information as part of disclosure proceedings in litigation further to a court order would be acting properly in the course of a profession; and a public relations consultant transmitting the information at the behest of the issuer properly to an appropriate newspaper would be acting in the course of her duties.

12–18 The FCA gives two examples of behaviour which it considers would fall within this head of behaviour in MAR[45]:

> "(1) disclosure of inside information by the director of an issuer to another in a social context; and
> (2) selective briefing of analysts by directors of issuers or others who are persons discharging managerial responsibilities."

The former, it is suggested, is akin to information being passed casually at a social gathering; and the latter relates to the problem of directors talking to representatives of some of their institutional investors and others in small groups in a way which constitutes the passage of information which is still inside information due to the smallness of the group in question. Disclosure will not constitute market abuse, however, if the disclosure is part of a body's proper functions or if it is made to a proper authority such as a government department,

---

[44] Nevertheless, there was an attempt at a press relations offensive with a profile in the Financial Times (Financial Times, January 27, 2012, 'The outsider who has run foul of the FSA').
[45] MAR,1.4.2E.

the Bank of England, the Competition Commission, the Takeover Panel or any other such regulatory body.[46] A part of the acid test for proper disclosure in this context is whether or not the disclosure was part of the approved procedure on the market in question—for example, in relation to the code on takeovers or as required by the UKLA's Listing Rules[47]—because such a circumstance would tend to suggest that the disclosure was properly made. Otherwise, the person making the disclosure would have to demonstrate that the disclosure was made in the proper discharge of their ordinary duties. Other specific examples are given in MAR.[48]

(3) Use of inside information in breach of standard of reasonable behaviour on the market: "misuse of information"

The third form of behaviour draws on s.118(2) and (3) of the FSMA 2000 in the following terms, further to s.118(4) of the FSMA 2000[49]:

12–19

> "The third is where the behaviour (in falling within subsection (2) or (3))—
> (a)
>> (a) is based on information which is not generally available to those using the market but which, if available to a regular user of the market, would be, or would likely to be, regarded by him as relevant when deciding the terms on which transactions in qualifying investments should be effected, and
>> (b) is likely to be regarded by a regular user of the market as a failure on the part of the person concerned to observe the standard of behaviour reasonably expected of a person in his position in relation to the market."

It is required, therefore, that three things have occurred. First, the information must not be generally available. Secondly, the information must be of a type which would have been regarded as relevant information by a regular user of the market when deciding whether or not to make an investment in the relevant securities. Thirdly, on the balance of probabilities a regular user of the market—akin, therefore, to a reasonable person in this context—must consider the defendant's actions to have been a failure to observe proper market conduct. It is suggested that this last requirement is one way of formulating the notion that the defendant must act with integrity—as under the *Principles for Businesses* rulebook—in that the notion of integrity is being measured by reference to the reasonable, regular market user. Clear examples of situations in which information should be disclosed or not dealt on include any circumstance in which FCA regulation requires disclosure of information or the withholding of that information respectively[50]; similarly information which would ordinarily be disclosed on a RIS (such as a change in rating by a ratings agency) should be disclosed.[51]

---

[46] MAR,1.4.3C.
[47] See Ch.39.
[48] MAR,1.4.6G and 1.4.7G.
[49] cf. Financial Services and Markets Act 2000, s.118(9).
[50] MAR,1.5.7(1)E.
[51] MAR,1.5.7(2)E.

12–20 The FCA gives examples of behaviour which it considers would fall within this head of behaviour in MAR. Dealing in qualifying securities on information which is not generally known, even if it is not strictly inside information, is considered by the FCA to be market abuse.[52] Indeed, any dealing based on information which is not generally owned, even if it is not inside information, is considered by the FCA to be market abuse.[53]

12–21 It is not required that the user of the information was an insider nor a regulated person: this could therefore apply to an ordinary tippee. One clear example given of market abuse in MAR is that in which the director of a target company in a takeover offer tells a friend at lunch that the company is subject to such an offer, and that friend then places a bet at fixed odds with a bookmaker that the company will be subject to a bid: this constitutes market abuse on the basis of misuse of information.[54] Similarly, if the same process occurred, in relation to a bet placed by a friend after lunch, but in relation to a "non-contractual icing" of takeover negotiations—that is, where the parties agreed in private to discontinue the takeover without publicising that information—then there would also be market abuse.[55]

12–22 It is not only that the behaviour relates directly to the securities but rather it can also be that the behaviour is carried on by reference, for example, to derivatives whose value is derived from those securities. Thus market abuse can be committed by people who speculate indirectly on the performance of those securities but who are nevertheless acting in a way which is abusive and which also depends on the performance of those securities. Thus, in s.118A(3) of the FSMA 2000, "the behaviour that is to be regarded as occurring in relation to qualifying investments" includes "behaviour which occurs in relation to anything that is the subject matter, or whose price or value is expressed by reference to the price or value of the qualifying investments" or behaviour which "occurs in relation to investments (whether or not they are qualifying investments) whose subject matter is the qualifying investments".[56]

(4)   Causing a false or misleading impression: "manipulating transactions"

12–23 The fourth form of behaviour constituting market abuse is akin to the disclosure of inside information offence, as set out in s.118(5) of the FSMA 2000 in the following terms:

> "The fourth is where the behaviour consists of effecting transactions or orders to trade (otherwise than for legitimate reasons and in conformity with accepted market practices on the relevant market) which—
> (a)   give, or are likely to give, a false or misleading impression as to the supply of, or demand for, or as to the price of, one or more qualifying investments, or
> (b)   secure the price of one or more such investments at an abnormal or artificial level."

---

[52] MAR,1.5.3(1)G.
[53] MAR,1.5.3(2)G.
[54] MAR,1.5.10(1)E.
[55] MAR,1.5.10(2)E.
[56] Financial Services and Markets Act 2000, s.118A(3).

The essence of this head of behaviour is artificiality. That is, if the dealer can justify the transactions—for example, if there is some pre-existing investment strategy which required the dealing to be made, or if it was part of a pre-existing legal obligation—then the dealing will not constitute market abuse. Otherwise, if transactions are made either with a view to giving a "false or misleading impression" as to the market demand for or price of securities, or to fix that price at an artificial level,[57] then there will be market abuse.[58] An example given in MAR of such behaviour is the acquisition of securities just before close of trading with a view to making the closing price of those securities seem markedly higher than otherwise it would have been.[59] Similarly, so-called "wash trades", in which securities appear to be bought and sold but in relation to which there is no change in beneficial ownership, will be market abuse when their object is to make it appear that there is a demand for those securities which does not exist, and at a price at which there is no market.[60] Another form of orchestrated market abuse in this context is the abuse of a dominant position in the market for particular securities so as to manipulate the market price of those securities.[61]

(5) Employing fictitious devices or contrivances: "manipulating devices"

The fifth form of behaviour constituting market abuse is akin to the disclosure of inside information offence,[62] as set out in s.118(6) of the FSMA 2000 in the following terms:

> "The fifth is where the behaviour consists of effecting transactions or orders to trade which employ fictitious devices or any other form of deception or contrivance."

12–24

Evidently the use of deception, fictitious devices and contrivances will constitute market abuse when they are conducted, in the view of the FCA, to take a benefit from the resultant, anticipated effect on the value of the securities in question. The FCA gives a number of examples in MAR of this sort of behaviour, as set out in the following paragraphs.

First, taking advantage of access to a regular media channel to communicate opinions which are calculated to affect the price of securities so as to lead to a beneficial effect for positions already held by the person making those comments.[63] This first example is difficult. In most circumstances when asked to make a comment, a person is likely to praise securities which she expects to perform well and to cast doubt on securities which she expects to perform poorly. That would be the case if the interviewee were simply telling the truth. It would be reasonable to suppose that such a person would also have structured her portfolios to mirror those views. This exercise in truth-telling may then influence

12–25

---

[57] MAR,1.6.10E.
[58] Examples are given at MAR, 1.6.15E.
[59] MAR,1.6.2(1)E; MAD art.1.2(c).
[60] MAR,1.6.2(2)E.
[61] MAR,1.6.4(1)E.
[62] See para.14–01.
[63] MAR,1.7.2(1)E.

the market value of those securities. Consequently, giving an honest opinion would tend to influence the price of those securities in the manner and in the direction indicated by the interviewee's comments. This, it is suggested, ought not to constitute market abuse because it is a feature and a result of ordinary trading. If this were to be considered to be market abuse then that would be to require all interviewees to hedge their comments and to dissemble so that they did not inadvertently cause a movement in market prices simply by voicing a genuinely-held opinion. By contrast, a maverick view (which was not genuinely held) expressed on such media which was done with a view to moving a market solely for the purposes of taking a benefit from a position on the securities in question would constitute market abuse. Such an interviewee would be speaking solely to move a market in a way which would realise a gain for her. Again, the artificiality involved in this situation, and the concomitant market manipulation involved, would be significant.[64]

12–26   Clearer FCA guidance would be required, it is suggested, if what the FCA wanted was to dissuade respected market participants from voicing their genuinely-held views about securities in the media; whereas people who deliberately misstate their views solely to move a market for personal gain would clearly be manipulating a market. The difficult case would be a person who voiced a genuinely-held belief in the strength of a given company with the result that his previous acquisition of shares in that company rose steeply in value after he tipped them or praised them in the media: here a market would have been manipulated, a personal gain would have been realised, but there would have been no artificiality in the views expressed. It is suggested that honesty ought not to be penalised if there is no intention to realise a gain which would not otherwise have been realised in tolerably predictable market conditions. Thus voicing support for a share in which one has already invested ought not to be market abuse if one is simply giving voice to a genuine belief that a particular share is a good bet. It would be an odd trader who did not back her own tips; or, rather, who did not invest in accordance with her own views of future market performance. The FCA would either have to ban such people from talking; or accept that one will invest in securities which one believes will rise, and that if the media interviews market participants then they will voice their opinions.

12–27   Discretion would be required, however, it is suggested, in relation to unknown takeovers currently in negotiation and similar events. An interviewee would need not to let slip any inside information to which he was privy either directly—by telling the world in a slip of the tongue that a takeover was in the offing—or indirectly—by hinting knowingly that the companies in question are involved in activities which are likely to help their prospects—because that would be to move a market. Genuinely inadvertent slips would be disastrous and embarrassing for secret negotiations, but need not be thought to be market abuse. Evidently, a professional with that sort of information would be well-advised to avoid media interviews so as to avoid the risk of such slips. This genuine error should be contrasted with a deliberate "slip" which was made with a view to driving the market.

---

[64] MAR,1.7.2(1)E.

Secondly, transactions which are performed to hide the beneficial ownership of property, for example to avoid transparency obligations under Pt 43 of the Companies Act 2006 (as discussed in Chapter 38), will be presumed to constitute market abuse.[65] Thirdly, "pump and dump" transactions in which misleadingly positive rumours about securities in which a long position has been taken, so as to increase the price of those securities with a view to selling them off when the price rises sufficiently, are market abuse.[66] Fourthly, "trash and cash" transactions in which a short position is taken, the inverse to the preceding example, with a view to depressing the price of the securities, will constitute market abuse.[67]

12–28

Frequently, such manipulating devices will involve the dissemination of false information, particularly when linked to dealing around the time of that dissemination of information by the same person or connected people.[68] It is suggested, that this need not be restricted to disseminations of false information; instead, it might also involve the dissemination solely of positive information with the concomitant suppression of negative information (particularly if it was information required to be disclosed by ordinary market practice or regulation), so as to have the same effect as disseminating literally false information.

12–29

(6) The dissemination of information giving a false or misleading impression: "dissemination"

The sixth form of behaviour constituting market abuse is akin to the disclosure of inside information offence, as set out in s.118(7) of the FSMA 2000 in the following terms:

12–30

> "The sixth is where the behaviour consists of the dissemination of information by any means which gives, or is likely to give, a false or misleading impression as to a qualifying investment by a person who knew or could reasonably be expected to have known that the information was false or misleading."

Akin to the preceding head of behaviour, disseminating false information will constitute market abuse. There is nothing in the drafting of this subsection which requires that this was done with the effect of generating a profit nor that it was even done with a view to generating such a profit. Simply acting in a planned manner so as to create a false impression as to the securities will constitute market abuse under this head.[69]

There are clearly issues as to the behaviour of journalists in such contexts. Newspaper stories, as is discussed in relation to insider dealing,[70] can drive the price of securities. Prior knowledge of a newspaper or other significant journal publication may therefore be inside information. Similarly, the abuse of journalistic sources can also disseminate false stories or can generate interest in securities and possibly create a market where none otherwise existed. Therefore,

12–31

---

[65] MAR,1.7.2(2)E.
[66] MAR,1.7.2(3)E.
[67] MAR,1.7.2(4)E.
[68] MAR,1.7.3E.
[69] See MAR,1.8.3E.
[70] See para.14–31.

the question arises as to the potential liability of journalists themselves for market abuse. Section 118A(4) of the FSMA 2000 provides that the dissemination of information by a person acting in the capacity of a journalist is to be assessed by taking into account the codes governing her profession unless she derives, directly or indirectly, any advantage or profits from the dissemination of the information.[71]

(7) Failure to observe standard of behaviour reasonably expected of a person in that market: "misleading behaviour and distortion"

12–32 The seventh form of behaviour constituting market abuse is akin to the disclosure of inside information offence, as set out in s.118(8) of the FSMA 2000 in the following terms[72]:

> "The seventh is where the behaviour (not falling within subsection (5), (6) or (7) [the three preceding types of behaviour])—
> (a)   is likely to give a regular user of the market a false or misleading impression as to the supply of, demand for or price or value of, qualifying investments, or
> (b)   would be, or would be likely to be, regarded by a regular user of the market as behaviour that would distort, or would be likely to distort, the market in such an investment,
> and the behaviour is likely to be regarded by a regular user of the market as a failure on the part of the person concerned to observe the standard of behaviour reasonably expected of a person in his position in relation to the market."

One of the examples which MAR gives of this form of market abuse is the movement of physical commodity stocks to give the appearance that there is a greater supply of that commodity than is actually the case.[73] Similarly, the movement of an empty cargo ship with a view to creating the impression of an increased supply would constitute market abuse.[74] Much depends on the market in question and the likely impact of particular types of distortion on regular users of that market, as well as the status of the person effecting that distortion the information and the regulatory requirements of the market in question.[75] Thus, for example, behaviour in compliance with the requirements imposed on holders of long positions in the "metal market aberrations regime" will not constitute distortion.[76]

12–33 It is not only that the behaviour relates directly to securities markets or some other, physically-settled market, but rather it can also be that the behaviour is carried on by reference, for example, to derivatives whose value is derived from those securities or commodities. Thus market abuse can be committed by people who speculate indirectly on the performance of those securities or commodities but who are nevertheless acting in a way which is abusive and which also depends on the performance of those securities or commodities. A clear manipulation strategy would be to acquire a series of cash-settled call options,

---

[71] Financial Services and Markets Act 2000, s 118A(4).
[72] cf. Financial Services and Markets Act 2000, s.118(9).
[73] MAR,1.9.2(1)E.
[74] MAR,1.9.2(2)E.
[75] See generally MAR,1.9.4E.
[76] MAR,1.9.3C.

exercisable over a period of time, which set the strike price for the securities at a much lower price than the buyer knows those securities will reach once her inside information is released into the market so as to increase the price of those securities. In this way, without actually acquiring a single security, the buyer of the options will receive a cash settlement amount under each option equivalent to the amount she would have received if she had actually bought securities at the price specified in the option and then actually sold them on the open market.[77] Thus, in s.118A(3) of the FSMA 2000, "the behaviour that is to be regarded as occurring in relation to qualifying investments" includes "behaviour which occurs in relation to anything that is the subject matter, or whose price or value is expressed by reference to the price or value of the qualifying investments" or behaviour which "occurs in relation to investments (whether or not they are qualifying investments) whose subject matter is the qualifying investments".[78] This would cover financial derivatives, such as options, used to speculate on the price of securities.

The line between the civil offences and the criminal offences of market abuse

What emerges from this discussion is that the sorts of activity which might be   **12–34**
punishable by the FCA are broadly similar to the offences set out in Part V of CJA 1993 and in s.397 of the FSMA 2000 which are considered in Chapter 14. The concern of both the market abuse code and the criminal law dealing with market integrity is that any information provided to the market is not misleading and that inside information is not misused. The market is based on free and open access to information: the integrity of the market is therefore predicated on the quality of that information and on the manner in which it is made available to the market and used by that market. The purpose of the FCA civil penalties in relation to market abuse is to give the FCA powers as regulator to intervene in this form of activity given the difficulty which has been experienced in generating prosecutions through the criminal law thus far.

C.   Territorial limitation of market abuse

Section 118A of the FSMA 2000 provides that: **12–35**

> "(1)   Behaviour is to be taken into account for the purposes of this Part only if it occurs—
>   (a)   in the United Kingdom, or
>   (b)   in relation to—
>   (i)   qualifying investments which are admitted to trading on a prescribed market situated in, or operating in, the United Kingdom,
>   (ii) qualifying investments for which a request for admission to trading on such a prescribed market has been made, or
>   (iii) in the case of section 118(2) and (3), investments which are related investment in relation to such qualifying investments."

---

[77] For a discussion of options, see A.S.Hudson, *The Law on Financial Derivatives*, para.2–30 et seq.
[78] Financial Services and Markets Act 2000 s.118A(3).

Thus the behaviour must take place in the United Kingdom; or if the behaviour does not take place in the UK then the investments must have been admitted to trading in the UK, or they must be subject to an application for admission to trading, or they must be related to such investments. Alternatively, it is sufficient that they are admitted to trading on a prescribed market or subject to an application to do so, or are related to such investments. It is further provided that a market is within the UK for the purposes of subs.(1):

> "as it applies in relation to section 118(4) and (8), a prescribed market accessible electronically in the United Kingdom is to be treated as operating in the United Kingdom."

Therefore, trading on-line in another jurisdiction is treated as being within the UK if it can be accessed from within the UK

5.   THE DEFINITION OF TERMS IN THE MARKET ABUSE CODE

A.   The meaning of the term "insider"

12–36   The type of person who must abuse the inside information is an "insider". Section 118B of the FSMA 2000 provides that:

> "For the purposes of this Part an insider is any person who has inside information—
> (a)   as a result of his membership of an administrative, management or supervisory body of an issuer of qualifying investments,
> (b)   as a result of his holding in the capital of an issuer of qualifying investments,
> (c)   as a result of having access to the information through the exercise of his employment, profession or duties,
> (d)   as a result of his criminal activities, or
> (e)   which he has obtained by other means and which he knows, or could reasonably be expected to know, is inside information."

Therefore, one is an insider if, first, one has inside information and, secondly, if one has that inside information as a result of one of the offices or activities in paragraphs (a) through (e) above. The issues concerning whether or not one is an insider are considered in relation to the similar concept in the criminal offence of insider dealing in Chapter 14.[79] A part of this definition of an "insider" is the definition of what constitutes "inside information", which is considered in the next paragraph.

"Inside information"

The general definition of "inside information"

12–37   Section 118C(2) of the FSMA 2000 provides that "inside information" is defined in the following way for the purposes of the market abuse provisions[80]:

---

[79]   See para.14–36.
[80]   Financial Services and Markets Act 2000, s.118B(1).

"(2) In relation to qualifying investments, or related investments, which are not commodity derivatives, inside information is information of a precise nature which—

    (a) is not generally available,

    (b) relates, directly or indirectly, to one or more issuers of the qualifying investments or to one or more of the qualifying investments, and

    (c) would, if generally available, be likely to have a significant effect on the price of the qualifying investments or on the price of related investments."

There are therefore four elements to this definition which are conjunctive. The first requirement that the information be of a "precise nature" excludes rumours and similar information. The remaining three requirements require that the information not be generally available, that it relates to listed companies or securities, and that it would have a significant effect on the price of those securities if generally known. There is reference to misuse of inside information being performed by an "insider".

Inside information in relation to commodities

12–38 It would be market manipulation to seek to give a false impression of the amount of a commodity held by making a ship seem to be loaded with a large amount of such a commodity. This tells us something about the particular nature of commodities transactions where, unlike most ordinary securities transactions, some physical, underlying property is transferred. Thus s.118C(3) of the FSMA 2000 provides that:

"(3) In relation to qualifying investments or related investments which are commodity derivatives, inside information is information of a precise nature which—

    (a) is not generally available,

    (b) relates, directly or indirectly, to one or more such derivatives, and

    (c) users of markets on which the derivatives are traded would expect to receive in accordance with any accepted market practices on those markets."

Therefore, commodity derivatives markets may have their own access to different forms of information. An observant stevedore or shipping clerk might have access on the quayside to valuable information not available to the public. Thus inside information in such contexts may be specific to the particular market in question. Section 118C(7) of the FSMA 2000 provides that in this context, deciding whether or not for the purposes of s.118C(3)(c) a person is "to be treated as expecting to receive information relating directly or indirectly to one or more such derivatives in accordance with any accepted market practices" one must consider whether or not that information is "routinely made available to the users of those markets", or is "required to be disclosed in accordance with any statutory provision, market rules, or contracts or customs on the relevant underlying commodity market or commodity derivatives market."

Inside information gleaned by those responsible for executing orders

12–39 Just as commodities markets (as just considered) may have particular personnel who have access to specialised forms of information which would be price sensitive if generally known, then those personnel who are responsible for executing orders may similarly have access to information as to the performance of particular companies by dint of knowing the volume of business in a particular security and so forth. Consequently, s.118C(4) of the FSMA 2000 provides that:

> "(4) In relation to a person charged with the execution of orders concerning any qualifying investments or related investments, inside information includes information conveyed by a client and related to the client's pending orders which—
>
> (a) is of a precise nature,
>
> (b) is not generally available,
>
> (c) relates, directly or indirectly, to one or more issuers of qualifying investments or to one or more qualifying investments, and
>
> (d) would, if generally available, be likely to have a significant effect on the price of those qualifying investments or the price of related investments."

This provision relates specifically to the execution of client orders. There is a reference to information conveyed by a client, which may include information as to the client's own investment strategies but also potentially to any inside information which that client may divulge. There is alternatively a reference to the client's pending orders. In either circumstance, the information must be "likely to have a significant effect" on qualifying investments.

Whether or not information is "precise"

12–40 It has been a requirement of some of the provisions considered thus far that the information in question must be "precise" if it is to be inside information. In this regard, s.118C(5) of the FSMA 2000 provides that:

> "(5) Information is precise if it—
>
> (a) indicates circumstances that exist or may reasonably be expected to come into existence or an event that has occurred or may reasonably be expected to occur, and
>
> (b) is specific enough to enable a conclusion to be drawn as to the possible effect of those circumstances or that event on the price of qualifying investments or related investments."

This definition needs to read in the context in which the term "precise" is used in s.118C to define "inside information" and then how that term is used in the market abuse code. That is, the inside information must relate to one of the types of entity described in s.118 of the FSMA 2000 (as considered above) by one of the types of person described in s.118. Those types of behaviour were much more tightly drawn than the definition of "precise" which refers generally to "circumstances" and not to any particular quality of circumstance. So, "precise" does not identify whether it is financial information relating to one company or any unpublished information relating to a market sector generally which are covered. In consequence, the statutory language would permit any of these possible interpretations.

Whether or not information will have a "significant effect"

12–41 It has been a requirement of some of the provisions considered thus far that the information in question must be such as to have a "significant effect" on the price or value of qualifying securities if it is to be inside information. In this regard, s.118C(6) of the FSMA 2000 provides that:

> "(6)   Information would be likely to have a significant effect on the price if and only if it is information of a kind which a reasonable investor would be likely to use as part of the basis of his investment decisions."

For the purposes of defining "significant effect" in the market abuse code the test is a version of the reasonable investor test found in relation to the general duty of disclosure in s.87A of the FSMA 2000 in relation to information which is necessary in a prospectus to enable an investor to make an informed assessment about securities.[81] Therefore, in deciding whether or not information would have a significant effect on the value of the securities we are required to consider whether or not a reasonable investor would be likely to use that information as a part, but not the sole factor, in his investment decision-making, not simply that he might do so.

Generally availability of information

A key aspect of information being inside information is that it is, in effect, privy   **12–42**
to insiders. Once information is generally available, it is no longer inside information by that definition. That is, the information loses its "inside" quality once it is known generally. However, diligent and perfectly lawful hard work by market analysts is likely to be able to predict market pressures impacting on companies and in turn on their profitability, or on the likelihood of mergers between certain types of entity. That is, the content of information can be guessed at before it is actually known. So, to take two random examples, the effect of widespread flooding in England which ruins crops is likely to raise the cost of raw materials for food production companies and so squeeze their profit margins; or the trend for mergers between large financial institutions with useful synergies might lead analysts to predict mergers of that sort. This could be the result of common-sense analysis, and not necessarily abuse of inside information. These predictions might take place at the same time as the managers of those companies are wrestling with exactly these issues. If the market analysts then learn the sort of information which might be gleaned at a meeting between institutional investors and the finance directors of public companies, and so advise their traders to make investments at a time which would have caused suspicions of insider dealing in other people, then the question arises as to the possibility that there has been market abuse. Section 118C(8) provides that:

> "(8)   Information which can be obtained by research or analysis conducted by, or on behalf of, users of a market is to be regarded, for the purposes of this Part, as being generally available to them."

So, analysis which unearths information which is not generally available to the market is nevertheless to be treated, correctly, as having been generally available to the analyst and his principals. The key question is as to the source of the

---

[81] See para.36–01.

information which went into that analysis: if the source was a legitimate source not tainted by being inside information as defined generally in s.118C, it is suggested, then that an investment made purely on that analyst's advice will not have been made using inside information. The source of the information which comprised the prediction is therefore the key question.

6. THE FCA'S POWERS IN RELATION TO MARKET ABUSE

A. The power to impose penalties in cases of market abuse

The circumstances in which penalties will be imposed

12–43 Section 123 of the FSMA 2000 provides the FCA with the power to "impose a penalty of such amount as it considers appropriate" on a person who has engaged in market abuse or who has encouraged another person to engage in market abuse.[82] Section 129 of the FSMA 2000 provides the court with a power to give directions as to the nature of a penalty in the form of a fine which should be payable to the FCA in a case of market abuse. Further to s.123(1)(b) of the FSMA 2000, the FCA may impose a penalty on a person whom the FCA is satisfied has either "required" or "encouraged" another person to engage in behaviour which would have been market abuse if performed by that first person. This requirement or encouragement can be caused by an action or by an omission.[83] The FCA is empowered to direct a recognised investment exchange or clearing house to suspend any investigations which it might be making under its own rules when the FCA considers it expedient or desirable because the FCA may exercise one of its powers under the market abuse code. Instead of imposing a penalty by way of a fine, the FCA is empowered to publish a statement that the defendant engaged in market abuse.[84] Any action taken under s.123 must be given way of a decision notice with a right to refer the matter to the Market Tribunal.[85] The FCA is required to publish statements of policy in relation to its approach to penalties[86] and statements of procedure in relation to those same matters.[87]

Relief from the penalty

12–44 The penalty is not to be imposed if the FCA is satisfied that the defendant reasonably believed that she was not committing market abuse, nor encouraging or requiring others to do so.[88] Alternatively, the penalty is not to be imposed if the

---

[82] Financial Services and Markets Act 2000, s.123(1).
[83] Financial Services and Markets Act 2000, s.123(1)(b).
[84] Financial Services and Markets Act 2000, s.123(3).
[85] Financial Services and Markets Act 2000, s.127
[86] Financial Services and Markets Act 2000, s.124.
[87] Financial Services and Markets Act 2000, s.125.
[88] Financial Services and Markets Act 2000, s.123(2)(a).

FCA is satisfied that the defendant "took all reasonable precautions and exercised all due diligence" to avoid behaving in a manner which would constitute market abuse.[89]

B. The regulation of "inside information" under the Listing Rules' Model Code

The Official List is the list of the most significant companies whose securities are available to be marketed to the general investing public, and in consequence such listed securities are regulated differently by the FCA, acting as the UK Listing Authority ("UKLA"). In this context, UKLA regulates misuse of inside information under the listing rules by means of the Model Code in Annex 1 to Chapter 9 of the Listing Rules. The Listing Rules are considered in detail in Chapter 38. This code requires that the instrument in question be one which is traded on an existing market and in which there is a continuing market. The types of behaviour caught within this regime relate not only to dealings directly in securities but also to any behaviour which affects their value more generally.[90] Further, that behaviour may take place in another jurisdiction but nevertheless have an impact on instruments traded in the United Kingdom and so fall within the market abuse code.[91] Market standards will be of great importance in the application of the code, given the importance given over in that code to close consideration of the norms usually applied particular markets[92] in particular when seeking to apply the "reasonable user" test outlined above.[93]

12–45

Dealings with a listed companies' securities form the focus of the Model Code particularly when they are conducted in a prohibited period by the use of inside information by any person who is "discharging managerial responsibilities" or who is an "insider employee". The "prohibited period" provision relates to "any close period" or "any period when there exists any matter which constitutes inside information in relation to the company",[94] perhaps during the lead-up to an announcement of a merger or before an exceptional announcement involving profit forecasts via a recognised information service. The "close period" refers to the 60 day period before the preliminary announcement of the company's annual results or half yearly results (as appropriate), or 30 days before the preliminary announcement of quarterly results (if appropriate).[95] Therefore, dealings with

12–46

---

[89] Financial Services and Markets Act 2000, s.123(2)(b).

[90] MAR 1, 1.11.8E.

[91] MAR 1, 1.2.9G.

[92] MAR 1, 1.2.3E.

[93] cf. *Polly Peck v Nadir* [1992] 4 All E.R. 769 where an objective test of reasonableness is used in relation to a claim for knowing receipt but where that objectivity is tempered by making reference to a "reasonable banker" in relation to financial transactions and not simply to an average person who may or may not have any banking knowledge. The standard used by the legislation of a hypothetical "reasonable user" of the market is intended to replicate the "reasonable man" test used frequently by the common law to establish a level of objectivity but while also retaining some recognition of the particular context within which that defendant is operating; thus creating a test more akin to the "average trader on the Stock Exchange" than "the man on the Clapham omnibus".

[94] Listing Rules, Ch.9, Annex 1, para.1(e).

[95] Listing Rules, Ch.9, Annex 1, para.1(a).

listed securities within a "prohibited period" using inside information by any restricted person are prohibited[96] unless they have clearance to deal with those transactions.[97] There is an obligation on restricted persons discharging managerial responsibilities to take "reasonable steps to prevent any dealings by or on behalf of any connected person of his in any securities of the company on considerations of a short term nature".[98] Transactions by restricted persons which fall within this code must be made public in accordance with the Disclosure and Transparency Rules.[99]

12–47   In general terms, the Disclosure and Transparency Rules oblige an issuer to notify a recognised information service "as soon as possible"[100] of any inside information which "directly concerns the issuer",[101] unless the issuer (on its own initiative) considers the prevention of disclosure to be necessary to protect its own "legitimate interests".[102] The term "legitimate interests" is not defined but examples given in the Disclosure Rules of matters which may impact on a company's legitimate interests include negotiations which are train and the public awareness of which may affect them adversely, or contracts entered into by one part of a company (such as a management board) but which require ratification by another part of the company (such as a supervisory board).[103] Disclosure in general terms must be full disclosure and not selective disclosure[104] except in relation to the preservation of duties of confidentiality[105] or, impliedly, to protect a company's legitimate interests. When dealing with rumours or speculation about the company then the company must assess whether or not that speculation is of a type that the company is in possession of inside information by knowing the true state of affairs (impliedly assuming there is not already inside information which requires publication).[106]

C.   Market abuse in the City Code on Takeovers and Mergers

12–48   Section 120 of the FSMA 2000 permits this FCA code on market abuse to interact with the City Code on Takeovers and Mergers (or, the Takeover Code). Section 122(1) of the FSMA 2000 provides that if a person "behaves in a way which is described in the code as behaviour that, in the Authority's opinion, does not amount to market abuse that behaviour of his is to be taken, for the purposes of

---

[96] Listing Rules, Ch.9, Annex 1, para.3.

[97] Listing Rules, Ch.9, Annex 1.3, in accordance with the procedure set out at Listing Rules, Ch.9, Annex 1.4.

[98] Listing Rules, Ch.9, Annex 1, para.20.

[99] See Disclosure and Transparency Rules, s.3.1 generally; see also Market Abuse Directive art.6.

[100] This will be satisfied if the issuer acted as soon as was possible in the circumstance of factors which were only gradually coming to light: Disclosure and Transparency Rules, Ch.2, para.2.2.2R. A short delay in publication of the information will be acceptable if it is "necessary to clarify the situation": Disclosure and Transparency Rules, Ch.2, para.2.2.9G.

[101] Disclosure and Transparency Rules, Ch.2, para.2.2.1R.

[102] Disclosure and Transparency Rules, Ch.2, para.2.5.1R. See Market Abuse Directive ("MAD") art.6(1).

[103] Disclosure and Transparency Rules, Ch.2, para.2.5.3R.

[104] Disclosure and Transparency Rules, Ch.2, para.2.5.6R. See MAD art.6(3).

[105] Disclosure and Transparency Rules, Ch.2, para.2.5.7G.

[106] Disclosure and Transparency Rules, Ch.2, para.2.7.1R.

this Act, as not amounting to market abuse". Section 122(2) of the FSMA 2000 provides, however, that "[o]therwise, the [code] may be relied upon so far as it indicates whether or not that behaviour should be taken to amount to market abuse". The City Code is discussed in Chapter 42.

PART IV

CRIMINAL LAW

CHAPTER 13

CRIMINAL OFFENCES IN THE LAW OF FINANCE

CORE PRINCIPLES

The criminal law is significant in relation to the law of finance in two particular senses: the first relates to the criminalisation of particular types of activity (such as insider dealing and money laundering) with the intention of maintaining the integrity of financial markets, and the second criminalises failures to observe particular regulatory requirements so as to support the authority of the FCA to enforce compliance with FSMA 2000 and its regulatory rulebooks. This Part IV considers insider dealing, money laundering and fraud. This chapter considers the particular role of criminal law in financial markets and some specific offences under FSMA 2000.

1. INTRODUCTION

This short chapter considers how the criminal law and the law of finance overlap in outline, before later chapters consider the detail of the principal offences. This Part IV generally is concerned with the principal offences under the English criminal law which apply to financial activity. These offences fall into two types. First, there are offences under the general criminal law which are important in the context of the law of finance—in particular the law on criminal fraud and

13–01

theft—but general offences such as assault (which could, of course, occur on a trading floor) are not considered because they are not specifically related to the law of finance. Second, there are offences which were created specifically for the financial context: in particular the law on insider trading[1] and the general offences set out in the Financial Services and Markets Act 2000.[2]

13–02   It is one of the maudlin vicissitudes of life that there are bad people who do bad things, and that is why we require criminal law. Some of those bad people perform their bad deeds in the financial services sector. It is one of the maudlin vicissitudes of criminal law that the system which requires a police force to detect crime, a prosecution service to prosecute trials, and a judicial and jury system to try them, is simply not suitable to provide sufficient oversight to prevent criminal activity being perpetrated on rapidly-moving, cross-border financial markets. Therefore, the general criminal law—dealing with theft, fraud and so on—has had to be extended to fit the financial services context. In this sense, the general criminal law may apply to financial activity but it was not created specifically to deal with finance, and therefore a large number of criminal offences have had to be created specifically for the financial markets context.

13–03   There are two sorts of criminal law applying to the financial services context, beyond the general criminal law. First, there are those rules such as the code on insider dealing (dealt with in Chapter 14) which criminalise particular activities committed in the financial services context because they are considered to be the sorts of behaviour which in themselves require criminal sanction. Secondly, there are those criminal offences which are created principally by the Financial Services and Markets Act 2000 ("FSMA 2000") to ensure compliance with requirements of that Act such that, for example, there must be a prospectus published in approved form in certain circumstances and that financial promotion is not to be made without authorisation, and so on. This second category of offences, therefore, supports the broader regulatory goals of FSMA 2000 and of the regulatory handbooks. As is discussed in the next chapter, on *insider dealing*, much of this criminal law has proved insufficient to deal with all of the abuse at which it is aimed, and therefore it has had to be supplemented by enhancing the powers and the role of the Financial Conduct Authority ("FCA") and the Prudential Regulatory Authority ("PRA")—particularly in relation to market abuse—to investigate and prosecute financial crimes such as insider dealing.[3] Thus, the context of financial market activity requires that the regulatory authorities are closer to market activity than the organs of the criminal law and so stands in their place in some contexts to ensure proper regulation of those markets at all levels.

---

[1] See para.14–01.
[2] See para.13–09.
[3] Financial Services and Markets Act 2000, s.402.

2. CRIMINAL LAW AND THE LAW OF FINANCE

A. Inter-sections between financial regulation and the substantive criminal law

The criminal law is a significant part of the regulation of the securities markets, as is the creation of so-called "civil penalties" for market abuse in the FSMA 2000. By "regulation" in this sense, I do not mean the sort of day-to-day, minute-by-minute observation of financial markets which is conducted by the regulators, but rather an impact on the behaviour of market participants by identifying types of behaviour which will open their perpetrator up to criminal punishment, and the stigma which such activities would attract to any financial institution involved. The criminalisation of some financial activities is clearly of great importance in the creation of a culture of compliance with a basic set of ethical principles among market actors. The effect of criminalisation is therefore intended to be to prevent those activities from taking place and also to ensure the punishment of any contraventions of those basic ethical principles. However, the criminal justice system which puts the criminal law into action is a lumbering behemoth compared to the (comparatively) nimble financial regulatory authorities. The FCA is able to monitor the day-to-day activities of participants in financial markets and to intervene actively in those markets using its statutory powers of investigation and so forth; whereas the criminal law can only react to prosecutions begun by one of the appropriate organs of the State or the police force, and can only act by means of lengthy criminal trials which take place long after the acts which give rise to them. This lapse of time before prosecutions may cause a loss of confidence in the marketplace while the trial is being prepared, whereas comparatively quick action taken by the FCA can shore up confidence and prevent abusive behaviour. The criminal law is therefore concerned with punishment of criminals, whereas FCA regulation is concerned with the integrity of the marketplace in which those acts were committed. A modern society requires both punishment and markets acting with integrity.

13–04

Thus, to *enforce* an ethic each day in the marketplace requires a regulator imbued with powers to act; whereas the criminal law has enormous power as a residual means of punishment and censure but one which is only *reactive* to circumstances after the event. Not that this is to say that the old Financial Services Authority was always as invasive as one may have wished nor that it regulated investment firms sufficiently closely, but its powers certainly gave it that potential—and those powers have since been passed to the FCA and the PRA. However, there is a sense in which the criminal law is more frightening than the FCA to individual traders or to investment firms in that the criminal law stands aloof from the common morality of the trading floor and can, to put it crudely, send perpetrators to prison. The FCA works with investment firms, the FCA and the PRA consult in the creation of their rulebooks, and they are required by the FSMA 2000 to have an eye to the competitive position of the UK financial sector. Unlike the FCA, the criminal law does not produce rulebooks which are the product of long consultation with market participants, the criminal law does not feel the need to

13–05

appease nor to win the confidence of market participants, and the criminal law demands "obedience" as opposed to being satisfied with "compliance" as financial regulation does.

13–06 It comes as no surprise, therefore, to observe that when the criminal law intervenes in financial activity, otherwise than in relation to behaviour which constitutes a criminal offence in any event, it is not concerned with systemic questions (such as the preservation of the integrity of the financial system under insider dealing legislation) nor is it concerned to support individual, regulatory requirements under statute (such as the requirement that a prospectus be published before securities are offered to the public) so that there is a genuine motivation for market participants to observe those requirements. This chapter identifies some of the key offences set out in FSMA 2000 in relation to the conduct of securities transactions, in relation to selling financial services without authorisation, in relation to disseminating unauthorised advertisements for financial products, and so forth.

B. Criminal law and the broader context

13–07 Much of the purpose of the criminal law in the law of finance is either to achieve broader policy goals or to create the impression of the pursuit of broader policy goals. Two key examples—which receive separate treatment in the two chapters to follow this one—are *insider dealing* and *money laundering*. The law on insider dealing is concerned to protect the integrity of the market and to ensure that contracting parties on securities markets are acting on an even playing-field.[4] That is a broader policy goal than simply ensuring the integrity of authorised firms: it is a policy goal concerned to prevent the abuse of inside information. This species of criminal offence has two goals: to preserve the integrity of the stock markets and to ensure that market participants are acting without one of them having an unfair advantage over the other. Thus, the purpose of the law on insider dealing—as expressed in the EU directives and in the appropriate financial regulations—is to achieve larger social goals to do with economic efficiency. The criminal offences relating to market manipulation have similar economic goals.[5] The law on money-laundering was concerned to prevent financial institutions being used as conduits for criminal financing, in particular drug money when it was first introduced under the Drug Trafficking Act 1994, and latterly has broadened its concern in an attempt to prevent terrorist organisations using the financial system either to invest, raise or launder money, further to the Proceeds of Crime Act 2002 and various pieces of anti-terrorism legislation.[6] Again, the purpose of this species of offence is to deal with criminal justice and political priorities—in particular with money laundering in an attempt to strangle criminal use of property in the hope that that would prevent organised criminal and terrorist organisations from functioning effectively.

---

[4] See para.14–04.
[5] See para.14–71.
[6] See para.15–01.

As a question purely of public relations, introducing a criminal offence to deal **13–08** with a perceived abuse is a headline-grabbing means for public policymakers to gesture an intention to deal with a problem. As has been outlined above, the FCA has been empowered to act in areas such as prosecuting insider dealing cases[7]: thus illustrating the need for the traditional architecture of the criminal law to be supplemented by an organisation with know-how about financial markets. Thus, for all of the grand gestures associated with the criminal law, financial regulation plays a significant, quasi-criminal law role albeit one that is less likely to grab headlines. Just as the police and the Crown Prosecution Service attend the mainstream criminal justice system, the FCA attends the oversight of financial activity (as discussed in Part III of this book) broadly in parallel to the criminal justice system's goal of controlling unacceptable behaviour. And yet, as is discussed in the next chapter, very few prosecutions were brought for insider dealing by either part of the legal system before the summer of 2008, and it is not clear how successful financial regulators can actually be in controlling market abuse.

3. KEY CRIMINAL OFFENCES UNDER THE FSMA 2000

A. Offences surrounding the regulation of financial markets

The detail of financial regulation was discussed in Chapter 8. The ultimate **13–09** sanctions for failure to comply with Bank of England financial regulations— whether through the FCA or the PRA—are supplied by the criminal law. That is, to ensure that financial institutions and their employees comply with key financial regulations, it is made clear in the FSMA 2000 that a breach of certain regulations will constitute a criminal offence. Thus, by way of example, s.19(1) of the FSMA 2000 contains "the general prohibition"[8] to the effect that "[n]o person may carry on a regulated activity in the United Kingdom", nor may she purport to do so, unless she is either an authorised person or is exempt from the requirement for authorisation. Similarly, s.21 of the FSMA 2000 contains a prohibition on financial promotion without authorisation.[9] These two core provisions of the financial regulatory scheme are supplemented by the criminal law in that failure to obey either prohibition constitutes a criminal offence. Therefore, there are two forms of criminal offence in relation to financial activity: the first acts as a supplement to the core requirements of financial regulation— such as ss.19 and 21 of the FSMA 2000, the criminal offences relating to market abuse, and the offences considered in the next section—and the second type of criminal offence acts as a code of substantive criminal offences in themselves— such as the code on insider dealing and that on money laundering. The first type of criminal offence is intended to ensure obedience to the FSMA 2000 generally, and thus has shored up the powers of the regulatory bodies created by that Act.

---

[7] See para.14–07.

[8] As referred to in Financial Services and Markets Act 2000, s.19(2).

[9] The financial promotion code contains a central principle which provides that no person shall "in the course of business, communicate an invitation or inducement to engage in investment activity": Financial Services and Markets Act 2000 s.21(1).

The second type of criminal offence is a more traditional criminal offence because Parliament has identified undesirable activities in society and sought both to deter and to punish them with criminal offences because they are considered to be wrong in themselves.

B.   Offences seeking to reinforce the powers of statutory bodies under FSMA 2000

The offence of giving false or misleading information to the FCA in purported compliance with financial services regulation

13–10   The FSMA 2000 and the panoply of regulation to which it has given birth can only be effective if there is some suitable sanction which can be imposed on market participants in the event that they fail to comply with those regulations. To this end there is an offence of giving false or misleading information to the FCA in purported compliance with financial services regulation created further to s.398 of FSMA 2000:

> "(1)   A person who, in purported compliance with any requirement imposed by or under this Act, knowingly or recklessly gives the authority information which is false or misleading in a material particular is guilty of an offence.
> (2)   Subsection (1) applies only to a requirement in relation to which no other provision of this Act creates an offence in connection with the giving of information."

Ultimately, therefore, wherever the financial regulations effected further to the Act[10] impose an obligation on any person to provide information of any kind to the FCA or the PRA then an offence is committed if that information is either false (which would include it being simply incorrect in a general sense as well as fraudulently inaccurate) or is misleading; and also provided that the person seeking to comply with the regulation either knows that the information is false or misleading, or is reckless as to whether or not that is the case. The question of the information being "misleading" is a complex one. Information could be misleading if it is read by someone who is unschooled in financial markets and who therefore misunderstands it due to some ambiguity in its terminology even if that would not have fooled an experienced market participant. That the information is being provided to the regulator would mean that it would need to be misleading to a regulator, and not to any hypothetical alternative reader. That the information need not be deliberately misleading is suggested by the fact that offence is committed either if the information was provided knowing that it was misleading or alternatively being reckless as to whether or not it was misleading. The word "reckless" means "being heedless of the consequences of one's actions . . . incautious, rash", or "negligent in one's duties", or "inconsiderate of oneself or another".[11] Recklessness in criminal law requires that the defendant was aware of the harm which would result from the act but that he nevertheless

---

[10] This is, I consider, the proper interpretation of this provision. It is only of any effect if it extends to FCA and other regulations effected under a power created by the Act, and not simply to powers which are explicitly included in the Act itself.

[11] All three definitions are given in the *Shorter Oxford English Dictionary*.

acted so as to cause that harm.[12] Recklessness in this context would encompass someone either being aware that she had not checked the accuracy of the information nor considered whether or not it would be information which could mislead the FCA,[13] or simply be heedless as to whether or not it would be misleading.

The regulators have a number of statutory powers to investigate infractions of the Act. Therefore, it is also an offence to give false information to investigators under s.177(4) of the FSMA 2000.[14]   **13–11**

Offence of giving false or misleading information to the OFT

There is an offence of giving false or misleading information to the Office of Fair Trading ("OFT") under s.399 of the FSMA 2000 in the following terms: **13–12**

> "Section 44 of the Competition Act 1998 (offences connected with the provision of false or misleading information) applies in relation to any function of the Office of Fair Trading under this Act as if it were a function under Part I of that Act."

Thus the role of the Office of Fair Trading supplements the work of the FCA in relation to entities which are not regulated by the FCA in many contexts (where pawnbrokers were traditionally regulated by the OFT).

Offences committed by bodies corporate and partnerships, and the liability of officers

Under s.400 of the FSMA 2000:   **13–13**

> "(1)   If an offence under this Act committed by a body corporate is shown—
> (a)to have been committed with the consent or connivance of an officer, or
> (b)to be attributable to any neglect on his part,
> the officer as well as the body corporate is guilty of the offence and liable to be proceeded against and punished accordingly."

Thus, where any offence is committed by a body corporate with either the connivance or consent of an individual or in a way which is attributable to that individual's neglect, then that individual is also guilty of the offence committed by the body corporate.

---

[12] *R v G* [2004] 1 A.C. 1034; *Brown v The Queen* [2005] 2 W.L.R. 1558.
[13] It is not clear on the face of the legislation whether the information the informer considers that it *would* mislead the FCA or merely considers that it *might* mislead the FCA. I would suggest that recklessness would be satisfied if the defendant was aware that it could mislead the FCA.
[14] Investigations are at para.9–44.

C.   Offences in the securities markets relating to offers of securities to the public

13–14   The criminal law acts as the central plank to the law on issuing securities to the public by providing that approved prospectuses must be made available to the public. That a failure to have a prospectus approved constitutes an offence lets us know that issuers of securities must have a prospectus prepared and approved before an issue to the public is made. Oddly, the legislation does not provide any positively worded requirement to that effect: instead the legislation is drafted in the form of a negative in that we are told it is a criminal offence not to do something, and regulated persons have an obligation to obey the requirements of the Prospectus Rules. Section 85 of the FSMA 2000, as amended by the Prospectus Regulations 2005, provides that it is unlawful either to offer transferable securities to the public in the UK[15] or to request the admission to trading on a regulated market of transferable securities[16] unless an approved prospectus has been made available to the public before the offer or request, as appropriate, is made. There is a second offence which is made out when a request is made to admit securities to trading on a regulated market without an approved prospectus having been made available to the public first. These provisions are considered in detail in Chapter 36.

---

[15] Financial Services and Markets Act 2000 s.85(1).
[16] Financial Services and Markets Act 2000, s.85(2).

INSIDER DEALING

CORE PRINCIPLES

The offences relating to "insider dealing" and "market manipulation" arise under Part V of the Criminal Justice Act 1993 and the Financial Services and Markets Act 2000 ("FSMA 2000") respectively. Insider dealing has been criminalised in part so that there is no inequality of bargaining power between one party who has inside information which the other party could not have, and also so as to preserve a perception of market integrity among investors.

The principal offence of insider dealing arises where the defendant "deals in securities that are price-affected securities in relation to the information". The offence is focused on buying or selling securities on the basis of inside information. There is a dealing in securities whenever securities are bought or sold by the defendant, or where she procures such a purchase or sale. Information is "inside information" if it relates to securities, if it is specific and precise, if it has not been made public, and if it had been made public it would have had a "significant effect on the price" of securities. The defendant must be an insider who has access to this information by virtue of her employment or other professional duties, or must have the information from an "inside source".

It is also an offence to encourage another person to deal in securities or to disclose information improperly to another person.

The offences of market manipulation are contained in s.397 and 398 of the FSMA 2000. Market manipulation arises where a "statement, promise or forecast" is made which is "misleading, false, or deceptive in a material particular". The purpose of the offence is to prevent the market value of shares being artificially raised or lowered by the dissemination of rumour and so forth. It is an offence to encourage someone to enter into transactions or to refrain from transacting as a result of such a statement.

1.   INTRODUCTION

14–01   This chapter is concerned with the criminal offences relating to insider dealing and market manipulation.[1] These offences seek to punish people who use "inside information" about quoted companies which has not yet been made public when dealing in securities (that is, "insider dealing" under Part V of the Criminal Justice Act 1993 ("CJA 1993")[2]), or who seek to manipulate a market by making a misleading statement (that is, "market manipulation" further to s.397 of the Financial Services and Markets Act 2000 ("FSMA 2000")). Insider dealing is particularly difficult for the authorities to identify and there have consequently been very few prosecutions. Therefore, the insider dealing code has been supplemented by the FCA regulation of "market abuse"[3] and a power under FSMA 2000 to impose "civil penalties" on transgressors.[4] The old Financial Services Authority was empowered to commence prosecutions on its own cognisance without needing authority from the Director of Public Prosecutions or any other agency.[5] The aim of these extensions to the criminal law's insider dealing regime has been to move the burden of combating misuses of inside information to the FCA, as regulator for the securities markets in the UK, so that the FCA can work in tandem with the criminal law.

14–02   The law on "market abuse" generally can be thought of as forming a single topic covering the criminal law on insider dealing and market manipulation, together with the FCA in the regulation of market abuse. The regulation of market abuse is conducted by the FCA further to s.118 et seq. of FSMA 2000 and was considered

---

[1] Parts of this chapter are based on parts of Ch.26 of A.S. Hudson, *Securities Law* (London: Sweet & Maxwell, 2008). For an excellent account of the law on insider dealing see B. Hannigan, *Insider Dealing* 2nd edn (Longmans, 1994).

[2] See para.14–03.

[3] Market abuse was considered in detail in Ch.12.

[4] A form of quasi-criminal power to impose penalties which has been granted to the Financial Services Authority ("the FSA") by Pt VIII of the Financial Services and Markets Act 2000 as considered below.

[5] *R v Rollins* [2010] UKSC 39, [2010] 1 W.L.R. 1922; affirming the decision of the Court of Appeal [2009] EWCA Crim 1941, [2010] Bus. L.R. 734. See also *R. (Uberoi) v City of Westminster Magistrates' Court* [2009] 1 W.L.R. 1905, DC.

in Chapter 12.[6] In this book a division has been made between the criminal law and financial regulation because from a lawyer's perspective those two sources of law have different effects. From the perspective of the governance of securities markets generally, there is a common effort to prevent misuse of information so as to preserve the integrity of those markets by using both the criminal law and financial regulation.

2.   THE SCOPE OF THE INSIDER DEALING CODE

A.   The insider dealing provisions

The statutory provisions on the criminalisation of insider dealing are contained in Part V of the Criminal Justice Act 1993 ("CJA 1993"), comprising ss.52–64 and Schs 1 and 2 of that Act.[7] Part V was passed to enforce the provisions of the EC Insider Dealing Directive[8] the preamble to which set out the purpose of the legislation to be to provide an "assurance afforded to investors that they are placed on an equal footing and that they will be protected against the improper use of inside information". The concept "inside information" is also used in relation to market abuse[9] (considered later in this chapter) and in relation to the Model Code in the Disclosure and Transparency Rules (considered in Chapter 38).[10] The FCA has the authority to impose "a penalty of such amount as it considers appropriate".[11]

14–03

B.   The objectives of the insider dealing provisions

There are two statutory objectives underpinning the insider dealing code: first, the protection of the integrity of the securities markets and, secondly, ensuring that in any securities transaction there is no imbalance of information between the buyer and the seller of that security. These underlying objectives in the legislation are considered below.[12]

14–04

---

[6] See para.12–08 et seq.
[7] See generally B. Hannigan, *Insider Dealing* 2nd edn (Longmans, 1994); Rider and Ashe, *Insider Crime—The New Law* (Jordans, 1993); Rider, Alexander and Linklater, *Market Abuse and Insider Dealing* (Tottel Publishing, 2002).
[8] 89/592/EC [1989] O.J. L334/30.
[9] See para.12–37.
[10] See para.38–36.
[11] Financial Services and Markets Act 2000, s.123.
[12] See para.14–64.

3. THE INSIDER DEALING OFFENCES

A. The three offences

The offences in outline

14–05   There are three offences relating to insider dealing. The principal focus of the offence in s.52(1) CJA 1993 is on individuals who deal in "price-affected" securities using information which they gleaned as an "insider". The second offence relates to encouraging others to deal in price-affected securities. The third offence relates to disclosing inside information. There are then a range of defences to these offences. Each element of these offences is considered in turn in the sections to follow.

The penalty

14–06   The offences are triable either way.[13] The maximum penalty on conviction on indictment is seven year's imprisonment or a fine of any amount, or both.[14] The maximum penalty on summary conviction is six month's imprisonment or a fine not exceeding the statutory maximum, or both.[15]

B. The power of the Financial Conduct Authority

14–07   Further to the enactment of the Financial Services and Markets Act 2000 ("FSMA 2000"), the Financial Conduct Authority has the power to prosecute any allegations of insider dealing.[16] Thus, the day-to-day regulator of the securities markets is given an inquisitorial and prosecutorial power in relation to insider dealing, which operates in tandem (it is suggested) with its powers to regulate market abuse more generally (as was discussed in Chapter 12).

C. The principal offence of insider dealing in s.52(1) CJA 1993

The elements of the offence under s.52(1) CJA 1993

14–08   The principal offence of "insider dealing" is contained in s.52(1) CJA 1993. Each expression in that subsection is defined elsewhere in the Act, and therefore we shall begin with s.52(1) before considering each of its component terms separately. The principal offence in s.52(1) is expressed in the following terms:

---

[13] Criminal Justice Act 1993, s.61(1).

[14] Criminal Justice Act 1993, s.61(1).

[15] Criminal Justice Act 1993, s 61(1).

[16] Financial Services and Markets Act 2000 s.402. That the Financial Services Authority (the former incarnation of the FCA) has the power under the legislation to bring a prosecution on its own initiative was upheld by the Supreme Court in *R v Rollins* [2010] UKSC 39, [2010] 1 W.L.R. 1922; and also upheld by the Divisional Court in *R (Uberoi) v City of Westminster Magistrates' Court*[2009] 1 W.L.R. 1905, DC.

"(1)   An individual who has information as an insider is guilty of insider dealing if, in the circumstances mentioned in subsection (3), he deals in securities that are price-affected securities in relation to the information."

The elements of the offence are therefore as follows. First, the offence is committed by an individual (that is, a human being[17]). Secondly, that individual must have information as an "insider", as is defined below, as opposed to having that information in any other way. There are other offences dealing with non-insiders considered below.[18] Thirdly, the individual must "deal" in securities, as is defined below. Fourthly, the securities in which the individual deals must be "price-affected securities", as is defined below. Fifthly, those securities must be price-affected securities "in relation to the information", and not coincidentally price-affected due to some other factor. Thus, the insider must be dealing in relation to information which itself affects the price of the securities. Sixthly and furthermore, these activities must be performed in the circumstances set out in s.52(3):

"(3)   The circumstances referred to above [in s.52(1)] are that the acquisition or disposal in question occurs on a regulated market, or that the person dealing relies on a professional intermediary or is himself acting as a professional intermediary."

Each of these elements is considered in turn. The legislation defines most of these terms in ss.54 through 60 of the CJA 1993, and therefore later sections of this chapter cross-refer with those definitions. Before turning to those questions of definition, however, we shall consider the two inchoate offences relating to insider dealing which are contained in s.52(2) of CJA 1993.

D.   The two inchoate offences relating to insider dealing in s.52(2) of CJA 1993

Aside from the principal offence in s.52(1) of CJA 1993 considered immediately above, an individual with inside information may commit two further offences, as set out in s.52(2) of CJA 1993 in the following terms:

14–09

"(2)   An individual who has information as an insider is also guilty of insider dealing if—
(a)   he encourages another person to deal in securities that are (whether or not that other knows it) price-affected securities in relation to the information, knowing or having reasonable cause to believe that the dealing would take place in the circumstances mentioned in subsection (3); or
(b)   he discloses the information, otherwise than in the proper performance of the functions of his employment, office or profession, to another person."

There are two offences here in effect. They are described as being "inchoate" in that they are offences of encouraging behaviour or disclosing information, and therefore operate in parallel to the principal offence.

---

[17] The term "person" may include companies as well as human beings; whereas "individual" can refer only to a human being.

[18] See para.14–09.

14–10   The first offence is committed if the insider encourages another person to deal in price-affected securities. Typically, this may involve an insider using a relative or a controlled person to deal in securities effectively on her behalf. The conditions in s.52(3) are that the securities be traded on a regulated market (as defined below) or that the insider relies on a professional intermediary or is herself a professional intermediary.[19]

14–11   The second offence is committed if the insider discloses the information to another person. However, this offence will not be committed if the disclosure takes place in the ordinary conduct of the insider's employment: for example if an insider communicates information to a fellow employee of the same company in the ordinary performance of her duties. Thus, for the insider to leave a Dictaphone cassette containing reference to the information for her secretary to type up as part of confidential minutes of a board meeting would not fall within the offence; whereas for the insider to leave a Dictaphone cassette containing the information and instructions as to how to acquire shares in the company in almost any other context before the information becomes public knowledge would fall within the ambit of the offence, because the former use is in the ordinary course of the insider's employment whereas the latter would not be. On the terms of s.52(3)(b) the offence is committed simply by means of the disclosure. There is no requirement that the disclosure have been made with the intention of causing a dealing in securities. Instead the disclosure itself is sufficient to constitute the actus reus of the offence. Part V of the CJA 1993 is clearly intended to secure the orderly dissemination of information to the market generally, and not clandestine disclosure to associates, acquaintances or controlled persons.

E.   Dealing in securities

The definition of "dealing in securities"

14–12   It is important to know what the expression "dealing in securities" encompasses. That term is defined in s.55 of the CJA 1993 in the following terms:

> "(1)   For the purposes of this Part, a person deals in securities if—
> (a)   he acquires or disposes of the securities (whether as principal or agent); or
> (b)   he procures, directly or indirectly, an acquisition or disposal of the securities by any other person."

Significantly there is no restriction in the wording of the offence to circumstances in which the defendant must be acquiring or disposing of securities in the course of a business: therefore, this is not an offence directed solely at persons who are regulated by the FCA. Instead, the purpose of the offence is both to capture professional traders in the securities markets and also to capture infrequent, non-professional dealers in securities who are seeking perhaps to turn a quick, clandestine profit from a one-off opportunity because some inside information

---

[19]   Criminal Justice Act 1993, s.52(3).

has come into their possession. Consequently, a person deals in securities not only as an experienced "dealer" but also as an inexpert (even first-time) participant in a securities transaction.

Therefore, in s.55(1) an individual "deals" in securities whenever she either acquires or disposes of securities. Thus, the offence can be committed either by trying to lock in a profit on securities which are expected to decrease in value in the future by selling them before their market price falls, or by trying to acquire securities at a price which is lower than the level to which those securities are expected to rise in the future.

14–13

Acting as principal or as agent

An individual may commit the offence when acting either as principal or agent. Therefore, the individual does not have to be the principal who is dealing with the inside information: it would be enough if, for example, a Chief Executive Officer instructed a junior employee in the finance department to acquire securities on her behalf. What is required, however, for that junior employee to be "an individual" who commits the offence is that that junior employee must also have access to inside information and so satisfy the other elements of the offence. In this way, individuals who are used as dupes by an inside dealer may escape liability if they themselves had no inside information as to the performance of those securities. However, the question would need to be asked—in relation to the definition of "inside information"[20]—whether or not the Chief Executive Officer's instructions to acquire the securities were made in such a way or contained sufficient information that the junior employee thereby came into possession of inside information: if she did come into possession of such information then she would be an inside dealer herself. If the agent has no knowledge of the inside information, the principal remains liable as principal if she satisfies the remaining requirements of the offence.

14–14

Indirect dealings

The statutory draftspeople were alive to the possibility that the acquisition or disposal of securities might be arranged indirectly. Thus, if an insider, for example, used a wholly-owned "shell" company[21] to acquire securities on her own behalf then that would constitute "indirect" dealing in the securities.

14–15

There are a number of ways in which company or trust holding structures could otherwise be used to circumvent this legislation by suggesting that the insider was not performing the actions but rather that the company or the trustees were. Let us consider some property management structures. Suppose that, instead of being the sole shareholder in this shell company, the insider had settled the company's shares on trust so that the trustees held the shares and held the power

14–16

---

[20] See para.14–27.
[21] Where the term a "shell company" refers to a company which does not trade and which exists solely as a vehicle to hold assets on behalf of the company's shareholders or ultimate individual owners (for example through a group structure).

to direct the company's activities: it is suggested that this would be no different from the preceding example if the insider is the sole trustee or de facto controls the decisions of the trustees.

14–17 The more difficult situation, it is suggested, might be that where the insider is one of a number of participants in an investment fund which deals in securities at a time when the insider held knowledge as to price-affected securities, whether as a beneficiary under a trust or as a shareholder in an investment company. The reference in the previous sentence to the insider being "one of a number of participants", it is suggested, is a reference to a number of potential situations, including the situation where the insider is only one of the trustees of the investment fund or the situation where the insider is one only of a number of investor-beneficiaries. It is suggested that it need not matter whether or not these parties acted at arm's length from one another because the real mischief at which s.52(1) is directed is whether or not inside information has been misused. So, even if the investors had never met but if the insider had convinced the trustees to deal in the price-affected securities by telling them what she knew about the company in relation to which she had inside information, then the offence would have been committed. At that moment it is likely that the trustees may have become insiders too. Suppose the insider was an employee of the company. Even if the insider did not disclose the information involved but simply dropped her employee's security pass for the company in question on the desk in front of the trustees and winked like a pantomime villain and implored them to do as she was suggesting, continuing to wink all the while, then the offence would have been committed, it is suggested, because the insider would have procured a misuse of the inside information even if she had not carried out the investment herself directly.

14–18 The test, it is suggested, should be whether or not it is the insider's knowledge which is being used to drive the transaction forward. For example, is that knowledge the sine qua non[22] without which the transaction would not have taken place? Did the transaction only take effect because the participants were seeking to profit from the insider's knowledge? Or is there some genuine proof that the trustees were intending to make that investment in any event for other demonstrable reasons in innocence of the inside information held by the insider and without relying on the insider's advice? If not, then it is suggested that the insider—and any other participant who satisfied the requirements for the s.52(1) offence—should be taken to have committed that offence.

What constitutes acquisition and disposal of securities

14–19 The requirement of either acquisition or disposal of a security in the s.52(1) offence is not limited to the time at which a formal transfer of title is recorded in relation to that security with the appropriate registrar or by transfer of an instrument or certificate, as appropriate. Instead, the concepts of acquisition and

---

[22] "Sine qua non" means "the thing without which" the transaction would not have taken place. i.e. was knowledge of the inside information the only thing that prompted the insider to make the investment because the insider knew that she would be able to make a profit on that investment.

disposal include, in effect, any transfer of an equitable interest by virtue of a contract to acquire or dispose of the security. Those concepts emerge from s.55(2) and (3) in the following terms:

> "(2) For the purposes of this Part, 'acquire', in relation to a security, includes—
> (a) agreeing to acquire the security; and
> (b) entering into a contract which creates the security.
> (3) For the purposes of this Part, 'dispose', in relation to a security, includes—
> (a)agreeing to dispose of the security; and
> (b)bringing to an end a contract which created the security."

There is a transfer of an equitable interest in property when the absolute owner of the security enters into a specifically enforceable contract to transfer that security to its counterparty.[23] The rationale for the equitable interest passing is that once the contract is capable of specific performance then the counterparty is able to enforce the transfer of the security in equity; and because equity "looks upon as done that which ought to be done" equity will deem that the transfer of title takes effect automatically as soon as the contract is specifically enforceable: therefore, only an equitable interest in the property passes, because equity is not able to pass the common law title.[24] Consequently, when a contract to transfer property between parties is created and specifically enforceable it is correct to think that equitable proprietary rights in that property will pass automatically between the parties. Therefore, an insider will have "dealt" with the securities as soon as such a contract for their transfer has been created. What is problematic in s.55(2)(a) and (3)(a) is the idea that it is sufficient for an acquisition or a disposal to have taken place once there is an "agreement" in place. It is suggested that "agreement" in this context should be read as a synonym for "specifically enforceable contract"; alternatively it could be read as including a mere attempt to form what transpires subsequently to be at common law a non-enforceable agreement. Under the former analysis, if no formally valid contracts were created then the offence of encouraging insider dealing under s.52(2)(a) could still be made out.

The insider dealing provisions generally are not limited to activities undertaken solely by the insider and with her own hands: rather the insider dealing code extends more generally to activities performed by agents or trustees at the insider's behest. Thus s.55(4) and s.55(5) make provision as follows: **14–20**

> "(4) For the purposes of subsection (1), a person procures an acquisition or disposal of a security if the security is acquired or disposed of by a person who is—
> (a) his agent;
> (b) his nominee; or
> (c) a person who is acting at his direction,
> in relation to the acquisition or disposal.
> (5) Subsection (4) is not exhaustive as to the circumstances in which one person may be regarded as procuring an acquisition or disposal of securities by another."

---

[23] *Neville v Wilson* [1997] Ch. 144.
[24] A.S. Hudson, *Equity & Trusts*, 260.

An acquisition or disposal can be made through an agent. An agent will be a person acting on behalf of the insider. It is suggested that that agent need not be paid. A nominee, strictly defined, is a person who acts as trustee of a bare trust for the insider.

14–21 A trust with more than one beneficiary, or a discretionary trust, would be caught by s.55(4)(c) on the basis that an acquisition or disposal can be made by "a person who is acting at" the insider's "direction". As considered immediately above,[25] the structures through which such acquisitions or disposals might be made may be complex. Consequently, a question would arise as to whether or not a trustee under a discretionary trust holding securities for a group of potential beneficiaries, or a small board of directors of a company with a number of shareholders, could be said to be acting at the insider's direction. It is suggested that there need not be any legal right to compel the trustee how to act; but rather obeying someone's instructions as a question of fact, if not law, is sufficient. So, the answer to this question in any given set of circumstances is probably a question of fact: to whit, did those trustees or directors de facto take directions from the insider on which they acted in relation to the dealings in price-affected securities? It is suggested that those trustees or directors need not necessarily have tended to act at the insider's direction—although a pattern of such behaviour would clearly be evidentially useful in demonstrating the defendant's mens rea—because the offence need only be committed in relation to one securities transaction: just as an accomplice to murder need not be in the habit of doing whatever the murderer instructed, provided that the accomplice did so on the occasion of the murder so as to commit that single offence.

14–22 This offence does not require a pattern of behaviour. The argument which would be raised in defence by the insider would be that as a member of a class of objects of a discretionary trust, he could not have given legally-enforceable directions to the trustee because he would probably have had no individual power to do so;[26] and similarly that in relation to a company, a minority shareholder would ordinarily not have such a power over the company's directors. However, the term used in s.55(4) is "acting at his direction" and not "acting in obedience to his legally enforceable power". Therefore, the question would be whether or not the dealing was undertaken as a result of a direction given on that occasion by the insider which was based on the insider's inside information. The statute is drafted more broadly than simply occasions when one person can legally compel another person, and instead encompasses situations in which one person can in fact direct another person's actions. Direction does not pre-suppose legally enforceable compulsion, merely some influence.

Derivatives to acquire securities

14–23 What is noticeable is that, on its face, the definition of "dealing in securities" in s.55 of CJA 1993 is very limited. The statute refers specifically to "dispose of the security" or "agreeing to acquire the security": in each case a reference to "the

---

[25] See para.14–20.
[26] See A.S. Hudson, *Equity & Trusts*, p.154.

security", as opposed to the value which could be earned from a speculation derived from that security's market value. Since the enactment of the 1993 Act there has been a revolution in financial techniques whereby the economic equivalent of dealing in securities can be mimicked using derivatives such as cash-settled call options (whereby the buyer of that option is able to acquire the cash flow which he would have received if he had acquired those shares on the stock market).[27] The way in which derivatives will be caught is under s.55(2)(b) and (3)(b) respectively whereby "entering into a contract to create a security" or "bringing an end to a contract which created the security" will constitute a "dealing" in that security. In this sense, Sch.2 includes in its definition of "security" any options or futures or contracts for differences. The use of derivatives in this context is explained in the next paragraph and thereafter the meanings of s.55(2)(b) and (3)(b) are considered.

As is discussed in Chapter 40, there are two types of cash-settled option: call options and put options.[28] A cash-settled option pays the difference between the price which one party agrees to pay for the option and the market value of the underlying security at the time. No securities actually change hands: rather, this is a speculation on the profit which would have been made if the parties had actually acquired the underlying securities. So, an insider who wanted to "deal in price-affected securities" could acquire a cash-settled option which would pay her the profit which she would have earned had she actually acquired the securities and then sold them; alternatively she could acquire a cash-settled put option which would oblige the seller to pay her what she would have earned had the seller of the option been obliged to acquire the securities at their earlier, higher price. The insider could also use "physically-settled"[29] options in the same manner—either put or call—if she wanted to dispose of securities which she actually held at the time of creating the option. The option can also be structured so that the insider can exercise it at any time she chooses—either when the inside information is actually made public, or when she considers that "the heat has died down"[30] and no-one would notice her dealings. By effecting the option, however, the profit was locked in at a time when the information was price sensitive and therefore, it is suggested, that the mischief at which the insider dealing code is directed would be satisfied.

14–24

---

[27] A.S. Hudson, *Financial Derivatives*, para.2–44 et seq.

[28] These structures could use "forwards" as opposed to options, although the insider is more likely to use options because they do not compel him to go through with the transaction even if his guess is wrong and the price of the securities moves in another direction (as a forward would require), or if he gets cold feet and decides to renege on the insider dealings (as a forward would effectively require). Forwards compel the parties to buy or sell; whereas options give one party or the other the choice whether or not to exercise their rights.

[29] The concept of "*physical* settlement" is a derivatives market usage—it does not require that there are tangible securities, rather it denotes the fact that the parties intend to transfer title in securities (by registration or otherwise, as appropriate) rather than simply to speculate on underlying market movements without intending to transfer securities.

[30] Always assuming that the option was itself created during a prohibited period, even if its profits were only realised at some later date.

14–25 As discussed above, s.55(2)(b) and (3)(b) CJA 1993 provide respectively that creating or bringing to an end an option or a future or a contract for differences will constitute a dealing in securities for the purposes of Part V.

Securities to which Part V applies

14–26 The scope of the securities to which Part V CJA 1993 applies is set out in Sch.2 to that Act, by virtue of s.54 CJA 1993. The categories of securities which are covered in that Schedule are shares, debt securities, warrants, depositary receipts, options, futures, and contracts for differences.

F.   Inside information

The definition of "inside information"

14–27 The concept of "inside information" is of central importance to insider dealing.[31] An offence will only be committed when a person has inside information which is used to deal in price-affected securities. The consequence of that mismatch in knowledge is that the market is said to lose its integrity because it is rigged in favour of those insiders who are privy to such information. This discussion, however, is concerned with the criminal law context of that expression. For the purposes of Part V, the term "inside information" is defined in s.56(1) CJA 1993 in the following manner:

> "(1)   For the purposes of this section and section 57, 'inside information' means information which—
>
> (a)   relates to particular securities or to a particular issuer of securities or to particular issuers of securities and not to securities generally or to issuers of securities generally;
> (b)   is specific and precise;
> (c)   has not been made public; and
> (d)   if it were made public would be likely to have significant effect on the price of any securities."

The effect of this subsection is that it provides a definition for the purposes of qualifying s.57 and the concept of an "insider", and it focuses the definition onto a narrow range of securities. The definition of "inside information" is thus very limited in scope. The information must comply with all four of the probanda in s.56(1): in short, it must be precise information relating to only one company. A large amount of confidential information relating to securities markets will, therefore, be excluded from the ambit of this particular offence. This provision is susceptible to a number of different interpretations.

14–28 It is difficult to know how to interpret the expression requiring that the information "relates to particular securities". That could be taken either to mean securities of a particular type (e.g. all shares in the market), or to securities

---

[31] The notion of "inside information" is also used in the Model Code in the UKLA Listing Rules (as considered in Ch.40 in relation to securities transactions) and in relation to the regulation of market abuse.

sharing a particular feature, or relating to companies of a particular type or which are in a particular market sector, or it could mean only relating to securities of one company and of the same type (e.g. only ordinary shares, or only preference shares, or only bonds of the same denomination). Helping us to understand the intended scope of that expression is the next phrase in para.(a) which relates to "a particular issuer of securities", which would seem to limit the definition to securities of only one company, were it not for the following phrase in para.(a) which refers in the alternative "to particular issuers of securities", suggesting that there might be more than one issuing company. The final phrase of para.(a) tells us that the definition does not relate to "securities generally or to issuers of securities generally". Thus, we know it is not a reference to all issuers, but it may be a reference to more than one issuer where para.(a) provides "particular issuers of securities" as aforesaid.

So, we are somewhere between this provision applying to only one company at a time and it not applying to every issuing company. Where does one draw the line in between? It seems probable that the reference to "particular issuers of securities" in the plural was intended to cover information about a merger or takeover in negotiation between two issuing companies: in such a circumstance it would be sensible to cover information relating as it does to both of the parties to that mooted merger. However, beyond that example, it would be a difficult question to know when information relating to multiple issuers would be appropriate information to fall within the offence, given that information relating to the entire community of issuing companies is not. Might it be the case that information relating to a particular market sector would be suitable to make out the offence? If that information relates to a market sector (such as a frozen concentrated orange juice market, for example) then that would seem to be too broad to be the sort of information which constitutes the mischief at which this section was aimed because a number of people are likely to know about information which relates to a specific market sector; unless it is information relating to a revolutionary patent about to be developed by one particular company, but then that would probably be information, in truth, relating to that particular company and not directly to the whole market sector. Alternatively, information about a change of heart in the defence ministry of the Ruritanian government so that it would not honour contracts with A Plc and B Plc would be information pertaining to a limited number of companies (albeit more than one company) which might be information falling within s.56(1) of the CJA 1993. However, beyond those comparatively straightforward examples, the precise meaning of this provision is unclear in the absence of clear authority. **14–29**

The second requirement in the definition of "inside information" is that the information be "specific and precise".[32] Therefore, the information cannot relate to a general "nervousness" among management generally or "concerns" among many market analysts about market share; instead, the information would need to relate for example to the under-performance of a large, specific business unit before accounts are published, or knowledge of the imminent commencement of **14–30**

---

[32] The definition of "precise" information for the purposes of market abuse under s.118(C)(5) FSMA 2000 is considered below.

a class action law suit against a company. The precision required of the information colours the requirement of specificity in that it discounts general sentiment such as nervousness or optimism, and requires instead that the information relate to a particular feature of particular information such as accounting information or patents or litigation or some such activity which will have an effect on the value of securities but which will be known about only within an organisation before its publication. In Australia, the courts have required that the information should be "unequivocally expressed and discerned" and not require too much deduction on the part of its recipient.[33] The courts will tend to measure the significance of information by reference to whether or not its eventual publication did affect the market value of the securities.[34]

14–31   The third requirement in the definition of "inside information" is that the information "has not been made public". This is the principal test in practice. Once information is generally known in a marketplace then it loses its quality of being "*inside* information" because its possession is no longer limited to insiders. It is not made plain what would constitute making information public. Information may lie somewhere on a point between rumour and fact.[35] Clearly, once a recognised information service ("RIS") has transmitted the information as being fact, then it will cease to be inside information. What is more difficult to know is the effect of rumours in the market or speculative journalism: both of which would simply be a part of a rumour until they are confirmed as being fact. So, if the information was the subject of a speculative newspaper story—in which the writer was simply speculating and not reporting historical fact—then it would be difficult to know whether the market sentiment as to the value of the securities (an upward movement for a positive rumour; a downward movement for a negative rumour) reflected the publication of the aspect of the information which would affect the value of securities, in that a market rumour would already change the market valuation before a RIS or a newspaper carried the rumour as fact. If rumour were accepted as constituting publication, however, this might make matters too easy for an inside dealer to leak information so that it becomes a rumour before almost immediately dealing in the affected securities. If the insider timed matters correctly then she could claim that her dealing took effect after the rumour began to circulate; from a profiteering point of view, however, she would need to act sufficiently quickly so that she locked in her profit on the securities before the market began to react to the rumour and so deflated her profit bubble. Therefore, not accepting that rumours of this sort constitute publication makes it more difficult for a person who is contravening the spirit of the legislation to profit from that activity by relying on the intrinsically gossipy nature of real-time financial markets to mask her activities.

---

[33] *Ryan v Triguboff* [1976] 1 N.S.W.L.R. 588, at 596, per Lee J.; cited by B. Rider et al, *Market Abuse and Insider Dealing*, para.3.36.

[34] *Chase Manhattan Equities Ltd v Goodman* [1991] B.C.L.C. 897, at 931, per Knox J.

[35] In relation to takeovers, when a rumour about the possibility of a takeover is out in the marketplace, the regulator will usually require that some statement of some sort is made by the company. False information and false rumours in such situations will not constitute inside information: see *Charles Chan Sing-Chuk v Innovisions Ltd* [1992] 1 H.K.L.R. 254. See P. Wood, *Regulation of International Finance*, para.21–029.

The fourth requirement is that the information must be of a kind which "if it were made public would be likely to have significant effect on the price of any securities". This requirement clearly excludes mere tittle-tattle about corporate affairs. The proof of this requirement in any given case will generally be proven one way or another when the eventual publication of the information hits the market: the price will either have moved or not moved significantly as a result. The concept of a *significant* movement in the price or value of securities will depend on habitual movements in the price of the security in question and the market on which it is traded. Insider dealing relates to activity on any regulated market—there are some markets which are much more liquid than others. Therefore, a liquid stock market might see large movements in the price of a share in any average business day, whereas on an illiquid market we might not expect the price of a share to move significantly or very much at all except in exceptional circumstances. Therefore, a movement in the former type of market may need to be much larger than a movement in the latter market for it to constitute a "significant" movement. Similarly, a security with a high price may need to have a larger absolute movement in price to render that movement a significant, proportionate movement in price than a share with a smaller value. Thus a movement of 50 pence on a share worth £20 would be less dramatic than a movement of 50 pence on a share worth £2. Also, some securities will have a higher average turnover than other shares, and so an unusually large amount of activity in a fairly static security may add to the significance of the information. So, movements in the securities of companies trading in a new market sector—such as one driven by technology—may go through periods of volatile trading and so see the prices of securities move by large amounts regularly in many trading days, whereas other companies in more established markets might rarely see such movements except in times of general securities market turmoil.

14–32

The definition of "price-sensitive information"

It is not enough that the information be inside information of the sort described in s.56(2) of the CJA 1993, as considered immediately above, but rather it must also be "price sensitive information" relating to "price-affected securities". The definition of the term "price affected securities" is set out in s.56(2) in the following terms:

14–33

"(2)   For the purposes of this Part, securities are 'price-affected securities' in relation to inside information, and inside information is 'price sensitive information' in relation to securities, if and only if the information would, if made public, be likely to have a significant effect on the price of the securities."

Thus, as considered in the preceding paragraph,[36] the information must be information of a sort which would be "likely to have a significant effect on the price of the securities", where the term "significant" was considered in the previous paragraph. It is not required that there was in fact an effect on the price of the securities subsequently. Rather it is sufficient that it can be proven that this effect was "likely", even if it did not take effect, provided that it was information

---

[36] See para.14–33.

of a kind which could be anticipated to have this effect. Whether "likely" means that the significant effect on price must take effect "on the balance of probabilities" or be "almost certain" or simply be "more likely than not" is not entirely clear from the provision.

Questions of "price" and "value"

14–34   It is further provided by s.56(3) CJA 1993 that "for the purposes of [s.56] 'price' includes value". There may be a movement in the entire market or in a market sector, even if the securities of A Plc hold their value, which may make the static price of A Plc shares seem more or less valuable. So if the market increases in value on average by 10 per cent and the shares of A Plc retain the same price, then the shares of A Plc have the same "price" but they have a lower "value". It is suggested that the value of the securities in question is the more important criterion given the volatility of most securities markets, although price may well be the most useful indicator of value. The question of value necessarily raises the question as to the value of A Plc's shares compared to what? Comparison with a sharply rising market sector will make A Plc's shares seem less valuable than comparison with a share market across all sectors which may be comparatively static thus making A Plc's shares seem similarly valuable to their previous value. Thus inside information must be of a type which would affect the value and not only the price of securities—but that leaves the question as to what comparators may be used to measure the value of those securities. It is suggested that the statute gives no guidance here. Clearly, price will be the first indicator of value and a movement in price occasioned by publication of a given item of information would be a clear demonstration of the price sensitivity of that information. It is suggested that in measuring the value of securities the court would need to consider the number of securities involved—whether securities of only one company or of a number of companies, whether of one denomination or several—and the most appropriate standard against which to measure the value of securities in that context.

What manner of information relates to a particular issuer

14–35   The question arises what sorts of information can be said to "relate" to a particular issuer. Section 60(4) of the CJA 1993 provides that for the purposes of Pt V of that Act "information shall be treated as relating to an issuer of securities which is a company not only where it about the company but also where it may affect the company's business prospects". Thus information can relate to a company, for the purposes of the insider dealing code, provided that it is "inside information" (as discussed already), even if it relates to the company's prospects and not simply to the company itself. It is not clear whether or not this could relate to market conditions affecting a number of companies, or whether it could relate to a factor which will affect a company's prospects indirectly (such as pending litigation or a creditor's petition for bankruptcy), or whether it should be limited to factors relating specifically to one issuer but affecting its prospects directly. It is suggested that a natural and literal reading of s.60(4) would encompass all three of these types of possibility.

A person having information as an insider

A person may have access to price-sensitive information or to information which, if commonly known, would have a significant effect on the value of securities, but that person may not necessarily have that information as an insider. So, a careful market analyst may have spotted a weakness in companies in a particular sector in relation to a particular external factor—such as interest rate movements, or the price of timber, or some such—and so may be able to speculate successfully on future price movements. However, that person is not an insider and that information would not be inside information if it was gleaned from public sources. The insider dealing code is only concerned to criminalise misuse of information by insiders. Therefore, it is important to know who will be an insider and in what circumstances they will be deemed to be acting as an insider. Section 57 of the CJA 1993 provides:

> "(1)   For the purposes of this Part, a person has information as an insider if and only if—
>   (a)   it is, and he knows that it is, inside information; and
>   (b)   he has it, and knows that he has it, from an inside source."

Therefore, there are two requirements here. Importantly, only these requirements will be sufficient. First, the insider must know that the information is inside information. The definition of inside information was considered above in relation to s.56(1). The second requirement is that the insider knows that she has acquired the information from an "inside source". The test of knowledge which is appropriate in criminal law is that the insider must be subjectively aware that the information is inside information, as considered above.[37] This would mean that a new employee in the finance department of a company who filed away a draft press release with inside information on it, but who did not realise that this was information not yet generally known in the marketplace, and who then bought shares in the company on the strength of that information, would not have "known" that the information was inside information if he misunderstood the manner in which such information was released to the marketplace. The more difficult cases would revolve around employees who were insiders but who claimed to have no knowledge of the nature of the information but who might be considered to be disingenuous in their claims not to understand how such things worked. It is suggested that in practice these things are worked out only in the witness box. The question, in truth, is whether or not a judge or a jury (as appropriate) believes the defendant's claims not to have realised the nature of the information and the source of the information. Subjective tests of knowledge in the criminal law consequently come down to the nature and experience of the individual defendant, and to their credibility in the witness box.

The question as to what will constitute an "inside source" is set out in s.57(2) of the CJA 1993 in the following terms:

14–36

14–37

---

[37] See para.14–27.

"(2)   For the purposes of subsection (1), a person has information from an inside source if and only if—
(a)   he has it through—
(i)   being a director, employee or shareholder of an issuer of securities; or
(ii)   having access to the information by virtue of his employment, office or profession; or
(b)   the direct or indirect source of his information is a person within paragraph (a)."

Therefore, inside sources will concern information which has come through a director of the issuer, of an employee of an issuer, or a shareholder of an issuer; or alternatively if that person herself receives the information from her employment or her office or her profession; or the information came directly or indirectly from such a person. Let us consider each element in turn.

14–38   The first type of inside source under s.57(2)(a) requires that the defendant "has it through" being one of three categories of person. Under s.57(2)(b) it can also constitute an "inside source" if a third party has the information through a person listed in s.57(2)(a), which is what makes this definition so interesting. The expression "has it through" is really quite broad. That would seem to include being told the information verbally or in writing by such a person; or over-hearing such a person talking; or intercepting that person's written communications. The expression "has it through" does not require on its face that the insider communicated the information intentionally to the defendant. It would be within the literal sense of that expression that the defendant was a director's gardener, for example, who overheard her talking to work colleagues on the telephone. Again, this approach would be appropriate if the mischief of the legislation was to prevent people taking advantage of information they come to know before it is made available to the public through a RIS or a newspaper or appropriate website. Thus, we have to ask whether a complete stranger who overheard an employee of an issuing company talking on a mobile phone in an otherwise empty train carriage, and who could identify the issuing company from the employee's rucksack logo, would have had information through that employee if she bought the company's shares as soon as she detrained: on a literal interpretation of s.57(2)(a) that person would have had information from an inside source.

14–39   As to the three categories of person in s.57(2)(a)(i), the legislation seems very strict. Shareholders in large public companies are unlikely to have access to very much inside information if they are ordinary members of the public, although arguably not if they are institutional investors. Institutional investors are more likely to have access to insiders at the issuing company because public companies generally go to great lengths to court the respect of the all-powerful institutional investors, whereas ordinary members of the public who will each constitute merely one of thousands of investors are unlikely to have very much advance information simply by virtue of being shareholders (as opposed to having private links to directors of the issuing company, and so forth). Ordinary shareholders of large companies may have a short window of special knowledge after an annual general meeting has reached a vote: but shareholders of companies whose annual general meetings are filmed or recorded and broadcast live on-line would by definition be unlikely to have confidential information in that manner. The question would be, once information was learned by all of the shareholders in a large public company, whether such a body of shareholders constituted a section of the public such that the information had then been "published". Given the composition of the shareholding of large public companies—a combination of institutional investors and many private, individual investors—it is suggested that in its vernacular sense this should be taken to constitute publication. However, that shareholders are mentioned in this provision suggests that such a body of shareholders should not be taken to be "the public"; and that instead publication of information could only take place once it has been transmitted by a RIS, even though that has not been stipulated in the statute. Being the shareholder of a private company would be a different matter, but the securities of a private company would not be traded on a regulated market nor admitted to listing. The statutory definition of information being "made public" is considered below,[38] and includes a reference to information being readily available to those who are likely to deal in securities, but that is not necessarily limited to existing shareholders of the company.

The references to "directors" and "employees" in s.57(2)(a)(i) are more straightforward. That a person has information through being a director or an employee does not, on the words of that paragraph, require that that person's directorship or employment necessarily brought them into contact with this sort of information, not in this context at least. Instead, it seems, on a literal reading of the paragraph, that acquiring information at work before it has been published is sufficient to constitute an inside source. Therefore, employees in the post-room or secretarial staff or cleaners could constitute inside sources, and so anyone to whom they transmitted information could also have it from an inside source under s.57(2)(b).

14–40

The two types of insider on the case law

There is a little decided case law on insider dealing. In *Attorney General's Reference (No.1 of 1988)*[39] Lord Lowry distinguished between "primary insiders" and "secondary insiders" on the basis of the now repealed 1985 Company Securities (Insider Dealing) Act. Primary insiders are directors, employees and shareholders, and any person who has information by virtue of his employment, office or profession, as set out variously in relation to s.57 CJA 1993. Secondary insiders are those people who acquire their information from primary insiders. This distinction may still be made on the offences considered above if one has a mind to do so, although, it is suggested, that the development of the insider dealing legislation and the market abuse code have made this stark distinction less important than it might have been hitherto given the range of activities which now fall naturally within the statutory language, as considered already in this chapter.

14–41

---

[38] See para.14–42.
[39] [1989] 1 A.C. 971.

Information "made public"

14–42 The focus of the insider dealing code is on preventing insiders from abusing information acquired from inside sources which is unknown to the investing public at large so as to earn personal profits and with the result of affecting the integrity of securities markets. In this regard s.58 of the CJA 1993 provides that:

> "(1) For the purposes of section 56, 'made public', in relation to information, shall be construed in accordance with the following provisions of this section; but those provisions are not exhaustive as to the meaning of that expression.
>
> (2) Information is made public if—
>   (a) it is published in accordance with the rules of a regulated market for the purpose of informing investors and their professional advisors;
>   (b) it is contained in records which by virtue of any enactment are open to inspection by the public;
>   (c) it can be readily acquired by those likely to deal in any securities—
>   (i) to which the information relates; or
>   (ii) of an issuer to which the information relates; or
>   (d) it is derived from information which had been made public."

Thus s.58(1) provides that the courts have leeway to develop the meaning of this expression beyond the terms of s.58(2). It is in s.58(2) that the core definitions are set out. Publication of information takes place in one of four contexts.

14–43 The first context depends upon publication in accordance with the ordinary rules of a regulated market[40]—it is suggested that publication in accordance with such rules should relate to regulated markets on which those securities are traded, as opposed to the hypothetical rules of some regulated market on which the securities are not traded, because otherwise the underlying purpose of ensuring integrity in securities markets will be thwarted.

14–44 The second context relates to "records" made available for inspection by the public. This would include published accounts and information as to directors' remuneration. The difficulty here would be in relation to dealings with securities where the information is hidden in voluminous records where it is unlikely to be found easily by members of the public.

14–45 The third context requires simply that the information can be "readily acquired" by those who are "likely to deal" in those securities or in relation to that information. This may include information published through a RIS but there is no reason in theory why it should not also be published only in an analyst's report if that report is ordinarily circulated among those who are likely to invest. That investors must be "likely" to invest suggests a small community of committed investors, as opposed to a larger community of less expert investors who may "possibly" invest: a literal reading of the focus on "likely" permits only the smaller community.

14–46 The fourth context is a general traverse which deals with information being derived from information which has been made public: thus including an understanding of an issuing company's financial position which would be derived from a close analysis of published accounting information.

---

[40] e.g. para.36–01.

This issue of the level of diligence which can be demanded of the recipient of information while still making information public is considered in detail in relation to s.58(3) in the following terms:

14–47

> "(3)   Information may be treated as made public even though—
>   (a)   it can be acquired only by persons exercising diligence or expertise;
>   (b)   it is communicated to a section of the public and not to the public at large;
>   (c)   it can be acquired only by observation;
>   (d)   it is communicated only on payment of a fee;
>   (e)   it is published only outside the United Kingdom."

Thus a number of possible objections to information being considered to have been made public are removed. As considered above in relation to the fourth context in s.58(2), for example, it is no objection that information has been cunningly concealed within accounting or similar information such that analysts would have to sift through those accounts before the information came clearly to light. This would of course give insiders a window between the publication of those accounts and the analysts' discovery of the truth in which securities could be dealt with on the basis that information had technically been published even though the market could be expected to take a while to discover what the insiders already knew was hidden in the footnotes to the accounts. This would, of course, require a level of conspiracy but, after the amount of "creative accountancy" at play in the affairs of Enron, WorldCom and others, that cannot be discounted.[41]

Professional intermediary

The reference to a "professional intermediary" in Part V is defined in s.59 of the CJA 1993 in the following terms:

14–48

> "(1)   For the purposes of this Part, a 'professional intermediary' is a person—
>   (a)   who carries on a business consisting of an activity mentioned in subsection (2) and who holds himself out to the public or any section of the public (including a section of the public constituted by persons such as himself) as willing to engage in any such business; or
>   (b)   who is employed by a person falling within paragraph (a) to carry out any such activity."

Thus a professional intermediary is someone who carries on a specified type of business activity or who holds himself out as acting as such, or is alternatively employed by a person engaged in such an activity. The specified activities are defined in the following terms:

> "(2)   The activities referred to in subsection (1) are—
>   (a)   acquiring or disposing of securities (whether as principal or agent); or
>   (b)   acting as an intermediary between persons taking part in any dealings in securities."

---

[41] See A.S. Hudson, *Securities Law*, Ch.4.

Thus a professional intermediary is someone who deals in securities or whose business is to act as an intermediary between people who deal in securities, except in the following circumstances[42]:

> "(3) A person is not to be treated as carrying on a business consisting of an activity mentioned in subsection (2)—
>
> (a) if the activity in question is merely incidental to some other activity not falling within subsection (2); or
>
> (b) merely because he occasionally conducts one of those activities."

Consequently, despite the ostensible breadth of s.59(2), one is not dealing in securities or acting as an intermediary between people dealing in securities if that activity is merely incidental to some other activity: thus, publishing stock market prices and adverts from stockbrokers in a newspaper does not make the newspaper an intermediary even though it does provide prices and carry adverts which connect buyers and sellers of securities with one another. A further requirement under s.59(3)(b) is that the activity must be in the nature of a business to the extent that it must be more than an occasional activity.[43]

"Regulated market"

14–49 The term "regulated market" has a different meaning in Pt V of the CJA 1993 from that in the Markets in Financial Instruments Directive ("MiFID"; as considered in Chapter 12 in relation to market abuse). In relation to the insider dealing code s.60(1) of the CJA 1993 provides that for the purposes of Pt V "regulated market" means any market "however operated" which is identified as being a regulated market for the purposes of Pt V in the Insider Dealing (Securities and Regulated Markets) Order 1994.[44] That Order identifies the United Kingdom regulated markets as being "any market established under the rules of" The London Stock Exchange Limited, LIFFE Administration and Management, OMLX the London Securities and Derivatives Exchange Limited, virt-x Exchange Limited, and "the exchange known as COREDEALMTS" and OFEX.[45] The Schedule to that Order identifies a list of traditional Exchanges across the European Union and the EEA (such as Berlin, Amsterdam, Bologna, Madrid, Frankfurt, Stockholm and Rome) and newer markets (such as NASDAQ, EASDAQ, and the Nouveau Marche) as being regulated markets.[46]

---

[42] Furthermore, under Criminal Justice Act 1993 s.59(4) " . . . a person dealing in securities relies on a professional intermediary if and only if a person who is acting as a professional intermediary carries out an activity mentioned in subsection (2) in relation to that dealing".

[43] See para.9–15 in relation to a discussion of the definition of "business" in the context of FSMA 2000.

[44] SI 1994/187, as amended by the Insider Dealing (Securities and Regulated Markets) (Amendment) Order 1996, SI 1996/1561; the Insider Dealing (Securities and Regulated Markets) (Amendment) Order 2000, SI 2000/1923; and the Insider Dealing (Securities and Regulated Markets) (Amendment) Order 2002, SI 2002/1874.

[45] Insider Dealing (Securities and Regulated Markets) Order 1994, SI 1994/187, art.10.

[46] Further to Insider Dealing (Securities and Regulated Markets) Order 1994, SI 1994/187, art.9(1).

The meaning of the term "issuer"

Section 60(2) of the CJA 1993 provides that for the purposes of Part V the term "issuer" in relation to any securities "means any company, public sector body or individual by which or by whom the securities have been or are to be issued".

14–50

G.   Defences

Two types of defences

The two offences in s.52(1) and (2) CJA 1993 are subject to the defences set out in s.53 and in Sch.1 of that Act.[47] There are two classes of defences in relation to the insider dealing offences: the defences relating specifically to each s.52 offence which are set out in s.53, and the special defences in Sch.1 which are applicable to market makers, to market information, and to price stabilisation respectively. The general defences qualify s.52 CJA 1993, whereas the special defences are narrower in scope in that they are intended to excuse particular kinds of professional, financial services activities. Section 53(6) of the CJA 1993 provides that for the purposes of the defences in general, any reference to "a profit" includes a reference to "the avoidance of loss".[48]

14–51

The s.53 CJA 1993 defences

The general defences to a charge of insider dealing are set out in s.53 CJA 1993. There are defences relating separately to the s.52(1) and (2) offences. Each is considered in turn.

14–52

The defence to the s.52(1) insider dealing offence

The defence to the s.52(1) insider dealing offence is set out in s.53(1) CJA 1993. There are three alternative defences in s.53(1). Each is considered in turn.

14–53

First, that the defendant did not expect that the dealing would result in a profit. There are perhaps two ways of demonstrating this credibly: either by showing that the dealing was part of a larger transaction (perhaps to do with a hedging strategy[49]) and so not aimed at generating profit per se, or by showing that the dealing was not intended to make a profit of the magnitude it did because of the inside information but rather because of some other factor.

14–54

Secondly, that the defendant had reasonable grounds to believe that the information had been sufficiently widely disclosed. There is no statutory guidance on this concept. There is no guidance on the basis on which the

14–55

---

[47] Criminal Justice Act 1993 s.52(4).

[48] Economically they amount to a similar thing: avoiding losing money in an accounting sense amounts to earning money in the same amount—the total amount of money owned does not increase but nevertheless it constitutes positive value.

[49] Although a successful hedge would have to make a profit so as to balance out some loss made elsewhere.

defendant had this belief (mere disingenuousness (i.e. "surely everyone knew that?"), or having heard direct suggestions from a market participant, or having read the information herself in a newsstand publication) nor on how wide that dissemination should have been. Furthermore, the defence requires that "none of those taking part in the dealing would be prejudiced by not having the information".

14–56   Thirdly, the defendant must be able to prove that she would have acted as she had acted whether or not she had the information. This might be demonstrated by showing a pattern of speculative dealing in those securities, or by showing an investment strategy which demonstrated a credible role for those particular securities, or by showing that the investments were managed by an arm's length discretionary fund manager, or by showing that those securities formed part of a genuine hedging strategy.

The defence to the s.52(2)(a) encouragement to deal offence

14–57   The defence to the s.52(2)(a) encouragement to deal offence is set out in s.53(2) CJA 1993. There are three alternative defences contained in this subsection. First, that the defendant did not anticipate that the dealing would result in a profit due to the price sensitive nature of the information. The same issues arise in relation to this defence as arose generally in relation to s.53(1)(a) above. Secondly, that the defendant had reasonable grounds to believe that the information has been sufficiently widely disclosed. The same issues arise in relation to this defence as arose generally in relation to s.53(1)(b) above. Thirdly, the defendant must be able to prove that she would have acted as she had acted whether or not she had the information. The same issues arise in relation to this defence as arose generally in relation to s.53(1)(c) above.

The defence to the s.52(2)(b) disclosure of information offence

14–58   The defence to the s.52(2)(b) disclosure of information offence is set out in s.53(3) CJA 1993. There are two separate defences in this subsection. First, if the defendant can demonstrate that she did not anticipate that anyone would act on the disclosure by dealing on a regulated market or through a professional intermediary. Secondly, that even if the defendant did anticipate that there would be dealing but that she did not anticipate that those dealings would result in a profit attributable to the price sensitive nature of the information. This second defence raises similar issues to those considered above in relation to s.53(2)(a).

The special defences

14–59   Section 53(4) of the CJA 1993 provides that the special defences contained in Sch.1 act in addition to the defences already considered. There are three classes of special defences relating to market makers, to market information, and to price stabilisation respectively. Each is considered in turn. The first special defence relates to market makers[50] to the effect that[51] an individual is not guilty of insider dealing, by virtue of dealing in securities or encouraging another person to deal, if she shows that she acted in good faith either in the course of her business as a market maker or in the course of employing a market maker.

The second special defence relates to individuals who deal in securities using **14–60** inside information if she can demonstrate that that information was "market information",[52] and that "it was reasonable for an individual in his position to have acted as he did despite having that information as an insider at the time".[53] In this context, "market information" relates to a series of facts which are known about those securities[54]: that securities of a given kind are to be dealt in or that dealings are under negotiation, including the number of securities which are to be dealt in; or that the price at which securities are to be dealt in is under negotiation; and finally, the identity of the people who are likely to be involved in securities dealings. It is provided that what is "reasonable" depends upon the content of the information, the circumstances in which the information was acquired by the insider, and the capacity in which the insider was acting.[55] This paragraph does not help us to know what "reasonable" actually means, although it does tell us some of what we would need to take into account in considering whether or not a given defendant had acted reasonably. Clearly, if an insider was dealing with the information in the course of an employment then that would be reasonable. If the defendant was employed by a RIS and preparing the information for publication then that would be reasonable.

There are two further specific defences. The offences in s.52 of the CJA 1993 do **14–61** not apply to "anything done by an individual acting on behalf of a public sector body in pursuit of monetary policies ... with respect to exchange rates or the management of public debt or foreign exchange reserves".[56] Similarly an individual is not guilty of insider dealing if she was acting in conformity with price stabilisation rules under s.144(1) of the FSMA 2000.

H. The private law enforceability of contracts

Even if an offence has been committed that does not necessarily invalidate any **14–62** contract which has been created as part of its commission. Thus, s.63(2) of the CJA 1993 provides that: "No contract shall be void or unenforceable by reason only of section 52". Consequently the contract may still give rise to all of the

---

[50] "(2) A market maker is a person who (a) holds himself out at all normal times in compliance with the rules of a regulated market or an approved organisation[49] as willing to acquire or dispose of securities; and (b) is recognised as doing so under those rules."
[51] Criminal Justice Act 1993, Sch.1, para.1.
[52] Criminal Justice Act 1993, Sch.1, para.2(1)(a).
[53] Criminal Justice Act 1993, Sch.1, para.2(1)(b).
[54] Criminal Justice Act 1993, Sch.1, para.4.
[55] The term "reasonable" in art.2(1) is susceptible of many interpretations. If we were of a cynical cast of mind—like the philosopher Hume—we might consider it reasonable for a man in possession of valuable information to make a profit from it as soon as possible. However, in the context of securities regulation we must assume that such largesse is not the legislative intention.
[56] Criminal Justice Act 1993, s.63(1).

remedies available under contract law and will not permit a defendant to escape liability by claiming that the contract is void *ab initio* by reason of its illegality.

I. The territorial scope of the offence

14–63   The offence of insider dealing is committed either if the defendant was "within the United Kingdom at the time" when she is alleged to have committed the criminal dealing, or if the regulated market on which the dealing occurred is regulated "in the United Kingdom", or the professional intermediary was "within the United Kingdom" when any of the components of the offence were committed.[57] A defendant will not be guilty of an offence of insider dealing unless he was "within the United Kingdom at the time when he is alleged to have disclosed the information or encouraged the dealing"[58]; or "the alleged recipient of the information or encouragement was within the United Kingdom at the time when he is alleged to have received the information or encouragement".[59]

J. The rationale for the offences of insider dealing

Why criminalise insider dealing?

14–64   There is some debate among the commentators as to why insider dealing has been criminalised at all. There are two broad schools of thought on insider dealing. One school of thought considers that insider dealing is a victimless crime and comparatively rare, and therefore not worthy of criminalisation. The second school of thought considers insider dealing to be a cancer in the heart of our securities markets and a demonstration of a lack of market integrity.

14–65   The principal reasons for criminalisation are that if insider dealing is permitted then investors will not have confidence in the integrity of the market: that is, if insiders are permitted to take profits from their investments on the basis of the manipulation of information which is unknown to other investors, such that the insider can be confident that that information will drive the market price of that security either up or down significantly, then inside investors are able to earn profits from the lack of knowledge of outsiders. There is an ethical problem here in that some investors will be able to exploit the ignorance of other investors when those other investors could not possibly have known better: after all, for the insider to generate a profit, it is necessary that there are unwitting investors buying at the price before the information becomes public knowledge and after the information has become public knowledge, such that the unwitting investors were buying at prices which could only benefit the insiders. There is also an economic problem here. If some investors were allowed to take profits in circumstances in which they are manipulating the lack of knowledge of other investors then those other investors are likely to stop investing in securities markets because they will consider that those markets are rigged in favour of

---

[57] Criminal Justice Act 1993, s.62(1).
[58] Criminal Justice Act 1993, s.62(2)(a).
[59] Criminal Justice Act 1993, s.62(2)(b).

insiders. Consequently, there will be a drying-up of liquidity for companies and other bodies wishing to access capital markets by issuing securities because the number of investors will have greatly reduced. The goal of the EU in particular is to promote deep, liquid capital markets: that requires as many investors as possible to feel confident in investing in those markets.

The first school of thought considers that no-one loses anything from insider dealing. Rather, it is said, some of the sharper market participants simply make a well-earned profit due to their shrewd knowledge of the markets and of the people in them. It is said that having inside information is just like having some intellectual property, like a patent or a copyright: you have access to an idea or to knowledge to which other people do not have access, and that idea or knowledge can make you money.[60] Thus it is said that having some inside information to which no-one else has access is akin to having a patent: that is, an ability to make a profit which no-one else has. So, it is said, if you can take advantage of your copyright while the law prevents other people from taking similar advantage of that copyright, then why should possessors of knowledge about markets be criminalised if they turn a similar profit?

14–66

The second school of thought suggests, however, that we should observe that there is a distinction between intellectual property and insider dealing: copyrights and patents are the fruits of someone's labours and are necessary to ensure that that person and that person alone is able to benefit from their labours for an identified period, and in part acts as an encouragement to them and to other people to persist with their economically valuable labours with the promise of the protection of intellectual property law. By contrast, insider dealing lacks the quality of compensating honest, entrepreneurial toil because the inside dealer has not developed any economically valuable product or idea. Furthermore, encouragement of insider dealing activity will simply skew capital markets in favour of those insiders who have access to this sort of information at a time when economic expansion in the EU as a whole relies on capital markets to fund and support economic growth. It is feared that this will dissuade a large number of investors from investing in capital markets because they cannot know that the market is being operated honestly, nor that the price they will pay for securities reflects their genuine worth.[61]

14–67

Capital markets become skewed, it is suggested, precisely because two tiers of investors are created—one with the information and one without the information—such that one is able to take advantage of the other with the result that in the future the second tier of investors will be reluctant to participate in that capital market. It is a long-term risk to the securities markets that liquidity will thus be reduced, and not a short-term risk confined to any one transaction. It is

14–68

---

[60] See, for example, A. Boyle, *Shamans, Software and Spleens* (Harvard University Press, 1996).

[61] That is, if insiders know of information which will enable them to make profits in the future, then that must necessarily mean that the current market price does not constitute the price which the market place as a whole will pay for those securities because the insiders know (or expect with some confidence) that the market price will change sufficiently in the future (when the information becomes public) so as to make those insiders a profit. In this sense, those market values are not genuine prices because the insiders know that those prices will change in such a way that they will earn profits which are not transparent to the rest of the market.

not just that a particular issue of securities today will be skewed but rather that a number of investors will withdraw from the market permanently because they will have no confidence in it and so that they will withdraw their capital from future deals. That is why one talks of both market integrity and also about fairness between any two contracting parties buying and selling securities.

14–69   There is a problem of fairness between contracting parties. No-one doubts that insider dealing constitutes sharp practice, because one party is able knowingly to take advantage of the ignorance of the other as to the likely future performance of that security once the inside information is publicly known: all that differs is whether one thinks that life is to the swift and therefore that taking the benefits of such sharp practice is no matter, or whether one thinks that there is an ethic essential to properly functioning markets which means that one cannot hoodwink counterparties but rather that one can only take advantage of their ignorance if one is relying solely on one's own skill. It is a little like taking performance enhancing drugs in athletics. If one takes the drugs then one is likely to outperform a similar athlete who has not taken them, but the ethic involved suggests that that race was unfairly organised if one athlete was always more likely to win for reasons other than their skills or their dedication. A clean athlete deserves her success, whereas the doped athlete does not. It is this species of ethical argument which distinguishes the acceptability of a well-resourced, skilful and dedicated investment firm relying on their superior analysts to make excellent predictions about market movements and so to make money from counterparties, from the unacceptability of someone exploiting an unfair advantage acquired through misuse of inside information to make a profit from dealing with counterparties before the market has had time to react to the information or even to know about the information. The former dealer deserves their profit whereas the latter does not. The latter has simply cheated. And a market which is known both to favour cheats and to be peopled by large numbers of cheats will not attract the volume of investors and their funds that it would otherwise do.

The prevalence of insider dealing in some contexts

14–70   The former Chief Executive of the Financial Services Authority, John Tiner, at the time he stepped down from that post, published FSA research into the large volume of suspicious trading activity which had taken place in particular before announcements about takeovers.[62] It was his assertion that insider dealing occurs frequently, but that it is difficult to prove. Not uncommonly there are difficult-to-explain clusters of speculation around one particular security over a short space of time (often a large amount of activity within minutes) without any public disclosure of information: which tends to suggest collusion among inside dealers, but which is very difficult to prove constitutes insider dealing beyond a reasonable doubt. The use of complex derivative transactions and intermediaries to hide the true controlling minds of the dealing operations, as considered in the examples given above, makes it difficult for regulators to be able to identify with

---

[62] *Financial Times*, July 3, 2007.

certainty any insider dealing: i.e. if Z has lined up a series of put options which permit Z to sell shares in Target Plc at a given price, then it is easy for Z to sell those shares very quickly off-exchange. Unlike the Securities and Exchange Commission in the US, the FCA does not have the power to offer immunity from prosecution to whistleblowers and so the job of identifying insider dealers and proving the mens rea of one of the offences is made all the harder. The FCA is seeking to deal more strictly with regulated firms' procedures relating to market abuse to ensure that leaks of inside information are less likely. There were similar reports in the financial press some months earlier that the FCA had found suspicious patterns of trading in relation to a large number of large takeover transactions. Whereas some suggest that insider dealing is not so great a problem as is sometimes suggested,[63] what emerges from this research is that insider dealing and market abuse remain significant problems which do challenge the integrity of our securities markets.

The regulator's rationale for criminalising insider dealing

The rationale which was given by Margaret Cole of the Financial Services Authority in March 2007 for the criminalisation of insider dealing was the following, summarising the principal points in the academic commentary:[64]

    14–71

> "The key points are that insider dealing:
> - impairs the allocative efficiency of the financial markets; reduces market liquidity and increases the cost of capital. If a stock market is functioning efficiently, the share prices should reflect all available information and so provide reliable signals upon which investment decisions are based;
> - it jeopardises the development of fair and orderly markets and in doing so it undermines investor confidence. It can threaten to harm confidence by undermining investors' beliefs that the market is fair, leading them to withdraw their investment;
> - it is immoral by being inherently unfair on the basis of inequality of access to information;
> - it is contrary to good business ethics;
> - it damages companies and their shareholders/investors; and more recent US cases have emphasised the breach of fiduciary duty by employees using privileged information that belongs to a firm."

In an article,[65] McVea presented the arguments set out (primarily) by American economists of the free market school in favour of allowing insider dealing. In essence, the argument fell into three parts. The first argument was that markets are efficient and that they should be allowed to proceed as they consider best because that will ensure the optimal pricing and participation levels. There are said to be a number of reasons why insider dealing is a better method for disseminating information into securities markets (better, that is, than the securities regulations considered in Part X of this book requiring the provision of certain categories of "necessary information" in the form of prospectuses and

---

[63] See, e.g. Rider and Ashe, *Insider Crime* (Jordans Publishing, 1993), pp.1–7; Rider, Alexander and Linklater, *Market Abuse and Insider Dealing* (Tottel Publishing, 2002), p.93 et seq.; Wood, *Regulation of International Finance*, p.534 et seq.

[64] *http://www.fsa.gov.uk/library/communication/speeches/2007/0317_mc.shtml* [Accessed on January 17, 2013.] She meets the accusation that the regulator did "sweet FSA" about insider dealing.

[65] H McVea, "What's wrong with insider dealing?", (1995) 15 *Legal Studies* 390.

other filings). Among these reasons is the idea that traders are more likely to believe information transferred in this way between traders than the formal announcements issued by a company (even though, we should note, under securities regulations the people responsible for those formal statements would be personally liable for any mistakes or misrepresentations under statute). The second argument was that the information is the property of the company and therefore that it is up to the company how it deals with it. In consequence, the argument runs, the company's management should be able to use that information as it sees fit as an inducement to those managers to work hard and maximise their own profits. (However, the regulations in Part X make it clear that this information cannot be the sole preserve of the company when it is required to be published.) This argument is surprising given the fraud which has been uncovered at organisations like Enron and WorldCom in misusing information for personal gain, and the wilful behaviour of employees at Lehman Brothers and other banks in mispricing their assets so as to make it appear that profits are higher than it truth they are. Free market economists tend to ignore the real world in which fraud is committed intentionally to the detriment of shareholders and the broader economy, preferring instead to think of "the markets" as being abstract entities which always operate rationally and without individuals' foibles. The third argument is that regulation is simply not cost effective. What the financial crisis of 2007–09 showed us is that too little regulation can be even more expensive.

14–72   In a response,[66] Prof Campbell dismissed much of this economic theory as being simply "silly", which the financial crisis 2007–09 would suggest that it is. The notion that free markets are rational and that they should be left entirely to their own devices because their actors will always act in their own and everyone else's enlightened self-interest has been proved to be the bunkum it always was. Prof Campbell instead reminded us of the context in which free markets had direct effects on the real economies of emerging nations as well as established ones; and how the stock markets can distort those economies, especially if their prices are distorted by insider trading and so forth.

14–73   The principal objections to Mr McVea's arguments are that share trading involves not only "traders" who might learn from an experience in which they suffer at the hands of inside dealers, but rather share trading involves ordinary members of the public, their pension funds and the fates of companies which generate useful activity for the real economy. The underlying objective of the securities market reforms of the 1990s in the EU (which are not mentioned in either of these articles) was to deepen the pools of capital which are available to companies: that is, more people were being encouraged to invest in the securities markets so that there would be more capital available to companies in the EU to fund their activities. Ordinary members of the public were being encouraged to invest too. When securities trading is treated as being a game between professional traders with inside information and ordinary members of the public risking everything, then it is no longer enough to treat securities regulation as being simply another part of that game. A little experience of life on a trading floor in an investment bank demonstrates that traders know far more about the reasons for market

---

[66] D Campbell, 'What *is* wrong with insider dealing', (1996) 16 *Legal Studies* 185.

movements than anyone else, that banks will indulge in market manipulation (considered below) which distorts markets, and that there is an unacceptable amount of insider dealing and fraud (such as the Libor scandal[67]) between traders. The events discussed in detail in Chapter 45 relating to the financial crisis and its aftermath demonstrate that banks are capable of all sorts of fraud, as well as downright incompetence.

Judicial and regulatory rationales for the criminalisation of insider dealing

What follows in this section are judicial and regulatory rationales for the law on insider dealing. What emerges is a simple desire to prevent wrongdoing which is perceived to cause harm in capital markets and also the difficulty in mounting prosecutions in a field in which it is so difficult to establish proof of the offences. So, to begin with, the decision of the Court of Appeal in *R v McQuoid*[68] both provides us with a case study on the law on insider dealing and also gives us a judicial perspective on the purpose of insider dealing. In that case, McQuoid and his father-in-law, Melbourne, were both prosecuted for insider dealing. At the relevant time, McQuoid was general counsel of TTP Communications (TPP). Furthermore, at the relevant time, TTP was the target in a mooted takeover bid by the mobile phone manufacturer Motorola. The possibility of a takeover bid was told to McQuoid in confidence in May 2006. Two days before the takeover bid was publicly announced, Melbourne bought shares in TTP at 13 pence per share. Melbourne had not dealt in shares of any sort in the period leading up to that purchase and what is more he had never purchased shares in TTP before. On 1 June the takeover offer was announced. The price at which the bid was made was at an agreed price of 45 pence per share. As a consequence, Melbourne made a profit of approximately £48,900 on his share purchase. Three months later, Melbourne gave McQuoid a cheque for precisely 50 per cent of the profit he had realised from this share purchase of TTP shares. The jury found both men guilty. It was found that McQuoid had passed inside information to Melbourne. Furthermore, the Financial Services Authority (the regulator at the time) obtained a court order freezing the profits from the trade. McQuoid and Melbourne were both sentenced to eight months in prison. The Lord Chief Justice, Lord Judge, held the following in relation to the offence of insider dealing in explaining the purpose of insider dealing law:

14–74

"7.   In passing sentence the judge observed that the offence committed by the appellant was not to be treated as a victimless crime. We agree. The person who sold the shares in TTP at 13 pence may have been determined to sell on that date at that price, or at any price. However, he would not have sold at that price if he had known that the takeover was already agreed and would become public within 48 hours. But, as is always the case, only those very few people on the inside knew exactly what was going on.

8.   Insider dealing has been an offence in England and Wales since 1980. The current offence is created in Part V of the Criminal Justice Act 1993, which replaced the Company Securities (Insider Dealing) Act 1985, which in turn replaced similar

---

[67] See para.3–01.
[68] [2009] EWCA Crim 1301, on appeal to the Court of Appeal from the decision at first instance at Southwark Crown Court, unreported, March 2009.

provisions contained in sections 68 to 73 of the Companies Act 1980. Those who involve themselves in insider dealing are criminals: no more and no less. The principles of confidentiality and trust, which are essential to the operations of the commercial world, are betrayed by insider dealing and public confidence in the integrity of the system which is essential to its proper function is undermined by market abuse. Takeover arrangements are normally kept secret. Very few people are permitted to have advance knowledge of them. Those who are entrusted with advance knowledge are entrusted with that knowledge precisely because it is believed that they can be trusted. When they seek to make a profit out of the knowledge and trust reposed in them, or indeed when they do so recklessly, their criminality is not reduced or diminished merely because they are individuals of good character.

9. In the present case, as a result of this breach of trust, the appellant made a substantial profit for himself and a similar profit for his father-in-law. It is true that only one transaction was involved, but the profit arising from his single act of dishonesty was virtually £50,000. This fact demonstrates (if it needs to be demonstrated) that profits from even a single transaction of insider dealing can be very high indeed. We therefore emphasise that this kind of conduct does not merely contravene regulatory mechanisms. If there ever was a feeling that insider dealing was a matter [not] to be covered by regulation, that impression should be rapidly dissipated. The message must be clear: when it is done deliberately, insider dealing is a species of fraud; it is cheating. Prosecution in open and public court will often, and perhaps much more so now than in the past, be appropriate. Although those who perpetrate the offence may hope, if caught, to escape with regulatory proceedings, they can have no legitimate expectation of avoiding prosecution and sentence."

Three clear points emerge. First, this is not a victimless crime. Second, his lordship highlights the risk to the integrity and proper functioning of the securities markets posed by insider dealing, which is in tune with the regulation of market abuse, as considered in Chapter 12. Third, market abuse cannot be reduced to a mere regulatory activity but rather remains a significant criminal offence in its own right. It is "cheating" and a species of criminal fraud. A similar point was made in *R v Spearman*[69] by Hughes J. to the effect that:

"13. We have been referred to the fact that new legislation enables some insider trading to be dealt with by means of regulatory or disciplinary process. That does not mean that the activity ceases to be a criminal offence which is likely to be prosecuted and if prosecuted likely in appropriate cases to be met by substantial sentences of imprisonment. Overall insider trading is a serious matter. On a large scale it corrupts the whole of the market in capital."

Therefore, on this basis any sense that insider dealing should be reduced in significance (by taking it away from the criminal law) is to be rejected. The appeal made in *McQuoid* was predicated on the notion that the defendant's sentence should have been reduced because insider dealing has now been reduced to the level of a regulatory matter and is in that sense no longer to be considered as a serious crime: this idea was rejected by the Court of Appeal in *McQuoid* and the Court of Appeal in *Spearman*.

14–75 The US Supreme Court described insider dealing in the following terms in *US v O'Hagan*.[70] It was held that:

---

[69] [2003] EWCA Crim 2893.
[70] 117 S. Ct. 2199, 138 L. Ed. 2d 724 (1997). K. Krawiec et al., 'Don't Ask, Just Tell: Insider Trading After *United States v. O'Hagan*', (1998) 84 *Virginia Law Review* 153-228; D. Nagy, "Reframing the Misappropriation Theory of Insider Trading Liability: A Post-*O'Hagan* Suggestion" (1998) *http://www.repository.law.indiana.edu/facpub/615.*

"Under the traditional or classical theory of insider trading liability . . . when a corporate insider trades in the securities of his corporation on the basis of material, non-public information. Trading on such information qualifies as a deceptive device . . . because a relationship of trust and confidence [exists] between the shareholders of a corporation and those insiders who have obtained confidential information by reason of their position with that corporation. ... That relationship . . . gives rise to a duty to disclose (or to abstain from trading) because of the necessity of preventing a corporate insider from taking unfair advantage of uninformed stockholders. ... The classical theory applies not only to officers, directors, and other permanent insiders of a corporation, but also to attorneys, accountants, consultants, and others who temporarily become fiduciaries of a corporation."

Interestingly, this conception of insider dealing (or, "insider trading" in the USA) is predicated on an idea of conflicts of interest between the inside dealer's professional or fiduciary duties to the issuer of a company (and its shareholders) and her own personal interests in misusing inside information. The act is criminalised because it constitutes a breach of that duty and an exploitation of the conflict of interest.[71]

14–76 In a different jurisdiction, the decision of the European Court of Justice in *Criminal proceedings against Grongaard*[72] expressed the requirement that a national court must, in the light of the applicable national rules, take particular account of the fact that that exception to the prohibition of disclosure of inside information must be interpreted strictly; the fact that each additional disclosure is liable to increase the risk of that information being exploited for a purpose contrary to the (then applicable) Insider Dealing Directive,[73] and the sensitivity of the inside information. As considered below in relation to English case law, the law on insider dealing is to be interpreted strictly. Therefore, it is suggested, that in spite of the lack of case law on the interpretation of the provisions of Part V of the CJA 1993, those provisions should be read strictly.

The difficulties of enforcing the insider dealing code

14–77 It is one thing to create a code of insider dealing legislation, but it is another thing to enforce it. There have been successive legislative codes in place in relation to insider dealing but before 2009 there had been very few successful prosecutions. The purpose of this section is to consider the difficulties with prosecuting insider dealing from a number of different perspectives. The difficulties in bringing an insider dealing prosecution were highlighted in a speech on March 17, 2007 by Margaret Cole, then Director of Enforcement at the Financial Services Authority:[74]

"As both the SEC [Securities and Exchange Commission in the USA] and we know piecing together an insider trading case can be a complex, painstaking process. It is rare to find a "smoking gun;" virtually all insider trading cases hinge on circumstantial evidence. It is quite

---

[71] Under English law, such a profit taken from an unauthorised conflict of interest would require a fiduciary (for example, a director or a professional advisor) to hold that profit on constructive trust for the company: *Regal v Gulliver* [1942] 1 All E.R. 378.

[72] [2006] I.R.L.R. 214, E.C.J. (C–384/02).

[73] 89/592/EEC.

[74] *http://www.fsa.gov.uk/library/communication/speeches/2007/0317_mc.shtml*. She meets the accusation that the regulator did "sweet FSA" about insider dealing.

common for insider traders to come up with alternative rationales for their trading strategies that the staff must refute with inferences drawn from the timing of trades, the movement of funds and other facts and circumstances. ... In the majority of cases the prosecution will be unable to obtain direct evidence that a person possessed inside information and knew that it was information of that nature. The best that the prosecution can expect is to be able to invite the jury to infer proof of these elements from the circumstances: the fortuitousness of the timing, an unusually large purchase (or short-selling), the fact that the defendant had never traded in that stock or even market sector before, perhaps even some timely contact with a person who may have been in a position to pass-on price sensitive information. However, persuading a jury that they can be satisfied to the criminal standard that they are clear beyond a reasonable doubt of such guilty knowledge, even on the strongest circumstantial evidence, is likely to be extremely difficult..."

These ideas deserve a little thought. Suppose that two old school-friends, one a bank trader and the other the finance director of a public company, meet for a drink in the George and Vulture pub in the City of London. The finance director tells his friend about some inside information relating to his company. No records are made of their meeting and no-one overhears them. The next day, the bank trader conducts his usual business involving a huge number of trades on behalf of customers across a huge number of companies. Among those transactions, the trader arranges to buy a quantity of shares in that company for a trust which acts as a front for his married sister. It is unlikely that this transaction would be spotted by the authorities unless there was something unusual about the acquisitions made by the trader, although if he was careful to buy in accordance with a similar pattern of acquisitions (i.e. of the same size and longevity of trade) to the average trade conducted on behalf of his clients then nothing would stand out as being suspicious to a prosecutor.

14–78   In a market in which large volumes of transactions are conducted by huge numbers of participants, it is very difficult for investigators to identify which buyers and sellers may be acting on the basis of inside information and so forth. Often, unless directors of the company involved can be shown to have made large gains around the time that the inside information was manipulable, it will be difficult to prove that third parties are acting on the basis of insider dealing as opposed to acting on the basis of their native wits. Solicitor David McCluskey has given us the following insight to prosecutions for insider dealing[75]:

> "While most frauds rely on some form of secrecy, the environment of enforced confidentiality in which insider dealing takes place means that it is all but impossible to catch insider dealers 'in the act'. Absent a tip off, an investigation usually begins with what the rest of the market can already see: an unusual trading pattern just prior to an announcement. The FSA obtains a list of those who traded in advance of publication and the lists of 'insiders' from the institutions involved in the transaction. Investigators will usually begin with basic cross-matching of data between insiders and traders, looking for some correlation between them."

From these two sources it is clear that insider dealing prosecutions are difficult. This is an issue which we must bear in mind when considering the nature of these offences in the abstract. There is a practical issue of proving insider dealing. However, what has been obvious since the end of the critical period of the

---

[75] *http://www.petersandpeters.com/sites/default/files/publications/DMSJ23June_pg19.pdf*

financial crisis in 2009 is that when financial regulators have the desire to find insider dealing then it is certainly possible for them to do so, as is considered next.

Recent prosecutions: the new era

There were several prosecutions relating to insider dealing commenced in 2009 in the UK and in the USA. They illustrated a new enthusiasm in the Financial Services Authority (which has been renamed the Financial Conduct Authority since April Fool's Day 2013) for rooting out insider dealing. Anecdotally there had always been thought to be a large amount of insider dealing in the markets (see the quotation from John Tiner above as an example) but there had been few prosecutions. In both the USA and in the UK in the wake of the global financial crisis there has been a renewed focus on fighting financial crime.

14–79

Press reports suggest that insider trading prosecutions increased by 43 per cent in 2012 in the USA. Of particular significance were the convictions of Raj Rajaratnam, the founder of the Galleon hedge fund, and Rajat Gupta, a board member of Goldman Sachs and former head of McKinsey & Co, for insider trading. Gupta was found to have passed confidential information to Rajaratnam inter alia about Warren Buffett's plan to invest in Goldman Sachs.[76] Rajaratnam was convicted on fourteen counts of insider trading and given eleven years in prison in 2011, as well as a fine of US$92.8 million by the SEC and a criminal fine of US$63.8 million, based on profits taken from insider trading of approximately US$50 million. It was found that Galleon had taken large profits over time in part as a result of tips which Rajaratnam received from former business school classmates.[77] Recordings of telephone conversations with friends giving him tips were played in court and the more memorable extracts repeated in the Press. It was proved that phone calls took place, for example, between Gupta and Rajaratnam only 23 seconds after a conference call for board members which disclosed Buffett's investment in Goldman Sachs.[78] These sorts of pieces of evidence substantiated the convictions. Convictions of this significance appeared to signal a new era in insider trading law.

14–80

In the UK, six people were convicted for insider dealing in relation to a series of offences committed between 2006 and 2008.[79] The first defendant had been employed in the print room at investment banks and had passed on information about impending takeovers which they had encountered while printing documents. These six convictions came on top of the aggregate fourteen successful prosecutions for insider dealing which the Financial Services Authority had previously obtained. It marked a significant development in its attitude to financial crime. The scheme had been complex and its discovery had

14–81

---

[76] *Financial Times*, June 15, 2012, "Gupta found guilty of insider trading".

[77] *Financial Times*, October 13, 2011, "Rajaratnam sentenced to 11 years in jail".

[78] Other Galleon traders were also convicted of insider trading offences: see *Financial Times*, October 13, 2011, "Rajaratnam sentenced to 11 years in jail".

[79] *Financial Times*, July 23, 2012, "Six convicted of insider dealing in City".

required the scrutiny of "hundreds of trading accounts and telephone records".[80] James Sanders, a co-director of Blue Index, was imprisoned for four years (the highest sentence at the time) for insider dealing offences, together with his wife.[81] His actions were described by the judge as "repeated and flagrant acts of dishonesty" as confidential information was channelled through his sister-in-law who worked for Deloitte, the accountancy firm, in San Francisco.[82]

4. OFFENCES RELATING TO MISLEADING MARKETS

A. Introduction

14–82 The notion of criminalising activity which intentionally seeks to pervert or manipulate markets is not new to English criminal law.[83] Thus, the spreading of rumours calculated to cause movements in the price of goods or securities has long been criminalised as a species of fraud.[84] The offences relating to market manipulation in this context, however, relate specifically to the offences created by the Financial Services Act 2012. (These offences replace the old s.397 of the FSMA 2000 which is repealed). The offences considered in this chapter are specific to financial services activity; whereas there are also offences relating to fraud enacted in the Fraud Act 2006, considered in Chapter 16, which apply generally.

B. Making misleading statements to procure a transaction

14–83 Section 89 of the Financial Services Act 2012 ("FSA 2012") provides for a general offence of making misleading statements with a view to inducing someone to enter into a transaction.[85] The circumstances in which the offence can take place (in effect, the actus reus) are the following, as set out in s.89(1), there must be a person who:

> "(a) makes a statement which P knows to be false or misleading in a material respect,

---

[80] *Financial Times*, July 23, 2012, "Six convicted of insider dealing in City". It is impossible to tell whether the fact that the defendants were not traders nor City professionals made their crimes easier to identify.

[81] *Financial Times*, June 20, 2012, 'Blue Index head jailed for insider dealing'.

[82] The sister-in-law was reportedly (*ibid*) the subject of an enforcement action by the SEC in the USA, thus indicating the cross-border co-operation between US and UK regulators.

[83] See also the Australian offences: *Australian Securities Commission v Nomura International Plc* [1998] F.C.A. 1570.

[84] Among the common law offences applicable here are conspiracy to defraud: *R. v De Berenger* (1814) 105 E.R. 536 (where false rumours about Napoleon's death were spread with a view to increasing the price of bonds artificially), and *Scott v Brown* [1892] 2 Q.B. 724 (where a conspiracy was hatched to make it appear that there was a market for shares whereby one of the conspirators bought shares on the exchange at a high price). There was an overlap between monopolisation and market manipulation in relation to the law on fraudulent misrepresentation: see *Salaman v Warner* (1891) 65 L.T. 132, 7 T.L.R. 454; *Sanderson & Levi v British Mercantile Marine & Share Co, The Times* July 19, 1899: cited in P. Wood, *Regulation of International Finance*, para.20–010.

[85] All of the events must have taken place in the UK.

(b)   makes a statement which is false or misleading in a material respect, being reckless as to whether it is, or

(c)   dishonestly conceals any material facts whether in connection with a statement made by P or otherwise."[86]

Any of these three forms of behaviour will constitute the first element of the offence. Therefore, it is required the defendant may have done any of three things to be guilty of this offence, and that she had the mens rea set out in s.89(2). The three forms of actus reus are as follows. First, she must have made a statement, knowing that it is false or misleading in a material respect. Therefore, it is not enough that there is an omission nor silence: for this offence it must be a statement. That statement could be verbal or, it is suggested, it could be an assertion made in writing, in an interview, or in any other sense in which an affirmative form of words are used to convey information to others. Notably, there is no context in which the statement must have taken place: therefore, a statement made in the shower would appear to be caught (provided that it satisfies the requirements of subsection (2)).

A statement may be false or alternatively it may be misleading. It is suggested that those two terms are not comfortable synonyms for one another, and therefore the word "or" should be considered to be disjunctive and not conjunctive. A false statement need not necessarily mislead: in circumstances in which I tell you that it is not raining but you can hear the rain thundering off the metal roof over our heads, my statement would be false but it would not mislead you. Similarly, my statement that human beings have survived exposure to a particular poison may be true but it may also mislead you into thinking that all humans can withstand it. Those two terms are sufficiently different to be distinct. The only issue would then be whether the provision was intended to cover statements which are both misleading and also false: but, had that been the intention, then the statute would have used the word "and".   **14–84**

Second, a statement must have been made which was false or misleading (as before) but the defendant need only be reckless as to whether it is false or it is misleading. Recklessness may be demonstrated by reference to the reasonable person and it may be demonstrated by the person making it not having checked their facts, not have considered the use to which the listener would put that information, and so forth.   **14–85**

Third, the defendant must have been dishonest in concealing facts. Dishonesty in the context of criminal law requires that the defendant was aware that honest people would consider her behaviour to have been dishonest, as well as her behaviour having been dishonest by the standards of honest people. Importantly, then, the defendant must also have concealed facts. This provision is very broad indeed. Bankers, senior executives in banks, PR employees in banks, and so forth all conceal facts—or "spin" facts—constantly, so that the reputation of the institution in the eyes of the markets is not harmed. Concealments of facts may,   **14–86**

---

[86] The principal difference from the repealed s.397(1) in this regard is that there is no explicit reference to a "promise" or a "forecast" although it is suggested that both terms would be encompassed under "statement is most circumstances". The principal difference is in relation to the mens rea of dishonesty and so forth. Section 397 was repealed by s.95 of the FSA 2012.

clearly, also happen in very private settings—for example, between lawyers discussing a transaction, between corporate financiers and clients, and so forth.

The offence is then committed, further to s.89(2), in the following terms where the following "mens rea" is present:

> "P commits an offence if P makes the statement or conceals the facts with the intention of inducing, or is reckless as to whether making it or concealing them may induce, another person (whether or not the person to whom the statement is made)—
>
> (a)   to enter into or offer to enter into, or to refrain from entering or offering to enter into, a relevant agreement, or
>
> (b)   to exercise, or refrain from exercising, any rights conferred by a relevant investment."

There are therefore several elements to this aspect of the offence. First, the defendant must have intended that another person was induced to act. The intention must have been to induce, whether by means of a statement or a concealment, the second element. Second, then, the ultimate intention must have been to induce another person to enter into an agreement or to realise an investment. Importantly, it can be any person who is induced to act, provided that the defendant intended that person to act. The inducement is therefore an inducement to enter into an agreement, or refrain from doing so; or an inducement to exercise any rights under an investment, or refrain from so doing.

There are three defences provided for in s.89(3). The defendant must be able to show that:

> "the statement was made in conformity with
>
> (a)   price stabilising rules,
>
> (b)   control of information rules, or
>
> (c)   the relevant provisions of Commission Regulation (EC) No.2273/2003 of December 22, 2003 implementing Directive 2003/6/EC of the European Parliament and of the Council as regards exemptions for buy-back programmes and stabilisation of financial instruments."

C.   Creating misleading impressions

14–87   It is a criminal offence to intend to create a false or misleading impression to induce another person to do any one of a number of acts in relation to an investment, knowing or being reckless that the impression is false. Importantly, s.90(3)(b) provides that the intention must be that a gain or a loss results, as opposed to being an intention that the third party is induced to act. Section 90 of the FSA 2012 provides that:—

> "(1)   A person ("P") who does any act or engages in any course of conduct which creates a false or misleading impression as to the market in or the price or value of any relevant investments commits an offence if—
>
> (a)   P intends to create the impression, and
>
> (b)   the case falls within subsection (2) or (3) (or both)."

Therefore, the defendant must intend to create the relevant impression. Section 91(2) provides that:

"(2)   The case falls within this subsection if P intends, by creating the impression, to induce another person to acquire, dispose of, subscribe for or underwrite the investments or to refrain from doing so or to exercise or refrain from exercising any rights conferred by the investments."

Therefore, the purpose of creating the impression under (1) is to have any of the outcomes specified in (2). In essence, the purpose is to mislead another person into dealing in specified way with a specified type of investment, with the ultimate intention of creating a gain or a loss as set out under s.91(4). So, s.91(3) provides that:

"The case falls within this subsection if—
(a)   P knows that the impression is false or misleading or is reckless as to whether it is, and
(b)   P intends by creating the impression to produce any of the results in subsection (4) or is aware that creating the impression is likely to produce any of the results in that subsection."

And thus the results specified above are set out in s.91(4):

"Those results are—
(a)   the making of a gain for P or another, or
(b)   the causing of loss to another person or the exposing of another person to the risk of loss."

The concepts of gain and loss are then defined in subss.(6) through (8). The terms "gain" and "loss" are defined confusingly as things which "extend only to gain or loss in money or other property of any kind":[87] it is oddly drafted in that it can extend *only* to particular types of property, but those types of property are "property of *any* kind". The gain or loss can be temporary (e.g. a short-term movement in a rate or price) or it can be permanent.[88] The concept of a gain is extended so that it "includes a gain by keeping what one has, as well as a gain by getting what one does not have";[89] and similarly a loss includes "not getting what one might get, as well as a loss by parting with what one has".[90] It is a defence for the defendant to show that the defendant "reasonably believed that D's conduct would not create an impression that was false or misleading", and it is also a defence to show that the defendant acted as it acted for stabilising prices in conformity with price stabilisation rules.[91]

D.   Making misleading statements in relation to benchmarks

The principal change in the FSA 2012 made in reaction to the Libor scandal   **14–88**
(discussed in Chapter 45) was to create a criminal offence of making a false statement in relation to the setting of a benchmark rate, such as the London Inter-Bank Offered Rate ("Libor"). In that instance, fourteen traders and other employees at Barclays (by the time of writing, although other banks have since

---

[87]   Financial Services Act 2012, s.90(6)(a).
[88]   Financial Services Act 2012, s.90(6)(b).
[89]   Financial Services Act 2012, s.90(7).
[90]   Financial Services Act 2012, s.90(8).
[91]   Financial Services Act 2012, s.90(9).

admitted involvement among their staff) induced the people who submitted quotes for fixing Libor to the BBA to misquote the rates at which Barclays had been dealing (for the most part so as to make money on outstanding transactions). While this would probably have fallen under the Fraud Act 2006, there was great political will to create a new criminal offence to deal specifically with the situation in which market rates are fixed by traders and others. Section 91 provides as follows:

> "A person ("A") who makes to another person ("B") a false or misleading statement commits an offence if—
> (a)   A makes the statement in the course of arrangements for the setting of a relevant benchmark,
> (b)   A intends that the statement should be used by B for the purpose of the setting of a relevant benchmark, and
> (c)   A knows that the statement is false or misleading or is reckless as to whether it is.""

The offence is therefore comprised of three elements, all of which must be proven. There must be a false or misleading statement which is made in the course of setting a benchmark (where the "benchmarks" are defined by order). The defendant must also intend that the statement should be used by the submitter for setting the benchmark. Finally, the defendant must either know that the statement is false or misleading, or the defendant must be reckless at to that state of affairs.

14–89 There is then a second offence for anyone else to do "any act" or to "engage in any course of conduct" which "creates a false or misleading impression as to the price or value of any investment or … interest rate" with an intention to do so and so that that impression "may affect the setting of a relevant benchmark", knowing that the impression is false or misleading and knowing that that impression "may affect the setting of a relevant benchmark".[92]

14–90 It is a defence further to s.91(4) for the defendant to show:

> "(a)   that D acted or engaged in the conduct—
> (i)   for the purpose of stabilising the price of investments, and
> (ii)   in conformity with price stabilising rules,
> (b)   that D acted or engaged in the conduct in conformity with control of information rules, or
> (c)   that D acted or engaged in the conduct in conformity with the relevant provisions of Commission Regulation (EC) No 2273/2003 of December 22, 2003 implementing Directive 2003/6/EC of the European Parliament and of the Council as regards exemptions for buy-back programmes and stabilisation of financial instruments."

These defences reproduce closely the defences in relation to s.89.

---

[92] Financial Services Act 2012, s.91(2).

CHAPTER 15

MONEY LAUNDERING

CORE PRINCIPLES

Money laundering is the process of seeking to transform money or other property derived from criminal activities into money which appears to be legitimate: in that sense the money is said to have been "laundered" because it is washed clean of its criminal stigma. Money laundering is a criminal offence under the Proceeds of Crime Act 2002 (as amended by other legislation). More generally, it is an offence to conceal, disguise, convert, or transfer property, or to remove property from the UK, under s.327 of the 2002 Act. The property which is dealt with in this way must be "criminal property": that is, property which is a benefit taken from "criminal conduct" or is suspected to be such. Many of the decided cases have related to the defendant's "suspicion" that the property was derived from criminal conduct. While these cases have differed in approach, it appears that the suspicion must be based on reasonable grounds.

There are further offences. First, the offence of participating in money laundering activities. Secondly, the offence of "tipping off" someone whose activities are under investigation for money laundering. Thirdly, conspiracy to launder money.

The Serious Crime Act 2007 created the Serious Organised Crime Agency to investigate this species of crime. The Terrorism Act 2000 (as amended) created offences in relation to money laundering for terrorist purposes. The Money Laundering Regulations 2007 impose obligations on various forms of person who handle money (and who might therefore be used as conduits for other people's money laundering activities): credit institutions, financial institutions, auditors, independent legal professionals, trust or company service providers, estate agents, high value dealers and casinos. Each of these people has obligations under the Regulations to conduct due diligence work in relation to their customers, and to keep records about their transactions.

There is a duty to make disclosure to the authorities imposed on people acting in the course of a business in the financial sector (including bankers, employees of investment firms and so forth). This aspect of the money laundering is controversial in that it appears to encourage professionals to over-report their clients' affairs; while the harm at which the law is directed (though palpable) has been questioned by many commentators.

1. INTRODUCTION

A. What is "money laundering"?

15–01 This chapter considers a range of finance-related crime which is not strictly limited to the activities of authorised firms and financial markets as they are considered in *Section Two* of this book. Instead the principal theme in this chapter is the use of the financial system by criminals either to fund their illegal activities or to try to conceal the fruits of those same illegal activities so as to put them beyond the reach of the authorities. The main criminal offences which are considered here relate to "money laundering".[1] Money laundering was defined in the explanatory notes to the Proceeds of Crime Act 2002 as being "the process by which the proceeds of crime are converted into assets which appear to have a legitimate origin, so that they can be retained permanently or recycled into further criminal enterprises". Money laundering was defined by HM Treasury in the UK in the following terms in a strategy document dealing with governmental policy on money laundering[2] as:

> "a term generally used to describe the ways in which criminals process illegal or 'dirty' money derived from the proceeds of any illegal activity (e.g. the proceeds of drug-dealing, human trafficking, fraud, theft, or tax evasion) through a succession of transfers and deals until the source of illegally acquired funds is obscured and the money takes on the appearance of legitimate or 'clean' funds or assets."

Money laundering, then, is often a sophisticated process which involves using the complexity of modern, globalised financial markets' infrastructure to the criminal's advantage so as to spirit money away from its source: more particularly to spirit "dirty" money away from its criminal source and attempt to transform it into legitimate assets.

The verb "laundering" refers to the process of trying to "wash" the dirty money **15–02** clean of its criminal stigma by a series of ostensibly harmless transactions. A good example of a money laundering scheme would be a criminal stealing money from a sterling-denominated bank account in London, perhaps by hacking into the London bank's computer systems, and then paying that money into a bank account in New York, before changing that money into US dollars and then dividing it into a number of irregular amounts, converting it into different currencies again and then paying each amount into different bank accounts in different jurisdictions. Each time the money is paid into a new bank account, there will always be money belonging to another person already in that bank account. Usually each bank account in well-organised criminal schemes will be owned by a different "dummy"[3] company controlled by some associate of the criminal so that the legal process of tracing that money becomes complicated, as discussed in Chapter 23.[4] The recipient of the money will then be wound up so as to complicate the tracing process even further. In the meantime, the money will have been moved onwards again and again and again. There are a number of jurisdictions in the world—principally Switzerland and some of the so-called offshore, island jurisdictions—which will either permit money to be held in bank accounts for which the owner is not recorded and the identity of accountholders kept secret, or which will permit money to be held on trust without the need for any beneficiary to be identified.[5]

---

[1] The literature on money laundering includes: R. Forston, "Money Laundering Offences under POCA 2002" in W. Blair and R. Brent (eds), *Banks and Financial Crime* (OUP, 2008), p.155 et seq. For a less linear approach see P. Alldridge, *Money Laundering Law* (Hart, 2003).

[2] *Anti-Money Laundering Strategy*, October 2004, HM Treasury.

[3] A dummy company is a company which carries on no trade but rather simply exists to hold assets for the people who control it.

[4] See this sort of process used in cases such as *Agip (Africa) Ltd v Jackson*; *El Ajou v Dollar Land Holdings* [1994] 2 All E.R. 685; [1994] 1 B.C.L.C. 464, [1994] B.C.C. 143.

[5] See A.S. Hudson, *Equity & Trusts*, s.21.2.5.

15–03   Once the money has been passed through enough dummy accounts and shell companies—that is, accounts and companies which have no ostensible purpose other than to facilitate this sort of money laundering—or even through legitimate accounts, the money can be invested in ostensibly legitimate activities so that the criminals can ultimately have the use of their money in the open air. Hence the use of the metaphor of "laundering" because it is hoped that enough washing of the money through different accounts and people will mean that the money becomes "clean" and so loses its stigma and taint of being connected to criminal activity. So, in *The Sopranos* television series Tony Soprano, a mafia boss, had a bar business, a pork butcher business, refuse collection businesses, and so on. These businesses were useful to Soprano's criminal activities because they (generally) traded legitimately and because they dealt in cash from anonymous, random members of the public so that any laundered money could more easily be folded into the businesses' books. Similarly in *R. v Saik*[6] the defendant had allegedly conspired to use his bureau de change business to launder the proceeds of drug trafficking by mixing drug money with ordinary money paid in by the public to acquire foreign currency. The problem with money laundering is that the source of the money, however, is criminal activity. Alternatively, it may be that the money is intended to be used for criminal activity or terrorism even though its source was entirely legitimate. In this instance, the purpose of the laundering would be to hide the original "investor" in the criminal activity. No one investing in international terrorist activity wants to be identified as such, and so their contribution must be concealed by laundering it.

15–04   Consequently, this chapter is not concerned with examining the operation of a financial market like securities or derivatives or bank lending. Instead the concern is to identify how the criminal law and criminals' use of the financial system interact because the ensuing web of regulation and criminal offences impose a number of obligations on banks when dealing with money from suspicious sources. Those obligations are our principal focus in this chapter. We shall consider in general terms the Proceeds of Crime Act 2002, which created the Asset Recovery Agency to expropriate the proceeds of a criminal lifestyle in relation to all forms of criminal activity; however, that Act also contains the principal offences relating to money laundering. It is supplemented and has been amended in this context by the other legislation discussed in this chapter. In particular the Serious Organised Crime Agency ("SOCA")[7] was created by the Serious Organised Crime and Police Act 2005 ("SOCPA 2005") to field reports of suspicious transactions, as considered below. The concern about money laundering and in particular about drug trafficking was the original source of concern for much money laundering legislation.[8] Latterly, international and national terrorism became a grave cause for concern. The particular context of international terrorism was dealt with by the Terrorism Act 2000 and subsequent legislation. The Money Laundering Regulations 2007 are the most recent development in this field.

---

[6] [2006] UKHL 18.

[7] It does seem possible that the name was chosen because the acronym sounds like the word "soccer".

[8] Money laundering was first criminalised by means of the Drug Trafficking Offences Act 1986, and latterly the Drug Trafficking Act 1994.

B. Policy issues surrounding the criminal law's treatment of money laundering and the proceeds of a criminal lifestyle

Given the policy priority which has been reassigned to counter-terrorism and to combating organised crime in the UK, particularly since the events of September 11, 2001 in New York, there is no surprise that the criminal law in relation to money laundering and the use of other "criminal property" has been revamped. The creation of SOCA replaced its forerunner (the National Criminal Intelligence Service) which was considered not to have been sufficiently effective in dealing with organised crime. Money laundering is perceived by policy makers to be the means by which "terrorists" acquire their funding, augment their funding through investment and conceal their assets. The term "terrorist" is one which in UK public policy terms includes home-grown bombers of municipal transport systems, criminals who commit acts of murder and sabotage for ideological ends, and insurgent military and paramilitary forces in various other jurisdictions around the world where the UK or its allies have military personnel in theatre. Therefore the criminal law in this area has been able to become more wide-ranging in its drafting and in its practical application than might otherwise have been possible. Of particular importance in the UK is the impact on banks of the obligations which they bear to report to the authorities any suspicious payments which are deposited with them by their customers. The approach taken by the legislation in the UK is to require the banks to assess the risk that the payment in question may have derived from a tainted source, as opposed simply to requiring banks to report payments over a given amount: this means that the banks are more likely to over-report transactions which they might otherwise have overlooked to ensure that they are not made subject to the strict penalties which may be imposed on them by the authorities, as discussed below.

15–05

As Forston points out anecdotally[9] it does seem that banks are reporting transactions which do not necessarily need to be reported so that they will not be at risk of failing to report appropriate transactions, with the effect that Forston identifies of private transactions being disclosed to the authorities in a way that compromises the confidentiality which people would ordinarily require in their financial affairs. Government and the legal system have been able to penetrate much further into the private realm as a result of this legislation than would otherwise have been the case. As with the discussion of insider dealing in the previous chapter, this leads some to wonder whether or not this architecture of observation is necessary to combat the ills which it has identified or whether it simply satisfies the expansionist agenda of those in the legal system who would prefer carte blanche to observe the citizenry more closely with CCTV on our streets, longer detention without charge in police stations, tracking of internet activity, and so on.

15–06

This is a policy dilemma which is difficult to square. Those charged with preventing further terrorist attacks in the UK, and there is no questioning that there have been terrorist attacks, would clearly like all the legal tools at their

15–07

---

[9] R. Forston, "Money Laundering Offences under POCA 2002" in W. Blair and R. Brent (eds), *Banks and Financial Crime* (OUP, 2008), p.156.

disposal which it is possible to devise. Contrariwise, the enlarged reach of the state into private lives and private affairs threatens ever more abrogations of the private lives of ordinary citizens. Gage L.J. has said that "[t]here is no doubt that the money laundering provisions of the Proceeds of Crime Act 2002 are draconian".[10] Similarly, Ward L.J. recorded the applicant before him as considering that money laundering regulation was "a raft of legislation of which Dracon, the Athenian legislator, would have been proud"; while also recognising on the other side of the argument "SOCA's view [that] the 2002 Act is a sharp but essential modern weapon in the fight against organised crime which gives SOCA and other law enforcement bodies the ability to counter-attack, and then pursue and recover the proceeds of the criminal activity".[11] As to money laundering specifically, the terrorist activities carried out by British citizens in the UK on 7/7 using rucksacks bought on the high street do not suggest the involvement of sophisticated international financiers; whereas, training operatives from many nations to fly aeroplanes into densely populated business districts does. The use of money laundering legislation began with the fight against international drug dealers, and so the struggle against the use of international financial systems to invest and conceal large amounts of money is directed at activities other than terrorism. It is impossible to know to what extent organised crime does in fact use the financial system to hothouse its assets precisely because any such activities will be clandestine even if they are real.[12] However, much of the benefit of this legislation is that, aside from the headline grabbing policy considerations of international terrorism and the drug trade, the existence of legislation which can expropriate the ill-gotten gains of criminals is in itself a genuinely useful mechanism in the management of the criminal justice system. Indeed, the existence of mechanisms in the criminal law to deal with any criminals attempting to conceal or invest their ill-gotten gains is a timely comparator to the civil law mechanism of tracing (discussed in Chapter 23) to recover property or its traceable proceeds for the victims of crime. Also legislation dealing with offences connected to terrorist activity and the interrogation of terrorists are not new to the 21st century. These issues form a deeply troubling background to the law considered in this chapter.

2.   MONEY-LAUNDERING OFFENCES IN THE PROCEEDS OF CRIME ACT 2002

A.   The scope of the Proceeds of Crime Act 2002

15–08   The Proceeds of Crime Act 2002 ("POCA 2002"; as amended by the Serious Organised Crime and Police Act 2005 ("SOCPA 2005")) has three principal objectives for our purposes: first, to criminalise the receipt of any benefit from "criminal property", which includes money laundering; secondly, to criminalise "tipping off" a money launderer; and thirdly, to require the disclosure of specified

---

[10] *R. v Gabriel* [2006] EWCA Crim. 229, at [29].

[11] [2007] Bus. L.R. 1317, 1321, at [9].

[12] For a summary of both the sceptics' case and the first steps being carried on towards research into this phenomenon, see B. Rider, "An insider paradox?", (2008) Vol.29 *The Company Lawyer* p.1.

types of dealing to the authorities. The POCA 2002 therefore has a much broader ambit than dealing solely with money laundering: the term "*money* laundering" in the context of the principal legislation is not limited to dealings with money but includes assets of any type, as is considered below.

B. The principal offences of money laundering in s.327(1) POCA 2002

It is an offence under s.327(1) of POCA 2002 to do acts related to concealing or abetting money laundering. Section 327(1) provides:

15–09

> "A person commits an offence if he—
> (a) conceals criminal property;
> (b) disguises criminal property;
> (c) converts criminal property;
> (d) transfers criminal property;
> (e) removes criminal property from England and Wales or from Scotland or from Northern Ireland."

Therefore, there are five offences contained within this subsection, all of which relate to "criminal property" (as is defined in the next section). As Lord Nicholls put it, "the property in question must emanate from a crime".[13] These offences will relate to the "laundering" of criminal property in that they bite if a person conceals, disguises, converts, transfers or removes the criminal property: all of these activities are the sorts of techniques which were discussed at the beginning of this chapter when defining the meaning of "money laundering". This subsection sets out the various forms of actus reus constituting each offence; the definition of "criminal property" in s.340(3) is considered below[14]; and the mens rea in this context, it is suggested, is supplied by the requirement that the defendant know or suspect that property is "criminal property" under s.340(3).

Let us take a simple example of money laundering. This example will focus solely on the actus reus of the offence; the mens rea will be considered below. Suppose that armed robbers steal cash from a security van which they ambush in a narrow London street. Clearly anyone who participates in this theft will commit criminal offences relating to the Theft Acts, possession of firearms, offences against the person of the security van guards, and so on. Those offences do not concern us except to the extent that they demonstrate that the property was derived from a criminal activity: namely, theft. Suppose further that the robbers drive back to their shared mock-Tudor house in Essex and hand the money to the ringleader's mother to hide in the attic. The ringleader's mother would therefore commit the offence of "concealing" the money if she put it in the attic behind the water tank in a black bin liner. If she instead sliced open some of the roofing insulation in the attic and put the banknotes inside that insulation then she would be guilty of "disguising" it as insulation as well as "concealing" it.[15] If the

15–10

---

[13] *R. v Saik* [2006] UKHL 18, [23]; relying on *R. v Montila* [2004] 1 W.L.R. 3141.
[14] See para.15–14.
[15] It is provided in s.327(3) that concealing the property includes "concealing or disguising its nature, source, location, disposition, movement or ownership or any rights with respect to it".

ringleader's mother packed some of the banknotes into a number of suitcases before going on holiday with some of her female relatives to Spain, then she would have committed the offence of "removing" the property from the jurisdiction. If she then tried to exchange comparatively small amounts of the sterling banknotes for euros while in Spain, she would then have committed the offence of "converting" the money. If she had placed some of the banknotes in her bank account in Chingford in Essex and then transferred those amounts to a bank account in Switzerland, she would then have committed the offence of "transferring" the money. It is suggested that on a literal interpretation of the word "transfer" simply the act of taking the banknotes out of the security firms boxes to place them in bin liners before putting them in the attic would constitute "transfer". This term "transfer" could, however, be interpreted to relate only to a transfer between bank accounts or some similar part of laundering the property. A literal interpretation would involve any movement of the property from one location or bag or container to any other location, bag or container: this would have the beneficial effect of capturing within the actus reus of the offence anyone who assisted the laundering activity, with the question of such a person's knowledge of the true nature of the activity to be decided.

15–11 A similar example of these offences using bank accounts, as in the example given at the start of this chapter, would be as follows. Again, this discussion focuses on the actus reus of the offence. Suppose that a computer hacker, Clyde, penetrated the firewalls on the computer systems of a bank and used information taken from an unwitting internet user to gain unlawful access to her bank account. Suppose Clyde then transferred £20,000 from his deposit account into a brand new deposit account opened by his conspirator, Bonnie, which contained no other money. If Bonnie then paid that money into her previous current account and mixed it with another £100 belonging to her and already deposited in her current account, then she would have committed the offence of "concealing" that money because she would have confused the identity of the original £20,000 with the £100 already held in that account. Under civil property law, this holding of £20,100 will be treated as a mixture of the £20,000 and of the £100 which could not be traced at common law, but rather only traced using the specialist tracing rules in equity—these principles are discussed in detail in Chapter 23. What this demonstrates is that the nature of the money will have been masked by changing it into a mixture of moneys, and therefore "concealment" would be a reasonable interpretation of this situation. It could also be said that Bonnie has attempted to "disguise" the money. It would be even easier to make out the concealment and disguise offences if Bonnie transferred the £20,000 into a bank account owned by a company, X Ltd, because that would be an attempt to conceal the money from anyone tracing through Clyde's original theft of the money and also disguising the money.[16]

15–12 It might be argued that "disguise" suggests cloaking the money in some way, and not simply moving it beyond the reach of those pursuing the money; whereas mixing the money with other money would suggest a disguise of the money by

---

[16] Clyde would himself be guilty of the actus reus of money laundering on these grounds by transferring the money to Bonnie at the outset.

changing its denomination and thus making it more difficult to identify. This is where, it is suggested, that the sort of complex money laundering transactions identified at the start of this chapter would constitute "disguise". So, if Bonnie transfers the money into an account held by X Ltd, which is a company controlled by Bonnie to launder money, then that is an attempt to disguise the money stolen by Clyde as being money belonging to a different legal person. Once the money is paid away from X Ltd to Y Ltd, also controlled by Bonnie, and X Ltd is wound up, then there is clearly an attempt to disguise the money. It is suggested though that any mixture of moneys would constitute a "disguise" because it is an attempt to exchange one identity of that property for another identity. On a different point, there is no need for X Ltd to be a shell company operated by Bonnie; it would be sufficient that X Ltd was a legitimate business and thus that Bonnie was attempting to wash the dirty money by making it appear to be part of the funds of a legitimate business, which is the money launderer's ultimate goal. While these activities could fall under a number of the other heads in s.327(1), there is an important general question addressed here about the way in which these offences should be interpreted.

If Bonnie then transferred the money into a different currency she would be guilty of "converting" the money. If in so doing she transferred the money to a different bank account, then she would be guilty of "transferring" the funds. And if she transferred the money into a bank account in another jurisdiction then she would have "removed" the money. It is suggested that in relation to a criminal tactic of moving money or other property away from the hands of the criminal, this literal approach to these offences would be a beneficial way of preventing criminals from benefiting at all from their criminal activities. There is a possibility that these offences would then bleed into the same sorts of activity covered by handling stolen goods and conspiracy, but that it is suggested is not a reason to deny these words their ordinary meaning.

15–13

C.   The definition of "criminal property"

The definition of "criminal property"

For an offence of "money laundering" to be made out, "the property in question must emanate from a crime. The criminal provenance of the property is a fact necessary for the commission of the offence."[17] In the language of the statute, it must be "criminal property".[18] The expression "criminal property" is defined in s.340(3) of the POCA 2002 in the following terms:

15–14

"(3)   Property is criminal property if—
  (a)   it constitutes a person's benefit from criminal conduct or it represents such a benefit (in whole or part and whether directly or indirectly), and
  (b)   the alleged offender knows or suspects that it constitutes or represents such a benefit."

---

[17] *R. v Saik* [2006] UKHL 18, at [23], per Lord Nicholls; relying on *R. v Montila* [2004] 1 W.L.R. 3141.
[18] Proceeds of Crime Act 2002 s.327(1).

There are therefore two requirements here: the fact that it constitutes a benefit, as considered first; and secondly a requirement that the defendant has knowledge or suspicion about that fact, which is considered afterwards.

15–15   The first half of the definition of what constitutes "criminal property" is therefore something which is a "benefit from criminal conduct". It is suggested that a "benefit" in this sense would clearly encompass three things: any "gain" which is attributable directly to that criminal activity; any "benefit in kind" which flows from that criminal activity; and also some thing which "represents such a benefit". The next three sections will therefore consider under these headings what constitutes a benefit from criminal activity, before the last two sections consider the requirements of knowledge and suspicion. What must be observed from the outset is that the property must be criminal property at the time when the allegedly criminal acts were performed.[19]

Gains from criminal activity; who must take the benefit?

15–16   The most straightforward example of criminal property in this sense, then, would relate to gains made by the defendant. We shall first consider what might be meant by a gain in this context and then consider who must make this gain. Gains taken directly from a criminal activity can be easily identified: the very car that was stolen; the money that was stolen from a bank account; the cash that was received from purchasers of illegal narcotics, and so on. Indirect gains from the criminal activity would include the cash proceeds from the sale of a stolen car: that is, not the car itself, which is the direct result of the theft, but rather the cash that is derived from its theft. A gain in this sense would be any *enrichment* of the criminal which flows from the crime either directly or indirectly. A gain in this sense could also include the avoidance of a loss. For example, if Irene faced a default interest payment under a contract to deliver a 100 bearer bonds to Tony which Irene did not own, then Irene's theft of 100 such bearer bonds would constitute a "gain" in this sense even if it simply meant that Irene broke even on her transaction with Tony because it would be a gain on the position if she had been required to pay default interest.

15–17   Next, let us consider who can make the gain and so commit the offence. There is no requirement in s.340(3)(a) that it must be the criminal who takes the benefit. That provision merely requires that it is "a person's benefit": the indefinite article suggesting that it need not be any person in particular.[20] In s.340(4) it is provided explicitly that "it is immaterial who carried out the conduct" or "who benefited from it". The benefit could be taken by any person flowing from the crime.

15–18   It is unclear as to the level of distance from the criminal activity which means that the offence is not committed. In other words, what is the level of proximity required for an offence to be committed? For example, if the criminal's nephew received a better birthday present after the crime than was affordable the previous

---

[19] *R. v Loizou* [2005] EWCA Civ 1579; noted by D. Ormerod [2005] Crim. L.R. 885.

[20] Indeed, if it were otherwise, then the criminal could simply set up a company to which the benefit was passed and claim that the benefit accrued to a different person; or else just have the benefit transmitted from the outset to a close relative with the same result.

year—an iPhone compared to a single movie on DVD—does that constitute a gain from the criminal activity? The nephew has clearly improved his lot but it is difficult to calculate to what extent he has derived a benefit: he would have got some sort of present, it is to be assumed, but is it possible to prove that this year's present would otherwise have been the same as last year's present and so constitute the cash difference in the two presents, or confiscation of the iPhone? It is suggested, that such a small item would be difficult to attribute directly to the crime, whereas a transfer of £300,000 worth of bearer bonds to the nephew acquired with the proceeds of a £10 million robbery of bearer bonds would be more obviously attributable to the crime. Consequently, it is suggested that the offence should be interpreted in accordance with a notion that the property must be understood as being reasonably attributed to the proceeds of the crime at issue.

Benefits in kind from criminal activity

The acquisition of property from crime need not simply lead to a cash gain once that money is sold off. For example, if Irene stole a computer chip from Tony that enabled her to operate a computer system which earned her £100,000 in profits, then a part of those £100,000 profits would be derived from the criminal property. The question would then be identifying the amount of profit which is attributable to the computer chip. Other benefits might accrue, and they might accrue to people other than the criminal. So, the criminal's family would see a rise in their standard of living if they moved to a better home and had more moveable goods in their house. A clear example of a benefit in kind accruing from a crime would include the ability to acquire expensive services, such as a chauffeur, but that sort of service would be difficult to identify as "property" unless it constituted a transferable service which could be turned to account. Thus, demonstrating the commission of the criminal offence is made difficult when there is no identified property at issue. Whereas, the ability to acquire a lease over a Chelsea riverside apartment would constitute the acquisition of property and therefore would both fall within the criminal offence and be capable of restitution under civil law. **15–19**

It is suggested that among the benefits which might flow from money laundering would be the avoidance or evasion of tax. Not having to pay a tax as a result of the laundering scheme would mean that the defendant has drawn an indirect benefit from the arrangement. If tax is purportedly evaded (as opposed to being lawfully "avoided"), that tax remains payable. However, that does not affect the question whether or not a benefit was taken in the time between the tax being evaded and eventually being paid (if at all). Instead, for the purposes of the criminal liability for money laundering only, if one evades tax then one has accrued a benefit at that moment and that should be enough to impose liability for the offence of money laundering by way of receipt of a benefit derived from criminal activity. Even if the later imposition of the tax when the truth is discovered is coupled with a payment of interest, then that does not change the fact that the defendant realised a benefit in the short term at the very least in the form of an opportunity to earn profits from the money involved at a rate above the rate of statutory interest. Even if those ill-gotten gains were to be recovered **15–20** by means of a constructive trust[21] or expropriated further to POCA 2002 then the defendant would still have had a benefit at the time of taking the money and not accounting to HM Revenue and Customs for it, which should found liability under s.327.[22]

A thing which represents a benefit; must the property be separately identifiable?

15–21   In the previous section, being able to acquire a lease over a riverside Chelsea apartment from the proceeds of the crime constitutes a straightforward item of property derived from the crime. However, there may be other items of property (including profits from investment or business activities) which do not have such a straightforward nexus with the crime. An example of property which might constitute such an indirect benefit from the crime might be profits from ticket sales for admission to an exhibition of Salvador Dali's early work if a stolen copy of Dali's *Girl at a Window* was on show and constituted the only painting which art critics and the bulk of the foot traffic to the exhibition considered to be worthy of attention. In such a situation, it could be said that the excess profits attributable to the pull of *Girl at a Window* is property indirectly derived from the theft of that painting. However, it would be difficult to identify precisely which profits were derived from that painting and which came from the presence of the exhibition more generally.

15–22   This raises a different question: is it necessary to identify separate property, as it is in civil law to bring a claim based on tracing, or is it sufficient to constitute the criminal offence that there is known to be *some* property which is derived from the crime, even if there is no separate property which is so derived? It is suggested that the offences in s.327(1) require only that there is a "benefit" for there to be a criminal offence made out. Therefore, the mischief of the offence is made out provided that the defendant has taken *some* benefit from criminal conduct. That wording does not require that there must be any particular property which constitutes that benefit, as long as some benefit can be attributed to *some* property in an identified parcel of property.[23] The requirement that a benefit is taken is not the same as a requirement that specific property be acquired.

---

[21] cf. *Attorney General for Hong Kong v Reid* [1994] 1 A.C. 1 and liability for the receipt of a bribe or, it is suggested, from Lord Templeman's judgment that any unconscionable activity involving criminal actions should take the form of a constructive trust over the property in question.

[22] For another perspective, see P. Alldridge and A. Mumford, "Tax evasion and the Proceeds of Crime Act 2002" (2005) 25 *Legal Studies* 353. In support of the approach taken in the text see R. Forston, "Money Laundering Offences under POCA 2002" in W. Blair and R. Brent (eds), *Banks and Financial Crime* (OUP, 2008), p.166.

[23] For a similar approach see *R. v I, K* [2007] EWCA Crim. 491, where it was held that "a simplified paradigm case" of under-declaring tax by £250,000 would cheat the public purse of £100,000 in income tax and £25,000 in VAT, and therefore that the taxpayer had received a benefit of £125,000 in that year as a result (at [21]). Therefore it was held that the offences further to s.328 should encompass cheating the Revenue. For a different view see Alldridge and Mumford, *op cit.*: this view is difficult to support for the reasons given in the text; the wording of the provision does not support this analysis. In support of the approach taken in the text see R. Forston, "Money Laundering Offences under POCA 2002" in W. Blair and R. Brent (eds), *Banks and Financial Crime* (OUP, 2008), p.166.

Indeed, if this analysis were not correct, then it would be very difficult to bring **15–23** prosecutions for money laundering at all precisely because money launderers mix tainted money with legitimately sourced money so that there are mixtures produced. If the property had to be separately identifiable then few prosecutions could be made out precisely because the launderer will usually mix tainted and untainted property. Such a narrow interpretation would neuter the effect of the legislation. A person takes a benefit from having a combination of moneys paid into her account—it is not necessary for there to be a benefit that money from one source is separately identifiable from money from another source. It is provided in s.340(6) that if the defendant obtained "a pecuniary advantage as a result of or in connection with conduct, he is to be taken to obtain as a result of or in connection with the conduct a sum of money equal to the value of the pecuniary advantage". This provision supports the analysis that no specified money or other property be identifiable separately from other property. Furthermore, civil law does not require that the property be anything more than traceable to a part of a mixture (as with equitable tracing[24]) for a proprietary remedy to be made available. Therefore, it is suggested that there is no evident reason why the criminal law should be required to do so.

Knowledge that there is a benefit from criminal activity

The alternative definition of "criminal property" under s.340(3) is that "the **15–24** alleged offender knows . . . that it constitutes or represents such a benefit". This would clearly be the case if the defendant had actual knowledge of the criminal activity. What is less clear is whether having constructive knowledge—that the defendant ought to have known, or that a reasonable person would have known—is would also fall within this provision. This issue is addressed, it is suggested, by the next section.

In dealing with a prosecution relating to conspiracy to launder criminal property, **15–25** Lord Nicholls considered the question whether a person can "know" that property is the proceed of crime unless she participated in the crime; whereas otherwise she can merely suspect that that is the case.[25] His lordship came down squarely, for the purposes of conspiracy under s.1(2) of the Criminal Law Act 1977, in favour of the test of knowledge being limited strictly to actual knowledge. As is discussed below, in relation to money laundering a person can be found guilty if she had more general, constructive knowledge in the form of "suspicion" because that is dealt with separately in s.340(3). In coming to this conclusion, Lord Nicholls recognised the difference in approach on this question between *R. v Ali*[26] dealing with the question of conspiracy to launder criminal property where it was suggested that to "know" meant simply to "believe"; whereas in *R. v Montila*[27] in

---

[24] See para.23–13.
[25] *R. v Saik* [2006] UKHL 18, at [25]: recognising a different in approach here between *R. v Ali* [2006] 2 W.L.R. 316, 335, at.[98] where it was suggested that to "know" meant simply to "believe"; whereas in *R. v Montila* [2004] 1 W.L.R. 3141 to meaning of the word to "know" meant to have actual knowledge.
[26] [2006] 2 W.L.R. 316, 335, at [98].
[27] [2004] 1 W.L.R. 3141.

relation to this substantive offence the meaning of the word to "know" was taken to require that the defendant had actual knowledge. The nature of "suspicion" is considered next.

Suspicion that there is a benefit from criminal activity

15–26   The second circumstance in which the defendant will be taken to have had sufficient knowledge of the source of the property is the circumstance in which "the alleged offender ... suspects that it constitutes or represents such a benefit". The concept of "suspicion" has been considered frequently in the House of Lords and in the Court of Appeal in recent years, in relation to offences which are closely related to those in s.327(1) of POCA 2002 but not the same offence. Those cases have usually been in relation to conspiracy offences where the defendant must have suspected that the property which was the subject of the conspiracy would derive from criminal conduct. The principal issue in these cases has been whether or not the criminal conduct must actually have taken place before the conspiracy was formed so that there is some criminal property in existence; and furthermore whether it must have been reasonable that the defendant would have suspected that there had been a crime in the circumstances. This section therefore serves as a central repository for the discussion of "suspicion" in various offences considered in this chapter.

15–27   The precise definition of the term of "suspicion" has travelled through the various levels of courts from a very general conception into a narrower conception and then to a test based in part on reasonableness. For the purposes of s.93A of the Criminal Justice Act 1988 it has been held in *R. v Da Silva*[28] at first instance that a person may be "suspecting" of another person's engagement in criminal conduct if that person has "the imagining of something without evidence or on slender evidence, inkling, mistrust". This definition was taken by the trial judge from a dictionary definition of "suspecting". It suggests that one's understanding of whether or not another person is engaged in criminal conduct can actually be quite slight: if you need only have an "inkling" or an "imagination of something without evidence" then it is likely that one will be taken to have suspected another's criminal conduct. The appeal in *R v Da Silva*[29] concerned the conviction of a woman who had assisted her husband to retain the benefit of money transfers by deception – the issue was whether she should be taken to have suspected that those funds were derived from criminal conduct.[30] It was held that it had been reasonable for the trial judge to use a dictionary definition of the word "suspecting" when directing the jury. As with *K Ltd v National Westminster Bank Plc*,[31] the particular concern related to the definition of "suspicion" which

---

[28]   [2006] EWCA Crim. 1654; [2007] 1 W.L.R. 303, CA.

[29]   [2007] 1 W.L.R. 303.

[30]   The money transfers were obtained fraudulently on behalf of non-existent workers at the AMT coffee concession which the couple operated at Kings Cross station.

[31]   [2006] EWCA Civ 1039, [2007] 1 W.L.R. 311.

encompassed the defendant merely having an "inkling" of something or a "fleeting thought". As Longmore L.J. approached this question in the Court of Appeal in *R v Da Silva*:[32]

> "It seems to us that the essential element in the word 'suspect' and its affiliates, in this context, is that the defendant must think that there is a possibility, which is more than fanciful, that the relevant facts exist. A vague feeling of unease would not suffice. But the statute does not require the suspicion to be 'clear' or 'firmly grounded and targeted on specific facts', or based upon 'reasonable grounds'. To require the prosecution to satisfy such criteria as to the strength of the suspicion would, in our view, be putting a gloss on the section."

It is enough to convict someone on the basis that they must have had a suspicion of something if they have an inkling of it. Significantly, a suspicion is not something reasonable or necessarily even particularly rational. One suspects something automatically without having to think it through reasonably in advance. Importantly, however, those suspicions must more than merely fanciful: so, while they do not need to be reasonably held they must be based in some sort of reality. It was considered that this provision was intentionally broad given the breadth of the money laundering code in general.

A different approach from that of Longmore L.J. was taken by Lord Hope in *R. v Saik*.[33] Lord Hope's approach considered that reasonableness was a part of "suspicion". This has had the effect of making prosecutions more difficult, just as Longmore L.J. feared it would, because it must also be demonstrated that the suspicion was reasonable in the circumstances. By requiring that someone had reasonable grounds for their suspicion means that their thoughts must be based on something more solid than a mere inkling or irrational supposition. Lord Hope expressed himself as follows[34]:

15–28

> "... the assumption is that the person has a suspicion, otherwise he would not be thinking of doing what the statute contemplates. The objective test is introduced in the interests of fairness, to ensure that the suspicion has a reasonable basis for it. The subjective test—actual suspicion—is not enough. The objective test—that there were reasonable grounds for it—must be satisfied too."

Therefore, as a result of Lord Hope's dicta, the defendant must have actual suspicion and also there must have been a reasonable basis for having that suspicion, as well as the property being used for criminal purposes.[35] Why there is such an assumption, as Lord Hope suggests, that the person has a suspicion in all circumstances in less clear. If the defendant was genuinely an idiot then she might not think there was anything wrong and therefore there would not be any subjective suspicion. What seems to be suggested here is that there is a *presumption* of suspicion, because we cannot know the subjective contents of

---

[32] [2006] EWCA Crim. 1654; [2007] 1 W.L.R. 303, CA.
[33] [2006] UKHL 18; [2007] 1 A.C. 18. That case related to an offence of conspiracy to launder money, and therefore it was not exactly the same offence as that under s.237 of POCA 2002.
[34] [2006] UKHL 18, at [52].
[35] See, for example, Hooper L.J. and D. Ormerod (eds), *Blackstone's Criminal Practice*, 18th edn, (OUP, 2007), p.995 for support of this restrictive analysis of *Saik*.

someone else's mind, and then the question is whether or not it is reasonable that a person would have had such a suspicion in these circumstances.[36]

15–29   It is suggested that this sort of suspicion ought therefore to be satisfied by any situation in which there was constructive knowledge of the facts set out in s.237(1): that is, that the defendant ought to have known, or that a reasonable person would have known, or that the defendant wilfully shut her eyes to the obvious, or that the defendant wilfully failed to make the enquiries which an honest or reasonable person would have made in the circumstances. These are the formulations associated with civil liability for unconscionable receipt, as discussed in Chapter 26. Criminal liability usually requires that the defendant appreciate her own mental state, whereas civil law is generally content with a demonstration that a reasonable person would not have acted as the defendant did; although the judgment in *K v National Westminster Bank, HMRC, SOCA*[37] suggests that the civil and criminal standards should be the same in relation to notions of "suspicion".[38] Section 340(3)(b) requires simply that there was suspicion, and it is suggested that the court should be satisfied if a reasonable person would have had suspicions.[39]

15–30   In *Shah v HSBC Private Bank (UK) Ltd*[40] Longmore L.J. followed his own judgment in *Da Silva* to the effect that the bank would have had a reasonable suspicion if it had been more than fanciful that the claimant was involved in money laundering, and that those suspicions did not need to be based on reasonable grounds. The claimant argued there could not be a reasonable suspicion if its actions had been based entirely on the automated response of a computer program. However, the bank demonstrated that its internal systems involved different bank officers processing the suspicious transaction report. The Court of Appeal held, on the facts, that the claimant should be allowed to take the matter to full trial (instead of the court at first instance having awarded summary judgment to the defendant dismissing the claimant's actions). This case is considered in greater detail below.

---

[36] See D. Ormerod, [2006] Crim. L.R. 998. See also *R. v Singh* [2003] EWCA Crim. 3712, at [34], per Auld L.J., as considered by Lord Hope [2006] UKHL 18, at.[67].

[37] [2006] EWCA Civ 1039.

[38] [2006] EWCA Civ 1039, at [16], per Longmore L.J.

[39] Scott L.J. took this view in *Polly Peck v Nadir (No.2)* [1992] 4 All E.R. 769 that it would be sufficient to demonstrate knowledge (for the purposes of civil liability for knowing receipt) if a reasonable bank acting in the circumstances ought to have been suspicious that the payments passed through its accounts had come originally from a breach of fiduciary duty. The factual matrices are thus very similar to money laundering: the defendant in Polly Peck had taken about £45 million in breach of fiduciary duty, and in the criminal sense by theft, and had then paid it through the defendant Central Bank of Northern Cyprus so as to exchange it for lire and pay it into a bank in Northern Cyprus. Therefore, it is suggested that suspicion could be demonstrated both by proof that the defendant had actually had suspicions; but also by the demonstration that a reasonable person would have had suspicions and therefore that the defendant must have done too.

[40] [2010] EWCA Civ 31, [2010] Bus. L.R. 1514.

D.   Exemption from the s.327(1) offence

There are three exemptions from liability under the offence in s.327(1) in the later subsections of that section. Each is considered in turn.   **15–31**

Authorised disclosure

The first category of exemptions under s.327(2) of POCA 2002 provides that: **15–32**

> "(2)   a person does not commit such an offence if—
>   (a)   he makes an authorised disclosure under section 338 and (if the disclosure is made before he does the act mentioned in subsection (1)) he has the appropriate consent;
>   (b)   he intended to make such a disclosure but had a reasonable excuse for not doing so;
>   (c)   the act he does is done in carrying out a function he has relating to the enforcement of any provision of this Act or of any other enactment relating to criminal conduct or benefit from criminal conduct."

A disclosure is an authorised disclosure under s.338(1) if it is a disclosure to a constable, a customs officer or a nominated officer by the alleged offender that property is criminal property. The disclosure must be made before the alleged offender does the prohibited act; or if the prohibited act is committed before the disclosure is made then the disclosure must be made on that person's "own initiative and as soon as is practicable after he first knows or suspects that the property constitutes or represents a person's benefit from criminal conduct"; or if the disclosure is made after the prohibited act has been committed then the defendant must have had a reasonable excuse for not making the disclosure beforehand.[41]

Events taking place outside the UK

The second exclusion from the statute arises in the following circumstances under s.327(2A):   **15–33**

> "Nor does a person commit an offence under subsection (1) if—
>   (a)   he knows, or believes on reasonable grounds, that the relevant criminal conduct occurred in a particular country or territory outside the United Kingdom, and
>   (b)   the relevant criminal conduct—
>   (i)   was not, at the time it occurred, unlawful under the criminal law then applying in that country or territory, and
>   (ii)   is not of a description prescribed by an order made by the Secretary of State."

In this provision, the "relevant criminal conduct" is "the criminal conduct by reference to which the property concerned is criminal property".[42] Thus, the actus reus of removing the property from this jurisdiction to another country under s.327(1)(e) must be deemed to have taken place in the UK as the property was taken across the border.

---

[41]   Proceeds of Crime Act 2002, s.338(2).
[42]   Proceeds of Crime Act 2002, s.327(2B).

Deposit-taking bodies

15–34   The most likely people to contravene s.327(c) and (d) relating to transferring and converting criminal property are deposit-taking banks. Therefore, an exemption is provided for such bodies in s.327(2C) in the following terms:

> "(2C)   A deposit-taking body that does an act mentioned in paragraph (c) or (d) of subsection
> (1) does not commit an offence under that subsection if—
> (a)   it does the act in operating an account maintained with it, and
> (b)   the value of the criminal property concerned is less than the threshold amount
> determined under section 339A for the act."

The threshold amount is £250 at present.[43]

E.   The offence of participation in money laundering arrangements in s.328

15–35   There is a separate offence under s.328 of the POCA 2002 for any person who "enters into or becomes concerned in an arrangement" which she "knows or suspects facilitates (by whatever means) the acquisition, retention, use or control of criminal property by or on behalf of another person". Therefore, the actus reus relates to entering into an arrangement, which would include a contract at one end of the spectrum or any other consensual pattern of behaviour at the other, which enables another person either to acquire, or to retain, or to use, or to control any criminal property. An arrangement could include a bank passing money through its accounts when its officers suspect that the property might be criminal property. If money was held in the account then that would be "retention"; if money was simply exchanged for foreign currency then that would constitute "use"; or if the money was paid into an account over which the criminal was a trustee then that would constitute an example of "control". The mens rea is either to "know" or to "suspect" that any component of that actus reus was being effected: these terms were considered above. As Laddie J. has explained this provision[44]:

> "The purpose of s.328(1) is not to turn innocent third parties like [banks] into criminals. It is to put them under pressure to provide information to the relevant authorities to enable the latter to obtain information about possible criminal activity and to increase the prospect of being able to freeze the proceeds of crime. To this end, a party caught by s.328(1) can avoid liability if he brings himself with the statutory defence created by s.328(2) [of making an authorised disclosure, for example where the bank is operating an account]".

There are exemptions from the commission of the offence, which mimic the exemptions in relation to the s.237(1) offences considered immediately above. First, if the defendant makes an authorised disclosure under s.338, as considered above.[45] Second, if the person believed that the offence took place outside the

---

[43] Proceeds of Crime Act 2002, s.339A(2).
[44] *Squirrell Ltd v National Westminster Bank Plc* [2006] 1 W.L.R. 637, at [16].
[45] Proceeds of Crime Act 2002, s.328(2).

UK, as considered above.[46] Thirdly, a deposit-taking institution does not commit the offence, in the manner considered above.[47] Furthermore, in *Bowman v Fels*[48] the Court of Appeal held that just because a lawyer discovers or suspects involvement with criminal property in the course of advising a client in legal proceedings that does not mean that the lawyer commits an offence under s.328(1) because that provision "is not intended to cover or affect the ordinary conduct of litigation by legal professionals".[49] This decision, it is suggested, is an important element of ensuring that the legislation does not prejudice the human rights of litigants or defendants to criminal proceedings by requiring their legal counsel to breach the constraints of legal privilege to make disclosure to SOCA.

F.   The offence of acquisition, use or possession in s.329

There is a further offence in the following terms in s.329(1) of the POCA 2002:   **15–36**

> "(1)   A person commits an offence if he—
>   (a)   acquires criminal property;
>   (b)   uses criminal property;
>   (c)   has possession of criminal property."

There is no requirement of dishonesty in this context; mere suspicion is enough.[50] The concept of "suspicion" was considered above.[51] There is no offence committed if an authorised disclosure is made under s.338 of POCA 2002, or otherwise as discussed above in relation to s.327 of POCA 2002,[52] and also if the act he does is performed in furtherance of any requirement of the POCA 2002.[53]

G.   The obligation to make disclosure to the authorities

The offence of failure to make disclosure in s.330

Sections 330, 331 and 332 of the POCA 2002 provide for a range of criminal   **15–37** offences in the event that there is a failure to disclose instances of money laundering, where the defendant knows or is suspicious of or has reasonable grounds to believe that money laundering offences have taken place. As the offences are drafted, it appears to be sufficient that that there was knowledge or suspicion of certain acts, but no necessary requirement that money laundering has actually taken place. This reinforces the concern of some commentators, as outlined at the beginning of this chapter, that POCA 2002 will encourage over-disclosure because bankers and others will be concerned about inadvertently committing an offence.

---

[46] Proceeds of Crime Act 2002, s.328(3).
[47] Proceeds of Crime Act 2002, s.328(5).
[48] [2005] 1 W.L.R. 3083.
[49] [2005] 1 W.L.R. 3083, at [83], *per* Brooke L.J.
[50] Proceeds of Crime Act 2002, s.329(3)(c).
[51] See para.15–26.
[52] Proceeds of Crime Act 2002, s.329(2), (2A), (2C).
[53] Proceeds of Crime Act 2002, s.329(2).

The scope of the offence in s.330: failure to disclose: regulated sector

15–38   Under s.330 of the POCA 2002 a person commits an offence if four conditions are satisfied.[54] First, if she knows or suspects, or else if she has reasonable grounds for knowing or suspecting, that another person is engaged in money laundering.[55] Secondly, if the information or other material on which her knowledge or suspicion is based, or which gives reasonable grounds for such knowledge or suspicion, came to her in the course of a business in the regulated sector.[56] The "regulated sector" is defined at great length in Sch.9 to POCA 2002 so as to cover banks ("credit institutions") and most of the sorts of activities which are regulated by the Bank of England as discussed in Chapters 8 and 9. Thirdly, that she can identify the person who is involved in the money laundering or alternatively that she can identify the whereabouts of any of the laundered property; or alternatively that she believes, or it is reasonable to expect her to believe, that the information or other material "will or may assist in identifying that other person or the whereabouts of any of the laundered property".[57] Fourthly, she must make disclosure of these matters as soon as is practicable after obtaining the information or other material; disclosure must be made to a nominated officer, or a person authorised for the purposes by SOCA to receive such disclosures.[58]

Exclusions from the offence in s.330, under Sch.2 to POCA 2002

15–39   The offence is not committed if the defendant had a reasonable excuse for not making the required disclosure[59]; or she is a professional legal adviser or an accountant, auditor or tax adviser[60]; or if the information came to her in privileged circumstances[61]; or if she both did not suspect money laundering and had not been given the requisite training[62]; or if she knew or believed that the offence was being committed in another jurisdiction.[63] Furthermore, "in deciding whether a person committed an offence under this section the court must consider whether he followed any relevant guidance" issued by "a supervisory authority or any other appropriate body" and which had been approved by the Treasury, and which had been "published in a manner it approved as appropriate in its opinion to bring the guidance to the attention of persons likely to be affected by it".[64]

---

[54] Proceeds of Crime Act 2002, s.330(1).
[55] Proceeds of Crime Act 2002, s.330(2).
[56] Proceeds of Crime Act 2002, s.330(3).
[57] Proceeds of Crime Act 2002, s.330(3A).
[58] Proceeds of Crime Act 2002, s.330(4).
[59] Proceeds of Crime Act 2002, s.330(6).
[60] Proceeds of Crime Act 2002, s.330(6).
[61] Proceeds of Crime Act 2002, s.330(6).
[62] Proceeds of Crime Act 2002, s.330(7).
[63] Proceeds of Crime Act 2002, s.330(7A).
[64] Proceeds of Crime Act 2002, s.330(8).

Further offences of failure to make disclosure

There is then a requirement for nominated officers to make disclosure further to **15–40** s.331 and s.332 of the POCA 2002. The provisions of s.330 are effectively applied mutatis mutandis to the nominated officers who are required to pass on the information disclosed to them in relation to s.330 to SOCA.

H.   The criminal offence of tipping off in s.333A

Clearly it would be prejudicial to criminal investigations if the criminal or the **15–41** money launderer were informed that investigations were being conducted into their affairs. Consequently, the offence of tipping off was inserted in the POCA 2002 in the form of new s.333A, which replaced the old offence in s.333 of that Act. It is an offence if any person discloses[65] any information (relating to money laundering) which came to them in the course of activities in the regulated financial sector and which had been reported in connection with s.330 of the POCA 2002 (which was considered above).[66] To make out the offence it must also be the case that "the disclosure is likely to prejudice any investigation that might be conducted following the disclosure"[67] and also that "the information on which the disclosure is based came to the person in the course of a business in the regulated sector".[68] There is a further offence of disclosing the fact that an investigation is either being contemplated or actually carried out; and that that disclosure is "likely to prejudice that investigation"; and that "the information on which the disclosure is based came to the person in the course of a business in the regulated sector".[69]

I.   Investigations in s.341

The Serious Crime Act 2007 created powers which were inserted into Part 8 of **15–42** the POCA 2002 to carry on investigations into criminal property. It is an offence further to s.342 of the POCA 2002 to prejudice an investigation which is carried out under s.341.

J.   Conspiracy to launder money

There has been a large amount of case law on the question whether a person has **15–43** formed a criminal conspiracy to launder money, further to s.1(2) of the Criminal Law Act 1977.[70] The approach taken by Lord Hope in *R. v Saik*[71] was that the

---

[65] Proceeds of Crime Act 2002, s.333A(1)(a).
[66] Proceeds of Crime Act 2002, s.333A(2).
[67] Proceeds of Crime Act 2002, s.333A(1)(b).
[68] Proceeds of Crime Act 2002, s.333A(1)(c).
[69] Proceeds of Crime Act 2002, s.333A(3).
[70] D. Ormerod, "Making sense of mens rea in statutory conspiracies" (2006) *Current Legal Problems*; D. Ormerod, "Proceeds of Crime: approach to appeals against conviction of conspiracy to commit money laundering offences brought on the basis of the decision of the House of Lords in *Saik*" (2008) Vol.7 Crim L.R. 567–571.

defendant must have had actual suspicion and also there must have been a reasonable basis for having that suspicion. As Lord Nicholls held in *R. v Saik*[72] for there to be a conspiracy to commit a money laundering offence:

> "where the property has *not* been identified when the conspiracy agreement is reached, the prosecution must prove the conspirator *intended* that the property would be proceeds of criminal conduct".[73]

So, it is clear that whether or not the property has been identified when the conspiracy is formed, the crime of conspiracy can still be made out[74]: it is enough that there is a conspiracy relating to property which will be laundered from criminal conduct in the future. There must be a present intention that future property will be laundered in the manner described in s.327.[75] However, if the property is identified at the time that the conspiracy is formed, then the "prosecution must prove the conspirators 'knew' the property was the proceeds of crime".[76] Lord Nicholls held that to "know" in this sense is to have actual knowledge.[77]

3. OFFENCES COMMITTED BY BANKS UNDER THE PROCEEDS OF CRIME ACT 2002

15–44   It is an offence for a bank to deal with criminal property further to s.328 of the 2002 Act unless the bank makes an authorised disclosure of that fact to the Serious Organised Crime Agency and has received an appropriate consent.[78] The context of the regulation of money laundering is considered later in this chapter. So, in *K Ltd v National Westminster Bank Plc*[79] the Court of Appeal considered the principle that if a bank processes a customer's cheque so that it transferred criminal property into another person's account then that facilitates the use or control of that property and is thus an offence under s.328 of the 2002 Act. It is an authorised disclosure under s.335 if a bank informs SOCA that it suspects that it is being asked by its customer to facilitate the use or control of criminal property; while any disclosure of this fact to the customer would constitute a tipping off offence under s.333 of the 2002 Act, unless that is done through a professional legal adviser further to s.333(2)(c) of that Act as part of legal proceedings within s.333(3)(b).[80] It was held that the First Protocol to the European Convention on Human Rights, relating to freedom to enjoy one's possessions, had no part to play in resisting the powers of SOCA and the disclosure regime under the 2002 Act in

---

[71] [2006] UKHL 18, at [52].

[72] *R. v Saik* [2006] UKHL 18, at [23]; relying on *R. v Montila* [2004] 1 W.L.R. 3141.

[73] See above.

[74] *R. v Saik* [2006] UKHL 18, at [24], per Lord Nicholls.

[75] See also *R. v Ali* [2006] 2 W.L.R. 316, 351, relied upon by Lord Nicholls, *R. v Saik* [2006] UKHL 18, at [24].

[76] *R. v Saik* [2006] UKHL 18, at [25], per Lord Nicholls.

[77] See para.15 25 above.

[78] The procedure for making disclosure and acquiring consent is set out in Proceeds of Crime Act 2002 s.335 and s.338.

[79] [2006] EWCA Civ 1039; [2007] Bus. L.R. 26.

[80] *R. v Da Silva* [2006] 1 W.L.R. 303, [2006] 4 All E.R. 900, CA, applied.

that the debt constituted by the bank account is not being cancelled, and thus the "money" is not being taken by the state, but rather access to that account is merely being delayed. More significantly the court held that there was, in terms, no power to compel SOCA to disclose the basis for refusing to allow the customer's account to be operated by the bank.

Similar issues arose in *R. (UMBS Online Ltd) v SOCA*[81] as to the effect of blocking a bank account on the basis "no more than a suspicion, not even reasonable suspicion" that criminal property was passing through that account. UMBS operated a credit union organised under Swedish law which was advertised as being beyond financial regulation, it operated also through a New Zealand entity which conducted its business over the internet and which had a presence in the UK through ten employees in an office in Wembley in north London. The UMBS organisation was investigated by the Swedish tax authorities and UMBS's bankers made a disclosure to SOCA and its accounts in the UK were blocked as a consequence. The bank therefore refused to perform the UK office's payment requests. A claim for judicial review was brought against SOCA. The question then arose as to the powers of SOCA under the Serious Organised Crime and Police Act 2005 ("SOCPA 2005"). Ward L.J. held that SOCA "should not withhold consent [to allow operation of the customer's account] without good reason".[82] However, the particular problem which Ward L.J. identified was the lack of transparency which SOCA exhibited in not giving reasons for its actions nor for its decisions whether or not to permit the operation of a bank account, and more particularly the fact that the SOCPA 2005 does not empower the court to compel disclosure of information and reasons from SOCA. There is indeed a slight whiff of Josef K in Kafka's novel *The Trial* in having one's bank account frozen (and thus access to one's money blocked) by a state agency in circumstances in which that agency gives no reasons for its actions and decisions. In line with much criminal law practice the concern is the idea that if disclosure of all information was required of SOCA then this might harm any investigation which SOCA was conducting.[83] Nevertheless, it was held that the bank had performed its duties appropriately in making disclosure to SOCA. As a result, the customer was entitled to ask SOCA to review the matter and on these facts SOCA had acted unlawfully in refusing to carry out that review. The Court of Appeal held that there should be a right to apply for judicial review; no further decision on the merits of the substantive law was available at the time of writing. However, Sedley L.J. did memorably describe the architecture of money laundering law in the following terms[84]:

15–45

"In setting up the Serious Organised Crime Agency, the state has set out to create an Alsatia—a region of executive action free of judicial oversight."

The Court of Appeal was concerned that it was very difficult within the SOCPA 2005 architecture to prove any abuse of power by SOCA.

---

[81] [2007] EWCA Civ 406, [2007] Bus. L.R. 1317.

[82] [2007] EWCA Civ 406, [2007] Bus. L.R. 1317 at [36].

[83] See, e.g. *R. (Energy Financing Team Ltd) v Bow Street Magistrates' Court (Practice Note)* [2006] 1 W.L.R. 1316, 1326, per Kennedy L.J.

[84] [2007] EWCA Civ 406; [2007] Bus. L.R. 1317, at 58].

15–46   In the case of *Shah v HSBC Private Bank (UK) Ltd*[85] the question of suspicion was very significant. The claimant had business interests in Zimbabwe and bank accounts with the defendant bank. The bank made a suspicious activity report to the authorities. In its communications with the claimant, the bank did not disclose that it had made such a report (as it was precluded from doing under statute). In consequence, the claimant was not able to make payments into nor out of those accounts. One of the ramifications of this action was that rumours spread to Zimbabwe, and in particular to the regulatory authorities in Zimbabwe, that the claimant was suspected of money laundering. In consequence, the Zimbabwean authorities froze the claimant's accounts in Zimbabwe. The claimant suffered losses of US$300 million as a result. The judge at first instance had awarded summary judgment to the bank: that is, the claimant's case had been dismissed without the need for a full trial because the bank's arguments were considered to be so overwhelming. The award of summary judgment was appealed to the Court of Appeal. Longmore L.J. followed his own judgment in *Da Silva* to the effect that the bank would have had a reasonable suspicion if it had been more than fanciful that the claimant was involved in money laundering, and that those suspicions did not need to be based on reasonable grounds. The bank would therefore have a good defence to the claimant's action if it could show that it had had such a suspicion. The claimant advanced the interesting argument, inter alia, that the bank could not be said to have formulated a reasonable suspicion if it had simply reacted to a computer program identifying a pattern of transactions which triggered its response automatically. Should the suspicion be based on the conscious thought processes of a human being within the bank? Or, alternatively, could it be said that the pre-programming of the bank's computer systems to identify a particular pattern of behaviour in itself constituted a conscious thought process which made it easier not only for the bank to form suspicions but also to comply with its legal obligations to identify suspicious transactions? The bank brought evidence that its internal systems involved three different bank officers processing the report of a potentially suspicious transaction. His lordship did consider that "there must (arguably) come a time when [the claimant] is entitled to have more information about his affairs than he has yet been given": this equivocal statement in itself demonstrates both how much the courts would like to give bank customers access to information and yet how little they are actually able to order. However, the Court of Appeal dismissed the finding of summary judgment and required the matter to proceed to trial.

15–47   Oddly, however, from the perspective of private law liability Rix L.J. held in *Abou-Rahmah v Abacha*[86] that even if a bank is conscious of a transaction which is believes may involve money laundering that it is nevertheless inequitable for that bank to have to account in restitution for amounts paid away in breach of trust as part of that transaction nor is it precluded from relying on the defence of change of position: this, it is suggested, is part of the courts' refusal to accept the self-evident truth that money laundering regulation imposes positive obligations on banks which ought not to be circumscribed by traditional case law principles.

---

[85] [2010] EWCA Civ 31, [2010] Bus LR 1514.
[86] [2006] EWCA Civ 1492, [9]; [2007] Bus. L.R. 220.

4. TERRORISM ACT 2000

A. The scope of the Act

The Terrorism Act 2000 (as amended by the Anti-terrorism, Crime and Security Act 2001 ("ACSA 2001")) deals, inter alia, with money laundering and "terrorist property". "Terrorism" is defined in s.1 of the Terrorism Act 2000 so as involve "violence against a person" or "serious damage to property" or "[endangering] a person's life', or creating a serious risk to the health or safety of the public", or "is designed seriously to interfere with or seriously disrupt any electronic system", and it must also be intended to influence the government or to intimidate the public, and it must also be intended to advance a "political, religious or ideological cause".[87] Therefore, the offences set out below relate to the use of property—particularly laundering property, for the purposes of this chapter—which involves from these forms of terrorism.

15–48

B. The money laundering offence in s.18

It is an offence under s.18 of the Terrorism Act 2000 either to enter into an arrangement or to become concerned in an arrangement which "facilitates the retention or control by or on behalf of another person of terrorist property". It is a defence to show that one "did not know and had no reasonable cause to suspect" that that arrangement related to terrorist property.

15–49

C. The duty to disclose information in s.19 et seq

Further to s.19 of the Terrorism Act 2000, there is a duty on a person to disclose information to a constable as soon as is reasonably practicable either her belief or suspicion that money laundering under s.18 has taken place (and in ss.15 through 17 of that Act, which are beyond the scope of this book). The defendant must have received the information in the course of a trade or profession, except in the regulated financial sector.

15–50

The duty to disclose in the regulated financial sector in this context is set out in s.21A of the Terrorism Act 2000. That provision closely resembles that under s.330 of the POCA 2002 set out above. Simply put, if the defendant knows or suspects or has reasonable grounds for knowing or suspecting that another person has committed an offence under s.18 of the 2000 Act, and if the information came to her in the course of a business in the regulated financial sector, and if she does not disclose the matter to a constable as soon as possible, then she commits an offence.[88] There is a further offence in the regulated financial sector under s.21D of the 2000 Act if a disclosure is made that an investigation is being or might be conducted.[89]

15–51

---

[87] Terrorism Act 2000, s.1.
[88] Terrorism Act 2000, s.21A.
[89] Terrorism Act 2000, s.21D.

D.   General powers under the Act

15–52   Investigations that terrorist property is involved may be carried out further to powers set out in s.38 of the 2000 Act. It is also an offence to do any act outside the UK which would have been an offence if committed inside the UK.[90]

5.   MONEY LAUNDERING REGULATIONS 2007

A.   Introduction

15–53   The Money Laundering Regulations 2007 ("the MLR")[91] implemented the EC Third Money Laundering Directive 2005.[92] These regulations are then implemented and supplemented by the FCA in its Money Laundering Sourcebook in relation to authorised firms and collective investment scheme providers. These regulations are concerned generally with the general regulatory objectives of promoting market confidence and public awareness, and of protecting consumers and reducing financial crime.[93] This section is slightly out of place in a chapter on criminal offences connected to money laundering but it seems useful to collect the entire discussion of money laundering in one place.

B.   The purpose of the Money Laundering Regulations 2007

The purpose of the regulations

15–54   The purpose of the MLR 2007 is to impose standards of behaviour governing "know your client" regulation in relation to customers. The entities which are governed by these regulations are the sorts of entities through which large or small amounts of cash, or in some cases securities, could be passed and so laundered more efficiently than in other contexts. The "know your client" regulation at issue here is a requirement that the regulated entities confirm the identity of their customers and keep records in an appropriate fashion through their appropriately trained staff. The intention, in effect, is to erect a structure for observing client conduct in effect so that a documentation trail will be prepared for any subsequent prosecution or investigative activity. It is in the legislation considered earlier in this chapter that disclosure to SOCA was required for the sorts of institution considered here.

The scope of people covered by the regulations

15–55   The MLR 2007 apply to credit institutions, financial institutions, auditors, independent legal professionals, trust or company service providers, estate

---

[90]   Terrorism Act 2000, s.63.

[91]   SI 2007/2157. These regulations replaced the Money Laundering Regulations 2003.

[92]   Directive 205/60/EC of 2005, which came into effect on October, 26 2005.

[93]   Money Laundering Sourcebook, 1.2.2G.

agents, high value dealers and casinos.[94] These people are referred to as the "regulated persons" for the purposes of this section.

C. Customer due diligence

The scope of the due diligence provisions

The regulated persons are required to conduct due diligence in relation to their customers. This must be done by using documents, or dates, or other pieces of information which have been acquired from a reliable source. In particular this means identifying their customer and verifying their identity, to prevent their identity being misused for money laundering purposes, whether the customer is acting as the beneficial owner or not.[95] Beneficial ownership in relation to companies means control of more than 25 per cent of the voting power in that company directly or indirectly; in a partnership ownership of more than 25 per cent of the capital or profits of that partnership; in a trust more than 25 per cent of the equitable interest in the trust property.[96] It is suggested that these specifications, however, are poorly expressed in relation to alterations of control or ownership, for example, by cancellation or issue of shares or the exercise of a trustee's discretion in favour of a beneficiary: in any of these ways control could easily be shifted to another person. There is an exception for bond trustees in having to conduct this sort of due diligence.[97]

15–56

The operation of the customer due diligence provisions

There must be ongoing monitoring of a business relationship with a customer, so that know-your-client regulation is not limited to an initial form-filling exercise.[98] Casinos have specific obligations as to the establishment and verification of the identity of customers.[99] In the event that verification of the customer's identity cannot be made, then in general terms the regulated person must not enter into the transaction, as described in the regulations.[100]

15–57

Shell banks and anonymous accounts

Regulated persons may not carry on correspondent banking with "shell banks"[101] nor with any bank which itself deals with shell banks, nor must banks deal with

15–58

---

[94] Money Laundering Regulations 2007, reg.3.
[95] Money Laundering Regulations 2007, reg.5.
[96] Money Laundering Regulations 2007, reg.6.
[97] Money Laundering Regulations 2007, reg.12.
[98] Money Laundering Regulations 2007, reg.8.
[99] Money Laundering Regulations 2007, reg.10.
[100] Money Laundering Regulations 2007, reg.11.
[101] Where a "shell bank" is a bank which requires no physical presence for that bank in the institution in which it is incorporated: Money Laundering Regulations 2007, reg.16(5). Ironically, such institutions are supposed to be organised more commonly in jurisdictions with attractive beaches than not.

anonymous accounts—in each case because it cannot be known who the human beings are who are ultimately controlling these shell companies and anonymous accounts.[102]

D.   Record-keeping, procedures and training

15–59   Regulated persons are required to ensure that they keep appropriate records of their dealings with their customers. This in turn requires that the regulated persons have staff who are suitably trained in their responsibilities to maintain such records.

E.   Supervision and registration

15–60   Each category of regulated person has a particular regulator assigned to it for the purposes of keeping records and obeying the MLR 2007. Among others, entities regulated by the FCA (as discussed in Chapter 8) are overseen by the FCA; the Office of Fair Trading oversees consumer credit financial institutions and estate agents; the Commissioners for HM Revenue and Customs oversee "money service businesses"[103] (which transmit money or changes its currency) not overseen by the FCA, and "high value dealers"; and casinos are overseen by the Gambling Commission. These regulators must then keep registers of regulated people and maintain supervision of them for the purposes of the MLR 2007.

F.   Enforcement

15–61   Officers of the designated supervisory authorities (as outlined immediately above) have powers further to reg.37 of the MLR 2007 to require information from regulated persons, and the attendance before them of "relevant and connected persons".[104] Where such an officer has a reasonable suspicion that premises are being used by such a person for the purposes of his "business or professional activities" then the officer may seek entry to those premises without a warrant and inspect them, provided that she does so having produced evidence of her authority to do so and provided that she does so at a reasonable time.[105] Alternatively, a warrant may be acquired from a Justice of the Peace is that person is reasonably satisfied on the basis of a statement under oath from an officer that there is information on those premises which reasonably falls within reg.37 or where the officer's access has been obstructed or where a person has failed to comply with a requirement imposed on them under reg.37. Failure to

---

[102] Money Laundering Regulations 2007, reg.16.
[103] The Commissioners must refuse to register an applicant which fails to pass a "fit and proper person" test for carrying on this form of business: Money Laundering Regulations 2007, reg.28.
[104] Money Laundering Regulations 2007, reg.37.
[105] Money Laundering Regulations 2007, reg.38.

comply with mandatory powers bestowed on supervisory regulators may result in a civil penalty[106] or liability for a criminal offence.[107]

---

[106] Money Laundering Regulations 2007, reg.42.
[107] Money Laundering Regulations 2007, reg.45.

CHAPTER 16

FRAUD IN THE CRIMINAL LAW

CORE PRINCIPLES

The Fraud Act 2006 provides for a number of criminal offences relating to fraud by false representation, fraud by failure to disclose information, and fraud by abuse of position. The offence of fraud by way of false representation requires that the false representation be made dishonestly with the intention that the representor make a gain for herself with the other person being exposed to the risk of loss. The offence of fraud by way of a failure to disclose information involves a dishonest failure to disclose information which the defendant was under a legal duty to disclose, and that the defendant intended to make a gain or to cause or risk loss to another person as a result. The offence of fraud by way of abuse of position applies to people who occupy a position which requires them to safeguard the financial interests of another person, and who dishonestly abuse that position with an intention to make a gain or to cause or risk loss to another person as a result.

1. INTRODUCTION

This chapter is concerned with the various provisions of the Theft Acts and the Fraud Act 2006 which relate (or which might relate) to financial transactions. These fraud and other dishonesty offences are part of the general criminal law and not created specifically for the financial services context. The Fraud Act 2006 creates criminal liability for fraud and obtaining services dishonestly. In relation to the law of finance, the Fraud Act 2006 potentially creates a large number of

16–01

offences outwith FSMA 2000 connected principally to the fraudulent sale of investments or financial instruments or other financial services.

2.   FRAUD ACT 2006

A.   The scope of the Fraud Act 2006

16–02   There are a number of offences created by the Fraud Act 2006. The general scope of the Act is set out in s.1 of the Fraud Act 2006, which provides that:

> "(1)   A person is guilty of fraud if he is in breach of any of the sections listed in subsection (2) (which provide for different ways of committing the offence).
> (2)   The sections are—
>   (a)   section 2 (fraud by false representation)
>   (b)   section 3 (fraud by failing to disclose information), and
>   (c)   section 4 (fraud by abuse of position)."

There are therefore three different means of committing criminal fraud.[1] Each form of the offence is considered in turn in the sections to follow.

B.   False representation

The core of the false representation offence

16–03   The first offence relates to fraud by means of a false representation. This offence requires a dishonest making of a false representation coupled with an intention that that representation would make a gain for the representor or a loss for some other person. Thus, s.2(1) of the Fraud Act 2006 provides that:

> "(1)   A person is in breach of this section if he—
>   (a)   dishonestly makes a false representation, and
>   (b)   intends, by making the representation—
>   (i)   to make a gain for himself or another, or
>   (ii)   to cause loss to another or to expose another to a risk of loss."

There are therefore two requirements for the commission of this offence. The first requirement is that a false representation is made dishonestly. In criminal law, the requirement of dishonesty is a requirement that the defendant not only failed to act as an honest person would have acted, but also that the defendant appreciated that honest people would have considered her behaviour to have been dishonest. That means that the defendant must have realised that her actions would have been considered to be dishonest by other, honest people. This idea is sometimes

---

[1] Strictly, s.1 suggests that there is only one offence, as opposed to three different offences, but that the offence may be committed in any of three different ways. It is unclear, however, whether on an indictment, if the offence had been committed by a composite of the three different methods, that should be recorded as one single offence (presumably attracting a higher sentence due to the combination of illegal actions) or whether that should be recorded as three different counts of fraud. The section as drafted suggests that only one offence is committed, even though it may be committed in three different ways.

rendered as a realisation by the defendant that she was breaching the ordinary mores of society. Furthermore, under the second requirement, the defendant is required to have had an intention of either making a gain for herself or a loss for some other person by means of the representation. The following sections consider what is meant by "gain", "loss", "risk of loss", and "representation" in this context.

It is suggested that this offence would cover the situation in which bank traders were called upon to submit quotations of the rates at which they had dealt on the open market so that a third party could prepare a benchmark rate like the London Inter-bank Offered Rate ("Libor"), but where those traders intentionally misquoted the rates at which they were dealing so that the Libor measurement would be higher or lower than its true level so as to benefit their trading positions. In such a situation, those traders would have made a representation (in the form of the rates at which they purported to have traded) dishonestly (in that they were aware that it would have been considered dishonest by honest people) with a view to making gains for themselves personally (in the form of their own bonuses) and for their employer (in the form of the bank's profits on financial instruments dependent on those rates). In the Libor scandal, discussed in Chapter 3, traders misquoted rates to fellow employees of the same bank so that those other employees would pass on the misquoted rates to the British Bankers Association (which is not a public body nor a regulator) for the purpose of preparing the official Libor figures against which many, many financial instruments were priced. For example, derivatives instruments around the world are priced relative to Libor, and even the rates fixed for some variable rate domestic mortgages are priced according to Libor. Nevertheless, a specific offence was created to cover the misquotation of benchmark rates, as considered in Chapter 12 on market abuse.[2]

16–04

The concept of "gain" in this context

Section 5(2) of the Fraud Act 2006 provides that the term "gain" will "extend only to gain . . . in money or other property". There would be an intention to make a gain in the financial context, for example, if the defendant sold a security to another person so that the defendant made a profit on the sale price over the purchase price of that security. Similarly, if the defendant sold an investment to another person, relying on a false representation, on the basis that that person would make a commission from the investment then the defendant would also be making a gain by means of earning that commission. Thus a trader within a firm could personally commit this offence if that trader sold investments on the basis of false representations on her own account in order to improve her standing within her own firm and so earn a commission or bonus on her salary.

16–05

---

[2] See para.14–88.

The concept of "loss" and "risk of loss" in this context

16–06   Section 5(2) of the Fraud Act 2006 provides that the term "loss" will "extend only to . . . loss in money or other property". It is suggested that this definition should be taken to mean that a devaluation in the value of property would constitute a "loss" in that the money value of that property would be less than otherwise would have been the case. It is enough in relation to "loss" in s.2(1)(b)(ii) of the 2006 Act that the defendant intended to expose another person to a risk of loss. That does not require that a loss resulted from the defendant's activity: but rather that there was a risk of loss.[3] In relation to financial transactions, there will generally be a risk that the investment may "go down as well as up", in the time-honoured phrase (unless the investment has a guaranteed return). Therefore, the offence would be made out, on this analysis, on every occasion in which the other elements of the offence can be proved.

16–07   The concept of "risk of loss" is a difficult one in the financial services context. As Lord Nicholls put it: "all investment involves risk".[4] Thus, any representation which is made by the seller of financial services in selling an investment runs the risk that the buyer of that product will realise a loss. Consequently, there is always an implied intention to expose a client to a risk that there might be a loss. It could be argued that the intention of the seller of financial services is that the client earn a profit or (if hedging) control a risk of loss, and therefore that a seller of financial services who is behaving properly would not have as her principal intention the intention of exposing a client to a risk of loss, even if there is always some risk of a loss arising bound up in financial products. Unless the legislation were read in this latter fashion—to the effect that there is ordinarily no principal intention to expose the client to a risk of loss which is likely to result in a loss—a literal reading of that legislation could lead to all financial services sales being taken to be criminal fraud!

16–08   The difficult question, then, is whether or not there is a risk of loss sufficient to constitute a criminal fraud. Clearly, if a seller intended to cause a client a large loss by, for example, selling the client securities for a high price which the seller knew to be worthless and which the seller owned on her own account, then there would be an intention both to cause a loss and to expose the client to the risk of loss. The difficult question more specifically, then, is where the seller does not know with certainty that the buyer will suffer a loss but is aware that there is a level of risk in the investment. It is suggested that the most appropriate means of deciding whether or not the seller's actions were sufficient to constitute the mens rea for criminal fraud would be to ask whether or not—by reference the regulatory Conduct of Business Rules—the level of risk imposed on that client was unsuitable for a client of that classification, whether a retail client or a professional counterparty. Thus, it would be possible to identify objectively, by reference to the conduct of business regulations, how a person of that client's level of expertise ought to have been treated by the seller and what level of risk would have been appropriate (and thus also inappropriate). Exposing the client to

---

[3] Fraud Act 2006, s.5(1).

[4] *Royal Brunei Airlines v Tan* [1995] A.C. 378.

an inappropriate risk of loss, as measured by conduct of business regulation, would, it is suggested, be an appropriate means of identifying when an inappropriate level of risk had been taken in relation to any given client and so escape the logical conundrum created in relation to a literal interpretation of this provision as applying to all bilateral, speculative transactions in the financial services context (as outlined in the previous paragraph).

Whether a "representation" has been made

Section 2(3) of the Fraud Act 2006 provides that a "representation" will have been made in the following circumstances:

16–09

> "(3)   'Representation' means any representation as to fact or law, including a representation
>   as to the state of mind of—
>   (a)   the person making the representation, or
>   (b)   any other person."

Thus the representor may be making a representation as to the legal nature of an investment, or as to the legal capacity of the issuer of securities, or as to some factual, market information.

It is also provided in s.2(4) of the Fraud Act 2006 that "a representation may be express or implied". Thus a representation made be inferred from the circumstances. Thus a trader could be taken to have made a representation to acquire a particular investment if she advocates an investment strategy to a client, without specifically advocating the purchase of a particular investment, if the result would be that that particular investment would be the only investment which the client would seek to acquire on the basis of that representation. For example, if the trader identified a range of five investments knowing that in practice only one of them would be possible for the client in the circumstances. Many such representations are made by electronic means in modern financial markets. In this sense, s.2(5) of the Fraud Act 2006 provides that:

16–10

> "(5)   For the purposes of this section a representation may be regarded as made if it (or
>   anything implying it) is submitted in any form to any system or device designed to
>   receive, convey or respond to communications (with or without human intervention)."

Thus communications on electronic noticeboards or by means e-mail or on a web-site can also constitute representations in this sense. It is common practice for traders to distribute inducements to invest among their customers by circular email or web posting.

Whether a representation is a "false representation"

In deciding whether or not a representation is a false representation, s.1(2) provides:

16–11

> "(2)   A representation is false if—
>   (a)it is untrue or misleading, and
>   (b)the person making it knows that it is, or might be, untrue or misleading."

There are therefore two requirements: that the representation must be untrue or misleading; and the representor must know of its falsity, or suspect that it might be false. In the financial services context there may be many types of false representation, for example, about the trading prospects of a company whose securities are being sold. Thus, it might be said, for example, that a company has an exclusive contract to exploit a silver mine with valuable deposits of silver which might encourage investors to invest in that company's shares on the basis that its prospects for profits are strong. If that company did not have such a contract then that representation would have been false; and similarly if an expert geologist's report incorrectly attested that the mine contained workable silver deposits when it did not, then that representation would also be untrue. In the former context, the representation would only be "false" in the sense defined by s.1(2)(b) if the representor knew that the company had no exclusive contract to exploit the silver deposits. In the latter context, if the representor did not know that the geologist's expert report was wrong then the representor would not have had the necessary knowledge for the representation to have been a false representation. A requirement that a person must act "knowingly" in the criminal law is a requirement that the defendant had "actual knowledge" of the requisite circumstances which constitute the offence.[5] Thus, the prosecution would be required to demonstrate that the defendant was "consciously" aware of all of the elements of the offence.

C.   Failure to disclose information

The scope of failure to disclose information

16–12   The second offence relates to fraud by means of failure to disclose information. Section 3 of the Fraud Act 2006 provides that:

> "A person is in breach of this section if he—
> (a)   dishonestly fails to disclose to another person information which he is under a legal duty to disclose, and
> (b)   intends, by failing to disclose the information—
>   (i)to make a gain for himself or another, or
>   (ii)to cause to another or to expose another to a risk of loss."

There are two facets to this offence. First, working in reverse order, there is a requirement that the defendant intends to make a gain, or to make a loss for another person, or to expose another person to a risk of loss. Secondly, there is the question of dishonest failure to disclose information. The requirement of dishonesty is a requirement that the defendant not only failed to act as an honest

---

[5] *Westminster City Council v Croyalgrange Ltd*, 83 Cr. App. Rep. 155, 164, per Lord Bridge. However, there is authority which suggests something more akin to private law notions of knowledge. Thus in *Warner v Metropolitan Police Commr* Lord Reid suggested that in the criminal law an allegation of knowledge would be made out if one were "wilfully shutting one's eyes to the obvious": [1969] 2 A.C. 256, 279. That is, the defendant would not need to have been consciously aware of all of the circumstances but rather it would be sufficient if the defendant could be shown to have avoided such knowledge by shutting his eyes to the obvious. There is no indication in the statute as to which approach would be the better one in this context.

person would have acted, but also that the defendant appreciated that honest people would have considered her behaviour to have been dishonest. It is also required that the failure to disclose information was a failure to disclose information which the defendant was under a legal duty to disclose. In the financial services context it is suggested that there are two general circumstances in which there would be a legal duty to disclose information: first, where a contractual or express fiduciary duty requires such disclosure; and, secondly, where financial regulation requires the provision of information, for example, under disclosure and transparency rules[6] or under the listing rules.[7]

The concepts of "gain" and "loss"

The definitions of "gain" and "loss" are set out below.[8] It is enough in relation to "loss" in s.3(b)(ii) of the 2006 Act that the defendant intended to expose another person to a risk of loss. That does not require that a loss resulted from the defendant's activity: but rather that there was a risk of loss. In relation to financial transactions, there will generally be a risk that the investment may "go down as well as up", in the time-honoured phrase (unless the investment has a guaranteed return). Therefore, the offence would be made out, on this analysis, on every occasion in which the other elements of the offence can be proved.

16–13

D.   Fraud by means of abuse of position

The third offence relates to fraud by means of abuse of position. Section 4 of the Fraud Act 2006 provides that:

16–14

"(1)   A person is in breach of this section if he—
    (a)   occupies a position in which he is expected to safeguard, or not to act against, the financial interests of another person,
    (b)   dishonestly abuses that position, and
    (c)   intends, by means of the abuse of that position—
        (i)to make a gain for himself or another, or
        (ii)to cause loss to another or to expose another to a risk of loss."

In this context the defendant must have occupied a position in which she is expected to safeguard the financial interests of another person. This requirement is considered first.

A person expected to safeguard the interests of another

A clear example of the situation in which a person would be expected to safeguard the interests of another person would be that of a trustee of a unit trust who is required to safeguard the trust property. A general example would be that of any fiduciary whose duties involve management of assets, such as a trustee

16–15

---

[6] See para.36–57.
[7] See para.37–01.
[8] See para.16–17.

with powers of investment over trust property.[9] A fiduciary is a clear example of a person who is required not to act against the financial interests of his beneficiary. Thus Millett L.J. has described fiduciary office in the following terms:

> "A fiduciary is someone who has undertaken to act for or on behalf of another in a particular matter in circumstances which give rise to a relationship of trust and confidence. The distinguishing obligation of a fiduciary is the obligation of loyalty. The principal is entitled to the single-minded loyalty of his fiduciary. The core liability has several facets. A fiduciary must act in good faith; he must not make a profit out of his trust; he must not place himself in a position where his duty and his interest may conflict; he may not act for his own benefit or the benefit of a third person without the informed consent of his principal. This is not intended to be an exhaustive list, but it is sufficient to indicate the nature of fiduciary obligations. They are the defining characteristics of the fiduciary."[10]

This would appear to be the axiom of what is intended by s.4, although a natural interpretation of the section would encompass other, non-fiduciary relationships—perhaps established by contract—which require similar duties of loyalty. However, fiduciary relationships are the most obvious examples of relationships in which one person is required to act in the interests of another.

Abuse of position

16–16   To commit the offence the defendant must then abuse that position. Under s.4(2) of the Act:

> "[a] person may be regarded as having abused his position even though his conduct consisted of an omission rather than an act."

Thus an omission to safeguard property would constitute a commission of the offence, as well as actions taken which cause loss to the victim of the crime. The clearest example of this sort of offence was the conviction of rogue derivatives trader Kweku Adoboli who had been employed by UBS in its back office in London before he was promoted to the derivatives trading desk. He caused losses of US$2.3 billion for UBS. His position was clearly one in which he was expected to promote the interests of UBS—and in that sense it is not too much of an expansion of the sense of the statute to say that a trader is intended to safeguard and not act against the interests of the bank when acting for it. He abused his conduct by entering into a series of risky trades beyond the scope of his authority within the bank, and then hid those transactions through his knowledge of the bank's systems: he had created fictitious trades to hide his losses, and exceeded his US$ 100 million trading limits. His losses had begun with a single loss of US$ 400,000 (on a portfolio under his management of US$ 40 billion at age 27) which he chose to hide from his superiors. Part of the abuse of the bank's systems involved holding profits off the books so that they could be used to off-set future losses. He claimed that he regularly exceeded his day-trading limits and that management were aware of this, to the effect that this

---

[9] See para.21–24.
[10] *Bristol and West Building Society v Mothew* [1998] Ch. 1 at 18, per Millett L.J.

could not be considered to be an abuse of his position if management connived in it. However, management could not have connived at the dishonest concealment of losses of that size, even if they had turned a blind eye to occasional excesses in his trading limits.[11]

The concepts of "gain" and "loss"

The definitions of "gain" and "loss" are set out below.[12] It is enough in relation to "loss" in s.4(1)(c)(ii) of the 2006 Act that the defendant intended to expose another person to a risk of loss. That does not require that a loss resulted from the defendant's activity: but rather that there was a risk of loss.   **16–17**

E.   The definition of "gain" and "loss"

The terms "gain" and "loss" are defined in s.5 of the Fraud Act 2006 in the following terms[13]:   **16–18**

> "'Gain' and 'loss'—
> (a)   extend only to gain or loss in money or other property;
> (b)   include any such gain or loss whether temporary or permanent;
> and 'property' means any property whether real or personal (including things in action and other tangible property)."

These definitions were considered in relation to the various aspects of the offence above. A statutory gloss to the term "gain" is given in s.5(3) in the following terms:

> "'Gain' includes a gain by keeping what one has, as well as a gain by getting what one does not have."

In this sense it is a gain not to lose an asset or some value which might otherwise have been lost. Thus, falsifying the fact that an asset had passed a limit identified, for example, in an option which ought to have required the defendant to transfer that asset to another person would constitute a gain if the defendant is thereby able to keep that asset by claiming falsely that the limit had not been crossed.

Similarly in s.5(4), the term "loss" is further defined in the following terms: **16–19**

> "'Loss' includes a loss by not getting what one might get, as well as a loss by parting with what one has."

In this sense, "loss" includes a lost opportunity and is not restricted to an out-of-pocket loss.

---

[11] See *Financial Times*, November 20, 2012, "Rise and fall of Adoboli the 'family' man": *http://on.ft.com/19ahd0J*.
[12] See para.16–17.
[13] Fraud Act 2006, s.5(1).

F.   Use of "articles" for fraud

16–20   It is an offence to have in one's possession or under one's control any "article" which is intended for use in relation to a fraud.[14] For these purposes, the term "article" includes "any program or data held in electronic form".[15] Thus an article would include, by way of example, a software program intended to be used as a pricing formula in inducing investors to purchase fraudulent investments; a software program intended to be used to sell fraudulent investments to a financial institution by triggering that institution's automatic electronic buy/sell systems; or a database of customers who were to be contacted with inducements to invest in fraudulent investments. It is also an offence to make, adapt, supply or offer to supply such an article.[16] Such a person must be shown to have acted knowing that the article was designed or adapted for use in a fraud or must have intended that the article would be used in connection with a fraud.[17] So, a person who constructs such a software program would be guilty of an offence, for example, provided that the mens rea is satisfied.

G.   The liability of employees and agents

16–21   An individual employee of a business—whether that business is conducted by a sole trader or by a company—may be personally liable for a crime committed in the conduct of that business if she knowingly commits the criminal offence.[18] Alternatively, the director of a company,[19] or any person purporting to act as such, is guilty of an offence if an offence under the 2006 Act was committed with her consent or connivance.[20] It is unclear whether or not traders who are not at the level of director within a company would be liable for a criminal offence under s.12 of the Fraud Act 2006: it is suggested that they would not appear to fall within this particular provision and instead would need to be demonstrated to have committed one of the offences elsewhere in the Act, as considered above.

H.   Fraud under private law

16–22   The private law liabilities in relation to fraud are considered in Chapter 24, in relation to the tort of deceit,[21] the tort of negligence,[22] and proprietary liability in relation to property acquired by means of fraud.[23]

---

[14] Fraud Act 2006, s.6(1).
[15] Fraud Act 2006, s.8(1).
[16] Fraud Act 2006, s.7(1).
[17] Fraud Act 2006, s.7(1)(a) and (b).
[18] Fraud Act 2006, s.9 and s.10.
[19] Or a secretary, manager or similar officer of a body corporate: Fraud Act 2006, s.12(2).
[20] Fraud Act 2006, s.12(2).
[21] See para.24–01.
[22] See para.25–01.
[23] See para.21–43.

3. Theft

A. Officer of a company publishing false information

The s.19 offence

Under s.19 of the Theft Act 1968 it is a criminal offence for an officer of a company to publish information about the company with the intention of misleading investors or creditors as to that company's financial position. Section 19 provides that:

> "Where an officer of a body corporate or unincorporated association (or person purporting to act as such), with intent to deceive members or creditors of the body corporate or association about its affairs, publishes or concurs in publishing a written statement or account which to his knowledge is or may be misleading, false or deceptive in a material particular, he shall on conviction on indictment be liable to imprisonment for a term not exceeding seven years."[24]

Therefore, where any document is published in relation to an offer of securities or in relation to an application for the listing of securities, any officer of the company commits an offence if she concurs in the publication of such a document containing statements which are either false or misleading. Furthermore, in relation to any possible claim brought by an investor in a company it is provided that "[f]or the purposes of this section a person who has entered into a security for the benefit of a body corporate or association is to be treated as a creditor of it".[25]

Penalty

The maximum punishment which the court may impose under this provision is seven year's imprisonment. The defendant has a defence if she acted merely negligently. The prosecution bears the burden of proving that the accused knew that the untrue statement was false and that the defendant had the intent to deceive or defraud any of the people mentioned in the section.

Case law on theft in these circumstances

In *R. v Kyslant*[26] it was held that a statement is false within the meaning of s.84 of the Larceny Act 1861 (which preceded the Theft Act 1968, s.19) if in its context it conveys a misleading impression even if it is literally correct. In *R. v Kyslant* Lord Kyslant, the chairman of the Royal Mail Steam Packet Company, had signed a prospectus in relation to the debenture stock of that company relating to an issue of £2 million, five per cent debenture stock. The prospectus showed a table of dividend paid between 1911 and 1927 and varying between four to eight per cent and contained the following statement:

16–23

16–24

16–25

---

[24] Theft Act 1968, s.19(1).
[25] Theft Act 1968, s.19(2).
[26] [1932] 1 K.B. 442 (Court of Criminal Appeal); see further *R. v Bishirgian* [1936] 1 All E.R. 586 (Court of Criminal Appeal).

"The interest on the present issue of debenture stock will amount to £100,000. Although this company in common with other shipping companies has suffered from the depression in the shipping industry, the audited accounts of the company show that during the past 10 years the average annual balance available has been sufficient to pay the interest on the present issue more than five times over."

In actual fact from 1921 onwards the company had operated at a loss and maintained its dividend distribution only out of the successful recovery of taxes and other claims on the Treasury, the use of reserves, capitalised profits and similar transactions, but not out of trading profits: a fact which was not disclosed in the prospectus. Lord Kyslant was found guilty under s.84 of the Larceny Act 1861, and convicted. In the Court of Criminal Appeal, Avory J.[27] held:

"The falsehood in this case consisted in putting before the intending investors, as material on which they could exercise their judgement as to the position of the company, figures which apparently disclosed the existing position, but in fact hid it. In other words, the prospectus implied that the company was in a sound financial position and that the prudent investor could safely invest his money in its debentures ... a statement which was utterly misleading when the fact that those dividends had been paid, not out of current earnings, but out of funds which had been earned during the abnormal period of the ward, was omitted."

Under s.84 of the Larceny Act 1861 it was doubtful whether the phrase "public company" which occurred in that provision included a private company, as formerly defined by the Companies Act 1948, s.28(1). It is suggested that it does include such an entity by analogy with *R. v Davies*,[28] decided on s.20(1)(ii) of the Larceny Act 1916 (now repealed). Section 19 of the Theft Act 1968 avoids this ambiguity by omitting the reference to a "public company".

---

[27] [1932] 1 K.B. 442, at 448.
[28] [1955] 1 Q.B. 72.

PART V

CONTRACT

Chapter 17

FORMATION OF CONTRACTS

Contract law is at the heart of the law of finance. This chapter considers how contracts are formed, and in particular some of the issues which arise in relation to the creation of contracts in the financial context. In investment banks there are a number of different types of professional who are important in the creation of financial transactions, but they do not always communicate with one another: the result can be a failure to form a common understanding about their transactions. The process of offer and acceptance, and the passage of consideration, are complicated in relation to complex transactions by the negotiation process: it is not unknown for the transaction to transform to such an extent that it assumes a completely different complexion without all of the human beings involved in the discussions appreciating the change. Consequently, the likelihood of the rescission of contracts on the basis of mistake is heightened. A case study to this effect is included at the end of this chapter. In the meantime there is an analysis of the way in which investment banks are structured and how contracts are formed within and between them.

1. INTRODUCTION

17–01   Contract law is central to the law of finance. As was explained in Chapter 4, contract law is one of the central concepts of English substantive law which is co-opted by the context in which financial transactions operate to create the law of finance.[1] Contracts are created between market counterparties entering into financial speculation, contracts are entered into between financial advisors and ordinary clients, contracts are entered into between groups of investors and the fiduciaries who manage their pooled investments. Contracts allocate the risks which parties agree to take in relation to their transaction[2]; contracts express the power relations between the parties; and each party seeks to win the negotiation battle to have their preferences expressed in the contract. Some contracts are used in a standard form in particular financial markets so that all participants assume either identical or largely similar obligations as between one another. Contracts express each parties' rights and obligations. Contract law provides the principles which resolve disputes as to the interpretation, implementation or termination of these contracts. This Part V of this book sets out the principal elements of the law of contract as they apply to the law of finance, and then later, contextual parts of this book in *Section Two: Specific Financial Techniques* apply those principles to particular types of financial product.

17–02   This chapter presents an analysis of the general English law of contract relating to the creation of contracts, identifying some issues of particular importance to financial transactions. In the corporate and inter-bank contexts, of particular importance to contracts created between traders employed by financial institutions is the question as to when a valid contract has been created in the to-and-fro of telephone conversations between traders, and particularly if the

---

[1] See para 4–01.
[2] See para.1–47 et seq.

traders fail to agree on an issue which in a perfect world their legal department would have wanted to be agreed in advance. At the other end of the spectrum from high turnover speculative trading are complex corporate finance transactions which take a very long time to put in place and which involve a large number of different types of professional retained by different institutions. In the to-and-fro of complex negotiations, the nature of the financial product may change either marginally or markedly. In a number of situations the resultant product has not matched the expectations of the parties, and has raised questions as to whether or not a valid contract has been created because it has not seemed as though there was a genuine meeting of minds. A separate set of questions arise in relation to the important and numerous contracts between financial institutions (whether banks, investment houses, or insurance companies) and ordinary, retail customers and small businesses – these types of business are considered in particular detail in Chapter 31. The composition of retail banks and the way in which contracts are made by them is considered below. The legal principles at issue in these sorts of cases (and in all cases in between) are the foundations of contract law, but they are of pivotal importance in financial transactions. There are also numerous questions about the use of unfair contract terms or standard market documentation in relation to inexpert clients which call into play questions as to what FCA conduct of business rules require over-and-above the ordinary law of contract. It is these sorts of issues which are considered in this Part V. In this chapter we consider when a contract has been created, whereas in the next chapter we consider whether or not that contract will be valid and the legal effect of any mistakes made in its creation. This chapter considers the role of standard market terms and master agreements in the creation of many financial contracts.

2. THE NATURE OF THE NEGOTIATION PROCESS IN COMPLEX FINANCIAL TRANSACTIONS

This section considers the deal-making process between the employees of financial institutions (referred to here as "traders") who are empowered to transact either with retail customers (i.e. inexpert customers, such as ordinary members of the public) or with market counterparties (i.e. other financial institutions and similar entities). This information is an essential prologue to the issues which are raised when financial institutions create contracts.

17–03

A. The composition of investment banks

Financial institutions like investment banks employ three tiers of professional in relation to their trading activities. In the so-called "front office" are the traders who sit on the trading floor and who are separated into different trading teams which focus on particular markets. Each trading team will answer to middle management and in turn that middle management will answer to senior management, the number of tiers of management depends on the size of the financial institution and its preference as an institution for risk management. Each

17–04

trading team will have limits placed on the number and aggregate value of transactions which they can enter into. As was discussed in Chapter 8 the financial institution as a whole will be required to account to its regulator periodically for its exposure to certain markets and to provide regulatory capital as a result. Each trading team and each trader will also be subject to the institution's own, general policies and procedures as to credit risk, legal risk, and so on. Consequently, each trading team is governed both by external regulatory factors and internal credit control factors.

17–05   The second tier of professional sits in the "middle office", or the "operations" area as it often known. All of the trades executed by the traders are processed in the operations department. It is in the operations area that a watch is kept over payment flows and the credit lines of traders. When a transaction is entered into, for example, requiring payment of "Libor plus 50 basis points on a notional amount of £10 million" on April 1 each year for ten years, then someone has to "remember"[3] to make that payment, to calculate the appropriate amounts, and to manage the accounts through which those payments are made. Within the middle office are many, many payment systems. In a perfect world all of the many thousands of obligations owed by the bank could be funnelled through one account. However, in practice, payments in different currencies must be passed through different accounts; payments booked by different trading teams will be made separately; payments booked in different branches or in different jurisdictions by the same institution will be paid separately; payments made in relation to different financial products will also be paid separately. This is important because when financial institutions deal with one another across thousands of different transactions, they would prefer to set off all the amounts they owe one to another and thus only be required to pay the small, net amount rather than having to make and receive those many thousands of payments in gross. This set-off referred to as "payment netting" and is discussed in Chapter 19 of this book.[4] Netting is also important if one party goes into insolvency because one's obligations to pay an insolvent person, and one's losses in relation to amounts that the insolvent person owes to you, can be set off under r.4.90 of the Insolvency Rules 1986.[5] What prevents payment netting between solvent parties in many circumstances is simply the fact that in the hurly-burly of high volume trading activity there is not enough time to calculate a net amount for transactions in different currencies and executed through different payment systems. The middle office is responsible for all of this essential operation in the financial engine room.

17–06   The third tier of employee is more diffuse and is commonly referred to as the "back office". In the back office are the following principal types of professional: credit management specialists; treasury; risk management specialists; lawyers; documentation specialists; "regulatory compliance" specialists; analysis departments; and general management. Different institutions will have different names for these departments: I am concerned with the general function, whatever name

---

[3] Or, rather, program a computer to remember.
[4] See para.19–13.
[5] See para.22–91.

it is given. Smaller institutions (such as hedge funds) might not have the resources to have all these various departments, and therefore one or two people might be attempting to fill all of these roles. The credit management department in a financial institution is responsible for assessing not only the overall credit exposure of the bank to its many clients and to its many markets, but also identifying matters such as the amount of "credit support" by way of taking security—as considered in Chapter 22[6]—which is required for any given transaction with any given counterparty. The treasury department in a bank is responsible for measuring the bank's liquidity: that is the balance between its cash in hand across all of its activities measured against its exposures and its obligations to its regulators to cover all of those liabilities. These functions will be important in setting credit lines across the institution. The risk management specialists are either simply credit managers or in larger institutions are people who take a more general view of the institution's entire risk profile across all of its markets and who consider future threats and opportunities. The lawyers in this example are people who advise on legal issues and on the execution of the more complex, one-off transactions entered into by the institution. Lawyers who are employed "in-house" by a financial institution often liaise with "outside counsel" in the form of large law firms which specialise in finance law work. By contrast, "documentation specialists" (sometimes known as "special execution" depart-ments) deal with the more commoditised work of drafting and passing on in a mechanical way standard form contracts in high volume business areas. Sometimes the documentation specialists have no legal qualifications or no legal professional qualifications, and as such are much cheaper to employ than fully qualified lawyers. By contrast again, regulatory compliance specialists deal not with substantive law questions but rather with compliance with FCA and other financial regulation, as was discussed in Chapter 8. The analysis departments are concerned, in this sense, with the analysis of markets looking for opportunities and predicting future trends. There have been difficulties when institutions have sold their analysis to customers, particularly when that analysis has seemed to advocate the likely profitability of instruments which that institution has already bought for on-sale to customers. Typically now analysis is separated between, first, analysis provided to inform the institution's own traders as to likely market trends and, secondly, analysis provided to outsiders, possibly being sold to customers. General management, for present purposes, is concerned with the oversight of, and interference with the day-to-day activities of,[7] all other departments.[8] In complex financial institutions there are a large number of people creating contracts with counterparties at one time and binding the institution into

---

[6] See para.22–01.

[7] It is one of the maudlin vicissitudes of life in any corporate entity (or even any public-sector entity like a university) that there are dozens of people whose job is (or who consider their job to be) interfering with the activities of the people who make the money, manufacture the products, teach the classes, and do all the real work. They are known as "middle management" or "administrators". There was a legend about the manager of a tractor factory in the Soviet Union who had become so enraged by all of the bureaucracy with which he had to deal, and which stopped his factory from doing any real work, that he decided that the only solution was to "kill all of the people producing the paper".

[8] This category of "general management" spends most of its time trying to find things for everyone else to do, which ironically will divert them from the important business of making money and dealing with customers. See generally the peerless *http://www.dilbert.com*.

those transactions. If those transactions raise any of the issues considered in this book, that raises the further question as to how the wrongs of the individual can be attributed to the entire institution, as is discussed in Chapter 18.[9]

B. The composition of retail banks

17–07 Financial institutions like retail banks deal with ordinary members of the public and small businesses, as opposed to other financial institutions. Their operations are less complex. There are high-street offices and there are internet sites which conduct business directly with the ordinary (or, "retail") customer. However, within those large, high-street institutions policy will be set at the corporate level for the products and prices which can be made available to retail customers. The standard terms on which those institutions will insist on doing business will be formulated at the corporate level. There may be questions on occasion as to whether or not any particular employee in a high-street branch has exceeded her authority to act in relation to retail customers and whether or not the customer is able to set transactions aside. There may also be questions of unfair contract terms and so on, as considered in the next chapter.[10] The organisation at the corporate level will then take deposits or other payments from its retail customers and seek to invest them or turn them to account so as to generate profit for the organisation as a whole. The regulation of ordinary banking is considered in Chapter 27.

C. The trading process between traders

17–08 Contracts in financial transactions entered into between financial institutions for speculative and similar trading purposes can be created entirely orally, as is considered below. There are transactions, such as mortgages over land, which must be created in the formally valid manner required by statute,[11] but those issues in relation to particular products are considered in *Section Two* of this book. For the majority of cases relating to financial trading activity, then, the material terms of the contract will be established once the traders have reached agreement by telephone. This is the modus operandi for financial derivatives, foreign exchange, securities and similar trading which is conducted in high volume primarily between expert financial institutions. By contrast, corporate finance transactions, involving large, complex transactions to raise finance usually for corporate entities, are usually not completed until the lawyers have agreed all of the details of the transaction together with the financiers and any other professionals involved. In retail banking, other procedures requiring the customer to complete application forms, and (where appropriate) to receive independent financial advice, must be completed. In each situation there will be a different point in time when the contract is understood by the parties to have come into full force and effect.

---

[9] See para.18–31.
[10] See para.18–39.
[11] Law of Property Act 1925, s.85. See para.49–04.

Returning to speculative trading activity, the cases which generate legal **17–09** difficulties are those situations in which the traders' discussions will not constitute all of the material terms of the contract such that there will not be a contract created until a written confirmation of the transaction is agreed.[12] There are situations, of course, in which mistakes are made between traders.[13] Therefore, as a second stage, it is usual for all trades to be double-checked by someone in the middle office operations area: that is, a person responsible for the processing of payments through the correct accounts and so forth. The operations area will be responsible for including in the documentation the details of the accounts into which payments are to be made and so forth.

It is important to note that this second level of the negotiation process has moved **17–10** on to documentation from the verbal discussions of the traders. There is no doubt that a contract to pay money and to provide financial services can be made verbally and without further formality[14]; however, many of the problems which arise in the context of complex transactions (such as financial derivatives) are based either on mistakes made by the traders,[15] or misrepresentations,[16] or commonly are based on those important legal issues (such as the governing law of the contract, or the appropriate tax structure, or the detail of the credit support documentation) which are typically too specialist to be discussed between the traders. This last issue is the most important in relation to documentation and the creation of complex transactions like derivatives contracts. Traders will always negotiate the economic effect of their transactions but they will generally not discuss issues relating, for example, to the governing law of a contract, the need for specific events of default, nor the practicalities of netting payments, unless the transaction is sufficiently important for lawyers already to have been involved in the negotiating process. When the product is a high-volume, frequently traded transaction, it is unlikely that specific legal advice will have been taken on it. Thus the traders may well not appreciate that even though a transaction seems to be identical to all of the others that were contracted in the past, there may well be a particular legal issue which arises for the first time in the circumstances of that particular transaction. The agreement between the traders will not have anticipated that issue and therefore it may well be held that there was no valid contract if a material term of the agreement was not considered by the traders. Thus, conflict may arise in relation to some disagreement over these sorts of terms and the question will therefore be as to whether or not, in any particular context, such terms will constitute material conditions of the contract and so enable rescission of the contract.[17] Importantly, while in theory a contract can be created verbally, it is the intention of the parties to inter-bank transactions that their agreements will eventually be reduced to writing.

Third, the transaction will require credit clearance, which is a multi-level process. **17–11** At the first level, the trader will require a credit limit within which she is

---

[12] See para.41–08.
[13] The issue of mistake in the creation of contracts is considered in para.18–03.
[14] See para.17–14.
[15] See para.18–03.
[16] See para.24–01 or 25–01.
[17] Rescission is considered at para.20–28.

permitted to deal with the counterparty. In circumstances in which the trader exceeds such a limit there will be an issue as to that trader's authority to bind the institution. The issue of authority is considered in Chapter 18.[18] At the second level, a large transaction will in itself require clearance from the bank's own credit department in accordance with the bank's own internal procedures. The third level involves the form of credit support which will be required. In many circumstances there will not be a contract unless the seller can acquire suitable guarantees[19] or collateral[20] from the buyer, and often vice-versa. Again, a question of authority to bind the institution will arise.[21]

17–12   Fourth, a legal advisor will be involved in those transactions which are out-of-the-ordinary. Questions will arise in relation to products with unusual features, in relation to counterparties with unusual structures, and in relation to credit support. Once more there will be issues as to whether or not all the material conditions of a contract have been agreed between the parties before that transaction can be said to be a binding contract. Thus the discussion between the traders will, necessarily, not always constitute a contract in itself if there are key terms of the transaction which remain outstanding.

17–13   This introduction to the negotiation process is intended to underpin the following straightforward, legal analysis of the means by which a contract is brought into existence. Through the course of this chapter, regular reference will be made to practicalities of transacting between financial institutions in the marketplace. Therefore, while the legal principles are settled, the manner in which traders and their institutions form contracts in practice makes the application of those principles more problematic

3.   OFFER AND ACCEPTANCE

17–14   A contract is created under English law when there has been an offer made, when that offer has been accepted, when consideration passes between the parties and once the parties intend to affect legal relations.[22] The requirements of offer and acceptance constitute familiar concepts of creating and evidencing agreement between the parties. This section, and the section immediately following, will consider the question of reaching such an agreement and also the problem of revoking offers or acceptance to avoid the creation of a binding contract. The next chapter will consider questions of the validity of the contract once made. The requirement of consideration is peculiar to Anglophile legal jurisdictions and is considered in detail below.

---

[18] See para.18–31.
[19] See para.22–77.
[20] See para.42–01.
[21] See para.18 31.
[22] There need not be payment of money upfront to constitute consideration, but rather it is sufficient to demonstrate consideration that the financial institution will deduct fees and commissions over the life of the parties' future dealings and transactions: *Investors Compensation Scheme Ltd v West Bromwich BS* [1999] Lloyd's Rep. PN 496, 504, per Evans-Lombe J.

A.   Offers and mere invitations to treat in marketing material

An offer to contract must be distinguished from a mere invitation to treat. An invitation to treat is an inducement to a potential counterparty to deal with person making the invitation but will not in itself be an offer. So, in an ordinary shop a sign in the window offering "Hudson's *Law of Finance*, dead cheap at £42" would be, prima facie, a mere invitation to treat and not an offer to sell that book for £42. Rather, when a passer-by enters the shop and suggests to the shop-keeper her willingness to buy that book for that price, it is the passer-by who is taken to make the offer and the shop-keeper to accept it. That it is a mere invitation to treat means that if the shop-keeper refused to sell the book for £42 but rather decided to refuse to sell it for less than £45, then the passer-by would not be legally entitled under ordinary contract law to enforce a contract at £42.[23]

17–15

The key distinction between a binding offer and an invitation to treat is that an offer must be specific to the intended counterparty and not be an overly general statement. The offeror must intend to make an offer which, if accepted, would bind her to the agreement.[24] An offer of a financial product should be distinguished from a "mere puff"; that is, a statement which is too vague to constitute an offer to enter into a contract.[25] In Chapter 34, for example, we consider "pathfinder prospectuses" which are often circulated among expert investors prior to an issue of bonds to assess the interest of those investors, and so to help fine-tune the terms on which the issue will be made: this is not an offer to enter into a binding contract until a future date at which the bond will be issued; so the pathfinder prospectus is a mere puff or an invitation to treat, depending on its terms. Therefore, as considered below,[26] advertising material which merely outlines the form of product which might be available to buyers is not necessarily an offer to put in place such products either at all or not on the precise terms indicated in that advertising material.[27]

17–16

B.   Whether an offer has been made at all

In transactions in which the parties have been involved in detailed negotiations, possibly including changes as to their mutual understanding of the transaction and its pricing,[28] it may be difficult to know which stage in those discussions constituted an offer which the counterparty could be taken to have accepted. When legal advisors are engaged in a lengthy negotiation leading to a single set of documentation which is to be signed by both parties before a contract is

17–17

---

[23] *Timothy v Simpson* (1834) 6 C. & P. 499; *Fisher v Bell* [1961] 1 Q.B. 394.

[24] *Storer v Manchester C.C.* [1974] 1 W.L.R. 1403.

[25] *Weeks v Tybald* (1605) Noy 11; *Lambert v Lewis* [1982] A.C. 225.

[26] See para.17–17.

[27] The difficulty with this analysis would be where a seller seeks to present its proposals not in the abstract but rather by specific reference to the circumstances of the target of its advertising. In any event, it is important to ensure that a clear line is drawn by the seller between marketing on the one hand and financial engineering directed specifically at the target on the other: *Bankers Trust v Dharmala* [1996] C.L.C. 18.

[28] On which see *Peekay v ANZ* below.

created, then no offer will have been made until the terms of the contract are complete. However, it is commonly the case in relation to transactions between expert traders that advice is only taken on specific issues about which the traders are not confident, and that otherwise outside legal counsel is not involved. In derivatives markets, even though the expectation is that all transactions will be documented, very many transactions remain undocumented—as is discussed in Chapter 41. More to the point, the market generally operates entirely on the basis of the traders reaching an agreement and many transactions maturing before any documentation is signed. Thus, the discussions may only take place between the traders without a legal analysis of the key issues. Consequently, the point at which an offer is made or an agreement is reached between the traders is a moot point, but not one which typically prevents the institutions involved from booking the transaction involved as though it was properly completed. Clearly, in more volatile markets, the longer discussions continue the more likely it is that the seller will not wish to be bound by pricing assumptions which may have gone out of date as a result of those market movements. In such a circumstance it is important to know whether or not an offer to provide a structure on particular terms has been made at all.

17–18   What is required is that one construe the precise terms of the correspondence between the parties. Where the seller has used language such as "we *may* be able to provide" or "it is hoped that market movements would make it possible" then it would appear that the seller has not committed itself to provide anything, but rather has expressed its agreement to contract to be subject to some future contingency.[29] Therefore, one analysis is that there is no clear offer at this stage, particularly if no price has been mentioned. The question then is whether the potential buyer makes an offer on approaching the seller in response to the marketing material. Alternatively, it might be argued that there is something about the circumstances which means that the seller could be interpreted as having made an offer (perhaps because the parties have dealt on similar terms before) which is perhaps deemed to have been repeated when the buyer expresses interest.[30] The question as to which party is deemed to make an offer and when that offer was deemed to have been made will therefore depend upon the circumstances. In the cut-and-thrust of a discussion between traders on the telephone this may not be important: what is most important in that situation is whether or not the traders had a meeting of minds at some point in their discussions so that a contract was made between them. However, it is in relation to the less common circumstances, for example where marketing material or an outline for a product to be sold in the future, is circulated among prospective buyers that the question of when an offer was made and when it was accepted becomes more important. If a trader circulates marketing material about a financial instrument which, it realises a little too late, contains a mistake which would cost her bank a large amount of money, then it would be important to know if she was merely making an invitation to treat (which would not be a contractual offer and which could not therefore be accepted by another trader so as to bind

---

[29] *Gibson v Manchester City Council* [1979] 1 W.L.R. 294; *Harvey v Facey* [1893] A.C. 552; *Harvela Investments Ltd v Royal Trust Co of Canada Ltd* [1986] A.C. 207.
[30] *Pharmaceutical Society of Great Britain v Boots* [1953] 1 Q.B. 401.

her to a contract) or whether she was deemed to be making an offer (which would form a valid contract if it was accepted by another trader at another institution). The law on mistake might save the trader by allowing her to set the contract aside (as discussed in the next chapter) but it would be easier to show that there was never a valid contract in the first place.

Such cases may be complex. The proper analysis of any arrangement may not be obvious. One decided case illustrates this problem. There had been a promotion by an oil company that any customer buying four gallons of petrol would be entitled to one promotional coin commemorating the World Cup.[31] In such a situation it is difficult to know whether the oil company was offering to sell four gallons of petrol and also one coin for the contractual price, or whether the purchase of the four gallons of petrol entitled the buyer to be made a gift of such a coin once the petrol had been paid for, or whether the entire promotion was merely an invitation to treat. The specificity of the benefit to which the customer was entitled—to whit, one coin—led the majority of the House of Lords to hold that an offer had been made although the precise basis of the right to the coin (whether by means of contract for sale or enforceable gift) was left uncertain even by those members of the House of Lords who felt that there had been a contractual offer made.[32] Clearly, the seller of such products must be astute to explain that any pricing or other information is not intended to make any offer of any particular structure nor of any outcome at any identified price to the recipient of any such material.[33]

17–19

C. Contracts created through on-going discussion

Many contracts are created as a result of lengthy negotiation in which the client's needs and the financial institution's expertise mould an appropriate solution to the situation. This may happen on the high street with retail customers when, for example a mortgage is sold to the customer to enable her to buy a house. However, it is more likely that the product which is sold to that customer is in truth an "off-the-shelf" product which the mortgagee has already devised, which exists in a computer pricing model on the salesperson's computer, and which is simply priced according to the amount which the customer wants to borrow. With large corporate clients, however, the financial products which are used—such as share issues, syndicated loans, and so on—are less likely to be ready-packaged in this way and are more likely to require lengthy consideration and structuring. Consequently, in the large scale corporate context, it is not always the case that one party will make an offer to the other. Rather, parties will frequently develop their transactions through ongoing discussion, as opposed simply to taking a product "off the shelf" as one would with a retail customer on the high street. Such a transaction will be a legally-binding contract provided that it can be demonstrated that the parties have come to an agreement sufficient to include all

17–20

---

[31] *Esso Petroleum Ltd v Commissioner of Customs and Excise* [1976] 1 W.L.R. 1.

[32] See also *Pharmaceutical Society of Great Britain v Boots* [1953] 1 Q.B. 401 as to the point in time at which an offer is made.

[33] *Harris v Nickerson* (1873) L.R. 8 Q.B. 286; *Re Charge Card Services Ltd* [1989] Ch. 497.

of the material terms of the transaction.[34] Once the intention to create a contract has been sufficiently established, whether or not it is possible to identify an offer separately from its acceptance, the court will enforce the contract where possible.[35] In limited circumstances, the courts will supplement the parties' recorded agreement with terms necessary to achieve their commercial objectives or to give business efficacy to their transaction, as considered below.[36] It will depend on how material are the terms which have been omitted before it is possible to know whether or not it is feasible to seek to give effect to the transaction.

D. Contracts created during lengthy negotiation but not all terms agreed

17-21 It does happen in financial transactions that contracts are negotiated at length but that the parties want to begin their transaction before the final form of the contract is agreed or before all of the terms which are expected to be agreed between the parties are finalised. In such situations it is possible that the parties might fail to agree on a matter which was intended to be a condition of the contract, with the effect that no contract has in fact been agreed between the parties such that any purported performance of that agreement would be set aside. Thus, it could be held that there is no legal liability created which can be imposed on either party where the parties were found not to have ever had a meeting of minds but where commercial exigencies forced them to begin performing their transaction in the hope that a contract could yet be finalised.[37]

17-22 Alternatively, it may be that the parties agree to begin performance of their agreement on the basis that the remaining conditions or other terms of their contract will be agreed latterly. The agreement is described as being "subject to contract" in these circumstances. If the parties have agreed to begin transacting before the contract is completed (as frequently happens in financial derivatives markets) then the transaction would probably be taken to be governed by a valid contract consisting of the terms which the parties had actually agreed between them, on the basis that the parties clearly intended to complete those contractual provisions at a later date.[38] If the parties were not considered to have manifested such a common intention to begin performing their contract, confident in their ability to finalise a contract in the future, then it would be found that there were no legal obligations created between the parties and therefore that neither party could be subjected to an order for specific performance and so forth.[39]

17-23 This approach is necessary for the efficacy of financial transactions. It is common for parties to wish to transact high volume transactions in the foreign exchange,

---

[34] *Hussey v Horne-Payne* (1879) 4 App. Cas. 311.

[35] *Brown v Gould* [1972] Ch. 53.

[36] In relation to implied contractual terms: *Pagnan v Feed Products* [1987] 2 Lloyd's Rep. 601.

[37] *Perry v Suffields Ltd* [1916] 2 Ch. 187; *Pagnan v Feed Products* [1987] 2 Lloyd's Rep. 601.

[38] *Branca v Cobarro* [1947] K.B. 854; *Clipper Maritime Ltd v Shirlstar Container Transport Ltd, The Anemone* [1987] 1 Lloyd's Rep. 546.

[39] *Winn v Bull* (1877) 7 Ch.D. 29.

derivative and similar areas. What would be required clearly is evidence of a mutual agreement between the parties that they were prepared to begin transacting even though no written agreement had been signed and even though some terms were not agreed. In essence then the parties would only be bound by contractual terms which they had agreed to and only in circumstances in which they had demonstrated that they had assumed the risk of beginning to transact without a written agreement. So, for example, two banks may begin to speculate on equity options even though their lawyers had not, for example, agreed in advance the detail of the security to be provided between them nor the governing law of the contract. If both of those banks had knowingly agreed to perform equity options business without a signed contract having been completed, then it would be unfair on the party which made money on their transactions to have those transactions cancelled because the other party sought to argue that no contract had been formed. It is suggested that in this instance the parties could have agreed to contract purely verbally and therefore no signed contract would be necessary in any event, and therefore their interim transactions should be enforced by contract law. Here both parties have voluntarily assumed the risk of there being no signed contract in place. On the other hand, if the parties are bound to perform transactions which have not been successfully reduced to writing, then the parties would be bound to transactions by which they had not freely agreed to be bound. This would introduce uncertainty to financial transactions because the parties would not know whether or not they would be bound by pre-contractual discussions, even if they had deliberately refrained from signing a contract until some important details were ironed out. It is suggested that in this latter context, no unfinished contractual terms should be enforced nor should the remainder of the contract which had been agreed. The acid test should be whether or not the parties had agreed to take the responsibility of being subject to an order for specific performance to force them to carry out those obligations which have been agreed. So, in the example set out above, if one of the banks had only agreed (and made that plain) to enter into the equity options on the basis that there was some other business need it had for those transactions, but if it made it clear that those transactions were intended to be subject to completion of the written contract subsequently, then there would be no agreement formed. It should not be forgotten that a regulated firm must conduct suitable conduct of business formalities in its dealings with a new customer and therefore, it is suggested, any contract which is subject to compliance with FCA regulation or money laundering regulation should not be enforced if those regulations are not complied with.

E. Acceptance in financial derivatives transactions: the battle of confirmations

To take effect as a contract, the offer must be accepted. This is a surprisingly difficult issue in relation to many financial markets: especially over-the-counter derivatives, which are created privately between the parties off-exchange. For example, financial derivatives transactions of this sort are usually expected to be confirmed by a "confirmation" once they have been formally agreed by the

17–24

traders on the telephone. The standard form of confirmation—as is considered in Chapter 41[40]—assumes that the parties will both sign one document. However, it is common for no confirmation to be signed by the parties and instead for the parties (with a deadening sense of futility) to send one another their own standard wording for such confirmations. Thus the context in which acceptance of an offer is most problematic is that in which both parties seek to accept in accordance with their standard terms, perhaps in relation to a conduct of business letter drafted in a form which that party considers to be either commercially desirable or necessary to satisfy its regulators. It may be that the two acceptance letters each constitute a counter-offer to the extent that their terms are in disagreement. Where the parties proceed to perform the contract without negotiating those terms, it may be either that the parties are taken to have accepted those terms impliedly[41] or that it will emerge latterly that there was no agreement between the parties as to those issues such that there was no binding contract ever entered into between them.[42]

17–25   In relation to a battle of forms over the precise wording of the confirmation to be entered into between the parties, this is a frequent problem in derivatives markets, albeit that it is a problem which rarely causes difficulties provided that both parties continue to pay and receive payment without dispute. The courts have tended to look to the final salvo in the negotiation process as constituting the terms of the contract[43]—that is, unless the parties subsequently demonstrate that there was no agreement between them.[44] Equally, where the documents continue to fly between the parties' lawyers after their operations departments have begun to make payments as though the contract were complete, under the general law of contract it would not usually be permissible to alter the terms of the contract once it was in force.[45] However, given the standard market practice that the documentation of derivatives, and thus the completion of agreement of their precise terms, follows the commencement of the performance of such contracts, it is likely that such terms would be accepted as forming part of the agreement.

F.   The creation of contracts and their objective interpretation

17–26   The legal principles governing the interpretation of financial contracts are considered in detail in Chapter 19. The Supreme Court in *Rainy Sky SA v Kookmin Bank*[46] summarised the principles in the following form:

---

[40] See para.41–08.

[41] *B.R.S. v Arthur V. Crutchley Ltd* [1967] 2 All E.R. 285.

[42] *Butler Machine Tool Co Ltd v Ex-Cell-O Corp (England) Ltd* [1979] 1 W.L.R. 401.

[43] *Zambia Steel & Building Supplies Ltd v James Clark & Eaton Ltd* [1986] 2 Lloyd's Rep. 225. cf. *Butler Machine Tool Co Ltd v Ex-Cell-O Corp (England) Ltd* [1979] 1 W.L.R. 401.

[44] cf. *Johnson Mathey Bankers Ltd v State Trading Corp of India* [1984] 1 Lloyd's Rep. 427.

[45] *Jayaar Impex Ltd v Toaken Group Ltd* [1996] 2 Lloyd's Rep. 437.

[46] [2011] 1 W.L.R. 2900.

"the ultimate aim of interpreting a provision in a contract, especially a commercial contract, is to determine what the parties meant by the language used, which involves ascertaining what a reasonable person would have understood the parties to have meant."[47]

The Supreme Court stressed the "irrelevance of the parties' subjective intentions".[48] Moreover, where there is more than one reasonable interpretation of a contractual provision "it is generally appropriate to adopt the interpretation which is most consistent with business common sense".[49] In *Rainy Sky* (relying on *Society of Lloyds v Robinson*[50]) the Supreme Court identified the need to ignore technicalities in the contractual language and also to ignore pre-contractual negotiations. What is overlooked, however, is the way in which financial contracts are created in stages. Financial transactions are established in two stages. First, the traders reach agreement between themselves. At that moment there is potentially a binding contract. Second, the lawyers translate those commercial terms into a written contract. This will also potentially constitute a binding contract. What is at issue is whether or not the agreement reached between the traders is thus invalidated, or whether it was never binding in the first place: that question is moot in most circumstances because the question is only likely to arise once the invalidity of the oral agreement has been superseded by some problem requiring the written form. The issue is whether or not the oral form of the agreement included within it all of the terms which the parties required to be completed for there to be a binding contract. The more difficult problem is whether the parties realised that their contract was incomplete when the traders hung up their telephones, or whether the parties only realised that their contract was not complete at a later date when other problems came to light (such as the need for a governing law or a provision as to the detail of the calculation agent's powers).

There is a second species of problem. Not only are contracts created in stages but, rather than focus on the "reasonable commercial person" as the Supreme Court did, it must be recognised that the commercial wishes of traders are in fact translated into documentation and thus into legal concepts by lawyers; and the protocols which any financial institution uses will be created with lawyers and regulatory compliance specialists. Therefore, the reasonable commercial person does not really have any control over the process: instead, it is her goals which are translated into contractual language. Consequently, it is not the reasonable commercial person who should constitute the sole reference point for the interpretation of a contract. Instead, it should be the intentions of the lawyers who drafted the contract and, if the contract is in standard form, the intentions of the trade association which created that contract (assuming the contracting parties'

17–27

---

[47] [2011] 1 W.L.R. 2900, 2907, at [14], per Lord Clarke. See also Lord Steyn, "Contract law: fulfilling the reasonable expectations of honest men" 113 L.Q.R. 433.

[48] [2011] 1 W.L.R. 2900, at [19].

[49] [2011] 1 W.L.R. 2900, at [30]. Interestingly, all of this focus on the intentions of commercial people, and the need not to get overly-focused on technicalities, tends to overlook the fact that it is lawyers who will draft commercial contracts and therefore the technicalities are probably inserted intentionally and, moreover, that the intentions of those commercial people are necessarily mediated through the advice of their lawyers.

[50] [1999] 1 W.L.R. 756.

intentions were in parallel with that of the trade association), as an expression of the underlying intentions of the "commercial people".

G.   The formation of a contract through performance, not offer and acceptance

17–28   The courts may infer the existence of a contract in appropriate circumstances. The proof of offer and acceptance may be inferred where the parties demonstrated the existence of a contract by beginning its performance. This is particularly important where there is no written agreement in place between the parties but where the parties instead start to perform their contracts, as in complex financial transactions like derivatives. In *RTS Ltd v Muller GmBH*[51] the Supreme Court held that the key question is the following: "Leaving aside the implications of the parties' failure to execute and exchange any agreement in written form, were the parties agreed upon all the terms which they objectively regarded or the law required as essential for the formation of legally binding relations?" The court will not impose a contract on the parties: therefore, the parties must clearly have reached a contract of their own. Significantly, a contract may come into existence "not as a result of offer and acceptance, but during and as a result of performance".[52] Consequently, the suggestion is that offer and acceptance do not need to be proved; but rather that performance will demonstrate sufficient intention to effect legal relations. It is suggested that the process of offer and acceptance is simply inferred in such circumstances, although the precise words used by Lord Clarke (delivering the judgment of the Supreme Court) suggest that offer and acceptance are not necessary. That both the parties simply begin to perform their contract means that "it would be unrealistic to argue that there was no intention to enter into legal relations".[53] Where contracts are executory, this may be more difficult to demonstrate.[54]

4.   CASE STUDIES: THE EFFECT OF CONFUSION IN THE TRANSACTION PROCESS

A.   The decision in *Peekay Intermark Ltd v Australia and New Zealand Banking Group Ltd*

17–29   While the law considered in this chapter is somewhat trite contract law, there are issues considered here which arise frequently on trading floors. This section considers a decided case in the English High Court[55] which deals with problems as to the creation of derivatives contracts between traders, account managers,

---

[51] [2010] UKSC 14, [2010] Bus LR 776
[52] [2010] UKSC 14, [2010] Bus LR 776, at [50].
[53] [2010] UKSC 14, [2010] Bus LR 776, at [50].
[54] [2010] UKSC 14, [2010] Bus LR 776, at [50].
[55] *Peekay Intermark Ltd v Australia and New Zealand Banking Group Ltd* [2005] EWHC 830 (Comm).

financial intermediaries and non-market counterparty customers. When considering the creation of high-volume derivatives contracts it is important to understand that those contracts are generally created by means of fast-moving negotiations between traders in which, while the majority of transactions will be created and performed without a hitch, there will often be mistakes, misunderstandings and misrepresentations made between those traders. In relation to low-volume, structured derivatives the negotiations between the parties will take some time and the product at issue may change its nature considerably during those negotiations: this is because the product is generally constructed by traders and marketed by account managers, such that there may be mismatches between the understandings of those traders and account managers and the customers who rely on them.

An illustration of these issues arose in *Peekay Intermark Ltd v Australia and New Zealand Banking Group Ltd*.[56] In 1998 a short-lived market arose in Russian government bonds. Latterly a banking moratorium was declared in Russia, but at this time those bonds were trading at a discount to their face value which meant that the bonds appeared to be cheap compared to that face value although they carried high risks. The Australia and New Zealand Banking Group Ltd ("ANZ") marketed products to a range of its customers which related to Russian bonds known as "GKOs". The particular client who commenced this litigation was Peekay Intermark Ltd ("Peekay"), acting through its director and controlling shareholder Mr Pawani. The facts of the case are long and involved, and reading the judgment in full repays the effort. Briefly put, the facts were as follows. Pawani had considerable investment experience, including dealing in derivatives, and was described as a "sophisticated individual and an experienced trader". We are told nothing of ANZ's approach under the applicable conduct of business regulation to their decision to sell complex products to Peekay via Mr Pawani. The original form of the product was described in ANZ's literature as being a "Note giving GKO Returns Hedged back In USD" [sic], and was in turn a form of product inspired originally by products sold by Credit Suisse First Boston. However, ANZ developed a different form of product which was a "deposit" rather than a "note". The "Indicative Term Sheet" sent to Pawani indicated that the product was a hedged "note" in relation to which Peekay would acquire a beneficial interest in the GKO held for it by ANZ, whereas in fact Peekay would acquire no such right under the product which was ultimately put in place, with the result that Peekay was exposed to Russian rouble risk if a banking moratorium was declared, as opposed to being hedged in US dollars.

17–30

What is clear is that the account manager who consulted with Pawani had not appreciated that the traders who were constructing the product had changed the nature of the product from a "note" to a "deposit". It was clear that Pawani had not read any of the documentation which ANZ sent to him in any detail because he was relying on the verbal representations made to him by the bankers. At the time of agreeing verbally with the account manager that Peekay would acquire this investment, Pawani contended that he had seen no other documentation. Subsequently, however, ANZ issued further documentation explaining in passing

17–31

---

[56] [2005] EWHC 830 (Comm).

that the product was a "deposit". It was not clear at what stage this realisation bore in on Pawani. The account manager did not see Pawani's acceptance letter, which showed that he considered the company was acquiring a "note" rather than a "deposit". However, the judge at first instance made it clear that Pawani's evidence lacked credibility in a number of particulars. Nevertheless what was found on the facts as to the documentation trail was the following:

> "[The account manager] said that when she first saw this Contract Note (apparently in the course of proceedings), she was 'mystified, shocked and perplexed all in one'. She described it as 'a very sloppy operational effort', and 'completely bizarre', adding, 'It's got wrong written all over it', and that it should never have gone out to the customer"... There was no such thing as a USD GKO."[57]

The passage just quoted from the decision in *Peekay Intermark Ltd v Australia and New Zealand Banking Group Ltd* demonstrates that within financial institutions the documentation process will happen at speed as the products are being developed and as on-going discussions are being conducted between a number of different people both acting on behalf of financial institutions and acting as financial intermediaries advising customers. In this case, Peekay contended that it had been induced to enter into this contract on the basis of negligent misrepresentations made to it as to the nature of the product. On these facts, it was held that the nature of the product had indeed been misrepresented to Pawani, acting on behalf of the claimant company, Peekay. Even though it was not clear exactly to what extent Pawani had been misled, and even though Pawani was acknowledged to have had experience in derivatives trading, it was clear that the nature of the product as sold was materially different from the product as originally described to Pawani. Consequently, it was held that Peekay had been induced to enter into the contract by the misrepresentation and consequently that Peekay was entitled to damages equal to the difference between the actual return on the product and the original investment.[58] (This decision was overturned by the Court of Appeal, as discussed below.)

17–32 Two things happened in the course of the transaction which are significant in relation to the discussion of the contract process. First, there was no single confirmation put in place which documented the parties' intentions. Secondly, there were at least two groups of marketing material which conflicted as to the nature of the investment at issue, and latterly a "Risk Disclosure Statement" after the contract had been created orally. As the judge held, "[w]hat was on any view most unsatisfactory was that there was no documentation correctly recording the terms of Peekay's investment". In derivatives markets, it is commonly the case that there are a large number of transactions—usually with only a short period from "start date" to "exercise date"—but sometimes, as with *Peekay v ANZ*, there are more complex products which are undocumented or subject to documentation which omits a number of significant legal provisions which the traders do not know they should settle between them. This is a key area of risk in the creation of derivatives in particular.

---

[57] [2005] EWHC 830 (Comm), at [46].
[58] [2005] EWHC 830 (Comm), at [97].

The role of the legal advisor in these contexts ought to be to address the manner in which financial institutions conduct the detail of their business (ensuring that traders, account managers, intermediaries and customers have a meeting of minds formed with free consent), as opposed to reliance on the mere existence of the protocols which may theoretically be in place within such institutions. The demeanour of witnesses, their credibility in front of a trial judge, and the impression of chaos which is frequently given by documentation trails of the sort in *Peekay v ANZ* is of course very important in litigation.[59] It is easy to forget, in the struggle to create mathematically complex products and legally exhaustive documentation, that a simple matter such as good faith in transacting and clarity in the conduct of business will contribute both to the creation of effective contracts and as to credibility in the witness box (should matters reach that stage).

17–33

B.   The reversal by the Court of Appeal

The decision of Siberry QC at first instance was reversed by the Court of Appeal.[60] In a nutshell, the Court of Appeal considered that Pawani was at fault for not having read the contract closely so as to notice that the nature of the product had changed, and consequently it was held that Peekay could not maintain an action for misrepresentation against ANZ. The Court of Appeal held, in essence, that the buyer should have read the documentation because if he had, as an "experienced investor", he would have realised that the nature of the product had changed.

17–34

The Court of Appeal focused on different aspects of the facts from the trial judge. The leading judgment was given by Moore-Bick L.J., with whom Collins J concurred; with a short judgment in agreement being delivered by Chadwick L.J. It was considered to be significant by Moore-Bick L.J. that a five-page risk disclosure statement had been included with the documentation sent to Pawani; that the original discussion between ANZ's account manager, Balasubramaniam, and Pawani contained merely a general description of the investment and not something which would ordinarily constitute a misrepresentation; that Pawani should have realised that this was a "derivative"; that it could be inferred (although there was no finding of fact to this effect) that Pawani would have understood the transaction better if he had read the documents;[61] that Pawani was arguing that a document induced him to enter into a transaction when that

17–35

---

[59] For further illustrations of this phenomenon see *The First National Bank of Chicago v Ackerley Communications Inc* 2001 US Dist LEXIS 20895 where the trial judge found the "straightforward testimony" of one party "infinitely more believable than the hedged and cagey answers given by" the other party. See also *Bankers Trust v Dharmala* [1996] C.L.C. 18 in relation to the defendant's employee who was considered to be honest and so unlikely to have made misrepresentations any more than "inadvertently".

[60] [2006] EWCA Civ 386.

[61] However, because there is no evidence of a regulatory survey into the client's expertise when entering into this transaction, it cannot be known whether or not the client would have had sufficient expertise to understand the terms of this particular transaction.

document explained clearly on its face that he was acting under a misconception;[62] and that while the court would be slow to interfere with the trial judge's finding of fact, his lordship had nevertheless made an inference from the facts that it was Mrs Balasubramaniam's description of the product which had induced Pawani to sign the contract later and that this was an inference which the Court of Appeal was entitled to reject. Moore-Bick L.J. did recognise that the documentation which was sent to Pawani, as a record of his discussions with Mrs Balasubramaniam was "about as inaccurate as it is possible to be".[63]

17–36   One of the more difficult issues for the Court of Appeal was the decision in *Redgrave v Hurd*[64] in which documents were provided to the plaintiff which would have revealed the true facts about a purchase to him if he had read them. As Moore-Bick L.J. himself summarised the principle in that case: "where a person induces another to enter into a contract by misrepresentation it is no answer to say that the person to whom it was made had the means of discovering the truth".[65] On that basis, just because Pawani had the means of discovering the truth, that does not cure the misrepresentation which was made originally by the employees of ANZ with whom he spoke. As Sir George Jessel M.R. held in *Redgrave v Hurd*[66]:

> "If a man is induced to enter into a contract by a false representation it is not a sufficient answer to him to say, "If you had used due diligence you would have found out that the statement was untrue. You had the means afforded you of discovering its falsity, and did not choose to avail yourself of them." I take it to be a settled doctrine of equity, not only as regards specific performance but also as regards rescission, that this is not an answer unless there is such delay as constitutes a defence under the *Statute of Limitations*."

And furthermore, Jessel MR held:[67]

> "... when a person makes a material representation to another to induce him to enter into a contract, and the other enters into that contract, it is not sufficient to say that the party to whom the representation is made does not prove that he entered into the contract, relying upon the representation. If it is a material representation calculated to induce him to enter into the contract, it is an inference of law that he was induced by the representation to enter into it, and in order to take away his title to be relieved from the contract on the ground that the representation was untrue, it must be shewn either that he had knowledge of the facts contrary to the representation, or that he stated in terms, or shewed clearly by his conduct, that he did not rely on the representation ... Where you have neither evidence that he knew facts to shew that the statement was untrue, or that he said or did anything to shew that he did not actually rely upon the statement, the inference remains that he did so rely, and the statement being a material statement, its being untrue is a sufficient ground for rescinding the contract."

---

[62] It is not clear that it was the document which induced him to enter the contract alone, but rather that conversations which he had had with agents of the defendant bank had originally induced him to enter into the transaction.

[63] [2006] EWCA Civ 386, [17].

[64] (1881) 20 Ch. D. 1.

[65] [2006] EWCA Civ 386, [31]. This case is taken to be authority in *Watersheds Ltd v Da Costa* [2010] Bus. L.R. 1, at [44], per Holroyde J. for the proposition that "even if a false statement has been made it can be nullified if it is correctly so that the representee is aware of the true position before he enters into the agreement".

[66] (1881) 20 Ch. D. 1, at 13.

[67] (1881) 20 Ch. D. 1, at 21-22.

Therefore, at first blush ANZ could not argue that Pawani should have been diligent enough to find out the truth. Nevertheless, the Court of Appeal in *Peekay v ANZ* used two ways of eluding this clear principle. First, relying on the principle in *L'Estrange v Graucob*[68] it was held that a person is to be held to the terms of a contract which he has signed. Secondly, the Court of Appeal considered that the case before them related to a "correction" rather than a straightforward misrepresentation and therefore *Redgrave v Hurd* and other, more recent cases[69] were capable of being distinguished. Moore-Bick L.J. held that *Peekay* was different because the final form of the documentation "corrected" the misrepresentation, but Parwani did not spot this. Therefore, his lordship considered that there was a distinction between cases of misrepresentation and cases of corrections on the one hand, and cases where a document corrected the misrepresentation (but the claimant did not notice) on the other. This, it is suggested, is a distinction without a difference: the issue is not whether there was a correction of the product or simply a misrepresentation without a correction; rather, the issue is whether or not there was a misrepresentation which induced Pawani to enter into the contract. In all situations, the principle in *Redgrave v Hurd* should hold good: it was not open to the defendant to argue that the claimant should have read all of the documentation and realised that he had been the victim of a misrepresentation.

What is particularly interesting is that the Court of Appeal took the view that Mr Pawani should have understood that this was "a derivative", although it is not clearly exactly in what sense it was a derivative: it is common for traders to develop novel products and to give them interesting names, but that does not mean that someone who does not work in an institution which is a derivatives dealer would necessarily recognise their esoteric features. Indeed, the entire purpose of the Conduct of Business regulation introduced by the Financial Services Authority Handbook was that sellers of derivatives were expected to classify the level of expertise of their clients and to treat them suitably as a result. As is discussed in Chapter 17, the Conduct of Business Sourcebook now in force imposes the following obligations on regulated financial institutions selling derivatives among others: an obligation to classify their customers' expertise according to the regulatory standards and to treat them accordingly;[70] an obligation to ensure that all communications with the customer are "fair, clear and not misleading";[71] an obligation to act "in the best interests" of the customer;[72] and an obligation to ensure "best execution" of any transaction for a customer.[73] On these facts, ANZ clearly did not provide "fair, clear and not misleading" communications from its various personnel and in various pieces of documentation, all of which contradicted one another. There is no evidence as to the regulatory requirements of suitable treatment, nor whether the final form of the product was suitable for this client. On these bases, it is suggested, the Court

17–37

---

[68] [1934] 2 K.B. 394.

[69] Relying on *Assicurazioni Generali v Arab Insurance Group* [2002] EWCA Civ 1642, [2003] 1 All E.R. (Comm) 140 and *Flack v Pattinson* [2002] EWCA Civ 1820 (unreported).

[70] MiFID, art 19(4); COBS, 3.2.1(1)R.

[71] MiFID, art 19(2).

[72] MiFID, art 19(1); COBS, 2.1.1R.

[73] MiFID, art 21.

of Appeal erred in finding that the obligations to ensure that the terms of the transaction were properly understood rested solely with the client: on the contrary, financial regulation imposes positive obligations on financial institutions to treat their clients much better than that. This issue segues into the next section: in essence, the question is whether ordinary principles of contract law should be adapted so as to cater for these regulatory requirements.

The interaction of regulatory obligations and ordinary contract law

17–38   As discussed at the end of the previous section, there is an issue as to whether or not the ordinary principles of English contract law should take account of the positive obligations imposed on regulated financial institutions by financial regulation. Ordinary contract law does not impose obligations on commercial people in ordinary circumstances unless those parties have voluntarily assumed those obligations. However, the circumstances are not normal if one of the contracting parties is governed by a statutory, regulatory code which obliges that person to conduct itself in a particular way in the creation of contracts. In those situations, it is suggested, the regulated person should have its regulatory obligations recognised not only by the regulator but also by the courts in assessing whether or not a misrepresentation, in the example considered immediately above, has been made. If the regulated entity bears an obligation to ensure that all communications are fair, clear and not misleading, then it is unacceptable for that entity to rely upon a contract founded on a series of wilfully self-contradictory conversations and documents. Rather, the common law should accept that not only does *Redgrave v Hurd* prevent a defendant from arguing that the plaintiff should have discovered the true facts, but also that the defendant's regulatory obligations oblige it to treat a client in the plaintiff's position differently. The client in *Peekay v ANZ* was not a market counterparty, and therefore was entitled to more careful treatment than the incompetent internal machinations of that investment bank. The principle in *L'Estrange v Graucob* ought not to outweigh *Redgrave v Hurd* in that context: that is, sellers of derivatives may not hold their clients (where they are not market counterparties) to the terms of contracts which have been created in breach of regulatory standards and also subject to a misrepresentation.

17–39   The case of *Bankers Trust v Dharmala (No.1)*[74] is a good indication of how a judge may use financial regulation to develop principles of substantive law. In that case Bankers Trust sold two interest rate swaps to Dharmala. Dharmala was an Indonesian financial institution but not one which dealt in swaps. The swaps generated large losses for Dharmala. Dharmala claimed, inter alia, that it had not understood the risks inter alia posed by potential movements in US interest rates and that Bankers Trust should have explained the risks to it. By measuring the level of expertise of Dharmala against the applicable code of financial regulation, Mance J. was able to decide that Dharmala was not an inexpert client and so Bankers Trust was not required to have treated Dharmala as such. If Dharmala had been inexpert then Bankers Trust would have been obliged to explain all of

---

[74] [1996] C.L.C. 252.

the risks associated with the swaps to its traders. Thus, the decision on the substantive law flowed directly from the application of the financial regulations. However, there are other cases in which the regulations could have been used to establish whether or not a common law test has been satisfied, such as the decision of Gloster J. at first instance in *JP Morgan v Springwell*[75] where a full inquiry was not made to see whether or not an "experienced" but not professional investor had been treated suitably in accordance with the then regulatory requirements. Other cases have undertaken such an exercise, however, and been able to establish objectively how a financial institution (or other regulated entity) should have behaved in the circumstances.[76] This issue is considered in detail in Chapter 3.

D. Discrepancies between the verbal discussions and the documentation

Differences in the understanding of a contract

Distressingly frequently there will be, as considered earlier in this chapter, discrepancies between two traders' understandings of the deal they are contracting for, or between the trader's and the client's understandings of that deal, or between the verbal understanding that was reached and the documentation (if any) which is signed by the parties. These difficulties were referred to above. The problem will be in establishing what are the proper terms of the contract in such a situation and indeed whether or not the parties were either operating under a common mistake, or whether one of them was operating on the basis of a misrepresentation, or whether the purpose of the contract has been frustrated. Discrepancies may arise as a result of failing to record the oral contract accurately in writing, or including in the documentation provisions (perhaps in a standard form passage hidden unread towards the end of the document) which the parties had never discussed verbally but which has the effect of significantly transforming the bargain between them, or by mistakenly using the wrong standard form agreement for the transaction at issue. **17–40**

If one of the parties has contracted on the basis of a mistake, and if the other party was aware of that mistake, then the equitable remedy of rectification may be available so that the documentation will be rewritten by the court to reflect the proper position.[77] In New York it has been held that the written documentation is decisive of the matter, even where a party intended to buy an amount of currency but mistakenly signed a contract in which it undertook to sell that same amount of currency.[78] However, it has been held in New York that where there was not only a document effected by means of a mistake but also a series of contradictory telexes between the parties, then the parol evidence rule (that oral evidence may **17–41**

---

[75] [2008] EWHC 1186.
[76] *Investors Compensation Scheme v West Bromwich Building Society* (1999) Lloyd's Rep PN 496; *Loosemore v Financial Concepts* (2001) 1 Lloyd's Rep. 235; *Seymour v Christine Ockwell*(2005) P.N.L.R. 39.
[77] *Powercor Australia Ltd v Pacific Power* [1999] VSC 110.
[78] *Intershoe Inc v Bankers Trust Co* 77 NY 2d 517.

not be admitted if it contradicts written evidence) may be set aside.[79] Indeed it may be possible, if the parties have exchanged a series of electronic messages and telexes suggesting they were to create an asset *swap* on the one hand and also signed a confirmation suggesting they were to create a *repo* on the other hand, that the court will hold that there was simply never a meeting of minds between the parties sufficient to form a contract.[80]

17–42 The English law approaches to rectification[81] and to mistake[82] are considered in subsequent chapters. Ordinarily the courts will not interfere with the parties' written intentions as expressed in their documentation except in relation to mistake or where rectification is appropriate. Exceptionally, perhaps, in *Boom Time Holdings Ltd v Goldman Sachs*[83] the Court of Appeal did effectively alter the parties' contractual documentation to achieve what it considered to be a just result. The defendant calculation agent had reached its calculations in relation to a barrier call option over shares in P Ltd. P Ltd had issued bonus shares: something which had not been anticipated in the parties' contractual documentation. The parties had not stipulated their contractual expectations nor had they stipulated in detail the manner in which the calculation agent would carry out its calculations.[84] Under a contract which did not take into account the possibility of P Ltd issuing bonus shares, it was held by the Court of Appeal that an alteration in the knock-out price and the rebate procedure was necessary to give effect to the genuine intentions of the parties and so achieve "economic equivalence" between the parties' expectations and their contractual documentation.

Interpreting contracts where there is a manifest error in the documentation

17–43 There are two possible solutions to the interpretation of a document when there is a clear error in it. Either the parties can seek a formal order for rectification or the court can be asked to issue an order that the contract is to be interpreted in accordance with the meaning which it was self-evidently intended to have. So, when an error has been made in the creation of a financial contract, then the general law will deal with it by interpreting the contract appropriately. Such a question arose in *State Street Bank and Trust Co v Sompo Japan Insurance Inc*[85] in front of Morritt C where, in essence, the parties had left out, in error, a right for the appropriate party to be paid an amount under a total return swap where there had been a failure under a connected agreement. It was contended that the purpose of the agreement was to provide for such a payment in such a circumstance but there was no provision in the appropriate agreement requiring

---

[79] *BNE Swedbank SA v Banker* 794 F. Supp 1291 (SDNY).
[80] *Lehman Bros Inc v Canadian Imperial Bank* 2000 US Dist LEXIS.
[81] See para.18–12.
[82] See para.18–03.
[83] Unreported February 25, 1997, per Colman J.; reversed on appeal [1998] EWCA Civ 169.
[84] See para.19–70 on the need for stating clearly the commercial intentions underpinning a contract.
[85] [2010] EWHC 1461 (Ch).

that payment be made.[86] Morritt C considered the authorities on interpretation in this context.[87] In *East v Pantiles (Plant Hire)*[88] it had been held that there was no need to obtain an order for rectification in circumstances where there had been a self-evident mistake and that rather the ordinary principles of interpretation could supply the solution by interpreting the contract as it was intended to have been drafted. In *Chartbrook Ltd v Persimmon Homes Ltd*[89] Lord Hoffmann considered an error in the formula to be used to calculate the amount to be paid in relation to a land transaction. Lord Hoffmann accepted the proposition set out by Brightman L.J. in *East v Pantiles* to the effect that:

> "Two conditions must be satisfied: first, there must be a clear mistake on the face of the instrument; secondly, it must be clear what correction ought to be made in order to cure the mistake. If those conditions are satisfied, then the correction is made as a matter of construction."

Lord Hoffmann held that it was possible for the mistake to emerge from a consideration of all of the documents in a transaction, and as such it need not be evident on the face of a single document. Emboldened by these principles, Morritt C considered the many documents in *State Street Bank* and noted that the treatment of payments in the accounts was different from the form of words used, which suggested that the latter was the result of an oversight. Consequently, his lordship held that the appropriate construction was clear from the documents taken as a whole and in consequence his lordship ordered that the documents should be interpreted accordingly.

5. SUITABLE TREATMENT OF COUNTERPARTIES

English law does not have a general requirement of good faith in the making of contracts although there are a number of legal and equitable doctrines which, when combined, might be said to amount to something similar. There will frequently be situations in which an expert seller is providing expert advice to an

17–44

---

[86] In practice it will happen, particularly in relation to bespoke master agreements and confirmations, that the parties agonise at some length over the events of default and over other details, but that they then fail to provide that in the event that the contract is in-the-money then the appropriate party must actually make a payment. Such a little thing, and so easy to overlook in the busyness of practice. I recall the silence and the creeping sense of horror over the telephone when I once pointed out just such an omission in a form of bespoke master agreement used by a boutique firm of solicitors who were expert in the area of finance law. We agreed to begin the drafting process from scratch and we worked successfully and collaboratively together on it. If we work together on these contracts with a view to reducing the risks for all involved then all will be well.

[87] His lordship considered the following: *Schuler AG v Wickman Machine Tool Sales Ltd* [1974] A.C. 235, [1973] 2 All E.R. 39, [1973] 2 W.L.R. 683; *East v Pantiles (Plant Hire)* [1982] 2 E.G.L.R. 111, (1981) 263 EG 61; *The Antaios* [1985] A.C. 191, [1984] 3 All E.R. 229, [1984] 3 W.L.R. 592; *City Alliance Ltd v Oxford Forecasting Services Ltd* [2001] 1 AER (Comm) 233; *Holding & Barnes Plc v Hill House Hammond Ltd (No.2)* [2001] EWCA Civ 1334; *Dalkia Utilities Services Plc v Celtech International Ltd* [2006] EWHC 63 (Comm), [2006] 2 P & CR 173, [2006] 1 Lloyd's Rep. 599; *KPMG v Network Rail Infrastructure Ltd* [2007] EWCA Civ 363, [2007] Bus. L.R. 1336, [2008] 1 P & CR 187 and *Chartbrook Ltd v Persimmon Homes Ltd* [2009] UKHL 38, [2009] A.C. 1101, [2009] 4 All E.R. 677.

[88] (1981) 263 EG 61.

[89] [2009] UKHL 38, [2009] A.C. 1101, [2009] 4 All E.R. 677.

inexpert buyer as to the performance of a complex financial instrument—anything from a domestic mortgage to an interest rate swap. In such situations, where the transaction loses money for the buyer, it is likely that the buyer will wish to allege that there was some mis-selling involved in the transaction[90] or that the seller breached some general duty to treat that client suitably. It is suggested that the clearest evidence of having acted suitably in relation to any given customer is to demonstrate that the transaction complied with conduct of business regulation in identifying that client's level of expertise and then providing suitable financial products. If, as was discussed in Chapter 9, the seller was acting in a fiduciary capacity in relation to the customer, then the seller's obligations of good faith will rest on her fiduciary office.[91] The closer the relationship between the financial institution and the client, and the more likely the buyer is to rely on the seller's advice, then the higher will be the obligation on the seller to treat the buyer suitably. In such a situation, the buyer may seek to argue that it was unduly influenced by the seller,[92] that the seller made an actionably negligent misstatement while acting in its professional capacity,[93] or (in some circumstances) that the seller breached some fiduciary duty to the buyer and so obviated any authorisation to benefit from their relation by way of commission or other profits.[94]

17–45 What is also difficult to identify is the amount of disclosure which the seller must make as to the risk associated with the product which is being sold. FCA regulation, as was discussed in Part III of this book, provides for a range of positive obligations for example in relation to financial institutions disclosing their commissions[95] and in relation to issuers of securities and voting control over their shares under transparency obligations regulation.[96] It is typically the case that private law will not impose positive obligations except in exceptional situations, whereas financial regulation exists not only to provide for minimum standards but also to impose obligations on regulated persons.[97] In general terms, the contract law position relating to disclosure relates back to whether or not failure to disclose some material factor related to the contract would itself be a misrepresentation. It is only in relation to insurance law[98] and fiduciary law[99] that there is a requirement of good faith. What is clear is that fraudulent statements actually made entitle the buyer to rescind the contract and recover damages at common law,[100] whereas innocent misrepresentations would entitle the buyer to rescind the contract in equity and recover an indemnity.[101] The greater difficulty

---

[90] Considered in Ch.26.
[91] See para.5–01.
[92] *Barclays Bank v O'Brien* [1994] 1 A.C. 180.
[93] *Hedley Byrne v Heller* [1964] A.C. 465.
[94] *Boardman v Phipps* [1967] 2 A.C. 46.
[95] See para.10–16.
[96] See para.36–57.
[97] See para.9–01 et seq.
[98] *Banque Financiere v Westgate Insurance* [1990] 2 All E.R. 947: in that sense disclosure is necessary for all matters which would affect the decision of a prudent insurer in deciding whether or not to insure that risk. See also *Bank of Nova Scotia v Hellenic Mutual* [1989] 3 All E.R. 628.
[99] See Ch.5.
[100] *Derry v Peek* (1889) 14 App. Cas. 337.
[101] *Newbigging v Adam* (1886) 34 Ch.D. 582; *Whittington v Seale-Hayne* (1900) 82 L.T. 49.

is whether or not the seller is obliged to explain to the buyer all of the risks associated with the transaction before the transaction is completed. The Misrepresentation Act 1967 does not, prima facie, cover omissions. Under common law there is no general principle that such matters be disclosed either[102] although there may be relationships, such as the provision of advice by a fiduciary or by someone in the course of their profession acting for the claimant, where disclosure would be required.[103]

Mance J. has adopted the approach that in deciding the level of disclosure appropriate to any given situation it is important to have regard to two things.[104] First, the applicable regulatory norms, in particular those rules governing the obligations on a financial institution to identify the level of expertise of its client[105] and, secondly, the level of understanding which could be expected of such a client as to the matter at issue. In the case of *Bankers Trust v Dharmala*[106] the matters complained of related to the seller failing to explain to the buyer the risks of loss associated with a complex interest rate swap if there were a movement in US Federal Funds rates.[107] In that case, because the buyer was a financial institution it was held that the seller did not owe a general obligation to explain all of such risks to that buyer although there may have been such an obligation if the buyer had not been a financial institution and therefore classifiable as a client with some expertise under conduct of business regulation.

17–46

6.   STANDARD FORM CONTRACTUAL TERMS

A.   Use of standard form contracts

The question of standard form contractual terms is particularly significant in financial markets given that so many contracts in derivatives, foreign exchange, commodities and other markets are created under the terms of such contracts. This is a separate question from the rules of exchanges which bind all participants on many markets. There is an assumption, enthusiastically pursued by many market participants it would seem, that once a standard form of contract exists there is no further need for contracting parties to examine the terms that are appropriate for their own particular transaction. For example, in financial derivatives markets, inexpert counterparties frequently sign the standard ISDA Master Agreement because they are told by the seller that they must sign it or else no business will be conducted with them.[108] In such a situation, the inexpert

17–47

---

[102] *Keates v Cadogan* (1851) 10 C.B. 591.
[103] *The Unique Mariner* [1978] 1 Lloyd's Rep. 438; *Lloyds Bank v Egremont* [1990] 2 F.L.R. 351; *BCCI v Ali* [2000] 3 All E.R. 51.
[104] *Bankers Trust v Dharmala* [1996] C.L.C. 18.
[105] See para.10–13.
[106] *Bankers Trust v Dharmala* [1996] C.L.C. 18.
[107] [1996] C.L.C. 18
[108] See para.41–01.

buyer will be bound by the terms of the contract[109] in the absence of any undue influence by the seller.[110] This will be so even if the counterparty has not even read the terms of the contract.[111] Such an occurrence is common when expert counterparties deal with hedge funds or other similar entities which have a great appetite for speculation using derivatives but who have insufficient funding or insufficient will to investigate the legal niceties required of them by regulated counterparties.[112] It has been held that if a market counterparty signs a confirmation to agree that all of the terms of the standard form of ISDA master agreement are to be incorporated by reference into the confirmation, then all of the terms of that master agreement are to be deemed to be so incorporated.[113] This is so even if the signing party did not have a copy of that master agreement to hand and was unaware of its terms. (The terms of the standard form derivatives contracts are considered in detail in Chapter 41.)

B. Unfair contract terms

17–48 The most critical point relating to standard form contract arising out of the foregoing discussion is the extent to which they could be said to constitute unfair contract terms. Such an unfair term may be unenforceable under the unfair contract terms legislation, which is considered in detail in Chapter 18.[114]

7. CONDITIONS AND WARRANTIES

17–49 When drafting a contract for a complex transaction it is important to be able to distinguish between those provisions of the agreement which are so fundamental to the parties' purpose that any breach of them will cause the contract to be treated as having been terminated, and other provisions of the contract the breach of which would be satisfactorily remedied by a payment of damages or an order for specific performance of that obligation. In Chapters 19 and 20 we begin the discussion of the manner in which contracts must be performed and may be terminated, and that discussion requires that we can distinguish between these forms of contractual provision. This discussion is intended to highlight the importance of this process of identifying the level of significance of each contractual provision in this discussion of the formation of contracts. Allusion has been made on a number of occasions in the foregoing discussion to those terms which are material *conditions* of the contract and to those terms which are mere

---

[109] *L'Estrange v F. Graucob Ltd* [1934] 2 K.B. 394; *Levison v Patent Steam Cleaning Co Ltd* [1978] Q.B. 69; *the Polyduke* [1978] 1 Lloyd's Rep. 211; *Singer (UK) Ltd v Tees & Hartlepool Port Authority* [1988] 2 Lloyd's Rep. 164.

[110] See para.24–39.

[111] *L'Estrange v F. Graucob Ltd* [1934] 2 K.B. 394; *Levison v Patent Steam Cleaning Co Ltd* [1978] Q.B. 69; *the Polyduke* [1978] 1 Lloyd's Rep. 211; *Singer (UK) Ltd v Tees & Hartlepool Port Authority* [1988] 2 Lloyd's Rep. 164. cf. *McCutcheon v David MacBrayne Ltd* [1964] 1 W.L.R. 125.

[112] Indeed such a principle may seem to militate against the suggestion that there is a contract between the parties at all on the basis that there cannot have been a meeting of minds in relation to a contract which both parties know has not been read by the more inexpert of them.

[113] *Credit Suisse Financial Products v Societe Generale d'Enterprises* Unreported July 14, 1996.

[114] See para.18–39.

warranties, whereby a breach of the former category would give ground for the contract being rescinded whereas the latter would not. The test for deciding whether or not any contractual term is a condition precedent rather than a mere warranty is that the term must go "to the root of the matter, so that failure to perform it would render the performance of the rest of the contract a thing different in substance from what the defendant had stipulated for".[115] Furthermore, it is important to ascertain whether or not breach of that term would affect "the substance and foundation of the adventure which the contract is intended to carry out".[116] By contrast, a warranty is a term of a contract which, when breached, "gives rise to a claim for damages but not to a right . . . to treat the contract as repudiated".[117]

It is not possible in the abstract to delineate all of those terms which will and those which will not constitute conditions and those which would be mere warranties. The question of categorisation can be resolved only on a case-by-case basis and then usually by proper construction of the documentation. As Blackburn J. held in *Bettini v Gye*[118]:

17–50

> "Parties may think some matter, apparently of very little importance, essential; and if they sufficiently express an intention to make the literal fulfilment of such a thing a condition precedent, it will be one . . ."

In standard form agreements, there will usually be a provision which identifies a range of matters as being of the essence of the contract, including the parties' capacity and authority to contract, the absence of litigation and so forth.[119] Where the parties have expressly identified a particular provision as being fundamental to their contract, then that term will be considered to be a condition of the contract such that a failure to perform it will release the non-defaulting party from any obligation to perform a relevant part of the contract.[120] Alternatively, if the parties have not expressly specified that any particular term is a condition, the court will imply that status in accordance with the test set out above as to whether or not the term is sufficiently fundamental to the contract.[121]

It is therefore important to identify any term the breach of which is considered by the parties to constitute a condition of the contract such that its breach ought properly to terminate that contract automatically.[122] Similarly, even if a term is a mere warranty, then it would be important to identify the size of the loss which

17–51

---

[115] *Bettini v Gye* (1876) 1 Q.B.D. 183, 188; *Graves v Legg* (1854) 9 Exch. 709, 716.

[116] *Bentsen v Taylor, Sons & Co* [1893] 2 Q.B. 274, 281, per Bowen L.J.

[117] Definition used in Sale of Goods Act 1979 s.61(1). See also *Bunge Corporation v Tradax Export SA* [1981] 1 W.L.R. 711, 724.

[118] (1875) 1 Q.B. 183, at 187.

[119] See para.19–28 et seq and 19–48 et seq.

[120] *Financings Ltd v Baldock* [1963] 2 Q.B. 104; *Bunge Corp v Tradax Export SA* [1980] Lloyd's Rep. 294; *Lombard North Central Plc v Butterworth* [1987] Q.B. 527; unless the circumstances point to the opposite conclusion, *L.G. Shuler AG v Wickman Machine Tool Sales Ltd* [1974] A.C. 235; *Antaois Compania Naviera SA v Salen Rederierna AB* [1985] A.C. 191.

[121] *Hongkong Fir Shipping Co Ltd v Kawasaki Kisen Kaisha Ltd* [1962] 2 Q.B. 26; *Photo Production Ltd v Securicor Transport Ltd* [1980] A.C. 827; *Bunge Corporation v Tradax Export SA* [1980] Lloyd's Rep. 294.

[122] See para.19–48.

might be expected to flow from its breach. This is particularly important in circumstances in which the loss which might result is the cost of closing out a hedge which the courts might not otherwise consider to fall within the foreseeable loss under that contract.[123] Recent case law on this topic is considered in detail in Chapter 41.[124] The role of conditions in the termination of contracts is considered in greater detail in Chapter 20 below.

---

[123] See para.20–13.
[124] See para.20–13.

CHAPTER 18

VALIDITY AND PERFORMANCE OF CONTRACTS

CORE PRINCIPLES

This chapter considers two things: the circumstances in which contracts may be rendered invalid, and the principles governing the interpretation and performance of contracts.

The interpretation of contracts is conducted on an objective basis in which the principal focus is on the words of the contract, but the parties are allowed to adduce evidence about "anything at all" which illustrates the context in which the contract was made. The English law approach to the interpretation of contracts begins with an analysis of the terms of the contract; but, where the terms of the contract are unclear, the court reads those terms in the light of the context in which they were originally created. The five principles identified in *Investors Compensation Scheme v West Bromwich BS* were that the perspective of the reasonable person must be taken; reference may be had to absolutely anything; no question as to the negotiations nor the subjective intentions of the parties may be admitted; the meaning of words must be that perceived by the reasonable man; and words must be given their ordinary meaning.

Mistakes are common on trading floors. These errors and confusions can form themselves into claims for mistake, misrepresentation, frustration of contract, and on occasion simply questions of interpretation or rectification of a contract. Mistake operates to avoid a contract at common law when it is a common mistake which is relevant to the subject matter of that contract. Mutual mistakes will nullify consent; whereas misunderstandings or miscommunications will negative consent. Unilateral mistakes will not ordinarily cause a contract to be set aside, unless some advantage is taken by one party of the other. Mistakes of fact and mistakes of law are both actionable, on the basis of case law involving interest rate swaps.

There are categories of transaction which are invalid in themselves. Gaming and wagering contracts require authorisation under the Gaming Act 2005 to be enforceable as such. Some species of speculative contract may appear to be gaming contracts, except for the saving provisions in FSMA 2000. Insurance contracts may only be sold by authorised persons: some forms of financial transactions resemble insurance contracts so closely that there are questions as to whether or not those transactions ought in fact to be considered to be gaming.

The use of agents to transact, which is common in many transactions when institutions act on behalf of corporate and other clients, raises questions as to the authority of those agents to bind their principals if they purport to go beyond the terms of their agency. Agents may have ostensible authority when they are acting in a way which could reasonably be understood by third parties as being within the authority of the agent in the circumstances.

The Unfair Contract Terms Act 1977 and its attendant regulations are significant when non-expert clients of a financial institution transact on the basis of the financial institution's standard terms. If that is the case, the financial institution may not restrict its liability for negligence. Transactions will be ineffective where they were found to be unfair or to require exorbitant payment. Litigation which has sought to define bank charges as being "unfair" under this legislative code has failed.

1. INTRODUCTION

The bulk of financial law practice is concerned with contracts. The bulk of finance is concerned with the creation and performance of contracts. Finance law is involved in establishing the terms of those contracts and also in resolving disputes when those contracts go wrong. This chapter is concerned with the legal principles governing the performance of contracts—in particular their interpretation—and also with issues which may cause contracts to be found to be invalid. One of the principal difficulties with the performance of financial contracts in practice is with mistakes. Mistakes, errors and confusions can be made at any stage during the creation of a contract or during its operation. They come in the form of fraudulent or negligent misrepresentations, misunderstandings, errors in drafting, clumsiness by traders or operations personnel, confusions as to the proper interpretation of standard contractual language, and so forth. Each of these different types of confusion have different legal analyses. **18–01**

The first section of this chapter is concerned with the interpretation of contracts. The English law approach is to analyse contracts objectively by reference to the context in which the transaction was created and not simply by reference to the wording of the document. This may be particularly significant in relation to financial transactions which rely so heavily in practice on standard wording which may not necessarily reflect with precision the commercial intentions of the parties' traders and financial engineers when putting a particular transaction in place. Questions as to the interpretation of contracts can also overlap at the edges with questions as to the rectification of contracts: that is, a question as to how the contract should be interpreted or construed can be confused with a question as to a mistake in a contract which needs to be rectified. Given the complexity of the law on mistake in England and Wales, it is common for parties to seek damages under tort or under another part of contract law (such as misrepresentation or failure of consideration) instead. When thinking about mistakes, what may be a "mistake" in colloquial terms may actually be based on a misrepresentation by one party to the other, a complete failure to agree on the meaning of a particular contractual provision which only comes to light after the contract has been completed, or the failure of some third party to act in a manner which the parties had predicted. Each of these different factual scenarios—while they are about a "mistake" on their face—raise different legal issues. Therefore, this section of this chapter is concerned with ironing out confusions, disagreements and mistakes which arise in the performance of contracts. **18–02**

This second half of this chapter is concerned with those phenomena which may cause a contract to be rendered invalid or unenforceable, and as such it is closely tied to the previous chapter on the *Formation of Contracts*. There are three distinct heads under which a contract may be found to be invalid. First, on the **18–03** basis that there was some factor about the manner in which the contract was created which caused it to be invalid: for example where there has been a mistake in the formation of the contract, where the creation of the contract was induced by some misrepresentation or by some fraud, or where there is some legal pre-requisite to the creation of that type of contract which was not performed. Secondly, where one or other of the parties did not have the legal capacity to create a contract of that sort, or where one or other of the parties acted through an agent who lacked the authority to create that contract. Thirdly, where there is something about the terms of the contract or of the manner of its creation which renders its enforcement unfair or unconscionable under statute, for example further to the Unfair Contract Terms Act 1977.

18–04   There are two types of validity at issue in this chapter. The first is invalidity on the basis of some default in the parties' pre-contractual negotiations, such as one party making a misrepresentation to the other, or the parties operating under a mistake as to the nature or effect of their contract. These issues concern the validity of contracts because they may give rise to a right to avoid the contract, or to recover damages or other remedies which will render the profitability of a financial transaction nugatory. The second is invalidity on the basis of some substantive rule of law which rules that the contract is unenforceable, either because that contract is void under gaming legislation, or unfair contract legislation, or insurance legislation, or rules against unconscionable bargains; or because that contract is outwith the capacity of one of the parties to execute it, or because it is outwith the authority of one of the individuals who purports to execute it.

2.   THE INTERPRETATION OF CONTRACTS

A.   The English law approach in outline

18–05   The interpretation of contracts is central to the operation of financial markets. Clearly each contract depends upon its own terms, and so describing the law which governs such exercises in interpretation is a little like trying to describe the taste of water. Nevertheless, there are a number of cases which have set out the principles which govern the interpretation of contracts.[1] It is easiest to understand there as being two different methods of interpreting of contracts, with most judges taking a position somewhere between these extremes. At one extreme is the literalist approach which concentrates solely on the written terms of a contract without considering any other information as to the circumstances in which that contract was made. At the other extreme is the subjectivist approach which insists on reading the contract in the light of all of the background circumstances, the intentions of the contracting parties when they created the contract, their objectives and so forth. Classically, the English law approach was literalist (and consequently focused solely on the precise terms of the contract without

---

[1] There are two excellent (and very readable) books on the subject: Sir Kim Lewison, *The Interpretation of Contracts*, 4th edn (Sweet & Maxwell, 2007); and Prof Gerard McMeel, *The Construction of Contracts*, 2nd edn (OUP, 2011).

considering anything else),[2] but the modern approach is a hybrid of the two approaches which begins with a literalist approach and then considers the relevant background circumstances if the literalist approach does not produce a ready solution to the interpretation of the contract.[3] In that sense, English law has moved from a literalist, purely objective approach to an approach which is predominantly objective but which also recognises context. This section will consider the general principles by reference to which contracts fall to be interpreted by courts in England and Wales (and also by courts in other jurisdictions, by way of illustration and comparison).

B. The central principles in *Investors Compensation Scheme v West Bromwich Building Society*

The five core principles governing the interpretation of contracts

The central principle in interpreting contracts under English law is generally taken[4] to be contained in the five-fold division of the principles set out in the judgment of Lord Hoffmann in the House of Lords in *Investors Compensation Scheme v West Bromwich Building Society* in the following terms[5]:

18–06

> "The principles may be summarised as follows.
>
> (1)   Interpretation is the ascertainment of the meaning which the document would convey to a reasonable person having all the background knowledge which would reasonably have been available to the parties in the situation in which they were at the time of the contract.
>
> (2)   The background was famously referred to by Lord Wilberforce as the 'matrix of fact', but this phrase is, if anything, an understated description of what the background may include. Subject to the requirement that it should have been reasonably available to the parties and to the exception to be mentioned next, it includes absolutely anything which would have affected the way in which the language of the document would have been understood by a reasonable man.
>
> (3)   The law excludes from the admissible background the previous negotiations of the parties and their declarations of subjective intent. They are admissible only in an action for rectification. The law makes this distinction for reasons of practical policy and, in this respect only, legal interpretation differs from the way we would interpret utterances in ordinary life. The boundaries of this exception are in some respects unclear. But this is not the occasion on which to explore them.
>
> (4)   The meaning which a document (or any other utterance) would convey to a reasonable man is not the same thing as the meaning of its words. The meaning of words is a matter of dictionaries and grammars; the meaning of the document is what the parties using those words against the relevant background would reasonably have been understood to mean. The background may not merely enable the reasonable man to choose between the possible meanings of words which are ambiguous but even (as

---

[2] See for example *Sirius International Insurance Co v FAI General Insurance Ltd* [2004] 1 W.L.R. 3251.

[3] *Investors Compensation Scheme v West Bromwich Building Society* [1998] 1 W.L.R. 896, [1998] 1 All E.R. 98; *Rainy Sky SA v Kookmin Bank* [2011] 1 W.L.R. 2900.

[4] *BCCI v Ali* [2001] 1 A.C. 251.

[5] *Investors Compensation Scheme v West Bromwich Building Society* [1998] 1 W.L.R 896, [1998] 1 All E.R. 98 at 115.

occasionally happens in ordinary life) to conclude that the parties must, for whatever reason, have used the wrong words or syntax (see *Mannai Investment Co Ltd v Eagle Star Life Assurance Co Ltd*[6]).

(5)   The 'rule' that words should be given their 'natural and ordinary meaning' reflects the common sense proposition that we do not easily accept that people have made linguistic mistakes, particularly in formal documents. On the other hand, if one would nevertheless conclude from the background that something must have gone wrong with the language, the law does not require judges to attribute to the parties an intention which they plainly could not have had. Lord Diplock made this point more vigorously when he said in *Antaios Cia Naviera SA v Salen Rederierna AB, The Antaios*:[7]

> '... if detailed semantic and syntactical analysis of words in a commercial contract is going to lead to a conclusion that flouts business common sense, it must be made to yield to business common sense.' "

Importantly, then, the parties' subjective states of mind and intentions are not the focus of the court's deliberations, but rather an objective assessment of the contract is. The Supreme Court in *Rainy Sky SA v Kookmin Bank* summarised the principles in the following form:

> "the ultimate aim of interpreting a provision in a contract, especially a commercial contract, is to determine what the parties meant by the language used, which involves ascertaining what a reasonable person would have understood the parties to have meant."[8]

Later, the Supreme Court stressed the "irrelevance of the parties' subjective intentions"[9] and where there is more than one reasonable interpretation of a contractual provision "it is generally appropriate to adopt the interpretation which is most consistent with business common sense".[10] Again, this is an objective approach.

18–07   One might have thought that contract law ought to be concerned with identifying the parties' intentions, but that is not how the English law approach to the interpretation of contracts works. The contract, in effect, takes on a life of its own (and a meaning of its own) which is distinct from the subjective views of the parties. Lord Steyn explained this point in *Sirius International Insurance Co v FAI General Insurance Ltd* in the following terms:[11]

> "The aim of the inquiry is not to probe the real intentions of the parties but to ascertain the contextual meaning of the relevant contractual language. The enquiry is objective: the question is what a reasonable person, circumstanced as the actual parties were, would have understood the parties to have meant by the use of specific language. The answer to that question is to be gathered from the text under consideration and its relevant contextual scene."

Of course, it may be that the parties have different objectives in the creation of a contract and therefore the establishment of an actual, subjective common intention would be difficult. As is argued in Chapter 19, in complex financial

---

[6] [1997] 3 All E.R. 352, [1997] 2 W.L.R 945.

[7] [1984] 3 All E.R. 229 at 233, [1985] A.C. 191 at 201.

[8] [2011] 1 W.L.R 2900, 2907, at [14], per Lord Clarke. See also Lord Steyn, 'Contract law: fulfilling the reasonable expectations of honest men' 113 L.Q.R. 433.

[9] [2011] 1 W.L.R 2900, at [19].

[10] [2011] 1 W.L.R 2900, at [30].

[11] [2004] 1 W.L.R 3251. Also in *Deutsche Genossenschaftsbank v Burnhope* [1995] 4 All E.R. 717.

transactions created under master agreements, it is advisable to agree a statement of the objectives of the contract in the wording of the contract itself so as to guide the court's interpretation at a later date.[12]

The perspective of the reasonable person

Lord Hoffmann made it clear in *Investors Compensation Scheme v West Bromwich Building Society* that the interpretation of contracts is to be conducted from the perspective of a reasonable person, albeit one who has knowledge of the circumstances in which the contract was created. This concept has been expressed as the 'familiar way of expressing the judicial process of inference from admissible primary evidence'.[13] It is not clear, however, whether the reasonable person should have expertise in financial practice or whether they should simply be a reasonable member of the public. Lord Goff suggested in the House of Lords in *President of India v Jebsens (UK) Ltd*[14] that it should be "reasonable persons in the shoes of the contracting parties."[15] The principle that the court should identify the meaning as it would be perceived by "the reasonable man" suggests that words need not be given their ordinary meaning but rather some deeper truth intended by the transaction and its documentation should be recognised instead.

18–08

This means that in relation to standard form contractual language the parties' particular intention in creating that contract are not necessarily as important as the terminology they use, even if that terminology was devised by a trade association many years before. This does mean that terms of art in standard documentation can be interpreted in the context of their intended meaning in that context and not their ordinary meaning: so, in financial transactions terms such as "pledge", "swap" and so forth can be given their technical meanings and not their ordinary, colloquial meanings. Briggs J. held in *LB Re Financing No.3 (in administration) Ltd v Excalibur Funding No.1 PLC*[16] that when construing a document, such as a trust deed in relation to a bond issue, that "the court's task when addressing issues of construction is to ascertain the meaning which the instrument would convey to a reasonable person having all the background knowledge which would reasonably be available to the audience to whom the instrument is addressed".[17] Briggs J. thus helpfully paints in some of the qualities to be attributed to "the reasonable man" in such situations, including technical knowledge of the purpose of that transaction.[18]

18–09

---

[12] See paras 19–81 and 19–85; and in particular in relation to derivatives contracts in para.41–24.
[13] *Zeus Tradition Marine v Bell* [1999] CLC 391.
[14] [1991] 1 Lloyd's Rep 1, 9.
[15] But what sort of reasonable persons would wear someone else's shoes?
[16] [2011] EWHC 2111 (Ch).
[17] [2011] EWHC 2111 (Ch), at [42].
[18] *LB Re Financing No.3 Ltd (In Administration) v Excalibur Funding No.1 Plc* [2011] EWHC 2111 (Ch).

Reference to "absolutely anything" in the background circumstances

18–10   The reference which Lord Hoffmann made in *Investors Compensation Scheme v West Bromwich Building Society* to the interpretation of unclear or ambiguous contractual terms by reference to the background circumstances includes "absolutely anything" which is relevant to the interpretation of the contract.[19] As a result of the introduction of this principle, however, litigants and their advisors began to seek to adduce mountains of evidence relating to the circumstances in which their contracts had been created originally, with the effect that litigation became difficult to manage.[20] For example, Lightman J. related how in *Wire TV Ltd v Cabletel (UK) Ltd*[21] he was confronted with a "flood" of evidence much of which was legally inadmissible and which required half a day hearing argument simply as to the admissibility of evidence. As a result, Lord Hoffmann was required to qualify this central principle in his own judgment in the later case of *BCCI v Ali*:[22]

> "When . . . I said that the admissible background included "absolutely anything which would have affected the way in which the language of the document would have been understood by reasonable man", I did not think it necessary to emphasise that I meant anything which a reasonable man would have regarded as relevant. I was merely saying that there is no conceptual limits to what can be regarded as background. It is not, for example, confined to the factual background and can include the state of the law ... or proved common assumptions which were in fact quite mistaken. But the primary source for understanding what the parties meant is their language interpreted in accordance with conventional usage..."

Nevertheless, as Douglas Adams put it: a common mistake that people make when trying to design something completely fool proof is to underestimate the ingenuity of complete fools.[23] In this instance, that means that Lord Hoffmann's attempt to be clear about what he meant by "absolutely anything" was taken by many to include matters which bore no direct relevance to the contract itself. In fairness to litigators, the reference to "absolutely anything" is an open invitation both to swamp one's opponents with documentation and to make reference to any and all facts which might possibly convince the judge to decide in your favour. Nevertheless, we have to understand the reference to "absolutely anything" to be a reference to absolutely anything which may be relevant to the interpretation of the contract from within a very broad background of material.

18–11   Indeed, as Saville L.J. put it in *National Bank of Sharjah v Dellborg*[24]:

> "It is difficult to quarrel with the general proposition that when interpreting an agreement the court is trying to work out what the parties intended to agree, rather than analysing words in a vacuum. ... However, where the words used have an unambiguous and sensible meaning as a

---

[19] *Investors Compensation Scheme v West Bromwich Building Society* [1998] 1 W.L.R 896, [1998] 1 All E.R. 98, 115.

[20] Indeed the case management process under the Civil Procedure Rules became an important part of applying Lord Hoffmann's principles in practice by excluding inadmissible evidence.

[21] [1998] C.L.C. 244, 257.

[22] [2002] 1 A.C. 251, 269.

[23] Adams, *Mostly Harmless* (Pan, 1992).

[24] Unreported, July 9, 1997; quoted in Lewison, 9.

matter of ordinary language, I see serious objections in an approach which would permit the surrounding circumstances to alter that meaning."

This sensible approach reflects the idea that it will only be relevant to consider the background circumstances when the written terms of the contract do not yield up a clear answer. Indeed in Australia the principle is that the surrounding circumstances may only be consulted once it can be demonstrated that there is some provision in the contract which is ambiguous.[25] Similarly, Lord Phillips MR suggested in *MSC Mediterranean Shipping v Owners of the Ship 'Tychy'*[26] that the court should consider why it is that extrinsic evidence should be taken into account at all and what precisely that would achieve, before considering it. In short, there must be a real problem of interpretation before background evidence is considered.

The exclusion of pre-contractual negotiations from the relevant background

While Lord Hoffmann held that "absolutely anything" may be included in the quest for the proper interpretation of the contract, nevertheless the pre-contractual negotiations between the parties are excluded under contract law and the law of evidence. This does have the difficulty in relation to complex financial transactions that it is precisely the negotiations between traders in financial institutions, or between a trader on the one hand and the finance director (or similar) of a corporate client on the other, which would illustrate how the documentation developed and which avenues of negotiation were accepted or rejected to achieve the final document. This, it is suggested, ought not to exclude an examination of the buyer's commercial objectives, as considered above. There have been authorities in which the judges have restricted the admissible background evidence to agreed facts about market practice.[27] Market practice (or a preference to deal differently from market practice) may be significant in identifying the parties' intentions and thus in establishing their objectives in drafting the documentation (whether following the standard wording or not) in the way that they did. In relation to negotiations about the amendment of a standard market document this may be significant in demonstrating that the parties had a specific concept in mind when they intentionally deviated from the standard language.

18–12

The natural and ordinary meaning of words

The principle that words are to be given their ordinary meaning is predicated on the idea that one should not assume that an error has been made in a document such that the document requires an ordinary word to be read in a peculiar fashion. Rather, each word should be given in its ordinary meaning on the assumption that has not been such an error. In short, one should assume that a word is to be given

18–13

---

[25] *LMI Australasia Ltd v Baulderstone Hornibrook Ltd* [2003] NSWCA 74.
[26] [2001] 2 Lloyd's Rep. 403, 409.
[27] *Galaxy Energy International v Assuranceforeningen Skuld* [1999] 1 Lloyd's Rep. 249.

its ordinary meaning, and not assume that it is to be given a stylised meaning. This fifth principle does present the difficulty that if the court is both supposed to identify the deeper truth of the document and also to deal with words according to their surface meaning, then the court is ultimately going to have to choose which of the two readings is more appropriate on the facts of any given case. Moreover, in so doing, the court is expected to give effect to business common sense in its reading of contractual provisions.[28]

18–14 This last point does present some difficulty: commercial people generally leave it to their lawyers to decide on the precise wording of a transaction and therefore commonly if one is to read that provision in accordance with business common sense that might be something slightly different from the approach taken by the lawyers who drafted it: lawyers will tend to think in legal concepts, whereas businesspeople think variously in their own registers. This is particularly true in relation to complex transactions like derivatives in which financial engineers and quantitative analysts tend to rely on mathematical explanations of their commercial intentions, which lawyers then attempt to translate into an entirely different language. Much is left out of the legal conceptualisation of the parties' commercial intentions, particularly given that none of the mathematical formulae which will have been used to create the product are ordinarily included in the contract. Therefore, there will always be a debate not only as to what business common sense would require in any given circumstances, but also as to whose business common sense is relevant in the first place: the financial engineer's, the accountant's or the lawyer's?

Interpretation in accordance with commercial common sense

18–15 When questions of interpretation come to court it is usually because there is some ambiguity in the wording of the contract, particularly when the parties seek to apply that wording to circumstances which had not been anticipated when the contract was drafted. (Occasionally, of course, questions of interpretation also come before a court because litigants are either hopeful that they might be able to overturn a well-drafted contract which is disadvantageous to them, or hopeful that they can delay its performance.) When faced with an ambiguous provision, there are at least two possible readings of it. So, in an effort to identify the better reading, the court may consider the commercial ramifications of both readings and then ask which of those readings accords with commercial common sense: i.e. which of them were the parties more likely to have intended when their contract was drafted.

18–16 This idea was considered by the Supreme Court in *Rainy Sky SA v Kookmin Bank*.[29] It was held by Lord Clarke (delivering the judgment of the court)[30] that "if the language is capable of more than one construction, it is not necessary to conclude that a particular construction would produce an absurd or irrational

---

[28] See the approach to commercial common sense taken by the Supreme Court in *Rainy Sky SA v Kookmin Bank*[2011] 1 W.L.R 2900, as considered below.

[29] [2011] 1 W.L.R 2900. See also *Barclays Bank Plc v HHY Luxembourg SARL* [2011] 1 B.C.L.C. 336, [25]–[26].

[30] [2011] 1 W.L.R 2900, at [43].

result before having regard to the commercial purpose of the agreement". Therefore, there is no need to demonstrate that the construction which is being argued for is absurd before turning to consider what commercial common sense requires. Of course, in practice, there will be two parties (claimant and defendant) advancing competing readings of the same contract. Where neither reading would flout common sense and therefore each reading is possible, then the court should "adopt the more, rather than the less, commercial construction".[31] Therefore, the notion of commercial common sense is a sort of tie-breaker where both readings are possible on the facts of any given case. So, on the facts of that case, there were performance bonds issued in relation to shipbuilding contracts which were ambiguously worded. The court followed the more commercially sensible of the interpretations in the context of that transaction.[32]

Commercial common sense does not mean interpolating provisions the court would prefer to see

Longmore L.J. explained why the courts should not seek to supplement the parties' contract with provisions of their own:[33]   **18–17**

> "There are dangers in judges deciding what the parties must have meant when they have not said what they meant for themselves. This is particularly dangerous when the parties have selected from the shelf or the precedent book [or from standard contractual language published by a trade association[34]] a clause which turns out to be unsuitable for its purpose. The danger is then intensified if it is only one part of such a clause which is to be construed in accordance with "business commonsense". If the parties had addressed their mind to the question which crawls out of a number of standard terms they would have used for the particular requirement which they had in mind, it is by no means obvious that they would have selected a form which was as Draconian as the one unwisely but in fact chosen."

Here, his Lordship is pointing out how dangerous it can be for the courts not only to second-guess what the parties must have meant but also to try and improve upon their language.

C. Interpretation of a standard form master agreement so as to validate the contract

Financial markets operate in many circumstances on the basis of standard market contracts. If any doubt is cast on the effectiveness or enforceability of such a contract then this causes minor ripples of panic through the market's legal   **18–18**

---

[31] [2011] 1 W.L.R 2900, at [43]; applying *Barclays Bank Plc v IIIIY Luxembourg SARL* [2011] 1 B.C.L.C. 336, at [26], per Longmore L.J.

[32] This same approach was taken to the interpretation of contradictory jurisdiction clauses in a master agreement and other documentation in *UBS AG v HSH Nordbank AG* [2009] EWCA Civ 585; [2010] 1 All E.R. (Comm) 727 so as to concentrate the hearing of various claims in one jurisdiction in a manner which the court considered to be commercially sensible.

[33] *Royal and Sun Alliance Insurance Plc v Dornoch Ltd* [2005] 1 All E.R. (Comm) 590.

[34] Author's addition.

advisors.[35] When dealing specifically with the interpretation of the ISDA Master Agreement (the standard market agreement for derivatives, analysed in Chapters 41 and 43) in *BNP Paribas v Wockhardt*[36], Clarke J. relied on the following passages from *Perpetual Trustee Co Ltd v BNY Corporate Trustee Services Ltd* in finding that the parties' freedom of contract should be observed by the court:

> "... on general principles the court should not be astute to interpret commercial transactions so as to invalidate them, particularly when ... consequential doubt might be cast on other long-standing commercial arrangements"[37]

And also:

> "It is also desirable that, if possible, the courts give effect to contractual terms which the parties have agreed. Indeed there is a particularly strong case for party autonomy in cases of complex financial instruments ..."[38]

Therefore, when interpreting the ISDA Master Agreement the courts are expected to do so in a way which supports the validity of the contract where possible and which holds the parties to the terms of their agreement. Of course, such an approach can only go so far. This is an approach which cannot cross the mandatory rules of English law. The courts cannot simply construe a contract so as to effect the goals which the marketplace generally might consider desirable (as has appeared to be the case in many of the recent cases discussed in Chapters 41 and 43) when that might be to the straightforward disadvantage of one of the contracting parties or contrary to some goal of public policy. It cannot be that the standard master agreement is applied whatever might be wrong with it.

3. MISTAKE

A. The nature of mistakes in financial transactions

18–19   To err is human. For human beings to err when working under the highly pressured conditions of trading floors or corporate finance floors is not only possible, it is likely. In truth, many financial institutions operate in a sort of organised chaos most of the time. In recent years there have been many reports in the financial press of hedge funds and other institutions employing traders who do not keep accurate records of the deals which they have done. Indeed, complex transactions were frequently recorded on scraps of paper by busy traders, and mistakes were made in transcribing the detail of what has been agreed. There are

---

[35] The panic is felt primarily in the financial institutions, whereas any legal practitioner worth her salt smells an opportunity to earn more fees by explaining the new change in the law to clients and thus generating a little more work.

[36] [2009] EWHC 3116, [24].

[37] *Perpetual Trustee Co Ltd v BNY Corporate Trustees Services and another; Belmont Park Investments Pty Ltd v Corporate Trustee Services Ltd and another* [2009] EWHC 1912 (Ch) per Sir Andrew Morritt, QC.

[38] *Perpetual Trustee Company Ltd v BNY Corporate Trustee Ltd & Butters* [2009] EWCA Civ 1160, at 58, per the Master of the Rolls. On appeal also from *Butters v BBC Worldwide Ltd* [2009] B.P.I.R. 1315, [2009] EWHC 1954 (Ch), Peter Smith J.

legends from many parts of the financial markets of traders writing only in pencil and often on the backs of envelopes. The scope for making mistakes in such a chaotic environment is self-evident. The more established financial institutions have state-of-the-art computer systems for traders whereby traders enter the details of transactions electronically onto their computer screens and a deal will only be recorded if the trader completes all of the "fields" on the screen which have been identified in advance for that sort of trade by the operations and legal departments of that institution. Such computer systems are also capable of generating automatically the standard form of contract appropriate to that form of transaction, complete with the financial details of that specific transaction. However, even in such well-structured trading environments it is possible that the trader may enter the wrong details or that there is something about that particular transaction which makes the ordinary legal terminology for that transaction suddenly inappropriate. We are all familiar with the sight of traders in well-run banks screaming into telephones when a market panic is in process. It should never be forgotten that even in the calm of its back office, Barclays misreported 57.5 million transactions to regulators in one financial year: proof that mistakes can happen on an enormous scale in any banking institution.[39] The improvement in technology has not removed mistakes. In some cases it has created new forms of error. Automated trading systems can cause enormous problems when they go wrong.[40] On May 6, 2010 there was a report of a "flash crash"[41] in New York which caused a very serious fall in the Dow Jones index (of an unprecedented 600 points in a few minutes) before rebounding only a few minutes later.[42] The US regulators the SEC and the CFTC confirmed that this had happened. In *Vanity Fair*[43] there had been a report that this crash had been caused by a trader mis-typing "billions" instead of "millions" into his computer system which triggered a huge fall in the share price of the company in question (a 37 per cent fall in a matter of minutes in Proctor and Gamble) and which had a huge knock-on effect on other shares on that market.[44] This is known colloquially as a "fat finger" error (as if it was the trader's fat fingers which caused the wrong keys to be hit). So, tiny errors like this do happen more frequently than people would

---

[39] See the discussion of Barclays in Ch.45.

[40] The threats posed by automated trading systems and the algorithims which control them are discussed in S. Patterson, *Dark Pools* (Random House, 2012); E. Perez, *The Speed Traders* (McGraw Hill, 2011); D. Duffie, *Dark Markets* (Princeton University Press, 2012).

[41] See *http://www.economist.com/blogs/newsbook/2010/10/what_caused_flash_crash;* and see also *http://www.bloomberg.com/news/2012-05-07/flash-crash-story-looks-more-like-a-fairy-tale.html.*

[42] A "flash crash" occurs when an automated trading system or a human trader mistakenly causes a temporary, serious fall in prices which then rebound (as though someone had quickly rectified their error). Automated trading systems are programmed to buy or sell automatically when prices reach a given value: so when prices start to fall it is often automated systems which make the problem worse by making more sales automatically.

[43] See: *http://www.vanityfair.com/online/daily/2010/05/is-a-typo-responsible-for-yesterdays-stock-market-crash.html#entry-more*

[44] The reason for the fall was that the market believed that someone was seeking to sell a huge amount of Proctor and Gamble stock very quickly. This happened at the same time as markets were very jittery indeed in May 2010 about the effect of the collapse of the Greek economy (amidst rioting in Greece and the near collapse of the euro as a currency).

like to admit.[45] This story demonstrates the knock-on effects which those tiny mistakes can have on even the largest markets. It also shows how markets will stampede even though there was never any rational suggestion that there was anything wrong with Proctor and Gamble.[46]

18–20   We must not allow ourselves to succumb to the enthusiastic prejudice that simply because financial professionals are well-paid and well-shod they never make mistakes. It is not unknown for lawyers advising well-known corporate clients to fail to express precisely the legal rights and obligations which they want their respective clients to bear. To illustrate how easily these sorts of mistakes are made in financial markets, there is a remarkable incident explained in Kate Kelly's book, *Street Fighters*,[47] which tells of how Bear Stearns CEO Alan Schwartz and his team of senior managers had organised a short-term loan facility on Thursday March 13, 2008 with Hank Paulson (then US Treasury Secretary) and Tim Geithner (then of the Federal Reserve Bank of New York). At that time, Bear Stearns was teetering on the edge of bankruptcy. This loan transaction was possibly the most significant transaction in the history of Bear Stearns up to that moment. It was intended to stave off the threat of bankruptcy for a short while in the hope that Bear Stearns could find some new assets or a buyer for its business. The people at Bear Stearns thought the loan was to last for 28 days. In a telephone call between Schwartz, Paulson and Geithner on Friday March 14, 2008 it was borne in on Schwartz that the loan had only been made for two days: i.e. to tide Bear Stearns over the weekend, and not to last for the 28 days which Bear Stearns had claimed in its press releases which had been distributed to calm the markets. Remarkably, when agreeing the loan which was intended to keep their bank from bankruptcy while it secured its future, the bank's most senior employees had failed to identify that it was to last for only two days and not 28 days. One should never under-estimate the possibility that professionals will make mistakes about the most basic (and thus the most important) elements of banking business.

18–21   Equally it may be that traders and client account managers fail to make clear to their clients the precise nature of the product which is being sold to the client, even if negotiations continue for some time and even if the parties are in regular contact. As was discussed in the previous chapter,[48] in *Peekay Intermark Ltd v Australia and New Zealand Banking Group Ltd*[49] confusion arose over the course

---

[45] If you read any memoir by a bank trader they will admit to mistakes that they made or that others made: see for example McDonald, *A Colossal Failure of Common Sense* and Lewis, *Liar's Poker*, discussed in Ch.45.

[46] The investment bank Bear Stearns crumbled from a capital base of US$18 billion to nearly filing for bankruptcy protection over the space of one week in March 2008, based on market rumours. Ultimately that bank was sold to JP Morgan for a price of $2 per share (which was adjusted latterly to US$10 per share), after having traded at one stage at US$172 in January 2007. Either the market was very mistaken in 2007 when the share traded at $172, or something was very wrong when it was sold for $2 only 13 months later.

[47] Kate Kelly, *Street Fighters* (Penguin: New York, 2009), p.113. This book tells the story of Bear Stearns, one of the key investment banks on Wall St between the Great Crash of 1929 and its failure in March 2008.

[48] See para.17–26.

[49] [2005] EWHC 830 (Comm).

of lengthy negotiations as to the nature of the complex product which was being created by the bank for Peekay. What began as a "note" became a "deposit", which was at one stage to be "hedged" in US dollars and at another stage not so hedged. Ultimately the Russian banking moratorium meant that this product caused Peekay a large loss. Even the account manager within the bank had not appreciated that the nature of the product had been changed by the bank's financial engineers. It was held that the nature of the product had been misrepresented to the client and that the client company was thus entitled to damages equal to the difference between the actual return on the product and the original investment.[50] No contract was ever reduced to writing; instead the parties were relying on a series of letters and messages which contradicted one another. Having considered some of the types of mistake which may arise in financial markets, we shall turn to the approach which English law takes to mistakes in contracts.

B.   The categories of mistake under English law

Unilateral and common mistake

For the purposes of English contract law it is important to distinguish between cases in which one party to the contract makes a mistake ("unilateral mistake") and those in which both parties make a mistake ("common mistake"). In general terms a common mistake in entering into a transaction will enable that contract to be rescinded[51]; whereas a contract entered into under a unilateral mistake will not be rescinded[52] unless the party who was not operating under that mistake was aware that the other party was so operating.[53] In effect, therefore, it is a mutual failure to generate a meeting of minds which occasions a right to terminate the transaction, and that in relation to a unilateral mistake it is only if that mistake was known to the other party that there will be a right to terminate the transaction. The first question is knowing what is meant by a mistake. In life, we all make mistakes of various kinds at different times, but not all of them have legal consequences.

18–22

Common mistake: mutual mistake

The first category of mistake is a "common mistake" in the form of a mutual misunderstanding where both parties are mistaken as to some legally relevant facts in relation to the contract. This was described as "mutual mistake" by Lord Atkin in *Bell v Lever Brothers*.[54] Ordinarily, this sort of mistake is taken to nullify consent between the parties in the purported creation of a contract between them.

18–23

---

[50] [2005] EWHC 830 (Comm), [97].
[51] *Cundy v Lindsay* (1878) 3 App. Cas 1.
[52] *Riverlate Properties Ltd v Paul* [1975] Ch. 133.
[53] *Webster v Cecil* (1861) 30 Beav 62; *Hartog v Colin & Shields* [1939] 2 All E.R. 566.
[54] [1932] A.C. 161

If this sort of mistake is operative on the minds of the parties in the creation of their contract, then the contract is deemed to be void *ab initio*.[55]

Common mistake: misunderstanding or miscommunication

18–24　The second category of mistake arises where there has been some misunderstanding between the parties, usually due to some breakdown or error in communication, which means that there is no effective agreement between the parties. In this category of mistake, both of the parties are acting under a misapprehension as to the nature of their agreement such that there is no meeting of minds between them. Therefore, this is also a form of common mistake because it is operative on the minds of both parties. This category of mistake is ordinarily taken to negative any consent between the parties. If such a mistake is operative on the parties in the creation of their contract, then the contract is deemed to be void ab initio. However, most mistakes of this type will relate to the interpretation of the contract, and so will tend to be litigated as such: that is, either as to the contents of the original contractual offer or as to the objective interpretation of the terms of the contract. The doctrine of mistake will apply only when there has been a mutual misunderstanding.

18–25　An example of a common mistake of this sort arose in *Raffles v Wichelhaus*[56] in which the parties had contracted for the sale and purchase of cotton but they had intended different ships both called "The Peerless" to carry that cargo.[57] It was found that there was no contract because there had never been a meeting of minds about a key term of the contract: that is, the identity of the ship which would carry the cargo in which they would trade. Such a dispute could revolve in practice around whether or not it was reasonable for the claimant to have formed the misconception it had. For example, if a seller sold a product based on the FTSE-100 and the buyer claimed not to understand that that meant the British FTSE-100 as opposed to another index, then it would not be reasonable for the buyer to be so disingenuous in its claim.

The theoretical basis for avoiding contracts for common mistake

18–26　The theoretical basis for avoiding contracts on the basis of either form of common mistake is that there was never a genuine meeting of minds due to this underlying misconception between both parties. Mistake therefore goes to the question of consent. The categories of common mistake are frequently divided into two, with a distinction being drawn between: common mistake which operates so as to nullify consent, and mistakes in communication which negative consent.[58] To say that consent is nullified means that there was sufficient consent in the first place but that it was erased by the mistake; whereas to say that consent is negatived means that the miscommunication prevented there being consent in

---

[55] *Bell v Lever Brothers* [1932] A.C. 161.

[56] (1864) 2 H & C 906.

[57] It is ironic perhaps that there were two ships which were both considered to be "peerless" by their proud owners.

[58] *Bell v Lever Brothers* [1932] A.C. 161, 224, Lord Atkin.

the first place. So, for example, where the parties both believed incorrectly that a particular security would form part of an index, then their consent is nullified by their common mistake. However, if their traders had communicated with one another in a confused fashion with both traders speaking at odds with one another as to which security was meant, then that would mean there had been a mistake of a sort which prevented there having been any consent between the contracting parties. The legal effect of both kinds of common mistake is the same: the contract is void *ab initio*.[59]

Unilateral mistake

The third category of mistake is "unilateral mistake" where only one party to the transaction is operating on the basis of a mistake, but the counterparty is not. At the simplest level, a unilateral mistake will not justify setting the contract aside at common law. So, for example, if the claimant contended that it had not understood that the FTSE-100 index only included the price of one hundred securities, and not the share price of every security traded on the London Stock Exchange, then that would be the claimant's mistake alone and so not a good ground for terminating the contract. As a simple matter of logic, there would be a contract between the parties, but the claimant would have entered into a binding contract on the basis of its own error and therefore that would not be a good ground for terminating that contract. In that sense, the buyer must beware.

18–27

Beyond those sorts of simple mistake in which the misconception was the claimant's error alone, this can be a complex category. It is suggested that if the counterparty has fraudulently or negligently misled the mistaken party, then that is a matter for the law on misrepresentation which is considered below: clearly, English law will not allow one party to take advantage of its counterparty by deliberately misleading them with a false representation. Otherwise, it will be important to know whether or not the mistake is a legally relevant mistake in any event: because an irrelevant mistake will have no effect on the efficacy of the contract. For example, if one party was mistaken about the identity of the author of *Bleak House* that would not be relevant to its decision to enter into an equity option in London.

18–28

Assuming neither of those things to be the case, the authorities usually divide between mistakes as to the terms of the contract and mistakes as to the identity of the other party. Ordinarily, such a mistake may mean that there was no contract on the terms that the parties had purportedly agreed, but there may still be a contract between them. Much will depend upon the circumstances and, put crudely, whether or not one party seems to be taking advantage of the other.

18–29

So, for example, if a party makes an offer with a mistake as to its terms, and the counterparty is aware of that mistake when it takes advantage of it by accepting the offer, then that unilateral mistake will not prevent there being a contract but the terms of the contract would probably be what the party making the original offer intended them to be. Importantly then, the doctrine of mistake here may go

18–30

---

[59] *Bell v Lever Brothers* [1932] A.C. 161.

to the terms of the contract. This sort of mistake is a not unknown occurrence on trading floors where sharp-eyed investors take advantage of mistakes in offer documents by accepting them before they can be withdrawn. So, for example, where a seller offers a product to a buyer and is aware that the buyer mistakenly assumes that the transaction will be conducted on the same terms on which they have contracted many times before, then it has been held that the contract will be set aside.[60] Similarly then if purchasers of derivatives do so on the basis of a mistake in an offering document when they knew full well that the seller had made a mistake in that document, then the contract would be void. Notably, the common law approach is to find that the contract is void, and not to give effect to the contract in part.[61]

18–31   The following sort of situation arises commonly on trading floors. Suppose that a trader intended to offer a speculative opportunity on which of two indices would produce a greater return on the investment of a notional amount of money, but that the trader made a drafting error whereby the offer document promised that "the investor shall be paid *the full return* on the larger of the two indices" as opposed to (what the trader intended to offer) that "the investor shall be paid *the difference between* the returns on the two indices", where the difference between these two measurements was in the order of US$100 million in total. Suppose then that some professional investors accepted the offer immediately before the mistake was noticed by the trader. It is suggested that the investor should have known of the mistake because of the huge return which it promised and so should be prevented from relying on a contract formed by the acceptance of that offer. The reason for refusing to allow the enforcement of this contract is that it would be unfair to cause the offeror a loss which it never intended to risk and which the investors knew (or, more accurately from the point of proof, which a reasonable investor could be expected to have known) was only offered to them by means of a straightforward mistake.

18–32   However, where this principle would become more difficult would be in different circumstances in which the investors simply made a shrewd profit on a transaction in which, for example, the offeror's traders made an error of judgment in constructing a product in 2007 which opened the offeror up to a risk which in hindsight they would have preferred to avoid: perhaps where the product offered a large return in the event that inter alia the investment bank Lehman Bros would go into insolvency (perhaps in the form of a credit default swap), and the offeror's traders simply failed to anticipate that risk. In this situation there was no straightforward drafting error, but rather the traders simply did not anticipate that in a year's time Lehman Bros would have become bankrupt. This would be different, it is suggested, from the situation in which a trader simply mistakenly failed to amend standard language used in another offer document such that a loss

---

[60] *Hartog v Colin and Shields* [1939] 3 All E.R. 566. In that case, the defendant knew that the claimant had been relying on the parties' previous pattern of dealing in hare skins, and would therefore be prevented from taking advantage of the claimant when the contract at issue was effected on a different basis at a concomitantly poor price for the claimant.

[61] For example, the common law does not give effect to the contract to the extent that the parties would have contracted; nor is the contract merely voidable or capable of being enforced by the claimant. Rather, it is either void or not void.

of US$100 million resulted. The former was an error of judgment but an offer which the offeror nevertheless intended to make at that time; whereas the latter was an offer which the offeror could never have intended to make if it had been brought to its attention. In common with the "officious bystander test", if the offeror had been asked whether they intended to provide for the return on the larger of the two indices as opposed to the difference between those two, then it is likely that they would have rebuked the bystander by saying "of course not"; but this would not have been the case in the former example at the time of creating the contract.

Non est factum

The fourth category of mistake is supplied by the doctrine of *non est factum*. This doctrine provides that where there is a unilateral mistake by a party who signs a document, then that may constitute a good defence to an action for the enforcement of that contract where that party argues that it is "not his deed" on the basis that document was executed due to a fundamental misapprehension as to its nature.[62] Examples would be signing a deed of transfer which the transferor thought would transfer property to one identified person when in fact it transferred that property to someone else;[63] or having the contents of a document falsified by a third party after it had been signed.[64] The doctrine arose most commonly in relation to cases of fraud which induced the claimant into creating the contract.[65]

18–33

C.   The basis of the common law on mistake

The decision of the House of Lords in *Bell v Lever Brothers*[66] remains the leading case on mistake in English law. It is renowned for the fact that the five judges all delivered speeches which failed completely to agree with one another. The most satisfactory judgement was that of Lord Atkin, not least because it spoke to general principle and not simply to the facts of that particular case. In his Lordship's view, the result of a mutual mistake was that:

18–34

> "Whenever it is to be inferred from the terms of the contract or its surrounding circumstances that the consensus has been reached on the basis of a particular contractual assumption, and that assumption is not true, the contract is avoided; i.e. it is void ab initio if the assumption is of present facts and it ceases to find if the assumption is of future fact."[67]

---

[62] On which see *Foster v Mackinnon* (1869) L.R. 4 CP 704; *Saunders v Anglia Building Society* [1971] A.C. 1004; *United Dominions Trust Ltd v Western* [1976] Q.B. 513.

[63] *Saunders v Anglia Building Society* [1971] A.C. 1004.

[64] *United Dominions Trust Ltd v Western* [1976] Q.B. 513.

[65] *Foster v Mackinnon* (1869) LR 4 CP 704; *Saunders v Anglia Building Society* [1971] A.C. 1004; *United Dominions Trust Ltd v Western* [1976] Q.B. 513. But see *Lloyds Bank v Waterhouse* (1991) 10 Tr L.R. 161, in which it was held that if the case involves the making of a misrepresentation or fraud, and if no third party is involved, then it should be treated as a case of misrepresentation.

[66] *Bell v Lever Brothers* [1932] A.C. 161.

[67] *Bell v Lever Brothers* [1932] A.C. 161, 218.

In a passage which made this doctrine sound similar to the doctrine of frustration of contract, his Lordship held that "when the new state of facts makes the contract something fundamentally different in kind from the contract in the original state of facts" then there is an actionable mistake.[68]

18–35   The basis for an action for mistake was summarised in the following terms by Lord Phillips in *The Great Peace*[69]:

> "... The following elements must be present if common mistake is to avoid a contract: (i) there must be a common assumption as to the existence of a state of affairs; (ii) there must be no warranty by either party that that state of affairs exists; (iii) the non-existence of the state of affairs must not be attributable to the fault of either party; (iv) the non-existence of the state of affairs must render contractual performance impossible; (v) the state of affairs may be the existence, or a vital attribute, of the consideration to be provided or circumstances which must subsist if performance of the contractual adventure is to be possible."

Therefore, this modern statement of the doctrine appears to base it primarily on grounds of impossibility which are similar to frustration of contract. As is considered below, many other instances of mistake can be solved by use of the equitable remedy of rectification or by the proper interpretation of the contract on an objective basis.

D.   The requirement that there be an operative mistake

18–36   The mistake must have been operative on the minds of the contracting parties and must have induced them to enter into the contract.[70] Thus, in *Oscar Chess v Williams*,[71] where two parties contracting for the sale of a car in circumstances in which some unknown third party had altered the log book's entry as to the date the car was made, the contract was not rescinded for mistake because neither party had sought to rely on that date in the creation of the contract. Thus any mistake on which a party seeks to rely must be material to the price, commercial viability, or operation of that contract.

E.   Mistakes of fact and mistakes of law

18–37   That parties are entitled to rely on a mistake of law in seeking to rescind their contracts has been upheld by the House of Lords in *Kleinwort Benson v Lincoln CC*.[72] In *Lincoln* a bank sought to recover moneys paid to the respondent local authority under interest rate swap agreements which the House of Lords in *Hazell v Hammersmith & Fulham*[73] had held to be beyond the powers of the local authority and therefore void ab initio. The claim for recovery of payments was based on a contention that those payments had been made under a mistake of law:

---

[68] *Bell v Lever Brothers* [1932] A.C. 161, 217. This was also the approach in *The Great Peace* [2003] Q.B. 679.

[69] [2003] Q.B. 679, [76].

[70] *Bell v Lever Bros* [1932] A.C. 161.

[71] [1957] 1 W.L.R. 370.

[72] [1998] 4 All E.R. 513.

[73] [1992] 2 A.C. 1, [1991] 2 W.L.R. 372, [1991] 1 All E.R. 545.

i.e. the assumption that local authorities had had the capacity to enter into interest rate swaps. Lord Goff, speaking for the majority in *Kleinwort Benson v Lincoln CC*, held there could be restitution of money paid under a mistake of law (thus repealing the long-established common law rule to the contrary). One interesting argument raised by the appeal was whether a mistake of law must be a mistake as to decided case law or legislation, or whether it was sufficient that there was a common perception in a marketplace that the law would assert a particular rule if a pertinent question was ever brought before a court. Thus, it was argued that the swaps market had generally believed that local authorities could enter into swaps agreements. The House of Lords held that payments made under a settled understanding of the law among market participants, which is subsequently departed from by judicial decision, are irrecoverable on grounds of mistake of law.[74]

There remains a large amount of uncertainty as to precisely which factors which will constitute a mistake of law. The very fact that common law and equity develop on a case-by-case basis means that it is impossible to be certain as to the law in any given case. Consequently, it is important to know precisely what types of mistake of law will be permissible in the future but (it is suggested) there is insufficient definitive, detailed judicial guidance at the time of writing.   **18–38**

F.   The inter-action of the doctrine of mistake with other doctrines

What has emerged from the foregoing discussion is that the doctrine of mistake is a very narrow doctrine. It is even narrower if one accepts the removal of the equitable doctrine of mistake by the Court of Appeal in *The Great Peace* as discussed below.[75] This short section discusses how cases involving mistakes in a colloquial sense are frequently argued on other bases.   **18–39**

The relegation of the doctrine of mistake behind the interpretation of contracts

There is a line of authority which suggests that most questions about mistake can be resolved by the proper interpretation of the contract between the parties. It may be that something which the claimant alleges is a mistake is in fact just a condition precedent to the contract, or may be resolved by an implied term of the contract, or may otherwise be resolved by interpreting what the parties' contract must be taken to have meant. So it has been suggested in *Associated Japanese Bank International Ltd v Credit du Nord SA*[76] that it is only if the contract is silent on a particular issue that the doctrine of mistake will come into play at all. Other approaches to the law on mistake have suggested that what contracts ordinarily do is to allocate risks between the parties, and as such a contract will have   **18–40**

---

[74] This decision was followed by the House of Lords in *Deutsche Morgan Grenfell Group Plc v Inland Revenue Commissioners and the Attorney General* [2006] UKHL 49; [2007] S.T.C. 1 in relation to overpayments of advance corporation tax under a mistake of law.
[75] [2003] QB 679.
[76] [1989] 1 W.L.R 255, 268.

allocated the risk that there has been a mistake.[77] The example which is typically given of this sort of allocation of risk is in relation to the sale of goods in which it is usual for the contract to identify which party bears the risk of the goods being damaged in transit and so forth.

The inter-action of mistake, conditions precedent and implied contractual terms

18–41 A condition precedent is a term of such fundamental importance that failure to perform it is said to absolve the non-defaulting party from any obligation to perform the contract.[78] The test for deciding whether any contractual term is a condition precedent rather than a mere warranty is that the term must "[go] to the root of the matter, so that failure to perform it would render the performance of the rest of the contract a thing different in substance from what the defendant had stipulated for".[79] As Blackburn J. held in *Bettini v Gye*[80]:

> "Parties may think some matter, apparently of very little importance, essential; and if they sufficiently express an intention to make the literal fulfilment of such a thing a condition precedent, it will be one . . ."

Furthermore, it is important to ascertain whether or not breach of that term would affect "the substance and foundation of the adventure which the contract is intended to carry out".[81] Typically what is really being argued in a claim revolving around a mistake is that it was really part of the parties' common intention that the circumstances should be *x* when in fact they have transpired to be *y*, and therefore that because the circumstances are *y* there should not be a contract at all. In essence, then, the claimant could be thought of as arguing that in truth there was an implied term of the parties' agreement that the position would be *x*, or, alternatively, that there was a condition precedent that the position would be *x* before the contract could be effective, and not that there was a "mistake" in the *Bell v Lever Bros* sense of that word.

The inter-action of rectification of contracts and mistake

18–42 The equitable remedy of rectification is available to amend the terms of a contract to reflect the true intentions of the contracting parties.[82] Rectification will be available in circumstances of common mistake[83] but will only be available in relation to an unilateral mistake in cases of fraud or similar unconscionable

---

[77] *Amalgamated Investment & Property Current Ltd v John Walker & Sons Ltd* [1977] 1 W.L.R 164.
[78] *Bettini v Gye* (1876) 1 Q.B.D. 183.
[79] *Bettini v Gye* (1876) 1 Q.B.D. 183 at 188; *Graves v Legg* (1854) 9 Exch. 709, 716.
[80] (1875) 1 Q B 183, at 187.
[81] *Bentsen v Taylor, Sons & Co* [1893] 2 Q.B. 274, 281, per Bowen L.J.
[82] *M'Cormack v M'Cormack* (1877) 1 L.R. Ir. 119; *Frederick E. Rose (London) Ltd v William H Pim Jnr & Co Ltd* [1953] 2 Q.B. 450.
[83] *Murray v Parker* (1854) 19 Beav 305; *Mackenzie v Coulson* (1869) L.R. 8 Eq. 368.

behaviour.[84] This remedy of rectification differs from the doctrine of mistake in that the contract is kept in existence, albeit on terms which are considered to reflect the intention of the parties better. The Court of Appeal expressed a limited enthusiasm for the rectification of negotiated commercial agreements in *BP Exploration Co (Libya) Ltd v Hunt*.[85] Nevertheless, the remedy of rectification depends upon the finding of a common mistake in the terms on which the contract was created and requires the claimant to prove that mistake.[86] This remedy is considered in Chapter 20.

The inter-action of mistake and misrepresentation

Lord Atkin gave an example in *Bell v Lever Brothers*[87] of one party selling another an oil painting which both parties mistakenly believed was the work of an old master. In such situation, his Lordship held that the buyer would have no action based on mistake unless there had been a representation or warranty made to it as to the identity of the artist. Therefore, even though there might have been a common mistake that would not necessarily found an action in law. Consequently, a large number of situations in which mistakes have been made by both parties to the contract would nevertheless need to be argued on the basis of misrepresentation. Once the claimant suggests that its misconception was based on a statement made by the defendant then the claim will proceed on the basis of misrepresentation as considered above. Given the many uncertainties as to the basis of the doctrine of mistake, the law on misrepresentation offers a more predictable outcome. In practical terms, in trying to prove common mistake it is necessary to demonstrate that the defendant (who is probably resisting the litigation in part because it stands to take some profit from the transaction) and the claimant were both operating on the basis of the same mistake.

18–43

G. Mistake in equity

The principles of equity provide that a defendant will be prevented from acting unconscionably or that a defendant will be prevented from taking unconscionable advantage of the claimant.[88] So, it has been contended by various judges that equity will intervene so as to prevent a defendant from taking unconscionable advantage of a mistake was made by the claimant. Ordinarily, to render this an *unconscionable* advantage it would be necessary that the defendant was aware of the claimant's mistake.

18–44

The leading case in this context is *Cooper v Phibbs*[89] in which the House of Lords ordered that the equitable remedy of recession would be available in a case

18–45

---

[84] *Whitley v Delaney* [1914] A.C. 132; *Monaghan CC v Vaughan* [1948] I.R. 306; *A. Roberts & Co Ltd v Leicestershire CC* [1961] Ch. 555; *Thomas Bates & Son Ltd v Wyndham's (Lingerie) Ltd* [1981] 1 All E.R. 1077.

[85] [1983] 2 A.C. 352.

[86] It should be remembered that meeting the standard of proof for this equitable remedy is difficult.

[87] [1932] A.C. 161.

[88] See Hudson, *Equity & Trusts*, 1.1; *Earl of Oxford's Case* (1615) 1 Ch Rep 1.

[89] (1867) L.R. 2 HL 149.

of common mistake.[90] In *Cooper v Phibbs*[91] parties to a lease had created the lease agreement on the mistaken assumption that the purported lessee did not already have an equitable interest in the demised property. On discovering the existence of this equitable interest, the lessee sought to rescind the lease contract on the ground that both parties to it had been operating under a common mistake as to the lessee's property rights. The House of Lords held that the contract could be rescinded on the basis of the parties' common mistake.

18–46   Purportedly following this approach, the judgment of Denning L.J. in *Solle v Butcher*[92] is the clearest modern statement of this doctrine, which was rejected by the Court of Appeal in *Great Peace Shipping*.[93] In a well-known passage, Denning L.J. held the following, in relation to his understanding of the decision of the House of Lords in *Bell v Lever Brothers*, explaining the distinction between contracts which, in his Lordship's opinion, would be *void* at common law and then contracts which would be *voidable* in equity[94]:

> "Let me first consider mistakes which render a contract a nullity. ... once a contract has been made, that is to say, once the parties, whatever their inmost states of mind, after all outward appearances agreed with sufficient certainty in the same terms on the same subject matter, then the contract is good unless and until it is set aside for the failure of some condition on which the existence of the contract depends, or for fraud, or on some equitable ground. Neither party can rely on his own mistake to say it was a nullity from the beginning, no matter that it was a mistake which to his mind was fundamental, and no matter that the other party knew that he was under a mistake.
>
> Let me consider mistakes which render a contract avoidable, that is, liable to be set aside on some equitable ground. Whilst presupposing that a contract was good at all, or at any rate not void, the court of equity would often relieve a party from the consequences of his own mistake, so long as it could do so without injustice to third parties. The court, it was said, had power to set aside the contract whenever it was of opinion that it was unconscientious for the other party to avail himself of the legal advantage which he had obtained.[95] ... It is now clear that a contract will be set aside if the mistake of the one party has been induced by a material misrepresentation of the other, even though it was not fraudulent or fundamental; or if one party, knowing that the other is mistaken about the terms of the offer, or the identity of the person by whom it is made, lets him remain under his delusion and concludes a contract on the mistake in terms instead of pointing out the mistake.
>
> A contract is also liable in equity to be set aside if the parties were under a common misapprehension either as to facts or as to their relative and respective rights, provided that the misapprehension was fundamental and that the party seeking to set it aside was not himself at fault.[96]"

In essence, Denning L.J. was of the view that if the misapprehension was fundamental to the parties' agreement and that the party seeking to set aside the agreement was not personally at fault, then the contract could be set aside in equity. Equity would not hold that the contract was void *ab initio*, but rather that it was voidable; whereas the common law would find a contract based on common mistake of void *ab initio*, but would not avoid a contract based on a unilateral mistake.

---

[90] See also *Earl of Beauchamp v Winn* (1873) L.R. 6 HL 223, 233.
[91] (1867) L.R. 2 HL 149.
[92] [1950] K.B. 671.
[93] [2003] Q.B. 679.
[94] [1950] K.B. 671, 691–693.
[95] *Torrence v Bolton* (1872) L.R. 8 Ch 118, 124.
[96] *Lansdown v Lansdown* (1730) Mos 364, 2 Jac & W 205.

The Court of Appeal (in the judgment of Lord Phillips) in *Great Peace Shipping*,[97] however, was clearly of the view that this was an undesirable development in equity. Denning L.J. had based his judgement in part on *Smith v Hughes*,[98] which was not directly on point in this context. The clear preference of Lord Phillips was to limit the doctrine of mistake to the common law categories. His judgment involved a close reading of the various cases referred to by Denning L.J. which sought to distinguish or limit each one to its particular circumstances.

18–47

Latterly, however, Lord Nicholls delivering judgement in the House of Lords in *Bank of Credit and Commerce International SA v Ali (No.1)*[99] lent support to the idea of equity having a role to play in this context. In a section in his Lordship's judgement headed "sharp practice", he made reference to the situation in which one party knew of the other party's mistake (in that case seeking a release without disclosing the existence of a claim) which his Lordship considered to be "unacceptable sharp practice".[100] This suggests that the courts should intervene so as to prevent such sharp practice. An equitable doctrine of mistake is ideally suited to doing this.

18–48

3. MISREPRESENTATION

A. The principles relating to misrepresentation in contract law

This section considers the principles dealing with misrepresentation in contract law; whereas Chapter 24 deals with fraudulent misrepresentation in tort, and Chapter 25 deals with negligent misrepresentation in tort. The Misrepresentation Act 1967 provides the recipient of a representation ("the representee") with a right to rescind a contract if a fraudulent misrepresentation was made to her which induced her to enter into the contract; whereas if the representation was negligent or innocent, then the court has a discretion under that Act to award the representee damages in lieu of rescission.[101] The representor must intend that the representee will rely on the representation,[102] and the representee's reliance on that representation must have been reasonable. For example, the representee must not have had actual knowledge that the representation was false. The representation must therefore have played some meaningful part in inducing the representee's acquisition of the financial instrument in question. There is a presumption that a material misrepresentation will have induced the representee's entry into the contract.[103]

18–49

[97] [2003] Q.B. 679.
[98] (1871) L.R. 6 QB 597.
[99] [2002] 1 AC 251.
[100] [2002] 1 A.C. 251, at [32].
[101] See generally *Chitty on Contracts*, para.6–001 et seq.
[102] See para.25–10.
[103] e.g. *Smith v Chadwick* (1884) 9 App. Cas. 187.

B. Representations of fact and of opinion

18–50   It is common for marketing material in relation to financial instruments to make representations as to the attractiveness of the investment involved, of the market to which it relates, and to the future prospects of the entire enterprise. The question is whether the law on misrepresentation will apply only to misrepresentations of hard fact or whether more speculative comments as to future events will also found liability. A representation must be substantially false or incorrect to become a misrepresentation.[104] A misrepresentation in contract law will generally be limited to representations of fact and therefore will not usually extend to statements of opinion.[105] Thus, ordinarily, there will be a misrepresentation if there was a statement in a prospectus issued by a company which was seeking investors in a new issue of shares which asserted as a fact that "the company has earned profits of £10 million from the sale of widgets in Ruritania in the last financial year" when that was not the case. It would not seem to apply, however, to a statement of opinion in the same prospectus such as "the company has the strongest reputation of all suppliers of widgets in Ruritania" even if the reputation of the company seems to be poor. The latter statement is phrased as a statement of opinion and therefore (on a literal interpretation of it) it could be said not to constitute a misrepresentation in contract law terms. Interestingly, this statement of opinion might be the sort of ambiguous misstatement which might found liability in tort, as considered in Chapter 25. However, if the opinion was not honestly held—for example, because the company's management knew that it was currently defending a class action law suit brought by all of its customers for widgets in Ruritania alleging that the products were defective and the company's sale techniques were dishonest—then such a statement of opinion which is not honestly held will be treated as a statement of fact,[106] and as such may constitute a misrepresentation.[107]

C. Implied representations

18–51   Marketing materials and other documents in relation to financial instruments may be made by people who are reluctant to state facts baldly for fear of making a mistake, and therefore a form of words may be hit upon which suggests that such-and-such is the case without actually saying it explicitly. Will such suggestions constitute actionable misrepresentations if the inferences to which they lead turn out to be false? Suppose that a prospectus for the issue of shares in an advertising agency contained a photograph of the creative department which devised all of the money-making ideas with the caption: "Here is our fantastic creative team who are the foundation of our success, who hold the key to our future, and who are committed to this business in perpetuity". The inference would be that that creative team is expected to be with the advertising agency in the future. That is impliedly represented by the caption. Implied representations,

---

[104] See, e.g. *Avon Insurance v Swire* [2000] 1 All E.R. (Comm) 573.
[105] *Hummingbird Motors Ltd v Hobbs* [1986] R.T.R. 276.
[106] *Smith v Land and House Property Corp* (1884) 28 Ch.D. 7.
[107] *Esso Petroleum Co v Mardon* [1976] Q.B. 801.

which are not actually stated explicitly but which are intended to create an impression in the representee's mind, will be treated as representations. So, suggesting that the creative genius behind a company's activities will remain with the company, when in fact it is known that that person is intending to resign from the company, will be a representation[108] which could be acted on if incorrect. The question is what interpretation a reasonable person would have put on any representation in any case.[109]

D.   Omission of information

The further question arises: will the omission of information found liability for misrepresentation in the same way as an incorrect statement? The cases have moved in different directions in relation to the omission of information. In *Percival v Wright*[110] a seller of shares withheld inside information from the buyer of those shares when he knew that that information would affect the future value of the shares when it became known. The shares indeed fell in value and the buyer sued on the basis of misrepresentation. It was found that the seller had not made a misrepresentation by withholding that inside information. (Under modern prospectus law it is likely that such information could not have been concealed, depending upon clearance having been given to pass on the information).[111]

18–52

It is suggested that in a circumstance in which the seller knows such information and yet cannot reveal it for regulatory reasons, then that seller ought not in good conscience to go ahead with the sale. If the buyer suffers loss as a result of the failure to pass on the information, then the seller ought to be liable for the buyer's loss whether or not the information was confidential or inside information. Otherwise, the seller is effectively exploiting the inside information to cause the buyer loss. Ordinarily, in circumstances in which the omission is intended to conceal facts from potential investors then it is suggested that that would constitute a misrepresentation.[112] Similarly, when information is withheld with the intention of misrepresenting the condition of the financial instrument which is being sold, then that will constitute a misrepresentation.[113] In this vein, the principle was established in *Oakes v Turquand*[114] that a misrepresentation will have been made if the representor made a statement which omitted information with the result that it created a false or a misleading impression as to the true position in the buyer's mind.

18–53

---

[108]   *Spice Girls Ltd v Aprilia World Service BV, The Times*, April 5, 2000.
[109]   *Geest Plc v Fyffes Plc* [1999] 1 All E.R. (Comm.) 672.
[110]   [1902] 2 Ch. 421.
[111]   See para.36–01.
[112]   See *Chitty on Contracts*, para.6–015.
[113]   See *Goldsmith v Rodger* [1962] 2 Lloyd's Rep. 249.
[114]   (1867) L.R. 2 H.L. 325; *Barwick v English Joint Stock Bank* (1867) L.R. 2 Ex. 259.

E. Fraudulent misrepresentation under contract law

18–54   A fraudulent misrepresentation is made, as set out in *Derry v Peek*,[115] when the seller of a financial instrument made a false representation "knowingly . . . without belief in its truth, or recklessly, careless whether it be true or false".[116] The test is subjective, requiring that the seller did not honestly believe the statement to be true according to its meaning as understood by the seller, albeit erroneously, at the time when the statement was made.[117] So, in *Niru Battery Manufacturing Co v Milestone Trading Ltd*[118] it was held that no claim lay for fraud in circumstances in which an account officer of the defendant bank honestly, if naively, arranged presentation of a letter of credit even though the goods involved had not been delivered. It has been held that a misrepresentation as to the purpose for which debentures were issued will similarly found liability, thus extending the scope of liability to statements as to future intention.[119] More generally predictions as to the future which do not disclose some existing intention to deceive will not constitute an actionable misrepresentation: for example where a person makes a promise to marry in the future but subsequently changes her mind.[120] The liability for fraud in tort is considered in detail in Chapter 24. Questions as to causation and so forth in relation to fraudulent misrepresentation are considered in that discussion.

F. Negligent misrepresentation under contract law

18–55   A negligent misrepresentation is one which is made carelessly or without reasonable grounds for believing that it was true. The manner of demonstrating the existence of a duty of care in relation to a negligent misrepresentation is set out in Chapter 25 in relation to the tortious doctrine in *Hedley Byrne v Heller*.[121] The quantum of damages in relation to negligent misrepresentation under contract law is set out in s.2(1) of the Misrepresentation Act 1967. The measure of damages for fraudulent misrepresentation is an amount sufficient to put the representee in the position which he would have been in had the misrepresentation not been made.[122]

---

[115] (1889) 14 App. Cas. 337.

[116] *Derry v Peek* (1889) 14 App. Cas. 337, 376, per Lord Herschell.

[117] *Akerhielm v De Mare* [1959] A.C. 789, PC.

[118] [2004] Q.B. 985.

[119] *Edgington v Fitzmaurice* (1885) 29 Ch.D 459.

[120] *Wales v Wadham* [1977] 1 W.L.R. 199.

[121] [1964] A.C. 465. See para.23–34.

[122] *Doyle v Olby (Ironmongers) Ltd* [1969] 2 Q.B. 158. It is not a measure of damages to put the representee in the position he would have been in had the representation been true: see *Chitty on Contracts*, para.6–049.

G. Rescission

The Misrepresentation Act 1967 provides the recipient of a representation ("the representee") with a right to rescind a contract if a fraudulent misrepresentation was made to him which induced him to enter into the contract; whereas if the representation was negligent or innocent, then the court has a discretion under that Act to award the representee damages in lieu of rescission.[123] The availability of rescission is considered in Chapter 20.

18–56

H. The efficacy of contracts under s.20 FSMA 2000

Section 20(2) of the FSMA 2000 provides that:

18–57

> "The contravention [of the requirement of authorisation under s.19] does not . . .
> (b)   make any transaction void or unenforceable . . ."

Importantly, therefore, it is not open to a person to argue that having failed to acquire authorisation under s.19 of the FSMA 2000 automatically makes any contract void. Rather, that contract may still be enforceable depending on the position under ordinary contract law. Consequently, the non-defaulting party may seek to enforce its rights under that contract or to seek damages in the manner discussed in Chapter 20.[124] The ramifications of s.20, and the power to enforce a contract further to s.28(3) of the FSMA 2000, were considered in Chapter 9.

5. CATEGORIES OF CONTRACT WHICH WILL BE VOID

A. Gaming and wagering

For reasons of public policy, gaming, betting and wagering contracts are null and void under private law.[125] No amount purportedly won on a gaming or wagering contract is recoverable either at law or in equity.[126] Gaming is regulated under the Gambling Act 2005. That Act requires any person who provides facilities used for the purposes of gambling to be licensed so to do.[127] If a person who provides facilities for gambling is not so licensed, then that person commits an offence.

18–58

---

[123] See generally *Chitty on Contracts*, para.6–001 et seq.

[124] See generally, *Phoenix General Insurance Co of Greece SA v Halvanon Insurance Co Ltd* [1988] 1 Q.B. 216 for the equivalent position under the old insurance law; and see also *Re Cavalier Insurance Co Ltd* [1989] 2 Lloyds Rep. 430; and *Box, Brown and Jacobs v Barclays Bank* [1998] Lloyds Rep. Bank 185 where an illegal deposit contract was nevertheless held to be valid in private law.

[125] Gaming Act 1845 s.18: "All contracts or agreements, whether by parole or in writing, by way of gaming or wagering, shall be null and void . . . no sum shall be brought or maintained in any court of law and equity for recovering any sum of money or valuable thing alleged to be won upon a wager . . .". See generally Treitel, "Gaming and Wagering", *Chitty on Contracts*, Guest et al (ed.), 28th edn (London: Sweet & Maxwell), Ch.38.

[126] Treitel, "Gaming and Wagering", Ch.38. Similarly agents are not entitled to recover sums from principals under such arrangements: Gaming Act 1892 s.1, reversing, inter alia, *Read v Anderson* (1884) 13 Q.B.D. 509.

[127] Gambling Act 2005 s.33.

Gaming under the 2005 Act includes "playing a game of chance for a prize", betting ("where something is staked to be lost or won on the result of a doubtful issue")[128] or a lottery.[129] With the development of new speculative, financial products, the question always arises whether or not those products are gaming or wagering contracts such that they would not be legally enforceable. The reason why speculative financial products are frequently claimed to be gaming or wagering contracts is that the amount payable under such a transaction involves taking a bet on the movement of some market price index. As this situation was described by Hawkins J.

> ". . . two persons, professing to hold opposite views touching the issue of a future uncertain event, mutually agree that, dependent upon the determination of that event, one shall win from the other . . . a sum of money".[130]

That is a definition of gaming, but it could equally well describe the parties' motivations in a speculative foreign exchange transaction or a cash-settled share option. The Gambling Act 2005 requires any person who provides facilities used for the purposes of gambling to be licensed so to do.[131] If a person who provides facilities for gambling is not so licensed, then that person commits an offence. As mentioned above, gambling in this context includes "playing a game of chance for a prize", betting ("where something is staked to be lost or won on the result of a doubtful issue"[132]) or a lottery.

18–59   Under the Financial Services and Markets Act 2000, contracts falling within s.412 of that Act are not "void or unenforceable because of s.18 of the Gaming Act 1845".[133] The definition of contracts which are covered by the 2000 Act are defined in the following terms[134]:

> "This section applies to a contract if—
> (a)   it is entered into by either or each party by way of business;
> (b)   the entering into or performance of it by either party constitutes an activity of a specified kind or one which falls within a specified class of activity; and
> (c)   it related to an investment of a specified kind or one which falls within a specified class of investment."

Therefore, it is required that all of the preceding three requirements must be satisfied. It is suggested that a contract will be entered into "by way of business" where the selling of the financial derivative is part of one of the parties' business activities. That will encompass financial derivatives even where they are entered into for speculative purposes because, it is suggested, all clients who are not private investors will be acting by way of business and the sellers of financial

---

[128] *Attorney General v Luncheon & Sports Club Ltd* [1929] A.C. 400, 406, per Lord Dunedin.
[129] Issues relating to fraudulent payments made through bank accounts by means of cheques dishonestly tendered within the context of the predecessor legislation were considered in *AIC Ltd v ITS Testing Services Ltd* [2006] EWCA Civ. 1601; *Grosvenor Casinos Ltd v National Bank of Abu Dhabi* [2008] 2 Lloyd's Rep. 1, [2008] Bus. L.R D95.
[130] *Carlill v The Carbolic Smoke Ball Company* [1892] 2 Q.B. 484, 490, per Hawkins J.
[131] Gambling Act 2005 s.33.
[132] *Attorney General v Luncheon & Sports Club Ltd* [1929] A.C. 400, 406, per Lord Dunedin.
[133] Financial Services and Markets Act 2000 s.412(1).
[134] Financial Services and Markets Act 2000 s.412(2).

derivatives will be acting in the business of selling such products. In *Morgan Grenfell v Welwyn Hatfield DC*,[135] Hobhouse J. held that interest rate swaps were not gaming contracts because they fell within s.63 of the now-repealed Financial Services Act 1986 on the basis that the transaction had a genuine commercial purpose. Alternatively, it will be sufficient that there was a genuine intention to make a profit or to avoid a loss.[136]

The question remains then: what if there was wagering as part of the transaction? Is it still possible that the transaction could be found to be a wagering contract? As Hobhouse J. has held:

> "[i]f there was an element of wagering in what [the parties] did, it was merely a subordinate element and was not the substance of the transaction and does not affect the validity and enforceability of the transaction."[137]

Therefore, it is suggested that a contract will not be a gaming contract if its principal purpose is not gaming.

Where the transaction serves some genuine commercial end other than speculation or where the transaction results in the physical delivery of a commodity or a security or whatever, then it is less likely that the transaction will be assumed to be a gaming or wagering contract because it will be assumed that the receiving party had a genuine intention to take title in those physically delivered assets.[138] Where the parties have an election between physical and cash settlement it would be necessary to demonstrate a genuine intention to take delivery of the underlying assets as part of some commercial purpose and that the right to take delivery was not merely a sham.[139]

B. Financial instruments and insurance contracts

If a financial instrument were construed to be an insurance contract, then the seller of that contract would commit a criminal offence if not registered as an insurance company[140] or if not acting in the course of authorised banking business.[141] Therefore, it is important to know whether or not any contract would be construed to be an insurance contract. This issue has been particularly significant in relation to credit derivatives which, broadly-speaking, pay out an amount to the buyer if an underlying product, usually a bond, fails to pay out an obligation, such as the coupon payments on a bond. The issue in relation to credit derivatives is discussed in Chapter 40.[142] The definition of what constitutes

18–60

18–61

18–62

---

[135] [1995] 1 All E.R. 1.

[136] Financial Services Act 1986 Sch.1, para.9, being one of the approaches adopted in *City Index v Leslie* [1992] 1 Q.B. 98, 110, per McCowan L.J.

[137] *Morgan Grenfell v Welwyn Hatfield DC* [1995] 1 All E.R. 9.

[138] *City Index v Leslie* [1992] 1 Q.B. 98, 112. See also James, *The Law of Derivatives* (London: Lloyds of London Press, 1999), p.24; and *Spreadex Ltd v Battu* [2005] EWCA Civ. 855.

[139] *Universal Stock Exchange v Strachan* [1896] A.C. 166; *Garnac Grain v Faure* [1966] 1 Q.B. 650; *Libyan Arab Foreign Bank v Bankers Trust Co* [1989] Q.B. 728, 764, per Kerr J.

[140] Insurance Companies Act 1982 s.2(1) and 14.

[141] Insurance Companies Act 1982 s.2(4).

[142] See para.40–49.

"insurance business" is not set out in detail in the legislation itself and so must be divined from the case law. As a general rule of thumb, it is less important which labels the parties attach to their transaction[143] than to establish the true nature of the transaction.[144] As to the essence of the activity which might attract the label of "insurance business" that has been identified as being connected with "first, the negotiation and conclusion of contracts and, secondly, the execution of those contracts by, in particular, paying claims".[145] On this basis one could be taken to conduct insurance business simply by negotiating or touting for insurance business without actually concluding contracts.[146]

6. CONTRACTS PERFORMED THROUGH AGENTS

A. Introduction

18–63   Financial transactions are frequently contracted through intermediaries, are always signed by two or more human beings on behalf of the parties, and are frequently entered into by entities whose financial backers, whose identity, or the level of whose support may be unknown to their counterparty.[147] This section is concerned with the common and difficult problem which arises in all of these contexts in financial markets: that of agency. In essence the problem is this: if an agent commits some wrong or improvidently purports to execute a transaction which is beyond her authority, will the contract be enforceable? The problems related to agents can arise in a number of ways. At the simplest level when a corporate officer signs a contract on behalf of his or her employer, that person is always acting as an agent of the employer and so raises questions as to their ability to bind the employer to the transaction. Further, suppose that a financial institution is contracting with an agent on behalf of a principal, such as a large corporate body which is using an intermediary solely to assist it with its complex financial transactions, when might that transaction be ineffective?[148]

18–64   There may be questions as to the authority of the agent—whether an ordinary employee or a financial intermediary—to bind the principal to that agreement. If a third party is dealing with the agent, it will ordinarily not be able to see the contract between the principal and the agent, and so cannot know the extent of the agent's powers. Briefly put, it is impossible for the counterparty to know whether or not the agent is purporting to bind its principal to types of transaction to which the principal had not agreed to become bound. Similarly, if the principal

---

[143] *Hampton v Toxteth Co-operative Provident Society, Ltd* [1915] 1 Ch. 721.

[144] *Prudential Insurance Company v IRC* [1904] 2 K.B. 658; *Fuji Finance Inc v Aetna Life Insurance Co Ltd* [1995] Ch. 122.

[145] Legh-Jones, Longmore, Birds, Owen (eds), *MacGillivray on Insurance Law* (London: Sweet & Maxwell, 1997), p.933; *R. v Wilson* [1997] 1 W.L.R. 1247.

[146] Lowry and Rawlings, *Insurance Law: doctrine and principles* (Oxford: Hart, 1999), p.355; *Scher and Ackman v Policyholders' Protection Board* [1993] 3 All E.R. 408; *R. v Wilson* [1997] 1 W.L.R. 1247.

[147] Elements of this discussion are culled from A. Hudson, *The Law on Financial Derivatives*.

[148] Sometimes very well known or very, very large investment funds may wish to maintain their secrecy and to conceal their financial transactions, and therefore may act through agents so as to conceal their own identity.

seeks to repudiate the contract, it will be important to know whether or not the principal can be deemed to have authorised the transaction and to what extent the principal will bear liability for any consequent loss suffered by the counterparty. In such situations it is clearly important to know how to effect such a contract, how to comply with the appropriate financial regulation and also how to create effective credit support structures. This section considers how transactions with agents may and may not be given effect.

B. Authority to act on behalf of another

An outline of the law of agency

The law of agency arises in general principles of the law of contract being a contract between a principal and its agent. While the law of agency is built on the common law of contract it has also been supplemented in relation to commercial agents by an EU directive[149] identifying who acts on behalf of a principal in the sale of goods.[150] The law of agency has two aspects: the first is the relationship between the principal and agent themselves (the internal aspect) and the second is the relationship between the agent and the third parties with whom the agent acts for the principal (the external aspect).

18–65

There is no particular formality necessary to constitute someone an agent,[151] except in relation to land.[152] However, given that many financial contracts are entered into in the form of a deed,[153] it is important to note that such an agent is also required to be appointed by deed[154] unless the financial contract by deed is itself executed in the presence of the principal.[155] It is possible to imply a contract of agency from the behaviour of the principal and the agent[156] although it is suggested that it would be rare in financial markets for parties to act one on behalf of another without a contract to that effect, particularly in the context of the conduct of business code introduced by the Financial Services and Markets Act 2000.[157] The one context in which this may become important is in contexts in which an agent has frequently acted of behalf of a principal in previous transactions but has no express contractual authorisation for a particular transaction which, perhaps, loses money for the principal: in such a situation the former pattern of transacting between principal, agent and counterparty may enable the counterparty to show that it was reasonable for it to believe that the agent was able to bind the principal again[158] perhaps where the principal knew

18–66

---

[149] Commercial Agents (Council Directive) Regulations 1993 (SI 1993/3053): cf. SI 1993/3173 and SI 1998/2868.

[150] Principally, in the context of derivatives, in relation to physically settled commodities transactions.

[151] *Heard v Pilley* (1869) 4 Ch. App. 548.

[152] Law of Property Act 1925 s.53.

[153] Law of Property (Miscellaneous Provisions) Act 1989 s.1.

[154] *Berkeley v Hardy* (1826) 5 B. & C. 355.

[155] *Ball v Dunsterville* (1791) 4 Term Rep. 313.

[156] *Garnac Grain Co Inc v HMF Faure and Fairclough Ltd* [1968] A.C. 1130.

[157] See para.10–01.

[158] *Pole v Leask* (1863) 33 L.J. 155.

that the agent was so acting but failed to warn the counterparty.[159] This question of the external authority of the agent is considered below.

Internal authority—liability between principal and agent

18–67 The first question is that of the liability of principal and agent between one another. In general terms, the liabilities of the principal and the agent will be dependent upon the terms of the agency agreement between them on the ordinary principles of the law of contract. Whereas 19th century cases were prepared to allow agents some largesse in interpreting the terms of their agency,[160] more recent cases have emphasised the possibility of communications technology enabling agents to establish the detail of their authority.[161] Therefore, it would be difficult for an agent to argue that a failure in the performance of its duties should be excused on the basis that it did not understand the precise nature of its obligations.

External authority—liability between agent and third party

18–68 The most significant question in this context relates to the doctrine of "ostensible authority": that is, the circumstances in which an agent appears to have authority from the actions of its principal and itself, such that one can assume that it has the requisite authority. Clearly, the authority which an agent is granted by its principal is a matter of private contract between agent and principal and therefore will not be known to any third party contracting with the agent as a matter of fact. Prudent practice on the part of the counterparty would be to insist on disclosure of the agency agreement to satisfy itself as to the extent of the agent's powers. As a matter of contract theory the principal would be entitled to repudiate any action of its agent which overreached its agency. However, the doctrine of ostensible authority provides that a counterparty would be able to enforce any contract entered into with the agent in circumstances in which the principal in some way represented to the counterparty that the agent had authority to act in the way that it did.[162] This doctrine has been explained as being a form of estoppel: effectively estopping the principal from reneging on an agreement entered into by its agent in circumstances in which the counterparty was reasonably entitled to rely on the agent's ostensible authority.[163] Therefore, if a financial institution operated its business so that Alf appeared to be in charge of a particular activity on its premises, a counterparty would be entitled to rely on an agreement entered into with Alf as being binding on that financial institution.[164]

18–69 What is more difficult is to decide whether or not an officer of a bank will have the ostensible authority to bind that bank, for example by purporting to sign a

---

[159] *Burnside v Dayrell* (1849) 3 Exch. 224.
[160] *Ireland v Livingston* (1872) L.R. 5 H.L. 395.
[161] *Woodhouse A.C. Israel Cocoa Ltd SA v Nigerian Produce Marketing Co Ltd* [1972] A.C. 741; *European Asian Bank AG v Punjab and Sind Bank (No.2)* [1983] 1 W.L.R. 642.
[162] *Freeman & Lockyer v Buckhurst Park Properties (Mangal) Ltd* [1964] 2 Q.B. 480.
[163] *Rama Corporation Ltd v Proved Tin and General Investments Ltd* [1952] 2 Q.B. 147.
[164] See, e.g. *Barrett v Deere* (1828) Mood & M.200.

contract on its behalf. The authorities are not entirely in agreement. In one decided case, an employee of a bank has been held to have had his actual authority enlarged when a customer reasonably believed that that person had the authority to enter into contracts technically outwith his actual authority. He had authorised loans to the customer when writing letters to that customer suggesting that he had such authority although that was unsubstantiated by any other officer of the bank.[165]

Contrariwise, the Court of Appeal has held that in general terms an officer of a bank cannot act outwith his authority nor make representations outwith that authority.[166] In that case, though, it was held that a counterparty may rely on that officer's signature on the basis that the officer in question had suggested that he did have the authority to enter into that contract when in fact he did not. On those facts, the Court of Appeal was both mindful of the general principle that one should not go outside one's authority, and yet aware of the fact that if someone has actual authority to enter into contracts of one kind it may not be obvious to third parties that that officer's authority precludes him from entering into other types of contract when the officer himself suggests that he can do so. **18–70**

What is important is that the representation as to the agent's authority must be made by the principal.[167] However, the difficulty remains that it may be the officer herself who makes the representation, purportedly on behalf of her principal, that she has the authority to do what she is attempting to do.[168] This returns us to the question: can the counterparty rely on that agent's assertion that it has the authority so to act? In essence, it is suggested that this issue would appear to resolve itself in the question whether or not the counterparty could be said to have acted reasonably in supposing that the agent had the authority claimed. An example of this situation might be in relation to an employee of a derivatives counterparty who had executed derivatives contracts on behalf of her employer on a number of occasions in the past on which those contracts had been honoured and performed without comment by her employer: in such a context, it is suggested that it would be reasonable for a counterparty to rely on that employee's assertion of her own authority to act on behalf of her employer as its principal given that the employer had honoured those transactions in that past. **18–71**

Nevertheless, the more prudent course of action for a market counterparty would be to procure documentary evidence—typically in the form of a decision of the board of directors under the entity's constitution—expressing formally the agent's ability to act. It is suggested that a counterparty in possession of such documentation ought not to be able to rely on ostensible authority where it has **18–72**

---

[165] *First Energy (UK) Ltd v Hungarian International Bank Ltd* [1993] 2 Lloyd's Rep. 194.
[166] *Egyptian International Foreign Trade Co v Soplex Wholesale Supplies Ltd (The Raffaella)* [1985] 2 Lloyd's Rep. 36.
[167] *AG for Ceylon v Silva* [1953] A.C. 461.
[168] In general terms, the authority to make representations on behalf of the principal will generally be taken to equate to authority to claim authority for oneself: *British Thomson-Houston Co Ltd v Federated European Bank Ltd* [1932] 2 K.B. 176. cf. *United Bank of Kuwait v Hammond* [1988] 1 W.L.R. 1051, where it was suggested that one cannot grant oneself an authority which one does not have; also *Suncorp Insurance and Finance v Milano Assuricurazioni SpA* [1993] 2 Lloyd's Rep. 225, 232, per Waller J.

notice of the extent of the agent's authority. Furthermore, in line with contract law theory the more attractive approach generally might be to accept that if the principal has expressly limited its agent's authority, then that agent ought not to be able unilaterally to extend that actual authority.[169] The position on the decided case law is therefore in an equivocal state.

C. LIABILITY OF THE PRINCIPAL AND OF THE AGENT TO THE COUNTERPARTY IN CONTRACT

18–73   Under the principles of the law of agency the agent creates a contractual nexus between the counterparty and its own principal, and therefore the principal will take both the benefits and the burdens associated with the law of contract in relation to that agreement.[170] The counterparty is therefore, in effect, contracting directly with the principal, subject to what is said below about the extent of ostensible authority.[171] The agent is, in general terms, equally liable under the terms of the contract, unless the contract expressly excludes the agent's own liability.[172] Exclusion of liability may be impossible where the agent's behaviour estops it from denying its liability under the contract: this is more likely in cases of undisclosed principals where the counterparty is led to believe itself to be contracting solely with the agent.[173] So, if an agent enters into a deed not expressed as being on behalf of another person, the agent will itself be liable under that deed.[174] Otherwise the agent's liability on instruments such as cheques, bills of exchange or promissory notes will only arise if the agent signs such an instrument.[175]

18–74   The principal may choose, of course, to ratify the acts of its agent: for example if the agent had executed a contract which created an unexpected profit for the principal.[176] Alternatively, vicarious liability may apply to principals for the acts of agents especially in relation to fraud[177]; and will apply to employers where torts are committed by employees (who are agents).[178] The appropriate test is usually one of the extent and nature of the control exercised by the principal over

---

[169] *United Bank of Kuwait v Hammond* [1988] 1 W.L.R. 1051, 1066, per Lord Donaldson M.R. This approach would put the onus on the counterparty to investigate fully the agent's power to sign on behalf of its principal. It is suggested that this would not be an impossible burden for financial institutions with their documentation, compliance, credit and legal departments.

[170] *Duke of Norfolk v Worthy* (1808) 1 Camp. 337; *Siu Yin Kwan v Eastern Insurance Co Ltd* [1994] 2 W.L.R. 370.

[171] See above.

[172] *Yeung Kai Yeung v Hong Kong and Shanghai Banking Corporation* [1981] A.C. 787, 795, per Lord Scarman.

[173] *Pacol v Trade Lines Ltd (The Henrik Sif)* [1982] 1 Lloyd's Rep. 456; *Arctic Shipping Co Ltd v Mobilia A.B. (The Tatra)* [1990] 2 Lloyd's Rep. 51.

[174] *Appleton v Binks* (1804) 5 East 148; *Chapman v Smith* [1907] 2 Ch. 97.

[175] Bills of Exchange Act 1882 ss. 89(1), 91(1).

[176] *Bolton Partners v Lambert* (1889) 41 Ch.D. 295.

[177] *Colonial Mutual Life Assurance Society Ltd v Producers and Citizens Assurance Co of Australia* (1931) 46 C.L.R. 41. See also, below *Houldsworth v City of Glasgow Bank* (1880) 5 App. Cas. 317, 326, per Lord Selbourne; and *Lloyd v Grace, Smith & Co* [1912] A.C. 716, 734, per Lord Macnaghten. cf. *Ellis v Sheffield Gas Consumers Co* (1853) 2 E. & B. 767.

[178] *Hutchinson v The York, Newcastle and Berwick Rly* (1850) 5 Exch. 343.

the agent in such a context.[179] What is important in the context of vicarious liability relating to agents who are not employees is the need to show that they were acting within the scope of their authority.[180] So, where an estate agent made fraudulent statements to a potential buyer of land, liability would attach to the seller only if the agent were authorised to make the statements which had been made.[181] Similarly, in the financial context it would be necessary to show that the employer had authorised a trader to make statements which were fraudulent misrepresentations on the basis that in general terms a principal is not liable for the acts of an agent otherwise than in relation to fraud.[182] It is therefore important when dealing through agents to ensure that any agents are themselves expressed to be personally liable in contract for any breaches of duty or defaults under that contract on their own account and also that the principal is contractually expressed to be so liable whether or not there has been fraud.

7.   UNFAIR CONTRACT TERMS

A.   Unfair Contract Terms Act 1977

When constructing documentation for a financial transaction, the parties will seek to limit their own liabilities, to protect themselves against the possibility of loss, to make it easier for the contract to be terminated if their counterparty fails to perform, and so on. Wherever possible, a powerful financial institution dealing with an ordinary customer or even another financial institution will try to weigh the contractual terms in its favour. It may, for example, grant itself powers to terminate the transaction which its counterparty does not have, or it may impose liabilities on its counterparty to pay penalties or interest on the happening of certain events. The question will arise in such circumstances whether or not those terms should be void as being unfair contract terms. The principal legislation dealing with unfair contract terms in England and Wales is the Unfair Contract Terms Act 1977 ("UCTA"), which is considered here, and regulations created in 1994 and in 1999 which are considered below. The unfair contract terms legislation is in fact limited to contractual terms which seek to limit one party's liabilities. It is important to recall (from Chapter 10), as considered below, that the obligations in the *Conduct of Business* regulations may not be excluded by contract by a regulated firm.

18–75

---

[179] *Performing Rights Society v Mitchell and Booker* [1924] 1 K.B. 762; *Argent v Minister of Social Security and Another* [1968] 1 W.L.R. 1749. cf. *Mersey Docks and Harbour Board v Coggins and Griffith (Liverpool) Ltd* [1947] A.C. 1 where it was suggested that this liability may attach where employees are lent to another employer.

[180] *Ellis v Sheffield Gas Consumers Co* (1853) 2 E. & B. 767.

[181] *Kooragang Investment Pty Ltd v Richardson and Wrench Ltd* [1982] A.C. 462. cf. *Armagas Ltd v Mundogas SA, The Ocean Frost* [1986] A.C. 717.

[182] *Nottingham v Aldridge* [1971] 2 Q.B. 739.

Exclusion of liability for negligence

18–76   This discussion will assume that the contract in question relates to a financial transaction. Under s.2(2) of UCTA, a person acting in the course of a business (such as a bank) will not be able to restrict its liability for negligence unreasonably in a written agreement. Section 2(2) provides as follows:

> "In the case of other loss or damage [which is not liability for death or personal injury resulting from negligence], a person cannot so exclude or restrict his liability for negligence except in so far as the term or notice satisfies the requirement of reasonableness."

The form of negligence which the Act seeks to cover is negligent breach of any obligation arising under the contract, except where it is reasonable to exclude one's liability.

18–77   Furthermore, s.13 of UCTA extends the application of s.2 to any circumstance in which the seller seeks to restrict its duties under the contract in respect of its tortious and non-tortious obligations. It has been held that this might extend as far as provisions which seek to exclude rights to set-off.[183]

Standard form contracts

18–78   The question is then as to the position under the standard form contracts used to document financial transactions generally, and specifically contractual provisions entered into between the parties as to remedies for specific breaches of the contract and termination events. The issue could be raised by a form of standard document used by a party who enters into financial contracts in the course of its business. Such standard form contracts are governed in s.3 of the UCTA in the following terms:

> "(1)   This section applies as between contracting parties where one of them deals as consumer or on the other's written standard terms of business."

In corporate finance, many institutions use a standard form of agreement in relation to derivatives, stock-lending, repo's, foreign exchange and so on by building on an industry standard contract[184]; whereas in retail finance, the customer will always be a consumer and in any event the use of standard form contracts governs everything from opening bank accounts to taking out mortgages. Therefore, standard terms are very common. The question is whether or not any exclusion clause in those standard terms will be ineffective on the basis that it is an unfair contract term. In this sense, s.3 continues:

> "(2)   As against that party, the other cannot by reference to any contract term—
> (a)   when himself in breach of contract, exclude or restrict any liability of his in respect of the breach; or
> (b)   claim to be entitled—
> (i) to render contractual performance substantially different from that which was reasonably expected of him, or

---

[183] *Stewart Gill Ltd v Horatio Myer & Co Ltd* [1992] Q.B. 600.
[184] See para.19–03.

(ii)in respect of the whole or any part of his contractual obligation, to render no
performance at all,
except in so far as (in any of the cases mentioned above in this subsection) the
contract term satisfies the requirement of reasonableness."

The first issue is whether or not any given exclusion of liability clause in a
contract could be said to constitute a standard term used by that particular entity
in question which would entitle the buyer to refute any provision in that contract
which "claimed to be entitled to... render a contractual performance
substantially different from that which was reasonably expected".[185] It is
submitted that this provision is only likely to be efficacious in the financial
context where the buyer has been required, as a result of inequality of bargaining
power, to execute the seller's standard form documentation. Where the contracts
are negotiated between parties of equal levels of expertise, and those provisions
are either market standard or, as is usual, negotiated between the parties, it is
difficult to see how the buyer could claim the protection of s.3 of UCTA. Again,
it is suggested that identifying the parties' appropriate levels of expertise depends
on an assessment in line with the client classification principles in the *Conduct of
Business Sourcebook* as discussed in Chapter 10 of this book.

The test of "reasonableness"

Sections 2 and 3 of UCTA establish the idea that an exclusion of liability **18–79**
provision in a contract will be valid if it is "reasonable". This word "reasonable"
is the draftsperson's default setting when it is too difficult to define in advance
exactly what will be permitted and what will not be permitted: instead the court is
asked to consider the facts and decide whether or not the exclusion of liability
clause would be reasonable in the circumstances which confront it. Section 11
provides that the requirement of reasonableness

"is that the term shall have been a fair and reasonable one to be included having regard to the
circumstances which were, or ought reasonably to have been, known to or in the
contemplation of the parties when the contract was made."[186]

There is no requirement that the parties have expressly discussed the exclusion of
liability term so that it was expressly in their contemplation. Rather, it is to be
considered whether or not that term was reasonable with regard to the general
circumstances of the contract, or in the alternative if it was within the
contemplation of the parties. It is suggested that a financial institution dealing in
relation to its own customers would need to make the exclusion plain from the
outset and would need to consider the context of the conduct of business rules in
the next section.

In *Smith v Eric S Bush*[187] Lord Griffiths outlined the following principles as being **18–80**
useful considerations when evaluating the level of reasonableness. First, whether
or not the parties were of equal bargaining strength. Secondly, whether or not it

---

[185] Unfair Contract Terms Act 1977, s.3(1).
[186] Unfair Contract Terms Act 1977, s.11(1).
[187] [1990] 1 A.C. 831; [1989] 2 All E.R. 514.

would have been possible or reasonable to have acquired similar advice in the circumstances for reasonable cost and convenience: such that, for example, if it were impossible to acquire alternative services then the exclusion of liability would be unreasonable, and vice versa. Thirdly, the level of difficulty associated with providing that advice or service: such that if the advice being given or service being performed was very complex then exclusion of liability would be more reasonable than if the service was a comparatively minor one in relation to which the exercise of care and skill was reasonable. Fourthly, the ramifications of finding that the exclusion clause was reasonable or unreasonable for the contract between the parties.

No exclusion of obligations under the conduct of business rules

18–81   The *Conduct of Business Sourcebook* provides explicitly that:

> "A firm must not, in any communication[188] relating to designated investment business seek to:
> (1)   exclude or restrict; or
> (2)   rely on any exclusion or restriction of
> any duty or liability it may have to a client under the regulatory system."[189]

Thus the obligations created, inter alia, by COBS and the rest of the *FCA Handbook* may not be excluded by the firm in communications with it clients nor by way of contract.

Exemption for sales of securities

18–82   Should there be any dealing in financial services which has English law as its governing law but which is not governed by FCA regulation, then the UCTA regime will apply. However, the UCTA regime has a specific exemption in Sch.1 for a range of transactions including "any contract so far as it relates to the creation or transfer of securities or of any right or interest in securities".[190] Therefore, straightforward sales of bonds or shares would be exempt. Also exempt would be options to acquire or to sell (call or put options respectively) securities of any sort. The term "securities" is defined in Part X as including shares, bonds, options to acquire the same, and other securitised assets including securitised derivatives and securitisation products considered in Chapter 44. Not included within this exemption, it is suggested, would be derivatives such as interest rate swaps which do not relate to securities.

---

[188] It is not clear whether "any communication" is intended to cover the initial conduct of business agreement between the parties as well as later communications, or not. It is suggested that if it were not covered then this provision would be of no practical effect because it would be circumvented by an ordinary exclusion of liability clause.
[189] COBS, 2 1.2R.
[190] Unfair Contract Terms Act 1977 Sch.1, para.1(e).

B.   Unfair Terms in Consumer Contracts Regulations 1994

The application of the regulations in general

There are regulations concerning consumer contracts effected under the Unfair **18–83**
Terms in Consumer Contracts Regulations 1994[191] which extend to a broader
range of contractual terms than UCTA.[192] The 1994 Regulations cover set-off
clauses and clauses which seek to restrict liability to penalties in respect of
contracts between consumers and suppliers. The Regulations apply to standard
terms and not to contractual terms which have been negotiated between
counterparties. The terms must be found to be unfair and to require exorbitant
payment, or must be demonstrated to have been created otherwise than in the
course of fair dealing. In the context of financial products this would appear to
capture complex products sold by reference to financial risk and pricing models
which then require exorbitant payment as a result of market movements, such as
financial derivatives. From the scope of Sch.3 of the Regulations, it would appear
that the sale and marketing of financial products in many circumstances would be
caught within the scope of the provision of advice relating to, and the supply of,
financial services. As such, the comments made previously about the reality of
documentation which is negotiated between the parties will apply.[193]

If a seller's standard terms were imposed on the buyer, then the Regulations **18–84**
would appear to be capable of application. In other circumstances where the
buyer contends that it has been the subject of unscrupulous imposition of
contractual provisions, it is suggested that the general remarks made in Chapter
10 about suitable conduct of business would apply. That is, if there has been some
breach of conduct of business regulation, that will only increase the likelihood
that a transaction will be found to have contained unfair contract terms. In
particular, the seller would face potential liability for undue influence, where
terms have been foisted on the buyer, or as to misrepresentation or deceit, where
terms are agreed as a result of some negligence or guile on the part of the
seller.[194]

The question of "suitability" has grown up around this species of issue. The **18–85**
corporate client would argue that there is a duty of care on the part of the bank to
ensure that the product being sold to it is suitable for it and that the context in
which it is sold has not been unsuitable in itself. Ought there to be a duty of care
at common law extending beyond that usually owed to one requiring the bank to
ensure that the product is appropriate for the particular client? The *Conduct of
Business* rulebook suggests that there must be. This argument proceeds on the
basis that only the banks know how the products work and therefore that it is

---

[191] SI 3159/1994.

[192] See Brownsword and Howells, "The Implementation of the EC Directive on Unfair Terms" [1995]
JBL 243, 248.

[193] There is a further issue on the Regulations (r.3(3)), that the "core provisions" of the agreement
will not be subject to revision by the Regulations. In the context of financial derivatives it is not
immediately obvious which terms are the "core provisions". The issue of material and collateral terms
is considered in Ch.19.

[194] See Cranston, *Principles of Banking Law* (Oxford, 1997) p.159 et seq.

unfair for them not to treat their inexpert customers with care and in good faith. There has been assertion in some cases that the banks have provided copies of their bespoke computer programs to clients when selling them products.[195] These programmes are sophisticated models which estimate the movements of the markets which will underpin the hedging or speculative transaction. What is not clear is whether or not the client is able to operate the model so that it can predict the effect of the product with an expertise that approaches that of the bank.[196] This is an issue which should be considered in the general terms of business documentation entered into between the parties.

Unfair requirements of interest

18–86 The decision of the House of Lords in *Director General of Fair Trading v First National Bank*[197] considered whether or not a bank's reliance on one of its standard terms was fair or not under the 1994 Regulations. The term in question provided that the consumer would be liable to pay interest until payment even after a judgment had been awarded against the consumer. The traditional approach under *In Re Sneyd*[198] and *Economic Life Assurance Society v Usborne*[199] was that a judgment finalised the amount that was owed and so wrapped unpaid interest up with the repayment of capital.[200] It was held that the provision was not however "unfair". The House relied on the principle that the parties should be entitled to rely on their own freedom of contract, and the amount of interest to be paid under this term after judgment was not unreasonable because it caused no imbalance between the parties' rights and obligations.[201]

C. Unfair terms in consumer contracts

The operation of the regulations in general terms

18–87 Further to the Unfair Terms in Consumer Contract Regulations 1999, enacting the appropriate EC Council Directive,[202] "unfair" terms are not binding on the consumer.[203] Those regulations apply where there have been individually negotiated terms between one party acting in furtherance of its business as a seller or supplier and another party acting as a consumer. These regulations apply,

---

[195] See for example the claim made in *The Proctor and Gamble Company v Bankers Trust Company and BT Securities Corp*, Civil Action No. C–1–94–735 (S.D. Ohio).
[196] The truth of course is that, even if the client can operate the program, the assumptions which underpin it (as to future interest rate movements, etc) are subject to violent change. An unexpected event of the magnitude of the Gulf War, for example, will radically alter any market predictions without being capable of being incorporated into model.
[197] [2001] UKHL 52.
[198] (1883) 25 Ch.D. 338.
[199] [1902] A.C. 147.
[200] An alternative approach was taken in *Ealing London Borough Council v El Isaac* [1980] 1 W.L.R. 932.
[201] See on this last point, Lord Millett at [57].
[202] 93/13/EEC [1999] OJ L95/29.
[203] Unfair Terms in Consumer Contract Regulations 1999 (SI 1999/2083), reg.8(1).

however, only to natural persons and not to corporations,[204] unlike the 1977 Act.[205] In consequence, their applicability will be limited in relation to complex financial contracts but may have greater application in relation to retail transactions.

Whether bank charges are "unfair"

A particularly high-profile series of cases has arisen in relation to bank charges and the unfair contract terms legislation. Unfortunately, the public discussion of this litigation proceeded on the basis that the courts were going to consider in the abstract whether or not the charges which high street banks and building societies levied on their ordinary customers for overdrafts and so forth (and which contributed as much as 30 per cent of their profits annually) were "unfair" in general terms. In fact, the litigation proceeded on the very narrow and technical basis as to whether or not those charges fell within the main bargain entered into between the parties when an account was opened, or whether those charges were outside the contemplation of the customers when they opened their accounts and consequently not part of the main bargain. Under the precise wording of the regulations, it was only open to the courts to consider the "unfairness" of those charges if they were not part of the main bargain between the parties or if the contract had been particularly badly worded. The reason for this arrangement in the legislation was that it derived from EU legislation which had taken the approach that the parties were free to enter into whatever contract they liked and therefore that they could include seemingly unfair terms if they wanted. It was only if there were collateral terms outside the main contract which the parties had not discussed as part of the main bargain, or if the contract was badly worded, that the courts should consider the unfairness of those terms because they might not have been something which the customer would have understood and thought about at the time of making the contract. What this statutory approach clearly fails to anticipate is that it is the banks (in this context) who draft the contracts and therefore they include all manner of potentially fair and unfair terms within those agreements which the customer has little option but to accept, or else take their business to another bank with very similar terms and conditions in their contracts. Ultimately, the Supreme Court held that the bank charges were part of the main bargain between the banks and their customers, and consequently that they could not be challenged on the ground of unfairness under the terms of the regulations. This decision is considered below. Unfortunately, the press reported this decision as the Supreme Court finding that bank charges were fair, which was something that the judges were at pains to point out was not the question in front of them. There were, however, a few minor skirmishes in the case law before that main case reached the courts.

18–88

The knotty problem of bank charges was first raised before the High Court in *Office of Fair Trading v Abbey National Plc.*[206] The issue was whether or not the charges which banks charged on current accounts when a customer, for example,

18–89

---

[204] Unfair Terms in Consumer Contract Regulations 1999 reg.3.
[205] *R & B Customs Brokers Ltd v United Dominions Trust Ltd* [1988] 1 W.L.R. 321.
[206] [2008] EWHC 875.

wrote a cheque when overdrawn were "unfair" within reg.5 and reg.6 of the 1999 Regulations. Regulation 5(1) provides that:

> "a contractual term which has not been individually negotiated shall be regarded as unfair if, contrary to the requirement of good faith, it causes a significant imbalance in the parties' rights and obligations arising under the contract, to the detriment of the consumer."

Furthermore, reg.6 provides that:

> "In so far as it is in plain intelligible language, the assessment of fairness of a term shall not relate:
> (a)   to the definition of the main subject matter of the contract, or
> (b)   to the adequacy of the price or remuneration, as against the goods or services supplied in exchange."

The problem faced by the banks was that the charges which they levied on their overdrawn customers bore no relation to the cost of any service which they were providing to their customers, and therefore were not exempt from the 1999 Regulations as a part of the "price or remuneration" for such a service. Therefore, the charges could be "unfair" within the terms of the Regulations. As is considered in Chapter 19, the charges that were levied did not, however constitute unenforceable penalty clauses at common law.[207]

18–90   In the further case of *Office of Fair Trading v Abbey National Plc*[208] the question at issue was whether or not charges levied on current accountholders while their accounts were overdrawn were "not capable of amounting to" penalties under the common law under the terms of the 1999 Regulations. The payment of a charge which was referable to the commission of some wrongdoing—that is, using the account once it had gone overdrawn—was therefore penal in that sense.[209] This was so even if the accountholder acquired benefits, such as the continued facility of a bank account. Some of the banks' general terms and conditions for current accounts were held not penal and others penal, although for the most part the facts were adjourned for further argument at further hearings.

18–91   The decision of Andrew Smith J. in the first case relating to *The Office of Fair Trading v Abbey National Plc*[210] was appealed to the Court of Appeal.[211] In this appeal, *The Office of Fair Trading v Abbey National Plc*,[212] the Court of Appeal agreed with Andrew Smith J. This was the beginning of the newsworthy part of the litigation. The principal question in the appeal was whether or not the four types of bank charges[213] fell to be interpreted as being matters which fell within

---

[207]   See para.19–39.
[208]   [2008] EWHC 2325.
[209]   Applying *Cooden Engineering Co Ltd v Stanford* [1952] 2 All E.R. 915.
[210]   [2008] EWHC 875.
[211]   [2009] EWCA Civ 116.
[212]   [2009] EWCA Civ 116.
[213]   The four types of bank charges were: "unpaid item charges" where purported payment is made when the customer's account is overdrawn and the bank refuses to make payment; "paid item charges" where purported payment is made when the customer's account is overdrawn but the bank nevertheless makes payment; "overdraft excess charges" where a customer exceeds her overdraft limit; "guaranteed paid item charge" where a cheque is honoured because it was offered with a cheque guarantee card even though the account was overdrawn.

the main subject matter of the contract. Under reg.6(2), as set out above, if the charges related to matters which were outside the main subject matter of the contract then they could be taken into account when deciding whether or not those charges were fair. The banks wanted to argue that the levying of these charges was part of the main subject matter of the contract and therefore that (under reg.6(2)) they could not be considered in deciding whether or not the charges were "fair". The Court of Appeal held, in essence, that when customers entered into contracts with banks they were not focused on the detailed terms and conditions relating to bank charges and therefore those charges were not part of the main subject matter of the contract: therefore, those charges could be part of the courts' consideration of "fairness" under reg.6. In essence, those charges were held to be unfair because the banks levied them without reference to any cost to themselves of providing banking services.

The Court of Appeal took it as read that ordinary customers would not be aware **18–92** of these charges nor that they would be focused on them. Sir Anthony Clarke M.R. held that "[i]t seems unlikely in the extreme that the typical customer reads [the lengthy express terms and conditions]":[214] although no evidence for this was adduced by his lordship. This, it is suggested, stretches credulity. Customers would probably be aware that using their account when overdrawn would attract a charge, something his lordship tacitly acknowledged.[215] What is objectionable here is the level of the charge which the bank levies so as to earn the £2.56 billion in profits which banks earned from these charges in 2006. Therefore, it is suggested, assuming that customers do not focus on such details nor that they can differentiate between the charges levied for different banking services is a useful means of allowing the court to proceed such that the "substance of the contract must be analysed as a package"[216], and so treat the charges as being unfair. Similarly, the court assumed that the language used in the agreements was not "plain and intelligible language" and that simply using such language would not be "a sufficient protection for consumers on its own".[217] There is, however, no empirical proof for either of these manifestations of ignorance or stupidity on the part of bank customers to the effect that they could not appreciate the risks bound up in plain English: instead it is just *assumed* by the Court of Appeal and by the academic commentary cited by the Court of Appeal. What is clear also is that the Court of Appeal's focus was only on what the customer would consider to be the main subject matter of the contract: given the £2.5 billion in profits at stake for the banks, it is suggested that the banks' focus would certainly be on the levying of charges as part of the contract. Indeed, among bankers, a "good customer" is in fact a customer who is late in making payments (so as to incur those ever-so-profitable bank charges) but one who always makes payment eventually (so that the bank does not have to write off defaults). Nevertheless, the Court of Appeal followed the principle that the unfair contract terms legislation is aimed in part at least at consumer protection and therefore focussed on the customers' expectations only.

---

[214] [2009] EWCA Civ 116, at [95].
[215] [2009] EWCA Civ 116, at [94].
[216] [2009] EWCA Civ 116, at [97], per Clarke M.R.
[217] [2009] EWCA Civ 116, at [97], per Clarke M.R.

18–93   The outcome is unobjectionable: the banks were clearly "gouging" their customers: i.e. charging as much as they felt they could so as to earn huge profits from profligate or hard-pressed customers' transactions, even though the banks suffered no commensurate loss in operating those accounts. On the contrary, those accounts were the most profitable for the banks because of the charges levied on those customers. The circumlocutions used by the Court of Appeal were necessary to come to that conclusion because otherwise reg.6(2) would have excluded consideration of these bank charges in a discussion of whether or not those charges were "fair". So, a fair result is reached by stretching the statutory language slightly, even though the court had no proof for its empirical assertions about the beliefs or practices of bank customers. Indeed, the suggestion made by Sir Anthony Clarke M.R. that a range of banking services should be seen "as a package" (as cited above) almost gave the game away by seeing the charges as being as one with the provision of the rest of an entire banking service.

18–94   The Court of Appeal focused on the interpretation of the Directive which gave rise to the 1999 Regulations and in particular to the interpretation put on that Directive by the House of Lords in *Director General of Fair Trading v First National Bank*.[218] Of particular importance was the finding that the two objectives of the Directive were the "promotion of fair standard contract forms to improve the functioning of the European market place" and the "protection of consumers throughout the European Community".[219] This underlying policy buoyed up the Court of Appeal in *Office of Fair Trading v Abbey National Plc*[220] by permitting it to find that the bank charges were outwith the main subject matter of the contract so that they could be folded into an enquiry as to whether or not they were "fair" or not, and therefore to find that they were "unfair". This is in spite of the assertion made by Treitel and others that the regulations were not intended to regulate prices (such as the level of bank charges) nor to interfere with freedom of contract.[221]

18–95   The Supreme Court overturned the decisions of the Court of Appeal and of Andrew Smith J. in *Office of Fair Trading v Abbey National Plc*.[222] This was one of the first high-profile cases to be heard by the new Supreme Court and as such it garnered a large amount of press attention: something which the judges refer to in their judgments. To rehearse the background again: to demonstrate that the bank charges could be challenged on the ground that they were unfair, the Office of Fair Trading (in effect, acting on behalf of bank customers) had to show that the bank charges were separate from the main bargain entered into between the parties. By contrast, the banks needed to show that the bank charges were part of the bargain and therefore that they were not something which could be scrutinised on grounds of their unfairness. The Supreme Court was in agreement as to the outcome, even if there were some minor differences in the reasoning taken by the judges. Lord Walker and Lord Phillips (with at least one of whom everyone else agreed) began with the EU legislation which had decided that the parties should

---

[218] [2001] UKHL 52.
[219] [2001] UKHL 52, at [31], per Lord Steyn.
[220] [2009] EWCA Civ 116, at [36], per Clarke M.R.
[221] [2009] EWCA Civ 116, at [43], per Clarke M.R.
[222] [2009] UKSC 6; [2009] 3 W.L.R 1215.

have freedom of contract and that they should be bound by the terms of their contracts, and therefore that it was only in relation to terms which had not been part of the main agreement that there could be any finding of unfairness. The alternative approach would have been to prioritise customer protection by allowing the courts to evaluate the fairness of any contractual term, whether part of the main agreement or collateral to it—but that was not the approach which the legislation took.

In essence, Lord Walker held that the banks and their customers contracted for a package of banking services. The bank charges were not payments for distinct services, nor were they levied so as to discourage customers from going overdrawn without permission. Nor did it matter that the majority of customers never went overdrawn and therefore that the majority of customers never incurred those charges.[223] Instead, bank charges were part of the payment structure for the entire package of services which were provided to customers. The bank charges were part of the "price or remuneration for the banking services provided" and furthermore this had been done in "plain intelligible language".[224] As such, those bank charges were part of the main transaction and therefore could not be assessed for their fairness within reg.6.

18–96

Interestingly, Lord Walker held the following[225]:

18–97

> "I do not see how it could have come to the conclusion that charges amounting to over 30% of the revenue stream were 'not part of the core or essential bargain'."

What this suggests is that Lord Walker is looking at this problem entirely from the perspective of the banks. It only matters to the banks that this is 30 per cent of their revenue stream; but that is of no direct interest to their customers, and it ought not to influence an objective finding whether or not these provisions were part of the core or essential bargain.[226] The question ought to have been what were the factors which were within the contemplation of both parties when they created their contract. Simply to focus on the importance of this transaction for the banks is inadvertently to highlight how it is the banks which draft all of the contracts and therefore that the customers have no power in the process at all.[227]

---

[223] Approximately 42 million people never went overdrawn, while approximately 12 million people did.

[224] [2009] UKSC 6; [2009] 3 W.L.R 1215, at [51]. The decision in *Office of Fair Trading v Foxtons Ltd (No.2)* [2009] EWHC 1681 (Ch) related to an agreement which was not written in plain and intelligible language.

[225] [2009] UKSC 6; [2009] 3 W.L.R 1215, at [47].

[226] More peculiar yet is an earlier, oddly gendered passage in which Lord Walker held that it "depends partly on whether one's perception of the average customer who incurs unauthorised overdraft charges is that he is spendthrift and improvident, or that she is disadvantaged and finding it hard to make ends meet": [2009] UKSC 6; [2009] 3 W.L.R 1215, at [2]. Why are men spendthrifts, while women find it hard to make ends meet?

[227] Interestingly also, Baroness Hale suggested that customers spend money from their accounts "with our eyes open because we want the product in question more than we want the money" ([2009] UKSC 6; [2009] 3 W.L.R 1215, at [93]): this approach overlooks the more critical fact that customers spend their money because they *need* the product in question, and not simply because they *want* it. People go overdrawn often through circumstance: they run out of money and *need* money, and then are stuck with large banking charges which bear no correlation to the cost of processing that

18–98   One of the key themes of this book has been how within a modern law of finance it is the business of the law to intervene in circumstances in which financial institutions are imposing unfair, unconscionable or oppressive terms on customers: that was the purpose of a range of rules stretching from conduct of business regulation (discussed in Chapter 10) through to the law on unconscionable activity and fraud (discussed in Pts II and VII). This nervousness about interfering in "free markets" must be put to bed in the wake of the global financial crisis of 2007–09 in which the effects of allowing banks free rein to innovate and to deal as they wish are clear for all to see: the trillions of pounds needed to shore up our banks in 2008/09 dwarf the billions which the banks have made in levying arbitrary charges on their customers. Indeed, this obsession with protecting freedom of contract and thus free markets now seems a little old-fashioned, overly ideological and even naïve. Customers need protection from banks, just as national economies need protection from banks.

D.   The FCA Unfair Contract Guide

18–99   The FSA published a statement of good practice "Fairness of terms in consumer contracts" in 2005 which relates to the 1999 Regulations. It is not part of the *FCA Handbook* nor is it a set of guidance principles as under that Handbook. Written before the implementation of MiFID in 2007, the statement highlights the need for regulated firms to take into account consumers' legitimate interests in the formation of contracts; that fairness to customers is a part of prudent business management and not contrary to it; and that firms should look to the general effect of their contractual terms in plain, intelligible language and not dwell on technical interpretations of them.

18–100   The FCA Unfair Contract Guide ("UNFCOG") sets out the FCA's approach to unfair contract terms after MiFID. The Guide is not intended to be a definitive guide to the operation of the 1999 Regulations, but rather gives general guidance to regulated firms as to the FCA's policy in that regard. The Guide provides a summary of the regulations to the effect that:

> "[t]erms are regarded as unfair if, contrary to the requirement of good faith, they cause a significant imbalance in the parties' rights and obligations to the detriment of the consumer".[228]

The FCA may consider the "fairness of a contract" within the terms of the Regulations if a complaint is made to it by a consumer.[229] The FCA might as a result look at the contracts which are used in a particular area of business or it

---

unauthorised overdraft. Instead, banks are using their customers' economic weakness to gouge them for profits which amount approximately to £2.6 billion annually. The PPI misselling scandal (discussed in Ch.45) and the profits taken from bank charges show how the banks use their ordinary, retail customers unconscionably as cash cows to capitalise the rest of their businesses, in particular their proprietary trading activities.

[228] UNFCOG 1.3.2G.
[229] UNFCOG 1.4.1G.

may look at the contracts used by a variety of firms in a particular business sector to consider their fairness.[230] The wider the number of complaints, the wider the review would be.[231]

---

[230] UNFCOG 1.4.3(1)G.
[231] UNFCOG 1.4.3(2)G.

CHAPTER 19

MASTER AGREEMENTS AND COMMON CONTRACTUAL TERMS AND CONDITIONS

CORE PRINCIPLES

Master agreements

This chapter considers some of the most important terms and some of the principal issues which arise in the operation of contracts in financial transactions. One of the key aspects of financial transactions is the use of "master agreement" structures. Master agreement structures are used to bring all of the parties' many transactions under the umbrella of one master agreement so that they will constitute "a single agreement" for insolvency, netting, termination and other purposes. A master agreement generally takes the form of standard market terms which the parties may amend or extend by means of a schedule attached to the master agreement that is negotiated from party to party. The master agreement constitutes the general provisions on which the parties conduct all of their business of the specified types: in particular, it enables the parties to terminate their transactions in the event that their counterparty breaches any one of the many events of default identified in the master agreement or appended to it in the schedule. Each individual transaction (and there may be thousands of them) which is contracted beneath the master agreement umbrella is documented by means of a "confirmation": that confirmation will frequently be in standard form and will provide that it is intended to constitute a single agreement together will all other confirmations, the master agreement and the schedule. This documentary architecture is then supplemented by any "credit support documentation"—such as a guarantee or a collateralisation agreement—which is used to support either all or some of the transactions entered into between the parties under the master agreement umbrella. Master agreements are used in relation to a number of areas of business in particular: stock-lending, repos, foreign exchange, and in particular financial derivatives (which are discussed in Chapter 41).

The use of standard form contracts is widespread in financial markets. This raises questions of unfair contract terms and questions as to whether or not the parties intended to create terms different from the standard terms but nevertheless failed to amend those provisions. When documentation from different marketplaces is combined—for example, as with swaps which are embedded in bond documentation—there is always the danger of mismatches such that payments in one context are made in a different way or on a different date from other payments.

Commonly used contractual provisions

This chapter considers frequently used terms in financial contracts so as to provide a central reservoir from which contextual analyses of those terms in particular market sectors can be conducted in later chapters of this book. Many of these terms are "events of default" breaches of which will cause the contract to be terminated. First, it is important to divide between "conditions" (which are contractual terms the breach of which justify the termination of the entire agreement) and "mere warranties" (which are less important contractual terms the breach of which can be remedied by damages without the need to terminate the entire contract). Secondly, failure to pay or to perform a contractual obligation will usually be conditions of the contract, which are sometimes remedied by payment of default interest under the terms of the contract. It is important that default interest clauses are not deemed to be penalty clauses or else they will be void. Thirdly, there are many forms of disruption which may affect a contract but it is a question for the interpretation of the contract whether that justifies termination of the agreement or not. These disruptions may be a brief or a grievous disruption of trading on an exchange, or force majeure such as a civil war or a national emergency or an act of terrorism and so on. It is advisable for the parties to specify in their contracts the maximum amount of volatility which they considered to be acceptable before the purpose behind their contract would have been frustrated and so be terminable.

Fourthly, among the events of default which commonly arise are events of insolvency, ranging from actually going into bankruptcy right the way through to insolvency proceedings being merely commenced by a disgruntled creditor or shareholder. There are also "cross default" provisions whereby contract x may be rendered capable of termination because of a default under a different contract y, whether committed by the counterparty or some affiliate of that counterparty. Similarly, "cross acceleration" provisions in a contract enable contract x to be terminated because a counterparty was required to pay its obligations under another debt y earlier than they were otherwise due. In each case, the early termination is intended to allow the non-defaulting party to terminate its agreement with the defaulting party once it is able to anticipate a future loss which is indicated by failure of some other contract in which the defaulting party is involved.

In loan contracts there are a number of common covenants (that is, conditions which if breached will cause the borrower's loan repayment obligations to be repayable immediately and the loan contract terminated). Loan contracts may involve one lender or a syndicate of lenders, or (for present purposes) may involve issues of bonds. These covenants are considered in Chapter 32 In relation to different forms of lending agreement. In this chapter they are placed in the context of the general law of contract. First, negative pledge clauses are important in that they prevent a borrower from pledging its assets to any other purpose which might prevent them being available to the lender in the event of a failure to repay the loan. In loan contracts relating to syndicates of lenders or to bond investors, all of the creditors are to stand in equal step ("pari passu") with one another. Secondly, the maintenance of the credit worth of the borrower is significant. If there is a "material adverse change" in the credit worth of the borrower, then that will typically constitute a breach of the loan contract. Credit worth will have deteriorated if the borrower's credit rating is downgraded by the ratings agencies, but usually such a ratings downgrade will come after the borrower's credit worth has self-evidently deteriorated and will therefore not offer much protection to the lender. Therefore, a lender would prefer to have the power to terminate a loan contract if there has been some deterioration in one of the indicators of a company's financial health (as discussed below) or publicly available information indicates such a deterioration in credit worth.

This chapter also considers the law relating to the remedies of specific performance of contracts, the rectification of contracts, and the circumstances in which contracts may be treated as having been frustrated in its later sections.

1. INTRODUCTION

19–01 This chapter is concerned with the manner in which financial contracts are performed, and with the identification of terms which justify the termination of contracts. It is concerned at first with issues which often occur when drafting financial contracts. The kernel of this chapter is in relation to the distinction to be made between conditions of a contract, which permit the termination of that contract if they are breached, and other terms which do not permit the automatic termination of the contract. As is evident from many of the standard form contracts for various types of financial product which are considered in various chapters of *Section Two* of this book, most standard form contracts are concerned with allowing the parties to terminate their dealings at the first sign of trouble, and therefore knowing whether or not termination is permitted is a key aspect of contract law in those contexts. Later sections of this chapter consider the doctrine governing the frustration of contract and the relevant rules on specific performance. This chapter can therefore be considered as a counterpart to the next chapter which considers the general law applicable to claims brought on termination of a contract, in particular claims for damages for breach of contract, money had and received and proprietary claims. This chapter therefore considers some of the more common terms found in financial contracts so as to form a central reservoir of definitions of these terms which will appear and reappear in *Section Two: Specific Financial Techniques* in this book.

2. ISSUES WITH DRAFTING CONTRACTS FOR FINANCIAL TRANSACTIONS

A. Introduction

19–02 A large amount of the law in this book relates to contract law, and a large amount of financial practice is to do with creating contracts. The principles of contract law that are of particular importance are discussed in this Part V of this book, and then are applied to particular contexts in the appropriate chapters in *Section Two: Specific Financial Techniques* of this book. What this particular section aims to do is to identify some of the key issues which arise frequently when drafting contracts in practice. For the most part, they are entirely practical and pragmatic issues. It seemed useful to have one place in which these issues were collected together. The most sustained analysis of financial documentation outside this chapter is in Chapter 41 in relation to the documentation of derivatives, where examples of these issues are worked through; although there are discussions of each standard market agreement in each appropriate chapter in Section Two of this book. This section is intended to provide the reader with a grounding in some of the basic issues and the basic jargon which are necessary for an understanding of the transactional issues which arise in relation to the financial products which are considered in Section Two of this book.

B. Construction of financial contracts

The analysis of a financial transaction depends upon the parties' contractual language which will ordinarily be binding[1] (especially where the parties are market professionals relying on legal advice), except in circumstances entitling the parties to rectification or where there has been undue influence or mistake. That is, if the parties have deliberately structured their bargain in one way, then the words used to express that bargain should be effected by the court.[2] Lord Steyn has observed that the trend in the judicial interpretation of contracts has been towards a purposive, commercial interpretation of those contracts.[3] The courts have set themselves against the sort of artificial literalism which characterised judicial interpretation in the 19th and early 20th centuries.[4] Interpretation is to be carried out on the basis of the meaning which would be conveyed to a reasonable person with all of the background knowledge available to the parties at the time that the contract was created.[5] Words are to be given their ordinary meanings, except where the context requires a particular meaning known to the parties in the context of their contract at the time of creating that contract.[6] In the context of financial contracts, as will emerge, most contracts between market professionals are conducted on the basis of market standard contracts which contain a large amount of jargon which call for restrictive interpretations in line with market practice. The difficulty with market practices which are not conducted on exchanges under the umbrella of clear market rules (that is, all so-called "over-the-counter" markets) is that they are difficult to prove or establish because different financial institutions often deal in different ways.

19–03

---

[1] See, e.g. the approach of Lord Steyn in *Equitable Life v Hyman* [2002] 1 A.C. 408, 460, where his lordship refused an interpretation of the terms of pensions investment contracts by which the directors of Equitable Life sought to reorganise the investment activities of pension fund schemes in the face of the structure set out in the contracts in reliance on some purportedly loose drafting.

[2] See *Equitable Life v Hyman* [2002] 1 A.C. 408.

[3] *Mannai Investments Co Ltd v Eagle Star Life Assurance Co Ltd* [1998] A.C. 749, 700. See also *Investors Compensations Scheme Ltd v West Bromwich BS* [1998] 1 W.L.R. 896, 912, per Lord Hoffmann, and *Equitable Life v Hyman* [2002] 1 A.C. 408, at [135], per Lord Woolf M.R.

[4] *Mannai Investments Co Ltd v Eagle Star Life Assurance Co Ltd* [1998] A.C. 749, 771, per Lord Steyn. With characteristic wit see also *Sirius International Insurance Company v FAI General Insurance* [2004] UKHL 54, at [19], per Lord Steyn, where his lordship referred to the sort of literalism discussed by William Paley (1838) such as the actions of "the tyrant Temures [who] promised the garrison of Sebastia that no blood would be shed if they surrendered to him. They surrendered. He shed no blood. He buried them all alive. This is literalism. If possible it should be resisted in the interpretative process."

[5] *Investors Compensations Scheme Ltd v West Bromwich BS* [1998] 1 W.L.R. 896.

[6] [1998] 1 W.L.R. 896. See also Nicholls, "My Kingdom for a Horse: The Meaning of Words" (2005) 121 L.Q.R. 577; McMeel, "The rise of commercial construction in contract law" [1998] L.M.C.L.Q. 382.

Furthermore, the interpretation of contracts should be considered in the light of the pressured atmosphere considered in Chapter 17 in which financial contracts are created.

C. The use of "master agreement" documentation structures

What is a master agreement structure?

19–04 It is common in situations in which parties are likely to conduct a large amount of repeat business of a similar type with one another for those parties to attempt to put in place some over-arching contractual documentation which will govern all of those different transactions, and also to have individual documents to confirm the terms of the individual trades. These over-arching documents are generally referred to as "master agreements"; whereas the documents dealing with individual transactions are referred to as "confirmations". A master agreement "structure" will involve bonding together the master agreement, any document used to amend the market standard terms of such a master agreement by any two parties, *all* of the confirmations documenting individual transactions, and any credit support documents (such as a guarantee or a collateral agreement) so that *all* of these documents taken together constitute a "single agreement" for contract law and insolvency law purposes. The single agreement philosophy is considered below. Master agreement structures are used in a number of financial markets and familiarity with the terms of the standard market contract for any given market is a key part of a lawyer's knowledge base in advising clients in those markets. The most detailed discussion of a master agreement in this book is the analysis of the ISDA Master Agreement structure across Chapters 41 through 43 of this book.[7]

In this book I will discuss the detail of the provisions of standard market documents for these sorts of transactions, where a standard market document exists and is generally available on the markets: for example, financial derivatives, *stock-lending, repos* and foreign exchange. Other forms of financial product which do not have a standard form of agreement, and where the parties' legal counsel tend to rely on their own, in-house documentation, will not be the subject of any specific terms because those documents are not constructed in a standard way and because they are not generally available. Instead, I will discuss the typical structures and common legal issues which are used in those markets: for example, in relation to bonds, syndicated lending, ordinary lending, and securitisations.

19–05 The principal reason why I decided to include a section in this chapter on the "performance and terms of contracts" on master agreements specifically was the readily apparent fact that most master agreements have the same basic objectives, very similar mechanisms for anticipating and resolving disputes between parties, and the same underlying philosophies. Their role has become very important in many financial markets as risk management tools and in the legal analysis of the products which they govern. Therefore, this section collects in one place a

---

[7] See also A.S. Hudson, *The Law on Financial Derivatives*, 5th edn (London: Sweet & Maxwell, 2012), Ch.3 on the terms of the ISDA Master Agreement.

distillation of the key issues surrounding master agreements. The law discussed in the remainder of this chapter—relating to the identification of conditions in contracts and the right to terminate those contracts—is of great importance because the role of most master agreements in essence is to enable the parties to terminate their transactions as quickly and painlessly as possible.

As is discussed below, there are a number of reasons why master agreements have become used in a number of markets: they make it possible to set off across a range of transactions, even on insolvency; they standardise risks across markets if they are used widely in the same form; and they go some way towards commoditizing complex financial products. These issues are discussed below. Before considering those policy issues, it is worth considering the circumstances in which master agreements are generally used. **19–06**

The reasons for using a master agreement

Master agreements are used most commonly in situations in which: first, the parties intend to conduct a large number of transactions of the same type; secondly, there are a large number of risks created by that type of product which the parties want to control across the whole of their transactions; and thirdly, in situations in which there is a standard master agreement used in relation to a particular product, even if the parties only intend to transact once. These motivations are considered in turn. **19–07**

Reasons for using a master agreement (1): the parties intend to transact a high volume of business

Master agreements came into use because parties intended to conduct a large amount of business between one another such that it was a waste of time to keep replicating long contracts for each individual transaction, particularly if those transactions might have expired before the contracts were executed. Furthermore, the real risks which the parties were seeking to control in their contracts, beyond a simple failure to pay, went far beyond the efficacy of one single transaction and therefore it would be important to allocate all of those risks across all of the parties' business between each other in a contract which served as a foundation for all of those transactions. For example, if the parties intend to conduct a large amount of foreign exchange business between one another, then they will have two principal legal concerns: first to ensure that each individual transaction has been contracted for appropriately, and secondly that the relationship between both parties across all of their transactions is protected from all of the many credit and other risks which may face them. These risks are considered next. Equally, very complex financial transactions—such as *interest rate swaps* and exotic, speculative financial derivatives—may require overarching documentation, particularly if it is thought that there may yet be a number of derivatives contracted over time between the parties, to protect the parties from the broad range of risk that was discussed in Chapter 1. There are other forms of complex financial transaction—such as securities issues or securitisations—which do not **19–08** use master agreement structures because there is no market standard for their construction and because each of them is very different on its own terms.

Reasons for using a master agreement (2): risk management

19–09 Market trade associations frequently advocate and co-ordinate the creation of standard market agreements—for example in relation to derivatives, capital markets, stock-lending, repos, foreign exchange, and so on—because a large amount of the risk which faces financial markets can be either reduced or controlled if participants in those markets know that the risks which they face have a legal framework and also if it can be known that across those markets most participants are dealing with those risks in the same way. This is said to ease *systemic risk*.

19–10 The key concern surrounding *systemic risk* is that new markets like derivatives markets or securitisations might carry within them a risk which cannot yet be identified (an "unknown unknown"[8]). This might cause one or more large financial institutions to fail and so set off a chain reaction in which the pressure of one institution's failure causes default in other institutions when they are not paid what they are owed by the first institution to fail. The risk is that the financial system might collapse or at least go through a profound trauma—as with the global financial crisis of 2007–09 in which governments had to intervene to save a number of financial institutions. Therefore, trade associations promote standard means of conceiving of the parties' legal issues so that it can be known both that participants in the marketplace have a reasoned and reasonable basis for their contracts, so that it can be known that most participants in a market face similar problems if a systemic event does occur, and so regulators can know how those market participants will be required to solve their legal issues under the terms of those documents.

19–11 What is important to remember is that there is no obligation on contracting parties whatsoever to use these standard form agreements. There is no regulatory principle to that effect nor is there any legislation enshrining these standard agreements. The markets which are at issue are over-the-counter markets: that is, markets outside formal exchanges. Products which are traded on exchanges will be governed by the rules of those exchanges. That is not what is at issue here. Therefore, the goal of the trade associations, with regulatory support no doubt, is to encourage parties when contracting privately to use standard form agreements. By introducing standard forms of agreement it is expected that the risks which are posed by financial products will become standardised, and consequently that (in legal terms at least) the products themselves will become commoditised. That is, it is expected that these one-off transactions created privately between parties off-exchange will have a large number of features which are the same and therefore that the legal analysis of the products which become so uniform that those contracts will become effectively commodities with as few features distinguishing them from one another as is possible. This is an interesting

---

[8] See para.31–02 on "unknown interests" and para.1–54 on "systematic risk".

example of free markets seeking to create their own uniformity: it is a sign of the free choosing to mould their own freedom into recognisable, uniform patterns.

Risk management in master agreements

There are four ways in which master agreement structures address risk. First, the transactions to which master agreements relate are created by traders verbally, as discussed in Chapter 17.[9] Consequently, the role of confirmations is both to confirm the existence of that contract and also to set out in writing the sorts of contractual terms which the parties' legal advisors would want to have agreed between them (as to governing law, market disruption, and so forth) but which the traders are unlikely to have discussed in the course of their transaction. Therefore, the confirmation reduces risk by establishing a contractual resolution of a number of issues which might otherwise arise.

19–12

Secondly, the parties are contractually typically required to pay in gross any amounts owed in relation to any confirmed transaction, but that would be an expensive way of doing business across the high volumes of such transactions that are likely to be in existence between market counterparties at any given time. Therefore, the parties need to provide for *payment netting* which will reduce their gross obligations to a single net amount. Usually, the master agreement provides that this payment netting takes place across all transactions of a particular type which are to be settled in the same currency on the same day. The only contractual limit on this provision is the extent of the parties' operations systems: so financial institutions will have one system which deals with interest rate swaps, one which deals with equity options, and so on—that is why the payment netting provision is usually limited to transactions of a particular type. That payment netting is limited to transactions in a particular currency, and perhaps transactions settled through a particular branch in a given jurisdiction, would also be a question of operational practicality. It would be expensive if parties owed amounts reciprocally to one another and were required to make those payments in full, whether that was under the same transaction, such as a *swap*, or under different transactions, but such that payment was to be made in the same currency on the same day. Payment netting provisions thus provide that the parties can set off the amounts which they owe reciprocally and then one party will be required only to pay the net amount. Consequently, the volume of the parties' obligations to one another is reduced for capital adequacy purposes and for the purposes of finding sufficient cash money or other assets to meet those obligations in gross.

19–13

Thirdly, the key provisions in any master agreement relate to the circumstances in which the parties can terminate their transactions. The greatest concern among those who constructed the master agreements relates to the risk of the insolvency of the counterparty and in particular to the need to set off any amounts owed between the parties in the event of the insolvency of one of them: this is referred to as "*close-out netting*". There are concerns under many systems of law as to whether or not amounts owed to an insolvent person can be off-set against amounts owed by that insolvent person, as is discussed in Chapter 22 the position

19–14

---

[9] See para.17–08.

under English law has been resolved.[10] A master agreement typically functions by identifying *events of default* which, if they occur, will entitle the non-defaulting party to commence the termination procedure. Typically, the termination procedure will entitle the non-defaulting party to set off amounts which are owing under all outstanding transactions under the master agreement so that it identifies one single, net amount which is to be paid by one party to the other in final settlement under the transaction. Some of the most common events of default are considered below.[11]

Warning notice: "master agreements can go down as well as up"

19–15   Three notes of warning should be sounded, however. First, master agreements will not salve all of the parties' ills: they are only ever compromise documents which constitute an uneasy consensus between the lawyers for the large financial institutions who in fact will have brought them into being at the behest of the sponsoring trade association. So, if a transaction is effected which is not within the standard type anticipated by the standard master agreement, then the parties will need to re-think their contract from the roots upwards. A good finance lawyer will always think the transaction through from the beginning and not become simply a slave to a standard market contract. If the goal of many finance lawyers is to wear bespoke suits, it is a surprise to find that so many of them are content to take their contracts off-the-peg.

19–16   Secondly, master agreements will not supplant the general, substantive law if for some reason that contract is void or otherwise ineffective. So, in *Westdeutsche Landesbank v Islington*[12] it was held by the High Court, Court of Appeal and House of Lords that once a party is found not to have the capacity to enter into that contract, then the purported contract is void ab initio and none of its terms are effective in any way. Consequently, the master agreement can have none of the effects which were hoped for it. Instead, the parties must anticipate the possibility of this sort of failure and construct their arrangements so as to minimise the effect of this loss or so as to ensure that the substantive law will give them the outcome that they seek, as is discussed in Chapter 42 *Collateralisation*. Often people think that I am being controversial when I say this,[13] but it is self-evidently the truth: an invalid contract will have no effect, and so nobody should be surprised when the general law (as discussed in this book in detail) decides the outcome of the parties' dealings. That is the effect of living under the rule of law, and I do not hear many people questioning that as a goal for democracies. Much of this law was considered in the previous chapter and its ramifications are considered in the next.

19–17   Thirdly, by way of example of what has gone before, standard market agreements can only hope to serve the standard case and therefore they tend to focus on transactions entered into by corporate entities and their attendant credit risks.

---

[10]   See para.22–91.
[11]   See para.19–48.
[12]   [1996] A.C. 669.
[13]   Das, *Swaps financing*.

Consequently, the most important provision in a master agreement (judged simply by its length) is usually the provision which defines the events which will be taken to constitute the "bankruptcy" of either party so that the counterparty may terminate all outstanding transactions. However, that does not cover situations in which trusts, for example, might reduce their capital or in which one of the beneficiaries might call for a large amount of the capital to be advanced to her: the trust would continue in existence but the credit worth of that trust would effectively have fallen away. Standard agreements generally only deal with ordinary companies, and nothing more exotic than that. Therefore, a transactional lawyer needs to think around and behind the standard market agreement and not simply shelter under it with everyone else as though it were an umbrella of words. Those who took the visionary step of standardising and commoditising legal risk in this way did not expect that they were dealing with all-comers in all situations. That is not the point of a master agreement. Other detailed issues with master agreements are highlighted generally in Chapters 41 through 43.

Reasons for using a master agreement (3): the master agreement is the standard document

When a master agreement is put in place for a one-off transaction that may simply be because the parties need a form of documentation on which they can agree and which they believe caters reliably for the risks which they face. So, for example, in a *bond* issue with an *embedded swap* (which would be used to alter the effect rate of interest paid by the issuer of that bond) it is usual to have the bond contract supplemented by a standard ISDA master agreement and confirmation for derivatives (which could be suitable for contracting thousands of swaps instead of just one) because that is considered to be the most appropriate format for documenting that swap.

19–18

D.   Issues with standard form contracts

Standard form contracts, "boiler-plate" clauses and novel situations

As was set out immediately above, the principal danger with contracts being effected in standard form is that this is the enemy of thought. A good lawyer thinks a transaction through from first principles, as opposed simply to relying on the standard documentation that is being used by the herd. Typically, the good lawyer will not need to take hours and hours over this with transactions which are intended to be and indeed are entirely ordinary, and thus appropriate for standard treatment. However, sticking slavishly to the standard form without thinking through the transaction creates an enormous legal risk: the risk is that the contract fails to meet the needs of the contracting parties in that particular context, or that signing a standard form contract in spite of there being peculiar characteristics about this transaction might demonstrate that the parties had no meeting of minds, or that the contract might simply be ineffective. The clearest example of

19–19

this sort of risk arose in the local authority swaps cases[14] in which contracts which the parties believed to be valid turned out to have been beyond the powers of the local authorities. Because a standard form of documentation and of credit support had been used, there was no impetus for the parties to construct a form of credit support which might have survived the failure of the principal transaction or to have ensured the severability of some parts of the transaction from others.[15] Whenever a novel twist on a standard transaction is used, this should set bells ringing in the lawyer's mind: after all, innovation is the lifeblood of financial practice and commercial innovation cannot be expected to consider all the legal risks in the white heat of the trading floor.

Standard form contracts, "the battle of forms", and no meeting of minds

19–20   In many financial transactions it is usual for large financial institutions to have a fixed position on the form of contract which they require before they are prepared to transact business, or to have in mind a menu of terms which are obligatory for them, terms which are merely preferred, and terms which are desirable but easily given up in negotiation. This position results from institutions taking professional advice, usually on entry to a new market, which hardens into the fixed view of each institution as they contract ever more business of that type. The larger the transaction, the more likely it is that outside professional advice will be taken each time; but the more that business is done in high volumes, the more likely it is that such advice will not be taken and instead that the institutions will rely on their own employees to document transactions.

19–21   The result of this process of high volume documentation is that each institution will frequently—for example in high volume financial derivatives business[16]— send their standard form documentation to their counterparty, so that each party is simply sending their own documentation out and not reading the documentation that is sent to them. There is then a stand-off, with no documentation having been signed. Because traders do not discuss the detailed legal terms of a transaction, it is unlikely that specific issues such as the governing law of the transaction, the presence of insolvency set-off provisions and so on will have been agreed between the parties. The risk then is that the parties will only have demonstrated that there was no meeting of minds between them when they sent out their contradictory standard contractual terms to one another.

Standard form contracts and unfair terms

19–22   As considered above in Chapter 17, it is common for financial institutions to use standard terms when dealing with other financial institutions, and usual practice for standard terms to be used when dealing with retail customers (that is, ordinary members of the public). When such terms are used, there are enhanced risks that an expert party is seeking unduly to influence an inexpert party, or that those

---

[14] On which see A.S. Hudson, *Swaps, Restitution and Trusts* (London: Sweet & Maxwell, 1999) generally.

[15] See A.S. Hudson, *Financial Derivatives*, 3–126 et seq.

[16] See para.17–24.

terms constitute unfair contract terms. This issue is considered in Chapter 18. One particularly remarkable occurrence on trading floors is the party which receives a financial institution's standard form contract and simply signs it and sends it back by fax[17] or email within minutes of its receipt. This will happen most frequently when a large financial institution is dealing with a small hedge fund when that hedge fund does not have sufficient resources to spend on employing legally qualified staff nor on taking outside counsel. This standard form contract is usually sent in its lengthiest form, possibly by fax, containing all of those provisions which that institution does not necessarily need to have in its contract but which are often included as "bargaining chips".[18] In such a situation the possibility of there having been no meeting of minds is raised, as is the possibility of there being found to be unfair contract terms which are being enforced on one party by the other.

E. Termination of financial contracts: the point of many contracts

The purpose behind the very existence of many contracts is the facilitation of the termination of dealings between the parties. Many of the "master agreements"— dealing for example with financial derivatives,[19] repos,[20] and stock-lending[21]— discussed in *Section Two: Specific Financial Techniques* of this book are put in place to cover all of the transactions entered into between the parties. They do not document individual transactions because that task is usually performed by deal tickets and the use of "confirmations".[22] The real purpose of a master agreement—which forms a single agreement by binding all of those confirmations into one contract—is to ensure formal legal niceties so that the parties can set off their obligations in the event of an insolvency or some other termination event. The commercial purpose for having a master agreement in place is so that the parties can terminate their transactions very quickly and neatly both by establishing what will constitute "conditions" of the parties' transactions, and by providing for express termination provisions which include mechanisms for bringing the parties' transactions to an end. For example, the master agreement which governs most derivatives contracts in the marketplace is made up primarily of "events of default" and "termination events" which organise the termination of all of the parties' outstanding transactions as covered by that master agreement. The other standard terms are primarily representations made by the parties to one another which will entitle the non-defaulting party to terminate the transaction if they turn out to be false. Other documentation used in these types of transactions is for credit support—again, protecting the parties against the default of the other.

19–23

---

[17] Once upon a time, everything was done by fax. It was a simpler age.
[18] That is, as terms which the parties will readily surrender to make it seem as though they are negotiating genuinely.
[19] See para.41–01.
[20] See para.50–14.
[21] See para.50–01.
[22] See para.41–08.

The role of the lawyer in this context is to be suspicious of the other party, and to be paranoid and thus conscious of all of the things which could possibly go wrong with the transaction.

F.   Mismatches in hybrid transactions

19–24   One of the key issues with complex financial transactions is ensuring that the various conventions for the various marketplaces or jurisdictions or institutions are matched. For example, in relation to complex financial derivatives such as "embedded swaps"—in which an interest rate swap is bound into a bond transaction so that the issuer of the bond can pay an effective rate of interest which is preferable to that which would otherwise be required under a bond transaction without an interest rate swap—it would be all too easy to have terms in the various documents which clash with one another. So, it is important that all of the events of default under the bond transaction will constitute events of default under the swap transaction so that nothing will cause the termination of one transaction but leave the other transaction continuing in existence. It is also important that payment day conventions for one transaction are the same as the conventions for the other transactions; and so on. If there were mismatches, then payments might be made under one transaction but not be required under the other, and so on. Different marketplaces have different conventions both for their standard market contractual terms and for their commercial practices (how payments are made, at what stage in the process, days on which markets are open or closed, and so on)—so these differences need to be catered for. This is a very practical matter indeed. There are also purely legal questions such as ensuring that the tax and regulatory effects of the hybrid transaction are as the parties wish them to be.

G.   Failure of contract and the role of the general law

19–25   The law relating to remedies for failure of contract is considered in Chapter 20. The risk once a contract fails—that is, once a contract has been held to be invalid—is that all of the parties' carefully crafted documentation and credit support structures cease to have any effect.[23] At that stage the general law deals with the way in which the failed contract is to be unwound. This presents a range of risks which are beyond the control of the parties: risks that the courts will decide on the treatment of their situation in ways that they will not like.[24]

---

[23] See for example *Westdeutsche Landesbank v Islington* [1996] A.C. 669, as discussed in A. Hudson, *Swaps, Restitution and Trusts* (London: Sweet & Maxwell, 1999), especially at p.111 et seq. in relation to the failure of the contract.

[24] See for example *Westdeutsche Landesbank v Islington* [1996] A.C. 669; [1996] 2 All E.R. 961, 965. See A. Hudson, *Swaps, Restitution and Trusts*, p.160.

H. Avoiding insolvency through contract and property structures

The principal concern in complex financial transactions is the ability to set off amounts which are owed mutually between the parties. The problem in a case of insolvency is that the insolvent person will both not be able to pay any amounts it owes and will also still seek recovery of amounts owed to it. Therefore, it is important for the solvent party to be able to set off these amounts so that only a smaller net sum is owed by one party to the other. In this way the systemic risk of the failure of a large financial institution can be reduced because the losses in effect across the market will be smaller, net losses and not losses in gross. Insolvency set-off is discussed in Chapter 22.

19–26

3. Frequently Used Contractual Terms Permitting Termination

A. Introduction

This section considers in outline some frequently occurring terms in standard market contracts. These terms are all considered in some detail in Chapter 41 in relation to derivatives documentation by way of worked examples which are considered in all chapters of this book dealing with financial products that have master agreements: here there is a summary of those terms in the abstract. These provisions are all defensive in nature in that they enable the parties to exit the transaction comparatively easily. The lay-out of this section begins with distinguishing between conditions and warranties, and thus between terms which may cause the termination of the agreement automatically and terms which may not.

19–27

B. Conditions and mere warranties

Express conditions grant rights to termination

Conditions of a contract are, strictly speaking, those terms which cut to the heart of the contract so that any breach of that condition entitles the non-defaulting party to terminate the contract. Conditions stand aside from the other terms of the contract which may impose obligations on one or other of the parties but which do not require that the contract is treated as having been terminated: this second class of contractual terms is referred to as "mere warranties". The process of deciding whether any given contractual term is a condition or a warranty is one which requires a close reading of any given term to decide what is the better interpretation to be placed on it. A well-drafted contract would make it clear whether or not any given term in a contract is a condition or a warranty; and such a provision will be decisive of the matter.[25] It is a matter for the parties to decide

19–28

---

[25] *Bettini v Gye* (1875) 1 Q.B. 183; *Financings Ltd v Baldock* [1963] 2 Q.B. 104; *Hongkong Fir Shipping Co Ltd v Kawasaki Kisen Kaisha Ltd* [1962] 2 Q.B. 26; *Photo Production Ltd v Securicor Transport Ltd* [1980] A.C. 827; *Bunge Corp v Tradax Export SA* [1980] Lloyd's Rep. 294; *Lombard North Central Plc v Butterworth* [1987] Q.B. 527.

whether or not they consider a term to be important: to some parties to financial transactions, matters such as the delivery of a document may be vitally important for their own regulatory or tax purposes. As Blackburn J. held in *Bettini v Gye*[26]:

> "Parties may think some matter, apparently of very little importance, essential; and if they sufficiently express an intention to make the literal fulfilment of such a thing a condition precedent, it will be one . . ."

Therefore, when we come to consider many of the standard market contracts in *Section Two* of this book, we shall see that it is usual for those contracts in standard form to identify some matters as being of the essence of the contract and therefore as being conditions; and the parties using those standard form agreements in particular circumstances may alter the standard language so as to elevate other contractual terms to the level of being conditions. Precise specifications as to how a contract is to be performed will be conditions if the parties provide to that effect, no matter how pedantic those provisions may seem to other minds; and the parties will be able to terminate the contract if such conditions are breached, even if the parties' real reason for relying on their right to terminate the agreement is based on the fact that the contract would no longer be profitable for them.[27] However, in some cases the fact that the parties refer to a term as being a "condition" will not always be decisive of the matter if the contract has been poorly drafted and the better interpretation to be placed on that term is that it is in fact a mere warranty.[28] This is unlikely in relation to standard form contracts and, one would hope, in relation to other documentation in financial markets even if it is drafted under pressure and in haste.

Conditions precedent and conditions subsequent

19–29　Conditions may specify that the enforceability of a contract is contingent of the performance of some act by the parties. A condition precedent is a condition which must be performed before the contract comes into effect. An example of a condition precedent would be: "the Buyer shall make a payment of £10,000 by way of a premium to the Seller before any obligation on the Seller to pay any amount to the Buyer shall come into effect". So, in this example (as an option), there is no obligation on the seller of that option to perform its obligations until the buyer has paid the "premium". Alternatively, the condition could be a "condition subsequent" which might occur after the contract had been formed and after the parties had begun to perform the terms of that contract, but which would cause the contract to be terminated. An example of a condition subsequent would be: "this contract shall be effective unless any obligation to make a payment under this contract shall become subject to a withholding tax". If a withholding tax was later introduced to apply to a contract of this sort, then the contract would no longer be enforceable. A well-drafted contract would then specify the manner in which the contract would be terminated. It is common to provide that the

---

[26] (1875) 1 Q.B. 183, at 187.

[27] *Arcos Ltd v EA Ronaasen and Son* [1933] A.C. 470.

[28] See for example the speech of Lord Reid in *L Schuler AG v Wickman Machine Tool Sales Ltd* [1974] A.C. 235.

parties' obligations are subject to their counterparty having performed certain actions (such as making payment or delivering appropriate, specified documentation) or having a specified status (such as appropriate capacity to act, or having granted its agents appropriate authority to act, or not being insolvent). In other words, if those conditions have not been satisfied, then the contract is void and unenforceable. Those requirements would need to be specified to be conditions of the contract, and not merely warranties which would not justify terminating the entire contract.

Denning L.J. set out the following analysis of whether something described in a contract as a "condition precedent" is properly to be described as such, where the facts at issue related to whether or not a lender was required to provide a credit to the plaintiff on the satisfaction of a condition precedent[29]:   **19–30**

> "What is the legal position of such a stipulation? Sometimes it is a condition precedent to the formation of a contract, that is, it is a condition which must be fulfilled before any contract is concluded at all. In those cases the stipulation 'subject to the opening of a credit' is rather like a stipulation 'subject to contract'. If no credit is provided there is no contract between the parties. In other cases, a contract is concluded and the stipulation for a credit is a condition which is an essential term of the contract. In those cases the provision of the credit is a condition precedent not to the formation of the contract, but to the obligation of the seller to deliver the goods. If the buyer fails to provide the credit, the seller can treat himself as discharged from any further performance of the contract and can sue the buyer for damages for not providing the credit."

This approach suggests that the court will have to consider the substance of what the contract provides and decide whether the condition relates to the contract being effective at all or simply whether breach of that condition brings the contract to an end.

The identification of terms as conditions if they are not expressly defined to be such

Therefore, as considered above, a term will be a condition if it is specified in the contract as being a condition.[30] However, the question then must be how to identify a condition in a contract if it is not expressed to be a condition. The test for deciding whether or not any contractual term is a condition rather than a mere warranty is that the term must go "to the root of the matter, so that failure to perform it would render the performance of the rest of the contract a thing different in substance from what the defendant had stipulated for".[31] Furthermore, it is important to ascertain whether or not breach of that term would affect "the substance and foundation of the adventure which the contract is intended to carry   **19–31**

---

[29] *Trans Trust SPRL v Danubian Trading Co Ltd* [1952] 2 Q.B. 297, 304.
[30] *Lombard North Central Plc v Butterworth* [1987] Q.B. 527.
[31] *Bettini v Gye* (1875) 1 Q.B. 183, 188; *Graves v Legg* (1854) 9 Exch. 709, 716.

out".[32] By contrast, a warranty is a term of a contract which, when breached, "gives rise to a claim for damages but not to a right ... to treat the contract as repudiated".[33]

The interpretation of intermediate terms

19–32   There will often be terms, in poorly-drafted contracts where conditions are not expressly identified, which are not clearly in one camp or the other. For example, in *Hong Kong Fir Shipping v Kawasaki Kisen Kaisha*[34] the Court of Appeal held that the late provision of a ship with an inappropriate crew did not constitute a breach which justified terminating the contract, but rather only permitted the recovery of damages because the breach did not render the contract otiose. Terms of this sort are referred to as "innominate" or "intermediate" terms because they are neither obviously conditions nor warranties. Their effect falls to be determined by analysing each term in its own context. What emerges from the judgment of Diplock L.J. is that a contract which contains very wide-ranging obligations to make a ship "seaworthy" includes important tasks and comparative minor tasks, just as an obligation to maintain a "suitable portfolio" of investments could be said to involve minor decisions and major decisions, such that the particular breach which is complained of by the claimant will fall to be considered in its own terms because the term as a whole encompasses things which could be conditions or which could be warranties.

19–33   This approach could be understood as part of a drift in some of the cases to encourage parties to carry out their contractual obligations by not assuming that terms are conditions so as to terminate those contracts, such as the decision of the Court of Appeal in *Cehave NV v Bremer Handelsgesellschaft mbH (The Hansa Nord)*[35] which suggested that one should not be able to rely on branding an intermediate term as a condition so as to terminate a contract because of adverse market conditions.[36] The courts here could be understood as distinguishing between trivial breaches of the contract (which will not justify termination of the contract) and fundamental breaches of the contract (which will justify such a termination). It is suggested, however, that the clear identification of a term as being a condition of the contract in the contract itself will not be unpicked by the court.

The principles governing the categorisation of uncertain terms between being conditions and warranties in master agreements

19–34   It is not possible in the abstract to delineate all of those terms which will and those which will not constitute conditions and those which would be mere warranties. The question of categorisation can be resolved only on a case-by-case

---

[32] *Bentsen v Taylor, Sons & Co* [1893] 2 Q.B. 274, 281, per Bowen L.J.

[33] Definition used in Sale of Goods Act 1979 s.61(1). See also *Bunge Corp v Tradax Export SA* [1981] 1 W.L.R. 711, 724.

[34] [1962] 2 Q.B. 26.

[35] [1976] Q.B. 44.

[36] [1976] Q.B. 44, 70, per Roskill L.J.

basis and then usually by proper interpretation of the documentation. In standard form agreements, there will usually be a provision which identifies a range of matters as being of the essence of the contract, including the parties' capacity and authority to contract, the absence of litigation and so forth.[37] Where the parties have expressly identified a particular provision as being fundamental to their contract, then that term will be considered to be a condition of the contract such that a failure to perform it will release the non-defaulting party from their obligations under the contract.[38] Alternatively, if the parties have not expressly specified that any particular term is a condition, the court will imply that status in accordance with the test set out above as to whether or not the term is sufficiently fundamental to the contract.[39] It is therefore important to identify any term the breach of which is considered by the parties to constitute a condition of the contract such that its breach ought properly to terminate that contract automatically.[40] Similarly, even if a term is a mere warranty, then it would be important to identify the size of the loss which might be expected to flow from its breach, which would be capable of compensation in damages (as considered in the next chapter). This is particularly important in circumstances in which the loss which might result is the cost of closing out a hedge which the courts might not otherwise consider to fall within the foreseeable loss under that contract.[41]

The efficacy of termination clauses

It is usual in financial agreements to provide for circumstances in which the parties are entitled to terminate the contract. The clearest means of doing this would be to make the matters identified in the events of default provisions into express conditions under the terms of the contract. In Chapter 41 we consider in detail the termination provisions which are used in derivatives documentation: those provisions are concerned to terminate the contract if either party fails to pay, or goes insolvent, or commits a breach under some other transaction, and so forth. The general question arises whether or not a termination provision will always be valid. In *Nuova Safim SpA v The Sakura Bank Ltd*[42] it was held that those derivatives termination provisions were effective. However, the decision of the Court of Appeal in *Rice v Great Yarmouth BC*[43] caused concern among contract lawyers when it held that a term purporting to permit termination for "any" breach could be picked apart in the way suggested in *Hong Kong Fir Shipping v Kawasaki Kisen Kaisha*[44] (considered above) by distinguishing

19–35

---

[37] See para.41–50.

[38] *Financings Ltd v Baldock* [1963] 2 Q.B. 104; *Bunge Corp v Tradax Export SA* [1980] Lloyd's Rep. 294; *Lombard North Central Plc v Butterworth* [1987] Q.B. 527; unless the circumstances point to the opposite conclusion, *L.G. Shuler AG v Wickman Machine Tool Sales Ltd* [1974] A.C. 235; *Antaois Compania Naviera SA v Salen Rederierna AB* [1985] A.C. 191.

[39] *Hongkong Fir Shipping Co Ltd v Kawasaki Kisen Kaisha Ltd* [1962] 2 Q.B. 26; *Photo Production Ltd v Securicor Transport Ltd* [1980] A.C. 827; *Bunge Corp v Tradax Export SA* [1980] Lloyd's Rep. 294.

[40] See para.43–09.

[41] See para.43–38.

[42] [1999] C.L.C. 1830; [1999] 2 All E.R. (Comm) 526.

[43] *The Times*, July 26, 2000.

[44] [1962] 2 Q.B. 26.

between trivial breaches of the contract and fundamental breaches of the contract. Market practice has tended to be to provide that only "material" breaches will grant a right to terminate the entire contract; although it is suggested that if the contract expressly identifies an explicit mechanism for terminating a contract on the happening of specified events, then that contractual mechanism should be put into effect provided that it causes no other harm.

4. Commonly Used Master Agreement Provisions

A. Introduction

19–36   This section considers some of the most significant species of contractual provision which are found in master agreements, all of which the parties would ordinarily consider to be central to the efficacy of such a contract and therefore as being conditions of the contract. The aim of this section is to provide a central discussion of these types of provision in their most general form, before they are considered in the context of various different types of financial product in *Section Two: Specific Financial Techniques* in this book.

B. Failure to pay or deliver

The commercial purpose of failure to pay provisions

19–37   Failure to make a payment or failure to make a delivery of a commodity or a security or other property are clearly fundamental breaches of any financial transaction created for the sole purpose of receiving payment or delivery of property. The contract may do one of three things. Failure to pay or to deliver would need to be contractually required by an identified date and/or in a specified manner before there could be said to have been any "failure"—a contract must make that plain. First, it may provide that this failure immediately terminates the contract and so the non-defaulting party is not obliged to perform any further obligations itself. Secondly, in the alternative, the contract may provide that there is no automatic termination but that instead the defaulting party must make its payment or delivery as specified in the contract together with a payment of a penalty, calculated usually in the form of an amount of interest on the total value of the transaction. Thirdly, in the alternative, the contract may specify that the contract remains in effect and that instead the parties are required to enter into some form of arbitration: this is unlikely in this instance, although possible in relation to other forms of default. In either case default interest may be payable or any credit support structure could be drawn upon if the defaulting party failed to make payment or to deliver.

Whether failure to pay is a condition of the contract

19–38   If a contract provides expressly that failure to make payment on time is a condition of the contract, then late payment will entitle the non-defaulting party to terminate the contract.[45] If a contract specifies that delivery of some property, whether a chattel or a security or some other instrument, is "of the essence" of that contract, then late delivery of that property would entitle the non-defaulting party to terminate the contract[46] and to claim damages for any breach of contract caused by that breach.[47] It would be clearly of the essence of a cash-settled financial transaction that the parties pay one another because receiving and making payment is the sole purpose for creating such a transaction. Therefore, such a term would be a condition of that sort of contract. However, the parties commonly provide in financial transactions that late payment or late delivery can be excused provided both that payment or delivery is made within a contractually specified number of business days after the due date, and also that default interest of some sort is payable. The question of default interest is considered in the next section.

Default interest and penalty clauses

It is common to provide in financial contracts for the payment of default interest in the event that a party pays any amount due under the contract late or makes any delivery late. Penalty clauses are not enforceable under English contract law: a penalty clause is a clause which aims to punish the defaulting party or to deter the defaulting party from breaching the contract,[48] for example, by requiring her to pay the non-defaulting party a large amount of money.[49] What would be valid is a clause which either provides that the non-defaulting party is entitled to recover its losses resulting from the defaulting party's breach or which provides that the defaulting party must pay an amount which is a reasonable estimate of the loss which the non-defaulting party is likely to suffer.[50] Therefore a contractual provision which imposed an obligation on a party who failed to perform her obligations to "pay £10,000 forthwith as censure for the breach of contract" would be void as being a penalty clause. However, a clause which provided that the defaulting party must "compensate in full the counterparty for any losses or expenses caused by the default" would be valid, as would a provision which required that the defaulting party must "compensate the defaulting party for the cost of acquiring a replacement transaction, the cost of unwinding any associated hedging transaction and the cost of funding any transaction terminated further to the default", because those provisions estimate the losses suffered by the non-defaulting party. If a penalty clause is void that does not affect the non-defaulting party's right to recover their loss by way of damages for breach of contract. So, a clause which purported to grant a party a right to recover any arrears owed to it and also to recover any amounts which

19–39

---

[45] *Lombard North Central Plc v Butterworth* [1987] Q.B. 527, CA.

[46] *Bunge Corp, New York v Tradax Export SA, Panama* [1980] 1 Lloyd's Rep. 294, 305 and 309, per Megaw and Browne L.JJ.; accepted in *Lombard North Central Plc v Butterworth* [1987] Q.B. 527, per Mustill L.J.

[47] *Lombard North Central Plc v Butterworth* [1987] Q.B. 527.

[48] *Lordsvale Finance Plc v Bank of Zambia* [1996] Q.B. 752; *Cine Bes Filmcilik Ve Yapim Click v United International Pictures* [2003] EWCA Civ 1669.

[49] *Lombard North Central Plc v Butterworth* [1987] Q.B. 527.

[50] *Lombard North Central Plc v Butterworth* [1987] Q.B. 527.

would have fallen due in the future was found to be a penalty clause; although that party was entitled to recover the arrears and also the future payments under common law damages because the counterparty had announced that it would not make payment in the future and thereby had committed a repudiatory breach of the contract.[51]

19–40 The question is then: when will a clause in a financial agreement constitute a void penalty clause or a valid clause seeking default interest? In addressing this question one must have regard to the principle set out in the House of Lords in *Dunlop Pneumatic Tyre Company v New Garage and Motor Company Ltd*.[52] The approach set out in that case for distinguishing between valid clauses and void penalty clauses has been summarised by Colman J. in *Lordsvale Finance Plc v Bank of Zambia*[53] as:

> "a matter of construction to be resolved by asking whether at the time the contract was entered into the predominant contractual function of the provision was to deter a party from breaking the contract [and so be void] or to compensate the innocent party for breach",

and so be valid. Assisting this process, in the words of Colman J., can be addressed in the following way: "[t]hat the contractual function is deterrent rather than compensatory can be deduced by comparing the amount that would be payable on breach with the loss that might be sustained if breach occurred".[54] This approach was approved in *Cine Bes Filmcilik Ve Yapim Click v United International Pictures*[55] by Mance L.J. and in *Murray v Leisureplay Plc*[56] by Arden L.J.

19–41 Mance L.J. in *Cine* also approved the dicta of Colman J. in *Lordsvale* to the effect that there may be perfectly valid clauses which do not necessarily identify a precise means of calculating the loss to the parties provided that the clause—such as a clause in *Lordsvale* to increase the rate of interest payable—can be explained as being "commercially justifiable" or as a calculation as part of a liquidated damages clause, and not simply directed at deterring the other party from breach of the contract. Therefore, a default interest provision would need to be addressed at some commercially reasonable rate which would meet some cost to be suffered by the non-defaulting party, such as funding the late payment or delivery. Another approach suggested by Lord Woolf in *Philips v Attorney General for Hong Kong*[57] is that the courts should promote legal certainty by enforcing the contract which the parties had agreed between them. The only objection to this blow for the principle of freedom of contract is that it is a matter of policy which deters penalty clauses in English contract law, and not a lapse in its affection for free markets.

---

[51] *Lombard North Central Plc v Butterworth* [1987] Q.B. 527. But see G. Treitel, "Damages on rescission for breach of contract" [1987] L.M.C.L.Q. 143.
[52] [1914] UKHL 1.
[53] [1996] Q.B. 752, at 762.
[54] [1996] Q.B. 752, at 762.
[55] [2003] EWCA Civ 1669.
[56] [2005] EWCA Civ 963, [13], per Arden L.J.
[57] (1993) 61 VL.R. 49.

The principles governing the identification of a term as being a condition, a termination of a contract provision, and a penalty clause

This section summarises the principles set out in the preceding sections relating to the identification of a term as being a condition of a contract, and as to the enforceability of default interest provisions. Mustill L.J. set out these propositions very clearly in the following dicta in his lordship's judgment in *Lombard North Central Plc v Butterworth*[58] (the numbering is taken from the judgment):

19–42

"1.   Where a breach goes to the root of the contract, the injured party may elect to put an end to the contract. Thereupon, both sides are relieved from those obligations which remain unperformed.

2.   If he does so elect, the injured party is entitled to compensation for (a) any breaches which occurred before the contract was terminated and (b) the loss of his opportunity to receive performance of the promisor's outstanding obligations.

3.   Certain categories of obligation, often called conditions, have the property that any breach of them is treated as going to the root of the contract. Upon the occurrence of any breach of condition, the injured party can elect to terminate and claim damages, whatever the gravity of the breach.

4.   It is possible by express provision in the contract to make a term a condition, even if it would not be so in the absence of such a provision.

5.   A stipulation that time is of the essence, in relation to a particular contractual term, denotes that timely performance is a condition of the contract. The consequence is that delay in performance is treated as going to the root of the contract, without regard to the magnitude of the breach.

6.   It follows that where a promisor fails to give timely performance of an obligation in respect of which time is expressly stated to be of the essence, the injured party may elect to terminate and recover damages in respect of the promisor's outstanding obligations, without regard to the magnitude of the breach.

7.   A term of the contract prescribing what damages are to be recoverable when a contract is terminated for a breach of condition is open to being struck down as a penalty, if it is not a genuine covenanted pre-estimate of the damage, in the same way as a clause which prescribes the measure for any other type of breach. No doubt the position is the same where the clause is ranked as a condition by virtue of an express provision in the contract.

8.   A clause expressly assigning a particular obligation to the category of condition is not a clause which purports to fix the damages for breaches of the obligation, and is not subject to the law governing penalty clauses."

In all of one's study of law, there is nothing to match a clear summary by a judge of all of the relevant principles. This summary, it is suggested, draws together all of the principles made thus far about the ability of contractual provisions to trigger termination of a contract.[59]

---

[58] [1987] Q.B. 527.

[59] In *Office of Fair Trading v Abbey National Plc* [2008] EWHC 2325 the question was whether or not charges levied on current accountholders while their accounts were overdrawn were "not capable of amounting to" penalties under the common law under the terms of the 1999 Regulations. The payment of a charge which was referable to the commission of some wrongdoing—that is, using the account once it had gone overdrawn—was therefore penal in that sense (applying *Cooden Engineering Co Ltd v Stanford* [1952] 2 All E.R. 915). This was so even if the accountholder acquired benefits, such as the continued facility of a bank account. Some of the banks' general terms and conditions for current accounts were held not penal and others penal, although for the most part the facts were adjourned for further argument at further hearings.

A. Contractual provisions relating to the performance of the contract

The calculation agent

19–43   The role of the calculation agent is significant in complex transactions: the calculation agent must calculate the amount (if any) that is to be paid between the parties, the market value of the transactions, whether any collateral is required to be paid, and so on. It is common for one of the parties to be the calculation agent: usually the seller of the financial instrument. In a contract it is usual to identify a calculation agent for any such calculations and to provide that the calculations which she carries out shall be considered to be correct and binding on the parties in the absence of manifest error or dishonesty. A corrupt calculation agent could clearly refuse payment to be made even if a transaction is in-the-money. More common is a situation in which both parties disagree with each other and the calculation agent as to the appropriate calculation, and therefore the contract provides a mechanism for appointing a third party who deals in such instruments regularly to perform the calculation, or else for three other parties to perform those calculations and for an average of their results to be binding between the parties. Much of this issue would be removed if the parties would include a clear pricing formula for their transaction in the documentation itself, instead of leaving it to the calculation agent. In the Court of Appeal in *Socimer International Bank Ltd v Standard Bank London Ltd*[60] it was held that a person acting in a position of, in effect, a calculation agent (in that the defendant was required to calculate the market value of securities under a "forward" in relation to securities transactions) will be bound "as a matter of necessary implication, by concepts of honesty good faith, and genuineness, and the need for the absence of arbitrariness, capriciousness, perversity and irrationality".[61] Therefore, the calculation agent may not act entirely as it wishes in establishing the market value of financial instruments. This is particularly important in derivatives transactions (such as forwards) considered in Chapter 40 where the value of the transaction to each party will change depending on market fluctuations.

Market disruption, extraordinary event and frustration

19–44   Market disruption arises, for example, when an exchange on which a share is traded ceases to operate for an identified period of time. The question is how the parties are to proceed in the event that the market disruption either takes only a short period of time to resolve itself and so causes only a slight disruption to the parties' transaction, or which effectively terminates the transaction. An extraordinary event would involve something fundamental interfering with the parties' transaction, such as the merger or nationalisation or liquidation of either party, or constituting some material adverse change in the ability of the contract

---

[60] [2008] EWCA Civ 116; [2008] Bus. L.R. 1304.
[61] [2008] EWCA Civ 116; [2008] Bus. L.R. 1304, at [66], per Rix L.J. This principle was applied in *Barclays Bank Plc v Unicredit Bank AG* [2012] EWHC 3655 (Comm) to assess whether or not a power to terminate a CDO had been used in a commercially reasonable manner.

to function normally. It is a problem that the event will cause such a serious disruption that the assumptions underpinning the transaction cease to reflect the parties' commercial intentions. This may involve the frustration of the contract, as considered below.[62] The difficulty here is whether or not one wants to have the contract terminate automatically. Generally a non-defaulting party would want the contract to terminate at once. Therefore, that is what contracts usually provide. Occasionally, however, the contract may nevertheless be profitable for the non-defaulting party: in which case she may prefer to elect whether not to terminate it, if the contract so allows.

Force majeure clauses

A force majeure clause permits the parties to terminate a transaction when there is **19–45** some sufficiently serious alteration to the circumstances in which the contract was made and in which it was expected to be performed. Often these clauses are limited to acts of god, war and so forth. They may refer more generally to any phenomenon which would constitute a frustration of a contract—that is, one which negates its commercial purpose.[63] A force majeure clause provides that in the event that it is unlawful, impossible or impracticable to perform obligations under the master agreement, then either party may set in train the close-out procedure only if a "waiting period" has elapsed to see if that force majeure event has ceased to exist. Common examples of a more general form of force majeure provision would be political events (such as terrorist attacks or an outbreak of civil war), or economic events (such as the closure of an exchange by a government or governmental authority which makes it impossible to acquire a price, or the extinction of the validity of a currency), or regulatory events (such as a declaration by a regulatory authority that a party was no longer able to carry on a type of business, or possibly a declaration by a tax authority that a given product is to be treated differently for tax purposes).

Exceptional volatility

Exceptional volatility is a great problem when it disrupts the parties' expectations **19–46** for their transaction. It may be that trading on an exchange is disrupted or that market events mean that the result of their transaction is something other than that for which they contracted. The contract may provide that the transaction is to be treated as being frustrated (and thus terminated) or else it may provide another mechanism for giving effect to the contract (for example, by carrying out any calculations on the next date when that market is deemed to be trading normally again). One type of provision which arises in some commercial contracts is an obligation that the parties will use "reasonable endeavours" or "their best endeavours" to rectify any loss or defect in the performance of the contract, such as transferring the contract to some other person. The concern would be that the defaulting party would make a pretence of salvaging the situation but would instead drag its feet. It has been held that "in the absence of any context

---

[62] See para.19–76.
[63] See para.19–76.

indicating to the contrary should be understood to mean that the purchaser is to do all he reasonably can to ensure" that the desired effect is achieved.[64] An example of this provision is the "termination event" procedure under derivatives contracts.[65]

B.   Protection against credit risk

19–47   The provision of credit support is discussed in detail in Chapter 22 *Taking Security*.

C.   Events of default commonly found in financial contracts

Contractual terms providing for termination of the contract

19–48   The treatment of termination clauses under general contract law is considered below.[66] As considered above, the occurrence of events of default typically trigger the termination provisions of a master agreement, as does breach of "covenant" in the language of loan transactions. The detailed provisions of master agreements in relation to derivatives,[67] stock-lending,[68] repos,[69] and foreign exchange spot and options trades[70] are considered elsewhere in the appropriate chapters of this book; and the contexts of loan covenants in relation to ordinary lending[71] and syndicated lending[72] are considered in the appropriate chapters of this book. Indeed, the particular types of events of default which are used in particular species of financial agreement form a significant part of the discussion in *Section Two* of this book. This section is intended only to give an introduction to some of those provisions before the considerably more detailed discussions of events of default in derivatives contracts and in loan contracts, for example, later in this book. From transaction to transaction, however, within particular species of financial product, there is enormous difference in the detail of the events of default as the parties seek to anticipate the particular risks associated with dealing with that counterparty in that market in that jurisdiction for that purpose at that time.

---

[64] *IBM United Kingdom Ltd v Rockware Glass Ltd* [1980] F.S.R. 335, 339; *Rhodia International Holdings Ltd v Huntsman International LLC* [2007] EWHC 292 (Comm).
[65] See para.43–23.
[66] See, for example, *Law Debenture Trust Corp v Elektrim Finance BV* [2005] EWHC 1999 (Ch) and para.19–56 et seq.
[67] See para.43–01.
[68] See para.50–01.
[69] See para.50–01.
[70] See para.36–01.
[71] See para.31–01.
[72] See para.32–01.

Cross default

A cross default provision anticipates a counterparty's likely failure to perform its obligations by providing that if that counterparty, or possibly any entity affiliated to that counterparty, should commit a default under *another* financial transaction of a specified kind, then that other default will trigger the termination of the contract containing the cross default provision. So if Miranda deals in *swaps* with Rowan, then Miranda will be concerned that if Rowan defaults in his obligations with other counterparties in other swaps contracts then Rowan is all the more likely to default in the future in swaps contracts with her: therefore, Miranda will provide by means of a cross default provision that Rowan's default under a swaps contract with a third party constitutes an event of default under all of the swaps contracts between Miranda and Rowan so that that Miranda can exit her contracts (she hopes) before Rowan goes into insolvency. The cross default which triggers this termination will need to be identified with sufficient clarity, and may amount simply to an acceleration of another obligation under another contract and not necessarily a complete default.

19–49

Acceleration of obligations

The acceleration of obligations, which is common in loan contracts, means that a contracting party is required to pay its obligations earlier than they would otherwise become due.[73] In loan contracts, if a borrower breaches one of the terms of the contract, then the loan is "accelerated" so that its obligations become repayable immediately and any credit support (a guarantee or something similar) may be called in by the lender. This is the principal means by which term loan contracts are terminated: instead of waiting for the time at which the loan would otherwise be paid off, once an event of default has occurred the loan is repayable immediately and the lender is entitled to recourse to any of the contractual mechanisms available to it. For other parties dealing with a borrower, knowing that obligations have been accelerated serves as fair warning that the borrower is probably in financial difficulties. The principles governing acceleration of loan contracts are considered in detail in Chapter 32,[74] including consideration of the relevant case law.

19–50

The concept of "cross acceleration" is used in master agreements so that the party which has not had its obligations accelerated (the non-defaulting party) may rely on the fact that its counterparty has had its obligations accelerated under another contract so as to terminate its agreement with its counterparty. The theory is that, if one's counterparty has its obligations accelerated under another agreement, then that counterparty is probably in financial difficulties and therefore all of the transactions which are outstanding under the master agreement should be terminated forthwith. So, if Maria had lent money to Boswell under a contract with a cross acceleration provision to the effect that it was an event of default for either party to have its obligations under any other indebtedness accelerated, then

19–51

---

[73] *Cheyne Finance Plc* [2007] EWHC 2116 took the expression "when they become due" to include anticipation of future events and not only events which had already come to fruition.
[74] See para.32–33.

if Boswell was required under his contract with Cleo to pay any amount earlier than it was otherwise due under that contract, Maria would be entitled to rely on that being an event of default under *her* contract with Boswell and so terminate her contract with Boswell by requiring him to pay all of his obligations immediately.

Wrongful acceleration

19–52   It is possible that a bank may open itself up to liability to pay damages in circumstances in which it sought to accelerate a contractual obligation (typically a loan) wrongfully. The cases relating to wrongful acceleration are considered in Chapter 32.[75]

Illegality and unenforceability

19–53   When contracts become unenforceable, the parties are thrown back on the general law to resolve disputes between them: these provisions are considered in the next chapter. That a contract becomes "illegal" means that its performance offends against the criminal law or against financial regulation, and therefore that it cannot be performed. The private international law consequences of contracts becoming illegal by other systems of law are considered in Chapter 6. Master agreements typically provide that if a contract becomes illegal, that will trigger the termination procedure under the contract unless the parties are able to circumvent that illegality.[76]

D.   Behaviour vitiating the contractual intention

Confusion, fat fingers and mistake

19–54   As is discussed in Chapter 17, it is common for mistakes to be made on trading floors whether because of the complexity of negotiations leaving the parties confused as to their final agreement,[77] or simple error inputting details into a computer, or offers of transactions being sent to potential customers containing erroneous terms, or the parties being at odds with one another. There have been a spate of so-called "fat finger" cases in which traders—whether or not in possession of unusually fat fingers we do not know—simply hitting the wrong keys on their keyboards or getting the terms of their transactions wrong and so inputting information as to a transaction which was wrong. The law on mistake is considered in Chapter 18. In practice one or other of the parties may be unwilling to litigate when their reputation might be threatened if their mistake were to come to light. On other occasions the mistake may have arisen from traders thinking

---

[75] See para.32–39.
[76] See para.43–23.
[77] See para.17–26.

that all of the legal issues had been resolved, or that they would be the same as in previous transactions, when in fact those issues were not resolved or were to be treated differently.

Misrepresentation: negligence and fraud

The legal treatment of misrepresentations which induce a person to enter in to a contract is considered in Chapters 24 and 25.

19–55

5.   COMMON LOAN COVENANTS

Loan covenants are considered in detail in Chapters 32 and 33 (relating to ordinary loans and to syndicated loans respectively). This discussion is intended merely to introduce the principal forms of loan covenant and the legal issues which they create. Loan covenants divide between covenants as to the condition of the borrower (its capacity, its continued solvency, its credit rating, and so forth); covenants as to the borrower's performance of its loan contracts generally (payments being made on time under this loan contract, no cross default on any other loans, no acceleration of payments under this loan or any other loan, and so on); covenants as to the continued feasibility of the loan (absence of any illegality, absence of any adverse tax treatment of the loan payments, and so on); and covenants governing the purposes for which the loan moneys may be used.

19–56

A.   Negative pledge

The nature of a negative pledge clause

If an *unsecured loan*[78] is made such that the lender has no rights to any identified assets of the borrower, as discussed in Chapter 22, then the lender will be concerned that the borrower will contract to transfer all of its assets to a third party after the unsecured loan has been made, with the result that the lender will not be able to recover its loan money because there will be insufficient property left. Consequently, unsecured lenders frequently include a provision in the loan contract which prevents the borrower from agreeing to transfer substantial parts of its assets to anyone else. Such a provision is known as a "negative pledge clause", which is a slight misnomer—the clause provides that the borrower will not "pledge" its assets to anyone else. Negative pledge clauses are in effect intended to ensure that the borrower retains priority to the borrower's assets among unsecured creditors in the event that there is a breach of duty under the unsecured loan contract. A negative pledge clause is a weak way of taking security because the lender does not have recourse as of right to any particular assets owned by the borrower or any third party: better mechanisms are set out in Chapter 22. When making loans, the lender will conduct a credit assessment of the borrower and will assess the likely risk of the borrower failing to make

19–57

---

[78] An unsecured loan is a loan made without the lender having any sort of security, such as a charge over the borrower's assets or property held on trust.

repayment: the reliance on a negative pledge clause is a result of the assessment that no further security is necessary but that the borrower's assets are sufficiently limited that some restriction on their use is required.

19–58 If a loan is made with the benefit of a *floating charge* in favour of the lender, that means that the lender has no property rights in any specific property before the charge crystallises.[79] Consequently, the lender will be concerned that the borrower might grant a fixed charge, for example, to some other person over the same assets as the floating charge and thereby leave the lender with a weaker right. Therefore, a lender may include a negative pledge in such a loan contract to prevent the borrower from granting any such rights over the assets which are intended to satisfy its obligations under the floating charge.[80]

19–59 Given that a negative pledge clause is a clause by which the borrower undertakes not to subordinate any of its assets to a secured interest of any other person, this would mean literally that the borrower would have to remain static and not use any of its assets at all. This is not what a negative pledge clause is intended to do. If the borrower is a trading entity then it will need to use its assets for the purposes of that trade: buying raw materials and selling finished products if it is a manufacturer, for example. Therefore, a negative pledge clause will need to identify those types of assets which can and cannot be used in the course of the trade without breaching the negative pledge provision. What a negative pledge clause is ordinarily worded to preclude is the creation of any "security interest" over any asset: but that would be to leave the borrower free to sell or to give away its assets. Furthermore, in the real world when a negative pledge clause comes to be negotiated, there may already be assets which are mortgaged to third parties or which are otherwise ring-fenced from the borrower's use. Therefore, negative pledge clauses must preclude selling assets, transferring assets away, creating any security interest over assets, but then define what types of assets may be dealt with by the borrower.

19–60 The Loan Market Association advocates the following sort of negative pledge clause by its members (but here it has been slightly simplified for the purposes of this discussion):

> "No [borrower, nor any member of the same group of companies as the borrower] shall . . . create or permit to subsist and Security over any of its assets. No [borrower, nor any member of the same group of companies as the borrower] shall . . .
> - sell, transfer or otherwise dispose of any of its assets on terms whereby they are or may be leased to or re-acquired by an Obligor;
> - sell transfer or otherwise dispose of any of its receivables on recourse terms;
> - enter into any arrangement under which money or the benefit of a bank or other account may be applied, set-off or made subject to a combination of accounts; or
> - enter into any other preferential arrangement having a similar effect
> - in circumstances where the arrangement or transaction is entered into primarily as a method of raising [the amount of debt ('financial indebtedness') of the borrower]."

---

[79] *Clough Mill v Martin* [1984] 3 All E.R. 982.

[80] *AIB Finance Ltd v Bank of Scotland* [1994] B.C.C. 184 has held that this negative pledge clause will not, however, constitute notice of the floating charge to any subsequent rightholder in relation to those assets.

There are therefore two elements to this definition. First, that no security interest—whether a charge, pledge, mortgage, trust or other structure discussed in Chapter 22—may be created over any of the borrower's assets. Secondly, a prohibition on sales or transfers of any assets, including arrangements whereby those assets may be sold and then leased back by the borrower, or any of the debts which are owed to the borrower (its "receivables") shall be transferred away, or any transaction which sets assets off against amounts owed to another person, or any transaction which grants a priority to someone else ahead of the lender (a "preferential arrangement"). The limitation in the final proviso—that pledges only matter if they are intended to increase the amount of the borrower's debt—raises questions as to what exactly constitutes "debt" in this context and may have the unfortunate effect that some ordinary business transactions are excluded if for example they increase the size of the borrower's ordinary overdraft or require the borrower to undertake to buy more raw materials to increase production. It would be usual to subject this provision to a "threshold term" so that obligations of only a small amount do not count, and that threshold would differ for borrower's who frequently deal in large projects one at a time—such as shipbuilders—which would be different from borrowers who deal in high volumes of small transactions—such as a restaurateur.

Enforcing a negative pledge clause

Breach of a negative pledge clause would ordinarily be expressed as constituting an event of default under a loan contract. Therefore, if there is a failure to observe the negative pledge provision—which would include the borrower going into insolvency and thereby transferring assets to its creditors—then the underlying contract would be terminated, as discussed above. As Professor Cranston (as he then was, now Mr Justice Cranston) sets out, there are then three avenues of action open to the lender.[81] First, seek an injunction to prevent a breach of the negative pledge clause, if the lender learns of a likely breach in time. An injunction could be sought against a third party who receives property which was intended for the use of another person.[82] However, it is suggested that the equitable remedy of injunction would not have effect against a third party purchaser who acquired those assets in good faith without having notice of the lender's rights under the "equity's darling" principle.[83] Otherwise, the third party could be liable for damages in tort in the event that the third party had interfered with the contract between the parties by procuring the transfer of the assets to it with, importantly, an intention to cause economic harm to the lender.[84] The tort of interference with contract is thus a limited doctrine, which developed originally in relation to traders seeking to divert opportunities towards themselves and away from parties who had already entered into contracts.[85] In the financial context it

19–61

[81] R. Cranston, *Principles of Banking Law*, 2nd edn (OUP, 2002), pp.317–318.

[82] See R. Cranston, *Principles of Banking Law*, 2nd edn (OUP, 2002), p.319; relying on *De Mattos v Gibson* (1858) 45 E.R. 108, at 110, per Knight Bruce L.J.

[83] See, for example, the dicta of Lord Browne-Wilkinson in *Westdeutsche Landesbank v Islington* [1996] A.C. 669.

[84] *Mainstream Properties Ltd v Young* [2005] EWCA Civ 861.

[85] e.g. *Lumley v Gye* (1853) 2 E. & B. 216.

would similarly require an intention on the third party's part to defeat the effect of the negative pledge provision. Secondly, seek specific performance of a negative pledge clause which is drafted so as to entitle the lender to equivalent assets of the sort which were the subject of the negative pledge provision.

19–62   The third avenue of action would be to draft the negative pledge so as to provide for "automatic security" such that the assets which are subject to the negative pledge become vested in the lender immediately on the occurrence of a breach of that provision (in the manner considered above in relation to "automatic early termination" in para.19–44). This last provision—the automatic security clause—would need to make it plain over which property precisely the rights were to come into existence or else there would be no property right for want of certainty of subject matter.[86] The property which would form part of this fund would also need to be property in which the borrower already held property rights, or else the purported proprietary right would fail as being "after-acquired" property.[87] From a contractual standpoint there is little difference between an automatic security clause and a floating charge if both were drafted so that both applied to a given pool of security and both crystallised at a contractually specified time on the happening of a contractually specified event. Alternatively, the provision could be drafted as an express trust over defined assets (provided those assets were defined) with a power for the borrower as trustee to use the assets for identified, ordinary business purposes during the life of the loan, but such that the power did not extend to the transfer, sale or re-hypothecation of those assets to any other person or purpose. As will be evident, turning the negative pledge into a type of security which is not simply predicated on the borrower observing its contractual obligations is a matter of attempting to transform that clause into one of the structures which provides security, as considered in Chapter 22. Otherwise, a "pure" negative pledge clause simply seeks to shore up an ordinary contract of loan which was contracted on the basis of a normal credit assessment of the borrower and relies effectively on the good faith of the borrower in striving to obey her contractual commitments to her bank.

B.   Pari passu clauses

19–63   A pari passu clause is a near cousin of the negative pledge clause just considered. The expression "pari passu" means "in equal step": in legal parlance, if people are in equal step that means that no single person has any advantage over anyone else.[88] This provision is used in relation to loan transactions in particular so that no one unsecured lender is entitled to any advantage over any other unsecured

---

[86] See para.21–13.
[87] See, e.g. *Re Brooks ST* [1939] Ch. 993: on which see A. Hudson, *Equity & Trusts*, 7th edn (Routledge, 2012), s.5.6.2. See also *Tailby v Official Receiver* (1888) 13 App. Cas. 523; *Re Lind* [1915] 2 Ch. 345; *Performing Rights Society v London Theatre* [1924] A.C. 1, *Norman v Federal Commissioner of Taxation* (1963) 109 C.L.R. 9. cf. *Re Ralli's WT* [1964] 2 W.L.R. 144, where the right of a remainder beneficiary is sufficient to constitute a property right even though the vested rights to property would only come into existence in the future.
[88] See *Merchant Bills Corp Ltd v Permanent Nominees Australia Ltd* (1972–1973) A.L.R. 565, cited in *Kensington International Ltd v Republic of the Congo* [2003] EWCA Civ 709.

lender; and therefore that no secured loans are to be created. Breach of this pari passu provision will be specified to be a breach of contract.

C.   Credit worth, "material adverse change" and the financial condition of the counterparty

The purpose of a credit measurement provision in a financial contract

Financial measurement of profit and loss, and of the risks associated with investments are key to financial transactions. Making an investment decision involves measuring the credit risk associated with the entity in which or through which the investment is made, and balancing that with the expected return; lending money is one of the key investments which banks make and therefore identifying the credit risk associated with a borrower is important; entering into complex financial transactions with a counterparty involves a decision as to the credit risk associated with that counterparty and the concomitant profit which is expected to flow from that transaction, and whether or not it is worthwhile. Therefore, financial measurement techniques are key to the commercial decision whether or not to enter into a transaction; and consequently financial contracts will often incorporate those credit calculations: indeed it is surprising that so many transactions are created without the inclusion of such material. Analysis of the financial information generated as to the performance of a company is therefore vital to a decision about whether or not to invest in it. Credit decisions as to the condition of the borrower in large scale corporate transactions are typically made by reference to a series of financial and accounting measurement models.[89] It is usual for one or more of these mechanisms for calculating credit worth to be included in the loan covenants so as to establish the financial condition which is required for that entity to remain of a sufficient credit worth for the lender to wish to remain in business with it. Credit decisions are a combination of science (using mathematical and accounting models) and art (using more general appreciation of the borrower's market, business plan, and particular strengths). The lawyer's intention is that if the borrower's financial condition deteriorates so as to fall below the contractually specified minimum for the acceptable mathematical ratio, then that will constitute an event of default.

19–64

Measuring financial performance: the principal models

Sometimes this sort of provision is referred to as a "credit downgrade clause" and the breach of the identified ratio would be specified in the contract as constituting a "material adverse change" in the borrower's financial condition. The purpose of such a provision is that the non-defaulting party is entitled to terminate its contract with the counterparty if the counterparty's credit worth "deteriorates in a material way": a material way in this sense means deterioration to a sufficiently

19–65

---

[89] There is a full discussion of the considerations which inform these financial measurements in the "Financial Analysis and Planning" chapter in Brealey, Myers and Allen, *Corporate Finance—International Edition*, 8th edn (McGraw-Hill, 2006), p.782 et seq.

serious extent. As discussed in this section, a well-drafted contract will provide that there has been a material adverse change if the credit worth of the counterparty falls below a contractually-specified level in one of the credit measurement models set out below. It is common in many financial contracts simply to provide that there will be an event of default if the "credit worth [of the entity] becomes materially weaker". The weakness that is referred to here is very unclear. A well-drafted contract would make it plain what "material" deterioration constitutes by reference to an identified mathematical, accounting model. The models considered here are "interest coverage", "debt coverage ratio", and general cash flow ratios. The principal issue here, it is suggested, is whether the measurement relates to capital items on the balance sheet, or to income items on the profit and loss account or the company's cash flow. The trouble with taking purely a capital measure is that it is capable of being manipulated. Balance sheets are prepared once a year, and so a company's position can be organised appropriately just in time. What was made startlingly clear by Lehman Brothers was that its balance sheet had been manipulated quarterly by means of a "repo 105" account through which an enormous transaction was entered into so that US\$ 50 billion of bad assets were sold temporarily to a third party, only to be bought back a few days later. This meant that the balance sheet was improved temporarily (because the bad assets were taken off the balance sheet at the moment of valuation) before those assets were knowingly added back to the balance sheet. If a picture had been taken across the year of the movements of cash and other assets within the company, then this transaction would not have been able to hide the company's true position.[90] With that in mind, let us consider some of the more common measures of credit worth.

19–66   The "interest coverage" of the borrower is a measurement of the amount of profit which the borrower has left to meet the interest costs on its borrowings after calculation of EBIT ("Earnings Before Interest and Tax"). This calculation therefore demonstrates the amount of free profit which the borrower has to meet the cost of its debt (its interest payments and any capital repayments). A company with too much debt or too much debt at a high rate of interest will therefore have a poor "interest coverage" ratio, in the form of little cash left over to pay for new debt and/or to invest in its business activities. The available profit which the borrower has left over is typically identified on a profit and loss statement after the entity's EBIT, or some analysts prefer to identify it by reference to the borrower's EBITDA ("earnings before interest, tax, depreciation and amortisation"). These amounts are simply identified from a company's standard profit and loss account as the statement of that entity's profit before subtraction is made of the amounts needed to pay for bank interest, tax, depreciation and amortisation (being measurements of the reduction in value of assets as they have become one year older). The question of depreciation is often treated by accountants as being flexible and therefore capable of manipulation, which is why most financial analysts prefer the cash-flow statements referred to below—they give a more accurate picture of how much "cash" the borrower actually has, beyond any

---

[90] This transaction is explained in detail in the Anton Valukas Report titled "In re Lehman Brothers Holdings Inc" for the United States Bankruptcy Court Southern District of New York (Chapter 11 Case No. 08-13555), March 11, 2010, especially at p.6.

clever manipulation of its annual profit and loss account.[91] Given that the lender is considering lending new capital to the borrower under a new loan contract, it is suggested that the weakness of EBITDA is that it does not consider the amount of free cash that is left once *existing* interest and taxation costs have been met. The difficulty with reference to the measurement of cash flow is in differentiating between borrowers who have poor liquidity (that is, they cannot access cash quickly) and borrowers who are insolvent (that is, they are unable to meet their debt obligations because they have insufficient assets, and not simply because they have a temporary inability to access cash).

Analysts will also look to the "debt coverage ratio" which is expressed as a ratio **19–67** of the borrower's long and short term debt and any regular periodical payments it has to make (such as leases), when compared to the aggregate of the borrower's debt and leases and its equity. In effect this ratio expresses the level of the borrower's debt and leasehold liabilities when compared to its equity share capital. It is generally thought that a borrower with too much debt is a poor credit risk simply because it already has too much debt. It is common for companies in continental Europe to rely on bank debt more than is the case in the UK where there is generally a greater amount of share capital. Similarly, some family companies are reluctant to issue new shares so as to dilute the shares owned by the family, and so a family company will tend to have more debt; whereas another type of company might be more relaxed about the idea of raising more capital from shareholders without the need to take on more debt with the contractually compelled cost of making interest payments, while shares only carry the ordinary shareholders' legally unenforceable hope that there will be sufficient profit to pay out a dividend. Therefore, any of these types of mathematical ratios must be understood in the broader context of the particular idiosyncrasies of the particular borrower. The "ratio" is usually expressed as a percentage, and therefore a loan contract would specify the level of debt to equity which would be acceptable under this ratio. This also prevents the borrower from bleeding money out of the entity by paying out dividends, buying in shares, or lowering its profits. The most significant actors in this rating game in financial markets are the ratings agencies, whose activities are discussed in Chapter 25 in detail.[92]

The measures of performance which are less easy to manipulate are those which **19–68** focus on the company's cash flow across the accounting year, as opposed to taking an annual "snap shot" of the level of profit and loss or the assets on the balance sheet at the end of the accounting year. Securities regulation requires that information is given at six month intervals as opposed simply to annually, and loan contracts could require cash flow statements even more frequently than that. A cash flow ratio would measure the cash inflows and outflows across the specified period. Thus, cash inflow from trading activities[93] could be expressed as a ratio to the cost of sales (including salaries, rent, and so forth) and the cost of

---

[91] See T. Smith, *Accounting for Growth*, 2nd edn (Century, 1996).

[92] See para.25–51.

[93] By limiting this to trading activities, one can exclude the sort of material (such as depreciation cost) which can be manipulated by accountants in reaching the final profit and loss, because the profit can be inflated by including amounts which are not derived directly from trading activities.

funding (debt interest and so forth), over the specified time period. A loan contract could express such a cash flow ratio to express the profitability or instead the liquidity of the borrower.

19–69   One very significant question about such measurements is the provenance of the numbers which are used. These calculations can be based on "book values" (that is, the amounts specified in the accounts) or they can be based on "market values" (that is, the then market value of the borrower's assets and liabilities). In derivatives markets, for example, all amounts are "marked to market", meaning that the parties calculate a market value for the asset in question at that time. The advantage of a market value is that it gives a clear idea of what the assets are worth in the market at that time, but those same values are subject to very sharp, short-term variations. By contrast, particularly for the borrowings of a manufacturing company, the "book value" of those assets may give a more steady and reliable statement of the company's worth, but only if the calculation methodology is adequate for the lender's purposes.

Material adverse change

19–70   As was outlined above, material adverse change clauses are clauses which entitle the non-defaulting party to identify an event of default if the financial condition of a counterparty has deteriorated beyond a contractually identified mark. A well-drafted material adverse change clause will identify the precise level at issue and the precise methodology that will be used to calculate that change. However, commonly banks prefer to allow themselves some flexibility to assess whether or not they consider that there has been a material adverse change without needing to rely on detailed mathematical models. Detailed models would prevent a bank which is convinced that X Plc will go into insolvency in five months' time from terminating a contract today just because the six monthly financial statements have not quite triggered the level of deterioration necessary to terminate the contract. Therefore, in syndicated lending it is common for a group of banks to reserve to themselves the ability to identify when a given level of deterioration of credit worth has occurred.[94] It is suggested that no borrower who can possibly avoid it ought to cede such control of that calculation to its bankers.[95]

19–71   Where there is discretion in a bank to identify whether or not it believes that there has been a material adverse change, then the question arises whether or not the bank is required to act in good faith in its use of that term. It is suggested that the precise wording of the bank's discretion would be very important: if the bank was expressed to be required to act in "good faith" then that would impose different obligations on it from a requirement that it act in a "commercially reasonable manner" because a commercially reasonable manner would require nothing more than that the bank act as any other reasonable bank would in the circumstances,

---

[94] See, e.g. P. Wood, *International Loans, Bonds, Guarantees, Legal Opinions*, 2nd edn (Sweet & Maxwell, 2007), p 106.

[95] It an irony in many corporate finance transactions that banks have worse credit ratings and certainly worse returns on capital than many of the companies from whom it insists on extracting these sorts of contractual provisions. The banks' bargaining power is often out of alignment with their own credit worth.

whereas acting in good faith would require that the bank consider the position of the borrower. Merely that the bank be required to act otherwise than "dishonestly" would, it is suggested, set this bar very low indeed. If the borrower's credit worth had fallen to some extent, then a bank would not need to be defrauding its borrower if it called for termination of the loan on grounds that the bank considered the credit worth had fallen "materially".[96] If the credit worth had not fallen at all because all measurements of profitability had remained stable throughout the period of the loan, then the bank would be acting disingenuously at least in calling in the loan.

The courts have given some little assistance in this area. A reduction of 20 per cent in the net asset value of a company over a period of only four months has been found to be a material adverse change in that company's credit worth.[97] If the material adverse change clause provides expressly that the existence of the material adverse change is to be measured by reference to a company's financial statements, then the lender is limited to conducting its assessment of a material adverse change only by reference to a survey of those financial statements, and cannot therefore seek to rely on other information.[98] There have been a number of recent cases on the ability of banks to rely on "acceleration" clauses, as considered above. What is clear from cases like *BNP Paribas SA v Yukos Oil Co*[99] is that the banks can also look to non-financial information when assessing whether or not there has been a material adverse change sufficient to justify accelerating the borrower's payment obligations under a bond. The company faced enormous tax obligations which the Russian government was imposing on the company, which in turn meant that the company faced the possibility of insolvency. In that case there was a broader backdrop. The arrest of the company's chief executive, in a context of great concern about the attitude of the Russian government to natural resources companies which had been passed from state ownership into private ownership by a previous regime, suggested that there had been a material adverse change in the affairs of the company, even if its principal business of selling oil remained potentially as robust as before. Indeed the doubling of the price of oil between 2005 and the time of writing suggested that the oil business itself was otherwise in fine health.

19–72

Liability for misapplication of a material adverse change provision

If a party which is empowered to declare the existence of an acceleration of obligations under a loan contract or a bond agreement does so incorrectly, then

19 73

---

[96] The law on insurance has a concept of "materiality" in relation to material matters which must be disclosed to the insurer by the customer. In the common law, a matter is material if it is information which the insurer would have wanted to know when making its decision: *Container Transport Interantional Inc v Oceanus Mutual Underwriting Association (Bermuda) Ltd* [1984] 1 Lloyd's Rep. 467. See also *Lambert v Co-operative Insurance Society* [1975] 2 Lloyd's Rep. 485; on which see R. Merkin (1976) 39 M.L.R. 478.
[97] *Lewis v Farin* [1978] 2 All E.R. 1149.
[98] *Re TR Technology Investment Trust Plc* (1988) 4 B.C.C. 244.
[99] [2005] EWHC 1321.

that person will be liable to the borrower for damages in contract.[100] There would be no question of an action in tort in these circumstances because the relationship between the parties is contractual.[101]

6.   PERFORMANCE OF PAYMENT OBLIGATIONS

A.   Impact of failure to pay

19–74   Failure to pay under a cash-settled transaction or failure to deliver under a physically-settled transaction will constitute a fundamental breach of the contract.[102] Breach of such a fundamental term of the contract will entitle the non-defaulting party to terminate the master agreement and all relevant transactions under that agreement.[103] Under the terms of the financial agreements either a late payment will be subject to payment of default interest on the outstanding amount or else it will trigger termination of the agreement, possibly with a penalties clause. Under the general law there are two possibilities for the non-defaulting party: seeking damages for breach of contract or alternatively seeking specific performance of that obligation. The courts will be less likely to award specific performance in relation to *cash-settled* contracts (where there is only an obligation to pay money) because contractual damages will frequently be sufficient remedy.[104] The position may be different in relation to foreign currency transactions or physically-settled transactions, however, because the other party to the transaction will require either an amount in a foreign currency or the physical delivery of a security, a commodity or some other asset. If one is awaiting the delivery of a physical asset then cash damages may not be sufficient remedy if one has need of that asset: perhaps to use in the conduct of a business, perhaps to complete some contractual obligation to one's own client, or otherwise. If possession of the physical asset was required, however, simply to secure a speculative profit by selling the asset off, then damages would only be sufficient if they were equal to the profits which would have been earned. The position in relation to contractual damages is considered in Chapter 20.[105]

B.   Date of due payment

19–75   Each jurisdiction and each market in each jurisdiction will have conventions as to the manner in which and the dates on which payments will be made and not made. Knowing and becoming accustomed to these conventions is an important part of becoming an expert in that market. In the abstract there is little than can be said about payment conventions. What is important is that there are no mismatches between payment conventions either within a financial contract or between that financial product and any other instrument to which it has a

---

[100] *Concord Trust v Law Debenture Trust Corp Plc* [2005] UKHL 27, at [41], per Lord Scott.
[101] *Concord Trust v Law Debenture Trust Corp Plc* [2005] UKHL 27 at [38], per Lord Scott.
[102] ISDA, Master Agreement, 1992, s.2(a)(i).
[103] ISDA, Master Agreement, 1992, s.5(a)(i).
[104] *Hutton v Watling* [1948] Ch. 26; [1948] Ch. 398.
[105] See para.20–03.

connection. Similarly, it is important that business day conventions in some jurisdictions which do not meet the usual timetable of the New York, Tokyo and London market centres are catered for in the documentation. Further, there are also conventions as to delivery of some products, including date of delivery after completion of a contract to deliver, which must be matched between the derivatives documentation and the appropriate market convention.

7.   FRUSTRATION OF CONTRACT

A.   Express contractual provision

From time-to-time financial markets move in unexpectedly violent ways—either booming or crashing. This can lead to a large amount of speculative profit, or in relation to transactions which are created to track financial markets this can cause a large amount of unexpected loss. So, if, for example, a product was created which was expected to turn a profit if interest rates rose, so as to offset a loss the investor might lose elsewhere in its portfolio, then it would be doubly harmful if interest rates moved unexpectedly violently. One of the parties may seek to cancel the transaction on the basis that its performance has frustrated its original purpose. The doctrine of frustration of contract may apply to avoid a contract on the basis that its commercial purpose is not capable of performance. In general terms it may be difficult to identify such an underlying purpose of the contract and so demonstrate that the underlying purpose of the contract has indeed been rendered impossible. Complex financial transactions would benefit from some explicit statement of the central purpose of the contract. For example, the parties would be well-advised to make clear the parameters within which they consider the value of their transaction moving, or the purposes for which the transaction was created. Were the contract to make this link between the purpose of the transaction and the expected movement of the underlying market clear, then it would make it possible to demonstrate that any unexpected performance of the transaction was outwith the contractual expectation of the parties and consequently frustrating to their contractual purpose. **19–76**

B.   The requirements for frustration of a contract

Impossibility of performance

Frustration of a contract will not be permitted simply because one or other of the parties has suffered loss or would rather not be bound by it. Often in financial transactions when frustration is sought one party will have made a large profit and the other party will have made a large loss: therefore, one party will be seeking to set the contract aside and the other to affirm it. If both parties were in the same position it is likely that they would simply agree to set the contract aside: in which case no further issues would arise. So, more than being an inconvenience it is a requirement that the contract no longer reflects the parties' contractual purpose and that it is impossible to perform it. **19–77**

19–78   An example of frustration of contract would arise where the subject matter of the contract was destroyed,[106] although there are cases where such destruction has not done so.[107] In contracts which are to be settled by payment of money through bank accounts, it is unlikely that the subject matter of the contract will have been destroyed—unlike buying a house, for example—and therefore the test in the financial context will require some consideration. The test is primarily whether or not the act of destruction has led to the subject matter of the contract becoming "for business purposes something else",[108] that is something other than that for which the parties intended to contract.[109] In this sense we might think of the termination of a stock exchange's ability to quote a price as being equivalent to "destruction" and in the absence of quoting a price, any product linked to that exchange would have become something other than what the parties had originally expected. Again, it is suggested that a statement—not usually included in financial contracts—making plain the purpose of the contract would be necessary in such circumstances. It is not necessary that the entirety of the subject matter of the contract be destroyed; rather, it is sufficient that part only of the subject matter is destroyed provided that the commercial purpose of the contract is frustrated.[110] Nor is it necessary that the destruction of that property have been at fault of one or other of the parties.[111] Where there has been some allocation between the parties of the risk of the failure of the purpose of the contract, then that may impact on the ability of the claimant to have the contract set aside.[112] For example, if the contract provided that the buyer forego a premium payable under an option regardless of the performance of the underlying asset.

19–79   These principles were framed primarily in relation to contracts for the sale or shipment of goods but the notion of identifying the commercial purpose of the contract remains significant for financial transactions albeit that it is more difficult to identify the underlying purpose of a financial transaction created otherwise than for straightforward speculation in the absence of an express contractual provision to that effect.

Impossibility of acquiring the price of the underlying asset

19–80   Where an index ceases to be published or where a stock exchange ceases to conduct trading, then the prices required to drive a range of options and forwards products (as well as the prices of securities quoted on that exchange) would be unavailable. In such circumstances three possibilities present themselves, depending on the terms of the applicable contract. First, the cessation might be considered to be so slight, such as a half hour interruption to trading that this

---

[106] *Taylor v Caldwell* (1863) 3 B. & S. 826.

[107] *Redmond v Dainton* [1920] 2 K.B. 256 where the destruction of leased premises did not rescind the tenant's obligation to pay rent.

[108] *Asfar & Co v Blundell* [1896] 1 Q.B. 123, 128.

[109] *Asfar & Co v Blundell* [1896] 1 Q.B. 123, 128, where a shipment of dates were waterlogged such that there were no longer of suitable quality; *The Badgary* [1985] 1 Lloyd's Rep. 395. cf. *Horn v Minister of Food* [1948] 2 All E.R. 1036.

[110] *Taylor v Caldwell* (1863) 3 B. & S. 826; *Appleby v Myers* (1867) L.R. 2 C.P. 651.

[111] *Lewis Emanuel & Sons Ltd v Sammut* [1959] 2 Lloyd's Rep. 629.

[112] *Victoria Seats Agency v Paget* (1902) 19 T.L.R. 16; *Clark v Lindsay* (1903) 19 T.L.R. 202.

interruption could be ignored.[113] Second, the contract may provide for an alternative means of reaching the price, so that a price could be generated in any event by the person acting as calculation agent for that transaction. Third, the unavailability of the price may be considered to be sufficient to frustrate the contract, depending on the terms of the contract itself.[114] In relation to shipping contracts the detention of a ship[115] or its seizure[116] have both led to frustration of a contract, as has the unavailability of the cargo to be loaded onto the ship due to industrial action.[117] It may be that the subject matter of a contract is rendered unavailable by a change in regulation or even governmental regulatory practice.[118] Alternatively, situations like the Gulf War begun in 2003 may make it impossible to move goods, to publish an index or otherwise to deal in a given jurisdiction for a given period of time because the price of oil moved so markedly and because of the general effect on financial markets.[119]

It is also possible that performance of the contract may be rendered more onerous as a result of some material change in circumstance in which case the contract may be frustrated.[120] The test is whether or not the contract is rendered "as a matter of business a totally different thing" by the relevant events.[121] Again, such an analysis may be made easier by the inclusion in the contract of a maximum volatility clause[122] or similar provision specifying the purpose of the transaction. In the absence of such a contractual provision it will be a matter of degree whether or not the performance of the contract is to be considered to be too onerous in the circumstance, for example where a devaluation of a currency leads to an unexpectedly large movement in interest rates.[123] On this question of degree, the following discussion relating to the line between frustration of purpose and some mere inconvenience becomes important. Nevertheless, there may remain a question as to whether or not the whole of the contract falls to be set aside or whether it is only some balancing payment which is required.[124]

19–81

---

[113] *Bunge Corp v Tradax Export S.A.* [1981] 1 W.L.R. 711, below.
[114] For example, in relation to terms specifying that time was of the essence: *Martindale v Smith* (1841) 1 Q.B. 389; *Hartley v Hymans* [1920] 3 K.B. 475; *Bunge Corp v Tradax Export S.A.* [1981] 1 W.L.R. 711.
[115] *The Adelfa* [1988] 2 Lloyd's Rep. 466.
[116] *Bank Line Ltd v Arthur Capel & Co* [1919] A.C. 435.
[117] *The Nema* [1982] A.C. 724.
[118] *B.P. Exploration (Libya) Ltd v Hunt* [1983] 2 A.C. 352.
[119] *The Evia (No.2)* [1983] 1 A.C. 736; *The Wenjiang (No.2)* [1983] 1 Lloyd's Rep. 400; *The Chrysalis* [1983] 1 W.L.R. 1469.
[120] *Metropolitan Water Board v Dick, Kerr & Co* [1918] A.C. 119; *Acetylene Co of GB v Canada Carbide Co* (1922) 8 Ll. L. Rep. 456.
[121] *Bank Line Ltd v Arthur Capel & Co* [1919] A.C. 435, 460.
[122] See para.19–85.
[123] cf. *Multiservice Bookbinding v Marden* [1979] Ch. 84 where it was held that such a shift will be immaterial if agreed by commercial parties who were properly advised.
[124] *Countess of Warwick SS Co v Le Nickel S.A.* [1918] A.C. 724; *The Agathon* [1982] 2 Lloyd's Rep. 211, below.

Frustration affecting only one party's performance

19–82   It is also possible that the frustration would affect only one party's performance under the contract: something which would be catered for in a well-drafted contract. This raises the question whether the contract is frustrated or whether it is simply a case of one party's ability to perform their obligations under it. The resolution of this question will depend upon whether or not that frustration goes to the "common object" of the parties.[125]

Distinguishing between impracticability and abnegation of purpose

19–83   In relation to many contracts it might be possible, with payment of huge sums of money or through extraordinary efforts, to overcome any event of frustration. However, the question for the doctrine of frustration will always be what amount of effort is reasonable to expend to overcome the frustration of the contract and at what point the parties are entitled simply to have their contract set aside. While some cases have held that mere impracticability would found a good claim for frustration,[126] the weight of the authorities provides us with a requirement that there be a level of impossibility which cuts to the heart of the purpose of the contract.[127] For example, a claim that "a wholly abnormal rise or fall in prices" should have been considered to have caused a contract to be frustrated has been rejected by the House of Lords as not being sufficiently impossible.[128] It is on this basis that it is suggested that financial contracts, particularly those used for non-speculative purposes, require some core statement of their purpose and some indication of the rate movements which the parties would consider acceptable and what would constitute absolute impossibility in the context.[129]

19–84   Where a contract has been rendered illegal, whether by virtue of a change in the law or in regulatory practice, then it may nevertheless be considered frustrated.[130] However, restrictions on the movement of capital will not necessarily constitute frustration,[131] nor will something which is only a peripheral interference with the performance of the contract,[132] nor something which relates only to currency fluctuations where the parties have been sufficiently advised as to the effect of their contract.[133]

---

[125] *Hirji Mulji v Cheong Yue SS. Co Ltd* [1926] A.C. 497, 507; *Krell v Henry* [1903] 2 K.B. 740.
[126] *Horlock v Beal* [1916] A.C. 486.
[127] *British Movietonenews Ltd v London & District Cinemas* [1952] A.C. 166; *Davis Contractors Ltd v Fareham U.D.C.* [1956] A.C. 696.
[128] *Davis Contractors Ltd v Fareham UDC* [1956] A.C. 696. 185; *Multiservice Bookbinding v Marden* [1979] Ch. 84.
[129] See para.19–85.
[130] *Fibrosa Spolka Ackcyjna v Fairburn, Lawson Combe Barbour Ltd* [1943] A.C. 32; *Denny v Mott* [1944] A.C. 265.
[131] *Libyan Arab Foreign Bank v Bankers Trust Co* [1989] Q.B. 728. cf. *Wahda Bank v Arab Bank Plc* [1996] 1 Lloyd's Rep. 470.
[132] *Denny v Mott* [1944] A.C. 265.
[133] *Multiservice Bookbinding v Marden* [1979] Ch. 84.

Maximum volatility provisions

The use of express contractual provisions which identify the parties' purpose in contracting for the financial product in the first place has the effect of making it plain when the purpose of that contract has been frustrated. Similarly, stating plainly the extent to which the parties anticipate markets moving, and thus the maximum amount of volatility on which they have based the presumptions underpinning the pricing and structuring of their financial transactions, has the beneficial effect of making it plain when unforeseen market movements can cause the transaction to be terminated rather than enforceable in a way which causes unexpectedly large losses to one party or another. So, for example with derivatives contracts where the amounts to be paid by either one of the parties depends upon the movement of markets, then it is possible that those markets will move significantly further than either party had expected or intended and therefore that one of the parties may suffer an exceptional level of loss. To guard against such a situation, the parties are advised to include a term which either identifies the amount of loss which the parties had within their expectations or which provides the basis on which the calculation agent can identify a loss which would have been expected under ordinary market conditions. In the light of the market collapses in 2008, this sort of provision would seem even more attractive than ever.

19–85

8. SPECIFIC PERFORMANCE

A. Specific performance in general terms

The doctrine of specific performance is an equitable remedy which entitles one party to a contract to require its counterparty to perform its obligations under that contract. In relation to transactions which require the physical delivery of an asset of a particular quality at a particular time, the doctrine of specific performance will be appropriate where it is the intention of the recipient of those assets that it take possession of them; as opposed to, for example, a transaction exercisable either in cash or by physical delivery in relation to which the buyer wishes only to receive a cash return rather than to take physical possession of the assets for some other commercial purpose. Whether the physical assets or simply a cash return are required is significant, as considered in the next section, because specific performance will not be available where cash damages would otherwise constitute a sufficient remedy.[134]

19–86

In relation to foreign exchange transactions a similar analysis to that for physically-settled transactions may hold true. Where cash damages would be payable in sterling and where the buyer wishes to take delivery of that foreign currency, the buyer would prefer to take delivery of the requisite amount of foreign exchange rather than cash damages in sterling. Clearly, this preference would be dependent on the exchange rate between sterling and the applicable foreign currency and possibly on the reason for seeking the foreign exchange. In

19–87

---

[134] *Hutton v Watling* [1948] Ch. 26; [1948] Ch. 398.

relation to the latter it may be that the client requires the foreign currency, for example, to meet a contractual obligation, to one of its own clients. The operation of specific performance in relation to cash transactions is considered in the following section.

B. Specific performance in money transactions

19–88 The significance of specific performance in the commercial context is its availability only in respect of circumstances in which damages are not an appropriate remedy.[135] Therefore, specific performance will not usually be available for an executory contract simply to pay an amount of money.[136] However, as considered above, in respect of a transaction in which physical delivery of a chattel or security is required, specific performance will be available where damages would not be a sufficient remedy.[137] If one is awaiting the delivery of a physical asset then cash damages may not be sufficient remedy if one has need of that asset: perhaps to use in the conduct of a business, perhaps to complete some contractual obligation to one's own client, or otherwise. If possession of the physical asset was required, however, simply to secure a speculative profit by selling the asset off, then damages would only be sufficient if they were equal to the profits which would have been earned.

19–89 The general rule in relation to contracts for the payment of money is that common law damages will typically be sufficient remedy. Therefore, a stream of cases in relation to contracts for loan witnessed a denial of specific performance on the basis that an award of damages would be adequate compensation for the lender. However, in *Beswick v Beswick*[138] an uncle agreed to transfer his business as a coal merchant to his nephew provided that his nephew would retain him as a consultant and pay an annuity to his widow. The nephew refused to make this payment to his aunt in the event. Therefore, his aunt sought an order for specific performance in her capacity as administratrix of her husband's estate. Even though the award was only an award for money, it was held that damages would be an insufficient remedy (being only nominal damages on the facts of that case) because it would have been impossible to predict the value of an annuity in the future and thus inappropriate to seek to reduce it to an award of damages. Therefore, there are situations in which contracts for the payment of money will be specifically enforceable.

19–90 In relation to financial transactions generally, that would seem to include a financial product in which it would be impossible to know what the future value of that product would be—and so impossible to compute damages with any accuracy—and therefore that only a delivery of the financial product at issue would be appropriate. Alternatively, it could be said that if financial institutions calculate the likely profit and loss of a financial product by marking them to their market value on an ongoing basis, then damages could similarly be computed on

---

[135] [1948] Ch. 26; [1948] Ch. 398.
[136] *South African Territories Ltd v Wallington* [1898] A.C. 309; *Beswick v Beswick* [1968] A.C. 58.
[137] *Cohen v Roche* [1927] 1 K.B. 169.
[138] [1968] A.C. 58.

the same basis. One issue which would also emerge at this point would be whether or not cash damages would be sufficient to provide the function which the financial product was expected for perform: for example, hedging the buyer's exposure to an identified market. Again, calculating in advance the damages necessary to replicate that hedge would be impossible: the question is whether or not a rough-and-ready amount could be estimated on a mark-to-market basis. Where it *is* relatively easy to acquire a replacement transaction in the market, specific performance will not be ordered because damages sufficient to acquire a replacement transaction from another provider would be sufficient[139]; whereas the unavailability of a replacement transaction will make specific performance appropriate.[140] Another possible approach in circumstances where only a part of the property specified in the contract can be supplied by the defendant, might be for an order either for rescission or for specific performance of the contract to be coupled with damages.

C.   Non-availability of specific performance

There are a number of circumstances in which a defendant will be able to rebut a claim for specific performance beyond its non-availability due to damages being a sufficient remedy (as was considered immediately above). First, before ordering specific performance of a contract, it is a logical pre-requisite that the contract be valid in the first place, as considered in the preceding chapter. Similarly, the contract must not have become void, for example on grounds of fraud or ultra vires.[141] Second, in cases in which the plaintiff has exerted a misrepresentation over the defendant which has induced the defendant to enter into the transaction, the court will not make an order for specific performance in favour of the plaintiff. Where the claimant has been so induced by a misrepresentation, that claimant will be entitled to rescind that contract.[142] In similar vein where one of the contracting parties was unduly influenced to enter into the transaction, that party will be entitled to rescind the contract.[143] Where there has been a mistake which has operated to induce a defendant to enter into a contract, it would be inequitable in many circumstances to entitle the plaintiff to enforce that contract against the defendant.[144] However, where only one party to a contract is acting under a mistake (unilateral mistake), the contract, typically, will not be rescinded.[145] The parties are entitled to rely on a mistake of law in seeking to rescind their contracts.[146]

19–91

Third, the claimant will be required to seek to protect its rights with sufficient speed. The proper approach is to consider the subject matter of the contract and to

19–92

---

[139] *Cuddee v Rutter* (1720) 5 Vin. Abr. 538.
[140] *Duncuft v Albrecht* (1841) 12 Sim. 189; *Kenney v Wexham* (1822) 6 Madd. 355; *Sullivan v Henderson* [1973] 1 W.L.R. 333.
[141] *Cannon v Hartley* [1949] Ch. 213.
[142] See para.20–28.
[143] *Barclay's Bank v O'Brien* [1993] 3 W.L.R. 786; *TSB v Camfield* [1995] 1 W.L.R. 430.
[144] Considered at para.25–10.
[145] *Riverlate Properties Ltd v Paul* [1975] Ch. 133.
[146] *Kleinwort Benson v Lincoln C.C.* [1998] 4 All E.R. 513.

decide on that basis whether or not specific enforcement of the contract has justly to be denied as a result of the parties' delay.[147] Thus, where a party fails to act under its rights under a rent review clause within reasonable time, it will be unable to require its landlord to carry its obligations to demand only a lesser rent in the meantime.[148] Fourth, the court has a statutory discretion to decide that on the facts in front of it, while specific performance might ordinarily be available, an award of cash damages would be a sufficient and suitable remedy for the harm which the applicant would suffer by reason of the respondent's failure to perform its specific obligations under the contract.[149]

9. RECTIFICATION OF CONTRACTS

19–93   Rectification is available to amend the terms of a contract better to reflect the true intentions of the contracting parties.[150] Rectification will be available in circumstances of common mistake[151] but will only be available in relation to a unilateral mistake in cases of fraud or similar unconscionable behaviour.[152] Rectification may also be available in respect of voluntary settlements to reflect the settlor's evident intention.[153]

19–94   The Court of Appeal considered the ability of contracting parties to rectify an agreement on the basis that it did not correctly reflect their common intention in the case of *BP Exploration Co (Libya) Ltd v Hunt*.[154] Hunt argued, inter alia, that a provision of the signed agreement failed to reflect the true intention of the parties and that this true intention could be found in an earlier and non-binding Heads of Agreement letter (which was found to be equivalent to a draft of the final form of the contract) exchanged between the parties. Accordingly, they requested rectification of the signed agreement. The Court of Appeal made several comments about the availability of rectification in denying Hunt's application.

19–95   First, all complex commercial transactions are preceded by draft versions which gradually isolate ambiguities and disagreements between the parties, a court would generally be reluctant—as a matter of policy—to conclude that an informal document should be treated as a superior statement of the parties' agreement than the final and executed document. Any other policy would undermine the certainty that parties expect when they sign final agreements—if

---

[147] *Lazard Bros & Co Ltd v Fairfield Properties Co (Mayfair) Ltd* (1977) 121 Sol. Jo. 793, *United Scientific Holdings Ltd v Burnley B.C.* [1978] A.C. 904.

[148] *United Scientific Holdinsgs Ltd v Burnley B.C.* [1978] A.C. 904.

[149] Senior Courts Act 1981 s.50.

[150] *M'Cormack v M'Cormack* (1877) 1 L.R. Ir. 119; *Frederick E. Rose (London) Ltd v William H Pim Jnr & Co Ltd* [1953] 2 Q.B. 450.

[151] *Murray v Parker* (1854) 19 Beav 305; *Mackenzie v Coulson* (1869) L.R. 8 Eq. 368.

[152] *Whitley v Delaney* [1914] A.C. 132; *Monaghan CC v Vaughan* [1948] I.R. 306; *A Roberts & Co Ltd v Leicestershire CC* [1961] Ch. 555; *Thomas Bates & Son Ltd v Wyndham's (Lingerie) Ltd* [1981] 1 All E.R. 1077.

[153] Alternatively, the court may order the delivery and cancellation of documents, or in relation to "*ne exeat in regno*".

[154] [1983] 2 A.C. 352.

"the relevant document is a legally binding document, it is appropriate to hold the parties to the objectively ascertained meaning of the words used".

Second, the only way to obtain rectification is to show that, as a matter of fact, there was a common mistake which resulted in there being no legally binding force to the signed agreement.[155] The claimant bears the burden of proving that there has been a mistake which is common between the parties. The Court of Appeal refused to accept that there was a mistake simply on the basis of a disparity between the wording of the draft letter and the wording of the executed document. It was not enough that there was ambiguity between the wording in the two different documents. The Court of Appeal held that it would be necessary to show something with "the objective status of a prior agreement", either written or oral, which provides the evidence of a continuing intention clearly different to that of the executed agreement, thereby proving the common mistake.

19–96

Ordinarily the courts will not interfere with the parties' written intentions as expressed in their documentation except in relation to mistake or where rectification is appropriate. Exceptionally, perhaps, in *Boom Time Holdings Ltd v Goldman Sachs*[156] the Court of Appeal did effectively alter the parties' contractual documentation to achieve what it considered to be a just result. The defendant calculation agent had reached its calculations in relation to a barrier call option over shares in P Ltd. P Ltd had issued bonus shares: something which had not been anticipated in the parties' contractual documentation. The parties had not stipulated their contractual expectations nor had they stipulated in detail the manner in which the calculation agent would carry out its calculations.[157] The Court of Appeal held that in relation to a contract which did not take into account the possibility of P Ltd issuing bonus shares, an alteration in the mechanism by which cash settlement amounts were to be calculated was necessary to give effect to the genuine intentions of the parties and so achieve "economic equivalence" between the parties' expectations and their contractual documentation.

19–97

---

[155] It should be remembered that meeting the standard of proof for this equitable remedy is difficult.
[156] Unreported February 25, 1997, per Colman J.; Unreported reversed on appeal February 6, 1998. See the discussion of this case in A. Hudson, *Financial Derivatives*, para.5–28.
[157] See A.S. Hudson, *Financial Derivatives*, para.3–37A on the need for stating clearly the commercial intentions underpinning a contract.

CHAPTER 20

TERMINATION OF CONTRACTS

CORE PRINCIPLES

Damages for breach of contract are paid in an amount sufficient to put the claimant in the position which she would have occupied but for the breach of contract. There are two principal mechanisms for the measurement of damages for a breach of contract. First, the claimant may receive by way of damages the difference between the contractual performance for which she contracted and the performance which she actually received. Alternatively, secondly, the claimant may be awarded damages which are sufficient to meet the "cost of cure". However, it is possible that if the loss is suffered but it is impracticable to provide for damages to cure the cost, then damages may be purely nominal; unless something to the contrary was made a condition of the contract. By contrast, damages for tort are measured according to the claimant's out-of-pocket loss: that is, an amount to put the claimant in the position she would have been in but for the tort and not to compensate her for any loss of opportunity nor any economic loss.

A number of further questions arise. First, as to who is liable for that breach of contract—which will require a close reading of the appropriate contract. Secondly, as to whether or not the breach of contract caused the claimant's loss. Thirdly, whether or not the loss is too remote from the breach of contract so as to fix the defendant with liability for it: that is, the loss in question must arise naturally from the breach of contract or must have been within the contemplation of the parties. In relation specifically to financial contracts, it would be advisable for that contract to make plain the quantum of damage which the parties would expect to recover or the purposes for which the contract is being created (and therefore the loss which may be within the contemplation of the parties).

The measure of damages for fraudulent misrepresentation is an amount sufficient to put the representee in the position in which she would have found herself had the misrepresentation not been made. So, for example, the measure of damages for a fraudulent misrepresentation in relation to an allotment of shares is prima facie the difference between the actual value of the shares at the time of allotment and the sum paid for them. Damages in relation to fraud under the tort of deceit are such as "to make reparation for all the damage flowing directly from the transaction". The effect of s.2 of the Misrepresentation Act 1967 is that there is no difference in the availability of damages between the representation being fraudulent and merely negligent.

At common law, when money has been transferred as a result of some unjust factor—such as failure of consideration, mistake, undue influence, or some other such factor—then the claimant will be able to recover the cash equivalent of sums paid by it to the defendant by means of a personal claim in restitution, traditionally known as "a claim for money had and received", so as to reverse the unjust enrichment acquired by the defendant (although the doctrine is at root equitable).

Rescission is a general equitable doctrine which permits the courts to achieve a restitutio in integrum: that is, to restore parties to the position which they had occupied originally. Rescission will be awarded in cases of mistake, misrepresentation or to set aside an unconscionable bargain. When seeking rescission of a contract on grounds of mistake, the mistake must be made by both parties in entering into a transaction.

A claimant may seek to establish a proprietary right by seeking to convince the court to recognise it by way of constructive trust, resulting trust or further to a tracing action.

1. INTRODUCTION

20–01   This chapter considers the principles governing the termination of contracts under the general common law. It surveys liability for damages for breach of contract; liability for fraudulent and for negligent misrepresentation; and liability for money had and received at common law. All of these different legal concepts have a role to play in relation to contracts which have failed or been terminated for one reason or another. Failure of a contract may, of course, arise in a number of contexts.[1] Those contexts could be divided between a straightforward failure to perform the contract where performance of the contract would nevertheless be lawful, and cases in which the contract is not performed because its performance is prohibited by law or by a court order.

Aside from the ordinary law of contract, there will be the terms agreed between the parties and contained in their contract. The principal objective of many financial contracts is to provide the parties with a means of ending their contracts on the happening of identified events. A well-drafted financial contract will contain two forms of termination provision. First, provisions permitting termination of the contract on grounds agreed between the parties.[2] A lawful termination of the contract in accordance with such contractual terms will not in itself constitute a breach of that contract provided that it is done in accordance with the terms of the contract[3]: so, the act of terminating a contract will not give rise to an obligation to pay damages. Secondly, the contract will contain provisions which identify the core, material terms of the contract,[4] the damage which is foreseeable from failure to perform the contract,[5] and so forth. Such contractual terms are the "conditions" of the contract, as discussed in Chapter 19. These provisions will be important to identify when there has been a sufficiently significant breach of the contract to justify termination of the agreement more generally and also to identify the level of damages which might be appropriate in relation to such a breach of contract. This chapter will assume that there has been a breach of contract and will concern itself with the ramifications of such a breach.

20–02

2.   DAMAGES FOR BREACH OF CONTRACT

A.   The measure of damages

Damages for breach of contract are paid in an amount sufficient to put the claimant in the position which she would have occupied but for the breach of contract. The central statement of the principle in this context was that made by Parke B. in *Robinson v Harman*[6]:

20–03

> "The rule of the common law is, that where a party sustains a loss by reason of a breach of contract, he is, so far as money can do it, to be placed in the same situation, with respect to damages, as if the contract had been performed."

---

[1] The issue of breach of an operative contract should be contrasted with the issue of failure of consideration (or absence of consideration) which is considered in detail in *Restitution*.
[2] See para.19–48.
[3] *Bridge v Campbell Discount Co Ltd* [1962] A.C. 600, below; *United Dominions Trust (Commercial) Ltd v Ennis* [1968] 1 Q.B. 54.
[4] See para.19–28.
[5] See para.20–13.
[6] (1848) 1 Ex. 850, 855.

The purpose behind this statement is that a payment of money in the form of damages can remedy a breach of contract. The tension in this statement clearly is that a contract is formed so that the parties will carry out their obligations, but that breach of those obligations can apparently be remedied simply by payment of money[7] (subject to what is said below about the doctrine of specific performance). As Lord Lloyd put it,[8] the authorities do "not say that the plaintiff is always to be placed in the situation physically as if the contract had been performed, but in as good a situation financially, so far as money can do it". That is, it will often be good enough to give the claimant money, and not simply to require the defendant to do what she undertook originally to do. The central tension from the perspective of the law of finance in this sense is that many transactions are intended only to require the payment of money between the parties; except for those few market contexts in which performance of the contractual obligations is particularly significant. An example of this latter type of contract in which performance would be significant would be physically-settled options to acquire commodities, such as copper, where the buyer of that option requires physical delivery of copper to on-sell to a client of her own: in that circumstance it is suggested that this purpose must be made clear in the contract so as to ensure that any breach of contract is not remedied solely in money or that loss may include further matters such as delivery of copper. The buyer's better option in that instance would be to make timely delivery a condition of the contract.

20–04　There are two principal mechanisms for the measurement of damages for a breach of contract. First, the claimant may receive by way of damages the difference between the contractual performance for which she contracted and the performance which she actually received. This remedy is therefore a measurement in money of the claimant's disappointed loss of expectation. So, if the claimant had contracted to receive two law textbooks for £40 each but had only received one, then the claimant would be entitled to damages of £40, plus interest on the judgment. Secondly, the claimant may be awarded damages which are sufficient to meet the "cost of cure".[9] The cost of cure is an amount which would pay for the performance which the claimant had actually received to be remedied so as to conform to the condition which the defendant was supposed to have supplied under the terms of the contract. So, if the claimant had contracted to buy a four-tier wedding cake and the defendant only delivered a three-tier cake, then damages would be the cost of acquiring a fourth tier for that cake. Alternatively, in either example the claimant might be entitled to receive specific performance, as considered in Chapter 19, to enforce the receipt of the second textbook that was ordered or the creation of a fourth cake tier.

---

[7] See the comments of Lord Millett, dissenting, to this effect in the House of Lords in *Alfred McAlpine Construction Ltd v Panatown Ltd* [2001] A.C. 518.

[8] *Ruxley Electronics and Construction Ltd v Forsyth* [1996] A.C. 344; quoting Viscount Haldane LC in *British Westinghouse Electric and Manufacturing Co Ltd v Underground Electric Railways Co of London Ltd* [1912] A.C. 673, 689.

[9] See above.

In *Ruxley Electronics and Construction Ltd v Forsyth*[10] a householder had **20–05** contracted with builders to build a swimming pool of a specified depth but in breach of contract the builders constructed the swimming pool a few inches shallower than was specified in the contract. The householder refused to pay and so the builders sued: therefore the householder counterclaimed for damages for breach of contract. It was held by the House of Lords that the householder was not entitled to recover damages for the cost of reconstructing the swimming pool from scratch but rather was only entitled to damages (in this instance £2,500) for his loss of amenity. As Lord Jauncey held[11]:

> "Damages are designed to compensate for an established loss and not to provide a gratuitous benefit to the aggrieved party from which it follows that the reasonableness of an award of damages is to be linked directly to the loss sustained."

Lord Lloyd cited the following principles from Cardozo J.[12] as summarising the principle here[13]:

> "... first, the cost of reinstatement is not the appropriate measure of damages if the expenditure would be out of all proportion to the benefit to be obtained, and, secondly, the appropriate measure of damages in such a case is the difference in value, even though it would result in a nominal award."

Thus, it is possible that if the loss suffered but it is impracticable to provide for damages to cure the cost, then damages may be purely nominal.

However, as was suggested by some of their lordships, the position might have **20–06** been different if the householder had had a penchant for diving from a diving board and so had needed the swimming pool to be of a given depth or else it would have been useless for his purpose. If this term had been included as a condition of the contract[14] then this would have entitled the householder to cancel the contract. As to the availability of damages, Lord Mustill[15] suggested that it is a matter for the parties in their contract to specify a particular type of performance if they wish it and therefore that damages would be necessary to cure the defendant's failure to meet that contractually specified level of performance.[16] This does seem to cut against the principle set out by Blackburn J. in *Bettini v Gye*[17] to the effect that the:

> "Parties may think some matter, apparently of very little importance, essential; and if they sufficiently express an intention to make the literal fulfilment of such a thing a condition precedent, it will be one ..."

Clearly, if the parties express that something is to be a condition of their contract, then it would be unfortunate if the court decided that the performance of that

---

[10] [1996] A.C. 344.
[11] *Ruxley Electronics and Construction Ltd v Forsyth* [1996] A.C. 344.
[12] *Jacob & Youngs v Kent* 129 NE 889.
[13] *Ruxley Electronics and Construction Ltd v Forsyth* [1996] A.C. 344.
[14] See para.19–28.
[15] [1996] A.C. 344.
[16] See also *Radford v De Froberville* [1977] 1 W.L.R. 1262, 1270, per Oliver J.
[17] (1875) 1 Q.B. 183, at 187.

condition to the letter is nevertheless not essential. In relation to the swimming pool, one can see why the court took the view that removing the tiling and plumbing, digging through the base of the swimming pool, excavating a few inches further, reconstituting the base of the pool, and then re-tiling and re-plumbing it all, would be an overly pedantic given the limited harm that had actually been caused. It is suggested, however, that in cash-settled financial transactions the difficulty in remedying the harm will be limited because all that will be required is the payment of a larger sum of money or the transfer of securities or similar intangible assets. There is nothing here which would be as difficult as reconstructing a swimming pool. There may be greater difficulty in remedying physically-settled transactions if, for example, acquiring further physical commodities to complete a transaction would involve disproportionate expense; or if further shares needed to complete an order could simply not be obtained because an issue had been over-subscribed. Nevertheless, it is suggested that the need to perform the transaction could not outweigh the difficulty involved in its performance where all that is required is a further accounting for cash or liquid securities. It could also be argued that in most circumstances all that would be required would be compensation in damages, unless the transaction had been created deliberately so as to hedge a particular exposure or to acquire specific assets which were in turn to be on-sold to the claimant's own customers.

B. Liability for breach of duty

20–07   When seeking to attribute liability for breach of a contractual duty, it is important to understand what the duty was exactly, before one can assess whether or not it was broken and whether or not damages are available for any consequent loss. Therefore, it is important to look to the terms of the contractual duty itself. To take a simple example: if my duty is to build a house with four walls and I only build a house with three walls, then I have breached my duty; whereas if my contractual duty was to provide my client with a raincoat, I cannot be held liable for breach of duty if my client goes out into the rain without putting the coat on. Similarly, if my duty is solely to provide information to a client so that she could make decisions about her investment portfolio for herself, then my liability will be limited to the loss which flows from a breach of that duty to provide information but not from the client's own stupidity in choosing a bad investment over a good one; whereas if my duty was to construct a risk management device (a "hedge") for a client's investment portfolio, then if I failed to create an appropriate hedge my liability to pay damages would be for all loss which flows from my breach of duty to create such a hedge. If one's obligations are to provide a viable portfolio then one's potential liability is for any loss that flows from the breach of the duty to provide such a portfolio, but arguably not if the loss flowed from some other factor such as a disruption of the market on which the investment was made (unless the contract expressly included such a market disruption within the factors which the defendant should cover).

So, in *South Australia Asset Management Corp v York Montague Ltd*[18] loans had been made on the basis of negligent valuations of the property which was to be put up as security for those loans. The valuers' contractual liability was taken to be to provide information as to the value of the secured property. The lenders contended that because the market had fallen, the property had become worth even less than the value at the time of the valuers' errors: therefore the damages were contended to be at the level of the total loss suffered by the lender in the form of the defective valuation and also the fall in the market value of the secured property. It was held that the valuers were liable in damages in contract for their breach of duty of care to provide information to the lenders. The amount of the damages which the valuers owed was the difference between the negligent valuation of the property and the actual value of the property, but did not include any other amounts.

20–08

Thus, a defendant may be liable only for loss which followed from their breach of contract, and not necessarily from market factors driving the value of the property. This is important in the financial context because of course most financial markets do move markedly. It is likely that a product which causes loss after a breach of contract might well do so because of unexpected market conditions, and therefore the total loss suffered by the claimant might be more than the loss directly attributable to the breach of contract. That total loss will only be recoverable in contract in damages if it resulted from the defendant's contractual duty.

20–09

There would be a difference if the defendant had warranted the result which the claimant would receive from the performance of the contract.[19] If, for example, a seller had guaranteed that a financial product would provide a suitable hedge for her client's risks, then the seller would be liable for damages for breach of that warranty if the product failed in its designed purpose. Thus, Lord Hoffmann held in *South Australia Asset Management Corp v York Montague Ltd*[20] that the lenders who had relied on the valuations given to them could not recover interest on the damages because that would be to give them a remedy as if they had not entered into the loan transactions at all but instead had lent the money to someone else, as opposed to them having entered into the transactions but without suffering the loss which the false information had caused them.[21] There was no evidence that they could have obtained such rates of interest elsewhere. The amounts of loss which are to be compensated by damages must be proved by the claimant. So, a lender would have to be able to demonstrate that if she had not

20–10

---

[18] [1997] A.C. 191; [1996] 3 All E.R. 365; [1996] UKHL 10.

[19] *South Australia Asset Management Corp v York Montague Ltd* [1997] A.C. 191.

[20] [1997] A.C. 191, [34].

[21] Lord Hoffmann summarised the decision of the Court of Appeal in *Banque Bruxelles Lambert SA v Eagle Star Insurance Co Ltd* [1995] Q.B. 375 to the effect that "in a case in which the lender would not otherwise have lent . . . he is entitled to recover the difference between the sum which he lent, together with a reasonable rate of interest, and the net sum which he actually got back": [1997] A.C. 191, [6]. That decision was the subject of the appeal in *South Australia Asset Management Corp v York Montague Ltd*.

entered into an investment which caused her loss then she would have done something more remunerative than simply placing her money on deposit with a bank.[22]

20–11   The more difficult question might be to identify precisely what is was that was bargained for. Suppose that an interest rate swap is entered into which the seller represented would prevent the buyer suffering an interest rate cost of £1 million, such that that representation was made a condition of the contract. Suppose then that market rates moved such that the swap was worthless and the buyer's interest rate cost rose to £1.5 million. Where the purpose of the swap was to hedge the cost of £1 million then the buyer would be entitled to be put into the position which was within the understanding of the contract; to whit, to be compensated for £1 million in interest cost and not £1.5 million.[23] Only if the contract had provided that the buyer would suffer no interest cost at all would the seller be obliged to pay damages equal to the £1.5 million interest cost imposed on the buyer.[24] That would depend upon how the contract was worded. Consequently, the claimant is only entitled to damages which will compensate her for the failure to perform the contract and not to damages which will compensate her for all of the loss which she may have suffered. Therefore, a contract must ensure that losses beyond the precise scope of the contract are brought expressly within the ambit of the conditions of the contract. Alternatively, a seller of a financial transaction would be well advised to express in the contract the precise purposes for which the contract is effected so that its potential exposure to damages is limited. Where the seller is able, in a contract with a sufficiently expert client,[25] to restrict its role to being that of an advisor who leaves the final choice of financial product to the buyer, then the buyer's entitlement to damages will be limited to loss which flows strictly from that narrow assumption of responsibility.[26]

C.   Causation

20–12   The issue is then whether the breach of contract caused the claimant's loss. A claimant will only be entitled to recover damages for a breach of contract if the breach of contract caused the claimant's loss.[27] Suppose a contract which specified that the seller was to sell the buyer a car with a V6 engine that had a top speed of 138 miles per hour, but that in fact the seller actually provided a car with an ordinary 16 valve engine with a top speed of only 110 miles per hour. Imagine then that the car failed to stop on a wet country road because the tyres on the car had a manufacturing fault and burst, with the result that the car crashed causing enormous damage. There may have been a breach of contract but that breach of contract (providing the wrong sort of car) would not have caused the buyer's loss

---

[22] *Swingcastle Ltd v Alastair Gibson* [1991] 2 A.C. 223, 239, per Lord Lowry.

[23] *Banque Bruxelles Lambert SA v Eagle Star Insurance Co Ltd* [1997] A.C. 191; *Nykredit Bank v Edward Erdman Group* [1997] 1 W.L.R. 1627.

[24] See above.

[25] See para.10–13.

[26] *Banque Bruxelles Lambert SA v Eagle Star Insurance Co Ltd* [1997] A.C. 191.

[27] *Monarch Steamship Co Ltd v A/B Karlshamns Oljefabriker* [1949] A.C. 196.

because the loss was caused by a manufacturing fault with the tyres. Therefore, on those facts, the seller would not be liable for the buyer's loss, but rather the buyer would have to proceed against the manufacturer of the tyres. The issues surrounding causation in financial transactions were considered in the previous section.

D. Remoteness

There may be situations in which there has been a breach of contract which **20–13** caused the claimant's loss, but in which that loss was nevertheless so remote or unlikely that damages may not be awarded. The reason for not awarding damages in such situations is that the loss suffered by the claimant would not have been within the contemplation of the parties which formed their contract. This may be problem in financial transactions where unexpected movements in financial markets cause damages which might be considered to be remote. The central principle in this context was set out in *Hadley v Baxendale*[28] in the judgment of Alderson B:

> "Where two parties have made a contract which one of them has broken, the damages which the other party ought to receive in respect of such breach of contract should be such as may fairly and reasonably be considered either arising naturally, i.e. according to the usual course of things, from such breach of contract itself, or such as may reasonably be supposed to have been in the contemplation of both parties, at the time they made the contract, as the probable result of the breach of it. Now, if the special circumstances under which the contract was actually made were communicated by the plaintiffs to the defendants, and thus known to both parties, the damages resulting from the breach of such a contract, which they would reasonably contemplate, would be the amount of injury which would ordinarily follow from a breach of contract under these special circumstances so known and communicated. But, on the other hand, if these special circumstances were wholly unknown to the party breaking the contract, then she, at the most, could only be supposed to have had in her contemplation the amount of injury which would arise generally, and in the great multitude of cases not affected by any special circumstances, from such a breach of contract."

Thus, damages are available to the extent that they arise "fairly and reasonably" either "naturally" from the circumstances of the contract or if they might reasonably have been supposed to be within the contemplation of the parties. The question will always be whether the loss was sufficiently foreseeable in that there was some serious or very substantial possibility of such loss.[29]

So, if a cook contracts to prepare a meal for a customer then it is reasonable to **20–14** suppose that that person will eat it and that any bad meat included in the meal may cause illness and loss: that would be a natural result of that transaction. Similarly, if a financial institution purports to create an investment portfolio entirely on its own cognisance for a client which includes a share in a company which subsequently goes into insolvency, then the loss suffered by the client flows naturally from the act of creating a portfolio with a poor share included in it.

---

[28] (1854) 9 Exch. 341, Court of Exchequer.
[29] *Hadley v Baxendale* (1854) 9 Exch. 341; *Koufos v C. Czarnikow Ltd ("The Heron II")* [1969] 1 A.C. 350; *The "Ile aux Moines"* [1974] 1 Lloyd's Rep. 262.

20–15 Alternatively, if the manufacturer of an iron bar knew that the buyer was intending to use that iron bar as a ceiling joist and that the manufacturer then failed to manufacture that joist to the contractual specifications, then it would be within the contemplation of the parties that the loss resulting from the collapse of that ceiling would be recoverable in proceedings for breach of the contractual warranty as to the strength of the iron bar. Thus, if a financial institution sold a financial product to an inexpert corporate counterparty having discussed with its trader the fact that that corporate counterparty intended to use that product to hedge against movements in interest rates, then if that product was designed in breach of contract in such a way that it did not perform as the client had been led to expect, then the loss of the hedge would be within the reasonable contemplation of the parties. However, if an expert client had simply put in an order for a financial product to speculate on interest rates—in fact hoping that it would provide a perfect hedge but not discussing this matter with the seller—then it would not have been within the reasonable contemplation of the parties that the client stood to lose an exceptional amount related to the hedge as a result of this breach of contract.

E. The measurement of damages for breach of a financial contract

Identifying the anticipated loss in a well-drafted contract

20–16 The identification of the damage which has been suffered in a financial transaction can be difficult because the market value of financial products can change minute-by-minute and it is not always clear at what stage a claimant would have realised its profits on an investment or whether a sale of the assets would have been possible. Consequently, it can be difficult to prove loss. The best mechanism for identifying loss is to make it plain in the contract how loss should be calculated and what benefits the parties' expected to flow from the agreement. The old-fashioned method for drafting a contract began with recitals and with the legend "whereas the parties intend" to do such-and-such: this methodology had the benefit of making it plain what the underlying purpose of the contract was intended to be. Such elegant solutions have been lost to modern drafting in financial transactions.

20–17 A well-drafted master agreement or confirmation agreement would make plain the parties' anticipated measure of loss in the event of some failure of performance so as to include express reference to the cost of acquiring replacement transactions as a measurement of the loss caused by failure to perform and also the cost of unwinding hedging positions.[30] The issue in relation to financial contracts will be whether or not the common law mechanisms for calculation of damages for breach of contract will be equivalent to the loss which the claimant will have suffered, for example including the cost of unwinding hedging arrangements which have not been considered to be foreseeable in the

---

[30] See para.43–38.

local authority swaps cases.[31] Common law damages will mimic the calculation of loss by reference to the cost of replacement contracts envisaged, for example in the derivatives context, by the ISDA Master Agreement where its standard wording requires that the calculation agent identifies the cost of creating replacement contracts and the most appropriate method for calculating its value.[32]

Physically-settled transactions require some short consideration. At common law the central measure of damages is the loss to the claimant with the aim of compensating that claimant for its loss.[33] The measure of damages for breach of contract will be that necessary to put the claimant in the position it would have been in had the contract been performed[34] but not to put the claimant in a better position than it would have been in but for the breach.[35] To establish a claim for damages it is therefore necessary for the claimant to demonstrate that a loss has resulted from the breach of contract and not simply that the contract has been breached.[36] Therefore, if there is a failure to make a delivery under a contract, it is important for the claimant to demonstrate that it has suffered some loss as a result of that failure to make delivery.[37] As a consequence it is necessary that any documentation explain that payment or delivery on time is of the essence of the contract so as to make the consequent loss evident.

20–18

Effects of breach of contract: specific performance

The equitable remedy of specific performance is considered in the next chapter.[38]

20–19

3.   Damages in Tort

This chapter is principally concerned with liability in contract law, as opposed to liability in tort. However, a word on the basis of liability for damages in tort would be appropriate. Damages for tort are measured according to the claimant's out-of-pocket loss; that is, an amount to put the claimant in the position she

20–20

---

[31] *Kleinwort Benson v Birmingham C.C.* [1996] 4 All E.R. 733, CA; *Peregrine Fixed Income Ltd v Robinson* [2000] C.L.C. 1328, [2000] Lloyd's Rep. Bank 304; *Australia and New Zealand Banking Group v Société Générale* [2000] 1 All E.R. (Comm) 682 (CA), [2000] C.L.C. 833, [2000] Lloyd's Rep. Bank 304.

[32] *Dunkirk Colliery Co v Lever* (1878) 9 Ch.D. 20; *W.L. Thompson Ltd v Robinson (Gunmakers) Ltd* [1955] Ch. 177; *Charter v Sullivan* [1957] 2 Q.B. 117. Specifically with reference to the acquisition of replacement transactions: *The Elena D'Amico* [1980] 1 Lloyd's Rep. 75; *Murray v Lloyd* [1989] 1 W.L.R. 1060.

[33] *Tai Hing Cotton Mill Ltd v Kamsing Factory* [1979] A.C. 95, 104.

[34] *Robinson v Harman* (1848) 1 Ex. 850, 855; *Phillips v Ward* [1956] 1 W.L.R. 471.

[35] *Perry v Sidney Phillips & Son* [1982] 1 W.L.R. 1297. cf. *Harbutts "Plasticine" Ltd v Wayne Tank & Pump Co Ltd* [1970] 1 Q.B. 447 whereby it may even be possible to claim damages which would have the effect of putting the claimant in a better position than if the contract had not been breached, provided that such a measure of damages is necessary to compensate the claimant's loss.

[36] *The Balaeres* [1993] 1 Lloyd's Rep. 215, 232.

[37] Where late delivery is accepted and a profit is made on re-sale of the asset in question, this may be set against the damages recoverable (*Wertheim v Chicoutimi Pulp Co* [1911] A.C. 301) unless, it is suggested, the contract provides to the contrary.

[38] See para.19–86.

would have been in but for the tort[39] and not to compensate her for any loss of opportunity nor any economic loss.[40] It is only in contract law that such opportunity cost will be recoverable.

4. DAMAGES FOR MISREPRESENTATION

A. The quantum of damages for fraudulent misrepresentation

20–21 The measure of damages for fraudulent misrepresentation is an amount sufficient to put the representee in the position in which she would have found herself had the misrepresentation not been made.[41] Lord Browne-Wilkinson in the House of Lords in *Smith New Court Securities Ltd v Scrimgeour Vickers (Asset Management) Ltd*[42] held as follows:

"(1)   The defendant is bound to make reparation for all the damage directly flowing from the transaction.

(2)   Although such damage need not have been foreseeable, it must have been directly caused by the transaction.

(3)   In assessing such damage, the plaintiff is entitled to recover by way of damages the full price paid by him, but he must give credit for any benefits which he has received as a result of the transaction.

(4)   As a general rule, the benefits received by him include the market value of the property acquired as at the date of acquisition; but such general rule is not to be inflexibly applied where to do so would prevent him obtaining full compensation for the wrong suffered.

(5)   Although the circumstances in which the general rule should not apply cannot be comprehensively stated, it will normally not apply where either (a) the misrepresentation has continued to operate after the date of the acquisition of the asset so as to induce the plaintiff to retain the asset or (b) the circumstances of the case are such that the plaintiff is, by reason of the fraud, locked into the property.

(6)   In addition, the plaintiff is entitled to recover consequential losses caused by the transaction.

(7)   The plaintiff must take all reasonable steps to mitigate his loss once he has discovered the fraud."

It was held that, while there was a duty on the claimant to mitigate their loss, where, in this case, investments had been acquired as part of a long-term investment strategy, there was no obligation on the claimant to sell the shares immediately when that would not have been a sensible strategy because of the low price which could have been acquired for those shares after the second fraud had been discovered. In any event, the claimant is entitled to recover the difference between the price at which the shares were acquired and the real value

---

[39] *Lim v Camden & Islington Area Health Authority* [1980] A.C. 174, 187. cf. *Junior Books Ltd v The Veitchi Co Ltd* [1983] 1 A.C. 520.

[40] *Cattle v Stockton Waterworks Co* (1875) L.R. 10 Q.B. 453; *Spartan Steel and Alloys Ltd v Martin & Co Ltd* [1973] Q.B. 27. cf. *Heldley Byrne v Heller* [1964] A.C. 465.

[41] *Doyle v Olby (Ironmongers) Ltd* [1969] 2 Q.B. 158. It is not a measure of damages to put the representee in the position he would have been in had the representation been true: see *Chitty on Contracts*, para.6–049.

[42] [1996] 4 All E.R. 769.

of those shares. Therefore, the claimant was entitled to recover the loss suffered even though the additional loss caused by the discovery of the second fraud had not been foreseeable.

The measure of damages for a fraudulent misrepresentation in relation, for example, to an allotment of shares is prima facie the difference between the actual value of the shares at the time of allotment and the sum paid for them.[43] The plaintiff is entitled to recover all the actual damage flowing directly from the fraudulent misrepresentation.[44] This principle means that in some cases the value as at the date of allotment will not be applied, for example in circumstances in which the plaintiff suffers further losses beyond any reduction in the value of the shares by reason of the fraud.[45] An action for breach of contract may attract damages for loss of other opportunities;[46] however, damages for the tort of deceit only compensate out-of-pocket loss and therefore no damages in respect of prospective gains can be recovered.

20–22

B. Damages for fraudulent misrepresentation do not depend on foreseeability

Damages in relation to fraud under the tort of deceit are such as "to make reparation for all the damage flowing directly from the transaction".[47] There is no requirement in a claim for fraudulent misrepresentation that the damage must have been foreseeable provided that it was caused by the transaction.[48] There is an obligation on the claimant to mitigate her loss on discovery of the fraud.[49] However, in the event that the transaction is profitable for the victim of the fraud, then that victim would be required to account when claiming its damages for the benefits which it had realised from the transaction: therefore, a claimant would only be entitled to the difference between the damage (including any cost of funding the loss of the transaction) and the profits realised.[50]

20–23

---

[43] *McConnel v Wright* (1903) 1 Ch. 546, CA; *Davidson v Tulloch* (1860) 3 Macq. 783; 22 D. HL 7.

[44] *Doyle v Olby (Ironmongers) Ltd* [1969] 2 Q.B. 158, CA.

[45] *Smith New Court Securities Ltd v Scrimgeour Vickers (Asset Management) Ltd* [1997] 1 B.C.L.C. 350, HL.

[46] That is, the claimant will not be able to receive damages for the profit which he expected to make from the transaction (i.e. loss of bargain) but rather only to receive damages for other profitable opportunities (such as acquiring securities which would have been acquired but for the misrepresentation inducing investment in these securities): *East v Maurer* [1991] 1 W.L.R. 461. The issue in relation to securities transactions would be identifying such alternative transactions, given the breadth of investment opportunities in securities markets, and demonstrating that particular investment strategies would have been followed, as opposed simply to claiming that one might have been able to realise a given market return.

[47] *Smith New Court Ltd v Scrimgeour Vickers* [1997] A.C. 254, 267, per Lord Browne-Wilkinson.

[48] [1997] A.C. 254, 267; *Downs v Chappell* [1997] 1 W.L.R. 426.

[49] See above.

[50] See above.

C.   Damages for negligent misrepresentation

20–24   The effect of s.2 of the Misrepresentation Act 1967 is that there is no difference in the availability of damages between the representation being fraudulent and merely negligent.[51] Section 2(1) of the Misrepresentation Act 1967 provides that:

> "Where a person has entered into a contract after a misrepresentation has been made to him by another party thereto and as a result thereof he has suffered loss, then, if the person making the misrepresentation would be liable to damages in respect thereof had the misrepresentation been made fraudulently, that person shall be so liable notwithstanding that the misrepresentation was not made fraudulently, unless he proves that he had reasonable ground to believe and did believe up to the time the contract was made that the facts represented were true."

The difference lies between the two forms of misrepresentation. In relation to fraudulent misrepresentation, damages are calculated in accordance with the loss that flows from the misrepresentation, regardless of whether or not that loss was foreseeable.[52] For negligent misrepresentation, damages are limited to foreseeable loss.[53]

5.   EFFECTING RESTITUTION OF PAYMENTS AT COMMON LAW

A.   The outline of the law of unjust enrichment and "money had and received"

20–25   At common law, when money has been transferred as a result of some unjust factor—such as failure of consideration, mistake, undue influence, or some other such factor—then the claimant will be able to recover the cash equivalent of sums paid by it to the defendant by means of a personal claim in restitution, traditionally known as "a claim for money had and received", so as to reverse the unjust enrichment acquired by the defendant.[54]

20–26   The doctrine of money had and received is therefore said to form part of the law of unjust enrichment[55]; itself a part of English law as a result of the decisions of the House of Lords in *Lipkin Gorman v Karpnale*[56] and *Woolwich Equitable Building Society v IRC*.[57] In those cases the concept of "unjust enrichment" was embraced as forming part of English law as a distinct doctrine.[58] (At the time, this doctrine was known simply as "restitution".) The aim of the doctrine of unjust enrichment is, first, to isolate an enrichment; secondly, to decide whether or not

---

[51] Except in relation to the requirement of writing for fraudulent misrepresentation under Statute of Frauds (Amendment) Act 1828, s.6.

[52] *Doyle v Olby (Ironmongers) Ltd* [1969] 3 All E.R. 344; *Smith New Court Securities v Scrimogeour Vickers (Asset Management) Ltd* [1996] 4 All E.R. 769.

[53] *The Wagon Mound (No.1)* [1961] A.C. 388.

[54] *Westdeutsche Landesbank v Islington* [1996] A.C. 669.

[55] *Westdeutsche Landesbank v Islington* [1996] A.C. 669, per Lord Goff.

[56] [1991] 2 A.C. 548, [1991] 3 W.L.R. 10.

[57] [1993] A.C. 70, [1992] 3 W.L.R. 366.

[58] That is in spite of the dicta of Lord Diplock in *Orakpo v Manson Investment Ltd* [1978] A.C. 95; [1977] 3 W.L.R. 229 which had previously upheld the orthodoxy that there was no such doctrine in English law.

that enrichment was generated in a manner which was unjust; and, thirdly, to deploy a response which restores the value lost by some other person. The scope of the doctrine is nevertheless potentially broad. There is a potential overlap between the imposition of proprietary rights to prevent unconscionable behaviour, as considered later in this chapter, and the restitution of unjust enrichment. The aim of unjust enrichment is to provide responses which require a defendant to give up an enrichment received at the plaintiff's expense. Its derivation is often traced to the American *Restatement of Restitution*[59] which states[60]: "a person who has been unjustly enriched at the expense of another is required to make restitution to the other". The appropriate remedy is then one which requires the defendant to give up to another an enrichment received at the other's expense or its value in money; that is "with gains to be given up, not with losses to be made good".[61] The aim is therefore not compensation for loss suffered, but rather reparation by return of value. The case law has seen the law of restitution develop out of "the ties of natural justice and equity".[62] Indeed the law of unjust enrichment is best thought of, it is suggested, as being a branch of equity, as was the ratio decidendi in *Moses v Macferlan*,[63] which has become confused by an enthusiasm for a more rigid taxonomy among some academic commentators.[64]

B. The basis of the claim for money had and received

The leading case in this context is the decision of the House of Lords in *Westdeutsche Landesbank v Islington*.[65] In that case, the bank had made payments to the local authority under a ten year interest rate swap before the parties learned that the contract was void ab initio. The bank had paid money to the local authority under the void contract, and sought restitution of those sums. As is discussed below, the bank wanted to assert a proprietary remedy but no members of the House of Lords were prepared to hold that a proprietary remedy would be available. Lord Goff held that the roots of the doctrine were in the speech of Lord Mansfield in *Moses v Macferlan*[66] to the effect that the "gist of the action for money had and received"[67] is that "the defendant, upon the circumstances of the case, is obliged by the ties of natural justice and equity to refund the money".[68] On the facts of that case there had been an unjust factor (i.e. the money had been paid under a mistake and there had been a failure of consideration) and therefore the bank was entitled to recover the amount which it had paid to the local

20–27

---

[59] See, for example, Goff and Jones *The Law of Restitution*, 5th edn (London: Sweet & Maxwell, 1999), p.13.

[60] American *Restatement of Restitution*, para.1.

[61] Birks, *Introduction to the Law of Restitution* (Oxford, 1989), p.11.

[62] *Moses v Macferlan* (1760) 2 Burr. 1005, 1012.

[63] (1760) 2 Burr. 1005, 1012.

[64] See *http://www.alastairhudson.com/englandsdreaming/englandsdreamingindex/html.*

[65] [1996] A.C. 669.

[66] (1760) 2 Burr 1005, 1012.

[67] [1996] 2 All E.R. 961, 980. *South Tyneside M.B.C. v Svenska International Plc* [1995] 1 All E.R. 545.

[68] *Westdeutsche Landesbank v Islington* [1996] A.C. 669; [1996] 2 All E.R. 961, 980.

authority. Importantly, the bank was entitled only to a personal claim in restitution (which is what the claim for money had and received is) so that it could receive an amount of money equal to the amounts which had been paid to the local authority. If the local authority had gone into insolvency (which it had not) then the bank would have had no security against the local authority because it had only personal rights against it.[69] Because an action for money had and received is a personal claim, it is no defence for a bank to resist it on the basis that all of the money paid to it has since been paid out of the account: the claim is a personal one against the defendant and not a proprietary claim which could be defeated by the property having been dissipated.[70]

6.   RESCISSION

A.   The ordinary principles of rescission

20–28   Rescission is a general equitable doctrine which permits the courts to achieve a restitutio in integrum: that is, to restore parties to the position which they had occupied originally. In the law of contract, the parties are returned to their original positions by having their contract set aside. In short, rescission will be awarded in cases of mistake, misrepresentation or to set aside an unconscionable bargain.[71] Rescission applies only to contracts which are voidable. Where a contract is void ab initio, there is no question of rescission on the basis that such a contract is taken never to have existed.[72] There is only a question as to the rescission of a contract if that contract is capable of being affirmed by either party. This chapter will consider rescission in its strict sense of setting aside contracts which are merely voidable, that is capable of being declared void but not void ab initio. The Misrepresentation Act 1967 provides the recipient of a representation ("the representee") with a right to rescind a contract if a fraudulent misrepresentation was made to her which induced her to enter into the contract; whereas if the representation was negligent or innocent, then the court has a discretion under that Act to award the representee damages in lieu of rescission.[73]

B.   The court's discretion to award damages in lieu of rescission in relation to a negligent misrepresentation

20–29   The court has discretion to award damages in lieu of rescission in relation to negligent misrepresentation further s.2(2) of the Misrepresentation Act 1967, in the following terms:

> "Where a person has entered into a contract after a misrepresentation has been made to him otherwise than fraudulently, and he would be entitled, by reason of the misrepresentation, to rescind the contract, then, if it is claimed, in any proceedings arising out of the contract, that

[69] *Guinness Mahon & Co Ltd v Kensington & Chelsea RLBC*, CA, *The Times*, March 2, 1998.
[70] *Bavins Junior and Sims v London and South Western Bank* [1900] 1 Q.B. 270.
[71] *TSB v Camfield* [1995] 1 W.L.R. 430.
[72] *Westdeutsche Landesbank v Islington* [1994] 4 All E.R. 890, per Leggatt L.J., CA.
[73] See generally *Chitty on Contracts*, para.6–001 et seq.

the contract ought to be or has been rescinded, the court or arbitrator may declare the contract subsisting and award damages in lieu of rescission, if of opinion that it would be equitable to do so, having regard to the nature of the misrepresentation and the loss that would be caused by it if the contract were upheld, as well as to the loss that rescission would cause to the other party."

Given that cash-settled financial transactions are generally concerned with the cash to which each party is entitled, then the nature of the contract would frequently be appropriate for an award of damages instead of rescission because the loss would be only a loss of money. However, there may be situations in which the representee required the securities to be delivered to it physically so that it could satisfy some other obligation (for example, supplying securities of that type to its own customers), or where the investor genuinely sought to participate as a shareholder in the company at issue, when it would be inequitable to compensate the representee solely by means of cash damages. However, of course, rescission of the contract would not in itself satisfy those objectives of the representee.

C. Rescission in cases of money had and received

The form of recovery which Lord Goff favoured in his speech in *Westdeutsche Landesbank v Islington* was one which returned the parties to the positions which they had occupied originally.[74] In that case, as considered above, a bank paid money to a local authority on the mistaken assumption that their contract was valid, when in fact it was void ab initio. This rescission approach would appear to achieve two goals. On general restitutionary grounds, it has a superficial attraction in that it terminates the unjust enrichment which the local authorities enjoyed at the expense of the banks. However, it would not necessarily restore to the banks the whole of the loss which they had suffered by entering into the transaction, including the cost of hedging arrangements.[75] The second goal achieved by the rescission approach is the avoidance of seeming to enforce the void contract by an award of lost opportunity cost to the parties. In the case of cash-settled derivatives, any award of damages[76] would be equivalent to performance of the contract.[77]

20–30

The central issue is the ability of common law or equitable remedies to restore the parties to the positions which they occupied before they purported to enter into the deep discount swap transaction in *Westdeutsche Landesbank v Islington*.[78] Given the nature of the property, all that would be required is a reverse payment of an equal amount of the same currency. As Lord Goff considered the position,

20–31

---

[74] [1996] 2 All E.R. 961, 966.
[75] See on this the discussion of the defence of passing on in *Kleinwort Benson v Birmingham C.C.* [1996] 4 All E.R. 733, below.
[76] Providing they are payable in the contract currency.
[77] *Morgan Stanley v Puglisi Consentino* [1998] C.L.C. 481.
[78] [1996] A.C. 669.

"... in the present case, there ought to be no difficulty about that at all ... because the case is concerned solely with money."[79] The restitution-by-rescission approach simply requires that:

> "... each party should pay back the money that it has received—or more sensibly strike a balance, and order that the party who has received most should repay the balance ... with an appropriate order for the payment of interest."[80]

It is suggested, that in those circumstances the most suitable method of achieving this result would be to effect an equitable set-off in respect of the moneys which remained outstanding.

Rescission and mistake

20–32   When seeking rescission of a contract on grounds of mistake, the rule is that a mistake made by both parties in entering into a transaction will enable that contract to be rescinded.[81] Whereas, where only one party to a contract is acting under a mistake, the contract will not be rescinded[82] unless the party who was not operating under a mistake was aware that the other party was so operating.[83]

Rescission and misrepresentation

20–33   For the purposes of rescission based on misrepresentation, there is an important distinction to be made between fraudulent misrepresentation and innocent misrepresentation. A fraudulent misrepresentation will render a contract void where that misrepresentation was made with an intention that it should be acted upon by the person to whom it was made.[84] The type of fraud required is that sufficient to found a claim in the tort of deceit: as considered in Chapter 24, that is a misrepresentation made knowingly, or without belief in its truth, or with recklessness as to whether or not it was true.[85] At common law, an innocent misrepresentation will found a claim provided that it has become a term of the contract. Section 1 of the Misrepresentation Act 1967 provides further that rescission will be available in cases of innocent misrepresentation in a situation in which that misrepresentation has induced the other party to enter into the contract. Therefore, a party to a contract who had made an innocent misrepresentation would give the other party to the contract a good defence to an action for specific performance of that contract.

20–34   It is necessary for an award of rescission that it is possible to return the parties to the position which they occupied before the creation or performance of the

---

[79] [1996] 2 All E.R. 961, 966.
[80] [1996] 2 All E.R. 961, 966.
[81] *Cundy v Lindsay* (1878) 3 App. Cas. 459.
[82] *Riverlate Properties Ltd v Paul* [1975] Ch. 133.
[83] *Webster v Cecil* (1861) 30 Beav. 62; *Hartog v Colin & Shields* [1939] 2 All E.R. 566.
[84] *Peek v Gurney* (1873) L.R. 6 H.L. 377.
[85] *Derry v Peek* (1889) 14 App. Cas. 337.

contract: an inability to do so would negate the possibility of rescission.[86] It may be the case that in some instances it will be impossible to restore the parties to the position which they had occupied originally because the property which was passed (perhaps sensitive information or know-how) is not capable of being compensated by a monetary remedy. However, the general proposition remains true that rescission will be effected if appropriate value can be restored.[87] Furthermore, it is possible for the court to award damages rather than rescission in cases of misrepresentation under s.2(2) of the Misrepresentation Act 1967 which provides that:—

> "Where a person entered into a contract after a misrepresentation has been made to him otherwise than fraudulently, and he would be entitled, by reason of the misrepresentation, to rescind the contract . . . the court . . . may declare the contract subsisting and award damages in lieu of rescission . . ."

Therefore, a contract can be affirmed by a court where it appears that damages would provide adequate remedy and make rescission unnecessary.

Rescission will be available then where, for example, a seller of derivatives **20–35** misallocates a private, retail customer as being an expert customer (particularly where it has never dealt with that person before), procures her signature on its standard conduct of business agreement for expert customers without providing her with all of the supporting documentation, and fails to explain the full extent of the risks of the complex web of derivatives and repos sold to her in circumstances in which the paucity of information given to her induced her to believe there was only limited risk and thus to enter into the contract.[88] That was the factual matrix which gave rise to rescission in *Morgan Stanley v Puglisi Consentino*.[89] This decision on the combination of regulatory and common law norms in developing a standard of suitable behaviour in the selling of derivative products will be, it is suggested, the future of the availability of rescission in this area.

D. Loss of the right to rescind in general terms

In a situation in which the plaintiff has affirmed the transaction in full knowledge **20–36** of the factor which is subsequently relied upon to make out a claim for rescission, that plaintiff will not be entitled to claim rescission of the contract.[90] In *Peyman v Lanjani*[91] the defendant had carried out a fraudulent impersonation of someone else to obtain a leasehold interest in a restaurant. The plaintiff knew of the fraud,

---

[86] *Erlanger v New Sombrero Phosphate Co* (1873) 3 App. Cas. 1218; *Clarke v Dickson* (1859) E.B. & E. 148; *Lagunas Nitrate Co v Lagunas Syndicate* [1899] 2 Ch. 392; *Steedman v Frigidaire Corp* [1932] WN 248; *Thorpe v Fasey* [1949] Ch. 649; *Butler v Croft* (1973) 27 P. & C.R. 1. cf. *Urquhart v Macpherson* (1878) 3 App. Cas. 831.
[87] *Newbigging v Adam* (1886) 34 Ch.D. 582; *Spence v Crawford* [1939] 3 All E.R. 271.
[88] *Morgan Stanley v Puglisi Consentino* [1998] C.L.C. 481, see para.7–16 for a detailed discussion of this case.
[89] [1998] C.L.C. 481.
[90] *Peyman v Lanjani* [1985] Ch. 457.
[91] [1985] Ch. 457.

but did not know that it gave him a right to rescission, when he agreed to become the defendant's manager. It was held that the plaintiff could not rely on rescission in these circumstances where he had known of the fraud but nevertheless entered knowingly into the transaction. In such circumstances, the plaintiff is deemed to have waived her rights in respect of the claim for rescission.[92]

20–37   In a number of circumstances, affirmation can take the form of implied affirmation. Therefore, affirmation can take the form of an express agreement to waive the right of rescission, or it can be merely implied from the circumstances.[93] Therefore, it is possible for a sufficient delay in activating the right of rescission to raise the inference of affirmation of the contract. Alternatively, that delay, or some action performed in furtherance of the contract, might be deemed to be acquiescence in the continued validity of the transaction. As above, it would be important that the plaintiff had knowledge both of the factor giving rise to the claim for rescission and knowledge of the right to rescind at the time of affirmation.

7.   PROPRIETARY CLAIMS ON TERMINATION OF A CONTRACT

20–38   When a contract is terminated, if the contract contained proprietary rights for one or other of the parties ("the secured party")—whether in the form of a trust or a mortgage or otherwise—then the secured party may be able to have recourse to those property rights, as discussed in Chapter 23 *Taking Security*. The problem arises that if the contract has been found to be void ab initio then the secured party will not be able to rely on the terms of the contract because if the contract did not exist then none of its terms existed.[94]

20–39   Alternatively, a claimant may seek to establish a proprietary right which is not contained in a contract but rather by way of seeking to convince the court to recognise it by operation of law. As considered above, this was the situation in *Westdeutsche Landesbank v Islington*[95] where a bank transferred money to a local authority under an interest rate swap contract which was subsequently found to have been void ab initio. The bank sought to recover the moneys which had been paid to the local authority by way of an equitable proprietary claim in resulting trust, or in constructive trust, or in equitable tracing. These doctrines are considered in Chapters 21 and 23 respectively.

20–40   It was held in *Westdeutsche Landesbank v Islington* that resulting trusts were limited to cases in which two or more parties had contributed to the purchase price of property, or where some trust was found to have been incompletely constituted. Neither of these possibilities was the case in *Westdeutsche Landesbank v Islington*. It was held that a constructive trust arose only in circumstances in which the defendant had had knowledge of some factor which

---

[92] *Clough v London & North Western Rail Co* (1871) L.R. 7 Ex. Ch. 26.

[93] Lapse of time will not necessarily preclude this application: *Life Association of Scotland v Siddal* (1861) 3 De. G.F. & J. 58; *Charter v Trevelyan* (1844) 11 Cl. & F. 714; *Leaf v International Galleries* [1950] 2 K.B. 86.

[94] *Westdeutsche Landesbank v Islington LBC* [1996] A.C. 669.

[95] [1996] A.C. 669.

should have affected her conscience at the time of having the property in her possession. As Lord Browne-Wilkinson held:

> "[t]here was therefore never a time at which both (a) there was defined trust property and (b) the conscience of the local authority in relation to such defined trust property was affected. The basic requirements of a trust were never satisfied."[96]

It was held, finally, in relation to a claim for equitable tracing both that there had **20–41** not been any proprietary right over the moneys and furthermore that the bank had in any event lost its right to trace into the local authority's bank accounts because those accounts had gone overdrawn after the money had been paid into them. This was said to offend against the principle that there must be identifiable trust property before there can be a valid trust: the overdraft on the account proved that the property which had been in that account had ceased to be there and that money was, as a matter of fact, impossible to trace after it had left that account.[97] As Lord Browne-Wilkinson held, in reliance on *Re Goldcorp Exchange Ltd (in receivership)*,[98] "[o]nce there ceased to be an identifiable trust fund, the local authority could not become a trustee" of the money it had received from the bank.

---

[96] [1996] A.C. 669; [1996] 2 All E.R. 961, 988–989.
[97] See above. There is an exception to this principle in the case of personal liability imposed under constructive trust on a person who dishonestly assisted in a breach of trust.
[98] [1995] 1 A.C. 74.

PART VI

PROPERTY

CORE PRINCIPLES

The trust enables a simultaneous separation of ownership of property between the legal title of the trustees and the equitable proprietary interests of the beneficiaries. The trustees owe fiduciary obligations to the beneficiaries which are governed by the terms of any trust instrument or, in the absence of a provision in such an instrument, by the general law of trusts.

Express trusts must have some person who has the rights of a beneficiary in the trust property. For the effective creation of an express trust there must be certainty of intention to create a trust, certainty as to the subject matter of the trust, and certainty as to the beneficiaries of the trust. In the absence of express provision in a trust instrument, the trustees' obligations to invest the trust fund are governed by the Trustee Act 2000: those obligations require the trustees to ensure that the investments are suitable in the particular context of the beneficiaries, and to ensure that the investments are sufficiently diversified in the context of that trust. The trustees have the right to invest the trust property as though they were its absolute owners subject to a general duty to take reasonable care and skill. These obligations are subject to anything to the contrary in the trust instrument.

The courts will imply the existence of trusts in some circumstances, principally in the form of constructive trusts. Constructive trusts are imposed on the defendant by operation of law in circumstances in which the legal owner of property has knowingly acted unconscionably in relation to that property in contravention of the claimant's equitable proprietary rights. Thus, constructive trusts will be imposed inter alia over unauthorised profits earned by the trustees from their fiduciary office, or over bribes received by a fiduciary (where that category of fiduciary office has been generously interpreted), or where the defendant has acted fraudulently or otherwise unconscionably in relation to property.

1.   Introduction—The Nature of the Trust

21–01 The trust is a device with an ancient provenance[1] which requires that the legal owner of property observe the equitable interests of beneficiaries either because those rights have been created intentionally by an express trust or more generally because a court of equity considers that good conscience requires that the legal owner should hold the property on trust.[2] Trusts can therefore be used as a means of providing responses to unconscionable behaviour by securing rights over property. Express trusts, however, are used commonly in financial transactions as property management vehicles because they are endlessly flexible and because they enable the beneficiaries to be shielded from the insolvency of the trustee. This chapter analyses the trust both as a property management vehicle, as a means of taking security and as a means of ensuring conscionable treatment of property.

21–02 The following definition of a trust is given in Geraint Thomas and Alastair Hudson's *The Law of Trusts*[3]:

> "The essence of a trust is the imposition of an equitable obligation on a person who is the legal owner of property (a trustee) which requires that person to act in good conscience when dealing with that property in favour of any person (the beneficiary) who has a beneficial interest recognised by equity in the property.[4] The trustee is said to 'hold the property on trust' for the beneficiary. There are four significant elements to the trust: that it is equitable, that it provides the beneficiary with rights in property, that it also imposes obligations on the trustee, and that those obligations are fiduciary in nature."

Trusts were created originally by courts of equity and therefore the beneficiary is said to have an "equitable interest" in the trust property; whereas the trustee will be treated by the common law as holding the "legal title" in the trust property, thus enabling the trustee to deal with the trust property so as to achieve the objectives of the trust.[5] In general terms we can observe that a trustee is the

---

[1] See A.S. Hudson, *Equity & Trusts*, 7th edn (Routledge, 2012), s.1.1.

[2] I have written a number of books on trusts law, so readers are referred for greater detail to A.S. Hudson, *Equity & Trusts* and to G.W. Thomas and A.S. Hudson, *The Law of Trusts*, 2nd edn (OUP, 2010) generally. For those unfamiliar with this area, I have also written a brief introductory guide which explains all of the main principles in an accessible way: A.S. Hudson, *Understanding Equity & Trusts*, 4th edn (Routledge, 2012).

[3] G.W. Thomas and A.S. Hudson, *The Law of Trusts*, para.1 01. In that book, from pp.1 through 26, Prof Thomas and I analyse the effects of this definition in greater detail than is necessary at this stage of this book.

[4] The nature of this form of "conscience" has been the subject of scholarly debate for centuries. See A. Hudson, *Equity & Trusts*, ss.1.1 and 32.2.

[5] The distinction between equity and common law is considered in A. Hudson, *Equity & Trusts*, s.1.2.

officer under a trust who is obliged to carry out the terms of the trust and who owes strict fiduciary duties of the utmost good faith to the beneficiaries.[6]

That the beneficiary has an equitable proprietary interest in the trust property means that even if the trustee should go into insolvency, the beneficiary retains those property rights regardless of the claims of unsecured creditors in the insolvency. Thus, by way of example, a trust could be used when seeking to take security against the possibility of the insolvency of a counterparty in a stock-lending transaction (whereby securities are to be transferred to a counterparty, so as to enhance the level of security in that transaction, subject to an obligation to transfer back securities of like kind in the future). The transferor would be concerned that the counterparty might go into insolvency before transferring securities back. The parties' contract could be drafted so as to provide that the counterparty holds the securities on trust throughout the life of the transaction. If the counterparty did indeed go into insolvency before transferring the securities back, the trust would have the effect of ensuring that the counterparty remained trustee over the securities and so the transferor would retain its equitable proprietary rights in the trust property throughout the life of the trust, regardless of the claims of any of the counterparty's creditors.

21–03

Trusts fall broadly into two types: trusts which are created intentionally by one or more parties for the benefit of identified beneficiaries (express trusts) and trusts which are created by operation of law regardless of the intentions of all of the parties (constructive and resulting trusts). Each type of trust will be considered in turn but, from the perspective of taking security and for property management purposes, express trusts are the most important category of trust. In the creation of an express trust there are a number of formalities to be obeyed.

21–04

The most important recent statement of the core principles of trusts law was made by Lord Browne-Wilkinson in *Westdeutsche Landesbank v Islington* in the following terms:

21–05

> "Equity operates on the conscience of the owner of the legal interest. In the case of a trust, the conscience of the legal owner requires him to carry out the purposes for which the property was vested in him (express or implied trust) or which the law imposes on him by reason of his unconscionable conduct (constructive trust)."[7]

Thus express trusts should be understood as being rooted in the need for the trustee to acknowledge ties of good conscience in relation to the beneficiaries. The most significant aspect of the express trust is this division in ownership between the common law ("legal") rights of the trustees and the equitable interests of the beneficiaries. The constructive trust is similar in that it prevents unconscionable behaviour by a person who has the legal title in property.

In commercial situations, for example that in *Westdeutsche Landesbank v Islington*, it is important for the parties to know which of them has which rights in

21–06

---

[6] See below at para.11.27. On the nature of trustee's obligations and powers see A. Hudson, *Equity & Trusts*, Chs 8 through 10 generally. The idea of good conscience requiring a trustee to act in the best interests of the beneficiary appears to have been present in *Gresley v Saunders* (1522) Spelman Rep.21–31.

[7] [1996] A.C. 669; [1996] 2 All E.R. 961, 988.

the property which is dealt with as part of a contract. A proprietary constructive trust will give a proprietary right to the beneficiary. That is, a right in the property itself which is enforceable against any other person. If the trustee went into insolvency then the trust property would not form part of the trustee's estate because the beneficial ownership of that property rests with the beneficiaries.[8] If there were no valid trust then there would be only rights *in personam* for the claimant (or, personal rights), as opposed to *in rem* (or, proprietary) rights. A mere *in personam* right would entitle the successful plaintiff to a claim in money only and not to any specific property. In cases of insolvency this would mean that the plaintiff would have no secured rights but only a *pari passu* debt claim with other unsecured creditors. The *in rem* right attaching to a beneficiary under a trust comes into operation from the moment that the proprietary right is validly created, under an express trust,[9] or at the moment when the defendant has knowledge of the factor which fixes her with liability under a constructive trust.[10]

A.   The creation of express trusts

Introduction

21–07   Express trusts can be created intentionally by the parties or express trusts can be deemed by the courts to have been created. An express trust is created when the absolute owner of property ("the settlor") declares or demonstrates an intention that a trustee or trustees shall hold identified property on trust for an identified beneficiary or beneficiaries. The trustee holds the legal title in that property; whereas the beneficiary acquires an equitable proprietary interest in it. It is typically the case that intentional express trusts in financial transactions are created in the form of a trust instrument in documentary form, although for trusts over most forms of property this is not necessary. The usefulness of a trust instrument is that the powers and obligations of the trustees are described (in a well-drafted instrument) in detail, as opposed to being inferred by reference to the general law of trusts. Constructive trusts and resulting trusts arise by operation of law—that is, not depending on the intention of the parties but rather by court order. The ways in which trusts come into existence are explored in this section.

The constitution of trusts

21–08   A valid declaration of trust over personal property will not require any formality under the law of trusts, provided that it can be demonstrated that the settlor intended to create an immediate trust over the property.[11] However, in relation to property to be made subject to a trust on death, in relation to trusts of land,[12] and

---

[8] See *Re Goldcorp* [1995] A.C. 74.
[9] An express trust is validly created either on a valid declaration of trust by the settlor (*Richards v Delbridge* (1874) L.R. 18 Eq. 11) or at the time when legal title in the trust property is transferred to the trustee (*Milroy v Lord* (1862) 4 De G.F. & J. 264).
[10] *Westdeutsche Landesbank v Islington* [1996] 2 All E.R. 961, 988.
[11] *M'Fadden v Jenkyns* (1842) 12 L.J. Ch. 146.
[12] Law of Property Act 1925 s.53(1)(b).

in relation to certain other property such as shares,[13] there will be statutory formalities to be satisfied before a valid trust will be created. Therefore, it is important to consider any statutory formalities relating to a specific item of property necessary for its transfer at common law to the trustees. For the effective constitution of the trust, the legal title in the trust fund must be transferred to the trustee[14] while the equitable interest passes to the beneficiaries. In general terms a trust is not capable of being undone once it has been created[15] unless there is some term to that effect in the trust or unless the clear purpose of the trust cannot be performed.[16]

21–09

An intention to make an outright transfer of property or to create a charge over property may not be reinterpreted as a trust simply to make it valid.[17] Therefore, when taking security over property by way of a trust, the parties to a transaction must ensure that their intention in providing security is made clear and appropriately structured.[18]

21–10

In cases of fraud, equity will not permit common law or statute to be used as an engine of fraud such that it may impose a trust even though there was no valid declaration of that trust.[19] Similarly, in circumstances in which a trust is purportedly created for an illegal purpose, such as to defraud creditors, or as a sham, then no valid trust will be created and the trust property will be considered to be owned absolutely by the settlor.[20] This is particularly significant in insolvency proceedings where trusts used to put property beyond the reach of insolvency creditors will be ineffective.[21] Furthermore, in circumstances in which a property-holder has made an assurance to a claimant that she will acquire rights in that property, equitable estoppel will grant rights to that claimant if she can demonstrate that she has acted to her detriment in reliance on that assurance.[22]

Requirements of certainty in the creation of an express trust

21–11

To create a valid express trust, the terms of that trust must be sufficiently certain.[23] There are three forms of certainty which the courts require for a trust to be valid[24]: certainty of intention to create a trust; certainty of the identity of the subject matter comprising the trust fund; and certainty as to the beneficiaries (or

---

[13] Uncertificated Securities Regulations 2001.
[14] *Milroy v Lord* (1862) 4 De G.F. & J. 264.
[15] *Paul v Paul* (1882) 20 Ch.D. 742.
[16] *Re Cochrane's Settlement Trusts* [1955] Ch. 309.
[17] *Milroy v Lord* (1862) 4 De G.F. & J. 264.
[18] See for example the problems raised in *Clough Mill v Martin* [1984] 3 All E.R. 982 where insufficient certainty of intention to create a trust led to a finding that the claimant had no fixed security rights.
[19] *Rochefoucauld v Boustead* [1897] 1 Ch. 196; *Lyus v Prowsa Developments Ltd* [1982] 1 W.L.R. 1044.
[20] See, for example, *Midland Bank v Wyatt* [1995] 1 F.L.R. 697.
[21] See *Midland Bank v Wyatt* [1995] 1 F.L.R. 697 and its analysis of the "claw-back" provision in Insolvency Act 1986 s.423.
[22] *Gillett v Holt* [2000] 2 All E.R. 289; *Yaxley v Gotts* [2000] 1 All E.R. 711; *Jennings v Rice* [2003] P. & C.R. 100; *Thorner v Major* [2009] UKHL 18.
[23] *Knight v Knight* (1840) 3 Beav. 148; *Knight v Boughton* (1840) 11 Cl. & Fin. 513.
[24] *Knight v Knight* (1840) 3 Beav. 148; *Knight v Boughton* (1840) 11 Cl. & Fin. 513.

"objects") of the trust. The intention to create a trust can be inferred from the circumstances: encompassing situations in which a man reassures his girlfriend that the bank account from which they pay for all their joint expenses will be "as much yours as mine"[25]; situations in which money from customers awaiting delivering of their goods is paid into a separate bank account[26]; and also situations in which commercial parties fail to make clear the precise legal nature of their common holding of future cash flows derived from boxing promotion contracts.[27] Thus in financial transactions, the finding of an express trust is not dependent on the parties consciously naming their arrangement as a trust— instead, the court may choose to infer a trust from circumstances in which an identified fund of property has been segregated with the intention that its legal owner shall hold that fund for the benefit or use of other people. One of the most significant cases in this area is *Re Kayford* [28]in which a mail order company was on the brink of insolvency when its accountants took the view that a separate bank account should be established for pre-payments which were still being received from customers so that those pre-payments would not be mixed with the company's general funds. When the company later went into insolvency, even though the precise legal nature of the arrangement had not been established by the company's management, it was held by Megarry J. that the act of putting money into a separate bank account should be interpreted as being the creation of an express trust. Therefore, the establishment of such a trust is not dependent upon any specific form of words (although best practice would involve the drafting of a trust instrument which made the situation clear), but rather on the proper interpretation of the circumstances.

21–12   The financial crisis 2007–09 gave rise to a large amount of litigation on the basis that customers of insolvent financial institutions sought to establish that assets held by the insolvent party were actually held on trust for them: the principal advantage of such a trust being that it continues in effect in spite of the trustee's insolvency. The insolvency of Icelandic bank Kaupthing gave rise to exactly such litigation in relation to its UK investment banking subsidiary "KSF". So, in *Brazzill v Willoughby*, [29] when KSF's Icelandic parent company, Kaupthing, went into insolvency in October 2008, the UK regulator the Financial Services Authority issued an order that KSF must set up an account into which it would pay amounts equal to deposits which it took from its customers in case KSF should go into insolvency itself. Relying inter alia on *Re Kayford*, Smith J. held that the establishment of this account should be interpreted as being a trust in favour of those customers. The terms of the Authority's order were argued to be unclear on the nature of the customers' rights, but it was found that the use of the term "trust" in the regulator's order bolstered the conclusion that the parties' intention in creating that separate account should be interpreted as constituting a trust, even though otherwise the terms of the arrangement had been unclear.

---

[25] *Paul v Constance* [1977] 1 W.L.R. 527.
[26] *Re Kayford* [1975] 1 W.L.R. 279.
[27] *Don King Productions Inc v Warren* [1998] 2 All E.R. 608, Lightman J.; affirmed [2000] Ch. 291, CA.
[28] [1975] 1 W.L.R. 279.
[29] [2009] EWHC 1633 (Ch), [2010] 1 B.C.L.C. 673.

Similarly, in *Mills v Sportsdirect.com Retail Ltd*[30] a corporate customer had entered into a repo transaction with KSF. Unusually for a transaction of that type, because the customer was concerned about KSF's financial position, the securities which were a part of that deal were passed to a specific subsidiary of KSF as nominee to be held for the purposes of that deal. The parties were vague about the precise legal nature of this aspect of the transaction: although, significantly, their various traders and other employees did use language to the effect that the securities would be "ringfenced", that they were in the customer's "box", and that they were owned by the customer. The customer sought to argue that this constituted a trust over those securities which would survive the insolvency of KSF. Lewison J. held that these discussions between the parties (no matter how vague they had been) together with the transfer of the securities into a nominee account, were sufficient to demonstrate an intention to create a trust.

That there must be certainty of objects (or, beneficiaries) simply requires that **21–13** there must be someone in whose favour the court can decree performance of the trust: if there were no person entitled to the trust fund as beneficiary then the trust would be void.[31] This is referred to as the "beneficiary principle", being a requirement that there must be an ascertainable beneficiary or beneficiaries with appropriate proprietary rights for a trust to be valid.[32] Consequently, a trust may not be created for an abstract purpose[33] in which no person takes at the very least some direct or indirect benefit.[34] That either of the parties to a collateral structure would be able to take title in the property comprising the trust fund would satisfy this beneficiary principle. Equally it would be no objection to the validity of such a trust that the parties' interests would only vest in them absolutely on the happening of a contingency, such as the performance or non-performance of either party of its obligations under a transaction at a given date.[35]

The particular problem of certainty of subject matter in financial transactions

There must be sufficient certainty as to the subject matter a trust for that trust to **21–14** be valid. This is a strict principle which has nevertheless tended to cause finance lawyers to be overly sanguine. The principle of certainty of subject matter requires that the property in the trust fund be separate and distinct from all other

---

[30] [2010] EWHC 1072 (Ch), [2010] 2 B.C.L.C. 143.
[31] *Denley, Re* [1969] 1 Ch. 373.
[32] *Leahy v Attorney General for New South Wales* [1959] A.C. 457; as explained by Goff J. in *Re Denley* [1969] 1 Ch. 373.
[33] *Leahy v Att Gen for New South Wales* [1959] A.C. 457.
[34] This area is contested among the trusts law cases and trusts law scholars. Some judgments such as *Re Denley* [1969] 1 Ch. 373, Goff J., have suggested that it is sufficient that there is someone who will take an indirect benefit at least from the trust property, whereas other decisions have suggested that to be a beneficiary under a valid trust (capable of validating that trust as a result) you must have immediate possession of your rights as a beneficiary, as in *Leahy v Att Gen for New South Wales* [1959] A.C. 457.
[35] See for example *Re Ralli's Will Trusts* [1964] 1 Ch. 288.

property; if the property is not segregated then the trust will be void.[36] A clear example relating to commodities investments arose in the decision of the Privy Council[37] in *Re Goldcorp*.[38] The facts of that case related to contracts entered into by a bullion exchange with its clients to the effect that it would not simply recognise in those customers' orders an obligation to acquire bullion for those customers but rather that it would actually procure and hold all of the bullion identified in the customer's order in its vaults. However, despite these well-drafted contracts which obliged the exchange to hold bullion to their customers' order, the exchange began to breach its contractual obligations by taking its customers' money and nevertheless only holding about as much bullion as was required to meet its delivery obligations on a normal working day. In time the exchange went into insolvency and when the customers came to take possession of their bullion, the bulk of them found that there was insufficient bullion there to meet their claims. The decision divided clearly between those claimants who did have bullion segregated and identified as being held for them as a matter of fact, and those claimants who as a matter of fact did not have any such bullion identified as being held for them. Only customers with bullion held separately to their account could claim successfully to have valid rights under trust, whereas customers without bullion held separately to their account could not have rights under trust because there was no certainty as to what the subject matter of that trust would be. Because the successful customers had rights under trust, their property rights were held on trust for them by the exchange regardless of the insolvency and regardless of the rights of any unsecured creditors.

21–15 This principle was upheld even though the customer's contracts purported to grant them all rights in theory in some specific bullion. It was held that because, as a matter of fact, no bullion had been segregated to the account of some of them, that those people could not rely on the terms of the contract, which suggested that that would be the case.[39] Their remedy lay only in contract law—which was of no practical effect because the exchange had gone into insolvency and therefore would have had insufficient funds to pay damages. The distinction between there being a valid trust and there not being a valid trust—on the basis of certainty of subject matter—turned on there actually being or not being segregation of the trust property on the facts, regardless of what the documentation was drafted to provide. Thus, a well-drafted trust document which purports to grant rights in segregated property will not create a valid trust if in fact the property which is to be held on trust is held as an unsegregated part of a larger fund of property.

21–16 There is a short line of authority which suggests that there is no need to segregate intangible property to be held on trust from other intangible property of like kind

---

[36] *Westdeutsche Landesbank v Islington LBC* [1996] 1 A.C. 669. cf. *Harland v Trigg* (1782) 1 Bro. C.C. 142; *Wynne v Hawkins* (1782) 1 Bro. C.C. 142; *Pierson v Garnet* (1786) 2 Bro. C.C. 226; *Sprange v Barnard* (1789) 2 Bro. C.C. 585; and *Palmer v Simmonds* (1854) 2 Drew 221.
[37] As recognised by Lord Browne-Wilkinson, *Westdeutsche Landesbank v Islington L.B.C.* [1996] 1 A.C. 669.
[38] [1995] 1 A.C. 74.
[39] See *London Wine Co (Shippers) Lrd, Re* [1986] PCC 121 on the same point.

where it can make no difference[40] which property is held on trust and which property is not.[41] There is Court of Appeal authority which has been taken to suggest that there is no need to segregate ordinary shares in a company from other shares of the same class in the same company.[42] In that case, however, the principal concern of Dillon L.J. was to prevent an employer from unconscionably denying his obligation to transfer 50 ordinary shares to an employee as required by that employee's contract of employment, which was done by purporting (weakly) to distinguish that case from earlier cases.[43] It was in a later decision of the High Court that it was explicitly suggested for the first time that there was no need to segregate intangible property such as securities from other property for there to be a valid trust created a part of that fund.[44] So, where a stockbroker contracted in terms that he would hold a given number of securities for his customers but failed to segregate the claimants' securities from other, identical securities, it was held that the trust could be valid in any event because the identical nature of the securities meant that there was no difference in quality between one item of property and another, albeit that Neuberger J. reached this conclusion reluctantly due to the precedent he was bound to follow.[45] However, this latter approach has been doubted by most trust law commentators[46] and is contrary to subsequent Privy Council[47] and House of Lords[48] authority, as well as being in contravention of earlier Court of Appeal authority.[49] Indeed, in relation specifically to trusts taken over money there is earlier Court of Appeal authority to the effect that money held in a bank account, a form of intangible property, must be held in an account separate from all other money for there to be a valid trust over that money.[50] While these two streams of authority cannot be satisfactorily reconciled, it is suggested that the weight of judicial authority was with the *Re Goldcorp* line of cases before the Lehman Brothers cases considered below.[51]

---

[40] Thus it has been suggested that this rule would be inappropriate in cases of insolvency where there are more claims to property than there is property to satisfy those competing claims: see A. Hudson, *Equity & Trusts*, s.3.3.

[41] *Hunter v Moss* [1994] 1 W.L.R. 452.

[42] *Hunter v Moss* [1993] 1 W.L.R. 934, Rimer QC, Deputy Judge of the High Court; [1994] 1 W.L.R. 452, CA.

[43] See, doubting this decision, Hayton, (1994) 110 L.Q.R. 335.

[44] *Re Harvard Securities, Holland v Newbury* [1997] 2 B.C.L.C. 369.

[45] *Harvard Securities Ltd, Re; Holland v Newbury* [1997] 2 B.C.L.C. 369.

[46] See *Underhill and Hayton on Trusts and Trustees* (Butterworths, 2002), p.79, where *Hunter v Moss* is clearly disapproved; *Lewin on Trusts* (London: Sweet & Maxwell, 2000), p.32, doubting this decision; Hudson, *Equity & Trusts*, p.87 et seq, especially p.90, where this case is again disapproved; Thomas and Hudson, *The Law of Trusts*, para.3.25 et seq. The only commentator giving houseroom to the contrary view is Dr Martin in *Hanbury and Martin Modern Equity* (London: Sweet & Maxwell, 2005), p.101.

[47] *Re Goldcorp* [1995] 1 A.C. 74.

[48] *Westdeutsche Landesbank v Islington* [1996] A.C. 669. See also the position in Australia in *Herdegen v Federal Commissioner of Taxation* (1988) 84 A.L.R. 271 which is in accordance with the English senior courts.

[49] *MacJordan Construction Ltd v Brookmount Erostin Ltd* [1992] B.C.L.C. 350, CA. Thus the doctrine of precedent ought to have compelled the Court of Appeal in *Hunter v Moss* to have decided differently.

[50] *MacJordan Construction Ltd v Brookmount Erostin Ltd* [1992] B.C.L.C. 350, CA.

[51] *Westdeutsche Landesbank v Islington L.B.C.* [1996] 1 A.C. 669.

21–17   In Australia, a recent decision of Supreme Court of New South Wales in *White v Shortall*[52] rejected the approach in *Hunter v Moss*. In that case the parties had an intention to contract and the defendant had an intention to declare a trust over a holding of 1.5 million shares such that 222,000 of those shares would be held on trust for the claimant. The inference which the court was prepared to make to validate the trust was that, in effect, the trust took effect over the entire holding of 1.5 million shares but such that the trustees had a power to elect which 222,000 shares out of that entire holding were to be treated as being held for the claimant. In effect, the claimant and the defendant were treated as being beneficiaries under one trust in the ratio 1500: 222. The court looked closely at the arguments used by Dillon L.J. in *Hunter v Moss* when purporting to justify granting a trust in that case. Dillon L.J. had sought to justify dispensing with the need for certainty of subject matter on the basis that most of the authorities had concerned chattels and on the basis that executors of a will trust do not know the property which they are to hold on trust and yet such trusts are valid. Neither argument holds water in that executors know that they hold on trust any property owned by the testator at the time of death, and that there is no reason in principle for distinguishing between tangible and intangible property except that it led conveniently to the answer Dillon L.J. wanted to reach and even then only if one misread the earlier decision of the Court of Appeal in *MacJordan v Brookmount*.[53] In *Re Harvard Securities*[54] Neuberger J. was clear that he was bound by the doctrine of precedent to follow *Hunter v Moss* although (if one reads his judgment tolerably closely) it seems that he did not wish to do so. This is indeed a slender reed on which to base an argument that trusts over intangible property do not require certainty of subject. Doctrinally, the decision in *Hunter v Moss* must be wrong and should not be relied upon.

21–18   This topic, it is suggested, teaches us an important lesson about the law of finance. There is an enthusiasm among many finance commentators to validate financial transactions. The difficulty in separating intangible financial instruments like shares, and particularly instruments like bonds when held as collateral assets, means that this issue is particularly significant in financial transactions when proprietary rights are sought over intangible financial instruments. And yet many of the commentators have clutched onto the decision in *Hunter v Moss*—which, if one actually reads it, is weakly argued, unlike *Re Goldcorp*—as though there were no alternative authorities and as though there had been absolutely no dissent about that decision.[55] There have in fact been many articles and treatises which have criticised this decision.[56] The basis for criticising this decision is simply that you cannot have property rights when you do not know to which property those rights relate.[57]

---

[52] [2006] NSWSC 1379.

[53] [1992] B.C.L.C. 350.

[54] [1997] 2 B.C.L.C. 369.

[55] See for example the excellent writings taking this straightforwardly positivist approach of P. Wood, *The Law of International Finance*, p.316; and J. Benjamin, *Interests in Securities* (OUP, 2000) 2.86.

[56] See Hayton, *Underhill and Hayton on Trusts and Trustees* (Butterworths, 2002), p.79, where *Hunter v Moss* is clearly disapproved of; Hayton, "Uncertainty of subject-matter of trusts" (1994) 110 L.Q.R. 335; *Lewin on Trusts*, p.32, doubting this decision; A. Hudson, *Equity & Trusts*, p.87 et seq, especially p.90, where this case is again disapproved of; G. Thomas and A. Hudson, *The Law of*

The effect of the financial crisis on certainty of subject matter

The financial crisis demonstrated that a number of investment banks had been knowingly breaching their financial regulatory obligations under the Financial Services Authority's Client Asset Sourcebook ("CASS")[58] with a staggering regularity and seeming lack of concern. The CASS regulations obliged investment banks to segregate their clients' assets into separate accounts so as to protect those clients against the insolvency of the banks. It was accepted in the cases discussed below that these regulations created a trust over client assets, even though the poorly drafted regulations had not made that legal categorisation nor its terms at all clear. Those banks—in particular Lehman Brothers—seemed in essence to use all of these client assets as a pool with which to increase the amount of capital available to them for a combination of proprietary trading and trading for their clients. However, many of the banks (particularly Lehman Brothers) had breached their regulatory obligations and had not segregated client money in this fashion. Investment banks of this sort will have huge numbers of clients with many billions of dollars in assets under management at any given time. Similar to the facts in *Re Goldcorp*, the issue was whether or not there had been sufficient certainty of subject matter to create trusts in favour of those customers. In *Re Global Trader Europe Ltd (in liquidation)*[59] Park J. had held that, in relation to another insolvent financial institution, that if there had been a failure to segregate assets for the benefit of a group of customers, then there could be no trusts in favour of those customers; although customers who had been fortunate enough to have had assets segregated to their accounts would have trusts in their favour over those accounts, just as in *Re Goldcorp*.

21–19

Perhaps the most significant case was *Re Lehman Bros International (Europe)(No.2)*[60] in which Briggs J. considered Lehman Brothers' practice of holding client assets in a central pool for long periods of time rather than in segregated accounts. His lordship held that this lack of segregation meant that each client of the bank with assets in that pool could not have a trust in their favour precisely because their moneys were held in a central, mixed pool without any assets being segregated to their account. However, this issue was appealed successfully to the Court of Appeal (under the name *Re Lehman Brothers International (Europe) (in administration) v CRC Credit Fund Ltd*[61]) in which it was held that there was one, large trust fund constituting the entire pool in favour of all of the clients as beneficiaries, with each client having a share in accordance with their rights against the bank (until amounts were segregated to the accounts of specific clients). In practice, this meant that the clients had valid trust rights in the Lehman Brothers insolvency. The Court of Appeal was able to take this view

21–20

Trusts, para.3.25 et seq.; Ockleton, "Share and share alike?" [1994] 5 C.L.J. 448. The only commentator giving houseroom to the contrary view is Dr Martin in *Hanbury and Martin Modern Equity*, p.101 and Martin, "Certainty of subject matter: a defence of *Hunter v Moss*" (1994) *Conveyancer*, p.223.

[57] See, e.g. Ockleton, "Share and share alike?" [1994] 5 C.L.J. 448.
[58] These regulations are discussed in Ch.9 at para 9–40.
[59] [2009] EWHC 602 (Ch), [2009] 2 B.C.L.C. 18.
[60] [2009] EWHC 3228 (Ch).
[61] [2010] EWCA Civ 917.

because the regulations were so ambiguously drafted as to the precise nature of the regulatory trust and because the Court of Appeal made very little reference to any case law. In essence it was held by the Court of Appeal that a single '*White v Shortall* trust' took effect over all the client assets: the entire pool of assets held by Lehman Brothers was treated (without demonstrating any intention to that effect on the part either of Lehman Brothers' clients or the draftsperson of the CASS regulations) as a single trust fund in which all of the outstanding customers had equitable interests in proportion to their rights against Lehman Brothers.

21–21   The Supreme Court in *Re Lehman Brothers International (Europe) (in administration) v CRC Credit Fund Ltd*[62] upheld the decision of the Court of Appeal on slightly different grounds. In essence, the Supreme Court approached this case strictly on the basis of the interpretation of the "statutory trust" in the CASS regulations and of the EU Markets in Financial Instruments Directive ("MiFID") on which they are based, and not on the basis of general trusts law as it is considered in this book;[63] albeit that CASS "is erected on the foundation of the general law of trusts"[64] according to Lord Walker. The majority, primarily through the judgment of Lord Dyson, chose to adopt an interpretation which offered the largest amount of protection to the largest possible number of clients of the bank.[65] Lord Dyson held that the statutory trust was to take effect on receipt of the money as suggested by the wording of the statute. Lord Dyson argued, because CASS was implemented to effect the requirements of MiFID in relation to client money, that the intention of CASS should be interpreted to be to safeguard client assets as MiFID required in its recitals. Lord Dyson held that *all* client money is deemed to be held on trust and therefore that all client money is to be protected by the statutory scheme in relation to a distribution of assets on the event of the bank's insolvency. In essence, then, once all client money is deemed to be subject to the trust then all of that money is deemed to be held aside from the general assets of the bank in its insolvency and instead to be distributed according to the CASS rules. Importantly, though, all clients with assets held by the bank under CASS are entitled to share in such a distribution, on a close textual analysis of the provisions of CASS. Moreover, Lord Dyson also advanced a purposive argument on the basis that it was the purpose of MiFID and CASS to protect *all* clients and not simply those who were fortunate enough to have assets set aside for them in fact. In that sense, this decision tells us nothing about general trusts law and as such should not be interpreted as having affected it. It was held by the majority that because the regulations require that "all" client money is to be held on the statutory trust, then segregation would not be a pre-requisite for a client to participate in the allocation of the sums held by Lehman Brothers because all sums are necessarily held on the terms of the statutory trust anyway. Lord Dyson acknowledged the difficulties (or, in truth, the chaos) which this would cause in allocating amounts between clients of the bank on this basis. Lord Walker's dissenting judgment doubted the large "single trust"

---

[62]   [2012] UKSC 6, [2012] Bus. L.R. 667.
[63]   e.g. per Lord Clarke, [2012] UKSC 6, [2012] Bus. L.R. 667 at [110].
[64]   [2012] UKSC 6, [2012] Bus. L.R. 667at [84].
[65]   e.g. per Lord Dyson, [2012] UKSC 6, [2012] Bus. L.R. 667, at [148].

trust approach.[66] In this vein, Lord Walker held that "a trust without segregation is a very precarious form of protection" which could be taken to be an acceptance that such a trust is a possibility in English trusts law, or else as a reason for rejecting the possibility of such a trust. Interestingly, Lord Walker held that "the majority's decision [in the Supreme Court] makes investment banking more of a lottery than even its fiercest critics have supposed"[67] because the absence of a need for segregation means that it is unknowable which client will get how much property from the general pool of property in advance.[68]

A slightly different, but related, problem arose in *Re Lehman Brothers International (Europe)(In Administration)*[69] in which Lehman Brothers had been in the practice of dumping all the securities and other assets from each region of the world into a central "hub" subsidiary of the bank from which the bank would make investments or fulfil client orders. Much of this hub activity was in breach of the CASS regulations because assets which were held for clients should have been held in segregated accounts for those clients and kept distinct from the bank's own assets. Here the Court of Appeal followed *Hunter v Moss* and held that there could be a trust over these unsegregated, intangible assets, even though the bank (as trustee according to this judgment) was entitled to use the assets for its own benefit and even though no assets were held to the account of any given customer in a segregated account. Clearly, the decisions of Briggs J. (at first instance in *Lehman Brothers*) and Park J. (in *Global Trader*) were in accordance with principle. The fault lay entirely with the reprehensible business practices of Lehman Brothers in mismanaging client assets.

21–22

The rights of beneficiaries

The rights of the beneficiaries under a trust exhibit two characteristics simultaneously: first, a proprietary right in the trust fund[70] and, secondly, personal rights against the trustees in relation to the proper management of the trust's affairs so that the beneficiaries may sue the trustees personally to recoup any loss caused by a breach of trust.[71] In both cases it is equity which recognises the beneficiaries' claims against the trust property and against the trustees personally; whereas the common law recognises the trustees as also being owners of the trust property to the extent that the trustees hold to the legal title in any property held on trust. All of the beneficiaries (constituting the entire, possible

21–23

---

[66] [2012] UKSC 6, [2012] Bus. L.R. 667 at [82].

[67] [2012] UKSC 6, [2012] Bus. L.R. 667 at [85].

[68] Lehman Brothers itself was correctly criticised by judges at all levels for its "shocking underperformance" and its regulatory non-compliance "on a truly spectacular scale". That none of these issues have yet led to criminal prosecutions is an affront to our jurisprudence and to the rule of law itself.

[69] [2011] EWCA Civ 1544.

[70] *Green v Spicer* (1830) 1 Russ. & M. 395, *Younghusband v Grisborne* (1844) 1 Col. 400; *Saunders v Vautier* (1841) 4 Beav. 115.

[71] Principally a right to recover any loss caused by a breach of trust, but also duties in relation to the provision of information, obedience to the terms of the trust and so forth, as considered in the next section relating to the *Duties of Trustees*.

equitable interest) may, if they are acting together and sui juris, direct the trustees how to deal with the trust property under the rule in *Saunders v Vautier* [72]

Types of express trust and special purpose vehicles

21–24   Thus far we have considered the express trust to be simply a binary arrangement between trustee and beneficiary. However, there can be a number of different beneficiaries with different rights. At one level it is possible to make the beneficiaries' rights contingent on different events. For example, a trust could be set up to provide that when a seller transfers shares to a buyer those shares are to be held on trust absolutely for the seller until the buyer makes payment and on trust absolutely for the buyer once payment has been made in full. In this example a third party could be established as trustee of the property, or either the seller or buyer could act as trustee—in either event the trustee is obliged to observe the terms of the trust and to ignore any conflict with their own personal interests. Trusts can therefore be used in Special Purpose Vehicle structures, whereby a trust is inserted as a property management vehicle in a more complex structure. Thus in Eurobond transactions, the interest payments which investors are entitled to be received are formally to be paid through a trustee, so that that trustee can be used to act on behalf of all of the investors as a group in the event that the bond issuer fails to make a payment to the investors as it is required to do.[73] In securitisation transactions, the assets which are to be securitised, as discussed in Chapter 44, may be held on trust.[74] Thus when a number of contracting parties want to have assets held either so that they can all ensure that they have proprietary rights in them, or so that they can disguise their ownership of those assets behind the ostensible rights of the trustee as a functionary acting on their behalf, or so that they can use the trustee to act on their behalf but subject always to the power to impose fiduciary obligations on the trustee, a trust will be used.

21–25   Trusts can also take the form of discretionary trusts. In a discretionary trust the trustees have the power, in whatever form the trust instrument provides, to select which beneficiaries[75] receive what proportion of the trust property.[76] Consequently, there are questions as to whether or not those beneficiaries under the discretionary trust have rights in the trust property before the trustees decide to exercise their discretion in the beneficiary's favour. Once the trustees' discretion has been exercised then clearly the beneficiaries to whom identified property has been advanced will have absolute rights in the property which has been transferred to them; whereas beneficiaries to whom no property has been advanced will have no rights in any property (assuming that the trustees have not breached any of their duties).

---

[72] (1841) 4 Beav. 115.

[73] See para.34–22.

[74] See para.44–11.

[75] The term "objects" is more commonly used in relation to those who are among the class of people who may benefit from a discretionary trust, but for ease of reference in this section the term "beneficiaries" will be used instead even though, strictly, many of those objects of the discretionary trust may be not be passed property by the trustees.

[76] A. Hudson, *Equity & Trusts*, s.4.1.

The question then is as to what rights if any the beneficiaries (or, technically, "objects") have in a discretionary trust before the trustees exercise their discretion. Before the discretion is exercised then none of the objects have any rights in any identified property.[77] If the power obliges the trustee to use up all of the trust property by distributing it among the beneficiaries, and if no further beneficiaries can be added to the class of beneficiaries (known as an exhaustive trust), then those beneficiaries will be able to act together and rely on the principle in *Saunders v Vautier* to direct the trustees how to use the trust property.[78] There are two circumstances in which this analysis would not apply. First, if the class of objects cannot be completely defined because the trust instrument permits future, currently unknown members to be added to the class within the trust's perpetuity period[79]; and, secondly, if the trustees are not obliged to exhaust the whole of the trust property.

21–26

Individual objects of a discretionary trust power will not have individual rights to any of the trust property because their rights are in competition with one another: that is, if one object of the trust receives trust property then that is property which cannot be paid to another object of the trust. Indeed it has been suggested in one decided case that the distinct nature of each object's claims to the trust property means that no object can be recognised as having an interest in possession before any identified property has been advanced to her.[80] This is particularly so if the trustees are not obliged to exhaust the whole of the trust property in favour of the objects of the power, although if the class of potential beneficiaries remains open[81] then even if there is only one object alive at the time then that person will not be able to exercise *Saunders v Vautier* rights because she could not prove that she would constitute the entirety of the equitable interest in the trust property.[82]

21–27

B. The duties of trustees

The duties of trustees to observe the trust instrument

Trustees owe fiduciary duties to the beneficiaries. The manner in which trustees are obliged to carry out their fiduciary duties is the core of the trust—the trustees owe those duties to the beneficiaries in relation to the trust fund. In circumstances

21–28

---

[77] *Murphy v Murphy* [1999] 1 W.L.R. 202. It could be said that collectively they must constitute all of the people who could possibly acquire rights in the property at any time in the future. In consequence it could be argued that all of the objects of the discretionary trust power—provided that they constitute all of the possible objects of that power and provided that they are all acting in concert—should be able to exercise the rights which the absolutely entitled beneficiaries would be entitled to under the principle of *Saunders v Vautier* under a fixed trust.

[78] *Re Smith* [1928] Ch. 915; *Re Nelson (note)* [1928] Ch. 920.

[79] *Re Trafford's Settlement* [1985] Ch. 32, 40 *per* Peter Gibson J.

[80] *Gartside v IRC* [1968] A.C. 553, 606 *per* Lord Reid, 617 *per* Lord Wilberforce.

[81] That is, if some future objects may yet join the class of objects.

[82] *Gartside v IRC* [1968] A.C. 553. Nevertheless, the logic of the *Saunders v Vautier* principle requires that all of the objects acting together will constitute the entirety of the potential equitable interest and that such a group may call for the trust property in circumstances in which the trustees are empowered to exhaust the whole of the fund and in which there cannot be any further members of the class of objects. As before, this requires that the discretionary trust power be an exhaustive power.

in which an express trust has been created in a trust instrument, it would be expected that the trust instrument would describe all of the duties and powers of the trustees. Each trustee is bound by all of the obligations in the trust instrument.[83] In general terms, a trustee does not have powers which are more extensive than those set out in the trust instrument.[84] In circumstances in which there is no trust instrument, or in circumstances in which the trust instrument is silent on a particular point, then the provisions of the Trustee Act 1925 and of the Trustee Act 2000 provide many of the trustees' obligations, together with the general obligation in the case law to act (in the words of the old cases) as a prudent person of business would act in the circumstances if acting on behalf of someone for whom she feels morally bound to provide.[85]

The duties of trustees under the Trustee Act 2000

21–29   The obligations set out in the Trustee Act 2000 relate primarily to the obligations of trustees when making trust investments. The provisions of this Act are excluded by any provision of the trust instrument to the contrary. The Trustee Act 2000 ("TA 2000") provides that "a trustee may make any kind of investment that he could make if he were absolutely entitled to the assets of the trust": this is referred to in the legislation as the "general power of investment".[86] Therefore, the trustee is not constrained, by statute, as to the investments which are made simply because she is a trustee, unless the trust instrument provides that that is the case. The TA 2000 provides for a statutory duty of care which imposes a duty of "such skill and care as is reasonable in the circumstances".[87] The TA 2000 requires that the trustees have regard to something described in the statute as the "standard investment criteria"[88] when exercising their investment powers: that is, it is suggested, whether making new investments or considering their existing investments.[89] The "standard investment criteria" to which the trustees are to have regard comprise two core principles of prevailing investment theory which relate, first, to the need to make "suitable" investments and, secondly, to the need to maintain a diverse portfolio of investments to spread the fund's investment risk. We shall take each of these in turn. The trustees are required to consider:

"(a)   the suitability to the trust of investments of the same kind as any particular investment proposed to be made or retained and of that particular investment as an investment of that kind, and

(b)   the need for diversification of investments of the trust, in so far as is appropriate to the circumstances of the trust.[90]"

---

[83] *Clough v Bond* (1838) 3 My. & Cr. 490. Unless that would be to the apparent benefit of the beneficiaries and not in breach of some other mandatory rule (such as a rule of illegality).
[84] See above.
[85] *Speight v Gaunt* (1883) 9 App. Cas. 1; *Learoyd v Whiteley* (1887) 12 App. Cas. 727.
[86] Trustee Act 2000, s.3(1).
[87] Trustee Act 2000, s.1(1).
[88] Trustee Act 2000, s.4(1).
[89] Trustee Act 2000, s.4(2).
[90] Trustee Act 2000 s.4(2).

The term "suitability" is one familiar to investment regulation specialists[91] which requires that, in general terms, investment managers are required to consider whether or not the risk associated with a given investment is appropriate for the client proposing to make that investment. In consequence, the investment manager could not sell, for example, complex financial derivatives products to inexpert members of the general public who could not understand the precise nature of the risks associated with such a transaction. Under the terms of the TA 2000, the trustee is required to consider whether the trust fund for which she is making an investment would be dealing in a suitable manner in making the proposed investment. It is presumed that the trustee would be liable for breach of trust in the event that an unsuitable investment were made which caused loss to the trust.[92] The FCA Conduct of Business regulations might give us some guidance as to what suitable behaviour would involve, remembering always that the steps which are required of any service provider:

> "... will vary greatly, depending on the needs and priorities of the private customer, the type of investment or service being offered, and the nature of the relationship between the firm and the private customer and, in particular, whether the firm is giving a personal recommendation or acting as a discretionary investment manager."[93]

Having categorised each client in this manner, the service provider is then required to treat them in a manner which is commensurate with their expertise and also to ensure that the investments sold to them are suitable for their purposes. Therefore, the requirement under s.4(3)(a) of the TA 2000 that the trustee is required to consider whether the trust fund for which she is making an investment would be dealing in a suitable manner in making the proposed investment will differ depending on the nature of the trust. Where the trust is a small family trust with a comparatively weak risk appetite, the investments to be made should be of low risk, whereas investments made on behalf of a trust fund created by two corporations who are expert in financial services (a not uncommon structure for highly-leveraged hedge funds) could be considerably more adventurous, and so intended to take much greater risks. It is presumed that the trustee would be liable for breach of trust in the event that an unsuitable investment were made which caused loss to the trust.[94]

Secondly, the trustees must pay heed to "the need for diversification of investments of the trust, in so far as is appropriate to the circumstances of the trust".[95] Two points arise from this provision. First, the question as to the amount of diversification necessary is dependent on the nature of the trust. A trust which requires the trustees to hold a single house on trust for the occupation of a named beneficiary does not require that the trustees make a range of investments: rather, the trustees are impliedly precluded from making a range of investments. Secondly, a trust with only a small amount of capital could not afford to buy a large number of investments.

21–30

---

[91] See para.10–14.
[92] *Target Holdings v Redferns* [1996] 1 A.C. 421; [1995] 3 W.L.R. 352; [1995] 3 All E.R. 785.
[93] FSA, Conduct of Business Rules, para.5.3.4.
[94] *Target Holdings v Redferns* [1996] 1 A.C. 421; [1995] 3 W.L.R. 352; [1995] 3 All E.R. 785.
[95] Trustee Act 2000 s.4(2)(b).

21–31   Therefore, the need for diversification itself is bound up with need to dilute the risk of investing in only a small number of investments. This is frequently referred to as "portfolio theory" and is predicated on the theory that if an investor invests in a number of investments in different markets, the impact of any individual market or investment suffering from a fall in value is balanced out by the investments made in other markets which will not have suffered from that particular fall in value. So, if a trust fund was comprised of £10 million, for example, diversification would require that the trustees do not simply invest in shares in a single company. Equally, diversification would require that the trustees do not invest in a number of companies which all deal in the same market, for example computer manufacture, because if there were a fall in that market then the entire value of the trust would fall. Therefore, diversification would involve acquiring shares in a number of companies in a number of different markets. However, diversification would also require investment in a number of different types of investments—for example, bonds, derivatives, land, foreign exchange and commodities, as well as shares—so that if there were a fall in UK share markets then the investments in other markets would balance out the fall in the trust's investment in shares. The assumption is that in modern marketplaces there will be volatility in all investment markets and therefore that this volatility—meaning that investments may increase and decrease greatly in value over comparatively short periods of time—carries with it the risk of investments falling in value. Investment professionals rely on volatility to generate profits: if different investments within markets, as well as the markets generally, rise and fall in value then a skilful investment professional will take advantage of opportunities to buy investments when they are cheap and to sell them when they have risen in value. In previous centuries it was generally supposed that investments would move slowly in value; this assumption fell away in the late 20th century. Thus the requirement expressed by judges such as Hoffmann J.[96] that trustees take account of "modern portfolio theory" when making investments so that a range of different investments will insulate the trust against the fall in any individual market or investment.

21–32   However, when thinking about the appropriate level of diversification it is also important to consider the size and nature of the trust. As was considered above, if the trust instrument clearly requires that the trustee invest in only a limited form of investments, then the trustee would be in breach of trust if she sought to diversify the trust's investments into any other forms of investments which were not permitted by the precise terms of the trust instrument. If the settlor's intention that, for example, a trust was invested only in "technology companies in the UK" failed to anticipate a period in which technology companies lost lots of money due to changes in the technology marketplace, then it would seem illogical to require that the trustee continue to obey the terms of the trust instrument and thus lose the trust a lot of money. Instead, s.33 of the Trustee Act 1925 might give the trustees an "excuse" for committing a technical breach of trust so as better to protect the trust fund. Nevertheless, if the trust fund were comprised of only £10,000 in free cash, then it would unreasonable to expect that a trustee would be

---

[96] *Nestlé v National Westminster Bank Plc* [2000] W.T.L.R. 795.

able to diversify the trust's investment portfolio as broadly as a trust containing £10 million because clearly the larger trust can afford many more different types of investment and can better afford the fees involved with buying that number of investments. Therefore, diversification in relation to the trust fund containing £10,000 will necessarily require the trustees to diversify only to the extent that the trust can afford to do so. Thus a trust fund comprising £10 million may include hundreds of different investments in its portfolio, whereas a trust fund including only £10,000 may have only six or seven different, carefully-selected investments in different markets. These questions are impossible to decide in the abstract. Rather, they must be considered on a case-by-case basis by reference to these principles.

The duties of trustees under the case law

The detailed duties of the trustees are manifold.[97] The principal duties for present purposes can be summarised as follows. First, the trustees bear a duty to obey the terms of the trust unless directed to do otherwise by the court. Secondly, the trustees bear a duty to safeguard the trust assets, including duties to maintain the trust property, as well as to ensure that it is applied in accordance with the directions set out in the trust instrument.[98] This obligation would ordinarily require a trustee of securities to ensure that voting rights are properly exercised, that any distributions in relation to the securities are properly collected and so forth. It is common in collateral arrangements to exclude the trustees' liability to carry out these obligations (as considered in Chapter 42). Thirdly, the trustees bear a duty to act even-handedly between beneficiaries, which means that the trustees are required to act impartially between beneficiaries and to avoid conflicts of interest.[99] Fourthly, the trustees bear a duty to act with reasonable care, meaning generally a duty to act as though a prudent person of business acting on behalf of someone for whom one feels morally bound to provide.[100] Fifthly, the trustees bear a duty to distribute the trust property correctly in accordance with the terms of the trust.[101]

21–33

Sixthly, and at the heart of the law of trusts, the trustees bear duties to avoid conflicts of interest, not to earn unauthorised profits from the fiduciary office, not to deal on one's own behalf with trust property on pain of such transactions being voidable, and the obligation to deal fairly with the trust property.[102] This rule is a strict rule which developed from the rule in *Keech v Sandford*[103] in which case a

21–34

---

[97] See, generally G. Thomas and A. Hudson, *The Law of Trusts*; A. Hudson, *Equity & Trusts*, Ch.8.
[98] Hudson, *Equity & Trusts*, para.8.3.3.
[99] *Re Tempest* (1866) 1 Ch. App. 485, 487, *per* Turner L.J; *Re Lepine* [1892] 1 Ch. 210, 219 *per* Fry L.J; *Stephenson v Barclays Bank Trust Co Ltd* [1975] 1 W.L.R. 882, [1975] 1 All E.R. 625; *Cowan v Scargill* [1985] Ch. 270; *Nestlé v National Westminster Bank Plc* (1988) [1993] 1 W.L.R. 1260.
[100] *Speight v Gaunt* (1883) 9 App. Cas. 1; *Learoyd v Whiteley* (1887) 12 App. Cas. 727.
[101] *Ashby v Blackwell* (1765) Eden 299; *Clough v Bond* (1838) 3 My. & Cr. 490; *Eaves v Hickson* (1861) 30 Beav. 136. cf. *Re Smith* (1902) 71 L.J. Ch. 411.
[102] *Nocton v Lord Ashburton* [1914] A.C. 932; *Boardman v Phipps* [1967] 2 A.C. 46; *Tito v Waddell (No.2)* [1977] 3 All E.R. 129; *Re Thompson's Settlement* [1985] 2 All E.R. 720; *Clark Boyce v Mouat* [1994] 1 A.C. 428.
[103] (1726) Sel. Cas. Ch. 61.

trustee sought to renew a lease which previously he had held on trust for an infant beneficiary. The beneficiary, being an infant, was not able to take out the new lease in his own name and therefore the trustee took out the lease in *his* own name. It was held that the lease should be held on constructive trust for the beneficiary not because there had been any suggestion of fraud or unconscionable behaviour on the part of the trustee but rather because the court considered that it should act strictly in preventing even the possibility that there might be any unconscionable benefit taken by a trustee. This principle was expressed in the following manner by Lord Herschell in *Bray v Ford*[104]:

> "It is an inflexible rule of a Court of Equity that a person in a fiduciary position... is not, unless otherwise expressly provided, entitled to make a profit, he is not allowed to put himself in a position where his interest and duty conflict. It does not appear to me that this rule is... founded upon principles of morality. I regard it rather as based on the consideration that, human nature being what it is, there is danger, in such circumstances, of the person holding a fiduciary position being swayed by interest rather than by duty, and thus prejudicing those whom he was bound to protect. It has, therefore, been deemed expedient to lay down this positive rule."

The trustees will only be permitted to take any profit or benefit if it is expressly envisaged by the trust instrument. Therefore, a trustee would not ordinarily be permitted to rehypothecate any trust property or to consider its own interests in its dealings with that property: in collateral agreements, therefore these obligations are commonly excluded.

21–35   Seventhly, the trustees bear a duty to preserve the confidence of the beneficiaries.[105] That is, not to allow any confidential information to become known to third parties.

21–36   Eighthly, the trustees bear a limited duty to account and to provide information to the beneficiaries. That is, unless there is something to the contrary in the trust instrument, the trustees bear only a limited obligation to give information to beneficiaries in relation to administration and management of the trust fund and in relation only to that part of a trust fund in which those beneficiaries have a proprietary interest.[106] The Privy Council decision in *Schmidt v Rosewood*[107] held that the court has an inherent discretion out of which access to information can be ordered: this decision may have the effect that the court have a general jurisdiction to order access to information whenever it considers that to be appropriate.

21–37   The trustees may be controlled by the beneficiaries by means of an application to the court. The court has an inherent jurisdiction to make orders in relation to the administration of a trust. The court may make orders by way variously of giving

---

[104] [1896] A.C. 44.
[105] *Bristol & West Building Society v Mothew* [1998] Ch. 1; *Prince Jefri Bolkiah v KPMG* [1999] 1 All E.R. 517; *Marks & Spencer Plc v Freshfields Bruckhaus Deringer* [2004] 3 All E.R. 773.
[106] As implied accepted in *O'Rourke v Derbyshire* [1920] A.C. 581; *Re Londonderry* [1965] Ch. 918; unless the court chooses to exercise its inherent discretion as to the management of trusts, perhaps: *Schmidt v Rosewood Trust Ltd* [2003] 2 W.L.R. 1442.
[107] [2003] 2 W.L.R. 1442; Pollard, 2003.

directions,[108] assuming administrative control,[109] by judicial review (in a private law sense) of the trustees' actions,[110] or by setting aside any exercise of a power of a trustee made by taking into account irrelevant considerations or failing to take into account relevant considerations.[111]

Breach of trust

Liability for breach of trust is considered in detail in Chapter 26. If the trustees were to commit a breach of trust which causes loss to the trust, then the beneficiaries have three remedies available to them: first, specific restitution of the property which had formed part of the trust fund before the breach of trust; secondly, a personal right against the trustees to have the trust fund reconstituted in cash; and thirdly, a personal right against the trustees to general equitable compensation for all losses consequent to the breach of trust.[112] Trustees are entitled to have their liabilities for breach of trust[113] and for the commission of any tort limited by the terms of the trust instrument.[114] Such liability exclusion clauses are equitable devices and not contractual provisions.[115] Trustees can limit their liability for negligence and gross negligence, but it appears that they may not limit their liability for dishonesty or fraud.[116]

21–38

2.   TRUSTS IMPLIED BY LAW

A.   Constructive trusts in general terms

Constructive trusts arise by operation of law. A constructive trust comes into existence by operation of law at the moment that the legal owner of property has knowledge of some factor which affects her conscience.[117] Such an "institutional" constructive trust means that "as from the date of its establishment the

21–39

---

[108] *Re Buckton* [1907] 2 Ch. 406, 414; *McDonald v Horn* [1995] 1 All E.R. 961, 970. A protector of a trust may make a similar application: *Re Omar Family Trust* [2000] W.T.L.R. 713; *Re Hare Trust* (2001) 4 I.T.E.L.R. 288, as may a beneficiary.

[109] *Talbot v Earl of Radnor* (1834) 3 My. & K. 252; *Re Gyhon* (1885) 29 Ch.D. 834; *Re Blake* (1885) 29 Ch.D. 913.

[110] *Re Beloved Wilkes's Charity* (1851) 3 Mac. & G. 440. In general terms see G. Thomas and A. Hudson, *The Law of Trusts*, Ch.20.

[111] *Re Hastings-Bass* [1975] Ch. 25, *Abacus Trust Company (Isle of Man) v Barr* [2003] 2 W.L.R. 1362; *Burrell v Burrell* [2005] EWHC 245, [2005] All E.R. (D) 351; *Pitt v Holt* [2013] UKSC 26.

[112] *Target Holdings v Redferns* [1996] 1 A.C. 421.

[113] *Target Holdings v Redferns* [1996] 1 A.C. 421, considered in detail in Ch.18.

[114] *Armitage v Nurse* [1998] Ch. 241; *Taylor v Midland Bank Trust Co* (2000) 2 I.T.E.L.R. 439; *Bogg v Raper*, The Times, April 22, 1998; *Wight v Olswang*, The Times, May 18, 1999.

[115] *Re Duke of Norfolk Settlement Trusts* [1982] 1 Ch. 61.

[116] *Walker v Stones* [2001] Q.B. 902.

[117] *Westdeutsche Landesbank v Islington* [1996] A.C. 669. Peter Millett Q.C. sitting as a High Court judge in *Alec Lobb Ltd v Total Oil GB Ltd* [1983] 1 W.L.R. 87, 94 referred to a general equitable doctrine providing relief for unconscionable conduct: "It is probably not possible to reconcile all the authorities, some of which are of great antiquity on this head of equitable relief, which came into greater prominence with the repeal of the usury laws in the nineteenth century. But if the cases are examined it will be seen that three elements have almost invariably been present before the court has interfered. First, one party has been at a serious disadvantage to the other, whether through poverty, or

beneficiary has, in equity, a proprietary interest in the trust property". The proprietary interest is then "enforceable in equity against any subsequent holder of the property (whether the original property or substituted property into which it can be traced) other than a purchaser for value of the legal interest without notice".[118]

21-40   An example of a constructive trust coming into existence would be as follows.[119] Suppose that a bank is required to make a payment to its customer but it mistakenly makes that payment a second time due to clerical error. Suppose then that the customer goes into bankruptcy soon after receipt of the second, mistaken payment such that its assets are frozen by its trustee in bankruptcy. The bank will wish to establish some proprietary right in the money to establish itself as a secured creditor in the customer's bankruptcy. On the current state of the authorities, the only argument open to it would be that it was a beneficiary under a constructive trust, there being no express trust declared over this mistaken, second payment. If the customer had known before it became bankrupt that the second payment had been made under a mistake then its conscience would be affected so that it would be required in good conscience to hold the second payment on constructive trust for the bank.[120] However, if the customer had not known before the time of its bankruptcy that the second payment had been made under a mistake, then the customer would not be taken to hold that second payment on a constructive trust for the bank because its conscience would not have been affected at the material time.[121] If the constructive trust came into existence before the bankruptcy, then the constructive trust would establish the bank as a secured creditor in the bankruptcy, but not otherwise.[122] On this basis, on the facts of *Westdeutsche Landesbank v Islington* itself, the local authority was not taken to have been a constructive trustee of the money it received from the bank because it had not known that the contract under which those payments were made was void.

B.   Fiduciaries earning unauthorised profits

The liability of fiduciary for earning unauthorised profits from her fiduciary office

21-41   This form of constructive trust is considered in detail in Chapter 26. In essence, a fiduciary who takes unauthorised profits from her fiduciary office will be

---

ignorance, or lack of advice, or otherwise, so that the circumstances existed of which unfair advantage could be taken ... Secondly, this weakness of the one party has been exploited by the other in some morally culpable manner ... and thirdly, the resulting transaction has been, not merely hard or improvident, but over-reaching and oppressive."

[118] See above.

[119] It is derived from the explanation of the decision in *Chase Manhattan Bank NA v Israel-British Bank (London) Ltd* [1981] 1 Ch. 105 delivered by Lord Browne-Wilkinson in *Westdeutsche Landesbank Girozentrale v Islington L.B.C.* [1996] A.C. 669, HL.

[120] *Westdeutsche Landesbank Girozentrale v Islington L.B.C.* [1996] A.C. 669, HL.

[121] [1996] A.C. 669, HL.

[122] *Re Goldcorp* [1995] 1 A.C. 74.

required to hold those profits on constructive trust for the beneficiaries of his fiduciary office from the moment of their receipt.[123] This principle is predicated on the need to prevent fiduciaries from permitting any conflict between their personal interests and their fiduciary offices.[124] The only defence on the authorities is to demonstrate that the profits earned by the fiduciary were authorised. The English authorities have been reluctant to find authorisation on the facts, particularly where the fiduciary has indulged in subterfuge or simply sought to divert profits to herself.[125]

The self-dealing principle

The self-dealing principle is considered in Chapter 28.   **21–42**

The fair-dealing principle

The fair-dealing principle is considered in Chapter 28.   **21–43**

The possible conflict of interest of market makers

The position of market makers is considered in Chapter 28.   **21–44**

C.   Constructive trust imposed over bribes or other unlawful profits

A fiduciary who receives a bribe or unlawful commission in the course of her   **21–45** fiduciary office will hold that bribe or commission on constructive trust for the beneficiaries of that fiduciary office.[126] Where any fiduciary commits an unlawful act in relation to property belonging beneficially to another person then the profits will be held on constructive trust for that beneficial owner.[127] This form of proprietary constructive trust requires that any profits made or substitute property acquired with the original property which is held on constructive trust are similarly to be held on constructive trust.

This principle was set out by the Privy Council in *Att Gen Hong Kong v Reid*.[128]   **21–46** The former Director for Public Prosecutions for Hong Kong had accepted bribes in relation to the prosecution of individuals within his jurisdiction. The bribes which he had received had been profitably invested. Lord Templeman held that a proprietary constructive trust is imposed on the recipient of the bribe as soon as

---

[123] *Boardman v Phipps* [1967] 2 A.C. 67. See A. Hudson, *Equity & Trusts*, s.12.5.

[124] Some of their lordships held that the trust was founded on this proprietary nexus between the information and the profit, rather than simply finding that the status of fiduciary required property to be held on trust. Perhaps this indicates the role of the law on constructive trusts as being a part of property law rather than a law of personal obligations.

[125] *Regal v Gulliver* [1942] 1 All E.R. 378; *IDC v Cooley* [1972] 2 All E.R. 162.

[126] *Attorney General for Hong Kong v Reid* [1994] 1 A.C. 324; *Tesco Stores v Pook* [2003] EWHC 823; *Daraydan Holdings Ltd v Solland International Ltd* [2004] 3 W.L.R. 1106.

[127] [1996] A.C. 669.

[128] [1994] 1 A.C. 324; [1994] 1 All E.R. 1

the bribe is received. This means that the employer is entitled to any profit generated by the cash bribe received from the moment of its receipt. Therefore, a constructive trust was imposed over the investments made with these bribes. Similarly, Lord Templeman held that the constructive trustee is personally liable to the beneficiary for any decrease in value if any property acquired with the bribe as well as for any increase in value in the bribe. This principle has been applied to junior employees in companies who have received bribes. Thus, a security guard was held liable under constructive trust principles in relation to a bribe paid to him by armed robbers so that he would disable security equipment at his employer's premises.[129] Consequently, a fiduciary office may be imposed on employees even when they are not holding high office within their own organisation: the principle is whether or not that employee is performing a task which is suitably sensitive in the context. Therefore, even junior employees in financial institutions who take bribes or other unlawful payments—including secret commissions or other benefits or emoluments—so as to pass on customers' confidential information or so as to provide benefits to the payer of the bribe will be liable to hold those bribes and any property acquired with those bribes on constructive trust.[130]

21–47   The decision of the Privy Council in *Reid* has, however, been purportedly overturned by the Court of Appeal in *Sinclair Investments (UK) Ltd v Versailles Trade Finance Group Plc*.[131] In that case, a Ponzi scheme had been created by the defendant who borrowed money from investors and then created a large number of dummy transactions to make it appear that bona fide investments were being made. It was held that a bribe paid to a fiduciary would not be held on trust because it could not be said to be a part of the trust fund, but rather was something for which the fiduciary would be required to account by means of a personal account to the beneficiaries. The moneys taken from the claimants had been used to contribute to a fund which acquired a valuable property. The claimants contended that, further to *Reid*, that property should be held on constructive trust. The Court of Appeal held instead that the claimant should be entitled only to a debt claim against the defendant for an amount equal to the amount of the bribe because there was no basis for a property right to be imposed in the circumstances The upshot of this approach is that the fiduciary is able to keep any profit learned from the bribe, and thus to benefit from her wrongful action.

21–48   Agents acting for their clients must avoid conflicts of interest in the form of undisclosed commissions. So, where an agent was retained to act as broker for a cohabiting couple in relation to the mortgage over their home, he was acting as a fiduciary in that context and would be treated as having acted on a conflict of interest where he acquired a mortgage for the couple based in part on the

---

[129] *Brinks v Abu-Saleh* [1999] C.L.C. 133.

[130] Similar principles apply in relation to secret commissions. See, however, the approach in *Hurstanger Ltd v Wilson* [2007] 1 W.L.R. 2351 based on fraud.

[131] [2011] EWCA Civ 347. Lewison J. reached the same conclusion at first instance: [2010] EWHC 1614 (Ch). See also *Dyson Technology Ltd v Curtis* [2010] EWHC 3289 (Ch) in relation to the judgment of Lewison J.

commission which he stood to earn from that mortgage.[132] The onus was on the agent to make full disclosure of the commissions which he stood to earn to the customer. In this instance an award of equitable compensation was considered sufficient to right the agent's breach of fiduciary duty.

D. Constructive trusts and fraud

In general terms, with the exception of fraudulent misrepresentation,[133] the commission of fraud will constitute a form of unconscionable behaviour which will found a constructive trust. As was held by Lord Browne-Wilkinson in *Westdeutsche Landesbank v Islington*[134]:

21–49

> "... when property is obtained by fraud, equity places a constructive trust on the fraudulent recipient".

In line with the general principle underpinning constructive trusts, then, a fraudulent act must be an unconscionable act such that any profits acquired from that fraud ought to be held on constructive trust for the victim of the fraud. This approach has been applied in four cases in the High Court[135]; but it has not been followed in two other High Court decisions on the basis that fraudulent misrepresentations are ordinarily voidable at the election of the victim of the fraud and therefore ought not to be give rise to a constructive trust automatically.[136] However, in relation to fraudulent misrepresentations it has been held that there will not be a constructive trust over any property passed under that contract.[137] In *Lonrho v Al Fayed (No.2)*,[138] Millett J. held:

> "A contract obtained by fraudulent misrepresentation is voidable, not void, even in equity. The representee may elect to avoid it, but until he does so, the representor is not a constructive trustee of the property transferred pursuant to the contract, and no fiduciary relationship exists between him and the representee. It may well be that if the representee elects to avoid the contract and set aside a transfer of property made pursuant to it, the beneficial interest in the property will be treated as having remained vested in him throughout, at least to the extent necessary to support any tracing claim."[139]

---

[132] *Hurstanger Ltd v Wilson* [2007] EWCA Civ 299; [2007] 1 W.L.R. 2351.

[133] Considered immediately below.

[134] [1996] A.C. 669, 716. Applied in *Twinsectra v Yardley* [2000] W.T.L.R. 527, 567; and *Niru Battery Manufacturing Co v Milestone Trading Ltd* [2002] EWHC 1425; [2002] All E.R. (Comm) 705, 722, *per* Moore-Bick J.

[135] *Twinsectra v Yardley* [2000] W.T.L.R. 527, 567, *per* Moore-Bick J.; *Collings v Lee* (2001) 82 P. & C.R. 27; *JJ Harrison (Properties) Ltd v Harrison* [2002] 1 B.C.L.C. 162; [2001] W.T.L.R. 1327; *Niru Battery v Milestone Trading* [2002] EWHC 1425.

[136] *Box, Brown & Jacobs v Barclays Bank* [1998] Lloyd's Rep Bank 185, Ferris J. See generally *Sinclair Investment Holdings SA v Versailles Trade Finance Ltd* [2004] All E.R. (D) 158, *per* Strauss QC (sitting as a Deputy Judge in the High Court) considering the conflicting authority but, in interlocutory proceedings, only needing to decide that there was a triable issue.

[137] *Daly v Sydney Stock Exchange Ltd* (1986) 160 C.L.R. 371, 387. cf. *Collings v Lee* (2001) 82 P. & C.R. 3. Although the opposite was accepted, without close analysis, in *Darydan Holdings Ltd v Solland International Ltd* [2004] EWHC 622, at [88], *per* Lawrence Collins J.

[138] [1992] 1 W.L.R. 1; [1991] 4 All E.R. 961.

[139] *Lonrho v Al Fayed (No.2)* [1992] 1 W.L.R. 1; [1991] 4 All E.R. 961; 11; 971.

Thus, because the transaction procured by means of the fraudulent misrepresentation may be affirmed by the victim of the fraud, it has been held that there ought not to be a constructive trust imposed over the proceeds of the fraud because that would preclude the right to affirm the transaction.[140] This principle has been applied in *Re Ciro Citterio Menswear Plc (in administration)*.[141] There may be other factors which would justify the imposition of a constructive trust, for example if the director was also committing criminal offences relating to insider dealing collateral to the loan contract, as in *Guinness Plc v Saunders*.[142]

21–50   At first blush, the principle that profits from a fraudulent misrepresentation will not be held on constructive trust would appear to contradict the principle set out by Lord Browne-Wilkinson in *Westdeutsche Landesbank v Islington*, as quoted above, that a person who perpetrates a fraud will be required to hold any property acquired by virtue of that fraud on constructive trust for the representee.[143] Indeed there have been cases in which the acquisition of property by fraud had led to the imposition of a constructive trust. So, in *Collings v Lee*[144] where an estate agent defrauded clients by transferring land to himself acting under an alias, it was held that there had been no intention to transfer the property to the agent and further that the agent had been in breach of his fiduciary duties so as to constitute him a constructive trust of the property. Similarly, in *JJ Harrison (Properties) Ltd v Harrison*[145] a director of a company was held to be a constructive trustee of property which he had fraudulently obtained from the company.[146]

E.   Proprietary rights under void contracts

21–51   One of the perennial worries for any lawyer dealing with complex financial products is the concern as to whether or not one of the contracting parties has the capacity to enter validly into the contract. The fear is that the contract will be found to be "ultra vires": that is, beyond the powers of the contracting parties. The impact of the ultra vires rule is that a contract entered into by an entity beyond its powers is treated as having always been void (known as being "void

---

[140] However, as considered below, it is not necessary that the imposition of a constructive trust should preclude affirmation of the transaction because, being a bare trust, the beneficiary can terminate the trust using the principle in *Saunders v Vautier* and affirm the transaction instead.

[141] [2002] 2 All E.R. 717.

[142] [1990] 1 All E.R. 652.

[143] This approach has not been followed, for example, in *Halifax Buildings Society v Thomas* [1996] Ch. 217; *Box, Brown & Jacobs v Barclays Bank* [1998] Lloyd's Rep. (Bank) 185, Ferris J.; *Shalson v Mimran* [2003] W.T.L.R. 1165, 1200, *per* Rimer J., (sub nom *Shalson v Russo* [2003] EWHC 1637, at [106]) for the reasons given in the main text to follow. See *Sinclair Investment Holdings SA v Versailles Trade Finance Ltd* [2004] All E.R. (D) 158 and *Shalson v Russo* [2003] EWHC 1637, at [106] for considerations of the conflict positions.

[144] (2001) 82 P. & C.R. 27.

[145] [2002] 1 B.C.L.C. 162, [2001] W.T.L.R. 1327.

[146] See also *Russell v Wakefield Waterworks Co* (1875) L.R. 20 Eq. 474, 479, *per* Lord Jessel M.R.

ab initio").[147] The result of the majority decisions in the House of Lords in the local authority swaps cases, such as *Westdeutsche Landesbank v Islington*,[148] is that it impossible for parties to retain a proprietary interest in property transferred under a commercial contract which is found to have been void ab initio. The restatement of the core rules of equity in the speech of Lord Browne-Wilkinson in *Westdeutsche Landesbank v Islington*[149] created a test that a proprietary claim in equity will only be upheld in circumstances in which the defendant had knowledge of the factor which is alleged to impose the office of trustee on her, thus affecting her conscience. However, the proprietary interest only comes into existence once the defendant has the requisite knowledge.

F. The continued failure to react to the decision in Westdeutsche Landesbank v Islington on systemic risk

In *Westdeutsche Landesbank v Islington* the interest rate swap contract between the parties was held to have been void ab initio and therefore it was held that there was no contract between the parties at all: that is, none of the terms of the master agreement, nor of the confirmations, nor of any credit support agreement entered into between the parties would be of any effect whatsoever. The parties were therefore, entirely correctly, thrown back on the general law to decide whether or not they were entitled to any rights in property. Given that there was no viable express contract between the parties, the House of Lords in *Westdeutsche Landesbank v Islington*[150] was unanimous in holding that neither any amount of money paid in advance by the bank in that case nor any of the periodic amounts payable under the interest rate swap were to be held on resulting or constructive trust, and thus none of those payments were able to attract compound interest. While there were two dissenting opinions in that case, it is important to note that Lord Goff and Lord Woolf dissented only on the availability of compound interest: the former asserting that it ought to have been available on the grounds of justice, the latter asserting that commercial people would expect that it would be made available. The court was unanimous, however, on the more significant question as to the lack of availability of a proprietary remedy where the underlying contract failed either due to mistake or lack of capacity or failure of consideration at a time when neither contracting party knew of those factors. The persistent failure of the derivatives markets to alter the manner in which they take collateral so as to accommodate this unanimous view of the senior English courts, as to the non-availability of proprietary rights in the event that a derivatives contract fails, is a continued source of enormous systemic risk and something which continues to astonish this writer.

21–52

---

[147] See for example, *Hazell v Hammersmith & Fulham* [1992] 2 A.C. 1; *Westdeutsche Landesbank v Islington* [1996] A.C. 669.
[148] [1996] A.C. 669; [1996] 2 All E.R. 961.
[149] See above.
[150] See fn.131, above.

G.   Resulting trusts

21–53   Resulting trusts arise either where two or more parties have contributed to the purchase price of property so that each is recognised as having on resulting trust an equitable interest in that property proportionate to the size of their contribution, or where some portion of the equitable interest remains unallocated and so that interest passes back on resulting trust to its last owner.[151] Constructive trusts arise where the conscience of the legal owner of property is affected by knowledge of some factor, such as the fact that a payment has been made to it under a mistake, in relation to the property at issue.[152]

H.   *Quistclose* trusts

21–54   *Quistclose* trusts, which are used significantly to take security in loan transactions, are discussed in Chapter 22[153] and in Alastair Hudson, *Equity & Trusts*, in Chapter 22.

---

[151]   See fn.131, above.
[152]   See fn.131, above.
[153]   See para.22–24.

CHAPTER 22

TAKING SECURITY AND INSOLVENCY

[633]

CORE PRINCIPLES

Taking security

"Taking security" is the process of seeking to use one or more of a number of legal structures to protect oneself against the risk that one's counterparty may go into insolvency or fail to perform its contractual obligations, or that one's contract may otherwise be unenforceable, or against any of the other risks discussed in Chapter 1. The menu of legal techniques which may be used are considered in turn in this chapter.

A transfer of title under contract means that the secured party acquires absolute title in assets put up to secure her exposure under a transaction: typically, other assets of the same kind would need to be retransferred to the counterparty once the transaction has been properly performed. This structure is similar to the "personal collateral" structure considered in Chapter 44. By contrast, a *Romalpa* clause provides that the secured party retains absolute title in property which is used by both parties for a transaction in common, even if that property passes into the counterparty's possession.

As considered in Chapter 21, trusts provide that the secured party acquires the equitable proprietary interest of a beneficiary in property set aside to provide security, and the counterparty acts as trustee of that property such that the trust continues in existence regardless of the counterparty going into insolvency. More specifically a *Quistclose* trust provides that a lender retains an equitable interest in money transferred to a borrower under a loan contract provided that that loan contract contained a term which required the borrower to use the money only for a specified purpose.

Mortgages grant a proprietary right to the secured party such that the secured party (the "mortgagee") may seek a sale of that property, or possession of that property, or foreclosure, or the appointment of a receiver (depending on the nature of the secured property). Mortgages are most commonly taken out to secure loans to buy land, although they may be used over chattels. Superficially similar to mortgages, charges provide the secured party with a right to petition the court to seek an order for the sale of the charged property in the event that the chargor fails to make payment to the secured party (the "chargee"); charges do not, however, grant the chargee a property right before a sale is ordered. Charges take effect in equity, and may take effect either over specified property (a "fixed charge") or over a changing, floating pool of property (a "floating charge").

Pledges ordinarily involve a transfer of possession (but not of ownership) in property until a contractual obligation is performed, and if that obligation is not performed then the secured party may seek ownership of the pledged property in lieu of performance (as with a pawnbroking contract). The term "pledge" is used in some markets' jargon to connote an outright transfer of the ownership of property, as opposed to a mere transfer of possession. Liens are similar to pledges in that liens transfer possession of property to the secured party so that the secured party may apply to the court for an order for sale of that property if the counterparty fails to make a contractually required payment.

[634]

Guarantees do not provide security by way of making property available to the secured party, but rather constitute a contractual undertaking by some third person to meet the unpaid obligations of one party to a transaction to its counterparty. Guarantees must comply with certain formalities (such as the need for the guarantee to be in writing) so as not to be a mere indemnity.

Insolvency

Section 323 of the Insolvency Act 1986 provides that a company is insolvent when it cannot pay its debts as they become due. The question as to whether or not a company is insolvent – particularly deciding whether it will be able to meet its future liabilities or not – is a complex one. There are two principles of insolvency law which might call the validity of contracts into question: the *pari passu* principle (which requires that all unsecured creditors are treated the same) and the anti-deprivation principle (which prevents any assets being taken from the estate of an insolvent person).

A key aspect of seeking security in complex, high-volume financial transactions is the ability to set off amounts owed reciprocally between the parties in the event that one party goes into insolvency. Further to r.4.90 of the Insolvency Rules, set-off between two parties, where one of them is insolvent, is mandatory when there are mutual debts between them. In relation to set-off between more than two parties, matters are more complex. The House of Lords held that set off between multiple parties in a clearing house arrangement would offend against the pari passu principle. The Settlement Finality Regulations have ensured that clearing houses will be valid. The Supreme Court has held latterly that set-off and "flip" provisions in a master agreement will not offend the anti-deprivation principle even if that means that the amount owed by the insolvent person's counterparty is thereby reduced.

1.   INTRODUCTION

A. The concepts underpinning the taking of security

The importance of taking security in financial transactions

Taking security is a key part of commercial transactions; particularly when dealing in financial markets. The expression "taking security" refers to the use of any one or more of the techniques considered in this chapter to protect oneself against the risk that one's counterparty will fail to perform its contractual obligations, or that the transaction will be unenforceable for some other reason, or that the transaction will generate a loss in some other way. The concept of risk in financial transactions was discussed in Chapter 1.[1] This chapter considers how the risk of a counterparty failing to perform its obligations can be controlled by providing "security". Under English law, security may be taken in a number of

22–01

---

[1]   See para.1–47 et seq.

different ways using common law devices or equitable devices which may give rise to proprietary rights or to merely personal rights depending on the structure and the circumstances.

Proprietary and personal rights

22–02   Let us begin by explaining some of the terminology. These terms will be considered in greater detail below but a working knowledge of them from the outset will be useful. A "proprietary right" in this context means a right over property, whether in the form of "absolute title" (that is, outright ownership of all of the possible rights in an item of property), or title recognised by common law (such as the rights of a trustee under a trust), or equitable rights (such as the rights of a beneficiary under a trust).[2] A proprietary right is important because the holder of a right in property can enforce that proprietary right against any third party even if some other person who is using or who has possession of the property goes into insolvency, or purports to transfer that property to a third party, or something of that sort. A proprietary right also gives rise to a range of remedies which are not available to the holder of a purely personal right. It is the opposite of a "personal right", in that a personal right does not grant any rights to property but rather only a right to recover damages or compensation, or to perform some other action short of granting rights in identified property. There have been circumstances in which the term "proprietary right" has been used by the courts to describe circumstances in which the claimant has only a contingent right to property but nevertheless does have some right which may crystallise into a full property right over an identified pool of property at some point in the future.[3] This is, it is suggested, an inaccurate use of the term. If the term "security" were to be used to cover all of the various techniques whether they are proprietary or personal in nature then it becomes a very broad term indeed and would be of little practical use. Similarly, the term "proprietary" right has been used by the courts to cover such a broad range of subtly but significantly different techniques that it may be of little practical use: so we will need to tease apart these differences in this chapter and to keep the proper distinction between proprietary and personal rights clearly in mind.

Structuring security

22–03   The term "structure" is important too. It denotes the practice of financial lawyers of choosing between a range of possible legal techniques to achieve an objective (in relation to taking security that may include selecting between a trust, a charge, a mortgage, a pledge, a contract to pay money, and so on) and then drafting and organising that arrangement so as to be properly analysable as having particular characteristics and as imposing appropriate rights and obligations between the contracting parties. The resulting phenomenon is colloquially known as a "structure". It is a key part of a finance lawyer's practice to organise structures

---

[2] See A. Hudson, *Equity & Trusts*, 6th edn (Routledge-Cavendish, 2009), Ch.2 for a full discussion of these concepts.

[3] For example *Re Spectrum Plus* [2005] UKHL 41; [2005] 2 A.C. 680, considered below.

which will achieve her client's goals, which will minimise liability to taxation, which will avoid regulatory problems, which will be commercially viable, and which will above all be legally enforceable in all jurisdictions and under all systems of law under which they need to be enforceable.[4] Above all, lawyers should take care to decide exactly what sort of proprietary or personal right is intended and organise their client's affairs accordingly; as opposed to using vague expressions like "security interest" or "hypothecation" which merely beg the question exactly what type of proprietary or personal right is intended.[5]

Credit risk management and the identification of appropriate security

The term "security" for the purposes of this chapter means *protection against risk*.[6] A contracting party is seeking protection against any one or more of a number of potential risks connected to any financial transaction. Much of the activity within financial institutions which is not concerned with creating or marketing products is concerned with the evaluation and assessment of risk. Of particular importance is credit risk management whereby financial institutions evaluate the risk of each counterparty failing to perform its obligations: this assessment of credit risk is intimately linked with the process of taking security in that the form and size of the security that is required will be relative to the perceived risk of the counterparty's non-performance of its obligations. There are other risks, such as risk that the market will collapse or move so markedly that the financial products at issue will become worthless or will cause the parties loss. Security will often be required so as to control these forms of non-counterparty risk too. The various species of risk were considered in Chapter 1.

22–04

The value of the security acquired could take a number of different forms: whether that is the entire, gross amount owed to the secured party; or a net exposure which the secured party has to its counterparty across a number of transactions, taking into account amounts owed to the secured party and amounts which the secured in turn owes to its counterparty; or an amount which the secured party calculates off-sets the perceived credit risk that the counterparty will not perform its obligations in relation to an underlying transaction or transactions; or some other amount which the parties negotiate between them.[7] By way of illustration, suppose that Alpha Bank owes US$100,000 to Beta Bank and that Beta owes US$80,000 to Alpha across all of their relevant transactions. If Alpha was concerned with its gross obligations, then Alpha would seek protection in the amount of US$80,000. However, seeking to match the net

22–05

---

[4] That is, in all jurisdictions in which the parties are acting or in which the transaction needs to be performed.

[5] See for example *Lowe v National Bank of Jamaica* [2008] UKPC 26 where the term "hypothecation" left an issue between the parties as to exactly what right the claimant had been intended to have.

[6] As opposed to the term "security" as used in Pt 10 of this book to refer to shares, bonds and so forth, which is an entirely different use of the same word.

[7] Where this last example involves a measurement by the secured party's credit department of an amount, typically a proportion of the net exposure of the secured party to the counterparty, which it estimates will be sufficient to offset the risk to it of doing business with the counterparty.

exposure in this instance would require protection to be provided to Beta in the amount of US$20,000, being the net exposure which Alpha owes to Beta across these contracts. In an ordinary personal collateral structure[8] it would be this net exposure which would be covered. Alternatively, the credit department at Beta might decide that the risk of Beta doing business with Alpha would be met if Alpha paid a percentage of that exposure in advance: say US$10,000, being an amount which Alpha's credit department thinks would assuage its credit concerns about doing business with Beta according to its estimate of the likelihood of Beta's default. This would be an entirely commercial decision.

This chapter will consider the various forms of protection offered by the law against a range of possible financial risks.

B. The core techniques in taking security

22–06   The legal techniques for taking security in commercial transactions fall broadly into four categories. The first category is security by means of taking title in some property. This group of techniques includes the trust,[9] transfer of title provisions[10] and retention of title provisions.[11] In each of these situations the legal technique identifies a proprietary right of some sort in some asset to which the rightholder can have recourse if its counterparty fails to perform its obligations under the contract. Further examples of this category are mortgages[12] under which the rightholder acquires a proprietary right in the mortgaged property.

22–07   The second category is comprised of a weaker form of security by means simply of contract: that is, a personal obligation to pay money in the event of some failure to perform an obligation under the contract. This is said to be a "weaker" form of security in that the rightholder does not have any identified asset to which it can have recourse on the default of its counterparty; rather, it is reliant on both the counterparty's ability and willingness to pay, either of which may have been the cause of the original failure to perform under the contract. Within this category are events of default,[13] guarantees to make payment,[14] some collateralisation obligations to transfer value to a collateral fund,[15] and some liens.[16]

22–08   The third category is comprised of quasi-proprietary rights: that is, a group of rights which purport to grant title in assets but which are nevertheless dependent on some contractual right crystallising so as to transform that right into a proprietary right. Thus a floating charge gives the rightholder rights of a given value over a fund but those rights are dependent on the counterparty maintaining

---

[8] See para.42–33 et seq.
[9] See para.21–01.
[10] See para.21–13.
[11] See para.21–20.
[12] See para.21–30.
[13] See para.19–48.
[14] See para.21–77.
[15] See para.42–33.
[16] See para.21–68.

that fund appropriately.[17] This contrasts, for example, with a trust arrangement in which a trustee holds the trust fund (particularly where a third party custodian is selected to act as trustee, as considered below) rather than the counterparty itself retaining management control of the security assets.

The fourth category comprises doctrines such as the pledge and the lien which grant only rights of possession, not ownership, of property but with the ability to petition the court for permission to sell the property so as to recover money owed to the creditor. **22–09**

C.   Collateralisation

The techniques associated with collateralisation are discussed in detail in Chapter 42 of this book. Collateralisation is used to take security in derivatives transactions, and comprises one of a number of hybrids of the techniques discussed in this chapter. **22–10**

D.   Transactions with different forms of entity

Different issues arise with different forms of entity when seeking to take security. Where the borrower is a member of a group of companies, then there is a question as to which entity will be the borrower under the transaction. Each company within a group of companies is treated by company law as being a separate legal person and therefore an obligation will only be enforceable against the company which is a party to the agreement.[18] Therefore, within groups of companies it is important to identify the company or companies which either hold the group's most valuable assets or which conduct the group's principal trade: these are the companies which have the most valuable assets which could be provided as security and therefore it is these companies which should either be the contracting entities or the entities which are extending any guarantee or other credit support as part of the transaction. There is always a risk, in consequence, that there may be a reconstruction of the group of companies such that the assets which are to be used to provide securities are moved to another company within the group. Consequently, the reconstruction of the counterparty entity will typically be an event of default triggering the termination of the agreement between the parties. It should also be an event which triggers any credit support arrangement between the parties. **22–11**

In relation to partnerships, the partnership property is owned by the partners in a manner defined by the partnership agreement: this may include a right for partners to take property out of the partnership's property, for example if they leave the partnership. Consequently, the termination of a partnership or the reconstitution of a partnership once a significant partner leaves or a new partner joins that partnership may have a significant effect on the credit profile of that partnership. Similarly, in relation to trusts it is possible for a beneficiary to **22–12**

---

[17] See para.21–50.
[18] *Salomon v A Salomon & Co Ltd* [1897] A.C. 22; *Adams v Cape Industries Plc* [1990] Ch. 433.

exercise a power to remove its share of the trust capital, or similarly for a trustee to exercise a power or discretion effectively removing a large amount of the trust's capital. In relation both to ordinary partnerships and to trusts there is no requirement that any filing or public provision of information is made as to their financial positions. When dealing with these sorts of entity—or indeed any entity which is not a company providing financial information in the ordinary manner—it is important to consider carefully the credit risks associated with that entity and the most appropriate manner in which credit support may be provided.

2. TRANSFERS OF ABSOLUTE TITLE

22–13   Taking security by means of a transfer of title is comparatively straightforward in conceptual, legal terms. What is envisaged is that the party requiring security ("the secured party") is transferred absolute, unencumbered ownership of all of the rights in property by way of an outright gift or assignment (referred to in this book as "absolute title"). In line with the secured party's calculation of its credit risk under the transaction, that property will be of a value which covers, to the secured party's satisfaction, its exposure to its counterparty. In the event that the counterparty does fail to perform its obligations, or more specifically in the event that the counterparty becomes insolvent, then the secured party is the absolute owner of that property and so title in that property will reduce the exposure which the secured party has to the counterparty's failure to perform.

22–14   Given that the property is transferred outright in this context, the secured party can have no obligation to account for that property in the counterparty's insolvency—always assuming that no question of a transfer at an undervalue with a view to defrauding the counterparty's creditors is deemed to have taken place under English insolvency law.[19] If there had been such a transfer at an under-value with a view to putting assets beyond the reach of insolvency creditors, then the court would be empowered to unpick the transaction and restore the status quo ante so that the creditors can have recourse to those assets in the transferor's hands.[20]

22–15   The assumption made here is that the secured party has no obligation at law or in equity as part of the law of property to account to the counterparty nor to make any re-transfer of the specific transferred property to the counterparty. If there was an obligation to hold the original property on trust or to hold that original property separately from all other assets, then the secured party would owe proprietary obligations to its counterparty. In this context, however, the transfer of absolute title to the secured party means that the secured party becomes the absolute owner of that property without any proprietary obligation to account to the counterparty in relation to that property. There may, however, (as in personal collateral structures) be a *contractual* obligation to make a transfer of property of a like kind or of equivalent value (whether in money or money's worth) to the counterparty in the event that the counterparty performs its obligations under a derivatives contract, or to make a re-transfer of property of a like kind or of

---

[19] Insolvency Act 1986, s.423.
[20] Insolvency Act 1986, s.423.

equivalent value to the extent that the counterparty has performed its obligations under that contract. It is important that this is merely a contractual obligation to make a transfer because the counterparty will have no proprietary right to any specific assets held by the secured party and therefore will have no claim in property law generally nor in the law of trusts specifically to any such property. Rather, the secured party would owe merely a personal obligation to transfer property of a particular type or cash of a given value to the counterparty, such that there was no specified property which was to be so transferred (even if the secured party happened to hold such property in a distinct account in readiness to perform this contractual obligation). A contractual obligation of this sort is said to be "merely a contractual obligation" because it offers no security against the counterparty's inability or unwillingness to perform its obligations: the law of contract will give the counterparty a right of enforcement but no further right (except perhaps a right to damages) if performance is rendered impossible in practice for example if the counterparty has gone into insolvency. This chapter is therefore concerned with mechanisms for the protection of a party to a transaction in the event that the law of contract offers no viable remedy or recourse as a matter of fact, or lest the law of contract should offer no such remedy or recourse at some time in the future.

The reason for starting this discussion of taking security with this elementary mechanism for taking security is that it is a feature of some collateral security structures and stock lending. Under the ISDA Credit Support Annex, the parties may outright transfers of money or securities (as stipulated in the contract) one to another equal to the payee's net exposure to the payer at the time of calculating the requirement to post collateral.[21] In that contract, the parties usually transfer any amount of money or money's worth required to be transferred under the terms of that contract by means of an outright transfer, such that the recipient is able to treat the property as being absolutely its own, even if it is required to account for the amount of any distribution which the transferor would otherwise have received on any securities transferred under that agreement. The standard market documentation is considered in detail in this regard in Chapter 42.[22] However, a number of other legal structures may also be used in collateralisation: those structures are considered in the remainder of this chapter.

22–16

3.   TRUSTS

The preceding chapter considered the law of trusts in detail.[23] The reader is referred to that discussion. For the purposes of taking security, as was considered in detail above,[24] a trust permits a number of different people to have different

22–17

---

[21] The expression "to post collateral" is the jargon used in the ISDA documentation and refers to the obligation of a party to transfer property (that is, the collateral property) to its counterparty in a form stipulated in the contract and in an amount calculated by reference to the provisions of that same contract.

[22] See para.42–33 et seq.

[23] I have written a number of books on trusts law, so readers are referred to G. Thomas and A. Hudson, *The Law of Trusts*, 2nd edn (OUP, 2010) and generally A. Hudson, *Equity & Trusts*. For

rights in the same property simultaneously. A beneficiary under an ordinary express trust[25] has an equitable proprietary interest in the trust property which will continue in full effect even if the trustee or any of the other beneficiaries go into insolvency. Thus, if a person fears the insolvency of its counterparty before that person returns or advances specified property under a transaction, then that person can have a trust declared over that property so that the counterparty acts as trustee over that property in the beneficiary's favour. If the trustee then goes into insolvency, the beneficiary retains a proprietary right in that property ahead of unsecured creditors in the insolvency. The trust can be structured so that a number of different people have rights in the trust property and so that the rights of some or all of those beneficiaries are contingent on the happening of some event, such as payment being made in full under a financial transaction. Trusts do not require registration under English law and therefore have no filing requirements, except for what is said in Chapter 40 relating to transparency obligations for listed companies. It would be usual in financial transactions to constitute a trust in a trust instrument in writing although there is no legal pre-requisite to create a trust in writing for most forms of property.[26] It is possible, however, that an express trust could be inferred from the circumstances even in relation to a financial transaction. For example, in decided cases where accountants have created a separate bank account to hold customer's prepayments to a company for goods lest the company should go into insolvency before those goods are delivered, it has been held that the intentions of those accountants should be interpreted as having created an express trust even though the accountants had no conscious appreciation that that was the legal effect of their actions.[27] Thus it is important to understand also that trusts will be imposed either because that is the best interpretation of the parties' intentions[28] or because the court considered that the defendant had acted unconscionably in relation to the property at issue.[29] This second form of trust is a constructive trust and operates entirely by operation of law, regardless of the wishes of the defendant. All of these issues were considered in Chapter 22.

---

those unfamiliar with this area, I have also written a brief introductory guide which explains all of the main principles in an accessible way: A. Hudson, *Understanding Equity & Trusts*, 4th edn (Routledge, 2012).

[24] See para.21–01.

[25] That is, as opposed to a discretionary trust, considered at para.21–21.

[26] See para.21–08.

[27] *Re Kayford* [1975] 1 W.L.R. 279.

[28] *Re Kayford* [1975] 1 W.L.R. 279.

[29] *Westdeutsche Landesbank v Islington* [1996] A.C. 669.

4. "LENDING" AND TRANSFER ARRANGEMENTS

A. The legal analysis of transfers of property

Distinguishing between outright transfers and retaining equitable proprietary rights

It commonly happens in financial markets that the market jargon masks the precise legal analysis of the transaction. So, for example, in "stock-lending arrangements" it has been held by an Australian court[30] that the "lending institution" actually transfers securities outright to the "borrowing institution", subject to a personal obligation on the borrowing institution to return securities of like kind at an identified date in the future; even though the market use of the word "lending" occasionally suggests that the lending institution retains proprietary rights in the securities in the same way that I retain proprietary rights in my lawnmower if I "lend" it to my next-door neighbour for her to use once to mow her lawn. More usually the term "lend" refers to an outright transfer of property as in Chapter 33 in "Ordinary Lending". Part of the role of the finance lawyer is to see through the market jargon and to analyse or to structure the transaction according to its true nature. This section aims to distinguish between structures which actually involve the transfer of title or the retention of title or something in between.

22–18

Suppose that Alex transfers an amount of US$10,000 to Barbara. If the transferor's intention is that Barbara is to become the absolute owner of that money, then Barbara becomes the absolute owner of the US$10,000 and Alex is left with no property rights at all in that US$10,000. If, however, the parties' mutual intention was that Barbara would hold that US$10,000 in a separate bank account so that the whole of the money is to be transferred absolutely to Barbara if Alex fails to make a payment under another transaction between them, and so that the whole of the money shall be returned to Alex if Alex makes payment properly and on time under that other transaction, then the best analysis of this transaction would be that Barbara is to hold the US$10,000 on trust because neither party is entitled to absolute title in the property until it is known whether or not Alex has made payment on time. Barbara cannot take the money for herself until Alex's payment has not been made: therefore, before that time she cannot be an absolute owner of the money, but rather only a trustee over it.[31] Thus, even though the money has been transferred into Barbara's possession, no non-contingent, beneficial rights of ownership have been transferred to her.

22–19

Romalpa clauses—retention of title

Suppose instead that the property in question in the previous example was a mechanical component over which Alex held both the patent and absolute title. If Alex delivered the component to Barbara so that it could be attached to a machine

22–20

---

[30] *Beconwood Securities Pty Ltd v Australia and New Zealand Banking Group Ltd* [2008] F.C.A. 594.
[31] See para.21–08.

to manufacture computer components subject a production and profit-sharing contract, and if the contract provided that Alex would remain the absolute owner of that component, then no property rights in the component would pass to Barbara: instead, it would be said that Alex had retained absolute title in that component. The same structure could be used in relation to commodities or to financial instruments. A retention of title clause in this manner means that the absolute owner remains the absolute owner of that property; whereas it would be possible using the example of the trust over the US$10,000 above that Alex could have retained the equitable interest in the money, using Barbara as a bare trustee for Alex as the sole beneficiary. These types of structures are considered in greater detail in the sections to follow because they are important parts of taking security.

22–21   An example of this sort of arrangement in commercial law is the *Romalpa* clause[32] in which a contractual provision enables the titleholder to property to retain common law rights in that property even if possession of the property is transferred to another person during the performance of the contract. So, in relation to a contract in which property is to be used as part of the contractual purpose, that property will remain the property of the provider both at common law and in equity.[33] This analysis remains possible provided that the property does not become mixed with other property so as to be indistinguishable: in such a circumstance this could only leave equitable tracing rights for the claimant[34] because bailment at common law would generally be impossible over a mixture.[35] It is a matter for the construction of the contract as to the rights which the provider of the property was intended to acquire. In general a retention of title under a *Romalpa* clause would prevent another party to that contract from passing good title to a third party.

Distinguishing between a merely personal right to recovery and a proprietary right to recovery

22–22   When property is transferred from Alex to Barbara, as in the examples given immediately above, with an obligation that Barbara is obliged to make a transfer of similar property back to Alex, it very important to know whether Barbara owes Alex proprietary obligations or merely personal obligations. The difference between the two types of obligation is identified by analysing the terms on which the transfer was made. If Barbara was required to transfer back exactly the same property that Alex had transferred originally, then Barbara would owe Alex proprietary obligations in relation to that property and Alex would thus retain proprietary rights in the property. Whereas, if Barbara's obligation was merely to make a transfer to Alex of property of a like kind, but not the actual property originally transferred to her, then Barbara owes merely personal obligations to

---

[32] *Aluminium Industrie Vaassen BV v Romalpa Aluminium Ltd* [1976] 1 W.L.R 676.

[33] [1976] 1 W.L.R. 676. Indeed no question of trust or equity arises at all.

[34] *Agip (Africa) Ltd v Jackson* [1991] Ch. 547; *El Ajou v Dollar Land Holdings* [1994] 2 All E.R. 685.

[35] *South Australian Insurance Co Ltd v Randell* (1869) L.R. 3 P.C. 101; *Chapman Bros Ltd v Verco Bros Ltd* (1933) 49 C.L.R. 306; *Coleman v Harvey* [1989] 1 N.Z.L.R. 723.

Alex because Barbara is under no obligation to retain the original property nor any other property until the moment when the re-transfer is required to take place.

Thus in an ordinary loan, the borrower is entitled to spend the loan moneys and is obliged only to make payment in the loan's currency at the date when the loan contract requires repayment. If the borrower fails to make repayment, then the lender's rights are purely personal rights to damages for breach of contract, unless the lender had also taken some proprietary rights under a mortgage or a trust or otherwise. When we consider taking collateral, by way of security, in Chapter 42 in relation to financial derivatives, these concepts are particularly important. There is a fundamental difference in principle *from the debtor's perspective* between an obligation merely to transfer different property from the original property which was posted by a counterparty and an obligation to hold the original property transferred by the counterparty on trust before re-transferring that same property. The former obligation is merely a personal obligation akin to a debt, which provides no security protection in an insolvency; whereas the latter is a proprietary right whereby the creditor will hold the debtor's collateral property to the debtor's account if the underlying derivatives contract is performed. From the perspective of the creditor the distinction is that in the former arrangement it owes (absent any contractual provision to the contrary) merely a personal obligation to account to the debtor for the collateral transferred to it; whereas in the latter context the creditor will owe fiduciary duties in relation to the safekeeping of that property.

22–23

B. *Quistclose* trusts

The competing analyses of the Quistclose trust

There is a particular form of security which is used in relation to loans known as a *Quistclose* trust.[36] A *Quistclose* trust is created by operation of law whenever the parties to a loan include a term in the loan to the effect that the loan moneys can only be used for a specified purpose. A *Quistclose* trust is generally analysed by trusts lawyers[37] on the basis that if the borrower were to go into insolvency, then a trust would be implied over the loan moneys so that those loan moneys are held on trust for the lender and are not therefore to be distributed among the insolvent person's estate. So, in *Barclay's Bank v Quistclose Investments Ltd*[38] Rolls Razor Ltd borrowed money from Quistclose. A condition was placed on the loan to the effect that the money was only to be used to pay a dividend to Rolls Razor's preferred creditors. The loan moneys were paid into an account held with Barclays Bank. Rolls Razor went into insolvency before the dividend was paid. Barclays Bank sought to offset the money in the bank account against Rolls Razor's overdraft on its general account with Barclays Bank. The House of Lords upheld a resulting trust over the loan moneys such that Quistclose was held to have an equitable interest under a trust in those loan moneys, such that the loan

22–24

---

[36] Derived from the decision in *Barclay's Bank v Quistclose Investments Ltd* [1970] A.C. 567.
[37] A. Hudson, *Equity & Trusts*, Ch.22; G. Thomas and A. Hudson, *The Law of Trusts*, Ch.9.
[38] [1970] A.C. 567.

moneys could not be distributed among any of the unsecured creditors (such as Barclays Bank) in Rolls Razor's insolvency. As Lord Wilberforce held:[39]

> "There is surely no difficulty in recognising the co-existence in one transaction of legal and equitable rights and remedies: when the money is advanced, the lender acquires an equitable right to see that it is applied for the primary designated purpose:[40] when the purpose has been carried out (i.e., the debt paid) the lender has his remedy against the borrower in debt: if the primary purpose cannot be carried out, the question arises if a secondary purpose (i.e., repayment to the lender) has been agreed, expressly or by implication: if it has, the remedies of equity may be invoked to give effect to it, if it has not (and the money is intended to fall within the general fund of the debtor's assets) then there is the appropriate remedy for recovery of a loan."

This passage means that there is no problem with having obligations at common law (i.e. to repay the loan) and obligations in equity (i.e. to hold the money on trust until it is used for the purpose specified in the loan contract). Thus, if the purpose is performed then the lender has rights against the borrower at common law under the terms of the contract (i.e. "has his remedy in debt"). The "secondary obligation" arises in equity either on the express terms of the contract or impliedly from the circumstances. The "remedies of equity" in this context are the "secondary trust" which requires that the loan money is held on trust if it is not used for the specified purpose.[41] Therefore, this model of the *Quistclose* trust is predicated on a reading of the particular contract at issue, then giving effect to the terms of the contract at common law, before equity intervenes with a remedy to ensure that the lender has an equitable interest in the loan moneys in the event that they are misused by the borrower (for example, if the borrower goes into insolvency and the assets are intended to be distributed among the borrower's unsecured creditors).

22–25   Most of the academic discussion, and later judicial understandings of this doctrine, have focused on it being a form of resulting trust and the problems which are attendant on that. However, another way of conceiving of a *Quistclose* trust, from a banker's perspective, is that the inclusion of a term which imposes a condition on the borrower's use of the loan moneys will grant the lender of that money an equitable interest in those moneys, unless and until the money is used for the specified purpose at which point the equitable interest must cease to exist.[42] Thus, a form of security can be taken in relation to lent moneys by the inclusion of such a term in the loan contract. Its proper analysis will depend upon the precise terms of any given contract.

22–26   Nevertheless, the courts persist in attempting to define the *Quistclose* trust as though it is a single legal technique independent of the terms of the loan contract

---

[39] [1970] A.C. 567, 581-582.

[40] *In re Rogers*, 8 Morr. 243, *per* both Lindley L.J. and Kay L.J.

[41] Interestingly, though, Lord Wilberforce expressed this in terms of being a general "equitable right", albeit that the House of Lords accepted the appeal before them which was predicated on the idea that this was a resulting trust.

[42] If the loan contract's condition once satisfied did not cause the equitable interest to terminate, then the loan itself would be impossible to perform because the borrower would not effectively be able to spend the loan moneys. Instead, once the loan moneys are used for the specified purpose in accordance with the loan contract, then the lender's proprietary rights in those moneys must disappear, and instead the lender is left with rights in the law of contract.

which created it. So, a further analysis of the *Quistclose* trust would consider it to be a form of retention of an equitable interest by the lender. The minority speech of Lord Millett in the House of Lords in *Twinsectra v Yardley* suggested that the *Quistclose* trust should be considered to be akin to a retention of title by the lender such that the lender effectively retains an equitable interest in the property throughout the transaction, such that the property is held on resulting trust for the lender.[43] His Lordship held that:

> "...the *Quistclose* trust is a simple, commercial arrangement akin...to a retention of title clause (though with a different object) which enables the borrower to have recourse to the lender's money for a particular purpose without entrenching on the lender's property rights more than necessary to enable the purpose to be achieved. The money remains the property of the lender unless and until it is applied in accordance with his directions, and in so far as it is not so applied it must be returned to him. I am disposed, perhaps predisposed, to think that this is the only analysis which is consistent both with orthodox trust law and with commercial reality."[44]

The lender could therefore be taken to retain the equitable interest in loan moneys throughout the life of the contract.[45] This raises the following paradox: how do you retain property which you gave away? If the lender transfers the property to the borrower, then how can the lender be said to have retained it? Alternatively, to quote precisely from Lord Millett, if the lender retains the property rights, then how can they be returned to him? Think of it this way: you ask to borrow my lawnmower, but I refuse to lend it to you. Then, the next day, I come to your door and ask you to return my lawnmower to me. You would look at me in puzzled amazement and say: "But you kept it, you jackass, so how can I return it to you?" The *Twinsectra* model does not work literally because, as drafted by Lord Millett, the money is both retained by the lender and also returned to the lender later on. Lord Millett's model can only make sense if it is the common law title which passes to the borrower (so that the borrower can spend the money for the specified purpose) and then it is some part of the equitable interest which is retained by the lender and another part of the equitable interest which is returned to him. But why make it so complicated?

It all turns on the drafting of the contract: if the contract contains an express trust **22–27** with the parties' equitable interests laid out, then there is no possibility of it being a resulting trust. It should be noted that the decided cases in England and Wales have focused on the *Quistclose* arrangement arising by operation of law, and not by an express trust. This raises two issues. First, there are commentators[46] and courts in Australia[47] which have expressed the view that the *Quistclose* trust should be analysed as an express trust (formed by inference from the loan

---

[43] Lord Millett was clear that the trust was still a resulting trust.

[44] [2002] 2 All E.R. 377, 398–399.

[45] [2002] 2 All E.R. 398, at [80]. This approach was followed in *Re Margaretta Ltd, Freeman v Customs and Excise* [2005] All E.R. (D) 262, per Crystal QC (sitting as a Deputy Judge in the High Court), at [15] et seq.

[46] See, for example, A. Hudson, *Equity & Trusts*, s.22.4.3.

[47] *Re Australian Elizabethan Theatre Trust* (1991) 102 A.L.R. 681, 691, per Gummow J.

contract[48]) with a power for the borrower to use the money for the purpose specified in the loan, as opposed to being a resulting trust. Secondly, it is suggested that the parties would be ill-advised to create a loan with the principal means of taking security in that arrangement being by means of a trust doctrine which is created by implication by the court—and which differently constituted courts seem to be interpreting differently from one another—as opposed to being specified in detail by the parties. Instead, it is suggested, that the parties would be better advised to use an express trust which they create by means of detailed provision in their loan agreement. Indeed, the lender would be better advised—if it is so concerned about the credit worth of the borrower—to hold the loan money in a separate account so that title in the money is retained absolutely by the lender until such time as it is to be applied for the contractually specified purpose, at which point *the lender* should make the payment directly to the intended recipient instead of paying it to a borrower whom it does not trust.[49]

The utility of a Quistclose trust when the loan moneys have been paid away

22–28   The real significance of the *Quistclose* trust in practice is often something different, however. What is little discussed in the decided case law is the following practical problem. Suppose that a lender lends money to a borrower subject to a contractual provision that the money be used for only a specified purpose. Then suppose that the borrower spends the money on some other purpose. Once that money has been spent, it is perfectly possible that the money will be impossible to locate—it may have been paid overseas, or it may have been paid rapidly through a series of bank accounts and mixed with other money. Suppose then that the original loan money has become inextricably mixed with other moneys in a bank account.[50] In this context the lender's only remedy would be by virtue of an equitable tracing action into the mixed fund in which the traceable proceeds of the original loan moneys rest.[51] Such a tracing action into a mixture can only be brought in equity.[52] Such an equitable tracing claim can only be brought if the claimant had some equitable proprietary interest in the loan moneys from the outset.[53] An ordinary loan contract will not create an equitable interest. So, it is only the *Quistclose* trust which creates an equitable interest for the lender and therefore the *Quistclose* trust will enable the lender to commence that equitable tracing action. No other claim would grant any property right in such a mixed fund. Tracing is considered in Chapter 24.

---

[48] As in *Re Kayford* [1975] 1 W.L.R. 279, where an express trust was formed by inference from the parties' actions.

[49] See A. Hudson, *Equity & Trusts*, s.22.4.7.

[50] In this context, "fund" is the word which property lawyers tend to use to encompass any holding or mixture of property which may include a bank account, or a trust fund, or even a heap of tangible property.

[51] The doctrine of loss of the right to trace will clearly be at issue here.

[52] See para.23–06.

[53] *Westdeutsche Landesbank v Islington* [1996] A.C. 669; *Boscawen v Bajwa* [1996] 1 W.L.R. 328; [1995] 4 All E.R. 769.

5. USING SECURED RIGHTS TO RECOUP LOSSES IN CASH

Security devices can seek to retain property rights so that the secured party can **22–29** seize identified property and become the owner of that property so as to offset her losses, as has been the focus so far. Alternatively, a property right could be used so as to provide a means of recouping the secured party's losses, by the simple means of giving the secured party some property which could be sold so as to recoup her losses. The sections to follow in this chapter are concerned less with taking ownership over property, and more instead with using property to generate enough cash to recover the secured party's losses. So, the next section considers mortgages—which grant the mortgagee a right in the secured property—and charges—which strictly do not grant the chargee a right in the secured property until there is a court order to that effect. Both mortgages and charges instead allow the charged property to be sold so as to generate an amount in cash to offset the amount which the chargor owes to the chargee. Similarly, equitable liens entitled the secured party to retain possession of property until she is paid what she is owed, or else she can apply for a court order to sell the property and recoup the amount which she is owed. In these cases, the ordinary purpose of the contracting parties is to use the security device to recover an amount of money which the secured party is owed, as opposed to providing property which the secured party would prefer to own outright. Selecting an appropriate method of security will usually revolve around identifying the property at issue and the secured party's commercial needs, and structuring the arrangement accordingly.

6. MORTGAGES AND CHARGES

A. The distinction between mortgages and charges

Mortgages and charges are subtly distinct concepts. A mortgage grants a **22–30** mortgagee a proprietary right in property as security for a loan so that the mortgagee may enforce its security by means of sale, repossession, foreclosure or appointment of a receiver, always provided that the mortgagor is entitled to recover unencumbered title of the mortgaged property once the loan has been repaid; whereas a charge, which may be fixed or floating, provides a chargee with a contingent right to seize property in the event that the chargor fails to perform its obligations in relation to an underlying contract, and then to seek an order of the court to permit sale. These doctrines are considered in detail below. The distinction between the two concepts, strictly, is as follows. A mortgage grants the mortgagee a proprietary right in the mortgaged property, whereas a charge creates no right in property but rather creates only a right to apply for a judicially-ordered sale of property if an underlying contractual obligation is not performed.[54] As Slade J. has expressed the distinction: a mortgage involves a conveyance of the mortgaged property to the mortgagee subject to the mortgagor's equity of redemption, whereas a charge makes no such conveyance and grants merely

---

[54] *Swiss Bank Corp v Lloyds Bank* [1982] A.C. 584 at 594; [1980] 2 All E.R. 419 at 426; *Ladup Ltd v Williams and Glyn's Bank Plc* [1985] 2 All E.R. 577; [1985] 1 W.L.R. 851.

contingent rights over the property in the event that the underlying obligation is not performed.[55] Mortgages may take effect at law or in equity as legal mortgages or as equitable mortgages respectively, whereas charges take effect only in equity. Charges in turn may be fixed or floating, as considered below. These distinctions between the two doctrines are meaningful but have often been overlooked in the decided cases. First, we shall consider mortgages.

B. The nature of the law of mortgages

22–31   Mortgages may be taken over land and over chattels. The principal features of a mortgage are that the mortgagee (the secured party) acquires a right of ownership in the mortgaged property which acts as security for a loan or other transaction between mortgagor and mortgagee, however equity protects the mortgagor's right to recover his property without the encumbrance of the mortgage on the discharge of the mortgagor's obligations to the mortgagee (known as the "equity of redemption").[56] A mortgage contract which purports to exclude or unconscionably limit the equity of redemption will be void. Therefore, a mortgage is a combination of a contract (most commonly a contract of loan) and a property right. As considered below, the rules relating to mortgages of land will apply to mortgages of personalty in general terms, with the exceptions considered below.[57]

22–32   A contract of mortgage is governed primarily by questions of contract law as to its formation, its terms, and its termination. The mortgage of land differs from an ordinary contract of loan in that the mortgagee acquires the rights of a mortgagee over identified assets of the mortgagor. The mortgage is said to be a proprietary interest in the mortgaged property, for example in relation to land, because the mortgagee's right can be registered at the Land Registry as such (if it is a mortgage over land), and because the mortgagee acquires the rights set out below.[58]

---

[55] *Re Bond Worth Ltd* [1980] Ch. 228 at 250. See, however, the obfuscation provided by Lord Hoffmann in *Re BCCI (No.8)* [1998] A.C. 214 where his Lordship appeared to speak generally of charges, describing them as ensuring that "the owner of the property retains an equity of redemption to have the property restored to him when the liability has been discharged". It is suggested that these remarks be read as a general description of the role of charges in insolvency proceedings and not as a commentary on the distinction between mortgages and charges.

[56] Law of Property Act 1925 s.116.

[57] See generally McGhee, *Snell's Equity*, 31st edn (London: Sweet & Maxwell, 2005) 777; McCormack, *Secured Credit under English and American Law* (Cambridge University Press, 2004); Goode, *Legal Problems of Credit and Security*, 3rd edn (London: Sweet & Maxwell, 2003); Falcon Chambers, *Fisher and Lightwood's Law of Mortgage*, 11th edn (Butterworths, 2002); Bridge, *Personal Property Law*, 3rd edn (OUP, 2002); Cousins, *Mortgages*, 2nd edn (London: Sweet & Maxwell, 2001); Smith, "Securities", in Birks (ed.), *Private Law* (OUP, 2000) p.455 et seq.; Gleeson, *Personal Property Law* (FT Law & Tax, 1997); Sykes and Walker, *The Law of Securities*, 5th edn (Law Book Co, 1993); Palmer, *Bailment*, 2nd edn (Law Book Co, 1991) Ch.22 "Bailment"; Tyler and Palmer, *Crossley Vaines on Personal Property*, 5th edn (Butterworths, 1973), p.447.

[58] The mortgage must be distinguished from a mere pledge, considered later in this chapter. A pledgee of property can obtain a sale of the pledged property on application to the court or otherwise under the terms of the contract containing the pledge, which is ostensibly similar to the mortgagee's power to obtain sale, but importantly a pledgee cannot acquire foreclosure in the way that a mortgagee can: *Harrold v Plenty* [1901] 2 Ch. 314, Cozens-Hardy J. (where his lordship considered, inter alia, that

C.   The mortgagee's remedies in general terms

A mortgagee of land has four principal remedies, variously the rights to: sale, **22–33** foreclosure, possession, and the appointment of a receiver.[59] A mortgagee of chattels has two remedies: sale and foreclosure. By contrast an equitable chargee under a mere charge has only two remedies: sale and the appointment of a receiver. The purpose of this discussion is to summarise the key principles as they relate to taking security so as to explain the nature and extent of the secured party's rights. The detail of the statute and the case law is considered in the sections to follow.

The mortgagee's power of sale under s.101 of the Law of Property Act 1925

The mortgagee's power of sale contained in s.101 of the Law of Property Act **22–34** 1925 ("LPA 1925") applies both to mortgages of land and of chattels, as well as to charges and to liens,[60] provided that the right has been created by deed. The mortgagee acquires statutorily provided powers of sale over the mortgaged property by one of two routes. The first is the specific power of sale set out under s.101 LPA 1925 on the following terms:

> "(1)   A mortgagee, where the mortgage is made by deed, shall, by virtue of this Act, have the following powers, to the like extent as if they had been in terms conferred by the mortgage deed, but not further (namely):—
>
> (i)   A power, when the mortgage money has become due, to sell, or to concur with any other person in selling, the mortgaged property, or any part thereof ... as the mortgagee thinks fit ..."

Thus, for this power of sale to be exercisable the mortgage must have been contained in a deed and the mortgage money must have become due. This power is subject to the provisions of s.103 LPA 1925 which require that there have been notice given by the mortgagee of arrears together with three months arrears,[61] or that some interest is in arrears and has continued to be so for two months,[62] or that there has been a breach of some other provision in the mortgage contract.[63] The mortgagee has a power to sell free from any rights or interests to which the mortgage has priority.[64]

---

deposit of a share certificate would suggest an intention to create a mortgage and not simply a pledge). A pledge merely gives a right of possession and not a right of ownership, whilst also securing the plegor's obligation to make payment.

[59] See generally Harpum, *Megarry and Wade on the Law of Real Property*, 6th edn (London: Sweet & Maxwell, 2000), Ch.19.

[60] As considered in the next section.

[61] Law of Property Act 1925 s.103(1).

[62] Law of Property Act 1925 s.103(2).

[63] Law of Property Act 1925 s.103(3).

[64] Law of Property Act 1925 s.104(1).

The power of sale under s.91 LPA 1925

22–35 There is a second, statutory means of seeking a sale of mortgaged property whereby "[a]ny person entitled to redeem mortgaged property may have a judgment or order for sale instead . . ." under s.91(1) LPA 1925. In short, any person entitled to redemption may apply to the court for the property to be sold. The mortgagor may also seek a sale as a person with an interest in the property under s.91 of the LPA 1925, and in times of recession mortgagors who were trapped in negative equity situations would seek a sale of the property rather than take the risk that the market value of the property would fall further while the redemption value of the mortgage stayed static or increased (as unpaid interest rolled up).[65] The case law surrounding this provision is considered in detail in Alastair Hudson, *The Law and Regulation of Finance*.[66]

The right of foreclosure

22–36 The right of foreclosure is a right to terminate the mortgage contract and to vest the mortgagee with absolute title in the mortgaged property.[67] The right of foreclosure arises once the mortgage moneys have become due at common law.[68]

The right of possession

22–37 At common law, a mortgagee may seek possession of the mortgaged property "even before the ink is dry on the contract".[69] In relation to land, this enables the mortgagee to go into possession of the land. Relief may be available in relation to mortgages of land where the mortgagor can demonstrate a reasonable likelihood of being able to repay the mortgage debt in the future.[70]

The right to appoint a receiver

22–38 Section 101(1) LPA 1925 provides the mortgagee with a power once the mortgage money has become due to appoint a receiver over the income from the mortgaged property. Section 101 was set out above.[71]

---

[65] *Palk v Mortgage Services Funding Ltd* [1993] 2 W.L.R. 415.

[66] See para.49–14.

[67] *Heath v Pugh* (1881) 6 Q.B.D. 345 at 360. The Law Commission has recommended the abandonment of the use of foreclosure in relation to domestic mortgages because of the ostensible harshness of taking ownership of a home away from its occupants, rather than seeking sale or possession.

[68] *Williams v Morgan* [1906] 1 Ch. 804.

[69] *Four Maids Ltd v Dudley Marshall Ltd* [1957] Ch. 317; *Western Bank v Schindler* [1977] Ch. 1; *National Westminster Bank v Skelton* [1993] 1 All E.R. 242.

[70] Administration of Justice Act 1970, s.36; Administration of Justice Act 1973, s.8.

[71] See para.21–34.

D.   Equitable mortgages

Mortgages may arise in equity, and so the mortgagee would be entitled to   **22–39**
equitable rights only. An equitable mortgage can arise in one of four
circumstances. First, it might be that the mortgage is taken out over a merely
equitable interest in property.[72] Secondly, it might be that there is only an
informally created mortgage insufficient to create a legal mortgage, for example a
mortgage of over land which does not comply with ss.85 and 86 of the LPA 1925.
Thirdly, the charge might be created as merely an equitable charge, for example
in circumstances in which property is charged by way of an equitable obligation
to pay money.[73] Fourthly, in relation to land, an equitable mortgage takes effect
by way of deposit of title deeds.[74] Equitable mortgages are considered in detail in
Alastair Hudson, *The Law and Regulation of Finance*.[75]

E.   The nature of charges

The manner in which a charge takes effect

Charges, as opposed to mortgages, take effect only in equity.[76] This section will   **22–40**
consider charges which do not take effect by way of mortgage. Charges grant a
right to seize property in the event that the chargor does not perform some
underlying obligation, for example to pay money under a contract of loan;
importantly, though, a mere charge classically does not grant the chargee an
immediate right in the charged property in the manner that a mortgage grants the
mortgagee such an immediate right of ownership in the mortgaged property.[77] As
the editors of *Fisher and Lightwood's Law of Mortgage* put it:

> "A charge is a security whereby real or personal property is appropriated for the discharge of a
> debt or other obligation, but which does not pass either an absolute or a special property in the
> subject of the security to the creditor, nor any right to possession. In the event of non-payment
> of the debt, the creditor's right of realisation is by judicial process."[78]

---

[72] Ordinarily it is considered that such a circumstance would not give rise to obligations under the
Bills of Sale Act 1882 (see Tyler, *Crossley Vainer on Personal Property*, 449), although a document
might be required to transfer an equitable interest further to s.53(1)(c) LPA 1925 as part of a larger
transaction disposing of personalty.

[73] *London County and Westminster Bank v Tomkins* [1918] 1 K.B. 515.

[74] *Tebb v Hodge* (1869) L.R. 5 C.P. 73; *Russel v Russel* (1783) 1 Bro. C.C. 269.

[75] See para.49–30.

[76] *Re Coslett Contractors Ltd* [1998] Ch. 495. Explained in Gleeson, *Personal Property Law*, p.235,
to be the case because title may not be divided at common law. However, of course, title at common
law may be held in common, for example by trustees.

[77] It should be noted that the judges are not always so discriminating between charges and mortgages,
often using the terms synonymously. See, for example, Slade J. in *Siebe Gorman v Barclays Bank*
[1979] Lloyd's Rep. 142, 159 where the terms are used interchangeably in the following passage: " . . .
a specific charge on the proceeds of [the book debts] as soon as they are received and consequently
prevents the mortgagor from disposing of an unencumbered title to the subject matter of such charge
without the mortgagee's consent, even before the mortgagee has taken steps to enforce its security."

[78] Falcon Chambers, *Fisher and Lightwood's Law of Mortgage*, p.25.

It should be noted that, as is discussed below,[79] a charge which is created by way of a deed will grant the chargee a power of sale once the mortgage money has become due.[80] Other forms of charge—such as floating charges and charges not created by way of deed—do not attract such a power to the secured party. Buckley L.J. explained how charges provide security only once an order of the court is made entitling the chargee to seize the charged property so as to turn it to account:

> "An equitable charge which is not an equitable mortgage is said to be created when property is expressly or constructively made liable, or specially appropriated, to the discharge of a debt or some other obligation, and confers on the chargee a right of realisation by judicial process, that is to say, by the appointment of a receiver or an order for sale."[81]

An equitable charge, then, grants the secured party some right by virtue of the parties' contract to sell the assets provided by way of security,[82] whether that property is held at the time of the creation of charge or whether it is only capable of first coming into existence once the specific property comes into the hands of the chargor.[83]

22–41 The nature of a charge was identified in the following terms by Millett J. in *Re Charge Card Services Ltd*[84]:

> "Similar definitions of equitable charge are to be found in *National Provincial and Union Bank of England v Charnley*.[85] It is sufficient to cite the language of Atkin L.J.,[86]...
>
> > 'It is not necessary to give a formal definition of a charge, but I think there can be no doubt that where in a transaction for value both parties evince an intention that property, existing or future, shall be made available as security for the payment of a debt, and that the creditor shall have a present right to have it made available, there is a charge, even though the present legal right which is contemplated can only be enforced at some future date, and though the creditor gets no legal right of property, either absolute or special, or any legal right to possession, but only gets a right to have the security made available by an order of the court.
> >
> > Thus the essence of an equitable charge is that, without any conveyance or assignment to the chargee, specific property of the chargor is expressly or constructively appropriated to or made answerable for payment of a debt, and the chargee is given the right to resort to the property for the purpose of having it realised and applied in or towards payment of the debt. The availability of equitable remedies has the effect of giving the chargee a proprietary interest by way of security in the property charged.'"

---

[79] See para.21–47.

[80] Law of Property Act 1925 s.101(1). See para.21–34.

[81] *Swiss Bank Corp v Lloyds Bank* [1982] A.C. 584, 594, per Buckley L.J.

[82] *Rodick v Gandell* (1852) 1 De G.M. & G. 763; *Palmer v Carey* [1926] A.C. 703.

[83] In which case there will be no such right until the property is taken legally into possession by the chargor: *Holroyd v Marshall* (1862) 10 H.L. Cas. 191; *National Provincial Bank v Charnley* [1924] 1 K.B. 431.

[84] [1987] Ch. 150, 176.

[85] [1924] 1 K.B. 431.

[86] [1924] 1 K.B. 431 at p.449.

Thus a charge grants a contingent right as opposed to an immediate proprietary right. Instead, specific property is "appropriated" for the purposes of securing payment of a debt.

The statutory power of sale over charges created by way of deed

The power of sale under s.101 LPA 1925 applies to charges and liens because s.103 LPA 1925 extends the definition of the term "mortgage"[87] so that it "includes any charge or lien on any property for securing money or money's worth".[88] The right to sell under s.101 is contingent on the charge having been created by way of a deed.[89] A deed under s.1 of the Law of Property (Miscellaneous Provisions) Act 1989 is a document which has been signed and delivered as a deed. Under s.101 LPA 1925, provided that the charge has been created by way of a deed, the chargee has a power to sell the charged property when the mortgage money has become due. The various positions in relation to charges and liens not created by deed are considered in the next section.

22–42

The judicial power of sale in relation to charges not created by way of deed

There is a judicial power of sale in relation to charges not created by way of deed. The judicial power relates to charges falling outside the statutory power under s.101 LPA 1925. Thus a chargee has a right to apply to the court to seek a right to seize the charged property and to sell it so as to realise the amount owed to her.[90] Any surplus realised on sale will be held on constructive trust for the chargor.[91] Charges are created by agreement of the parties, whether by means of contract, settlement, will or by the appropriation of personalty for the discharge of the chargor's obligations to the chargee. There is no specific formality for the creation of a charge over personalty.[92] Rather, the court will look to the intention of the parties. By contrast, a charge by way of a contract over land or an interest in land must be contained in a single document signed by the parties containing

22–43

---

[87] In turn, a "legal mortgage" is defined to mean "a mortgage by demise or subdemise or a charge by way of legal mortgage and 'legal mortgagee' has a corresponding meaning . . .": Law of Property Act 1925, s.101(1).

[88] Law of Property Act 1925, s.101(1).

[89] Law of Property Act 1925, s.101(1).

[90] *Johnson v Shippen* (1703) 2 Ld. Ray. 982; *Stainbank v Fenning* (1851) 11 C.B. 51; *Stainbank v Shepard* (1853) 13 C.B. 418. This doctrine is also considered in the following cases: *Swiss Bank Corp v Lloyds Bank Ltd* [1982] A.C. 584 at 595; [1980] 2 All E.R. 419 at 425, CA; [1982] A.C. 584; [1981] 2 All E.R. 449, HL; *Carreras Rothmans Ltd v Freeman Mathews Treasure Ltd* [1985] Ch. 207; [1985] 1 All E.R. 155 at 169; *Re Charge Card Services Ltd* [1987] Ch. 150 at 176; [1989] Ch. 497 CA; *Re BCCI (No.8)* [1998] A.C. 214; [1997] 4 All E.R. 568, HL; *Re Cosslett Contractors Ltd* [1998] Ch. 495 at 507, per Millett L.J.

[91] cf. Law of Property Act 1925, s.103.

[92] *Cradock v Scottish Provident Institution* (1893) 69 L.T. 380, affirmed at (1894) 70 L.T. 718, CA.

all of the terms of that contract.[93] A charge over property which the chargor did not own at the time of purporting to create the charge will not be effective.[94]

22-44   What is significant about a charge taking effect only in equity is that it is specifically enforceable by virtue of the contract: it is therefore the equitable remedy of specific performance which gives rise to the right as an equitable right.[95] A floating charge is an example of an equitable charge, arising only in equity rather than at common law. The existence of such a charge may be deduced from the circumstances provided that the property to be subject to the charge, provided that it is a fixed charge, is sufficiently ascertainable.[96]

Whether or not a charge creates a "proprietary" right

22-45   Ordinarily, as considered above, a charge does not technically create a proprietary right for the chargee but rather creates a right to judicial process which will then empower the chargee to seize the charged property if an underlying debt or other obligation has not been satisfied in good time or in accordance with the terms of the appropriate contract.[97] The exception to this rule would be a charge created by way of a deed which grants the chargee a statutory power of sale under s.101(1) LPA 1925 to sell the charged property, which is an ability to realise the secured right which is not dependent upon judicial process. Nevertheless, there are two recent decisions of the House of Lords in which it has been suggested that charges in general create proprietary rights,[98] in spite of the position under the earlier case law which has distinguished between charges and other structures which create proprietary rights such as trusts and mortgages. This, of course, raises an interesting jurisprudential question as whether or not these decisions of the House of Lords should be deemed to have changed that earlier position, even though their Lordships did not explicitly discuss those earlier cases nor explicitly overrule them; or whether the decisions of the House of Lords should be considered not to be binding on this particular issue because they were per incuriam the earlier cases; or whether there Lordships should be taken to have signalled impliedly a change in the nature of what constitutes a "proprietary rights" under English law. It is suggested that a "proprietary right" which is contingent on some action being taken by a court before the rightholder is able to exercise it, is not the same as a vested proprietary right which the rightholder can exercise without any further process of law.

22-46   The study of common law legal systems is based on the identification of shifts in opinion dealing with ostensibly similar questions across different generations of

---

[93] Law of Property (Miscellaneous Provisions) Act 1989, s.2.

[94] *Re Earl of Lucan, Hardinge v Cobden* (1890) 45 Ch.D. 470. cf. *Re Brook's ST* [1939] 1 Ch. 993. However, where consideration is given for the grant of the charge, then there is authority for the charge taking effect at the time stipulated in the contract: *Wellesley v Wellesley* (1839) 4 Myl. & Cr. 561.

[95] *Walsh v Lonsdale* (1882) 21 Ch.D. 9.

[96] In *Re Nanwa Gold Mines Ltd* [1955] 1 W.L.R. 1080. cf. *Moseley v Cressey's Co* (1865) L.R. 1 Eq. 405.

[97] *Swiss Bank Corp v Lloyds Bank* [1982] A.C. 584, 594, per Buckley L.J.

[98] *In Re BCCI (No.8)* [1998] A.C. 214, 226, per Lord Hoffmann; *In Re Spectrum Plus Ltd* [2005] UKHL 41; [2005] 2 A.C. 680, at [138] and [139], per Lord Walker.

judges or by the same judges in subtly different contexts. Lord Hoffmann demonstrated a robust attitude to such technical niceties when he held that:

> "the law is fashioned to suit the practicalities of life and legal concepts like 'proprietary interest' and 'charge' are no more than labels given to clusters of related and self-consistent rules of law."[99]

It was recognised by Lord Hoffmann in *Re BCCI (No.8)*[100] that, while a charge may be described as creating a proprietary right, nevertheless a "charge is a security interest created without any transfer of title or possession to the beneficiary".[101] Thus, any proprietary right is not achieved by means of a transfer of title (by which it is assumed his Lordship meant a transfer of outright title, as opposed merely to a transfer of an equitable interest) nor by means of a transfer of possession. Nevertheless, it is suggested that it is only in relation to a fixed charge that there could be said to be such a proprietary right. Thus Lord Scott has held that:

> "the essential characteristic of a floating charge, the characteristic that distinguishes it from a fixed charge, is that the asset subject to the charge is not finally appropriated as a security for the payment of the debt until the occurrence of some future event."[102]

Thus, in relation to a floating charge, there is no appropriation of any property subject to the charge until the event happens which is defined in the terms of the charge as crystallising that right. Consequently, it is suggested, there cannot be a right in any identified property before crystallisation occurs under a floating charge. By contrast, in relation to a fixed charge, there must necessarily be some property which is segregated or separately identified so that it can be subjected to a valid fixed charge: consequently, it might be possible to think of this fixed charge as creating a right in property. However, even in relation to a fixed charge the property right is contingent on the underlying debt not being paid and an application being made to seize the charged property: therefore, if the chargee's right under a charge is a proprietary right, it is not a proprietary right equivalent to the rights of a beneficiary under a bare trust (which comes into existence at the time of the creation of the trust[103]). As Lord Walker has expressed the operation of a fixed charge:

> "Under a fixed charge the assets charged as security are permanently appropriated to the payment of the sum charged, in such a way as to give the chargee a proprietary interest in the assets."[104]

Thus, the chargee is considered to have rights permanently appropriated so as to be subjected to the charge. The element, it is suggested, which is missing from this definition is the contingent nature of even a fixed charge: there is no right, unless something to the contrary is made clear in the terms of the charge, to seize

---

[99] *In Re BCCI (No.8)* [1998] A.C. 214, 227, per Lord Hoffmann.
[100] [1998] A.C. 214, 226, per Lord Hoffmann.
[101] [1998] A.C. 214, 226.
[102] *In Re Spectrum Plus Ltd* [2005] UKHL 41; [2005] 2 A.C. 680, at [111], per Lord Scott.
[103] *Saunders v Vautier* (1841) 4 Beav 115.
[104] *In Re Spectrum Plus Ltd* [2005] UKHL 41; [2005] 2 A.C. 680, at [138], per Lord Walker.

the charged property unless and until there has been some default under the payment obligation under the charge. By contrast, in relation specifically to mortgages, the mortgagee has a right of possession at common law "even before the ink is dry on the contract".[105] However, under a fixed charge, the chargor should be considered to be bound by the obligation not to re-hypothecate the property.

F. Fixed charges

The nature of a fixed charge

22–47   The purpose of a fixed charge is to secure a right for the secured party (the "chargee") to be paid an amount of money, such that if the money is not paid then the chargee can apply to the court for permission for a sale of the charged property. A fixed charge takes effect over identified property and is fixed and thus limited to that identified property. A fixed charge grants contingent quasi-proprietary rights to the rightholder, in the manner considered immediately above, entitling the rightholder to take full proprietary rights over the charged property once the contingency has been satisfied, the contingency being that the chargor must have defaulted in some obligation specified in the terms of the charge.[106] The essential nature of a charge has been expressed in the following terms:

> "... any contract which, by way of security for the payment of a debt, confers an interest in property defeasible or destructible upon payment of such debt, or appropriates such property for the discharge of the debt, must necessarily be regarded as creating a mortgage or charge, as the case may be. The existence of the equity of redemption is quite inconsistent with the existence of a bare trustee-beneficiary relationship."[107]

Thus the distinction between a fixed charge and, for example, a trust is that the interests of a beneficiary under a trust are not capable of being expunged simply by payment of a debt, whereas that is precisely the nature of the property rights under a mortgage or charge. The equity of redemption is precisely that expression of the need for a mortgage or charge to be valid that the chargor be able to extinguish those property rights in the chargee by discharge of the debt.[108]

Certainty of subject matter

22–48   In relation to a fixed charge, it is necessary that the charged property is sufficiently identifiable.[109] Therefore, the reader is referred to the discussion of

---

[105] *Four Maids Ltd v Dudley Marshall Ltd* [1957] Ch. 317; *Western Bank v Schindler* [1977] Ch. 1; *National Westminster Bank v Skelton* [1993] 1 All E.R. 242.

[106] A fixed charge may also be over future property, for example future book debts: *Siebe Gorman & Co Ltd v Barclays Bank Ltd* [1979] 2 Lloyd's Rep. 142.

[107] *Re Bond Worth* [1980] 1 Ch. 228, 248, per Slade J. See also *Re George Inglefield Ltd* [1933] Ch. 1.

[108] See, e.g. *Reeve v Lisle* [1902] A.C. 461; *Samuel v Jarrah Timber Corp* [1904] A.C. 323.

[109] *Illingworth v Houldsworth* [1904] A.C. 355, 358, per Lord Macnaghten.

certainty of subject matter (in relation to trusts) in Chapter 21.[110] Without such certainty as to the identity of the subject matter of the charge, that charge cannot be valid as a fixed charge, unless its proper analysis is as a floating charge, as considered below.

The remedies of the chargee

The remedies of a chargee are sale and the appointment of a receiver. An equitable chargee will not be entitled to foreclosure[111] nor to possession[112]: these two remedies arise only in relation to mortgages.[113]

22–49

G.   Floating charges

The operation of a floating charge

A floating charge comes into existence by virtue of some contractual provision which grants the chargee rights of a given value over a fund of property which is greater in size than that right or which contains property the identity of which may change from time-to-time.[114] A floating charge "crystallises" at the time identified in the terms of the charge itself. Crystallisation is the moment in time at which the chargee's rights change from being contingent rights over a fluctuating fund of property into rights of a contractually identified value over identified property. Crystallisation, then, is, the point in time at which the secured party is entitled to take possession of a part of the charged property. By contrast with a fixed charge, in which the rights attach to identified property, a floating charge has a defined value which takes effect over a range of property but not over any specific property until the point in time at which it crystallises.[115] A floating charge is different from a fixed charge in that the chargor is entitled to deal with the property over which the charge floats—that is, by selling it, using it, replacing it with assets of like kind—without needing the permission of the chargee, unlike a fixed charge which restrains the chargor from dealing with the charged property without accounting to the chargee.[116]

22–50

An illustration of a floating charge structure would be as follows, based on the facts of the case of *Clough Mill v Martin* [117] A supplier of yarn had entered into a contract with a clothes manufacturer under which the supplier was granted proprietary rights in any unused yarn and, significantly, in any clothes made with that yarn until it received payment from the clothes manufacturer. It was held by

22–51

---

[110] See para.21–08.
[111] *Tennant v Trenchard* (1869) 4 Ch. App. 537; *Re Lloyd* [1903] 1 Ch. 385 at 404, CA.
[112] *Garfitt v Allen* (1887) 37 Ch.D. 48, 50.
[113] See para.21–30.
[114] Such as a stock of goods held in a warehouse by a manufacturer where some of those goods will be shipped out and other goods added to the fund from time-to-time.
[115] *Re Yorkshire Woolcombers Association* [1903] 2 Ch. 284; *Illingworth v Houldsworth* [1904] A.C. 355; *Evans v British Granite Quarries Ltd* [1910] 2 K.B. 979; *Re Bond Worth* [1980] 1 Ch. 228.
[116] *Royal Trust Bank v National Westminster Bank Plc* [1996] B.C.C. 316.
[117] [1984] 3 All E.R. 982.

the Court of Appeal that there was insufficient intention to create a trust over any particular stock of clothing. In part, the court considered the fact that the identity of the property over which the supplier's proprietary rights were to have taken effect changed from time to time and that those proprietary rights took effect over a stock of property larger than the value of the rights which the supplier was to have received. Therefore, it was held that the charge could only be a floating charge of an identified value over the clothes and yarn. It need not matter that the charge is expressed by contract to be a fixed charge if in fact the court considers that it can only be a floating charge due to the changeability of the fund of property held subject to it.[118]

The definition of a floating charge

22–52   A floating charge will usually be identified by reference to the following factors set out by Romer L.J.:

> "(1) If it is a charge on a class of assets of a company present and future; (2) if that class is one which, in the ordinary course of business of the company, would be changing from time to time; and (3) if you find that by the charge it is contemplated that, until some future step is taken by or on behalf of those interested in the charge, the company may carry on its business in the ordinary way so far as concerns the particular class of assets I am dealing with."[119]

Therefore, a floating charge enables the owner of that property to continue to use it as though unencumbered by any other rights.[120] The only difficulty then arises as to how to deal with the property once the chargee seeks to enforce its rights.[121] Another formulation of the difference between a fixed and a floating charge was set out by Lord Macnaughten in the following terms:

> "A [fixed, or] specific charge ... is one that without more fastens on ascertained and definite property or property capable of being ascertained and defined; a floating charge, on the other hand, is ambulatory and shifting in its nature, hovering over and so to speak floating with the property which it is intended to effect until some event occurs or some act is done which causes it to settle and fasten on the subject of the charge within its reach and grasp."[122]

What, perhaps, that statement does not encapsulate however is the acid test for the distinction between floating and fixed charges: whether or not the chargor is

---

[118]   *Re Armagh Shoes Ltd* [1984] B.C.L.C. 405; *Re Brightlife Ltd* [1987] Ch. 200.

[119]   *Re Yorkshire Woolcombers Association Ltd* [1903] 2 Ch. 284, 295, per Romer L.J.

[120]   *In Re Spectrum Plus Ltd* [2005] UKHL 41; [2005] 2 A.C. 680, at [111], per Lord Scott.

[121]   In this sense there is a narrow line in many cases between a floating charge and either a fixed charge or a trust. For example, a provision which purported to create a trust over "the remaining part of what is left" from a fund would not be sufficiently certain to create a trust nor a fixed charge because the identity of the precise property at issue could not be known: *Sprange v Bernard* (1789) 2 Bro. C.C. 585. The alternative analysis of such provisions is then that they create a mere floating charge such that the person seeking to enforce the arrangement would acquire only a right of a given value which related to a general pool of property without that right attaching to any particular part of it. Such a structure would be weaker than a proprietary trust right in the event of an insolvency because the rightholder could not identify any particular property to which the right attached: *Re Goldcorp* [1995] 1 A.C. 74.

[122]   *Illingworth v Houldsworth* [1904] A.C. 355, 358, per Lord Macnaghten.

entitled to deal with the property as though the charge did not exist, something which is a feature of a floating but not a fixed charge.

The form of right constituted by a floating charge

That the rights of the chargee do not bite until the charge itself has crystallised creates a complex form of right.[123] The right is necessarily contingent on the chargor committing some default under the terms of the contract giving rise to the charge. The chargor is able to dispose of the property in the fund and deal with it in the ordinary course of events.[124] Once that default has been committed, it is said that the charge will crystallise at that time but, simply as a matter of logic, it is not always clear even then over which property this charge bites. Suppose that there is more property in the fund than is necessary to discharge the value specified in the contract giving rise to the charge: in that case it cannot be the case that the chargee can acquire property rights in that surplus. Similarly, in the event that there is less than the amount required to discharge the charge in the fund and, perhaps, if there were more than one such claim against the fund, it could not be said that the chargee necessarily has property rights in the fund which could necessary take priority in an insolvency. However, the floating charge would give rise to some rights in the holders of those rights against that general fund.[125]

22–53

H. The registration of charges

The requirement of the registration of a book debt as a charge

Certain types of charge created in relation to companies require registration to be effective. The importance of identifying an agreement as being or not being a book debt is that such a charge may require registration under s.860 and s.861 of the Companies Act 2006 ("CA 2006").[126] Section 860(1) provides that:

22–54

> "(1)   A company that creates a charge to which this section applies must deliver the prescribed particulars of the charge, together with the instrument (if any) by which the charge is created or evidenced, to the registrar for registration before the end of the period allowed for registration."

If a company fails to comply with s.860(1) then an offence is committed by the company and by every officer of the company who is in default.[127] The charge may be registered by "any person interested in it".[128] The types of charge which require registration are defined in s.860(7) in the following manner:

---

[123] *Re Woodroffes (Musical Instruments) Ltd* [1986] Ch. 366.

[124] *Wallace v Evershed* [1899] 1 Ch. 891.

[125] *Cretanor Maritime Co Ltd v Irish Marine Management Ltd* [1978] 1 W.L.R. 966.

[126] It was said by Lord Sainsbury during the Parliamentary debates on what would become the Companies Act 2006 that the new provisions in ss.860 and 861 of that Act were intended to re-enact the old ss.395 and 396 of the Companies Act 1985 (now repealed) albeit in different words but without effecting the underlying purpose of those old provisions: *Hansard*, HL Vol.686, col. 480 (November 2, 2006).

[127] Companies Act 2006, s.860(4).

[128] Companies Act 2006, s.860(2).

"This section applies to the following charges . . .
- (a) a charge on land or any interest in land . . .,
- (b) a charge created or evidenced by an instrument which, if executed by an individual, would require registration as a bill of sale,
- (c) a charge for the purpose of securing any issue of debentures,
- (d) a charge on uncalled share capital of the company,
- (e) a charge on calls made but not paid,
- (f) a charge on the book debts of the company,
- (g) a floating charge on the company's undertaking or property . . ."

It is further defined in s.861(5) that the term "'charge' includes mortgage.

I. Charges over book debts

The nature of a book debt as a security

22–55   One particular, recurring problem with taking charges in the context of financial transactions is that of taking charges over book debts. A "book debt" is simply a debt which is held on one party's books. So, if, for example, a bank holds an account in favour of a customer, is it possible for that bank to take a charge over that account? (There is even a question as to whether or not bank accounts constitute book debts for this purpose.[129]) There have been two particular issues in the decided cases concerning this form of arrangement. The first issue is how a charge can be taken over a debt, in particular a debt which may only be paid in the future.[130] The second issue is this: if a bank holds an account for its customer, which is therefore a debt owed by the bank to its customer while that account is in credit, can that bank take a charge over that account even though the account is in itself a debt which it owes to its customer? A "book debt" need not refer only to bank accounts—although that is the clearest example in relation to financial transactions—but rather can refer to any debt accrued in the course of a business and owed to the proprietor of that business.[131]

Registration of book debts

22–56   The importance of identifying an agreement as being or not being a book debt is that such a charge may require registration under s.860 and s.861 of the Companies Act 2006 ("CA 2006"). A "charge on the book debts of the company" is a registrable charge under s.860(7)(f) of the CA 2006. It has been held that a "customer's balance with a bank is not within the expression 'all book debts and other debts'",[132] although the authorities which have advanced this proposition

---

[129] *In Re BCCI (No.8)* [1998] A.C. 214, 227, per Lord Hoffmann.
[130] As has been recognised since the decision of the House of Lords in *Tailby v Official Receiver* (1888) 13 App. Cas. 523.
[131] *Shipley v Marshall* (1863) 14 C.B.N.S 566; *Independent Automatic Sales Ltd v Knowles and Foster* [1962] 1 W.L.R. 974. cf. McCormack [1989] L.M.C.L.Q. 198; McCormack, *Reservation of Title*, 2nd edn (Sweet & Maxwell, 1995), p.105 et seq. This question is considered at the end of this chapter in relation to set-off and netting, specifically in relation to set-off on insolvency; whereas this section considers the possibility of a charge over such book debts in general terms.
[132] *In Re Brightlife Ltd* [1987] Ch. 200; *Northern Bank Ltd v Ross* [1990] B.C.C. 883.

have been doubted in general terms.[133] Lord Hoffmann in *Re BCCI (No 8)*[134] refused to rule definitively on the question whether or not an ordinary bank deposit constituted a "book debt" of that bank, but he did not disapprove (and perhaps could be read as having approved) the judgment in *Northern Bank v Ross*[135] to the effect that "in the case of deposits with banks, an obligation to register [under s.860] is unlikely to arise".

The particular problem of future book debts

A further issue arises in relation to taking security over book debts which are not yet payable: known as, "future book debts". As a consequence, the possibility arises that a registrable charge may be created over future book debts; that is, some obligation which has not yet become payable.[136] This type of asset include debts which remain uncollected but which are recorded as assets on the company's books. For example, in a bank's accounts, a mortgage which is owed to the bank and which has twenty years left to run would be recorded in the bank's accounts as an asset which is expected to pay interest for another twenty years and to repay the capital of the loan by the end of the twenty year period. The question is how to deal with such a future debt for the purposes of taking security. Clearly, from a credit risk perspective, a debt owing £x over the next 20 years is less attractive than £x in cash today because there might be a default over the remaining twenty year term and because the bank would have the use of the money in the meantime. Nevertheless, that future debt does have some value today.

22–57

A number of questions arise in relation to such future debts. The first question is whether or not charges over such uncollected debts are registrable under s.860 of the Companies Act 2006; the further question is whether or not such charges should grant priority rights in an insolvency. These issues have arisen on the decided cases. The core issue has been whether or not the charge is a fixed or a floating charge.[137] A charge over book debts is usually analysed as a floating charge because the chargor is normally entitled to use the money or other assets in that account, with the result that the chargee can only be said to have a charge over a floating pool of property held in that account, such that there is only a floating charge over that account. In relation to a package of receivables or other debts, the identity of the property held subject to the charge is capable of change and thus the charge would be a floating charge. Consequently, many commercial parties have sought to dress up a floating charge over book debts as a fixed charge in the hope of attracting the priority a fixed charge accords to the chargee in an insolvency. However, the chargor will typically want to retain the ability to use the money held in that account. Therefore, to attempt to achieve this effect,

22–58

---

[133] See *In Re BCCI (No.8)* [1998] A.C. 214; *In Re Spectrum Plus Ltd* [2005] UKHL 41; [2005] 2 A.C. 680.
[134] *In Re BCCI (No.8)* [1998] A.C. 214, 227.
[135] [1990] B.C.C. 883.
[136] *Tailby v Official Receiver* (1888) 13 A.C. 523; *Independent Automatic Sales Ltd v Knowles and Foster* [1962] 1 W.L.R. 974.
[137] See para.21–40.

the charge will often be structured so that the chargee has a fixed charge over the book debts but so that the chargor also has a right to use the property held in that account unencumbered by the charge. The House of Lords in *Re Spectrum Plus Ltd*[138] has doubted the feasibility of such structures, as considered below.[139] This case, and the cases which preceded it are considered below.

22–59   There had previously been a line of cases which had approved structures of this general type, including the now-overruled decision of Slade J. in *Siebe Gorman & Co Ltd v Barclays Bank*[140] and the decision in *Re Brightlife*.[141] These cases[142] created problems for banks and their customers. On the one hand, it was important for the customer that it be free to use all the money in its bank account as part of its circulating capital; but, on the other hand, it became advantageous for the banks to have some form of control over the customer's use of its bank account to retain the rights attributable to a fixed charge.[143] In consequence a new form of charge structure was created which purported to create two charges: one which imposed a fixed charge on the uncollected book debts and a floating charge over the proceeds of those debts once collected. In consequence the bank would have a proprietary right in all of the debts which remained to be collected in, but the customer would have free use of all of the cash when it had actually been collected in. This structure was held to constitute a fixed charge when it came before the Court of Appeal in *Re New Bullas Trading Ltd*.[144]

22–60   The decision in *Re New Bullas Trading Ltd* was disapproved of by the Privy Council in *Agnew v IRC ("The Brumark")*.[145] Lord Millett advocated an analytical approach whereby the court should, first, consider the rights and obligations which the parties granted each other under their agreement and then, secondly, seek to categorise the charge only after such an identification of the true

---

[138] [2005] UKHL 41; [2005] 2 A.C. 680.

[139] See para.21–55.

[140] [1979] 2 Lloyd's Rep. 142.

[141] So, in *Re Brightlife* [1987] Ch. 200 a company purported to grant a fixed charge over its present and future book debts and a floating charge over all its other assets to its bank. While the company was not entitled to factor or otherwise deal with the debts it had collected, it was entitled to pay all uncollected debts into its general bank account. It was held that, on a proper construction of the parties' agreement, this general bank account was outwith the scope of the fixed charge and therefore it was held that the debts paid into the general bank account were subject only to a floating charge.

[142] *Siebe Gorman & Co Ltd v Barclays Bank* [1979] 2 Lloyd's Rep. 142; *Hart v Barnes* [1983] 2 V.R. 517; *Re Brightlife* [1987] Ch. 200; *Supercool Refrigeration and Air Conditioning v Howerd Industries Ltd* [1994] 3 N.Z.L.R. 300. cf. *Siebe Gorman & Co Ltd v Barclays Bank Ltd* [1979] 2 Lloyd's Rep. 142; *Re Keenan Bros Ltd* [1986] B.C.L.C. 242.

[143] It is suggested that some form of *Quistclose* trust, as considered above, would have been a better method of controlling the customer's use of their account.

[144] [1994] 1 B.C.L.C. 485. Nourse L.J. held that uncollected book debts were more naturally the subject of a fixed charge because they rested immobile on the chargor's books until they were paid off, and that it was only once they were paid off that their cash proceeds were more likely to be applied to the circulating capital of the enterprise and so subject only to a floating charge. In consequence, Nourse L.J. held that it was not open to the company to argue that it was entitled to remove the proceeds from the ambit of the fixed charge simply because they were entitled to use them as part of its circulating capital on the terms of the contract with the chargee.

[145] [2001] 2 A.C. 710; [2001] 3 W.L.R. 454; [2001] UKPC 28; [2001] 2 B.C.L.C. 188, 199, per Lord Millett.

intentions of the parties.[146] Using this approach to the construction of the parties' agreement, the acid test would then be whether the assets were under the free use of the chargor such that they could be subtracted from the security offered to the chargee, or whether they were under the restrictive control of the chargee so that they could not be subtracted from the chargee's security.[147] The central question is, on analysis of the agreement, whether the chargor is entitled to free use of the proceeds for its own benefit: if so, the charge is only a floating charge. The approach of Lord Millett in *Agnew* was approved in the House of Lords in *Re Spectrum Plus Ltd*.[148]

The book debt and its proceeds capable of being subject to separate security interests

The preceding discussion still leaves open the question whether or not the cash proceeds of a book debt can be subject to a separate charge from the uncollected book debt itself. This requires some mental alchemy: that is, can the money which is expected to be received on payment of a debt be separated from the debt itself? Lord Millett held in the Privy Council in *Agnew v IRC* that the "[p]roperty and its proceeds are clearly different assets."[149] Thus, it was accepted that a book debt and the proceeds of that book debt are capable of constituting separate items of property and capable of being subjected to different charges in different ways. In this instance, one by way of a fixed charge and the other by way of a floating charge.

22–61

A "specific charge" over book debts: Re Spectrum Plus Ltd

The House of Lords in *Re Spectrum Plus Ltd*[150] considered a transaction in which the issuing company created a charge "by way of specific charge" in the form of a debenture in favour of the National Westminster Bank over the company's book debts to secure the money owed by the company to the bank. The issue arose, inter alia, whether this charge over present and future book debts was a fixed charge—as the bank contended—or whether it constituted merely a floating charge. Significantly, the company was prevented from dealing with the uncollected book debts but, once the debts had been collected, there was no control placed on the company's ability to use those debts in the terms of the debenture.

22–62

Consequently, it was held that the receipts derived from the book debts held in the company's account were free to be used by the company. Therefore, regardless of the bank's attempts to have the charge drafted so as to appear to be a fixed charge, the charge was properly to be analysed as a floating charge because the assets

22–63

---

[146] [2001] 2 B.C.L.C. 188, 201; where his lordship drew a parallel with the case of *Street v Mountford* [1985] A.C. 809 in which the courts look for the true intentions of the parties in the analysis of leases and licences before allocating any particular agreement to either category.
[147] [2001] 2 B.C.L.C. 200.
[148] [2005] 2 A.C. 680.
[149] [2001] 2 B.C.L.C. 188, 203; [2001] 2 A.C. 710; [2001] 3 W.L.R. 454; [2001] UKPC 28.
[150] [2005] 2 A.C. 680.

were not required to be held for the purposes of the charge but rather could be dealt with by its customer. This decision, quoted above on numerous occasions, approved the decision of the Privy Council in *Agnew v IRC*.[151]

7. PLEDGES

22-64   Pledges grant the pledgee ("the secured party" or creditor) a right to possession of the pledged property but not to ownership of those assets. The secured party retains possession of that property until the pledgor performs its obligations under the contract between the parties. So, if the pledgor had agreed to pay £*x*, for example, then the pledge would entitle the pledgee to retain possession of the pledged property until the debt of £*x* is paid. If the pledgor failed to perform its obligations in full, then the secured party may seek the authorisation of the court to sell the pledged property as thus offsetting the pledgor's failure to pay. A pledge can take effect either by the actual delivery of property into the possession of the secured party, with the intention of providing that property as security for some contractual obligation; or the pledge can be inferred from the circumstances in which a debtor has delivered property into its creditor's possession as disclosing such an intention to provide the possession of that property by way of security.[152]

22-65   The secured party in a pledge transaction (before the secured party seeks to enforce its security) has no ownership of the pledged property; and even though in commercial practice it is often described as having a "special property" in the pledged assets,[153] nevertheless that does not constitute ownership of proprietary rights in the pledged property.[154] The type of property which may be the subject matter of a pledge is therefore restricted to property over which possession can be transferred, such as chattels and documents evidencing title over property (such as bills of lading or bearer securities). The detail of the manner in which pledges are created at common law has been described in the following way:

> "At common law a pledge could not be created except by a delivery of possession of the thing pledged, either actual or constructive. It involved a bailment. If the pledgor had the actual goods in his physical possession, he could effect the pledge by physical delivery; in other cases he could give possession by some symbolic act, such as handing over the key of the store in which they were. If, however, the goods were in the custody of a third person, who held for the bailor so that in law his possession was that of the bailor, the pledge could be effected by a change of the possession of the third party, that is by an order to him from the pledgor to hold for the pledgee, the charge being perfected by the third party attorning to the pledgee,[155] that is acknowledging that he thereupon held for him; there was thus a change of possession

---

[151] [2001] 2 A.C. 710.

[152] *Official Assignee of Madras v Mercantile Bank of India Ltd* [1935] A.C. 53 at 58.

[153] See, e.g. *Matthew v TM Sutton Ltd* [1994] 4 All E.R. 793.

[154] One significant distinction on the authorities between a pledge, in the form of a pawn arrangement, and a mortgage in this context is that if the arrangement grants the secured party an immediate right to take ownership of the secured property then that would constitute a mortgage, whereas if the parties' contract merely suggested that the secured party would have certain rights and powers in the future after the happening of some contingency then that would be merely a pledge: *Mills v Charlesworth* (1890) 25 Q.B.D. 421, per Lord Esher.

[155] That is, by way of attornment the person in possession of the pledged property can acknowledge that henceforth it holds that property to the order of another person, with the pledgee's concurrence.

and a constructive delivery; the goods in the hands of the third party became by this process in the possession constructively of the pledgee."[156]

Therefore, a pledge can take effect by means of constructive delivery of possession or by means of attornment.[157] Alternatively, a "trust receipt" can be given in circumstances in which the pledgee permits the pledgor to sell the pledged assets subject to the pledge obligations so that the pledgor acts as the pledgee's agent in effecting that sale.[158] The pledgor then becomes trustee of the sale proceeds for the pledgee.[159]

The precise rights of the secured party in a pledge transaction will turn on the manner in which they are expressed in the pledge agreement. A pledge agreement may provide,[160] quite simply, that the secured party is entitled to absolute title in the pledged assets in the event of non-performance by its counterparty, thus establishing a different case to that set out immediately above. Significantly, such an arrangement may not be a pledge as ordinarily so-called because in this example the secured party would acquire an absolute interest in the property as opposed to merely a right of possession of that property. An ordinary pledge usually only grants possession of the property, prior to a court order entitling the pledgee to take absolute title in satisfaction of the debt. More commonly, a contract would provide that the secured party is entitled to take absolute title in the pledged assets only up to the value of any amount owed to it by its counterparty. Within this second analysis, the pledge contract might provide that the pledgee takes no proprietary title until some default of the pledgor identified in the agreement, and has merely a possessory interest until that time. As witness to this analysis it was held in *The Odessa*[161]:

22–66

> "If the pledgee sells he does so by virtue of and to the extent of the pledgor's ownership, and not with a new title of his own. He must appropriate the proceeds of the sale to the payment of the pledgor's debt, for the money resulting from the sale is the pledgor's money to be so applied."

It is suggested that that analysis must necessarily be contingent on the precise terms of the pledge agreement and the form of rights which they purport to grant to the secured party.[162]

There are then two options: either the secured party is entitled to take title in the assets themselves or is entitled only to sell the assets and take such proportion of those sale proceeds as is required to offset the counterparty's outstanding obligations. In deciding which is applicable, recourse must be had to the precise terms of the pledge agreement.

22–67

---

[156] *Official Assignee of Madras v Mercantile Bank of India Ltd* [1935] A.C. 53 at 58.

[157] That is, the person in possession of the pledged property can acknowledge that henceforth it holds that property to the order of another person, with the pledgee's concurrence.

[158] *North Western Bank Ltd v Poynter* [1895] A.C. 56; *Re David Allester Ltd* [1922] 2 Ch. 211.

[159] *Re David Allester Ltd* [1922] 2 Ch. 211.

[160] This is the way in which so-called "pledges" in many derivatives documents are structured.

[161] [1916] 1 A.C. 145, 159.

[162] See generally N. Palmer and A. Hudson, "Pledge", in Palmer and McKendrick (eds), *Interests in Goods*, 2nd edn (London: Lloyd's of London Press, 1998).

8. LIENS

22–68   Liens typically arise by operation of law without the need for the consent of both parties—with the exception of contractual liens—and entitle the rightholder to retain property in her possession until a payment to which she is entitled from the owner of the property is made to her. A lien therefore secures payment without necessarily transferring title initially, although the rightholder may be entitled to sell the property to generate funds to make the payment owed to it. A common law lien is predicated on possession of the property at issue and constitutes a right to detain that property until payment, whereas an equitable lien confers a right to apply to the court for sale and arises irrespective of possession, as considered below. Diplock L.J. described the common law lien as a "primitive remedy" of a "self-help" variety whereby the claimant has a right exercisable over goods already in his possession and operates as a defence to the other party's claim for recovery of those goods.[163] It is said to be primitive in the sense that it reeks of brute force and the common sense notion that if you owe me x and I have property of yours in my possession equal to the value of x, then I should simply keep your property unless you make payment of x to me.

A.   Possessory lien

General lien

22–69   The possessory lien falls into two types. The *general lien* enables someone who is already in possession of property to retain that property as security for payment of some obligation owed to it. There are particular contexts in which the common law has accepted that such general liens will arise: in relation to solicitors,[164] bankers,[165] stockbrokers[166] and factors[167] due to a market practice which accepts that such professionals are entitled to retain goods lodged with them by their customers to ensure payment of their fees.[168] That possession may either be a legal possession of that property or simply possession of property as a matter of fact. Importantly the lien is a right only to detain property pending satisfaction of an obligation and not a right to sell it.[169] If the rightholder wishes to sell the property to recover amounts owed to it by the counterparty, then she must apply to the court for permission to effect such a sale.[170]

---

[163] *Tappenden v Artus* [1964] 2 Q.B. 185.
[164] *Barratt v Gough-Thomas* [1951] Ch. 242.
[165] *Brandao v Barnett* (1846) 12 Cl & Fin. 787.
[166] *Re London and Globe Finance Corp* [1902] 2 Ch. 416.
[167] *Kruger v Wilcox* (1755) Amb. 252.
[168] *Plaice v Allcock* (1866) 4 F. & F. 1074.
[169] *Hammonds v Burclay* (1802) 2 Ea. 227.
[170] *Larner v Fawcett* [1950] 2 All E.R. 727.

Particular lien

Under a general lien, there need not necessarily be any link between the property detained and the account on which the obligation to make payment arises. This is to be distinguished from a *particular lien* which entitles the rightholder to detain property to secure payment in relation to specific services tendered in connection with that property.

22–70

A particular lien, like a general lien, arises at common law by operation of law. In relation to a particular lien it is typically the case that the lien will only arise if the rightholder was required to improve or to maintain the property in some way beyond simply acting as bailee of it by way of simply holding it for safekeeping.[171] Holding property for safekeeping might be considered to be a trust.[172] The distinction between a bailment and a trust is that in the former the custodian would merely take possession of the property without any acquisition of property rights; whereas in the latter a trustee is vested with the legal title in the property,[173] a trustee holds the equitable interest in that property for the beneficiaries of the trust,[174] and a trustee is also encumbered with the fiduciary obligations which are ordinarily associated with trusteeship.[175]

22–71

It has been suggested by some commentators that a common law lien is similar to a pledge in that it is a right to ensure payment which bites both on the pledgor's failure to pay and on the basis that possession of goods has been lodged with the plaintiff.[176] Indeed it is also difficult in many circumstances to draw clear lines between liens and vested property rights. Nevertheless, it is suggested that the following distinction is the key: a lien does not grant any present right in property to the rightholder whether at common law or in equity until the court makes an order entitling the rightholder to sell the property at issue and refuting its obligations to return that property to its previous owner.[177]

22–72

B.   Contractual lien

A contractual lien arises by virtue of some contractual provision. Importantly, the lien arises in relation to property which is already in the secured party's possession so that the secured party is able to retain that property in discharge of an obligation owed to it by the owner of that property.[178] While the law relating to the interpretation of liens is frequently equivocal, on the balance of the authorities it does appear that such a contractual lien is not exercisable unless and until the rightholder is in possession of the property to be detained.[179]

22–73

---

[171] *Re Southern Livestock Producers Ltd* [1964] 1 W.L.R. 24.
[172] See para.21–01.
[173] See para.21–02.
[174] See para.21–02.
[175] These duties were considered above at para.21–24 et seq.; see generally G. Thomas and A. Hudson, *The Law of Trusts*.
[176] Gleeson, *Personal Property Law*, p.247.
[177] *Larner v Fawcett* [1950] 2 All E.R. 727, below.
[178] *Re Cosslett (Contractors) Ltd* [1998] Ch. 495, Millett L.J.
[179] cf. *George Barker (Transport) Ltd v Eynon* [1974] 1 W.L.R. 462.

C. Equitable lien

22–74 An equitable lien does not arise out of contract and therefore arises without the need for the common intention of the parties.[180] An equitable lien is a manifestation of a jurisdiction accepted by courts of equity to detain property by imposing an equitable charge over it.[181] That equitable charge in turn grants the chargee a right to apply to the court for an order for sale of that property by means of a writ in the Chancery Division of the High Court endorsed with a claim to be entitled to an equitable lien,[182] and otherwise in the manner considered above in relation to equitable charges.[183] Oddly, for a lien, therefore, the equitable lien does not depend upon pre-existing possession of property but rather can be best understood as being a part of the equitable jurisdiction under which the court will award an equitable lien when it is deemed appropriate to do so. Ordinarily, the courts will award equitable liens in a narrow range of well-established contexts.[184] Examples of equitable liens include an equity to secure the discharge of indebtedness,[185] the solicitor's lien on property recovered,[186] a trustee's lien in relation to her expenses,[187] and in relation to contracts for the sale of land there are the vendor's lien over the purchase money and the concomitant purchaser's lien over any deposit advanced.[188] The equitable lien is predicated on there being some obligation to pay money or to do some similar act. Equity will impose a charge in such circumstances to reflect this obligation.

22–75 There may be circumstances in which the imposition of an equitable lien will resemble the creation of a right under proprietary estoppel principles where the plaintiff has acted to her detriment in relation to the defendant's property in reliance on a representation made to her that she would thereby, for example, acquire some interest in that property.[189] However, the distinction would be that under proprietary estoppel principles the plaintiff may acquire some right in the property[190] whereas under an equitable lien the plaintiff will acquire only the rights of a chargee to apply for sale of the property, as already mentioned.

22–76 An equitable lien will be extinguished in circumstances in which the secured party has taken some other right as security for the transaction.[191] So, where a vendor of land has received part payment or taken security for the payment in

---

[180] *In Re Welsh Irish Ferries Ltd* [1986] Ch. 471.

[181] [1986] Ch. 471; *In Re Kent & Sussex Sawmills Ltd* [1947] Ch. 177.

[182] *Bowles v Rogers* (1800) 31 E.R. 957; *Re Stucley* [1906] 1 Ch. 67.

[183] See para.21–40 et seq.

[184] Not in relation to sales of goods, where a statutory lien applies: Sale of Goods Act 1979 s.41.

[185] *Re Bernstein* [1925] Ch. 12 at 17; *Re Bond Worth Ltd* [1980] Ch. 228 at 251.

[186] See *Snell's Equity*, para.42–05.

[187] Trustee Act 1925, s.30(2); *Re Beddoe* [1893] 1 Ch. 547.

[188] *Mackreth v Symmons* (1808) 15 Ves. 329 at 340, 33 E.R. 778 at 782; *Rose v Watson* (1864) 10 H.L. Cas. 672 at 684.

[189] *Re Basham* [1986] 1 W.L.R. 1498; Hudson, *Equity & Trusts*, Ch.13 "Equitable Estoppel".

[190] Although in a number of cases the plaintiff has acquired only a personal equitable right to compensate her detriment: *Baker v Baker* (1993) 25 H.L.R. 408, CA; *Sledmore v Dalby* [1996] 72 P. & C.R. 196; *Gillett v Holt* [2001] Ch. 210, CA; *Campbell v Griffin* [2001] EWCA Civ 990, [2001] W.T.L.R. 981; *Jennings v Rice* [2002] EWCA Civ 159.

[191] *Mackreth v Symmons* (1808) 15 Ves. 329.

some other way, the lien may not be available.[192] In a similar fashion to other equitable remedies, the equitable lien will be extinguished by delay and laches.[193]

9. GUARANTEES

A. The distinction between guarantees and indemnities

The formalities required for a guarantee

A guarantee is a promise made by a guarantor to a creditor to honour the performance of the obligations of some other person, the primary debtor, which are owed to that creditor. An important distinction must be made between a guarantee and an indemnity. A guarantee is a form of secondary liability in that the guarantor is only liable to make payment if the primary debtor would have been liable to make payment. In such a circumstance, the guarantor is assuming the obligation of the primary debtor where that primary debtor defaults in the performance of its obligations. By contrast, an indemnity is a promise to make good any loss which the creditor suffers under a transaction whether or not the primary debtor would have been liable to make payment in relation to that loss. In this latter instance, it is the creditor's loss which is being compensated in general terms, and not the primary debtor's failure to perform some obligation which it was at law and in equity obliged to perform. The distinction, considered below, is a matter of construction of the terms of a contract.[194]

22–77

The distinction between a guarantee and an indemnity is significant because a guarantee is required to be made in writing[195] whereas an indemnity has no such formality in its creation.[196] Further to statute,[197] "[n]o action shall be brought . . . whereby to charge the defendant upon any special promise to answer for the debt, default or miscarriage of another person" unless there is evidence of that promise in writing.[198] Therefore, the contract of guarantee may be created orally, provided that it is evidenced in writing subsequently. The type of evidence required is a signed note or memorandum although it is more usual in financial markets to include all of the terms of the guarantee in one contract signed by all of the relevant parties.

22–78

As such a guarantee will create a contract between the guarantor and the creditor, provided that it is properly structured. Where a guarantor agrees to guarantee the performance of a party to a contract by paying any shortfall in their contractual obligations, that guarantor is obliged to make payment without receiving any

22–79

---

[192] See *Parrott v Sweetland* (1835) 3 My. & K. 655.

[193] See *Snell's Equity*, para.42–05 et seq.

[194] *Yeoman Credit Ltd v Latter* [1961] 1 W.L.R. 828; *Heald v O'Connor* [1971] 1 W.L.R. 497; *General Produce Co v United Bank Ltd* [1979] 2 Lloyd's Rep. 255.

[195] Statute of Frauds 1677, s.4; *Harburg India Rubber Comb Co v Martin* [1902] 1 K.B. 778, CA; *Pitts v Jones* [2008] 2 W.L.R. 1289.

[196] *Birkmyr v Darnell* (1704) 1 Salk. 27; *Argo Caribbean Group v Lewis* [1976] 2 Lloyd's Rep. 289.

[197] See above.

[198] That is so whether the promise arises in contract or in tort: *Kirkham v Marter* (1819) 2 B. & Ald. 613.

payment or other obligation in return. In consequence, there is a risk that there would be no consideration moving between the promisee and the promisor such that guarantees are created by deed, so removing the need for consideration.[199] Where consideration is required because no deed is executed, it is common to express such consideration as taking effect by means of forbearance on the part of the creditor from suing the primary debtor in the event that the guarantor performs the primary debtor's obligations.[200]

22–80   The distinction between a guarantee and an indemnity is a narrow one despite its importance.[201] It has been suggested by some commentators that the development of a different principle at common law in relation to indemnities is, in part, an attempt to circumvent the Statute of Frauds 1677.[202] What is clearly required for a guarantee is that there be some person who is liable as primary debtor and that the guarantor is liable only if that primary debtor defaults in the performance of some obligation owed to the creditor. However, in the event that a guarantor agrees to compensate the creditor for any loss suffered by the creditor from the transaction, whether or not it was owed by the primary debtor, there will be only an indemnity. There are authorities on which the guarantor's promise to "put the creditor in funds in the event of the primary debtor's failure to perform", rather than to assume all of the obligations of the primary debtor, have been interpreted as having constituted a mere indemnity and not a guarantee because that provision indicates a mere duty to compensate the creditor's loss and not necessarily to assume enforceable liabilities which the primary debtor has repudiated.[203] Similarly, if a parent company were to agree to assume all of the liabilities of one of its subsidiaries such that the subsidiary maintained no further obligation to the creditor, then there would be no guarantee because the parent would either be taking an assignment of the transaction or it would be offering an indemnity to the creditor.[204]

22–81   Obtaining a performance bond from a third party in the event that a counterparty to an agreement fails to perform some delivery obligation may nevertheless be a guarantee where it supplements the obligation of that counterparty and does not merely compensate the creditor for general loss.[205] Such a structure has similarities to a letter of credit.[206] Furthermore, the creditor will be obliged to account for any surplus recovered from the guarantor under such a performance obligation as well as entitled to recover any shortfall in the primary debtor's obligation from the guarantor.[207]

---

[199] *Hall v Palmer* (1844) 3 Hare. 532; *Macedo v Stroud* [1922] 2 A.C. 330.

[200] *Crears v Hunter* (1887) 19 Q.B.D. 341.

[201] *Yeoman Credit Ltd v Latter* [1961] 1 W.L.R. 828.

[202] Treitel, *The Law of Contract*, 10th edn (London: Sweet & Maxwell, 1999), p.166.

[203] *Guild & Co v Conrad* [1894] 2 Q.B. 885, 892. Also see *Thomas v Cook* (1828) 8 B. & C. 728; *Wilkes v Dudlow* (1874) L.R. 19 Eq. 198; *Re Hoyle* [1893] 1 Ch. 84.

[204] *Goodman v Chase* (1818) 1 B. & Ald. 297.

[205] *Trafalgar House Construction (Regions) Ltd v General Security and Guarantee Co Ltd* [1996] A.C. 199.

[206] Smith, "Security", in Birks (ed.), *Private Law* (OUP, 2000), 455.

[207] Smith, "Security", 455; *Cargill International SA v Bangladesh Sugar and Food Industries Corp* [1998] 1 W.L.R. 461.

Guarantees forming part of a larger transaction

The foregoing formalities apply to guarantees which stand alone and not to guarantees which form part of a larger transaction. Thus, for example, the credit support documentation in financial derivatives transactions is intended to constitute one single agreement together with the master agreement, its schedule and all attendant confirmations.[208] In consequence, a guarantee executed as part of a master agreement would potentially be part of a larger transaction. In circumstances in which an intermediary introduced clients to a stockbroker on condition that the intermediary would receive half the profits or bear half the losses, as applicable, it has been held that such a guarantee to meet those losses payable by the stockbroker constituted part of a larger transaction.[209]

22–82

One further category of guarantee which does not attract the foregoing formalities requirements is a guarantee provided by a *del credere* agent, that is a guarantor who guarantees the solvency of the counterparty and nothing more.[210] It may be that a guarantee is given by a parent company that its subsidiary will not go into insolvency during the life of the master agreement. Such a guarantee would be different from a guarantee from that holding company that it would meet directly all of the obligations of the subsidiary in relation to individual transactions.

22–83

B. Enforceability of guarantee

Informal guarantee unenforceable, not void

Where the formalities in relation to the creation of a guarantee are not performed, the contract is not automatically void but rather is not capable of enforcement.[211] Therefore, where the guarantee is itself secured by some pledged or deposited asset by the guarantor, that security will not in itself be void simply because the guarantee is not enforceable.[212] It would be possible that a guarantor would be estopped from reneging on a contract for want of formality where that contract had been partly performed in reliance on, for example, an assurance that some item of property would be available to the creditor to secure its transaction.[213] A contract of guarantee may, in certain circumstances relating to obligations beyond simply payment of money but perhaps relating to the provision of an annuity, be specifically enforceable.[214]

22–84

---

[208] ISDA, *ISDA Multi-currency Master Agreement* (ISDA, 1992), s.1(c).

[209] *Sutton & Co v Grey* [1894] 1 Q.B. 285.

[210] *Couturier v Hastie* (1852) 8 Ex. 40.

[211] *Leroux v Brown* (1852) 12 C.B. 801; *Elias v George Sahely & Co (Barbados) Ltd* [1983] 1 A.C. 646, 650.

[212] *Thomas v Brown* (1876) 1 Q.B.D. 714; *Low v Fry* (1935) 152 L.T. 585.

[213] *Yaxley v Gotts* [2000] 1 All E.R. 711.

[214] *Beswick v Beswick* [1968] A.C. 58; Treitel, *The Law of Contract*, p.170, fn.12.

Other contexts in which a guarantee will be unenforceable

22–85   Under the general law of contract, a guarantee will not be enforceable if it has been procured by means of fraud,[215] misrepresentation[216] or undue influence.[217] Similarly, guarantees entered into on the basis of mistake will be unenforceable where such mistake goes to the heart of the contract.[218] When the obligations of the primary debtor are discharged, the obligations of the guarantor are similarly discharged.[219] This position may be different under an indemnity where the contract of indemnity identifies some loss outwith the obligations of the primary debtor to pay for which the party providing the indemnity is nevertheless entitled to pay.

Rescission for non-disclosure

22–86   The common law on guarantees has developed a limited obligation to make disclosure to the guarantor. Principally this obligation requires that disclosure be made in relation to any aspect of the transaction which would cause the guarantor to bear a greater obligation or risk than it would otherwise have anticipated.[220] However, this obligation will not relate simply to questions of the credit risk arising from the transaction and will relate only to the intrinsic commercial aspects of the contract.[221] In relation to complex financial contracts this is clearly an important limit on the enforceability of a guarantee where it can be shown that the guarantor had not understood all of the risks which it was guaranteeing. In many transactions the ordinary process of identifying the competence of the buyer of such a product will determine the level of information as to the risks of the transaction which will be required to remove the seller's liability for, inter alia, undue influence.[222] Failure to ensure that the risks are adequately communicated to the guarantor will entitle the guarantor to rescind the contract of guarantee.

Alteration in the nature of the guarantor's obligation

22–87   In the previous paragraph it was suggested that there is a limited duty of disclosure to the guarantor of its obligations under the contract of guarantee. One context in which changing circumstances will be important and entitle the guarantor to rescind the contract of guarantee is where the circumstances of the transaction change such that guarantor is found to bear substantially different

---

[215] *Barton v County Natwest Ltd* [1999] Lloyd's Rep. 408.
[216] *Lloyds Bank v Bundy* [1975] Q.B. 326; *Lloyds Bank v Waterhouse* [1993] 2 F.L.R. 97; *Barclay's Bank v O'Brien* [1994] 1 A.C. 180.
[217] *Barclay's Bank v O'Brien* [1994] 1 A.C. 180.
[218] [1994] 1 A.C. 180; *Associated Japanese Bank (International) Ltd v Credit du Nord SA* [1989] 1 W.L.R. 255.
[219] *Western Credit v Alberry* [1964] 1 W.L.R. 945.
[220] *Levett v Barclays Bank Plc* [1995] 1 W.L.R. 1260; *Credit Lyonnais Bank Nederland v Export Credit Guarantee Department* [1996] 1 Lloyd's Rep. 200.
[221] [1996] 1 Lloyd's Rep. 200.
[222] *Bankers Trust v Dharmala* [1996] C.L.C. 18.

liabilities from those originally undertaken in relation to the contract of guarantee as originally envisaged by it. Therefore, if the creditor and the primary debtor were to vary their contract in some material way, then there would be an entitlement in the guarantor to rescind its guarantee.[223] For example, if an amendment is made to a loan contract for which a guarantee is provided, then the guarantor will be released from its obligations if what results is a materially different guarantee obligation from the one for which the parties originally contracted.[224]

The question arises: in what circumstances will an alteration in the market on which a financial transaction is based be such that the contract of guarantee can be taken to have been rescinded on this basis? For example, if there were an unexpectedly sharp movement in interest rates, would a guarantee over an interest rate swap be unenforceable on the basis that such a movement in market rates was outwith the volatility which the parties could have expected? It is suggested that the discussion of the doctrine of frustration would apply in this circumstance whereby the parties would have to demonstrate that there was some clearly expressed understanding of the risks which would and which would not be borne by each of them in their contract. It is suggested that the courts will look to the expertise of the parties in relation to such financial instruments when deciding whether or not those parties ought to have understood that interest rate swaps are subject to movements in interest rates of whatever magnitude; where such a party is considered sufficiently expert to understand the risk, it will be considered bound to perform its contract whatever those market movements.[225]

22–88

Furthermore, the creditor will owe duties of good faith to the guarantor in relation to the realisation of any security; for example, where land has been provided by way of mortgage as part of the guarantee and that land is sold at an unreasonably low price by the mortgagee to one of its associates.[226]

22–89

C.   A "letter of comfort"

A letter of comfort is not a guarantee but it is given usually by a parent company suggesting that one of its subsidiaries is expected to be able to meet its obligations. While it gives no legal protection to the recipient of the letter, a letter of comfort is thought in financial markets to constitute a statement on which the provider of the letter is placing its reputation. The market uses letters of comfort where one or other of the parties is unwilling to provide a full guarantee. The letter of comfort is not a legally binding document but does provide some comfort to a contracting party that the company providing the letter is not distancing itself commercially from the contracting entity's financial obligations.

22–90

---

[223] *Holme v Brunskill* (1878) 3 Q.B.D. 495; and also to recover any relevant security transferred under the guarantee *Bolton v Saloman* [1891] 2 Ch. 48; *Smith v Wood* [1929] 1 Ch. 14.
[224] *Triodos Bank NV v Dobbs* [2005] EWCA Civ 630.
[225] *Bankers Trust v Dharmala* [1996] C.L.C. 18, below.
[226] *China and South Sea Bank v Tan Soon Gin* [1990] 1 A.C. 536.

10. INSOLVENCY AND INSOLVENCY SET-OFF

A. Introduction

22–91 The principal concern in commercial, financial transactions is that one's counterparty will go into insolvency. An insolvent person will not be required to make payment to a solvent contracting party. This puts the solvent party in a difficult situation. The solvent party will be unable to recover amounts which are owed to it by the insolvent person, and yet the insolvent party may be able to recover amounts which are owed to it by the solvent party depending on the system of law governing that insolvency.

22–92 The English insolvency law position is that, where there are mutual debts owed, a set-off between those mutual debts will be mandatory further to r.4.90 of the Insolvency Rules in the event of the insolvency of either of those parties, provided that the right to set-off is contained in the contract. Rule 4.90 of the Insolvency Rules 1986 provides as follows:

> "(1) This rule applies where, before the company goes into liquidation there have been mutual credits, mutual debts or other mutual dealings between the company and any creditor of the company proving or claiming to prove for a debt in the liquidation. (2) An account shall be taken of what is due from each party to the other in respect of the mutual dealings, and the sums due from one party shall be set off against the sums due from the other. (4) Only the balance (if any) of the account is provable in the liquidation, alternatively (as the case may be) the amount shall be paid to the liquidator as part of the assets."

The rule therefore requires that there must have been mutual credits,[227] mutual debts or other mutual dealings between the insolvent party and its solvent counterparty, before the company goes into liquidation.[228] If that initial requirement is satisfied the more difficult issue of valuation of the amounts owed mutually commences. These amounts must be capable of being conceived of as debts owed between the parties.[229]

22–93 That set-off will be available wherever there are mutual debts owing between parties to a contract is clear from the decisions of the House of Lords in *Stein v Blake*[230] and *Re BCCI (No.8)*.[231] The absence of such a provision entitling the parties to set off on insolvency would preclude the entitlement to act off on insolvency.[232] However, if the contract contains a set-off clause which purports to include set-off between people who are not parties to the contract or between parties between whom there are no mutual debts, then that set-off provision will not be enforceable for insolvency purposes.[233]

---

[227] *Rose v Hart* (1818) 8 Taunt. 499.

[228] *Bank of Credit and Commerce International S.A. v Prince Fahd Bin Salaman Abdul Aziz Al-Saud* [1997] B.C.C. 63.

[229] *MS Fashions Ltd v Bank of Credit and Commerce International S.A. (No.2)* [1993] Ch. 439, 446 per Dillon L.J; *Re ILG Travel Ltd* [1996] B.C.C. 21. See on this R. Goode, *"Principles of Corporate Insolvency Law"*, 2nd edn (London: Sweet & Maxwell, 1997), p.188.

[230] [1996] 1 A.C. 243.

[231] [1998] A.C. 214.

[232] *Re BCCI (No.8)* [1998] A.C. 214, per Lord Hoffmann.

[233] *British Eagle v Air France* [1975] 2 All E.R. 390.

B.   The concept of insolvency in law

When is a company insolvent?

To begin at the beginning, it is important to identify on what basis an entity will be found to be insolvent. The principal legislation governing the law on corporate insolvency is the Insolvency Act 1986 ("IA 1986") and the Enterprise Act 2002.[234] The ordinary test for whether or not an entity is insolvent is contained in s.123 of the Insolvency Act 1986 to the effect that an entity is insolvent when it is unable to meet its debts when they become due:

22–94

> "(1)   A company is deemed unable to pay its debts—
>   (a)   if a creditor (by assignment or otherwise) to whom the company is indebted in a sum exceeding £750 then due has served on the company, by leaving it at the company's registered office, a written demand (in the prescribed form) requiring the company to pay the sum so due and the company has for 3 weeks thereafter neglected to pay the sum or to secure or compound for it to the reasonable satisfaction of the creditor, or
>   (b)   if, in England and Wales, execution or other process issued on a judgment, decree or order of any court in favour of a creditor of the company is returned unsatisfied in whole or in part, or …
>   (e)   if it is proved to the satisfaction of the court that the company is unable to pay its debts as they fall due.
> (2)   A company is also deemed unable to pay its debts if it is proved to the satisfaction of the court that the value of the company's assets is less than the amount of its liabilities, taking into account its contingent and prospective liabilities."

In the Court of Appeal in *BNY Corporate Trustee Services Ltd v Eurosail-UK 2007-3BL Plc*,[235] Lord Neuberger approved the characterisation of s.123(1) as being a "cash flow test" (in which the measure of the solvency of the entity depends upon its ability to meet its obligations from cash flow) and s.123(2) as being a "balance sheet test" (in which the obligations rest on a measurement of the entity's structural assets and liabilities as valued at the time of creating the balance sheet account). This allows a balance to be struck between an entity's present and future liabilities on the one hand and its present and likely future wherewithal to meet those liabilities, as is considered next. As the market value of those assets increases, a financial institution will appear to be better able to meet it obligations, provided that those assets are sufficiently liquid to be able to sold so as to meet those obligations. (The specific context of bank insolvency under the Banking Act 2009 is considered in Chapter 29.)

Identifying whether an entity is insolvent and valuing contingent, future liabilities

The question of when a company becomes insolvent is a complex one because it depends upon a valuation of that company's likely future cash flow, not just its current worth, and also a valuation of its capital assets. The question of valuing contingent, future liabilities as part of the insolvency process is a complex one.

22–95

---

[234] The principal legislation is reinforced by the Insolvency Rules 1986 and other regulations.
[235] [2011] Bus. L.R. 1359, [2011] 1 W.L.R. 2524.

Any individual, let alone a trading organisation, will have amounts which are owed today, amounts which it is known are owed in the future, and also amounts of income which will be earned in the future. The insolvency of financial institutions is particularly complex because the assets which they own (including currencies, securities, and other financial instruments) fluctuate in value, and therefore it will be difficult to establish from time-to-time whether or not those institutions should be considered to be solvent or insolvent at today's date. By way of example, the decision of Morritt C in *BNY Ltd v Eurosail Plc*[236] concerned a collateralised debt obligation ("CDO")[237] which had been guaranteed by Lehman Bros subsidiaries and which had therefore collapsed in value due to the insolvency of Lehman Bros in September 2008. The entity which had issued the bonds under the CDO programme was simply a special purpose vehicle ("SPV") created solely for that purpose and without any other assets or business beyond the CDO. Because the transaction had been guaranteed by Lehman Bros subsidiaries, the claimants sought to have the SPV declared insolvent. The issue in this particular appeal concerned the difficult question whether or not the issuer was insolvent. Specifically it revolved around whether or not future obligations to make payment rendered that entity insolvent if at the time of taking the valuation that entity would not have been able to meet them. Of particular significance in relation to s.123 of the Insolvency Act 1986 in establishing whether or not an entity is insolvent is paragraph (d) which requires the court to take "into account [that entity's] contingent and prospective liabilities". This required a review of the authorities.

22–96 Previously, in relation to earlier legislation, Nicholls L.J. had posited an example in *Byblos Bank SAL v Al-Khudhairy*[238] of a company which had £10,000 in assets and a future obligation to repay a loan of £100,000, and had held that "when taking into account its future liabilities, such a company does not have the present capacity to pay its debts and as such it 'is' unable to pay its debts".[239] What this approach did not consider was whether or not that entity would have been able to raise the £90,000 difference in the time between the date of valuation and the date of required payment. Under different legislation again, in 1869, it had been held in *Re European Life Assurance Society*[240] that the reference a company's "debts" was expressed to be a reference to debts which were actually due at the time when the valuation was taken. So, when Briggs J. considered the Insolvency Act 1986 in *In re Cheyne Finance plc (No 2)*[241] in the context of when the debts must become due, his lordship held that he was not bound by the judgment of Nicholls L.J. because the 1986 Act relates to balance sheet liability in which the court is not limited to the entity's "present" ability to meet its obligations as had been the case in *Byblos Bank*.

---

[236] [2010] EWHC 2005 (Ch), [2010] Bus. L.R. 1731.
[237] See para 47 01.
[238] [1987] B.C.L.C. 232.
[239] [1987] B.C.L.C. 232 at 247.
[240] (1869) LR 9 Eq 122.
[241] [2008] Bus. L.R. 1562, [30] et seq.

So, similarly, in *BNY Ltd v Eurosail Plc*[242] Morritt C considered he was not **22–97** bound by the approach of Nicholls L.J. in *Byblos Bank* because that related to different legislation and that taking into account the contingent and prospective liabilities of the entity did not require his lordship simply to base his approach on a "commercially illogical" face value of those future or contingent obligations (because those values could vary over time and because the present value of an instrument differs from the value of waiting for its maturity (due to the "time value of money"[243])).[244] In consequence, on the facts it was held that because there was no obligation to bring into account the face value of the future obligations of the SPV in relation to payments under the CDO then the SPV entity was not insolvent at the material time. Whereas, if those future obligations had been brought into account at that time at their face value then the entity would have been insolvent.

The Court of Appeal in *BNY Corporate Trustee Services Ltd v Eurosail-UK* **22–98** *2007-3BL Plc*[245] approved the judgment of Morritt C. One significant point which was made in the Court of Appeal was that the purpose of s.123(2) of the 1986 Act was to deal with entities with incurable problems with future or contingent debts: this meets the point made above that an entity may be able to find sufficient funds to meet a future obligation even if it is not in funds at the time of valuing its assets and liabilities. Therefore, the question was whether or not that entity could reasonably be expected to meet its obligations.

C. Insolvency set-off

Derham has defined "set-off" as being "the setting of money cross-claims against **22–99** each other to produce a balance".[246] Common to all claims for set-off are two basic requirements.[247] First, both of the claims must be claims for money or in relation to property which the applicable party is entitled to convert into money. Secondly, the right to set-off under a contract must operate in favour of both parties and arise from mutual rights and obligations. This is referred to as a requirement of "mutuality" more generally in the operation of set-off.[248]

Insolvency set-off (sometimes referred to in market parlance as "close-out **22–100** netting") is the circumstance in which one party to a number of transactions goes into insolvency and the solvent party seeks to set off the amounts which are owed between the various parties across their contracts so that only a small, net sum is actually owed between them. Suppose Xavier Bank and Yvonne Bank entered into a series of 10 speculative financial transactions between them so that on a net

---

[242] [2010] EWHC 2005 (Ch), [2010] Bus. L.R. 1731
[243] Where the "time value money of money" refers to the mathematical, financial theory that, for example, being paid £5 immediately is worth something different from a promise to pay £5 in one year's time.
[244] [2010] EWHC 2005 (Ch), [2010] Bus. L.R. 1731, [31].
[245] [2011] Bus. L.R. 1359, [2011] 1 W.L.R. 2524.
[246] Derham, *The Law of Set-off* 4th edn (OUP, 2010), p.1.
[247] See Goode, *Principles of Corporate Insolvency Law*, 2nd edn (Sweet & Maxwell, 1997), p.174.
[248] See, e.g. Goode, *Principles of Corporate Insolvency Law*, 2nd edn (Sweet & Maxwell, 1997), p.174.

balance Yvonne owed £5 million more to Xavier than Xavier owed to Yvonne, but so that in gross Xavier owed £100 million to Yvonne and Yvonne owed £105 million to Xavier. Some codes of insolvency law prevent the insolvent Yvonne from making any payments (other than through a court-managed insolvency process) but still require Xavier to pay all that it owes to Yvonne: in such a situation, Xavier is required to pay £100 million but will not receive the £105 million that is owed to it: a total loss of £205 million. Whereas, if insolvency set-off was permitted then Xavier would be able to subtract the amounts owed to it from the amounts which it owes, with the result that it would only suffer a loss of the balance of £5 million which Yvonne owes to it. If Xavier had used any of the other security devices considered in this chapter (in particular a trust) then it might also be able to protect itself against even that loss. Therefore, the availability of set-off on insolvency is very important in financial transactions, especially between parties who conduct a large amount of business between one another and in relation to transactions like financial derivatives.

22–101 Under insolvency law in this jurisdiction, set-off is *required* to be made on insolvency further to s.323 of the Insolvency Act 1986.[249] Section 323 provides that:

> "(1) This section applies where before the commencement of the bankruptcy there have been mutual credits, mutual debts or other mutual dealings between the bankrupt and any creditor of the bankrupt proving or claiming to prove for a bankruptcy debt.
>
> (2) An account shall be taken of what is due from each party to the other in respect of the mutual dealings and the sums due from one party shall be set off against the sums due from the other.
>
> (3) Sums due from the bankrupt to another party shall not be included in the account taken under subsection (2) if that other party had notice at the time they became due that a bankruptcy petition relating to the bankrupt was pending.
>
> (4) Only the balance (if any) of the account taken under subsection (2) is provable as a bankruptcy debt or, as the case may be, to be paid to the trustee as part of the bankrupt's estate."

Thus, set-off on insolvency is mandatory and it is not possible to contract out of the set-off.[250] Significantly, under statute, only the balance is provable in the insolvency as a debt owed to the bankrupt person. It is also a requirement that the counterparty did not have notice that a bankruptcy petition was pending at the time that these rights and obligations were created: therefore, the contracts must not have been created so as to extract assets from the insolvent party in the event that the insolvency happened. Under r.2.85 of the Insolvency Rules 1986, when an administrator gives notice of an intention to make a distribution then an account shall be taken in respect of any mutual dealings. More significant for present purposes is the obligation to make such a set-off in relation to mutual dealings between the parties under r.4.90 of the Insolvency Rules.

22–102 The central purpose of the provision is set out in r.4.90(3) in the following terms:

---

[249] *Stein v Blake* [1996] A.C. 243.

[250] *National Westminster Bank Ltd v Halesowen Presswork & Assemblies Ltd* [1972] A.C. 785; *Cushla Ltd* [1979] 3 All E.R. 415, approved in *Stein v Blake* [1996] A.C. 243.

"(3)   An account shall be taken of what is due from each party to the other in respect of the mutual dealings, and the sums due from one party shall be set off against the sums due from the other."

This is the provision which sets out not only the parties' right to set off mutual debts owed between them but more to the point provides that they "shall" effect set-off. It is this principle which was indeed held in *Re BCCI (No.8)*[251] to require that a set-off must be effected in relation to transactions falling within this provision. Nevertheless, it has been a long-standing principle of insolvency law in this jurisdiction that set-off must be effected in insolvency cases.[252] Moreover, parties are not permitted to contract out of this mandatory principle that where there are mutual debts and mutual dealings then a set-off must be effected in the event that one of the parties goes into insolvency.[253] The jurisdiction for set-off on insolvency proceeds on an equitable basis so as to achieve justice between the parties,[254] hence its broad interpretation and application[255] in particular by reference to the detailed Insolvency Rules.[256]

The pre-requisite for the application of this statutory set-off is contained in r.4.90(1) of the Insolvency Rules:[257]   **22–103**

"(1)   This Rule applies where, before the company goes into liquidation there have been mutual credits, mutual debts or other mutual dealings between the company and any creditor of the company proving or claiming to prove for a debt in the liquidation."

It is therefore required that there must have been mutual credits, mutual debts or other mutual dealings between the parties.[258] It was always a requirement under the common law that there must have been mutual credits,[259] mutual debts or other mutual dealings between the insolvent party and its solvent counterparty, before the company went into liquidation.[260]

---

[251] [1997] 4 All E.R. 568, [1998] A.C. 214.

[252] *Ex p. Barnett, In re Deveze* (1874) 9 Ch. App. 293, 295, per Lord Selborne; *Mersey Steel and Iron Co Ltd v Naylor, Benzon & Co* (1884) 9 App Cas 434, 438, per Lord Selborne; *National Westminster Bank Ltd v Halesowen Presswork & Assemblies Ltd* [1972] A.C. 785, per Viscount Dilhorne, and see now *Re BCCI (No 8)*[1997] 4 All E.R. 568, [1998] A.C. 214, as considered below.

[253] *National Westminster Bank Ltd v Halesowen Presswork & Assemblies Ltd* [1972] A.C. 785 in reliance on *Ex p. Barnett, In re Deveze* (1874) 9 Ch. App. 293 and *Mersey Steel and Iron Co Ltd v Naylor, Benzon & Co*(1884) 9 App Cas 434,

[254] *Bailey v Finch* (1871) L.R. 7 Q.B. 34; *Mathieson's Trustee v Burrup, Mathieson & Co* [1927] 1 Ch. 562.

[255] *BCCI (No.8), Re* [1998] A.C. 214.

[256] See in particular r.4.90 considered below, para 13–61.

[257] This formulation of the rule was substituted by SI 2005/527, r 23.

[258] Hoffmann L.J. held in *MS Fashions Ltd v Bank of Credit and Commerce International SA (No.2)* [1993] Ch. 425, 432 that there were three principles here: the mandatory principle that a set-off must be performed so that neither party can sue in gross; the retroactivity principle to the effect that these calculations are deemed to take place at the same time as the winding up order takes effect; and the hindsight principle that valuations must estimate contingent future obligations, as discussed in the text above.

[259] *Rose v Hart* (1818) 8 Taunt. 499.

[260] *Bank of Credit and Commerce International SA v Prince Fahd Bin Salaman Abdul Aziz Al-Saud* [1997] B.C.C. 63.

22–104 It is then provided by r.4.90(8) that "only the balance (if any) of the account owed to the creditor is provable in the liquidation": that is, only the net balance owing between the parties is required to be brought into account in the insolvency. Rule 4.90(4) provides that the amounts which are brought into account are not just amounts which are actually owing at the time, but also "contingent" amounts which might be owed in the future.[261] Briggs J. held in *Lomas v JFB Firth Rixson Inc*[262] held that this is permissible because r.4.90(4)(c) provides that an amount which is "capable of being ascertained" by reference to "a matter of opinion" can be brought into account. However, this does leave an amount of uncertainty because, as has been illustrated by cases like *Peregrine Fixed Income Ltd v Robinson Department Store Plc*,[263] the courts may not necessarily accept the parties' valuation methodologies even if they are included in their contract if it is considered that that methodology is not "commercially reasonable".[264]

Principles of insolvency law which might obviate a contract

22–105 Insolvency law is astute to prevent arrangements which seek unconscionably to reduce the assets which would be available for distribution in an insolvency by creating contractual provisions which purport to entitle solvent counterparties to take assets from, or to reduce their obligations to, the insolvent person. Two particularly significant principles in this regard are the pari passu principle and the anti-deprivation principle. They have arisen in high profile finance law cases because parties to financial transactions commonly include terms in their contracts which purport to reduce their obligations to an insolvent counterparty by means of a set-off or by entitling them to seize identified forms of asset. The question is then whether such a recalculation of the amounts owed between the parties contravenes these principles. Those principles are considered here.

The pari passu principle

22–106 The pari passu principle requires that all unsecured creditors are treated in the same manner such that no unsecured creditor is given an unfair advantage over any other unsecured creditor. English courts have refused to give effect to arrangements which would contravene the pari passu principle, including situations in which the parties had sought to provide for a set-off arrangement in their contract so as to elevate a person who would otherwise have been an unsecured creditor to the status of a secured creditor.[265] In consequence,

---

[261] *Charge Card Services Ltd, Re* [1987] Ch. 150. See also *Secretary of State for Trade and Industry v Frid* [2002] EWHC 3192, [2003] 2 B.C.L.C. 284.

[262] [2011] 2 B.C.L.C. 120.

[263] [2000] Lloyd's Rep Bank 304.

[264] This idea is somewhat ironic if it involves the court replacing commercial parties' actual contractual agreement with its own view of what should have been in that contract. In that case the parties' standard market documentation had included the loss of a hedge in the calculation of a loss, but the inclusion of this amount in the parties' calculations was refused by the court. Therefore, an area of uncertainty here (unless the parties include their calculation methodology in their contract) is as to the matters which the courts will permit to be included for these purposes.

[265] *British Eagle International Airlines Ltd v Cie Nationale Air France* [1975] 1 WLR 758.

unsecured creditors are usually eager to contest the validity of the property rights of the secured creditors, and the pari passu principle will distribute any assets pro rata among the unsecured creditors if their actions contesting the secured creditors' property rights are successful.

The anti-deprivation principle

The "anti-deprivation" principle provides that it is unlawful to seek to withdraw an asset from the estate of an insolvent person: for example, by taking an asset away to give to a particular unsecured creditor after in the insolvency. The rationale which is given in the cases is that such a withdrawal would be a "fraud on the bankruptcy laws".[266] This is a case law principle which the Supreme Court has recognised underpins insolvency law, and even the context in which the modern legislation was enacted.[267]

22–107

The decision of the Supreme Court in *Belmont Park Investments Pty Ltd v BNY Corporate Trustee Services Ltd*[268] is the leading authority on the nature of the anti-deprivation principle. The Supreme Court considered a form of collateralised security including a credit default swap[269] issued by a subsidiary of Lehman Brothers ("LBSF") in the wake of the collapse of the investment bank in September 2008. Lehman Brothers sought protection under Chapter 11 of the United States Bankruptcy Code, which constituted an Event of Default under the ISDA Master Agreement in place between the parties. Among the documents, and typical for a CDO,[270] were an ISDA Master Agreement, trust deeds relating to the powers and obligations of the trustee in the management of the issuer's duties, and documentation governing the rights of investors who acquired the "notes"

22–108

---

[266] *Higinbotham v Holme* (1812) 19 Ves Jun 88, 92.

[267] *Belmont Park Investments Pty Ltd v BNY Corporate Trustee Services Ltd* [2011] UKSC 38, [2011] 3 WLR 521.

[268] [2011] UKSC 38, [2011] 3 WLR 519. On appeal from *Perpetual Trustee Co Ltd v BNY Corporate Trustee Services Ltd* [2009] EWHC 1912 (Ch), [2009] 2 BCLC 400, Morritt C, and then from *Perpetual Trustee Co Ltd v BNY Corporate Trustee Services Ltd* [2009] EWCA Civ 1160, [2010] Ch 347, [2010] Bus LR 632.

[269] As Morritt C described the product at first instance, [2009] EWHC 1912 (Ch), [1]: "For the purpose of the issues before me the essential elements of the Dante Programme were: (1) the issue of notes to investors by a special purpose vehicle (the issuer) formed by a Lehman company in a tax-friendly jurisdiction; (2) the purchase by the issuer with the subscription money paid for the notes of government bonds or other secure investments (the collateral) vested in a trust corporation; (3) a swap agreement entered into by a Lehman company and the issuer under which the Lehman company paid the issuer the amounts due by the issuer to the noteholders in exchange for sums equal to the yield on the collateral; (4) the amount by which the sum payable under the swap agreement by the Lehman company exceeded the yield on the collateral represented the premium for the, in effect, credit insurance provided by the noteholders; (5) the amount payable by the Lehman company to the issuer on the maturity of the notes (or on early redemption or termination) was the initial principal amount subscribed by the investors less amounts calculated by reference to events defined as credit events occurring during a specified period by reference to one or more reference entities, thereby giving effect to the effective insurance aspect of the programme; (6) the collateral was charged by the issuer in favour of the trust corporation to secure its obligations to the noteholders and the Lehman company on terms which changed their respective priorities on the occurrence of certain specified events, including the insolvency of the Lehman company; (7) each of the transactions summarised above (except the purchase of the collateral) is governed by English law."

[270] See Ch.43 for a discussion of these derivatives products.

issued by the issuer (referred to here as "noteholders").[271] Naturally, after these insolvency proceedings began, no payments were made to the noteholders under the collateralised security. Consequently, the trustee triggered the termination procedure over the security and some of the noteholders sought to rely on a provision in the documentation which purported to give them a preferential right to the insolvent company's assets by virtue of clause 5.5 of the supplemental trust deed which directed the trustee as to the order in which it should distribute the scheme's assets in the event of a default. Here, there had been an event of default under the ISDA Master Agreement, inter alia, when the Lehman Brothers group of companies went into insolvency such that there was a failure of credit support under that agreement, and therefore the trustee was obliged by clause 5.5 of the trust deed to observe the noteholder priority provisions. What was difficult here was that the priorities to the assets in question "flipped" in favour of the noteholders on the happening of such an event of default: therefore, the noteholders became entitled to these assets before other creditors in the event of insolvency. The creditors who were disadvantaged by this provision argued that its effect was to withdraw assets from Lehman Brothers' estate contrary to the anti-deprivation principle.[272]

22–109   It was held by the Supreme Court that the insolvency legislation must be read in the context of pre-existing anti-deprivation and pari passu principles which were taken to constitute a bedrock of principle on which the insolvency legislation had been built. In that sense, the anti-deprivation and pari passu principles were to be considered as mandatory principles of law. However, on these facts, it was held that this documentation was not contrary to either of those principles because the documentation had been created in good faith and with no specific intention to avoid the insolvency legislation. It was important that the master agreement which contained these "flip" provisions had not been drafted in the expectation that the counterparty was about to go into insolvency or in the shadow of a looming insolvency, but rather that the parties had included those provisions as part of their ordinary contracting process far ahead of the insolvency.[273]

22–110   It was held by the Supreme Court, in particular in the judgment of Lord Collins, that the standard market agreement for derivatives transactions had been created in a commercially reasonable manner which, significantly, was not intended to elude the insolvency legislation.[274] Moreover, the court was to apply the substance and not the form of the parties' contract, and to interpret their

---

[271] All of these documents used in derivatives transactions are considered in detail in Ch.44.

[272] Goode, '*Perpetual Trustee* and Flip clauses in Swap Transactions' (2011) 127 L.Q.R. 1, 34.

[273] There are two objections to this outcome in principle, as explored in the text to follow. First, the flip clause was created in case there would be an insolvency at some point in the future—that the precise circumstances were not known at the time of drafting the clause does not mean that the clause was not drafted so as to avoid any insolvency should it ever arise. Second, the effect of the flip clause was to change the identity of the person who was entitled to the assets in question on the happening of the insolvency (from all the unsecured creditors to one, newly secured creditor) and therefore was in breach of the principle that assets should not be taken from an insolvent person's estate on the happening of their insolvency. It is suggested that the Supreme Court was concerned to reach an outcome which upheld the validity of these sorts of provisions in the derivatives markets while the effects of the most serious financial crisis in living memory worked its way through the system.

[274] This documentation is discussed in detail in Ch.41.

agreement in a commercially sensitive manner. What is less clear is the precise type of situation which will be taken to constitute "bad faith" in such circumstances. Presumably, a contract entered into the day before the insolvency with such a provision in it would run the risk of being found to be in bad faith, but it is unclear how much earlier than that would be acceptable. Here the parties had no idea that LBSF would go into insolvency when they entered into their contract; but what if it was only their carelessness which led them to miss the evident fact that Lehman Brothers would go into insolvency in time?

D. Multiparty set-off, clearing houses and the pari passu principle

The problem with multiparty set-off

There is a more complex situation in which the pari passu principle is an issue: **22–111** that is the situation in which there are more than two parties to a contract who are seeking to assert set-off between them all. When one of the parties to such a multiparty arrangement goes into insolvency, how will the set-off still function normally under insolvency law? Of particular importance in this regard are clearing house arrangements (such as those which are to be used in derivatives transactions in the future) in which all of the members of the clearing house may seek to set off the amounts which they owe between one another. As was considered above, r.4.90 of the Insolvency Rules requires the existence of mutual debts owed between the parties before set-off can be permitted.[275] With the multi-party agreements it is sometimes the case that there are not necessarily any obligations owed mutually between each party and every other party, even though each party would give consideration by entering into the netting agreement in the first place. So, in a multi-party netting agreement between A, B, C and D, if A and B owe separate amounts of money to each other and in turn C and D owe separate amounts of money to each other, then there is no mutual debt between A and C nor B and D, and consequently there can be no set-off between them all.[276] Therefore, the contractual nexus between the parties must make it clear that A, B, C and D owe mutual debts between one another.

The English courts refused at one time to give effect to multi-party netting **22–112** agreements on the basis that they would offend against the pari passu principle because the solvent party "cannot manufacture a set-off by directing that the deposit be applied to discharge someone else's debt, even though it may, as between itself and the debtor, have a right to do so".[277] In *British Eagle*

---

[275] Insolvency Rules 1986, r.4.90.
[276] *Re BCCI (No.8)* [1998] A.C. 214, 223, per Lord Hoffmann.
[277] *British Eagle International Airlines Ltd v Cie Nationale Air France* [1975] 1 W.L.R. 758. The way in which the derivatives market has sought to ensure a form of set-off which includes all of A, B, C and D is to create multi-party netting agreements which draw the separate transactions under the umbrella of one contract which will in turn set off all of the transactions under all of the master agreements in existence between those parties. There is nothing remarkable about the parties agreeing to set amounts off on this basis while they are all solvent. The issue arises when one of them goes into insolvency.

International Airlines Ltd v Cie Nationale Air France[278] the House of Lords applied the proposition that the divestment of an insolvent's assets was against public policy because it would have permitted the parties to contract out of the statutory pari passu principle.[279] In that case a clearing house scheme had been created within which airlines would set off amounts owed between themselves on a monthly basis in relation to sums owed for sales of tickets for travel on one another's aircraft. This scheme constituted a contract between all of the members. Clearing took effect through the clearing house itself in that the members of the scheme had to settle their accounts with the clearing house and they were paid by the clearing house. When British Eagle went into liquidation it owed large sums under the terms of this scheme. The majority of the House of Lords held, in considering the question whether or not British Eagle should be required to perform its contractual payment obligations under the clearing house arrangement in spite of its insolvency, that such an order would give preference to members of the clearing house to the straightforward disadvantage of the airline's other unsecured creditors. It was held by the majority of the House of Lords that it would be contrary to public policy to allow the parties to this clearing house arrangement to contract out of the statutory requirement that in the event of an insolvency all of the assets of an insolvent person must be distributed among the unsecured creditors on a pari passu basis. It was held by Lord Cross, speaking for the majority, that if this advantage was conferred on one category of unsecured creditors, to the detriment of the other category of unsecured creditors, then it would infringe the pari passu principle in insolvency law.[280] Therefore, it was held that this multiparty netting arrangement would not enforceable in the insolvency.[281]

22–113 In a strong dissenting speech, Lord Morris held that there were contractual debts in existence between the members of the clearing house, including a requirement to set-off, which should be enforced.[282] Central to Lord Morris's argument was the contention that the liquidator should be bound by the terms of the agreement into which the British Eagle had entered some time before the insolvency (viz. to effect set-off of any amounts owed to it through the clearing house arrangement), and that to argue otherwise was for the liquidator to seek to alter the terms of that

---

[278] [1975] 1 W.L.R. 758, [1975] 2 All E.R. 390, HL.

[279] See Cranston, *Principles of Banking Law* (Oxford, 1997), 321, where *British Eagle* is identified as the leading authority in cases of multi-lateral netting where there are non-mutual claims.

[280] Goode has criticised this decision for failing to observe the commercial expectations of the parties: Goode, *Principles of Corporate Insolvency Law* 2nd edn (Sweet & Maxwell, 1997), 182. In this, the House of Lords has acted similarly to *Westdeutsche Landesbank v Islington LBC* in imposing legal principle in a way which went against the parties' commercial understanding of their agreement.

[281] In that case it was possible under the clearing scheme agreement that the member airlines would still have a right of action against one another. The terms of that agreement had changed before it became an issue before the High Court of Australia in *International Air Transport Association v Ansett Australia Holdings Ltd* (2008) 234 C.L.R. 151 by which time such proceedings could only be commenced by the clearing house.

[282] There were debts in existence albeit that the rules of the scheme operated so as to novate those debts into obligations with the clearing house. Within the statutory language then in force, this was held to be sufficient to constitute the "property" of the insolvent person which could be distributed among the members of the scheme.

contract after the event. This would have had the result of calling the property into the insolvent's estate for general distribution.

As Lord Hoffmann confirmed in the House of Lords in *Re BCCI (No.8)*, the availability of mutual set-off in these circumstances is restricted to claims between contracting parties and not to claims in respect of third parties, for fear that this would "subvert the fundamental principle of pari passu" as established in *British Eagle*. On the facts of *Re BCCI (No.8)*, therefore, the separate legal personality of borrower and depositor could not be overlooked to give effect to set-off. As his lordship held:[283]

22–114

> "[The appellant] cannot manufacture a set-off by directing that the deposit be applied to discharge someone else's debt, even though it may, as between itself and the debtor, have a right to do so. This is the very type of arrangement which the House declared ineffective in *British Eagle*."

Therefore, the set-off must be clearly operational between two contracting parties specifically and cannot benefit the obligations owed by some third party to that set-off arrangement. For example, Alpha Plc cannot claim to set-off a payment it owes to an insolvent entity against another payment owed by the insolvent entity to one of Alpha Plc's wholly-owned subsidiaries because that subsidiary is a different legal person from Alpha Plc. There would need to be some contractual *nexus* which connected the debts owed between Alpha Plc, its subsidiary and the insolvent entity. This may have implications for margin-credit agreements in the derivatives area, which are considered below.

The impact of the decision in *British Eagle* in respect of financial transactions like derivatives was that executory contracts would not be capable of being rescinded, or alternatively amounts owed under them set off, on the insolvency of one counterparty in such a multi-party netting arrangement. This would have been so even if there had been a clause purporting to create a form of close-out netting.[284] The practical solution has come in the form of the Financial Markets and Insolvency (Settlement Finality) Regulations 1999 considered next.

22–115

Settlement Finality Regulations and clearing houses

The central policy in relation to the future of derivatives regulation is the clearing of derivatives transactions through a central counterparty structure.[285] To facilitate clearing it is important that multi-lateral netting under a clearing structure will be enforceable if one of the members goes into insolvency. Many of these uncertainties about the operation of set-off under the case law have been resolved by statutory instrument. The Financial Markets and Insolvency (Settlement Finality) Regulations 1999,[286] as amended on several occasions,

22–116

---

[283] [1998] A.C. 214, 223.
[284] The only qualification to this argument, under the executory analysis, is that no asset must have passed under the contract to the insolvent.
[285] para.16–79 et seq.
[286] SI 2979/1999.

implement the EC Settlement Finality Directive.[287] The purpose of these Regulations (the "Settlement Finality Regulations") is to ensure that set-off provisions will be effective in the event of an insolvency, especially in relation to central counterparty, clearing houses and collateral structures. In effect, their goal was to reverse the effect of the decision in *British Eagle* in relation to insolvency set-off agreements.

22-117   The regulations operate as follows. Any unincorporated association or corporate body may apply to be officially designated as the "operator" of a "designated system" which will clear payments between its members.[288] Investment exchanges and clearing houses approved under the FSMA 2000 will be deemed to be appropriate bodies for this purpose.[289] The operator of that system shall provide the designating authority with information it may require as to its membership, activities on the system, and so forth.[290] This information gathering power is very important in times of economic crisis because it enables regulators to proceed on an informed basis in their responsibilities relating to an otherwise opaque market like that for privately-contracted, over-the-counter derivatives. The authority may then publish information or "give advice".[291]

22-118   Significantly, for the purposes of insolvency set-off through clearing structures and the provision of collateral, reg.13 and those following modify insolvency law. To that effect, reg.14 provides that:

> "(1)   None of the following shall be regarded as to any extent invalid at law on the ground of inconsistency with the law relating to the distribution of the assets of a person on bankruptcy, winding up, [administration,] sequestration or under a protected trust deed, or in the administration of an insolvent estate [or with the law relating to other insolvency proceedings of a country or territory outside the United Kingdom]—
>
> (a)   a transfer order;
>
> (b)   the default arrangements of a designated system;
>
> (c)   the rules of a designated system as to the settlement of transfer orders not dealt with under its default arrangements;
>
> (d)   a contract for the purpose of realising collateral security in connection with participation in a designated system [or in a system which is an interoperable system in relation to that designated system] otherwise than pursuant to its default arrangements; or
>
> (e)   a contract for the purpose of realising collateral security in connection with the functions of a central bank."

Therefore, unlike in *British Eagle*, the default arrangements of the clearing house or collateral arrangements will not be affected by the pari passu principle in insolvency law. And in consequence, under reg.15:

> "(2)   If, in England and Wales or Northern Ireland, a bankruptcy, winding-up or administration order has been made or a creditors' voluntary winding-up resolution has been passed, the debt—
>
> (a)   is provable in the bankruptcy, winding-up or administration or, as the case may be, is payable to the relevant office-holder; and

---

[287] Directive 98/26/EC.

[288] The Financial Markets and Insolvency (Settlement Finality) Regulations 1999, Reg.3.

[289] The Financial Markets and Insolvency (Settlement Finality) Regulations 1999, Reg.6.

[290] The Financial Markets and Insolvency (Settlement Finality) Regulations 1999, Reg.10.

[291] The Financial Markets and Insolvency (Settlement Finality) Regulations 1999, Reg.12.

> (b)   shall be taken into account, where appropriate, under section 323 of the Insolvency Act 1986 … or Rule 2.85 of the Insolvency Rules 1986 … (mutual dealings and set-off) or the corresponding provision applicable in the case of winding up or administration;
>
> in the same way as a debt due before the commencement of bankruptcy, the date on which the body corporate goes into liquidation … or enters into administration … in the case of a partnership, the date of the winding-up order."

Thus set-off in relation to mutual dealings is encompassed within these regulations. However, such a provision is not effective if created after the insolvency.[292]

---

[292] The Financial Markets and Insolvency (Settlement Finality) Regulations 1999, Reg.20.

CHAPTER 23

TRACING AND PROPRIETARY CLAIMS

CORE PRINCIPLES

It is an important part of English property law that a property owner may recover property taken from her, or that she may trace her original property rights into substitute property, for example, if her original property was sold and used to buy shares. Tracing is the process of identifying property which has been acquired by the defendant and which is traceable back to property previously owned by the claimant. So, tracing would enable the claimant to try to establish rights in those shares. The question as to the remedy which the claimant acquires in the traced property is a separate question from the tracing process, because the tracing process is simply the detective work of identifying property against which the claimant may bring a claim. The tracing process is particularly important to achieve recovery of property in financial transactions when money has been laundered or other property taken in breach of contract or in breach of fiduciary duty.

A "following" action entitles the claimant to recover the original property which was taken from it. If that property has been substituted for other property—for example, if that property was money which has been used to acquire a chattel—then "common law tracing" will permit an action against that substitute chattel, provided that there has been no mixture of any of that property with any other property.

The most common tracing action in financial contexts relates to situations in which money or financial instruments are mixed in an account such that common law tracing will provide no action. In such circumstances tracing can only be conducted in equity (known as "equitable tracing"). To bring an action for equitable tracing it is important that the claimant had some equitable proprietary right in the original property on which the tracing process is based. Equity will provide a range of tracing techniques if the trustee has combined the traced property with her own personal property: this is, in effect, an extension of liability for breach of trust. However, where the mixture is a combination of the property derived from innocent people, then the process is more complex. There is old authority relating to tracing into current bank accounts which provides that the first money to be paid into the mixed account is to be deemed to be the first money to leave the account. The artificiality of this approach has caused High Court judges in recent cases to seek to circumvent that rule by finding that any property acquired from a mixed fund should be treated as having been acquired by all contributors to the mixture in proportion to the size of their contribution. The question then arises as to the form of equitable remedy which would be appropriate once tracing has been completed.

The possible remedies for equitable tracing include a constructive trust, an equitable lien, an equitable charge, or subrogation. The defences to a tracing action include change of position, estoppel by representation, and the rights of a bona fide purchaser of the property. Each is considered in the text to follow.

1. INTRODUCTION—THE USE OF TRACING IN FINANCIAL TRANSACTIONS

23–01   Tracing is the process by which a claimant seeks to establish title to property taken from her or to establish title to property which has been substituted for that original property. In financial transactions and in banking relationships this enables a claimant to trace the movement of funds through successive bank accounts where it can be shown that each bank account contains value which was derived from the original property in which the claimant had property rights. As such it is a particularly important weapon in the litigator's armoury when dealing with money laundering and similar forms of complex, financial fraud. Tracing will apply to cases involving honest mistakes[1] as well as fraudulent schemes, although explaining tracing in its essence is easier with examples involving fraudulent schemes. A good example of the sort of claim at issue arose in *Agip (Africa) Ltd v Jackson*[2] where accountants fraudulently took money from the claimant's bank accounts and paid that money through a number of different bank accounts, changed the currency of that money, mixed the original money with other money in a series of bank accounts so as to make the original money unidentifiable, paid the money through a number of different jurisdictions, and had the bank accounts owned by a series of dummy companies which were wound up once the payments had passed out of their accounts. Clearly, after this succession of transactions which were orchestrated solely to make the task of tracking the money down very difficult indeed, if English property law rested solely on protecting property rights to the original money held by the claimant company then it would be impossible to enforce property rights against money launderers such as these accountants.[3] What tracing does, however, in the manner discussed in this chapter, is to begin with the claimant's property rights in the original money and then traces those property rights through the succession of accounts, funds and mixtures into which that money or substitutes for that money have passed. If this tracing process is successful, the claimant is then able to establish one of a number of potential remedies against any funds which can be shown to contain any traceable residue of the original property.

This tracing process is a significant contribution to commercial litigation by common law systems because it permits ownership of one item of property to be traced into other items of property which constitute the sale proceeds of that original property, or which were acquired with the original property, and so on. Otherwise, any system of property law (such as classical civil code conceptions of property law) which is limited to recognising only title in the original property which was owned outright by the claimant and, if that original property becomes impossible to locate or to recover for some reason, then the claimant would be able only to bring personal claims in damages for the loss suffered as a result of the loss of that property against any person responsible for that loss. In practice in relation to money laundering and fraud in financial transactions, the person who committed the wrong will have disappeared, or will have gone into bankruptcy, or will be resident in a jurisdiction where legal proceedings cannot be commenced. Hence the importance of being able to establish property rights over assets held in a jurisdiction in which an order of an English court (for our purposes) can be enforced. Tracing, by contrast to civil code conceptions of property, entitles the successful claimant to enforce proprietary rights against the substitute property in whoever's hands it rests or in whatever form it takes.

23–02

This topic is considered in detail in Alastair Hudson, *Equity & Trusts*.[4]

---

[1] *Re Diplock* [1948] Ch. 465.

[2] [1991] Ch. 547; [1991] 3 W.L.R. 116; [1992] 4 All E.R. 451.

[3] This would be essential if the money launderer had gone into insolvency, or if its front companies had been deliberately wound up as part of the scheme, or if the original property was beyond legal enforcement (for example in a jurisdiction in which an English writ could not be enforced).

[4] A. Hudson, *Equity & Trusts*, 7th edn (Routledge, 2012), s.19.6.

2. The Different Types of Tracing Action

A. The structure of this chapter

23–03 As outlined above, tracing is the process by which a claimant seeks to establish property rights in some property in which she either had property rights previously or which constitutes the traceable proceeds of that original property.[5] It is important to recognise that there are different types of tracing which will be appropriate in only particular types of situation. This section sketches those distinctions, the sections following then examine the principles underpinning these tracing actions in detail, before the section on "remedies" below[6] identifies which type of claim will be appropriate for which type of circumstance.

B. Following and clean substitutions at common law

23–04 Establishing title in the very property which the claimant owned previously is known as a "following" action.[7] This type of action is concerned with the straightforward, physical return of property to its rightful owner. It operates most clearly in relation to chattels, so that if my car is taken from me, I can use a following action to identify my particular car (from its registration number and its chassis number) in someone else's driveway. There has been no substitution of the property and certainly no inextricable mixture of that property with any other property. A following claim would be unlikely to be useful in relation to actions to recover money or intangible securities, unless that money or those securities had always been held by the defendant in an account entirely separate from all other property and provided that the money or securities are identifiable as being the property originally owned by the claimant. This type of action is best understood, it is suggested, as being a subset of the common law tracing action, considered next.[8]

23–05 A common law tracing action may apply more generally to substitutions of property, and so is not limited to recovery of the original property owned by the claimant. So, if the claimant's money is taken and paid into a new bank account, not having been commingled with other property, then interest earned on that money is added to the account, there would be a combination of the original money with the interest received but no mixture with other property: a common law tracing action would be appropriate to take title to this account holding the original money and the interest on it.[9] Therefore, if the property claimed constitutes clean substitutions of the original property—that is, where the property claimed is either the original property, or if a substitute for the original property it has not been mixed with any other property—then a claim in common

---

[5] For more detailed accounts of the principles considered in this section see A.S. Hudson, *Equity & Trusts* Ch.19 "Tracing"; G.W. Thomas and A.S. Hudson, *The Law of Trusts* (OUP, 2004), Ch.33 "Tracing and proprietary claims".

[6] See para.22–28.

[7] *Foskett v McKeown*; after L. Smith, *The Law of Tracing* (Clarendon Press, 1997).

[8] cf. *Jones, F.C. (a firm) v Jones* [1996] 3 W.L.R. 703.

[9] See *Jones, F.C. (a firm) v Jones* [1996] 3 W.L.R. 703, which is considered in greater detail below.

law tracing would be appropriate. The more difficult circumstance is that in which the original property has been inextricably commingled with other property entirely so that one item of property cannot be distinguished from the other, such as two funds of money being combined in a bank account. This context is considered next.

C. Tracing into mixtures in equity

Only equitable tracing can permit a tracing action into a mixture of property, that is in circumstances in which the claimant seeks to establish proprietary rights in a fund of property which either has the original property or the proceeds of such property inextricably mixed with property from another source. Examples of this sort of mixture in the financial context would be combinations of money in a bank account or combinations of non-segregated securities of the same type. To bring a tracing action in equity, however, the claimant must demonstrate a pre-existing equitable interest in the original property, whether by means of the original property having been held on express or constructive trust for the claimant or by means of it having been held subject to some other fiduciary relationship.

23–06

Tracing is only the process of identifying the property against which the claim will be brought, before selecting the appropriate remedy which will be enforced over that property.[10] The advantages of such a proprietary claim, as opposed to a personal claim for money had and received,[11] are the claimant acquires priority over unsecured creditors in an insolvency by means of property rights in identified property, and that a proprietary claim will lock in rights to assets whose market value increases. The cases concerning mixtures have arisen most frequently in relation to banking transactions in which money drawn from more than one source is mixed in a bank account such that the claimant is seeking to establish some rights over the money held in that account.[12] Each of these forms of tracing claim is considered in detail in the sections to follow. First, we begin with common law tracing.

23–07

3. COMMON LAW TRACING

A. The limitations of common law tracing in financial transactions

Common law tracing will be of limited use in many financial transactions because typically in open market transactions money and securities will be turned to account or transferred before the machinery of litigation can practically be begun. Thus, if two financial institutions contract to sell assets but by mistake the wrong securities are transferred from one party to the other, it is likely that those

23–08

---

[10] *Boscawen v Bajwa* [1996] 1 W.L.R. 328.
[11] See para.20–27.
[12] *Agip v Jackson* [1990] Ch. 265, 286, per Millett J., CA; [1991] Ch. 547; *El Ajou v Dollar Land Holdings* [1993] 3 All E.R. 717; appealed [1994] 2 All E.R. 685; *Lipkin Gorman v Karpnale* [1991] 2 A.C. 548.

securities will be transferred or mixed with other securities before the mistake can be unravelled. Common law tracing will only be available if the property which is sought by means of the tracing action had remained unmixed with other property. In relation to money held in bank accounts, it is even less likely that the money will have remained unmixed in transactions between market counterparties. By way of example, in *Lipkin Gorman v Karpnale*[13] the plaintiff law firm sought to recover money taken from it by one its partners and gambled at the defendant's casino. It was held that the plaintiff could trace at common law into a distinct account in which some of the misappropriated money remained identifiable and unmixed with other moneys; but that the plaintiff could not trace into the casino's general accounts after the remaining money because money which had been paid into those general accounts had become mixed with other moneys.

23–09   Thus, if any money claimed has been paid into a general account or mixed with other money, common law tracing will be unavailable. It should be recalled that equitable tracing into mixtures is only possible if there has been some pre-existing fiduciary relationship granting the claimant an equitable interest in the property which is sought. The same principle applies to securities and other assets.

23–10   Equally, then, seeking to recover property from money launderers or similar actors will be difficult at common law, if the claimant has no pre-existing equitable interest in the property sought. By way of example, in *Agip (Africa) Ltd v Jackson*[14] money had been taken from a company's bank accounts by accountants who executed forged money transfer orders and then laundered that money through a series of bank accounts. Actions were brought, inter alia, at common law. It was held that common law tracing was only possible in relation to clean substitutions of the company's original money into identified bank accounts, but not into bank accounts in which the original moneys had been mixed with other money.[15] Consequently, it can be seen that common law tracing is a comparatively brittle head of claim which can be precluded if the property at issue is commingled with other property.

B. Circumstances in which common law tracing will apply to financial transactions

23–11   The principal need for common law tracing is in circumstances in which there is no fiduciary relationship which granted the claimant an equitable interest in the original property. Common law tracing has been used in relation to investment transactions. A good example of this was the decision of the Court of Appeal in

---

[13] [1991] 3 W.L.R. 10; [1992] 4 All E.R. 512; [1991] 2 A.C. 548.

[14] [1991] Ch. 547; [1991] 3 W.L.R. 116; [1992] 4 All E.R. 451.

[15] This approach was supported by Sir Peter Millett writing extra-judicially: Millett, "Tracing the Proceeds of Fraud" (1991) 107 L.Q.R. 71—where his lordship argued that the proper approach for English law would be to do away with common law tracing completely on the basis that it is of restricted potential use, and of no use where property is mixed or no longer separately identifiable.

FC Jones & Sons v Jones.[16] In that case, £11,700 was paid from a partnership bank account to Mrs Jones, who was the wife of one of the partners. Mrs Jones held that money in a separate bank account. She invested the money in financial instruments—namely potato futures contracts—and made a large profit. Ultimately she held a balance of £49,860 in that bank account which had never contained any property other than the original £11,700 or the profits made on that original £11,700. It transpired that the partnership had technically committed an act of bankruptcy under the 1914 Bankruptcy Act and therefore all of the partnership property was deemed to have passed retrospectively to the Official Receiver. Therefore, the Official Receiver, acting on behalf of the partnership, sought to trace into the entire £49,860. It was held that all the money was to be paid to the Official Receiver on the basis of a common law tracing claim. In the judgement of Millett L.J., the plaintiff was allowed a proprietary common law claim on the basis that the money at issue was separately identifiable.[17] It was held that the right was a proprietary right to claim whatever was held in the bank account, whether that amount was more or less than the original amount deposited and it was immaterial whether or not those amounts constituted profits on the original money.

Notably, the claimant in *FC Jones & Sons v Jones* would not have been able to bring an equitable tracing claim on these facts because there was no pre-existing equitable interest in the money at issue: therefore, the extension of common law tracing on these facts was the only means of providing the Official Receiver with a remedy. Ordinary securities market counterparties will not stand in fiduciary relationships with one another—their relationship will be purely contractual[18]— and therefore only common law tracing will be available if property is taken by one party from the other. So, as in *Jones v Jones*, profits from trading in futures may be traceable at common law if held distinct from other property. **23–12**

4. EQUITABLE TRACING

A. The principles underpinning equitable tracing

Equitable tracing is able to permit the claimant to trace into mixed funds of property. It is a pre-requisite for an equitable tracing claim that the plaintiff had some equitable interest in the original property, or that the person who transferred that property away had some fiduciary relationship with the plaintiff, such as being a trustee or acting as the claimant's agent or as the claimant's partner or as a director of the claimant company.[19] If there is no such equitable interest, then equitable tracing will not be available and the claimant is instead thrown back on common law tracing, as considered above. So, if property is taken from, for example, a trust account in breach of trust and then paid into another account **23–13**

---

[16] [1996] 3 W.L.R. 703; [1996] 4 All E.R. 721.

[17] It was held that there could be no claim in equity against Mrs Jones because she had never stood in a fiduciary relationship to the partnership.

[18] That is, assuming that no party stands as agent or trustee or partner or director, and so forth, in relation to one another.

[19] *Re Diplock's Estate* [1948] Ch. 465; *Boscawen v Bajwa* [1996] 1 W.L.R. 328.

where it is mixed with other money, then equitable tracing will permit a claim into that mixed fund because the beneficiaries had an equitable interest in that original fund. The rationale for this rule historically is that an equitable interest was necessary to invoke the jurisdiction of a court of equity: the principle has lived on in spite of the fusion of the common law courts and the courts of equity by means of the Judicature Act 1873; instead the principles of these two systems of law remain distinct at present.

23–14 The discussion to follow will divide between the tracing process as applied to particular types of financial activity—principally tracing into mixed funds where there has been no breach of trust, tracing specifically into bank accounts, tracing through fiduciaries who have committed a breach of trust by mixing trust money with their own money, and circumstances in which the right to trace can be lost—before then considering in turn the remedies and the defences available. As was outlined above, tracing strictly is simply the process of identifying against which property the action will be brought. It is then a separate question, as considered below in the section on remedies, as to exactly what sort of remedy will be imposed.[20] Equity has a large range of remedies, four of which can be used in tracing actions. The selection of the remedy will depend upon the nature of the property and the context.[21]

B. Equitable tracing into mixed funds generally

23–15 The general principle is that in equity when two or more people have contributed property to a mixed fund—whether of chattels or intangible assets held in a common account—then each of those people is entitled to trace into that mixture and to claim a pro rata share of the mixture in proportion to their contribution to it.[22] The tracing process is the detective work of identifying into which fund the traceable proceeds of the claimant's property passed, and is distinct from the question as to which equitable remedy is appropriate once that detective work has been completed. Remedies are discussed at the end of this chapter. It is not required that the defendant who is in possession of the property at the time that the action is brought has acted unconscionably. Rather the purpose of equitable tracing is to vindicate the property rights of the original owner of property by tracing those rights.

23–16 Thus in *Re Diplock*[23] a payment was made under a will trust by its trustees to a medical charity as the trustees thought they were empowered to do under the terms of the trust. It transpired that the clause of the will trust which purported to grant that power was void under charities law. The trustees therefore sought to recover the value which had been transferred to the charity. The charity was entirely innocent of the invalidity of the trust provision but nevertheless it was obliged to account to the trust under its tracing action. Because the beneficiaries of the trust had had an equitable interest in the trust property from the outset, they

---

[20] See para.22–28.
[21] See para.22–28.
[22] *Re Diplock's Estate* [1948] Ch. 465.
[23] [1948] Ch. 465.

were able to trace in equity. Their money had passed into the account of the charity. The beneficiaries were therefore entitled to identify the account into which their property had passed and to trace into that account. The charity was not required to have acted unconscionably to be liable in an equitable tracing claim—rather it was sufficient that it was in possession of property into which the claimant was entitled to trace in equity.

Similarly in *Foskett v McKeown*[24] a trustee took money from the trust fund and used it to pay two-fifths of the premiums on a life assurance policy which he had taken out over his own life in favour of his children. The trustee then committed suicide. The beneficiaries of the trust were entitled to trace in equity because they had a pre-existing equitable interest. It was held that the beneficiaries were entitled to trace their moneys into the life assurance premiums and thus into the lump sum pay-out which was acquired by those premiums on the trustee's death. Because the trust had contributed two-fifths of the premiums it was held that the beneficiaries were entitled to trace into two-fifths of the lump sum pay-out. Thus tracing will operate in relation to transactions which pay out a capital amount in response to periodical payments. This principle would therefore also apply to financial derivatives, bonds, shares, annuities and so forth which also acquire a capital amount and income profits through periodical payments.

23–17

C. Equitable tracing into current bank accounts

Different principles apply in relation to mixtures in current bank accounts due to the legacy cast by some old authorities. The question with payments into a mixed account is how to trace into that account. The old authorities related specifically to current bank accounts: it is not clear whether the courts would now seek to limit them to that particular context. As will emerge below, more modern authorities have sought ways round the old rule.

23–18

As we have seen in general terms, each contributor to that mixture will be deemed to be a proportionate owner of the whole mixed account.[25] When considering how one seeks to trace into a current account containing a mixture of different moneys from different people, and also how one traces through payments which are made out of that mixture, one has to apply the approach in *Clayton's Case*.[26] (This discussion pre-supposes that the contributors to the mixed fund are innocent of any breach of fiduciary duty themselves; whereas mixtures of trust property with a trustee's own property in breach of trust are considered in the next section). The issue as part of the tracing process, as opposed to the question of which equitable remedy may eventually be imposed, is the question of identifying which part of mixed fund of money is to be the subject of the claim. The approach taken in *Clayton's Case* was to deem the first money to have been paid into the account to be the first money to have been paid out of the

23–19

---

[24] [2000] 3 All E.R. 97.
[25] *Re Diplock's Estate* [1948] Ch. 465; *Barlow Clowes v Vaughan* [1992] 4 All E.R. 22; *Russell-Cooke Trust Co v Prentis* [2003] 2 All E.R. 478; *Commerzbank AG v IMB Morgan Plc* [2004] EWHC 2771.
[26] (1816) 1 Mer. 572.

account, the second money paid in to be the second money paid out, and so on until all moneys have been accounted for.

23–20 A worked example will illustrate the principle. If the defendant took £100,000 from Trust A and paid it into an empty bank account on March 1 and if the defendant then took £200,000 from Trust B and paid it into that same account on March 2, and then if on March 3 £50,000 was spent on X Plc shares which trebled in value before the remaining money was then invested on March 4 in a company, Y Plc, which is now insolvent, the question would be which shares could be traced into by the beneficiaries of Trust A and which by the beneficiaries of Trust B. The approach in *Clayton's Case* would be that the first money paid into the account—being the money from Trust A—would be deemed to be the first money to be paid out of that account. The result would therefore be that Trust A could trace one half of its money into the X Plc shares (which were bought first in time and which were bought for £50,000, half of the amount contributed by Trust A). The X Plc shares are now worth £150,000 because their market value has tripled. Because Trust A would be deemed by *Clayton's Case* to have acquired all of these X Plc shares, the beneficiaries of Trust A now happen to own proprietary rights in property which is much more valuable now than it was on the date of its acquisition. The successful claimant is treated as being the owner of the property whatever its value happens to be. Thus, the remaining half of the money from Trust A money and all of the money from Trust B would then be deemed to have been spent on the worthless Y Plc shares: being the second money in, that is deemed to be the second money to be paid out. This is the exact opposite of an approach which sought to compensate claimants for their loss (like common law damages or equitable compensation) or a proprietary approach which treats the parties as being owners in common of the property in the account.

23–21 While *Clayton's Case* has not yet been overruled, it is clear from decisions in the wake of the Court of Appeal's decision in *Barlow Clowes v Vaughan*[27] that the majority of English courts would prefer to resile from the *Clayton's Case* principle[28] because its results often appear arbitrary. Take the worked example set out in the preceding paragraph. There is no reason why Trust A should be deemed to own the whole of the valuable X Plc shares when both Trust A and Trust B had contributed to the fund from which those shares were bought. On the date of the purchase, the moneys were taken from an account which held money from both A and B: therefore, it is somewhat arbitrary to assign all of the equitable interest in the X Plc shares to one contributor to that fund as opposed to the other.

---

[27] [1992] 4 All E.R. 22.
[28] *Barlow Clowes v Vaughan* [1992] 4 All E.R. 22; *El Ajou v Dollar Land Holdings (No.2)* [1995] 2 All E.R. 213, 222, Robert Walker J.; *Re Lewis's of Leicester* [1995] 1 B.C.L.C. 428; *Sheppard v Thompson* Unreported, December 3, 2001; *Russell Cooke Trust Co v Prentis* [2003] 2 All E.R. 478; *Commerzbank AG v IMB Morgan Plc* [2004] EWHC 2771.

At the time of writing, however, *Clayton's Case* has not been formally overruled in England, merely criticised and sometimes distinguished.[29] In other jurisdictions,[30] the courts have preferred to find that the contributors to a common fund should be treated as acquiring an equitable interest in any property bought using money from that fund in proportion to their proportionate contribution to the mixture. Using a proportionate share approach in the worked example given above, Trust A would acquire one-third of any property bought from the fund (in proportion to its contribution of £100,000 to a total fund worth £300,000) and Trust B would acquire two-thirds of any property bought from the fund.

23–22

In *Barlow Clowes v Vaughan*[31] the Court of Appeal expressed a preference for a "rolling charge" approach in relation to a mutual investment fund to which investors had contributed not only differing amounts of money but also had contributed for differing lengths of time. The rolling charge, if the court had felt able to apply it to the precise facts before them, would have sought to account both for the aggregate amounts constituted by each investor and also for the time-value of their contribution.

23–23

That English law is demonstrating a movement away from *Clayton's Case* and towards simply dividing the mixed fund proportionately between the contributors to that fund emerges from recent decisions of the High Court. So, in *Russell-Cooke Trust Co v Prentis*[32] Lindsay J. held that the *Clayton's Case* approach was still binding but that it was also capable of being - distinguished on the facts of any given case. As this point was put by Woolf L.J. in *Barlow Clowes v Vaughan*[33]:

23–24

> "There is no reason in law or justice why his depredations upon the fund should not be borne equally between [the parties]. To throw all the loss upon one, through the mere chance of his being earlier in time, is irrational and arbitrary, and is equally a fiction as the rule in *Clayton's Case*. When the law adopts a fiction, it is, or at least it should be, for some purpose of justice. To adopt it here is to apportion a common misfortune through a test which has no relation whatever to the justice of the case."

Latterly in *Commerzbank AG v IMB Morgan Plc*[34] the same approach to authority of *Clayton's Case* was taken by Lawrence Collins J. in a case in which a fraudulent investment scheme was operated through a correspondent bank account held by Commerzbank such that money was taken from the public and mixed in the bank account. It was held that it would have been unjust and

---

[29] The courts in Canada and in Australia have preferred to apply a proportionate share approach whereby each contributor to the mixed fund is deemed to take a proportionate share in any property acquired with money from that fund: *Re Ontario Securities Commission* (1988) 52 D.L.R. (4th) 767 (Sup Ct) in Canada and *Re French Caledonia Travel Service Pty Ltd* (2003) 204 A.L.R. 353, per Campbell J., in Australia; as have the courts in the USA, see *Re Walter J Schmidt & Co*, 298 F 314, 316 (1923), per Learned Hand J.

[30] See *Re Ontario Securities Commission* (1988) 52 D.L.R. (4th) 767 (Sup Ct) (Canada); *Re French Caledonia Travel Service Pty Ltd* (2003) 204 A.L.R. 353, per Campbell J. (Australia); *Re Walter J Schmidt & Co*, 298 F 314, 316 (1923), per Learned Hand J. (USA).

[31] [1992] 4 All E.R. 22.

[32] [2003] 2 All E.R. 478.

[33] [1992] 4 All E.R. 22, 44.

[34] [2004] EWHC 2771.

impracticable to have applied *Clayton's Case* on these facts: unjust because it would have produced arbitrary results between the investors, and impracticable in that it would have required a difficult exercise to decide which payments in and out of this account were derived from which investors and made in which order. Therefore, the approach in English law at the time of writing seems to be that, in relation to mixtures of innocent participants' money, *Clayton's Case* is to be applied, although the court may choose to apply a proportionate share approach instead if the application of the first-in-first-out approach appears to the court to be "arbitrary and irrational".

D. Where a contributor to the mixed fund has committed some breach of fiduciary duty

23–25　There is a different approach in circumstances in which a contributor to the mixed fund has committed some breach of fiduciary duty to obtain the property paid into the fund—whereas the preceding sections were concerned with cases in which the contributors to the mixed fund were all innocent of any breach of fiduciary duty. Where a contributor to the fund is a fiduciary who has committed a breach of duty, the courts have taken tended to assume everything against the malfeasing trustee. So, in *Re Hallett's Estate*[35] a solicitor ("the trustee") was holding property, in the form of bearer bonds, on trust for his client. The trustee mixed the trust property with his own holding of identical bearer bonds, before selling all of the bonds. The trustee then dissipated part of the sale proceeds on his own living expenses while investing the rest successfully. The court sought to protect the position of the beneficiary of this trust arrangement, mindful that the trustee would otherwise have committed a breach of trust in selling the bonds and then dissipating the bulk of the sale proceeds. The court therefore chose to assume that the trustee had acted honestly and so used the trust's share of the sale proceeds to make the successful investments with the effect that the trustee was therefore deemed to have used his own share of the sale proceeds on his personal living expenses. In that case, it is suggested, the court acted so as to reach the most convenient result: that is, one which justified entitling the claimants to trace into the valuable assets. In cases in which there has been breach of fiduciary duty, the courts tend to assume everything in favour of the beneficiaries. This sometimes leads to different approaches being taken to that in *Re Hallett*. So, in *Re Oatway*[36] it was decided that the beneficiaries could elect whether they wanted to enforce a charge over the mixed fund or to have unauthorised investments acquired out of that fund assimilated into the trust fund. The approach here was different from that in *Hallett's Estate* but it had the same objective of protecting the beneficiaries against any loss caused to them by a breach of trust when the trustee mixed trust property with his own, personal property.

---

[35] (1880) 13 Ch.D. 695.
[36] [1903] 2 Ch. 356.

E. Loss of the right to trace in equitable tracing actions

The right to trace can be lost. A tracing action will fail against a bank account if that account has gone overdrawn since receiving the money which is being traced. The rationale is that if the account has fallen to zero since the traced moneys entered it, then the traced moneys have by definition left that account. Equally, if the account falls in value below the amount of money which was paid into it in the form of the traced moneys, then the maximum amount which can be traced from that account is the lowest level to which the account fell after receipt of the traced moneys: the rationale for this principle is that that lowest balance is the largest amount which could represent the traced moneys. Both these principles hold true even if more money is added to the account later: no property claim can be brought against later additions to the account because by definition they were not derived from the traced moneys. It is still possible, however, to trace onwards into whichever account that money has passed subsequently.[37]

23–26

The question of loss of the right to trace is of particular importance when considering the problem of tracing through electronic bank accounts. In *Bishopsgate Investment Management v Homan*[38] money was taken from pension funds in breach of trust. The beneficiaries under those pension funds sought to recover the sums taken from their trusts on the basis of an equitable tracing claim. The money had been passed into bank accounts which had gone overdrawn between the time of the payment of the money into the account and the bringing of the claim. On the basis that the accounts had gone overdrawn (and therefore were said to have none of the original property left in them) it was held that the beneficiaries had lost their right to trace against those accounts because the property had disappeared. The same principle was upheld in *Westdeutsche Landesbank v Islington LBC*[39] to the effect that the specific property lent by a bank as part of an interest rate swap could not be traced into because it was not capable of identification once the bank accounts into which the moneys had been paid had subsequently been run into overdraft on a number of occasions. All of the money lent by the bank had been dissipated and was therefore untraceable. Even though other moneys had subsequently been paid into that bank account, because the account had already gone overdrawn no property claim could be brought against that account.

23–27

---

[37] If the account has fallen in value below the value of the property being traced, then the claim can only be brought for the highest intermediate balance.

[38] [1995] Ch. 211.

[39] [1996] A.C. 669.

5. REMEDIES IN EQUITABLE TRACING ACTIONS

A. The four principal remedies

23–28   The four principal remedies, once the equitable tracing process has been completed so as to identify the target property,[40] are the constructive trust,[41] the charge,[42] the lien[43] and subrogation.[44] Each will be considered in turn in the paragraphs to follow. What is important to note is that there is very little judicial authority on the applicability of remedies in this area. Consequently, it is difficult to know which remedy one *should* be entitled to. What one can know is how these remedies function as general concepts of the general law and therefore what will be done in this section is to consider in what circumstances each form of remedy would be most suitable for the claimant's objectives. This topic is considered in detail in Alastair Hudson, *Equity & Trusts*.[45]

B. Constructive trusts as remedies in equitable tracing actions

23–29   A constructive trust will grant a claimant proprietary rights in the property which is held on constructive trust. Thus, a constructive trust would be a desirable claim in a situation in which the claimant wishes to become the owner in equity of the assets which are held on trust. For example, if the mixed fund contained securities which were expected to increase in value, then if the claimant were the owner of an equitable interest in those securities she would own those proprietary rights in the securities whether they held their value or increased markedly in value. If the trust fund contained money in a sterling denomination then a constructive trust would have no particular advantage over the other remedies considered here. If the trust fund contained money in a denomination other than sterling and which was expected to increase markedly in value against sterling, then the claimant would wish to have a constructive trust over that non-sterling amount. A constructive trust is also malleable in its form and therefore it would be appropriate[46] to hold a mixed fund on constructive trust in whatever proportions the parties had contributed to the mixture.

23–30   Constructive trusts will be available in general terms, under the authority of *Westdeutsche Landesbank v Islington*,[47] at any time at which the defendant had knowledge of some factor which affected her conscience in relation to the traced property. The logic of that proposition would mean that a constructive trust would be available in relation to a tracing claim if the defendant had mixed the property unconscionably. Lord Browne-Wilkinson, delivering the leading speech in the

---

[40] By the expression "the target property" is meant the property which the claimant has traced her original property rights into and against which she is seeking to impose an equitable remedy.

[41] *Westdeutsche Landesbank Girozentrale v Islington L.B.C.* [1996] A.C. 669, HL.

[42] *Re Tilley's WT* [1967] Ch. 1178.

[43] *Diplock's Estate, Re* [1948] Ch. 465, below.

[44] *Boscawen v Bajwa* [1996] 1 W.L.R. 328.

[45] A. Hudson, *Equity & Trusts*, s.19.6.

[46] In that there is no objection in principle to so holding.

[47] [1996] A.C. 669.

House of Lords in *Westdeutsche Landesbank v Islington LBC*[48] explained that a constructive trust would only come into existence at the moment that the recipient counterparty appreciated that the payment had been made to it mistakenly and that therefore in good conscience it would be required to return that money. Until that moment of realisation, however, there could be no constructive trust.

However, the imposition of constructive trusts in tracing claims does not appear **23–31** to depend on the demonstration of unconscionable behaviour on the part of the defendant. Instead there are a number of cases in which remedies in equitable tracing claims have been ordered against defendants who have not acted unconscionably. As was considered above in relation to *Re Diplock's Estate*[49] the defendant in a tracing action will be held liable under that equitable tracing action regardless of her good or bad conscience. The focus of the courts in equitable tracing cases is to recover the traceable proceeds of the claimant's property.[50] Consequently, the court are concerned to protect the rights of the claimant by permitting her to trace those property rights into the hands of even an innocent defendant.[51]

An illustration of this tendency was given by the Court of Appeal in *Allan v Rea* **23–32** *Brothers Trustees Ltd*[52] it was held that if property was taken from one pension fund in breach of trust and paid into a second pension fund then the beneficiaries under the first pension fund would be entitled to trace into the second pension fund even though neither of the trustees involved had knowingly permitted these moneys to pass between the funds in breach of trust. A constructive trust was imposed over the traced property in that case. It was no objection that the trustees of the second fund had not acted knowingly and unconscionably in the receipt of that money.[53] Similarly in *Clark v Cutland*[54] when one of the shareholders organised the diversion of a company's assets into his personal pension fund it was held that the company was entitled to trace into that pension fund.[55] It was held further that an appropriate proportion of the value taken from the pension fund should be held on constructive trust for the company. Indeed, many cases involving equitable tracing have focused on the need to vindicate the property rights of the original beneficial owner of the property as opposed to responding solely to some unconscionable behaviour.[56]

---

[48] [1996] A.C. 669.
[49] [1948] Ch. 465.
[50] *Foskett v McKeown* [2001] A.C. 102.
[51] See *Re Diplock; Diplock v Wintle* [1948] Ch. 465; *Foskett v McKeown* [2001] A.C. 102 where neither defendant was required to have acted unconscionably.
[52] *Allan v Rea Brothers Trustees Ltd* [2002] EWCA Civ 85, where this issue emerges at [46].
[53] *Allan v Rea Brothers Trustees Ltd* [2002] EWCA Civ 85, at [52], per Robert Walker L.J.
[54] [2003] 4 All E.R. 733, [2003] EWCA Civ 810.
[55] Applying *Foskett v McKeown* [2001] 1 A.C. 102; *Allen v Rea Bros Trustees Ltd* [2002] EWCA Civ 85, (2002) 4 I.T.E.L.R. 627.
[56] *Foskett v McKeown* [2001] 1 A.C. 102.

C. Charges as remedies in equitable tracing actions

23–33 An equitable charge will be available to give effect to a proportionate share in a mixed fund of property without the need to segregate out any specific property to the claimant's account. Instead, the charge will secure a right to be paid an amount of money equal to the value which was lost to the trust. In the event that the money is not paid, the claimant will be entitled to seize property to the value of the amount owed to it. A charge would be appropriate as a remedy if the claimant wished to be paid in money and did not want to acquire title in the mixed property. In a tracing action, the benefit of a charge to the claimant would be to grant her a right to be paid whatever amount of money has been awarded by the court further to the tracing claim so as to recover the beneficiaries' loss, but with the added benefit of a security interest over the charged property which can be seized by order of the court if the defendant fails to make payment. Thus, charges grant a right to seize the charged property in the event that the defendant does not perform her obligations to pay money or to transfer property to the claimant. Importantly, though, a mere charge does not grant the chargee an immediate right in the charged property in the manner that a mortgage grants the mortgagee such an immediate right of ownership in the mortgaged property.[57] Charges were discussed in detail in Chapter 22.

D. Liens as remedies in equitable tracing claims

23–34 A lien is a possessory claim which entitles the claimant to petition the court, in the event that the amount owed to it is not paid, to turn the property to account in the amount of the property owed to it.[58] This remedy would be appropriate in relation to property which could be detained in this fashion, and so would be unlikely to assist in many securities transaction cases. Liens were discussed in detail in Chapter 22.

E. Subrogation as a remedy in equitable tracing claims

23–35 Subrogation is an equitable remedy which "works to revive extinguished rights of action and then to transfer them from one party to another"[59] where the court considers it to be equitable to do so. So, in *Boscawen v Bajwa*[60] mortgage moneys were mistakenly advanced by a financial institution to acquire land, when in fact the sale had not been completed. Consequently, the freeholder's solicitor mistakenly used those mortgage moneys to redeem the freeholder's

---

[57] It should be noted that the judges are not always so discriminating between charges and mortgages, often using the terms synonymously. See, for example, Slade J. in *Siebe Gorman v Barclays Bank* [1979] Lloyd's Rep. 142, 159 where the terms are used interchangeably in the following passage: " . . . a specific charge on the proceeds of [the book debts] as soon as they are received and consequently prevents the mortgagor from disposing of an unencumbered title to the subject matter of such charge without the mortgagee's consent, even before the mortgagee has taken steps to enforce its security."

[58] *Hammonds v Barclay* (1802) 2 East 227.

[59] Mitchell, *The Law of Subrogation* (Clarendon Press, 1995), p.5.

[60] Mitchell, *The Law of Subrogation*, p.5.

mortgage with a second financial institution. The first institution's money was traced into the discharge of the freeholder's mortgage. The remedy was that the first institution was subrogated to the rights of the second institution as mortgagee. That is, the redeemed mortgage was revived and the freeholder owed all of his obligations instead to the first institution: the first institution acquired a mortgage over the land by way of equitable subrogation. Thus, if property from a securities transaction was used to discharge an obligation to a third party, the claimant could be subrogated to the rights under that debt owed to the third party so that the debt would be revived and owed to the claimant instead

6. DEFENCES

A. Change of position

The foundations of change of position

The defence of change of position will be available to a defendant who has received property and, on the faith of the receipt of that property, suffered some change in their personal circumstances.[61] If there has been sufficient change of position in good faith, the defendant will have a defence to the tracing claim. The most concise judicial statement of the manner in which the defence of change of position might operate was set out by Lord Goff[62]:

> "Where an innocent defendant's position is so changed that he will suffer an injustice if called upon to repay or to repay in full, the injustice of requiring him so to repay outweighs the injustice of denying the plaintiff restitution."

23–36

Thus the court is required to consider which outcome would be more unjust: either allowing the defendant to keep the property given the harm that would cause to the claimant, or forcing the defendant to return the property to the claimant if the defendant had acted in some way in reliance on having received that property.[63]

The general principle on which the Court of Appeal in *Niru Battery Manufacturing Co v Milestone Trading Ltd* has described the defence of change of position, in the words of Sedley L.J., were in terms that:

> "courts ... are not tied to a single rigid standard in deciding whether a defence of change of position succeeds. They are to decide whether it is equitable to uphold the defence. Since the doctrine of restitution is centrally concerned with the distribution of loss among parties whose rights are not met by some stronger doctrine of law, one is by definition looking for the least unjust solution to a residual problem".[64]

23–37

---

[61] *Lipkin Gorman v Karpnale* [1991] 2 A.C. 548.

[62] [1991] 2 A.C. 548.

[63] *Scottish Equitable v Derby* [2000] 3 All E.R. 793, High Court; [2001] 3 All E.R. 818, Court of Appeal.

[64] *Niru Battery Manufacturing Co and anor v Milestone Trading Ltd and ors* [2003] EWCA Civ 1446, at [192], per Sedley L.J.

This explanation of the defence of change of position suggests that it may operate on the basis of equitable notions of fairness.[65] Similarly, in *Dextra Bank and Trust Co v Bank of Jamaica* the keynote of the defence of change of position has become its transformation into a general, equitable form of defence which is:

> "...founded on a principle of justice designed to protect the defendant from a claim to restitution in respect of a benefit received by him in circumstances in which it would be inequitable to pursue that claim, or to pursue it in full".[66]

Thus restitution—understood as being a general conception of recovery or return of property—has become equated by the courts with general notions of equity and as such need not be based on restitution of unjust enrichment.

Bad faith in change of position

23–38   It has been held by Sedley L.J. in *Niru Battery Manufacturing Company v Milestone Trading Ltd*[67] that the defence of change of position is not dependent upon the demonstration of an absence of bad faith in equal and opposite manner to the obligation to prove dishonesty in a claim for dishonest assistance.[68] Bad faith will, however, prevent a finding of a change of position defence. In *Barros Mattos v MacDaniels Ltd*[69] Laddie J. accepted the proposition that the defence of change of position would not be available to someone who had acted illegally.

That the change of position may take place before receipt of the property

23–39   In *Dextra Bank and Trust Co v Bank of Jamaica*,[70] the Privy Council held that incurring a future liability in reliance on the receipt of property could constitute a change of position. In this case a fraudster had induced D to make loans to him on the basis that the loan would be used in a foreign exchange transaction with B. B forwarded an amount in Jamaican dollars to the fraudster, believing it was making payment to D, before D made any payment. The fraudster absconded with the money. In seeking to resist a tracing claim brought by D, B claimed that its payment to the fraudster had been made by way of a change of position to in reliance on the payment which D was to make in the future: the problem being that B was claiming that it was changing its position in reliance on an event

---

[65] The same use of words has been applied in *Credit Suisse (Monaco) SA v Attar* [2004] EWHC 374, at [98], per Gross J.

[66] *Dextra Bank and Trust Co v Bank of Jamaica* [2002] 1 All E.R. (Comm) 193, at 38.

[67] [2003] EWCA Civ 1446.

[68] [2003] EWCA Civ 1446, at [179]. In *Niru Battery v Milestone Trading*, Niru had agreed to buy lead ingots from Milestone and so Milestone had obtained financing from CAI to acquire that lead by means of commonly used financial instruments known as "warehouse warrants". To pay for the release of the warrants, Milestone in turn acquired further finance from BS and SGS. CAI sold the warrants when it became concerned about the market value of lead and so Milestone was not able to fulfil its obligations to Niru. In proceedings for restitution it could not be demonstrated that any party had acted dishonestly, with SGS being liable in negligence and CAI only for unjust enrichment.

[69] [2004] 3 All E.R. 299; [2004] EWHC 1188.

[70] [2002] 1 All E.R. (Comm) 193.

which had not yet taken place. Nevertheless, the defence was allowed because the payment was clearly reliant on the anticipated receipt. In consequence, it is suggested, that in relation to interest rate swap transactions it would be possible to take into account future payments as part of a change of position. Similarly, payment of a premium under an option could be connected to the subsequent payment of a cash-settled amount under a call option. That a change of position can take place before the property is received has been accepted in *Commerzbank AG v Price*.[71]

B. Estoppel by representation

The second defence to an equitable tracing claim is that of estoppel by representation. Estoppel by representation will be made out in circumstances in which the defendant to a tracing action can demonstrate that some representation has been made to her, that that representation was deliberately or innocently false, that the claimant knew the representation would be acted upon, that the defendant then acted to her detriment in reliance upon the representation, and that there was no defence to the estoppel.[72] The defence of estoppel by representation arose in *National Westminster Bank Plc v Somer International*[73] where Somer received notice from the claimant bank that a payment had been made into its US dollar account which Somer mistakenly believed to be an amount which it was expecting to receive from a specific client. In fact, the payment had been made into that account by the bank by mistake, instead of being paid into an account owned by another of the bank's customers. In reliance on the receipt of the money, Somer shipped goods to its client believing that the payment was a payment for those goods. Subsequently, the bank sought to recover the mistaken payment. It was held that Somer was entitled to an estoppel by representation because the bank had represented to it that the money belonged to Somer, that Somer had acted to its detriment in reliance on that representation, and that Somer was therefore entitled to retain moneys paid to it by the bank equal to the value of the goods shipped to its customer.

23–40

Whereas the doctrine of estoppel by representation had previously operated merely as a rule of evidence,[74] the Court of Appeal in *National Westminster Bank Plc v Somer International* held that the doctrine of estoppel by representation operated on generally equitable principles such that, if the court considered the retention of the whole of the payment to be unconscionable, it would be possible to limit the defendant's remedy to compensation for the detriment which it had suffered. Therefore, on these facts, Somer could retain only an amount equal the value of the goods which it had shipped in reliance on the representation.[75] This mooted development is, however, at odds with earlier authority and the flexibility

23–41

---

[71] [2003] EWCA Civ 1633.
[72] See generally the various forms of estoppel by representation applied in *Jordan v Money* (1854) V HLC 185, 10 E.R. 868 and *National Westminster Bank Plc v Somer* [2002] Q.B. 1286, CA.
[73] [2002] Q.B. 1286, CA.
[74] *Avon County Council v Howlett* [1983] 1 W.L.R. 605.
[75] *Scottish Equitable v Derby* [2001] 3 All E.R. 818 applied.

of the older, purely evidential form of the estoppel by representation consequently awaits confirmation by a higher court.[76]

C. Bona fide purchaser for value without notice

23–42   The third defence arises when the defendant can demonstrate that it was a bona fide purchaser for value of rights without notice of the claimant's rights, then this will grant it a defence in equity.[77] In general terms the rights acquired should be legal title in the property, although it is suggested that this aspect of the doctrine is not always followed slavishly.

---

[76] See *Avon County Council v Howlett* [1983] 1 W.I.R. 605 at 622 per Slade L.J.

[77] *Westdeutsche Landesbank v Islington* [1996] A.C. 669.

PART VII

WRONGS

CHAPTER 24

FRAUD AND UNDUE INFLUENCE

[713]

CORE PRINCIPLES

The tort of deceit (or, the tort of fraudulent misrepresentation) arises on the making of a false representation in circumstances in which the defendant knew that that representation was untrue, or alternatively where the defendant was reckless as to the truth or falsity of that representation. The defendant must have intended that the claimant would rely on that statement and the claimant must then have relied on the representation. The defendant will be liable to compensate any losses suffered by a claimant in reliance on the false representation made by the defendant. The claimant is entitled to damages so as to put her in the position which she would have occupied if the misrepresentation had not been made.

Undue influence is significant when financial products are sold to inexpert customers so that inappropriate influence may have been exerted over the customer by the seller so as to sell her unsuitable products which may then cause the customer loss. Undue influence has become particularly important in relation to banks seeking to enforce their security over domestic homes under mortgage contracts where one cohabitee has unduly influenced or made a misrepresentation to another cohabitee so as to gull that other cohabitee into signing the mortgage contract or into agreeing to act as surety in relation to that mortgage. If there has been undue influence or a misrepresentation exerted between the cohabitees then this may lead to the mortgage contract being set aside so that the bank loses its security for the loan, further to the decision in *Barclays Bank v O'Brien* and related cases. The mortgagee will not be bound by any undue influence or misrepresentation where the mortgagee has taken "reasonable steps" to find out the signatory's rights. It is suggested that a particularly important light is shone on the doctrine of undue influence as an equitable doctrine by the "*Bundy* categories" of undue influence which are considered at the end of this chapter.

1. INTRODUCTION

24–01 It is one of the maudlin vicissitudes of life that wherever there is money, there will be some fraud, stealing and lying. The history of financial markets has been littered with examples of thieves and liars, among the straight-backed, steadfast and honest bankers. The several scandals discussed in Chapter 45 are testament to that state of affairs continuing to be the case. This chapter considers the private law context of fraud; whereas Chapters 13 through 16 considered its criminal law context. Financial markets are motivated by the urge to make profit from market movements. Profits are made from being sharper or better informed or cleverer than the person from whom one buys or to whom one sells, or simply by being expert enough to design a product for which an inexpert customer is prepared to pay a fee. There is, however, a narrow line somewhere between taking legitimate advantage of one's own superior skill, research and timing, and simply unconscionably exploiting a counterparty by telling untruths, allowing her to operate under a misapprehension or misleading her. This chapter considers the private law approach to the tort of fraudulent misrepresentation (often known as the tort of deceit), and also a line of very importance case law dealing with undue influence in banking transactions at the turn of the 21st century.

2.   THE TORT OF DECEIT—FRAUDULENT MISREPRESENTATION

A.   The elements of the tort of deceit

The tort of deceit is frequently referred to as the "tort of fraudulent misrepresentation", or sometimes simply as fraud.[1] To make out a claim in deceit the defendant must have made a false representation in circumstances in which the defendant knew that that representation was untrue, or alternatively the defendant must have been reckless as to the truth or falsity of that representation. In either event, the defendant must have intended that the claimant would rely on that statement. The claimant must then have relied on the representation. If the claim is made out successfully, then the defendant will be liable to compensate any losses suffered by a claimant in reliance on the false representation made by the defendant. These elements of the tort of deceit are considered in detail in this chapter. If the representation was not deceitful—in the sense of not having been made in the knowledge that it was false or being reckless as to its falsity—then liability may arise under the tort of negligence, as considered in the next chapter.

24–02

Fraud is demonstrated when a person makes a representation knowing that it is untrue, or not believing it is true, or being reckless as to its truth or falsity. The test was classically stated by Lord Herschell in *Derry v Peek*[2] in the following terms[3]:

24–03

> "First, in order to sustain an action of deceit, there must be proof of fraud and nothing short of that will suffice. Secondly, fraud is proved when it is shown that a false representation has been made (i) knowingly, (ii) without belief in its truth, or (iii) recklessly, careless whether it be true or false. Although I have treated the second and third as distinct cases, I think the third is but an instance of the second, for one who makes a statement under such circumstances can have no real belief in the truth of what he states. To prevent a false statement from being fraudulent, there must, I think, always be an honest belief in its truth."

The application of this test to various forms of financial activity is the business of the sections to follow.

B.   The need for a false misrepresentation

The nature of a false representation

The defendant must have made a false representation to attract liability under the tort of deceit. The misrepresentation may be explicit or it may be inferred from the circumstances. The most straightforward example of a false representation is a representation which the representor knows to be false and which is made the intention of deceiving the representee so as to gull that representee into creating a contract. An inferred misrepresentation would arise where the defendant intended to create a false impression in the mind of the claimant and the representee

24–04

---

[1] This tort is sometimes referred to simply as "fraud". See generally *Clerk and Lindsell on Torts*, Ch.18.

[2] (1889) 14 App. Cas. 337.

[3] (1889) 14 App. Cas. 337, 376.

inferred that the representation was being made. So, for example, in relation to a prospectus made in relation to an issue of securities it is sufficient to render a representation into a false representation if the defendant intends that the claimant investor will garner an impression from that representation which is untrue.[4] The status of inferred representations was complex under the older authorities. These distinctions are considered in greater detail in the sections to follow.

That a false representation can be made impliedly and not simply explicitly

24–05   There are authorities under the general law of tort to the effect that a false representation must be made actively: which means that the representor must have intended to mislead the representee and also that the representation was actually made, as opposed to being merely implied. Consequently it was held that "mere silence, however morally wrong, will not support an action of deceit".[5] Therefore, it was the case that a defendant could not be held liable for deceit if she failed to mention some fact the absence of which would cause a misapprehension in the mind of the representee: the rationale was that a failure to mention a fact does not constitute a representation of that fact. These cases, it is suggested, should not be followed today in the financial context.

24–06   This narrow approach to misrepresentations was at odds, however, with even the 19th century cases on the preparation of prospectuses in the issues of securities (principally shares in the 19th century). By way of example, the old cases on the preparation of prospectuses created what is referred to as a "golden rule" which imposed an obligation disclosure on those preparing prospectuses which meant that careful omissions of facts, or weasel words taking care not to state a misrepresentation literally even if the misrepresentation was nevertheless implied, would not be sufficient to avoid liability precisely because there was an obligation to make disclosure of all material facts. As is considered in Chapter 38, the Prospectus Rules provide that the people responsible for a prospectus will be required to provide all of the information which would ordinarily be required by a reasonable investor and his professional advisors when making a decision whether or not to invest in the securities in question. Therefore, the application of this sort of abstruse common law reasoning would in any event tend to be inappropriate in a financial sector governed by positive obligations to make disclosure.

24–07   There are contexts in the general law of tort in which omissions of material have been taken to constitute false representations. A clear example of this principle arose in *Peek v Gurney*[6] where it was held by Lord Cairns that "a partial and fragmentary statement of fact" can have the effect that "the withholding of that which is not stated makes that which is stated absolutely false".[7] So, withholding

---

[4] See *Moens v Heyworth* (1842) 10 M. & W. 147, quoted in *Clerk and Lindsell on Torts*, para.18–04.
[5] *Bradford Third Equitable Benefit Building Society v Borders* [1941] 2 All E.R. 205, 211, per Lord Maugham.
[6] (1873) L.R. 6 H.L. 377
[7] (1873) L.R. 6 H.L. 377, 403.

a part of the truth with a view to creating a false impression will constitute a false representation. An example of this sort of implied representation might arise in a situation in which shares were offered in a company which had recently settled litigation in secret with an agreement to pay four-fifths of its annual profit to the other party, if the prospectus for those securities stated that "there is no litigation outstanding at present which will affect future profits" and thus suggested that there were no reasons why litigation would lead to future reductions in profits. Literally it would be true that there was no litigation outstanding at the time that the representation was made because that litigation had been settled before the statement was made; but it would deceive an investor as to the obligation which the company faced to pay away four-fifths of its profits in the future.

The principle that implied, non-explicit misrepresentations should attract liability was approved by the House of Lords in *Smith New Court Securities Ltd v Scrimgeour Vickers (Asset Management) Ltd*,[8] in the context again of false statements made in a prospectus in relation to the issue of securities. Lord Steyn held that if only a partial account of the truth is given such that the true position is hidden then "a cocktail of truth, falsity and evasion is a more powerful instrument of deception than undiluted falsehood".[9] Meaning that if half-truths are sprinkled in amongst the facts, then the representee is all the more likely to be misled. The statement becomes all the more plausible, it is said. Lord Chelmsford held in *Peek v Gurney* that "half the truth will sometimes amount to a real falsehood".[10] Therefore, a statement in a prospectus which discusses the issuing company's exploitation of a patent, and which makes play of the profit which is expected to generate, without making mention that that patent is under legal challenge or that there is pending litigation brought by customers who have suffered harm as a result of the patented process, would constitute a false representation if the intention was to present a purely positive impression as to the patented process. Failing to mention the legal challenges and stressing only the possible profits which are expected to flow from the patent would create a misleading impression as to the company's prospects. (The nature of half-truths is considered in greater detail in the next chapter in relation to the tort of negligence.[11])

24–08

Whether statements merely of opinion or belief can be fraudulent

Ordinarily deceit will relate to statements of fact which turn out to be false. Nevertheless, a statement of opinion may constitute a fraudulent misrepresentation. As Bowen L.J. put it in *Edgington v Fitzmaurice*[12] "the state of a man's mind is as much a fact as the state of his digestion". Thus, it was held that the

24–09

---

[8] *Smith New Court Securities Ltd v Scrimgeour Vickers (Asset Management) Ltd* [1994] 4 All E.R. 225.

[9] [1994] 4 All E.R. 225.

[10] (1873) L.R. 6 H.L. 377, 392; see also Lord Cairns at 403: "such a partial and fragmentary statement of fact, as the withholding of that which is not stated, makes that which is stated absolutely false".

[11] See para.25–01.

[12] (1885) 29 Ch.D. 459, 483. See also *Clydesdale Bank Ltd v Paton* [1896] A.C. 381, 394, per Lord Herschell and at 397, per Lord Davey.

purposes for which debentures were said to be being issued—namely to expand the business through the acquisition of buildings and moveable assets—could constitute a misrepresentation if those were indeed not the genuine purposes for issuing the debentures—just as in that case the directors did not actually intend to buy land and moveables, but rather intended to defray some of the company's pressing liabilities with the debenture capital. Consequently, deliberately misstating an opinion so as to mislead the representee would constitute a fraudulent misrepresentation. *Edgington v Fitzmaurice* was a clear case in which the opinion stated was intentionally false and its purpose was to make investors believe that they were making an investment which would improve the business, rather than simply attempting to bail the business out of difficulties. A more difficult situation would be that in which the statement was made in good faith but was nevertheless false.

24–10 A genuinely-held belief in the truth of a proposition will ordinarily not be a fraudulent misrepresentation because fraud requires knowledge that a representation is false, or recklessness as to its truth or falsity: thus a genuinely-held belief could only be fraudulent if it was made recklessly. Recklessness in this context has been held to encompass simply indifference as to whether or not the statement is true or false.[13] Thus it would be feasible to suppose that one could have a foolish indifference to the truth of a genuinely held but foolish opinion. It is more likely that such a statement would be found to be negligent—as considered in the next chapter—because it is difficult to fix a defendant with fraud if she is really a fool. As Lord Herschell held in *Derry v Peek*[14] "[t]o prevent a false statement from being fraudulent, there must, I think, always be an honest belief in its truth", suggesting that an honest fool would not be found to be dishonest. So in *Thomas Witter Ltd v TBP Properties Ltd*[15] it was held by Jacob J. that a careless failure to check whether or not a profit forecast was accurate could not be proved to have been dishonest and therefore no liability lay in fraud.

24–11 On the other hand, it could be said that foolishness could be carried recklessly to lengths which would call into question that person's honesty.[16] Recklessness has been held to constitute indifference as to whether or not the statement is true or false.[17] It may be that a statement is so evidently false that the person who made it would seem to be impossible to believe if they claimed to have believed that it was correct. Of course if it is an opinion which it can be proven is not honestly held by the representor, then it would be fraudulent.[18] This must be especially so if investors are expected to act upon that statement. The case of *Derry v Peek* itself concerned a company which asserted in its prospectus that the company had the right to operate trams by steam power rather than by horses, whereas in fact it was only able to use steam power if the Board of Trade authorised it so to do. In the event, the Board of Trade refused its permission. The plaintiff shareholder brought an action for fraud against the directors on the basis that the statement in

---

[13] *GE Commercial Finance Ltd v Gee* [2005] EWHC 2056, at [104], per Tugendhat J.
[14] (1889) 14 App. Cas. 337.
[15] [1996] 2 All E.R. 573.
[16] *Anderson v Pacific Insurance Co* (1872) L.R. 7 C. & P. 65, 69, per Willes J.
[17] *GE Commercial Finance Ltd v Gee* [2005] EWHC 2056, at [104], per Tugendhat J.
[18] *GE Commercial Finance Ltd v Gee* [2005] EWHC 2056, at [104], per Tugendhat J.

the prospectus had formed the basis of the contract for purchase of the shares. It was held that the directors were not liable for fraud because they had made the statement in the prospectus to the effect that the company could use steam power in the honest belief that it was true. Latterly in *Niru Battery Manufacturing Co v Milestone Trading Ltd*[19] it was held that no claim lay in deceit in circumstances in which an account officer of the defendant bank honestly, if naively, arranged presentation of a letter of credit even though the goods involved had not been delivered.

Continuing obligations

As considered in Chapters 35 through 39, there are many contexts in which securities regulation imposes continuing obligations on issuers to provide information and to ensure that any changes in that information are relayed to a recognised information service ("RIS") or prompt the preparation of supplementary prospectus. Under the general law of tort, in relation to continuing representations[20] there is an obligation to correct the representation before that representation is acted on by the claimant.[21]

24–12

C.   The defendant's state of mind

The meaning of fraud

The forms of representation which may give rise to liability have been considered above; this section considers the state of mind which the defendant must have in greater detail. Lord Herschell held in *Derry v Peek*[22] that:

24–13

> "there must be proof of fraud and nothing short of that will suffice. . . . fraud is proved when it is shown that a false representation has been made (i) knowingly, (ii) without belief in its truth, or (iii) recklessly, careless whether it be true or false".

As mentioned above, a statement will not be fraudulently made if the maker reasonably believed in its truth or accuracy.[23] It is not enough to prove that the defendant had been guilty of gross negligence, nor that he had made the statement without any reasonable grounds for believing it to be true. What must be demonstrated is a fraudulent state of mind. The test is a subjective one, as is shown in the following passage from the judgement in *Akerhielm v De Mare*[24]:

> "The question is not whether the defendant in any given case honestly believed the representation to be true in the sense assigned to it by the court on an objective consideration of its truth or falsity, but whether he honestly believed the representation to be true in the sense in which he understood it albeit erroneously when it was made. This general proposition is no doubt subject to limitations. For instance, the meaning placed by the defendant on the

---

[19] [2004] QB 985.

[20] See *Clerk and Lindsell on Torts*, para.18–16.

[21] *Briess v Woolley* [1954] A.C. 333.

[22] (1889) 14 App. Cas. 337.

[23] *Niru Battery Manufacturing Co v Milestone Trading Ltd* [2004] Q.B. 985.

[24] [1959] A.C. 789, 805 (P.C.).

representation made may be so far removed from the sense in which it would be understood by any reasonable person as to make it impossible to hold that the defendant honestly understood the representation to bear the meaning claimed by him and honestly believed it in that sense to be true."

The defendant in an action for deceit will escape liability if she can prove that she did believe the fact stated, even though her belief was not based on reasonable grounds, for, if she believed the statement, fraud is negatived.[25] Again she will escape liability if she can prove that the plaintiff was not, in fact, misled. An example of this would be where the claimant knew the statement to be false when she acquired the investment or financial product at issue.[26] However, it has been held that the defendant cannot avail herself of the "audacious plea"[27] that the plaintiff might easily, by inquiry or otherwise, have ascertained that the statement was untrue. The onus is on the person making the statement to make a correct statement, not on the listener to check on all the facts.

D. The defendant must have intended that the claimant would act on the representation

24–14   The defendant must have intended that the claimant would act on the representation for an action to lie in deceit.[28] It is sufficient that the defendant realises that the claimant will rely on the false representation.[29] Thus in preparing a prospectus, it will be sufficient to found liability on this part of the tort of deceit if the maker of the statement realised that the claimant would rely on that statement. This raises an issue as to when it is reasonable to assume that a person will rely on a statement. In *Possfund Custodian Trustee Ltd v Diamond*[30] Lightman J. considered that the issue of shares ought not to be treated as though it was limited to any particular group of investors; whereas in *Al-Nakib Investments (Jersey) Ltd v Longcroft*[31] the issue was intended to be a rights issue to a limited class of potential subscribers and therefore that its duty of care was owed only to that limited class of subscribers. Thus at common law the context in which a representation is made will be important.[32]

---

[25] *Derry v Peek* (1889) 14 App. Cas. 337; *Akierhelm v De Mare*, above.

[26] As, e.g. in *JEB Fasteners Ltd v Marks Bloom and Co* [1981] 3 All E.R. 289; [1983] 1 All E.R. 583 (CA).

[27] *Aaron's Reefs v Twiss* (1896) A.C. 273, per Lord Watson.

[28] *Peek v Gurney* (1873) L.R. 6 H.L. 377.

[29] *Shinhan Bank Ltd v Sea Containers Ltd* [2000] 2 Lloyd's Rep. 406.

[30] [1996] 2 All E.R. 774.

[31] [1990] 3 All E.R. 321.

[32] See generally *Raiffeisen Zentralbank Osterreich AG v The Royal Bank of Scotland* [2010] EWHC 1392 (Comm), Christopher Clarke J. on the nature of what will constitute a representation on which another person relies, in turn relying on *MCI WorldCom International Inc v Primus Telecommunications Inc* [2004] EWCA Civ 957. See also *Standard Chartered Bank v Ceylon Petroleum Corporation* [2011] EWHC 1785 (Comm). These cases analysed the facts in front of them for evidence of an actionable misrepresentation without making an meaningful contribution to the substantive law itself.

E.   The claimant must have been influenced by the representation

The claimant must have relied upon the representation when acquiring the   **24–15**
securities in question. As Lightman J. put this matter in relation to offers of
securities:

> "For the purpose of the torts of deceit and negligent misrepresentation, it is necessary to
> establish a material misrepresentation intended to influence, and which did in fact influence,
> the mind of the representee and on which the representee reasonably relied.[33]"

Significantly, the representation need only have been one of a number of
factors which caused the claimant to act as he did, provided that it was a material
inducement.[34] The statement must have been an inducement in the sense, in this
context, of deceiving the claimant.

F.   The standard of proof

The standard of proof for deceit is the ordinary test of the balance of   **24–16**
probabilities.[35] There have, however, been judicial statements suggesting that the
more serious the allegation of fraud then "the higher the degree of probability that
is required",[36] which is a qualification which has been approved in relation
specifically to securities transactions.[37]

G.   Liability for fraudulent misrepresentation under the law of contract

This chapter has been concerned with liability in tort. Liability for fraudulent   **24–17**
misrepresentation may also arise under the law contract further to the
Misrepresentation Act 1967. Those issues were considered in Chapter 20.[38]

H.   The measure of damages for fraudulent misrepresentation

The test for the quantum of damages: Smith New Court v Scrimgeour Vickers

When a fraudulent misrepresentation has been made in the manner considered   **24–18**
above, the measure of damages is that appropriate to claims in tort. The claimant

---

[33] *Possfund Custodian Trustee Ltd v Diamond* [1996] 2 All E.R. 774; [1996] 1 W.L.R. 1351; [1996] 2
B.C.L.C. 665, per Lightman J.

[34] *J.E.B. Fasteners Ltd v Marks Bloom & Co* [1983] 1 All E.R. 583, 589, per Stephenson L.J.; and see
Paul & Vincent v O'Reilly (1913) 49 Ir. L.T. 89. See generally, *Clerk and Lindsell on Torts*,
para.18–32.

[35] *Hornal v Neuberger Products Ltd* [1957] 1 Q.B. 247.

[36] *Ibid*, 258, per Denning L.J.

[37] *Smith New Court Securities Ltd v Citibank NA* [1997] A.C. 254, 274, per Lord Steyn.

[38] See para.20–03 et seq in relation to damages for breach of contract and para.20–21 for damages for
misrepresentation.

is entitled to be placed in the position which she would have occupied if the misrepresentation had not been made.[39] The issue arose before the House of Lords as to the measure of damages in connection with a purchase of shares induced by a fraudulent misrepresentation in *Smith New Court Securities Ltd v Scrimgeour Vickers (Asset Management) Ltd*.[40] Here an investor in shares had been induced to make an offer for the purchase of shares on the basis that there were two other bidders for those shares. It was found at first instance that there had been fraudulent misrepresentations made to the investor with damages calculated on the difference between the price paid and the real value of the shares. The issue before the House of Lords was as to the appropriate quantum of damages in this regard, and further issues arose as to whether all of the representations had been actionable.

24–19   There had been two separate frauds perpetrated. The first was a representation by R on behalf of Citibank that induced the claimant to acquire the shares from Citibank at a price of £23,141,424. The second was committed by G against the issuer of the shares, F, which caused F to lose a large amount of money. Neither the issuer of the shares nor G were parties to the action; rather, the action concerned the damages payable in respect of the first fraud. The announcement of the second fraud caused a large fall in the value of the shares. This fall led the claimant to research the circumstances of the acquisition of the shares in the first place. It was at this time that the first fraud was uncovered. The first fraud was made up of three representations by R: that there were other bidders for the shares; that other bids had been received and would be made known to the claimant; and that those bids were higher than in fact they were. Thus the value of the shareholding had been artificially increased.

24–20   It was held by Lord Browne-Wilkinson that the impact of the second fraud on the issuer of the shares had created a "false market" in those shares. However, it was also found that the first fraud had had no impact on the open market value of the shares. The central objective in making an award of damages in relation to a tort was restated to be put the injured party in the same position as if the wrong had not been sustained.[41]

24–21   The 19th century rule relating to the date of valuation being the transaction date was held not to be a rule capable of *universal* application in the modern context,[42] although it was probably good law in the *majority* of contexts.[43] However, the usefulness of this rule is identified as being the lack of any requirement of proof of causation. In taking another date at the appropriate valuation date there will be, from case to case, difficulties in demonstrating the causal nexus between the damages sought and the movements in the value of the appropriate security. Lord

---

[39] *Smith New Court Securities Ltd v Scrimgeour Vickers (Asset Management) Ltd* [1994] 4 All E.R. 225; the correct measure is the difference between what the purchaser paid and the price which, absent the misrepresentation, the shares would have fetched on the open market.

[40] [1996] 4 All E.R. 769.

[41] [1996] 4 All E.R. 769, 774, per Lord Browne-Wilkinson; *Livingstone v Rawyards Coal Co* (1880) 5 App. Cas. 25, 39, per Lord Blackburn.

[42] [1996] 4 All E.R. 769, 778, per Lord Browne-Wilkinson.

[43] [1996] 4 All E.R. 769, 778, per Lord Browne-Wilkinson, 793, per Lord Steyn.

Browne-Wilkinson ordered that the damages recoverable would be the difference between the contract price and the amount actually realised by the plaintiff on disposal of the shares.[44]

Lord Steyn approached the question of the damages recoverable by analogy to a **24–22** racehorse acquired on the basis of a false representation that it was a champion when it was in fact a greatly inferior performer. In his lordship's opinion if the horse died as a result of some extraneous factor, the claimant would not be entitled to recover the entire value of the horse. It would only be open to such a claimant to recover the difference between the real value of the horse at the time it was bought and the price that was actually paid.[45] Similarly, with respect to shares which are acquired as a result of some false representation (affecting their precise value) but which become entirely worthless due to some extraneous factor (affecting their having any effective value at all), the investor would be entitled to recover only the difference between the real value of the shares and the price paid for them. Such an investor would not be entitled to claim repayment of the total price paid for the shares by arguing that the property had become worthless.

Lord Browne-Wilkinson set out seven principles which are to inform decisions in **24–23** this area[46]:

"(1) The defendant is bound to make reparation for all the damage directly flowing from the transaction.

(2) Although such damage need not have been foreseeable, it must have been directly caused by the transaction.

(3) In assessing such damage, the plaintiff is entitled to recover by way of damages the full price paid by him, but he must give credit for any benefits which he has received as a result of the transaction.

(4) As a general rule, the benefits received by him include the market value of the property acquired as at the date of acquisition; but such general rule is not to be inflexibly applied where to do so would prevent him obtaining full compensation for the wrong suffered.

(5) Although the circumstances in which the general rule should not apply cannot be comprehensively stated, it will normally not apply where either (a) the misrepresentation has continued to operate after the date of the acquisition of the asset so as to induce the plaintiff to retain the asset or (b) the circumstances of the case are such that the plaintiff is, by reason of the fraud, locked into the property.

(6) In addition, the plaintiff is entitled to recover consequential losses caused by the transaction.

(7) The plaintiff must take all reasonable steps to mitigate his loss once he has discovered the fraud."

Therefore, the inflexibility of the old rule in *Doyle v Olby (Ironmongers) Ltd*[47] is not be to applied rigidly in future cases. This is particularly the case in those instances where to tie the measurement of damages to the date of the transaction would fail to take account of continuing misrepresentations or the inability of the injured party to dispose of the securities. Incidental loss is similarly recoverable. However, the Court of Appeal has recently exposed itself as reluctant to consider

---

[44] [1996] 4 All E.R. 769, 778, per Lord Browne-Wilkinson,780, per Lord Browne-Wilkinson.

[45] [1996] 4 All E.R. 769, 778, per Lord Browne-Wilkinson, 789 et seq, per Lord Steyn; citing *Twycross v Grant* (1877) 2 C.P.D. 469, 544, per Cockburn C.J.

[46] [1996] 4 All E.R. 769, 778, per Lord Browne-Wilkinson, 769, 778, per Lord Browne-Wilkinson.

[47] [1969] 2 Q.B. 158.

the ambit of consequential loss as extending too widely in financial transactions. For example, the cost of unwinding hedging transactions or of acquiring replacement transactions in connection with interest rate swaps has been held to be outwith the nexus of consequential or incidental expense.[48]

24–24   This approach was followed in *Parabola Investments Ltd v Browallia Cal Ltd*[49] where an investor, Gill, was induced by the fraudulent misrepresentations of the defendant's agent to invest with them, and therefore that investor was entitled to recover

> "all its losses which flow directly from that fraud, which consist not only of the depletion of its trading fund and loss of profits it would otherwise have made on that fund in the period of the fraud, but the loss of profits it has suffered up until the trial. As a consequence of having been deprived of that fund and only had a smaller fund with which to trade, Tangent has continued to suffer from the adverse effects of the fraud up until the trial".[50]

Therefore, the claimant was also able to recover its opportunity cost in this instance. The investor had been a successful investor in equities and derivatives who acted through the claimants, which were special purpose vehicles created for his investment activities. Bomford, the third defendant who was employed by the defendant financial institution as a trader, traded on behalf of Gill but gave him false information about the profitability of the transactions which he was creating. He knowingly misled Gill and continued to trade on his account because he knew that Gill relied entirely on the profit and loss statements which Bomford gave to Gill directly, as opposed to any other material. In this way, the claimant entity lost money and thus robbed Gill of any opportunity to trade profitably in another way. The award of damages was that set out immediately above.

The duty to mitigate one's loss

24–25   One further important issue is the duty to mitigate loss once the fraud comes to the attention of the injured party. The injured will generally be required to take steps to mitigate that loss by selling the securities.[51] Otherwise there will be a requirement to bring the value of the asset into account in valuing the damages which are to be awarded in respect of the deceit or fraudulent misrepresentation.[52] On the facts of *Smith New Court v Scrimgeour Vickers*, it was held that the claimant had acquired the shares as part of a long-term, market-making risk position and therefore should not be held to be subject to a duty to mitigate loss because the purpose for which the shares had been acquired locked the claimant into them.[53] It was held further that the plaintiff would only have been able to have disposed of the shares at a loss. Consequently it was held that it would not

---

[48] *Kleinwort Benson v Birmingham C.C.* [1996] 4 All E.R. 733,
[49] [2009] EWHC 901 (Comm). This decision was upheld on appeal: [2010] EWCA Civ 486, [2010] Bus LR 1446.
[50] [2009] EWHC 901 (Comm).at [209].
[51] *Doyle v Olby (Ironmongers) Ltd* [1969] 2 Q.B. 158.
[52] [1996] 4 All E.R. 769, 778, per Lord Browne-Wilkinson.
[53] [1996] 4 All E.R. 769, 780, per Lord Browne-Wilkinson.

have been "sensible" to have disposed of them.[54] It would appear that the duty to mitigate on this latter basis is thus rendered a weak duty. Where, as a result of fraud, the purchaser has been induced into the purchase, it is likely that there will only be a possibility of a sale at a loss. Therefore, in broad terms, the disposal of the shares would never be a sensible financial decision even though the law may have considered it necessary to mitigate loss. Perhaps these dicta of Lord Browne-Wilkinson are intended to be restricted to the facts of cases such as *Smith New Court* where the securities had more than halved in value between purchase and discovery of the fraud.

3. THE LAW OF FRAUD IN RECENT FINANCE CASES

A.   Introduction

One of the more significant aspects of the law on fraud in the context of financial transactions is that much of the case law has been brought not because the claimant genuinely believed that the defendant had acted fraudulently, necessarily, but rather because the defendant financial institution has excluded its liability for carelessness, negligence and similar breaches of duty, and therefore the only line open to the claimant is to seek to prove fraud so as to recover damages. It is a regrettable feature of this area of the law that the use of exclusion of liability clauses (even though they are precluded in relation to a financial institution's regulatory liabilities by COBS 2.1.2R) means that customers—no matter how inexpert—cannot recover damages for loss which have been caused by the carelessness or negligence of the financial institution in whose expertise they were required to repose so much confidence.

24–26

B.   Actual fraud

There are, of course, instances of actual deceit on the part of traders where it is possible to prove that there was conscious deceit on the part of the defendant. Often this is in the form of hiding losses and then lying about the fact, as with Leeson in relation to the collapse of Barings Bank. In *Parabola Investments Ltd v Browallia Cal Ltd*[55] the Court of Appeal upheld the finding of the trial judge that a trader who worked for the defendant had deliberately made a series of fraudulent misrepresentations, including concealing trading losses from the other parties, so giving rise to liability for damages for fraudulent misrepresentation.[56] The trial judge simply considered the trader to have been a liar.

24–27

---

[54] [1996] 4 All E.R. 769, 780, per Lord Browne-Wilkinson.

[55] [2010] EWCA Civ 486.

[56] Toulson L.J. quoted Flaux J.'s assessment of that trader's performance in the witness box during the trial in the following way, it had been: "'a disastrous three days in the witness box for Mr Bomford, during which he was exposed not just as a fraudster throughout ... but also as a persistent and inveterate liar in almost everything he said": [2010] EWCA Civ 486, at [3].

C.   Fraud in complex financial transactions

Introduction

24–28   This section considers recent cases on the law of fraud in financial transactions, principally in the wake of the financial crisis. The context in which those transactions were created is considered in detail in Chapter 45—especially the litigation relating to Barclays[57] and Goldman Sachs.[58] What emerges from these cases is a limited application of the test in *Derry v Peek* and instead a focus in long High Court judgments on finding evidence of actual fraud (as opposed to recklessness or carelessness as to the truth of a representation). In all of these cases, the claimants were obliged to try to prove fraud because the defendant financial institutions had excluded their liability for negligence by an express provision in the parties' contracts. We shall begin with a case involving Barclays.

Fraud and hyper-complex, over-rated derivative products

24–29   The decision of Hamblen J. in *Cassa di Risparmio della Repubblica di San Marino SpA v Barclays Bank Ltd*[59] related to a very complex series of collateralised debt obligation ("CDO") products which a small financial institution organised in San Marino had asked Barclays to structure for it. In essence, the claimant wanted to be able to on-sell those CDOs to its own customers so as to give them exposure to the CDO and credit default swap ("CDS") markets. Somewhat optimistically perhaps it hoped to acquire exposure to these markets at minimal risk while acquiring a comparatively high investment return. So, the structured product was to be rated at AAA but was to pay a rate of return which was higher than that ordinarily paid on such a product. It was alleged that on Barclays' own internal risk modelling methodology "at their dates of issue the CDOs had a probability of default over their lives of around 30 per cent (equivalent to single 'B' or 'junk')".[60] The claimant alleged that it had been induced to enter into the transaction to buy the various "notes"[61] and to enter into the restructuring of those notes on the basis of fraudulent misrepresentations made to it by various employees of Barclays which those people could not reasonably have believed to be true. Ultimately, Hamblen J. held that none of the allegations of fraud had been proved on these facts.

24–30   At first blush, that a product could be rated at the highest investment grade, AAA, and in hindsight be considered to have been equivalent to "junk" at the same time, would naturally lead an investor to wonder whether or not the seller had acted so recklessly that their behaviour should be considered to constitute fraud.

---

[57] para 57–37.
[58] para 57–29.
[59] *Cassa di Risparmio della Repubblica di San Marino SpA v Barclays Bank Ltd* [2011] EWHC 484 (Comm).
[60] [2011] EWHC 484 (Comm), at [5].
[61] The term "notes" is commonly used by English judges to describe a very wide range of financial instruments which are sold to third party investors.

Further to the decision of the House of Lords *Derry v Peek*,[62] it is sufficient for a defendant's actions to be considered to be fraudulent if that person acting knowingly deceitfully or was reckless as to the truth. Here, the argument would have been that Barclays was reckless as to the credit quality of the CDO which it had constructed. Barclays could have been held to be liable if they were considered to have acted so recklessly that they could not reasonably have believed that rating to be true or their product to be sufficiently safe.

However, Hamblen J. did not carefully match the facts in front of him against the detail of the common law test. *Derry v Peek* was cited and quoted from in only three paragraphs of a judgment made up of 566 paragraphs. The methodology which Hamblen J. used was to consider each allegation of misrepresentation one-at-a-time with the result that he found them to have been unproven on the facts; whereas a very recent High Court decision was cited and quoted from on seventeen occasions.[63] That High Court decision of Gloster J. in *JP Morgan v Springwell* had not applied the precise test in *Derry v Peek* forensically either. If his lordship had taken all of the circumstances in the round, then, it is suggested that it would have been more difficult to find that there was no recklessness in the *Derry v Peek* sense of that term in constructing this product, where Lord Herschell considered that an allegation of fraud would be made out if "a false representation has been made ... recklessly, careless whether it be true or false".[64] One of the principal problems with this case was that it had to be argued on the basis of fraud, due to the presence of an exclusion of liability clause in the parties' contract,[65] as opposed to being argued on the basis simply of negligence.

24–31

The CDO structure in this case was very complex and therefore it required a large amount of work by Barclays to construct it: in that sense it is a good example of a product which could not have been constructed by the buyer, in which the buyer was reliant on the expertise of the seller, but which the buyer had nevertheless ordered in broad terms.[66] Consequently, it could be said on the one hand that the buyer was entirely reliant on the seller, but at the same time it could be said that the seller was occupying a middle ground between merely executing an order and yet being required to bring its own discretionary expertise to bear on the organisation of the structure. When the CDO and CDS markets collapsed, this structure collapsed in value too.

24–32

The buyer contended that there had been dishonesty in the creation of this structure and that fraudulent misrepresentations had been made to it by the salesman, F, at Barclays with whom the claimant had dealt before, and by the employee who was responsible for structuring the product, A, amongst others. The lengthy judgment considered the facts in some detail and each of the allegations of fraud, but there was little analysis of the authorities. Consequently,

24–33

---

[62] (1889) 14 App. Cas. 337.

[63] As considered in section E below: it is questionable whether these recent High Court decisions are applying the law on fraud with sufficient precision to the factual circumstances before them.

[64] (1889) 14 App. Cas. 337, 368.

[65] The context of exclusion of liability clauses is considered immediately below in this section of this chapter.

[66] The buyer approached the seller asking for a product of this sort to be put together, and then the seller used its expertise and prior experience to construct such a product.

this case does not easily lend itself to a brief discussion because it turned on its own facts. In essence, Hamblen J. did not find that any of the allegations of fraud had been made out and therefore Barclays was found not to be liable for fraud. Many of the allegations related to conversations had over lunch in San Marino, telephone conversations, emails and so forth in which it was alleged that F had suggested that in his experience no AAA rated product had ever failed and therefore the claimant contended that these sorts of statements amounted to representations about the unlikelihood of this CDO structure failing. As is well-known in the wake of the global financial crisis, the credit rating agencies typically rated complex structures at AAA as a result of clever structuring by quantitative analysts, even though those ratings in some cases crumbled from AAA to junk status in a few months in 2008–09. Reading between the lines, Hamblen J. was simply unconvinced by the allegations made by the claimant that, inter alia, this extremely complex structure concealed from it the idea that reference entities within the structure might have weaker credit profiles than the AAA rating indicated, and furthermore that there was no clear representation that there would be no loss or that the product was something other than what it was—a very complex set of derivative instruments with a risk of failure.

24–34   Nevertheless, there are oddities on the facts. Once the structure had begun to fail, Barclays agreed to repurchase two out of three products from the claimant and one of the alleged misrepresentations related to whether or not Barclays was to make any profit out of these repurchases. In relation to A, his lordship relates that this individual was a junior member of the structuring department at Barclays and that, remarkably, he had no knowledge of whether or not Barclays would take a profit from the transaction. Furthermore, he was too junior to have any face-to-face interaction with clients in the ordinary course of events with the result that he could not have made meaningful representations in any event. It is not clear on the facts as related by his lordship how much contact A did have with the claimant. What is difficult to believe is that A would have had *no* idea about the likely profit that would flow from such a series of transactions; although it is perfectly reasonable to suppose that a junior employee might have refrained from making dishonest statements to a client or from dishonestly creating a CDO structure. What is peculiar is the notion that such a person could be considered to have been squirreled away in the bowels of the bank creating CDO structures with the result that he was so completely shielded from the commercial context in which these products operated. No explicit point is taken about whether or not A was too junior to have bound the bank vicariously, or whether his role was so strictly limited to the quantitative analysis of products that his role was explicitly ring-fenced away from the process of identifying whether or not those products were suitable for any given client, or whether he simply spoke the truth on each occasion he had contact with a client. At first blush, that A was responsible for "structuring" this CDO assumes that A must have known what was going into it and whether or not it could in good conscience have been considered to be a AAA product. On that basis, it seems difficult to argue that Barclays was not vicariously reckless as to the quality of the CDO which it was selling as a top, investment grade product. However, in effect, Hamblen J. maintained that, taking each individual allegation separately, there was no individual allegation which involved a smoking gun of conscious dishonesty: despite the dicta of Lord Herschell in *Derry v Peek*.

Complete refusal to be bound from the outset among market counterparties

The issue arose in *IFE v Goldman Sachs*[67] as to whether or not Goldman Sachs bore any legal responsibilities to its client in relation to a financing agreement and bond issue connected to a proposed takeover of Finelist by Autodis. In the documentation connected to the bond issue Goldman Sachs asserted that it bore no responsibilities towards the claimant. Indeed this disclaimer of liability was in the form of a document titled "Important Notice". The reports, which had been prepared by third parties, on which the claimant had relied in making its investment contained inaccuracies but Goldman Sachs, as lead manager, had made it plain in the documentation that it assumed no responsibility for the contents of those reports. The issue arose whether this was an unfair contract term in the form an exclusion of liability clause and whether or not Goldman Sachs had any responsibility at common law for the misrepresentations in the reports on which the claimants had relied. It was found at first instance that the parties were of equal bargaining strength.[68] It was held in effect that it was open to Goldman Sachs to exclude its liability in this fashion by expressly stating that it made no representation as to the accuracy of the reports, and that the equivalent bargaining strength of the parties meant that the principles about unfair contract terms did not apply. On appeal[69] the Court of Appeal held that the inclusion of the disclaimer of liability in the form of the "Important Notice" prevented there being a representation inferred from these circumstances.[70] This case proceeded entirely on the basis of common law liability; but in any event it is keeping with the argument made above as to the suitable treatment of customers because both parties were market counterparties. It is suggested that the claimant was a financial institution which was capable of forming its own view both about the reliability of the reports and about the documentation which it had signed, unlike inexpert investors in some of the cases considered above.

24–35

Cases in the wake of the Enron collapse

In the wake of the Enron collapse, a number of cases were commenced, inter alia, against professional advisors to Enron claiming range of similar entitlements to those just considered. So in *Mahonia Limited v JP Morgan Chase Bank*[71] the

24–36

---

[67] [2006] EWHC 2887 (Comm).
[68] There was also an issue under the terms of the bondholders' agreement as to whether or not the claimant had waived its right to bring this action as the agreement purported to provide on its face. It was held that the agreement was indeed to be interpreted on the basis that the bondholders including the claimant had waived their rights against Goldman Sachs.
[69] *IFE v Goldman Sachs* [2007] EWCA Civ 811.
[70] It was held by Waller L.J. that the Important Notice constituted a contractual term between the parties with which the claimant should be deemed to have agreed.
[71] [2004] EWHC 1938 (Comm).

claimant alleged that a number of swaps contracts and a letter of credit should have been held to have been unenforceable and that the claimant was entitled to damages at common law severally on the basis that Enron's method for accounting for these products was unlawful under US GAAP, on the basis that the bank's in-house counsel had made a false misrepresentation that the transaction was a swap when it was allegedly a disguised loan to Enron, on the basis that the defendants were parties to a fraudulent conspiracy to obtain the letter of credit, and alternatively on the basis that the transactions were otherwise illegal under US securities law. On the facts, however, it was held by Cooke J. that the defendants were entitled to believe that accounts had been prepared by reasonable and reputable accountants and that consequently there had been no breach of US GAAP nor of US securities laws. Furthermore, on the facts, it was held that the bank's in-house counsel had made no such actionable representation during a taped telephone conversation between officers of the parties and that there was no evidence of such a conspiracy. Therefore, none of the claims were made out on the facts.

D. Hypothetical examples of fraud in financial transactions

Knowingly selling a poor investment

24–37   Allegations have been made in relation to American investment banks which sold derivatives which took speculative positions on the housing market in the USA continuing to rise, while those investment banks themselves took positions on their proprietary account[72] (and on behalf of other clients) which assumed a steep fall in the US housing market.[73] The most high-profile case of this sort, discussed in Chapter 45,[74] was the "Timberwolf" transaction concocted by Goldman Sachs. While that structure has not yet been taken to court in this jurisdiction, there is a hypothetical argument to be considered as to whether or not there should be a liability for fraud here. The question is whether the marketing of CDOs to clients while the selling institution was itself taking the exact opposite position on the very same CDOs constituted fraud. It is unclear whether this would constitute fraud in a legal sense or mere sharp practice. On the one hand, the investment banks were advising clients to invest in the securities at the same time as they themselves considered them to be a bad bet. And yet it could be said that restaurants selling food which is high in saturated fats are not liable to customers who choose to eat it. It would only be if the restaurateur intentionally or recklessly encouraged a customer to eat food on the basis that it was healthy when in truth the restaurateur knew it to be harmful (or even comprised of food which was dangerously past its "use by" date) that there could be liability. So, in relation to an investment bank, it might only be if the bank were selling products

---

[72] i.e. investing the bank's own money on its own account.
[73] In July 2010 Goldman Sachs agreed to pay a fine to the SEC in the USA of approximately US$500 million (about 15 days' trading receipts) connected with its mis-selling of an "Abacus" CDO product when it knew that the hedge fund which had originated the transaction was speculating on the securities in that CDO showing a loss.
[74] See para.45–29.

to inexpert clients that the issue of the bank needing to explain the risks to the client would arise. Otherwise, if dealing with another market professional, it might be thought that the client could make up its own mind about the transaction. Unless there were some hidden feature of the transaction, or some knowledge not known to the client, or an appreciation on the part of the seller that the buyer was acting on the basis of a mistake, then an action ought to lie. There were exchanges of emails within Goldman Sachs to the effect that "that was one shitty deal" in describing the product that was sold to clients in those circumstances.

And yet the test for fraud requires knowledge that there was an untrue statement **24–38** or recklessness as to whether or not that statement was true: therefore, a claim for fraud in these circumstances would require that such a false statement could be identified. It is not sufficient that the investment bank has acted unconscionably. The principle that implied, non-explicit misrepresentations should attract liability was approved by the House of Lords in *Smith New Court Securities Ltd v Scrimgeour Vickers (Asset Management) Ltd*.[75] Consequently, the claimant client might seek to show that there was an implication that the product would be profitable for the client, or else (it would be said) why would the investment bank have developed it? The real reason for the creation of the product, it would be alleged, would be to earn a profit for the investment bank, for which it was necessary to find a patsy to stand on the other side of the deal. That would be said to constitute an implied statement which was false. The investment bank would counter-argue that the selling of the product was akin to offering a game of poker to a friend: that friend might win or lose. There is no implied promise that the friend should win the poker game, just as one market professional does not promise another that a speculative investment (on which each stands on opposite sides) will yield a profit. Instead, a market professional is understood to take an informed choice on that chance.

This is where the argument that the bank was "careless" as to the accuracy of its **24–39** statements might be different in relation to an inexpert client because an inexpert client might be expected (in the absence of understanding all the risks associated with a product) to infer a representation as to the likely profitability of an investment product. In such a situation, internal correspondence rejoicing at selling a "shitty deal" to a retail customer might tend to suggest that the bank traders knew that their representations were being relied upon and that the customer had failed to read into them any appreciation of the more general risks. That the regulatory standards differentiate between different types of customer should, it is suggested, feed into the analysis of whether or not the bank should be deemed to have been "reckless" or "careless" in the context in that failing to take care in relation to a market professional counterparty which can assess the risks for itself is a forgivable treatment of that person precisely because it can assess the risks for itself; whereas the opposite is true of a retail customer who cannot assess those risks, as the market professional ought to have known if it had conducted its "know your client" duties properly.

---

[75] *Smith New Court Securities Ltd v Scrimgeour Vickers (Asset Management) Ltd* [1994] 4 All E.R. 225.

24-40 It would, however, give rise potentially to a claim that there had been a breach of the standard of "integrity" in the PRIN rulebook if an investment bank knowingly sold a product which it considered likely to generate a loss for its client. The utility of the concept of integrity is that it enables a regulator to publish a statement of censure or impose a fine without having to be able to point to one specific fraudulent misrepresentation. Instead, it is enough that one can identify inappropriate or "sharp" practice, particularly when the internal emails suggest that there was a conscious "taking advantage" of counterparties.

E. Problems with the development of the law on fraud in financial transactions cases

24-41 There is a tendency, it is suggested, in recent High Court cases on finance law to focus far more on recent judgments and less on tracing the highest authority for a legal principle to decisions, for example, of the House of Lords in *Derry v Peek* before applying the principle set out in the highest authority to the facts of the case. In the judgment of Hamblen J. in *Cassa di Risparmio della Repubblica di San Marino SpA v Barclays Bank Ltd*,[76] for example, there are many more references to the judgment of Gloster J. in *JP Morgan v Springwell*, which was not even a case exclusively on fraud, than to the principal authority on the law on fraud as set out by the House of Lords in *Derry v Peek*: there were seventeen references to the former case and only four to the latter in the judgment of Hamblen J.[77] The loss of respect for the doctrine of precedent is impoverishing our finance law by removing much of the certainty from it and by removing observance of centuries of careful jurisprudential development. Much was overlooked in *Cassa di Risparmio*, including the precise test set out by Lord Herschell which would find fraud in cases of culpable carelessness and also the failure to consider sufficiently carefully the regulatory obligations of the seller of that financial product. Instead, the High Court is reluctant to impose a finding of fraud on a bank unless proof of actual deceit is presented, something which is not the basis of the law in this area.

4. EQUITABLE FRAUD AND UNDUE INFLUENCE

A. Undue influence and the meaning of equitable fraud

24-42 Undue influence is significant in financial transactions, particularly (but not exclusively) in retail financial transactions, because when financial products are sold to inexpert customers it is easy for the expert seller to exert inappropriate influence over the customer thus sell the customer unsuitable products which may cause the customer unanticipated loss. The sense in which the term "fraud" is used by equity in this context is not in the sense of deceit considered at common

---

[76] *Cassa di Risparmio della Repubblica di San Marino SpA v Barclays Bank Ltd* [2011] EWHC 484 (Comm).
[77] See also *Deutsche Bank v Khan* [2013] EWHC 482 (Comm), a case on misrepresentation decided by Hamblen J. in a very similar fashion, referring to his own judgments.

law above, but more generally in relation to "any breach of the sort of obligation which is enforced by a court that from the beginning regarded itself as a court of conscience".[78] Equity has always considered fraud to be a term with infinite possible meanings. The very role of equity from Lord Ellesmere's judgment in the *Earl of Oxford's Case*[79] was stated as being to "correct men's consciences for frauds, breach of trusts, wrongs and oppressions".

The area of undue influence has become particularly significant in relation to banks seeking to enforce their security over domestic homes under mortgage contracts where one cohabitee has unduly influenced or made a misrepresentation to another cohabitee so as to gull that other cohabitee into signing the mortgage contract or into agreeing to act as surety in relation to that mortgage. If there has been undue influence or a misrepresentation exerted between the cohabitees then this may lead to the mortgage contract being set aside so that the bank loses its security for the loan. In the words of Lord Hobhouse in *Royal Bank of Scotland v Etridge (No.2)*[80] the basis of the equity in these situations is that there has been "an equitable wrong committed by the dominant [cohabitee] against the other which makes it unconscionable for the dominant party to enforce his legal rights against the other". These principles are considered in the sections to follow. The structure of the discussion is to summarise the high-level principles on undue influence first, and then to go over those principles again but delving in much more detail into the three key House of Lords decisions in this area and the many Court of Appeal decisions which have altered the effect of those high-level principles. This is a good illustration of how common law and equitable principles are both sensitive to context and how they can change subtly but significantly over the course of litigation.

24–43

B. Undue influence and mortgage contracts

The principles underpinning undue influence in mortgage contracts

Where there has been undue influence or a misrepresentation exercised by a mortgagor over a signatory to a mortgage contract or over a surety of a mortgage transaction (referred to in this discussion as "the cohabitee"), and if the mortgagee has not taken reasonable steps to ensure that the cohabitee has received independent legal advice as to the nature of the transaction, then the mortgagee will be taken to have had constructive notice of the undue influence or misrepresentation. In such a situation, the cohabitee can set the mortgage aside against the mortgagee.[81] Whereas previously it was necessary to demonstrate that there was some manifest disadvantage to the cohabitee to the transaction such that the mortgagee would be fixed with notice of the undue influence or misrepresentation, that is no longer a requirement.[82] However, there must be

24–44

---

[78] *Nocton v Lord Ashburton* [1914] A.C. 932, 954, per Viscount Haldane L.C.
[79] (1615) 1 Ch. Rep. 1.
[80] [2002] A.C. 773, at [103].
[81] *Barclays Bank v O'Brien* [1994] 1 A.C. 180; *Royal Bank of Scotland v Etridge* [1998] 4 All E.R. 705, CA.
[82] *Royal Bank of Scotland v Etridge (No.2)* [2002] A.C. 773, HL.

something about the transaction which would cause the mortgagee to be put on notice.[83] An example of a situation in which there will generally be something about the transaction which ought to put the mortgagee on notice is the situation in which the claimant was acting as a surety for another person's borrowings without any direct interest in the subject matter of that loan.[84]

The categories of undue influence

24–45   There are two categories of undue influence: actual undue influence and presumed undue influence. The following test for the application of the doctrine of undue influence was derived from *Bank of Credit and Commerce International SA v Aboody*[85] and is that applied in the House of Lords in *Barclays Bank v O'Brien*:

> "Class 1: actual undue influence.... Class 2: presumed undue influence... the complainant only has to show, in the first instance, that there was a relationship of trust and confidence between the complainant and the wrongdoer of such a nature that it is fair to presume that the wrongdoer abused that relationship...[86]
>
> Therefore, the doctrine of undue influence divides into two. First, situations in which there has been de facto undue influence. Actual undue influence requires evidence of some influence exercised over the claimant. Secondly, circumstances in which undue influence is presumed. Notice of presumed undue influence will arise (seemingly) in situations in which there is a manifest disadvantage to the claimant, or where there is a special relationship between the claimant and the mortgagor which ought to put the mortgagee on notice.[87] In circumstances in which there transaction is ostensibly unremarkable and to the financial advantage of the claimant, then no claim would stand against the defendant third party.[88]"

Actual undue influence

24–46   Clearly, the line between permissible pressure and undue influence will be a difficult one to draw in many circumstances. For example, it is clear that where a person is induced to enter into a mortgage to avert the prosecution of his son in relation to the forgery of bills held by the mortgagee, that mortgage will be set aside on grounds of undue influence.[89] Other cases have involved a demonstration of de facto control of one person by another in circumstances of religious

---

[83] [2002] A.C. 773, HL.

[84] *Perry v National Provincial Bank* [1910] 1 Ch. 464; *Royal Bank of Scotland v Etridge (No.2)* [2002] A.C. 773, HL; *Greene King Plc v Stanley* [2002] B.P.I.R. 491.

[85] [1992] 4 All E.R. 955.

[86] Lord Hobhouse identified the source of this division in the following manner: "The division between presumed and actual undue influence derives from the judgments in *Allcard v Skinner*. Actual undue influence presents no relevant problem. It is an equitable wrong committed by the dominant party against the other which makes it unconscionable for the dominant party to enforce his legal rights against the other. It is typically some express conduct overbearing the other party's will. It is capable of including conduct which might give a defence at law, for example, misrepresentation.": *Royal Bank of Scotland v Etridge (No.2)* [2002] A.C. 773, at [103].

[87] *Barclays Bank v O'Brien* [1994] 1 A.C. 180; *CIBC v Pitt* [1993] 3 W.L.R. 786—in the manner considered below.

[88] *CIBC v Pitt* [1993] 3 W.L.R. 786; *Leggatt v National Westminster Bank* [2000] All E.R. (D) 1458, CA.

[89] *Williams v Bayley* (1866) L.R. 1 H.L. 200.

observance[90] or simply where an older man has control over a younger man.[91] Therefore, influence need not be physical but it must be unjustified in that it seeks a benefit for the person exercising the influence which would not otherwise have been agreed to. The purpose behind the application of the principle is to prevent a person from relying on their common law rights where those rights have arisen as a result of some fraud or wrongful act on the part of that person. In the old cases it was necessary to demonstrate both that there was some benefit to the defendant[92] and some manifest disadvantage to the plaintiff.[93] The removal of these elements as being pre-requisites of the action is considered below.[94]

Presumed undue influence

The presumed undue influence category advances a more difficult proposition: that there are certain relationships which ought to warn third parties that some undue influence might be possible, such that those persons are deemed to have constructive notice of the undue influence. The aim of equity in this context is to provide particular protection for parties in one of the prescribed relationships. The problem then is to identify those relationships which ought to put the other party on notice, because "[a]t least since the time of Lord Eldon, equity has steadfastly and wisely refused to put limits on the relationships to which the presumption can apply".[95] It is required that there is a suitable degree of trust and confidence between the parties such that it could be presumed that one party would tend to rely on the other. It is not sufficient to demonstrate that one party is in a fiduciary relationship with that other.[96]

24–47

Thus, in the case of *Lloyds Bank v Bundy*,[97] Lord Denning held that an elderly bank customer who was cajoled into incurring injurious debts in favour of the bank at the advice of the bank manager was entitled to rely on a presumption of undue influence between banker and a customer in the position of that particular customer. Lord Denning was concerned to protect the interests of a person who was vulnerable and who was in a situation in which he would tend to rely on the advice given to him by the bank. However, Lord Denning's formulation of the appropriate principles has been much criticised, as will emerge below.

24–48

The Court of Appeal upheld the finding of a county court judge that in a situation in which a man in his mid-forties convinced his parents, then in their seventies, to put their house up as security for a loan the son was taking out to acquire an interest in a public house, then there would be a relationship of trust and confidence between the son and the parents.[98] The most significant factor in that context was the comparative business experience and acumen of the son and the

24–49

---

[90] *Morley v Loughman* [1893] 1 Ch. 736.
[91] *Smith v Kay* (1859) 7 H.L.C. 750.
[92] *Allcard v Skinner* (1887) 36 Ch.D. 145.
[93] *Bank of Credit and Commerce International SA v Aboody* [1990] Q.B. 923.
[94] *Royal Bank of Scotland v Etridge (No.2)* [2002] A.C. 773.
[95] *Goldsworthy v Brickell* [1987] Ch. 378, 401, per Nourse L.J.
[96] *Re Coomber* [1911] 1 Ch. 723; *Goldsworthy v Brickell* [1987] Ch. 378.
[97] [1975] Q.B. 326.
[98] *Greene King Plc v Stanley* [2002] B.P.I.R. 491.

naivety of his parents. The issue therefore is in what circumstances will a presumption arise that there could be undue influence and thus place liability on a third party to the undue influence itself. As will be seen below, the onus of proof falls on the defendant to disprove that there was any undue influence in line with the presumption. The defendant is bound by any undue influence which arises in such a situation.[99]

Reasonable steps

24–50 The mortgagee will not be bound by any undue influence or misrepresentation where the mortgagee has taken "reasonable steps" to find out the signatory's rights.[100] "Reasonable steps" will be said to exist in circumstances in which the claimant has received, or even just signed a certificate asserting that she has received, independent legal advice as to the effect of the mortgage or surety they are signing.[101] This, in effect, means that the claimant's rights to resist repossession of the home are shifted into a claim in tort against the solicitor if the solicitor failed to give proper advice because the bank is absolved from liability by dint of obtaining a certificate (often signed only by the cohabitee, it is suggested by some of the judges) that independent legal advice has been given to all of the parties involved.

C. The case of *Barclays Bank v O'Brien*

24–51 The law on undue influence in the law of mortgages received a shot in the arm in the decision of the House of Lords in *Barclays Bank v O'Brien*.[102] As was mentioned above typically these cases have related to situations in which a cohabitee has been unduly influenced into co-signing or acting as surety for a mortgage over their home by their cohabitee, and whether as a result that person should be entitled to set the mortgage contract aside against the bank.

The facts in Barclays Bank v O'Brien

24–52 The facts of *Barclays Bank v O'Brien*[103] revolved around a misrepresentation and alleged undue influence exercised by a husband over his wife. The husband was a significant shareholder in a manufacturing company which had a substantial, unsecured overdraft. The husband arranged with the manager of the respondent bank for an overdraft facility for which the husband agreed to secure the company's indebtedness. The husband provided security by means of a second charge over the matrimonial home owned jointly by the husband and the appellant, his wife. The bank prepared the necessary documentation which

---

[99] *Barclays Bank v O'Brien* [1994] 1 A.C. 180.
[100] *Barclays Bank v O'Brien* [1994] 1 A.C. 180.
[101] *Midland Bank v Massey* [1995] 1 All E.R. 929; *Banco Exterior Internacional v Mann* [1995] 1 All E.R. 936; *Halifax Mortgage Services Ltd v Stepsky* [1996] Ch. 1; *Barclays Bank v Coleman* [2000] 1 All E.R. 385.
[102] [1993] 3 W.L.R. 786.
[103] [1993] 3 W.L.R. 786.

included a guarantee to be provided by the husband and a charge to be signed by both the husband and the wife. Mrs O'Brien was to act as "surety". Mrs O'Brien received no independent advice as to her rights even though the bank manager had required that she receive that. The husband signed the documentation without reading it and Mrs O'Brien was taken to the bank by her husband to sign as surety for the overdraft. It is important to note that Mrs O'Brien was a guarantor of the overdraft provided for her husband's business. She took no direct benefit from the guarantee which she signed.[104]

Importantly, Mr O'Brien lied to Mrs O'Brien about the size of the overdraft and, therefore, about the size of the guarantee she was signing. While Mrs O'Brien knew that she was creating a charge over the matrimonial home in favour of the respondent bank, she believed that it was for £60,000 rather than £135,000 and that it would only last for three weeks. This is important: Mrs O'Brien was the victim of a misrepresentation.

24–53

The decision in Barclays Bank v O'Brien

There were four significant issues in the leading speech of Lord Browne-Wilkinson: misrepresentation, agency, presumed undue influence, and manifest disadvantage to the appellant. First, the question of misrepresentation. Mrs O'Brien's successful appeal turned ultimately on the argument that she had been the victim of misrepresentation. It is very significant that on the facts of that case, Mrs O'Brien was the victim of a misrepresentation and it was on that basis that the House of Lords ultimately found that Mrs O'Brien was entitled to have the mortgage set aside. It is sufficient to show that there has been a misrepresentation effected by the mortgagor against the co-signatory which induced that person to sign the agreement. Again, where the mortgagee has failed to ensure that the co-signatory has received independent advice as to the effect of the transaction, the mortgagee will be fixed with constructive notice of that misrepresentation. Consequently, the co-signatory will be entitled to set aside the mortgage against the mortgagee.[105] The question of undue influence on the facts of O'Brien was unproven.

24–54

Secondly, the question of agency. There is a logical difficulty when setting aside a mortgage against a bank when the undue influence or misrepresentation has taken place between cohabitees without any employee of the bank being present. There is a need for the bank to be fixed with constructive notice of the undue influence or misrepresentation—this is a question which Lord Browne-Wilkinson resolved by finding that there was something about the transaction which ought to have put the bank on notice, as considered in the next section. Where the cohabitee who exerted the undue influence or made the misrepresentation was in some way acting as the agent of the bank, however, that would be sufficient to fix

24–55

---

[104] Although it might be said that she benefited indirectly from the continued solvency of her husband's business, the position has been taken that if she had no direct stake in the business taking the overdraft or borrowings then she had no direct benefit in the transaction.

[105] Subject to the extent of that person's reliance on the representations: *Barclays Bank v Rivett* [1999] 1 F.L.R. 730.

the bank with constructive notice because the undue influence or misrepresentation was carried out by an agent of the bank. On the facts of *Barclays Bank v O'Brien*, there was a suggestion that the bank's employees had dispatched Mr O'Brien on a mission to co-opt his wife as a surety for the overdraft, and thereby that Mr O'Brien had become their agent for these purposes.[106] Such a relationship of agency would, prima facie, fix the bank with notice of everything of which their agent had notice.[107] Thus it was held by Lord Browne-Wilkinson that:

> "if the wrongdoing husband is acting as agent for the creditor bank in obtaining the surety from the wife, the creditor will be fixed with the wrongdoing of its own agent and the surety contact can be set aside as against the creditor".

24–56   Thirdly, the question of presumed undue influence. Lord Browne-Wilkinson held that in cases involving husband and wife, the wife can demonstrate that there was a relationship of "trust and confidence" between them such that there is a presumption of undue influence. Importantly, in the case of *CIBC v Pitt*,[108] which was heard contemporaneously by the House of Lords, Lord Browne-Wilkinson held that this presumption will only arise in circumstances in which there is some manifest disadvantage to that co-habitee. On the facts of *O'Brien*, it was held that, because Mrs O'Brien was acting as surety in a transaction under which she took no direct, personal benefit, it must be presumed that she might have been the subject of some undue influence. It is suggested that this must be correct, or else all mortgagees would be required to enquire into the detail of the relationship between each married couple seeking to take out mortgages with them.[109]

24–57   Fourthly, whether or not there was a manifest disadvantage to the appellant, Mrs O'Brien. On the facts in *O'Brien* the creditor was held to have been put on inquiry in that the transaction was to the financial disadvantage of Mrs O'Brien and that there is a substantial risk in transactions of that kind that the husband has committed a legal or equitable wrong in procuring the wife to act as surety. It should be noted that the need for manifest disadvantage has since been doubted—it is considered below in relation to the decision of the House of Lords in *Royal Bank of Scotland v Etridge (No.2)*—but was nevertheless central to the decision of the House of Lords in *CIBC v Pitt* which is considered next.

The concurrent appeal in CIBC v Pitt

24–58   The decision of the House of Lords in *Barclays Bank v O'Brien* can only be understood fully if it is read in the light of the concurrent appeal in *CIBC v Pitt*[110] which was heard by the same House of Lords at the same time as *O'Brien*. *CIBC*

---

[106] The problem with this argument, of course, is that it is unlikely that the terms of Mr O'Brien's agency could have included lies or threats, misrepresentation or undue influence. The suspicion of agency in *O'Brien* arose from the fact that it was the bank which had proposed the surety arrangement to support the problem of an overdraft for Mr O'Brien's company.

[107] [1986] 2 All E.R. 54.

[108] [1993] 4 All E.R. 433.

[109] See also *Northern Rock BS v Archer* [1999] Lloyd's Rep. Bank 32.

[110] [1993] 4 All E.R. 433.

v Pitt illustrates the importance of there being something unusual about the transaction before the bank will be fixed with notice of the undue influence.

CIBC v Pitt concerned a straightforward mortgage over property rather than a **24–59** provision of a guarantee by a cohabitee. Mr Pitt had told the appellant that he wished to borrow money on the security of the house to finance speculation on the stock market. The appellant, Mrs Pitt, was unhappy with this suggestion and expressed these reservations to her husband. Mr Pitt wanted to borrow the money and so exerted undue influence on Mrs Pitt so that she would agree to the loan. Mrs Pitt did not read any of the documentation and only saw the first and last pages of it in any event. The solicitors who acted for the couple were also solicitors for the bank. The appellant, Mrs Pitt, did not receive any independent advice as to the transaction. She alleged that she had entered into the transaction as a result of her husband's undue influence and as a result of her husband's misrepresentation of the loan to her. The trial judge found that there had been undue influence but no misrepresentation.

What the appellant could not demonstrate on the facts was that the financial **24–60** institution was affected by the undue influence of the husband. Importantly, on the facts in *Pitt* there was nothing to indicate that this transaction constituted anything other than a normal loan taken out by a husband and a wife which was secured by a charge over their matrimonial home.[111] It was held that, unlike the facts in *O'Brien* where Mrs O'Brien was acting to her manifest disadvantage as a surety, there was no similar factor in *Pitt* which ought necessarily to raise a presumption of undue influence given that the bank was found to have been extending money on an ordinary secured loan transaction which indicated no necessary disadvantage to Mrs Pitt. Therefore, there is no necessary link between there having been some undue influence exerted between cohabitees and a right for the wronged party to set aside the mortgage contract.

Royal Bank of Scotland v Etridge (No.2)—moving away from manifest disadvantage?

The decision of the House of Lords in *Royal Bank of Scotland v Etridge (No.2)*[112] **24–61** is of central importance to the operation of undue influence in these contexts now, building on *O'Brien* and *Pitt*. Different members of the House of Lords, however, took different approaches. What emerges most clearly from *Royal Bank of Scotland v Etridge (No.2)* is that transactions where some person is required to act as a surety will be an example of a situation in which such a person might have been the victim of some undue influence or misrepresentation because they are guaranteeing another person's performance of the transaction without taking any direct benefit themselves *qua* surety.

Lord Nicholls suggested in *Royal Bank of Scotland v Etridge (No.2)*[113] that the **24–62** test of manifest disadvantage was no longer required but that the suggestion made in *Barclays Bank v O'Brien* that there be some notion of fixing mortgagees with

---

[111] *Leggatt v National Westminster Bank* [2000] All E.R. (D) 1458.
[112] [2002] A.C. 773.
[113] [2002] A.C. 773; [2001] 4 All E.R. 449.

notice in circumstances in which a co-habitee stands to suffer some financial disadvantage would remain an important factor. The approach in *CIBC v Pitt* was therefore approved. What emerges also that the principal focus of Lord Nicholls's speech is on the position of sureties in particular and not signatories to mortgages in general.

24–63   In the same appeal, Lord Hobhouse was generally supportive of the approach taken by Lord Browne-Wilkinson in *Barclays Bank v O'Brien* but was critical of the use of the constructive notice test on the basis that it would be necessary to apply this test differently in different situations.[114]

24–64   Lord Scott's approach is somewhat different again. His lordship's approach was focused more clearly on the cohabitee failing to give free consent to a contract if she has acted under undue influence or some misrepresentation. The approach taken here is more akin to a contract lawyer's approach on the possibility of setting aside a contract between two people where one has unduly influenced the other. The injustice of enforcing such a contract *between those two people* is self-evident. However, the property lawyers faces a more complex job when seeking to set aside a right to repossess the co-habitee's home because of some undue influence exercised over her by a third party, such that the contract between the mortgagee and the third party should be set aside in toto. The addition of the third person to the matrix complicates the neat contractual theory of free consent.

24–65   The further question asked by Lord Scott, so as to deal with this question of fixing the mortgagee with responsibility (in the form of losing its proprietary rights to repossession) for a private wrong committed between the mortgagor and his cohabitee, is that of asking whether or not the mortgagee had knowledge of that wrong. The test of knowledge requires that the mortgagee was fixed with the knowledge itself—although it is not made clear whether or not that includes constructive knowledge where the bank is taken to have known of any factors which it would have discovered but for wilfully and recklessly failing to make the enquiries which a reasonable bank would have made or but for wilfully closing its eyes to the obvious—and not simply that it has constructive notice or imputed notice via some agent.[115] Lord Scott did, however, agree with Lord Nicholls's core assumption that if there is some special feature in the transaction, then that will fix the mortgagee bank with knowledge of any undue influence.[116]

24–66   Briefly put, that three of their lordships weighed in with lengthy speeches, each of which set out lengthy summaries of the applicable tests in slightly different terms, did not help to introduce the certainty which they had desired. In effect, the law stays much the same as it was under the *O'Brien* principle, except that the requirement of manifest disadvantage has been removed. There is a reinforcement of the principles, considered below, that independent legal advice ought to be addressed to ensuring that the co-habitee understands the agreement before

---

[114] [2001] 4 All E.R. 449, 484.
[115] [2001] 4 All E.R. 449, 509.
[116] [2001] 4 All E.R. 449, 509.

agreeing to become a co-signatory to it or before agreeing to act as a surety. These issues are considered next in relation to the mortgagee's means of discharging their duties.

D.   Mortgagee's means of avoiding having the mortgage contract set aside

Watering down O'Brien—the bank is obliged merely to urge the taking of independent advice

As Lord Browne-Wilkinson held in *O'Brien*, the mortgagee can be discharged from constructive notice where the mortgagee had taken "reasonable steps" and where the mortgagee had not acquired actual notice of the matters complained of. The most important question on the cases has therefore become that of delineating the circumstances in which the mortgagee is able to restrict its own liability by means of taking "reasonable steps". In general terms, this has been approved by the House of Lords in *Royal Bank of Scotland v Etridge (No.2)*.[117] The lesson to be drawn from the cases which came between *O'Brien* and *Etridge* was that the Court of Appeal was prepared greatly to reduce the banks' duties necessary to avoid the contract being set aside.

24–67

So, in *Massey v Midland Bank*,[118] Ms Massey had been persuaded by her partner to charge her property as security for his overdraft with the mortgagee. The bank interviewed them together but Ms Massey was advised by the mortgagee to seek independent advice. This advice was given to Ms Massey in her partner's presence. The Court of Appeal held that the mortgagee was required only to see that advice was sought by the spouse, not ensure that the advice was properly given. As Steyn L.J. held: "[i]n these circumstances nothing more was required of the bank than to urge or insist that Miss Massey should take independent advice". This is an incredibly significant restriction on the underlying principle set out by Lord Browne-Wilkinson in *O'Brien*. In that case it was held that there will be presumed undue influence where the transaction is to the manifest disadvantage of the co-habitee, and that the mortgagee will have constructive notice of any misrepresentation or undue influence exercised over that person unless they have advised that person seek independent advice.

24–68

In *Massey*, in the judgment of Steyn L.J., the two questions which must be considered are: whether or not the mortgagee was put on inquiry as to the circumstances in which the co-habitee agreed to provide the security, and, if so, whether or not the mortgagee took reasonable steps to ensure that the agreement of the cohabitee to the charge had been properly obtained. This test was followed by differently constituted Courts of Appeal in *Banco Exterior Internacional v Mann*[119] and was the approach taken in *Bank of Boroda v Rayarel*.[120]

24–69

---

[117] [2002] A.C. 773.
[118] [1995] 1 All E.R. 929.
[119] [1995] 1 All E.R. 936.
[120] [1995] 2 F.L.R. 376.

Banking practice shifting to the formality of a certificate

24–70   Banking practice has developed to require the co-signatory, co-habitee, or surety to sign a certificate attesting to the fact that they have taken independent advice. In *Banco Exterior Internacional v Mann*, an issue arose in circumstances in which the solicitor advised both the borrower, the cohabitee, and the company for which the loan was sought, with the result that it was said to be unclear whether or not the cohabitee had received independent legal advice. Morritt L.J. held that the position must be considered from the mortgagee's point of view. On the facts of *Mann*, the mortgagee had been shown a certificate that the cohabitee had received legal advice and therefore considered that it had taken reasonable steps and consequently that this suggested that the cohabitee had agreed to the mortgage. Therefore, the co-habitee need not have actually received independent legal advice. Rather it is enough for the mortgagee to demonstrate that the co-habitee has attested that such advice has been taken; provided that the mortgagee had no actual notice of the cohabitee not having received such advice.[121]

24–71   In *Royal Bank of Scotland v Etridge (No.2)*, Lord Scott held that a solicitor should give advice to the cohabitee, and that there should be written confirmation that such advice had been given so that the mortgagee could form a reasonable belief that the signatory or surety had understood the effect of the transaction.[122] In that same appeal, Lord Hobhouse was clear that there must be "true independent advice" given by a solicitor which would lead to "real consent" to the contract.[123] It is suggested that this cannot be satisfied by an entirely formalistic process of signing certificates if there had not been any proper advice actually given. However, the question remains whether the solicitor assumes liability for any wrongdoing if she fails to give adequate advice to the cohabitees but nevertheless signs a certificate to suggest that she has done so. In such circumstances, clearly, the bank would be required to inquire behind every certificate if they still retained liability for the effect of any undue influence which the inadequate advice failed to resolve; and in effect the purpose of permitting the bank to escape liability by taking reasonable steps would be obviated. In that same appeal, Lord Nicholls suggested that the bank should obtain in every case a written confirmation from the solicitor that the solicitor had explained the transaction to the co-habitee armed with the "necessary financial information" supplied to it by the mortgagee.[124]

24–72   It is important to note, however, that what this development in the law has done is to shift responsibility from the bank to make enquiries onto the solicitor giving advice. As such the claimant acquires rights to sue the solicitor in the event that advice is negligently given under the tort of negligence. From the perspective of the cohabitee that will be an inferior form of remedy compared to the possibility

---

[121] Indeed, the rule in *Mann*, if followed to its logical conclusion, would seem to circumvent the initial thrust of *O'Brien* that the mortgagee is required to look into certain matters where there is presumed undue influence.

[122] *Royal Bank of Scotland v Etridge (No.2)* [2001] 4 All E.R. 449, 509ff.

[123] [2001] 4 All E.R. 489.

[124] [2001] 4 All E.R. 473.

of a quasi-proprietary remedy[125] which sets aside the entirety of the mortgage[126]: the claim in negligence is a purely personal claim to received common law damages which will not in itself protect the claimant's rights in her home. Thus a proprietary right is lost, to be replaced by a purely personal right in money. It could be said that the bank is better able to bear the risk and the cost associated with providing proper advice to the parties than are the ordinary retail customers with no necessary understanding of the legal effects of mortgage contracts.

The liabilities of the solicitor giving advice, particularly when advising more than one party

In *Midland Bank v Serter*,[127] the Court of Appeal held that where the solicitor had represented the mortgagee, mortgagor and the cohabitee, the mortgagee was not bound by constructive notice of any undue influence where the cohabitee had signed a certificate acknowledging receipt of legal advice. Even in circumstances in which it is the mortgagee which directs the solicitor to advise the cohabitee, the solicitor acts as solicitor to the cohabitee, owing that person all of the duties of a solicitor.[128] The bank is then entitled to rely on the advice which the solicitor gives to the cohabitee, even if the solicitor in fact breaches the obligation to the cohabitee and favours the mortgagee or the mortgagor instead by not passing information as to the nature of the transaction to the cohabitee.[129] Where the solicitor undertakes the task of advising the cohabitee, the solicitor is deemed to be independent and the mortgagee is entitled to rely on the appropriate advice having been given by the solicitor.[130]

24–73

In the Court of Appeal decision in *Barclays Bank v Thomson*[131] the bank obtained a mortgage over T's family home, lending the money to T's husband. The bank instructed a solicitor to act on its behalf in the mortgage transaction: including giving advice to T. The solicitors had explained to T the effect of the mortgage on the family home in the husband's absence. It was held that the bank was entitled to rely upon the solicitor's assurance that T had been properly advised. As a result, the bank was not to be imputed with any notice of any undue influence or misrepresentation which was active on T. Therefore, it was found that the bank was able to avoid a finding of constructive notice by receiving a representation that T had received legal advice. The onus has therefore shifted from the mortgagee making inquiries as to whether or not there are rights in some cohabitee, to ensuring that a cohabitee certifies that some independent legal advice has been given.[132]

24–74

---

[125] The nature of which is considered in A. Hudson, *Equity & Trusts*, para.20.5.

[126] A.S. Hudson, *Equity & Trusts*, para.20.4.8.

[127] [1995] 1 F.L.R. 367.

[128] *Midland Bank v Serter* [1995] 1 F.L.R. 367; *Banco Exterior v Mann* [1995] 1 All E.R. 936.

[129] *Halifax Mortgage Services Ltd v Stepsky* [1996] 2 All E.R. 277.

[130] *Banco Exterior v Mann* [1995] 1 All E.R. 936.

[131] [1997] 4 All E.R. 816.

[132] cf. *Halifax Mortgage Services Ltd v Stepsky* [1996] 2 All E.R. 277.

24–75   As Hobhouse L.J., delivering a dissenting judgment, stressed in *Banco Exterior v Mann*[133] a solicitor can only be truly independent if, in relation to a potentially disadvantageous transaction, she advised the cohabitee not to sign. Nevertheless, in *Halifax BS v Stepsky*[134] it was held that the mortgagee should be absolved from any responsibility to procure truly independent advice in such circumstances by means of ensuring that the solicitor had actually given impartial advice to a cohabitee while also acting as advisor to the mortgagee. In *Stepsky* there was a suggestion that the solicitor had sought to cajole the cohabitee to sign the agreement against the cohabitee's better interests. In circumstances in which a solicitor is clearly involved in a conflict of interest in acting for the bank, for the mortgagor and for the cohabitee, then the solicitor will not be able to give independent advice on which the mortgagee can rely to discharge its liability.[135] Therefore, where the solicitor is advising the bank as to a complex financial transaction and is found to have placed improper pressure on the mortgagor to agree to that transaction, it has been held that that provision of advice cannot be suitable to discharge the bank's obligation to take reasonable steps.[136]

E.   Setting aside the contract

24–76   In circumstances in which the claimant had knowledge of a part of the mortgage or surety, but did not know the full amount of the liability, the claimant will nevertheless be entitled to have the mortgage set aside in toto.[137] The only exception to that principle will be where the claimant has nevertheless taken some benefit from the transaction—in which case the claimant will be required to account to the defendant for that benefit.[138]

5.   THE *BUNDY* CATEGORIES OF UNDUE INFLUENCE

A.   Introduction

24–77   In the decision of the Court of Appeal in *Lloyds Bank v Bundy*[139] Lord Denning set out a series of categories in which transactions between a bank and its customer could be set aside. The first three categories were accepted by his lordship without discussion: "fraud, misrepresentation, or mistake", all of which are considered Pts V and VII of this book. As Lord Denning put it, even though there is a general rule that the common law will not interfere with the bargain struck between banks and their customers, yet nevertheless[140]:

---

[133] [1995] 1 All E.R. 936.
[134] [1996] 2 All E.R. 277.
[135] *National Westminster Bank Plc v Breeds* [2001] All E.R. (D) 5.
[136] [2001] All E.R. (D) 5.
[137] *TSB Bank v Camfield* [1995] 1 All E.R. 951, *Castle Phillips Finance v Piddington* [1995] 70 P. & C.R. 592.
[138] *Midland Bank v Greene* [1994] 2 F.L.R. 827; *Dunbar Bank Plc v Nadeem* [1997] 1 All E.R. 253.
[139] [1974] EWCA Civ 8; [1975] Q.B. 326.
[140] [1975] Q.B. 326.

"... there are exceptions to this general rule. There are cases in our books in which the Courts will set aside a contract, or a transfer of property, when the parties have not met on equal terms—when the one is so strong in bargaining power and the other so weak—that, as a matter of common fairness it is not right that the strong should be allowed to push the weak to the wall. Hitherto those exceptional cases have been treated each as a separate category in itself. But I think the time has come when we should seek to find a principle to unite them."

Lord Denning accepted that bargains could be interfered with when there was "fraud or misrepresentation or mistake". However, there were five further categories, all of which were said to revolve around a general principle.

B.   The general principle

The general principle which underpins all of these cases is an inequality of bargaining power which the Court of Appeal was not prepared to countenance in general terms. As Lord Denning described the principle[141]:   **24–78**

"The fundamental rule is that if the parties have made an agreement, the Court will enforce it, unless it is manifestly unfair and unjust; but if it be manifestly unfair and unjust, the Court will disregard it and decide what is fair and just."

The principle was expressed by his lordship more fully in the following passage[142]:

"Gathering all together, I would suggest that through all these instances there runs a single thread. They rest on 'inequality of bargaining power'. By virtue of it, the English law gives relief to one who, without independent advice, enters into a contract or transfers property for a consideration which is grossly inadequate, when his bargaining power is grievously impaired by reason of his own needs or desires, or by his own ignorance or infirmity, coupled with undue influences or pressures brought to bear on him by or for the benefit of the other. When I use the word 'undue' I do not mean to suggest that the principle depends on proof of any wrongdoing."

By way of example, in the case of *The Port Caledonia and The Anna*[143] a rescuer refused to help drowning people by throwing them a rope unless he was paid £1,000: clearly this was a case in which the venal "rescuer" was relying on a position of bargaining strength so as to extort money from the claimant. There are five categories identified by Lord Denning, as considered in each of the sections to follow.

C.   The five categories of undue influence

(1)   Duress of goods

The first category is "duress of goods" which arises when: **24–79**

---

[141] [1975] Q.B. 326; referring to *Akerblom v Price* (1881) 7 Q.B.D. 129, 133, per Brett L.J.
[142] [1975] Q.B. 326.
[143] (1903) P. 184.

"a man is in a strong bargaining position by being in possession of the goods of another . . . [and] the owner is in a weak position because he is in urgent need of the goods. The stronger demands of the weaker more than is justly due: and he pays it in order to get the goods. Such a transaction is voidable. He can recover the excess.[144]"

It was suggested that it was "the inequality of bargaining power—the strength of the one versus the urgent need of the other—renders the transaction voidable and the money paid to be recovered back".[145]

(2) Expectant heir

24–80   The second category is that of the "expectant heir" which arises when[146]:

"A man is so placed as to be in need of special care and protection and yet his weakness is exploited by another far stronger than himself so as to get his property at a gross undervalue. The typical case is that of the 'expectant heir'. But it applies to all cases where a man comes into property, or is expected to come into it—and then being in urgent need—another gives him ready cash for it, greatly below its true worth, and so gets the property transferred to him.[147] Even though there be no evidence of fraud or misrepresentation, nevertheless the transaction will be set aside ... Kay J. said[148]:

'The result of the decisions is that where a purchase is made from a poor and ignorant man at a considerable undervalue, the vendor having no independent advice, a Court of Equity will set aside the transaction.'"

The keynote here is that a person must have been placed in a position of weakness and has an "urgent need" which causes her to agree to sell her property quickly at a price which is lower than the property is actually worth.

(3) Undue influence

24–81   The third category is "undue influence" as considered already in this chapter. However, the conceptualisation of this doctrine which is used by Lord Denning is that set out in *Allcard v Skinner*[149] whereby the defendant "has been guilty of some fraud or wrongful act—expressly so as to gain some gift or advantage from the weaker" or where "the stronger has not been guilty of any wrongful act, but has, through the relations which existed between him and the weaker, gained some gift or advantage for himself". The categories of undue influence used by Lord Denning include "parent over child, solicitor over client, doctor over patient, spiritual adviser over follower". The general principle on which Lord Denning relied was that stated by Lord Chancellor Chelmsford in *Tate v Williamson*[150]:

---

[144] *Astley v Reynolds* (1731) 2 Stra. 915; *Parker v Bristol & Exeter Railway Co* (1851) 6 Exch. 702; *Steele v Williams* (1853) 8 Exch. 625; *Green v Duckett* (1883) 11 Q.B.D. 275.
[145] *Maskell v Horner* (1915) 3 K.B. 106.
[146] [1975] Q.B. 326.
[147] *Evans v Llewellyn* (1787) 1 Cox Eq. Cas. 333.
[148] *Fry v Lane* (1888) 40 Ch.D. 312, 322.
[149] (1887) 36 Ch.D. at p.171.
[150] (1861) L.R. 2 Ch. App. 55, 61. See also *Tufton v Sperni* (1952) 2 T.L.R. 516, CA.

"Wherever the persons stand in such a relation that, while it continues, confidence is necessarily reposed by one, and the influence which naturally grows out of that confidence is possessed by the other, and this confidence is abused, or the influence is exerted, to obtain an advantage at the expense of the confiding party, the person so availing himself of his position, will not be permitted to obtain the advantage, although the transaction could not have been impeached if no such confidential relation had existed."

Therefore, again, the principle is that advantage must have been taken of the claimant by the defendant to constitute undue influence on this model. The discussion in *Royal Bank of Scotland v Etridge (No.2)*[151] (considered above) which suggested that "manifest disadvantage" need not be proven to establish undue influence had not countenanced that the doctrine was itself based on an advantage being taken of one person by another person, as opposed to being merely an evidential requirement for demonstrating undue influence. That the defendant must have taken advantage of the claimant demonstrates that the doctrine of undue influence is an equitable doctrine concerned to prevent an unconscionable advantage being taken by the defendant so as to acquire property or some other benefit from the claimant.

(4)   Undue pressure

The fourth category is that of "undue" pressure. What Lord Denning described as being "the most apposite" example of this head of claim was the decision in *Williams v Bayley*.[152] Lord Denning described the transaction in the following terms[153]: **24–82**

"... a son forged his father's name to a promissory note, and, by means of it, raised money from the bank of which they were both customers. The bank said to the father, in effect:

'Take your choice—give us security for your son's debt. If you do take that on yourself, then it will all go smoothly: if you do not, we shall be bound to exercise pressure.'"

Thereupon the father charged his property to the bank with payment of the note. The House of Lords held that the charge was invalid because of undue pressure exerted by the bank. Lord Westbury held[154]:

"A contract to give security for the debt of another, which is a contract without consideration, is above all things a contract that should be based upon the free and voluntary agency of the individual who enters into it."

As Stuart V.C. held[155]: "when an agreement, hard and inequitable in itself, has been executed under pressure on the part of the party who executes it, the Court will set it aside".

---

[151] [2001] 4 All E.R. 449.
[152] (1866) L.R. 2 H.L. 200.
[153] [1975] Q.B. 326.
[154] *Williams v Bayley* (1866) L.R. 2 H.L. 200, at p.218.
[155] *Ormes v Beadel* (1860) 2 Giff. 166, 174; *D. & C. Builders Ltd v Rees* (1966) 2 Q.B. at p.623.

(5)   Salvage agreements

24–83   The fifth category is that of "salvage agreements" which arise in circumstances in which "a vessel is in danger of sinking and seeks help" with the result that "the rescuer is in a strong bargaining position" and the "vessel in distress is in urgent need". The result of this situation is that the parties "cannot be truly said to be on equal terms".

D.   The decision on the facts of *Lloyds Bank v Bundy*

24–84   Lord Denning's judgment in *Lloyds Bank v Bundy* is a classic of his lordship's spare but passionate prose style. From the first two sentences, I would suggest, we know who will win. It is the story of a case as though told by Dickens[156]:

> "Broadchalke is one of the most pleasing villages in England. Old Herbert Bundy was a farmer there. His home was at Yew Tree Farm. It went back for 300 years. His family had been there for generations. It was his only asset. But he did a very foolish thing. He mortgaged it to the bank. Up to the very hilt. Not to borrow money for himself, but for the sake of his son. Now the bank have come down on him. They have foreclosed. They want to get him out of Yew Tree Farm and to sell it."

Old Herbert Bundy agreed to sign away his farm and ancestral family home when the bank manager came calling with a briefcase full of paperwork on which he wanted Herbert Bundy to sign his name in favour of his hopeless but beloved son. On the facts in *Lloyds Bank v Bundy* it was held that the old man who signed away his home, Yew Tree Farm, did so solely to help his son's business, did so on the advice of the bank manager who called at his house with contracts which he encouraged the old man to sign while he waited and without independent advice, did so in a relationship of trust and confidence in the bank manager, and did so because of his natural affection for his son.

24–85   It is important to note that Cairns L.J. did not concur with Lord Denning, but rather concurred with Sir Eric Sachs (formerly Sachs L.J.) so that it is Sachs L.J. who gives the majority decision of the court. Sachs L.J. based his decision on *Allcard v Skinner*[157] and on whether or not there was a special relationship between the old man and the bank. The fact that Mr Bundy was faced by three people in his living room at Yew Tree Farm who were "anxious" for him to sign the agreements and the fact that he had no independent advice was held to constitute a circumstance in which there was pressure placed on him sufficient for him to be entitled to have the agreements he signed set aside. Notably, it was not necessary to demonstrate that the bank manager had acted in any way wrongfully.

24–86   For all the talk from the new Chief Executive of the Financial Conduct Authority about a new approach to financial regulation, nothing quite matches the approach taken by Lord Denning. In his lordship's view, the courts should be able to rewrite contracts when they have been procured by undue influence, including a person's lack of experience, then those contracts should be set aside. As his

---

[156] [1975] Q.B. 326.
[157] (1887) 36 Ch.D. 145.

lordship put it, when a contract is "manifestly unfair and unjust, the Court will disregard it and decide what is fair and just". The experience of ordinary customers in the PPI and interest rate swap mis-selling cases across the entire gamut to the experience of market counterparties disadvantaged under the Libor mis-selling scandal leads us inevitably to the conclusion that the courts must have the power to set contracts aside when they have been procured or perverted by misfeasance by a financial institution. Similarly, regulators should be empowered to intercede in circumstances in which there has been widespread mis-selling (as with PPI or interest rate swaps) or even just individual mis-selling. Either the Ombudsman or the FCA should be empowered to cancel contracts, with the financial institution then having to bear the cost and delay of an appeal to the courts from there. What Lord Denning has reminded us is that our law should be built on conscience, and when banks act unconscionably then their contracts should be cancelled immediately and any loss suffered by their clients should be compensated.

CHAPTER 25

NEGLIGENCE AND OTHER LIABILITY IN TORT

CORE PRINCIPLES

The tort of negligence provides a successful claimant with damages for any loss suffered as a result of the defendant's breach of a duty of care. There are five requirements for a successful claim based on the tort of negligence: there must have been a breach of a duty of care; that breach of duty must have caused damage to the claimant; that damage must have been foreseeable; there must have been sufficient proximity between the parties; and it must be "fair, just and reasonable" for the court to impose that liability. These elements are considered in turn in the discussion to follow, beginning with a discussion of the nature of the tort of negligence and the concept of the "duty of care" on which it is based.

In general terms there can be no recovery for purely economic loss under the tort of negligence, except in relation to the doctrine in *Hedley Byrne v Heller* (outlined below). It is not enough that there is a duty of care and that there is loss: rather, that loss must have been foreseeable. The court will consider "what a reasonable person in the circumstances of the defendant ought to have foreseen". The requirement of proximity will need the relationship between the parties to make the imposition of liability reasonable. There are authorities which require that a claim for negligence must be "fair, just and reasonable".

The tort of negligence in relation to financial transactions is based on the decision of the House of Lords in *Hedley Byrne v Heller*. For liability to arise, there must be a special relationship between the parties such that the seller of the financial instrument ought to have known that its customer was relying on it and that the customer was relying on the seller to exercise skill and care in making the statement. Thus, whenever advice or any statement connected to a financial institution's business is made to a customer and that customer relies on that statement and suffers loss as a result, then the financial institution will be liable in damages for that customer's loss. The interpretation of whether or not a financial institution acted appropriately in relation to its customer will be informed by the FCA Conduct of Business regulations.

In relation to takeovers it was held in *Caparo v Dickman* that accountants and auditors preparing and certifying accounts were not liable in negligence to a company which relied on those accounts when deciding to take over the company which was the subject of the accounts. When this principle is applied to prospectuses prepared in relation to issues of securities, an interesting development arises. The cases have differed in relation to claims by investors who relied upon prospectuses when acquiring securities: it has been held that prospectuses prepared specifically for a small group of investors could not be relied upon by people outside that group, whereas in another case it has been held that general investors in the "after market" may rely upon prospectuses so as to found liability in tort for those who prepared the prospectus. With the introduction of positive obligations on those who prepared prospectus under the prospectus regulations, it must now be the case that those who prepare prospectuses will be liable in tort to any investor who relies on the contents of such a mandatory prospectus when acquiring investments.

Damages are available in negligence so as to compensate the claimant for any loss she has suffered as a result of that negligence so as to return her to the position she was in before the tort was committed. This is often referred to as her "out-of-pocket" loss. She is not, however, entitled to any future profit she might have earned but for the commission of the tort. The position in relation to contractual damages is different, as was discussed in Chapter 20.

Three other torts are considered in this chapter. First, a person who commits a breach of statutory duty which causes another person loss will be liable in tort for damages, provided that the statute can be interpreted as creating such a right which would exist distinct from the common law duty of care. Second, the tort of defamation may give rise to actions for libellous or slanderous statements made on financial markets. The defences of justification or fair comment will, however, preclude actions where the comment has been made honestly and appropriately. Third, the tort of misfeasance in a public office may impose liability on a regulator in damages where an officer of that regulator knowingly causes loss to the claimant or recklessly does so. These principles are considered at the end of the chapter.

1.   Introduction

There are two principal species of tort which are considered in this chapter: first, **25–01** the application of the tort of negligence generally and, secondly, the tort of negligent misstatement specifically. The tort of negligent misstatement is a subset of the tort of negligence but it has its own particular principles and is of particular significance to financial transactions. The tort of negligent misstatement is the most common source of liability in tort in relation to financial services because the most common source of liability in that context is based on advice given or statements made (in prospectuses or otherwise) by sellers of financial services to their customers. In relation to the tort of negligence more generally, there may be tortious liabilities in negligence where no "statements" were made and where, perhaps, something more than merely economic loss was suffered.[1] The tort of fraudulent misrepresentation (the tort of deceit) was considered in the previous chapter. The tortious liabilities here are generally supplemental to claims in the law of contract which were considered in Part V. At the end of this chapter there are also brief discussions of the torts of breach of statutory duty, of defamation and of misfeasance in a public office.

---

[1] An excellent distillation of the principles of the tort of negligence is set out in P. Giliker and S. Beckwith, *Tort*, 2nd edn (London: Sweet & Maxwell, 2004).

2. THE TORT OF NEGLIGENCE

A. The scope of the tort of negligence

25–02   The tort of negligence provides a successful claimant with damages for any loss suffered as a result of the defendant's breach of a duty of care. There are five requirements for a successful claim based on the tort of negligence: there must have been a breach of a duty of care; that breach of duty must have caused damage to the claimant; that damage must have been foreseeable; there must have been sufficient proximity between the parties; and it must be "fair, just and reasonable" for the court to impose that liability. These elements are considered in turn in the discussion to follow, beginning with a discussion of the nature of the tort of negligence and the concept of the "duty of care" on which it is based.

B. The duty of care

25–03   The law of negligence is based on there being a duty of care and on that duty of care having been breached so as to cause loss to the claimant. The history of the tort of negligence is well known. The speech of Lord Atkin in *Donoghue v Stevenson*[2] is taken as the foundation of the modern law of negligence when his lordship identified a "neighbour principle" underpinning the duty of care in the sense that "[y]ou must take reasonable care to avoid acts or omissions which you can reasonably foresee would be likely to injure your neighbour".[3] In the decisions in *Hedley Byrne v Heller and Partners*[4] (about which much more is said below) and *Home Office v Dorset Yacht*[5] this principle was qualified; with Lord Reid observing in the latter case that Lord Atkin's dicta should be applied as a statement of general principle rather than literally as though a form of statute.[6] The later decision of the House of Lords in *Anns v Merton LBC*[7] was to seek to identify a high-level, general principle centred on whether or not there was a relationship of sufficient proximity between the parties such that there was reasonable foreseeability of loss, and then whether or not there were any reasons to disapply liability. This led to economic loss being permitted in a widening range of circumstances,[8] including in the case of *Anns v Merton LBC* itself.

25–04   The approach in *Anns v Merton LBC* did not find favour with common lawyers and so a new orthodoxy took hold following the decision of the House of Lords in

---

[2] [1932] A.C. 562.
[3] [1932] A.C. 562, 580.
[4] [1964] A.C. 465.
[5] [1970] A.C. 1004.
[6] [1970] A.C. 1004, 1027.
[7] [1978] A.C. 728, in particular Lord Wilberforce's two stage test at 751–752. See, as to its application in relation to claims against accountants and auditors arising from alleged inaccuracies in accounts, *Scott Group Ltd v McFarlane* (1978) 1 N.Z.L.R. 553 (New Zealand Court of Appeal); *JEB Fasteners Ltd v Marks, Bloom and Co (a firm)* [1981] 3 All E.R. 289; [1983] 1 All E.R. 583 (CA); *Twomax Ltd v Dickson, McFarlane & Robinson* 1983 S.L.T. 98.
[8] See the building case of *Junior Books v Veitchi Co Ltd* [1983] 1 A.C. 520, and the cases in fn.66, above.

Caparo Industries Plc v Dickman.[9] In consequence, liability in tort for negligence is now to be imposed only by reference to existing categories in the case law, rather than by reference to a general, overarching principle. As Lord Bridge summarised the kernel of the test for making out the tort of negligence in *Caparo Industries Plc v Dickman*[10]:

> "What emerges is that, in addition to the foreseeability of damage, the necessary ingredients in any situation giving rise to a duty of care are that there should exist between the party owing the duty and the party to whom it is owed a relationship characterised by the law as one of 'proximity' or 'neighbourhood' and that the situation should be one in which the court considers it fair, just and reasonable that the law should impose a duty of a given scope on the one party for the benefit of the other."

Quoting the dicta of Brennan J. in the High Court of Australia in *Sutherland Shire Council v Heyman*,[11] Lord Bridge held that the law should develop incrementally in future from the existing categories of the law of tort. This should now be considered as the central statement as to how the tort of negligence operates.[12] The various elements of the tort are considered in the sections to follow. It should be recalled that in Chapter 3 we discussed the effect of regulatory standards on establishing whether or not there was a positive duty of care in existence between people and whether or not that duty had been breached: it is suggested that that regulatory context should be borne in mind when considering the existence of a duty of care at common law.[13] First, however, we shall consider the limits imposed on the availability of damages in the tort of negligence for economic loss. Numerous cases concerned solely with banks' duties of care when operating their customers' accounts are considered in para.30–15 et seq.

C. No economic loss—when this general tort will apply in financial contexts

In general terms there can be no recovery for purely economic loss under the tort of negligence.[14] A claimant may only recover damages for her loss as a result of some loss or harm suffered as a result of some harm caused to her property or some personal injury or something of that sort. However, if the loss is a loss purely of money without any other harm, then no action will lie in negligence in general terms. This idea needs to be considered in a little more detail. Damages for negligence are in themselves money; damages awarded for loss of property

25–05

---

[9] See in particular: *Governors of the Peabody Donation Fund v Sir Lindsay Parkinson & Co Ltd* [1985] A.C. 210 H.L.; *Caparo Industries Plc v Dickman* [1990] 2 A.C. 605.

[10] [1990] 2 A.C. 605.

[11] (1985) 60 A.L.R. 1, 43.

[12] One theme in the development of the duty of care not discussed in the text is the mooted development of an approach in which the courts focus solely on the binary question whether or not there is a duty of care and not on the standard of care nor the level of breach which is required to create liability: *South Australia Asset Management Corp ("SAAMCO") v York Montague Ltd* [1997] A.C. 191.

[13] See *Loosemore v Financial Concepts* [2001] Lloyd's Rep. PN 235 as an example of a case where breach of FIMBRA rules constituted a breach of the duty of care in the tort of negligence.

[14] *Spartan Steel & Alloys Ltd v Martin & Co (Contractors) Ltd* [1973] Q.B. 27.

are in a sense measuring an economic loss and identifying the damages necessary to compensate that loss. However, "pure economic loss" refers to the circumstance in which it is only money which the claimant has lost; as opposed to a situation in which the claimant suffers personal injury and then some *consequent* economic loss, or suffers damage to some property of hers and then some *consequent* economic loss. These consequent economic losses are linked to some substantive, non-monetary harm. The key exception to this principle against recovery of pure economic loss is the tort of negligent misstatement predicated on the principle in *Hedley Byrne v Heller*, considered in detail below.[15] There have been other cases which have exceptionally permitted pure economic loss; but those cases have usually been predicated on the notion that there was a very close relationship between the parties which was similar to a direct contractual relationship,[16] and those cases have been limited to their own facts.[17]

25–06 The limitation of the cases in which economic loss will be available will be important in financial cases. In financial transactions it will be very rare that the parties' losses are not purely economic losses, or that those losses are not speculative profits which are expected to flow from a transaction. There are circumstances, however, in which transactions are "physically settled" (e.g. where commodities are delivered as part of the transaction) and in which circumstance it may be that the underlying chattels are required by the claimant, as opposed to being replaceable simply with money. Alternatively, a slightly more adventurous argument could be made in relation to foreign currency transactions, remembering that a foreign currency is not strictly legal tender in the UK.[18] It may be that if a foreign exchange transaction was to be settled by delivery of a "physical" payment in another currency, because a foreign currency would be considered to be a chattel because it is not legal tender in England and Wales, the loss would therefore have been a loss of a chattel and not strictly a loss of money, and so arguably not a purely economic loss.

D.   Damage must have been caused to the claimant

The requirement that the defendant must have suffered loss

25–07 The liability in tort is not based on morality: one is not punished simply for one's wrongs (as in criminal law) but rather one is liable only to compensate anyone who suffers loss and damage as a result of a breach of a duty of care. It is possible, after the decision in *White v Jones*[19] for liability in negligence to arise in favour of third parties on the basis of what Lord Goff referred to as "transferred

---

[15] See para.24–26.

[16] *Junior Books v Veitchi* [1983] 1 A.C. 520. In that case a sub-contractor who installed specialist flooring to its own design negligently, was held to be liable for the economic loss caused to the claimant by way of lost profit because (even though there was no direct contractual link between the parties) their relationship was almost as close as a contractual relationship and the defendant had not been interfered with in any way.

[17] *D & F Estates Ltd v Church Commissioners* [1989] A.C. 177.

[18] See para.2–25.

[19] [1995] 2 A.C. 207.

loss". In that case a solicitor had negligently failed to make changes to a will at the instigation of the testator and thereby caused loss to the people who were to have been named in the will as a result of those changes. It was held that those intended legatees were entitled to sue for damages to recover their loss in negligence. In relation to financial transactions it is therefore possible that if a financial institution acts negligently it will be liable in tort to third parties who suffer loss as a direct result of that negligence. Similarly, in *Gorham v British Telecommunications Plc*[20] the widow of a deceased employee of BT was entitled to damages for the loss which she suffered as a result of the employee being negligently misadvised about a choice between two available pension plans with the result that the widow received less than otherwise she would have done after her husband's death. It is an important part of the claimant's duties, however, in relation to all torts—including negligence and the tort of conversion—to mitigate its loss by taking reasonable action to ensure that it suffers no further harm than that flowing from the commission of the tort.[21]

Types of indirect harm caused by the defendant in financial transactions

The following sorts of circumstance could easily arise in financial transactions, creating difficult problems for the law of tort. They arise from the complex nature of financial institutions and from the great variety of services which they offer to their many clients. The harm caused may be indirect, in that it may not necessarily be caused by a direct interaction between bank and client. This section simply describes some of the potential problems. **25–08**

The first type of liability might result straightforwardly from the different activities within investment banks. Investment banks carry on a huge number of different activities at once, through different departments in different office buildings, often in different jurisdictions, and through employees who may never even have met. Consequently, it is very possible that an investment bank may be acting for a client through one department or subsidiary company (perhaps recommending a portfolio of investments in shares, including one company in particular) while at the same time offering corporate finance advice to that company through a different department or subsidiary where that corporate finance advice might cause the company's shares to decrease in value. As a result, the bank would have both created a portfolio which caused the customer loss and it would also have concealed the knowledge that those shares were about to fall in value. The customer could claim that the investment bank had acted fraudulently if advisors in both the investment advice and in the corporate finance departments had known of both transactions: that is, if the bank was both finding investors for the company while at the same time advising the company to employ a strategy which would cause its share price to fall.[22] Alternatively, if the investment bank had acted through two completely different departments or subsidiaries whose employees had never met, let alone discussed their distinct businesses, then the claimant would have to argue that the loss it suffered was caused solely by the **25–09**

---

[20] [2000] 1 W.L.R. 2129.
[21] See, e.g. *Uzinterimpex JSC v Standard Bank Plc* [2008] Bus. L.R. 1762.
[22] See *Killick v Pricewaterhouse Coopers* [2001] Lloyd's Rep. PN 18.

defective investment portfolio which included those shares, and not by any collusion within the bank.[23] The complexity of the investment bank might very well mean that the department advising ordinary investors is acting at odds with the department (possibly required by securities law to observe secrecy) advising on corporate finance transactions. Identifying the appropriate special relationship might therefore be difficult.

25–10 The second type of liability might result from a formal, statutorily required document—such as a prospectus in relation to an issue of securities[24]—in which statements are made on which investors are expected to place reliance. This raises liability under *Hedley Byrne v Heller*—considered below—and which is considered in great detail in relation to securities prospectuses in Chapter 41. In short, because securities regulation requires the publication of these documents, it will not be open to the person who prepared those documents to argue that the person who relied upon their contents was not in a relationship of sufficient proximity of the person making the statement: if the documents are required to be published and their correctness to be maintained under the terms of the regulations, then the persons responsible for the statements made in those documents will be liable in tort to anyone who relies upon them. Therefore, the common law may need to be shaped by the regulatory requirements in this field.

25–11 The third type of liability might result from an investment bank preparing investment analysis for its clients which is sold to those clients as part of the bank's services. In the event that there was any error in that analysis, then an action might lie in contract or in negligent misstatement. Suppose the analysis contains negligent mistakes—perhaps reversing the names of two different companies, one of which is expected to earn large profits and the other of which is expected to realise large losses. The question would be whether or not this sort of material would found an action in negligence if it came into the possession of third parties who had not entered into a contract with the bank (and who would therefore have no action in contract), and if it was relied upon by those third parties when making investment decisions, then an action for negligent misstatement might be commenced if it was considered to be reasonable foreseeable that those third parties would come into possession of the investment advice. The investment bank in this instance would contend successfully that there would no relationship of proximity between it and the third party who relied on that analysis if the documents were prepared solely for the benefit of a limited class of people (here, its clients).[25] In this situation, it is supposed (as with sales of economic analysis to customers generally) that there is no regulatory obligation to publish that information and therefore that it cannot be assumed that third parties will rely on advice which was prepared for the eyes of selected customers only. If the analysis, however, was designed deliberately to misinform the bank's own customers so that the bank would be able to sell its customers securities which it already owned and which it considered to be a bad risk for the future, then the investment bank would be liable for fraud, in the manner

---

[23] An action may also lie in contract, but that issue is considered in Ch.20.

[24] On which see Ch.38.

[25] See, for example, *Al-Nakib Investments (Jersey) Ltd v Longcroft* [1990] 3 All E.R. 321.

considered in the previous chapter. The more difficult case is that in which no fraud can be proved (because there are no recordings or other records of meetings between employees within the bank to show a clear conspiracy) but in which the bank advises its own customers to buy securities from it but which cause a loss for those customers. In such a circumstance the bank may be in breach of contract and it may have been negligent provided that the loss was considered to be foreseeable (as considered next). The law relating to negligent misstatement is considered in detail below.

E. Foreseeability

It is not enough that there is a duty of care and that there is loss: rather, that loss must have been foreseeable. The court will consider "what a reasonable person in the circumstances of the defendant ought to have foreseen".[26] Therefore, there is only a duty of care to avoid causing loss to another person if that loss was reasonably foreseeable. In financial transactions, a contracting party to a transaction will clearly be entitled to damages (aside from a claim in contract) if a negligently sold transaction performs unexpectedly (due perhaps to a market crash) and thus causes loss to the claimant. Loss may be unrecoverable either if the loss is unforeseeable (but the defendant personally is not unforeseeable); or if the defendant is an unforeseeable defendant. Categories of defendant whose loss is unforeseeable will not be able to recover damages. As discussed below, the common law will find that a person who was not intended to receive the defendant's advice, or who could not be intended to receive that material or that service, will be insufficiently proximate to the defendant or that her loss was unforeseeable.[27]

25–12

F. Proximity

Strictly, tort lawyers separate out the idea of "proximity" from the idea of "foreseeability". Proximity is a question as to the closeness of the relationship between the claimant and the defendant; whereas, foreseeability concerns the question whether or not the type of harm which the defendant suffered was foreseeable, albeit that the notion of foreseeability must be measured in the context of the parties' relationship. This concept is particularly important in relation to liability under *Hedley Byrne v Heller*[28] which is considered in detail below.[29] Proximity will often be decided by whether or not the court considers that the relationship between the parties makes the imposition of liability reasonable.[30]

25–13

---

[26] Giliker and Beckwith, *Tort*, 2nd edn (London: Sweet & Maxwell, 2004), p.35.
[27] See, for example, *Al-Nakib Investments (Jersey) Ltd v Longcroft* [1990] 3 All E.R. 321.
[28] [1963] 2 All E.R. 575, [1964] A.C. 465.
[29] See para.24–26.
[30] *Alcock v Chief Constable of South Yorkshire* [1992] 1 A.C. 310, at 410, per Lord Oliver.

G. "Fair, just and reasonable" to impose liability

The extent of the "fair, just and reasonable" requirement

25–14 In a few cases, such as the speech of Lord Bridge in *Caparo v Dickman* and the Court of Appeal in *Goodwill v British Pregnancy Advisory Service*,[31] it has been required that the claim for negligence must be "fair, just and reasonable", as well as satisfying the elements considered above. It is unclear on the authorities the extent to which this "fair, just and reasonable" requirement will be used to obviate claims which otherwise would have been effective. Balcombe L.J. considered that this requirement was merely a part of deciding whether or not there was proximity between the parties[32]: that is, if there was insufficient fairness in imposing liability that would be because there was insufficient proximity between them.

Circumstances in which liability may not be "fair, just and reasonable"

25–15 In spite of the doubts considered above about whether or not this requirement is really a separate one, I would suggest that in financial cases it might have a significant role to play.[33] So, for example, there may be situations in which there is sufficient proximity between the parties because they were within one another's contemplation but in which it may nevertheless be considered unfair, unjust and unreasonable to impose liability. Consider a transaction between Mortgage Bank had created 100,000 mortgage contracts with customers who transpired to be "sub prime" risks and many of whom failed to make their repayments. Suppose that Mortgage Bank then sold these mortgage contracts to other banks, and that those buyers in turn sold those mortgage contracts on to Profit Bank: there was therefore no direct contractual nexus between Mortgage Bank and Profit Bank. Assume that Profit Bank had also been involved in the sub-prime mortgage market in the US at the same time, selling exactly the same sorts of mortgages to the same sorts of customers. Suppose then that Profit Bank contended that Mortgage Bank had breached its duty of care to Profit Bank by selling mortgages to inappropriate customers and by failing to enforce the mortgage contracts sufficiently vigorously. There is sufficient proximity between these parties because Profit Bank has acquired securities which Mortgage Bank put up for sale; but on the facts we may argue that it is unreasonable to impose liability on Mortgage Bank for a course of action which Profit Bank itself was involved in when it sold mortgages to the same types of customer. Profit Bank was already exposed to that market of its own volition, and therefore it may be unreasonable to hold Mortgage Bank liable for further losses it suffered as a professional counterparty in the same market.

---

[31] [1996] 1 W.L.R. 1397, 1406, per Gibson L.J.

[32] *Marc Rich & Co AG v Bishop Rock Marine Company (The Nicholas H)* [1994] 1 W.L.R. 1071.

[33] The reservations expressed by some commentators on the law of tort nothwithstanding: see, e.g. Markesinis, Johnston and Deakin, *Tort Law*, 6th edn (OUP, 2008), pp.177–178.

In financial transactions generally we may also look to the FCA Conduct of Business principles[34] for demonstration that even if a claim in tort might otherwise be made out, according to those conduct of business principles the seller would not ordinarily have been required to do anything more than she had done in dealing with that customer in that context, and therefore that it would not have been reasonable to impose liability on a financial institution. This is most likely in relation to transactions between market counterparties where it might be thought reasonable for such parties to be able to make informed decisions as to the risks associated with a transaction or an investment without needing to suggest that there was a duty of care owed to them by another market counterparty. As was discussed in Chapter 3, it is suggested that the *FCA Handbook* stands as a statement of what is considered to be reasonable behaviour in the UK financial markets, whether in the form of rules or of guidance notes, being the statement of requisite behaviour for regulated persons on those markets.

25–16

Whether there will be a duty of care in financial transactions: JP Morgan Chase Bank v Springwell Navigation

The older authorities have expressed an equivocal attitude to the level of care owed by banks when advising their customers in investment transactions, in a way that it is suggested would be difficult to maintain in a world peopled by FCA Conduct of Business regulation (as considered in Chapter 10), and an extensive zone of fiduciary liability where investment advice is offered to a customer in circumstances in which the bank is doing more than simply taking a customer's order and instead is providing advice (as considered in Chapter 5[35]). So, to demonstrate this equivocation: Salmon J. in *Woods v Martins Bank Ltd*[36] has held that in relation to investment advice a bank manager owes duties of care and skill in relation to a customer with little or no investment experience; whereas in *Banbury v Bank of Montreal*[37] the House of Lords considered that "it would be difficult to establish that advising on investments was part of the business of banking". The modern context of finance law, however, suggests that duties of care will be more easily identified in financial transactions between a bank or an investment firm and their customers. It is suggested that the general need for investment (especially in the form of pensions and to repay mortgages) for much of the population and the growth of formal financial regulation, means that investment advice takes place in a very different climate from that in 1918 when *Banbury* was decided. This change will be demonstrated in this section by reference to a recent decision of Gloster J.

25–17

It has been held that if a customer is sufficiently expert or sufficiently commercially knowledgeable to understand the concept of "risk-return" calculations[38] in investment, then there will not be a duty of care owed by a financial institution to that client in relation to any alleged misstatement in that

25–18

---

[34] See para.10–01.
[35] See para.5–04.
[36] [1959] 1 Q.B. 55.
[37] [1918] A.C. 626.
[38] See para.1–53.

customer's investment portfolio. In this regard, the decision of Gloster J. in *JP Morgan Chase Bank v Springwell Navigation Corp*[39] concerned a company, Springwell, which was the vehicle through which P and his family conducted their speculative investment business. The defendants, Chase and other group companies, provided Springwell with investment advice through various traders and other employees in various departments. Springwell had a portfolio of about US \$700 million, and Chase provided advice as to the structure of that portfolio. Chase recommended, inter alia, large numbers of emerging market investments including ruinous investments in securities issued by the government of the Russian Federation ("GKOs"): these products were complex derivatives, and a large amount of these investments were acquired using leverage (in effect, high-risk borrowings). The Russian banking moratorium in 1998 meant that the GKOs became effectively worthless. Springwell sued Chase, inter alia, for negligent misstatement resulting from the advice given as to the contents of its investment portfolio.

25–19   Gloster J. found that, although P and the other family members had no specific expertise in financial derivatives and had no other advisors, nevertheless P was commercially astute enough not to have needed to have all of the risks explained to him. This conclusion seems somewhat remarkable in the context of financial regulation requiring non-expert counterparties to have their best interests considered by financial institutions when dealing with them.[40] Gloster J. considered that "even if" P had had the conduct of business agreement explained to him, he would not have done anything differently: surely the point is that unless P had had the effect of that contract explained to him he could not have known, as an inexpert investor, whether or not he should have changed his mind. It was held that in this context no duty of care arose between the parties because there was nothing in the contracts nor in the context which justified the existence of such a duty of care here. It is suggested that this is a peculiar reading of the financial regulations in effect at the time. It illustrates the determination of the common law courts to impose duties of care only when they consider it to be appropriate on the facts of any given case, as opposed to having a sufficiently clear understanding of what circumstances will give rise to a duty of care in the abstract. It is suggested that under the FCA Conduct of Business Sourcebook, with its prohibition on the exclusion of a financial institution's liabilities to its customers, Chase would now be required to ensure that a non-market counterparty would be entitled to have all of the risks associated with complex financial derivatives products explained to her so that that customer could make an informed decision to continue with that investment strategy, as opposed to making a pig-headed but ignorant decision to do so.[41]

25–20   Springwell argued on appeal to the Court of Appeal[42] that there were three particular representations which should have been treated differently at first instance: that is representations to the effect that the investments would be conservative, that they would be liquid, and that there would be no currency risk.

---

[39] [2008] EWHC 1186 (Comm).

[40] See para.10–16 et seq.

[41] See para.10–16 et seq.

[42] *JP Morgan v Springwell* [2010] EWCA Civ 1221.

It was held, however, that individual expressions could not be lifted "like a fish out of water" so as to demonstrate a misrepresentation, but rather the entire context of the dealings between the parties and the context in which those representations were made must be considered.[43] Having considered these statements in the round, the Court of Appeal upheld the judgment of Gloster J., including a reliance on the individuals who operated the claimant company having sufficient understanding of investment products to form a view on the investments at issue. However, the Court of Appeal did not consider closely the regulatory obligations of the bank in relation to conduct of business and "know your client" rules to decide whether or not in that context the bank had acted appropriately. Instead there is a single phrase in the court's judgment finding that "Chase fulfilled its obligations", without any more analysis than that.[44]

The interest rate swap misselling cases

In the wake of the financial crisis there were several claims brought by the owners of small businesses which had been allegedly mis-sold interest rate swaps and similar derivatives products. At the time of writing, those cases have not yet gone to trial, and the litigation process appears to be particularly drawn out. Such litigation as there has been is discussed at para.40–77. In essence, the claimants have found that derivatives which were marketed to them as a means of controlling their interest rate and similar risks have incurred tremendous losses for them as a result of market movements in the wake of the financial crisis. Some of the claims relate specifically to mismatches between the terms of those businesses' borrowing and the terms of the derivatives: including differences in the duration of those products and differences between the notional amount of the swap and the amount of the buyer's underlying loan. In some cases it has been alleged that the buyer was obliged to enter into the swap as a condition precedent to being granted the loan that it was seeking. There is a common complaint that the fees and break costs associated with these derivatives were not explained to the customers. In essence, the banks are alleged to have breached their regulatory obligations under COBS (discussed in Chapter 10) and, as argued in Chapter 3, that should found a claim at common law on the basis that COBS constitutes the manner in which a reasonable bank should act when dealing with an inexpert customer. That issue is considered next.

Whether a duty of care will be based on the defendant's regulatory obligations

In relation to the establishment of any duty of care at common law, there have been cases in which the courts have examined the regulatory obligations of regulated firms when deciding whether or not that firm should be treated as

25–21

25–22

---

[43] *JP Morgan v Springwell* [2010] EWCA Civ 1221 at [112] et seq, per Aikens L.J.
[44] [2010] EWCA Civ 1221, at [125], per Aikens L.J.

owing its client a duty at common law.[45] In the *Principles for Businesses* rulebook, considered in Chapter 9, all regulated firms are required to conduct their businesses with due skill, care and diligence, and to obey conduct of business regulation in their treatment of their customers.

25-23 One line of authority suggests that the common law should maintain its traditional principles and not be bound by the content of any particular regulatory rule. So, in *Beary v Pall Mall Investments*[46] it was suggested that the common law should continue to apply its own principles. However, in *Loosemore v Financial Concepts*[47] the court considered the appropriate conduct of business regulation in formulating the terms of the common law duty. Similarly, in *Gorham v British Telecommunications Plc*,[48] a pensions provider argued that its duty of care to its client in a claim for negligence should be *limited* to extent of its narrow regulatory duties. The Court of Appeal held that the obligations would not be limited in this fashion when the common law duty of care extended further.

25-24 Nevertheless, it is suggested, that where those principles call, for example, for "reasonableness" or for the finding of a duty of care then the courts should look to regulatory standards when deciding what is reasonable or whether there should be a duty of care or not. Other cases have taken a subtly different approach. So, in *Seymour v Christine Ockwell*[49] it was held that regulatory principles could inform the finding of a common law duty on the basis that they "afford strong evidence as to what is expected of a competent advisor in most situations". Importantly, the content of those regulatory rules would not be decisive of the common law claim in themselves because they are merely "evidence" of what is required of the defendant at common law. The position would appear to be that the courts will consider the extent of a defendant's common law duties by reference to the defendant's regulatory obligations, although the defendant will not be able to limit its obligations by relying on a narrow set of obligations in the appropriate context if the common law imposes a higher requirement.

H. Liability for omissions; especially omissions by regulators

Ordinarily no liability for an omission in tort

25-25 In general terms there is no liability in tort for pure omissions: that is, there is ordinarily no liability in tort for a failure to do something when one had no other obligation to do it.[50] Regulated firms will be liable for any failure to comply with their obligations under the FCA regulations as considered in Chapter 10, but that is not the same as liability in tort.[51] In the tort of negligence there will only be a

---

[45] See for example: *Investors Compensation Scheme v West Bromwich Building Society* (1999) Lloyd's Rep. PN 496; *Loosemore v Financial Concepts* (2001) 1 Lloyd's Rep. 235; *Seymour v Christine Ockwell* (2005) P.N.L.R. 39.
[46] [2005] EWCA Civ 415.
[47] [2001] 1 Lloyd's Rep. 235.
[48] [2000] 1 W.L.R. 2129.
[49] [2005] P.N.L.R. 39.
[50] *Smith v Littlewoods Organisation Ltd* [1987] A.C. 241, 271, per Lord Goff.
[51] See para.10–01.

liability connected to a failure to act if the defendant was under some prior obligation to act at all. Lord Bridge suggested[52] that liability would attach in this circumstance only in a context in which the defendant had "promised to make another person better off"[53]: which is exactly what might be expected in a financial transaction. As it is argued in para.25–43 below, where there is a regulatory obligation to act, a failure to do so might found liability in negligence.

The potential liability of statutory regulators

More particularly, the question arises as to the liabilities of regulators who fail to prevent the loss suffered by investors. Such an obligation might arise under statute. This issue arose in *Yuen Kun Yeu v Att Gen of Hong Kong*[54] where the Commissioner of Deposit-Taking Companies in Hong Kong negligently granted a licence to accept deposits to a fraudulent enterprise which took the claimants' deposits from them. The claimants contended that the defendant Commissioner had acted negligently in failing either to deny a licence or to control the enterprise once it had begun to trade fraudulently: that is, it was claimed that the defendant had committed a negligent omission. The Privy Council held that there was insufficient proximity between the Commissioner and the investors who relied on the good-standing of the fraudulent enterprise, and therefore that there was no liability in negligence on these facts. This does seem to be a remarkable finding. If a regulatory body is required to consider the suitability of an entity for authorisation to conduct financial services business, then it is odd if no liability at all attaches to that entity in tort if the regulator is negligent in failing to investigate the condition of that entity with sufficient assiduity to spot an ill-concealed motive for fraud, or a pattern of fraudulent trading soon after commencement of business. The Privy Council's approach only makes sense if it is considered too expensive for the regulator to owe damages equal to the losses suffered by all investors stemming from the negligent authorisation of such an investment firm: that is, this decision only makes sense as a policy decision because otherwise the investors in the marketplace would have been within the contemplation of the FCA in the UK given its statutory obligations to enhance investor protection.[55]

25–26

The potential liability of non-statutory regulators

There have been cases, however, in which non-statutory regulators have been held liable for omissions in the discharge of their duties. In *Watson v British Boxing Board of Control*[56] where boxer Michael Watson alleged that the Board, which regulated professional boxing, had been negligent when it failed to draft adequate rules so as to provide for adequate medical support at the ringside so that when Watson suffered a brain haemorrhage during a brutal bout with Chris

25–27

---

[52] *Curran v Northern Ireland Co-ownership Housing Association* [1987] A.C. 718.
[53] Giliker and Beckwith, *Tort*, p.38.
[54] [1988] A.C. 175.
[55] Financial Services and Markets Act 2000 s.5(1); see para.8–10.
[56] [2001] 2 W.L.R. 1256.

Eubank there was inadequate medical support to prevent him from suffering brain damage. The Court of Appeal held that the Board was liable to Watson in damages because there was sufficient proximity between the parties and because Watson was one of a limited class of people who were affected by the rules. So, a regulatory body (even if it is not created or empowered by statute) may be liable in tort for failing to provide for adequate rules, as well as for the inadequate performance of its obligations. Similarly, a regulatory body may be liable for the negligent failure of one of its agents. Thus, the Welsh Rugby Union Ltd was held liable for the failure of a referee which they had appointed to deal appropriately with a serious injury to a player who ended up confined to a wheelchair as a result: the referee had permitted scrums to continue unsafely.[57] The rareness of such events was considered by the Court of Appeal to negate any concern that this would open the floodgates to other such claims.

Potential liability for the regulator under FSMA 2000

25–28   The obligations of the Financial Conduct Authority ("FCA") under the Financial Services and Markets Act 2000 ("FSMA 2000") include an obligation to secure the protection of consumers, and the reduction of financial crime[58] such that any negligent failure to do that is an omission to carry out an act required of the FCA by statute. The protection of market confidence[59] cannot be achieved if the FCA bears no obligation to those who transact with regulated entities. The stronger argument would seem to be that, if there was nothing which ought to have made the regulator suspicious when the application for authorisation was granted, then the fraud perpetrated by the shysters running the enterprise was a *novus actus interveniens* which would break the chain of the regulator's liability in negligence. Otherwise, it is suggested that it would be an opiate on the conscience of public regulators like the FCA if they are not kept on their mettle by the prospect of being personally liable for any loss which may flow from any negligence in the carrying out of their statutory duties. The FCA also bears obligations, and thus potentially liability, as a public body under public law: the potential liability for the FCA under judicial review principles is outlined in Chapter 9 of this book.[60]

3.   THE TORT OF NEGLIGENT MISREPRESENTATION

A.   Introduction

25–29   This important section concerns liability in the tort of negligence for financial transactions. In particular it focuses on the tort of negligent misrepresentation because this is the principal area in which negligence is manifested in financial transactions. One of the contexts in which negligent misrepresentation has been particularly important in the financial context has been in relation to issues of

---

[57] Financial Services and Markets Act 2000.
[58] Financial Services and Markets Act 2000 s.2(2).
[59] Financial Services and Markets Act 2000 s.2(2).
[60] See para.9–62.

shares accompanied by a prospectus, where that prospectus contains misrepresentations which have been made negligently: those cases are considered in detail in Chapter 39, and only in outline in this chapter.[61] In general the focus of this chapter will be on the sorts of situations in which financial advice is given by a financial professional to a customer relating to investment advice or the structuring of complex financial products, or the making of statements (such as those in a prospectus) which will be relied upon by investors on financial markets generally. The elements of this tort are considered in detail below. The claimant's remedy in such situations is common law damages, as discussed below.[62]

B.   The principle in *Hedley Byrne v Heller*

The decision in Hedley Byrne v Heller

The seed from which the law on negligent misrepresentation grew was the decision of the House of Lords in *Hedley Byrne v Heller*.[63] In this case the claimant obtained a reference from one of its client's bankers: the claimant, an advertising agency, was concerned that it was about to assume a large financial obligation paying for advertising for that client whom it feared might not be able to repay it in the future. The bank gave a reference suggesting that the client would be able to pay; although negligently it had failed to realise that this was not the case when the references were given. The House of Lords held that the bank should be liable for damages for its negligent misstatement to the claimant. Lord Reid held that in this case there was a special relationship between the parties because the bank ought to have known that the claimant was relying on the bank and that the claimant was relying on the bank to exercise skill and care in making the statement. As Lord Morris put it[64]:

25–30

> "I consider that it follows and that it should now be regarded as settled that if someone possessed of a special skill undertakes, quite irrespective of contract, to apply that skill for the assistance of another person who relies on such skill, a duty of care will arise . . . Furthermore if, in a sphere in which a person is so placed that others could reasonably rely on his judgment or his skill or on his ability to make careful inquiry, a person takes it on himself to give information or advice to, or allows his information or advice to be passed on to, another person who, as he knows or should know, will place reliance on it, then a duty of care will arise."

Thus a duty of care will arise simply on the basis of one person voluntarily making a statement to another person in a context in which it is reasonable to place reliance on that statement. It has been suggested by some commentators that this means that the claimant is acquiring an equivalent to a contractual indemnity without having negotiated for such an indemnity.[65] In the financial context in particular this is a somewhat facile point: typically the client will have no option but to sign the seller's standard contract and so cannot include such a

---

[61]   See para.9–62.
[62]   See para.24–44.
[63]   [1963] 2 All E.R. 575, [1964] A.C. 465.
[64]   [1963] 2 All E.R. 575, [1964] A.C. 465.
[65]   e.g. Weir [1963] C.L.J. 216.

term in the contract; and more significantly if a financial institution with all of its professional advisors on hand chooses to make a statement in circumstances in which other people can reasonably rely on it, then it has assumed that liability and it is consequently perfectly reasonable that it should sound in tort.

The ramifications of this principle for the law of finance

25–31   The ramifications of this principle for the law of finance are clear: whenever advice or any statement connected to a financial institution's business is made to another person (in particular someone less expert in financial matters) and that other person relies on that statement and suffers loss as a result, then the financial institution will be liable in damages for that other person's loss. One line of defence for the financial institution will be that provided by the Conduct of Business regulations: if the other person is a market counterparty expert in financial matters, then it would be unlikely for it to have been reasonable for that other person to have placed complete reliance on the first financial institution's statements. An interesting set of circumstances arose in *Bankers Trust v Dharmala (No.2)*,[66] where a financial institution, with no expertise in interest rate swaps and dealing primarily in a jurisdiction without sophisticated financial markets, acquires complex interest rate swaps from an investment bank which is expert in those products (and which has a reputation for putting highly sophisticated products in place). It was held that there is no obligation on the expert bank to explain all of the risks to the less expert institution because its ranking under conduct of business regulation would nevertheless mean that it could reasonably be supposed that it could assess those risks for itself. So, by extension, such an institution would not be able to claim that it was reasonable for it to rely entirely on the statements made by such an expert investment bank so as to found a claim on negligent misstatement.[67]

Special relationships with financial institutions in the business of providing advice

25–32   Special relationships are easy to demonstrate in financial transactions when a financial institution is giving advice or selling a product to a client as part of its business: in such a circumstance the client will place reliance on the statements of that financial institution due both to its perceived and its broadcast expertise.[68] Financial institutions in the business of providing financial advice broadcast their prestige in their advertising generally and in their marketing of particular products and services: this, it is suggested, puts them in a special relationship with any customer who relies on that institution's advice precisely because it is

---

[66] [1996] C.L.C. 518.

[67] See generally *Raiffeisen Zentralbank Osterreich AG v The Royal Bank of Scotland* [2010] EWHC 1392 (Comm), Christopher Clarke J. on the nature of what will constitute a representation on which another person relies, in turn relying on *MCI WorldCom International Inc v Primus Telecommunications Inc* [2004] EWCA Civ 957. See also *Standard Chartered Bank v Ceylon Petroleum Corp* [2011] EWHC 1785 (Comm). These cases analysed the facts in front of them for evidence of an actionable misrepresentation without making an meaningful contribution to the substantive law itself.

[68] See, e.g. *Riyad Bank v Ahli United Bank* [2005] 2 Lloyd's Rep. 409.

suggesting that it has expertise on which customers may rely. It is only when clients contact an institution merely to make an order, without receiving any advice (as was discussed in relation to conduct of business regulation[69]) that there would not be a special relationship because no statement is made by the institution in that context. So, if I telephone Profit Bank and give them an instruction to buy me a given number of shares in X Plc, then Profit Bank owes me no duty of care in negligence because it has not induced me to buy those shares; whereas if I contact Profit Bank as an ordinary customer seeking advice on investments in shares and Profit Bank advises me to buy shares in X Plc then their purported expertise and advice would have induced my investment and so would attract prima facie liability under the *Hedley Byrne* principle if that investment caused me loss. The argument that would be raised here, of course, is that it is only when the financial institution actually offers the customer advice in this latter context precisely because the act of giving the advice constitutes the proximate relationship and not the inducement in the advertisement.

In *Mutual Life and Citizens' Assurance Co v Evatt*[70] an insurance company gave investment advice to a client who relied on that advice and consequently suffered loss. It was held by the Privy Council that this insurance company was not in the business of providing investment advice—rather it was in the business of selling insurance—and therefore the *Hedley Byrne v Heller* principle ought not to apply. Lord Morris and Lord Reid, wisely, dissented on the basis that this advice was provided in the course of a business transaction, even if it was not the defendant's principal business. It is suggested that, as Lord Morris held in *Hedley Byrne v Heller*, if a professional person gives advice while acting as a business person (as opposed, for example, to making a statement at a social function) then that person assumes the liability that someone who can rely on her statements reasonably in the context may suffer loss as a result of relying on those statements. The views of Lord Morris and Lord Reid were followed in *Esso Petroleum v Mardon*[71] and in *Howard Marine and Dredging Co Ltd v Ogden & Sons Ltd.*[72]

25–33

In *Investors Compensation Scheme Ltd v West Bromwich BS*[73] an independent financial adviser had taken out advertisements in national newspapers targeting retired people encouraging them to invest in products which would leave investors secure in their homes while providing them with a secure future income. The newspaper advertisements focused instead by inference on the fast cars and yachts which might be within the reach of investors. Sales staff reassured potential investors that the investments were "sure fire winners" and that they were "completely safe". The investors suffered large losses and sued inter alia on the basis of negligent misstatement. Evans-Lombe J. did not dismiss the advertisements and comments by sales staff as being "mere puffs", but rather treated them as meaningful representations. Clearly the investors were not intended to be sophisticated investors whereas the defendant financial advisers were professionals. This was significant in his lordship's finding that the

25–34

---

[69] See para.10–01.
[70] [1971] A.C. 793.
[71] [1976] 1 Q.B. 801.
[72] [1978] 2 All E.R. 1134.
[73] [1999] Lloyd's Rep. PN 496.

investors relied on the expertise of the defendant and its sales staff. It was held that the statements made by the sales staff were made without an honest belief in their accuracy and consequently that they constituted actionable misrepresentations.[74]

Cases in which responsibility is assumed in financial transactions

25–35   Where a financial institution assumes responsibility for a person's business affairs—whether or not as a fiduciary—then that institution will be liable under *Hedley Byrne* for any statements made or services rendered.[75] So, in *Henderson v Merrett Syndicates Ltd* it was held that if agents assumed responsibility for the affairs of investors—such as "Names" on the Lloyds Insurance market—then the actions of those people would constitute a special relationship founding liability under the *Hedley Byrne* principle.[76] As Lord Goff held, it must be an objective test as to whether or not liability must be taken to have been assumed by the defendant given the circumstances of the parties' interaction, as opposed to a purely subjective or voluntary assumption of liability (or more likely exclusion of liability) by the financial institution.[77] Advising a person on the form of pension they should take out would also constitute a special relationship sufficient to found liability under *Hedley Byrne*.[78] In these cases the courts have based liability on the defendants' assumption of liability,[79] in line with the dicta of Lord Morris as quoted above. In effect, when a financial institution or financial advisor gives advice, that person assumes the responsibility for any loss suffered by someone who reasonably relies on that advice and so suffers loss.[80] This general principle has been encapsulated in the speech of Lord Oliver in *Caparo v Dickman* in relation to financial transactions, as set out in the next section.

The encapsulation of this principle in Caparo v Dickman

25–36   While the principle underpinning liability in tort for negligent misrepresentation is contained in the decision in *Hedley Byrne v Heller*,[81] that principle has been conceptualised usefully for financial purposes in subsequent cases. The position was expressed in the following terms by Lord Oliver in *Caparo Industries Plc v Dickman*[82]:

---

[74] Relying inter alia on *Cornish v Midland Bank* [1985] 3 All E.R. 513.

[75] *Spring v Guardian Assurance Plc* [1995] 2 A.C. 296, 318, per Lord Goff.

[76] *Henderson v Merrett Syndicates Ltd* [1995] 2 A.C. 145.

[77] [1995] 2 A.C. 145, 181. See also *Caparo v Dickman* [1990] 2 A.C. 605, 637, per Lord Oliver; and *Williams v Natural Life Health Foods Ltd* [1998] 1 W.L.R. 830, 835, per Lord Steyn.

[78] [2000] 1 W.L.R. 2129. Similarly, *Wheldon v GRE Linked Life Assurance Ltd* [2000] 2 All E.R. (Comm) 914.

[79] See, for example, P. Giliker and S. Beckwith, *Tort*, p.91.

[80] A different, more traditional approach was taken in *IFE Fund SA v Goldman Sachs* [2006] EWHC 887 (Comm) where in relation to a syndicated loan arrangement it was held that an investment bank owed no duty of care to lenders in relation to whom it had assumed no obligations.

[81] [1963] 2 All E.R. 575, [1964] A.C. 465.

[82] [1990] 2 A.C. 605.

"What can be deduced from the *Hedley Byrne*[83] case, therefore, is that the necessary relationship between the maker of a statement or giver of advice (the adviser) and the recipient who acts in reliance on it (the advisee) may typically be held to exist where (1) the advice is required for a purpose, whether particularly specified or generally described, which is made known, either actually or inferentially, to the adviser at the time when the advice is given, (2) the adviser knows, either actually or inferentially, that his advice will be communicated to the advisee, either specifically or as a member of an ascertainable class, in order that it should be used by the advisee for that purpose, (3) it is known, either actually or inferentially, that the advice so communicated is likely to be acted upon by the advisee for that purpose without independent inquiry and (4) it is so acted on by the advisee to his detriment. That is not, of course, to suggest that these conditions are either conclusive or exclusive, but merely that the actual decision in the case does not warrant any broader propositions."[84]

The decision in *Caparo v Dickman* itself was concerned with an audit report on which the claimant relied when deciding whether or not to launch a takeover bid for the company which was the subject of that audit report. The context of statements made in takeover cases is considered in outline next, and cases relating to the preparation of prospectuses governing securities issues is considered thereafter. Both of these contexts are considered in much greater detail in Chapter 39.[85]

The emphasis on pragmatism, not general principle, in subsequent cases

The approach of many common law courts following *Caparo v Dickman* has been to take a practical approach to the question whether a duty of care exists, and to find that the evolution of "lower level principles" on a case-by-case basis in tort is a more useful approach than relying on "high abstractions" and general principles. This tendency is particularly evident in the judgment of Lord Hoffmann in *Commissioners of Customs & Excise v Barclays Bank*,[86] where his lordship cast doubt on the usefulness of the:

25–37

"tendency, which has been remarked upon by many judges, for phrases like 'proximate', 'fair, just and reasonable' and 'assumption of responsibility' to be used as slogans rather than practical guides to whether a duty should exist or not. These phrases are often illuminating but discrimination is needed to identify the factual situations in which they provide useful guidance. For example, in a case in which A provides information to C which he knows will be relied upon by D, it is useful to ask whether A assumed responsibility to D.[87] Likewise, in a case in which A provides information on behalf of B to C for the purpose of being relied upon by C, it is useful to ask whether A assumed responsibility to C for the information or was only discharging his duty to B.[88] Or in a case in which A provided information to B for the purpose of enabling him to make one kind of decision, it may be useful to ask whether he assumed responsibility for its use for a different kind of decision.[89] In these cases in which the loss has been caused by the claimant's reliance on information provided by the defendant, it is critical

---

[83] [1964] A.C. 465.

[84] [1991] 2 A.C. 605 at 638. See also Lord Bridge at 620–621 and Lord Jauncey at 659–660 (esp. at 660E "the fundamental question of the purpose"). See also *James McNaughton Papers Group Ltd v Hicks Anderson & Co (a firm)* [1991] 1 All E.R. 135. cf. *Morgan Crucible Co Plc v Hill Samuel Bank Ltd* [1991] 1 All E.R. 148.

[85] See para.39–17 et seq.

[86] [2007] 1 A.C. 181.

[87] *Hedley Byrne & Co Ltd v Heller & Partners Ltd* [1964] A.C. 465 : *Smith v Eric S Bush* [1990] 1 A.C. 831.

[88] *Williams v Natural Life Health Foods Ltd* [1998] A.C. 830.

[89] *Caparo Industries Plc v Dickman* [1990] 2 A.C. 605.

to decide whether the defendant (rather than someone else) assumed responsibility for the accuracy of the information to the claimant (rather than to someone else) or for its use by the claimant for one purpose (rather than another). The answer does not depend upon what the defendant intended but, as in the case of contractual liability, upon what would reasonably be inferred from his conduct against the background of all the circumstances of the case. The purpose of the inquiry is to establish whether there was, in relation to the loss in question, the necessary relationship (or 'proximity') between the parties and, as Lord Goff of Chieveley pointed out in *Henderson v Merrett Syndicates Ltd*,[90] the existence of that relationship and the foreseeability of economic loss will make it unnecessary to undertake any further inquiry into whether it would be fair, just and reasonable to impose liability. In truth, the case is one in which, but for the alleged absence of the necessary relationship, there would be no dispute that a duty to take care existed and the relationship is what makes it fair, just and reasonable to impose the duty."[91]

This does not meant that the notion of something being fair just and reasonable has no utility at all. As his lordship continued[92]:

"It is equally true to say that a sufficient relationship will be held to exist when it is fair, just and reasonable to do so. Because the question of whether a defendant has assumed responsibility is a legal inference to be drawn from his conduct against the background of all the circumstances of the case, it is by no means a simple question of fact. Questions of fairness and policy will enter into the decision and it may be more useful to try to identify these questions than simply to bandy terms like 'assumption of responsibility' and 'fair, just and reasonable'. In *Morgan Crucible Co Plc v Hill Samuel & Co Ltd*[93] I tried to identify some of these considerations in order to encourage the evolution of lower-level principles which could be more useful than the high abstractions commonly used in such debates."

As was held in *Bankers Trust v PT Dharmala Sakti Sejahtera*,[94] "the ultimate decision whether to recognise a duty of care, and if so of what scope, is pragmatic"[95]; this approach was applied latterly in *JP Morgan Chase Bank v Springwell Navigation Corporation*,[96] as was considered above.

C. Liability for negligent misrepresentations in accounts prior to a takeover: *Caparo Industries v Dickman*

The appeal in Caparo Industries v Dickman

25–38   The appeal in *Caparo Industries Plc v Dickman*[97] related to a claim brought by a claimant which had acquired shares in a target company, Fidelity Plc, as part of a takeover. The claimant contended that it had relied on Fidelity's accounts for the accounting year 1983–84, which had been audited by the accountants Touche Ross and which showed a pre-tax profit of £1.3 million. After acquiring a controlling shareholding in the target company, the claimant discovered that the company's financial position ought to have demonstrated a loss of £0.4 million.

---

[90] *Henderson v Merrett Syndicates Ltd* [1995] 2 A.C. 145, 181.
[91] [2007] 1 A.C. 181, [35].
[92] [2007] 1 A.C. 181, [36].
[93] *Morgan Crucible Co Plc v Hill Samuel & Co Ltd* [1991] Ch. 295, 300–303.
[94] [1996] C.L.C. 518.
[95] [1996] C.L.C. 518, [50].
[96] [2008] EWHC 1186 (Comm).
[97] [1990] 2 A.C. 605.

Consequently, the claimant sought to establish a breach of a duty of care in negligence on the part of the accountants when acting as the auditors of the company. The claimant argued that, as a person intending to acquire a controlling shareholding in the company, the accountants owed it a duty of care when auditing the company's accounts. Lord Bridge held that:

> "[i]f a duty of care were owed so widely, it is difficult to see any reason why it should not equally extend to all who rely on the accounts in relating to other dealings with a company as lenders or merchants extending credit to the company".[98] Therefore, it was held that on policy grounds a general duty of care ought not to be imposed on auditors in such situations.[99]

The claim brought in *Caparo v Dickman* asserted a very wide duty of care in relation to those contemplating the takeover of companies. An assertion which was considered by the House of Lords simply to extend too far. What emerges from Lord Bridge's speech, however, is a range of issues beyond this narrow focus on the context of takeovers and the wider policy considerations. Lord Bridge also held that the salient feature of cases following *Hedley Byrne v Heller*,[100] relating to the liability of those making misstatements in tort to those relying on those statements and suffering loss as a result, was that the defendant "knew" either that the advice or statement made would be communicated to the claimant directly or indirectly, and further that the defendant "knew" that the claimant was very likely to rely on that advice or statement. Significantly, then, the *Hedley Byrne* line of cases had referred to situations in which the claimant was a person within the contemplation of the person responsible for the statement.

25–39

The effect of the change in principle in Caparo Industries v Dickman

In applying the *Anns v Merton LBC* principle (which has since been discredited) in *JEB Fasteners Ltd v Marks, Bloom & Co*[101] Woolf J. held that where accounts had been prepared in a situation in which a takeover of the company was a possible and foreseeable means of obtaining finance, then the accountants owed a duty of care to the claimant who subsequently did take the company over and suffer loss as a result of having relied, inter alia, on misstatements in those accounts. As a result of the decision in *Caparo Industries Plc v Dickman*, such an approach became untenable. So, in *McNaughton Papers Group v Hicks Anderson*,[102] accounts were prepared specifically for the target company, MK, and therefore were not considered to be statements on which the claimant could rely as having created a duty of care once the claimant had taken over the target company in reliance on misstatements made in those accounts. The rationale for this decision was that the purpose for which the statements were made (here, as part of accounts prepared for the benefit of MK alone) precluded any other person from relying on them to found a duty of care.

25–40

---

[98] [1990] 2 A.C. 605.
[99] Approving *Al Saudi Banque v Clark Pixley* [1990] Ch. 313.
[100] [1964] A.C. 465.
[101] [1981] 3 All E.R. 289.
[102] [1991] 1 All E.R. 134.

25–41   In slightly different circumstances in *Morgan Crucible Co Plc v Hill Samuel Bank Ltd*,[103] the directors and financial advisors of the target company had made express representations in the course of a contested takeover forecasting a 38 per cent increase in pre-tax profits at a time when an identified bidder for the company had emerged. The purpose behind these and other representations had been to induce the bidder to make a higher bid. The bidder relied on those statements. The Court of Appeal held that there was therefore a relationship of sufficient proximity between the bidder and those who had been responsible for the statements to found a duty of care in negligence. The decision in *Caparo Industries Plc v Dickman* was distinguished on these facts on the basis that in *Caparo* no identified bidder had emerged at the time when the statements had been made, whereas in *Morgan Crucible Co Plc v Hill Samuel Bank Ltd* an identified bidder had emerged and the statements had been made to induce a reaction from that particular bidder.

D.   The application of the *Caparo* doctrine to prospectuses put into wide circulation

25–42   It is important, for present purposes, to consider how the *Caparo* principle—relating on its facts to takeover cases—would apply in situations in which the statements made in prospectuses are likely to be put into wide circulation either among a limited class of investors or made available to the public generally. The principle in *Hedley Byrne v Heller* was summarised for the purposes of negligent misrepresentations made in prospectuses used in the issue of securities by Lightman J. in *Possfund v Diamond*[104] in the following terms:

> "In 1963 the House of Lords in *Hedley Byrne v Heller & Partners Ltd*[105] established that at common law a cause of action exists enabling the recovery of damages in respect of a negligent misrepresentation occasioning damage and loss where the necessary proximity exists between the representor and representee. It is clearly established (and indeed common ground on these applications) that in a case such as the present, where the defendants have put a document into more or less general circulation and there is no special relationship alleged between the plaintiffs and the defendants, foreseeability by the defendants that the plaintiffs would rely on the prospectus for the purposes of deciding whether to make after-market purchases is not sufficient to impose upon the defendant a duty of care in such a situation requires a closer relationship between representor and representee, and its imposition must be fair, just and reasonable."

So, such a relationship is not a given: although one was found on these facts. The decided cases relating specifically to issues of securities relating to negligent misrepresentation have divided into two camps. The first relates to statements made in relation to takeovers on which a company has relied when acquiring shares in the target company. The second relates to representations made in a prospectus in connection with offers of securities either to a limited pool of targeted investors or to the public at large. Each context is considered in turn. The

---

[103] [1991] 1 All E.R. 148.
[104] *Possfund Custodian Trustee Ltd v Diamond* [1996] 2 All E.R. 774; [1996] 1 W.L.R. 1351; [1996] 2 B.C.L.C. 665, per Lightman J.
[105] [1963] 2 All E.R. 575; [1964] A.C. 465.

common law, for the most part, has taken the view that if a statement was intended only to be made to a limited group of people, then no-one else should be entitled to rely upon it for the purposes of the doctrine in *Hedley Byrne v Heller*.[106] In the context of inaccurate statements in offer documents, the requisite proximity is likely only to be established as between the maker of the relevant statement and persons to whom the document is specifically directed (for example, shareholders on a rights issue) and for its specific purpose (for example, subscription for shares[107] or purchase of shares in the case of an offer document issued for the purpose of an offer for sale). It is unlikely to be established as between the maker of the statement and persons who purchased securities in the market albeit in reliance of the offer document but to whom the document was not directed.

As mentioned above, the decided cases on this issue have divided between whether damages should only be available to investors which were expressly within the contemplation of the person making the statement, or whether damages should also be available to purchasers of the securities in the "after market" if they were within the contemplation of the person making the statement, or whether a statement made in a prospectus is deemed to be actionable by anyone who actually suffers a loss as a result of relying on it. So, in *Al-Nakib Investments (Jersey) Ltd v Longcroft*,[108] when an issue of securities was intended to be limited to a defined class of places, it was held that there was no duty owed to purchasers of securities outwith the class intended to benefit from the placement of securities; whereas, in *Possfund Custodian Trustee Ltd v Diamond*,[109] Lightman J. held that those responsible for the preparation of a prospectus owed liabilities not only to the initial subscribers for shares but also to purchasers in the after-market who sought to rely on the terms of that same prospectus. Lord Bridge held in *Caparo v Dickman* that:

> "[t]he situation is entirely different where a statement is put into more or less general circulation and may foreseeably be relied on by strangers to the maker of the statement for any one of a variety of different purposes which the maker of the statement has no specific reason to anticipate."[110]

25-43

What is significant, as discussed in Chapter 36, is that securities regulation makes the publication of a prospectus obligatory either when securities are being offered to the public or when securities are to be admitted to trading on a regulated market. Consequently, in those contexts it is suggested that the niceties of the distinctions between these two cases (and the many others which came before them) are of no further relevance: the issuer of the prospectus is required to make a prospectus generally available to the public in the form required by the Prospectus Rules. Those Prospectus Rules also specify those people who are to

25-44

---

[106] By extension, it is sufficient that the expert knew that the statement or advice would be passed on to third parties such as the claimant: *Riyad Bank v Ahli United Bank* [2005] 2 Lloyd's Rep. 409.

[107] Note *Caparo Industries Plc v Dickman* [1990] 2 A.C. 605.

[108] [1990] 3 All E.R. 321.

[109] [1996] 2 All E.R. 774.

[110] [1990] 2 A.C. 605; [1990] 1 All E.R. 568, 576. Approving *Scott Group v Macfarlane* [1978] 1 N.Z.L.R. 553, 566, per Richmond P.

be considered to be responsible for the contents of that prospectus. These common law issues are considered in much greater detail in Chapter 39. In that discussion it is suggested that the decision of Lightman J. in *Possfund Custodian Trustee Ltd v Diamond*[111] is the only possible approach in relation to statements made in connection to securities issues which are governed by the Prospectus Rules, and that the other cases are now necessarily out-of-date and at odds with UK financial regulation. The approach taken by Lightman J. in *Possfund* was to recognise the "changed market practice and philosophy" relating to the preparation of prospectuses "namely to inform and encourage after-market purchasers". Thus, it was held that a duty of care was owed to purchasers in the after market who relied on the prospectus. This was even before the Prospectus Rules required the preparation of prospectuses with a certain minimum content so as to inform and encourage purchases in the after-market. The common law must therefore move forward, it is suggested, in line with that new regulatory practice and common market consensus.

E.   Proximity in financial transactions

25–45   It is a requirement of the tort of negligence that there must be sufficient proximity between the defendant's actions and the claimant's loss. In particular, relating to the law of finance, the question has arisen in relation to securities transactions as to the proximity between misrepresentations made in a prospectus and reliance placed on those misrepresentations by investors who were not, arguably, within the contemplation of the people who prepared the prospectus. The principles on the decided cases were set out by Lightman J. in the following terms:

> "The law has drawn a distinction between representations made to specific persons for specific purposes and representations to the public (or sections of the public e.g. investors). In the case of the former, in general it is sufficient to establish a duty on the part of the representor that he should reasonably have foreseen that the persons concerned would rely on his representation for the purposes in question. But in the latter, generally it is necessary to establish a proximity between the representor and representee beyond the mere foreseeability of reliance by the representee to render it fair, just and reasonable that such a duty be imposed in respect of the representation."[112]

The test is therefore whether it is fair, just and reasonable for the defendant to be fixed with liability for the statements made in the prospectus in the context of the particular offer of securities. It is suggested that, given that the prospectus regulations[113] require the publication of a prospectus to be made available to the public at large whenever shares are to be offered to the public or are to be admitted to trading on a regulated market,[114] then it cannot be appropriate to exclude liability on the basis that it would be fair, just or reasonable to do so.

---

[111]   [1996] 2 All E.R. 774.
[112]   *Possfund Custodian Trustee Ltd v Diamond* [1996] 2 All E.R. 774; [1996] 1 W.L.R. 1351; [1996] 2 B.C.L.C. 665, per Lightman J.
[113]   See para.36–06.
[114]   Financial Services and Markets Act 2000, s.85.

What is fair, just and reasonable is to reinforce the statutory and regulatory principles. The cases relating specifically to prospectuses are considered below.[115]

F. The burden of proof

The burden of proving each ingredient of liability in tort for negligent misstatement is borne by the claimant.

25–46

G. Concluding remarks

It is suggested that the law on the tort of negligence ought to accept that the presence of a duty of care exists in circumstances in which statute or regulation imposes a positive obligation on a person which that person negligently fails to perform properly thus causing loss and damage to the claimant. Instead, the courts have been reluctant to accept the presence of a liability for damages in negligence whenever there is a risk that this will lead to a large number of claims: this is the "floodgates" argument, to the effect that claims should be resisted if they would open the floodgates to many, many more such claims. The regulatory handbook is a compilation of regulations which must be complied with before permissions are made available, and of regulations which impose positive obligations on regulated persons to act. If a person is under a positive obligation to act then, it is suggested, that person should be taken to owe a duty of care to any person with whom she transacts or who will be foreseeably affected by the performance of that regulatory duty. The duty of care need not extend beyond the scope of that positive obligation imposed by those regulations. But if that person bears an obligation to perform an act, or to refrain from an act, and a failure to comply with that regulation causes loss and damage which cannot be remedied by any other means, then it is suggested that there is no good reason not to infer the existence of a right to sue for negligence in those circumstances. There is no question that the defendant is not reasonably to be subjected to liability because the FCA regulations require compliance—so, no new positive obligation is being imposed on this person by the common law. The number of people who may bring such a claim are within the expectation of the FCA when it drafted its regulations and when the EU legislature drafted the underpinning directives.

25–47

4. DAMAGES IN TORT FOR NEGLIGENT MISREPRESENTATION

Tortious damages are available so as to compensate the successful claimant for loss she has actually suffered so as to return her to the position she was in before the tort was committed—often referred to as her "out-of-pocket" loss—as opposed to being entitled to any future profit she might have earned but for the

25–48

---

[115] See para.39–17.

commission of the tort.[116] Lord Blackburn set out the core principle in the following dicta in *Livingstone v Rawyards Coal Co* such that the defendant it entitled to[117]:

> "... the sum of money which will put the party who has been injured, or who has suffered, in the same position as he would have been in if he had not sustained the wrong for which he is now getting his compensation or reparation."

In the case of financial transactions, this is an amount of money which returns the claimant to the position which she was in before the tort was committed: thus the position before an investment was bought, or a financial product put in place, or a portfolio constructed.

5. NEGLIGENCE, FINANCIAL TRANSACTIONS AND REGULATORY "SUITABILITY"

A. The concept of suitability

25–49 More recent cases in England and Wales have begun to make reference to the suitability of the products sold to customers by financial institutions. The concept of suitability is not a natural common law concept. And yet claims had been advanced on the basis of a failure at common law to treat customers suitably or to sell them suitable financial products as part of a larger claim relating to misrepresentation or misstatement. A key example of this tendency is *Titan Steel Wheels v Royal Bank of Scotland* [118] where the claim was framed in the language of suitability, although the judgment did not consider the financial regulation in effect at the time which includes suitability. That decision is considered first.

B. Liability in negligence for mis-selling complex financial instruments

Introduction

25–50 This section considers the drift in the cases dealing with liability in negligence for mis-selling financial instruments. Many of those cases have limited themselves to finding fact on the cases in front of them but not to applying the detail of the common law principles to those facts. The decisions in *Titan Wheels v Royal Bank of Scotland*, in *Camerata Property Inc v Crédit Suisse Securities (Europe) Ltd* and in *JP Morgan v Springwell* were particularly focused on the facts before them and ignored the regulatory context in which the sellers of those instruments were operating: both of these cases were considered in relation to fraud in the previous chapter, where it was clear that the detail of the decision in *Derry v Peek* was not applied to the facts. By contrasts, other cases have looked more closely at

---

[116] The exception to this may appear to be damages for loss of income as a result of personal injury, where there is some amount for loss of future income.

[117] (1880) 5 App. Cas. 25, at 39.

[118] [2010] EWHC 211 (Comm).

the regulatory context, such as *Rubenstein v HSBC*. In general terms, where the courts examine a financial institution's regulatory obligations, then it appears more likely that that institution will be held to be liable for breach of duty in tort.

When a seller will be liable: Titan Steel Wheels v Royal Bank of Scotland

The judgment of Steel J. in *Titan Steel Wheels v Royal Bank of Scotland* [119] suggests nothing less than impatience with the claimant's assertions that it had been sold unsuitable products by the defendant bank. The claimant was seeking damages in tort for losses caused by negligently sold foreign exchange instruments. The conduct of the trial seems to have displeased the trial judge, with the number of days of the hearing taking longer than expected, with the defendant bank's failure to disclose all of its evidence as to recorded telephone conversations between the parties' agent having been relied upon by the claimant as suggesting skulduggery, and most significantly of all with the documentation supplied to the claimant indicating on its face that the bank did not accept any responsibility for any representations and so forth made as part of the negotiation process. In essence the claimant had three contentions.

25–51

First, that the bank's trader was not merely providing products but rather that he was providing advice to the claimant's finance director and that in consequence the defendant bank owed the claimant a duty of care at common law. The claimant, Titan Wheels, was a manufacturer of steel wheel products for motor vehicles which was sensitive to foreign exchange movements because most of its income was in euro while its expenses were mostly in sterling. Consequently, Titan had used forward rate agreements to control its exposure to movements in those currencies. In this case it had entered into a structured product which contained barrier elements which knocked in and knocked out the parties payment obligations. Eventually this product realised a large loss for the claimant, although it had proved profitable in the short-term. Indeed, Steel J. found that the claimant could have used a much simpler product but for the fact that it sought to earn a profit on its foreign exchange activities (of about £250,000 in one year): this was a factor for which Steel J. remarkably placed responsibility at the feet of the claimant for prioritising a desire for profit, as opposed to blaming the defendant for encouraging the use of an overly risky product.

25–52

The Terms of Business letter which purported to be the entirety of the basis of the parties' contract (thus displacing any pre-contractual negotiations) made it plain inter alia that the bank was providing services on an "execution" basis and that it was therefore not providing advice. This meant that the bank was seeking to avoid liability for any decision which the claimant might make and instead claimed that it was only providing products which the customer had requested.[120]

25–53

---

[119] [2010] EWHC 211 (Comm).
[120] The distinction is as follows. If you buy food from a takeaway shop, then you simply ask for what you want and the shop provides you with no advice. Here, the bank is arguing that the customer gave it an order and it simply provided what was asked for. By contrast, if one went into an expensive restaurant and asked the chef to advise you what to eat and then the chef cooked it for you, that would

The recorded conversations suggested that on occasion the bank's trader was advocating the comparative advantages of the structured product over the products which the client had previously held, although the client's finance director was also keen to change the existing products.

25–54   It was very important to Steel J. that all of the documentation supplied by the bank made it clear that the bank was not offering investment advice and that the claimant should seek professional advice if it was unsure. Indeed, the claimant had bought complex financial products from other banks. However, this does not answer the point that the trader may have overstepped the bounds of the parties' relationship by offering advice to the client so that its employer should be liable for any inducement constituted by that advice. Furthermore, it does not address the fact that the bank is relying on its standard terms and that the assertion in a confirmation that the bank is not acting as an advisor after a transaction has been completed does not change the fact that the bank may have actually given advice in creating that transaction. A confirmation seeks to confirm the legal terms of a pre-existing transaction: as such there is something disingenuous about it, a little like a revisionist history which seeks to assert what should have been agreed in the past. Contractual terms and certainly significant inducements may have arisen before the confirmation is put in place: hence, a confirmation merely confirms the pre-existence of a contract. So, silence as to a particular point in the confirmation does not in itself demonstrate that there was no significant inducement on the part of a bank.

25–55   Second, it was contended that the structured product sold to the claimant was unsuitable in that it was too complex for the claimant's purposes and that by extension the defendant had breached its regulatory obligations in selling it to the claimant. Steel J. focused on the claimant's somewhat contrived arguments which were based on the history of the legislation relating to the bank's obligations and its suggestion that Titan Wheels was to be considered to be a "private person" on this basis. Its arguments would have been better directed at the requirements in the regulatory code currently in effect in COBS, discussed above and also in Chapter 10,[121] that it must classify its client appropriately, that it must explain the risks associated with a product to a non-professional counterparty, that it must act in the best interests of the client, that it must ensure best execution for the client, and that all of its communications must be fair, clear and not misleading—where the last three of these obligations appear to be fiduciary obligations.[122] Significantly, the defendant would not have been able to contract out of these obligations in the way that Steel J. found that it was otherwise entitled to do in relation to its ordinary common law obligations.

25–56   Third, that the finance director had insufficient authority to bind the claimant company to this transaction. This point was not pursued in detail. In essence, the

---

be a different relationship in which the chef had both provided advice and prepared a specific meal. The bank was seeking to argue that it had not provided advice nor cooked up any specific instrument for the claimant.

[121] See the discussion in Ch.10 as to the nature of the obligations under the Conduct of Business Sourcebook.

[122] See Ch.5 generally.

finance director who was conducting these transaction appears not to have been a board member of that company and it was asserted that he would have had to get the approval of at least one director at board level in relation to a transaction of this complexity. It is suggested that as part of its general "know your client" regulatory obligations the defendant bank should have inquired into the authority of this individual as well as inquiring into his intrinsic knowledge and expertise of complex derivatives as opposed to relying on the fact that he had entered into lots of these transactions before. Having entered into previous transactions does not in any way demonstrate that that person understands what they involve, merely that they have contracted them before. The purpose of conduct of business regulation is to protect the buyer from its own ignorance by requiring at the very least a warning as to the risks involved in circumstances in which the client is not an expert counterparty. However, the common law approach is that of caveat emptor: something which is observable in the judgments of the Court of Appeal in *Peekay Intermark Ltd v ANZ*,[123] of Gloster J. in *JP Morgan v Springwell* (latterly affirmed by the Court of Appeal),[124] and the Court of Appeal in *IFE v Goldman Sachs*[125]—all of which were relied upon by Steel J. in *Titan Wheels* (and which are discussed below).

The heart of the matter is this. The common law, in particular as exercised through the agency of Commercial Court judges, takes the view that the documentation entered into between parties is decisive of the relationship between them, but that fails to acknowledge that in financial transactions there is a context beyond the traditional concerns of the common law with holding parties to the terms of the agreements which they have signed: in financial transactions the regulated parties are bound by conduct of business regulation out of which they are not permitted to contract. What is remarkable (and familiar) about the transcripts of the telephone conversations which are recorded by Steel J. in his judgment is just how incoherent they are in a context in which the seller is obliged to make communications to its customer under COBS which are "fair, clear and not misleading". The courts did not consider these regulatory requirements in assessing the standards expected of a financial institution in this context. **25–57**

The nub of the problem is this: if a corporate client is told that it is being treated as an intermediate customer and that there are risks with its products, does it understand what it is being told? My favoured illustration of the weakness in this approach is by way of analogy with a dog being offered a biscuit. If you say the word "biscuit" to a dog that dog will jump around excitedly knowing that it is in for a treat. What the dog does not know is the nature of the biscuit, how that biscuit is made, what its ingredients are, whether that biscuit will be injurious to its health over time, or anything of that sort. The dog's reaction to the word "biscuit", I assume, is an immediate response to the memory of a pleasurable sensation that follows the use of that word as its owner heads for the appropriate **25–58**

[123] [2006] EWCA Civ 386.
[124] [2008] EWHC 1793 (Comm); confirmed at [2010] EWCA Civ 1221. Reliance is also placed on *Trident Turboprop (Dublin) Ltd v First Flight Couriers Ltd* [2008] EWHC 1686, relying ultimately on *Henderson v Merrett* [1995] 2 A.C. 145, [1994] 3 All E.R. 506, [1994] 3 W.L.R. 761.
[125] [2007] EWCA Civ 811, [2007] 2 Lloyd's Rep 449.

cupboard in the kitchen. The same is true of corporate finance directors when proffered the financial alchemy associated with a financial derivative. The finance director's primitive understanding that its financial risks will be minimised and that it may earn profit on the side masks its ignorance of the risks and assumptions which are wrapped up in the black box of the financial engineer's financial derivative products. Like a dog in a kitchen at snack time, corporate finance directors are prone to jump about excitedly when they hear the words "derivative" and "hedge", they are bound to rely on what the trader tells them, and the fact that they have a history of investing in such products does not mean that they have understood them any more than a dog has understood the nature of the biscuits which it has eaten in the past. A similar phenomenon was observable among fund managers in small financial institutions before the summer of 2007 when they heard the words "CDO", "structured" and "AAA".[126] The purpose of financial regulation is to protect customers from these dangers. Indeed, interestingly, the proposal for the MiFID II directive is aimed primarily at reinforcing the entitlement of intermediate counterparties to receive clear advice from the sellers of complex investment and hedging products about the risks which they are assuming. The English common law has yet to accept that these financial regulations constitute a new dimension in contract law as it applies to financial transactions because it imposes positive obligations on regulated firms and those firms may not contract out of those obligations. In essence, *Titan Wheels* was decided in complete ignorance of the obligations imposed on the defendant by the Conduct of Business Sourcebook.

How closely does a regulated firm need to inquire into the expertise of the customer at common law?

25–59   The practices of banks in selling complex products to customers was evident from *Bankers Trust v Dharmala (No.2)*. Similar issues relating to the creation of investment portfolios were raised by *JP Morgan Chase v Springwell*.[127] In *Springwell*, individuals acted on behalf of a family investment company which accepted investment advice from Chase, a large financial institution. Some passing reference was made to the applicable conduct of business regulation by Gloster J. in finding that the individuals who made the decisions for the family company had sufficient commercial knowledge and acumen to appreciate the risks of the investments which were being proposed to the family company, even though they had no financial qualifications nor experience as employees of financial institutions themselves. Rather, their high-risk approach to investment in foreign exchange markets generally contributed to a sense that they should be treated as being sufficiently knowledgeable. In turn, this finding was used to rebut any suggestion that they had been influenced into a course of dealing against their will or contrary to Chase's obligations to treat them suitably. It was held therefore that no duty of care was owed by Chase to this client company.

---

[126] See, for example, the sort of factual circumstances which surrounded the litigation in *Cassa di Risparmio della Repubblica di San Marino SpA v Barclays Bank Ltd* [2011] EWHC 484 (Comm), considered below.
[127] [2008] EWHC 1186.

This is an odd finding because it was based in part on an finding by Gloster J. after listening to 12 days of evidence that the individuals would not have acted any differently even if they had had the extensive documentation for the transaction explained to them: however, how could one know that, if the individuals making the company's decisions had had the risks explained to them, then they would not have acted differently on the basis of that knowledge?

The claimant company in *JP Morgan Chase v Springwell* contended that in advising investment in risky Russian government bonds (just as in *Peekay v ANZ*[128]) there had been negligent mis-selling in tort, negligence in tort in general terms, breach of fiduciary duty, and breach of the contract between the parties. The claimant assembled all of the possible arguments which could found a right to compensation to recover the loss it suffered on those Russian bonds, and argued them at once. The court will not allow double recovery for one loss, but this litigator's tactic of arguing everything at once is standard practice because the litigator cannot know in advance which claim will eventually come up to proof at trial. The legal principles underpinning these issues are discussed in detail in the remainder of this chapter.

25–60

Springwell argued on appeal to the Court of Appeal[129] that there were three particular representations which should have been treated differently at first instance: that is representations to the effect that the investments would be conservative, that they would be liquid, and that there would be no currency risk. It was held, however, that individual expressions could not be lifted "like a fish out of water" so as to demonstrate a misrepresentation, but rather the entire context of the dealings between the parties and the context in which those representations were made must be considered.[130] Having considered these statements in the round, the Court of Appeal upheld the judgment of Gloster J., including a reliance on the individuals who operated the claimant company having sufficient understanding of investment products to form a view on the investments at issue. Again, however, the Court of Appeal did not look closely at the regulatory obligations of the bank in relation to conduct of business and "know your client" rules to decide whether or not in that context the bank had acted appropriately. Instead there is a single phrase in the court's judgment finding that "Chase fulfilled its obligations", without more analysis than that.[131]

25–61

By contrast in *Morgan Stanley UK Group v Puglisi Cosentino*[132], the claimant bank sold a complex derivative to the defendant. The bank was held to have been in breach of the conduct of business regulations then in force in advising the defendant to enter into such a transaction as an inexpert private customer. The documentation which was faxed to the customer identified him as an "expert customer" despite the fact that he was a retail customer, despite the fact that Morgan Stanley had not dealt with him before and despite the fact that he had not

25–62

---

[128] [2006] EWCA Civ 386.

[129] *JP Morgan v Springwell* [2010] EWCA Civ 1221.

[130] *JP Morgan Chase Bank v Springwell Navigation Corp* [2010] EWCA Civ 1221, at [112] et seq, per Aikens L.J.

[131] [2010] EWCA Civ 1221, at [125], per Aikens L.J.

[132] [1998] C.L.C. 481.

dealt before in the precise forms of complex derivatives and repo products which had been recommended to him by Morgan Stanley.[133] The bank sought to enforce the contract. However, Longmore J. found for the defendant customer because it was found that the defendant would not have entered into the transaction if he had received proper advice and an appropriate risk warning in accordance with the conduct of business regulations. This case also illustrated how important it is that the procedure by which documentation is provided to the customer and signed by the customer is conducted appropriately. Here, the wrong documentation had been sent and insufficient consideration had been given to client care on the whole. Longmore J. referred to the concept of "suitability" in his judgment. It is suggested that the most significant issue here is the double-barrelled concept of suitability: first, the means by which the product is sold must be suitable and, secondly, the substance of the product which is sold must itself be suitable.

Gross negligence outwith an exclusion clause—Camerata Property Inc v Credit Suisse Securities (Europe) Ltd

25–63   In *Camerata Property Inc v Credit Suisse Securities (Europe) Ltd*[134] Andrew Smith J. considered an exclusion of liability clause which provided that a financial institution would not be liable for any loss suffered by its client as a result of following its investment advice except in the event of its gross negligence. The claimant was a company organised in Belize which was owned by a private individual who had been advised to invest in "structured notes", that is investments involving derivatives, which had fallen sharply in value as a result of the collapse of Lehman Brothers.[135] The financial institution contended that it had conducted a survey of the competence of the investor and concluded both that the investor had sufficient competence to understand the risks associated with such investments and that the particular investment in question was suitable for him. The note had been issued by Lehman Brothers, a fact which was not disclosed to the individual investor by the financial institution. The question arose as to whether or not it had been grossly negligent (so as to circumvent the exclusion of liability provision) for the defendant financial institution to have failed to predict the failure of Lehman Brothers in September 2008. The claimant had raised concerns when Bear Stearns had collapsed in March 2008 but the defendant did not advise any alteration in the investment (through the relationship manager allocated to the claimant). Between March and September 2008, Lehman Brothers' credit rating fell (particularly in June 2008 in rating

---

[133] There were also questions about his ability to speak English, even though the seller did on occasions provide Italian speakers with whom he could communicate, let alone his ability to understand the products themselves in whatever language.

[134] [2011] EWHC 479 (Comm); [2011] 2 B.C.L.C. 54.

[135] We are told the following about the private individual by Smith J.: "Mr Ventouris, who is Greek, is a wealthy man. He is in his thirties and has shipping experience: he holds a Captain's B certificate and he is qualified as a chief officer of an ocean-going vessel. He studied for the degree of Master of Business Administration in Maritime Studies from Leicester University through a distance learning programme, which included some accountancy and economics." He ran the shipping business which had been begun by his father.

downgrades by S&P and Fitch)[136] but the defendant failed to advise any change in the investment in regular discussions with the claimant, and it failed to inform the claimant that it was Lehman Brothers which had issued the underlying note. While Smith J. considered that it was unclear whether or not gross negligence was a concept known to the common law in this context, it was his lordship's view that to establish gross negligence the claimant would have to establish more than ordinary negligence. It was held further that it was "fair and reasonable" within s.11 of the Unfair Contract Terms Act 1977 in these circumstances for the financial institution to limit its own liability to gross negligence by means of an limitation of liability clause.

Furthermore, on these facts it was held that even if the individual relationship manager had been grossly negligent in failing to analyse the material provided to him by the client, that had not affected the advice which he had given and therefore it was not relevant for deciding whether or not that relationship manager should be deemed to be personally liable. It was held that before September 2008 that there was no reason for the relationship manager to have had concerns about Lehman Brothers. However, it is suggested that there were well-known concerns about Lehman Brothers in the marketplace before September 2008—not least when two different rating agencies lowered its credit rating in June 2008—albeit that participants in the marketplace generally did not perhaps consider that institutions of the size of Lehman Brothers were at risk of default, let alone insolvency. Nevertheless, the approach taken by Smith J. was, in effect, to consider what could be expected of the reasonable financial advisor, and on that basis it was held that a reasonable investor advisor could not have been expected to behave differently in these circumstances.[137] Moreover, his lordship was unconvinced that the actions of the relationship manager or of the financial institution had caused the claimant any loss specifically, as opposed to the downturn in that investment causing that loss.[138]

25–64

Smith J. did lavish a large amount of attention on the "know your client" inquiries which the financial institution made of the claimant. The client had identified a low level of risk tolerance among its investment preferences. It is interesting, however, that in the many pages of the judgment which are devoted to considering that individual's level of expertise and his attitude to risk, the written answers to the bank's questionnaires are not taken as being definitive of this matter in the way, for example, that exclusion of liability clauses are generally taken by the courts to be definitive of the extent of the bank's liability. Instead,

25–65

---

[136] [2011] EWHC 479 (Comm); [2011] 2 BCLC 54, at [223].

[137] Interestingly, however, no evidence was adduced as to what a reasonable banker would have done in these circumstances [2011] EWHC 479 (Comm); [2011] 2 B.C.L.C. 54, at [189]. However, the market was not considered by his lordship (on the basis of evidence adduced as to market performance) to have considered Lehman to have been likely to default between March and September 2008.

[138] More specifically it was held that the individual controlling the claimant had not asked specifically about the identity of the issuer of the note: however, on this specific point it is suggested that it is not a question of the customer having to ask specific questions to elicit information (after all, the customer may not know enough to know what questions to ask) but rather a question as to the nature and extent of the responsibilities of the seller at common law and under conduct of business regulation.

his lordship considered that the individual was "clearly intelligent and financially astute"[139] and that he had showed a lively interest in the investments, even though he had expressed himself on the bank's questionnaires to be interested only in conservative investments. It is suggested that this judicial attitude is skewed in favour of finding in favour of the banks because it means that a customer cannot place a limit on the sort of risk which he is prepared to take in any given situation, but rather the court will investigate other factors to decide whether or not the bank acted reasonably as opposed to whether or not the customer got what he expressly bargained for. This is significant on these facts, it is suggested, because it appears that the relationship manager paid very little attention to the information that was given by the client on the questionnaires. Nevertheless, his lordship placed a great deal of attention on the impression which arose in cross-examination to the effect that the claimant was in fact interested in more adventurous investments than his avowed focus on "low risk" and "conservative" investments in the questionnaires suggested.[140] This, in the final analysis, was held to justify a finding that the relationship manager and the financial institution had acted reasonably.

Remoteness of loss

25–66   The question will always arise in relation to any loss suffered as a result of negligently unsuitable investment product which causes loss to a customer: did the loss result from the customer being sold the wrong type of product, or did the loss result from market conditions beyond anyone's control? If the loss could be showed to have resulted from circumstances beyond anyone's control, then the defendant seller of that investment product would be able to escape liability on the basis that the loss was too remote from the breach of duty. In cases in which the seller is negligent in failing to understand the nature of the investment product, or in which the seller is negligent in failing to assess the customer's risk appetite and level of expertise under COBS, then the question of remoteness becomes more critical. All will depend upon the facts of the case.

25–67   An example of a case in which the seller was very negligent on both of the accounts just mentioned was *Rubenstein v HSBC*.[141] In that case, a solicitor, Rubenstein, sought to invest the proceeds of the sale of his matrimonial home (approximately £1.5 million) temporarily by way of a deposit of some sort with HSBC. He was advised by HSBC to invest in a "bond" which was being issued by a fund operated by AIG: AIG was the insurance company (discussed in Chapter 45) which collapsed due to the exposure of its financial products group to the CDO market in 2008. This fund invested so as to acquire a higher rate of return than ordinary money market funds: of the two funds operated by AIG which were suggested to the claimant, he was advised to take the more

---

[139] [2011] EWHC 479 (Comm); [2011] 2 B.C.L.C. 54, at [114].
[140] [2011] EWHC 479 (Comm); [2011] 2 B.C.L.C. 54, at [114] through [125], especially at [125] where his lordship refers to his impression of Mr Ventouris as opposed simply to focusing on his avowed preferences as expressed clearly in the forms given to him for that purpose by the financial institution.
[141] [2012] EWCA Civ 1184.

adventurous of the two, with the longer date to maturity, and the riskier investment class. The investment advisor had failed to understand the nature of the investment fund and so reassured the claimant that the bond was the same as a deposit account in that the cash deposit could be recovered at any time and that deposit would not fall in value. The investment made in 2005 was carried out at a time when there was no evidence of any particular risk (appreciated by any of the parties) with these products, although the bond was not a deposit and in time the fund suffered great losses. Importantly, a deposit would have attracted a rate of interest and would have been recoverable by the customer at the end of the term, whereas an investment in the form of a "bond" (as in this case) in a fund makes a variable return and the investor suffers the risk that the investment stake might be lost. The market crash hit in the autumn of 2008. When the claimant sought to recover his investment, he was informed that there had been such volatility in the market that it was impossible to identify a value for his investment at that time. AIG had many customers seeking to recover their investments early. Realising an early termination on the fund meant that the fund's assets were sold at a loss. All of the investors suffered a loss as a result and the claimant suffered various losses further to his inability to recover his deposit when he had sought to do so. The claimant alleged negligence on the part of the defendant in recommending that fund.

The judge at first instance held that there was negligence on the part of the HSBC investment advisor in relation to the promotion of this particular fund which was so different from the deposit which the claimant had sought. The reasons were that the advisor had suggested that this investment was not the same as a deposit, and that the advisor had not investigated the other funds which were on offer.[142] The trial judge made regular reference to the defendant's COBS obligations. However, it was found that the loss which the claimant had suffered was too remote from the market conditions which had caused the loss. The defendant had argued, in effect, that the loss was caused by market hysteria and not the acts of the defendant's advisor. **25–68**

This matter was appealed to the Court of Appeal.[143] The Court of Appeal overturned the trial judge's finding the loss was too remote from the defendant's act. Rix L.J., delivering the judgment of the court, focused on the breach of COBS 5.3.5R to the effect that the defendant had not identified the appropriate classification of its customer and then identified a suitable investment for that customer. His lordship also relied on the fact that the advisor had negligently misled the claimant as to the terms and nature of the bond. However, it was in relation to the question of proximity that the court overruled the court at first instance. The defendant sought to rely on the judgment of Flaux J. in *Camerata Property Inc v Crédit Suisse Securities (Europe) Ltd (No.2)*,[144] where it was held **25–69**

---

[142] [2011] EWHC 2304 (QB).
[143] [2012] EWCA Civ 1184.
[144] [2012] EWHC 7 (Comm), [2012] P.N.L.R. 15.

that the cause of loss had been the collapse of Lehman Brothers as opposed to any negligent advice given by the defendant. However, on these facts the Court of Appeal held that:[145]

> "In the context of statutory protection for the consumer [under FSMA 2000], it seems to me that a bank must reasonably contemplate that, if it misleads its client as to the nature of its recommended investment, and thereby puts its client into an investment which is unsuitable for him, when it could just as easily have recommended something more suitable which would have avoided the loss in question, then it may well be liable for that loss."

On these particular facts, the defendant's advisor had failed to give proper advice. He had failed to inform himself about the nature of the investment and thus he failed to inform the claimant. Instead, he allowed the claimant to believe that he was acquiring an investment akin to a cash deposit which could be accessed at any time and which would retain its value, as opposed to an investment product into which the claimant would be locked and the value of which could fall as well as rise. Without that advice, the claimant would not have made that investment. Therefore, it was held that the loss was not too remote from the defendant's negligent act. The bank was therefore liable in negligence.

25–70   The court also considered the dicta of Lord Hoffmann in *SAMMCO*[146] to the effect that there is a distinction between an obligation to provide someone with information so that they can make a decision for themselves, and an obligation to provide someone with advice as to the course of action which they should take. This useful division suggests that a claimant must look closely at the terms of the defendant's obligations and ask: was the defendant obliged merely to give me all necessary information (in which case their liability will turn on whether or not they gave me suitable information) or was the defendant obliged to give me advice as to the course of action to take (in which case their liability will turn on whether or not they advised a suitable course of action). Alternatively, the question might be whether the defendant actually purported to give advice as to the course of action to take, even though its regulatory obligations were limited to merely giving information, because if the defendant chooses to go beyond its remit then an inexpert customer is entitled to rely on that advice, so as to found liability under *Hedley Byrne v Heller*.

6.   Hypothetical Future Litigation Arising from the Global Financial Crisis 2008

A.   Banker's negligence and the sale of bad assets

The purpose of this section

25–71   In the previous chapter there was a discussion of hypothetical scenarios in which it was alleged that banks had made fraudulent misrepresentations when selling

---

[145] [2012] EWCA Civ 1184, at [123], per Rix L.J.
[146] *South Australia Asset Management Corp v York Montague Ltd* [1997] A.C. 191.

assets to their customers.[147] Those scenarios were based on press reports of banks selling assets which were known to be "bad" or "toxic" to customers, where the expressions "bad" or "toxic" mean that the selling bank knew or believed that those assets would generate large losses for whoever owned them. Nevertheless, it is alleged that those banks misrepresented the nature and profitability of those assets when selling them to investors. In the previous chapter it was therefore an issue whether or not the bank knew or was reckless as to the falsity of those representations. In this discussion it is assumed that knowledge or recklessness cannot be proved and therefore that a claim is being brought in negligence. The claim in negligence will be based on either a regulated firm or bank (hereafter, "the bank") making a negligent misrepresentation as to the terms or nature of assets when selling them to customers, or a bank negligently advising or procuring the sale of assets to the customer when those assets were unsuitable for that customer.

Much of this discussion will be predicated on factual scenarios considered in that previous chapter and so the reader may wish to cross-refer to that discussion.

Negligently allocating high-risk assets to non-professional investors

In circumstances in which a regulated firm has discretion over its customer's investment portfolio, then PRIN principle 9 requires that "a firm must take reasonable care to ensure the suitability of its advice and discretionary decisions for any customer who is entitled to rely upon its judgment".[148] In circumstances in which, for example, such a firm sold participations in CDOs related to US sub-prime mortgages at a stage at which the market had begun to assume that sub-prime mortgages in the US would begin to fail in large numbers in 2007, then it could be said that the firm had been negligent in making those investments because the market was aware of the problems with CDOs of that type and because even the financial press had begun to identify that that market was likely to suffer large losses. The previous chapter considered whether intentional selling of such products to inexpert investors would constitute fraud. Here it is suggested only that there was some negligence in this sale. A duty of care would exist because of the contract between the parties. Liability for breach of contract, as discussed in Chapters 19 and 20, may also apply, depending on the terms of the contract between the parties. Much would depend on the general level of knowledge in the marketplace at the time and whether at that point in the cycle those sorts of investments would be expected by reasonable professionals to generate losses. It is suggested further that even if there was doubt about whether or not losses would result, then in any event if the investments were being sold to inexpert investors for whom that level of risk would have been inappropriate then the need for a greater degree of prudence (in line with conduct of business rules, discussed in Chapter 10) would have required a reasonable firm to have recommended different investments.

25–72

---

[147] See para.24–27.
[148] See para.9–26.

Negligently selling sub-prime mortgages

25–73   The more difficult scenario relating to mis-selling centres on the very kernel of the 2008 financial crisis: selling mortgages to people who could not afford to repay them. This is important in two different ways. The mortgagors may themselves argue that the mortgagee banks were negligent in selling them mortgages knowing or suspecting strongly that those mortgagors would not be able to repay them at all or in full.[149] Third parties who invested in those mortgages or invested in securities (such as CDOs) built on those products may also claim that the losses which accrued to them were due to the negligence of the mortgagees or those selling the CDOs. In ordinary circumstances it would be unlikely that a claim for negligence would apply in such a situation unless the mortgagee had made some sort of core error in lending money on the basis of no real security—such as lending money for houses to be built of tissue paper in the sea. Instead, what appears to have occurred during the housing booms in the US and the UK is that mortgagees actively sought to lend money to mortgagors of weak credit worth because each new mortgage was an asset for a bank; and therefore the more mortgages there were, the more assets the bank had. The suggestion could more credibly be made that a bank had been negligent in selling mortgages if it had adopted an active policy of marketing its loans to people who would not previously have been considered to be good risks, particularly if the loans were made at more than the then market value of the homes bought with them to people at four or five times their incomes. The issue would be whether a duty of care is owed to third parties who acquired CDOs based on those mortgages. It is suggested that if the CDOs were based on the mortgages' performance—because the investors were buying bonds based on the income received on those mortgages, as explained in Chapter 44—then there must have been a duty of care owed by the banks who created the mortgages to the investors who bought CDO rights based on those same mortgages from those same banks, unless that liability was excluded between expert counterparties. It is less likely that the mortgagors would be able to bring such an argument based in tort, and more likely that any argument about misselling would be based in contract and in particular on a suggestion that the mortgagee exerted undue influence over the mortgagor.[150]

B.   Misstatement when selling bad assets

The issue in general terms

25–74   The discussion in this chapter of the principle in *Hedley Byrne v Heller* has focused on misstatements about securities and has identified two themes: first, that if an offer of securities is made to a limited class of people, then other people may not rely on any misrepresentation to found liability in tort; and, secondly, by contrast where a statement is made in a context in which it is reasonable to expect

---

[149] In terms of selling CDO's, it could be argued that the banks were negligent in not pricing into the product the risk of the failure of the underlying mortgages.

[150] See para.24–41.

that third parties will encounter it, or especially when regulations require the making and publication of statement, then third party purchasers of the securities will be entitled to sue in tort on the basis of losses suffered as a result of that misrepresentation. In relation to the financial crisis in 2008, a number of investments were sold by banks on the basis of market perception that housing markets and other markets (such as the credit markets) would continue to rise inexorably. Failure to predict the failure of these markets may constitute negligence, this is particularly so the closer that the investment was sold to the start of the collapse in the summer of 2007. In particular, the negligence would seem to be located specifically in the continuance of selling investments in markets which were thought to be likely to fail, not simply in the failure to predict that fall: after all, the growing concern in the market generally and in the financial press about housing and credit markets should have indicated to a firm that the risk of those markets was growing and therefore that there were categories of less expert investor for whom those risks had become inappropriate.

Bank selling investments in SIVs in which toxic assets had been hived off

As was considered in the previous chapter, there have been allegations made that **25–75** some banks have set up "special investment vehicles" (or "SIVs") into which they have passed so-called "toxic assets". The question considered here is whether or not they would be negligent in marketing those assets to clients given the fact that latterly they would have generated large losses for those clients. In particular, liability would depend on whether the bank had made negligent misrepresentations as to those assets. If the bank had not anticipated the level of risk associated with those assets then it is suggested that they were negligent in selling those assets to investors in the SIV within the *Hedley Byrne v Heller* doctrine if there was a special relationship of banker and client between the parties, if the client was relying on the bank's expertise, and if the representation induced the client to invest in those assets. That will depend upon whether or not the client was sufficiently inexpert to rely on the bank's advice, or sufficiently expert not to need that advice. It is suggested that the client classification process which the bank is required to undertake further to the conduct of business rules considered in Chapter 10 should have made the bank conscious of the extent of the client's likely reliance on its expertise.[151] In this sense, liability should follow the level of the client's expertise.

Manipulating retail credit-rating formula to enhance components of securitisations

As was said in the previous chapter, it is difficult to know on which side of the **25–76** line between negligence and fraud one should locate situations in which banks used accounting and credit rating techniques to repackage securitisation products so as to make them appear to be of a higher credit rating than otherwise they

---

[151] See para.10–23.

would have been. If a bank genuinely considered the accounting treatment of a securitisation to be a moot issue and therefore chose the more preferable of two possible treatments, then its liability would appear to lie in negligence and not in fraud. If I sell you what purports to be a BMW 320d but which is unbeknownst to me actually a BMW 318si, then I will have sold you something that is not what I have represented it to be. If a banker represents that a product which produced enormous losses as being something other than a product which could generate that level of loss, then she exhibited an unprofessional level of ignorance of the risks associated with that product. This would be particularly so if the product is sold during a period when informed market sentiment accepts that products which had previously been highly profitable had become very risk—such as CDOs in 2007 and 2008—then failure to factor in that level of risk would be negligent and selling those assets would be in breach of a professional investment manager's duty of care to an inexpert client under conduct of business regulation, as was discussed in the previous section.

C.   Rating agencies and their role in the global financial crisis of 2007–09

Liability of ratings agencies under negligent misstatement generally

25–77   Credit ratings agencies play a very important part in the conduct of securities markets, particularly bond markets, as is discussed in Chapter 34. The ratings agencies are private businesses which assign a credit rating to securities and to trading companies and governments. The independence of the ratings agencies is vital in the operation of the securities markets because the markets rely on the ratings that are given to these securities when deciding whether or not to invest in a security, as is explained in Chapter 34. Therefore, ratings agencies are making statements—the rating of the securities—which will be relied upon by the investing public when making decisions about those investments. Under the *Hedley Byrne v Heller* principle considered above, the ratings agencies may suggest that there was no special relationship between them and the investment public—after all the rating is sought from them by the companies which are being rated. However, it is beyond question that all professional investors and most inexpert investors will have been led by the rating in making their investment decisions: that is the business in which ratings agencies find themselves. Consequently, the investing public will have been within the contemplation of the ratings agencies when publishing ratings. Furthermore, the investing public will have been beyond any contractual nexus limiting the agencies' liability. While the ratings agencies may wish to limit their liabilities in relation to the general public, they must be taken to know that reliance is placed on their ratings. The particular problem arises in relation to complex products like CDOs which were rated highly but which subsequently failed. This issue is considered next.

Liability of ratings agencies when ratings fell from AAA to "junk" between July and August of 2008

Let us suppose hypothetically that there were complex financial products which were rated by ratings agencies in July 2008 on the optimistic basis on which these products had been rated for years previously to the effect that they were of a AAA credit quality (which is as high as a rating can go), and then in August 2008 those same products had fallen in quality to "junk" status (which is as low as a rating can go). For there to be such a fall in quality when since at least August 2007 the financial press and the general market sentiment had been that these products were likely to generate losses, it is suggested that rating these products at AAA was negligent, if not downright perverse. It suggests a blindness to the obvious: to whit, that these products had been over-rated and over-priced for some time. Given what is said in the prior section about the liability of rating agencies under the principle in *Hedley Byrne v Heller* it is suggested that the ratings agencies must be liability in tort to investors who acquired those products on the basis of the rating assigned to them. In *Camerata Property Inc v Credit Suisse Securities (Europe) Ltd*[152] an investment in bonds issued by a Lehman Brothers entity failed and lost the claimant money. The claimant argued that he had raised concerns with the defendant that when Bear Stearns had collapsed in March 2008 that this investment was risky, but the defendant had not advised any alteration in the investment. Latterly, between March and September 2008, Lehman Brothers' credit rating had fallen and so the claimant had repeated his concerns, but the defendant still persisted in its view that no change was necessary. Moreover, the defendant had failed to inform the claimant that it was a Lehman Brothers entity. Nevertheless, the defendant had excluded its liability for all defaults up to gross negligence and Smith J. was not prepared to find that this constituted gross negligence—therefore, no liability lay at common law.

25–78

6. THE TORT OF "BREACH OF STATUTORY DUTY SIMPLICITER" AND LIABILITY UNDER S.150 FSMA 2000

A. The tort of breach of statutory duty

A person who commits a breach of statutory duty which causes another person loss will be liable in tort for damages,[153] provided that the statute can be interpreted as creating such a right which would exist distinct from the common law duty of care.[154] The tort of breach of statutory duty is distinct from the tort of negligence. The tort of breach of statutory duty has been referred to by Lord Browne-Wilkinson as the tort of "breach of statutory duty simpliciter",[155] such

25–79

---

[152] [2011] EWHC 479 (Comm); [2011] 2 B.C.L.C. 54.
[153] *Groves v Lord Wimborne* [1898] 2 Q.B. 402; *X (minors) v Bedfordshire County Council* [1995] 2 A.C. 633; *O'Rourke v Camden LBC* [1998].
[154] *Gorringe v Calderdale Metropolitan Borough Council* [2004] UKHL 15; [2004] 1 W.L.R. 1057, at [3], per Lord Steyn.
[155] *X (minors) v Bedfordshire County Council* [1995] 2 A.C. 633. See generally *Clerk & Lindsell on Torts*, 19th edn (London: Sweet & Maxwell, 2006), para.9–06 et seq.

that all that must be demonstrated is that the defendant has committed some breach of her duties under statute (subject to any defences or questions of the limitation period for bringing an action). On a proper construction of the statute it must be demonstrated that the "statutory duty was imposed for the protection of a limited class of the public and that Parliament intended to confer on members of that class a private right of action for breach of the duty".[156]

25–80   By way of example, in s.85(4) of the FSMA 2000 it was clearly the intention of Parliament to provide a remedy for any person who has suffered loss as a result of a breach of either s.85(1) or 85(2) FSMA 2000 because the statute provides as such.[157] In the FSMA 2000 the intention to create a right to damages for breach of a statutory duty is generally explicit, whereas there are many non-financial services statutes where it has not been.[158] The remedy, where no specific criminal offence is created (such as s.85(1) of the FSMA 2000) or where no specific civil remedy is provided (such as in s.90 of the FSMA 2000) or where no specific civil penalty is created (such as in relation to market abused in s.118 of the FSMA 2000), is to sue for damages for breach of statutory duty,[159] unless the proper interpretation of the statute prohibits such an interpretation. It was held that the (now repealed) s.47 of the Financial Services Act 1986 did not create a civil right of action against the insurance company Norwich Union on behalf of investors (or "names") in the Lloyds insurance market who considered that Norwich Union had missold their investments to them primarily because s.47 provided for criminal liability but was not included within the list of civil liabilities in s.62 of that Act.[160]

B.   Liability under s.150 of the FSMA 2000

25–81   There is a significant right to damages provided for in s.150 of the FSMA 2000. Section 150(1) provides as follows:

> "A contravention by an authorised person of a rule is actionable at the suit of a private person who suffers loss as a result of the contravention, subject to the defences and other incidents applying to actions for breach of statutory duty."

Therefore, s.150 provides for a right to damages in accordance with the general principles of breach of statutory duty and thus confirms that that tort applies to certain activities under the FSMA 2000.[161] The claimant must therefore have suffered a loss, and that loss is to be remedied in damages at common law. The activities which fall within the tort must be committed by a person who has been authorised to act by the FCA under the FSMA 2000.

---

[156] *X (minors) v Bedfordshire County Council* [1995] 2 A.C. 633 at 731.

[157] See para.36–01.

[158] See *Clerk and Lindsell on Torts*, para.9–11.

[159] *Cutler v Wandsworth Stadium Ltd* [1949] A.C. 398.

[160] *Norwich Union Life Insurance Co Ltd v Qureshi* [1999] 2 All E.R. (Comm) 707.

[161] Financial Services and Markets Act 2000 s.150(1). Under a similar provision in the now repealed Financial Services Act 1986, a firm of independent financial advisers was held liable to compensate elderly customers who were missold pension investments by them for the losses which they suffered as a result: *Investors Compensation Scheme Ltd v West Bromwich BS* [1999] Lloyd's Rep. PN 496.

Furthermore, those activities must constitute a contravention of a "rule". The **25–82**
term "rule" is not defined in s.150 except in s.150(4) where it is provided that it
does not encompass any rules created under Pt 6 of the FSMA 2000 (relating to
offers of securities to the public and the other matters considered in Part X of this
book, which have similar rights to compensation in s.90 and in s.90A of the
FSMA 2000) or "a rule requiring an authorised person to have or maintain
financial resources".[162] The Rights of Action Regulations[163] provide that among
the rules which are included here are breaches of a rule prohibiting exclusion of
liability, breach of insider dealing rules, breach of client money rules, and breach
of fiduciary duties.[164] It is suggested that the term "rules" should be taken to
encompass any rule set out in the FSMA 2000 itself or any rule created by the
FCA or some other competent authority further to a power granted by the FSMA
2000. It is provided in s.150(2) that a specific rule may provide that s.150 does
not apply in relation to that rule.[165] Similarly, a rule may provide that "a
contravention of a rule which would be actionable at the suit of a private person is
actionable at the suit of a person who is not a private person".[166]

Where, for example, an investment is recommended to clients for whom it is **25–83**
wholly unsuitable, then that investor will be able to recover compensation for any
loss suffered as a result of that unsuitable investment. So, when a married couple
sold their family farm and sought advice on acquiring alternative accommodation, it was unsuitable for them to be sold investments in an unregulated, offshore
collective investment scheme.[167] The rule which was broken here in relation to
s.150[168] is the client classification principle under the Conduct of Business
Sourcebook. Liability in this case, interestingly, applied between a product
provider and a customer who had not met directly but rather who communicated
through a financial intermediary. In this instance the intermediary would be liable
in tort as well as the product provider who was aware of the nature of the
customer involved or who failed to comply with client classification principles.
The provision of any sort of advice by a finance professional would be actionable
if it went beyond the mere giving of information and is instead objectively likely
to influence the investor's decision whether or not to invest in a given financial
product.[169]

A "private person" for the purposes of s.150 is defined by the Rights of Action **25–84**
Regulations.[170] The first category of private person is "any individual" who is not
carrying on a regulated business activity under FSMA 2000.[171] The second
category of private person covers non-individuals (such as companies) who are
not "acting the course of a business of any kind".[172] It is suggested that

---

[162] Financial Services and Markets Act 2000 s.150(4).
[163] Financial Services and Markets Act 2000 (Rights of Action) Regulations 2001, SI 2001/2256.
[164] See above, reg.6.
[165] Financial Services and Markets Act 2000 s.150(2).
[166] Financial Services and Markets Act 2000 s.150(3).
[167] *Seymour v Caroline Ockwell & Co (A Firm)* [2005] EWHC 1137.
[168] That case related to s.62 of the repealed Financial Services Act 1986 which was similar in intent.
[169] *Walker v Scottish Equitable* [2007] EWHC 1858, at [97], per Henderson J.
[170] Financial Services and Markets Act 2000 (Rights of Action) Regulations 2001, SI 2001/2256.
[171] See above, reg.3.
[172] See above, reg.3.

partnerships and unincorporated associations should not be treated as falling within this definition because, lacking legal personality, they are not strictly "persons". The ability of any "private person" to bring a claim means that the claimant does not necessarily have to be an investor herself nor necessarily directly a customer of the defendant. Consequently, the surviving spouse of a customer could bring an action.[173]

7. DEFAMATION

A. Introduction

25–85   It is possible for a company to be the victim of defamation. Markets operate on the basis of rumour and innuendo. On share markets, when there is a good feeling in the marketplace generally about a company, its shares will increase in value. This will have a number of effects on that company, including making it possible for that company to raise capital more easily. However, when a company's share value falls on the basis of innuendo and rumour, then that will limit a company's ability to raise capital and may harm its business as a result, making it more vulnerable to takeover or to insolvency. If such innuendo were put into writing then it could constitute libel or if it were communicated verbally then it could constitute slander, and in either case it could give rise to liability in the tort of defamation.[174] A misstatement by a credit rating company about an individual (especially when that causes that person to lose banking services) may constitute defamation.[175] Companies may sue for defamation as well as individuals.[176]

B. The need for a defamatory statement

25–86   The first question in the tort of defamation would be whether or not the statement is defamatory. As Giliker and Beckwith put it: "a statement is defamatory if it harms a person's reputation".[177] In *Sim v Stretch*[178] it was held that a statement will be defamatory then if it would "tend to lower the plaintiff in the estimation of right-thinking members of society generally", and includes circumstances in which the claimant would thereby be "shunned or avoided" by those reasonable people,[179] or that people would attach a pejorative interpretation to the statement.[180] If a company's reputation was harmed, for example, by statements circulated among finance professionals in the professional marketplace or by statements made in a magazine which might also be read by non-professional

---

[173] This displaces the exclusion of potential claimants of that sort under the ancien regime: *Gorham v British Telecommunications Plc* [2000] 1 W.L.R. 2129.
[174] See Giliker and Beckwith, *Tort Law*, Ch.12, for a very clear discussion of this tort.
[175] *Smeaton v Equifax Plc* [2013] EWCA Civ 108.
[176] *South Hetton Coal Co v North-Eastern Association Ltd* [1894] 1 Q.B. 133; *McDonalds Corp v Steel (No.1)* [1995] 3 All E.R. 615.
[177] Giliker and Beckwith, *Tort Law*, p.361.
[178] [1936] 2 All E.R. 1237.
[179] *Youssoupoff v MGM Pictures Ltd* (1934) 50 T.L.R. 581.
[180] *Frost v London Joint Stock Bank Ltd* (1906) 22 T.L.R. 760, CA.

investors, such that those two types of investor "shunned or avoided" the claimant company's securities then that could constitute a defamation. Defamation could be couched in technical language so that only professionals would understand its meaning, or the defamation could be made in plain language so that it could also be understood by non-experts. It is a separate question, considered below, whether or not such a statement would attract a defence against liability. Clearly, ordinary analysis offered up by stock market analysts or by columnists in newspapers could be thought of as being defamatory whenever a company is criticised; but the defences will put many such statements outwith the scope of liability as considered below. In banking contexts, it has been held that there were libellous statements made by banks in saying that the funds in a customer's account were "not sufficient" to meet its obligations[181] and similarly that one must "present again" a customer's cheque. Other examples of bankers slandering their customers, as in *Tournier v National Provincial Bank*,[182] are considered at para.29–12.

C. That the statement must refer to the claimant

The second question in the tort of defamation would be whether or not the defamation refers specifically to the claimant. If the claimant is identified by name, then clearly that defamation is aimed at them. If the claimant is referred to in a manner that readers of a libel, for example, would know which company is meant, then that would be directed at the claimant. Whereas, if the statement is made at a marketplace generally then it would be more difficult to demonstrate that the defamation was intended to relate to one person or another.   **25–87**

D. That the statement must have been published

The third question in the tort of defamation would be whether or not the defamation had been published. Publication would have taken place if the defamation was disseminated through a RIS[183] or in a newspaper. It would be more difficult to know whether or not discussions between traders constitute publication. The principle is that communication of the defamation to someone other than the defendant or the claimant constitutes publication. Therefore, if the defendant was a trader who was simply discussing matters with another trader on the telephone before making the defamatory remark, then that would constitute publication. Traders' telephone conversations are taped and therefore proof of the defamation could be obtained if the tapes were acquired. Evidently, if the defamation was published on an electronic bulletin board or online "chat room" then that would also constitute defamation. An exception to this principle would arise perhaps where the only people who had access to that messaging system were employees of the same firm. In that latter sense, it could be said that the employer of the people who heard and who made the defamatory statement were   **25–88**

---

[181] *Davidson v Barclays Bank* [1940] 1 All E.R. 316.
[182] [1924] 1 K.B. 461.
[183] That is, a recognised information service.

all part of the same person and that there had been no publication of the statement, unless it is considered that the effect of the remark is equivalent to publishing it because (for example) the statement will influence the manner in which those employees advise their customers to buy or not to buy the securities of the claimant company.

E.   Defences to an action for defamation

The four defences

25–89   The fourth question in the tort of defamation would be whether or not any of the defences to defamation applied. The principal defences to defamation are: that the statement was justified (that is, that it was true); that the statement constituted "fair comment"; that the statement was made in privileged circumstances (such as between lawyer and client); or that an offer of amends has been made under the Defamation Act 1996 in relation to inadvertent defamation. The defences of justification and of fair comment are the most important here.

The defence of justification

25–90   The defence of justification will require that the defendant can demonstrate that the statement was simply true. In fact the authorities require only that the statement was "substantially true": that is, that it was based on truth, even if there is some minor error in it.[184] There is no actionable defamation if the defendant was simply telling the truth. The defendant would therefore be required to be able to prove her statement was based on fact: something which will be difficult to do if it is based on analysis and opinion, and not simply on financial information or statistics. If the statement was an analyst's statement which was based accurately on published information such as accounts and market statistics, then it is suggested that it would be justified.[185]

The defence of fair comment

25–91   The most significant defence in this area is that of fair comment.[186] As Giliker and Beckwith put it: it is concerned with the defendant proving that "she has exercised the right to criticise the claimant"[187] and thus has reasonably exercised her right to freedom of expression. The elements of the defence are as follows. The statement must have been made in the public interest. Thus a statement made

---

[184] *Alexander v North Eastern Railway Co* (1865) 122 E.R. 1221.

[185] Beyond the law on defamation, when a bank provides references as to a customer's credit worth it is not doing so as a fiduciary and therefore will owe liabilities only in negligence for any misrepresentation, and will owe no amount in damages to the customer for a negative reference if the information provided in that reference is accurate: *Turner v Royal Bank of Scotland* [2001] EWCA Civ 64. It is suggested that the same reasoning should operate as a defence to a claim for defamation by the customer.

[186] See generally *Reynolds v Times Newspapers Ltd* [2001] 2 A.C. 127; *Branson v Bower (No.2)* [2002] Q.B. 737.

[187] Giliker and Beckwith, *Tort Law*, p.378.

in a newspaper, such as the *Lex* column in the *Financial Times*, which is intended to inform the reading public about the business condition of certain companies and markets would be made in the public interest. Further, a comment must have been made which was "fair". A comment which is based on facts will be fair, even if it draws conclusions which are extrapolated from those facts. Thus a comment that a company had suffered a downturn in its orders based on a published fact would justify a comment to the effect that that company was likely to suffer a loss because the downturn was considered to be large enough to leave its cost of sales higher than its sales for the year. However, if the facts suggested that the company's orders had fallen by 10 per cent and that its profits were likely to be 10 per cent smaller than the previous year, that would not without more justify a comment to the effect that the company was therefore insolvent: a company trading in profit that is able to meet its obligations when due would not be insolvent. Finally, the comment must also be "honest". Thus, a statement that a company is insolvent which is intended to make that company's shares cheaper so that the defendant who made the statement can buy those shares at a good price, would not be honest. That would be market manipulation.[188] As Lord Nicholls has held,[189] with the support of more recent case law,[190] it is a requirement of the defence that the defendant can demonstrate that she genuinely believed in the truth of the comment.

8. TORT OF MISFEASANCE IN A PUBLIC OFFICE

25–92

A question arises as to whether or not a regulator may bear other liabilities in private law (beyond the potential for negligence considered above) to investors and other customers who suffer loss as a result of the fault of a financial institution which was to have been regulated by that regulator. There is a tendency in the Press to seek to blame the regulators in any instance of misfeasance by a financial institution as though regulators will, like some caped superhero, protect all consumers from harm in all circumstances. In *Three Rivers District Council v Bank of England (No.3*[191]*)* the Three River District Council sued the Bank of England for damages under the tort of misfeasance in a public office when the Bank of Credit and Commerce International ("BCCI") went into bankruptcy after a huge array of frauds and other misfeasance committed by officers of BCCI.[192] The council had been a depositor with that bank and therefore suffered loss when the bank failed because it could not recover the value in its bank accounts.[193] In essence, the council's claim was that the Bank of England ought not to have granted BCCI a licence to conduct banking business and (in effect) that it ought to have regulated BCCI in such a way that the council would not have suffered the losses which it did suffer.

---

[188] See para.14–71.

[189] *Cheng v Tse Wai Chun (Tse Wai Chun Paul v Albert)* [2001] E.M.L.R. 777, 797.

[190] e.g. *Branson v Bower (No.2)* [2002] Q.B. 737, 746.

[191] [2001] UKHL 16; [2003] 2 A.C. 1.

[192] *Three Rivers District Council v Bank of England* [1999] Lloyd's Rep. Bank 283.

[193] That is, strictly, the debt which the bank owed to the council as its customer would not be paid because the bank had gone into insolvency.

25-93   It was held by the House of Lords that the Bank of England may in theory be liable for the tort of misfeasance in a public office if one of its officers acted knowingly outside the scope of her powers with the intention that the claimant would suffer loss or harm, or alternatively if that officer were recklessly indifferent to the legality of her acts and the effects which they might cause for the defendant.[194] It is thus a two-level tort.[195] The first formulation will be difficult to make out in many circumstances because the officer must have acted in bad faith knowing that her actions would cause harm to the claimant and intending that that would occur. This has been referred to in the cases as "targeted malice".[196] Ultimately The House of Lords did not impose such liability on the Bank of England in relation to a claim brought by depositors with the latterly bankrupt and fraud-ridden Bank of Credit and Commerce International ("BCCI") against the Bank of England for granting authorisation to BCCI to conduct business as a bank. This litigation did not reach a satisfactory conclusion. The appeal considered here was concerned with establishing the basis on which the tort operated, but the complex matter of establishing whether or not it was borne out on the facts in relation to six thousand depositors with BCCI was not completed. The other streams of litigation arising out of these facts were concerned with complex interlocutory, procedural matters.

25-94   The Court of Appeal in the *Three Rivers* case had based liability somewhat differently on a finding of "dishonesty".[197] Akin to the House of Lords, the Court of Appeal recognised that the tort of misfeasance in a public office is not set in stone and that it is therefore capable of development; the Court of Appeal found that the proof of the tort depended on there being some "targeted malice" by the regulator such that harm or probable harm would result; and the Court of Appeal found that liability would sound in damages in tort if the regulator had actual knowledge of the activities which caused harm to the claimant or if the regulator demonstrated reckless indifference to the activities which caused harm to the claimant. However, this standard of knowledge and of recklessness was said to be akin to the objective notion of "dishonesty" set out by Lord Nicholls in *Royal Brunei Airlines v Tan*[198] which required that the court consider what an honest person would have done in the circumstances and ask whether or not the defendant behaved in that way.[199] However, the formulation of dishonesty used by the Court of Appeal suggested that the regulator must have had knowledge of the factors involved, and therefore the test was not completely the objective test set out in *Tan*. It was held that insufficient facts had been found before the matter came on before the Court of Appeal to determine whether or not there would have been such liability. Similarly, in *Hall v Governor and Company of the Bank of*

---

[194] *Three Rivers District Council v Bank of England* [2001] UKHL 16; [2003] 2 A.C. 1.

[195] See, however, the concerns of Lord Millett about this formulation: [2003] 2 A.C. 235.

[196] See, e.g. the example of *Roncarelli v Duplessis* (1959) 16 D.L.R. (2d) 698 used by *Winfield and Jolowicz on Tort*, 2006, 359, where the Prime Minister and Attorney General of Quebec intentionally sought revenge on the claimant for having provided bail for Jehovah's Witnesses during a political dispute with those public officials.

[197] [1999] Lloyd's Rep. Bank 478.

[198] [1995] 2 A.C. 378.

[199] See para.26–09 for a discussion of this test.

England,[200] relying on the *Three Rivers* decision in the Court of Appeal, it was held by Neuberger J. that, because no "dishonesty" could be found on the facts, the Bank of England could not be found to have committed misfeasance in its public office.

It is suggested that it would be unusual for a regulator to show "targeted malice" **25–95** towards consumers, but actual knowledge of factors which ultimately would cause loss to consumers is a much easier hurdle to cross. For example, if the FCA or the PRA could be demonstrated to have had sufficient knowledge of factors which contributed to the global financial crisis of 2008 (such as the misselling of mortgages, as discussed in Chapter 45) then it could be argued that the FCA or the PRA owed a duty to consumers to intercede and to require that financial institutions operate their mortgage business in an appropriate manner.

---

[200] [1999] Lloyd's Rep. Bank 478.

BREACH OF TRUST

CORE PRINCIPLES

The first category of breach of trust relates to the liability of trustees of express trusts for a breach of the terms of that trust. The trustee will be liable in whichever of the three following ways is appropriate in the circumstances: a proprietary liability to provide specific restitution of any property lost to the trust fund; or a personal liability to reconstitute the value of the trust fund in cash; or a personal liability to provide compensation for any loss resulting from the breach of trust.

The second and third categories of liability for breach of trust relate to the liabilities of third parties ("strangers") who have intermeddled with a breach of trust or a breach of some other form of fiduciary duty: they are dishonest assistance and unconscionable receipt. "Dishonest assistance" relates to a loss being caused by a breach of trust in circumstances in which the defendant dishonestly assisted that breach of trust in some way. A person is "dishonest" if she failed to act as an honest person would have done in the circumstances. "Unconscionable receipt" relates to a loss being caused by a breach of trust in circumstances in which the defendant acted unconscionably and received property from a trust fund with knowledge that the property had been passed to her in breach of trust. In this "knowledge" encompasses having actual knowledge, or having wilfully shut one's eyes to the obvious, or having wilfully failed to make the inquiries which an honest and reasonable person would have made. In either case, the defendant is liable to account personally to the beneficiaries for the loss suffered by the trust as a result of the breach of trust. The defendants are said to be "constructive trustees" in that, in effect, the defendants are construed to be express trustees and thus effectively made personally liable to account to the beneficiaries as though express trustees accounting for a breach of trust.

The liability of strangers in relation to breach of fiduciary duties has been particularly significant in relation to banking transactions, particularly where a director or a trader of a financial institution has committed an act of dishonesty or has acted knowingly in the context of a breach, and then whether or not their liability is to be imputed to the company or institution for which they worked. Recent cases have begun to rely on financial regulation to supply statements of what an honest banker should have done in the circumstances or as to information which a banker should have known in the circumstances due to positive obligations under conduct of business regulation.

1. INTRODUCTION

26–01   This chapter considers liability for breach of trust arising in financial transactions. A number of different claims are considered under the general heading "breach of trust". First, self-evidently, there is the liability of trustees of express trusts for a breach of trust which they committed or permitted to happen. There are, however, a number of other claims which flow from breaches of trust which may ensnare financial institutions and their employees. These liabilities are often referred to as breaches of trust but they refer more generally to breaches of fiduciary duties in general terms. Secondly, then, is the liability of a person who is not a trustee (referred to in the cases as a "stranger") who dishonestly assists in a breach of trust or other fiduciary duty (referred to as "dishonest assistance"). Thirdly, is the liability of a stranger who knowingly receives property in breach of trust (referred to as "unconscionable receipt") in circumstances in which she acted unconscionably in some way. The claims for both dishonest assistance and for unconscionable receipt are personal claims to account for the loss caused by the breach of trust or fiduciary duty. Fourthly, tracing actions to recover property passed away on breach of trust or other fiduciary duty: these actions were considered in detail in Chapter 23, and are therefore only summarised in this chapter. Fifthly, other proprietary claims to a constructive trust flowing from a misuse of fiduciary office, such as earning unauthorised profits. Each is considered in turn.

2. BREACH OF TRUST

A. Liability of trustee

The basis of liability for breach of trust

An express trustee will be liable to account to the beneficiaries for any loss suffered as a consequence of a breach of trust. The beneficiaries are only required to show some general causal connection, but explicitly not to satisfy a test of foreseeability akin to that at common law. Thus, in the leading case, *Target Holdings v Redferns*,[1] the claimants were gulled into lending money to a company by means of a fraudulent over-valuation of the land which was to be put up as security for the loan, with the result that a sale of the land could not repay the loan when the rogues absconded with the money. The defendant solicitors were innocent of the fraud but had acted as trustees for the loan moneys during the transaction. The solicitors had committed a technical breach of trust by misusing those trust moneys but had replaced the funds in time for the mortgage to be completed. The claimants sought to recover their loss from the defendant solicitors on the basis that there had been a breach of trust. It was held that there must be some causal link between the breach of trust and the loss for an action for breach of trust to stand. On these facts it was held that the loss was caused by the fraudulent over-valuation of the mortgaged land—in which the defendant solicitors had played no part—and not by the solicitors' breach of trust. Therefore, no action for breach of trust against the solicitors would stand.

26–02

Specific restitution: the proprietary remedy for breach of trust

Lord Browne-Wilkinson identified three possible remedies in connection with a breach of trust in *Target Holdings v Redferns*.[2] The first is the remedy of specific restitution of the original property making up the trust fund which was lost through the breach of trust. This is a proprietary remedy whereby the trustee is required to recover the precise property which previously formed part of the trust fund but which was transferred away in breach of trust. If that property cannot be recovered or identified, then this remedy will not be available. There are, distinct from the liabilities of the trustees for breach of trust, still tracing actions to impose property rights over any substitute property for that taken from the trust, or to establish property rights over any property with which the original trust property was mixed. Tracing actions are considered below.[3]

26–03

---

[1] [1996] 1 A.C. 421.
[2] [1996] 1 A.C. 421.
[3] Importantly, a tracing action is distinct from the liability of the trustees personally because the primary liability in relation to a breach of trust is against the trustee personally, and any further action is a secondary action.

Equitable compensation

26–04   The second remedy for breach of trust is a personal remedy requiring a payment of money by the trustee to the trust equal to the value of the amount lost by the trust fund due to the breach of trust.

26–05   The third remedy is a further personal remedy to pay equitable compensation to the trust to compensate the beneficiaries any further loss caused by the breach of trust. The remedy of equitable compensation in relation to breach of fiduciary duties generally was described in the following terms by Blackburn J.[4]:

> "... the correct approach to equitable compensation for breach of fiduciary duty is to assess what actual loss, applying common sense and fairness, has resulted from the breach, having regard to the scope of the duty which was broken. ... [T]he beneficiary is entitled to be placed in the position he was in before the breach occurred. This assumes that he can show that the breach was causally relevant to the course of action which has given rise to his loss in the sense that, but for the breach of duty, the beneficiary would not have acted in the way which caused his loss."

This remedy is therefore an equitable remedy in its purest sense. Lord Browne-Wilkinson identified two important ideas in relation to equitable compensation in *Target Holdings v Redferns*.[5] First, while there must be some causal connection between the breach and the loss that nevertheless does not include all of the common law architecture relating to causation, foreseeability, proximity and so forth. Secondly, the purpose of equitable compensation is to compensate the beneficiary for her loss to the extent that she has actually suffered a loss.

B.   Exclusion of liability for breach of trust

26–06   Trustees may limit their liabilities for breach of trust in the trust instrument.[6] Express provision in the trust instrument may exclude the trustees' liability in tort for any liability for negligence and so forth.[7] Such exclusion of liability clauses are treated by trusts law as being equitable devices and not contractual provisions.[8] It has been found on the decided cases that trustees can limit their liability for negligence and gross negligence, but they may not limit their liability for dishonesty or fraud.[9] Such clauses were considered in Chapter 5.

---

[4] *Nationwide v Balmer Radmore* [1999] Lloyd's Rep. PN 241, 278.
[5] [1996] 1 A.C. 421.
[6] *Target Holdings v Redferns* [1996] 1 A.C. 421, considered in detail in Ch.18.
[7] *Armitage v Nurse* [1998] Ch. 241; *Taylor v Midland Bank Trust Co* (2000) 2 ITELR 439; *Bogg v Raper, The Times* April 22, 1998; *Wight v Olswang* (1999) *The Times*, May 18.
[8] *Re Duke of Norfolk Settlement Trusts* [1982] 1 Ch. 61.
[9] *Walker v Stones* [2001] Q.B. 902.

3. DISHONEST ASSISTANCE AND UNCONSCIONABLE RECEIPT IN A BREACH OF TRUST

A. Personal liability to account as a constructive trustee

There are then two forms of personal liability to account as a constructive trustee **26–07** for involvement in a breach of trust—as considered respectively in the following two sections—either by way of receiving trust property knowing of the breach of trust or by way of dishonest assistance in the breach of trust. The remedy for both claims is the same. The defendant is personally liable to account to their beneficiaries for the loss caused by the breach of trust as a constructive trustee. That the remedy is a personal remedy means that there is no property held on trust by the claimant, rather it is sufficient that the equitable wrong[10] of dishonest assistance or of knowing (or unconscionable) receipt of the property has been committed. That the defendant is said to be a "constructive trustee" means that the defendant, in spite of being a stranger to the trust, is *construed* to be a trustee[11] and thus is made personally liable for her participation in the breach of trust just as an express trustee would be under *Target Holdings v Redferns*.

B. The significance of personal liability to account in financial transactions

It is common in financial transactions for fiduciary relationships to arise, as was **26–08** considered in Chapter 5 of this book. Trusts arise in relation to pension funds and unit trusts, as well as arising more generally as a vehicle for holding property or taking security—as considered in Chapter 21. Fiduciary relationships more generally arise in a large number of circumstances in which a financial institution acts in the affairs of clients either directly as trustee or indirectly assuming fiduciary responsibility in the manner considered in Chapter 5. A person, whether an individual trader or a financial institution acting as an intermediary, who assists in a breach of fiduciary duty will be personally liable to account to the beneficiaries of that fiduciary duty as a constructive trustee.[12] Thus, such a person would be personally liable to compensate the beneficiaries for the whole of that loss.[13] Importantly, then, when financial institutions as a corporate entity or their employees (such as their traders) as individuals participate in the management of their clients' assets, any breach of trust may impose liability on either the institution or its agents and employees for the whole of the loss caused to the

---

[10] This is the language used by Lord Nicholls in *Dubai Aluminium v Salaam* [2002] 3 W.L.R. 1913.

[11] In *Dubai Aluminium v Salaam* [2002] 3 W.L.R. 1913 Lord Millett suggested that language of constructive trust is unfortunate because no property is actually held on trust. However, it is suggested that the approach of Lord Nicholls is preferable because it recognises that a wrong is committed here in equity—either by means of the defendant dishonesty in assisting the breach of trust or the unconscionability or knowledge in receiving the trust property in breach of trust—and that the defendant is simply being deemed to be a trustee and subjected to the remedy to which an actual express trustee would be subjected under ordinary breach of trust principles.

[12] *Royal Brunei Airlines v Tan* [1995] 2 A. C. 378; *Dubai Aluminium v Salaam* [2002] 3 W.L.R. 1913; *Barlow Clowes v Eurotrust* [2006] 1 W.L.R. 1476, [2006] 1 All E.R. 333.

[13] *Royal Brunei Airlines v Tan* [1995] 2 A.C. 378.

beneficiaries of the fiduciary arrangements. Much is said in the judgments, particularly by Lord Nicholls,[14] about the particular context of breaches of fiduciary duty in investment transactions and the applicability of these claims in circumstances in which the defendant institution or trader takes unsuitable risks, and not simply when such a person is straightforwardly deceitful. Furthermore, there are issues as to the transmission of liability from dishonest or unconscionable traders to the institutions that employ them. Even more significant is the development of a notion that commercially unacceptable conduct (particularly when evidenced by a breach of regulatory principles) will satisfy the requirement of dishonesty, unconscionability or knowledge of the breach of trust, as appropriate. This bridge between substantive law and financial regulation is, as was discussed in Chapter 3, a significant part of the likely future of the law of finance. These issues are considered below at the end of this chapter.

C.   Dishonest assistance

The nature of dishonest assistance

26–09   A person, even if otherwise unconnected with the trust, who dishonestly assists in a breach of trust will be personally liable to account to the beneficiaries for any loss caused by that breach of trust.[15] The dishonest assistant himself will not need to be a fiduciary; it is enough that he assists the breach of some other person's fiduciary duty.[16] It is a pre-requisite that there have been a breach of trust.[17] There is very little commentary as to what will constitute "assistance" in a breach of trust—it seems that any act which facilitates the breach of trust will suffice. The bulk of the discussion in the case law has revolved around the question of what constitutes "dishonesty" in this context.

The test for dishonesty

26–10   The source of the current law on the meaning of "dishonesty" in relation to dishonest assistance is the decision of the Privy Council in *Royal Brunei Airlines v Tan*,[18] principally the judgment of Lord Nicholls. In that case a company carried on business as a travel agency and entered into a contract to sell the claimant airline's tickets on the basis that all receipts for ticket sales were to be held on trust by the company prior to being paid to the airline periodically. The defendant was the managing-director of the company who organised for trust money to be used to pay the company's debts. The issue arose whether or not the defendant was liable for dishonest assistance in the breach of trust committed by the company. It was held that the managing director had dishonestly assisted in that breach of trust: there was no requirement that the company as trustee had to be

---

14   [1995] 2 A.C. 378.
15   [1995] 2 A.C. 378.
16   [1995] 2 A.C. 378.
17   [1995] 2 A.C. 378.
18   [1995] 2 A.C. 378; *Twinsectra v Yardley* [2002] UKHL 12.

shown to have acted dishonestly. The principal issue was as to the nature of the test for "dishonesty". In this regard, Lord Nicholls held the following:

"...acting dishonestly, or with a lack of probity, which is synonymous, means simply not acting as an honest person would in the circumstance. This is an objective standard."[19]

The test of "dishonesty" in this context is actually a test asking whether or not the defendant did or did not do what an honest person would have done in the same circumstances. Thus, the court will ask what an objectively honest person would have done. As is considered below, in the financial context this also involves asking what would have been required of a financial professional by financial regulation.[20] That this test is clearly stated by Lord Nicholls to be an objective test means that it does not matter that the defendant may have thought that what she was doing was honest: instead the question is what an objectively honest person would have done in those circumstances. Interestingly, this test does not require that there is any active *lying* on the defendant's part.[21] Rather, it is sufficient that the defendant fails to live up to an objective standard of probity.[22] It is also not required that the assistant be proved to have been acting fraudulently, as indeed it could not be shown that the defendant in *Royal Brunei Airlines v Tan* was because he had intended to return the money to the trust fund: it is enough that an honest and reasonable person would not have behaved in the way that the defendant acted.

Dishonesty in investment transactions, and the suitability of the risk taken

Much is said in *Royal Brunei Airlines v Tan* about the concept of risk as it applies **26–11** in particular in investment transactions. There is a self-evident context in which a defendant may act dishonestly: that is if she advises an investment in breach of a fiduciary duty or trust which she knows is likely to cause loss. For example, if she already held securities which she knew would fall in value and was therefore keen to off-load them onto someone else; advising that the trust bought those securities from her in breach of trust would be dishonest. It would be dishonest because that would not be the action of an honest person in those circumstances and it is suggested that it would be contrary to requirements of integrity under FCA regulation. There are other contexts, however, which are more complex. For example, what if an investment advisor advised a customer to take a reckless risk in its choice of investments? Would that be dishonest? Furthermore, will such an advisor be dishonest if she advises the taking of a risk which is unsuitable in the

---

[19] [1995] 2 A.C. 378, 386.

[20] See para.9–01.

[21] cf. *Eagle Trust Plc v SBC Securities Ltd* [1992] 4 All E.R. 488, 499, per Vinelott J.; *Polly Peck International v Nadir (No.2)* [1992] 4 All E.R. 769, 777, per Scott L.J.

[22] This is to be contrasted with the action for knowing receipt which, in the judgment of Scott L.J. in *Polly Peck v Nadir (No.2)* [1992] 3 All E.R. 769, sets out a form of subjective test of whether or not the recipient "ought to have been suspicious" and thereby have constructive notice of the breach of trust in those particular circumstances.

context of FCA conduct of business regulation?[23] In addressing this type of issue, Lord Nicholls expanded his discussion of "dishonesty" in *Royal Brunei Airlines v Tan* in the following manner:

> "All investment involves risk. Imprudence is not dishonesty, although imprudence may be carried recklessly to lengths which call into question the honesty of the person making the decision. This is especially so if the transaction serves another purpose in which that person has an interest of his own."[24]

These dicta mean that an advisor who advises the taking of a risk which is reckless, or it is suggested an advisor who advises the taking of a risk which takes "imprudence" to "reckless lengths", may be taken to have acted dishonestly for the purposes of liability for dishonest assistance. This is especially so if that advisor stands to earn some personal commission from the transaction (in that that would be an example of "an interest of his own"). Therefore, the issue arises of the advisor who stands to profit from the transaction even if it is unprofitable for the buyer in circumstances in which the advisor recommends the taking of a large investment risk. The basis of this form of liability is that a third party:

> "...takes a risk that a clearly unauthorised transaction will not cause loss... If the risk materialises and causes loss, those who knowingly took the risk will be accountable accordingly."[25]

The test for dishonesty in this context is therefore a level of risk which the court considers to be too great. Therefore, an accessory may be liable where the risk taken, for example in respect of a securities investment, is considered by the court to have been too great, even though the market might consider the acquisition of that sort of security to be standard practice and even advisable in many circumstances. In terms of transactions such as that in *Bankers Trust v Dharmala*[26] where the losses generated are very large in cash terms, it will appear ex post facto that the risk taken would have been unacceptable. This is particularly so where the investment is being used as part of a portfolio investment strategy but then generates a loss which is large in terms of the total size of the portfolio, or which is disproportionate to the losses generated by the other assets making up the portfolio, or which is excessive and unsuitable for a customer of that profile in the context of FCA conduct of business regulation. On the basis that it is the court's decision on the level of risk that counts, it is therefore difficult to counsel an advisor as to the approach to be taken to the investment of trust property. It is not a failure to ascertain whether or not the investment is in breach of trust which is decisive of the matter, but rather whether or not the *level of risk* assumed is in breach of duty. As Lord Nicholls told us: "honesty is an objective standard". Therefore it is for the court to measure the level of risk and, consequently, the honesty of the third party. The outcome would seem to depend upon an objective assessment of "the circumstances known to the third party at the time". However, recklessness as to the ability of the trust to

---

[23] See para.10–01.

[24] [1995] 2 A.C. 378, 387.

[25] [1995] 2 A.C. 378, 387.

[26] [1996] C.L.C. 518.

invest must similarly be a factor to be taken into account in deciding on the honesty of the third party investment manager. Similarly, where the bank charges any fees in connection with the transfer, it may be liable for unconscionable receipt of a part of that money.[27] The liability for the seller is that of making good the whole of the claimant's loss where its property invested under some fiduciary relationship was found to have been invested imprudently or recklessly.[28]

The development of the test for dishonesty

In spite of the admirable clarity of the test for dishonesty in *Royal Brunei Airlines v Tan* there has been some discussion in subsequent cases as to the structure of that test. In the House of Lords in *Twinsectra v Yardley*[29] Lord Hutton suggested that the test for dishonesty should be a hybrid test combining elements of objectivity and subjectivity. This meant that the test for dishonesty required *both* that objectively an honest person would not have behaved as the defendant behaved (being the test in *Royal Brunei Airlines v Tan*) and also that the defendant appreciated that her actions would be considered to be dishonest by honest and reasonable people. The effect of this change to the test would have been that a defendant would have been able to resist a finding of dishonesty if her personal morality would not have considered the behaviour to have been dishonest or would not have recognised that other people would have thought it dishonest. In this way, a person with questionable morals would be able to rely on moral relativism to escape liability for dishonesty. In *Twinsectra v Yardley* itself, a solicitor escaped liability for dishonest assistance when he passed moneys in breach of trust to his client on the basis that he had not appreciated the nature of the fiduciary obligations on him and importantly on the basis that he had not appreciated that honest people would have considered his behaviour to have been dishonest.

26–12

This effect of Lord Hutton's test was put under the microscope in the decision of the Privy Council in *Barlow Clowes v Eurotrust*[30] when the defendant argued, in spite of assisting the unlawful transmission of large amounts of money out of investment funds in breach of fiduciary duty for Cramer, in a manner which the judge at first instance decided was dishonest, that his personal morality meant that he would never ask questions of a client and that he did not appreciate that such behaviour would be considered to be dishonest by honest people. The defendant relied explicitly on Lord Hutton's test in *Twinsectra v Yardley*. The unanimous Privy Council found that the test for dishonesty in this context should be an objective test in the manner argued for by Lord Nicholls in *Royal Brunei*

26–13

---

[27] The liability in respect of deposit-taking banks can be difficult to conceptualise. For example, where X Bank allows a cheque drawn on A's account to be paid to a third party's account, the bank may be liable for dishonest assistance. Where the third party's account was overdrawn, the credit of the cheque will make the bank potentially liable for knowing receipt where the funds are used to reduce the overdraft because in the latter instance the bank receives the money in discharge of the overdraft loan. See Oakley, *Constructive Trusts* (London: Sweet & Maxwell, 1997) p.186 et seq.

[28] *Royal Brunei Airlines v Tan* [1995] A.C. 378.

[29] *Twinsectra v Yardley* [2002] UKHL 12; approving *Abbey National Plc v Solicitors Indemnity Fund Ltd* [1997] P.N.L.R. 306.

[30] [2006] 1 W.L.R. 1476; [2006] 1 All E.R. 333.

Airlines v Tan.[31] The defendant was held to have been dishonest, relying principally on the finding of the judge at first instance (having heard lengthy evidence from the defendant) that he was simply dishonest and must have known that the money came from a tainted source.[32]

26–14   Importantly, an intervening decision of the House of Lords in *Dubai Aluminium v Salaam*[33] found that the test for dishonesty should be that set out by Lord Nicholls in *Royal Brunei Airlines v Tan*,[34] but without making reference to the decision in *Twinsectra v Yardley*. The leading speech was delivered by Lord Nicholls, not surprisingly approving his own judgment in *Royal Brunei Airlines v Tan*. In *Dubai Aluminium v Salaam* a partner in an accountancy firm had assisted a client to commit a breach of fiduciary duty, and the question arose, inter alia, whether or not he should have been held liable as a dishonest assistant in the breach of fiduciary duty.[35] It was found that the appropriate test was an objective one. The objective test approach in *Royal Brunei Airlines v Tan* has been supported latterly by a majority of the Court of Appeal in *Abou-Rahmah v Abacha*,[36] albeit that the phrasing used by Arden L.J. suggested that the defendant must not only be objectively dishonest but also must subjectively appreciate this interpretation of her behaviour. It is suggested that this is a straightforward misreading of the judgment of Lord Nicholls in *Royal Brunei Airlines v Tan*.[37]

26–15   Many of the more recent cases have seized on the following dicta in the judgment of Lord Nicholls in *Royal Brunei Airlines v Tan* as suggesting that the test need not be entirely objective:

> "when called upon to decide whether a person was acting honestly, a court will look at all the circumstances known to the third party at the time. The court will also have regard to personal attributes of the third party such as his experience and intelligence, and the reason why he acted as he did."[38]

---

[31]   See A. Hudson, *Equity & Trusts*, p.855 et seq. on this point.

[32]   In *Barlow Clowes v Eurotrust* [2005] W.T.L.R. 486 in the Privy Council Lord Hoffmann has suggested that the speeches delivered by Lord Hutton and Lord Hoffmann in *Twinsectra v Yardley* were not intended to add a subjective element to this test. So, in *Barlow Clowes v Eurotrust* itself, Henwood managed an investment fund, ITC, through which Clowes and Cramer invested a large amount of money on their own accounts in breach of trusts held by them for private clients. It was claimed that Henwood had dishonestly assisted the breach of those trusts by controlling the investment of trust property through ITC. Henwood contended that, relying on Lord Hutton's hybrid-subjective conception of dishonesty, his personal morality dictated that he would ask no questions of his clients and instead simply obey their directions, and that he had therefore not been dishonest. The judge at first instance found as a fact that he must have suspected the true source of the funds. It was held by a unanimous Privy Council that the correct test to apply was a purely objective test, with the result that Henwood could not rely on his own personal morality to preclude a finding that he had been dishonest. Consequently, he was held to have been dishonest. For the law relating to dishonest assistance, it is suggested this means that for the future the test will be one of objective dishonesty.

[33]   [2002] 3 W.L.R. 1913; [2003] 1 All E.R. 97.

[34]   [1995] 2 A.C. 378.

[35]   The case relates primarily to the transmission of liability to the partnership as a whole from the individual partner. This, it is suggested, is why so few commentators have noticed it in spite of the extensive discussion of the test of dishonesty.

[36]   *Abou-Rahmah v Abacha* [2006] EWCA Civ 1492; [2007] Bus. L.R. 220.

[37]   See A. Hudson, *Equity & Trusts*, s.20.3.

[38]   [1995] 2 A.C. 378, 391.

That second sentence is the only expression of that sentiment in a judgment of several pages and yet it has been used by some judges to allow a survey of the personal characteristics of the individual defendant.[39] Nevertheless, the authorities have recognised that, aside from that wrinkle, the test is intended to be objective. The following summary of the principles has been set out in *Aerostar Maintenance v International Ltd v Wilson* by Morgan J.[40]:

"The test as to dishonesty, distilled from the above authorities,[41] is as follows. Dishonesty is synonymous with a lack of probity. It means not acting as an honest person would in the circumstances. The standard is an objective one. The application of the standard requires one to put oneself in the shoes of the defendant to the extent that his conduct is to be assessed in the light of what he knew at the relevant time, as distinct from what a reasonable person would have known or appreciated. For the most part dishonesty is to be equated with conscious impropriety. But a person is not free to set his own standard of honesty. This is what is meant by saying that the standard is objective. If by ordinary objective standards, the defendant's mental state would be judged to be dishonest, it is irrelevant that the defendant has adopted a different standard or can see nothing wrong in his behaviour."

Therefore, the courts have accepted that one can look at the circumstances in which the defendant was operating at the time: for example, the amount of information which would have been available to the hypothetical honest person in those circumstances, and so forth. It is suggested that the court ought not to consider the defendant's specific, personal attributes—such as inattentiveness, stupidity, greed, and so forth—because they will introduce subjectivity to what is an objective test. Instead, in financial transactions, the court should consider the objective requirements which are placed on a regulated person by financial regulation (in particular by reference to conduct of business regulation) as a statement of what an honest person should have done in the defendant's circumstances.

The suggestion that the test for dishonesty in this context should be changed so as to be subjective is, it is respectfully suggested, absurd.[42] Let us focus on the liability of financial advisors for present purposes. Financial advisors working for authorised firms under FCA regulation are required to act with integrity. That is itself an objective standard objectively expressed in a code of financial regulation. These people are regulated by objective standards. Therefore, the case law tests in this regard should reflect the fact that the defendant is bound by an objective code of behaviour from the Principles for Businesses rulebook through to the Conduct of Business Sourcebook and beyond. The first and only place that the courts need to look for a statement of what a reasonable or honest banker

26–16

---

[39] *Starglade v Nash* [2010] EWCA Civ 1314; *Fiona Trust & Holding Corporation v Privalov* [2010] EWHC 3199 (Comm), at [1437], per Andrew Smith J.

[40] [2010] EWHC 2032 (Ch), at [184].

[41] Those authorities were: the decision of the Privy Council in *Royal Brunei Airlines v Tan* [1995] 2 A.C. 378, the decision of the House of Lords in *Twinsectra Ltd v Yardley* [2002] 2 A.C. 164, and the decision of the Privy Council in *Barlow Clowes International Ltd v Eurotrust International Ltd* [2006] 1 W.L.R. 1476. And in his lordship's opinion, correctly, "the two decisions of the Privy Council represent the law to be applied in this jurisdiction: see *Abou-Rahmah v Abacha* [2007] 1 All E.R. (Comm) 827 at [66]–[70]".

[42] See A. Hudson, *Equity & Trusts*, s.20.3; and new essays on the author's website.

should do in any given circumstance is set out in those regulations. Those regulations are objective. The test for honesty should therefore be objective too.[43]

D. Unconscionable receipt

The basis of unconscionable receipt

26–17   A person will be personally liable to account to the beneficiaries of a trust if she receives property knowing that it has been passed to her in breach of that trust and in circumstances where her behaviour is unconscionable.[44] This claim for "unconscionable receipt" is predicated on receipt of the property coupled with the appropriate level of knowledge and unconscionability. In finance law practice this claim will be important in circumstances in which a trader has acted dishonestly or knowingly in breach of trust[45] but receipt of the property has been made by the bank employing that trader when it receives that money into its control or possession.[46] In contradistinction to dishonest assistance, unconscionable receipt requires that there have been some receipt of property, whether cash or non-cash assets, which has been paid away in breach of fiduciary duty. Where a person receives trust property in the knowledge that that property has been passed in breach of fiduciary duty, the recipient will be personally liable to account to the trust for the value of the property passed away.[47] It is a defence to demonstrate the receipt was authorised under the terms of the trust or that the recipient has lawfully changed her position in reliance on the receipt of the property.[48]

The requirement of receipt

26–18   Whether or not there has been receipt will generally be decided in accordance with the rules for tracing claims.[49] In the decision of Millett J. in *Agip (Africa) v Jackson*,[50] his lordship held that:

> "... there is receipt of trust property when a company's funds are misapplied by any person whose fiduciary position gave him control of them or enabled him to misapply them."

Thus a financial institution will receive property when a customer pays money to it and that money is passed into its accounts,[51] or when a customer reduces its overdraft.[52]

---

[43] See A. Hudson, "The Liability of Trusts Service Providers in International Finance Law", in Glasson and Thomas (eds), *The International Trust*, (Jordans Publishing, 2006), p.638 et seq.
[44] *Re Montagu* [1987] Ch. 264; *Agip v Jackson* [1990] Ch. 265, 286, per Millett J.; [1991] Ch. 547 CA; *Lipkin Gorman v Karpnale* [1991] 2 A.C. 548; *El Ajou v Dollar Land Holdings* [1993] 3 All E.R. 717, appealed [1994] 2 All E.R. 685. See A. Hudson, *Equity & Trusts*, s.20.3.
[45] The distinction between these various claims is considered below.
[46] *El Ajou v Dollar Land Holdings* [1993] 3 All E.R. 717.
[47] per Scott L.J. in *Polly Peck International v Nadir (No.2)* [1992] 3 All E.R. 769.
[48] *Lipkin Gorman v Karpnale* [1991] 2 A.C. 548.
[49] *El Ajou v Dollar Land Holdings* [1993] B.C.L.C. 735.
[50] [1989] 3 W.L.R. 1367, 1389.
[51] *Polly Peck International v Nadir (No.2)* [1992] 3 All E.R. 769.
[52] *MT Realisations Ltd v Digital Equipment Co Ltd* [2003] 2 B.C.L.C. 117.

The requirement of unconscionability

It was held by Nourse L.J. in *Bank of Credit and Commerce International v Akindele*[53] that the defendant is taken to have acted unconscionably if his knowledge was such that it would have been unconscionable for him to retain any benefit taken from the receipt of the property; or that it would have caused the beneficiaries uncompensated loss without the defendant having a good defence or an absence of knowledge.[54] This approach was put more broadly still by Megarry V-C in In re Montagu's Settlement Trusts[55] to the effect that liability lies where "[the recipient's] conscience is sufficiently affected for it to be right to bind him by the obligations of a constructive trustee". This approach was also upheld in *Criterion Properties Plc v Stratford UK Properties LLC*[56] where the Court of Appeal preferred the flexibility of the notion of "conscionability".[57] Carnwath L.J. took a similar approach to Nourse L.J. in the Court of Appeal in *Charter Plc v City Index Ltd*.[58] Carnwath L.J. (with whom Mummery L.J. agreed) held that:

26–19

> "... liability for "knowing receipt" depends on the defendant having sufficient knowledge of the circumstances of the payment to make it "unconscionable" for him to retain the benefit or pay it away for his own purposes."

The notion of unconscionability is therefore linked to the requirement of knowledge. On this model of the test, it is not that the defendant has acted unconscionably in general terms which imposes liability, but rather it is a question as to whether or not the defendant had such knowledge of the circumstances so as to make his retention or dealing with the property unconscionable. The test is whether or not the defendant acted in good conscience.[59]

The test of knowledge

Liability for unconscionable receipt, as demonstrated immediately above, requires that the defendant had the requisite knowledge of the breach of trust as well as having acted unconscionably. The requirement of knowledge in this context is satisfied if the defendant has knowledge of any one of the kinds set out by Peter Gibson J. in three categories of knowledge discussed in *Baden v Societe*

26–20

---

[53] [2001] Ch 437, [2000] 4 All E.R. 221.

[54] It is suggested that Nourse L.J.'s formulation presents the difficulty that it focuses on the defendant having taken a benefit and thereby strays too close to rendering this doctrine a restitutionary doctrine concerned with the reversal of an unjust enrichment, whereas the purpose of this doctrine is to compensate the beneficiaries for any loss occasioned by a breach of trust.

[55] [1987] Ch 264, 273.

[56] [2003] 2 B.C.L.C. 129. Carnwath L.J., having been the trial judge in *BBCI v Akindele* acknowledged that the Court of Appeal had overruled his own preference for a test of dishonesty at first instance: [2001] Ch. 437, 455, per Nourse L.J.

[57] [2003] 2 B.C.L.C. 129, [38]. In that case the test of unconscionability was advocated in relation to a claim brought on behalf of shareholders that the directors of a company had knowingly committed breaches of duty in entering into arrangements which would prevent a takeover of that company by third parties.

[58] *Charter plc v City Index Ltd* [2008] 2 WLR 950.

[59] *Citadel General Assurance v Lloyds Bank Canada* [1997] 3 S.C.R. 805, 152 D.L.R. (4th) 385.

Generale,[60] those three categories of knowledge are: actual knowledge; wilfully shutting one's eyes to the obvious; and wilfully and recklessly failing to make inquiries which an honest person would have made.[61] As Scott L.J. held in *Polly Peck*,[62] these categories are not to be taken as rigid rules and "one category may merge imperceptibly into another".[63] Thus, first, a defendant will be taken to have had knowledge of a breach of trust if she actually knew of the breach. Secondly, she will be taken to have had knowledge of a breach of trust if she had shut her eyes to the obvious, for example by receiving large amounts of money from a suspicious source and simply choosing wilfully to ignore the source of those moneys. Thirdly, she will be taken to have had knowledge of a breach of trust if she wilfully and recklessly failed to make inquiries, for example by taking a suspiciously large amount of money from two large suitcases wielded by a new client, especially if she was a banker who had suspicions that her client had sourced these funds from criminal activity but who nevertheless refused to ask any questions about the source of the money.

26–21   While the decision of Peter Gibson J. actually contained five categories of knowledge, Megarry V.C. in *Re Montagu*[64] restricted those five categories to the three discussed above which required that the defendant had acted wilfully. In *Re Montagu* itself the defendant was found to have forgotten the facts which would have indicated to him that there had been a breach of trust and to have got himself into "an honest muddle". If the test had not required that he had acted wilfully, then the defendant would have been liable for unconscionable receipt. Because the test was limited to categories of wilfulness, however, the defendant was found not to be liable for unconscionable receipt. This development in the cases suggests that liability in this context should be thought of as liability for an equitable wrong: namely, the wrong of acting wilfully in receipt of property.

Knowing receipt in banking contexts

26–22   In a banking context, the Court of Appeal in *Polly Peck v Nadir (No.2)*[65] held that there was no requirement to prove a fraudulent misapplication of funds to found a claim on unconscionable receipt. It was enough to demonstrate that the recipient had had the requisite knowledge both that the funds were trust funds and that they were being misapplied. In deciding whether or not a banker acting as a conduit for moneys taken in breach of a fiduciary duty ought to have been suspicious of

---

[60] (1983) [1993] 1 W.L.R. 509.

[61] The original five categories are restricted to three by *Montagu, Re* [1987] Ch. 264.

[62] per Scott L.J. in *Polly Peck International v Nadir (No.2)* [1992] 3 All E.R. 769.

[63] per Millett J. in *Agip v Jackson* [1989] 3 W.L.R. 1367, 1389.

[64] [1987] Ch. 264.

[65] *Polly Peck International v Nadir (No.2)* [1992] 3 All E.R. 769. That case of concerned a claim brought by the administrators of the plaintiff company against the Central Bank of Northern Cyprus. It was alleged that the Central Bank had exchanged the sterling amounts for Turkish lire either with actual knowledge of fraud on the plaintiff company or in circumstances in which the Central Bank out to have put on inquiry as to the source of those funds. As such, it was said on behalf of the plaintiff that the Central Bank had been the knowing recipient of the funds taken from it in breach of the director's fiduciary duty, when the money had been under the control of the Central Bank, and that the Central Bank was therefore liable to account as a constructive trustee for those sums which had passed through its hands.

the source of those funds, Scott L.J. preferred to approach the matter from the point of view of the "honest and reasonable banker"[66] (although his lordship did express some reservations that this should not be considered to be the only applicable test in this context).[67] In *Polly Peck v Nadir (No.2)* a director of a group of companies organised for funds of about £45 million to be transferred from those companies and paid through a bank under his control to the defendant, which was the Central Bank of Northern Cyprus. The defendant bank transferred the sterling amounts into Turkish lire, such that the defendant bank received the sterling by paying it into its own accounts. While the money at issue was a very large amount of money, it was held both that there was nothing about the context of the transaction which ought to have made the defendant suspicious and that for the defendant as a central bank such a large amount of money was not completely unusual.

Defences

The only available defences against a claim for unconscionable receipt are bona fide purchaser for value without notice,[68] change of position,[69] or potentially passing on.[70] These defences are considered in Chapter 23 in relation to tracing.[71]

26–23

4. THE INTERACTION BETWEEN FINANCIAL REGULATION AND THE SUBSTANTIVE LAW ON PERSONAL LIABILITY TO ACCOUNT

A. The substantive law on dishonest assistance and unconscionable receipt using financial regulatory norms

Personal liability to account for dishonest assistance and for unconscionable receipt turn principally on proof of dishonesty or knowledge (or unconscionability) respectively. The test of "dishonesty" is predicated on a finding of what an honest person would have done in the circumstances. Given that this is an objective test, there would be nothing more useful than an objective statement of what constitutes honest behaviour in any given context. When the facts relate to a financial transaction there is just such a statement of what standard of behaviour will be appropriate in the form of FCA regulation. Similarly, questions as to what a regulated person ought to have known and as to what a regulated person ought to have inquired into, to establish knowledge, are addressed by money laundering and FCA regulation. Similarly, concepts of unconscionable behaviour could be

26–24

---

[66] *Polly Peck v Nadir (No.2)* [1992] 3 All E.R. 769, 778–780.
[67] It does appear, however, that the reasonableness of the recipient's belief falls to be judged from the perspective of the recipient itself.
[68] *Westdeutsche Landesbank Girozentrale v Islington LBC* [1996] A.C. 669, considered in *Restitution*.
[69] *Lipkin Gorman v Karpnale* [1991] 2 A.C. 548, considered in *Termination and Restitution*.
[70] *Kleinwort Benson v Birmingham C.C.* [1996] 4 All E.R. 733, considered in *Termination and Restitution*.
[71] See para.23–36.

interpreted so as to correlate, it is suggested, with the requirement of "integrity" in the Principles for Businesses rulebook.

26–25   A number of decided cases have begun to build bridges between substantive law and financial regulation, using the latter to inform the creation of the tests in the former.[72] The case of *Bankers Trust v Dharmala*[73] is a good example of how a judge may use financial regulation to develop principles of substantive law. Mance J. was required to adjudicate on a case in which BT had sold two interest rate swaps to D. The interest rate swaps were more complex than was required for the client's purposes. The client claimed not to understand that movement in Fed Funds Rates in the US would affect the performance and potential losses on the first interest rate swap. That interest rate moved, triggering a large loss, which caused BT to sell a replacement swap to D which in turn caused another large loss. D contended, inter alia, that BT had unduly influenced it into both transactions, that BT had misrepresented the terms of the transactions, and that BT should have explained all of the relevant risks to D. The substantive law issues therefore turned on the question whether or not D had sufficient expertise to understand the transaction. Mance J. looked to the then applicable financial regulation—the Bank of England London Code—for a statement of how BT should have treated D. On that analysis it was found that D was a financial institution and, while its employees were not experts in these products, they should have been treated as having sufficient knowledge to appreciate the interest rate risks associated with these interest rate swaps, even if those swaps had features which were unnecessary for D's needs. Whichever tests is at issue, the judge is left with the task of measuring the defendant's behaviour against some objective standard. The most obvious embodiment of objective standards in relation to the functions of financial advisors, in the United Kingdom, is contained currently in the *FCA Handbook*.

26–26   More generally, recent cases have considered the question, again in relation to fiduciary law and the personal liability of strangers to a trust, as to proving misfeasance in the substantive law by reference to objective standards of "commercially acceptable conduct", whether or not those statements are embodied in financial regulation specifically or in other indicia of commercially reasonable conduct. This movement was indicated most clearly in the decision of Knox J. in *Cowan de Groot Properties Ltd v Eagle Trust Plc*[74] where it was held that the defendant would be held to have acted dishonestly if he had been guilty of "commercially unacceptable conduct" in the particular context. The court was thus inviting us to identify what would constitute acceptable conduct in the commercial market at issue and then to ask whether or not the defendant had complied with such standards. The standards for commercially acceptable conduct in financial markets, particularly in the EU, are made clear in the appropriate EU legislation: norms which are embodied in English law by FCA regulation further to FSMA 2000. Thus, a person who treats a customer in a way which would be, for example, contrary to conduct of business regulation as

---

[72] See A. Hudson, "The Liabilities of Trust Service Providers in International Finance Law", in *The International Trust*, p.639.
[73] [1996] C.L.C. 252.
[74] [1992] 4 All E.R. 700, 761, per Knox J.

required by the FCA, would prima facie be acting unacceptably and so be at risk of being found to have acted dishonestly or unconscionably, as appropriate.

This approach in *Cowan de Groot v Eagle Trust* has been approved in a number of more recent cases.[75] So, where an investment advisor procured investments for beneficiaries in a market—here, a short-lived market in insurance and reinsurance losses—which was considered always to have been unsustainable by financial regulators, that advisor would have been a dishonest assistant in a breach of trust due to the level of risk involved.[76] The regulator found that the risk management procedures across the investment advising firm were "well below what would have been expected" from professional advisors in that general marketplace.[77]

26–27

It will also be important to consider the comparative expertise of the advisor and the person who was the victim of the breach of trust, in line with FCA regulation, which requires that such a measurement of the client's expertise be carried out. Where the client is inexpert and the advisor encourages the taking of a risk which is incommensurate with that client's level of expertise, then a finding of dishonest assistance is all the more likely.[78] So, where an investment advisor advised complex investments in real property in the UK through offshore companies, when the client had originally wished only to acquire accommodation for a child who was to study in the UK, and where that client had expertise only in running a successful business selling pottery but not in financial investments, then these factors would support a finding of dishonesty because selling those investments to that client was contrary to the appropriate regulatory codes of conduct.[79]

26–28

B.   Dissonances between substantive law and financial regulation

In *Polly Peck v Nadir (No.2)* Scott L.J. found that from the perspective of the honest and reasonable banker, there was nothing about the transaction which required that the defendant should have been taken to know about the breach of trust. In common with the decision of Millett J. in *Macmillan v Bishopsgate*,[80] it was found that there was no obligation on bankers to conduct inquiries into the source of payments. In the memorable phrase of Millett J., "account officers are not detectives" and therefore do not have any obligation to make inquiries as to the source of the property which their bank received. It is suggested below[81] that banking and money laundering regulation do impose positive obligations on bankers to inquire into the source of suspicious payments. Consequently, the attempt made by the courts to avoid imposing onerous obligations on financial

26–29

---

[75] *Cowan de Groot Properties Ltd v Eagle Trust Plc* [1992] 4 All E.R. 700, 761, per Knox J.; *Heinl v Jyske Bank (Gibraltar) Ltd* [1999] Lloyd's Rep. Bank 511, 535, per Colman J.; *Bank of Scotland v A Ltd* [2001] 3 All E.R. 58; *Sphere Drake Insurance Ltd v Euro International* [2003] EWHC 1636 (Comm); *Manolakaki v Constantinides* [2004] EWHC 749; *Tayeb v HSBC Plc* [2004] 4 All E.R. 1024.

[76] *Sphere Drake Insurance Ltd v Euro International Underwriting Ltd* [2003] EWHC 1636 (Comm).

[77] [2003] EWHC 1636 (Comm).

[78] *Manolakaki v Constantinides* [2004] EWHC 749.

[79] [2004] EWHC 749.

[80] [1996] 1 W.L.R. 387.

[81] See para.25–28.

practitioners is at odds with the development of banking regulation. This is an example of the dissonances which frequently emerge between substantive law and financial regulation where the former is operating on an ideology relating to the imposition of reasonable obligations and where the latter is operating on an ideology relating to the integrity of the financial system. This is the antithesis of the thesis advanced in Chapter 3 that the law of finance will tend to meld substantive law tests with the principles of financial regulation.

26–30   Money laundering[82] and similar "know your client" regulations[83] impose positive obligations on regulated entities to conduct due diligence into the sources of funds passed to them by their clients, particular in relation to new clients. As such, it would be much more difficult for financial advisors to plead ignorance not only of straightforward theft (as on the two decided cases considered thus far), but more generally of any breach of fiduciary duty by clients who are trustees or by themselves as advisors to trusts or to companies via their directors. It is suggested that English law in this sense is out of step with common market practice and out of step with the norms established by statutory financial regulation.[84]

C.   The transmission of liability to account from an individual to a corporate entity

26–31   The question is whether or not the company which employs the advisor would also be fixed with any knowledge or dishonesty of the advisor. In general terms, if the advisor were a controlling mind of the company, then that company can itself be held to have had the same mens rea as the individual advisor.[85] So, the Chief Executive Officer of a company may be its controlling mind or the managing director of a division within a large company may be part of its controlling mind, but a junior employee or a mere branch manager in a nationwide supermarket chain would not be.[86]

26–32   The controlling mind of a company is not necessarily the same person as the person who carries on the management of that company. However, it is important to consider from case-to-case and transaction-to-transaction who is the controlling mind of the company in that context. By way of example, in *El-Ajou v Dollar Land Holdings*[87] an investment manager in Geneva defrauded his client and passed his client's property to his co-conspirators. The money was then

---

[82] See generally Money Laundering Regulations 1993 (SI 1993/1933) including the appointment of a Money Laundering Reporting Officer responsible for the management of oversight in relation to money laundering by clients within each regulated person.

[83] See generally *FCA Handbook of Rules and Guidance: Business Standards—Money Laundering Sourcebook* and the *Principles for Businesses* on management and control. The focus here is on the need for an authorised person to maintain appropriate systems and controls to oversee the behaviour of clients and their traders' interactions with those clients.

[84] "Statutory" in the sense that many of these regulations are drawn from directly effective EU legislation, as considered above, or if not are created further to powers created by FSMA 2000.

[85] *Tesco Supermarkets v Nattrass* [1972] A.C. 153.

[86] [1972] A.C. 153.

[87] [1994] 2 All E.R. 685; [1994] 1 B.C.L.C. 464; [1994] B.C.C. 143.

laundered through numerous jurisdictions before the fraudsters met with the chairman of a property development company in London called "DLH". The chairman of DLH ordinarily took no part in the day-to-day management of the company, and yet he was the only employee who was responsible for bringing this stolen money into the company. The Court of Appeal held that the test for demonstrating that a company has knowledge of something is that "the controlling mind" or "the directing mind and will" of the company had knowledge of whatever has been alleged. On these facts, there were different people within DLH who acted as the directing mind and will of DLH in different contexts. In that case, it was necessary to identify the person who was the directing mind and will specifically in relation to the investment acquired from the fraudsters. On these facts, even though the chairman of the company ordinarily played no part in the day-to-day management of the company, he had been the person who had organised the investment in DLH and he had acted without any of the requisite resolutions of the board of directors in so doing. These factors suggested that the chairman was the directing mind and will in this particular context because he had assumed managerial control of this transaction. Consequently, he was held to be the controlling mind for the purposes of this transaction. Therefore, any knowledge which the chairman had about these transactions could be attributed to DLH. Therefore, DLH could be held to have had knowledge of the source of the investment because the chairman was found to have had that knowledge. The knowledge of the agent could be attributed to the company. The same principle was applied by the Privy Council in *Lebon v Aqua Salt Co Ltd*.[88]

Similarly, in the Privy Council in *Meridian Global Funds Management Asia Ltd v Securities Commission*[89] it was held that when deciding the obligation of a company which traded in securities to report that it held a given number of a particular type of share so as to comply with securities regulation, the knowledge which should be attributed to the company would be the knowledge of the people who were authorised to acquire those shares on behalf of the company. This approach is not limited to a single person or to a small group of people who run the entire organisation – which would tend to make it difficult to demonstrate knowledge in relation to a large organisation where a function like acquiring shares might be conducted at a much lower level within the company – but rather identifies knowledge in the hands of the individuals who could bind the company in those transactions. The same analysis holds in relation to the knowledge which is required to be proved in relation to a claim for unconscionable receipt. So, in *Crown Dilmun v Sutton*,[90] the controlling mind and managing director of a company learned of an opportunity to develop a football ground which he should have exploited for the benefit of that company: instead, he created a new company (the second defendant) to exploit that opportunity on his own account.

26–33

---

[88] [2009] UKPC 2, [2009] 1 BCLC 549; also applied in *Meridian Global Funds Management Asia Ltd v Securities Commission* [1995] 3 All E.R. 918, [1995] 2 B.C.L.C. 116; and in *Jafari-Fini v Skillglass Ltd* [2007] EWCA Civ 261.

[89] [1995] 3 All E.R. 918, [1995] 2 B.C.L.C. 116.

[90] [2004] 1 B.C.L.C. 468. This decision applied *Satnam Investments Ltd v Dunlop Heywood & Co Ltd* [1999] 1 B.C.L.C. 385; [1999] 3 All E.R. 652; *Criterion Properties Ltd v Stratford UK Properties Plc* [2003] 2 B.C.L.C. 129; [2003] 1 W.L.R. 218.

It was held that the knowledge of the director would be transferred to the second defendant because the director was the controlling mind of the second defendant also. Therefore, the receipt of profits from the development of the football ground which passed through the second defendant's bank accounts led to the second defendant being liable for knowing receipt of those profits (further to the constructive trust imposed over those personal profits further to *Boardman v Phipps*).[91] It has even been held that where information comes to the attention of one director of a company, that may be treated as knowledge held by the company even if that director did not inform other board directors of the facts.[92] To be able to fix the company with liability has the advantage of providing a defendant which is more likely to be able to make good the beneficiaries' loss than an individual employee.[93]

5. TRACING ACTIONS

26–34   The principal discussion of tracing actions in this book is set out in Chapter 23. This section serves as a very brief summary of the key principles. The personal liability of the trustees is the primary liability in the event of a breach of trust. The obligation on the trustee to recover the property, if any, which was passed away in breach of trust—referred to as "specific restitution"—is part of that primary liability. However, frequently that obligation of specific restitution will be impossible to perform if the original property cannot be recovered or if it has been mixed with other property. In this context a tracing action will be required. Common law tracing will permit the recovery of "clean substitutions" for the original property—that is, substitute property (such as profits earned from the investment of the original property) provided that the target property has not been mixed with any other property.[94] If the target property has been mixed with some other property, then tracing is only possible in equity. Equitable tracing requires a pre-existing equitable interest in the original property.[95] The remedies available in relation to equitable tracing over a mixture of property range between a constructive trust, an equitable lien, and an equitable charge. The defences range between change of position, estoppel by representation, and bona fide purchase for value without notice of the other party's rights.

---

[91] [1967] 2 A.C. 46.

[92] *Jafari-Fini v Skillglass Ltd* [2007] EWCA Civ 261.

[93] An employee will also be personally liable for any fraud which she commits in the course of her employment, over and above any liability attaching to her employer: *Standard Chartered Bank v Pakistan National Shipping Corp* [2003] 1 A.C. 959.

[94] *FC Jones v Jones* [1997] Ch. 159.

[95] *Westdeutsche Landesbank v Islington* [1996] A.C. 669.

6. CONSTRUCTIVE TRUSTS FOR MISFEASANCE IN A FIDUCIARY OFFICE

A. The liability of fiduciary for earning unauthorised profits from her fiduciary office

The basis of liability

A fiduciary who takes unauthorised profits from her fiduciary office will be required to hold those profits on constructive trust for the beneficiaries of her fiduciary office from the moment of their receipt.[96] This principle is predicated on the need to prevent fiduciaries from permitting any conflict between their personal interests and their fiduciary offices. As Lord Cohen held in *Boardman v Phipps*: "an agent is, in my opinion, liable to account for profits which he makes out of the trust property if there is a possibility of conflict between his interest and his duty to his principal".[97]

26–35

This rule is best illustrated by the decision of the House of Lords in *Boardman v Phipps*.[98] Boardman was solicitor to a trust and while on trust business he acquired confidential information as to an investment opportunity in a private company in which the trust held shares. Boardman invested personally in the company and took control of it before making it profitable, to the financial benefit of the beneficiaries. A majority of the House of Lords held that Boardman should hold his personal profits on constructive trust for the beneficiaries of the trust in a strict application of the rule in *Keech v Sandford*,[99] even though he had not used trust money to acquire these shares for himself and even though the trust had not suffered a direct loss.[100] The House of Lords was unanimous as to the significance of the principle that fiduciaries should not be permitted even the possibility of conflict of interest in such circumstances. A minority of the House of Lords approved the principle, although they wanted to absolve Boardman from liability on the basis that he had not acted in bad faith on the particular facts of that case.

26–36

Thus, a fiduciary will be constructive trustee of any unauthorised profits made from her office, even where the fiduciary has acted in good faith.[101] The rule is a strict rule that no profit can be made by a trustee or fiduciary which is not authorised by the terms of the office. A fiduciary who profits from that office will be required to account for those profits. The rule emerges from the old case of

26–37

---

[96] *Boardman v Phipps* [1967] 2 A.C. 67. See A. Hudson, *Equity & Trusts*, s.12.5.

[97] Some of their lordships held that the trust was founded on this proprietary nexus between the information and the profit, rather than simply finding that the status of fiduciary required property to be held on trust. Perhaps this indicates the role of the law on constructive trusts as being a part of property law rather than a law of personal obligations.

[98] [1967] 2 A.C. 67.

[99] (1726) 2 Eq. Cas. Abr. 741.

[100] By "direct loss" is meant that the trust was not out-of-pocket as a result of the transaction although the trust would clearly have generated more profit if the shares had been bought for the trust; that is, an opportunity lost rather than a direct, out-of-pocket loss.

[101] *Boardman v Phipps* [1967] 2 A.C. 67.

Keech v Sandford[102] in which it was held that a trustee who renewed a lease personally to protect the interest of an infant beneficiary was required to hold his interest under that lease on trust for the child. While there had been no allegation of fraud in that case, the Lord Chancellor considered that the rule should be "strictly pursued" because there were risks of fraud in allowing trustee's to take the benefit of renewed leases which they had previously held on trust.[103]

Authorisation for the profits

26–38   The defendant may avoid liability under *Boardman v Phipps* if she can demonstrate that she had authorisation for the profits being made. Authorisation could clearly be provided by express provision in the document creating her fiduciary office. Alternatively, authorisation could be inferred from the circumstances. So, in *Queensland Mines v Hudson*[104] where the defendant managing director of the plaintiff company profitably exploited some mining contracts on his own account, having first acquired the agreement of the board of directors of that company once the board had made an informed decision not to exploit those contracts on the company's own account, it was held that the decision to repudiate the contracts by the company entitled the director to pursue them on his own account without there being any conflict with his fiduciary responsibility to the company.

26–39   This decision appears exceptional when compared to the stringency of the decisions in two different Houses of Lords in *Boardman v Phipps* and in *Regal v Gulliver*.[105] So, in *Industrial Development Consultants Ltd v Cooley*[106] a managing director was offered a contract by a third party. The offer was made expressly on the basis that the third party would deal only with the managing director but not with his employer. Without disclosing this fact to his employer, the managing director left his employment and entered into a contract with the third party within a week, having led his employer to believe that he was retiring on grounds of ill-health. It was held that the managing director owed fiduciary duties to his employer throughout. He was therefore required to disclose all information to the company and to account for the profits he made under the contract on constructive trust principles.

26–40   Similarly, in *Regal v Gulliver*[107] it was held that where four directors of the plaintiff company subscribed for shares in a subsidiary company, which the board of directors had intended to be acquired by the plaintiff company itself, the directors' profits on these shares were profits made from their offices as directors. Therefore, they were required to account for them to the company. This decision illustrates the court's suspicion that this opportunity could have been exploited on behalf of the company rather than on behalf of the directors personally and, further, that fiduciaries cannot authorise one another to profit from their fiduciary

---

[102] (1726) 2 Eq. Cas. Abr. 741.
[103] See also *Re Biss* [1903] 2 Ch. 40
[104] (1977) 18 A.L.R.1.
[105] [1942] 1 All E.R. 378.
[106] [1972] 2 All E.R. 162.
[107] [1942] 1 All E.R. 378.

office. What emerges from this case is the unacceptability of fiduciaries purporting to grant each other authorisation to earn personal profits. In relation specifically to company directors, s.175(1) of the Companies Act 2006 provides that a "director of a company must avoid a situation in which he has, or can have, a direct or indirect interest that conflicts, or possibly may conflict, with the interests of the company." Taking profits from such a conflict of interest will lead to those profits being held on constructive trust, as in *Regal v Gulliver*. In the event that there is such a conflict, then the director can acquire authorisation in accordance with s.175(5) by agreement of the directors (provided, the case of public companies, that the company's constitution permits the directors to do so). Section 170 provides that the interpretation and development of this provision is to incorporate and move with developments in the case law principles outlined above.

The nature of the remedy

The profit taken by a fiduciary from any conflict of interest will be held on proprietary constructive trust for the trust by the fiduciary.[108] Consequently, anything acquired with those profits is similarly held on constructive trust. The beneficiaries of this constructive trust would be entitled to trace this property into any fund of property acquired in part with these profits.[109] If no property is left, then the fiduciary will be personally liable for an amount equal to those profits.[110]

26–41

The self-dealing principle

The determination to prevent fiduciaries benefiting from any conflict of interest is written into a large amount of the law relating to fiduciaries dealing with trust property. Thus, the self-dealing principle entitles the beneficiary to avoid any transaction in which the fiduciary is dealing with the beneficiaries of their power purportedly at arm's length on the fiduciary's own account. As before, this principle is based on the rule in *Keech v Sandford*[111] that even the possibility of fraud or bad faith being exercised by the trustee is to be resisted.[112] Megarry V.C. in *Tito v Waddell (No.2)*[113] enunciated the self-dealing principle in the following terms:

26–42

"if a trustee purchases trust property from himself, any beneficiary may have the sale set aside *ex debito justitiae*, however fair the transaction".

The right of the beneficiary is therefore to set aside the transaction. The same principle applies to purchases by directors from their companies[114] although most articles of association in English companies expressly permit such transactions.

---

[108] *Boardman v Phipps* [1967] 2 A.C. 67.

[109] [1967] 2 A.C. 67.

[110] *Sinclair Investments Holidays SA v Versailles Trade Finance Ltd (No.3)* [2007] EWHC 915; *CMS Dolphin Ltd v Simonet* [2001] 2 B.C.L.C. 704.

[111] (1726) 2 Eq. Cas. Abr. 741.

[112] *Ex p. Lacey* (1802) 6 Ves. 625.

[113] [1977] Ch. 106. cf. *Prince Jefri Bolkiah v KPMG* [1999] 1 All E.R. 517—with reference to "Chinese walls".

[114] *Aberdeen Railway Co v Blaikie Brothers* (1854) 1 Macq. 461.

Where the beneficiary acquiesces in the transaction, then that beneficiary is precluded from seeking to have that transaction set aside.[115]

26–43   The only advisable course of action for a fiduciary wishing to enter into such a transaction would be to acquire the leave of the court in advance of the transaction to acquire those interests. The court will require the fiduciary to demonstrate that the transaction is in the interests of the beneficiaries and that the fiduciary will not take any unconscionable advantage from the transaction.[116] Unsurprisingly, the fiduciary will not be able to avoid this principle simply by selling to an associate or a connected company or similar person—although the authorities on this point relate primarily to sales to relatives,[117] the trustee's children[118] and the trustee's spouse.[119] It is suggested that in any event such a transaction would be a sham transaction and therefore capable of set aside in any event[120] or treated as an attempt to effect a fraud on the power.[121]

The fair-dealing principle

26–44   The fair-dealing principle is similar to the self-dealing principle considered immediately above. The fair-dealing principle may validate acquisitions by fiduciaries of property held for their beneficiaries, provided that the fiduciary does not acquire any advantage in that transaction which is attributable to her fiduciary office.[122] Any unconscionably earned profits will be held on constructive trust. This principle also applies to fiduciary relationships such as acquisitions by agents of the interests of their principals.[123] To demonstrate that the transaction was not procured as a result of any abuse of position the fiduciary will be required to demonstrate that no details were concealed, that the price obtained was fair and that the beneficiary was not required to rely entirely on the fiduciary's advice.[124] The fair dealing principle is necessarily less strict than the self-dealing principle because the trustee is able to seek justification of the former by demonstrating that the transaction was not procured in bad faith.

B.   Market makers and conflicts of interest

26–45   The position of market makers in relation to the preceding discussion of conflicts of interest requires some careful thought. From the preceding discussion it is clear that if a fiduciary earns unauthorised profits from her fiduciary office then those profits will be held on constructive trust, and the same will be the case if the fiduciary purports to transact with the beneficiaries at arm's length on his own

---

[115] *Holder v Holder* [1968] Ch. 353.

[116] *Campbell v Walker* (1800) 5 Ves. 678; *Farmer v Dean* (1863) 32 Beav. 327.

[117] *Coles v Trecothick* (1804) 9 Ves. 234—which may be permitted where the transaction appears to be conducted as though at arm's length.

[118] *Gregory v Gregory* (1821) Jac. 631.

[119] *Ferraby v Hobson* (1847) 2 P.H. 255, *Burrell v Burrell's Trustee* 1915 SC 333.

[120] *Street v Mountford* [1985] 2 W.L.R. 877; *Midland Bank v Wyatt* [1995] 1 F.L.R. 697

[121] *Rochefoucauld v Boustead* [1897] 1 Ch. 196.

[122] *Chalmer v Bradley* (1819) 1 J. & W. 51; *Tito v Waddell (No.2)* [1977] Ch. 106.

[123] *Edwards v Meyrick* [1842] 2 Hare 60.

[124] *Coles v Bradley* (1804) 9 Ves. 234.

account. This aspect of fiduciary law developed before market practice in the securities markets moved towards market-making. The term "market maker" is defined in one dictionary of market terms[125] to mean:

> "A dealer firm that maintains a firm bid and offer price in a given security by standing ready to buy or sell at publicly quoted prices."

Therefore, a market maker is someone who publishes prices at which they will buy and sell securities (thus making a market in those securities) on that regulated market. A market maker does not simply take orders from customers and then fulfil those customers' orders by acquiring securities according to their instructions in the open market from third parties. Instead a market maker often sells securities which she already owns, or in which she has already established a short position. This is important. A market maker already owns the securities which are being sold to its clients, and therefore there is clearly a risk of a conflict of interest if the market maker is seeking to sell off stock which it already owns (as opposed simply to fulfilling orders which those same clients have decided to buy without the market maker's advice), because the market maker clearly has a vested interest in selling off the securities it already holds, as opposed to advising the acquisition of the best available investments in the best interests of the customer.

If that market maker is acting as a fiduciary then the following problem arises. If the fiduciary seeks to sell securities which the fiduciary already owns, then that fiduciary will have a conflict of interest because it would be trying to earn profits from its beneficiaries from its existing stock. If the advisor gave independent advice without seeking to sell its own stock to the beneficiaries, then this particular conflict of interest would not arise. Under the fair dealing principle, the fiduciary would be able to justify her actions if she had sold the securities at a fair price. What would be difficult to justify would be selling one specific type of security to customers which was owned by the fiduciary market maker, when there were other securities which the customer could have acquired which would have been preferable for the customer's risk profile. If the fiduciary makes a personal profit from the transaction—which would of course be the purpose of the transaction—then those profits would be held on constructive trust as discussed immediately above.

26–46

7. ELECTION BETWEEN REMEDIES

There is a difficulty of election between remedies.[126] To what extent can a claim for recovery of property be considered to be separate from the contractual claim in connection with which it arises? In valuing the appropriate restitution, is it possible to reach a valuation without reference to the underlying contract? The

26–47

---

[125] Downes and Goodman, *Barron's Dictionary of Finance and Investment Terms*, 7th edn (Barron's Educational Series, 2006).
[126] *Burrows* [1995] C.L.P. 103, 112–113; *Stevens* [1996] R.L.R. 117, 121—Election between alternative remedies.

conclusion to be drawn from *Tang v Capacious Investments*[127] is that where a plaintiff is required to choose between alternative remedies, he must make such election at the time when judgement is awarded in his favour. The plaintiff is not to be deemed to have made such an election simply by dint of accepting payment as restitution, unless he was in full cognisance of the options open to him.

---

[127] [1996] 1 A.C. 514; [1996] R.L.R. 11.

SECTION 2

SPECIFIC FINANCIAL TECHNIQUES

PART VIII

BANKING

Section Two: Specific Financial Techniques is the second half of this book. It relates to the particular *contexts* in which the substantive law *concepts* considered in *Section One: General Principles*.

The specific financial techniques discussed in this Part VIII build on the foundational legal concepts considered in Pts I through VII of this book by applying to the specific context of banking. In this context, banking refers to deposit-taking, the operation of bank accounts, the operation of payment systems, and the regulation of those activities. Chapter 27 outlines the fundamentals of banking law, its history, and explains how this Part VIII differs from the remainder of the financial techniques considered in this second half of the book. Chapter 28 then analyses prudential banking regulation (as distinct from the regulation of investment services, and as distinct from conduct of business regulation) from the international regulatory standards through to the UK regulations. The coverage of UK regulation includes prudential issues as to the solvency of banks and the Banking Act 2009 code relating to failed banks. Chapter 29 considers the centuries-old case law dealing with the banker-customer relationship outwith the regulatory context which forms the core of traditional banking law. Chapter 30 considers the banking payment systems across the full gamut from retail to commercial contexts. Chapter 31 then focuses specifically on the law relating specifically to retail banking. This chapter pays particular attention to the Banking Conduct of Business Sourcebook ("BCOBS") which governs banks' treatment of customers and is overseen by the Financial Conduct Authority. Too much finance law commentary concentrates on corporate finance, but Chapter 31 acts a central point which collects together the various sources of law dealing specifically with personal banking.

CHAPTER 27

FUNDAMENTALS OF BANKING LAW

CORE PRINCIPLES

Part VIII is concerned with what might be termed "traditional banking law", that is taking deposits, making payments and operating bank accounts. The discussion in this Part VIII divides between a survey of the regulation of banking business, the private law dealing with the relationship between banker and customer (including the maintenance of accounts), the various methods by which payments are made in banking transactions, and an account of the global banking crisis of 2008 together with its likely effects on banking business in the future.

1. THE SCOPE OF THIS PART VIII

A. The focus on "traditional banking"

This Part VIII of this book considers banking law in detail. By "banking law" is meant the law relating to the traditional activities of taking deposits, operating accounts and making payments. These are the traditional activities of banks, as opposed to investment firms, stockbrokers and so forth. Bankers ordinarily operate bank accounts, accept deposits into those bank accounts, deal with payments into and out of those accounts, and latterly have begun to provide services connected to those core activities, including the operation of electronic payment systems, the issue and operation of payment cards (whether credit cards, debit cards, charge cards, and so on), and the settlement of cheques. The definition of a bank for the purposes of EU law is "an undertaking whose business is to receive deposits or other repayable funds from the public and to grant credits for its own account" or "an electronic money institution".[1] This does

27–01

---

[1] Banking Directive 2006/48/EC, art.4.

not include investment activity, securities trading and so forth. So, the sense in which "banking" is being discussed in this Part VIII of this book is limited to traditional banking activities relating to accounts and payments. The electronic conduct of much banking business today has caused a sea-change in the activities of banks. Much of ordinary bank business involves receiving deposits from customers with one hand and then looking to lend that money out to other customers at a higher rate of interest. This approach to banking, which is solid and prudent, is much too simplified to explain the range of modern banking practice. Lending activities (including syndicated lending and bond issues) are considered in Part IX.

B.   The business of banking

27–02   Banking, even international banking, has been in existence for longer than we often care to remember. The first cross-border banking institution in the Western world appears to have been that run by the Knights Templar who were a religious order founded in 1118 and who helped to fund crusades, who exchanged money, who acted effectively as bankers to the Pope, and who even provided mortgages.[2] The Templars themselves took a vow of poverty and so used the riches which they had amassed solely for the purposes of the Order.[3] It is thought that the Italians formed the first institutions which we might now recognise as being banks.[4] Monte dei Paschi di Siena claims to be the world's oldest bank, founded in Siena, Italy in 1472. Those Italian bankers were said to have sat on benches at long tables to do their business, and the Italian word for bench, "banco", is said to have given rise to the English word "bank", the French word "banque" and (of course) the Italian "banco".[5] Much of the early exchange activity in the 17th century was centred on Amsterdam due to the advanced flows of credit and other information which the Dutch circulated at that time.

27–03   The activity of banking in London was divided between "merchant bankers" who dealt mainly in bills and other papers which acknowledged receipt of goods and finance provided to facilitate trade, and commercial banks.[6] In a trading city organised around a very busy riverside, London's principal need for financing was to give credit to purchasers of goods and to provide bills which enabled merchants to cover the cost of putting boats full of goods out to sea before those goods could be sold. These banks were known as "merchant banks" because many of the financiers who extended credit to other people were themselves merchants. Most of the early banking houses were run by wealthy individuals who came to know their depositors personally: such as Rothschild, Samuel

---

[2] See J. Weatherford, *The History of Money* (Three Rivers Press, 1997), p.64.
[3] There were tradable contracts in place even before this whereby Babylonian kings would provide mercenary soldiers and slaves on demand to whoever held those contracts: this is something which is akin to trading in derivatives: A. Hudson, *The Law of Financial Derivatives*, 4th edn (London: Sweet & Maxwell, 2006), p.12.
[4] See, for example, the very readable Valdez, *An Introduction to Global Financial Markets*, 5th edn (Palgrave Macmillan, 2007), p.15.
[5] S. Valdez, *An Introduction to Global Financial Markets*, p.15.
[6] See M. Holden, *The Law and Practice of Banking, Vol.1: Banker and Customer*, 2nd edn (Pitman, 1976), p.6.

Montagu and so on in London, and JP Morgan, Rockefeller and so on in New York. Having a bank account was once very rare because few people had the sort of disposable wealth which needed to be lodged with a bank as opposed to being measured in heirlooms and land or kept in a strongbox.[7] Therefore, early banking was built on individual customers trusting the individual who was acting as their banker, and the banker trusting the individual who wanted to write cheques and so forth. Today, banking is a mass market activity and banks seek to sell many more products (nominally through subsidiaries trading through the same premises) to ordinary citizens. Much of banking law has its roots in the practices of the old-fashioned banking system and therefore it is important to understand this context to understand the shape of those rules. Many of the 20th century cases were decided shortly after the Edwardian period when banking was still a comparatively exclusive activity.

The traditional business of banking is well described by the fictional character Mr Holder in the Sherlock Holmes story "The Beryl Coronet" when explaining the nature of his firm's business to Sherlock Holmes at 221B Baker Street[8]:

27–04

> "It is of course well known to you that in a successful banking business as much depends upon our being able to find remunerative investments for our funds, as upon our increasing our connection and the number of our depositors. One of our most lucrative means of laying out money is in the shape of loans, where the security is unimpeachable. We have done a good deal in this direction during the last few years, and there are many noble families to whom we have advanced large sums upon the security of their pictures, libraries, or plate."

So, a banker traditionally earned money by lending money to dependable people in return for satisfactory security and by charging them interest. Latterly, they also operated bank accounts for their customers by holding deposits, paying and collecting on cheques, and so forth. What is remarkable to the modern mind about Mr Holder's (fictional but credible) business, in Conan Doyle's story, is that he took possession of a very valuable coronet as security for a large loan and then, rather than leave the coronet in a heavily-guarded bank vault, took the coronet home and placed it in an insecure bureau in his bedroom from which it was stolen that same night. (Hence his need to consult Sherlock Holmes.) In 1892 when this story was written the business of banking was clearly both to take deposits and operate accounts (for which fees could be charged) and also to invest those deposits at a better rate of return than the interest which was paid to the depositor. The investments which a bank made were, inter alia, the loans which were made to its clients. The sort of security which was taken for this sort of loan, as discussed in Chapter 22, is reckoned to be rights in chattels, although it is not clear whether that is in the form of charges, trusts or liens. These sorts of chattels would have been heirlooms, with the "plate" being the valuable chinaware, silverware and so on which would have been passed down through a wealthy family. Two things are worthy of note. First, families at that time were much less likely to buy new chattels of this sort when they had valuable heirlooms, unlike

---

[7] Even in the 1970s, only half of the population in the UK had a bank account.

[8] A. Conan Doyle, "The Beryl Coronet", in *The Adventures of Sherlock Holmes*, first published in 1892 (now available in *The Adventures of Sherlock Holmes* (Penguin, 1991) at p.236; or *The New Annotated Sherlock Holmes*, Vol.1, L. Klinger (ed.), at p.322).

our modern obsession with shopping. Secondly, this sort of security is unsophisticated and therefore very unlike the complex financial models of collateralisation (considered in Chapter 42) which are part of modern financial markets. There is also something quaintly unprofessional to modern eyes about a senior partner in a banking firm like Holder taking a hansom cab home to Streatham, clutching a valuable coronet which is the only security for an enormous loan, and then "locking" it in a bureau which even casual acquaintances knew could be opened "by any key".

This form of banking is in essence the same as modern banking: money is deposited or lent for security with market value sufficient to cover the bank's exposure. What is different is the entire architecture of risk management mathematics, of detailed documentation of transactions, of agonising over the terms on which security is provided, of questioning the purpose for which the loan is to be used, of making funds available electronically, of compliance with money laundering and other regulation, and so forth. Banking has become more professionalised as a result, although the scope for catastrophic strategic errors and loss remains as became evident in the banking crisis of 2008.[9]

2. THE LIMITS OF "BANKING BUSINESS"

27–05   The term "banking business" or "banking" used in this book is restricted to the traditional activity of taking deposits from customers, making loans, operating accounts and so forth. It does not include giving investment advice, investing in securities and so forth. These activities are regulated separately by the Bank of England and so are treated differently in this book.[10] References to "banking law" are therefore references to the law relating to those forms of traditional banking business and not references to all of the investment and other activities in which banks of various types may become involved. The form of banking which is at issue here was defined in the following terms by Dr H.L. Hart when defining what constitutes a person as being a banker, that is[11]:

> "a person or company carrying on the business of receiving moneys, and collecting drafts, for customers subject to the obligation of honouring cheques drawn upon them from time to time by the customers to the extent of the amounts available on their current accounts."

Therefore, this Part VIII is limited to a narrow compass of banking activities; whereas later parts of this book consider other aspects of financial services activities beyond ordinary banking.

---

[9] See 57–01.

[10] At the time of writing, the financial regulations in the UK were contained in the Financial Services Authority rulebooks and guidance notes referred to collectively as the "*FSA Handbook*". As explained in Ch.8, the Financial Conduct Authority ("FCA") will create the *FCA Handbook* and the Prudential Regulatory Authority ("PRA") will create the *PRA Handbook*, both of which will come into effect from April Fool's Day 2013.

[11] H. Hart, *The Law of Banking*, 4th edn (1931), p.1. See also *Re District Savings Bank Ltd* (1861) 31 L.J. Bank 8; *Halifax Union v Wheelwright* (1875) L.R. 10 Ex. 183, at 193; *Re Birkbeck Permanent Benefit Building Society* [1912] 2 Ch. 183.

3. BANKING REGULATION

Chapter 28 considers "Banking Regulation". There are three tiers of banking **27–06** regulation. The first tier of banking regulatory principle is formulated at the international level, generally by means of the Bank of International Settlements and the creation of the Basel II regime, which is giving way to the Basel III regime. This international regulatory initiative is intended to shape the principles on which national regulation will be formulated and enforced. The second tier is compromised of the various banking directives effected by the European Union, as considered in Chapter 28. The third tier, as considered in Chapter 28, is UK regulation which implements the EU legislation and which, at the time of writing, has being comprised of an uncomfortable straddling of the roles of the Treasury and the various subsidiary entities of the Bank of England. The tri-partite division of banking regulation in the UK had the predictable effect that no single regulator has been able to take a hold of the market and to ensure that bank's business models were suitable in the light of the banking crisis of 2008. Of particular importance in Chapter 28 is the Banking Act 2009 which was introduced to provide for the special resolution regime effecting the takeover of failing banks, the insolvency of banks, bank administration, and related compensation schemes.

4. THE RELATIONSHIP OF BANKER AND CUSTOMER

Chapter 29 considers the private law governing the relationship between banker **27–07** and customer. Ordinarily, a banker will not owe fiduciary duties to her customer. However, there may be situations in which the bank has assumed a position of trust and confidence which would require the inference of a fiduciary relationship, or alternatively where a banker has failed to conduct its business with that customer suitably and so has rendered itself a fiduciary in any event. The ordinary business of banker and customer will, however, be governed by the law of contract. One particularly important aspect of the private law of banking relates to the fees which banks charge to their clients. Rather than banks being allowed to charge any fees which are recorded in their contracts, there are a number of rules of contract law which prevent banks from contracting for whatever they want. The use of standard contractual terms by banks means that ordinary customers arc at a disadvantage and are forced to sign up to whatever terms are put in front of them. Consequently, provisions purporting to allow banks to charge unfairly high fees will be unenforceable. Similarly, the consumer credit legislation will refuse to enforce unconscionable credit bargains. Therefore, private law will set aside inappropriate transactions on these grounds, or as discussed in Chapter 18 (in relation to the validity of contracts) and Chapter 24 (in relation to undue influence in the creation of contracts); and financial regulation also requires that business is conducted in a suitable manner, as discussed in Chapter 10.

Aside from private law questions of breach of contract or tort, there are also a **27–08** number of obligations owed by banks under the regulatory structure, as outlined above. So, money laundering regulation requires that banks make disclosure to the authorities of a variety of types of transaction which the bank may consider may be suspicious: the ugly syntax of that phrase is deliberate because the regulations are so widely drawn that bankers are likely to over-report transactions so as to protect themselves against the possibility that their clients' activities may transpire to have been illegal.

5.   BANK PAYMENTS

27–09   Chapter 30 considers "Bank payments". That chapter traces the species of bank payments which are possible in modern banking practice from traditional payment mechanisms such as payment by cheque, payment by means of letters of credit and by bills of exchange, through payments by means of payment card, funds transfers made in documentary form or electronically, through to e-money used on the internet. Much of that discussion is concerned with the commercial bases on which these different payment mechanisms have developed, but they create a number of legal issues and have generated a long case law over the centuries.

CHAPTER 28

BANKING REGULATION

CORE PRINCIPLES

Banking regulation in the EU is built on principles created under the umbrella of international organisations which bring together the regulators and central bankers of the world. The most significant set of principles are those set out in the "Basel II Accord", which was updated in November 2005, and the Basel III Accord which is due to replace it (once implemented in the EU in 2013). The Basel II Accord divides its focus between three "pillars": requirements for regulatory capital; supervisory review; and market disclosure. The basic principle is that banks should be required to set aside amounts of capital appropriate to the risks which they are taking in different market sectors: the idea is that if the bank were to fail then the capital which had been set aside would help to meet the cost of that failure.

The first, regulatory capital pillar identifies three key risks (although others are also addressed): credit risk, liquidity risk, and operational risk. The credit risk approach updated requirements for banks to set aside sufficient capital to guard against bank failures in accordance with new risk measurement models. (This approach clearly failed in the banking crisis of 2007–09.) A part of the problem was that risk valuation models did not accommodate the risk of a systemic market failure nor of individual firms mispricing their risks. The second pillar gave regulators greater powers to supervise banks. The third pillar urged transparency on banks in that banks were required to make more information publicly available than hitherto.

The EU regulation of banking practice is provided by means of a range of directives which implement those international models: currently EU law in this area is contained in the Second Consolidated Banking Directive 2006 and the Capital Adequacy Directive 2006. At the time of writing, these directives are due to be replaced by a new banking regulation which will introduce the Basel III methodology for bank capital and which is intended to regulate the size of bankers' bonuses so as to remove the incentive for individual traders to seek personal profit over common sense.

The UK regulation of banks has been collected into the Bank of England (through the Financial Conduct Authority, the Prudential Regulatory Authority and the Financial Policy Committee) and the Treasury, with each having had responsibility for the regulation of different aspects of banking, as was discussed in Chapter 8. The effect of the financial crisis has been a need to consolidate responsibility for banking regulation, but coupled with a need for banking regulation to be more aggressive in its control of systemic and other risks.

The Banking Act 2009 was passed to deal with bank failure and to grant powers to the regulatory authorities to organise the sale of a failed bank to a private sector purchaser, or to organise the break-up of a failed bank, or to nationalise a failed bank. The Act also deals with bank insolvency.

The Independent Commission on Banking, chaired by Vickers, suggested that retail banks need to be "ring-fenced" off from the investment bank operations of banking groups. The Financial Services (Banking Reform) Bill 2013 has laid the foundations for that proposal. However, neither of these documents explains what a "ring-fence" would actually be in legal terms.

1. INTRODUCTION

This chapter considers the regulation of banking. In this context, "banking" refers to deposit-taking and account management businesses operated by corporations which are recognised as being "banks" in English law, or "credit institutions" as they are referred to in the EU law parlance.[1] The definition of a "credit institution" in the Banking Directive is "an undertaking whose business is to receive deposits or other repayable funds from the public and to grant credits for its own account" or "an electronic money institution".[2] However, much of the policy context for banking regulation begins with international organisations creating regulatory initiatives such as "Basel II", considered below, and the initiative which is to replace it, "Basel III". The most successful international regulatory initiative has been that created by the EU in that its directives have legal effect within the member states of the EU and are either implemented by domestic legislation (as in the UK) or are simply directly effective (as in the Netherlands) in those states' domestic legal systems. The basis of the UK's banking regulation is thus set out by EU directives, as considered below. Those directives have been implemented into UK banking law and, together with other UK regulatory rules, constitute UK banking regulation. At the time of writing, a new banking regulation has been promulgated in the EU which aims to upgrade the regulatory scheme to comply with the Basel III initiative (considered below), to control "bankers' bonuses", and so forth. The bulk of this chapter will focus on the roots of banking regulation policy at the international level, the transmission of those international principles into EU law, and the regulation of banking in the UK. However, before coming to the UK context, this chapter will pass first through the international context of banking regulation and then the applicable EUC banking directives. Our discussion therefore begins with a consideration of international banking initiatives.

28–01

---

[1] In that sense, "banking" is different from "investment business", as was discussed in Ch.8.
[2] Banking Directive 2006/48/EC, art.4.

2.   International Regulatory Initiatives

A.   The context of international regulatory initiatives

28–02   The regulation of banking business in a perfect world (which this is not) would begin with enforceable regulation at the international level. The principal lesson from the financial crisis 2007–09 was that the regulation of international banking businesses requires international co-operation and co-ordinated international policies. In a perfect world with international regulation, those regulations would then filter down to the national level where regulators for particular jurisdictions would look to the protection of their own financial systems but in the context of a broadly supportive network of national regulators working harmoniously together so as to regulate cross-border banking activity effectively. There are, in fact, a number of international initiatives which are intended to shape regulatory policies across different jurisdictions. Of particular importance in the banking regulatory world is the "Basel II Accord", which is discussed immediately below, which was the product of many years of negotiation between the banking supervisory authorities making up the Committee on Banking Supervision (which has its Secretariat housed at the Bank for International Settlements ("BIS") in Switzerland). The Committee on Banking Supervision is comprised of the Group of Ten[3] and seeks to create a suitable framework for banking regulation which can be replicated around the world. The Basel Committee was established in 1975 by the central banks of the Group of Ten leading economies ("G-10") in an attempt to co-ordinate the financial sectors of those economies in the hope ultimately of preventing a systemic banking collapse. The Committee seeks to create a suitable framework for banking regulation which can be replicated around the world. It is expected that the members of the Group of Ten will adopt the terms of its accords into their own legal codes. The Basel II Accord is not in itself enforceable law but rather creates a context within which banking regulation in different jurisdictions can work collaboratively and, importantly, it provides the underlying principles for all banking regulation. That Accord has been replaced by the "Basel III Accord" which, at the time of writing, had yet to be incorporated into the EU banking law firmament.

28–03   International regulatory initiatives are "soft law". That means that they have no direct legal enforceability in themselves, although they inform legally enforceable regulatory rules and practices from jurisdiction to jurisdiction such as the EC Capital Adequacy Directive. Nevertheless, these initiatives are not strictly "law" in themselves because no court nor any other regulatory agency will enforce them directly. A large amount of the world's trade will, it is supposed, be effected in the shadow of a number of regulatory initiatives such as the World Trade Organisation's many rounds of talks aimed at creating rules for the regulation of international trade and to ensure (so far as is possible) open competition between trading nations around the world. There are other international initiatives, of course, under the auspices of the United Nations and similar bodies concerned

---

[3] Comprising regulators from bank supervisory authorities and central bankers from Belgium, Canada, France, Germany, Italy, Japan, Luxembourg, the Netherlands, Spain, Sweden, Switzerland, the UK, and the US. This group is oddly made up now of more than ten members.

with international security, the eradication of poverty, climate change, and so forth. Similarly, in the arena of financial regulation, these international bodies seek to create global principles to even-out differences between jurisdictions. Their principles tend to be created after many years of exhaustive negotiation. They also tend to be compromises between the various vested interests and temporary or long-term alliances between nation states or ethnic groupings. Consequently, these initiatives are lumbering agglomerations of disconnected ideas masquerading as a solution to the world's problems. Clearly, the path of international diplomacy cannot run straight nor could we rationally expect that it would move quickly. However, as the global banking crisis showed, once an ineffective banking regulatory system has been negotiated over a number of years at the highest level, the world stands stupefied when its product does not solve all problems.

B.   The Basel II Accord

The purpose of the Basel II Accord

The Basel II Accord ("Basel II") was generated after a number of years of work by the Committee on Banking Supervision within the Bank for International Settlements ("BIS"). Basel II, which was updated in November 2005, has been adopted into the law of the EU by means of the Capital Adequacy Directive, considered below. The Accord applies to "internationally active banks" on its own terms, although a broader application of its principles is anticipated by the Committee. The purpose of the Basel II accord was to create a framework which is more risk sensitive than its predecessor "Basel I" and also more closely in accord with the risk management processes of modern banks. The aim of Basel I had been to strengthen the capital requirements imposed on banks. Basel II updates those capital requirements by using a different risk measurement approach.

28–04

The three pillars

Basel II sets out three "pillars" in the form of requirements for: regulatory capital; supervisory review; and market disclosure. Each is considered in turn in the sections to follow.

28–05

C.   The first pillar: regulatory capital

The scope of the first pillar

The first, regulatory capital pillar relates to the calculation of the risk faced by banks and the maintenance of sufficient regulatory capital to meet and offset those risks. The Accord provides that[4]:

28–06

---

[4] Basel Committee on Banking Supervision, *International Convergence of Capital Measurement and Capital Standards—a revised framework*, November 2005, ("*Basel II*"), para.4.

"The fundamental objective of the Committee's work to revise the 1988 Accord has been to develop a framework that would further strengthen the soundness and stability of the international banking system while maintaining sufficient consistency that capital adequacy regulation will not be a significant source of competitive inequality among internationally active banks."

The Committee's focus was therefore on the integrity of the financial system. The existence of the Committee is itself recognition of the fact that the financial system at issue is a *global* financial system in which "internationally active" banks deal across borders and therefore transplant risks from one jurisdiction to another and from one marketplace to another. When attempting to regulate and to manage the risks associated with the global financial system there is a need, at the very least, for an internationally coherent approach to financial risk management. The aim of the first pillar, therefore, is to identify a methodology for calculating risks. The First Pillar methodology introduces "risk sensitive capital requirements", which go beyond what was in the Basel I Accord created in 1988.

The methodology of the first pillar: credit ratings and a worked example[5]

28–07   This first pillar identifies three key risks (although others are also addressed): credit risk, liquidity risk, and operational risk. The credit risk approach updated requirements for banks to set aside sufficient capital to guard against bank failures in accordance with new risk measurement methodologies. The discussion set out in the Basel II document proceeds through a discussion of the calculation of minimum capital requirements on the basis of three sorts of credit risk: the standardised approach, the internal ratings based approach and the securitisation framework.

28–08   The formulae for calculating the amount of different types of capital required in different circumstances are set out in some detail in the Basel II document.[6] In effect, different capital weightings are given to different types of business according to the credit risk assigned to the entity in question by the credit ratings agencies. For example, let us compare two types of security and let us suppose that one security is a bond issued by an OECD country which has attracted the highest possible rating of AAA, whereas the other security is a bond issued by a public company which is rated at only B+. The Basel II system identifies a risk weight for the two types of security (i.e. the higher the risk weight, the more risky the investment) and also identifies the amount of capital which must be held to cover each £1 million of exposure to that entity's security of that type. The table, extracted from the hundreds of pages of regulations looks as follows:

---

[5] As is discussed in Ch.45, credit ratings are assigned by the ratings agencies (which include Moodys, S&P, and Fitch) to the securities of government and corporate entities, with AAA being the highest rating (in the S&P framework) stretching down the alphabet to about C, or to ungraded level. So, in the example given in the text, AAA is the highest possible rating and B+ therefore much lower.
[6] The formulae are discussed in *Basel II* from pp.12 through 162 et seq.

OECD Country bond rated AAA	0%	0
Company bond rated B+	50%	40,000

What this tells us is that for each £1 million of exposure to government bonds in countries rated AAA (i.e. an assessment that the debt of that government has only a negligible risk that that government will not make its payments), there is no need to hold capital in reserve in case of loss; whereas for each £1 million of exposure to corporate bonds rated B+ there is a requirement that £40,000 is to be held in reserve. The safe government bond is thought to carry a risk of "zero" whereas the B+ bond has a risk which is expressed as being "50%".

An exposure by a bank to an investment in an AAA rated entity will require less **28–09** regulatory capital to cover it than an investment in a B+ rated entity because a credit rating of B+ indicates a much higher level of credit risk than an AAA rated entity. Similarly, markets in financial products such as credit default swaps will be treated as being much more risky than investments in the ordinary shares of FTSE-100 public companies traded on the London Stock Exchange: therefore, more capital will be required in relation to the credit default swaps than the FTSE-100 shares. Therefore, the risk profile of a bank's business is calculated by reference to the whole of its activities in accordance with these detailed formulae.

Interestingly, however, the bank is not required to hold cash equal to the exposure **28–10** of the corporate bond, but rather only £40,000 for every £1,000,000 of exposure to those bonds. Therefore, the banks' risks are not completely covered, only partially covered. In effect, the Basel II Committee assessed the likelihood of loss on the various types of investment which are set out across the hundreds of pages of principles in Basel II: that is, they assessed the risks associated with each type of investment. They are not assuming that the entire financial system will fail. The credit ratings agencies[7] will re-grade corporate and government securities from time-to-time: so if, for example, a company fell into loss and its prospects looked bad, then the credit rating given to that company would probably fall.

Waggishly, some commentators have referred (off the record) to this sort of **28–11** regulation as being "bus timetable law" because in effect the regulators are looking up the applicable risk weighting factor for each type of business just as one might look at a bus timetable for the time of a particular service to a particular part of town. Nevertheless, just because this regulation is numerical rather than legal does not make it any the less important. What is important, as considered below, is the identification of the presumptions which underpin these mathematical models. Those capital requirements are then considered in the light of operational risk and trading book issues. There is a sense in which capital regulation of this sort is not really regulation at all. What it is, in truth, is a system of compulsory insurance in the event that financial institutions go into insolvency in the future; as opposed to regulatory oversight of the actions that those

---

[7] See para.34–13.

institutions take before they get into difficulties. A regulator should prevent, control and censure inappropriate activity, instead of simply lining up sandbags in case the floods come. The regulators would argue that they are involved in oversight by stress-testing financial institutions and assessing the capital which has been put aside on an ongoing basis; but it still feels like it is activity directed at the aftermath of a crash and not at preventing that crash in the first place.

The limited scope of the inputs to risk calculation

28–12   Importantly, these risk assessments are based on "assessments of risk provided by banks' internal systems inputs to capital calculations".[8] This means that the regulators are primarily reliant on figures provided to them by banks which are based on the banks' own assessment of the risks that they face. This assessment is qualified by the Committee setting out "detailed requirements ... to ensure the integrity" of the banks' assessment models.[9] Rather than the regulators making plain the figures they require and the basis on which they should be calculated it is for the banks to assess and identify those risks for themselves. This means that regulatory risk assessment is being carried on entirely by reference to the risks which the banks believe they face. Consequently the regulators will be unlikely to identify any other risks because the calculations are being limited to things which the banks acknowledge as being risks; but not any others, such as systemic risk. Regulation cannot be carried on by reference to things which the banks acknowledge are risks because that means the regulators cannot be genuinely independent precisely because their decisions are predominantly fettered by the banks' own views.

The principal shortcoming of slavish reliance on mathematical models

28–13   The weakness with risk management models of this sort is that they cannot predict the future accurately: rather, they can only help us to understand from time-to-time what the future might be. Such risk measurement models are entirely dependent on the issues which we choose to put in them. If we fail to build into our projections for the future the collapse of Profit Bank or a long war between one country and another, then our risk models will simply fail to predict the future accurately, no matter how sophisticated their mathematics might be. When in 1995 I asked an analyst where in his mathematical model to identify the risks associated with a ten year interest rate swap he had taken into account a future war in Iraq, he told me (after looking at me blankly for a while) both that his model would accurately predict the future for the swap because it was based on the accept future interest yield curve[10] and also that no-one in the market thought that there would not be another war in Iraq within ten years. Interest rates have changed markedly over the intervening ten years in unexpected ways because of war and financial crises; and as is well known the US military entered

---

[8] *Basel II*, para.5.
[9] *Basel II*, para.5.
[10] That is, a market measurement of where market participants expect that interest rates will either raise or fall in the future.

[846]

Iraq again in 2003. That model did not accurately predict the future. No-one could sensibly expect that it would accurately predict the future precisely because it is the unexpected which makes profits on markets possible: if there was no volatility on markets then no-one would make profits because everyone would know what would happen next and all market prices would be in perfect synch with one another. The world is just not like that. And that is the danger with using mathematical models to claim to control risk on global financial markets—and this bit is important—*if* one genuinely expects that simply running the numbers in a mathematical model can accurately predict the future. What is important in risk management is using models to help to understand the result of certain sensitivities or eventualities coming to pass. One must be brave enough in regulation to "think outside the box": that means, to countenance things which may seem unlikely or unpalatable at the time so that one can be forearmed against the possibility of them arising in the future. This issue is considered in Chapter 45.[11] This approach clearly failed in the global banking crisis of 2008 in that a number of very large banks failed and were either nationalised, taken over so as to avoid their bankruptcy, or simply went into bankruptcy.

D. The second pillar: supervisory review process

The second pillar considers the "key principles of supervisory review, risk management guidance and supervisory transparency and accountability".[12] The aim of this second pillar then is to encourage banks to use better risk management systems and methodology. The role of a regulatory supervisor is to "evaluate how well banks are assessing their capital needs relative to their risks and to intervene, where appropriate".[13] Holding capital against risks is not enough if the banks are not able to assess and to manage the risks that they are running in the first place. A risk management approach is required within banks to oversee their boards of directors and management, assessment of sound capital levels, comprehensive assessment of risks, suitable monitoring and reporting, and appropriate internal control review.[14] The entire measurement of risk is predicated on the Value at Risk ("VaR") model so prized in financial theory. The VaR methodology considers the level of probability of an investor losing money based on a calculation considering the historical performance of the investment and the credit rating of the entity in which the investment is made, which in turn establishes the rate of return (or the interest rate) which is required for an investment with that level of risk.[15] The second pillar gives regulators greater powers to supervise banks: the issue in practice is whether or not regulators are actually sufficiently inquisitive in their oversight of banks.

28–14

---

[11] See also Taleb, *The Black Swan* (2007).
[12] *Basel II*, para.719.
[13] *Basel II*, para.721.
[14] *Basel II*, para.727.
[15] See, for example, Brealey and Myers, *Corporate Finance*, 8th international edn (McGraw-Hill, 2006), p.664; Morrison and Wilhelm, *Investment Banking* (OUP, 2007), p.27.

E. The third pillar: market discipline and disclosure of information

28–15   The third pillar urges transparency on banks in that banks are required to make more information publicly available than had been the case before then. The third pillar therefore sets out "a set of disclosure requirements which will allow market participants to assess key pieces of information on the scope of application, capital, risk exposures, risk assessment procedures, and hence the capital adequacy of the institution".[16] Ultimately, the test for the need for information to be disclosed is based on a measure of "materiality": that is, a consideration of whether or not the information is information which would have a material effect on the economic decisions of any person if that information was either stated or omitted.[17] There is a general disclosure principle in Basel II to the effect that all banks should have "a formal disclosure policy approved by the board of directors that addresses the bank's approach for determining what disclosures it will make and the internal controls over the disclosure process".[18] Among the matters which are to be disclosed are any differences between a bank's accounting policies and generally accepted accounting policies, all members of the bank's group of companies, any restrictions on transferring capital within the group, statements as to the bank's capital, and the group's current book value of interests in insurance entities.

F. The efficacy of the Basel II Accord

28–16   What should be observed is that the Basel II approach did nothing to prevent the banking crisis of 2008. On the one hand it could be said that the Basel II approach had not had time to bed in so as to prevent the onset of a crisis which had its roots in banking practices which were in train before the Accord came into effect. Nevertheless, it could be said that the Basel II Accord was so similar in structure to its predecessor in all relevant particulars that it would not have effected the occurrence of the global banking crisis in any event. While there are areas like credit default swaps and securitisations which remain effectively unregulated, these information-based models will be of no real effect. The global financial crisis of 2008 is considered in Chapter 45.

G. The Basel III Accord

The underpinnings of Basel III

28–17   The Basel III Accord builds on the Basel II platform considered above, via the developments which were made in the form of "Basel 2.5" reforms as a half-way

---

[16] *Basel II*, para.809.
[17] *Basel II*, para.817.
[18] *Basel II*, para.821.

house to full implementation of the Basel III Accord.[19] Basel III is in effect a tightening of the Basel II system to account for the impact of the financial crisis. In particular the new regime focuses on the mispricing of risk by banks (especially an underestimate of the banks' exposures and an overestimate of the value of the bank's own assets), the impact on bank's solvency of assets which are held off-balance sheet (especially securitisation products like CDOs[20]), and the availability of liquid assets to which a bank can have recourse in the event that the market ceases to operate like it did in the autumn of 2008. The BIS has summarised the Basel III Accord in the following terms:[21]

> "'Basel III' is a comprehensive set of reform measures, developed by the Basel Committee on Banking Supervision, to strengthen the regulation, supervision and risk management of the banking sector. These measures aim to:
> * improve the banking sector's ability to absorb shocks arising from financial and economic stress, whatever the source
> * improve risk management and governance
> * strengthen banks' transparency and disclosures."

In terms of the principal policy changes from the Basel II Accord, the BIS provides that:

> "The reforms target:
> * bank-level, or microprudential, regulation, which will help raise the resilience of individual banking institutions to periods of stress.
> * macroprudential, system wide risks that can build up across the banking sector as well as the procyclical amplification of these risks over time."

Therefore, in common with the reforms which were discussed in Chapter 8, there is an enhanced focus on micro-prudential regulation (that is, oversight of the financial condition of individual financial institutions) and on macro-prudential regulation (that is, oversight of the stability of the entire financial system). Again, this is the result of a financial crisis which hit two years after the Basel II Accord had been implemented.[22] The Basel III Accord is expected to be implemented into EU law in 2013.

The three pillars of the Basel III regime are as follows. Pillar 1: capital, risk **28–18** coverage and containing leverage; Pillar 2: risk management and supervision; Pillar 3: market discipline. Those pillars are reinforced versions of the Basel II structure. Each of the enhancements to the pillars is considered in turn.

---

[19] See generally S. Gleeson, *International Regulation of Banking* 2nd edn (OUP, 2012) which penetrates that accord more deeply than is possible in this chapter.

[20] As discussed in Ch.44, the purpose of collateralised debt obligations ("CDOs") was in part to move assets off the banks' balance sheet by transferring them to special purpose vehicles which would then bear those risks. In the financial crisis, some banks took too many of those risks back onto their balance sheets (as with Citigroup).

[21] *http://www.bis.org/bcbs/basel3.htm.*[Accessed March 6, 2013.]

[22] The Basel Committee's response to the financial crisis is set out at: *http://www.bis.org/bcbs/fincriscomp.htm.* [Accessed March 6, 2013.]

Pillar 1: capital, risk coverage and containing leverage

28–19 The principal feature of the Accord remains the retention of capital to offset the risk of loss. However, Basel III focuses more on equity share capital on than on other forms of capital: equity share capital is a more stable form of capital than other assets. The minimum of ordinary share capital is to be increased to 4.5 per cent of total risk-weighted assets, with a further "capital conservation buffer" making this rise to 7 per cent. The use of share capital to reinforce bank solvency means that private sector investors (in the form of shareholders) will therefore be more exposed to bank failure instead of public money being used to such an extent in the event of future bank failures. Regulators will also have discretion to enforce a further capital requirement on a counter-cyclical basis, in essence, to store up nuts for winter: a counter-cyclical capital requirement means that capital must be put aside during positive market conditions to guard against future downturns.

28–20 The risk coverage element includes two particular developments from Basel II. First, enhanced regulatory capital coverage for securitisation products and for aspects of firms' trading books in relation to derivatives and complex securities transactions. Second, amending the approach to counterparty risk (i.e. the risks which financial institutions assume from other contracting parties) and to exposures to central counterparties in derivatives transactions (as considered in Chapter 40).

28–21 The principal cause of the 1929 crash in New York was leverage: that is, an excess of borrowing over real capital. Similarly, the 2008 crash involved banks which were hugely over-leveraged taking large risks in relation to their investments. So, the first pillar involves a leverage ration which measures the financial institution's level of debt compared to its other assets and liabilities.

Pillar 2: risk management and supervision

28–22 The second pillar of Basel III builds on that in Basel II but with a renewed emphasis on securitisation products (which was so pivotal to the financial crisis, of course) and capturing off-balance sheet exposures (such as securitisations and some derivatives). Regulated firms also need to take greater care of concentrations of risk in particular markets under Basel III—another problem in the lead-up to the financial crisis. Also new to Basel III are policies relating to the control of employee compensation within banks (in particular the problem of "bankers' bonuses") and a new approach to firms' valuations of their own products and exposures (whereas firms like Lehman Brothers took optimistic valuations of their assets and liabilities before their insolvency).

Pillar 3: market discipline

28–23 A key feature of the changes to the third pillar is enhanced reporting of the detail of firms' regulatory capital practices and a different approach to off-balance sheet items (such as CDO products held outside the originating firm's balance sheet).

Global liquidity monitoring

Over-and-above the three pillars, regulators are required to look to the liquidity of **28–24** regulated firms. The credit crunch in 2007–08 meant that banks stopped lending money to one another with the result that banks began to run short of funds: that is, there was a shortage of liquidity. Consequently, a liquidity coverage ratio is introduced to require firms to hold high-quality, liquid assets against their liabilities so that they can pass 30-day stress tests created by the regulators to measure their ability to withstand particularly difficult market conditions.

3.   EU BANKING REGULATION

A.   The organisation of EU banking regulation

The regulation of banking at the EU level falls into line with the general **28–25** principles identified above in relation to investment activities and the general principles of EU law considered in Chapter 7. The development of banking regulation followed a slightly different path from that for investment services, but one which has always operated broadly in parallel to it at the background policy level.[23] The keynote of the regulation of "credit institutions"—as banks are referred to in EU parlance—was free movement of capital at the outset, and latterly has been the drive towards completion of the EU single market in 2005.[24] The passporting policy, considered in Chapter 7,[25] was adopted for the regulation of banking so that once a bank is authorised to act as such in its home Member State, then it will be able to establish branches to provide banking services in other Members States of the EU. The principal EU legislation dealing with banking regulation is now the Second Consolidated Banking Directive 2006 ("CBD 2006"),[26] which recast and replaced the Consolidated Banking Directive of 2000.[27] The CBD 2006 restates the principles of the 2000 Directive which in turn consolidated the provisions of the Second Banking Co-ordination Directive.[28] As discussed below, at the time of writing, new legislation is working its way through the Parliamentary pipework of the EU.

It has been held that as a matter of English law a predecessor to this legislation **28–26** (the 1977 Banking Directive) did not create directly enforceable rights for depositors in a bank to sue the Bank of England directly for alleged failures by

---

[23] See generally J. Usher, *The Law of Money and Financial Services in the European Community*, 2nd edn (OUP, 1999), which is now a good bit out of date; G. Walker, *European Banking Law* (BIICL, 2007).

[24] See para.7–14.

[25] See para.7–15.

[26] Directive 2006/48/EC (June 14, 2006).

[27] Directive 2000/12/EC. All of the commentary available to me on EC banking regulation discusses only the original Consolidated Banking Directive of 2000, not the 2006 restatement: G. Walker, "Bank regulation", in M. Howard and R. Masefield, *Butterworths Banking Law Guide* (LexisNexis, 2007), p.1, at 48 et seq; G. Walker, *European Banking Law* (BIICL, 2007); E. Ellinger, E. Lomnicka, R. Hooley, *Modern Banking Law*, 4th edn (OUP, 2002), p.53.

[28] Directive 89/646/EEC.

the Bank to regulate the entity holding their deposits appropriately.[29] Therefore, these regulations operate only at a level between the legislator and the regulator, not horizontally between consumers and the regulator.

B. Establishment and authorisation of banks: the Second Consolidated Banking Directive 2006

28–27   The Second Consolidated Banking Directive 2006 ("CBD 2006") is "the essential instrument for the achievement of the internal market" in relation both to credit institutions' freedom to establish themselves across the EU and their freedom to provide financial services.[30] A credit institution is in effect a bank which receive deposits.[31] The aim of the directive is to harmonise banking laws across the EU and to provide a "single licence" for banks to be passported from their home State across the EU. Furthermore, the directive is concerned to ensure competition between banks and to safeguard depositors.[32] Responsibility for "supervising the financial soundness of a credit institution, and in particular its solvency" lies with the home Member State.[33] At the regulatory level, the directive calls for increased regulatory co-operation at the national level.[34] The directive has the twin goals of depositor protection and of competition between "credit institutions" (which I will refer to here as "banks"). Its focus of the directive is on the establishment of banks and their prudential supervision.

28–28   Member States are required to provide for the means of authorising people to act as banks,[35] including a statement of the proposed banking operation, the businesses envisaged and the structural organisation of the bank.[36] An applicant is required to have 1 million euro by way of its own capital,[37] its capital may not fall below that level,[38] and it must have at least two directors.[39] Member States are required to prevent unauthorised people from acting as banks.[40] An approved bank within the EU then has a right of establishment in the other Member States of the Union.[41] This is done in the first place by notifying the competent authority of its home Member State that it intends to establish a branch in other jurisdictions.[42] The prudential regulation of a bank is the responsibility of the competent authority of that bank's home Member State.[43] The competent

---

[29] *Three Rivers District Council v Bank of England* [2001] UKHL 16; [2003] 2 A.C. 1.
[30] Directive 2006/48/EC, recital (3).
[31] Directive 2006/48/EC, art.4.
[32] Directive 2006/48/EC, recital (9).
[33] Directive 2006/48/EC, recital (21).
[34] Directive 2006/48/EC, recital (22).
[35] Directive 2006/48/EC, art.6.
[36] Directive 2006/48/EC, art.7.
[37] Directive 2006/48/EC, art.9.
[38] Directive 2006/48/EC, art.10.
[39] Directive 2006/48/EC, art.11.
[40] Directive 2006/48/EC, art.5.
[41] Directive 2006/48/EC, art.25.
[42] Directive 2006/48/EC, art.25(1).
[43] Directive 2006/48/EC, art.40.

authority is entitled to require information from regulated banks but is required to protect the confidentiality of that information.[44]

C. Capital requirements

The Capital Adequacy Directive 2006 ("CAD 2006")[45] is the fourth directive dealing with capital adequacy.[46] Capital adequacy regulation is a key part of banking regulation, governing as it does the level of capital which credit institutions ("banks") and investment firms (as defined in MiFID) are required to maintain to cover their business activities. The theory is that a minimum amount of capital held in this way, will enable a bank to rise out of difficulties in the event of its failure. The content of EU regulation in this context has been based on Basel II, discussed above. Its replacement regulations, considered below, have moved to the Basel III methodology.

28–29

D. The guarantee of bank deposits

The Deposit Guarantee Directive[47] requires Member States to create a scheme whereby 90 per cent of deposits up to £20,000 can be recovered. The Investor Compensation Scheme Directive[48] requires a similar scheme be put in place for investment services activity. The position was changed in the UK in 2008 such that deposits up to £50,000 with an institution (under one bank authorisation) would be guaranteed. At present, the level is £85,000.

28–30

E. Electronic money

The Electronic Money Directive 2000[49] deals with payments by means of electronic payment systems, as is discussed in Chapter 30. The aim of the directive was to co-rdinate and harmonise the law, regulations and administrative procedures governing electronic money institutions in different Member States, with a view to facilitating innovation and the use of electronic money services. The electronic money that is at issue is "an electronic surrogate for notes and coins". This electronic money is redeemable for tangible notes and coins whenever the customer wishes in accordance with the terms agreed between the parties.[50] Institutions which provide electronic money services require authorisation just like credit institutions (considered above) and so must have a minimum

28–31

---

[44] Directive 2006/48/EC, art.44 et seq.
[45] Directive 2006/49/EC. All of the commentary available to me on EC banking regulation discusses only the original Capital Adequacy Directive of 2000, not the 2006 restatement: G. Walker, "Bank regulation", in M. Howard and R. Masefield, *Butterworths Banking Law Guide* (LexisNexis, 2007), 1, at p.48 et seq; G Walker, *European Banking Law* (BIICL, 2007); E. Ellinger, E. Lomnicka, R. Hooley, *Modern Banking Law*, 4th edn (OUP, 2002), p.59.
[46] See Capital Requirements Regulations 2006 (SI 2006/3221).
[47] Directive 94/19/EEC.
[48] Directive 97/9/EEC.
[49] Directive 2000/46/EC.
[50] Directive 2000/46/EC, art.3.

capital of not less than 1 million euro. These institutions are required to have "sound and prudent management, administrative and accounting procedures and adequate internal control mechanisms".[51] Among the risks to which the institution should be responsive are "technical and procedural risks"[52] which would be particularly significant in electronic money business.

4. FUTURE DEVELOPMENTS IN BANKING REGULATION

28–32 At the time of writing, a draft regulation is processing through the EU legislative process. In essence, that regulation implements the Basel III structure considered above. The most newsworthy aspect of the draft regulation has been the proposal to restrict bankers' bonuses to the amount of their annual salary (or double their salaries if the shareholders agree to that).

28–33 The principles of EU banking regulation were considered in Chapter 7.[53] The EU Commission announced in September 2012 that it intended to introduce reforms to banking regulation across the EU to set up a single supervisory mechanism which will grant powers relating to financial stability and banking supervision to the European Central Bank (ECB); to reform the framework for banking regulation further to the establishment of the European Banking Authority (EBA); and a proposal for the implementation of an EU banking union and the creation of a single rulebook and a single supervisory mechanism for the EU.

28–34 The draft Commission outline for the regulation provides[54] that the ECB will be exclusively responsible for the prudential supervision of credit institutions.[55] The particular regulatory developments are intended to empower the ECB to:

- authorise and withdraw the authorisation of all credit institutions in the euro area;
- assess acquisition and disposal of holdings in banks;
- ensure compliance with all prudential requirements laid down in EU banking rules and set, where necessary, higher prudential requirements for banks, for example for macro-prudential reasons to protect financial stability under the conditions provided by EU law;
- carry out supervisory stress tests to support the supervisory review, and carry out supervision on a consolidated basis—such stress tests are a supervisory tool also used by national authorities to assess the stability of individual banks; they will not replace the stress tests carried out by the EBA with a view to assessing the soundness of the banking sector in the Single Market as a whole;
- impose capital buffers and exercise other macro-prudential powers;

---

[51] Directive 2000/46/EC, art.7.
[52] 2000/46/EC, art 7
[53] See para 7-86 *et seq.*
[54] *http://europa.eu/rapid/press-release_MEMO-12-662_en.htm* [Accessed January 30, 2013.]
[55] At the time of writing, the regulation was not available in draft form: *http://ec.europa.eu/internal_market/bank/legislation/index_en.htm.* [Accessed March 6, 2013.]

- carry out supplementary supervision over credit institutions in a financial conglomerate;
- apply requirements for credit institutions to have in place robust governance arrangements, processes and mechanisms and effective internal capital adequacy assessment processes
- carry out supervisory tasks in relation to early intervention when risks to the viability of a bank exist, in co-ordination with the relevant resolution authorities;
- carry out, in co-ordination with the Commission, assessments for possible public recapitalisations;
- co-ordinate a common position of representatives from competent authorities of the participating Member States in the Board of Supervisors and the Management Board of the EBA, for topics relating to the abovementioned tasks.

National regulatory authorities are intended to assist the ECB. They would prepare and implement the ECB acts under the oversight of the ECB, including day-to-day supervision activities. The ECB will be central to the supervision of monetary policy in the EU so as to cope with the shocks which the eurozone currency area has suffered since the financial crisis. The Commission has proposed that the "ECB will ensure a truly European supervision mechanism that is not prone to the protection of national interests and which will weaken the link between banks and national sovereigns". The solution to the eurozone crisis is therefore understood to be an increasing Europeanization of banking regulation: that is, more Europe, not less. The effect of the global financial crisis 2007–09 on banking regulation in the UK is considered in the following section in relation to the Banking Act 2009, and in Chapter 45 in relation to the lessons to be learned from the crisis.

5.   UK BANKING REGULATION

A.   The regulation of banking and building society deposit-taking activity

The scope of "banking" regulation in this chapter

This discussion focuses on the regulation of banking business: that is on deposit-taking, the management of accounts and similar services considered in this Part IX of this book. The general context of financial regulation of all financial services activity was outlined in Chapters 8 and 9 of this book. The general structure of financial regulation forms a backdrop to this discussion. It will be important in this chapter to distinguish between "retail banks" which take deposits, operate bank accounts, offer overdrafts and effect payments for ordinary customers and small businesses. By contrast, there are "investment banks" which sell investment products (such as securities and derivatives) including doing so on their own account, which engage in syndicated lending and foreign exchange transactions for very large corporate clients, and which operate across borders.

28–35

The difference is partly one of scale but it is also one of the nature of the risks which they take. Significantly, there are "universal banks" which engage in both sorts of banking and investment activity around the world and which therefore offer the risk of allowing risks from one market to bleed into other markets. These universal banks are often said to be too big to manage, as is discussed in Chapter 45.

The development of banking regulation in 1997

28–36   In October 1997 a Memorandum of Understanding ("MOU") was entered into between the old Financial Services Authority, the Treasury and the Bank of England in an attempt to clarify the manner in which they would approach overlaps in their regulatory competences. The initial MOU was replaced in March 2006 by a second MOU. The initial MOU explained that the Financial Services Authority would co-operate with the other two bodies and any overseas regulator, as appropriate. The 2006 MOU allocated responsibility between the three British institutions such that the Bank of England was identified as being responsible for three aspects of the integrity of the financial system: namely, the monetary system, the infrastructure of the financial system, and the banking payment system. The Bank of England remained responsible for acting as the lender of last resort to the banks. The Financial Services Authority was identified as being responsible for the regulatory matters set out in Chapters 8 and 9 which, in relation to banks, related specifically to authorisation to act as a bank, prudential supervision of banking operations, and so forth. The Treasury was identified as being responsible for the legislative structure of banking regulation and the general infrastructure of the system, as well as acting of course as the government ministry responsible generally for financial, fiscal and monetary affairs. What was perhaps unclear was exactly which one of these entities would take the lead and set policy once a bank was genuinely threatened with insolvency. When Northern Rock failed, there was only confusion between these three entities.

B.   The role of the Bank of England

28–37   The history and development of the Bank of England as a central bank was considered in Chapter 8. The role of the Bank of England then passed through a period of regulating banks and playing a role in the monetary stability of the UK, before its present role was readdressed in the Bank of England Act 1998 and the Banking Act 2009.

28–38   The first function of the Bank of England is "monetary". The Bank of England's Monetary Policy Committee acquired independent control over the setting of base interest rates (and thus of a key lever of monetary policy) under the Bank of England Act 1998. Section 11 of the Bank of England Act 1998 provides that:

> "In relation to monetary policy, the objectives of the Bank of England shall be—
> (a)   to maintain price stability, and
> (b)   subject to that, to support the economic policy of Her Majesty's Government, including its objectives for growth and employment."

A second function for the Bank of England was introduced by the Banking Act 2009 relating to the stability of the financial systems in the UK. Part 7 of the Banking Act 2009 amended the structure and functions of the Bank of England in this sense. Section 238 of the 2009 Act introduced a new s.2A to the Bank of England Act 1998, such that:

28–39

> "(1) An objective of the Bank shall be to contribute to protecting and enhancing the stability of the financial systems of the United Kingdom (the "Financial Stability Objective).
>
> (2) In pursuing the Financial Stability Objective the Bank shall aim to work with other relevant bodies (including the Treasury and the Financial Services Authority).
>
> (3) The court of directors shall, consulting the Treasury, determine and review the Bank's strategy in relation to the Financial Stability Objective."

Furthermore, a Financial Stability Committee is created by s.238 of the Banking Act 2009 which creates a new 2B of the Bank of England Act 1998, whereby:

28–40

> "(2) The Committee shall have the following functions—
>
> (a) to make recommendations to the court of directors, which they shall consider, about the nature and implementation of the Bank's strategy in relation to the Financial Stability Objective,
>
> (b) to give advice about whether and how the Bank should act in respect of an institution, where the issue appears to the Committee to be relevant to the Financial Stability Objective,
>
> (c) in particular, to give advice about whether and how the Bank should use stabilisation powers under Part 1 of the Banking Act 2009 in particular cases [which are considered at the end of this chapter],
>
> (d) to monitor the Bank's use of the stabilisation powers,
>
> (e) to monitor the Bank's exercise of its functions under Part 5 of the Banking Act 2009 (inter-bank payment systems), and
>
> (f) any other functions delegated to the Committee by the court of directors for the purpose of pursuing the Financial Stability Objective."

The Bank of England thus received an enhanced role in relation to the maintenance of the stability of the financial system. A central bank may play a role in this context in regulating the activity of deposit-taking banks specifically or financial activity more generally. The purpose of the Banking Act 2009 (as is discussed at the end of this chapter in detail) is to furnish the regulatory authorities in the UK with the powers necessary to dispose of a future banking crisis or the failure of a particular bank. In any event, one of the principal objectives of that legislation is to preserve the integrity of the financial system: consequently that has been written into the objectives of the Bank of England.

Private law liability of the Bank of England

Significantly it has been held by the House of Lords that the Bank of England may in theory be liable for the tort of misfeasance in a public office, as was discussed in Chapter 25,[56] if an officer of the Bank of England acted knowingly outside the scope of her powers with the intention that the claimant would suffer loss or harm, or alternatively if that officer were recklessly indifferent to the

28–41

---

[56] See para.25–62.

legality of her acts and the effects which they might cause for the defendant.[57] In that case the House of Lords refused to impose such liability on the Bank of England in relation to a claim brought by depositors with the latterly bankrupt and fraud-ridden Bank of Credit and Commerce International ("BCCI") against the Bank of England for granting authorisation to BCCI to conduct business as a bank. The reason for this refusal to impose liability was based on the impossibility of proving such knowledge or recklessness on the part of the Bank of England on those facts.

C. The nature of Financial Conduct Authority regulation of banks

Giving effect to Basel II through the FCA and PRA Handbooks

28–42   The "GENPRU" sourcebook sets out general prudential regulation for regulated activities generally.[58] There are specific principles relating to the prudential regulation of banks in the "BIPRU" sourcebook which governs the prudential regulation of banks, building societies and investment firms. That prudential regulation relates to the maintenance of adequate capital for those banks and the evaluation of the level of risk faced by each sector of their businesses. This methodology was described above in relation to the Basel II Accord. The BIPRU sourcebook is the means by which those regulatory principles are implemented into UK finance law. The FCA and PRA jargon refers to rules as to the capital requirements of institutions (the internal capital adequacy assessment process) and rules as to the supervisory review and evaluation process. Drawing on Basel II, the standardised credit risk approach is set out in Chapter 3 of BIPRU, the internal ratings based approach in Chapter 4 of BIPRU, credit risk mitigation in Chapter 5 of BIPRU, and the management of operational and market risk in Chapters 6 and 7 of BIPRU respectively.

Capital adequacy regulation

28–43   The regulation of capital held by banks is governed by the Capital Adequacy Directive, considered above. This directive was implemented to UK banking regulation by means of the Capital Requirements Regulations 2006.[59] The FSA is required by those regulations (as from January 1, 2007):

> "to take such steps, in going concern and emergency situations, as it considers appropriate—
> (a)   to co-ordinate the gathering and dissemination of relevant or essential information; and
> (b)   in co-operation with the relevant competent authorities [across the European Economic Area], to plan and co-ordinate supervisory activities."[60]

The focus here is on the co-ordination of regulation internationally, which was a particular problem in 2008 in the global financial crisis (considered in Chapter

---

[57]   *Three Rivers District Council v Bank of England* [2001] UKHL 16; [2003] 2 A.C. 1.
[58]   See para.9–47.
[59]   SI 1006/3221.
[60]   SI 1006/3221, reg.11.

30). The regulations also provide for new assessment methodologies for risk-weighting and for securitisation risk-weighting.

D. Freezing orders under Anti-Terrorism, Crime and Security Act 2001

The Treasury has power under s.4 of the Anti-Terrorism, Crime and Security Act 2001 ("ACSA 2001") to make a "freezing order"[61] by means of a statutory instrument[62] which prohibits people in the UK from "making funds available" to any person identified in the order, whether that is a foreign government or another person outside the UK.[63] The term "funds" here includes "gold, cash, deposits, securities . . . and other such matters as the order may specify".[64] While this legislation was thought to have been intended to deal with terrorist organisations or with states which might support the activities of terrorists against the UK, it is drafted sufficiently broadly that it may be used in general terms so as to freeze the assets of *any* person whose actions threaten the UK economy, or the property or life of UK citizen or resident. Freezing orders can last only for two years.[65] Two conditions must, however, be satisfied before this power is exercisable. First, the Treasury must "reasonably believe" that[66]:

    "(a)   action to the detriment of the United Kingdom's economy (or part of it) has been or is likely to be taken by a person or persons, or

    (b)   action constituting a threat to the life or property of one or more nationals of the United Kingdom or residents of the United Kingdom has been or is likely to be taken by a person or persons."

Secondly, if it is one person who is to take this action, then that person must either be the government of another country or a resident of another country.

This power was used by the UK government in 2008 when a number of Icelandic banks admitted insolvency, with the result that a large number of UK residents and a large number of UK local authorities and non-governmental organisations stood to lose large deposits of many millions of pounds. It was the first time that this power had been used in relation to a banking transaction. There was some surprise that the banks of Iceland were being treated as though "terrorist" organisations by dint of the use of this particular piece of legislation. The effect of freezing orders, therefore, is to give the Chancellor of the Exchequer acting through the Treasury enormous power to freeze the assets of foreign governments and foreign residents, individuals and companies; however, the requirement that the order take effect by means of a statutory instrument provides the possibility of Parliamentary oversight of its introduction.

28–44

28–45

---

[61] Anti-Terrorism, Crime and Security Act 2001, s.4.
[62] Anti-Terrorism, Crime and Security Act 2001, s.10.
[63] Anti-Terrorism, Crime and Security Act 2001, s.5.
[64] Anti-Terrorism, Crime and Security Act 2001, Sch.3, para.2.
[65] Anti-Terrorism, Crime and Security Act 2001, s.8.
[66] Anti-Terrorism, Crime and Security Act 2001, s.4(2).

E. Banks' duties in relation to money laundering and suspicious transactions

Introduction

28–46   The obligations of banks under money laundering regulation were considered in Chapter 15. In this section we focus specifically on banks' duties in relation to suspicious transactions entered into by their clients.

Banks' duties in relation to suspicious transactions

28–47   Section 93A of the Criminal Justice Act 1988 provides that it is a criminal offence for a bank to receive a payment on behalf of a customer about which it is suspicious without reporting the payment to the appropriate financial regulators. This provision is part of the money-laundering legislation which seeks to prevent money being passed on behalf of criminals through banks and other organisations. This creates a difficult problem for banks in practice. On the one hand, a bank cannot be too astute in its suspicions because it may be in breach of its contract with its customers if it refuses to accept payments on grounds that it fears they had been made in breach of money laundering regulation; on the other hand, it commits an offence if it does not make a report of the transaction.

28–48   So, whether or not a bank considers the behaviour of its clients to have been suspicious may have criminal law and regulatory consequences. For example, in *Tayeb v HSBC Bank Plc*,[67] a bank refused to accept a payment of slightly under £1 million into one of its customer's accounts through the computerised CHAPS payment system. The bank had been suspicious about the source of this payment. In this instance, the customer had in fact sold a valuable database and so had earned the money legitimately. Consequently, it was held that the bank had acted in contravention of its contract with its client by refusing to receive the payment and its concerns about its obligations under the 1988 Act would not be sufficient excuse.

28–49   For the purposes of s.93A of the Criminal Justice Act 1988 it has been held in *R. v Da Silva*[68] that a person may be "suspecting" of another person's engagement in criminal conduct if that person has "the imagining of something without evidence or on slender evidence, inkling, mistrust". This definition was taken by the trial judge from a dictionary definition of "suspecting". It suggests that one's understanding of whether or not another person is engaged in criminal conduct can actually be quite slight: if you need only have an "inkling" or an "imagination of something without evidence" then it is likely that one will be taken to have suspected another's criminal conduct. The *Da Silva* test does not require wilfulness and does not require that the signs of criminality were obvious, as was underlined in *K Ltd v National Westminster Bank Plc*.[69]

---

[67] [2004] EWHC 1529 (Comm); [2004] 4 All E.R. 1024.
[68] [2007] 1 W.L.R. 303, CA.
[69] [2007] 1 W.L.R. 311, CA.

Under s.328 of the Proceeds of Crime Act 2002 a banker will commit a criminal **28–50** offence if she knows or suspects that money in a customer's account is derived from criminal activity and if she fails to make an authorised disclosure of that fact under s.338 of the 2002 Act. So, where a banker cleared a cheque for a customer while knowing or suspecting that the money came from criminal activity, then she would have facilitated or controlled the use of that money. The question of whether or not a banker had knowledge or suspicion was decided by reference to the *Da Silva* test. However, where a banker makes the appropriate disclosure, this is an interference with the free flow of trade and a breach of the contract with the customer which has been sanctioned by Parliament in the 2002 Act. Again, the regulatory context in which bankers operate is very different from the standards currently established by the leading cases in the civil law. These principles were considered in greater detail in Chapter 15.

6. BANKING ACT 2009: BANK INSOLVENCY AND CRISIS MANAGEMENT

A. Introduction

The chronology and the key events of the financial crisis 2007–09 are considered **28–51** in Chapter 45. The crisis is often identified as having begun when two funds operated by the French bank BNP Paribas failed; but the failure of the UK bank Northern Rock perhaps indicated that high street banks which had formerly been considered to be solid and reliable, with conservative business models, could go into insolvency. Therefore, the television news pictures of ordinary depositors queuing out of Northern Rock branches into the high streets in August 2007 so as to withdraw their deposits marked the beginning of a banking crisis beyond the banking houses of the City of London. What followed was a "credit crunch" in which banks would not deal with one another, with the result that there was very little money in the system to be lent to ordinary businesses or to grease the wheels of ordinary commerce. The failure of Northern Rock marked a new chapter in UK banking law. It was the first time in the modern era of the statutory regulation of the financial system that a bank had failed. Significantly, it was also the first time a former mutual building society which had converted into being a bank had failed as a result of a transformation in its business model from the conservative business of taking deposits from customers and then lending money by way of domestic mortgages based on the institution's base of customer deposits, into a bank which borrowed money on financial markets far in excess of its capital base and which became hugely exposed to the property markets which crashed in the USA. What became clear was that the marketplace would not be able to clear up the Northern Rock mess as it had done with Barings Bank,[70] nor was the harm spread globally as it had been with the collapse of BCCI.[71] What became

---

[70] Barings Bank, a comparatively small banking operation with very little presence among the ordinary populace, was simply bought up by the Dutch financial services conglomerate ING in 1995 by ING assuming the obligations of Barings after the impact of Nick Leeson's trading on it.

[71] BCCI had been the world's seventh largest private bank with assets of more than US$20 billion, with its bases of operations centred on Karachi and London. However, it became clear by 1991 that it was involved with criminal activity and money laundering in several countries. It was clearly

immediately clear was that the government and the regulators were faced with a crisis for which they had no legal powers: they could not compel anyone to do anything under the law that was necessary at the time. Therefore, emergency legal powers had to be enacted. This section traces the development of those legal powers which culminated in the enactment of the Banking Act 2009. What emerges is that the Banking Act 2009 is, in effect, the playbook used by the politicians and the regulators in dealing with the Northern Rock crisis set out in statutory form.

B. The Banking (Special Provisions) Act 2008 and the Northern Rock crisis

28–52   Before the Banking Act 2009, there was a temporary measure—the Banking (Special Provisions) Act 2008 ("B(SP)A 2008")[72]—which was enacted in the wake of the Northern Rock crisis in 2008 so as to give the Treasury powers to nationalise banks or to compel the takeover of banks by a designated "body corporate" if they were in financial difficulties.[73] This was also the legislation which governed the failure of the Bradford and Bingley.[74] Before the B(SP)A 2008 was enacted, there were no powers for the regulatory authorities in the UK (nor in the USA) to enable them to intervene in cases of bank failure. The Act related to any "UK deposit taker", which was a reference to any bank regulated by the old Financial Services Authority within the meaning of the FSMA 2000 and the RAO.[75] The Treasury had two principal powers under the Act, in essence, to order the transfer of ownership of a bank or to order the transfer of a bank's property.[76] There are two purposes for which the powers in the B(SP)A 2008 may have been exercised: maintaining the stability of the UK financial system and protecting the public interest. The power of the Treasury was limited to circumstances in which the stability of the UK financial system faced a "serious threat".[77]

---

improperly regulated and its reach to 78 countries made it ideal for moving huge amounts of money around the world covertly. A huge amount of complex litigation has followed the collapse of this extraordinary bank. It has been suggested that its clientele included a Who's Who of the world's leading dictators and criminal organisations. BCCI was liquidated finally in July 1991.

[72] This Act "expired" on February 20, 2009 when the Banking Act 2009 received the Royal Assent.

[73] Northern Rock Plc Transfer Order 2008 (SI 2008/432).

[74] Bradford & Bingley Plc Transfer of Securities and Property etc Order 2008, SI 2008/2546; Bradford & Bingley Plc Transfer of Securities and Property etc (Amendment) Order 2009, SI 2009/320. See also: Heritable Bank Plc Transfer of Certain Rights and Liabilities Order 2008, SI 2008/2644; Kaupthing Singer & Friedlander Ltd Transfer of Certain Rights and Liabilities Order 2008, SI 2008/2674; Kaupthing Singer & Friedlander Ltd Transfer of Certain Rights and Liabilities (Amendment) Order 2009, SI 2009/308; Heritable Bank Plc Transfer of Certain Rights and Liabilities (Amendment) Order 2009, SI 2009/310.

[75] Banking (Special Provisions) Act 2008, s.1.

[76] As indicated by Banking (Special Provisions) Act 2008, s.2.

[77] The question arises whether or not there is a "serious threat" if a smaller bank like Barings were to go into insolvency again without threatening the entire financial system (in that no other banks would be expected to fail as a result) but so that other banks would suffer hardship and some loss from that bank's failure.

C.   The underlying approach of the Banking Act 2009

The emergence of the Act

The Banking Act 2009 was introduced as a Bill on October 8, 2008. The Bill was **28–53** published only three weeks after the collapse of Lehman Brothers: the largest corporate bankruptcy in history at that time. In truth the Bill bore the stamp of the run on Northern Rock in August 2007 and the Brown administration's difficulties in rescuing that bank, rather than being a reaction to the Lehman Brothers collapse specifically.[78] The way that the Act imbues regulators with powers, and presents them with a number of different means of dealing with banks in difficulties, is the result of the attempt to sell off Northern Rock which required a number of different strategies to be used before the bank was eventually taken into public ownership. Nevertheless, the Bill was not rushed through Parliament in the way that the Banking (Special Provisions) Act 2008 had been. The Banking Act did not receive the Royal Assent until February 12, 2009. The very shape of the Act is the result of the lessons learned during that crisis to do effectively with rescuing banks ("the Special Resolution Regime"), the insolvency of banks, the administration of banks in difficulties, and compensation for shareholders who lose their holdings as result of powers in the Act. The discussion to follow will concentrate in its early stages on these powers.

For present purposes the principal issue is the way in which the Act deals with **28–54** bank failure and the effects of the failure of the banking system in the event of a crisis like the crisis which began in 2007. A few points are worthy of mention at the outset. First, the Act creates powers for the UK regulatory authorities and provides a series of different methodologies which can be used to deal with banks which are in difficulties. Consequently, the Act does not prescribe particular forms of action but rather recognises that what the regulatory authorities require either in the event of a systemic banking collapse or in the event of the collapse of a single banking institution is a combination of legal powers to take action and also the flexibility to find the right solution in the particular circumstances. In all circumstances the underlying objective of the Act is to ensure the continued integrity and stability of financial markets (including the banking system). This may require the sale of the troubled bank in toto, or the break-up of that bank into parts, or the administration of that bank, or the insolvency of the bank, or taking that bank into public ownership. In essence then the Act describes methodologies and creates high-level principles for the preservation of the financial system.

The legislative methodology of the Act

The Act is interestingly constructed. Each Part of the Act is prefaced by an **28–55** "overview" section which summarises the provisions to follow. Being statutory provisions themselves and not simply side-notes, they are capable of being used

---

[78] The Explanatory Notes to the Act suggest that the Treasury had harboured ambitions to renovate the law on bank insolvency since the *Banking Reform – protecting depositors*discussion paper in 2007 but the factor which brought the legislation to a head was the Northern Rock collapse and the need for the B(SP)A 2008, followed by the BA 2009.

to interpret the provisions to follow. The principal Parts of the Act also contain a clear statement of the objectives of those provisions and the conditions on which the regulators are permitted to exercise their powers. It is a model of modern legislative drafting in its clarity of structure, even if there are moments when the detail of the provisions contains the usual ambiguities which attend all legislative drafting.

The composition of the Act

28–56 The Banking Act 2009 is divided (for present purposes) into seven parts.[79] The first part deals with the "Special Resolution Regime" concerning the takeover of banks which are in difficulties. The second part deals with "Bank Insolvency" which concerns the appointment and role of a liquidator in relation to a bank which is unable to meet its debts. The third part deals with "Bank Administration" concerning the administration of any part of a bank ("the residual bank") which remains unsold under the special resolution regime, and the attempt therefore to maintain the viability of that residual bank.[80] The fourth part amends the Financial Services Compensation Scheme (as discussed in Chapter 9) to account for the rights of people who are entitled to compensation in relation to the takeover of banks. The fifth part deals with Inter-bank Payments. The sixth part deals with the issue of banknotes. The seventh part deals with a miscellaneous category of issues, among which the most important are the modernisation of the governance of the Bank of England, provisions relating to the FSA, and various provisions relating to the support of banks. Each is considered in turn in the sections to follow, although our principal focus shall be on failed banks.

D. The Special Resolution Regime

In essence

28–57 This section sets out a potted summary of the Special Resolution Regime ("SRR"). The SRR sets out specific objectives for the UK regulatory authorities to pursue when considering their powers. The five objectives are: to protect and enhance the stability of the financial systems of the United Kingdom, and to protect and enhance public confidence in the stability of the banking systems of the United Kingdom; to protect depositors; to protect public funds; and to avoid interfering with any human rights to property.[81] The powers with which the regulatory authorities are imbued are the stabilisation powers, the bank insolvency procedure, or the bank administration procedure.[82] Thus the regulations are based on high-level principles in the form of the five objectives

---

[79] The last two parts were late additions to the Bill, and replaced a mooted second banking bill for 2009.

[80] The first three parts, which are the principal focus of this section, came into force on February 21, 2009 in accordance with the Banking Act 2009 (Commencement No.1) Order 2009 (SI 2009/296).

[81] Banking Act 2009, s.4(4)–(8).

[82] Banking Act 2009, s.4(2).

which the regulatory authorities must observe when exercising their powers. Any regulator exercising one of these powers must consult with the other regulatory authorities in the manner set out in the statute, as well as obeying the precise statutory limits on those powers. Significantly, the Act included (late in its passage) a requirement that a Banking Liaison Panel give advice on the manner in which the SRR should be used. In essence then, the SRR gives powers to the regulatory authorities and identifies the general goals which they must seek to achieve in whatever action they decide to take in the operation of those powers, and also requires them to have regard to the impact of their actions on the banking system generally.

The heart of the Banking Act 2009 is the introduction of the SRR. The problem **28–58** which was faced by governments in many countries during 2008, after the failure of Northern Rock in the UK in 2007, was the effective insolvency of a number of banks and the concomitant need to support those banks by lending money to the banking system to increase liquidity (to ease what was conceived at first as being a liquidity crisis), supporting private sector takeovers of failing banks, using public money to buy shares in failing banks (effectively nationalising them during what self-evidently became a solvency crisis in time), or allowing banks to go bankrupt. The underlying purpose of the SRR is to identify a procedure by which failing banks can be taken over either by banks in the private sector or by the State or by a "bridge bank" owned by the State.

The definition of "bank"

The Act refers to "banks". The definition of "bank" was a matter of some debate **28–59** in committee during the passage of the legislation. The core definition of "bank" is as follows:[83]

> "In this Part 'bank' means a UK institution which has permission under Part 4 of the Financial Services and Markets Act 2000 to carry on the regulated activity of accepting deposits (within the meaning of section 22 of that Act, taken with Schedule 2 and any order under section 22)"

Section 22 of the FSMA 2000 was discussed at para.9–10. In consequence, this definition covers all of the financial activities set out in Sch.2 of that Act relating to the acceptance of deposits. This constitutes an enlargement from the original bill. In effect, a bank constitutes anything which is a deposit-taking institution. While the definition of "banks" encompasses credit institutions in most definitions in EU law, the following categories of institution are excluded from the definition: building societies, credit unions and other institutions specified by Treasury regulation.[84] An institution does not cease to be a "bank" for these purposes simply because it loses its authorisation: an extension which enables the regulatory authorities to cater for the health of the system even if a particular institution needs to lose its authorisation.[85]

---

[83] Banking Act 2009, s.2(1).
[84] Banking Act 2009, s.2(2), providing that those regulations have been made by statutory instrument and approved by both Houses of Parliament: Banking Act 2009, s.2(5).
[85] Banking Act 2009, s.2(4).

The regulatory authorities

28–60 The regulators which have powers in relation to the operation of the Act are the Bank of England's regulatory authorities and the Treasury.[86] The regulatory authorities acting together prepared a report for the Chancellor of the Exchequer in July 2008 called *Financial Stability and Depositor Protection – Special Resolution Regime*,[87] which illustrates their approach to the relevant issues.

E.   The operation of the SRR

The five objectives which the regulatory authorities must pursue

28–61 There are five objectives set out in s.4 of the Act in relation to which the SRR powers are to be carried on. There is no significance in the order in which the objectives are set out: that is, one objective is not superior to another.[88] Those objectives are as follows:

> "(4)   Objective 1 is to protect and enhance the stability of the financial systems of the United Kingdom.
>
> (5)   Objective 2 is to protect and enhance public confidence in the stability of the banking systems of the United Kingdom.
>
> (6)   Objective 3 is to protect depositors.
>
> (7)   Objective 4 is to protect public funds.
>
> (8)   Objective 5 is to avoid interfering with property rights in contravention of a Convention right (within the meaning of the Human Rights Act 1998)."

The Treasury is empowered to produce a code of practice (as considered below) which will give guidance on the interpretation of these objectives.[89] The first two objectives are concerned to combat the instability which was brought not only to the international banking system but also directly into the 'real economy' in the UK. The first objective "to protect and enhance the stability of the financial systems of the United Kingdom" is concerned with the inherent good health of the financial system. The reference to the "financial systems", in the plural, is to all financial markets whether banking, securities markets, and so forth, when compared to the limited effect and application of the second objective to the banking system. The Act provides that among the financial systems which are to be maintained, is the "continuity of banking services".[90] By contrast, the second objective "to protect and enhance public confidence in the stability of the banking systems of the United Kingdom" encompasses both investor protection (such as the rights of bank customers and other investors) and also confidence in the banking system. The reference to "investors" here is uncomfortable given that the legislation relates only to deposit-taking institutions, which ordinarily have customers, and not to broader categories of investors, for example, in securities

---

[86]   Banking Act 2009, s.4(3).

[87]   CM 7459.

[88]   Banking Act 2009, s.4(10).

[89]   Banking Act 2009, s.5(2).

[90]   Banking Act 2009, s.4(9).

markets. The reference to the banking system is a reference not to financial markets generally but rather to banking and lending markets specifically.

What is unclear is what are the "financial systems" of the UK: do they mean only the Stock Exchange and the general speculative circus that is investment banking, or does it include pension fund activity, credit unions, and so forth, even though they are strictly outwith the definition of "bank" for the purposes of this legislation? Does that definition extend to the credit card facilities available in shops? Similarly, the expression "banking systems" presumably refers to the business activities of banks, building societies and credit unions as defined in the Act, but does it extend any further? There are no definition provisions in the Act in this regard. The underlying purpose here is to prevent the seizure of the systems for banking and finance in the UK as in 2008. Interestingly, the focus of this provision in relation to the banking system is only on "public confidence" and not with the intrinsic stability of the system itself: the problem in 2007–09 was the illiquidity and insolvency of the banking system itself and not simply with the lack of confidence of the public (except when queues of public waited outside Northern Rock offices to withdraw their savings). However, for the operation of the Banking Act in the future, it is suggested, it is important to retain as much flexibility as possible to ensure that the regulatory authorities can take appropriate action to stave off a future crisis. Therefore, the references to the financial systems and the banking systems should be interpreted broadly. **28–62**

The third objective to protect depositors reflects the core of government policy which was been to protect those members of the public who have deposits with banks and similar institutions. During the 2008 financial crisis it was a proud boast by the UK government that no depositor had lost any of their money in the UK, although depositors in Icelandic banks seemed likely to suffer a different fate. **28–63**

The fourth objective to protect public funds is significant in circumstances in which the funds of public or quasi-public bodies are on deposit with banks. Alternatively, it may relate to the application of public funds under the SRR to shore up failing banks. **28–64**

The fifth objective to "avoid interfering with property rights in contravention of a Convention rights" further to the Human Rights Act 1998 is unclear as to the identity of these human rights. There are human rights either to one's possessions under the First Protocol to the Convention or to the protection of family life. There were concerns raised by the shareholders in banks that nationalisation of banks in 2008 would equate to "theft" of their shares. This insupportable argument overlooked two facts. First, that shareholders take a risk when investing in companies that if the company goes into insolvency then they will lose all of their investment. Secondly, that if the government intervenes to recapitalise banks, and so preserve them from the bankruptcy which had already spectacularly overtaken very large banks like Lehman Brothers, then that is preserving the viability of those shareholders' investments which would otherwise have become worthless. Furthermore, it is suggested, government (or other regulatory) intervention to preserve the viability of individual banks and of the banking system as a whole should in itself be considered to be an activity of **28–65** such importance that it should be permitted to override any purported human right to an investment in a financial or banking institution which otherwise would be insolvent or "failing" in the sense discussed below and as defined in the Act.

28–66   The Treasury is empowered to create a code of practice—as opposed to a regulatory rulebook—to govern the use of these powers.[91] The matters on which the code should give guidance are as follows:

> "(a)   how the special resolution objectives are to be understood and achieved,
> (b)   the choice between different options,
> (c)   the information to be provided in the course of a consultation under this Part,
> (d)   the giving of advice by one relevant authority to another about whether, when and how the stabilisation powers are to be used,
> (e)   how to determine whether Condition 2 in section 7 is met,
> (f)   how to determine whether the test for the use of stabilisation powers in section 8 is satisfied,
> (g)   sections 63 and 66, and
> (h)   compensation."

The text of this code was not available at the time of writing. The regulatory authorities are to have regard to the code when exercising their powers in this context.[92] Before issuing the code of practice, the Bank of England must consult with the other regulatory authorities.[93]

The conditions precedent to the regulators being permitted to use its powers under the SRR

28–67   The two, general conditions which govern the regulator's use of its powers in this context are set out in s.7 of the Act in the following terms:

> "(2)   Condition 1 is that the bank is failing, or is likely to fail, to satisfy the threshold conditions (within the meaning of section 41(1) of the Financial Services and Markets Act 2000 (permission to carry on regulated activities)).
> (3)   Condition 2 is that having regard to timing and other relevant circumstances it is not reasonably likely that (ignoring the stabilisation powers) action will be taken by or in respect of the bank that will enable the bank to satisfy the threshold conditions."

These conditions are conditions precedent to the regulator being permitted to use its stabilisation powers. The first condition, that "the bank is failing, or is likely to fail, to satisfy the threshold conditions",[94] is a reference to s.41 of the FSMA 2000 provides that the "threshold conditions" are the conditions set out in Sch.6 to that Act.[95] The second condition is that "having regard to timing and other relevant circumstances it is not reasonably likely that (ignoring the stabilisation powers) action will be taken by or in respect of the bank that will enable the bank to satisfy the threshold conditions". Those threshold conditions require that a person carrying on a regulated banking activity must be a body

---

[91]   Banking Act 2009, s.5.
[92]   Banking Act 2009, s.5(4).
[93]   Banking Act 2009, s.6.
[94]   Banking Act 2009, s.7(2).
[95]   The threshold conditions for authorisation to conduct regulated activities were discussed in para.9–31.

corporate or a partnership, with its head office in the UK if it is a body corporate constituted under the law of any part of the United Kingdom. The resources of the person conducting that activity must be adequate in relation to the regulated activities that are being carried on. The regulator must be satisfied that the person conducting this activity is a fit and proper person who conducts their affairs soundly and prudently.[96] The regulator must consult with the Treasury before reaching a decision on the second condition.

Significantly, the regulator "shall treat Conditions 1 and 2 as met if satisfied that they would be met but for financial assistance provided by (a) the Treasury, or (b) the Bank of England (disregarding ordinary market assistance offered by the Bank on its usual terms)". The concept of "financial assistance" in this context includes giving guarantees or indemnities, and the assistance can be actual or contingent in general terms.[97] A Treasury order may, if made by statutory instrument with the consent of both Houses of Parliament, exclude any assistance from falling within this definition.[98]

28–68

The Banking Liaison Panel

Section 10 of the Act provides that a panel of people able to advise on the broader context of the impact of a use of the SRR is able to advise the Treasury on those matters. The Panel will be comprised of at least one person who is appointed by each of the regulatory authorities, and the Financial Services Compensation Scheme; and one or more people who represent the interests of banks, one or more people who have expertise in the law relating to the UK financial systems in the Treasury's opinion, and one or more people who have expertise in insolvency law.[99] It is provided in s.10(1) that:

28–69

> "The Treasury shall make arrangements for a panel to advise the Treasury about the effect of the special resolution regime on—
> (a)   banks,
> (b)   persons with whom banks do business, and
> (c)   the financial markets."

Therefore advice is taken in relation not only to the effect on banks and on financial markets more generally, but also on any "persons" (customers, companies and so forth) who conduct business with banks commercially, in their private capacities or otherwise. The particular matters on which the Panel may advise are:[100]

> "(a)   the exercise of powers to make statutory instruments under or by virtue of this Part, Part 2 or Part 3 (excluding the stabilisation powers, compensation scheme orders, resolution fund orders, third party compensation orders and orders under section 75(2)(b) and (c)),
> (b)   the code of practice under section 5, and

---

[96] Banking Act 2009, s.7(3).
[97] Banking Act 2009, s.257(1).
[98] Banking Act 2009, s.257(2), (3).
[99] Banking Act 2009, s.10(3).
[100] Banking Act 2009, s.10(2).

(c) anything else referred to the panel by the Treasury."

F. The three stabilisation options

28–70 The stabilisation options refer, in effect, to sales of the whole or part of a bank in difficulties in one of three ways. These different methods are referred to as the "stabilisation options" in s.7 and the following sections. There are three options to maintain stabilisation in this context. First, to find a private sector purchaser of the failing bank; or, secondly, to use a "bridge bank"; or, thirdly, to take the failing bank into "public ownership". Each option grants the regulatory authorities a power to act and each option is subject to conditions precedent being satisfied. They are considered in turn in the sections to follow.

(1) Private sector purchaser

28–71 The preferred market solution is for a failing bank to be taken over by another bank as opposed to it going into insolvency or into insolvent administration.[101] There are specific conditions in relation to a private sector purchaser taking over a bank, as set out in s.8 of the Act. The two general conditions in s.7 also apply in the manner considered above. The specific conditions for a private sector purchaser are that the regulatory authorities must consider the stability of the financial systems in the UK, the maintenance of public confidence in the banking system in the UK, and the protection of depositors ("Condition A");[102] and further that the Treasury must have recommended that the Bank of England exercise the stabilisation power and that in the Bank of England's opinion the exercise of that stabilisation power is "an appropriate way to provide that protection" ("Condition B").[103] Section 8(2) provides that:

> "Condition A is that the exercise of the power is necessary, having regard to the public interest in—
> (a) the stability of the financial systems of the United Kingdom,
> (b) the maintenance of public confidence in the stability of the banking systems of the United Kingdom, or
> (c) the protection of depositors."

The Bank of England, as the primary regulator in effect in this context, must consult with the Treasury before determining whether or not Condition A is met.[104] The key concept is one of *necessity* in protecting the "financial systems" and the banking systems" (as both terms were discussed above) and depositors.

---

[101] The problem with the process in 2008 is that there are now fewer genuine investment banks left in the USA and the UK on the traditional model because they have either been taken over by other banking groups or have voluntarily re-organised themselves. As a result there is a lack of competition between banks and also a reduction in the possibility that the banking markets will form different views of the same market conditions, with the result that future systemic failures are more likely because the reduced marketplace is likely to sleepwalk en masse into future repetitions of the securitisation and CDS failures of 2008 (as explored in Ch.57).

[102] Banking Act 2009, s.8(2).

[103] Banking Act 2009, s.8(5).

[104] Banking Act 2009, s.8(3).

The term "necessary" is not defined. The failure of Northern Rock constituted a necessary condition, it is suggested, in relation to that bank; just as the systemic failure in the autumn of 2008 suggested by the liquidity and latterly solvency crisis which affected the entire banking sector would also make it necessary to intervene in relation to a failing bank. This power is no small thing, of course. The state is intervening in the private affairs of a bank. However, the experience of 2008 tells us that without state intervention of this sort, the financial system may not be able to withstand another similar shock.

There is a further requirement, however, if the Treasury has already provided **28–72** financial assistance (as defined above[105]) to the bank in question.[106] In that circumstance, the Bank of England must ensure that Condition B is satisfied[107]:

> "Condition B is that—
> (a)   the Treasury have recommended the Bank of England to exercise the stabilisation power on the grounds that it is necessary to protect the public interest, and
> (b)   in the Bank's opinion, exercise of the stabilisation power is an appropriate way to provide that protection."

The Treasury's link with the bank in question necessarily makes it a person whose opinion is required. Again, the Act grants powers to the regulatory authorities but gives them great freedom to decide whether or not the transaction is in the public interest and is an appropriate way to provide protection.

To effect a private sector purchase, "all or part of the business" of the failing bank **28–73** may be sold to "a commercial purchaser", although there is no requirement that that person must be a "bank" within the terms defined in the Act.[108] It is suggested, however, that an unsuitable person not in the banking business ought to be refused permission to acquire a bank. So, for example, it is suggested that a business which operated commuter train services which were well-known for their unreliability ought not to be considered to be an appropriate person to operate a banking business if it had no experience of conducting regulated financial services business in the UK.

The transfer is effected by one or more "share transfer instruments" which **28–74** transfer ownership of the business in chunks or as a whole, or by one or more "property transfer instruments" which transfer the property of the failing bank.[109] Those instruments are made by the Bank of England.[110]

(2)   Bridge bank

The logic of the Act, it is suggested, is that the options work in sequence. The **28–75** most attractive solution to the condition of a failing bank is to have that bank acquired by a commercial purchaser, as considered above. If a private purchase of

---

[105] See para 29-60.
[106] Banking Act 2009, s.8(4).
[107] Banking Act 2009, s.8(5).
[108] Banking Act 2009, s.11(1).
[109] Banking Act 2009, s.11(2).
[110] Banking Act 2009, s.11(2).

that sort cannot be obtained, then a bridge bank structure is used. Within the terms of the Act, a "bridge bank" is a company which is "wholly owned by the Bank of England".[111] More generally, a bridge bank is a bank which is created temporarily to administer the assets of a failed bank. The manner in which that administration is carried out will depend upon the circumstances and the nature of the failed bank's assets. In practice this mechanism would only be used if there was no private sector purchaser prepared to take over the failing bank, just as with Northern Rock where no suitable commercial purchaser could be found despite a lengthy search. There are specific conditions in relation to a "bridge bank" taking over a bank, as set out in s.8 of the Act. The specific conditions precedent to a bridge bank exercising its powers are the same as that for a private sector purchaser.[112] Those specific conditions were discussed in the previous section.

28–76   The transfer is effected by one or more "property transfer instruments" which transfer the property of the failing bank to the bridge bank.[113] The power to make those instruments is vested in the Bank of England.[114]

28–77   The code of practice to be created by the Treasury further to s.5 of the Act applies to the bridge bank procedure in relation to:[115]

"(a)   setting objectives,
(b)   the content of the articles of association,
(c)   the content of reports under section 80(1),
(d)   different arrangements for management and control at different stages, and
(e)   eventual disposal."

(3)   Temporary public ownership

28–78   Cascading down the list of stabilisation options from a private sale to the use of a bridge bank, there is then a third option of taking the bank into public ownership. The iteration of the Northern Rock collapse saw public ownership as being the final option once a private sale and a break-up of the bank could not be achieved. Indeed, following the events of the autumn of 2008, the public support of banks lost a little of its stigma once so many banks were either taken into public ownership or were recapitalised by public money. The third stabilisation option of taking a bank into public ownership is, it is suggested, drafted too broadly. At one level, taking into public ownership could be said to constitute a purchase of all of the shares in a bank; or it could be a purchase of a majority share in a bank; or it could encompass an injection of capital into the bank which does not acquire a majority stake. This last variation would not render the state the majority owners of the bank, however, and would be a poor trade-off for investing public money to rescue a bank.

---

[111]   Banking Act 2009, s.12(1).
[112]   Banking Act 2009, s.8(1).
[113]   Banking Act 2009, s.11(2).
[114]   Banking Act 2009, s.10(2).
[115]   Banking Act 2009, s.12(3).

There are specific pre-conditions in relation to a bank being taken into **28–79** "temporary public ownership", as set out in s.9 of the Act. The Treasury must be satisfied that one of the following conditions is satisfied:

"(2) Condition A is that the exercise of the power is necessary to resolve or reduce a serious threat to the stability of the financial systems of the United Kingdom.[116]

(3) Condition B is that exercise of the power is necessary to protect the public interest, where the Treasury have provided financial assistance in respect of the bank for the purpose of resolving or reducing a serious threat to the stability of the financial systems of the United Kingdom."[117]

The Treasury is required to consult with the other regulatory authorities before making its decision.[118] It is important that the Act only envisages banks being taken into *temporary* public ownership and not permanent public ownership—a salve for the concerns of bankers that they will be owned in perpetuity by the government and not allowed to continue making catastrophic commercial errors in private. The limited utility of this power is illustrated by the wording of the first condition ("Condition A") to the effect that "the exercise of the power is necessary to resolve or reduce a serious threat to the stability of the financial systems" of the UK.[119] In relation to the second condition ("Condition B"), that "the exercise of the power is necessary to protect the public interest" in circumstances in which the Treasury has provided "financial assistance" either directly to the failing bank or generally "in respect of" that bank,[120] the definition of "financial assistance" is left opaque. It is suggested that such assistance should encompass either direct purchase of shares in the bank, or making loans available to that bank directly (that is, outside the ordinary process for the issue of gilts into the money markets to control money supply).

Temporary public ownership is carried out by means of the Treasury (not the **28–80** Bank of England) making "one or more share transfer orders" so as to acquire ownership of the share capital of the bank itself.[121] The transferee is then either a nominee of the Treasury or a company which is wholly owned by the Treasury.[122] At the time of writing, Northern Rock has been sold to the Virgin group after having been held in public ownership, and the state still owns significant shareholdings in the Lloyds banking group and in the RBS banking group.

The transfer mechanisms

This section defines the instruments and orders which were referred to above. A **28–81** "share transfer instrument" is an instrument which provides for shares in a failing bank to be transferred.[123] A "share transfer order" by contrast is an "order" which

---

[116] Banking Act 2009, s.9(2).
[117] Banking Act 2009, s.9(3).
[118] Banking Act 2009, s.9(4).
[119] Banking Act 2009, s.9(2).
[120] Banking Act 2009, s.9(3).
[121] Banking Act 2009, s.13(2).
[122] Banking Act 2009, s.13(2).
[123] Banking Act 2009, s.15.

provides for shares in a failing bank to be transferred.[124] It is not clear whether or not this "order" is required to be a court order or simply an order issued by the Treasury or a statutory instrument moved by the Treasury.

28–82 There are also "property transfer instruments" which provide that the trading books of failing banks are transferable when there is a sale to a private sector body or to a bridge bank. Property transfer orders may be made in similar fashion by the Treasury when there has been a bank taken into temporary public ownership.[125] The matters to be transferred are the "property, rights or liabilities" of those banks.[126] The purpose of such an instrument is that the assets and liabilities which the bank has created as part of its trading activities must be transferred along with the ownership of the business under the SRR process. As emerged with the break-up of Lehman Brothers in 2008 and thereafter was that some banks were prepared to buy parts of Lehman's trading books (in effect the profitable bits, or the bits which were thought to fit well with the solvent banks' existing businesses) but were not prepared to buy those parts of the business which included loss-making assets.[127] Therefore, the banks assets may be divided and some assets transferred separately from other assets.[128] There is then a separate question, to be specified in the instrument, as to whether the transferee takes those assets subject to the obligations of the failing bank or as a person unconnected with the prior transactions: that is whether there is a "succession" or whether the transferee is to be treated as being "connected" to the transferor.[129]

28–83 There is a further issue as to the events of default which will have been triggered by the SRR process being undertaken in relation to the bank: under most loan agreements and master agreements for most of the business in this *Section Two: Specific Financial Products* of this book that would have triggered termination of the agreement. Section 33(3) of the Act provides that the "property transfer instrument is to be disregarded in determining whether a default event provision applies".[130] The effect of this provision therefore appears to be an attempt to prevent counterparties to loan agreements and master agreements from terminating their contracts because a bank has been identified as a failing bank under the SRR.

---

[124] Banking Act 2009, s.16.

[125] Banking Act 2009, s.45.

[126] Banking Act 2009, s.33(1).

[127] Such partial transfers are to be conducted in accordance with the Banking Act 2009 (Restriction of Partial Property Transfers) Order 2009, SI 2009/322.

[128] One of the many possibilities in cases of this sort is to create a "bad bank" in which the bank's loss-making assets are separated away from the saleable assets, so that the remaining "good bank" with the saleable assets can be sold off or can continue to operate as before. Meanwhile, it is hoped that the bad assets may in time improve or that they may be sold at a great discount to a finance house which thinks it might be able to make a profit on some of the assets from among the detritus if the sale price is low enough. The solution followed in Ireland involved the separation of "bad" parts of banks off from the "good" parts of those banks, with the bad assets being run down and liquidated over time.

[129] Banking Act 2009, s.33(1).

[130] Banking Act 2009, s.38(7).

Compensation

When assets are taken over or taken into public ownership, the question of compensation arises for people who have lost assets in that process. Sections 49 through 62 of the Act provide for the valuation and award of compensation by experts appointed for that task. Compensation is provided by way either of a compensation scheme order; a resolution fund order, which entitles the transferors to participate in the proceeds of the resolution of a bridge bank structure or of a bank being taken into temporary public ownership;[131] or a third party compensation order, which establishes a scheme for paying out compensation.[132]

28–84

G.   Bank insolvency

Bank insolvency in general terms

Part 2 of the Act deals with bank insolvency. One of the great difficulties with the global financial crisis of 2008 was deciding whether banks were insolvent (that is, unable to meet their debts as they became due) or whether they were solvent but dealing in an illiquid market which made it seem temporarily as though they would have been unable to meet their debts as they would in time fall due. The concept of solvency and insolvency was considered in detail in Chapter 22.[133] Section 90 of the Banking Act 2009 gives an overview of the insolvency process under Part 2 of the Act as follows[134]:

28–85

> "(2)   The main features of bank insolvency are that—
> (a)   a bank enters the process by court order,
> (b)   the order appoints a bank liquidator,
> (c)   the bank liquidator aims to arrange for the bank's eligible depositors to have their accounts transferred or to receive their compensation from the FSCS,
> (d)   the bank liquidator then winds up the bank, and
> (e)   for those purposes, the bank liquidator has powers and duties of liquidators, as applied and modified by the provisions of this Part."

In the first place there must be a court order made for the insolvency process to begin[135] which must be made on an application from the regulatory authorities.[136] A liquidator is to be appointed with a view to liquidating the assets of the insolvent bank. To demonstrate insolvency, three particular grounds must be satisfied:[137]

> "(a)   Ground A is that a bank is unable, or likely to become unable, to pay its debts,
> (b)   Ground B is that the winding up of a bank would be in the public interest, and
> (c)   Ground C is that the winding up of a bank would be fair."

---

[131]   Banking Act 2009, s.49(3).
[132]   Banking Act 2009, s.49(4).
[133]   para 23–97.
[134]   Banking Act 2009, s.90(2).
[135]   Banking Act 2009, s.94.
[136]   Banking Act 2009, s.95.
[137]   Banking Act 2009, s.96(1).

So, first, the bank must either be unable to pay its debts or unlikely to be able to pay its debts. Two problems arise here: a bank can be treated as insolvent if it is considered "unlikely" that it will be unable to pay its debts, which raises problems as to the level of likelihood and whether that means a likelihood of a failure across the life of the debt or in the immediate future; and also that the bank must be "unable to pay its debts" possibly at any time and not (as the legend ordinarily has it) when the bank is "unable to pay its debts *as they become due*". Secondly, it must be in the public interest that the bank is wound up. Thirdly, the winding up must be "fair". Furthermore, the threshold conditions set out in s.7 of the Act must also be satisfied, as set out above. If those conditions are satisfied, then an insolvency order may be made further to s.98 of the Act where notice has been given under s.120 (for an application for an administration order or a petition for winding up order) and one of the regulatory authorities applies for a bank insolvency order, then the insolvency order "is treated as having taken effect when the application or petition was made or presented".[138]

28–86   A bank liquidator is then appointed in accordance with the Bank Insolvency (England and Wales) Rules 2009.[139] The insolvent bank is then liquidated in accordance with the objectives set out in s.99 of the Act:

> "(1)   A bank liquidator has two objectives.
> (2)   Objective 1 is to work with the FSCS so as to ensure that as soon as is reasonably practicable each eligible depositor—
>   (a)   has the relevant account transferred to another financial institution, or
>   (b)   receives payment from (or on behalf of) the FSCS.
> (3)   Objective 2 is to wind up the affairs of the bank so as to achieve the best result for the bank's creditors as a whole."

Importantly, under s.103 a bank liquidator "may do anything necessary or expedient for the pursuit of" the s.99 objectives.[140] Under s.99, the objectives of the bank liquidator are to work effectively with the Financial Services Compensation Scheme ("FSCS", which was discussed in Chapter 9) and "to wind up the affairs of the bank so as to achieve the best result for the bank's creditors as a whole".[141] To achieve the liquidation there are two phases. In the first phase, a "liquidation committee" is to be appointed once the insolvency order has been made[142] and that liquidation committee must consist of individuals appointed by the regulatory authorities and the FSCS.[143] The liquidation committee is required by s.102 to recommend that the bank liquidator pursue Objective 1 (in s.99) or Objective 2 (in s.100), in particular bearing in mind the desirability of working effectively with the FCSC. The liquidation committee is therefore focused in the first instance on paying back the depositors, or passing a "full payment

---

[138] Banking Act 2009, s.98(2).
[139] Bank Insolvency (England and Wales) Rules 2009 (SI 2009/356).
[140] Banking Act 2009, s.103(1).
[141] Banking Act 2009, s.99.
[142] Banking Act 2009, s.100.
[143] Banking Act 2009, s.100(2).

resolution" in the jargon.[144] Once that is done, a second form of liquidation committee is appointed by a meeting of the bank's creditors.[145]

Insolvency and investment banks

There is a further power in s.233 of the Banking Act 2009 for the Treasury to modify insolvency law as it relates to "investment banks" by means of Treasury regulation. The reference to "investment banks" is a reference to banks which safeguard or administer investments, or which deal in investments either as principal or agent.[146] Those regulations may establish a new procedure for investment banks where (i) they are unable, or are likely to become unable, to pay their debts ..., or (ii) their winding up would be fair".[147] Those Treasury regulations are required to observe the following principles:[148]

28–87

> "(a) identifying, protecting, and facilitating the return of, client assets,
> (b) protecting creditors' rights,
> (c) ensuring certainty for investment banks, creditors, clients, liquidators and administrators,
> (d) minimising the disruption of business and markets, and
> (e) maximising the efficiency and effectiveness of the financial services industry in the United Kingdom."

Otherwise, there is great lassitude in the nature of those obligations, their detail and the procedures which they require, including whether or not an insolvency order is made by a court or by other classes of person.[149]

H. Bank administration

The fundamentals of bank administration

The previous section considered the liquidation of banks. There may well be a part or parts of a bank, however, which continue to do business and which continue to have customers: this rump of a bank is known as "the residual bank". Part 3 of the Act provides for the way in which the residual bank's affairs are to be administered. Administration in this sense pre-supposes that these parts of the business will continue in effect as long as possible, or hopefully with a view to them being returned to "normal" (as that term is defined in the Act and discussed below). Administration of a bank is conducted in detail in accordance with Bank Administration (England and Wales) Rules 2009,[150] although the core legislative principles are set out in Part 3 of the Banking Act 2009.

28–88

An overview of Part 3 is presented in s.136 of the Act, to the effect that:

28–89

---

[144] Banking Act 2009, s.100.
[145] Banking Act 2009, s.100.
[146] Banking Act 2009, s.232.
[147] Banking Act 2009, s.233(1).
[148] Banking Act 2009, s.233(3).
[149] See Banking Act 2009, s.234 and s.235.
[150] Bank Administration (England and Wales) Rules 2009 (SI 2009/357).

"(2)   The main features of bank administration are that –

(a)   it is used where part of the business of a bank is sold to a commercial purchaser in accordance with section 11 or transferred to a bridge bank in accordance with section 12 (and it can also be used in certain cases of multiple transfers under Part 1),

(b)   the court appoints a bank administrator on the application of the Bank of England,

(c)   the bank administrator is able and required to ensure that the non-sold or non-transferred part of the bank ("the residual bank") provides services or facilities required to enable the commercial purchaser ("the private sector purchaser") or the transferee ("the bridge bank") to operate effectively, and

(d)   in other respects the process is the same as for normal administration under the Insolvency Act 1986, subject to specified modifications."

The administration process is to be used when a private sector purchaser or a bridge bank has acquired the failing bank under ss.10 and 11 of the Act. The Bank of England must seek an administrator for the residual bank so that the residual bank can continue in operation in the way that administrations are organised under the Insolvency Act 1986 scheme.

The objectives of the bank administrator

28–90   The objectives of the administration scheme are set out in ss.137 through 140 of the Act. Section 137(1) provides for the two objectives of the bank administrator:

"(1)   A bank administrator has two objectives—

(a)   Objective 1: support for commercial purchaser or bridge bank (see section 138), and

(b)   Objective 2: "normal" administration (see section 140)."

Importantly, Objective 1 takes priority over Objective 2.[151] The first objective, to support the commercial purchaser or the bridge bank, is set out in the following terms:[152]

"Objective 1 is to ensure the supply to the private sector purchaser or bridge bank of such services and facilities as are required to enable it, in the opinion of the Bank of England, to operate effectively."

28–91   The second objective, to seek the "normal administration" of the business, is set out in the following terms:[153]

"Objective 2 is to—

(a)   rescue the residual bank as a going concern ("Objective 2(a)"), or

(b)   achieve a better result for the residual bank's creditors as a whole than would be likely if the residual bank were wound up without first being in bank administration ("Objective 2(b)")."

---

[151] Banking Act 2009, s.137(2).
[152] Banking Act 2009, s.137(1)(a).
[153] Banking Act 2009, s.137(1)(b).

The normality implied in the concept "normal administration" is a reference to returning the bank back to being a going concern or at least allowing it to become an undertaking which is more likely to satisfy the creditors' needs more fully than a straightforward winding up would do.

The process for obtaining a bank administration order

The process for obtaining a bank administration order is that the Bank of England may apply to the court, nominating an identified person as the bank administrator.[154] The grounds for making a bank administration order on the application of the Bank of England are that the Bank of England intends to make a property transfer instrument or will apply for a property transfer order,[155] and that the residual bank is unable to pay its debts.[156] The administrator is then required to make proposals for the administration of the business[157] and to share information when a transfer has been made to a bridge bank.[158] Termination of administration may occur when there is deemed to have been a "successful rescue" of the residual bank.[159]

28–92

I.   Financial assistance to banks and the Asset Protection Scheme

Section 228 of the Banking Act 2009 provides a power for the Treasury to support banks in relation to the statutory powers considered thus far in this discussion. Section 228(1) provides:

28–93

> "There shall be paid out of money provided by Parliament expenditure incurred—
> (a)   by the Treasury for any purpose in connection with Parts 1 to 3 of this Act,
> (b)   by the Treasury, or by the Secretary of State with the consent of the Treasury, in respect of, or in connection with giving, financial assistance to or in respect of a bank or other financial institution (other than in respect of loans made in accordance with section 229), or
> (c)   by the Treasury in respect of financial assistance to the Bank of England."

The Treasury therefore has a very broad power to act in relation to bank failure as discussed thus far. It enables the use of public money to support financial institutions. Section 229 of BA 2009 provides that the Treasury may make loans to banks out of the National Loans Fund.

The first example of this power in action was the Asset Protection Scheme by which the Treasury provided support to Royal Bank of Scotland ("RBS") and the Lloyds Banking Group ("Lloyds"). RBS was one of the ten largest banks in the world but was effectively insolvent during the financial crisis but for public money; Lloyds had acquired HBOS during an intense 36-hour period in a deal

28–94

---

[154]   Banking Act 2009, s.142.
[155]   Banking Act 2009, s.143(1)–(2).
[156]   Banking Act 2009, s.143(3).
[157]   Banking Act 2009, s.147(2).
[158]   Banking Act 2009, s.148.
[159]   Banking Act 2009, s.153.

brokered by the government, where HBOS was effectively insolvent but for public money. Further to a Treasury press release of February 26, 2009:

> "The Asset Protection Scheme will play a central role in restoring confidence in the UK's biggest banks by providing protection against future losses on their riskiest assets. Banks will receive protection for a proportion of their balance sheets so that the healthier core of their commercial business can continue to lend to creditworthy businesses and households. In return for access to the Scheme, banks will be required to pay a fee and enter into legally binding agreements to increase the amount of lending they provide to homeowners and businesses. The Government will report to Parliament annually on the delivery of the agreements."

The implementation of the Asset Protection Scheme generated detailed negotiations between Treasury officials and senior management of the banks involved. The process was in effect a process of contract negotiation for the terms on which protection in the form of public money will be provided in practice, as well as a public relations minefield in which the management of the press reporting of the implementation of the scheme has operated in parallel to the legal machinations of the parties.

J.   The role of law in financial crisis management

28–95   The role of law in financial crisis management is significantly more limited than law school jurisprudence courses (with their focus on positivism and the rule of law) would suggest. Banking law merely provides powers to the various regulators to compel or prevent action: however, the decisions as to what action should be taken to resolve the situation are primarily political, economic and commercial. The law does not compel any particular course of action; instead, the law empowers the regulators and politicians to take any course of action which seems appropriate (or expedient) in the context. That the law empowers the politicians and the regulators means that whatever they choose to do will be protected against future legal complaint, provided that their actions were in compliance with the legislation. Crisis management is typically concerned with knowing what has worked in the past and being able to identify the right response for the circumstances: or, in the jargon, the authorities must identify the right tool for the job.[160] Of course, the law is supreme in that banks, their shareholders and others are required to obey the lawful commands of the person who holds those legal powers, but the law itself does not compel the power-holder to act in any given way. Instead, politics and economics tend to take over when crises occur, and law is simply the backdrop against which regulators and politicians decide how to act in the circumstances. Therefore, the UK Banking Act 2009 is just a play-book which presents the Bank of England with a series of options for crisis management, ensuring that the law will compel others to obey its lawful commands in practice.

---

[160] Policy papers in the wake of the financial crisis 2007–09 tended to talk of "the regulatory toolkit", by which was meant the range of legal powers which regulators had so as to deal with different types of problem or crisis.

K. Financial Services Compensation Scheme ("FSCS")

The FSCS is amended to account for people who have rights to compensation further to the failure of a bank under the Act, and was considered in Chapter 9.

28–96

L. Inter-bank payments

Part 5 of the Act relates to the inter-bank payment system. The legislation is elliptically expressed but the underlying purpose is to prevent the seizure experienced by the inter-bank lending system in 2008 whereby banks were not lending money to one another and whereby inter-bank payment systems interfered with the ordinary operation of the banking system. An overview of Part 5 is set out in s.181 of the Act: it provides that the Bank of England is able "to oversee certain systems for payments between financial institutions", including but not limited to the activities of banks, including clearing and other systems for processing payments. This is the first time that payment systems have been subject to regulation in this fashion.

28–97

The Bank of England can recognise payment systems as falling within Part 5 by means of a recognition order if a failure or defect in those systems would affect the stability of financial systems in the UK.[161] The principles on which the Bank of England must carry out its oversight[162] and a code of practice[163] are to be published by the Bank of England under the Act. The Bank of England may also require that the operator of the payment system publish rules for the operation of its system.[164] Powers for the Bank of England to empower individuals to carry out inspections of the operation of payment systems are set out in s.193 et seq. of the Act.[165]

28–98

7. THE REFORM OF BANKING: RING-FENCING

A. Introduction

The landscape of British banking needs to change in the wake of the financial crisis (in which several formerly staid banks either fell into insolvency or needed to be rescued) and in the wake of the range of scandals which have come to light relating to UK banks. Those scandals, discussed in Chapter 45, include the Libor misquoting scandal, the misselling of PPI and interest rate swaps, involvement in money-laundering for drug cartels and sanctions-busting, failure to segregate client assets, and misreporting transactions to the regulators. The ethics and reputation of modern banking have clearly never been lower. It is incumbent on Parliament to respond. The principal reaction of the Conservative-led Coalition Government was to convene the Independent Commission on Banking and, when

28–99

---

[161] Banking Act 2009, s.184.
[162] Banking Act 2009, s.188.
[163] Banking Act 2009, s.189.
[164] Banking Act 2009, s.190.
[165] Banking Act 2009, s.193.

the scandals kept coming, the Parliamentary Commission on Banking Standards to suggest legislative change. We begin with the report of the Independent Commission on Banking.

B. The Independent Commission on Banking: "the Vickers Report"

Introduction

28–100   In June 2010, the Conservative-led Coalition Government in the UK commissioned a report from the Independent Commission on Banking ("ICB") under the leadership of Sir John Vickers. The report was intended to consider the organisation and regulation of banks in the UK in the light of the financial crisis. The final report ("the Vickers Report") was published on September 12, 2011. In December 2011 it was announced that the proposals made in the report would be reduced to legislative form for introduction to Parliament in 2012. This timetable was delayed with the revelation of several banking scandals led to the creation of the Parliamentary Commission on Banking Standards (as considered in Chapter 45). That legislation takes the form of the Financial Services (Banking Reform) Bill 2013, which is considered in the next section of this chapter. In essence the Vickers Report recommended that banks in the UK should have "mandated services" which were essential to the operation of the economy for individuals and small- and medium-sized enterprises ("SMEs") which would be "ring-fenced" from other financial activities; that banks should be more "loss-absorbing" in the sense of holding more capital against the possibility of future losses or another liquidity crisis; and that there should be increased competition in the banking sector. The proposals are not intended to be implemented in full until 2019.

The principal proposed reform: ring-fencing

28–101   The proposal made in the Vickers Report is that retail banks would be ring-fenced off from other entities, and that among the activities which would be prohibited for them would be derivatives. The intention is that retail banks would be limited to deposit-taking, payment systems and similar services. The US experience of the Glass-Steagall division between investment banking and retail banking activities is that it co-existed with an extended period of calm in US banking markets compared with the Great Crash of 1929 and the global financial crisis of 2007–09 which book-ended it. The Glass-Steagall Act was introduced to deal with the problem of over-leveraged banking houses crashing and wiping out their accountholders' savings. Some commentators, such as Prof Elizabeth Warren,[166] have identified that period of calm in ordinary banking in the USA in the 20th century with the Glass-Steagall controls. In the wake of the repeal of Glass-Steagall by the Clinton administration in 1999, those same commentators have pointed to an unprecedented period of volatility in financial markets,

---

[166] Formerly Professor of Law at Harvard, now US Senator.

accompanied by the growth in financial derivatives.[167] As such, the separation of retail banking (where deposits are taken from individuals and SME's and loans and account services are operated for them) from investment banking (including speculative activity on the banks' "proprietary account": that is, speculating with their own money) has strong antecedents. The toxic combination of a real estate market crash in the USA and the amplification of that retail crash into global derivatives markets via CDOs and CDSs meant that the re-introduction of a separation of banking activities was inevitable. The questions for the ICB were, having indicated that it favoured some form of separation of retail banks from other operations: which form of separation of activities should be used; and how should be rights and obligations of the participants be structured? The report addressed the first of these questions and failed properly to address the second, as we shall explore.

The nature of the ring-fence

The Vickers Report advocates a "ring-fence" to separate risky elements of banks off from the mainstream, retail banks but the precise legal nature of that structure is more difficult to identify in that Report (and the Bill, considered below, does not define its terms any more clearly). The approach which the Report takes is to insulate the retail bank from the investment bank. As a piece of literature, the Report is peculiar. Rather than argue from first principles for a ring-fence, the Report deals with some of the arguments for other structures instead and presents its model of a ring-fence as the only remaining feasible argument. This is a convenient approach if, like the Report, you fail to discuss the precise legal nature of the thing which you are proposing. In essence, the ring-fence is intended to operate so as to quarantine the retail-banking activities of the ring-fenced entity ("RFE") off from other banks and other members of its corporate group. The idea is that the bank has its mandated activities "fenced off" from the non-mandated activities of other subsidiaries. At the crudest level, the RFE would need to be a separate legal entity within any corporate group. The Report describes the ring-fence in the following fashion:[168]

28–102

> "The purpose of the retail ring-fence is to isolate those banking activities where continuous provision of service is vital to the economy and to a bank's customers ..."

Thus, the objective is to ensure that economically vital banking activities will be separated off from other financial market activities. The report identifies some commercial senses in which the ring fence will operate. The RFE must not be dependent on the rest of the group for its solvency or liquidity. The RFE must have an independent board of directors: but that does not necessarily mean that the board of directors must be different people, only that under company law they reach decisions which are in the particular interests (as they see them) of the RFE.[169] The RFE must have an "appropriate relationship"[170] with the rest of the

---

[167] See para.45–01.
[168] Independent Commission on Banking, Final Report, p.35.
[169] Companies Act 2006, s.172; as discussed in Hudson, "Directors" in *Charlesworth's Company Law* 18th edn (Sweet & Maxwell, 2010), 328 et seq.

group of companies such that the RFE has its own culture appropriate to its clientele and specific activities. A question remains as to the manner in which dividends and other distributions should be made within the group from the RFE to the holding company, as considered below.

28–103 As to the legal nature of the ring fence, it is provided elsewhere in the Report, under the somewhat misleading sub-title "legal and operational links":

> "• Legal and operational links. Where a ring-fenced bank is part of a wider corporate group, the authorities should have confidence that they can isolate it from the rest of the group in a matter of days and continue the provision of its services without providing solvency support.
>
> • As a result:
>
> (a) ring-fenced banks should be separate legal entities—i.e. any UK regulated legal entity which offers mandated services should only also provide services which are not prohibited and conduct ancillary activities;
>
> (b) any financial organisation owned or partly owned by a ring-fenced bank should conduct only activities permitted within a ring-fenced bank. This organisation's balance sheet should contain only assets and liabilities arising from these services and activities;
>
> (c) the wider corporate group should be required to put in place arrangements to ensure that the ring-fenced bank has continuous access to all of the operations, staff, data and services required to continue its activities, irrespective of the financial health of the rest of the group; and
>
> (d) the ring-fenced bank should either be a direct member of all the payments systems that it uses or should use another ring-fenced bank as an agent."

The opening paragraph is not a description of how the ring-fence would work in legal terms; rather it is description of the outcome which the ICB would like to result from the operation of the ring-fence. The later paragraphs provide that ring-fenced entities must be distinct legal persons, that the ring-fenced entity's balance sheet should contain only permitted assets, that the ring-fenced bank has access to appropriate personnel and facilities within the group, and that the ring-fenced bank should have suitable access to payment systems. However, this leaves open a number of detailed questions as to the nature of the ring-fence, as considered in the next section.

The legal nature of the ring-fence

28–104 The report is laden with jargon and, from a lawyer's perspective, it is imprecise on many crucial areas of detail. Nowhere is this more true than in relation to the legal and operational nature of the ring-fence. There are a number of questions which remain outstanding from the extract from the report considered immediately above.

28–105 First, what is the nature of the "distinctness" of the RFE's status as a distinct legal entity? The principle in *Salomon v A Salomon & Co Ltd*[171] provides that each company is a distinct legal entity: distinct from the human beings who create and staff it, and significantly also distinct from other companies in the same group of

---

[170] Independent Commission on Banking, Final Report, para.3.90, p.74.
[171] [1897] A.C. 22.

companies.[172] Therefore, there is nothing remarkable in requiring banking groups to operate "mandated activities" through a separate company. This does not answer any of the more complex questions about the way in which the RFE is to be protected from being used as a guarantor for the debts of other group companies or from having its assets hypothecated by other group companies by being used as collateral against borrowings or as credit support in relation to derivatives transactions, and so forth.[173] Similarly, distributions and dividends, as well as inter-company loans and transfer pricing, can allow cash and other assets to be bled out of one company in a group for the benefit of other companies in that same group. So, how would these sorts of distributions be prevented? Or would the RFE in fact be prey to those sort of intra-group transactions? For the RFE concept to work properly, then it would be important to control the extent to which this could happen. If the purpose of the ring-fence is to protect the assets of the RFE so that its depositors and accountholders will not lose their money, then it is important to prevent any transfer of assets within the corporate group because any mechanism which permits intra-group transfers can be exploited so as to reduce the total assets held by the RFE. The only way to be sure that the RFE maintains the assets of its depositors and accountholders is if its assets are entirely protected from distribution to or appropriation by other group companies.

Second, to what extent can the RFE share operations systems, "middle office" personnel and so forth with other group companies? If the RFE is intended to function as a distinct legal entity then a question arises as to whether it is de facto a distinct legal person or whether it is simply de jure a distinct legal person. A de facto legal person would operate from distinct premises (at least operating on a Chinese wall basis) with distinct employees performing all of its operational, legal, strategic, compliance and other commercial activities, without overlap with other entities in the same corporate group. By contrast, a de jure legal person would have its transactions booked as thought a separate legal person, it would have separately minuted meetings of its board of directors and prepare separate accounts, but those accounts would be rolled up into the group accounts, its in-house lawyers would also be the in-house lawyers for other group companies, its operations systems would also be the operations systems for other group companies, and so on. A de jure distinct legal company would only be distinct in relation to its paperwork, but not in relation to the activities performed by its human personnel. Such a company is only a distinct person in theory; in the day-to-day practicalities of its operations that company would be the same as every other company unless those operations functions are separated out de facto.

28–106

---

[172] *The Albazero* [1977] A.C. 774; *Adams v Cape Industries Plc* [1990] Ch 433; *Atlas Maritime v Avalon* [1991] 4 All E.R. 783, [1991] 1 W.L.R. 917.

[173] The report appears to accept the notion of cross-subsidy between group companies: para.3.21, p.44 in rejecting narrow banking as a model. The report is ideologically wedded to the universal banking model and the economies of scale which it offers, instead of seeing the massification of universal banks (such as Citigroup with its US$60.8 billion of losses in 2008–09) offering all financial services from one banking group as being a part of the problem. Another model would have been to require the complete separation of each company so that they are not connected within groups at all. There is very little focus in the report in this context on the effect of ring-fenced entities on ordinary people and SME's, and too much focus instead on traditional arguments about economies of scale of the sort which led to the problem of too many banks being too big to fail.

This, it is suggested, is key to the operation of the RFE as a distinct entity without any inter-action with the non-mandated (or, potentially toxic) activities of other group companies.

28–107   Third, to what extent should Chinese walls operate to maintain confidential information within the RFE? There is a brief mention of "Chinese wall" arrangements in the report.[174] A proper Chinese wall, as explained by Lord Millett in *Bolkiah v KPMG*[175] is not a perfunctory exercise nor is it something which can be taken "off the peg" and used in all situations. The principal goal of a Chinese wall arrangement is that no information can pass from one entity to another; no professional advisors nor other personnel can work for the two entities either simultaneously nor at any later stage such that confidential information could pass. So, ordinary precautions involve separating the premises which each entity would use whether in the same building or, preferably, by using different buildings, so that the personnel from one cannot access the physical space, photocopying facilities, recreational facilities, computer servers, and so forth of the other entity. Furthermore, as Lord Millett pointed out in *Bolkiah v KPMG*, it is not enough to satisfy the duty to maintain a Chinese wall that one does one's very best to prevent information from passing between personnel or between entities, but rather one bears a strict obligation to make sure that it does not actually happen in fact, whether or not anyone is blameworthy for the occurrence: effectively, there is a strict liability in equity for allowing confidential information to move across a Chinese wall. Nevertheless, it is permissible to have, for example, a single firm of accountants or solicitors representing both sides to the same piece of litigation, provided that a proper Chinese wall arrangement is put in place. In terms of the RFE then, it is important to recognise that a Chinese wall requires this level of separation. If what is meant is that there can be overlaps in personnel and operating systems, then that is not a Chinese wall in the English law sense of that term.

28–108   Fourth, would there be circumstances in which the ring-fence would permit the use of financial derivatives? For example, would the ring-fenced entity be allowed to use interest rate swaps to manage the interest rate risks on its own balance sheet? It could be argued that the use of derivatives for clearly identified risk management purposes would not be a prohibited investment banking transaction because it would not be putting the ring-fenced entity's own balance sheet at risk (at least, not any more than any hedged position does). However, the report does not provide answers at this level of detail.

28–109   One of the arguments that was used to support the idea of a ring-fence, as opposed to complete separation of retail banks from investment banks, was the reputational cost which banks would wish to avoid in having a ring-fenced entity within their group fail. However, as Alan Greenspan observed in evidence to a Congressional committee in the wake of the financial crisis, financial institutions do not necessarily operate sensibly in their own enlightened self-interest (as he more than anyone would previously have expected). The mythical reputational

---

[174] Independent Commission on Banking, Final Report, p.138.
[175] [1999] 2 A.C. 46.

cost to a financial institution[176] is a poor substitute, from a lawyer's perspective, for legal rights and obligations being placed on the various parties to such a structure. Instead the "cost" of full separation is emphasised in the report over a safe system of bank organisation. Moreover, in the wake of the financial crisis, when the reputations of all financial institutions are at rock bottom, it is very questionable whether the threat of reputational cost is any sort of deterrent at all.

C.   Financial Services (Banking Reform) Bill 2013

Introduction

There are four principal provisions in the Financial Services (Banking Reform) Bill 2013 ("FS(BR)B 2013") for present purposes. This discussion is based on the first draft of the Bill which was presented to Parliament for its first reading in the House of Commons. Those provisions will (necessarily) change during the passage of the legislation through Parliament. The Bill is intended to make amendment to the FSMA 2000.

28–110

The protection of core services

First, the PRA will be required to oversee ring-fenced banks so as to ensure that there is a continuous supply of the "core services" which those banks supply to the economy – in essence, the acceptance of deposits, the operation of bank accounts and the availability of overdrafts, as defined in clause 4 of the Bill. The Treasury will be empowered to make regulations as to other forms of core services which, it is suggested, should encompass all of the payment, accounting, lending and clearing services without which economic life would not function. To this end, the PRA has a "continuity objective" which involves the management of risk and oversight of the micro-prudential condition of banks which ensures continuity of core services.

28–111

The ring-fence

Second, identified services will be "ring-fenced". The approach which is taken in the legislation is the ring-fencing of banks which conduct "core services". Therefore, the legislation looks to protect those core service providers—retail banks, in effect—from risks caused to them by other activities. By limiting the definition of "core services" only to the acceptance of deposits, making payments, and making overdrafts available means that only a very narrow range of banking services are covered by the ringfence. There will be many banking services including the operation of current accounts, ordinary lending, mortgages, insurance and mainstream investment products (such as unit trusts) which will continue outside that ringfence and therefore unprotected.

28–112

---

[176] In the wake of the global financial crisis it is difficult to see how the reputation of banks could be any lower in any event. If a banking group was close to failure, or if its retail subsidiary was failing, then it is likely that it would have taken some reputational cost already.

Excluded activities for ring-fenced banks

28–113 Third, the Bill excludes certain activities from the permitted activities of ring-fenced banks. These activities include "dealing in investments as principal" which is a reference to making investments on its own account (i.e. with its own money where it stands to make a loss from that investment). The Treasury may make regulations in this regard: in particular so as to permit the sorts of investments which a ring-fenced bank may make. The real question—which will only be decided by future regulation because it is not addressed in the Bill at this stage—is which sorts of investment will be permitted and which will be proscribed. For example, one of the underlying objectives of this policy is to protect retail banks from the risks associated with markets like derivatives. Therefore, it is to be expected that derivatives will be proscribed. However, there are some types of derivatives which can be used for benign purposes—like interest rate swaps which are used to offset undesirable price movements in existing obligations, and which do not expose the buyer to unnecessary risk—and which therefore might be permitted for retail banks just as they are currently permitted for building societies. The derivatives which are candidates for exclusion are derivatives which expose the retail bank to any unhedged risk of loss which does not meet an existing obligation (such as the risk of increasing loan interest rates). Moreover, that the ring-fenced bank must not be dealing as principal means that it is, apparently, acceptable for that bank to deal in derivatives provided that it is acting on someone else's behalf (i.e. in buying those products for a customer).

The regulations governing ring-fencing

28–114 A fourth provision of note is the power for "the appropriate regulator" in whichever context—whether conduct of business or micro-prudential regulation—to make regulations to provide for the ring-fencing arrangements. Very significantly indeed, clause 142H anticipates that the ring-fence will permit retail banks and investment banks (and other entities) to form part of the same corporate group. This means that the ring-fenced entity can form part of the same group as other entities which raises a number of risks. Draft clause 142H provides in the following terms for the required contents of ring-fencing rules drafted by those regulators:

> "Ring-fencing rules made for the group ring-fencing purposes must include—
> (a)   provision restricting the power of a ring-fenced body to enter into contracts with other members of its group otherwise than on arm's length terms;
> (b)   provision restricting the payments that a ring-fenced body may make (by way of dividend or otherwise) to other members of its group;
> (c)   provision requiring the disclosure to the appropriate regulator of information relating to transactions between a ring-fenced body and other members of its group;
> (d)   provision requiring a ring-fenced body to ensure that its board of directors (or if there is no such board, the equivalent management body) includes to a specified extent—
>   (i)   members who are treated by the rules as being independent of other members of the ring-fenced body's group,
>   (ii) members who are treated by the rules as being independent of the ring-fenced body itself, and

(iii)   non-executive members;

(e)   provision requiring a ring-fenced body to act in accordance with a remuneration policy meeting specified requirements;

(f)   provision requiring a ring-fenced body to act in accordance with a human resources policy meeting specified requirements;

(g)   provision requiring arrangements made by the ring-fenced body for the identification, monitoring and management of risk to meet specified requirements;

(h)   such other provision as the appropriate regulator considers necessary or expedient for any of the purposes in subsection (4)."

Two issues emerge in particular from this provision. First, it is permissible to have some directors in common of the ring-fenced bank and the non-ring-fenced entities.

Second, there is an attempt to restrict the risk of the assets and conservative business model of the ring-fenced entity being abused by other companies in the same group. Let us consider what those risks would be without that provision. The ring-fenced entity could otherwise be exposed to transfer-pricing or loans within the group such that entities which are exposed to "excluded activities" such as investing on their own accounts—unless the ring-fenced entity is prevented from contracting with non-ring-fenced entities within the same group on any terms which cannot be proved to be a term that would have been in a contract with a third party. Clearly, it is suggested, the ring-fence should require that retail banks and investment banks cannot sit in the same corporate group, or at least that they must contract as though arm's length counterparties at all times (subject to a claw-back of any assets thus transferred): it is not enough simply to require that the two types of entity must act through different companies.

28–115

There are other risks, however. The ring-fencing regulations must make it plain that the ring-fenced bank must not take on exposures to such entities by acquiring shares in them or otherwise indirectly funding their investment activities (through intermediaries who on-lend funds to those subsidiaries), and not simply by making them loans. Moreover, under most master agreement structures and under most loan contracts, cross default will mean that a ring-fenced bank will be obliged to repay its obligations earlier than would otherwise be the case if another entity within its corporate group goes into insolvency or merely suffers a material deterioration in its credit worth: therefore, the regulations will have to prevent ring-fenced banks from being infected in this fashion by the misdeeds of other members of its corporate group.

28–116

The ring-fence regulations will also have to make it plain how the insolvency of the corporate group will not affect the ring-fenced bank: for example, the many breaches of the CASS regulations which were discussed in Chapter 9 demonstrate that an assumption that banks will hold client assets separately from other moneys cannot be relied upon, with the result that clients of the ring-fenced entity may be at risk of loss in practice even if the regulations on their face purport to protect them. To do otherwise would be to place all of the risk of loss on the FSCS in its underwriting of those accounts. Therefore, there needs to be another mechanism for ensuring that the retail bank will have the funds both to meet its obligations and to refund its clients.

28–117

28–118   There is one last, very real risk: in practice in banking groups, traders and documentation personnel mistakenly record the wrong corporate entity as being a party to a transaction, with the effect that a ring-fenced bank might be transposed for an investment bank as a party to a transaction, which is something which must be covered in the regulations by providing for the avoidance of such transactions. The regulations must anticipate innocent breaches of the ring-fence, as well as advertent breaches. They must also contain sufficient flexibility to confront structured breaches of the spirit of the ring-fence and not simply breaches of the letter of the regulations.

CHAPTER 29

THE BANKER AND CUSTOMER RELATIONSHIP

CORE PRINCIPLES

The normal relationship between banker and customer is governed entirely by the law of contract, and is not a fiduciary relationship unless there is something particular about the context to justify the inference of a fiduciary relationship. By taking a deposit from a customer, the banker is understood to have undertaken to repay the amount of that deposit when the customer makes a demand for that money (classically, but typically not today) at the branch where the deposit was made. The advent of internet banking and automated teller machines (as considered in the next chapter) mean that demands for repayment of the deposit—referred to in ordinary parlance as "taking money out of the bank"—can now occur at different branches of the bank or outside bank premises entirely.

A bank owes a duty of confidentiality to its customers. This duty of confidentiality may be breached where statute (particularly banking regulation) so requires, where the bank is otherwise legally compelled to pass information to some other person, where there is a duty to the public to make disclosure, where the interests of the bank require disclosure, or where the disclosure is made with the customer's express or implied consent. The duty of confidentiality begins from the moment that a banker-customer relationship begins.

The banker is required to obey any mandate given to it by its customers that is within the scope of their contract: a mandate is an instruction to the bank to make payments, to honour cheques, or otherwise deal with the customer's account. Refusal to comply with a customer's instructions may give rise to damages, unless the bank has one of the pretexts for so doing identified in the case law discussed in this chapter. The customer's principal obligation (aside from any terms including in any specific banking contract) is to take reasonable care to prevent any fraud being exercised over their account.

A banker's obligations are also demarcated in part by the consumer credit legislation, the unfair contract terms legislation, money laundering regulation, and so on, as considered elsewhere in this book and as outlined below.

1. INTRODUCTION

29–01 The heart of banking law is the contractual relationship between banker[1] and customer.[2] Therefore, a customer will be required to rely on the law of contract for the most part in seeking to exert its rights against a bank. The first section of

---

[1] The word "banker" is used in the old cases on which traditional banking law is based. It is a slightly quaint usage which suggests a rich individual taking deposits from well-to-do Georgians and Victorians, and owing them personal obligations based on propriety in maintaining the depositor's

this chapter considers the nature of the banker-customer relationship as a contract in some detail; whereas the remainder of the chapter will focus primarily on the legal relationship constituted by various types of bank accounts. The old banking law cases create a number of esoteric rules relating to the treatment of banker's obligations towards their customers. Chapter 28 has considered the regulatory principles governing the activities of banks; whereas this chapter considers the private law context of the inter-action between banker and customer, those circumstances in which the bank may be subject to fiduciary duties, the types of accounts and services which are provided by banks, and so forth.[3]

2. THE PRIVATE LAW ANALYSIS OF THE RELATIONSHIP BETWEEN BANKER AND CUSTOMER

A. The commercial nature of the banker-customer relationship

The culture in which banks operate today is very different from the culture in which banks operated in many of the core cases on which banking law is based: those cases were decided in the early 19th century.[4] At that time, the culture of banking was a narrow business in which smaller private banks took deposits from and made loans to people who were from the upper classes or who were affluent members of the upper middle class. Today, banking is a mass market activity in which most adults in England and Wales have bank accounts and therefore their relationship with their bank is not the personal relationship which might have been the case in the early 19th century, unless one is so very rich as to do one's banking with the "private client" banking business of clearing or investment banks, as was considered in Chapter 27.[5]

29–02

B. The relationship of banker and customer is a debtor-creditor relationship, not a trustee-beneficiary relationship

When I was a very young boy, my mother took me to open an account with the National Savings scheme at the Post Office. I deposited my birthday money and received my savings account book with a credit in it. Some while later I returned to the Post Office with my mother to make a small withdrawal from the account so that I could buy Christmas presents. I was distressed to find that I was not given back the £5 note which I had deposited originally. The serial number on the

29–03

---

confidence and exquisitely good manners. We would think today about mass banking for the vast majority of the population, as opposed to personal banking. Therefore, we tend to think about "banks" as opposed to "bankers". However, I shall retain the quaint usage "banker" for the most part because it is used in the cases and in the Bills of Exchange Act 1882 s.2, and because I rather like it.

[2] *Foley v Hill* (1848) 2 H.L. Cas. 28, 9 E.R. 1002.

[3] The best discussion of this material in M. Hapgood (ed.), *Paget's Banking Law*, 13th edn (LexisNexis, 2007), Chs 7, 18 and 19; and in briefer compass, R. Cranston, *Principles of Banking Law*, 2nd edn (OUP, 2002), Ch.5.

[4] e.g. *Foley v Hill* (1848) 2 H.L. Cas. 28, 9 E.R. 1002.

[5] For example in London most of the private client offices aimed at these "high worth" individuals are located in the Mayfair area (especially in Berkeley Square), or else they are in Switzerland, Monaco and similar jurisdictions.

banknote I received from the cashier was not the serial number on the note which I had deposited. My mother reassured me that this was perfectly normal and that I should not be worried. This younger version of myself was clearly concerned that the adults were involved in some sort of swizz.[6] I had in fact had my first encounter with the risk associated with depositing money with banks: when money is deposited with a bank, that money becomes absolutely the property of that bank, and the bank records in its books that it owes a debt to its depositor equal to the amount of the deposit to the depositor. The depositor thus becomes one of the bank's creditors. That is why a bank account which is not overdrawn is said to be "in credit" because the depositor is a creditor of the bank; whereas when a bank account is overdrawn, and the bank has thus made a loan available to the depositor in excess of amounts which have been deposited with it by the depositor, it is said that the account is a "debit" in that the depositor owes money to the bank and is therefore its debtor.

29–04   It had been asserted in the early days of banking law that when a bank received a deposit from a depositor that it should be treated as a trustee of that deposit, so that it would not be entitled to use that money for any other purpose. In the earliest days of private banking, it might have been reasonable to suppose that bankers were holding money on trust when their customers were only a few very rich individuals who had forged a personal relationship with the banker and agreed to have the banker act in their financial affairs. However, even by the middle of the 19th century this would be contrary to the expectations and business model of bankers who aim to receive deposits and then to invest those deposits either by lending them to other customers at a higher rate of interest than the interest which is payable to the depositor, or to invest that money more generally on other markets, as was discussed in Chapter 27. The modern understanding of banking arrangements as being based on contract and not trust emerged in the early Victorian era. It was in *Foley v Hill* that Lord Cottenham LC described the inter-action of banker and customer in those terms[7]:

> "[M]oney placed in the custody of a banker is, to all intents and purposes, the money of the banker, to do with it as he pleases; he is guilty of no breach of trust in employing it; he is not answerable to the principal if he puts it into jeopardy, if he engages in a hazardous speculation; he is not bound to keep it or deal with it as the property of his principal; but he is, of course, answerable for the amount, because he has contracted, having received that money, to repay to the principal, when demanded, a sum equivalent to that paid into his hands."

A banker therefore owes only personal obligations to its customers (that is, its depositors) when it receives their deposits. In that sense, money transferred to a

---

[6] The word "swizz" denotes a con, trick, or fraudulent scheme; it was one used in a lot of the books set in boys' boarding schools which I read at the time: for example Buckeridge, *Jennings Follows A Clue* (Armada).

[7] (1848) 2 H.L. Cas. 28, 9 E.R. 1002, 1005. See also *Westminster Bank Ltd v Hilton* (1926) 43 T.L.R. 124, 126, per Lord Atkinson to the same effect, identifying also that the banker acts as the customer's agent in relation to the payment and collection of cheques.

bank is an outright transfer of money to the bank.[8] So, for example, when money is paid to a bank under a mistaken understanding that that bank is entitled to act as an authorised bank, the payers are not entitled to recover the amounts paid over on the basis of that being money had and received to the use of the payers precisely because the proper analysis of an ordinary deposit with a bank is that the bank takes that money absolutely and so it is not held to the use (nor on trust for) the depositor.[9] Similarly, when a bank provides references as to a customer's credit worth it is not doing so as a fiduciary and therefore will owe liabilities only in negligence for any misrepresentation, and will owe no amount in damages to the customer for a negative reference if the information provided in that reference is accurate.[10]

C.   General duties under private law

The general duties of a bank under general private law in England and Wales are those obligations which were set out in Chapters 16 through 26 of this book. They govern the power to make and to terminate contracts; liability for damages for breach of contract or for fraudulent misrepresentation or for negligent misrepresentation; the ineffectiveness of contracts created through undue influence, which has been a particular issue in relation to banking transactions as considered in Chapter 24; the creation and breach of fiduciary duties such as trusts; and so forth. This chapter is concerned with the particular obligations which have been created by equity and the common law to be borne specifically by bankers and their customers. The courts are reluctant to imply terms into a contract between bank and customer[11]: so, for example, a bank was found not to owe an implied contractual duty to inform a customer of a new type of account which would pay out interest which could have replaced that client's existing, non-interest bearing account[12]; similarly a bank did not owe its customer any obligation to provide advice to it or to provide information to it outside the terms of its agreed banker-customer relationship.[13] Ordinarily, the proper law governing a bank account is the law of the jurisdiction in which that account is held.[14]

29–05

---

[8] *Hirschhorn v Evans (Barclays Bank garnishees)* [1938] 2 K.B. 801, 815, per Mackinnon L.J. So a bank operating an account on behalf of a Lloyds insurance syndicate would not hold those moneys on trust (without something more in the arrangement to require that analysis): *Mann v Coutts & Co* [2003] EWHC 2138; [2004] 1 C.L.C. 301.

[9] *Box v Barclays Bank Plc* [1998] Lloyd's Rep. Bank 185.

[10] *Turner v Royal Bank of Scotland* [2001] EWCA Civ 64.

[11] *Fennoscandia Ltd v Robert Clarke* [1999] Lloyd's Rep. Bank 108.

[12] *Suriya & Douglas v Midland Bank Plc* [1999] Lloyd's Rep. Bank 103.

[13] *Fennoscandia Ltd v Robert Clarke* [1999] Lloyd's Rep. Bank 108.

[14] *Libyan Arab Foreign Bank v Bankers Trust Co* [1989] Q.B. 728, 746.

D.   Implied terms typically read into a banking contract by the common law

That a customer must make a demand on its bank before payment is due

29–06   A customer must make a demand of its bank before payment of amounts deposited with that bank become due. A number of cases have considered this issue. Notably in *N Joachimson v Swiss Bank Corp*[15] a partnership, which comprised enemy aliens during the 1914–1918 war, sought recovery of funds from its bank.[16] The issue arose before the Court of Appeal whether the partnership was required to have made a "demand" on its bank for repayment before that bank was required to make payment to its customer, or whether repayment was owed throughout the life of the contract just as a lender is entitled to enforce immediate repayment in relation to a borrower (as is demonstrated in Chapter 32).[17] It was held by the Court of Appeal that payment was only required to be made once a demand was made. The position was described by Atkin L.J. in the following way:

> "I think that there is only one contract made between the bank and its customer. The terms of that contract involve obligations on both sides and require careful statement. They appear upon consideration to include the following provisions. The bank undertakes to receive money and to collect bills for its customer's account. The proceeds so received are not to be held in trust for the customer, but the bank borrows the proceeds and undertakes to repay them. The promise to repay is to repay at the branch of the bank where the account is kept, and during banking hours. It includes a promise to repay any part of the amount due against the written order of the customer addressed to the bank at the branch, and as such written orders may be outstanding in the ordinary course of business for two or three days, it is a term of the contract that the bank will not cease to do business with the customer except upon reasonable notice. The customer on his part undertakes to exercise reasonable care in executing his written orders so as not to mislead the bank or to facilitate forgery. I think it is necessarily a term of such contract that the bank is not liable to pay the customer the full amount of his balance until he demands payment from the bank at the branch at which the current account is kept. Whether he must demand it in writing it is not necessary now to determine. The result I have mentioned seems to follow from the ordinary relations of banker and customer, but if it were necessary to fall back upon the course of business and the custom of bankers, I think that it was clearly established by undisputed evidence in this case that bankers never do make a payment to a customer in respect of a current account except upon demand."[18]

The principal point in this context is that banks are not required to make payment immediately; unlike the situation in which a bank has lent money to a borrower where the courts have held that the bank as lender is ordinarily entitled to insist on immediate repayment.[19] Bankers are not required to make immediate

---

[15] [1921] 3 K.B. 110.
[16] In both *Schering Ltd v Stockholms Enskilda Bank* [1946] A.C. 219, HL, per Lord Thankerton and *Arab Bank Ltd v Barclays Bank* [1952] 2 T.L.R. 920 it was suggested that "the effect of the outbreak of war upon contracts legally effected by it is to abrogate or destroy any subsisting right".
[17] See para.32–34; see *Brightly v Norton* (1862) 122 E.R. 116, 118.
[18] [1921] 3 K.B. 110, 127, per Atkin L.J. See also *Lloyds Bank Ltd v Margolis* [1954] 1 W.L.R. 644. A creditor claiming money in a debtor's account through the creditor by means of a garnishee order could not acquire rights against funds in that account without complying with contractual conditions precedent to accessing those funds: *Bagley v Winsome* [1952] 2 Q.B. 236.
[19] *Brightly v Norton* (1862) 122 E.R. 116, 118.

payment without demand or notice. The basis of this rule is, interestingly, a perception of the business of bankers at the time: that is, the law was shaped by an understanding of what bankers actually did in the world at the time, and not on the basis of what the law of contract should require of them nor even what the court thought was reasonable for them to do in the abstract. Thus, the law followed practice rather than the other way around.

The question arises as to what constitutes a "demand". The accepted definition of a "demand" is that "there must be a clear intimation that payment is required to constitute a demand",[20] but no further formality is required than that. The power of a bank to demand repayment of a loan on demand is considered in detail in Chapter 32.[21] Things which would constitute a demand include an instruction in writing signed by the customer being sent to the manager of the branch of the bank where the account is kept. It has also been held that the service of a writ for payment would constitute a demand.[22] What is not clear is whether turning up at one's bank and asking for payment purely verbally would constitute a "demand". Inserting one's bank card into an automated teller machine (or, "cashpoint", as discussed in the next chapter), entering one's PIN ("personal identification number") and selecting withdrawal of the amount held in the account must constitute a "demand" because entry of the PIN is an electronic signature prior to the giving of the instruction to make repayment to the customer.[23]

29–07

Importantly, then, in relation to the solvency of a bank, it does not owe the deposits made with it back to its customers until those customers make a demand of it for repayment. The time for the purposes of the limitation period for an action based on a demand begins when the bank acknowledged that it owed a debt.[24] A customer could not recommence the limitation period by making a fresh demand and so arguing that the right to sue the bank began afresh.[25]

The right to demand payment

As is discussed in detail in Chapter 32,[26] banks are legally entitled to demand immediate repayment of amounts owed by way of loan or in the form of charges from its customers. This power to demand payment immediately must be read in the light of the agreement between the parties as to the bankers' rights.[27] If the terms of the agreement are that an overdraft or some other loan is to be repayable on demand, then the bank may recover the amount immediately by demand even if the bank knew that the purpose of the loan was to pay for a specified

29–08

---

[20] *Re Colonial Finance, Mortgage, Investment and Guarantee Co Ltd* (1905) 6 SRNSW 6, 9; accepted in *Re A Company* [1985] B.C.L.C. 37, per Nourse J.

[21] See para.32–33.

[22] *N Joachimson v Swiss Bank Corp* [1921] 3 K.B. 110, 115, per Bankes L.J.

[23] It is difficult to see in *N Joachimson v Swiss Bank Corporation* [1921] 3 K.B. 110 why the parties had to argue the question up to the House of Lords: the point is not made entirely plain. It is assumed that the insolvency of the partnership meant that a formal demand could not have been made after that event.

[24] *Bank of Baroda v Mahomed* [1999] Lloyd's Rep. Bank 14.

[25] *Bank of Baroda v Mahomed* [1999] Lloyd's Rep. Bank 14.

[26] See para.32–34 et seq.

[27] *Titford Property Co Ltd v Cannon Street Acceptances Ltd* unreported May 22, 1975, per Goff J.

transaction which would take some time to be completed.[28] It is not open to the customer to argue that the loan should not recoverable immediately on demand just because the bank is deemed to have known that the loan was intended to be for a fixed amount.[29] (The situation is different in relation to term loans, as is considered in Chapter 32.)

The duty of confidentiality

29–09   Banks owe a duty of confidentiality to their customers. This duty is considered in detail below.[30]

E.   The fiduciary obligations of banks

When a bank will be a fiduciary

29–10   The concepts relating to fiduciary liability were considered in Chapter 5. Ordinarily, fiduciary concepts do not apply in relation to banking contracts. Following on from the discussion in the previous section, it follows that if a banker is a not a trustee simply as a result of being a banker, then a banker will not ordinarily be a fiduciary.[31] The banker will only be a trustee if there is something specific about the relationship to make that banker a trustee. So, for example, if a bank agrees to act as trustee for one of its customers then clearly that bank would therefore have become a trustee in that context;[32] or if money is received by a bank to be held for the benefit of a third party then the bank owes fiduciary duties to that third party.[33] The circumstances in which a bank may be held to be a fiduciary in general were set out in Chapter 5: they may arise when the bank acts as trustee or as agent for a customer; when the bank is also providing discretionary investment advice as well as acting as banker; when a bank receives property unconscionably as a result of some breach of trust or other fiduciary duty, and so forth. There are other situations in which a bank will be a fiduciary which relate, beyond the matters considered in Chapter 5, to confidentiality. The reader is referred back to that discussion.

---

[28] *Williams and Glyn's Bank v Barnes* [1981] Com. L.R. 205; *Lloyds Bank Plc v Lampert* [1999] 1 All E.R. (Comm) 161, CA.

[29] *Bank of Ireland v AMCD (Property Holdings) Ltd* [2001] 2 All E.R. (Comm) 894, Lawrence Collins J.

[30] See para.28–10.

[31] *Foley v Hill* (1848) 2 H.L. Cas. 28, 9 E.R. 1002.

[32] *Rowlandson v National Westminster Bank Ltd* [1978] 1 W.L.R. 798; [1978] 3 All E.R. 370.

[33] [1978] 1 W.L.R.; [1978] 3 All E.R. 370.

3.   The Bank's Duty of Confidentiality

A.   The core statement of the duty of confidentiality in *Tournier v National Provincial*

A banker's duties to its customers include a duty of confidentiality. When a bank deals with a person's finances that is generally taken by the customer to be dealing with that customer's confidential affairs. People tend to be touchy about the secrecy of their money. If we consider the same idea from another perspective, if a bank were to advertise its customer's financial affairs to businesses who might want to market goods and services to them directly, or were to make them known to the customer's enemies or rivals, then that would be unacceptable to almost all customers. In relation to commercial organisations, the confidentiality of their accounts, their cash flow, and their financial organisation is a significant part of their business and would be incredibly valuable to their business rivals if it became known. Therefore, for practical reasons and for reasons of propriety, bankers owe a duty to each customer to keep their financial affairs confidential.

29–11

The generally accepted,[34] central statement of the bank's duty of confidentiality was set out in *Tournier v National Provincial and Union Bank of England*[35] in the following terms:

29–12

> "In my opinion it is necessary in a case like the present to direct the jury what are the limits, and what are the qualifications of the contractual duty of secrecy implied in the relation of banker and customer. There appears to be no authority on the point. On principle I think that the qualifications can be classified under four heads: (a) where disclosure is under compulsion by law; (b) where there is a duty to the public to disclose; (c) where the interests of the bank require disclosure; (d) where the disclosure is made by the express or implied consent of the customer."[36]

(This particular case involved an allegation of slander and therefore a jury was required to decide on the effect of that slander.) There are therefore two central principles. First, that the bank owes a general duty of confidentiality to its customers when acting as banker in relation to their accounts. However, that duty may be overridden in any one of four circumstances (numbered (a) to (d) by Bankes L.J.) which are considered immediately below in relation to "limitations on the duty of confidentiality".

In *Tournier v National Provincial and Union Bank of England* the plaintiff, Tournier, was a customer of the defendant bank who had kept a large overdraft for some time and who was employed as a travelling salesman. A third party wrote a cheque to Tournier but instead of paying that cheque into his own account, Tournier indorsed the cheque in favour of a bookmaker. The defendant bank found out that the cheque had been indorsed in favour of a bookmaker by ringing the recipient bank. The manager of the defendant bank then telephoned Tournier's employers to find out his personal address and disclosed the fact that

29–13

---

[34]   See, e.g. *Turner v Royal Bank of Scotland* [1999] Lloyd's Rep. Bank 231, CA.
[35]   [1924] 1 K.B. 461.
[36]   [1924] 1 K.B. 461, 472–473, per Bankes L.J.

Tournier had had an overdraft, speculated that he must nevertheless be obtaining money from somewhere, and disclosed the fact that Tournier had indorsed a cheque in favour of a bookmaker. Tournier sued the defendant bank for slander and on the basis that the bank had breached its duty of confidence to him. A majority of the Court of Appeal held that the defendant bank had indeed breached its duty of confidentiality to the plaintiff while it was acting in its role as banker, and that it was therefore liable to Tournier in damages at common law.

B.   Limitations on the duty of confidentiality

The role of money laundering regulation

29–14   The principal limitation on the banker's duty of confidentiality relates to that banker's obligations under money laundering regulation to disclose suspicious transactions to the authorities. Clearly, this punches a large hole in the patina of confidentiality which bankers are otherwise supposed to maintain. These issues were considered in Chapter 15.

The commencement of the duty of confidentiality

29–15   There is a question as to when the duty of confidentiality arises, and therefore there is a question as to when a person becomes a customer and so protected by the duty of confidentiality. A person becomes a customer without doubt when she opens a bank account with a bank.[37] In *Importers Co Ltd v Westminster Bank Ltd*[38] the Privy Council held that:

> "... the word "customer" signifies a relationship in which duration is not of the essence. A person whose money has been accepted by a bank on the footing that they undertake to honour cheques up to the amount standing to his credit is, in the view of their Lordships, a customer of the bank ... irrespective of whether his connection is of short or long standing."

Therefore one becomes a customer on opening an account and on a bank agreeing to honour cheques on one's behalf. As Lord Davey held elsewhere, "there must be some sort of account, either a deposit or a current account or some similar relation, to make a man a customer of a banker".[39] The question then is as to any other sort of activity which would bring two people within the relationship of banker and customer. It has been held that if an agent of a bank offers investment advice to a person who does not hold an account with the bank, and then if the agent sent written instructions to the bank that it accept the agent's recommendation to that person, then the relationship of banker and customer existed from the moment that the bank accepted the agent's instructions in favour of that person.[40] It was accepted by Atkin L.J. in *Tournier* that information obtained about a customer even if not directly derived from the customer's

---

[37] *Ladbroke v Todd* (1914) 111 L.T. 43; *Commissioners of Taxation v English, Scottish and Australian Bank Ltd* [1920] A.C. 683.

[38] [1927] 2 K.B. 297.

[39] *Great Western Railway Co v London and County Banking Co Ltd* [1901] A.C. 414, 420.

[40] *Woods v Martins Bank Ltd* [1959] 1 Q.B. 55.

account should be covered by the duty of confidentiality if it nevertheless arose generally out of the relationship of banker and customer.

The following sections consider the four circumstances identified by Bankes L.J. in which the duty of confidentiality may be circumvented.

(1) Disclosure compelled by law

Disclosure will be permitted where it is compelled by the law more generally: particularly by statute. For example, as was already mentioned, when disclosure is compelled by money laundering regulation, then the duty of confidentiality will be circumvented. It is assumed that disclosure would be required "by law" if a court order required such disclosure. Furthermore, where a regulator or other government agency requires disclosure of information further to a statutory power held by that person, then that would compel disclosure too. For example, a banker assumed itself to be under a duty to make disclosure in *Libyan Arab Foreign Bank v Bankers Trust Co*[41] when disclosure was required of it by the Federal Reserve Bank of New York.

29–16

(2) Duty owed to the public

Many of the decided cases during the 20th century, including the *Joachimson* case, related to enemy aliens during time of war: that is, the law permitted the assets of citizens of enemy countries to be frozen during war, and thus bankers would be permitted to breach their duties of confidentiality where the holder of the account was such an enemy alien. It is suggested that suspecting that an account was held by a terrorist cell would encompass a "danger to the state or public"[42] sufficient to justify breaching the duty of confidence, although Bankes L.J. held in *Tournier* that disclosing information to the police because the customer was suspected of a crime would be unwarranted.[43] In relation to sufficiently serious circumstances, such as terrorism or at time of war, that such niceties as those suggested by Bankes L.J. would be considered to be less important in the eyes of law enforcement agencies. In relation to the collapse of the international financial institution Bank of Credit and Commerce International it was held that having access to that institution's accounts overrode the duty of banker-customer confidentiality.[44]

29–17

(3) The bank's interest

The only decided case in which a bank has sought to contend that it was breaching the duty of confidentiality in its own interest was *Sutherland v Barclays Bank Ltd*.[45] In that case a wife had been gambling and so the bank refused to pay on her cheques. The wife complained to her husband and her

29–18

---

[41] [1989] Q.B. 728; [1989] 3 All E.R. 252.
[42] *Weld-Blundell v Stephens* [1920] A.C. 956, 965, per Lord Finlay.
[43] [1924] 1 K.B. 461, 474.
[44] *Pharaon v Bank of Credit and Commerce International SA* [1998] 4 All E.R. 455.
[45] (1938) 5 LDAB 163, cited in *Paget's Banking Law*, para.8.5.

husband telephoned the bank. The banker explained to the husband that the reason for the failure to honour those cheques was that the wife was using them for gambling purposes. Du Parcq J. held that it was in the bank's interest to make the disclosure and also that the wife had impliedly consented to disclosure by involving her husband in the contretemps.

(4)   Authorised disclosure

29–19   When a customer authorises disclosure of information, either actually or inferentially, then the bank is permitted to breach its obligation of confidentiality.[46] Clearly, when a person waives her rights of confidentiality then she may not subsequently seek to rely on those rights against the person who had the benefit of that waiver.[47]

Other circumstances

29–20   It has been held by the Court of Appeal that when a bank made disclosure to a trustee in bankruptcy over a husband's estate that there were difficulties with the enforceability of a caution which the trustee in bankruptcy had entered over the wife's matrimonial home.[48]

4.   THE BANKING CONDUCT OF BUSINESS SOURCEBOOK ("BCOBS")

29–21   The Banking Conduct of Business Sourcebook ("BCOBS") was introduced in 2009 to extend formal regulatory principles of the proper conduct of business by banks in relation to their ordinary customers. Previously there had been two non-statutory, voluntary banking codes in existence which experience had suggested were simply not being observed properly by the banks in dealing with their customers. Indeed, there have been significant mis-selling scandals involving banks dealing with their retail customers (principally the PPI mis-selling scandal, in relation to which banks have been fined many billions of pounds). The BCOBS principles are considered in Chapter 31 in relation to retail customer banking. The remainder of this chapter will continue to focus on the older case law which formed the core of banking law before the introduction of the prudential regulatory principles considered in Chapter 28 and the conduct of business principles in Chapter 31.

---

[46]   See above.
[47]   *Turner v Royal Bank of Scotland* [1999] Lloyd's Rep. Bank 231.
[48]   *Christofi v Barclays Bank Plc* [2000] 1 W.L.R. 937.

5. THE OPERATION OF ACCOUNTS AND PAYMENTS THROUGH ACCOUNTS

A.   Introduction

This section considers a number of principles relating to the operation of bank accounts and relating to liabilities as to the making of payments through accounts. This discussion also serves as a preface to the next chapter in which the various forms of bank payment are considered. Strictly, payments are made through bank accounts not when payments are made to the payee's bank but rather only when that payment is credited to the payee's bank account.[49] It is suggested that this principle has an echo of the time when payment was actually made in coin and a record of that deposit of coin entered in the banker's books; whereas in the modern age the receipt of payment by the bank is merely an adjustment of the level of the value in bank accounts which should automatically oblige the recipient bank to account to its customer for the amount of that payment.

29–22

B.   Bank mandates

The meaning of a "mandate"

A "mandate" borne by a bank is a statement of the powers which a bank possesses when acting on behalf of each of its customers in operating their accounts and making payments under their customer's instructions; equally a mandate is expressive of the obligations which a bank has undertaken in relation to the operation of a customer's account. It is common, for example, for people to give powers to their banks to make a monthly payment to their mortgagee from their current accounts or to make periodical payments of rent to the customer's landlord, or to make periodical payments to insurers, in the form of a standard order or a direct debit. The customer's bank is thus given a mandate by the customer to make a payment to the intended recipient in the identified amount. In relation to more complex bank accounts—including bank accounts owned by companies—there will also be a need to identify by way of a mandate which individuals are permitted to sign cheques from that account and so forth. Among the mandates which are given by a customer to its bank are cheques written by that customer. On ordinary principles of the law of contract, a bank may act on oral instructions given to it by its customer even if the parties' relationship was otherwise set out in writing, and so the customer may not later bring proceedings against the bank for any loss caused by the bank performing that oral instruction.[50]

29–23

---

[49] *Tayeb v HSBC Bank* [2004] EWHC 1529; [2005] 1 C.L.C. 866, at [47].
[50] *Morrell v Workers Savings and Loan Bank* [2007] UKPC 3; [2007] Bus. L.R. Digest D57.

Loss suffered further to the honouring of fraudulent cheques

29–24   The question arises: what liability does a bank bear if it acts in relation to its customer's account and in so doing causes that customer loss? In answer to that question, if the bank was acting within the terms of its mandate then it had authority to act and would thereby suffer no liability,[51] provided there was no further factor beyond acting within the terms of the mandate. So, if the bank paid out on a cheque which was signed by a person who had authority to sign cheques under the mandate, then the bank would not be liable for any loss which flowed from the bank honouring that cheque.[52] The bank might, however, be liable, it is suggested, if it had had knowledge of a fraud in which that authorised signatory was embroiled even if it was nominally acting within the terms of its mandate. By contrast, if the customer fails to take sufficient care in relation to its account so as to prevent fraud—for example by leaving her cheque book lying around in full view of third parties, or in a company failing to have a system in place to prevent employees pilfering money from the company's accounts—then Lord Finlay held that:

> "if [the customer] draws the cheque in a manner which facilitates fraud, he is guilty of a breach of duty as between himself and the banker, and he will be responsible to the banker for any loss sustained by the banker as a natural and direct consequence of this breach of duty".[53]

A bank owes duties only to its customers in relation to cheque payments, but does not owe duties to payees of cheques who are not its customers.[54] The effect of fraudulent cheques is considered in the next section.

Payments discharging another person's debts

29–25   It happens occasionally that someone chooses to pay another person's debts for them. Suppose that Xavier chose to pay Zena on a debt which Yasmin owed to Zena. This may arise in a number of circumstances. It may be that Xavier simply wanted to help out his friend Yasmin and so paid her debt with her agreement. Alternatively, it may be that Xavier stands to take some direct or indirect benefit from the cancelling of Yasmin's debt with Zena so that Xavier can exert pressure over Zena or Yasmin. This sort of pressure could also have been exerted by means of the different mechanism of Xavier acquiring Zena's interest to the debt so that Xavier could seek to enforce the debt against Yasmin perhaps to force Yasmin closer to bankruptcy or to bully her into agreeing to a takeover or to enter into some other transaction. In this second class of circumstances Yasmin would

---

[51] *London Intercontinental Trust Ltd v Barclays Bank Ltd* [1980] Lloyd's Rep. 241; *Symons v Barclays Bank* [2003] EWHC 1249 (Comm).

[52] *London Intercontinental Trust Ltd v Barclays Bank Ltd* [1980] Lloyd's Rep. 241.

[53] *London Joint Stock Bank Ltd v Macmillan* [1918] A.C. 777, 789.

[54] *Grosvenor Casinos Ltd v National Bank of Abu Dhabi* [2008] EWHC 511 (Comm), per Flaux J., where sums in the region of £99 million had been gambled by an individual at a casino with losses of £18 million being suffered by that individual, but two bearer cheques in relation to about £6 million of that amount owed were not honoured even though the individual bearer had vouchsafed that the two bearer cheques he carried would be honoured. It was held that the holder's bank owed no such duties to any other person as were owed to its customer.

prefer that Xavier had not paid off her mortgage. It may be that Yasmin does not want her debt to be paid off at all (she may be contesting it or she may feel that the matter is perfectly under control).

Nevertheless, Equity provides that if one has one's debts paid by another person, then one may not retain that benefit[55]; and to look at the same issue from the other side, the payer who has discharged the debt is entitled to rely on their payment and the benefit connected to that payment.[56] What if a bank paid a customer's debt but did so wrongly, perhaps ignoring a necessary formality before payment was made? For example, if a bank pays one of its customer's debts out of that customer's account in breach of a mandate that two signatures were required, then that bank is entitled to rely on the same equitable principle as a defence against the customer's action for money had and received.[57] That means, the bank can argue that the customer benefited from having that debt discharged and therefore that the customer has a benefit in that amount which cannot be recovered from the bank on the basis that the bank did not obey the formal requirement. It is suggested that this principle is unfortunate in circumstances in which the customer did not want the debt paid at all (because it was contesting the amount of the debt or the quality of the service provided to it by a third party), or did not want the debt paid yet (so as to protect its cash flow) because the bank's actions may cause other losses to the customer (for example, using up the last of its funds which it had intended to use in another transaction). It is suggested that this principle should apply only if the bank had not failed to observe some formal requirement, if the bank had been given a mandate to make that payment, and if breach of the first two provisos did not cause the customer loss.

29–26

C.   The bank's liability to pay compensation in relation to a wrongful refusal of a payment order (including a cheque)

There will be a serious effect for a customer who is in business (and for retail customers potentially too) if its bank refuses to make payment in accordance with its agreement with its customer because that customer may lose business or suffer loss as a result of that payment not being made: a retail customer could lose her rented home, a trade customer could lose its own customers or suppliers, or the customer may suffer a worsening in her credit rating thus harming her ability to access financing in the future.[58] The House of Lords took the view that trading customers would be entitled to compensation in *Wilson v United Counties Bank Ltd* to the effect that:

29–27

> "... the refusal to meet the cheque, under such circumstances, is so obviously injurious to the credit of a trader that the latter can recover, without allegation of special damage, reasonable compensation for the injury done to his credit."[59]

---

[55] *Blackburn Building Society v Cunliffe* (1882) 22 Ch.D. 61.
[56] *AL Underwood Ltd v Bank of Liverpool and Martins* [1924] 1 K.B. 775.
[57] See para.20–27.
[58] *Kpohraror v Woolwich Building Society* [1996] 4 All E.R. 119.
[59] [1920] A.C. 102, 112, per Lord Birkenhead.

Where the customer is not in trade, it was at that time assumed that there was a need to prove damage or else that customer will only receive nominal damages.[60] However, the Court of Appeal recognised subsequently that retail customers can suffer harm, as indicated above, by lack of access to finance to buy their homes, services and so on.[61]

D. Fraud and forged payment instructions in relation to accounts

The effect of forged signatures

29–28 A forged signature on any bill of exchange (including a cheque) will be "wholly inoperative".[62] The question which is considered in the following section relates to the effect of a bank honouring a cheque or other bill or instruction which was honoured by a bank by making payment from the customer's account, and in relation to which the customer then seeks recovery of the money taken from its account against the bank.

The customer's duties in relation to fraud or forgery in relation to its own account

29–29 A customer owes two duties to its bank in relation to fraud and forgery over that account: first, to take reasonable care when drawing cheques so as to avoid fraud and, secondly, to inform its bank in the event that there is any forgery which comes to its attention.

29–30 In exercise of the first principle, Lord Finlay held as follows in *London Joint Stock Bank Ltd v Macmillan*[63]:

> "The relation between banker and customer is that of debtor and creditor, with a superadded obligation on the part of the banker to honour the customer's cheques if the account is in credit. A cheque drawn by a customer is in point of law a mandate to the banker to pay the amount according to the tenor of the cheque. It is beyond dispute that the customer is bound to exercise reasonable care in drawing the cheque to prevent the banker being misled. If he draws the cheque in a manner which facilitates fraud, he is guilty of a breach of duty as between himself and the banker, and he will be responsible to the banker for any loss sustained by the banker as a natural and direct consequence of this breach of duty."

In this case a clerk sought to defraud a partnership by writing out a cheque from the company's account, as he usually did, and sought a partner's signature deliberately when that partner was hurrying out of the office. The clerk had deliberately left blank spaces on the cheques so that he could obtain a partner's signature for an amount that appeared to be a petty cash amount but then add in figures later so that the cheque was in fact a cheque for a much larger amount. The bank cashed the cheque and the clerk absconded with the money. The question which arose was whether the partnership could recover its loss from the

---

[60] *Rae v Yorkshire Bank Plc* [1988] F.L.R. 1.
[61] *Kpohraror v Woolwich Building Society* [1996] 4 All E.R. 119.
[62] Bills of Exchange Act 1882, s.24.
[63] [1918] A.C. 777, 789.

bank or whether the bank was entitled to rely on the customer's duty to it to prevent fraud on its own bank account. The House of Lords found for the bank. As Lord Finlay put it.

> "It has been often said that no one is bound to anticipate the commission of a crime, and that to take advantage of blank spaces left in a cheque for the purpose of increasing the amount is forgery, which the customer is not bound to guard against. It has been suggested that the prevention of forgery must be left to the criminal law. I am unable to accept any such proposition without very great qualification. Every-day experience shows that advantage is taken of negligence for the purpose of perpetrating frauds.... As the customer and the banker are under a contractual relation in this matter, it appears obvious that in drawing a cheque the customer is bound to take usual and reasonable precautions to prevent forgery. Crime, is indeed, a very serious matter, but every one knows that crime is not uncommon. If the cheque is drawn in such a way as to facilitate or almost to invite an increase in the amount by forgery if the cheque should get into the hands of a dishonest person, forgery is not a remote but a very natural consequence of negligence of this description."

Thus, the partnership bore a responsibility to prevent fraud; with the result that negligent failure to prevent fraud made fraud all the more likely and therefore that the partnership would bear responsibility for the loss that resulted from this fraud. At the other end of the spectrum from the *Macmillan* case where blanks in which figures could be included were left, is the case of *Societe Generale v Metropolitan Bank Ltd*[64] in which the letter "y" was added to the word "eight" on a cheque so as to acquire seventy-two pounds fraudulently (being the difference between eight pounds and eighty pounds): in the latter case it was held that no bank would ordinarily be expected to spot the insertion of a single letter on a cheque and therefore that no liability should attach to the bank for a failure to notice that fraudulent addition. The difference between these cases could be said to be the difference between an obvious and a trifling fraud on a cheque; or alternatively the difference could be said to be that banks are more likely to escape liability in spite of being the professionals who ought to be better able to spot these sorts of fraud than their customers, even if their customers also bear responsibilities to avoid fraud.

Under the second principle, the customer bears an obligation to inform the bank as soon as possible once a fraud has come to its attention.[65] So, if a husband finds out that his wife has been fraudulently cashing cheques on his personal account but fails to inform the bank of the fraud, then he is not later entitled to rely on the forgeries because his silence led to him being estopped from relying on those forgeries.[66] It has been held that having merely constructive knowledge of the forgery—that is, knowledge of factors which would have made a reasonable person inquire into the payments and to find out that they are forgeries—would not be sufficient to establish liability.[67]

29–31

---

[64] (1873) 27 L.T. 849.
[65] *Greenwood v Martins Bank Ltd* [1933] A.C. 51.
[66] *Greenwood v Martins Bank Ltd* [1933] A.C. 51.
[67] *Patel v Standard Chartered Bank* [2001] Lloyd's Rep. Bank 229. See also *Price Meats Ltd v Barclays Bank Plc* [2000] 2 All E.R. (Comm) 346. cf. *McKenzie v British Linen Co* (1881) 6 App. Cas. 82 and *Morrison v London County and Westminster Bank Ltd* [1914] 3 K.B. 356.

29–32 It was held in *Tai Hing Cotton Mill v Liu Chong Hing Bank Ltd*[68] that the customer did not owe duties to take reasonable precautions in the management of its business generally to prevent fraudulent cheques being presented against its accounts and also to check its accounts periodically to seek out any such fraud. In that case an accounts clerk had forged the managing directors' signature on cheques drawn on the company's accounts equalling HK$5.5 million in the aggregate. The bank paid under the cheques from the company's accounts. The company sought to recover the money from the bank. The bank alleged that the company's internal control systems were inadequate to prevent fraud of this sort. It was held that the only duty which the customer bore was to exercise due care when drawing cheques not to permit fraud and also to notify its bank if it found fraud: this did not equate to the more extensive duties of maintaining internal systems to prevent fraud nor of establishing internal systems to seek out fraud. Thus, the customer's duties are more passive than active in the sense that the customer is not required to seek out fraud on its accounts.

E. Estoppel by representation

29–33 The doctrine of estoppel by representation was considered in Chapter 23. Where a person makes a representation to a bank, for example that cheques were genuine, then that person is estopped from arguing subsequently that those cheques are not genuine after the representation had caused the bank to pay on the cheques.[69]

F. The extent of the bank's duties to its customer in relation to misappropriation of funds from a customer's account

29–34 There are two different approaches to the factual situation in which an impostor (or some similar fraudster) purports to withdraw money from a customer's account. There are two points of view. On the one hand it could be said that bankers should bear a high standard to ensure that the person seeking to withdraw money is indeed the customer; or alternatively it could be said that it would be an obstacle to efficient banking business if the bank were held to such a high standard that each withdrawal had to be investigated too closely. In *Selangor United Rubber Estates Ltd v Cradock (No.3)*[70] and in *Karak Rubber Co Ltd v Burdon (No.2)*[71] a high standard was imposed on banks. It was held in *Selangor* that the bank would have knowledge of anything if its officers had knowledge of circumstances which would have put them on inquiry as to the presence of a fraudulent design. In *Karak* the manager of the bank was induced into paying out

---

[68] [1986] A.C. 80; [1985] 2 All E.R. 947, PC. Applied in *Yorkshire Bank v Lloyds Bank* [1999] Lloyd's Rep. Bank 191.
[69] *Bank of England v Vagliano* [1891] A.C. 107 (forgeries of bills which had the customer's signature endorsing their validity estopped the customer from pleading the invalidity of those bills later); *Brown v Westminster Bank Ltd* [1964] 2 Lloyd's Rep. 187 (fraudulent cheques had been asserted were genuine by the customer who was subsequently estopped from pleading their fraudulent nature).
[70] [1968] 2 All E.R. 1073; [1968] 1 W.L.R. 1555.
[71] [1972] 1 All E.R. 1210; [1972] 1 W.L.R. 602.

on a cheque which was presented as part of a takeover fraud in which fraudsters stole money from the target company to fund their intended takeover: it was held that a banker bore a contractual duty of care and skill as required of a reasonable banker and that due to the size of the amount in this case that the bank would be liable under its contractual duty of care to the customer. In *Gray v Johnston*[72] Lord Cairns emphasised the likely interference with ordinary banking business that would be caused if the test were set too high. More recent cases, such as the decision in *Barclays Bank v Quincecare Ltd*[73] and the decision of the Court of Appeal in *Lipkin Gorman v Karpnale Ltd*,[74] have emphasised the principle that banks proceed on the basis of trust and therefore that a banker should not be required to assume fraud but rather could be entitled to assume honesty and so need only make enquiries when the facts suggested something suspicious.[75]

On the one hand, this vaguely Pollyanna-like approach to banking business, which assumes that everyone is honest in an honest world, is inappropriate in an age of money laundering and similar regulation which in any event requires bankers to inquire into the nature of payments and to be astute in identifying payments connected with criminal activities. The common law should recognise that banks bear obligations to consider the nature of deposits and payments in any event, that the banks have sufficient resources and staff to bear such an obligation, and that therefore the banks should be expected to inquire reasonably into the bona fides of withdrawals and presentation of cheques to ensure there is no fraud. These common law principles are simply out of keeping with a world of money laundering regulation imposing positive obligations on banks to inquire into the sources of payments and with a world of rampant fraud (such as misusing credit card details and other "identity theft" crimes) on the internet. On the other hand, there is the practical problem that there are so many payments made through all of the accounts operated by a bank in any given day and so many cheques which fall to be cleared, that as a practical matter not all frauds will be spotted. In relation to credit card fraud, banks use software models to identify unusual payments in relation to client accounts so as to spot likely fraud. Their argument would be that there is little more that they can do in a world of so many payment systems and so many bank accounts. In the 19th century cases, there were many fewer people with bank accounts and all payments were made in cash or by paper cheque which made the identification of fraud or misfeasance more likely.

29–35

With this debate in mind, the common law principle was expressed slightly differently by May L.J. in *Lipkin Gorman v Karpnale*[76]:

29–36

"For my part I would hesitate to try to lay down any detailed rules in this context. In the simple case of a current account in credit the basic obligation on the banker is to pay his customer's cheques in accordance with his mandate. Having in mind the vast numbers of cheques which are presented for payment every day in this country, whether over a bank counter or through the clearing [system], it is in my opinion only when the circumstances are such that any

---

[72] (1868) L.R. 3 H.L. 1.
[73] [1992] 4 All E.R. 363.
[74] [1992] 4 All E.R. 409.
[75] *Barclays Bank v Quinecare Ltd* [1992] 4 All E.R. 363, 377, per Steyn J.
[76] [1992] 4 All E.R. 409, 421.

reasonable cashier would hesitate to pay a cheque at once and refer it to his or her superior, and when any reasonable superior would hesitate to authorise payment without enquiry, that a cheque should be paid immediately upon presentation and such enquiry made."

A similar approach was taken by Parker L.J. as to whether or not "a reasonable and honest banker knew of the relevant facts".[77] In this conceptualisation there is no necessary assumption of honesty, instead the emphasis is on whether or not there is anything about the cheque which would cause a reasonable banker to hesitate to pay the cheque. What is less clear is whether this conceptualisation requires a banker to be astute in seeking out cheques over which it would be reasonable to refuse immediate payment, or whether this process is entirely passive and it is only if a suspicious cheque comes to the banker's attention that something need be done. Again, it is suggested that this common law doctrine should fall into line with the regulation of money laundering and the obligation to identify suspicious transactions on an active basis. The regulatory context of money laundering is what is actually informing banking practice in any event.

G.   Payments made by mistake

29–37   There are three contexts in which mistake has already been considered in *Section One: General Principles* of this book. The first context is where a mistake is made in creating a contract: that is not significant here. The second context is where payment is made under a mistake by a bank and recovery of the money paid is sought by the customer from whose account the payment was made under the principles of money had and received: these principles were discussed in Chapter 20, and are considered below as a personal claim for money had and received. The third context is where payment is similarly made under a mistake and the customer or some other person seeks a proprietary remedy in relation to that mistaken payment: this was also considered in Chapter 20 and in Chapter 21, as is outlined below as a proprietary claim to recover money.

29–38   The following general principles were set out in *Barclays Bank v WJ Simms Son*[78] in this regard by Goff J.:

"(1) If a person pays money to another under a mistake of fact which causes him to make payment, he is prima facie entitled to recover it as money paid under a mistake of fact. (2) His claim may however fail if (a) the payer intends that the payee shall have the money at all events, whether the fact be true or false, or is deemed in law so to intend; or (b) the payment is made for good consideration, in particular if the money is paid to discharge, and does discharge, a debt owed to the payee (or a principal on whose behalf he is authorised to receive the payment) by the payer or by a third party by whom he is authorised to discharge the debt; or (c) the payee has changed his position in good faith, or is deemed in law to have done so."

The decision of the House of Lords in *Westdeutsche Landesbank v Islington*[79] clarified the approach to both personal and proprietary claims by establishing the

---

[77] [1992] 4 All E.R. 409, 441.
[78] [1980] Q.B. 677, 695, per Goff J.
[79] [1996] A.C. 669.

following principles.[80] Where money is paid from an account under a mistake, then the claimant customer may bring an action for money had and received to recover an amount equal to that mistaken payment from the bank, subject to what is said below. Where money is paid from an account under a mistake, the claimant may establish a proprietary right over a mixed fund containing that money or the traceable proceeds of that money under the tracing principles set out in Chapter 23 of this book. A constructive trust may be imposed over a mistaken payment if the recipient of that payment had knowledge of the fact that the payment was made under a mistake before the money is dissipated[81]; no proprietary claim may be brought over an account into which that money was made if the account subsequently went overdrawn after that money had been paid into it because it is said that no trace of that original money remained in that account at the time of bringing the proprietary claim. The particular problem of banks mistakenly making payments under cheques into their customers' accounts is considered in the next chapter.[82]

H.   Tracing payments

The law on tracing actions—whereby a claimant seeks to recover the value of property taken from it by tracing into substitute property or into mixtures of property containing the traceable proceeds of that original property—is considered in Chapter 23. This area of law has become particularly important in relation to banking transactions because of the ease with which money can be paid out of one bank account and passed at great speed into another bank account in another jurisdiction belonging to another person, and then transferred onwards again any number of times. Identifying where the proceeds of that original account have gone and seeking to bring a proprietary claim against the fund of money (or other property) where that money eventually came to a halt, is a complex process. The applicable principles are considered in full in Chapter 23 primarily by reference to banking transactions in any event.

29–39

I.   Unfair contract terms

The law on unfair contract terms was considered in detail in Chapter 18.

29 40

---

[80] Thus overruling *Sinclar v Brougham* [1914] A.C. 398; and also, it is suggested, *Fibrosa Spolka Akcyjna v Fairbairn Lawson Combe Barbour Ltd* [1943] A.C. 32.

[81] In relation to the law on mistake, knowledge must be had at the time of receiving the payment (*Kelly v Solari* (1841) 9 M. & W. 54, 58, per Lord Abinger) but it is suggested that there is no reason why knowledge could not be developed in relation to constructive trust at any time before the property is disposed of so that it becomes impressed with that trust.

[82] See para.30–15.

J.   Consumer credit legislation

29–41   The Consumer Credit Act 1974 (as amended by the Consumer Credit Act 2006) is intended to protect consumers in relation to consumer credit and hire purchase agreements which involve amounts of money not exceeding £25,000. The consumers covered by this Act include individuals, partnership and unincorporated associations, but not companies. People who are engaged in the statutorily specified forms of business are required to be licensed to conduct such business. Conducting such business without a licence is a criminal offence.[83] The principal forms of business specified in the statute are the provision of credit to consumers (such as loans or credit cards), hire purchase of chattels, credit brokerage, debt advice, and debt collecting. Among the most important provisions of the 1974 Act are those avoiding extortionate credit bargains,[84] another is the requirement that the "true cost" of the borrowing is made clear to consumers,[85] and yet another is the proper form of advertisements.[86] The operation and regulation associated with the 1974 Act is outwith the scope of this book. The regulation of consumer credit contracts under the 1974 Act is conducted by the Office of Fair Trading ("OFT"). This legislation is considered in greater detail in Chapter 31. Most aspects of mortgage business are now regulated by the FCA.

6.   BANKER'S RIGHTS RELATING TO THE TREATMENT OF MONEYS

A.   The banker's lien

29–42   A lien is a right to retain property owned by another person until that other person pays an amount which is owed in full. Bankers have a lien implied by the common law which attaches to all "commercial paper" (that is, instruments carrying a value, such as bonds) which are lodged with a bank in the ordinary course of its banking business.[87] The nature of liens in general terms was discussed in Chapter 22: they are a possessory right to restrain property until some other payment is made, rather than a proprietary right.

B.   Rights of appropriation

29–43   A difficult problem arises if money is purportedly to be paid into or out of a customer's account but if the customer does not make plain which account is intended. The customer has the right to nominate the account in the ordinary course of events,[88] although the banker will have a right to appropriate the funds to a suitable account if no such nomination is made by the customer.[89] It is open

---

[83]   Consumer Credit Act 1974, s.39.
[84]   Consumer Credit Act 1974, ss.137–139.
[85]   Consumer Credit Act 1974, s.20.
[86]   Consumer Credit Act 1974, s.43.
[87]   *Brandao v Barnett* (1846) 12 Cl. & F. 787.
[88]   *Deeley v Lloyds Bank Ltd* [1912] A.C. 756, 783, per Eve J.
[89]   [1912] A.C. 756, 783.

to the bank to open a new account if that is necessary to protect its security.[90] For example, in *Deeley v Lloyds Bank*[91] an amount would have been appropriated to an account which would effectively have paid off the mortgage debt on which the bank sought to base its security when dealing with that customer. (Keeping the mortgage debt in existence would have meant that the bank could have seized the mortgaged property if the customer failed to perform its obligations in the future, whereas paying off that debt would have extinguished that mortgage security.) It was held by the House of Lords that the banker was entitled to protect its position by simply creating a new account and paying the money into that new account so that the mortgage debt in the other account was not extinguished. The metaphor which was used in this case was that the banker was entitled to "rule off" the amounts in its books belonging to the previous account and so to create a brand new account in its ledgers under that "ruling off". (Indeed, that was a time of simple, schoolroom metaphors for banking, whereas now as new account would be made by a few keystrokes on a computer.[92]) This principle is based by Lord Shaw on the banker's natural inclination to protect its own position[93] but has not been extended beyond the operation of bank accounts in the case law.[94]

C.   Combination of accounts

A bank has a power to combine a customer's accounts in certain circumstances so as to meet a payment obligation of that customer. The obligation must be a payment instruction made by the customer to its bank. The most common example would arise if a customer wrote a cheque drawn on an account which had insufficient funds in it to meet the payment instruction embodied by the cheque, but if the customer had other accounts with the bank which contained sufficient funds to meet the payment obligation. In such circumstances the banker would be empowered to combine those accounts so as to make the payment in full. This may be done by creating an overdraft over the account on which the cheque was drawn and using the funds in the other account to secure that overdraft. Otherwise, the cheque would have to be dishonoured due to a lack of funds. The banker is ordinarily permitted to do this without notice to the customer, unless the parties had agreed that there would be no such combination of accounts.[95] Where a company was wound up and a cheque paid into that company's bank account after the winding up, the bank was allowed to combine the company's accounts.[96]

29–44

---

[90] *Deeley v Lloyds Bank Ltd* [1912] A.C. 756, 785, per Lord Shaw.
[91] [1912] A.C. 756, 785.
[92] This phenomenon was ridiculed by Fletcher Moulton L.J. in the Court of Appeal in this case, and seems to be treated with similar derision by *Paget's Law of Banking*, 227.
[93] *Deeley v Lloyds Bank Ltd* [1912] A.C. 756, 785, per Lord Shaw.
[94] *Re Diplock* [1948] Ch. 465, 555, per Lord Greene M.R.
[95] e.g. *Barclays Bank v Quistclose* [1970] A.C. 567 where the bank knew that the funds had been deposited for a specific purpose and so could not be used to set off amounts owed to the respondent bank.
[96] *National Westminster Bank Ltd v Halesowen Presswork and Assemblies Ltd* [1972] A.C. 785; [1972] 1 All E.R. 641.

D. Banker's right of set-off

29–45 Set-off is permitted in equity in circumstances in which there are amounts owed between parties which are connected in such a way that it would be inequitable to permit the claimant to receive what is owed to her without setting off an amount owed reciprocally.[97] In relation to banks the situation is often slightly different from that classic case, however, because it is usually the bank which is seeking to set off amounts. The problem can be understood in the following way. A banker, as considered above, is required to make payments on a cheque out of an account which is in credit.[98] What if the bank is owed money by that customer: is it entitled to set off the amounts it is required to pay out against the amounts which are owed to it (and thus not make payment in the amount of the set-off)? It has been held that a bank may have an equitable right to set off amounts held to its customer's account against amounts owed to it if the bank has a contractual right so to do.[99] In such situations, the terms of the contract between the parties are paramount, whether based on explicit contractual provision or an implied contractual term on ordinary principles of contract law.[100] It would, however, not be permissible for the bank willy-nilly to set off amounts between accounts held by a customer; nor, for example, could a bank seek to set off amounts paid into a customer's current account against a loan made by the bank to that customer, or else the customer would be constantly in danger of having the money held to her account in her current account taken from her at the bank's whim.[101] This returns, it is suggested, to the notion that set off is permitted only in equity in this context and only in circumstances where it would not be inequitable to set off amounts owed reciprocally between the parties. Banks have sought to argue, where they have lent money to X, that the bank should be entitled to set off amounts which are to be paid into an account which was allegedly held on trust for X against X's loan (but where the existence of that trust has not been yet been proven). However, the courts have refused to award set off in these circumstances because on the facts of the decided cases the existence of that trust (or, "nominee account" arrangement) was not proven and the court was not prepared to delay payment into that account while a mere suspicion of a trust arrangement was proved or disproved by lengthy litigation,[102] in particular where it was considered to be the bank's fault that it had not established the beneficial ownership of the account in the first place. More generally, if the customer is not the beneficial owner of the moneys held in that account then they may not be used to set off against some personal obligation of the customer because that would be to permit a trustee to use a beneficiary's property to discharge her own debts.

---

[97] c.g. *Hanak v Green* [1958] 2 Q.B. 9.

[98] *Bhogal v Punjab National Bank* [1988] 2 All E.R. 296; *BCCI v Al Saud* [1997] 6 Bank L.R. 121, CA.

[99] *Saudi Arabian Monetary Agency v Dresdner Bank* [2005] 1 Lloyd's Rep. 12: applying *Bhogal v Punjab National Bank* [1988] 2 All E.R. 296; *BCCI v Al Saud* [1997] 6 Bank L.R. 121, CA.

[100] *Saudi Arabian Monetary Agency v Dresdner Bank* [2005] 1 Lloyd's Rep. 12.

[101] *Bradford Old Bank Ltd v Sutcliffe* [1918] 2 K.B. 833, 847, per Scrutton L.J.

[102] *Re Willis Percival & Co, Ex p. Morier* (1879) 12 Ch.D. 491; *Re Hett, Maylor & Co Ltd* (1894) 10 T.L.R. 412; *Uttamchandani v Central Bank of India* (1989) 133 Sol. Jo. 262, CA.

7. BANK CHARGES

A. Demand

The right to make a demand for payment was considered above.[103] The role of demand in relation to recovery of loans and overdrafts is considered in Chapter 32.

29–46

B. Interest

The obligation to pay interest is ordinarily set out as a term of the contract. The obligation to pay default interest if there is some failure to perform obligations was considered in detail in Chapter 19.[104] A bank has been held to be entitled to compound interest until judgment where it could show that was a common usage in banking practice and that therefore a term should be implied into its agreement with its customer to that effect in relation to circumstances involving promissory notes issued in relation to a mortgage taken over a ship.[105] Where the setting of the rate of interest is left contractually to the discretion of the lender, it has been held that the lender's discretion should nevertheless not be treated as being entirely unfettered.[106] Rix L.J. has held that the bank's discretion "should not be abused" and that this discretion shall be "limited, as a matter of necessary implication, by concepts of honesty, good faith, and genuineness, and the need for the absence of arbitrariness, capriciousness, perversity and irrationality".[107] Banks must use objective criteria in making this decision—and it is common for banks to link their interest rates to a given spread above base rates as adjusted for the risk profile of each particular client.[108]

29–47

C. Bank charges and unfair contract terms

The context and detail of the unfair contract terms legislation—dealing with unreasonable exclusion of liability clauses—was considered in Chapter 18. The principal issue in that discussion in relation to bank related to exclusion of liability provisions contained in banks' standard contractual terms and imposed on consumers are a result. In the House of Lords in *Director General of Fair Trading v First National Bank*[109] it was held that the parties should be free to rely on the terms of their contract if the interest payable under that contract caused no

29–48

---

[103] See para.28–08.
[104] See para.19–39.
[105] *National Bank of Greece SA v Pinios Shipping Co No.1* [1990] 1 A.C. 637.
[106] *Paragon Finance Plc v Staunton* [2001] EWCA Civ 1466.
[107] *Socimer International Bank Ltd v Standard Bank London Ltd* [2008] EWCA Civ 116, at [66]. See also Arden L.J. rejecting the idea that "reasonableness" in this context should be linked to administrative law ideas of reasonableness which Rix L.J. accepted in the *Socimer* case: *Lymington Marina Ltd v MacNamara* [2007] EWCA Civ 151.
[108] *Socimer International Bank Ltd v Standard Bank London Ltd* [2008] EWCA Civ 116, at [66].
[109] [2001] UKHL 52.

imbalance in the parties' rights and obligations.[110] Nevertheless it was held that the contract was susceptible to an assessment of its fairness. In *Office of Fair Trading v Abbey National Plc*[111] the High Court considered the different, high profile question as to whether or not bank charges on ordinary customer's current accounts were "unfair" within the Unfair Terms in Consumer Contract Regulations 1999. It was held that the particular charges in issue were unfair because they had been arbitrarily levied and were not exempt as a part of the "price or remuneration" for any particular service: that is, the banks had simply chosen to charge £30 for a cheque written when overdrawn but could not demonstrate that the cost to them of processing such a cheque amounted to £30. The role of the 1999 regulations in preventing professionals from relying on "unfair" and "unintelligible" terms in their agreements was re-emphasised by the Court of Appeal in *Office of Fair Trading v Foxtons Ltd*.[112]

8. BANK ACCOUNTS

A. The nature of bank accounts

29–49 A bank account is a chose in action in which a customer deposits money with a bank and the bank recognises that money is credited to the customer's account. The banker owes contractual duties of creditor and debtor to its customer.[113] The banker and customer will agree contractual terms on which the banker will provide services to the customer, including the availability of cheque books, bank cards and so forth. Also important is the availability of overdraft facilities. Indeed, as any student or former student reading this book will know, the purpose of opening a bank account is often to acquire an overdraft facility from the bank without having any money to deposit into that account. As discussed below, an overdraft is a loan made by the bank to the customer which is often unsecured. Bank accounts may be either current accounts with overdraft facilities and the other services considered above, or deposit accounts in relation to which the parties' purpose is that the customer will make deposits and that the bank will credit the customer with amounts of interest on the amount of the deposit credited to it.

29–50 If we are being accurate, we must think of "amounts being credited to the customer's account" and strictly not of "money being held in an account". It is common to talk colloquially of "money" being "held" in a bank account but these metaphors are inappropriate.[114] There is no "money" strictly so called being held precisely because notes and coins are not kept separately for any individual customer, but rather only a book entry recording the balance of amounts which have been deposited into that account less amounts which have been withdrawn

---

[110] See on this last point, Lord Millett at [57].
[111] [2008] EWHC 875.
[112] [2010] Bus. L.R. 228.
[113] *Foley v Hill* (1848) 2 H.L. Cas. 28, 9 E.R. 1002.
[114] Just as most people talk of "the sun rising in the morning" when everyone knows, after just a moment's thought, that what happens is that the Earth orbits the sun and rotates on its axis: the sun does not move, let alone rise.

from that account, as discussed in Chapter 2. Similarly, nothing is "held" because that both suggests tangible property is being kept physically (as opposed to a mere book entry being made) and the bank does not act as a trustee in relation to that amount which is credited to the customer's account.

B.   Current accounts

A current account is the ordinary account held between banker and customer. As was said at the beginning of this chapter, the relationship of the parties is a relationship of debtor and creditor. Any money deposited becomes the property of the bank and the bank then owes a purely contractual obligation to account to the customer in accordance with the terms of their agreement for the money deposited with the bank. It is only when accounts go overdrawn, when the customer purports to withdraw more money than has been credited to that account, that matters change as is discussed below.

29–51

C.   Deposit accounts

A deposit account can be an account in relation to which the deposit can be withdrawn on demand, in relation to which the deposit can only be withdrawn on specified notice, or in relation to which the deposit can only be withdrawn after the effluxion of a fixed period of time. As with a current account, the deposit is a transfer of money to the bank which is repayable in accordance with the terms governing withdrawal of the money from the account. However, a deposit account may not go into overdraft because the purpose of a deposit account is for the bank to hold a credit to the customer's account to earn interest.[115]

29–52

D.   Overdrafts and loan accounts

An overdraft facility on a bank account is a form of loan made by a bank to the accountholder.[116] An overdraft is a permission granted to an accountholder to draw on the facility expressed by the bank account—with its payment cards, cheques, and so on—above the amount of any credit which the accountholder may have in that account, but always subject to a maximum amount which can be drawn down. Therefore, the bank is effectively advancing a loan to the accountholder to a maximum amount identified in the overdraft facility agreement. (The principal discussion of loans is set out in Chapter 32 below: the reader is referred to that discussion for a full analysis of the law relating to loans.)

29–53

As with ordinary loans, unless there is a contractual provision to the contrary it is open to the bank to terminate the overdraft on demand.[117] On the opening of a

29–54

---

[115] *Barclays Bank Ltd v Okenarhe* [1966] 2 Lloyd's Rep. 87, per Mocatta J.
[116] Banks are not obliged to make overdrafts available, nor even to consider whether or not to make them available, unless there is a specific contractual obligation which requires them to do so: as confirmed by *Office of Fair Trading v Abbey National Plc* [2008] EWHC 875 (Comm), at [78], per Andrew Smith J.
[117] *Lloyds Bank v Lampert* [1999] 1 All E.R. (Comm) 161.

bank account, the bank may agree to an overdraft facility being created which permits the customer not only to demand the withdrawal of amounts held to her credit in that account but which also permits the customer to draw down a loan by way of overdraft once all of the money credited to that account has been disposed of by the customer. It is common for corporate businesses, sole traders, and ordinary individuals to cruise a line between having their current accounts in credit at some times and in debit (where it is therefore overdrawn) at others. When an individual in employment receives her salary directly by means of a credit being made to her bank account she will often be in credit for a few days of that month before her ordinary living expenses cause that balance to dwindle so that she goes overdrawn. At the moment that she has exhausted the credit of her account balance, she is in a loan arrangement with her bank by spending money which is more than the amount deposited in that account. Such retail overdraft facilities used by individual customers are typically unsecured loans of a few hundred pounds. The terms of the contract establishing the bank account may set out the length of time for which the overdraft may be maintained and an agreement with the bank will establish the maximum amount of the overdraft.

29–55   When overdrafts are taken out for business purposes as a means of managing the cash flow of that business, it is possible that that overdraft will be much larger than an ordinary individual's overdraft and therefore that the bank may require some security in the event that the overdraft loan is not paid off in a timely manner. The more complex the business, the more likely it is that there will be a large number of bank accounts held by the business with its bank, and therefore it is likely that different accounts will be in overdraft frequently while other accounts used for other business purposes are kept in credit. For the bank, management of these sorts of complicated accounts are important and the banker will need to understand the terms of the customer's business very well to understand the nature of the various facilities. Where an agent opens a bank account for a principal whose identity had been disclosed to the bank, then the agent would not be liable to the bank for an overdraft on that account where there was no agreement between the parties that the agent would be so liable.[118] In relation to large-scale corporate banking business, there will be dedicated "account managers" (or sometimes "relationship managers") whose role within the bank is to liaise constantly with a small number of large corporate clients to keep those clients' banking needs under close supervision.

E.   Issues relating to joint accounts

The ownership of accounts held jointly

29–56   Where accounts are opened in joint names with the intention that money is to be used jointly, or even jointly and severally, the owners of the account will be joint tenants. However, a court will require evidence that the parties were intended to

---

[118] *Royal Bank of Scotland v Skinner* (1931) S.L.T. 382.

hold the property in the account jointly.[119] In *Re Figgis*[120] Megarry J. was called on to consider joint bank accounts which had been held for fifty years. The accounts were both a current account and a deposit account. Megarry J. held that a current account might be held in common for the sake of convenience so that bills and ordinary expenditure could be paid out of it. The deposit account was a different matter because money in that account would usually be held for a longer period of time and only used in capital amount for specific purposes. It would, however, be possible for either type of account to be deemed at a later stage to have become an advancement in favour of the wife if the circumstances of the case suggested that that was the better inference. Megarry J. therefore held that the equitable presumption should operate so as to presume the existence of a gift to the wife even though the account had only been operated by the wife during the First World War and during her husband's final illness.[121] A different result was reached on similar facts in *Marshal v Crutwel*[122] because in that circumstance the account had been opened merely for the sake of convenience and contained only money provided by the husband such that the court did not feel it could presume that there was intended to be a gift.[123]

Where property is paid into a bank account by a husband with the intention that that property shall be held on a joint tenancy basis by the husband and his wife, then the account is so held on joint tenancy and will pass absolutely to the survivor of the two.[124] Similarly, property acquired with funds taken from that joint bank account would belong to them both as joint tenants[125] unless they were expressly taken in the name of one or other of them.[126] The difficulty arises in situations where either the intentions of the husband are not made clear or in situations in which the husband transfers the bank account into the joint names of himself and his wife but continues to use the account for his own personal use. In the latter circumstance it would appear that the presumption of advancement is to be rebutted.[127] These same factual issues would arise in relation to any purported joint tenancy over a bank account but the question of the presumption of advancement will only arise in relation to jointly held bank accounts between husband and wife or father and child.

29–57

---

[119] *Macdonald v Tacquah Gold Mines Co* (1884) 13 Q.B.D. 535; *Hirschorn v Evans* [1938] 2 K.B. 801. Where there is no evidence that an account universal and put in one person's name was intended to be held beneficially for one person only and not for two people jointly, then the money in that account would be held on resulting trust to the sole intended beneficial owner and this would rebut a presumption of advancement if the other party was the beneficial owner's spouse: *Aroso v Coutts & Co* [2001] W.T.L.R. 797.

[120] [1969] Ch. 123.

[121] This presumption of advancement operates in circumstances in which husbands put property into the possession of their wives in circumstances in which it is unclear whether a gift, a trust or some other relationship is intended: *Bennet v Bennet* (1879) 10 Ch.D. 474.

[122] (1875) L.R. 20 Eq. 328.

[123] cf. *Re Harrison* [1918] 2 Ch. 59.

[124] *Marshall v Crutwell* (1875) L.R. 20 Eq. 328; *Re Figgis* [1969] Ch. 123.

[125] *Jones v Maynard* [1951] Ch. 572; *Rimmer v Rimmer* [1952] 2 All E.R. 863.

[126] *Re Bishop* [1965] Ch. 450.

[127] *Young v Sealey* [1949] Ch. 278.

Purported withdrawals by one accountholder only

29–58 The principal issue in relation to joint bank accounts is how the bank must deal with one accountholder purporting to deal unilaterally with the money credited to that account. In *Catlin v Cyprus Finance Corpn (London) Ltd*[128] Bingham J. was required to consider circumstances in which Mr and Mrs Catlin were joint holders of that account. Thus they were jointly the owners at common law of the chose in action which constituted that account. The bank accepted a withdrawal instruction from Mr Catlin alone and thus allowed Mr Catlin to spend the money in the account. It was held that Mrs Catlin, who had not consented to that withdrawal, was entitled to be compensated by the bank in the form of common law damages equal to her half share in the money credited to that account.[129] Nevertheless, the parties to a joint account may agree that one accountholder is entitled to withdraw amounts from that account alone.[130]

---

[128] [1983] Q.B. 759; [1983] 1 All E.R. 809.
[129] See also Goodhart (1952) 68 L.Q.R 446.
[130] *Hirschhorn v Evans (Barclays Bank garnishees)* [1938] 2 K.B. 801; *Fielding v The Royal Bank of Scotland Plc* [2004] EWCA Civ 64.

CHAPTER 30

PAYMENT METHODS

CORE PRINCIPLES

This chapter considers the various means by which payments are made, beyond the basic transfer of cash considered in Chapter 2. The discussion begins with cheques and their legal treatment as bills of exchange whereby the payer gives an instruction to her bank to make payment to the payee's bank and thus into the payee's account. The mechanism for payment is through the clearing system for cheques whereby the banks settle the payments with one another. A bank will be

[921]

liable in damages to its customer if it wrongfully dishonours a cheque on the basis of the (somewhat arcane) case law considered in this chapter.

1. INTRODUCTION: THE DEVELOPMENT OF MONEY

30–01 This chapter is a sequel to the last chapter which dealt with the legal nature of the banker-customer relationship. In this chapter we consider the detail of, and the legal issues associated with, the operation of bank accounts and the means by which payment is made through bank accounts or by means of credit cards and similar arrangements.

2. CHEQUES

A. Cheques are a type of bill of exchange

Introduction

30–02 Probably everyone reading this book is familiar with the concept of a cheque. As a means of facilitating payment, the cheque made commercial life much easier than it had previously been because payment could be made simply by completing a cheque, placing the name of the payee in the appropriate place on the cheque, filling out the amount that was to be paid from the payer to the payee in figures and in words, signing the cheque,[1] and passing the cheque to the payee. The payee will then "pay the cheque in" to her bank account. This opens up a second dimension in relation to cheques. The first dimension is the payer writing the cheque out in favour of the payee, whereas the second dimension is that in which the payee's bank seeks to "clear" the cheque by presenting it to the payer's bank, at which time the payer's bank will ordinarily agree to pass funds by debiting the payer's bank account and the payee's bank will then credit the payee's bank account in either case with the amount specified on the cheque. In this section we will consider the role of these four different people (payer, payee, and their two banks), the legal requirements for a valid cheque, and the means by which payment passes between the parties. The previous chapter considered that one of the core aspects of traditional banking practice is the business of honouring cheques drawn on a bank account held with the customer. In this section we shall consider how this process of cheques operates and the principal legal issues which it raises. First, however, we must consider the legal definition of a cheque.

---

[1] Strictly, dating it is not essential to it taking effect, although some banks may refuse to honour it without a date.

The meaning of a cheque being a "bill of exchange"

A cheque is a type of "bill of exchange".[2] A bill of exchange is defined in s.3 of   **30–03**
the Bills of Exchange Act 1882 in the following terms:

> "(1) A bill of exchange is an unconditional order in writing, addressed by one person to another, signed by the person giving it, requiring the person to whom it is addressed to pay on demand or at a fixed or determinable future time a sum certain in money to or to the order of a specified person, or to bearer."

Consequently, the features of a bill of exchange are as follows. First, it must be unconditional in the sense that there must not be any condition precedent before the bill is payable. Secondly, it involves a transfer of money's worth by one person to another in that the bill itself expresses one person as being payer and the other as being payee. Thirdly, the person expressed on the bill as being the person to whom it is addressed (the payee) is entitled to be paid. Fourthly, that payment date may either be on a fixed date, or at a time to be fixed in the future, or (within a given period of time) at whatever date the payee chooses to seek payment. Fifthly, the bill may either be paid to the original payee named on the bill itself, or that bill may be "indorsed" by the payee so that payment instead can be made to whichever person has the bill indorsed over to them, or to the "bearer" who is the person who has the bill in their possession.

The entirety of the law on bills of exchange is beyond the scope of this book. Instead this discussion will focus specifically on the law relating to cheques, a species of bill of exchange.

The meaning of a "cheque"

A cheque is a bill of exchange in that it is made in writing and drawn on the bank   **30–04**
account of the payer. The cheque is expressed as being payable to a payee. A "cheque" is defined in s.73 of the Bills of Exchange Act 1882 as follows:

> "A cheque is a bill of exchange drawn on a banker payable on demand. Except as otherwise provided in this Part, the provisions of this Act applicable to a bill of exchange payable on demand apply to a cheque.ErrorError"

That a bill of exchange is "drawn on a banker" means that the cheque is presented by the payer on the basis that it will be settled ultimately by the bank which holds the account for the payer from which payment will be made. That the cheque is "payable on demand" means that the payee is entitled to be paid on giving a demand for payment (where the concept of "demand" was considered in the previous chapter).

---

[2] The key practitioners texts in this area are: A.G. Guest, *Chalmers and Guest on Bills of Exchange and Cheques*, 6th edn (London: Sweet & Maxwell, 2005); Brindle and Cox (eds), *Law of Bank Payments*, 3rd edn (London: Sweet & Maxwell, 2004).

The two purposes of a cheque

30–05   It is generally expressed in the textbooks on banking law that a cheque has two purposes.[3] The first purpose is to enable the person on whose account the cheque is drawn to withdraw cash from her own bank account. So, a cheque which is made payable to "Cash" permits the bearer of that cheque to present it at the bank on which it is drawn and to receive the amount of cash entered on the cheque. In practice this use of cheques "made out to 'cash'" has been superseded by the various forms of bank cards considered later in this chapter. The second use of a cheque, as assumed so far in this section, is to transfer money's worth from one bank account to another, from the payer to the payee. It is said that this is a transfer of "money's worth" in the sense that the term "money" is discussed in Chapter 2 of this book: that is, there is no movement of notes and coins from the payer's bank to the payee's bank, but rather the payer's bank reduces the credit in the payer's bank account by the amount recorded on the cheque and the payee's bank increases the credit in the payee's bank account by a corresponding amount. Therefore, it is not "money" as classically understood which passes between accounts, but rather a book entry which is equal to an amount of money which is altered in value. Of course, this transfer does have the effect that the payee will ultimately be able to take that amount of money from her bank account in cash.

The first use of a cheque (making a cheque payable to "cash") raises questions as to whether or not there has been fraud by the bearer of the cheque (that is, the person who has the cheque in their possession), and as to whether or not there is sufficient credit in the account on which the cheque is drawn. The context of fraud was considered in Chapter 24. The issue of there being insufficient credit in the account is considered below.

The legal effect of a cheque being crossed or not crossed; indorsement

30–06   Historically, before 1992, a cheque was capable of being indorsed over to any number of people. Indorsement took effect by the payee both writing on the back of the cheque the name of the person to whom the benefit of the cheque was being passed and then signing the back of the cheque. As a result of the Cheques Act 1992, the vast majority of cheques in this jurisdiction are now "crossed" (as explained below) which means that such cheques may not be indorsed to third parties' benefit.[4] A cheque which is not crossed is a "negotiable instrument", whereas a cheque which is crossed is a mere payment order.

B.   The practicalities of dealing with cheques

30–07   The practicalities of dealing with cheques are therefore that the payee bank must present the cheque to the payer bank, and the payer bank must then consider whether or not the cheque is one which it is required to honour. In the distant past of banking practice, a clerk would be required to present himself at the offices of

---

[3]   e.g. A.G. Guest, *Chalmers and Guest on Bills of Exchange and Cheques*, p.615.
[4]   Bills of Exchange Act 1882, s.81A(1).

the payer bank (and indeed at the particular branch on which the cheque was drawn) to seek payment from the payer in relation to each of those cheques. Payment would have been made in cash and the clerk would then have been required to transport that cash back to its own branch of its bank. Clearly, this was inconvenient and involved security problems with clerks transporting large amounts of cash between banks. Therefore, the banks instead developed the practice of meeting in a particular building and clearing all of the various cheques owed between their customers (and therefore payable between themselves as bankers) and settling in cash at that stage. The clearing process has, however, become more sophisticated than that now, as is considered in the next section.

C. Clearing

The clearing system operates as follows. The payer must have originated a payment instruction (acting as "the originator") which is received by the payee and passed on to the payee's bank. The payee's bank then theoretically seeks payment from the payer's bank. This is only theoretically the case. In fact, the banks seek to clear all of the cheques outstanding between them. They do not effect transfers cheque-by-cheque; instead, they identify all of the amounts owed by one bank's customers to the other bank's customers and then calculate the net amount which is owed by one bank to another across all of those cheques. There is therefore a "netting" process carried on between these banks to identify that single amount payable in sterling on that particular date. In practice, this netting process is not settled bilaterally between two banks at a time, but rather is effected through an entity which effects multilateral netting across all of the banks in the clearing system. The benefit of netting is that it reduces the number of payments which need to be made between banks, as was discussed in Chapter 19.[5] Clearing is now carried on electronically not just in relation to paper cheques but also in relation to electronic payments (as discussed below). Where paper cheques are involved, the cheque must be physically transferred through the clearing system between banks. Electronic clearing takes effect by BACS or CHAPS, which operate as follows.

30–08

D. Collection

Payment on a cheque is made, as discussed in the next section, by presentment of that cheque to a bank and by means of the money payable on that cheque being collected by the payee's bank. Ordinarily this means that collection of the amount payable on that cheque is made through the clearing system, as just discussed. If the collecting banker delays in presenting the cheque with the result that that cheque is not paid upon and so causes its customer loss, then that collecting bank will be liable to its customer for that loss.[6] Where one bank acts as an agent of another in collecting a cheque, then the question has arisen whether that agent is entitled to be indemnified where the cheque is converted (that is, where the

30–09

---

[5] See para.19–13.
[6] *Lubbock v Tribe* (1838) 3 M.&W. 607; *Yeoman Credit Ltd v Gregory* [1963] 1 All E.R. 245.

cheque is paid over to a person who is not entitled to be the payee) against an action by the customer to recover its loss against that agent bank at common law.[7] In *Honourable Society of the Middle Temple v Lloyds Bank Plc*[8] Lloyds Bank acting as agent made a payment as instructed by its principal, a Turkish bank, which had the effect of converting a cheque to the claimant's detriment. It was held by Rix J. that Lloyds Bank should be entitled to an indemnity from the Turkish bank precisely because it was doing what it was instructed to do. In *Linklaters v HSBC Bank Plc*[9] HSBC Bank was acting as agent for BPE Bank when a cheque payable to Linklaters was stolen and presented for payment to BPE. BPE accepted the cheque and credited it to an account as instructed by the thief. It was held that while HSBC was prima facie liable for conversion of the cheque (but not liable in negligence to BPE), HSBC was nevertheless acting as BPE's agent and so was entitled to an indemnity against Linklaters' claim.[10]

E. Payment of cheques

30–10 Chalmers and Guest use the expression that the payer's bank makes payment in relation to the cheque by means of funds which are "lent" by the bank to the payer for this purpose.[11] The meaning of this expression is that the payer does not actually have any money in a literal sense; instead, all that the payer has is a bank account held by the bank whereby the bank acknowledges either that the payer has previously deposited funds with it equal to the amount of the cheque or that the payer has agreed a sufficiently large overdraft facility with the bank. Therefore, it is said (somewhat quaintly) that the bank is "lending" money to the payer with which the payee's account will ultimately be credited. Of course, if the payer's account was in credit and had sufficient funds to cover the amount in the cheque, then the bank is not "lending" money to the payer as much as recognising that the payer is a customer who is entitled to have its deposit of money returned to it or alternatively (within the terms of their agreement) used to settle cheques which the payer writes (up to an amount agreed between the parties). Therefore, the payer's bank is not "lending" money to the payer so much as using as much of its funds as is necessary to meet its contractual obligation to the payer (its customer) to settle the amount of the cheque.

---

[7] *Honourable Society of the Middle Temple v Lloyds Bank Plc* [1999] 1 All E.R. (Comm) 193.

[8] [1999] 1 All E.R. (Comm) 193.

[9] [2003] 2 Lloyds Rep. 545.

[10] *Linklaters v HSBC Bank Plc* [2003] 2 Lloyds Rep. 545, following *Honourable Society of the Middle Temple v Lloyds Bank Plc* [1999] 1 All E.R. (Comm) 193. Doubt was cast on the *Middle Temple* case in argument in *Linklaters v HSBC* on the basis of the decision in *Kai Yung* [1981] 1 A.C. 787 where it was suggested by Lord Scarman (at 799) that failure to check the accuracy of signatures against specimen signatures would have made the bank liable to contribute to the remedying of the customer's loss.

[11] Guest, *Chalmers and Guest on Bills of Exchange and Cheques*, pp.615–616.

F.   Liability for dishonoured cheques

The extent of the bank's liabilities for dishonoured cheques are considered in the next section.

3.   THE EXTENT OF THE BANK'S LIABILITIES TO OBEY ITS CUSTOMER'S INSTRUCTIONS

A.   The nature of the bank's general liabilities

The context of liabilities owed to customers

This section serves as a central reservoir for a discussion of a number of issues as to the nature of the bank's liabilities in the event that it fails to observe its customers' instructions which arise variously in this chapter (and which were discussed also in the previous chapter). This discussion relates solely to the obligation to obey a customer's instructions. The general duties of a bank in relation to negligence, breach of trust, breach of contract, and so forth were considered in detail in Chapters 17 through 26 of this book. The contractual basis of the banker–customer relationship was considered in the previous chapter. A bank's liabilities are predicated on the contract between the bank and its customer. A number of those terms are self-evidently implied into the contract between the parties, such as the absence of a liability to make payment on cheques if there are insufficient funds credited to the customer's account to meet that cheque. Except where suggested to the contrary in the remainder of this chapter, the liabilities of the bank to its customer strictly to do with the obligation to make those transfers applies mutatis mutandis to the other forms of payment structure in this chapter. Therefore, "dishonouring cheques" is an example of the sorts of liabilities which attend a bank more generally when acting on instruction from its customers. Furthermore, there have been many more cases on cheques than on the very modern forms of payment which are discussed below.

Liabilities in negligence in relation to mistaken cheque payments and concomitant liabilities to third parties

Banks may also owe duties at common law to people who are not their customers if, for example, they mistakenly make payments into their customers' accounts of moneys to which those customers are not entitled. If the customer receives money under a mistake, then that customer will be required to account to the payer for the amount mistakenly received on the basis of money had and received.[12] But what of the liability of the bank to that payer? Under s.4(1) of the Cheques Act 1957, if a bank receives payment for one of its customers in relation to an instrument (such as a cheque) under which its customer did not have good title, then the banker will not itself owe any liability to the payer provided that the bank has not acted negligently and provided that it has acted in good faith. Proof

---

[12] *Westdeutsche Landesbank v Islington* [1996] A.C. 669.

of negligence will generally be predicated on evidence as to ordinary banking practice,[13] but negligence will not be proven simply because a bank had a duty to take reasonable care.[14] In *Marfani & Co Ltd v Midland Bank Ltd*[15] Diplock L.J. held that what the court must do is:

> "to look at all the circumstances at the time of the acts complained of and to ask itself: were those circumstances such as would cause a reasonable banker possessed of such information about his customer as a reasonable banker would possess, to suspect that his customer was not the true owner of the cheque?"

Lord Dunedin[16] approved the approach of Isaacs J. who considered that "the test of negligence" in such circumstances would be whether or not the payment of the cheque into an account "was so out of the ordinary course that it ought to have aroused doubts in the bankers' mind, and caused them to make inquiry".[17] If banks choose not to inquire sufficiently closely then they take the risk of being held to be liable.[18]

30–14   These principles were set out in the 1920s; in the 21st century banks bear obligations to inquire into suspicious transactions in any event, as considered in Chapter 15. When a cheque is identified among the multitude as being problematic "albeit only as a result of an inquiry after fate" from among the many thousands of cheques which are cleared and is therefore referred to management, then it must receive individual attention.[19] As was made clear by the Court of Appeal in *Architects of Wine Ltd v Barclays Bank Plc*[20] "the courts should be wary of hindsight or of imposing on a bank the role of an amateur detective".[21] Yet again, the courts are persisting in this quaint notion that banks ought not to bear positive obligations to investigate the payments which are made through their systems even though they are required to keep a wary eye open by money laundering regulation and even though they have the computer systems and the staff to perform this sort of task.

B.   Dishonouring cheques

The dishonouring of cheques

30–15   The payer's bank may refuse to honour a cheque written by one of its customers: that is, the bank may refuse to transfer funds to the payee's bank. In the colloquial expression, that cheque "bounces" in that the payee's bank presents the cheque to

---

[13] *Marfani & Co Ltd v Midland Bank Ltd* [1968] 1 W.L.R. 956, 975.
[14] *Architects of Wine Ltd v Barclays Bank Plc* [2007] EWCA Civ 239; [2007] Bus. L.R. Digest D37.
[15] [1968] 1 W.L.R. 956, 972.
[16] *Commissioners of Taxation v English, Scottish and Australian Bank Ltd* [1920] A.C. 683, 689.
[17] *Commissioners of State Savings Bank v Permewan* (1914) 19 C.L.R. 457, 478. Approved *Lloyds Bank Ltd v Chartered Bank of India, Australia and China* [1929] 1 K.B. 40, 59, per Scruton L.J.
[18] *AL Underwood Ltd v Bank of Liverpool* [1924] 1 K.B. 775, 793, per Scruton L.J.
[19] *Honourable Society of the Middle Temple v Lloyds Bank Plc* [1999] 1 All E.R. (Comm) 193, 228, per Rix J.
[20] [2007] EWCA Civ 239; [2007] Bus. L.R. Digest D37.
[21] See above, at [12].

the payer's bank but it will bounce back to the payee if the payer's bank refuses to pay out under that account. This section considers the payer's bank's liabilities for failing to honour a cheque, and the circumstances in which that bank may refuse to honour that cheque.

Breach of contract if a bank fails to honour a cheque

At first blush, for a bank to dishonour a cheque is a breach of the bank's contractual obligations owed to its customer.[22] A bank is therefore prima facie under an obligation to pay on a cheque when that cheque is presented to it.[23] A bank which wrongfully refuses to pay on a cheque will therefore be liable in damages for breach of contract to its customer in the manner set out in Chapter 20.[24] So, in *Evans v London and Provincial Bank*,[25] where a bank wrongfully dishonoured a cheque which had been presented by a woman to pay for family groceries, it was held that the bank had to account to their customer in damages. However, because the woman could demonstrate no loss, it was held that she was entitled only to nominal damages of one shilling. This is in keeping with the case law considered in the previous chapter to the effect that loss is generally taken to have been suffered by a customer who is in trade due to loss of access to finance or loss of custom through a bank's wrongful failure to honour a payment instruction,[26] although later authority has taken the view that retail customers may also suffer loss in the same circumstances (such as loss of their home or loss of access to finance) even if there is no trade involved.[27]

30–16

As was discussed in Chapter 25, refusing to honour a customer's cheque may also be taken to be a defamatory statement in that it carries with it a statement (whether express, or implied by dint of refusal to honour the cheque) that that person does not have sufficient money (either in that bank account or generally) to meet the obligation under that cheque. As was discussed in Chapter 25, there is a defence to defamation if the statement is true, for example that the customer does not have sufficient funds in its account.

30–17

Countermands

A customer may withdraw an instruction to the bank to pay on a cheque (that instruction being embodied in the act of writing the cheque itself) by issuing a countermand; that is, an instruction that the cheque not be honoured. The bank is obliged to obey this instruction as with all other instructions which are within the terms of the parties' agreement between themselves. The bank is required to

30–18

---

[22] *Cunliffe Brooks & Co v Blackburn District Benefit Building Society* (1884) 9 App. Cas. 857, 864; *London Joint Stock Bank Ltd v Macmillan* [1918] A.C. 777, 824.
[23] [1918] A.C. 777, 824.
[24] *Marzetti v Williams* (1830) 1 B. & Ad. 415.
[25] *The Times*, March 1, 1917.
[26] *Wilson v United Counties Bank Ltd* [1920] A.C. 102, 112, per Lord Birkenhead.
[27] *Kpohraror v Woolwich Building Society* [1996] 4 All E.R. 119.

exercise due care and skill in this regard.[28] The problem comes when customers give ambiguous countermand instructions. In *Westminster Bank Ltd v Hilton*,[29] for example, the customer intended to countermand one cheque but mistakenly identified a different cheque. The bank countermanded the cheque which has been identified by its customer. The House of Lords held that the bank bore no liability for the loss which flowed from the wrong cheque being countermanded. It was held that the bank had a duty to act honestly and fairly in such circumstances, but nothing more.[30] The giving of a cheque therefore operates as a conditional payment only, unless the parties expressly or by implication otherwise agree, because a cheque is a revocable mandate by the customer to her bank which authorises the bank, as her agent, to make payment out of moneys standing to the credit of her account or which the bank is willing to advance to her.[31]

Circumstances in which cheques may be dishonoured without liability in damages

30–19   The payer's bank may refuse to pay out on a cheque in a number of circumstances. Given that the bank's obligation to pay on a cheque is a contractual obligation, then the terms of the contract between the parties will govern the extent of the bank's liabilities: which means that the bank will not be obliged to pay out on cheques when that payment would be in circumstances outwith the terms of the contract between the parties.[32] A bank will agree to pay out on cheques only if the customer has sufficient funds credited to its account[33]; or, if the parties had agreed that the customer would have an overdraft facility, to the extent that that overdraft facility has not been fully drawn down.[34] If a cheque is presented to the payer's bank which the payer has written then the analysis taken on the authorities is that the bank has the option whether or not to honour the cheque, and the presentation of the cheque is deemed to be a request by the payer to her bank to extend her an overdraft facility on its ordinary terms sufficient to meet the cheque.[35]

30–20   There is a problem with the honouring of cheques. It is illustrated by the facts of *Marzetti v Williams*.[36] The payer's account had a credit of £69 at 9.30am. The payer paid £40 in cash into that account at 11.00am. The payer therefore expected to have £109 in that account. However, the bank did not enter the credit of £40

---

[28] *Curtice v London City and Midland Bank Ltd* [1908] 1 K.B. 293; *Westminster Bank Ltd v Hilton* (1926) 43 T.L.R. 124.

[29] (1926) 43 T.L.R. 124.

[30] See also *Curtice v London City and Midland Bank Ltd* [1908] 1 K.B. 293.

[31] *In Re Romer & Haslam* [1893] 2 Q.B. 286 and *Bolt & Nut Co (Tipton) Ltd v Rowlands Nicholls & Co Ltd* [1964] 2 Q.B. 10; *Re Charge Card Services Ltd* [1989] Ch. 497.

[32] *Marzetti v Williams* (1830) 1 B. & Ad. 415, 424; *Bank of New South Wales v Laing* [1954] A.C. 135.

[33] *N Joachimson v Swiss Bank Corporation* [1921] 3 K.B. 110; *Bank of New South Wales v Laing* [1954] A.C. 135, 154.

[34] *Fleming v Bank of New Zealand* [1900] A.C. 577.

[35] *Barclays Bank v Simms* [1980] Q.B. 677; A.G. Guest, *Chalmers and Guest on Bills of Exchange and Cheques*, 635.

[36] (1830) 1 B. & Ad. 415.

until 4.00pm, and the payer presented a cheque for £87 at the bank's counter at 3.00pm. The bank refused to honour the cheque because the payer's account in the bank's ledgers at 3.00pm still stood at a balance of only £69. The problem therefore is what happens if payments have not cleared into the payer's account before the payer purports to write cheques to pay money out of that same account. It was held in *Marzetti*, importantly by the jury sitting in that case,[37] that the delay of over four hours (between 11.00am and 3.00pm) in failing to credit the account was an unreasonable delay. Perhaps the jury was comprised of irascible bank customers who themselves considered the service provided by their bankers to be unsatisfactory. It has been asserted that this would not be considered to be an unreasonable delay in modern banking practice.[38] This may seem surprising given a world of computer payments: at modern high street banks the cheques and pay-in slips are scanned when money is paid in, and so one might think that credit and debit could happen instantaneously. Of course, the reason why such credits and debits do not happen automatically is that the clearing system needs three business days at least to agree that payment should be made, as discussed above.

C.   Interest on cheques

In *Emerald Meats (London) Ltd v AIB Group Plc*[39] it was held that a term is implied into a contract between banker and customer to the effect that interest is payable to a customer in accordance with the bank's own standard practice. This does not require that the bank pay interest calculated from the immediate receipt of funds as receiving bank, but rather may permit the bank to wait until the fourth business day after receipt. The principle here derives from the principle in *Lloyds Bank v Voller*[40] to the effect that a bank is entitled to organise its business in a way which is profitable for it.   **30–21**

4.   FUNDS TRANSFERS AND MANDATES TO PAY

A.   Introduction

Transferring funds between accounts is a core activity for banks. There are banks which specialise in providing "cash management" services to other banks in relation to particularly complex transfers of funds between many different accounts. In this context we are concerned, it is suggested, less with thinking about "money" and more with thinking about funds which are credited to one account and which are then "moved" to another account by means of a debit from the payer account and a credit to the payee account. To put it crudely, as the value of one account goes down, the value of the other account goes up by an equal amount. The bank's duty to effect transfers of funds is part of its contractual   **30–22**

---

[37] The range of cases on which juries would sit was very different in 1830 from what it is today.
[38] E.P. Ellinger, E. Lomnicka and R. Hooley, *Modern Banking Law*, 3rd edn (OUP, 2002), 414.
[39] [2002] EWCA Civ 460.
[40] [2000] 2 All E.R. (Comm) 978, CA.

agreement with its customer and therefore is governed by the principles considered in the previous chapter and by reference to the principles considered thus far in this chapter relating to the extent of those obligations. In effect, because these duties are created by contract, then the extent of those duties are also governed by the terms of that same contract. The case law above in relation to the honouring of cheques, it is suggested, applies mutatis mutandis to the obligations of banks in relation to order to transfer funds between accounts.

B. Mandates to pay: standing orders and direct debits

30–23 A "mandate" is an instruction given by a customer to its bank which both compels the bank to carry out activities (such as transfers of funds between accounts, provided that they are within the terms of the contract between the parties) and may empower the bank to act as the customer's agent for that purpose.[41] As before, the heads of liability considered above in relation to the obligation to obey customer's instructions apply in this context. Common examples of mandates are standing orders given to banks by customers which instruct banks to transfer an identified sum of money on specified dates to an identified account of an identified person. Direct debits are similar payments made electronically after a once-and-for-all instruction is given by the payer in favour of the payee which is transmitted to the payer's bank. Direct debits are ordinarily capable of transfer by notice from the payer to its bank, although the termination of such a payment instruction would constitute a breach of contract between the payer and the payee.[42]

C. Paper-based funds transfers

30–24 The process in relation to paper-based funds transfers was considered above in relation to cheques.

D. Electronic funds transfers

30–25 It is common to use electronic funds transfer mechanisms to pay everything from employee's salaries to settling standing orders. The business of transferring "money" between accounts has been in many contexts for centuries now in fact a process of altering a bank's records as to the amount of money to be credited to an individual to reflect a payment out of that account or a payment into that account. At the surface level, the legal relationship between payer, payee and the banks holding the accounts of both those parties is the same in relation to electronic funds transfers as it was in relation to cheques. The payer gives an instruction to its bank to transfer funds to the payee via the payee's bank. The

---

[41] *Conservative and Unionist Central Office v Burrell* [1982] 1 W.L.R. 522, [1982] 2 All E.R. 1, at p.6, per Brightman L.J.
[42] *Esso Petroleum Co Ltd v Milton* [1997] 2 All E.R. 593.

difference is that payment is effected through an electronic system which therefore involves the presence of an entity which manages that electronic system.

Electronic payments are typically made through BACS Ltd or CHAPS Clearing Company Ltd. BACS was established in 1968 and stood originally for "Banks Automated Clearing Services". BACS operates a computer-based system for clearing credit and debit transfers in sterling, particularly standing orders and direct debit payments. Ordinarily BACS deals with very high numbers of transfers but in small amounts. The banks which belong to the BACS system have direct access to it and make payments through it as a result. The CHAPS system (the Clearing House Automated Payment System) starting operations in 1984 to make payment on the same day, as opposed to the three-day cycle on which BACS functions.

30–26

The Society for Worldwide Interbank Financial Telecommunication ("SWIFT") deals in cross-border payments between banks, and is "the almost universal system for transferring funds across international boundaries".[43] SWIFT is a non-profit organization established in Brussels and owned entirely by its member banks. The advantage of SWIFT for banks is that it deals in standard message formats which reduce ambiguity and thus the risk of mistakes, and its efficiency of operation is designed to knit with banking payment practices and systems.[44]

30–27

E. The banker's duty to take care in relation to transfers of funds

Banks owe a duty to take reasonable care and skill when carrying out funds transfers. So, for example, where a bank has exercised reasonable care and skill, and possibly acted through intermediary banks in the ordinary course of business, then it will face no liability. So, in *Royal Products Ltd v Midland Bank Ltd*,[45] Midland Bank received instructions from Royal Products, a Maltese company, to transfer £13,000 from Royal Products' account with Midland Bank in the UK to BICAL, a Maltese Bank. Midland Bank transferred those funds via a correspondent bank, Bank of Valletta in Malta, for onward transfer to BICAL. While Bank of Valletta knew that BICAL were in financial difficulties, it nevertheless transferred the funds on to BICAL but BICAL went into insolvency and no credit was made to Royal Products' account with BICAL in Malta. Royal Products proceeded against Midland Bank for payment of £13,000 from it. Webster J. held that Midland Bank bore no obligation to make that payment because it had acted with reasonable care and skill in dealing through Bank of Valletta and that this had been "an ordinary banking operation" in relation to which no particular breach of duty by Midland Bank could be identified.

30–28

---

[43] *Dovey v Bank of New Zealand* [2000] 3 N.Z.L.R. 641, 645.
[44] See generally Brindle and Cox, *Law of Bank Payments* (London: Sweet & Maxwell, 2004), Ch.3.
[45] [1981] 2 Lloyd's Rep. 194.

5.   PAYMENT, CREDIT AND DEBIT CARDS

A.   The context of payment, credit and debit cards

30–29   The context of so-called "plastic money" is similar to electronic payment, as considered above, in that the instruction given by a customer to its bank to make payment will be governed by the terms of the contract between customer and banker. The rules relating to the liability of banks in relation to customers were considered above. The extra factor in relation to card-based transactions is that there is a card which gives electronic instructions to the payer's bank via the operator of the card system to make that payment; and therefore there are people other than the payer, payee and banks engaged in the transaction whose legal obligations require explanation. The central case, describing the difference between the many forms of card is the decision of Millett J. in *Re Charge Card Services Ltd*.[46] What emerges from the dicta of Millett J. in that case is the following pragmatic evaluation of the treatment of different payment methods by the judiciary over the centuries:

> "As the cases cited to me demonstrate, the approach of the courts to this question has not been conceptual or based on any such supposed principle, but has been strictly pragmatic. As each new method of payment has fallen to be considered, its nature and the surrounding circumstances have been examined to see whether a presumption of conditional payment should be made. Indeed, only in this way is it possible to identify those special circumstances which may take an individual case out of the general rule applicable to payments by a particular method."[47]

Therefore, as will emerge from the discussion to follow, there has been little case law analysing the legal relationships between the parties to various forms of payment card specifically.

B.   Cheque cards

30–30   A cheque card (or "cheque guarantee card") is a card issued by a bank to its customer which purports to guarantee that the bank will honour a single cheque up to a maximum amount, beyond which the payee is taking the risk that the cheque will not be honoured. The card will bear a number which will correlate with the account which the payer has and which needs to be written on the reverse of the cheque to indicate the presentation of that guarantee card. The card will have an expiry date after which the guarantee represented by that card will no longer be effective. It was held in *Re Charge Card Services*[48] that:

> "The use of the cheque card in connection with the transaction gives to the payee a direct contractual right against the bank itself to payment on presentment, provided that the use of the card by the drawer to bind the bank to pay the cheque was within the actual or ostensible authority conferred upon him by the bank."[49]

---

[46] [1989] Ch. 497, CA.
[47] [1987] Ch. 150, 166.
[48] [1987] Ch. 150, Millett J.
[49] See also *First Sport Ltd v Barclays Bank Plc* [1993] 1 W.L.R. 1229.

Millett J. held further that[50]:

> "A cheque is a revocable mandate by the customer to his bank which authorises the bank, as his agent, to make payment out of moneys standing to the credit of his account or which the bank is willing to advance to him. The obligation undertaken by the bank to the supplier, which it enters into through the agency of its customer when he uses the bank card, is not to dishonour the cheque on presentation for want of funds in the account, so that it is obliged if necessary to advance moneys to the customer to meet it. If the cheque is met, the bank honours its own undertaking as principal to the supplier and, as agent for the customer, makes payment on its behalf out of his own moneys, whether or not these have been advanced to him for the purpose."

Therefore, a payee acting reasonably in relation to the card is entitled to enforce a direct contractual right against the bank to require payment of the cheque. In a difficult decision in *First Sport Ltd v Barclays Bank*,[51] the Court of Appeal has held that a bank was required to pay under a cheque to a payee even though a cheque had been stolen, the customer's signature forged on it and the cheque guarantee card used by the forger. The Court of Appeal relied inter alia on the fact that the terms under which the card was issued did not specify that payment would only be made if the cheque was signed by the customer and not by some other person. In effect, the court caused liability to lie with the person who had the deeper pockets and was therefore better able to absorb the loss. The approach of Evans L.J. was that even a thief could present the card validly, provided that the person seeking payment could not have realised that the thief was indeed a thief.

C.   Debit cards

Debit cards are similar in effect to cheques in that when payment is made through   **30–31**
a debit card then the amount paid is taken directly from the customer's bank account. A debit card is issued by the customer's bank for the purpose of permitting debits to be made directly from that account for goods, services and so on. There is no need for a cheque book as a result. That the debit card is being used by the customer is verified by the entry of the customer's four-digit personal identification number ("PIN") in relation to purchases made in person; otherwise, the card number and any other security information contained on the card itself can be used to pay for services over the telephone or over the internet. Generally, debit card transactions are conducted through an "Electronic Funds Transfer-Point of Sale" system: this system authenticates the card as being valid at first and then the customer enters her PIN to authorise the transaction.

---

[50] [1987] Ch. 150, 166, per Millett J. affirmed [1989] Ch. 497, CA.
[51] *First Sport Ltd v Barclays Bank* [1993] 1 W.L.R. 1229, 1234; [1993] 3 All E.R. 789, 794. See also *Charles v Blackwell* (1877) 2 C.P.D. 151. cf. *Smith v Lloyds TSB Group Plc* [2001] Q.B. 541, CA.

D. Charge cards

30–32   A charge card is similar in its use to a debit card, but the card is not necessarily issued by the customer's bank. There are also other differences. The principal difference between debit cards and charge cards is that a charge card creates an account between the card issuer and the customer whereby the customer is entitled to use that card to pay for goods and services up to maximum credit limit agreed between the card issuer and the customer. The balance on a charge card must then be discharged by the customer at the end of each monthly period identified in the contract between the parties. The customer is not permitted to keep a balance outstanding on the card beyond that monthly period. Charge cards are exempt from the consumer credit legislation.[52] The detailed operation of such cards are considered below in the dicta of Millett J. which take credit and charge cards together at the same time.

E. Credit cards

30–33   A credit card is similar to a charge card but with the important difference that a customer may maintain an amount outstanding on a credit card beyond each monthly period. The agreement between the parties, governed by the consumer credit legislation, will specify both the maximum amount of money which the customer may charge to that card in the aggregate, and the agreement will also specify the minimum amount which the customer is required to pay off each month on that card so as to reduce the balance owed to the card issuer. As with a charge card, the card is not necessarily issued by the customer's bank but rather is issued by a financial institution who may otherwise be acting as arm's length from the customer.

30–34   Credit cards with a credit limit under £25,000 are governed by the Consumer Credit Act 1974[53] (discussed in the Chapter 31) and by the Unfair Terms in Consumer Contracts Regulations 1999 (discussed in Chapter 18). The Consumer Credit Act governs the manner in which the card is supplied to the account holder, the limits which are placed on the account holder's liability for any misuse of the card by another person, and the liability of the supplier for any misrepresentation or breach of contract. It is an offence to supply an unsolicited token (or, credit card in this context) to a consumer.[54] Card issuers ordinarily bear the risk of misuse of the card, particularly where the likelihood of misuse due to loss or theft of the card has been reported to it.[55] Further to the Consumer Protection (Distance Selling) Regulations 2000 (SI 2000/2334), a consumer is entitled to a refund when her credit card has been used fraudulently.

30–35   The people involved in a credit card transaction are as follows, as described by Millett J. in *Re Charge Card Services*[56]:

---

[52] Consumer Credit Act 1974 s 16(5)(a).
[53] Consumer Credit Act 1974 s.14(1).
[54] Consumer Credit Act 1974 s.51.
[55] Consumer Credit Act 1974 s.84.
[56] [1987] Ch. 150, 158.

"On the use of the card, three separate contracts come into operation. First, there is the contract of supply between the supplier and the cardholder (either in his own right or as agent for the account holder); secondly, there is the contract between the supplier and the card-issuing company, which undertakes to honour the card by paying the supplier on presentation of the sales voucher; and, thirdly, there is the contract between the card-issuing company and the account holder by which the account holder undertakes to reimburse the card-issuing company for payments made or liabilities incurred by the card-issuing company to the supplier as a result of his or his cardholder's use of the card. There are thus three separate contracts and three separate parties, each being party to two of the three contracts but neither party nor privy to the third. While the legal consequences of these arrangements must depend upon the terms of the particular contracts employed, one would expect each contract to be separate and independent and to be entered into between principals. In particular, one would expect the card-issuing company to enter into both its contract with the supplier and its contract with the account holder as a principal in its own right and not merely as agent for the account holder and the supplier respectively. One would also expect the supplier to be entitled to be paid whether or not the card-issuing company is able to obtain reimbursement from the account holder, and the card-issuing company to be entitled to be paid whether or not the goods or services supplied by the supplier are satisfactory."

There are therefore three parties. Let us suppose that an ordinary person is buying shoes in a shop in London's West End using her credit card. Unconnected with the shop will be the "card issuer" which is a financial institution which issued the card to the shopper in the first place. The "account holder" is the ordinary customer who is entitled to use the credit card, and who is using it to buy shoes. The "supplier" is the company which owns the shoe shop in this example. The shoe shop will be owned by a company (probably part of a chain of shops owned by that company in the West End) and that company will have entered into a contract with the card issuer permitting it to use the card issuer's system to receive payment for its goods. The account holder and the supplier enter into a contract for the sale of shoes and tendering of payment is achieved by way of the account holder's credit card. The account holder has already entered into a contract with the card issuer. Strictly, the role of the card issuer will in turn be played by two separate companies: one is the financial institution who entered into the contract with the card issuer (possibly a bank, or possibly another regulated firm) and the other is the entity (such as Visa or MasterCard) which operates the system through which payments are made. The supplier has also already entered into a contract with the card issuer whereby the supplier agrees to accept payment by means of presentation of a valid card with a valid PIN. On presentation of the sales receipts to the card issuer, the supplier is entitled to payment, less the card issuer's fee. The card issuer then waits for payment to be made to it by the account holder in accordance with its agreement with the account holder. The supplier has the reassurance of immediate payment, whereas the card issuer aims to earn enough money from interest on late payments, other charges levied on the account holder, and fees from the suppliers, to amount to a sufficient profit across the business year. When dealing with a large number of accounts as card issuers do, the aggregate cash flow which it earns is enormous.

The comprehensive explanation given of the commercial operation of charge and credit cards by Millett J. in *Re Charge Card Services* was the following one[57]:
30–36

---

[57] [1987] Ch. 150, 168.

"... credit and charge cards are used mainly to facilitate payment of small consumer debts arising out of transactions between parties who may well not be known to each other, and the terms of which are usually not the subject of negotiation. The identity of the card-issuing company is necessarily a matter for agreement, since the card must be one which the customer is authorised to use and the supplier has the necessary equipment to accept. The machinery of payment by charge or credit card does not require the disclosure of the customer's address to the supplier, and in the absence of special precautions which are seldom taken, at least in the case of small transactions, and which were not taken in the present case, the supplier might well have difficulty in identifying the customer without the co-operation of the card-issuing company. The availability of the card as a method of payment is advantageous to both parties: the customer obtains free credit for a period longer than that which the supplier is prepared to give even to the card-issuing company, or than he himself would obtain from the use of a cheque, with or without a bank card; while the supplier obtains not only better security (as he hopes) but the convenience of having a single debtor in place of many, and the prospect of extra trade by reason of the credit facilities which he is able to extend (without providing them himself) to the customer. Finally, the terms on which the supplier is entitled to payment from the card-issuing company are quite different from those on which the card-issuing company is entitled to payment from the customer; and both differ from those on which the supplier would be entitled to payment from the customer if he were subject to any residual liability not discharged by the use of the card. The card-issuing company is liable to pay the supplier very shortly after the receipt of the sales vouchers and claim form, but is entitled to deduct its commission; while the customer is liable to pay the full face value of the voucher, but is entitled to much longer credit. If the customer is liable to pay the supplier on the failure or default of the card-issuing company, it is on terms more onerous than either, for he must be liable to make immediate payment of the full face value of the voucher. It is difficult to find any justification for imputing to the customer an intention to undertake any such liability.

The essence of the transaction, which in my view has no close analogy, is that the supplier and customer have for their mutual convenience each previously arranged to open an account with the same company, and agree that any account between themselves may, if the customer wishes, be settled by crediting the supplier's and debiting the customer's account with that company. That process does not depend on the company's solvency, and the customer must be discharged, at the latest, when the supplier's account with the company is credited, not when the supplier is paid. But once that point is reached, there is no logical place to stop short of the customer signing the voucher."

Thus in a credit card transaction, the risks borne by each party are mediated through the credit card provider. It has been held by the House of Lords in *Office of Fair Trading v Lloyds TSB Bank Plc*[58] that there is nothing in s.75 of the Consumer Credit Act 1974 to prevent credit card providers from being liable to cardholders (for damages for misrepresentation and so forth) in relation to transactions created outside the UK as well as within the UK. Indeed, the House of Lords considered that this analysis was in keeping with the general policy of that legislation to protect consumers whether transactions are entered into within the UK or outside it.

F.   Store cards

30–37   Store cards are not of a generic type but rather may either be charge cards or they may be credit cards but they are issued by a retail shop, usually a retail chain of stores. The card will entitle the customer to use the card in payment for goods from that store on terms to discharge the balance in identified time periods and within the confines of a maximum credit limit. The principal difference between a store card and either a charge card or a credit card simpliciter is that the store

---

[58] [2008] Bus. L.R. 450.

will not be managing the operation of the financial transactions embodied by the customer's use of the card even though it will have been the store company which procured the customer's agreement to use their credit facility, but rather a financial institution will operate the card on behalf of the store company.

G. "Cashpoint" (automated teller machine) cards

Automated teller machine cards (colloquially known most commonly in the UK, by the trade mark used by Lloyds TSB Bank for their machines, as "Cashpoint" cards) permit the holder of a bank account to withdraw cash from her bank account by means of an Automated Teller Machine ("ATM", or "Cashpoint"). The card issued to the customer is governed by the agreement between banker and customer. The customer is entitled to withdraw cash in an amount that is within the credit held to the customer's account, or within the customer's overdraft limit, and which is within any daily maximum placed on the customer's card. The card will itself have an expiration date, after which it will cease to be accepted by the Cashpoint machines. The card is initially verified once it is slotted into the Cashpoint and then the customer gives authorisation for the transaction by entering her PIN number on the Cashpoint's keypad.

30–38

H. Electronic voucher payment and pre-paid cards

Electronic cards are used more and more to replace the need for cash but not so as to debit a bank account nor to impact on a credit balance. Instead, pre-paid cards are means of paying for goods or services by presentation of the card to a vendor who "swipes" that card through a card reader which reduces the value stored on that card's memory by the cost of the goods or services bought with it. An example is the London Transport "Oyster" card which is bought for a flat fee from a large number of retailers (such as newsagents and Underground stations) and which has a given value attributed to it by being stored on the card's microchip memory. The Oyster card may be used to pay for travel on London Transport services (such as the Underground or London buses) by being swiped across the card reader at the entry to the service. The value on the Oyster card is reduced by a flat amount on bus travel, and by being swiped on exit from Underground stations according to the length and concomitant cost of the journey. Similarly, "pay-as-you-go" mobile phones can be "topped up" by increasing the amount of value attributed to them with which to make telephone calls or to send texts at bank Cashpoints and so forth. The extension of electronic payment and pre-paid card systems is thus proliferating widely. Each of these payment mechanisms involves a contract between customer and service provider, while also involving the participation of the entity which is providing the electronic payment service itself.

30–39

I.   Internet payments

30–40   Payments are made more commonly across the internet. For the most part payment takes effect by credit card payment, sometimes by direct debit from a bank account, and less often by arranging for a cheque to be sent by the buyer of services through the post. Therefore, these payment mechanisms are at root the same as the mechanisms considered so far.

6.   DOCUMENTARY CREDITS

A.   The context of documentary credits

The structure of a documentary credit

30–41   The law relating to documentary credits, and letters of credit in particular, are part of the law of sale of goods, and so are considered in this chapter only in outline as a means of effecting payment in many international trade transactions. A "documentary credit" is a right to receive an amount of money (and in that sense is a "credit" akin to money held in a bank account) which is embodied in a document (and hence is "documentary"). Documentary credits are a compromise between the interests of a seller of goods who wants to know that it will receive payment before it undertakes the exercise of shipping goods internationally, and the interests of a buyer of goods who wants to take delivery before making payment. A documentary credit stands aside from the contract of sale between the parties. It is a right in the shipper of goods to receive payment once delivery has been made in the manner specified in the terms of the documentary credit itself and, importantly, once documents (principally a bill of lading) have been delivered so as to evidence delivery of the goods.

30–42   In the abstract there would be at least two possible methods of organising payment in these sorts of situations. The parties could have payment for the goods held on trust by a bank acting as trustee such that the trustee will hold the equitable interest in the buyer's money on trust for the buyer unless and until the seller delivers goods of the right quantity and quality; and either the seller's goods could be held on trust for the seller until payment is made in full, or else the seller could simply retain absolute title in those goods until payment is made in full into the seller's bank account.[59] Trusts are not recognised in all jurisdictions in the world and therefore would be inappropriate to assert a right to money or rights over chattels in such jurisdictions, and furthermore commercial practice prefers that the right to receive payment under the documentary credit is kept separate from the underlying contract of sale. Mercantile practice has therefore developed documentary credits. A documentary credit is used to create either a revocable or (more usually) an irrevocable credit with a bank. A revocable credit would give the buyer the power to refuse to make payment, which would be a great risk for the seller and shipper of goods. Thus, an irrevocable credit with a bank in favour of the seller reassures the seller that it has

---

[59] See A.S. Hudson, *Equity & Trusts*, s.2.5.

the security of having a credit made available to it in case the buyer sought to refuse to accept delivery of the goods. A hypothetical example of this sort of transaction is set out in Brindle and Cox's *Law of Bank Payments*[60]:

> "In April, a seller based in Utopia contracts to sell some machinery to a buyer based in Ruritania. Delivery is to be made in December. The seller will have to start manufacturing the machinery in May in order to have it ready for delivery in December. There is no readily available market for the machinery. The seller therefore stands to suffer a heavy loss if the buyer refuses to take delivery of the machinery and pay the price. He can protect his position by agreeing with the buyer that payment will be made by an irrevocable credit, confirmed by a Utopian bank, such credit to be advised to him by the end of April. The buyer and seller agree upon the documents which are to be presented to the bank for payment. These are likely to include a bill of lading or some other transport document showing that the contract goods have been shipped, an insurance policy in respect of the goods and a commercial invoice."

An "irrevocable credit" in this sense would be an amount of money (or possibly other assets acceptable to the seller) which is held in a bank account by the issuing bank.

A legal analysis of the rights of the parties

There is, it is suggested, a narrow distinction between such an arrangement and a trust: the question would be whether or not the seller acquires rights against the money held in the bank account before delivery of the goods is made. For example, what would happen if the buyer sought to repudiate the credit and to take the money back again? Would the buyer or the bank be obliged to act as fiduciaries in accounting to the seller for the money formerly held in the account, or would the seller merely have rights in contract against the buyer for damages in breach of contract or specific performance, or against the bank for breach of contract? The answer to these questions in any given set of circumstances would turn on how the parties' arrangements were organised, and whether or not such an equitable interest in the moneys was explicitly excluded both by the documentation and by the parties' underlying intentions. In relation to documentary credits in practice, the bank will have excluded itself from any part in the contract of sale between the buyer and the seller and will be bound only by the terms of its obligations to the buyer under the documentary credit. Nevertheless, if the buyer acted as a fiduciary, would that be acting as a trustee such that the seller would acquire equitable proprietary rights in the money, albeit rights which were defeasible under the terms of the credit agreement itself if the goods were inappropriate? **30–43**

As was mentioned above, the answers to these questions would depend upon the terms of the contract which governs the documentary credit. If the contract were to provide that the bank owes no obligation to the seller, then that would prevent rights being created in contract law. This might be achieved by the credit agreement providing that the money held in the bank account is to remain absolutely the property of the buyer, and therefore that the relationship between buyer and bank is the ordinary contractual relationship between bank and **30–44**

---

[60] M. Brindle and R. Cox, *Law of Bank Payments*, p.652.

customer.[61] At this point, the seller would have no proprietary rights in the money held in that account. However, if the obligation to transfer the money in that bank account was both expressed in the credit agreement as being irrevocable by the buyer (apart from some identified events of default such as the goods being of the wrong type) and if the money were set aside in a bank account without being mixed with other moneys, then once goods of the right type were delivered by the seller, the seller would acquire specifically enforceable rights to have that money transferred to it and so would appear to have an equitable interest in that money from that moment.[62]

30–45   These sorts of problems have not been resolved by English commercial law, and instead a pragmatic approach is taken by the authorities[63] and by the commentators[64] to the effect that documentary credits generally and letters of credit in particular are widely used as part of international trade law and so ought simply to be treated as being effective. Of particular importance in relation to documentary credits is the letter of credit, which is considered next.

B.   Letters of credit

30–46   Letters of credit are the most common form of documentary credit in international trade. They constitute a very important form of financing for international transactions, typically for sales of goods. In essence a letter of credit is a right which entitles a shipper of goods to be able to insist on payment from a paying bank once documents evidencing delivery of those goods have been delivered to that paying bank. In *Re Charge Card Services*, Millett J. explained the background to letters of credit[65]:

> "Letters of credit are employed to finance international commercial transactions between traders who are normally known to each other, and the terms of which have been the subject of negotiation. The contract will usually provide merely for payment to be made by letter of credit, the identity of the issuing bank being left to be nominated by the buyer after the contract has been concluded, and being a matter of indifference to the seller. Even where the identity of the issuing bank is agreed between the parties, there is no prior contract between the issuing bank and the seller; its obligations to the seller arise under the letter of credit itself. The sole purpose of the letter of credit is to provide security to the seller to replace that represented by the shipping documents which he gives up in exchange for the credit. Finally, the terms on which the seller is entitled to payment must be identical to those to which he is entitled under the contract with the buyer."

The standard mechanism for structuring letters of credit is by means of the Uniform Customs and Practice for Documentary Credits ("UCP") which was published in a number of evolving versions between 1933 and 2007 by the International Chamber of Commerce. The current version is the "UCP 600", with

---

[61] *Foley v Hill* (1848) 2 H.L. Cas. 28, 9 E.R. 1002.
[62] This analysis flows from cases such as *Walsh v Lonsdale* (1882) 21 Ch.D. 9 and *Neville v Wilson* [1997] Ch. 144 where a specifically enforceable contract transfers the equitable interest in property which is to be transferred under the terms of that contract.
[63] e.g. *Hamzeh Malas & Sons v British Innex Industries Ltd* [1958] 2 Q.B. 127, 129, per Jenkins L.J.
[64] e.g. R. Goode, "Abstract Payment Undertakings", in Cane and Stapleton (eds), *Essays for Patrick Atiyah* (Oxford: Clarendon Press, 1991).
[65] [1987] Ch. 150, 168.

provisions relating to the electronic transmission of documentation in "eUCP". This standard form agreement is only efficacious under English law if it is expressly incorporated into the contract between the parties.

The purpose of a letter of credit, in essence, is that the seller has an irrevocable right to payment for the goods on the condition that a bill of lading in respect of those goods is delivered to the paying bank. A letter of credit arrangement is structured as follows. There is a contract of sale between seller and buyer at root, with the ordinary combination of conditions, warranties, and events of default in that contract. Of importance will be the provisions as to whether or not the buyer is able to repudiate the goods for being of the wrong type or insufficient quality, who bears the risk of spoilage of the goods while in transit, and how payment is to be made under the letter of credit. The letter of credit is based on a contract between the buyer and the "issuing bank". The issuing bank issues the letter of credit at the buyer's instruction. The issuing bank will ordinarily be in the buyer's home jurisdiction or else in some jurisdiction convenient to the buyer. That issuing bank will ordinarily have to make delivery and payment in another jurisdiction, and therefore the issuing bank will ordinarily contract with a bank in that other jurisdiction (a "correspondent bank") so that the correspondent bank will make payment ultimately to the seller in the specified payment currency from the funds passed to it by the issuing bank. Payment will then be made in accordance with the terms of the contract either by the issuing bank or by the correspondent bank (typically appointed for the purpose in the port to which the goods are to be delivered). The contract provides that payment is to be made by the appropriate bank once documents including a bill of lading are delivered at the destination port for shipment of the goods.

30–47

The letter of credit is a legal document separate from the contract between the parties which therefore has a legal life of its own: the letter of credit is ordinarily entitled to be settled distinct from the contract between the parties. Payment is therefore to be made regardless of the contract of sale between the parties, unless there was something expressly to the contrary in the parties' transactions. The extent of the obligation to pay is therefore to be derived from the terms of the letter of credit itself. Bankers will not be imputed with knowledge of market terminology and therefore will only be obliged to make payment under the credit if the documents are strictly in order,[66] The documents to be delivered are the original documents, and not copies.[67]

30–48

Fraudulent presentation of documents would also unravel the obligation to make payment.[68] The only circumstances in which an English court will grant an injunction to restrain payment being made on a letter of credit is in circumstances in which there has been clear and obvious fraud provided that the bank has notice

30–49

---

[66] *JH Rayner & Co Ltd v Hambros Bank Ltd* [1943] K.B. 37.
[67] *Glencore International AG v Bank of China* [1996] 1 Lloyd's Rep. 135; *Kredietbank Antwerp v Midland Bank Plc* [1996] Lloyd's Rep. Bank 219. English courts will sometimes listen to evidence of standard market practice in this context, as with opinions of the ICC Banking Commission: *Credit Industriel et Commercial v China Merchants Bank* [2002] 2 All E.R. (Comm) 427.
[68] *United City Merchants (Investments) Ltd v Royal Bank of Canada* [1983] 1 A.C. 168; *Czarnikow-Rionda Sugar Trading Ltd v Standard Bank London Ltd* [1999] Lloyd's Rep. Bank 197; *Banco Santander SA v Bayfern Ltd* [1999] Lloyd's Rep. Bank 239.

of this fraud.[69] Examples of such fraud would be where the documents are forgeries or where payment is sought where the claimant has no right to payment.[70] However, such an injunction will not be granted even where there is fraud of this sort if the letter of credit has already been negotiated by the beneficiary of the letter of credit.[71] This approach is surprising, it is suggested. A better approach would be that fraud unravels everything so that no payment can be enforced against the bank and so that credit is given to the seller. If the beneficiary is fraudulently seeking payment then no payment ought to be enforceable against the bank if the bank knows of the fraud. By extension, if the bank had no knowledge of the fraud then the bank ought not to be liable for making payment under an otherwise ostensibly valid letter of credit. The approach of commercial law is to enforce payment so as to maintain commercial certainty in the irrevocability of the credit, and then presumably to require the payer to proceed against the fraudster at common law: this approach does, however, require payment to be made to a fraudster to which she is not entitled and then for the payer to seek recovery against a person who has already committed fraud and who is likely as a result to abscond with the money and so be impossible to sue in practice. Nevertheless, English courts consider such letters of credit to be irrevocable to the extent that payment must be made even if there is some fraud involved.[72]

---

[69] *DCD Factors Plc v Ramada Trading Ltd* [2008] Bus. L.R. 654, [14], per Lloyd Jones J.
[70] [2008] Bus. L.R. 654, [14].
[71] *DCD Factors Plc v Ramada Trading Ltd* [2008] Bus. L.R. 654.
[72] *Kvaerner John Brown Ltd v Midland Bank Plc* [1998] C.L.C. 446, 449, per Cresswell J.

CHAPTER 31

RETAIL BANKING AND CONDUCT OF BUSINESS REGULATION

CORE PRINCIPLES

This chapter considers some specific problems relating to high-street banking. It is easy in an analysis of the law of finance to overlook the retail customer because so much of the excitement in practice is focused on corporate and speculative financial instruments. However, the sociology of financial services to individuals and to small businesses is fascinating and, as the financial crisis 2007–09 reminded us, the place of core customer deposits and retail business is at the heart of the role which banking plays in modern societies. Many of the legal issues which apply to retail banking have been considered in this book already: so this chapter will not repeat those analyses but rather it cross-references them in the discussion to follow so as to pull together a single discussion of retail banking across this book.

Its principal focus is on conduct of business regulation as it applies to high-street, retail banks by virtue of the Banking Conduct of Business Sourcebook ("BCOBS"). BCOBS emphasises the core regulatory principles that the bank is required to act in the best interests of its customer. The bank is required to communicate appropriately with its customer, and it is permitted an oddly wide range of promotional activities to people who are already its customers. Otherwise, as is the case with most FCA regulation, the customer is to be provided with sufficient information of the appropriate kind to make their own choices.

The second issue is the regulation of lending to ordinary citizens. The Consumer Credit Act 1974, which is merely outlined here, governs the provision of lending services to ordinary citizens. That Act created the Office of Fair Trading which licences all moneylenders. The function of regulating lending will pass to the Financial Conduct Authority in April 2013. Of particular importance in the real world for the poor, and for those who scrape by, are unlicensed moneylenders (known as loan sharks) and licensed payday loan companies, both of which charge extortionate rates of interest (albeit with different levels of violence in their recovery policies). The Office of Fair Trading has been seeking to improve the oversight and challenge to both forms of activity.

The third issue relates to problems with the application of contract law to ordinary, retail banking practice: why is it that banks assume they can unilaterally change the terms of their contract with their customer, regardless of the effect on that customer or the doctrine of specific performance. Even where there is an express contractual term to permit such a change, it is suggested that there are supervening regulatory principles which should govern the application of that power.

The fourth issue relates to the chimerical concept of identity theft. If money deposited into a bank account becomes absolutely the property of the bank, then why does the burden of any theft of money value "from that account" apply to the customer when it is in law the bank's money which has been stolen? In what circumstances should the customer's own fault interfere with that analysis?

1. INTRODUCTION

A. The scope of this chapter

31–01 The purpose of this chapter is to collect in one place references to the principal regulatory and legal principles which relate to private citizens when they are bank customers. This is referred to here as "retail banking". The principal focus of this chapter is on consumer protection through conduct of business regulation, and therefore it falls on the Banking Conduct of Business Sourcebook ("BCOBS"). Otherwise it is all-too-easy for a book on the law of finance to lapse into an exclusive focus on corporate banking clients and services, and the high-profile world of derivatives trading and so forth. However, the advent of the payment protection insurance ("PPI") scandal, which is discussed in detail in Chapter 45,[1] demonstrates that ordinary retail customers are used by their banks as a source of easy profit: millions of customers were sold add-on insurance (which was inappropriate for them) on a systematic scale by all high street banks. Similarly, the bank charges litigation which was discussed in Chapter 18, whereby customers had sought to claim that the charges which were levied on them, for unauthorised overdrafts and so forth, were unfair under the unfair contract terms regulations.[2] It was found that they were not unfair only on the basis that a strict application of the regulations did not permit a survey of their fairness to be undertaken. What the litigation highlighted was that the charges did not represent the cost of providing that service to the bank and, more significantly, that those bank charges constitute a significant part of the banks' profits. It seems that retail banking would not have been in profit in the 21st century without the bank charges and PPI charges which it generated. In other words, our banking system is built on extracting profit from customers who are too credulous, too financially challenged, or too disorganised to avoid those charges. In short, profit depends upon the expert taking advantage of the inexpert; the strong taking advantage of the weak.

B.   Changes in retail banking

The very breadth of financial techniques which relate to corporate clients and to cross-border banking and financial services can dominate an analysis of the law of finance. What has been revealed by the financial crisis of 2007–09 (as it is discussed in Chapter 45) is that even those banks which provided services to ordinary citizens on the high street in the UK were at risk from a financial crisis which might begin in on the other side of the world in the USA and be spread through the credit derivatives markets to the bank which holds their savings. Moreover, even banks which seemed to be ostensibly the safest and the most reputable in the UK might be engaged in systematic misfeasance ranging from mis-selling payment protection insurance ("PPI"), right through to the falsification of the London Inter-Bank Offered Rate ("Libor") which affected the rates at which mortgages and other financial instruments were payable by ordinary customers. While British banks historically had conservative business models (whereby they would take deposits and lend out a multiple of those deposits to appropriate customers), in the lead-up to the financial crisis there were banks like Northern Rock which had taken to using short-term funding on financial markets to fund a rapid expansion into other forms of financial instrument and other forms of business. They were funding long-term obligations with short-term money: a particularly risky strategy. When those short-term market dried up during the credit crunch in 2007–08, the weaker banks using that model went into insolvency.

31–02

---

[1] para.45–01.
[2] para.18–87.

C. The context of access to financial services for all citizens

31–03 The context of high street banking after 2009 is therefore very different from the calmer world in 2006 before the financial crisis. The market for financial services on the high street for ordinary citizens and small businesses is very different now from the way it used to be even 20 years ago. Self-evidently there have been enormous changes made by the introduction of ATMs, payment cards and internet banking, all of which mean that much of the traditional banking law relating to cheques and payments of cash over the counter in a bank branch has had to be reinterpreted for this new world. Similarly, as discussed in Chapter 45, HM Treasury figures show that there are still over one million adults who do not have access to banking services in the UK. Therefore, alternative financial services providers like credit unions and friendly societies are being encouraged to fill the gap, as is discussed in Part XIII of this book, by making small loans, quasi-bank accounts and other services available to people who cannot access mainstream banking services. However, there are many unsavoury means of accessing finance for the poor. In particular there are unlicensed moneylenders—colloquially known as "loan sharks"—who make the lives of many ordinary people a misery. Recently, the "payday loan" providers have begun to provide "services" which charge extraordinary rates of interest for short-term loans. Both of these sorts of lending are considered below. For the poor, there is a choice between reputable credit unions (where they exist) usually serving small geographic areas, and disreputable "loan sharks" or short-term internet lenders (both of whom charge astonishingly high rates of interest for small loans, albeit with markedly different levels of violence involved in their practices for recovering late payments).

D. Discussions of retail banking services elsewhere in this book

The scope of this section; the place of the individual

31–04 This short section is intended solely to identify other places in this book where issues relating to retail financial and banking services have already been discussed. Those discussions are not repeated here: rather cross-references are provided to enable a single discussion of retail financial services (a topic which is so often overlooked in the discussion of corporate and speculative activity and in the discussion of high-level regulatory policy). At one level, the whole of this book has been about the ability of ordinary people to acquire a "wherewithal to act" through finance from the beginning of Chapter 1. The discussion of money, similarly, in Chapter 2 had more to do with the notes and coins held by individuals than any corporate activity. Much of the discussion of financial regulation in the wake of the financial crisis (considered in Chapter 45) has been concerned with the protection of ordinary customers from the shenanigans of the corporate finance world and the speculative activities of financial institutions. The innovation of financial markets has often been focused on the creation of new financial instruments for corporations or for speculation, but there has always been a part of any retail or universal bank's attention which has been focused on finding ways to increase its core deposits from retail customers or to maximise the safe income stream that flows from levying charges on large numbers of retail customers for various aspects of their purportedly "free" banking service. In the modern age, the ordinary customer has become the bankroll for the financial speculators' adventures in complex mathematics, and she has become the bankroll for the bankers' failures through her taxes and increased charges. It is hoped by policymakers that the regulatory changes considered in Chapters 8, 9 and 28 will ameliorate that situation for the future; the nightmare scenario, which occurred in 2008, is analysed in Chapter 45.

Utility banking services: payment systems and deposit-taking

The concept of "utility banking" is one that is explored in Chapter 45. It refers to those services which are carried on by financial institutions (especially the main clearing banks) which are so pivotal to the operation of the economic and social life of the nation that they effectively constitute utilities like water or electricity. Examples are the payments system operated between banks, the activity of deposit-taking, and so forth. If banks do operate a utility function in this context, then it may be appropriate to subject them to public law models of regulation and supervision. **31–05**

The relationship between customer and banker

The traditional banking law principles governing the relationship between customer and banker were considered in Chapter 29. The legal principles governing payments systems and payment card systems were considered in Chapter 30. **31–06**

Lending

The law relating to ordinary lending is considered in Chapter 32. Those principles in Chapter 33 apply to retail customers as they apply to corporate customers. The law relating to overdraft loans and bank accounts was, however, considered in Chapter 29. **31–07**

Mortgages

The law relating to mortgages (under statute, the common law and in equity) is considered in Chapter 49 of Hudson, *The Law and Regulation of Finance*. Also included in that chapter is the very important discussion of the regulation of mortgage business by the FCA under the Mortgage Conduct of Business Sourcebook ("MCOBS"). **31–08**

Insurance

The law and regulation of insurance business are considered in Chapter 45 of Hudson, *The Law and Regulation of Finance*. **31–09**

2. THE BANKING CONDUCT OF BUSINESS SOURCEBOOK

A. Introduction

31–10   Once upon a time, retail banks operated on the basis of voluntary Banking Codes by reference to which they promised to treat their customers well, in accordance with the terms of those codes.[3] Nevertheless, banks continued to treat their customers poorly (as has been revealed latterly, by means of mis-selling both payment protection insurance to ordinary customers and unnecessarily complex interest rate swaps to small businesses, and by using unfair contract terms in their agreements). Then they caused a cataclysmic crash in the real economy from the summer of 2007 onwards. From November 1, 2009, however, the Banking Conduct of Business Sourcebook ("BCOBS") has provided for a code of principles governing the treatment of customers by banks in relation to ordinary banking business.[4] BCOBS falls to be interpreted in the same way as the rest of the *FCA Handbook*, as discussed in Chapter 9; whereas the earlier Banking Codes were only to be construed by reference to a "broad, purposive and common sense approach" and in a "non-technical way".[5]

31–11   This formalisation of banks' obligations is, it is suggested, a welcome development because it makes banks' obligations clearer and also because it offers more formal protection to customers. Unlike the old common law relating to banking transactions (discussed in Chapter 29, which still has effect, of course), the regulations impose positive obligations on banks across all of their dealings with clients, instead of being limited to those few matters which the common law considered important (such as confidentiality). The common law, by contrast only imposes obligations which the parties have agreed to assume (by way of contract) or which constitute established legal wrongs (such as negligence). That the regulation imposes positive obligations requires the banks to behave in the stipulated way whether they wish to do so or not. This marks a great change in the nature of the banker-customer relationship.

31–12   One of the principal changes wrought by BCOBS is the prevention of exclusion of liability clauses for banks in their contracts with customers in the same way that COBS prevents investment firms from excluding their liabilities for matters falling within the rulebook. This is an important development in ensuring that the conduct of business principles become obligatory in practice. It is the general practice of financial institutions to exclude their liabilities by contract wherever possible.

---

[3] Those codes were voluntary, as was illustrated by *R v Financial Ombudsman Service, Ex p. Norwich and Peterborough BS* [2002] EWHC 2379, considering by way of judicial review whether or not the ombudsman had considered the Banking Code appropriately in using it to decide whether or not the bank had acted fairly and reasonably within the scope of FSA regulation. It was found that this code did not govern the question whether or not the same rate of interest should be paid on superseded accounts as on ordinary current accounts

[4] The COBS rulebook considered in Chapter 10 related to investment business, as opposed to banking business.

[5] *R (Ex p. Norwich and Peterborough BS v Financial Ombudsman Service Ltd* [2002] EWHC 2379 (Admin), per Ousley J.

B.   Core principles relating to the treatment of bank customers

The application of BCOBS to banking business

BCOBS applies in the following manner[6]:   **31–13**

> "This sourcebook applies to a *firm*[7] with respect to the activity of *accepting deposits* from *banking customers* carried on from an establishment maintained by it in the *United Kingdom* and activities connected with that activity."

BCOBS applies to banking business, primarily to deposit-taking and, in parts, to payment services in compliance with the Payment Services Directive.[8] BCOBS requires that, further to principle 6 of PRIN, a firm must "pay due regard to the interests of its customers and treat them fairly" and furthermore that under principle 7 of PRIN a firm is required "to pay due regard to the information needs of its clients and communicate information to them in a way which is clear, fair and not misleading".[9] These principles apply to all communications and promotions.

Thus, in effect, the *FCA Handbook* architecture applies to banks in the same way   **31–14**
as the general financial services regulations considered in Chapter 9 in relation to banks needing to have appropriate internal systems and controls, as to the manner in which communications are to be made to their customers, and so forth. In essence, then, the financial services umbrella which has covered investment business under EU law and under the FCA rulebooks now also applies to ordinary banking business as a result of BCOBS. This is significant because mainstream banking business had previously been subject to lesser regulatory treatment than investment business.

Communications (including promotions) with customers

One of the most important aspects of BCOBS is its stipulation of the general   **31–15**
principles which govern banks' communications with their customers. There are three important regulatory requirements as to communications: first, relating to the explanation of risks; second, relating to the need for clarity in the content of communications; and, third, in ensuring that no important matter is hidden in the "small print" of an agreement.

Therefore, first and significantly, in relation to the need to explain risks to   **31–16**
customers, paragraph 2.3.1R provides that a firm must ensure that "each communication ... is accurate and, in particular, does not emphasise any potential benefits of a retail banking service without also giving a fair and prominent indication of any relevant risks".[10] The need to explain risks is particularly

---

[6] BCOBS, 1.1.1R.
[7] The sourcebook retains the FCA usage "firm" throughout, although the text will refer to "bank" as well as firm when quoting.
[8] BCOBS, 1.1.4R.
[9] BCOBS, 2.1.1G, and BCOBS, 2.2.1R.
[10] BCOBS, 3.2.1(2)R.

significant in the retail context. Ordinary members of the public may well not understand the fees associated with a service, or the risks of a particular type of service, or even the need for a service (such as mis-sold payment protection insurance). Indeed, a relative of mine was once sold an investment product by a high street bank on the basis that there was "no risk"—assuming my relative to be an idiot, the bank employee even wrote those two words down in block capitals on a piece of paper for her. Being an investment product, there was of course a risk that it would fail but the salesman's pitch was that there would not in practice be any failure to make payment. Remarkably, this was only a few months after the failure of Lehman Brothers. It was proved by the payment protection insurance scandal[11]—where billions of pounds of useless, needless insurance was sold to customers—that there is something rotten in high street banking, whereby too often ordinary customers are seen simply as easy marks for banks.

31–17 Secondly, the bank must ensure that each communication "is sufficient for, and presented in a way that is likely to be understood by, the average member of the group to whom it is directed, or by whom it is likely to be received".[12] This means that a bank may not simply rely on setting out everything which needs to be said but doing so in such technical or dense language that many clients would not be able to understand it. Instead, the obligation placed on the bank is to present both legal and commercial terminology in a sufficiently comprehensible fashion for ordinary customers, but such that no significant material is omitted and no important nuance lost. The bank is entitled to consider the intended targets of each banking product and to draft their communications appropriately.

31–18 Thirdly, the firm must ensure that each communication "does not disguise, diminish or obscure important information, statements or warnings". Thus, a warning or important information must not be, for example, hidden among the small print as many organisations used to tend to do: forms legendarily included inducements in a large font and then warnings, exclusion of liability language and so forth in much, much smaller font in a block of text hidden away at the bottom of a form. Hence, the vernacular usage of the term "hidden among the small print" in which commercial service providers would typically limit their own liabilities. Banks also bear obligations to include the name of the firm in communications with customers.[13]

31–19 The decision of the Court of Appeal in *The Office of Fair Trading v Abbey National Plc*[14] emphasised the approach of the Court of Appeal to the sorts of commercial information, such as bank charges, which it was held that an ordinary client would not consider. Given that judicial attitude, in relation to all of these requirements, it is suggested that banks need to ensure that they are very clear in explaining all of the risks and all matters which they assume those customers will have considered in their communications with customers. The Supreme Court took a different approach to the interpretation of the unfair contract terms legislation in this context: finding instead that the charges formed a part of the

---

[11] Discussed in Ch.45 in detail.
[12] BCOBS, 3.2.1(3)R.
[13] BCOBS, 3.2.1(1)R.
[14] [2009] EWCA Civ 116.

main bargain between the parties and were therefore not something which could be reviewed under the grounds of fairness under the regulations.[15]

C. Enabling customers to make informed decisions

As was highlighted in Chapter 3,[16] the underlying philosophy of financial services regulation is that customers are not protected against their own folly nor protected against the possibility of loss, but rather customers are to be provided with enough information of a suitable kind to enable them to make their own minds up. The focus is therefore on facilitating informed decision-making by consumers of financial services. In a capitalist marketplace we are all free to fail, provided that a professional has not taken inappropriate advantage of our ignorance. In this vein, BCOBS provides that:[17]

31–20

> "A firm must provide or make available to a banking customer appropriate information about a retail banking service and any deposit made in relation to that retail banking service:
> (1) in good time;
> (2) in an appropriate medium; and
> (3) in easily understandable language and in a clear and comprehensible form;
>   so that the banking customer can make decisions on an informed basis."

In effect, this principle rehearses some of the requirements of the central principles set out above, in particular relating to the need for the information to be provided in clear and comprehensible language. Rather than define what constitutes "good time" or the appropriate medium for communication, the bank is required to identify what would be the most appropriate time and the most appropriate medium for each customer by reference to the importance of the service to the customer and the convenience of the method to the customer as well (except in relation to distance selling, considered below).[18] The strength of this sort of high-level regulation is that it leaves it to the bank to identify the most appropriate method of dealing with its customers, and therefore forces the bank into an ethical as well as a legal consideration of what is suitable in its business practices as well as its treatment of individual customers. Consequently, the bank cannot be careless about the way it treats its customers, nor can it simply use a cheap, efficient, one-size-fits-all approach. A compliant bank will be required to generate considerate and appropriate ways of dealing with individual customers, or at least with particular, narrow classes of customer. The side benefit for the banks will be an increase in their public relations profile by dint of using more client-focused sales and operations techniques.

Ultimately, the weakness of this sort of regulation is that it will not prevent credulous customers from being attracted by glossy brochures and advertising blandishments to acquire products which may cause them loss in the longer term.

31–21

---

[15] [2009] UKSC 6; [2009] 3 W.L.R. 1215.
[16] para.3–10, and 8–17.
[17] BCOBS, 4.1.1R.
[18] BCOBS, 4.1.2G. As a form of high level principle, the firm is required to identify the way in which it will comply with this regulatory requirement, as opposed to the FSA spelling out in detail what boxes must be ticked to satisfy the requirement.

For example, a number of customers acquired savings products from banks which they were told would pay them a "guaranteed return" only for the collapse of Lehman Brothers to reveal for the first time that it was Lehman Brothers which was the originator of those products. This had not been revealed in any correspondence nor by any of the independent financial advisors involved. In consequence, the guarantees were worthless because the ultimate payer (a Lehman Brothers subsidiary) was bankrupt and the deposits were absorbed into the Lehman Brothers organisation just before the insolvency. In such situations, what is required is a clearer stipulation in the regulations that information about the originator of the financial product at issue and about the risks associated with the ultimate income-producing asset must be made plain to the customer. When a customer reads an advertisement promoting a bond with a guaranteed return, that sounds entirely plausible and desirable, particularly to customers who rely on interest for their income, perhaps to supplement a pension. However, if the customer were made aware that it is not simply a legally-binding promise by the nice salesman which will generate the income, but rather a complex securities transaction originated by a large, unknown-to-the-customer American investment bank, and that the bank is ultimately the source of the "guarantee", then the customer might be more wary of the investment. The word "guarantee" in this context actually means: the originator is confident that payment will be made; whereas the customer hears: payment will definitely be made and I have a legally-binding undertaking to that effect so I do not need to worry. There is an enormous difference between those two things and the high-level principles need to come down to specificities of this sort to ensure that customers are better protected.

31–22   For example, it is a particularly egregious feature of modern banking practice that, at the time of writing, several high street banks are offering "bonds" to their customers in a manner which makes them appear to be bank accounts. However, a bond does not attract the same protection in the form of the £85,000 guarantee offered by the FSCS in relation to all bank accounts, nor does it attract all of the same benefits of a bank account otherwise. And yet the leaflets and web-pages (for there are no complete sets of contractual terms available in the branches) which accompany those bonds do not make clear anywhere what exactly the difference between a "bond" and an "account" is in this context. Instead the "guaranteed"[19] bond interest is detailed, as is the length of the investment.

31–23   Instead the requirements of BCOBS extend only to a guidance note (not a rule) which goes only this far[20]:

> "The appropriate information rule applies before a banking customer is bound by the terms of the contract. It also applies after a banking customer has become bound by them. In order to meet the requirements of the appropriate information rule, information provided by a firm to a banking customer should include information relating to:
> (1)   the firm;
> (2)   the different retail banking services offered by the firm which share the main features of the retail banking service the banking customer has enquired about, or which have

---

[19]   The guarantee is, again, a mere promise that the interest will reach a particular amount; but it is not a guarantee that some third party will make any payment which the bank fails to make.
[20]   BCOBS, 4.1.4G.

the product features the banking customer has expressed an interest in, unless the banking customer has expressly indicated that he does not wish to receive that information;

(3) the terms and conditions of the contract for a retail banking service and any changes to them;

(4) the rate or rates of interest payable on any deposit, how and when such interest is calculated and applied and any changes to that rate or those rates;

(5) any charges at any time payable by or on behalf of a banking customer in relation to each retail banking service and any changes to those charges;

(6) a banking customer's rights to cancel a contract for a retail banking service;

(7) how a banking customer may make a complaint (at the time and in the manner required by DISP 1.2);

(8) the terms of any compensation scheme if the firm cannot meet its obligations in respect of the retail banking service;

(9) basic bank accounts but only if the firm offers a basic bank account and the banking customer meets the firm's eligibility criteria for such an account; and

(10) the timescales for each stage of the cheque clearing process"

What is clearly missing is a requirement that the customer have a complete set of the terms and conditions supplied to them, and a requirement that the precise nature of the product be made clear to them.

Among these guidance notes, it is suggested, the continued presence of the notion **31–24** that a customer may refuse to receive information takes no account of the fact that that customer may be acting in ignorance of things which, if brought to her attention, might change her mind. A dog will jump up excitedly at the word "biscuit", but it is only if the dog understands that what was actually said was "don't eat, poisoned biscuit" that the dog is likely to refrain from eating it. Similarly, retail bank customers can only make informed choices if they are provided with all of the information. The customer can then take the risk of not reading the information. However, if the information is not provided in the first place or if it is provided in a fashion that is incomprehensible to them, then such a customer cannot ever make a truly informed decision: the opportunity to do so has been withheld from them. The case law on undue influence (considered in Chapter 24[21]) requires that independent advice be given to customers in relation to mortgages before a mortgagee can escape liability for constructive notice of any undue influence between mortgagors and sureties. It is suggested that the only defensible position in this context in relation to banking services generally is if customers are given independent advice by reference to all of the necessary information, whether they would rather bother to read it in advance or not.

The guidance notes then provide for the following matters also to be borne in **31–25** mind:[22]

"The information required by the appropriate information rule may vary according to matters such as:

(1) the *banking customer's* likely or actual commitment;

(2) the information needs of a reasonable recipient having regard to the type of *retail banking service* that is proposed or provided and its overall complexity, main benefits, risks, limitations, conditions and duration;

---

[21] para.24–48.
[22] BCOBS, 4.1.5G.

(3)   distance communication information requirements (for example, under the distance communication *rules* less information can be given during certain telephone sales than in a sale made purely by written correspondence (see *BCOBS 3.1*)); and

(4)   whether the same information has been provided to the *banking customer* previously and, if so, when that was."

The same issues, it is suggested, arise as arose in relation to the previous guidance note.

D.   Provision of accounts and other information

31–26   After a banking product[23] has been sold, the bank owes obligations to the customer to provide the customer with a statement of their account on paper or in a "durable medium".[24] The bank must also provide a banking service once the contract has been created which is "prompt, efficient and fair".[25] That this requires to be stated in a regulatory rule is interesting because for most banks the purported virtues of customer care are an essential part of their marketing strategy in the early 21st century. The British Banker's Association document "A Statement of Principles: banks and businesses – working together" is incorporated by reference into the guidance notes.[26] In particular, in relation to customers who are in "financial difficulty"[27] the rules begin with a rehearsal of Principle 6 from PRIN to the effect that a bank is required to "pay due regard to the interests of its customers" and in particular that principle is said to apply to those customers who are in financial difficulty.[28] This guidance note, however, directs a bank to do nothing other than to *consider* their customer's interests. It does not prevent a bank from commencing bankruptcy proceedings, nor demanding the immediate repayment of an overdraft loan, and so on. To preserve some semblance of a market, a bank is required to provide a prompt and efficient service to a customer who wants to move to another bank.[29]

---

[23] I have used the market argot "banking product" which gives the (once consciously) illusory image that something tangible like a car is being created. A banking product may in fact be the taking of a deposit, where the "product" is the contract entitling the customer to receive interest, to use a bank card, and so forth. Nevertheless, it is still a market usage which grates on the ear, I find.

[24] BCOBS, 4.2.1R. After a straw poll of my relatives' banking arrangements, it seems that only two banks—NatWest and Lloyds TSB—provide regular, hard copy statements on a monthly basis of each bank account. The other banks and building societies tend to provide an annual statement for deposit accounts or else nothing at all (unless one turns up at the bank in person). This egregious breach of these obligations is quite remarkable.

[25] BCOBS, 5.1.1R.

[26] BCOBS, 5.1.3G.

[27] BCOBS, 5.1.4G.

[28] BCOBS, 5.1.4G.

[29] BCOBS, 5.1.5R.

E.   Cancellation rights

The customer has "a right to cancel a contract for a retail banking service … **31–27**
without penalty and without giving any reason within 14 calendar days".[30] The
principal exception to this rule is in relation to cash deposits.[31] The 14 day period
runs either from the "conclusion of the contract" or the date on which the terms of
the contract were sent to the customer.[32] The existence of the right to cancel and
the terms on which cancellation takes effect are to be notified to the customer in
good time after the creation of the contract.[33] The contract is terminated from the
time when the cancellation takes effect.[34]

F.   Distance marketing and e-commerce

The development of internet and telephone banking has led to the EU Distance **31–28**
Marketing Directive. BCOBS, implementing that directive, requires that the
prescribed information must be provided to a customer in relation to a "distance
marketing" arrangement "in good time" before a contract becomes binding on
that customer.[35] Distance marketing is anything which is done at a distance,
defined in the FCA Handbook glossary as something constituting "an organised
distance sales or service provision scheme". The central principle is that the
customer must know all of the terms in advance of forming an agreement and
know about her right to cancel;[36] that is, over-and-above the discussion in the
previous sections about making risks clear, ensuring that communications are
clear, fair and not misleading, and so forth. The full range of material which must
be provided is set out in the distance marketing disclosure rules set out in Annex
1 to Chapter 3 of BCOBS.

The key exceptions are where a service is being provided in succession to **31–29**
operations "of the same nature" performed between the parties before,[37] or where
the customer agrees to a brief summary of that information being provided on the
telephone before the full information is provided in hard copy before an
agreement is created.[38] This latter exception is, it is suggested, an egregious
exception to the central principle because it is over the telephone that customers
are more likely to be convinced to enter into agreements which, in the cold light
of day, they may not wish to create. Moreover, the permission for a summary to
be given may dissuade the customer from reading the subsequent hard copy
material properly, or may cause the customer to read it in such a way that the
customer assumes that the information correlates with her recollection of the
earlier telephone conversation. In either case, the customer may be encouraged

---

[30] BCOBS, 6.1.1R.
[31] BCOBS, 6.1.2(c)R.
[32] BCOBS, 6.1.4R.
[33] BCOBS, 6.1.5R.
[34] BCOBS, 6.3.1R.
[35] BCOBS, 3.1.2R.
[36] BCOBS, 3.1.2R , as implemented in BCOBS 3, Annex 1.
[37] BCOBS, 3.1.9R.
[38] BCOBS, 3.1.11R.

into a deal by a salesman's call which otherwise she might not have done so effectively in the way that boiler rooms cajole or coax people at home into buying poor investments. Unlike boiler rooms, however, a regulated firm must not seek to enforce "unsolicited services" against a consumer.[39] However, the financial promotion regulations (discussed in Chapter 11) do permit authorised firms to cold-call in some contexts, and this may have the same effect on an inexperienced customer. Similarly, further to the EC E-Commerce Directive, in e-commerce contexts, unsolicited emails may be sent by authorised firms in the UK provided they are clearly and unambiguously identified as such: the effect is not the prevention of unsolicited advertisements and promotions by email, but rather the legitimacy of such communications provided that they comply with the regulations as to their provenance, clarity and accuracy.

3.   LENDING AND THE RETAIL CUSTOMER

A.   Introduction

31–30   For working class Britain, and even for young professionals who feel themselves affluent but not yet in funds sufficient to enjoy the lifestyles they read about in magazines, short-term loans in comparatively small amounts (compared to loans for the purchase of cars or land, for example) are becoming a way of bridging the gap between their expectations and their means. The regulation of such lending activity has not, before April Fool's Day 2013, been the business of the principal financial regulator in the UK.[40] Instead, the Office of Fair Trading has had competence in this regard. This section considers the regulation of such lending activities and in particular the legal contexts of "payday" lenders and "loan sharks".

B.   Short-term loans and the Consumer Credit Act 1974

The provisions of the Consumer Credit Act 1974 in outline

31–31   The Office of Fair Trading ("OFT") was created by the Consumer Credit Act 1974 ("CCA 1974") to oversee consumer (as opposed to commercial) credit business. The OFT operates the licensing regime for moneylenders and others providing consumer credit. Operation without a licence in a prescribed activity constitutes a criminal offence.[41]

31–32   The OFT has several statutory functions involving it in preparing codes of guidance for compliance with the CCA 1974 and its regulations; adjudicating in complaints brought to it about the activities of licensed credit providers (for example, in relation to inappropriate recovery practices, inappropriate sales

---

[39] BCOBS, 3.1.15R
[40] See, for example, the work that is being done by Stella Creasy MP in relation to loan sharks in the Walthamstow constituency in East London at: *http://www.workingforwalthamstow.org.uk/category/ legal-loan-shark-campaign/* [Accessed March 14, 2013].
[41] Consumer Credit Act 1974, s.39.

practices, and so forth); and generally "superintending" the operation of those regulations.[42] The OFT also has a function of keeping the Secretary of State informed about social and commercial changes in the area of its remit over time.[43] "Consumer credit agreements" between an individual (i.e. not a company) and any other person (whether an individual or a company or other entity) in an amount of not more than £25,000 are covered by the CCA 1974.[44] This would include loans[45] of less than £25,000. An attempt to create small agreements of less than £50 will lead to them being treated as a single credit agreement.[46] Similarly, "credit token agreements"—including vouchers, cards, coupons, stamps and so forth—are covered by the CCA 1974. The activities of deposit-taking banks, mortgages over land, friendly societies, and so forth are exempt from the statute because they are regulated separately,[47] as considered elsewhere in this book. Anyone conducting a business in any of these non-exempt activities must be licensed by the OFT.[48] The licensee is required to be a "fit person" to hold that licence.[49] The ultimate powers of the OFT are the suspension and revocation of a licence on the basis that, assuming hypothetically that the licence had come to an end, the OFT was of the view that it would not have renewed the licence:[50] therefore, these powers are triggered where the licensee effectively acts in such a way that it would not have received a licence in the first place.

The OFT is then empowered to make regulations, as it does, about conduct of business in these contexts, which encompass the need for record-keeping and specifies the types of information which must be made available to the customer.[51] Many complaints which the OFT receives revolve around inappropriate conduct of business such as giving inadequate information about rates of interest, penalties, fees and so forth, and high-pressure techniques for recovering payment (including bombarding the customer with telephone calls, electronic messages, letters and so forth) as well as threats of various kinds.[52]

31–33

C. Payday lenders

As with any provider of a consumer credit agreement, so-called "payday lenders" or internet-based, short-term lenders or any other such lender are required to be licensed by the OFT. Payday lenders are a particularly sensitive species politically at the time of writing. They specialise in making small loans (usually of an amount equivalent to a week's or a month's wages) to borrowers which are

31–34

---

[42] Consumer Credit Act 1974, s.1.
[43] Consumer Credit Act 1974, s.1(2).
[44] Consumer Credit Act 1974, s.8.
[45] Consumer Credit Act 1974, s.9.
[46] Consumer Credit Act 1974, s.17.
[47] Consumer Credit Act 1974, s.16.
[48] Consumer Credit Act 1974, s.21.
[49] Consumer Credit Act 1974, s.25.
[50] Consumer Credit Act 1974, s.32.
[51] Consumer Credit Act 1974, s.26.
[52] See, for example, *http://www.oft.gov.uk/shared_oft/business_leaflets/consumer_credit/debt-letters.pdf.*

intended to be repaid very quickly and which therefore attract very high rates of interest so that the lender can recover a profit on its loan in the few days for which that loan is supposedly expected to exist. These loans are marketed at people who need a little money to tide them over until their salary reaches their bank account at the end of the money (hence the name "payday" lenders) and the concept is that the borrower will be glad of the money to fund their lifestyle for a few days until their wages reach them. The OFT estimates that this sector is currently worth £2 billion.

31–35 This type of loan is necessarily aimed at people who cannot acquire overdrafts on their current accounts to tide them over for that period of time. Clearly, the risk is that people who are desperate for money will borrow from anyone who will lend to them and that over time they will build up a package of debt which becomes semi-permanent and on which the interest rates rise particularly steeply. The interest rates charged by payday lenders are commonly at extraordinary levels of 2,000 per cent APR. The payday lenders' argument is that they are only intended to be very short-term loans and therefore should never reach those rates of interest (but if that were the case then the loans would be specified to be fixed term loans of a short period with a maximum APR much lower than 2,000 per cent).

31–36 The OFT has carried out extensive work into the condition of payday lenders as a sector, including providers such as wonga.com. The report expresses the OFT's intention to refer the anti-competitive practices of this sector to the Competition Commission.[53] The OFT discovered these lenders are not complying with the Consumer Credit Act 1974 on a widespread basis, not complying with the OFT's "Irresponsible Lending Guidance", and generally making loans to people who are not able to repay them and for whom those loans are generally unsuitable. It emerged that one third of payday loans are not repaid on time (thus incurring higher interest rates), that 28 per cent of loans are rolled over[54] at least once and that this provides one half of the sector's revenues. Moreover, 19 per cent of the sector's revenues come from that 5 per cent of loans which are rolled over more than four times and which thus incur the highest rates of interest generally. Thus, the sector has a vested interest in customers not repaying their loans on time. The sector's failure to administer complaints procedures properly is another cause for concern. The OFT has consequently made this sector a priority for its future work. At the time of writing, the Coalition government has announced that it will delay any thoughts of regulating payday lenders differently until movement towards voluntary codes have been decided upon. This is something which cuts against the findings of the OFT that this sector is a particular concern for it.

---

[53] OFT, "Payday Lending – Compliance Review Final Report", March 2013. *http://www.oft.gov.uk/ shared_oft/Credit/oft1481.pdf.* [Accessed March 14, 2013]

[54] By "rolled over" is meant that the original loan is replaced by a new loan, or that the loan period is extended—both at an interest cost.

D.   Unlicensed moneylenders: "loan sharks"

There are few things more disturbing in our ordinary lives than the phenomenon **31–37** of loan sharking. Ordinary people who are disenfranchised by the financial sector (which is currently, ironically, also harming their employment prospects through its impact on the real economy) have to seek money somewhere. If the high street banks do not consider them to be a suitable credit risk—particularly if they are one of the millions of people who have experienced a period of unemployment— then they may turn to unlicensed moneylenders. The term "loan sharks" is commonly applied to these people, the term perhaps deriving from the black-and-white George Raft film of the same name. Loan sharks lend small amounts of cash and they are habitually violent or menacing in recovering their money, arbitrarily increasing the rates of interest which they will require from borrowers before they will consider the debt to be settled. A good example of the sort of misery which is caused by loan sharking is provided in Ken Loach's film *Raining Stones*. Ken Loach has for many years been the chronicler of the plight of working-class Britons. In *Raining Stones*, a man needs to buy his daughter her first communion dress and so ill-advisedly he borrows money from a loan shark. The misery, violence and injustice which follow his decision to involve himself with an unlicensed moneylender is genuinely disturbing as this man, with his muscular, hairy forearms and gold signet rings, terrorises his family and his home.

The plight of ordinary people facing loan sharks is a deeply troubling one; **31–38** however, the legal analysis of their activities is, in theory, very straightforward. An unlicensed moneylender commits a criminal offence by lending money without a licence.[55] Where the moneylender is not licensed, no binding contract is created between lender and borrower.[56] It is common for such a person to commit several other criminal offences in the course of seeking to recover their money, of which the most obvious is obtaining money with menaces, although assault and criminal damages is not unknown as well.

Under s.21 of the Theft Act 1968 it is a criminal offence to make an unwarranted **31–39** demand[57] for money with menaces with a view to making a gain.[58] This offence is known more simply as "blackmail". The concept of "menaces" includes actions such as the threat of physical violence or causing harm to some other person or property.[59] It was held by Sellers LJ in *R. v Clear*[60] that "threats and conduct of such a nature and extent that the mind of an ordinary person of normal stability

---

[55] Consumer Credit Act 1974, s.39.

[56] Consumer Credit Act 1974, s.40, unless the OFT makes an order relating to that agreement.

[57] It is suggested that a menacing demand for money from an unlicensed moneylender must be an unwarranted demand; as opposed to the demand for repayment which a high-street bank might make in relation to an unauthorised overdraft.

[58] *R. v Hester* [2007] EWCA Crim 2127 where the general scope of the offence of blackmail is discussed.

[59] *R. v Tomlinson* [1895] 1 Q.B. 706. See *R. v Lawrence and Pomroy* 57 Cr. App. R. 64, relating to recovery of money.

[60] [1968] 1 Q.B. 670, 679. However, it has been held that, if the victim is known to be particularly vulnerable, then the menaces do not need to be objectively as bad as in other cases: *R. v Garwood* [1987] 1 All E.R. 1032.

and courage might be influenced or made apprehensive so as to accede unwillingly to the demand would be sufficient" for a jury to be asked to consider whether or not there had been menaces.[61] The concept of menaces is not limited to acts of physical violence,[62] but it must amount to menacing pressure of some sort.[63] It is also enough to use another person to offer the menaces on the loan shark's behalf.[64] The concept of "gain" in the statute includes "getting what one has not", but that would clearly involve extorting money from a borrower. With a somewhat metaphysical lilt, Lord Lane C.J. held (as quoted in *Archbold*) that "in the calendar of offences, blackmail was one of the ugliest and most vicious because it involved what one found so often, attempted murder of the soul".[65]

4. PROBLEMS OF CONTRACT LAW AND HIGH STREET BANKING

A. A simple question

31–40 This section examines a simple question: why do banks think that they are entitled to change the terms of their contracts unilaterally? And what rights should the customer have, not only to repudiate the contract, but also to insist on a return to the status quo ante (i.e. the terms of the parties' original contract)?

B. Why are banks able unilaterally to alter the terms of their contracts?

31–41 One particular issue has always puzzled me: why do banks think that they can unilaterally alter the terms of their contracts with their customers? The situation is well-known to all bank customers: periodically, a letter arrives through the post which contains a superficial brochure outlining the "new" terms of your account, loan or other financial "service". On some occasions, the bank will identify a clause in the original contract which empowered it to change the terms of its agreement, but this nevertheless raises the question whether or not the customer is obliged to accept whatever terms the bank chooses to impose: ranging perhaps from a power to cancel the contract by notice, to alter the amount of interest payable on an overdraft, and so forth. There are three principal problems here: first, banks' complete ignorance of the idea that a contract is an agreement between two people in which both people must have agreed to its terms; second, banks' refusals to supply their customers with the complete terms of their agreement; and third the banks' assumption that they know better than you do how your money should be treated.

---

[61] His lordship was considering what would be a sufficient concatenation of circumstances for a jury to be asked whether or not there was a case to consider.

[62] *Thorne v Motor Trade Association* [1937] A.C. 797, HL.

[63] *R. v Jheeta* [2007] EWCA Crim 1699.

[64] *R. v Lambert* [2009] EWCA Crim 2860.

[65] *R. v Hadjou* 11 Cr. App. R. 29, as summarised (without direct quotation marks) in *Archbold – Criminal Pleading, Evidence and Practice* (Sweet & Maxwell, 2005), para.21–259, p.1989.

First, banks' determination to reserve to themselves a power to change the terms of their contracts unilaterally. By way of example, the NatWest "Personal and Private Banking—Terms and Conditions" document (a pre-printed leaflet sent to all accountholders of that type) provides expressly that the contractual documentation which is provided to its customers does not constitute the entire agreement between the parties. This means that there are terms which purportedly form a part of that contract which are never seen by the customer because they are not included on the leaflet. If so, how can those terms possibly be binding on the customer under ordinary contract law theory?

31–42

Second, some banks' and financial institutions' refusal to supply customers with the complete terms of their contract. More egregious than the NatWest refusal to supply all of the terms of their contracts, I was once told by Direct Line (also owned by the same organisation as NatWest) that they "could not" (by which they meant "would not") supply me with a copy of the terms of the contract between us on the basis that "the terms are constantly changing so by the time we send you the terms of the contract then they will have changed". This is a statement which completely undermines the entire basis of contract law in England and Wales, and demonstrates a complete misunderstanding of the nature of a contract. A contract requires a meeting of minds as to *all* the terms of that agreement. It also completely ignores the regulatory obligation, considered below, that a financial institution must provide a copy of the terms of a contract to its customers.

31–43

Third, banks' assumption that their latest policy constitutes better knowledge as to how your money should be organised than your personal preference or the terms of your contract. So, on another occasion from those mentioned before, Lloyds Bank changed the nature of my bank accounts without telling me. They decide arbitrarily to move all the money from my current account into another account, with a "sweep up" facility that would keep my current account at a level of £1,000 by shifting money automatically between accounts. You can imagine my surprise on looking at my balance at a cashpoint, and the seemingly endless moments of panic as I wondered where all of my money had gone.[66] When I presented myself at my branch some moments later, the person who appeared from the recesses of the building after several minutes was very surprised that I was unhappy with this wheeze which they had supposedly invented for the convenience of their customers. No-one had thought to tell me that they were doing this. Banks' decisions to alter the way in which an account operates or how it is designated often results from (what the bank considers to be) rational decisions to change business practices; but that does not account for there having been a contract previously that the bank would operate the account in a particular manner, in reliance on which the customer deposited money with that bank. Breach of that contract by the bank should lead to the bank being liable to the customer in damages for any resulting loss. If one looks closely at most contractual documentation for any account (assuming that is produced) then the

31–44

---

[66] This sweep-up arrangement was particularly inconvenient for me at the time because it prevented me from making expenditure by way of cheque above the amount of the sweep-up facility without making myself overdrawn on that account, even though it had had more than sufficient money to cover those cheques in it beforehand.

precise contractual power which enables a bank to do this is generally missing. The account might be able to be cancelled, but not altered unilaterally into another type of arrangement altogether.

31–45 The simple point is that the power imbalance between high street banks and private customer means that the law of contract is ordinarily ignored by the banks on several occasions during their interaction with their customers. This must change.

C.   Three proposals to re-order the law on contract in relation to retail bank accounts

31–46 There follows three proposals to regularise the law in this area. First, banks must not be allowed to change the terms of contracts unilaterally. At present the logic would be that a bank reserves itself a right to change the terms of the account (even though the customer may not be presented with a term to that effect at the outset) and that the customer can always take their business elsewhere if they are unsatisfied. However, there is no reason why the customer should be obliged to suffer the annoyance of moving account (and the weeks before the funds are actually transferred, the direct debits and standing orders changed, and the new account up and running). The bank should be required by specific performance to carry out the banking contract which they formed with their customer at the outset. Where there is no express contractual term permitting banks to make this change, then the banks should not consider themselves to be at liberty to make that change simply because they consider the terms or the rate attaching to that service to be inconvenient for the future. Where there is an express contractual term permitting a change of the terms of the contract, then that must be interpreted in accordance with BCOBS and the ordinary principle that the bank must act with integrity and in its customer's best interests.

31–47 Second, any alteration of the terms of an account (even if made by some express contractual term) should be subject to a common law requirement of reasonableness and an equitable requirement of good conscience. Thus, when a bank exercises a right to change a rate, that rate of interest should not, for example, change from 1 per cent to 4 per cent within six months. The difference in those rates for a private customer can be the difference between solvency and insolvency. Before a bank can make such a change in rates, the customer must have it explained to them the maximum change in rates which is permitted under the contract before the contract is formed, with (importantly) the cash difference which is involved on an ordinary monthly repayment (and not simply the change represented in the form of an amount in percentage terms). For any contract in relation to which the bank considers itself entitled unilaterally to change any of the terms of the contract, there must be a cooling off period between the creation of the contract and its full effectiveness, together with the customer having been provided at the outset of the contract with information expressed in pounds sterling as to the maximum amount by which repayments can increase. Beyond that information, there is an implied maximum volatility in the amount payable on that account.

Third, the doctrine of specific performance should be used (and legislated for, if **31–48** necessary) far more aggressively than hitherto so that banks are held to the terms of their agreements with their customers. The doctrine of specific performance is appropriate (even though all that is at issue, at one level, is an amount of money ordinarily compensable by a payment in damages) because the provision of financial services involves more than simply money: it involves the provision of a service, of facilities and of a predictable means of being able to operate one's affairs which the bank has represented that it will provide under the terms of its contract with its customers. In this sense, banking is merely the provision of a basic service for most people which is nevertheless as essential to the operation of their lives as the provision of water to the home or electricity to the workplace.

5. THE CHIMERA OF IDENTITY THEFT

This section is, in effect, a parlour game for banking lawyers. What is suggested **31–49** here is that, if banking law is applied logically, then there is no such thing as "identity theft" at all. However, the concept of identity theft, which appears to place the status of victimhood on the customer whose account is penetrated, is a useful fiction for bankers both to reduce their costs and to prevent widespread fraud if the law were understood to operate not as a theft offence. So, the question is: on what basis, if any, can the concept of identity theft be supported?

In the internet age, everyone is encouraged to be concerned about "identity theft". **31–50** In essence, this is the fear that a person or persons unknown will gain access to our online accounts by pretending to be us and thereby "steal our money" or acquire service in our names or something of that sort. The "theft" of our identity is achieved by the simply process of learning our "username" and our "password". All of this commonly proceeds on the basis of a complete misunderstanding of how electronic money and other services operate. In particular, let us begin with the concept "identity theft" itself. For ease of reference, let us take as a definition of "identity theft" the following: a computer hacker (that is, a person who gains unlawful and unlicensed access to the computer records of the accountholder by penetrating the accountholder's computer or the bank's computer systems from a remote computer over the internet) misuses the accountholder's username and password so as to gain illegal access to the services attached to that account. It is possible, of course, that identity theft may occur without any computer hacking—the criminal may read the username and password over the accountholder's shoulder as they type, or they may find this information stored on a Post-it note stuck to that person's desk in an open-plan office, or they may find the accountholder's notebook with the information recorded inside. However, for the present, let us assume a faceless computer hacker gaining access to the victim's account (through spam emails, or computer viruses, or fake web-pages asking for information to be recorded in them, or otherwise) remotely from a distant computer over the internet.

While this may appear at first blush to be a little overly-pedantic, it is **31–51** nevertheless important. It is not the "identity" which is stolen. While there will be more than a knot of annoyance or worry on learning that someone else has gained access to our account, it nevertheless not our "identity" which is "stolen". We continue as the same people we were beforehand. We continue to cling to all of the badges of our identity which we have always held: outward appearance, sense of humour, personal history, a set of internal hopes and fears unknown to all but our closest confidants. All that has been used is our username and password. And those have not been "stolen" in the legal sense of have been appropriated as part of an intention permanently to deprive us of them (as defined in the Theft Act 1968). Instead, they have been misused by someone who is not entitled to use them. That person is committing an offence under s.2 of the Fraud Act 2006 by making a misrepresentation (in that they purport to be the accountholder and they use the username and password to acquire services or other value (including a transfer of "money" value between accounts perhaps)) so as to make a gain for themselves. They are not necessarily committing an offence of theft, however, as is considered next.[67]

31–52   The offence of theft requires that the defendant appropriates property with an intention permanently to deprive the victim of it. What is required is that there is an intention to make a permanent deprivation of property, whereas many so-called "identity thefts" have no intention to make such a permanent deprivation of property belonging at law to the claimant. Rather, to explain the criminal offence, we must do so on a different basis. It is a difficult question whether or not the victim's property is actually stolen. There are three problems, considered in turn: first, what is the property that is stolen; second, what is it that is permanently deprived; and, third, is the "money" actually the victim's money at all? This last point is key to our understanding of electronic money.

31–53   It is settled law that when money is deposited in a bank account, that money becomes the property of the bank.[68] To keep matters simple at first, let us assume a deposit of notes and coins, as opposed to an electronic payment. Immediately on depositing money there is an automatic transfer of ownership in that money at common law from the accountholder to the bank. In return, further to the contract between banker and customer, a debt is created between banker and customer equal to the amount of the deposit. The terms on which the customer may demand a payment of money from the bank or some other service from the bank (including the honouring of a cheque or the payment of an amount of money through the bank's payment systems to another person at the order of the accountholder) are then governed by the contract between the customer and the bank. Importantly, however, when the customer seeks to make a withdrawal "from" her account, she does not receive a repayment of her original notes or coins, but rather she receives an amount of notes and coins equal in value to the amount of her original deposit. This point was very important in the House of

---

[67] It would be a useful fiction to consider the username and password as being property because then its misuse could be considered to give rise to a theft. However, it is suggested, that it is more satisfying to think of this as being a fraud offence because there is clearly a fraudulent misuse of the value held in the bank account within the terms of the Fraud Act 2006, in a way which does not require the identification of an item of property the use of which is permanently appropriated from the accountholder.

[68] *Foley v Hill* (1848) 2 H.L. Cas., 28 Q.B., 9 E.R. 1002; see para.29–10.

Lords' decision in *Foley v Hill*[69] where the customer had sought to argue that the bank was the trustee of an amount deposited with it, such that the customer retained an equitable interest in those moneys. However, the House of Lords was adamant that on the deposit of money into a bank account there was no trust automatically declared over that money.[70] Instead, the bank acquires absolute title in that money and recognises that it owes a debt for an equal amount of money on demand to its customer. The customer is thus a creditor of the bank in the amount of the value of the money deposited in the aggregate with the bank. This is central to the idea of identity theft: if the customer does not retain property rights in the money which is deposited with the bank, then it becomes more difficult to identify how there can be any property of the accountholder which is stolen.

The property which the accountholder holds when a bank account is created is the chose in action constituted by its contract with the bank and the acknowledgement that automatically in return for its deposit of money with the bank that that chose in action constitutes a debt with a value equal to the amount of the deposit (and in the aggregate with any other deposits). There is no "money" owned by the accountholder as a result of her deposit in the sense of notes and coins continuing to be held for her by the bank. Instead, title in her notes and coins is relinquished and in its place she acquires a debt owed to her by the bank for the same amount. This distinction is crucial.	**31–54**

So, what happens when identity theft takes place? In short, a fraud is undoubtedly committed. If any property is appropriated, however, then it is the bank's property and not the accountholder's property. This is a very inconvenient analysis for the banks because the banks would prefer to persist with the idea that it is the customer who loses out when a computer hacker extracts "money" from a bank account. However, this is not the case. When the deposit is made, the customer relinquishes title in the deposit in favour of the bank. The bank therefore becomes the absolute owner of the money. This means that the bank conveniently increases its capital by the amount of that deposit and is therefore able to increase its own investment activities (whether in the form of lending money to other customers at interest, or using that capital to invest in securities markets and so forth on its own account). When the computer hacker gains access to the bank's assets—via the portal that is opened by means of the customer's account facility then it is the property of the bank which is diminished in value by the amount of the hacker's appropriation.	**31–55**

In *R v Preddy*[71] a perfectly logical but deeply inconvenient argument was run. In that case it was argued, entirely correctly at one level, that when a "theft" takes place in relation to a bank account, then there is no appropriation of property in the form of "money". The property involved in relation to bank accounts is not money, as discussed above, because any money passes absolutely to the bank and is replaced by a debt in the form of the bank account. Therefore, the property	**31–56**

---

[69] (1848) 2 H.L. Cas., 28 Q.B., 9 E.R. 1002.
[70] Although the parties could, extraordinarily, choose to create such a trust if they wanted. The point being that in the ordinary course of events that does not happen. Importantly, the bank would have to agree to act as trustee so as to change the ordinary legal analysis.
[71] [1996] A.C. 815.

involved is the chose in action constituted by the bank account. Consequently, when a computer hacker accesses a bank account and withdraws value from it and transfers that value to another account, both bank accounts continue to exist. All that has happened is that the value which is attached to one bank account has fallen, and the value which attaches to the other bank account has concomitantly increased. No money properly so-called passes between the accounts; rather the value of each account is altered. What is stolen is "value" not "money". Nevertheless, both items of property continue in existence. The property in question here is in fact the chose in action representing the account. Moreover, it is the value of the bank account which has been appropriated and not the bank account itself. Consequently, it becomes important to think of the value as being property in some way so as to preserve the integrity of the theft offence in this context. Of course, it is convenient to think of this as being a theft of "money" because clearly the defendant has acquired value to which she was not lawfully entitled by accessing another person's property (the chose in action represented by the bank account). However, the Fraud Act 2006 offers us more convenient and less fictional mechanisms for explaining the criminality of this conduct. What is important in the last analysis is that the criminal law can punish this activity.

31–57 The idea of "identity theft" in its current form—that a customer's property is stolen—is useful only for the banks who must otherwise bear the burden of the loss. Given that the banks can more usefully bear that burden, and that the only property which is taken belongs in property law to the banks, it is suggested that it is the banks which ought to bear that burden. Reasonably enough, perhaps, banks would claim that they ought not to be liable for the carelessness or misdeeds of customers who allow (or even facilitate) other people using their bank account facility to abstract value to themselves while allowing the accountholder to claim that the value of their bank account should remain the same throughout. Where an accountholder conspired with a hacker to access their account and transfer value from it to another account by pretending to be the accountholder, it would be unacceptable to allow that accountholder to retain the value of their account. However, the law of property would simply provide that any part of the value of the account (that is, the value represented by the debt between the parties) equal to the amount which was appropriated by the hacker would be held on constructive trust by the accountholder for the bank—in essence, that part of the debt would therefore be treated as being cancelled by means of an equitable set-off of the amount of value identified as being subject to the account and the amount deemed to be held on constructive trust.

PART IX

LENDING

Part IX considers a range of transactions concerned with lending money, whether under an ordinary contract of loan or by means of the issue of a security in relation to that loan. Lending in this context relates to ordinary bank lending as well as to syndicated lending from a number of lenders. Bonds are a means of acquiring loan funding by issuing transferable securities to a large number of lenders (who are also acting as investors in that they can sell their bonds on the open market). All of these forms of lending are organised around similar forms of loan agreements and loan covenants which permit termination of the loan agreement by means usually of "acceleration" of the borrower's repayment obligations. The covenants which trigger such acceleration clauses include events of default such insolvency, breach of contractual conditions and representations, covenants as to the financial condition of the borrower, cross default, material adverse change, negative pledge, and pari passu clauses. These types of provision build on the discussion of such general loan covenants in Chapter 19. The chapter on foreign exchange transactions considers the particular context of lending money in different currencies from sterling. The master agreement typically used in relation to foreign exchange business is structured on the basis set out in Chapter 19. The specific financial techniques discussed in this Part IX therefore build on the foundational legal concepts considered in Pts I through VII of this book.

CHAPTER 32

ORDINARY LENDING

CORE PRINCIPLES

An ordinary "term" loan involves an outright transfer of money from a lender to a borrower, subject to a contractual obligation on that borrower to pay periodical amounts of interest to the lender during the life of the loan and to repay the capital amount of the loan at the end of the loan period. The lender has no rights to any property unless it takes some security, as discussed in Chapter 22; therefore, if the borrower breaches its obligations, the lender only has personal rights in contract or in tort against the borrower, aside from any rights provided by a security agreement.

When a loan contract is terminated that is generally done by means of the "acceleration" of the borrower's repayment obligations: that is, by requiring the borrower to make repayment of all amounts owing under the loan immediately, instead of permitting the borrower to wait for the effluxion of the loan period. This acceleration provision is triggered by the occurrence of an "event of default" in the loan contract. The bulk of a loan contract is typically concerned with the drafting of these terms (or, "covenants"). Many of the loan covenants considered in this chapter have already been considered in Chapter 19 in the context of the general law of contract, and therefore reference should be had to that discussion first.

Loan covenants divide, broadly speaking for the purposes of this discussion, into five categories. First, covenants as to the condition of the borrower, which include covenants as to the borrower's capacity to act, its financial condition on the basis of accounting information, and its credit worth. The condition of the borrower will be of importance at the outset of the loan and will also constitute a set of continuing obligations during the life of the loan. Secondly, covenants as to the borrower's performance during the life of the loan, including the absence of any failure under other indebtedness ("cross default") and so forth. Thirdly, covenants as to the continued feasibility of the loan, including the loan not being declared ineffective, illegal or subject to an unexpected tax treatment. Fourthly, circumstances in which the loan will be accelerated and provisions governing the manner in which acceleration will be effective. At common law, lenders are entitled to demand repayment of the loan at any time, unless there is some express provision to the contrary. These cases are considered in detail in this chapter. Fifthly, negative pledge and pari passu provisions which provide, respectively, that no assets to be used in discharge of the loan are made available to third parties and that no lender is put in a better position than any other lender.

1. INTRODUCTION

32–01   This chapter considers the basic features of an ordinary loan transaction, albeit with a focus on corporate lending with its complex documentation, before the next chapter considers the more complex features of "syndicated lending". There are three types of loan considered in this chapter: first, an ordinary loan made by a bank to its customer; secondly, a loan in the form of an overdraft; and thirdly, a loan made subject to some security. In the second half of this chapter we shall consider some of the common terms (or, "covenants") in a loan contract. In particular there is a detailed analysis of the acceleration of obligations, which is the mechanism by which loan contracts are typically terminated. We begin with a working definition of a basic loan. The aim here is to break down the underpinnings of an ordinary loan to their absolute basics so as to understand the legal issues which they raise.

2. THREE BASIC TYPES OF LOAN

A. The mechanics of an ordinary loan

32–02   This section will seek to define a loan in its most pared down form, and then to identify the legal effect of those various elements. The core definition of a loan as it appears to a lawyer runs as follows. A loan is a contractual agreement between borrower and lender whereby the lender agrees to transfer an amount of money ("the loan capital") to the borrower outright subject to a contractual obligation on the part of the borrower to repay the loan capital at the termination of the loan agreement and a further contractual obligation on the borrower to pay periodic amounts to the lender calculated by reference to the capital amount ("interest") on identified dates during the life of the loan.

From a banker's standpoint a loan is an exchange of cash flows: at the outset **32–03** there is a transfer of a capital amount to the borrower, and in return the borrower pays a rate of interest calculated on the capital amount of the loan on regular payment dates, and finally a capital amount equal to the loan is repaid at the end of the transaction. The bank earns its profit from setting the amount of interest payable on the loan at an appropriate rate both to attract customers and to earn the profits (or, the rate of return) which it requires on its loan business. Loans can be made to large successful businesses, or to small high-risk businesses; loans can be made to individuals with high credit ratings or to individuals with low credit ratings; loans are also made to trusts, unincorporated associations, and so on and so on throughout society: a lender will identify its target market from within these various sorts of borrowers and fix the rate of interest that is charged accordingly, within the limits set by the appropriate consumer credit legislation. These calculations are made in accordance with the lender's own predictions for future interest rates and the likely effect of future economic movements on the customer in question. In the following sections, we shall consider how a lawyer understands these various elements of the loan contract primarily as a series of obligations to pay money.

B. The legal elements of an ordinary loan

An ordinary loan as a bundle of contractual obligations

A loan at its most basic level is a contractual agreement between borrower and **32–04** lender. In a basic loan contract it is the lender which assumes all of the risk of the borrower failing to make payments of interest or failing to make the repayment of the loan capital at the end of the transaction. Consequently, lenders are involved either in the business solely of identifying the credit worth of the borrower in question—possibly requiring references, or insisting on being that person's sole banker for current account and other purposes—or alternatively taking security of some sort for the loan, as considered below.[1] It is contract law which decides all of the questions as to the parties' various obligations, in the absence of any property right created by way of security.

The nature of the payment obligations in an ordinary loan

In the absence of any such proprietary security (as considered in the previous **32–05** section), the legal analysis of the flows of property between lender and borrower under a loan contract are as follows. The lender transfers the loan capital outright to the borrower. That money, therefore, becomes absolutely the property of the borrower. The only control on the manner in which the borrower is entitled to use that money is any specific contractual provision identifying the purposes for which the money may be used. A breach of such a specific purpose in the loan contract may lead either to a breach of contract remediable by payment of

---

[1] See para.31–11.

damages, or to the termination of the loan contract if the contract so provides, or to the creation of an equitable interest in the loan moneys by way of a *Quistclose* trust as discussed below.[2]

32–06 Assuming there is no breach of any such provision or that there is no such provision in the loan contract, then the borrower has two species of contractual obligation: first, a contractual obligation to repay the loan capital at the termination of the loan agreement, and, secondly, a contractual obligation to pay interest. The repayment of the capital is vital to the lender so that it can keep using that money in the future; the payment of interest is of high importance to the lender because that is the source of its profits. The obligation to "repay" the loan capital is a personal obligation to pay an amount equal to the amount which was loaned originally to the lender. The borrower is not required to pay back the very money which was lent originally. If the borrower was required to transfer bank the exact same money which had been originally lent then that would tend to lead to the interpretation that the borrower was intended to hold that original loan on trust for the lender: this would not be the purpose of an ordinary loan because the borrower would not be able to use the money for her own purposes if she was required to hold it on trust. There are transactions in which property other than money is "lent" between the parties for a variety of purposes which may exceptionally involve the retention of property rights, but that would be very rare indeed: see, in Hudson, *The Law and Regulation of Finance*, the discussion of stock lending and repos in Chapter 50, and of collateralisation in Chapter 42. This is different from the *Quistclose* arrangement considered below. Under an ordinary loan the loan moneys are transferred outright to the borrower such that the lender takes the risk that the borrower will pay it neither the interest which is payable under the contract nor the amount of the loan capital. The lender's rights are therefore purely contractual in nature, unless the lender has taken some proprietary security as part of the arrangement.

The termination of a loan contract and species of loan covenants

32–07 The termination of a loan may take effect in one of two ways. An ordinary loan will often be made for a contractually specified term (and thus is usually referred to as a "term loan"). The termination of a term loan which is properly performed by the borrower will be the expiry date identified as the end of the term. Alternatively, the terms of the loan contract which impose other obligations on the parties other than purely the payment of money (known as "loan covenants") will identify the types of activity which will constitute events of default. Consequently, if the borrower commits an event of default under the terms of the loan contract then the contract will either be considered to be terminated immediately, if the contract specifies that that is the case, or else the contract will provide for some other mechanism for unwinding the loan. In secured loan contracts[3] the termination of the loan will be linked in the contract to the realisation of the security which was provided by the borrower at the

---

[2] See para.31–16.

[3] A "secured" loan contract is a contract which is improved by the use of one of the techniques for taking security which were considered in Ch.23.

outset—whether in the form of collateral or property rights in identified assets or a guarantee, or whatever: the techniques of taking security were considered in Chapter 22. So, if the borrower breaches a condition of the loan agreement then the lender's rights under the security agreement will be activated immediately. If the loan is not secured then the lender will have recourse only to the general law for recovery of damages for breach of contract, or for money had and received at common law; or in tort for fraud or negligence, if appropriate. All of these general law remedies were discussed in detail in Chapter 20.

Clearly the drafting of the loan covenants will be very important in the practicalities of lending arrangements. Loan covenants are considered below.[4] In this context the lawyer is again acting as a risk manager in that she is taking the commercial risks identified by the lender and then rendering them into legal language and into legal structures which will ensure that the lender is repaid what she is owed either by the borrower's proper performance of her obligations or else by means of those legal structures. The principal loan covenants in commercial lending to large businesses in amounts of many millions of dollars are discussed in the next chapter in relation to syndicated lending. More generally loan covenants divide between covenants as to the condition of the borrower (its capacity, its continued solvency, its credit rating, and so forth); covenants as to the borrower's performance of its loan contracts generally (payments being made on time under this loan contract, no cross default on any other loans, no acceleration of payments under this loan or any other loan, and so on); covenants as to the continued feasibility of the loan (absence of any illegality, absence of any adverse tax treatment of the loan payments, and so on); and covenants governing the purposes for which the loan moneys may be used. All of these general covenants were outlined in Chapter 19 *Master agreements and common contractual terms and conditions*[5] and are considered in Chapter 33 in the particular context of syndicated lending. **32–08**

C.   Loans in the form of an overdraft

Overdrafts were considered in Chapter 29 in relation to core banking activities.[6] An overdraft is a loan, however, and therefore raises all of the issues which were identified with the ordinary loan set out above. **32–09**

The key distinctions, clearly, are that a single sum of money is not transferred at the outset of the transaction, instead the borrower may use as much of the facility as she requires; and often there is no simple term by the end of which the loan capital must be repaid, instead the value held in the account may rise and fall so that the loan is occasionally paid off by the account going into credit and then taken up again when the account goes into debit. Alternatively, overdraft facilities may be made subject to a maximum time period, especially if the bank is **32 10**

---

[4] See para.32–17.
[5] See para.19–56 et seq.
[6] See para.29–51.

concerned about the borrower's credit worth. Interest is raised in the form of ordinary interest and commonly in the form of bank charges which are charged for the use of the overdraft facility.

D. Secured loans

Taking security in loan contracts

32–11   The general legal principles relating to taking security were considered in Chapter 22. In essence, the expression "taking security" refers to any legal structure used by a bank, in the context of loan transactions, to protect itself against the failure of a borrower to make a payment to it or any other failure identified in a loan contract. Taking security may therefore divide between structures like guarantees which ensure that payment will be made by some other person to satisfy the borrower's obligations, or taking security may entitle the bank to seize property of a value which is sufficient to discharge the borrower's obligations in whole or in part. We shall consider guarantees first; and then in the two sections to follow we shall consider two forms of proprietary security which are used primarily in relation to loans: mortgages and *Quistclose* trusts.

Guarantees and sureties

32–12   The legal principles relating to guarantees were considered in Chapter 22.[7] The practicalities of obtaining guarantees in individual cases far exceed in their complexity the simplicity of the idea of guarantee. A guarantee in a loan contract operates in effect such that if the borrower fails to make payment under a loan contract then some other person (the guarantor) undertakes to make that payment on her behalf. Clearly, the primary commercial question in relation to guarantees is finding someone who will agree to pay another person's obligations. The detail of the distinction between a guarantee (with its attendant formal requirements) and a warranty was considered in Chapter 22.[8]

32–13   So, if a bank is dealing with a subsidiary company in a group of companies, then it will be usual practice to seek a guarantee from the principal trading company within that group because that is the entity which will usually have most of the group's cash flow, whereas loans are often taken out in large groups by a subsidiary company formed for the purposes of acquiring financing. Such a subsidiary has no assets except those provided by the main trading companies within a group. It should be remembered that, as a question of company law, if a contract is made with X Ltd then that contract is not binding on Y Ltd, even if Y Ltd is a member of the same group of companies with its shares being held entirely by the same holding company which owns all of the shares in X Ltd, unless Y Ltd itself is expressly made a party to that contract.[9] The doctrine of the separate personality of companies means that no one company is responsible for

---

[7] See para.22–77.
[8] See para.22–77.
[9] See para.4–32.

the obligations of another company, even if they are in common ownership, unless there has been some fraud or there is some other reason to lift the corporate veil.[10] A guarantee will similarly often not be accepted from a holding company because holding companies often have no assets of their own other than shares in their subsidiaries: they are usually merely a shell to facilitate the structure of the group of companies. Instead, it may be subsidiary companies within the group which actually own the valuable assets and which conduct business. A guarantee would only be taken from a holding company if that holding company has valuable assets of its own. Within groups of companies it is perfectly possible for the directors and other human beings who run the group of companies de facto to move assets around within a group so that one contracting company in time has no assets left against which the bank can bring an action. So, if one company within a group owned the valuable assets to which the lender ultimately wanted to have recourse, then the lender would need to ensure that those assets were not shuffled sideways into another company in that group which was not bound by the guarantee. Therefore, it is an important part of a guarantee agreement that such restructurings or movements of assets do not take place without the contractual obligations expressed by the guarantee moving, in effect, with those assets.

In non-commercial transactions, guarantees may be taken from one individual to guarantee the performance of another individual—so, a parent may provide a guarantee for the performance of an adult child who is, for example, a student. Surety relationships are also used in relation to loans. For example, in the well-known case of *Barclays Bank v O'Brien*[11] Mr O'Brien acquired an overdraft from the bank for the purposes of his business. The bank required security for the overdraft and so Mr O'Brien agreed that the overdraft should be secured over his matrimonial home. The bank required his wife, Mrs O'Brien, to agree to act as "surety" in relation to Mr O'Brien's repayment commitments, which meant that Mrs O'Brien agreed to surrender her interests in the matrimonial home to the bank so that the bank could enforce its security against the matrimonial home if Mr O'Brien should fail in his obligations. Thus the "guarantee" in this context was not a promise to pay money but rather was an undertaking not to prevent the bank from realising its security against property in which the surety may have had an interest. In the event, in that case, it was found that Mr O'Brien had made a misrepresentation to his wife, in circumstances in which the parties' relationship created a presumption of undue influence such that the bank was to be treated as having constructive notice of this fact, and therefore that the security interest was to be set aside.[12]   **32–14**

Mortgages

The regulation and law of mortgages were discussed in Chapter 22 to the extent that mortgages are used to provide security for lending. Mortgages are, of course,   **32–15**

---

[10] See para.4–33, and see generally A.S. Hudson, *Understanding Company Law* (Routledge, 2012), Ch.2.
[11] [1994] 1 A.C. 180.
[12] See para.24–39.

used most commonly in the United Kingdom to provide lending for ordinary people to acquire their homes in the private property sector. The mortgage itself grants a property right in the property acquired with the loan to the bank as "mortgagee". In the event that there is a default under the terms of the mortgage agreement or under the terms of s.101 of the Law of Property Act 1925, then the bank is entitled to rely on one of the remedies of a mortgagee to recover its money—usually by way of taking possession of the property or by way of forcing a sale of the property. In practice the regulation of mortgage lenders limits the theoretically huge largesse which the common law gives to the terms of mortgage contracts.

Quistclose trusts

32–16   *Quistclose* trusts are discussed in Chapter 22. In essence, when a loan contract specifies that the loan moneys are to be used only for a specified purpose, then the lender acquires an equitable proprietary interest in the loan moneys even after they have been transferred to the borrower. The precise nature of *Quistclose* trusts remain a matter for feverish debate among academics and judges alike. The first difference of view is whether a *Quistclose* trust means that the lender *retains* an equitable proprietary interest throughout the life of the loan,[13] or whether that equitable interest comes into existence only as a secondary matter once the loan moneys have been misused,[14] or whether the borrower is to be treated as holding the loan moneys on express trust through the transaction for the lender but with a power to use the moneys for the specified purpose.[15] What is significant about a *Quistclose* trust (regardless of the conceptual analysis which is placed on it) is that if the borrower goes into insolvency, then because there is a trust over the loan moneys those loan moneys are held on trust for the lender and therefore are not distributed among the borrower's creditors. Taken from the perspective of a banker, a *Quistclose* trust is one method of retaining some proprietary rights in the loan moneys once they have been paid to the borrower; and therefore this is different from the ordinary loan structure considered at the outset of this chapter. A *Quistclose* trust also grants the lender an ability to trace after the loan moneys into mixed accounts in the event that the loan moneys are transferred away by the borrower in breach of the term in the loan contract, because such tracing may only take place if the lender had an equitable proprietary interest in the loan moneys before they were misapplied by the borrower.[16]

---

[13] *Twinsectra v Yardley* [2002] 2 A.C. 164.
[14] A.S. Hudson, *Equity & Trusts*, s.22.4.2.
[15] See, e.g. *Re Australian Elizabethan Theatre Trust* (1991) 102 A.L.R. 681.
[16] See para.23–13; *Westdeutsche Landesbank v Islington* [1996] A.C. 669.

3. TYPES OF LOAN COVENANTS IN ORDINARY LENDING TRANSACTIONS

A. Introduction

This section considers those types of loan covenant which are commonly found in ordinary loans: the specific context of syndicated loans is considered in the next chapter. Importantly, many of these provisions have been considered in outline terms already in Chapter 19 of this book.[17] It would be useful to begin by attempting to categorise the types of covenants which are used in loan contracts. Loan covenants divide between covenants as to the condition of the borrower (its capacity, its continued solvency, its credit rating, and so forth); covenants as to the borrower's performance of its loan contracts generally (payments being made on time under this loan contract, no cross default on any other loans, no acceleration of payments under this loan or any other loan, and so on); covenants as to the continued feasibility of the loan (absence of any illegality, absence of any adverse tax treatment of the loan payments, and so on); and covenants governing the purposes for which the loan moneys may be used.

32–17

B. Covenants as to the condition of the borrower

The purpose of such covenants

In corporate contexts, the borrower will need to make covenants as to its own condition to satisfy the lender's credit risk concerns; whereas in retail contexts the institution is more likely to reach its own conclusions as to the borrower's credit worth by reference to credit reference agencies and on the basis of information provided by the borrower. The intention would be, in general terms, that if one of the covenants as to the condition of the borrower was breached then the loan would become immediately repayable, any guarantee or other credit support would be capable of being called in and the contract would be terminated. The lender will therefore wish to specify that these provisions are conditions of the contract—so that the contract can be terminated if any of the conditions are breached—and not merely warranties—which would entitle the claimant only to damages.[18] The borrower will be required to represent that all information provided is accurate and that the validity of the contract is predicated on the accuracy of that information.

32–18

Capacity and authority to act

It is important to know that the borrower has the capacity to enter into the transaction, and therefore that the contract is not beyond the powers of the borrower. The weakness in building a contract on the correctness of a representation by the borrower as to its capacity is that if the borrower does not

32–19

---

[17] See para.19–56.
[18] See para.19–28 et seq.

have the capacity to enter into the contract then it does not have the capacity to make that representation. Therefore, capacity is in truth a legal risk which the lender will need to investigate. A different issue is the authority of the signatory to bind the borrower to the contract, which rests on the principles of agency considered in Chapter 18.[19]

Solvency, insolvency and bankruptcy

32–20   The continued solvency of the borrower will evidently be a particularly significant aspect of loan contracts. As was discussed in Chapter 22, the insolvency of the borrower is one of the key credit concerns in the creation of financial transactions. Therefore, the solvency of the borrower will be a requirement of any contract of loan because a loan contract (without any credit support structure) entitles the lender only to a personal, contractual claim to be paid the amount of money which is specified in the contract by way of interest and repayment of capital: consequently, if the borrower were insolvent then the lender would not be able to recover its capital and earn the profits it had expected. A well-drafted loan contract, however, will not simply specify that there is a breach of covenant when the borrower is actually insolvent, but rather will use the structures considered in Chapter 17 to anticipate the possible future insolvency of the borrower: ranging from a credit downgrade, or simply a deterioration of credit worth by reference to identified credit rating criteria, through to the commencement of insolvency proceedings (by service of a petition or otherwise) of whatever type by either a creditor, or a shareholder or voluntarily by the borrower itself. Different types of entity go into different formal types of insolvency, administration or receivership once they become incapable of meeting their obligations as they become due; and human beings go into bankruptcy, as discussed in Chapter 22. These subtle differences in procedure need to be met appropriately in the documentation.

The financial condition of the borrower

32–21   The most significant aspect of a borrower's condition will be its financial condition: whether the employment status of an ordinary retail borrower or the accounting condition of a corporate borrower. In relation to publicly issued debt from public companies, like bonds discussed in Chapter 34, there will be a formal credit rating issued by one of the credit rating agencies.[20] This rating will also be relied on in relation to ordinary lending to such an entity. A large amount of information will be publicly available in relation to listed securities for large public companies. The situation is more complex in relation to loans with smaller companies with no publicly offered securities (as discussed in Chapter 35) because there will not be a regularly updated stream of such information, including interim financial reports and announcements of significant alterations to the entity's condition made through an RIS. With smaller entities, the lender will need to rely on audited accounts and other information which is requests

---

[19] See para.18–27.
[20] See para.34–13.

specifically from the borrower. Any inaccuracy in this information will constitute an event of default—whether that inaccuracy was inherent from the outset or arose latterly—and thus trigger the termination of the contract, or such other mechanism as the parties agree between them.

Information as to the financial condition of the borrower shall include its annual accounts (principally its profit and loss statement and its balance sheet), but these statements are manipulable[21] and therefore bankers tend to rely instead upon cash flow statements giving a picture of the entire accounting year and which therefore give a clearer picture of the movement of funds within the borrower's activities, as opposed to a snap-shot of the assets and liabilities of the entity at one particular date.

32–22

Calculating the credit risk of the borrower and establishing credit deterioration

Lending money is one of the key investments which banks make and therefore identifying the credit risk associated with a borrower is important. Therefore, a large part of financial theory relates to the calculation of credit risks. Credit decisions as to the condition of the borrower in large scale corporate transactions are typically made by reference to a series of financial and accounting measurement models.[22] It is usual for one or more of these mechanisms for calculating credit worth to be included in the loan covenants so as to establish the financial condition which is required for that entity to remain of a sufficient credit worth for the lender to wish to remain in business with it. Credit decisions are a combination of science (using mathematical and accounting models) and art (using more general appreciation of the borrower's market, business plan, and particular strengths). The lawyer's intention is that if the borrower's financial condition deteriorates so as to fall below the contractually specified minimum for the acceptable ratio, then that will constitute an event of default. Sometimes this sort of provision is referred to as a "credit downgrade clause" and the breach of the identified ratio would be specified in the contract as constituting a "material adverse change" in the borrower's financial condition. Measurements of the condition of the borrower divide between "income" measures; "capital" measures; and "income and capital measures". The income measures are concerned with the condition of the borrower's profit and loss account, and its cash flow position; whereas the capital measures are concerned with the "net worth" on the borrower's balance sheet, and thus the balance of its assets and

32–23

---

[21] See for example T. Smith, *Accounting for Growth*, 2nd edn (Century, 1996) which demonstrated the many techniques which can be used by accountants and financiers to massage annual accounts (lawfully) to enhance the appearance of the company. In particular, Smith focused on the need among public companies to make it appear as though they were generating constant earnings-per-share growth so as to comply with the objectives of the institutional investor community.

[22] There is a full discussion of the considerations which inform these financial measurements in the "Financial Analysis and Planning" chapter in Brealey, Myers and Allen, *Corporate Finance—International Edition*, 8th edn (McGraw-Hill, 2006), p.782 et seq.

liabilities when compared to the total about of debt which it has. Financial matters of this sort were considered in general terms in Chapter 19.[23]

32–24 The capital measurements typically relate to the net worth of the borrower and to its debt coverage. The net worth of a company is ordinarily the extent to which its assets exceed its liabilities.[24] Generally its equity share capital and any reserves are taken, having subtracted any material which would be of no effective value in the event of an insolvency (such as intangible assets like goodwill, deferred taxation, revaluations of assets and so on). This picture of the company is generally taken on an annual basis in the annual balance sheet and therefore is capable of some manipulation across the accounting year to ensure that the company's capital position is acceptable at the date of the balance sheet: just like brushing a scruffy child's hair before an annual photograph so that the child appears to be the model of decorum when the photograph is taken. The revaluation of the value of assets and so forth can adjust the net worth of a company at the margins.

32–25 Analysts will also look to the debt coverage ratio which is expressed as a ratio of the borrower's long and short term debt and any regular periodical payments it has to make such as leases, when compared to the borrower's debt and leases and its equity. In effect this ratio expresses the level of the borrower's debt liabilities when compared to its share capital. There are various forms of the debt coverage ratio. The general objective is to identify whether or not the borrower is solvent: i.e. does the borrower have sufficient cash and equity capital to meet the costs of its debt and the repayment of the loan capital? The most important aspect of any coverage ratio, however, is to identify the level of the borrower's liquid assets which can be used to meet any repayment obligations.

32–26 It is generally thought that a borrower with too much debt is a poor credit risk simply because it already has too much debt and therefore may not be able to generate enough income to meet its repayment obligations. A key part of borrowing money in corporate contexts is then to convince the lender that the borrower has a suitable strategy for using those loan moneys so as to generate enough extra profit from its business to meet the repayment obligations. It is common for companies in continental Europe to rely on bank debt more than is the case in the UK where there is generally a greater proportion of share capital. Similarly, some family companies are reluctant to issue new shares so as to dilute the shares owned by the family, and so a family company will tend to have more debt; whereas another type of company might be more relaxed by the idea of raising more capital from shareholders without the need to take on more debt with the contractually compelled cost of making interest payments, while shares only carry the shareholders' unenforceable hope that there will be sufficient profit to pay out a dividend. Therefore, any of these types of mathematical ratios must be understood in the broader context of the particular idiosyncrasies of the particular borrower. The "ratio" is usually expressed as a percentage, and therefore a loan contract would specify the level of debt to equity which would be acceptable under this ratio. This also prevents the borrower from bleeding money

---

[23] See para.19–64.
[24] As defined in *Barron's Dictionary of Financial Terms*.

out of the entity by paying out large dividends, buying back shares from its existing shareholders, or lowering its profits.

The income mechanisms include the "interest coverage" of the borrower which measures the amount of profit that borrower generates out of which it can sustain the cost of its debt (its interest payments and any capital repayments), which indicates the amount of free profit which the borrower has. This concept of "free profit" is typically relegated behind the entity's EBIT ("earnings before interest and tax") or its EBITDA ("earnings before interest, tax, depreciation and amortisation") which is recognised in a standard profit and loss account as the statement of that entity's profit before subtraction is made of the amounts needed to pay for bank interest, tax, depreciation and amortisation (these last two being measurements of the reduction in value of assets as they have become one year older). The question of depreciation is often treated by accountants as being flexible.[25] Given that the lender is considering lending new capital to the borrower under a new loan contract, it is suggested that the weakness of EBITDA is that it does not consider the amount of free cash that is left once *existing* interest and taxation costs have been met.

32–27

The measures of performance which are less easy to manipulate are those which focus on the company's cash flow across the accounting year, as opposed to taking a one-off, "snap shot" of the level of profit and loss or the assets on the balance sheet at the end of the accounting year. Securities regulation requires that information is provided by public companies at six-month intervals as opposed simply to being provided annually, and loan contracts could require cash flow statements even more frequently than that. A cash flow ratio would measure the cash inflows and outflows across the specified period. Thus, cash inflow from trading activities[26] could be expressed as a ratio to the cost of sales (including salaries, rent, and so forth) and the cost of funding (debt interest and so forth), over the specified time period. A loan contract could use such a cash flow ratio to measure the profitability and the liquidity of the borrower.

32–28

Prohibitions on restructurings of the borrower

Control of the financial condition of the borrower will also relate to changes in its capital structure: thus providing that mergers with other entities (particularly if the resultant entity is of a lower credit worth), or being taken over by another entity, or any other restructuring would constitute a breach of covenant. Similarly, large discretionary distributions (such as dividends) or other payments from capital would constitute a breach of covenant if the result of that distribution or payment caused a significant reduction in the capital base or alteration to the cash flow of the borrower. Whether or not a distribution would be "significant" or not would be something which would be identified by reference to contractually

32–29

---

[25] See T. Smith, *Accounting for Growth* (1996).
[26] By limiting this to trading activities, one can exclude the sort of material (such as depreciation cost) which can be manipulated by accountants in reaching the final profit and loss, because the profit can be inflated by including amounts which are not derived directly from trading activities.

specified leverage or coverage ratios, or whatever other credit calculation is specified by the parties, by reference to the size of the outstanding loan capital.

Provision of information

32–30   Clearly, a central part of the operation of these covenants would be the provision of sufficient information to the lender to know whether or not there has been a breach of contract. As was outlined above, in relation to entities with publicly issued debt, there will be a large amount of information in the public domain already—as considered in Part X in detail. The problem therefore relates to information not made public in that way or to the large number of borrowers who will not have any publicly issued debt. Therefore, reporting obligations are a key part of the covenants of a loan contract whereby the borrower is required to furnish the lender with specified types of accounting and other information on a timely and an accurate basis. Given that a breach of a financial covenant may well encourage the borrower to breach its reporting obligations, there is also the question of whether or not the contract should be deemed to be automatically terminated and any credit support agreement automatically triggered on the happening of a breach of covenant.

C.   Covenants as to the borrower's performance

32–31   There will be another cadre of covenants which relate to the borrower's performance of its obligations under the loan contract. The principal obligation will clearly be the obligation to make payments of interest on a timely basis and to make repayments of capital as required by the contract. Performance would also cover any credit support agreement which imposes payment obligations on the borrower, such as a collateral agreement.[27] In deciding whether or not a borrower is likely to be able to meet its future repayment obligations under a loan contract with one lender, Profit Bank, the borrower's failure to meet repayment obligations under loans with other lenders would signal a likelihood of future default in its loan with Profit Bank. Thus, the loan contract will specify that cross default under any other loans or cross acceleration of repayment obligations under another loan would constitute a default under the loan with Profit Bank. These standard form contractual terms were considered in Chapter 19.[28] The principles relating specifically to acceleration of loan obligations are considered below.[29]

D.   Covenants as to the continued feasibility of the loan

32–32   It is important to know that the loan contract itself will be capable of performance. The principal concerns of the parties to a loan contract, as to its commercial feasibility, relate to any supervening illegality of that contract under

---

[27] See para.42–01 et seq.
[28] See para.19–48.
[29] See para.31–35.

criminal law or regulatory principles such that the contract is declared to be void or unenforceable; or any change in its tax treatment, such as the introduction of a withholding tax on payments of interest requiring that tax is withheld before the interest is paid, or a change in the tax treatment of some facet of the loan, for example, under the UK "loan relationships" taxation scheme; or a declaration that the loan was not enforceable under contract law, as with the loans which Lord Goff recognised were being made to local authorities by banks hidden inside interest rate swaps in the *Westdeutsche Landesbank v Islington*[30] and other litigation.

E.   Acceleration of obligations

The role of acceleration of obligations in loan contracts

The acceleration of obligations in loan contracts means that the borrower is required to pay her obligations earlier than they would otherwise become due. If a borrower breaches one of the terms of a loan contract, then the loan is "accelerated" so that its obligations become repayable immediately and any credit support (a guarantee or something similar) may be called in by the lender. This is the principal means by which term loan contracts are terminated. Instead of waiting for the time at which the loan would otherwise be paid off, once an event of default has occurred the loan is repayable immediately and the lender is entitled to recourse to any of the contractual credit support mechanisms available to it under its loan contract.   **32–33**

Power of acceleration in loan contracts

This power of acceleration is clearly a very powerful one. Ordinarily the power of acceleration in a loan contract entitles the non-defaulting party to demand payment of everything owing to her immediately. This may cause enormous difficulties for the borrower, particularly if the borrower is already experiencing some difficulties which have prompted the acceleration in any event. It should be recalled that in the law on loans made by way of mortgage that the mortgagee is considered by the case law to have a right to repossession even before the ink is dry on the contract.[31] The mortgagee therefore has a great power to terminate the contract at will. It has taken the intervention of statute to introduce the concept that this power must not be exercised if the mortgagor is likely to be able to repay in a reasonable time.[32]   **32–34**

So, the question must arise generally in relation to covenants permitting acceleration as to whether they must be exercised reasonably or whether the rightholder has a power to act as she sees fit. The weight of the English authority is that a lender with a right to accelerate may accelerate the borrower's   **32–35**

---

[30] [1996] A.C. 669.
[31] *Four Maids Ltd v Dudley Marshall Ltd* [1957] Ch. 317; *Western Bank v Schindler* [1977] Ch. 1; *National Westminster Bank v Skelton* [1993] 1 All E.R. 242.
[32] See para.49–14.

obligations as she wishes and so may demand payment immediately, without giving the borrower any grace period nor time to find the money[33] (although a reasonable period to have its bank actually carry out the transfer should be allowed[34]), if the term in the contract permitted recovery on that basis. As Blackburn J. put it in *Brightly v Norton*[35]: "a debtor who is required to pay money on demand, or at a stated time, must have it ready, and is not entitled to further time in order to look for it". If a contract provides that repayment may be demanded immediately by the bank, then the bank is entitled to give such a demand even if the parties' negotiations prior to the grant of the loan had suggested that the loan facility would have been available for a longer period of time.[36] Thus, if a loan contract provides that the bank may require repayment on demand, then it is not open to the borrower to argue that that was contrary to the arrangement between the parties.[37] Consequently, assuming no provision to the contrary on the terms of the loan contract, a bank has been held to be entitled to send in receivers one hour after demanding repayment of £600,000 to it.[38] It was found in that case that ordinarily the lender should give time for payment to be made through its bankers—given that, with the best will in the world, no bank will make this payment immediately—but that if the borrower has acknowledged that it would not be able to pay in any event then it would not be necessary to allow such a period of time to elapse. The borrower would be well-advised to specify a grace period and to specify conditions limiting the circumstances in which the power can be exercised because, it is suggested, that if a loan agreement specified that the lender may not seek repayment immediately, then the lender would be bound by that express contractual provision.

32–36   The issue is whether or not the lender may insist on immediate repayment in all circumstances if there is no specific right to that effect in the contract. There have been cases where an absence to specify precisely that the banker could be paid on demand has meant that the banker was not entitled payment on demand. So, in the complex litigation in *Williams & Glyn's Bank Ltd v Barnes*[39] the parties had agreed that a loan facility would be available to the borrower until certain obligations had been paid when they fell due, but subject to the condition that this arrangement was subject to the "usual banking conditions". The bank took the phrase subject to the "usual banking conditions" to mean that it would be able nevertheless to demand immediate repayment; the borrower contended that the parties' arrangement was that the loan facility would be available for a longer period of time and not repayable until the discharge of the identified obligations. It was held that the bank was not entitled to rely on its opinion of what constituted "usual banking conditions" to introduce a right to repayment which

---

[33] *Bank of Baroda v Panessar* [1986] 3 All E.R. 751.

[34] *Shepherd & Cooper Ltd v TSB Bank Plc* [1996] 2 All E.R. 654.

[35] (1862) 122 E.R. 116, 118.

[36] *Lloyds Bank v Lampert* [1999] 1 All E.R. (Comm) 161, CA; *Bank of Ireland v AMCD (Property Holdings) Ltd* [2001] 2 All E.R. (Comm) 894.

[37] *Bank of Ireland v AMCD (Property Holdings) Ltd* [2001] 2 All E.R. (Comm) 894.

[38] *Shepherd & Cooper Ltd v TSB Bank Plc* [1996] 2 All E.R. 654.

[39] The case took 104 days in court. The full judgment (of about 700 pages) in *Williams & Glyn's Bank Ltd v Barnes* is unreported, but Ralph Gibson J. did deliver a shortened summary judgment which can be found at (1981) 10 *Legal Decisions Affecting Bankers* 220; (1981) Com. L.R. 205.

was not expressed on the face of the contract. It was argued on behalf of the customer in *Barnes* and accepted by Ralph Gibson J. that:

> "if a party enters into an arrangement which can only take effect by the continuance of a certain existing state of circumstances, there is an implied engagement on his part that he shall do nothing of his own motion to put an end to that state of circumstances under which alone the arrangement can be operative".[40]

That is, if the loan was made for a specified purpose, then the bank should not be entitled to terminate that loan arbitrarily so as to frustrate that purpose. As Ralph Gibson J. put it: "A reference to usual banking conditions cannot in my opinion override express terms of a contract or terms which are necessarily implied from those express terms". This approach was reinforced by the notion that the court will not freely alter the bargain struck between contracting parties.[41] Similarly, in *Cryne v Barclays Bank Plc*[42] the Court of Appeal refused to imply a term into a contract that the bank should be entitled to demand immediate repayment of a loan, by means of the appointment of a receiver so as to protect their security, when the loan contract did not state on its face that the bank had that right. In so doing, the Court of Appeal relied inter alia on the decision in *Barnes*.

On the one hand it could be argued in relation to term loan contracts that the general approach in the earlier cases seem unprincipled, in that if the parties have agreed to a loan which will be repayable at a given point in the future then the loan ought not to be repayable until that time. This is the approach taken in relation specifically to mortgage contracts over the home where statute has carved out a particular defence to possession of the mortgage property whenever the mortgagee should decide: the mortgagee is taken by some cases to have agreed to lend the money over a full term and therefore it should be forced to wait the full term for the return of its money.[43] Contrariwise, other authorities have taken the view that the mortgagee need not wait if its security is at threat. This is the alternative view on the ability of banks to be entitled to demand immediate repayment even on term loans. This alternative argument—which underpins English law currently—is that the credit risk which the banker was prepared to take at the outset was predicated on the notion that if the borrower's credit worth deteriorated before the end of the term then the bank must be allowed to protect its position by demanding immediate repayment of the loan, instead of being forced to sit on its hands until the end of that term when the borrower would possibly have gone into bankruptcy. The English approach is therefore protecting the literal contractual bargain struck between the parties and is also protecting the security which the banker demands so as to be able to conduct banking business and so oil the wheels of the general economy. The approach in cases like *Barnes* and *Cryne* does tally with one view of this traditional approach in that the banks

32–37

---

[40] Applying dicta of Chief Justice Cockburn in *Stirling v Maitland* (1864) cited with approval by the House of Lords in *Shirlaw v Southern Foundries* [1939] 2 K.B. 206.

[41] Relying on *Photo Productions v Securicor Ltd* [1980] A.C. 827; [1980] 1 All E.R. 556; [1980] 2 W.L.R. at 283, per Lord Diplock.

[42] [1987] B.C.L.C. 548.

[43] See para.49–25.

in those cases were being denied a right to automatic, immediate repayment because such a right was not expressly contained in their contract.

32–38   Where notice is required to be given as a pre-requisite for the implementation of the right of acceleration, then the courts will be astute in policing the manner in which notice was given and specifically whether it complied with the terms of the contract. However, provided that the demand is made in accordance with the terms of the contract and if it is sufficiently clear that it is a demand for payment (thus without the need for any specific form of wording) then that will be sufficient.[44]

Wrongful acceleration

32–39   If a bank wrongfully accelerates a debt obligation and thereby causes loss to the borrower, then the bank will be liable for damages to compensate the borrower's loss. Similarly, by analogy in that withdrawing a loan facility is equivalent to failing to lend, it is said that if a bank fails to lend to a customer then the customer may proceed against the bank.[45] In either event, the bank will be required to bear the burden of proving its loss. If the borrower could acquire funds elsewhere on similar terms, then the damages will be nominal. If funds could be acquired elsewhere but only on worse terms, then the damages would be the difference between the terms which the bank had offered and the best terms which could reasonably be acquired elsewhere.

32–40   These cases should be capable of clear distinction, it is suggested. There ought to be no obligation on a bank to lend to anyone on general principles of freedom of contract. A customer ought to be entitled only to demand that a loan is made either if the bank has already offered a loan in reliance on which the customer has acted to its detriment (perhaps by agreeing to undertake burdensome obligations on the basis that it had funding at the rate offered to it by the bank), or if the bank is already in a contractual nexus with a customer under which the customer has assumed obligations on the basis of its continued ability to draw down on that account. In either case it is suggested that the bank ought not to be obliged to carry out the loan if some event has happened in the meantime, such as the customer publicly acknowledging its inability to pay its debts as they become due, which would have constituted an event of default under that contract or a commercially compelling basis on which to deny a loan to a customer.

32–41   The question of liability for acceleration of obligations was considered in the *Elektrim* litigation. As is discussed in Chapter 34 in relation to bonds, a bondholder argued for acceleration of payment obligations in *Concord Trust v Law Debenture Trust Corporation Plc*.[46] (A bond is a form of borrowing, considered in Chapter 34, in which large numbers of lenders each lend a small amount and acquire a transferable security in return for their loan.) In that case the bond conditions provided that the trustee had a power give notice to the issuer of the bonds, Elecktrim, that payment was required immediately if 30 per cent of

---

[44] *Re a Company* [1985] B.C.L.C. 37; *Bank of Baroda v Panessar* [1986] 3 All E.R. 751.

[45] P. Wood, *The Law and Practice of International Finance*, 40.

[46] [2005] UKHL 27.

the bondholders had requested that action and if the trustee considered that the issuer's failure was "materially prejudicial to the interest of the bondholders". In essence, the lenders were giving notice of a demand for accelerated payment under the terms of the bond through the bond trustee where a condition had been breached. The same factual matrix was the subject matter of the litigation in *Law Debenture Trust Corporation v Elektrim Finance BV*.[47] The first event of default was said to be a breach of one of the conditions of the agreement, which provided that the bondholders were to have two nominees on the management board of Elektrim, when one of the bondholders' nominees was dismissed from that board. It was held at first instance in *Concord Trust* by Smith J. that this constituted material prejudice to the position of the bondholders, and therefore that the trustee was entitled to issue a notice that an event of default had occurred.[48] If a party which is empowered to declare the existence of an acceleration of obligations under a loan contract or a bond agreement does so incorrectly, then that person will be liable to the borrower for damages in contract.[49] There would be no question of an action in tort in these circumstances because the relationship between the parties is contractual.[50] No liability lay against the trustee in tort nor on the facts against the trustee in contract. It is a remarkable thing that the obligations of the trustee were considered to arise entirely at common law in this case, when the liabilities of a trustee lie of course in the law of trusts for breach of trust[51]—a phenomenon referred to by trusts lawyers as a "fusion fallacy". Hart J. in *Law Debenture Trust v Elektrim* concurred with the analysis of Smith J. and therefore held that the acceleration of obligations in event of default could be enforced by the bondholders. There were other events of default at issue in that second strand of this litigation relating to an expropriation of property by the Polish tax authorities and a failure to make payments of coupon in a timely manner, both of which were upheld on the facts. A further event of default would have been triggered if a petition for bankruptcy had been lodged, in that case, under Polish law: on the facts it was found that such a filing had taken place and therefore that the trustee was entitled to rely upon it.[52]

F.   Negative pledge

A negative pledge clause is a clause by which the borrower undertakes not to subordinate any of its assets to a secured interest of any other person: this means that the lender's claims against the borrower's assets will not be subordinated to any other person's claims. Negative pledge clauses were considered in detail in Chapter 19.[53]

32–42

---

[47] [2005] EWHC 1999 (Ch.).

[48] [2004] EWHC 270 (Ch.).

[49] *Concord Trust v Law Debenture Trust Corp Plc* [2005] UKHL 27, [41], per Lord Scott.

[50] [2005] UKHL 27, [38], per Lord Scott.

[51] See para.23–01 et seq.

[52] cf. *Martyn Rose Ltd v AKG Group* [2003] EWCA Civ 375; [2003] 2 B.C.L.C. 102, in which a petition was improperly presented.

[53] See para.19–57.

G. Pari passu clauses

32–43   A pari passu provision is a provision which stipulates that the borrower must not allow any creditor to acquire an advantage over any other creditor: thus all unsecured creditors have their rights in proportion to their respective rights in equal step. Pari passu provisions were considered in detail in Chapter 19.[54]

H. Consumer credit issues in relation to ordinary borrowing

Issues surrounding consumers' rights in ordinary lending

32–44   The context of legislation governing unfair terms was considered in Chapter 18, and the context in which that legislation applies to banking transactions generally was considered in Chapter 29. The Unfair Terms in Consumer Contracts Regulations 1999 will apply to any contract, including a loan, which is entered into by a "consumer" and which is entered into on standard terms: that is, is entered into on terms which have not been freely negotiated by the parties. Most corporate loans will be entered into on the basis of negotiation between the bank, the client and the parties' professional advisors, and therefore will not fall within those regulations. However, ordinary retail banking business will. This issue was considered in detail in Chapter 30.

There are many issues in relation to loans which raise questions of the consumer credit legislation, particularly dealing with unconscionable bargains. These issues were considered in relation to ordinary banking relationships in Chapter 29.

Hire purchase

32–45   Hire purchase agreements are outside the ambit of this book. Under a hire purchase agreement, the purchaser acquires property over time by means of periodic payments towards the purchase price, by payments of capital amount towards the purchase price, and by payments of interest for the facility to be put in place. These structures are commonly used in the acquisition of cars and other sorts of high value chattels. Many of the issues surrounding hire purchase agreements relate to the consumer credit legislation which governs the sorts of provisions which may be included in such agreements to protect consumers from exploitation. Those issues have already been considered in Chapter 30.

4. SUBORDINATED DEBT

32–46   This short section merely makes mention of the concept of subordinated debt. As was considered in Chapters 19 and 22 and above in this chapter, the concern of lenders is to ensure that the repayment of their loans is protected by taking security or by means of covenants in the loan contract which entitle the loan repayment to be accelerated. If a loan is not secured or if it is not possible to use

---

[54] See para.19–57, and particularly 19–63.

a negative pledge clause because (for example) there are already loans in place with such provisions in them, then any further loans would need to be made at a higher rate of interest to accommodate the concomitant lack of security. Alternatively, in complex circumstances (such as those considered in the next chapter) where there are many lenders it may be that some lender's rights against the borrower are subordinated behind the rights of other lenders. These are examples of subordinated debt. A lender with only subordinated debt will be an unsecured creditor in the borrower's insolvency and therefore will only be entitled to recover amounts in the insolvency one secured lenders (with "superior" debt) have been repaid. Hence the higher rate of interest payable in relation to such subordinated loans.

CHAPTER 33

SYNDICATED LENDING

Core principles

The principles relating to syndicated loans build on the principles relating to ordinary lending which were considered in the previous chapter. The reader is therefore referred to the previous chapter before reading this one.

Syndicated lending is a form of lending undertaken by groups of banks when a single borrower wants to borrow more money by way of a loan than any single bank is prepared to lend on its own. Syndicated lending is used typically where amounts equivalent to hundreds of millions of US dollars are sought by a corporate borrower. For the syndicate banks, this mechanism has the advantage of spreading the risk associated with such a large loan between them, but nevertheless allows each to participate in the profits that will be earned from receiving interest from the borrower. The borrower in this sort of transaction is usually a corporate borrower. The lenders are organised into a "syndicate" which provides the loan moneys. The loan moneys are typically provided by a series of separate loans from each individual lender directly to the borrower but subject to the same contractual terms agreed on behalf of all members of the syndicate; sometimes these syndicated loans will be contracted for collectively. Different banks may provide different amounts of the loan. The interest paid on the loan is therefore divided up between the lenders in proportion to the amount of money which each has lent.

There will be a lead bank or banks who will be responsible for the structure of the issue (referred to as the "arranger") and who may well assume greater liabilities than the other members of the syndicate once the transaction is put in place (either as an agent for the operation of the transaction on behalf of the other lending banks; or, if some security structure is provided, as a trustee). The other banks therefore act simply as lenders responsible for smaller parts of the total loan amount.

Importantly, many of the covenants which arise in syndicated loans are the same as those in ordinary loans: those covenants were considered in the previous chapter. Examples of these covenants include: core events of default, negative pledge clauses, pari passu clauses, covenants to provide information, financial covenants, and so forth. Some of these covenants require some amendment to cope with the number of lenders involved in syndicated loan business. There are other covenants, however, which apply only to syndicated loans, such as: syndicated agent clauses, "syndicate democracy" provisions; set-off, and so forth. Most of these provisions relate to the allocation of rights and responsibilities between the various lenders, and the role of a fiduciary (the "syndicate agent") to ensure the proper flow of moneys and performance of obligations between the members of the syndicate.

1. Introduction

33–01 Syndicated loans are best thought of as being ordinary loans with additional features which are provided typically to large companies in relation to very large amounts of money. Consequently, syndicated loans are predicated on all of the techniques and legal principles considered in the previous chapter. The reader should refer to that chapter before reading this one to understand the background inter alia to common loan covenants and the termination of loan agreements. The difference presented by syndicated loans is primarily based on the amount of money at issue and the size of the companies involved in the transactions. For example, the key cases discussed in detail in this chapter have involved one of the world's largest oil companies and one of the world's largest steel producers.[1] As a consequence of the loan being so very large, it is common for individual banks to balk at the prospect of assuming so large a risk. Loans of this sort usually range in size from hundreds of millions of US dollars (or their equivalent in other currencies) to billions of dollars. Clearly, a loan of this size would constitute an enormous risk for any individual bank when dealing with a single borrower because that bank would be assuming all of the risk that the borrower would default on its repayments, with the result that the bank would have loaned out a ruinously large amount of money to a bad credit risk. Therefore, in relation to such large loans a group of banks (in the form of a "syndicate") will club together so that each individual member of that syndicate will lend a part of the total loan amount separately. The term "syndicate" is not a specifically legal expression. It merely expresses the presence of a number of banks acting in concert as lenders. The company is therefore able to borrow the amount of money which it requires and the banks are able to acquire both an asset in the form of a loan to that company and a loan of a reasonable size. As is discussed below, a "lead bank" will organise the syndicate of banks which will provide the entire loan amount to the borrower by marketing the transaction to them on the borrower's behalf and a "syndicate agent" will ensure the proper conduct of the loan agreement. The typical documentation architecture for a syndicated loan and the possible permutations for providing a syndicated loan are considered below.

Much of the focus of finance lawyers in practice is on the large corporate transactions because that is the apex of financial market practice for the large, multinational law firms. The larger the transaction in monetary terms, the larger the amount of legal expertise that will be poured over it. This does not necessarily mean that a larger transaction is necessarily any more complex than an ordinary loan, simply that when more money is at stake it is natural for more care to be taken in analysing the detail of the transaction and in anticipating potential future problems. The syndicated loan market is no different. It should be accepted, however, that the presence of a number of banks acting as lender instead of a single bank acting as lender will in itself add a layer of complexity to the loan agreement.   **33–02**

Let us think briefly about the commercial position of the banks in these transactions. Each lending bank is effectively taking a speculative risk on the corporate borrower. While the lenders do not ordinarily acquire any shares in the borrower nor any other rights against the borrower, subject to what is said below about taking security, they therefore are taking a calculated risk on the ability of the borrower both to meet the enormous interest payments which are required during the life of the loan and to repay the loan capital at the end of the loan term.   **33–03**

---

[1] *BNP Paribas v Yukos Oil* [2005] EWHC 1321 (Ch.) and *Argo Fund v Essar Steel* [2005] EWHC (Comm) respectively.

Therefore, the lenders are taking a speculative risk on the borrower's business strategy, market positioning and so forth over the life of the loan. The purpose for which the money is required and the business plan which underpins the request for financing are therefore very significant indeed. Whereas it is common for the large banks who make these sorts of loans to seek to develop exclusive and close relationships with large companies, when a loan of this size is sought then those banks will prefer to loosen the leash on which they would ordinarily prefer to keep their relationship with their clients so as to enable the loan to be put in place. Of course, if the lead bank in any context was so jealous of its relationship with a company, then it might prefer to advise that company to borrow money by way of a bond issue instead of taking out a syndicated loan so that the group of people who will have privileged access to the company's strategic planning processes is limited. Bonds are considered in Chapter 34.

33–04 This chapter considers the manner in which syndicated loans may be structured and the principal legal issues which arise in relation to their documentation. A syndicated loan is in essence an ordinary term loan entered into for a fixed period of time, as discussed in Chapter 32, but with a number of lenders instead of there being just one lender. As with an ordinary term loan, a term loan will come to an end either when the expiry period ("the term") is reached or when an event of default specified in the contract occurs. On the happening of an event of default, the borrower's obligation to repay the loan is accelerated so that repayment must be made immediately and any rights to enforce security will crystallise. Therefore, many of the issues relating to syndicated loans are the same as for ordinary loans. So, in many places in this chapter there will be a cross-reference back to the discussion of a particular concept which was discussed in the previous chapter so as to avoid unnecessary repetition. The specific issues which arise only in relation to syndicated loans stem primarily from the fact that there are more lenders involved in a syndicated loan than in an ordinary loan and also relate to the lender's likely preference for more security to cater for the fact that a syndicated loan involves such a large sum of money.

The market association for syndicated lending is the Loan Market Association.[2] This association publishes a variety of documentation relating to syndicated lending, with a view to promoting the "liquidity, efficiency and transparency" of those markets.

2. THE STRUCTURE OF SYNDICATED LENDING TRANSACTIONS

A. The possible structures for a syndicated loan

Thinking about syndicated lending in the round

33–05 A syndicated loan could conceivably be structured in any one of a series of ways. This section considers the various, basic approaches. In setting up the law of finance it is important to consider not just "*the* one way" in which a market tends to structure a particular transaction but rather to consider first all of the possible

---

[2] *http://www.lma.eu.com/default.aspx*

legal techniques which could be used to structure a syndicated loan. There is a tendency (as was discussed in Chapter 31) for participants in financial markets to adopt a herd mentality and consequently to behave in the same way in relation to particular types of transaction. Consequently, it becomes easy to think of agreements like syndicated loans as being exactly the same, when in truth each has features which are unique to its own particular context. So, in this discussion we shall consider how a syndicated loan *could be* structured, as well as considering the ways in which they typically *are* structured. One of the key potential differences between structures revolves around whether the lenders act as one unit or whether they act as people with different rights and liabilities separate from one another. The texts on international finance law have tended to argue that a syndicated loan must correspond to one particular structure or another. The assumption is that there is only one way of structuring syndicated lending or of structuring a bond issue (as considered in the next chapter). This is simply not true, as the cases considered at the very end of this chapter illustrate. Syndicated loan transactions are over-the-counter arrangements and therefore the parties are free to design them as they see fit. Consequently, while there are common features to such lending arrangements and while the Loan Market Association publications will generally be influential, it is simply not the case that all syndicated loans are identical nor that they fit a single template. Therefore, it is important to think matters through from first principles.

Typical events of default in relation to syndicated lending

Before turning to the structure of syndicated loan agreements, it is worth reminding ourselves of a few of the basic principles governing a loan agreement: namely, the events of default which will cause the agreement to be terminated. The ordinary range of events of default contained in syndicated loan contracts is considered below. The principal events of default relate to the inaccuracy of any representation as to the quality or condition of the borrower at the outset of the transaction, any material adverse change in the condition of the borrower during the transaction, any failure of any guarantor or other credit support provider during the life of the transaction, any default in any other borrowing or other financial transaction, and any event signalling the upcoming insolvency of the borrower or its general inability to meet its obligations as they become due.   **33–06**

Structure 1: several lending liabilities with identically drafted documentary events of default

The first means of structuring a syndicated loan would be for the various lenders to remain distinct and to have separate rights and obligations from one another. They would therefore have "several" (or, "distinct") contractual rights. This is the most common structure in the marketplace. Effectively, there are therefore a number of distinct lenders making separate loans to the borrower, but on contractual terms negotiated for them by a lead bank. Thus, the lead bank would organise a syndicate on the basis that a number of different loans are made to the borrower which in the aggregate supply the borrower with all of the money that it   **33–07** needs. So, for example, if Metal Basher Plc wished to borrow £80 million to expand its production capacity in its factories in the Midlands, and if Profit Bank was unwilling to accept the entire risk of Metal Basher repaying all of its obligations, then Profit Bank might agree to provide £10 million by way of one loan itself and then agree to act as lead bank in sourcing seven further loans of £10 million each from seven other banks. Suppose that £10 million was then to be lent by Mammoth Bank to Metal Basher Plc as one of the syndicate of eight banks. Metal Basher Plc would have eight separate contractual arrangements with each of the eight banks whereby each would provide £10 million with the result that Metal Basher Plc would have borrowed a total of £80 million.

33–08 The question would then be as to the rights and obligations of the parties. On these facts Metal Basher Plc would owe obligations to pay identical amounts of interest to each of the lenders (because here each lender has made a loan of the same size) on the same payment dates during the life of the loan, and identical obligations to make repayment of the capital at the end of the loan term.[3] The eight lenders would have entered into the same form of contract with the same wording. There is a complication as to Profit Bank's role. Profit Bank would have contracted with Metal Basher both as a lender and also as the arranger of the transaction, thus attracting a fee for arranging the deal either directly from Metal Basher and/or from other lending banks. Profit Bank would probably have two separate capacities: first as the arranger of the syndicated loan and latterly as the agent of the syndicate of banks. The contracts which each lender would have signed would have been negotiated by Profit Bank as arranger of the transaction. Policing the payment of interest, observance of the covenants in the loan, and the maintenance of any security for the loan, would be performed by Profit Bank as the agent for the syndicate of eight banks. Profit Bank would occupy a fiduciary role in relation to the syndicate when acting as their agent: consequently, Profit Bank would not be permitted to allow any conflict between its own interests as a member of the syndicate and its fiduciary role as agent for the syndicate, it would not be permitted to earn any unauthorised profit from its fiduciary office, and so forth.

33–09 In the event, however, if the eight lending banks were making entirely separate loans then their rights and any action taken against Metal Basher would be separate rights and actions. On this model, Profit Bank would owe its fiduciary obligations to each lender separately and therefore Profit Bank would have nine different capacities: one as a lender, and eight different sets of obligations owed to eight different lenders. However, for the syndicate to be acting as a syndicate, then the parties' common understanding might be that all eight lenders may indeed be owed separate repayment obligations by Metal Basher Plc but nevertheless that they would have some form of contractual arrangement between themselves whereby Profit Bank in its capacity as agent would be acting for all of them collectively. The issue in this context would be if one lending bank (such as Mammoth Bank) sought to advantage itself over the other banks, for example, by

---

[3] If the facts had been different, and different loans of different sizes had been made, then the amounts of interest and capital payable would have been in proportion to the size of the loan that each lender had made to Metal Basher Plc.

seeking to enforce its security ahead of agreement by the syndicate as to how recovery of the parties' security should proceed.

The manner which an agreement between the lenders might work is considered next, but one point is worthy of consideration now. If the banks' events of default in their separate loan contracts were drafted identically but nevertheless placed in different loan agreements, then there would be nothing to prevent Mammoth Bank from enforcing its several rights against Metal Basher Plc without requiring permission from anyone else because its contractual rights would be distinct from the rights of everyone else in the syndicate. Only a contractual agreement that no single lender would be permitted to act independently of the other lending banks in the syndicate could prevent Mammoth Bank from acting in that way. Any such agreement would have to constitute a contract between the lending banks in the syndicate even if payments of interest or repayments of capital were in fact paid directly by Metal Basher Plc to the lending banks as opposed to being paid to Profit Bank as agent and then distributed by Profit Bank between the lenders. Therefore, control of how the lending banks will activate their rights will need to be governed either by means of a contract entered into between all of the members of the banking syndicate specifying in what circumstances any member of the syndicate will exercise its rights; or will need to be governed by each lending bank agreeing to exercise its rights only through Profit Bank as syndicate agent on behalf of each bank, with each syndicate bank agreeing to the same power for Profit Bank and Profit Bank agreeing with each bank how those powers would be exercised (considered next); or will simply need to be left ungoverned so that Mammoth Bank can act unilaterally in whatever way it pleases.

Structure 2: joint lending with joint events of default

The syndicated loan could be organised so that the lenders have separate rights but so that they agree to act as a genuine syndicate in the sense that they are prevented from activating their rights without the agreement of a specified majority of the members of the syndicate to take any particular course of action. In this scenario a contract between the lenders would identify how votes are to be organised and what majority is required for the activation of any right such as the identification of an event of default. In many syndicated loan arrangements, the lenders will lend different amounts and so will have contributed different proportions of the total loan amount required by the borrower. As such, each lender would have a voting power in proportion to the size of its participation in the syndicated loan amount.

33–10

In an alternative scenario, the relationship between the lending banks could be organised as a partnership such that the banks owed fiduciary duties to one another as described by the partnership contract between them. A partnership in the English law sense is an undertaking in common with a view to profit. Suppose the parties to the syndicated loan agreement are organised on the same commercial terms as in the hypothetical example in the previous section. The lenders' rights to seek recovery from Metal Basher would be exercisable only collectively by means of the partnership agreement. As a matter of practicality

33–11

this could be most conveniently exercised through the offices of the syndicate agent, Profit Bank, so as to prevent the lending banks from exercising their rights in different ways at different times. Profit Bank would therefore be acting as agent, and therefore as a fiduciary, for the banks in the syndicate. Any attempt by an individual lender, such as Mammoth Bank, to act unilaterally would be a breach of the partnership contract between the lenders, and so that unilateral act would be terminable, or else any profits earned through breach of the contract would be held on constructive trust for the other partners.[4] In such a collaborative structure, the parties would take a share in the interest payments made by the borrower in proportion to the size of their loan.

33–12   It is suggested that, whereas any individual commentator may describe the syndicate in a syndicated loan as being comprised of lenders making distinct loans or as having some interdependent rights, the proper analysis of the transaction in either event is a matter for the interpretation of any given transaction on its own terms. As emerges from the case studies at the end of this chapter, there is no single form of syndicated ban agreement in the world. For example, the existence of a partnership may be inferred from the circumstances, just as purely several liability may also be interpreted from the circumstances, or else either case may be specified explicitly in the documentation thus making such inference unnecessary. In any case, it is suggested, there will be a "mirror principle" in operation whereby the rights of any one lender mirrors the rights of all other lenders in their capacity as a lender.[5] This position will be secured by a form of pari passu provision whereby no single member of syndicate nor any other lender outside the syndicate would be entitled to have rights which granted it an advantage over other lenders.

The usual syndicated loan structure

33–13   Ordinarily lending banks will not want to be in partnership with one another because they will not want to owe one another the fiduciary obligations which come with a partnership; they will not want to share the "profits" of a business undertaking in the sense that is meant by partnership law; and they will not want to bear any potential obligation under partnership law to indemnify one another's losses in relation to the transaction. Therefore, even though the lenders' agent will collect the borrower's payments of interest before transmitting them on to the lenders, the agreement between the lenders will usually make it plain that they are not intending to be partners: to ensure that a partnership is not inferred from the circumstances, the lenders must make it plain that they are not sharing profits nor sharing losses, but rather are entitled only to a cash amount from the borrower (paid through the lead bank acting as syndication agent) as specified in the loan contract. It would be more likely that a partnership would be formed intentionally if for some reason the lending banks had little confidence in one another and so wanted the reassurance of having the fiduciary obligations of partners imposed on all of the members of the syndicate to provide a remedy in the event of any profit

---

[4] On which, see para.5–05.

[5] That is, the rights and obligations of the lead bank will be different whenever it functions as agent or arranger from the situation in which it operates purely as a lender (that is "qua lender").

being earned from a conflict of interest or other breach of duty. There are also circumstances in which the syndicate will be comprised of lenders with different types of rights and where some lenders have rights which are subordinate to other members of the syndicate (for example where the borrower goes into insolvency the subordinate members can only recover their losses once the senior members have recovered their losses from the borrower).[6] In such circumstances, the lenders will not be partners and will not have the same rights against the borrower, the syndicate agent and against one another.

One lender may be liable to another lender in syndicate if that first lender knowingly interfered with the other's right, for example, to have the proceeds of the sale of mortgaged land applied to repay the loan.[7] Therefore, unless the contract explicitly excludes such liability, the members of the syndicate may owe duties between themselves not to interfere with one another's separate contractual rights. Similarly, they may vary the terms of their agreement provided either that all of the contracting parties agrees to the change or that the contract expressly permits such a variation.[8] Consequently, it is only possible to speak in the abstract about the nature of the rights of participants in a syndicated loan arrangement precisely because those rights and obligations are specifically the creatures of the contracts which created them from case to case.

33–14

Taking security in joint and in several lending

The structure of the transaction and the extent to which the lenders acquire security for their loan will depend upon the terms of the loan. The pari passu "mirror principle" requires that no single lender acquires an advantage over the other lenders. Therefore, no security could be taken by any single lender in advance of any other lender. Where the borrower is a member of a group of companies, then there is a question as to which entity will be the borrower under the transaction. Each company within a group of companies is treated by company law as being a separate legal person and therefore a loan obligation will only be enforceable against the company which is a party to the loan.[9] Therefore, within groups of companies it is important to identify the company or companies which either hold the group's most valuable assets or which conduct the group's principal trade: these are the companies which have the most valuable assets and therefore it is these companies which should either be the contracting entities or the entities which are extending any guarantee or other credit support as part of the transaction. Security in lending transactions may be any of the security mechanisms discussed in Chapter 22; taking security in loan contracts was considered in detail in the previous chapter. The fact that a loan is ordinarily concerned with the payment of money (payments of interest and repayments of capital) means that a guarantee is often sought from companies other than the borrower for the lending in common with the other events of default considered below.

33–15

[6] *British Energy Power v Credit Suisse* [2008] EWCA Civ 53, [2008] 1 Lloyd's Rep. 413.
[7] *Swiss Bank Corp v Lloyds Bank Ltd* [1979] 2 All E.R. 853.
[8] *Redwood Master Fund Ltd v TD Bank Europe Ltd* [2002] EWHC 2703.
[9] *Salomon v A Salomon & Co Ltd* [1897] A.C. 22; *Adams v Cape Industries Plc* [1990] Ch. 433.

B. Case study: the syndicated loan agreement in *BNP Paribas v Yukos Oil*

33–16   This section considers the transaction in the case of *BNP Paribas v Yukos Oil*[10] as an example of how a syndicated loan may be structured. It was a case in which Evans-Lombe J. ultimately made an order for summary judgment in favour of the lending banks. The key provisions of this contract will emerge at appropriate stages of the discussion to follow. The contract (the "loan agreement") provided that if any event of default was breached, then the entire amount remaining outstanding under the loan agreement would become repayable immediately: an "acceleration of obligations" clause, as it is known in the jargon considered in the previous chapter. The Yukos Oil Company ("Yukos") is an enormous Russian oil company. Yukos had borrowed about US $470 million from a syndicate of banks. In October 2003 the Russian government commenced an investigation into Russian oil companies and into the immensely wealthy "oligarchs" who owned and managed them. The position of these oligarchs became somewhat precarious under the Putin regime after they had originally been allowed to acquire control of the enormous Russian oil companies by the Yeltsin regime as part of their assistance for the then Russian government. As a result of that investigation, the chief executive of Yukos, Mr Khodorkovsky, was imprisoned ostensibly in relation to tax violations, Yukos was subject to a tax bill for US $3 billion, and the assets of Yukos were frozen by the Russian government. The syndicate of banks sought to accelerate Yukos's obligations under the loan on the basis of clause 19.4 of the loan agreement on the grounds that there was some material fallacy in a representation made to the syndicate as to the financial prospects for Yukos, and under cl.19.27 on the basis that there had been a material adverse change in the fortunes of Yukos due to the freezing of its assets and the imposition of a very large tax bill on it. It was held that there had self-evidently[11] been a material adverse change once the Russian government had imprisoned the company's chief executive. The context of government interference with the business of oil companies by freezing their assets and the imprisonment of executives on the basis of alleged tax irregularities had caused enormous concern in the financial press, and so clearly constituted a material adverse change. Further to the decision of the House of Lords in *Concord Trust v Law Debenture Trust Corporation Plc*[12], Evans-Lombe J. would not imply a term into the contract to the effect that lenders would not make an invalid demand under a loan contract, nor would his lordship otherwise imply terms to restrict the lenders' rights to identify an event of default under the agreement.[13]

33–17   The loan agreement contained a large number of typical provisions for syndicated lending agreements. Clause 15 of the agreement provided for a number of representations which were made at the outset of the transaction by the borrower

---

[10] [2005] EWHC 1321 (Ch.).
[11] His lordship gave the order for summary judgment ex tempore at the end of the submissions to him and, as is made clear at the outset of his lordship's judgment, only give his written reasons at a later date because of the urgency of the original application before him.
[12] [2005] 1 W.L.R. 1591.
[13] [2005] EWHC 1321, [23].

to the effect that: no member of the Yukos group was subject to any proceedings which would lead to their insolvency; no litigation or similar action was then in process which would have a "material adverse effect" on Yukos; and there had been "no change in the business condition (financial or otherwise) prospects or operations" of Yukos since the financial statements which the lenders had required from Yukos had been prepared. Clause 19 contained the events of default which would terminate the loan agreement, which included provision that it would be an event of default if, in the opinion of the lenders, there was a "material adverse effect" on "the business, condition or production or export capacity" of Yukos. There would also be events of default if Yukos failed to pay any sum when it fell due; if Yukos or any of its affiliates failed to comply with any obligation specified in the agreements; if any statement in a financial document transpired to be incorrect in a material respect; if Yukos or any member of its group of companies admitted its inability to make any payment when due; if any form of insolvency proceeding was threatened against Yukos or any member of its group of companies; if there was any breach of the pari passu provision; or if "any event or circumstance occurred which in the reasonable opinion of [an identified person] had or might reasonably be expected to have a Material Adverse Effect".

Importantly, then, the syndicate and its agent had the power to identify when a material adverse change had occurred in relation to Yukos's business: the parties were not prepared to wait for an official downgrading of Yukos's credit worth or anything of that sort. There is therefore a large amount of "art" in identifying when such an event of default has occurred, even in relation to a US $470 million loan, and not simply "science" in the exact calculation of when such an event has occurred. This may seem surprising given the amount of money at stake. Nevertheless, it is a feature of even the most sophisticated financial agreements that there is often a large amount of flexibility and uncertainty in play, even if commercial lawyers always like to talk about their desire for certainty. So, in this litigation it is clear that there was a dispute between the parties as to whether or not an event of default had arisen at all. However, for the lenders to be able to move quickly so as to realise their security and so forth, there is no time to wait for "science" to catch up with the reality as bankers can "artfully" understand it. Formal calculation of Yukos's credit worth would have required waiting for official financial information so that analysts at the independent ratings agencies could calculate the necessary figures and publish an official view. When the chief executive of the borrower has been imprisoned and the company subjected to a tax bill which is many times larger than the loan, then common sense dictates that the borrower will probably be unable to meet its loan obligations in full in the future. **33–18**

The classification of the syndicate agent's obligations remains a matter for analysis on a case-by-case basis

In spite of the foregoing discussion of a usual syndicated lending arrangement, recent decided cases have illustrated the variety which is present in practice. It remains important for finance lawyers to analyse transactions from first **33–19** principles on each occasion even if there is an assumption that transactions of that sort correspond generally to a specific pattern. The case law demonstrates that a proper legal analysis of any transaction or market will proceed in accordance with law and not with market legend. For example, it is commonly said that there is a clear distinction between the agency obligations of a syndicated lending agent and the trust obligations of a bond trustee (considered in the next chapter). In the first place it must be acknowledged that simply because the market preference is for a syndicate agent to be merely an agent acting on behalf of the syndicate, there may nevertheless be situations in which the courts will find that the syndicate agent was in law acting as a trustee of moneys in favour of the members of the syndicate as beneficiaries. As is clear from *Uzinterimpex JSC v Standard Bank Plc*[14] the "agent" may be held to have been holding property on trust for the members of the syndicate and to have been acting as a trustee. Here, the bank participated in the tortious conversion of consignments of cotton in concert with the borrower. It was held that the syndicate agent should be treated as trustee of the sale proceeds received for the conversion of the cotton.[15] The court rejected the argument that the syndicate agent was acting in law only as an agent. Toulson J. considered that the transaction required the interpretation that the syndicate agent was in fact holding the money in this bank account on trust to be distributed in accordance with the terms of the syndication agreement.

33–20 While a syndicate agent may therefore be found to be acting as a trustee in some circumstances, there are also circumstances in which the syndicate agent will be able to limit its fiduciary and other obligations to the members of the syndicate. So, in *IFE Fund SA v Goldman Sachs International*[16] the syndicate agent had explicitly asserted in writing in a Syndicate Information Memorandum that it was not providing a warranty for the accuracy of any of the financial information which it had passed on to the syndicate in its role as syndicate agent. In this sense, the syndicate agent had acted solely as "arranger" in putting the transaction together and as "syndicate agent" only once the transaction had been finalised. The purpose of the disclaimers in a document titled Important Notice, however, were effectively intended to reduce the agent's responsibilities from being responsible for the bona fides of the transaction to being merely a go-between who brought the various parties together. This analysis of the role of a syndicate agent strips the role of much of its fiduciary content and instead puts the parties (lenders and borrower) in a position where they must look after their own positions instead of relying on the offices of the agent to organise everything for them. The "agent" in this context was merely a kind of matchmaker. It was held that the syndicate agent was not liable for damages at common law in relation to losses caused by inaccuracies in the information which it had passed on in its limited syndicate agent role. This is, in effect, a victory for the principle of exclusion of liability by way of contract for specific parts of a transaction. It was held that "a party involved in negotiations towards a commercial venture owes no positive duty of disclosure towards another prospective party".[17] Thus, even

---

[14] [2008] Bus. L.R. 1762.

[15] [2008] Bus. L.R. 1762, at [42].

[16] [2006] EWHC 2887.

[17] [2006] EWHC 2887, at [64].

though the syndicate agent would ultimately be acting as a form of agent (and thus as a fiduciary) for the syndicate, it bore no positive duties of due diligence before the creation of the transaction: its fiduciary obligations were thus limited. There was held to be nothing unfair in these contract terms because, following *Photo Production Ltd v Securicor Transport Ltd*,[18] the parties were "not of unequal bargaining power".

Therefore we can see that the presence of agency obligations does not mean that the syndicate agent will necessarily be liable for all loss suffered by the lenders or borrower. Similarly, that there were people involved in a transaction acting as syndicate agents, that does not mean that the syndicate agent will be liable to third parties who suffer loss from a larger transaction to which the syndicate agent's duties do not extend. This point was upheld in *JP Morgan Chase Bank v Springwell Navigation Corp*[19] where the presence of a "syndicate team" within the defendant investment bank, which was subject to some fiduciary duties when acting as syndicate agents, did not mean that every aspect of the bank's dealings with its customers were subject to fiduciary principles. Therefore, disputes between the parties fell to be decided only in accordance with contract law.

33–21

3.   THE PROCESS OF ARRANGING SYNDICATED LOANS

A.   The role of the lead bank in promoting the transaction

This section considers the mechanics of putting a syndicated loan agreement together. The transaction is commenced by the borrower seeking funding and by a bank which acts as "lead bank" in organising the terms of the transaction in negotiation with the borrower and in organising the syndicate of banks which will participate in the syndicate. The lead bank performs two different roles: the first as "arranger" of the transaction and the second as "agent" for the syndicate. It would be possible for the roles of arranger and agent to be performed by different people, but they are both more usually performed by the lead bank. The arranger acts as an equivalent to a "promoter" in share issues by seeking out participants for the syndicated loan. Having negotiated the borrower's requirements and the expected rate of interest and key covenants with the borrower, then the lead bank will market the proposed transaction to prospective members of the lending syndicate, usually by means of a document known as a "term sheet" or an "offer document". This document engages the lenders' interest and allows the lead bank to negotiate the precise terms of the transaction with the borrower, as to financial issues such as the rate of interest, and as to commercial issues relating to the covenants required in the agreement by the lenders and as to any security required for the transaction. There will therefore be a contractual nexus between the lead bank and the borrower, and a separate contractual nexus between the lead bank and the banks comprising the lending syndicate. Whether the lead bank should be considered to be an agent in either capacity is considered in the next section.

33–22

---

[18] [1980] A.C. 827, 843, per Lord Wilberforce.
[19] [2008] EWHC 1186.

B.   The role of the lead bank as "agent" in relation to the syndicate

33–23   The lead bank may be deemed to be acting in a fiduciary capacity as agent of the borrower when seeking to attract lenders to the syndicate, in that the lead bank is seeking to attract loan finance for the borrower at the borrower's direction in accordance with the contract between the borrower and the lead bank. This suggests that the lead bank is acting as agent, particularly given that the lead bank's role is to seek the best available deal for the borrower when acting consequently in the borrower's affairs.[20] Alternatively, the lead bank may be deemed to be the agent of the lending banks when negotiating the terms of the loan agreement on their behalf because the lead bank is acting on their behalf in securing both the existence and the precise terms of that transaction.[21] It has been held that the lead bank will occupy a fiduciary role in relation to the information document which it circulates to potential lenders in advance of an agreement being formed and when it negotiates the lenders' participation in the syndicated loan.[22] The lead bank will, however, prefer not be a fiduciary in general terms in this context. Consequently, the lead bank will typically only agree to act on the basis that it is not a fiduciary but rather that it is acting instead as an ordinary provider of financial services, albeit as an intermediary, on the basis of the ordinary law of contract. As was considered in detail in Chapter 29, a bank will rarely be considered to be a fiduciary unless there is something particular about the context of a transaction which suggested something to the contrary. On the basis that the lead bank will not be a fiduciary, it would be potentially liable in tort for any negligent misstatement made either to the lenders as to the condition of the borrower or made to the borrower (as considered in the next section); the lead bank may potentially be liable in tort for any fraudulent misrepresentation; or the lead bank may potentially be liable in contract for any misrepresentation or any other breach of contract: the general law relating to these heads of liability were considered in Chapters 20, 24 and 25.

33–24   The lead bank will ordinarily act as the agent of the lenders in collecting all payments of interest from the borrower. The lead bank will then pass on the payments to the lenders. It is suggested that on receipt of those payments that the "agent", as a fiduciary, will hold those payments on trust for the other banks in the syndicate until such time as those amounts are paid on properly to the banks making up the syndicate. The precise duties and powers of the agent will depend upon the structure of the agreement. So, in *British Energy Power v Credit Suisse*[23] there was a dispute as to whether the syndicate agent was able to act only as an agent of the members of the syndicate or whether it could act as a principal when dealing directly with the borrower and the rights of the various lenders. It was held that the agent may act "as a principal" in enforcing obligations under the agreement against the parties to it where the syndicate lending agreement bore that interpretation.

---

[20] *White v Jones* [1995] 2 A.C. 207 at 271.
[21] *Natwest Australia Bank v Tricontinental Corporation Ltd* [1993] A.C.L. Rep 45; discussed in O'Donovan, *Lender Liability*, 370.
[22] *UBAF Ltd v European American Banking Corp* [1984] Q.B. 713.
[23] [2008] EWCA Civ 53; [2008] 1 Lloyd's Rep. 413.

C.   The lead bank's potential liability for negligent misstatement

The lead bank plays a significant role in marketing a syndicated loan to the lenders. The lenders effectively take a speculative position in "investing" in the borrower by lending it money because they are taking a risk that the borrower will not repay its loan. A loan contract does not fall within the securities regulatory requirements considered in Part X of this book because loans do not fall within the definition of "securities" in that context. Therefore, while there are similarities between a bond issue and a syndicated loan, as considered below, it is only bonds which are securities and which must comply with securities regulation in many circumstances. Because syndicated loans do not fall under securities regulation, the liability of the lead bank for marketing the syndicated loan therefore arises under the general law. So in *Natwest Australia Bank v Tricontinental Corporation Ltd*[24] the lead bank failed to make disclosure of all material facts to the lenders when marketing the syndicated loan transaction to them. The borrower told the lead bank that its contingent liabilities were "normal" when in fact it faced contingent liabilities of US$46 million. Some officers of the lead bank were aware of the true position. The borrower defaulted on its repayment obligations and the lenders sought to recover their loss in damages in negligence from the lead bank. It was held that the lead bank had assumed responsibility to pass on all relevant information to the other lenders and therefore that the lead bank owed a duty of care to the lenders which it had breached.

D.   The borrower's right to borrow and the lenders' obligation to lend

Once a loan contract has been created (subject to the conditions precedent considered in the next section) then the lenders may face an obligation to lend money to the borrower in performance of its contractual obligations. It is usual in relation to a syndicated loan for the contract to provide that each lender makes the amount specified in the loan contract available to the borrower on the basis that the borrower is required to give five business days' notice to each lender that it wishes to draw down that money and furthermore that it makes plain whether it is drawing down the full amount or only a part of the total amount agreed with the lender. Consequently, there is a possibility that the lender may agree to lend money but at a later date refuse to advance that money to the borrower. Ordinarily, a borrower is not entitled to specific performance of the obligation to make the loan,[25] in part because damages would be a suitable remedy.[26] The borrower will not suffer a loss if it can obtain replacement funding elsewhere at the same rate of interest. If the borrower could only obtain funding at a lower rate of funding (presumably if the difference in rate was caused by the lender's refusal to lend, and not simply due to different lending policies at other banks), then that would constitute a loss which would be compensable by common law damages.

---

[24] [1993] A.C.L. Rep. 45.
[25] *South African Territories v Wallington* [1898] A.C. 309.
[26] See para.19–88.

However, it has been held that in "exceptional circumstances" the borrower may be entitled to specific performance of the loan agreement.[27] It is suggested that exceptional circumstances may arise if, after completion of the loan contract, market conditions deteriorated so markedly that the borrower could not acquire funding from any other bank due to a loss of market liquidity as in the global banking crisis of 2008, then that may constitute exceptional circumstances in which the bank should be required to perform its contractual obligations to lend at the contractually specified rate. The distinction here would be that the borrower could not acquire a replacement transaction and therefore that specific performance of the loan contract would be the only appropriate remedy.[28]

4. SYNDICATED LOAN COVENANTS

A. The principal discussion of loan covenants in the previous chapter

33–27 Loan covenants were discussed in detail in the previous chapter.[29] The discussion in this chapter therefore is only intended to highlight any additional features which arise in relation to syndicated loans, and to consider terms which are specific to syndicated loans. The reader is therefore referred to the previous chapter in relation to loan covenants and to Chapter 19 for general principles of contract law as to the operation of contracts, before considering this section.

B. Events of default relating to the giving of information

Covenants to provide information to the lenders

33–28 The loan contract ordinarily provides that the borrower is required to supply the syndicate with specified types of information about its condition, performance and prospects during the life of the loan. Most significantly the borrower will be required to provide financial information as to its profit and loss forecasts, balance sheet, and cash flow to the lenders on a half-yearly or even quarterly basis. The lenders may also require information as to any significant event which occurs in relation to that borrower's financial condition between the presentation of financial information and the creation of the syndicated loan contract. In relation to entities which have their securities posted on a regulated market or on the Official List, then there will be a large amount of information publicly available and the issuer of those securities will bear continuing obligations to make the markets aware of any significant change in their financial condition (as considered in Part X of this book): therefore, the lenders will have a large amount of information available to them through those mechanisms. However, if the borrower has no such securities in issue (which is rare given the size of these loans and thus the nature of the companies involved) or if they are not governed

---

[27] *Loan Investment Corp of Australasia v Bonner* [1970] N.Z.L.R. 100.
[28] See para.19–88 et seq.
[29] See para.32–17 et seq.

by the securities regulations set out in Part X of this book but rather by a looser form of regulation, then the lenders will require the provision of detailed information directly.

Financial covenants

The context of financial covenants was considered in detail in the previous chapter.[30]

33–29

Conditions precedent and representations

As was discussed in Chapter 19, it is common in financial contracts for the borrower to make a number of representations as to its financial condition, its capacity to act, and so forth.[31] The intention is that these representations constitute conditions precedent to the lenders' obligations to lend a fixed amount of money or to make a loan facility available to the borrower. That they are "conditions precedent" means that the lender bears no obligation to make money available to the borrower unless those conditions are first satisfied. Furthermore, if those representations transpire to have become false in any way or turn out to have been false at the time that they were made, then an event of default is committed.

33–30

C.   General events of default

These events of default and any law relating specifically to them were considered in general terms in the preceding chapter. The reader is thus referred to that discussion.[32] This discussion highlights the context of these provisions in relation to syndicated loans specifically.

33–31

Acceleration of obligations

As with any loan, in the event that a loan covenant is breached, then the borrower is required to repay the loan immediately. In that sense, the loan is "accelerated".[33]

33–32

Cross default

A default under another transaction would constitute a default under the loan agreement.[34] A cross default provision would encompass a breach of any other loan contract, bond issue or other financial transaction of a minimum size. For example, if an acceleration provision had been triggered under another loan, then the first loan contract would also have its acceleration provision triggered.

33–33

---

[30] See para.32–21 et seq.
[31] See para.19–28 et seq.
[32] See para.32–17.
[33] See para.32–33.
[34] See para.19–49.

Material adverse change

33–34   A material adverse change involves any deterioration in the financial condition or position of the borrower. An example of a material adverse change clause was given in relation to *BNP Paribas v Yukos Oil*[35] where the loan agreement provided that there would be an event of default if there was "any event or circumstance occurred which (in the reasonable opinion of [an identified person] had or might reasonably be expected to have a Material Adverse Effect". The identification of a "material adverse change" requires an exercise of an art of identifying a change in the condition of the borrower and also an identification that that change was sufficiently "material". So, that a company faces a US \$3 billion tax bill and has its CEO imprisoned will constitute a material adverse change.[36] However, where there are no financial statements available for a new start-up company, then it will be impossible to identify whether or not there has been a material adverse change because it could not be known what the position was before so as to identify whether or not it had changed materially.[37] A fall of 20 per cent in the net assets of the company has been held to be a material adverse change.[38]

Restructuring

33–35   The decision to make a loan and the covenants and security required as part of the transaction are based on the condition of the borrower at that time. If the borrower alters its capital structure, however, then the basis on which the loan was originally made is altered. Similarly, if the borrower is either taken over by another company, or takes over another company, or merges with another company, then the resultant entity will be different from the borrower to which the money was lent: therefore, the acceleration provision will be triggered if the credit worth of the resultant entity is materially weaker than that of the original borrower.

Negative pledge and pari passu clauses

33–36   Negative pledge and pari passu clauses were considered in Chapter 19.[39]

D.   Contractual mechanics specific to syndicated lending arrangements

The role of the syndicate agent

33–37   The lead bank, when acting as agent for the syndicate, will be a fiduciary but the extent of its obligations can nevertheless be limited by the terms of its agency.

---

[35] [2005] EWHC 1321 (Ch.).
[36] *BNP Paribas v Yukos Oil* [2005] EWHC 1321 (Ch.).
[37] *Re TR Technology Investment Trust Plc* (1988) 4 B.C.C. 244.
[38] *Levison v Farin* [1978] 2 All E.R. 1149.
[39] See para.19–57 et seq.

Consequently, the terms of the agency agreement will limit the lead bank's obligations in practice. The agent will be the agent of the lenders and not of the borrower. The loan contract will provide that when the borrower pays the interest payments to the agent on behalf of the syndicate then that satisfies the borrower's obligations to make that payment. The lenders are required to proceed against the agent. It is suggested that the lenders should specify in the terms of the agent's agency that it acts as trustee of the entire payment received from the borrower for the lenders as beneficiaries, in the proportions to which those lenders are entitled under the loan contract. While the lead bank will receive a fee for acting as agent, it will not wish to assume the sort of management obligations which are imposed on trustees in bond transactions (considered in the next chapter): that is, the agent will accept no obligations for the management of the borrower's payment obligations, to commence litigation against the borrower to enforce the obligation to make payment, and so forth. Similarly, the lenders will ordinarily choose to structure their contract so that they are not bound to form a consensus with the other lending banks when deciding how to proceed in relation to their individual rights under the loan agreement.

However, there are transactions in which the lead bank will owe fiduciary duties **33–38** to lenders precisely because those transactions are based on the common understanding that the lead bank will undertake duties negotiating with the borrower in the event of some default under the transaction. This possibility emerges from the discussion of *Argo Fund Limited v Essar Steel Limited*[40] set out below. For example, Tennekoon presents a broader commercial management role for the agent and was more accepting of the possibility that lead banks will be fiduciaries[41] than are other commentators such as Wood who see the lead bank as never occupying a fiduciary role.[42] However, as Lord Browne-Wilkinson put it in *White v Jones*[43] one becomes a fiduciary whenever one involves oneself in the affairs of another.[44] This definition is very broad but it does capture the essence of an agency relationship as imposing fiduciary duties: one owes fiduciary duties in any context in which one is acting on behalf of another in that other's affairs in a context in which that other is reposing trust and confidence in you to act selflessly in their interests, such as the context in which a lead bank is negotiating a loan agreement on behalf of a syndicate and in which it is collecting interest payments on behalf of that syndicate from the borrower. In some of the decided cases considered at the end of this chapter, the syndicate agent has been found to be a fiduciary.

Syndicate democracy

As was highlighted above in relation to some syndicated loan agreements, the **33–39** lenders' several rights will be tempered by a contractual provision between the lenders that they will only exercise their contractual rights (for example to

---

[40] [2005] EWHC 600 (Comm).
[41] Tennekoon, *The Law and Regulation of International Finance* (Butterworths, 1991), p.58.
[42] e.g. Wood, *Law and Practice of International Finance* (London: Sweet & Maxwell, 2008), p.96.
[43] [1995] 2 A.C. 207 at 271.
[44] See paras 5–04 and 5–05.

terminate the loan contract) if there is a contractually specified majority of lenders voting in favour of it. However, the lenders ordinarily do have separate rights to be repaid their loans (because the loan agreements are typically structured in that way) and therefore they would ordinarily have distinct rights under the law of contract to proceed against the borrower in the event of a failure to make payment. The extent of syndicate democracy will depend upon the terms of the loan contract.[45] An individual lender would be prevented from acting unilaterally only if the syndicated loan agreement were organised so that the lenders agreed only to act collectively to enforce repayment of their loans (for example, by terminating the loan agreement), as was discussed above at para.32–07.

5.   THE OPERATION OF SYNDICATED LOANS, LOAN PARTICIPATIONS AND LOAN TRANSFERS

A.   The purpose of this section

33–40   Law is the perfect social science. As with all social sciences, there are many theorists creating complex theoretical models and arguing over the likely performance of those models if they were implemented in practice. Lawyers create models in the form of statutes, in the form of common law principles effected through court judgments, and in the form of structures like contracts and trusts. There are therefore many examples of legal models at work in the world, and there are many other models available in textbooks, in academic articles and in other jurisdictions where things are done differently. What is also perfect about law as a social science is that when key actors take actions—especially judges, and to a lesser extent legislators and lawyers—they give detailed reasons for their actions in the form of written judgments which reflect on factual scenarios which have arisen in the real world and which reflect the consequences which were deliberately designed for those real-world scenarios in the form of remedies. Therefore, to understand how problems come before a court in England and Wales and how those problems are resolved there are thousands of case reports available annually detailing the mechanisms which English law uses to resolve disputes. This section considers cases on syndicated lending to illustrate the context in which issues arose and the way in which they were resolved by the English High Court. What is noticeable is the way in which a syndicated loan was used to provide the borrower with protection against unfortunate economic and political circumstances, all of which occurred outside the United Kingdom but which were nevertheless resolved by an English court under choice of law and choice of jurisdiction principles in the syndicated loan agreement. Our focus, therefore, will be on the cases of *Argo Fund v Essar* and others below. However, before we come to those case studies it is important first to explain some activities which are commonly conducted in relation to loans and their similarity to bonds.

---

[45] For example, the agreement may permit a majority of lenders to compel the compliance of the minority against their wishes: *Redwood Master Fund Ltd v TD Bank Europe Ltd* [2002] EWHC 2703.

B.   A comparison with bond transactions

Syndicated lending is superficially similar to bond issues in that a number of investors are found by the arranger to lend money to a borrower in return for periodical payments of interest, and repayment of the loan capital at the end of the transaction, or on the earlier happening of an event of default. However, the investors in a bond issue acquire a number of securities equivalent to the size of their investment and those securities can generally be disposed of easily on the open market (depending on the nature of the issuer); whereas participations in a syndicated loan involve a much larger investment by the lending banks and do not grant the lending banks securities. It is usual for syndicated loans to explain the extent to which the lending banks may transfer away their rights under the loan, so that the lenders may sell their participation in the loan transaction to third parties, albeit they would be required to sell into an illiquid market when compared to the liquid market for corporate bonds. Bond transactions are considered in the next chapter.

33–41

C.   Loan participations

A loan participation is different from a syndicated loan. In a loan participation, a single lender of a large amount of money will seek to transfer parts of that large loan to other lenders so as to spread the risk of the borrower failing to make repayment to those other lenders. This is similar to an insurer agreeing to insure a large risk but then seeking to reinsure that same risk with other insurers so as to reduce the amount of the risk which it is effectively shouldering on its own.

33–42

D.   Loan transfers

Loans as discussed in Chapter 32 and 33 of this book are not securities: that is, those loans cannot be traded on an organised market in the way that shares in public companies or bonds can be traded on open markets. (Securities are considered in Part X of this book.) Loans are contracts entered into between two parties. A loan will be capable of transfer, however, to a third party in the same way that the benefit of any chose in action can be transferred to a third party. The loan can therefore be transferred in exchange for money. A loan is transferred by assigning all or part of the lender's rights to another person. The loan contract itself may prevent such a transfer, for example if the borrower wished to control who would be its lender from time-to-time so that it can ensure that its lender is not a person with an aggressive policy on acceleration of loan obligations, and so forth.

33–43

A loan can be transferred either by way of a novation or simply by means of a transfer. A novation of the agreement would involve replacing the original lender with a new party such that the borrower and other parties could no longer enforce any rights against that original lender; instead, all of the rights and obligations would pass to the new party. In an ordinary transfer the original party does not

33–44

necessarily pass away its obligations to third parties (such as the borrower and the other lenders) when it transfers the benefit of its contractual right to the new party.

33–45   The benefit derived from a transaction which is expressed as being non-transferable may be transferred to a third party or settled on trust.[46] The contract is not transferred, because it is non-transferable, but rather the benefit that is derived from it has been held to be capable of being treated as an item of property in itself.[47]

E.   Case study: *Argo Fund Limited v Essar Steel Limited* and the secondary market

33–46   This section considers the transaction in the case of *Argo Fund Limited v Essar Steel Limited*[48] as an example of how a syndicated loan was structured in practice, and as an example the rights of those who acquire rights under syndicated loans by acquiring those rights in the secondary market as opposed to acting as a lender under the syndicated loan transaction. Essar Steel Limited ("Essar") is a very large Indian steel producer; whereas the Argo Fund Limited ("Argo") was a mutual fund resident in the Cayman Islands. Essar entered into a two-year syndicated loan for US$40 million over which Bayersiche Landesbank Girozentrale ("BLG") was the lead bank. The purpose of the loan was to consolidate Essar's obligations to its bondholders. The loan was taken out shortly before customs duties and US embargoes were imposed on Indian steel products which severely affected Essar's business. Consequently, Essar was unable to make its payments to the lending banks when they became due. Essar began negotiations with BLG on behalf of the other lenders (demonstrating that BLG occupied a fiduciary role as lead bank and agent in relation to the other lenders). Argo had acquired its rights by acquiring a participation in the syndicated loan on the secondary loan market. That means that Argo had bought its right to become part of the syndicate from a member of the loan syndicate, even though it had not been part of the original group of lenders, presumably because it considered loan repayments from Essar to be a good investment. Argo sought a right to enforce Essar's failure to pay as an acquirer of rights on the secondary market. Essar argued that the terms of the loan contract meant that only the original lending banks were entitled to enforce the events of default under the agreement. Clause 27 of the loan contract permitted transfers of lenders' contract rights and there was no limitation placed on the persons who could become transferees of those rights. However, that clause differentiated between a novation and a transfer. By contrast an assignment of the agreement which passed "all rights and benefits" under it would not necessarily release the original lender's obligations. It was held that on the proper construction of these agreements, Argo was a proper

---

[46] *Don King v Warren* [1998] 2 All E.R. 608.
[47] [1998] 2 All E.R. 608.
[48] [2005] EWHC 600 (Comm).

"bank or financial institution" which was capable of taking a transfer of an original lender's right and consequently capable of enforcing Essar's obligations to make payment against it.

F. Cases Studies: The liabilities of the syndicate agent in complex syndication structures

The syndicate agent may be acting as a trustee

Syndicated financing can be more complex than the sorts of straightforward lending by a group of banks that was considered above. For example, a syndicate may be assembled so as to pay performance guarantees in relation to the delivery of goods, as in *Uzinterimpex JSC v Standard Bank Plc*.[49] In that case, the bank acted as agent for a syndicate of banks providing a guarantee of payment in advance of delivery of a consignment of cotton. It was alleged that the bank had connived with the buyer in taking delivery of the cotton without proper documentation (in breach of contract), such that the buyer had been able to take the goods and resell them before having paid for them.[50] In this instance the bank was not proved to have acted dishonestly, but it was found that it had committed the tort of conversion in assisting the sale of the cotton contrary to the terms of the contract. In this instance, the bank acted as syndicate agent in such a way that it received "the entire proceeds for the sale of the cotton" which was paid into a "transaction account" held specifically for this arrangement by the bank before transmission of amounts on to the members of the syndicate. It was held that the bank as syndicate agent acted as trustee of these moneys while they were held in that account.[51]

33–47

In relation to the finding of a trust, the argument was raised that the bank was acting solely as "agent" and thereby solely in a ministerial capacity[52] in holding those moneys and then transferring them on to the members of the syndicate: as such, what was being argued was that the bank was not acting as a trustee at all but rather as a sort of steward passing the money out from the account. As was made clear in para.29–04 above, the House of Lords in *Foley v Hill*[53] held that a bank does not usually act as a trustee in relation to the operation of ordinary bank accounts. However, in this context Steel J. considered that the transaction required the interpretation that the syndicate agent was in fact holding the money in this bank account on trust to be distributed in accordance with the terms of the syndication agreement. That must be correct: as was explained in para.21–07 et seq., an express trust can be inferred from the circumstances without the parties' needing to use the term "trust". Here it was sufficient to find the existence of a

33–48

---

[49] [2008] Bus. L.R. 1762.
[50] See the discussion of letters of credits at para.30–45 et seq.
[51] [2008] Bus. L.R. 1762, [42].
[52] A "ministerial" capacity is one in which you are simply passing money on without taking any rights or obligations yourself: such as a bank paying out an ordinary standing order for one of its customers.
[53] (1848) 2 H.L. Cas. 28, 9 E.R. 1002.

trust that the bank had legal title in money which it was holding for the benefit of other people on terms defined in the contract.

33–49 Furthermore, it was not suggested that any liability was transmitted to the members of the syndicate as principals when their agent, the bank, sought to recover money from the seller without releasing the appropriate documentation relating to the cotton to the seller. Therefore, the bank would not appear to bear the obligations of an ordinary agent when acting on behalf of the syndicate (as would ordinarily be the case, as discussed in para.18–32 et seq).[54] This question of limiting the obligations of syndicate agents is considered in the next section.

The syndicate agent may exclude its liability for the accuracy of information

33–50 A further illustration of the obligations of a syndicate agent was set out in *IFE Fund SA v Goldman Sachs International*[55] in which Autodis, a large manufacturer of car parts, sought to take over Finelist. The syndicated financing in this case was in the form of "syndicated credit facilities" provided in "tiers". This meant that Autodis was given a right to draw on funds provided by a syndicate of lenders: akin to a series of overdrafts being provided by different banks. That the funding was in "tiers" meant that in the event of Autodis failing to make repayment of these loan facilities then the priority of each lender to have recourse to Autodis's assets or to any security put up by Autodis would be controlled by the terms of the contracts in place between the parties. Goldman Sachs was the syndicate agent. There was a "mezzanine facility" supplied by the claimant, IFE, which had priority ranking behind the "senior debt".[56] In this litigation, it transpired that Finelist's accounts had presented a false picture of its financial position and so IFE among others suffered loss when the transaction fell through. IFE sued Goldman Sachs (as the most attractive solvent defendant) for misrepresentation of Finelist's position.

33–51 On the facts, however, Goldman Sachs had explicitly asserted that it did not warrant the accuracy of any of the financial information which it had passed on to the syndicate in its role as syndicate agent. This explicit exclusion of liability was set out in the form of an "Important Notice" attached to the front of the "Syndicate Information Memorandum" which was circulated electronically and latterly in writing to the potential members of the syndicate before the transaction was finalised. It made it clear that all of the information had been acquired from third parties (the sponsors, Arthur Anderson the accountants, and so forth). The Important Notice explained that Goldman Sachs had not verified any of the information and that therefore it was making no representation nor warranty as to the accuracy of that information. Goldman Sachs thus acted as "arranger" in

---

[54] See e.g. [2008] Bus. L.R. 1762, [10] and [24], per Moore-Bick L.J.
[55] [2006] EWHC 2887. This decision was affirmed at [2007] 2 Lloyd's Rep. 449, [2007] EWCA Civ 811.
[56] If it makes it easier to picture, IFE effectively stood in the middle of the queue behind the senior lenders and in front of the junior lenders. In such transactions, because the junior lenders are only entitled to recover their security last, they will ordinarily receive a higher rate of interest on their loans to reflect the higher risk.

putting the transaction together and as "syndicate agent" once the transaction had been finalised: all in receipt of its usual fees for doing so. The purpose of the disclaimers in the Important Notice, however, were effectively intended to reduce Goldman Sachs's responsibilities from being responsible for the bona fides of the transaction to being a sort of matchmaker between borrower and lenders. It transpired that the accounts had been prepared without knowledge of fraudulent movements of money within Finelist so as to conceal its true financial position.

Toulson J. held that Goldman Sachs had therefore not made any representation as to the condition of Finelist and therefore could not be held liable for damages at common law on that basis. Therefore, a syndicate agent may explicitly exclude its liability for any of the information which it transmits as syndicate agent, even if it is also acting (as Goldman Sachs was) as the arranger of the transaction. Goldman Sachs had put the syndicate together and organised the syndicate's mezzanine financing of this transaction, but it avoided liability. There is therefore no obligation of due diligence as to the accuracy of all information passed on to the syndicate members on the part of an arranger nor of a syndicate agent when putting such a transaction together provided that that financial institution expressly excludes its liability; it is assumed (but not decided in this case) that a syndicate agent would not bear an obligation to conduct due diligence as to the accuracy of all information passed on to the syndicate members even if it had not excluded its liability. It seems that it was only if Goldman Sachs had "actual knowledge" that the information which it had transferred was inaccurate that it would have borne an obligation to bring that matter to the attention of the members of the syndicate.[57] Otherwise, "a party involved in negotiations towards a commercial venture owes no positive duty of disclosure towards another prospective party".[58] Thus, even though Goldman Sachs would ultimately be acting as a form of agent (and thus as a fiduciary) for the syndicate, it bore no positive duties of due diligence before the creation of the transaction. As was discussed in Chapter 5,[59] the obligations of a fiduciary are ordinarily very demanding but they can be excluded for anything short of dishonesty by express provision in the document setting out the fiduciary's obligations, as was effectively illustrated here.

33–52

Furthermore, it was held that there was nothing unfair in these contract terms because, in reliance on *Photo Production Ltd v Securicor Transport Ltd*,[60] where the parties were "not of unequal bargaining power" the intention of Parliament in relation to the unfair contract terms legislation was to allow them to apportion the risks between themselves. Here, the members of the syndicate were thus assuming the risk of the information provided to them being correct because Goldman Sachs had refused to provide any warranty as to its accuracy.

33–53

---

[57] [2006] EWHC 2887, [60].
[58] [2006] EWHC 2887, [64].
[59] See para.5–37 et seq.
[60] [1980] A.C. 827, 843, per Lord Wilberforce.

The presence of syndicate agency need not impose further private law liabilities

33–54   In *JP Morgan Chase Bank v Springwell Navigation Corp*[61] there was involvement by the "syndicate team" at various subsidiaries of JP Morgan Chase Bank with the investment entities used by a family of wealthy shipping magnates. The private law claims relating to these transactions were considered in Chapter 25,[62] in particular the question as to whether or not the bank owed a duty of care to clients: on these facts it was held that no such duty was owed even to private individuals because they had sufficient investment expertise to understand the risks for themselves.[63] No particular, actionable fiduciary or other duties attached to the bank because of the context of any syndicated investment structures. Thus, even the liabilities of an "agent" in relation to syndicated transactions may be quite limited; except where a trust or other fiduciary obligation is both necessitated by the context and not excluded by the syndicated loan documentation.

---

[61] [2008] EWHC 1186.

[62] See para.25–28 et seq.

[63] It is difficult to shake the sense that Gloster J. reached this decision in part because the claimants were so rich that it is thought that they must know the risks, as well as because they were self-assured and experienced enough not to need the risks explained to them. Nevertheless, they were placing their investment portfolio in the hands of professionals to invest in complex products. What perhaps sunk their claim was the fact that the losses were caused by the failure of the Russian banking market (a straightforward form of political risk) and not by the inherent complexity of the products in which they were investing.

CHAPTER 34

BONDS

CORE PRINCIPLES

A bond is a security by which investors make capital loans to the issuer of the bond and in return receive an income stream by way of interest, repayment of the loan at the end of the bond's life, and transferable securities in the form of bonds in an amount proportionate to the size of the loan.

A typical eurobond issue in London is documented by means of a "mandate letter" which sets out the role of lead managers of the issue; a "subscription agreement" detailing inter alia the banks' obligation to buy up any bonds which are not subscribed for by investors; a "management agreement" detailing the obligations between the banks managing the issue; and, significantly, a prospectus detailing the terms of the bond, the issuer's financial condition and so forth (a prospectus will be legally required if the bonds are to be offered to the public). The required contents of a prospectus are considered in Chapter 36.

Bond transactions usually contain a negative pledge provision (which requires that none of the issuer's assets are pledged to any other person), and a pari passu provision (which provides that all investors must be treated equally). Events of default under a bond agreement typically include failure to make payments of interest when due, a deterioration in the issuer's credit worth or credit rating, any event of insolvency relating to the issuer, cross default and cross acceleration in relation to any other debts owed by the issuer, and any corporate restructuring of the issuer. The covenants typically included in lending of this sort were considered in Chapter 32.

1. INTRODUCTION

A. The scope of this chapter

34–01   This chapter deals with bonds. It is divided into three parts: first, the structure of a typical bond issue; secondly, the common forms of documentation for a bond issue; and, thirdly, legal issues which arise in relation to bond issues.[1]

B. What is a bond?

34–02   A *bond* is a means of borrowing money by issuing the lender with a transferable security in return for the loan, as well as undertaking to pay interest on the loan and to repay the loan capital at the end of the loan term. Whereas an ordinary loan (considered in Chapter 32) consists of a contract whereby a lender advances capital to a borrower subject to contractual obligations to repay the capital in time and to pay periodic amounts of interest in the meantime, a bond is a means of acquiring loans from a number of investors in the securities markets. The "borrower" in a bond issue is in fact the "issuer" of the bonds, which may be a company or which may be a government (a so-called "sovereign" issuer). The "lenders" in a bond issue are in fact a group of investors each of whom contribute an amount of money towards the total "loan" and who in return receive absolute ownership of the number of bonds for which they have paid. The price of the bond is fixed in advance by the issuer. Ordinarily those bonds are transferable: which means that the bonds can be sold to other people in the "after market". Many investors in bonds are interested in the possibility of selling their bonds on the open market for a speculative profit; other investors are interested in the cash flow which will be paid by the issuer to the investors on regular payment dates. Bonds are a form of security and so can be traded (as discussed in Chapter 35) similarly to shares and other securities.

34–03   Investors in a bond issue acquire the right to receive the repayment of their loan at the expiry of the bond issue, and to receive a cash flow during the life of the bond. This cash flow during the life of the bond is a payment of interest which is calculated by reference to the number of bonds which the investor has acquired. A key part of the structuring and marketing of a bond before its issue is the identification of the amount of interest which the issuer will be required to pay to the market so as to convince investors that the bonds are worthy of their investment. The safer the company is perceived to be, the lower the rate of

---

[1] Among the literature on bonds see: R. Tennekoon, *The Law & Regulation of International Finance* (Butterworths, 1991), p.143 et seq.; P. Wood, "International Loans, Bonds, Guarantees, Legal Opinions", Vol.3 of *The Law and Practice of International Finance*, 2nd edn (London: Sweet & Maxwell, 2007); and M. Hughes, *Selected Legal Issues for Finance Lawyers* (Lexis Nexis, 2003), p.38 et seq.

interests needs to be; and therefore if the company is perceived to present a higher credit risk, then it is required to pay a higher rate of interest to investors. The cash flow which is paid to the investor is therefore the equivalent of interest on an ordinary loan, although in bond markets this form of interest is known as "coupon". It is known as "coupon" because in the early bond markets investors received "bearer bonds" (that is, bonds in a physical form, rather like a banknote) and those bearer bonds had small coupons attached to them. When the investors wanted to be paid their "coupon" they had to tear off the appropriate coupon for each payment date and deliver it to the issuer in return for each payment of interest on each bond.

The bearer bonds could be traded between bondholders simply by transferring the physical bond in return for a payment of money. Today bonds are issued in a "*dematerialised*" form, which means that the bondholder does not now receive bearer bonds but rather has her ownership of her bonds recorded on a register of bondholders electronically. The reason for shifting from a system of bearer bonds to a system of ownership being evidenced electronically was that it became a common occurrence for the (often bowler-hatted) couriers[2] who used to take these bearer bonds from bank to bank in the City of London to be robbed; and so it was decided that it would be more secure to maintain an electronic system of ownership without valuable bearer bonds needing to be transported around the City or elsewhere. Transfers of bonds are now recognised by the registration of the new owner on the electronic register of bondholders.

34–04

C. The management of bond issues

A bond issue is managed either by a single lead manager or a group of managers which will be investment banks. The number of managers will depend upon the size and complexity of the issue. It will be the responsibility of the lead manager to prepare a prospectus for the issue, to fix the issue price of the bonds and to organise their placement in the market. The bond issue will be extensively documented and will contain a series of provisions entitling the investors to terminate the issue early and recover their capital sums and other amounts in lieu of periodical interest. The documentation is considered below, whereas this section considers the practicalities of putting a bond issue in place.

34–05

There is a significant element of expertise in the structure of a bond issue. First, the issuer, as the investment banks' client, will have a view as to how much capital it requires for its own commercial purposes, possibly under advisement from one or more of the investment banks. For the investment banks themselves, the fees which are earned for acting as lead manager are the core earnings for their corporate finance departments. There is also prestige involved in being lead manager of a large, important bond issue, both existential prestige and the sort of

34–06

---

[2] These people used to be a feature of London City life, although latterly large numbers of such bonds would be moved by more secure means in armoured vans and so forth. Attempts to steal these bearer bonds from armoured vans by violent criminal gangs were a staple part of television cop shows like *The Sweeney* in the 1970s.

prestige which brings more business in the future.[3] The investment banks also want to get closer to large corporate and other clients so that they can know and advise on (and charge fees for) the shaping of those clients' financial needs: forging relationships with clients is a key part of an investment banker's life.[4]

34–07 The investment banker then has to match the client's needs for capital with the best strategy for acquiring funding for that client at that time—whether a loan or a bond issue or a share issue. Having identified a bond issue as the best means of proceeding, the investment banker must then decide in which jurisdiction the bonds should be issued. Often bonds are issued internationally to maximise the available market. The investment banker must decide what precise market is then the best source of capital: a small group of selected financial institutions, or a larger pool of smaller institutions, or a full-scale listing of the securities so that they can be offered to the widest possible investment market (across the entire EU and beyond if the regulations are complied with). These are sensitive commercial decisions which require gauging the precise mood of the market, whether or not there have been too many similar issues recently which would have soaked up a lot of investor capital, or whether bond markets are buoyant because of disturbance in the equity markets, for example. The decision is made more critical by the fact that the lead investment banks are usually required to buy up any securities which are left unsubscribed for once the issue has been made. Identifying the market is important, and therefore identifying the price at which the bonds will be offered (that is, identifying the rate of interest that will be paid on the bonds) and also the credit rating that will be given to those bonds by the credit ratings agencies.

D. Bonds as securities and the advantages of listing

34–08 Bonds are a form of security, as discussed in great detail in Part X of this book. An issue of any security—whether a bond or a share or some other sort—involves a large number of professionals to advise the issuer about the desirability, pricing, regulation and documentation problems surrounding that bond issue. The larger companies which issue bonds may have those bonds traded on regulated securities markets and admitted to the Official List in London or in other Member States of the EU. When a security is offered to the public or admitted to trading on a regulated market, there is a range of very detailed securities regulations which govern that issue: principally the Prospectus Rules and the Disclosure and Transparency Rules in the UK created by the Financial Conduct Authority ("FCA"). If the securities are admitted to the Official List,

---

[3] The process by which companies meet the investment banks which they might use for such an issue and by which they select the lead manager(s) is known as a "beauty parade" in which beautifully dressed bankers give complex "presentations", or "sales pitches", to explain why their firm is the most appropriate for the job. These presentations are rehearsed for days and the PowerPoint slides re-drafted for weeks before the beauty parade.

[4] I do not intend anything sarcastic in the expression "forging a relationship", although it is an interesting idiom which suggests false smiles and forced laughter over business lunches. Typically corporate financiers are much better dressed and much more polite than traders who work on dealing floors, because the corporate financiers have to schmooze their clients.

then the FCA Listing Rules apply to that listing. These regulations are long and complex, and place great demands on the issuer and its professional advisors. The principal advantage of having bonds offered to the public is that this opens up the widest possible market for those bonds; whereas issues which do not comply with those regulations may not be offered to the public and may not be traded on regulated markets like the London Stock Exchange. The other advantage of trading securities in this manner is that investors know that the issuer has been required to comply with the appropriate securities regulations and therefore that its affairs are likely to be in order, that a large amount of information will have been made publicly available further to the securities regulations, and that the FCA will oversee the continuing obligations relating to the accuracy of that information. The reader is referred to Chapter 35 for an introduction to UK securities law, which then directs the reader to appropriate parts of subsequent chapters of Part X of this book which deal with these regulatory issues.

E. The dematerialisation of bonds

As was outlined above, bonds are not issued in physical form, and they are therefore not transferred in physical form between traders in the bond markets.[5] Rather, bonds are held by the custodians Euroclear or Clearstream in the European markets. The right of the investor is not expressed in relation to any individual bond but rather is expressed in the form of a "global bond" or "global note" which is issued by the issuer. The investor receives an entry in a register organised by the custodian or some other person (here, the registrar) which evidences her acquisition of a given number of bonds. This effect of removing the tangible bonds from circulation is commonly dubbed "dematerialisation". The proprietary right of the investor is therefore in the chose in action against the registrar and not in any individual bond. "Dematerialisation" refers to this market practice of issuing bonds by means of an entry on a register and the issue of a global note, as opposed to the traditional bearer form. As we shall see, this dematerialised security raises a number of the problems of intangibility considered in Chapter 21 because the dematerialised nature of the bonds put up as collateral to secure financial transactions raises a number of difficult questions of English property law.[6]

34–09

F. Bonds and syndicated lending

There is a similarity between the issue of bonds and a syndicated loan. Briefly put, in a syndicated loan (as was discussed in Chapter 33) a number of lending institutions come together to assemble sufficient capital for the borrower and to share the risk of the borrower's failure; in a bond issue a number of lenders in the form of investors contribute in the aggregate as much capital as the borrower needs and so spread the risk of the loan. Both forms of transaction require complex documentation to allocate risks between lenders, managers of the

34–10

---

[5] Even though their documentation will frequently express the bonds to be bearer bonds.

[6] See para.21–15 et seq.

transaction and borrower, and to identify the events which will constitute defaults under the agreement. There is often also a fiduciary officer whose role is that of a pseudo-regulator for the transaction to ensure that all payments are made: so the role of eurobond trustee is compared by some commentators with that of the "syndicate agent" in syndicated loan transactions.[7] In syndicated lending the syndicate agent is a functionary who carries out the instructions of the borrower, arranging the availability of the credit and the making of payment. The syndicate agent represents the issuer and not the investor; whereas the trustee exists to represent the interests of the investors.[8] Further, the syndicate agent is responsible for making payment and for carrying out administrative obligations to do with the conversion of the global bond and so forth. The trustee, however, will bear all the usual fiduciary duties relating to the avoidance of conflicts of interest, due diligence and so forth[9] as well as taking title in the issuer's obligation to pay.

34–11   In a bond issue a security is issued to the investor by the issuer. The covenants contained in the legal documentation of these methods will be broadly similar (in that they will allow for early termination in certain circumstances, and so forth) but will contain significant differences (in that one method involves the issue of a security and that the other does not). The bond itself constitutes a personal claim exercisable by the investor against the issuer. The claim is both for the stream of interest payments to be made on the identified payment dates and for the repayment of the capital amount at the end of the issue. The bond itself is understood by law to constitute property and is therefore transferable and capable of being used as security for lending in itself. Bonds are transferred in the open market depending on the performance of the issuer and the attraction of that bond's rate of interest compared to prevailing market rates.

G. The use of a trustee

34–12   As is discussed below,[10] a trustee may well be used in a bond issue to provide some added security for bondholders in that the trustee will be empowered to act on behalf of the bondholders in the event that the issuer fails to make a payment.[11]

---

[7] Wood, *Law and Practice of International Finance*, 168 et seq.

[8] It is my opinion that the trustee does not represent the investors straightforwardly. There are a number of events of default in which the trustee is required to judge whether or not there has been breach: the trustee is required to act impartially in these circumstances and therefore could not be said to be partial on behalf of the investors in all circumstances.

[9] *Keech v Sandford* (1726) Sel. Cas. Ch. 61; *Aberdeen Railway v Blaikie Bros* (1854) 1 Macq. 461, HL; *Bray v Ford* [1896] A.C. 44; *Parker v McKenna* (1874) 10 Ch. App. 96; *Boardman v Phipps* [1967] 2 A.C. 46, and in relation to liability for breach of trust *Target Holdings v Redferns* [1996] 1 A.C. 421.

[10] See para.33–22.

[11] See, for example, *Law Debenture Trust Corporation v Elektrim Finance BV* [2005] EWHC 1999 (Ch.).

H. The role of credit rating agencies

Credit ratings agencies play a very important part in the conduct of securities markets, particularly bond markets. The ratings agencies—principally Moody, Standard & Poors ("S&P"), and Fitch—are private businesses which assign a rating to securities and to trading companies and governments. This rating, to use the best known methodology, rates the entities with the best credit risk as being "AAA" down through AA, A, BBB, BB, B, and so forth. The ratings are a combination of a purported "science" which is based on mathematical modelling of the entities' financial performance (or economy in the case of governments), and of "art", which is based on analysts' assessments of the prospects for that entity's business (or economy), its place in the global economy generally, and so forth. The independence of the ratings agencies is vital in the operation of the securities markets because the markets rely on the ratings that are given to these securities so that professional investors in particular can decide whether or not any given investment is likely to produce a high enough return given the risk associated with it. So, the interest rate payable on a bond will depend both on prevailing market rates at the time (together with expectations of where those rates will move in the future) and on the risk associated with the company issuing that bond: the higher the risk, the higher the rate of interest that investors will require from that bond issue to make taking the risk worthwhile.

34–13

Credit ratings agencies are independent (in the sense that they have always purported to reach their ratings without favour or bias) but they are paid by the entities which are being rated by them or by those entities' advisers. Therefore, it has been suggested that the ratings agencies have not always been as independent as they ought to have been because there is necessarily competition between the different agencies (which are commercial businesses) for the business of the various investment banks and their clients. In relation to securitisation issues it has been alleged that they have assigned questionably high ratings to products which have subsequently turned out to be valueless: these products are discussed in Chapter 47. Whether this will give rise to liability in tort under English law was considered in Chapter 25.[12]

34–14

2. The Documentation of Bond Issues

A. The scope of this discussion

This section considers typical documentation used for bond issues in London. First, we shall consider the different types of agreement which are put in place between the various actors. Then we outline some of the principal terms of those agreements—many of which were discussed in Chapter 19. Finally, we outline the appropriate principles for the listing of bonds under FCA securities regulation. It is important to remember that bond issues can have very many

34–15

---

[12] See para.25–51.

different terms and therefore that this discussion aims to discuss only the most basic form of transaction, with an indication of the sorts of terms which may be added in particular circumstances.

B. The typical documentation architecture for a London eurobond issue

The managers' interaction with the issuer

34–16   This section considers the structure which is usually deployed in a "eurobond"[13] issue in the London markets ("a London eurobond issue"). In a typical London eurobond issue the following forms of documentation will generally be found. First, a "mandate letter" which grants the power to the investment bank or banks which are leading the issue to act on behalf of the issuer. The purpose of this mandate letter is to bind the lead banks into the transaction, so that they will not involve themselves in any activities which would conflict with the issue, and to empower them to act on behalf of the entity which is issuing the securities because otherwise UK securities law and company law would prevent a person acting on behalf of a company which had not agreed to that action.

34–17   A key part of the relationship between the lead managers and the issuer will be the "subscription agreement" which sets out the terms on which the investment banks leading the issue undertake to buy any securities which are not subscribed for by arm's length investors once they are offered to them. This is a key part of the skill of investment banks in this context: identifying the issuer's needs for capital and then identifying the most likely market to provide that level of capital in a securities issue, as considered above. That the investment banks are usually obliged by the subscription agreement to acquire any securities which are left unpurchased means that they are putting their own money on the line when they advise the issuer. This agreement will also specify the fees which the lead managers are entitled to receive. It is usual for the liabilities of the managers to be "joint and several"—meaning that they are liable together for any obligation, or that any one of them may be liable for the whole of any obligation too in the event that any other managers cannot perform their obligations. The managers will require indemnity from the issuer against any misstatement in any of the marketing material (considered next) which results from information provided by the issuer, and therefore the issuer is required to warrant that the information provided is correct.

Documentation to market the issue to investors

34–18   Secondly, the issue will need to be marketed to investors. If the issue is not to be listed nor to be offered to the public nor to be admitted to trading on a regulated market, then there is no regulation as to the precise form that that marketing material must take; otherwise the issue will be governed by the FCA securities

---

[13] A "eurobond" is a bond issued outside the country of the issuer's origin; although some market participants use the term to refer to all bonds issued outside the US.

regulations considered in Chapter 35 et seq. There will be some form of prospectus (sometimes referred to as an "offering circular") sufficient to give prospective investors a clear picture of the issue and its attractions. The prospectus will typically be required by investors (absent any securities regulations requiring such information) to include financial statements and other information about the nature and quantity of securities to be issued and their commercial purpose for the issuer. Any misstatement made in that prospectus will be actionable under the law of tort, as considered in Chapter 25,[14] even if it is not governed by FCA prospectus regulation. If the issue is to be offered to the public or admitted to trading on a regulated market or listed then the securities regulatory issues considered below will be significant.

It is common for an issue which is being made to a limited range of investors to be preceded by a "pathfinder prospectus" which attempts to identify investors' interest ahead of the issue proper—the intention of such a document may not be to form an investment contract but instead merely to gauge interest prior to entering into legal relations, as is discussed in Chapter 17 in relation to "mere puffs" of this sort prior to the creation of binding contracts under English law.[15] The pathfinder prospectus will usually not form a contractual offer for the bonds because the issuer's intention is normally merely to assess the likely interest of the target investor community and thus to help the issuer to fine tune the terms of the issue before a full contractual offer is made subsequently. The subscription agreement will usually contain a power for the managers to terminate or postpone an issue in the event that they consider that market conditions have altered sufficiently to require such a delay. Typically, a market disruption will be required to permit such a delay, in the form of a correction in appropriate currency markets, or a political event affecting the transaction, or something of that sort; but the documentation of any given transaction may include other powers.

34–19

Obligations between the managers

Thirdly, there is the position between the managers which is required to be settled by a further agreement, which is usually referred to as a "managers' agreement". This agreement will identify the obligations of each manager in relation to the marketing of the issue and their separate obligations in relation to any expenses connected to the issue, which the managers are required to bear under the subscription agreement. As is considered below, a trustee is used in many bond issues and therefore a trust deed will be required to identify the powers of this trustee to act on behalf of the investors in the event of any identified default by the issuer. Bonds are issued under a global bond and there will need to be documentation drafted to conceptualise this dematerialisation of the issue.

34–20

---

[14] See para.25–44.
[15] See para.17–15.

Embedded swap documentation

34–21   As is considered in Chapter 40, it commonly happens that an issuer is required to seek capital in a jurisdiction in which it cannot acquire the best rates of interest (perhaps because it is little known in that place) or because market conditions mean that it cannot acquire the rate of interest which it would like. Therefore, the rate of interest which the investor is required to pay on the bond may be swapped for a rate of interest or a rate of interest on a different currency which is preferable for the issuer. This type of swap is embedded in the bond documentation (and is thus known as an "embeddo" in the marketplace) by means of a standard form swap agreement (as discussed in Chapter 41) being adapted so as to alter the effective interest rate[16] payable by the issuer of the bond and also in order to ensure that the terms of the swap agreement match the terms and conventions used in the main bond documentation.

C. The use of a trustee or a fiscal agent

The role of the trustee or a fiscal agent

34–22   A trustee may be used in the transaction or it may not, as the parties select.[17] The Yellow Book, which stood for securities regulation governing listed companies in the UK before the Financial Services and Markets Act 2000 ("FSMA 2000"), required the presence of a trustee. The FCA, which acts as the UK Listing Authority ("UKLA") in relation to listed securities, including bonds, creates and oversees the relevant regulations formally; however, the use of a trustee with powers and duties delineated by the bond documentation itself can also offer a more tailored means of protecting the specific investors in a particular bond issue. The UKLA's listing rules (discussed in Chapter 36) presently stop short of providing an unequivocal requirement that each debt security be accompanied by a trust deed creating a trustee empowered to protect the interests of investors (in the manner considered below). In the listing rules there is a requirement that among the "additional documents", which the UKLA may require to be lodged with it together with any application to the UKLA for the listing of any securities is: "in the case of debt securities, a copy of the executed trust deed".[18] Further, the listing rules contain a continuing obligation that, if there is no other obligation for the issuer to publish annual accounts, the trust deed contain a requirement that the trustee be informed annually as to whether or not there has been any event of default under the terms of the issue.[19] These provisions suggest that a trust

---

[16] The reference to the "effective interest rate" means the following: the issuer is still required to pay the interest specified in the bond documentation to the investors, but because of the swap the issuer will have a part of its interest rate cost met by the seller of the swap in accordance with that agreement thus effectively reducing its interest cost.

[17] See, for example, *Law Debenture Trust Corporation Plc v Elektrim Finance BV* [2005] EWHC 1999 (Ch.); *Concord Trust v Law Debenture Trust Corp Plc* [2005] 2 Lloyds Rep. 221. See also the detailed discussion in P. Rawlings, "The Changing Role of the Trustee in International Bond Issues" [2007] J.B.L. 43.

[18] Listing Rules, Ch.7, para.7.9(f).

[19] Listing Rules, Ch.23, para.23.32.

structure is expected but not explicitly required by the listing rules. The rules reflect the common market practice of using a trustee.

The role of the trustee then is to provide a form of "transaction specific" regulatory protection for the investors. The trustee has the power to intercede if there is any irregularity with the payment of coupon by the issuer to the investor, with the consequence that the bond issue is declared to be held on express trust by the trustee.[20] The bonds are held on trust by the trustee and in turn the investors acquire the rights of beneficiaries under that trust, so that the trustee can enforce the payment obligations of the issuer on their behalf. Strictly then, all payments are made through the trustee to the investors as beneficiaries. This structure, however, raises the problems considered in the two following sections. The obligations of bond trustees include the following. As was discussed in Chapter 32, there are a number of general covenants which are typical to all lending transactions, whether in the form of ordinary loans or bond issues: this discussion focuses only on the few relating specifically to bond transactions. In bond issues, there are two possible types of fiduciary: fiscal agents and bond trustees. Both types of fiduciary bear administrative duties and duties concerned with the onward transmission of interest payments to investors.

34–23

There is an important difference between the two, however. In general terms a fiscal agent acts solely as the agent of the issuer (acting as a conduit for payments and so forth) and does not therefore owe fiduciary obligations directly to the investors; whereas a bond trustee does owe obligations to the investors as part of its administrative responsibilities. The presence of a bond trustee is therefore more attractive to investors because the trustee acts as an impartial arbiter between issuer and investors. Which form of fiduciary is used is therefore a key commercial decision when putting a bond issue in place. Where a trustee is used, the issuer will typically covenant to provide all necessary information to the trustee, to observe pari passu and negative pledge clauses, to conduct its affairs in an appropriate manner, to comply with any and all appropriate listing and other financial regulations, and to ensure that no event of default under the bond documentation is in existence or may occur. For the issuer, the benefit of using a trustee is that the trustee is typically given the power, as considered below, to waive certain types of minor default by the issuer: in that sense, the trustee is a referee deciding whether or not breaches are significantly serious to be actionable by the investors. Of course, any fiduciary will bear the obligations considered in Chapter 5 of this book; and a trustee will bear the obligations discussed in Chapter 21. A number of issues arise in relation to the law of trusts in relation to bonds: one particular issue is that of certainty of subject matter and the property over which the trustee takes title, as considered below. The role of the bond trustee, and the difficulties which may arise in carrying out this refereeing function emerge from recent cases such as *Law Debenture Trust Corporation v Elektrim Finance BV* (considered in para.32–39) and of *Citibank v MBIA*.

34–24

The decision of Mann J. in *Citibank NA v MBIA Assurance SA*[21] considered the role of trustees in bond issues. The case related to the complex debt taken on by

34–25

---

[20] See G. Thomas and A. Hudson, *The Law of Trusts*, 2nd edn (OUP, 2009), Ch.50 generally.
[21] [2006] EWHC 3215.

Eurotunnel and in particular issues surrounding the restructuring of that debt under French insolvency law. Citibank acted as trustee under the deed of charge and the trust deed over the "Tier 3 bonds" which were at issue here; MBIA was a bondholder seeking to direct Citibank to vote in favour of a proposed restructuring of Eurotunnel's debt in those French insolvency proceedings. The bond documentation (which was contained in various documents) empowered MBIA (as the "note-controlling party") to direct Citibank how to vote in certain instances, including this sort of restructuring (in cl.8.1 of the trust deed). Citibank was unclear whether it could exercise its own discretion as to the suitability of the proposed restructuring or whether it was obliged to follow the directions given to it by MBIA. It was argued on behalf of the other parties that this proposed restructuring would transform the bonds into something commercially different and therefore that Citibank ought not to vote for them. Citibank therefore sought directions from the court as to how it should act. While the documentation empowered MBIA to instruct Citibank how to act, the bond documentation provided (in cl.10.1 of the trust deed) elsewhere that Citibank was not "required to have regard to the interests" of the bondholders in relation to "the exercise of such rights, powers or discretions" and that Citibank would bear no liabilities to the bondholders;[22] elsewhere again the documentation (in cl.12.2 of the trust deed) gave Citibank as trustee the right to exercise the lender's vote in relation to any such matter. Further to cl.12.2, Mann J. considered that Citibank had a broad power to act in relation to this proposed restructuring and that therefore there was no impediment to it following the instruction given to it by MBIA under the bond documentation. Furthermore, the limitation of liability here was held not to remove the existence of a viable trust.

34–26   This, it is suggested, does not answer the question whether the trustee, Citibank, was *free* to act as it wished or was *bound* to follow MBIA's instruction. The bond documentation both required Citibank to obey MBIA and yet elsewhere purported to give it freedom to act. Therefore, if it had freedom to act, it ought to have been entitled to refuse MBIA's instructions. Here, the resolution of the issues between the parties was that Citibank as trustee was free to consider itself bound by MBIA's direction. That correlated well enough with the commercial basis of this transaction in that MBIA was intended to be in control of the structuring of the Tier 3 bonds. The best understanding of this litigation is that the extensive documentation served only to confuse the obligations of Citibank. It is not that trusts law makes the role of a trustee unclear, but rather that overly-complex documentation obfuscates the obligations of a trustee by seeming to include contradictory rights and obligations. On this basis Mann J. is to be congratulated on finding a commercially sensible path out of the mire.

The problem of certainty of subject matter

34–27   The problem of English trusts law which arises is the following. To create a valid express trust under English law the property comprising the trust fund must be

---

[22] [2006] EWHC 3215, at [7] and [25] especially. In spite of the breadth of that provision, prudence will often encourage a careful trustee to seek the added cover of a court's agreement to its actions.

separately identifiable.[23] Therefore, where a beneficiary attempts to assert rights under the law of trusts over a trust fund comprising a portion of a total holding of intangible securities—such as bonds issued under a global note which recognises ownership by means of entry on a register—that trust will not be found valid unless the specific securities at issue are identified.[24] Therefore, any proprietary rights asserted over the trust fund would similarly fail.[25] There is authority, however, that with reference to a trust declared over a portion of a total holding of ordinary shares, there is no need to segregate those shares which are to be held on that trust.[26] It is suggested that this latter approach will only be effective where there is, for example, no issue of insolvency and a number of creditors seeking to claim rights in the shares which is greater than the number of shares available to be distributed among them.[27] In relation specifically to money, which might be thought to be the most obvious example of property which is interchangeable, there is a requirement that the fund be segregated within a bank account before any trust can be imposed equal to a liquidated sum held with other moneys in a bank account.[28] Such unenforceability of the trust structure would render ineffective any trust over bonds.[29] This issue was considered in detail in Chapter 21.[30]

This issue is considered in some detail by Tennekoon.[31] The analysis which Tennekoon propounds is that the bond is not the intended trust fund. Standard bond documentation provides that when a bond is sold in the open market both title to the bond and to the coupon stream passes on sale. If the bond were held on trust, then only an equitable interest would be disposed of on sale of the bond.[32] The trust fund is something other than the bundle of rights to receive coupon and

34–28

---

[23] *Re Goldcorp* [1995] 1 A.C. 74; *Re London Wine (Shippers) Ltd* [1986] P.C.C. 121; cf. Goode "Ownership and Obligation in Commercial Transactions", (1987) 103 L.Q.R. 433; Ryan, "Taking Security Over Investment Portfolios held in Global Custody", [1990] 10 J.I.B.L. 404.

[24] *Re Goldcorp* [1995] 1 A.C. 74.

[25] As Benjamin sets out, there is no obligation typically on the depositary to segregate the assets in the manner which English trusts law would appear to require: Benjamin, *The Law on Global Custody* (Butterworths, 1996), p.131. See also Prime, *International Bonds and Certificates of Deposit* (Butterworths, 1990), p.4 et seq. on the role of euro-currencies in this context.

[26] *Hunter v Moss* [1994] 1 W.L.R. 452, [1994] 3 All E.R. 215; see also (1994) 110 L.Q.R. 335. Also possibly *Re Stapylton Fletcher Ltd* [1944] 1 W.L.R. 1181 would be of some support as to the lack of need for segregation, although the case relates only to legal interests in the chattels at issue. See the discussion at paras 22–15 through 22–17 which sets out the position doubting the correctness of this approach.

[27] See *Westdeutsche Landesbank v Islington LBC* [1996] A.C. 669, [1996] 2 All E.R. 961 per Lord Browne-Wilkinson approving the decision in Re Goldcorp.

[28] *Mac-Jordan Construction Ltd v Brookmount Erostin Ltd* [1992] B.C.L.C. 350; *Re Jartray Development Ltd* (1982) 22 B.L.R. 134; *Rayack Construction v Lampeter Meat Constructions Co Ltd* (1979) 12 B.L.R. 30; *Nestle Oy v Lloyds Bank Plc* [1983] 2 Lloyds Rep. 658; *Concorde Constructions Co Ltd v Colgan Ltd* (1984) 29 B.L.R. 120. cf. *Swiss Bank v Lloyds Bank* [1979] 2 All E.R. 853, affirmed [1981] 2 All E.R. 449, whereby a claim to an unsegregated fund might nevertheless give rise to a charge.

[29] See, for a general commercial analysis of this issue Duffett, "Using trusts in international finance and commercial transactions" [1992] Journal of International Planning 23.

[30] See para.21–15.

[31] Tennekoon, *The Law and Regulation of International Finance* (London: Butterworths, 1991), 226 et seq.

[32] Requiring signed writing to effect the transfer: Law of Property Act 1925, s.53(1)(c).

principal which is personified by the bond itself. The issuer (or, borrower) gives an undertaking to pay coupon in the bond documentation both to the investors and to the trustee: that obligation is itself a chose in action which is capable of constituting a trust fund. Under English law there is no objection to constituting a trust fund with such an obligation.[33] There is long-standing authority that covenants in a trust deed can themselves constitute a trust fund.[34]

A structure to circumvent the certainty of subject matter problem

34–29 Given that the practice of the bond market is to issue bonds in the form of entries on a register acknowledging that the beneficiary has a right to one bond out of the total issue of bonds, but not allocating any given bond to any given investor, the best trust structure would be to identify the custodian as being the sole beneficiary under the trust of the claim vested in the eurobond trustee, and in turn to provide that the custodian's entire equitable interest is to be held on trust by the custodian for the investors as an homogenous beneficial class.[35] The chose in action against the registrar can itself be settled on trust, as outlined above. Professor Wood reduces the role of the trustee to that of a financial agent charged with the duty of supervising the issuer (or, keeping the issuer "honest").[36] That is to overlook the extensive rights in relation to breach of trust which a trustee has in this context as against the issuer, over-and-above the contractual rights expressed in the bond documentation, as discussed in Chapter 26. A trustee is a fiduciary responsible for the proper performance of the bond transaction, and not merely a payment agent.

The problem of enforceability

34–30 There is one final issue as to the role of the custodian of the global note as a trustee in itself. A trustee may or may not be appointed in respect of the global note. Further, the custodian may not be expressed to be a trustee and yet appear to have the trappings of a trustee in a jurisdiction where the trust concept is not recognised. The issue as to the enforceability of trustee obligations is therefore a question of the conflict of laws.[37]

---

[33] *Fletcher v Fletcher* (1844) 4 Hare 67; *Don King Promotions v Warren* [1998] 2 All E.R. 608; *Re Dairywise* [2000] 1 All E.R. 320.

[34] *Tomlinson v Gill* (1756). Amb. 330; *Fletcher v Fletcher* (1844) 4 Hare 67; *Lloyd's v Harper* (1880) 16 Ch.D. 290; *Les Affreteurs Reuinis SA v Leopold Walford (London) Ltd* [1919] A.C. 801.

[35] This is subject to the point made in relation to collateralisation in Ch.45 that Clearstream and Euroclear are resident in jurisdictions which do not recognise the legal efficacy of the trust. Therefore, there is the possibility that the bonds are resident in a jurisdiction in which the fiduciary obligations on the custodian are not enforceable. In consequence it appears that the trust will only be enforceable in England and Wales—this requiring a concomitant provision in the bond documentation.

[36] A long-held view: P. Wood, *Law and Practice of International Finance* (London: Clark Boardman, 1981), para.9.12(3)(b). See also P. Wood, *International Loans, Bonds, Guarantees, Legal Opinions*, 168 et seq. See also Tennekoon, *The Law and Regulation of International Finance*, 227.

[37] See A. Hudson, *Equity & Trusts*, s.3.5; Benjamin, *The Law on Global Custody* (Butterworths, 1996), 41 et seq.

D. Typical contractual provisions

Offer documents and prospectuses

The required provisions of a prospectus are set out in Chapter 36 if the issue falls under the FCA's prospectus regulations. If not, then the contents of the prospectus will need to be such as will entice enough investors but will be subject to the general law of tort as considered Chapter 25 generally and with specific reference to negligent misstatements in prospectuses in Chapter 39.

34–31

Transferability

If securities are to be listed, it is a requirement that they must be transferable.[38] From the perspective of an investor, it is a requirement that the bond which is acquired can be sold (and thus transferred) to other investors.

34–32

Negative pledge and pari passu status

The nature of negative pledge clauses is considered in detail in Chapter 19.[39] Briefly put, in relation to bond documents, a negative pledge clause will provide that the issuer will not permit any of its assets to be subject to any form of security right in favour of any other person. The intention is to ensure that the issuer's assets remain available to the bondholders in the event of any failure to perform by the issuer. The principal concern would be that new bonds were issued which would displace the status of the existing bondholders. It is feature of bond documentation that all of the bondholders stand pari passu: that is, no one bondholder is to have any advantage to be paid in advance of any other bondholder. There is also a further sense in which the pari passu clause operates: the bonds are to stand in line with all of the issuer's other unsecured debt obligations. Pari passu clauses are considered in Chapter 19.[40]

34–33

Events of default

The range of occurrences which may constitute events of default in bond documentation are legion: each bond issue will generate its own issues. The purpose of an event of default is to trigger the termination of the agreement between the parties—in this instance, between the bondholders and the issuer, and the trustee if any. The range of events of default in a bond document, however, will include the effect of the issuer's failure to pay any amounts when due, or its admission in writing that it will not be able to pay any amount due under the bond when it becomes due; any deterioration in the credit rating assigned to the bonds by a credit rating agency; any insolvency event relating to the issuer; and any corporate restructuring of the bondholder, especially a takeover of that entity by another entity or a merger with another entity.

34–34

---

[38] Listing Rules, 2.2.4R.
[39] See para.19–61.
[40] See para.19–63.

34–35 A credit rating is assigned to all bond issues by a credit ratings agency (such as Moodys or Standard and Poors) and a downgrade of that rating would only occur after a significant deterioration in the financial condition or prospects of the issuer: therefore, it is usual practice to link the credit rating of the bonds into the credit default language, not least because the credit rating of the bonds will have had a significant effect on the price of the bonds. Corporate restructuring is a difficult issue. The bondholders would be less concerned about the issuer acquiring another, smaller entity and subsuming it within the issuer's operations successfully so as to enhance its business; whereas if the issuer is subsumed into another entity so that it will not honour its bond obligations, then clearly that would constitute a serious problem. Furthermore, the resultant entity might be of a lower credit worth than the original issuer was.

34–36 As is set out below in relation to the *Elektrim* litigation,[41] in that instance the events of default included the presence of a person nominated by the bondholders on the Management Board of the Polish issuer, and any expropriation of property by a governmental, regulatory institution. These are example of events of default which were included because they reflected particular issues which concerned the bondholders about the condition and prospects of that particular issuer: concerns which, it transpired, were well-founded.

34–37 Among other events of default which are frequently included are cross-default and cross-acceleration provisions, as considered in Chapter 19 and in Chapter 32,[42] which provide that any default by the issuer under another specified transaction, or any requirement under any other indebtedness that the issuer should pay its obligations earlier than was otherwise required, would constitute an event of default under the bond document. This issue is considered next.

Acceleration of obligations

34–38 Breach of payment and other covenants under the terms of the bond transaction lead to the issuer being required to make payment earlier than would otherwise have been required by the terms of the parties' agreement (otherwise known as "acceleration of obligations"). The bond documentation, observing the supervisory role of the trustee, gives the eurobond trustee exclusive competence to call for acceleration of the bond obligations in the event of breach of a relevant condition of the agreement. The bond documentation will also provide for a range of obligations in relation to which the eurobond trustee has the discretion to judge whether or not the issuer is in breach. For example, there will be a range of events of default[43] which only cause acceleration of payment obligations if the eurobond trustee considers them to be materially prejudicial to the interests of the investors. Therefore, the eurobond trustee's role as arbiter between the parties may be an essential one. However, once accelerated payments are recovered from the issuer,

---

[41] See para.33–36; [2005] EWHC 1999 (Ch.).

[42] See para.19–49.

[43] Typically based on preventing the issuer from pledging prescribed assets as security for other obligations when they were to be retained solely to provide security for the bond transaction at issue.

those payments are necessarily held on trust by the eurobond trustee for the investors in accordance with their proportionate equitable intrests.

A case law example of the enforcement of events of default in bond documentation

A bondholder argued for acceleration of payment obligations in *Law Debenture Trust Corporation v Elektrim Finance BV*[44] in which case it was alleged that an event of default had taken place. The mechanics for the relevant events of default were that bondholders constituting owners in the aggregate of 30 per cent of the bonds in issue could give notice to the trustee and that the trustee in turn was empowered to notify the issuer and the issuer's guarantor that the redemption amount on the bond (that is, the full amount to be paid by the issuer in repayment of all of its obligations to the bondholders) was accelerated so that it was to be paid immediately. Among the conditions of the agreement were that the bondholders would have two nominees on the management board of the issuer, but one of those nominees was dismissed from that board, purportedly triggering an event of default. It had already been held in earlier litigation by Smith J. that this constituted material prejudice to the position of the bondholders—because the purpose of the contractual provision was to enable the bondholders to participate in the management of the issuer—such that the trustee was able at that time to issue a notice that an event of default had been committed.[45] Hart J. concurred with the analysis of Smith J. and therefore held that the acceleration of obligations event of default could be enforced by the bondholders. There were other events of default at issue, relating to an expropriation of property by the Polish tax authorities and a failure to make payments of coupon in a timely manner, both of which were upheld on the facts. A further event of default would be triggered if a petition for bankruptcy had been lodged, in that case, under Polish law: on the facts it was found that such a filing had taken place so that the trustee could rely on it.[46]

34–39

Enforcement proceedings

Competence to bring enforcement proceedings generally under the terms of the bond documentation is vested solely in the eurobond trustee. It is significant that the documentation will vest this competence in the trustee whereas an alternative analysis of the structure (in the absence of the usual specific documentary provision to the contrary) would be that the investor has a straightforward right in contract and in specific performance to enforce the issuer's payment obligations. The restriction of these rights to the exclusive competence of the eurobond trustee would appear to be akin to an express contractual agreement to take disputes to arbitration and not to go to court. However, it would appear right in principle that the eurobond trustee would hold this power to bring enforcement

34–40

---

[44] [2005] EWHC 1999 (Ch.).
[45] [2004] EWHC 270 (Ch.).
[46] cf. *Martyn Rose Ltd v AKG Group* [2003] EWCA Civ 375; [2003] 2 B.C.L.C. 102, in which a petition was improperly presented.

proceedings on trust for the investors. Therefore, it would seem clear that the investors could force the trustee to bring enforcement proceedings.

3. BONDS OFFERED TO THE PUBLIC OR LISTED

34–41   Bonds are securities and therefore fall within securities law as considered in Part X of this book. There are many types of investor which cannot be reached by limited offers made to small groups of expert financial institutions—not just ordinary members of the public but in many jurisdictions there are entities such as pension funds and investment funds which are prevented by law from investing in securities which are not listed or which have not been granted the appropriate regulatory approvals to be offered to the public. Any offer in the EU which is made to the public or which relates to securities which are intended to be admitted to trading on a regulated market must have a prospectus in approved form prepared and authorised and published before any offer takes place[47]; and if those securities are to be listed in the EU then the listing regulations apply. This is a large amount of regulatory compliance which is necessary to access a wider investor market than would otherwise be the case.

34–42   In an application for listing of debt securities, the applicant must lodge the required documents at least two business days prior to the FCA hearing the listing application.[48] These required documents include an application for listing in prescribed form,[49] and the prospectus must have been approved by the FCA.[50] On the day of the application the applicant must also produce a copy of the board resolution authorising the issue of the securities or written confirmation that the board has authorised the issue of the securities.[51] The issuer is required to keep copies of documents relating to the issue for six years after admission to listing: including any documents mentioned in the prospectus, any agreement to acquire assets in consideration for an issue of securities, the applicant's constitution at the date of issue, the annual report and accounts referred to in the prospectus, the last interim accounts prior to the date of admission, and any temporary or definitive documents of title.[52] An applicant may be required to produce those documents to the FCA if requested to do so.[53] The key principles relating to applications in general are considered in Chapters 36 and 37.

4. COVERED BONDS

34–43   The regulation of covered bonds is conducted by the FCA further to the Regulated Covered Bonds Regulations 2008.[54] A covered bond" is a bond in relation to which the right to be paid is "guaranteed to be paid by an owner from

---

[47] Financial Services and Markets Act 2000, s.85.
[48] Listing Rules, Ch.3, para.3.4.3R.
[49] Listing Rules, Ch.3, para.3.4.4(1)R.
[50] Listing Rules, Ch.3, para.3.4.4(2)R.
[51] Listing Rules, Ch.3, para.3.4.5R.
[52] Listing Rules, Ch.3, para.3.4.6R.
[53] Listing Rules, Ch.3, para.3.4.6R.
[54] SI 2008/346.

an asset pool it owns".[55] The FCA is required to maintain a register of issuers and a register of covered bonds.[56] An issuer of covered bonds must apply for admission to that register and if it does then it may not issue (nor purport to issue) covered bonds.[57] Furthermore, the asset pool must be maintained and administered in accordance with the record-keeping requirements of the regulations and so as to ensure that the asset pool is "of sufficient quality to give investors confidence that in the event of the failure of the issuer there will be a low risk of default in the timely payment of claims attaching to the bond".[58] What is interesting about this last requirement is that there is no requirement to ensure that the asset pool does in fact cover those obligations but rather is limited to giving investors confidence that that might be the case, which is a very different thing.

---

[55] SI 2008/346, reg.1.
[56] SI 2008/346, reg.7.
[57] SI 2008/346, reg.15.
[58] SI 2008/346, reg.17(2)(d).

PART X

STAKEHOLDING

This Part X considers the principles which govern the acquisition of investment stakes in companies and in governments by means of buying securities—principally shares and bonds—issued by those entities. Thus investors acquire a "stake" in the issuing entity either in the form of a share (as discussed in Chapter 4), or in the form of a bond which entitles the investor to a cash flow from the company. If the investor has a share then the investor has a stake in the form of ownership rights in the company if the company is wound up and voting rights, but more importantly has a right to a dividend (if one is declared) or to sell the share if she chooses; whereas the investor in a bond issue has a right to interest and to sell the bond, but no other right to ownership of part of the company. In either case, the investor has a "stake" in the performance of the company or other entity issuing the security. Chapter 37 sets out the principles of general law and of securities regulation which underpin this very important area of financial practice. Securities transactions create contracts between the issuer and subscriber for securities, and between people who buy and sell securities on the open market. Importantly, the prospectus which is required for most securities issues contains many representations which underpin those sale contracts. The specific financial techniques discussed in this Part X therefore build on the foundational legal concepts considered in Pts IV through VII of this book relating to contract and tort law in particular. Securities markets are a means for companies and governments to raise capital either from the public or from specialist, professional investors without using ordinary loans, as considered in the previous Part IX.

CHAPTER 35

THE FUNDAMENTALS OF UK SECURITIES LAW

CORE PRINCIPLES

Sources of UK securities law

UK securities law is based on a combination of EC securities directives (implemented into UK securities law by various Acts, statutory instruments and regulatory rulebooks discussed below), Financial Conduct Authority ("FCA") regulation in the *FCA Handbook*, and the general law of England and Wales (for the purposes of this book). This chapter explains the general principles on which securities regulation operates, before later chapters in this Part X fill in the regulatory detail.

The policies underpinning the EC directives

The underlying purpose of securities law is to regulate the provision of information through securities markets. The principal policies of the EC directives are to create a single market for securities in the EU; to permit issues of securities which have been authorised in one Member State to be deemed authorised in all Member States of the EU as though they had a "passport"; and to provide a liquid pool of capital across the EU. These policies are considered in detail in this chapter. The underlying policies of EU financial services legislation were set out in Chapter 7. Also of importance are the directives on market abuse and accounting practice.

Prospectus regulation

At the heart of securities law is the following rule in s.85 of the FSMA 2000. A prospectus in prescribed form must be authorised and published in relation to any issues of securities which are either to be offered to the public or in relation to which admission to trading on a regulated market is sought; other issues of securities do not require such a prospectus, although very few issues will fall outside this requirement unless they fall within one of the specific statutory exemptions. The regulatory focus is therefore on securities which are offered to the public, as opposed to private sales of securities or offers of securities which are limited to professional investors. Breach of the requirement in s.85 is a criminal offence. This is provided for by the amended Part 6 of the FSMA 2000, which implemented the EC Prospectus Directive. The FCA regulates prospectuses by means of the "Prospectus Rules". These regulations are considered in detail in Chapter 36.

Transparency obligations

Once securities are in issue there are requirements in prescribed cases for the issuing company to make information public about the people who have voting control as shareholders over it, and about the people who control those shareholders; and also to make public identified types of financial information about the company's performance. These rules are known as "transparency obligations" and are created further to Part 43 of the Companies Act 2006, which implemented the EC Transparency Obligations Directive. The FCA regulates transparency obligations through the Disclosure and Transparency Rules ("DTR"). These regulations are considered in detail in Chapter 36.

Listed securities

There is an important sub-set of securities regulations relating to "listed" securities; which are generally-speaking the securities in the largest public companies which are entered on the "Official List" maintained by the FCA. In this context the FCA is acting as the "UK Listing Authority" ("UKLA"), that is the "competent authority" for the purposes of the EC Consolidated Admissions and Reporting Directive. Listed securities have their own regulatory treatment over and above prospectus and disclosure and transparency rules in the UKLA Listing Rules. These regulations are considered in detail in Chapters 37 and 39.

Private companies may not offer securities to the public

Private companies are prohibited from offering their securities to the public. Therefore, this chapter relates only to public companies.

1. INTRODUCTION

A. Securities law within the law more generally

The components of securities law: securities regulation and the general law

35–01   "Securities law" as it is defined in this book is a fusion of securities regulation, of statutes aimed specifically at securities transactions, and of the general law of England and Wales as it relates to securities transactions. It is a topic which I analysed in detail in my book *Securities Law*.[1] Securities law is part of the law of finance in that the general principles underpinning financial services regulation in the UK also underpin securities regulation. So, all of the high-level principles discussed in Chapter 8 and in subsequent chapters apply to securities, such as the requirement that regulated firms act with "integrity", conduct of business regulation, financial promotion regulation, and market abuse regulation.

35–02   There are then regulations which apply specifically to securities transactions, which are referred to in this book as "*securities regulation*". Therefore, securities regulation can be thought of as a sub-set of *financial regulation* in that it is governed, first, by general financial regulation and, secondly, specifically by regulation applying specifically to securities markets. Securities regulation, as it is defined in this section of this book, is a system of rules derived ultimately from a group of EC securities directives (as set out below in relation to "The Sources of Securities Law") that govern the manner in which securities may be offered to the public or admitted to trading on regulated markets in the European Union, and the information which must be provided by the issuer and its professional advisors at the time of issue and on a continuing basis thereafter. These principles create "securities regulations" whereby the competent authority in each member state of the European Union is responsible for the regulation of offers of securities to the public in the manner described below.[2] Securities regulation can therefore be thought of as a tier of regulation which takes the general principles of financial regulation (such as the Markets in Financial Instruments Directive ("MiFID") and the Principles for Business rulebook) and applies them in a particular context, in common with regulations which have been prepared specifically for the context of securities transactions.

Securities law is not only made up of securities regulation, however, but rather is also comprised of the general law of England and Wales, and also some statutes enacted specifically to deal with securities transactions (such as the criminalisation of insider dealing by the Criminal Justice Act 1993, discussed in Chapter 14). In *Section One: General Principles* of this book, our focus was on those parts of the substantive law—principally contract law, tort law and equity—which apply to securities, and also the general principles of financial regulation applying to financial services business generally. While there are key cases in English general law which have dealt specifically with securities transactions, the bulk of the

---

[1] A.S. Hudson, *Securities Law*, 2nd edn (London: Sweet & Maxwell, 2013).
[2] See para.35–27 et seq.

general law does not deal with securities transactions specifically, and therefore the concepts of general law must be translated to the securities law context as with any other contextual analysis of English law.[3] Nevertheless, there are aspects of private law liability which are specific to securities business, having been created by the Financial Services and Markets Act 2000 ("FSMA 2000").[4] The securities regulation considered in relation to securities are set out in the next section.

B. The purpose of securities regulation in a nutshell

The regulation of securities markets is in fact the regulation of information. Securities markets are "markets" in that the participants in those markets are required to make their own choices about their investments; no regulator promises to protect them from their own stupidity nor their own bad luck. However, there is a problem in financial markets in that some investors clearly have more expertise, better information[5] and a stronger bargaining position than others. An investment bank is better able to make investment decisions than an ordinary member of public with no experience of financial markets. Therefore, the role of securities regulation is to ensure that all market participants have access to the same base level of information; and it is also to ensure that when an expert deals with an inexpert investor that expert must deal with that inexpert investor appropriately by providing her with suitable information and explaining all of the risks which such a person would need to understand. There is no promise that the inexpert investor will be protected from loss. All that is promised is that the inexpert investor will be given the information necessary to make her own informed choices. So, prospectus regulation specifies the level and type of information which must be made public by a person issuing securities; conduct of business regulation specifies how sellers must treat different categories of customer (ranging from the expert to the inexpert); transparency regulation specifies the types of information which issuers of securities must make available to the market; financial promotion regulation prevents inappropriate marketing information being circulated; and market abuse regulation prevents "inside information" from being misused to make unfair gains for some at the expense of others. These markets are also markets in the sense that in all markets some people gain and some people lose; all that finance law will do is to specify a minimum level of fair dealing that is required of all regulated market participants.

35–03

---

[3] Securities regulation, however, as distinct from the general law relating to securities, applies to the entire United Kingdom as a result of its derivation from the law of the EU.

[4] For example, s.90 and s.90A FSMA 2000, as considered at para.37–36 et seq.

[5] Both in the sense of greater expertise and access to a greater range of information sources, as well as greater skill in analysing that information.

2.   An Outline of Securities Law

A.   The purpose of this summary

35–04   This short section gives a very short, potted account of the principal aspects of securities law which are discussed in this book: it is hoped that this summary will serve as a map through the thicket of the law and regulation which can otherwise seem almost impenetrable to the novice. It is suggested that such a reader begin with this summary and then follow the pathways into the more detailed chapters which follow. Some jargon is used in this summary but those terms are considered in greater detail below, so it is suggested that the novice reader tries first to grasp the lie of the land before worrying about detail: the detail is considered in the chapters to follow.

B.   Offers of securities to the public and the requirement for prospectuses

35–05   Securities law relates to the issue of any and all types of security: shares, bonds, securitized derivatives, and so forth. Securities may be issued to the public generally or they may be issued to a smaller, private class of investors. Most regulation is concerned with issues of securities to the public, and that is the principal focus of this chapter. A distinction must be made between "public companies" and "private companies", where public companies have their shares issued to the public (and therefore are governed by the appropriate regulations) and private companies whose shares are not available to the public and not quoted on any regulated market. Private companies are prohibited from offering their shares to the public.[6] A "private company" is defined as being a company which is "not a public company".[7] Consequently, the bulk of the topic of securities law is related to trading in the securities issued by public companies, and therefore that will be the principal focus of this Part X.

35–06   When a public company wishes either to offer its securities to the public or to request the admission of its securities to trading on a regulated market, then a prospectus must be prepared, authorised by the Financial Conduct Authority ("FCA") and published further to s.85 of the Financial Services and Markets Act 2000 ("FSMA 2000").[8] The obligations relating to the form and content of that prospectus are set out in the FCA's Prospectus Rules contained in the *FCA Handbook* ("the Prospectus Rules"), as discussed in detail in Chapter 36. Failure to comply with s.85 is a criminal offence. If a public company wishes to have its securities admitted to the "Official List" (which comprises the securities of the most significant public companies, and which therefore has both an extra regulatory burden and a concomitant marketing advantage) which is maintained by the FCA when acting in its capacity as the UK Listing Authority ("UKLA"),

---

[6] Companies Act 2006, s.755.
[7] Companies Act 2006, s.4(1).
[8] Financial Services and Markets Act 2000, s.85.

then it must comply with the UKLA's Listing Rules ("Listing Rules"). If securities are to be listed then those securities must also be admitted to trading on a regulated market.

C. The obligation to make disclosure in the prospectus, under transparency regulation, and in relation to listed securities

The prospectus must comply with the general duty of disclosing all information which is "necessary" for an investor to make an "informed assessment" about whether or not to buy those securities, further to s.87A of FSMA 2000. Prospectuses therefore relate to issues of securities and the information which must be made available to the investing public. Once securities have been issued, there are then transparency obligations which require the publication of information about voting control of the issuer and about the financial condition of the issuer while those securities are in issue. The prospectus and transparency rules are considered in Chapter 36. If the issuer chooses to have its securities admitted to the Official List, then there are a number of obligations to provide information when applying for admission to that list and also continuing obligations necessary to maintain that listing, as dictated by the Listing Rules which are discussed in detail in Chapters 37 and 39.

35–07

D. Market abuse

Securities law also contains a range of regulation to do with "market abuse". In this regard there are criminal offences connected to insider dealing and other offences connected to making a false market in securities, as were discussed in detail in Chapter 14. The FCA also has powers to impose "penalties" in relation to market abuse connected to dealing with "inside information", as was discussed in Chapter 12. The Listing Rules also contain a code on market conduct which prohibits dealing with inside information. The common objectives of these regulations are to maintain the integrity of the market in the eyes of the investing public and to ensure that contracts between buyers and sellers of securities are conducted on an equal footing.

35–08

3. THE SOURCES OF SECURITIES LAW

Securities regulation is built on the architecture designed by the Lamfalussy process, discussed in Chapter 7,[9] whereby Directives are used at the EU level to create high-level, framework principles so as to allow the EU's legislature to respond more nimbly to market change than would be possible if the Directives contained all of the technical detail. Then the other tiers of the Lamfalussy architecture create the detailed regulations and oversee the stability of those structures. (The Lamfalussy process and its regulatory structure have been replaced by the reforms considered in Chapter 7 further to the Larosière

35–09

---

[9] See para.7–16.

Report[10]—however, the Directives created under the Lamfalussy process still remain in effect.) The regulation of securities markets in the UK is based on the EC securities directives, which set out the framework principles on which FCA *securities regulation* is built.[11] Those directives are supplemented by the Commission's technical regulations, which fill in the technical details. These directives were then implemented into UK securities law through Part 6 of FSMA 2000 (as amended by subsequent legislation), by various items of secondary legislation introduced under FSMA 2000,[12] and by means of the FCA's securities regulations contained in the *FCA Handbook*. The principal UK regulations of interest in this context are the Listing Rules, the Prospectus Rules, and the Disclosure and Transparency Rules, each of which is explained below.

35–10   Beyond the *securities regulations*, properly so-called, are the broader range of FCA *financial regulations* dealing principally with the regulation of the conduct of business (as updated by MiFID); advertisement of financial instruments by way of financial promotion; the control of market abuse (derived from the Market Abuse Directive); and the core principles governing the proper behaviour of financial services businesses. These areas of regulation are important to securities law but, because they have already been considered in detail in Part III of this book, they are only referred to specifically in relation to securities regulation in this Part X of this book when a particularly significant issue relating to them arises.

35–11   Securities law as a whole is then rounded out with the general law dealing with issues as diverse as misrepresentations in offering documents, the fiduciary duties of some participants in securities transactions, remedies for loss at common law, rights to recover property or to recover loss in equity, conflict of laws, and the many criminal offences relating to securities transactions including insider dealing, market manipulation, theft, fraud and so forth. Those general issues were also dealt with severally in *Section One: General Principles* of this book, and are discussed in this Part X only as necessary in relation specifically to securities law.

4.   EU SECURITIES REGULATION

A.   The historical development of EC securities regulation

35–12   The development of securities regulation in the EU was considered in Chapter 7. In essence, there had been a perception in the old European Economic Community that a large obstacle to the economic development of the Community was the absence of a single market for capital. Therefore, the Community sought to develop a single market for capital by breaking down the barriers between Member States by means of harmonising those separate regulatory codes. The beginnings of a serious legislative movement towards the modernisation of

---

[10] See para.7–55.
[11] See para.34–20.
[12] In particular the Prospectus Regulations 2005 (SI 2005/1433), repealing earlier statutory instruments, and The Financial Services and Markets Act 2000 (Market Abuse) Regulations 2005 (SI 2005/381).

securities regulations in the Community can be identified in the Investment Services Directive of 1993[13] ("ISD"),[14] but the ISD could not keep pace with the rate of change in securities markets.[15] It required the Financial Services Action Plan ("FSAP") of 1999[16] to reinvigorate the legislative agenda.

The so-called "Committee of Wise Men", chaired by Belgian central banker Baron Alexandre Lamfalussy, produced a final report in February 2001 (known as "the Lamfalussy Report") which, inter alia, suggested a new methodology for the creation of EC directives in the securities field. The Lamfalussy process comprised four levels of legislation, namely: framework principles, implementing measures, cooperation, and enforcement. The key to this methodology was to simplify the principal legislation in the form of high-level directives which set out the general, framework principles on which regulation was to be based, with the inclusion of more detailed rules in Technical Regulations to be published by the Commission.

35–13

However, as explained in Chapter 7,[17] the structure for EU regulation has been changed in the wake of the financial crisis 2007–09 and as suggested by the Larosière Report to stiffen the sinews of the regulatory process. The approach taken in the Lamfalussy process has similarly been set aside for the future in favour of a system which uses Regulations to create, ultimately, a single rulebook across the entire EU, instead of a patchwork quilt of high-level principles set out in Directives which are implemented differently in different Member States. The current securities regulations were created under the Lamfalussy process.

35–14

B.   The policy underpinning EC securities regulation

Harmonising capital markets and ensuring investor protection

The securities directives have developed the following principal policy objectives. First, the creation of efficient markets so that companies are able to access liquid capital by means of issuing securities and so that there are securities markets available to investors. Secondly, to ensure investor protection in these securities markets. To this end, the implementation of MiFID effected widespread changes in conduct of business regulation across the EU.[18] These policy objectives are based on two assumptions. First, a perception that the securities markets in the EU are too fragmented. Secondly, a determination embodied in the

35–15

---

[13] Directive 93/22/EEC [1993] OJ L141/27.
[14] This directive has since been superseded by the Markets in Financial Instruments Directive 2004.
[15] This directive has now been displaced by MiFID, as implemented in 2007. The ISD was created after a long period of time but failed to anticipate the rise of the derivatives markets in the 1990's. Market practice since the passage of the ISD in 1993 saw an explosion in the electronic trading of securities, great developments in trading platforms operated off-exchange, the growth of over-the-counter derivatives and securitisation products, and a large number of securities-related corporate governance scandals. Consequently, the markets changed rapidly very soon after the implementation of the ISD.
[16] COM(1999) 232.
[17] para.7–55.
[18] See para.3.60.

Financial Services Action Plan that the different strands of securities regulation practised previously in each separate Member State across the EU required harmonisation. What is at issue is the manner in which this objective of harmonisation has been pursued. Let us be clear about what it does not mean. The general law which may affect securities markets—such as contract law, tort law, fiduciary law, and so forth—is not to be harmonized in this process: therefore, the contract law of each Member State will remain idiosyncratically the contract law of each Member State, and so on. Rather, it is the regulation of securities by the competent regulatory authority of each Member State which is to be harmonised; and other issues—such as the criminalisation of insider dealing and the provision of a right to compensation in certain circumstances—which have been required by EC directives (as considered in this Part III). In relation to those matters which are to be harmonised, however, there are questions as to the extent to which there has actually been any harmonisation at all. This question requires a little attention.

35–16   The word "harmonisation" could mean either "equalisation", in the sense of making all of the securities regulation of each Member State exactly the same; or merely "approximation", in the sense of bringing those securities regulations closer together without needing to make them identical. Thus far, the EU has only achieved "approximation" through the establishment of minimum standards of regulation across the EU precisely because the securities directives grant Member States the power to create more stringent rules than are contained in the directives. However, with the detail of the Commission's Technical Regulations it is not only at the framework level that EC securities regulation has been brought closer together across the EU. In the Consolidated Admission and Reporting Directive ("CARD") the legislative objective is to promote the "co-ordination" of the securities laws of member states, as opposed to requiring their "harmonisa-tion". The municipal implementation of the directive in Member States requires the implementation of minimum standards, as opposed to the equalization of standards. Thus CARD's implementation takes account of "present differences in the structures of securities markets in Member States"[19] so as to enable member states to take into account "any specific situations with which they may be confronted"[20]; and so "co-ordination should first be limited to the establishment of minimum conditions".[21] The means by which the competent authorities of Member States give effect to the Transparency Obligations Directive can be "subject to requirements more stringent than those laid down" in the Directive.[22] This process of imposing more stringent requirements is known colloquially in the markets as "gold-plating".

35–17   So, it is difficult to harmonise securities regulations across the EU when the power granted to Member States in the directives themselves to make their own regulations more stringent than the base level identified in those directives. This means, for example, that the regulatory approach in the Republic of Ireland is different from that in the UK. The approach in the Republic of Ireland is to

---

[19] CARD, recital 5.
[20] CARD, recital 5.
[21] CARD, recital 6.
[22] Transparency Obligations Directive, art.4(1).

implement the directives by means of lengthy statutory instruments (of about 120 pages[23]), which are created further to powers contained in principal legislation (the Investment Funds Companies and Miscellaneous Provisions Act 2005), where it is those statutory instruments which contain all of the principal regulatory rules which are generally taken verbatim from the EC directives and then supplemented by comparatively brief rules and guidance notes published by Ireland's Financial Regulator. In the UK, by contrast, there are enabling powers in the FSMA 2000 and brief statutory instruments (typically only about 20 pages, such as the Prospectus Regulations 2005) granting powers to the FCA to create rules, whereby the FCA is then responsible for the maintenance of very, very detailed rulebooks which are hundreds of pages long and which form a casserole of rules, guidance notes, verbatim quotes from EC directives and UK legislation, verbatim reproduction of the detailed Commission technical regulations, and also a number of detailed instances in which UK regulation is more stringent or demanding than the directives require. The precise wording between many key provisions is also slightly different in the UK and in the Republic of Ireland, which may be surprising given that they are based on the same English translation of the EC directives, albeit that they are directed at the same general regulatory objectives.

Passporting issues of securities

Rather than require that all securities regulations across the EU are equal, what has been provided for instead in the securities directives is that an issue of securities which has been authorised in one Member State can be taken to be authorised in any other Member State. This is known as "passporting" the securities issue by granting those securities, in effect, a passport so that they can move throughout the EU. This became the key means by which a single market for securities was to be effected, and as such still underpins the Directives currently in force; although this is not the same as having a single market for securities which operates identically in all jurisdictions because it recognises the separateness of each Member State but allows issuers and issues to be offered to the public across borders. Thus, the distinction between the laws of different Member States remains, although their securities regulations are required to have the same minimum standards. However, the ability of jurisdictions to "gold-plate" their regulations means that, for example, admission to trading in one jurisdiction may be more demanding than admission to trading in another jurisdiction. Significantly, however, no discrimination can be permitted between the way in which any given jurisdiction deals with applications for authorisation between issues originating in its own jurisdiction or issues seeking to be passported in from another jurisdiction.

35–18

---

[23] e.g. the Irish Prospectus (Directive 2003/71/EC) Regulations 2005.

The macroeconomic policy underpinning securities regulation; and the importance of information

35–19   Securities regulation in the EU is based on macroeconomic objectives to do with the development of a viable, single market for securities which is understood by potential investors as protecting their interests. The enthusiasm for a single capital market is itself predicated on a perception that a viable, liquid market for capital without obstacles will encourage economic activity. These underlying assumptions are made clear in the directives. For example, in the first recital to the Transparency Obligations Directive 2004 it is provided that:

> "Efficient, transparent and integrated securities markets contribute to a genuine single market ... foster growth and job creation by better allocation of capital and by reducing costs. The disclosure of accurate, comprehensive and timely information ... builds sustained investor confidence and allows an informed assessment of their business performance and assets. This enhances both investor protection and market efficiency."

These goals are to be achieved by means of "transparency for investors through a regular flow of information",[24] whilst communicating with investors who own shares with voting rights about changes in the company's major holdings. The requirement for proper information to be provided to investors is considered in Chapter 36 *Prospectuses and transparency obligations* in relation respectively to the regulatory requirement that a prospectus in approved form accompanies any issue of securities (so that minimum levels of information are made available to the market) and to the requirement that issuing companies make enough information known to the market as to who owns controlling interests in its securities. It is through "harmonisation" of regulations dealing with these species of information that it is expected that an appropriate level of protection of those investors can be maintained.[25] The removal of barriers within and between Member States relating to issues of securities is to be effected by displacing national rules with Community-wide rules.[26]

C.   The six EC Directives relating to securities

35–20   There are six EC Directives which are of relevance to public issues of securities. First, the Consolidated Admission and Reporting Directive of 2001[27] which consolidates, as its name suggests, the principles in an earlier slew of directives. Secondly, the Prospectus Directive[28] which was implemented by the Prospectus Regulations 2005 and ultimately by means of the new prospectus rules which were effected by the old Financial Services Authority as of July 1, 2005, with that responsibility passing to the FCA on April Fool's Day 2013. Thirdly, the Transparency Obligations Directive[29] which was implemented in the UK in 2007

---

[24] Transparency Obligations Directive, recital 2.
[25] Transparency Obligations Directive, recital 5.
[26] Transparency Obligations Directive, recital 9.
[27] 2001/34/EC.
[28] Directive 2003/71/EC (2003) OJ L345.
[29] Directive 2004/109/EC (2004) OJ L390.

by Part 43 of the Companies Act 2006. These three directives are referred to here as the "securities directives", and are considered in outline in turn in the following sections. The two other directives relate to financial matters more generally but they have great bearing on securities markets. Fourthly, then, is the Market Abuse Directive, dealing with inside information and so forth, implemented in 2005; and, fifthly, the International Accounting Standards Directive, implemented in 2005 relating to the form of accounting information provided by companies. Finally, MiFID, as discussed in Chapter 7,[30] governs the whole of financial services activity. It would worthwhile first to consider the development in principle of the EC legislation in this context, given that the recent directives were developed as a result of recent policy developments.[31] Each directive is considered in turn.

D.   The Consolidated Admissions and Reporting Directive

The structure of CARD

The Consolidated Admissions and Reporting Directive[32] ("CARD") consolidated the four earlier "listing directives" (the Admission Directive,[33] the Listing Particulars Directive,[34] and the Interim Reports Directive[35]; as well as, effectively, the provisions of the later Public Offers Directive[36]). CARD itself has been amended by a number of later EC securities directives, principally to reflect the new focus on the regulation and publication of prospectuses.[37] Not all issues of securities are covered by CARD. Rather, CARD is limited to "admission to official listing on a stock exchange",[38] as opposed to private offerings or issues of securities in general terms outside the official list.[39]

35–21

---

[30] See para.2–37 et seq.

[31] A very full discussion of these developments is provided by N. Moloney, *EC Securities Regulation* (OUP, 2002), pp.1 53.

[32] 2001/34/EC. Hereafter "CARD".

[33] 79/279/EEC of March 5, 1979 "co-ordinating the conditions for the admission of securities to official stock exchange listing".

[34] 80/390/EEC of March 17, 1980 "co-ordinating the requirements for the drawing up, scrutiny and distribution of the listing particulars to be published for the admission of securities to official stock exchange listing". This Directive was latterly amended by the following Council Directives: No.82/148/EEC; No.87/345/EEC; No.90/211/EEC, the latter two relating to mutual recognition) and No.94/18/EC (extending the scope of art.6).

[35] 82/121/EEC of February 15, 1985 "on information to be published on a regular basis by companies the shares of which have been admitted to official stock exchange listing".

[36] Directive 89/298 of April 17, 1989 [1989] OJ L124/8, known colloquially as the "POD".

[37] Principally 2003/6/EC; 2003/71/EC; 2004/109/EC, and 2005/1/EC, as considered in the text to follow.

[38] CARD, art.1(a) and art.2.

[39] The transposition of these principles to UK securities regulation is considered in para.34–17.

The co-ordination objective

35–22   CARD takes account of "present differences in the structures of securities markets in Member States"[40] so as to enable member states to take into account "any specific situations with which they may be confronted".[41] Thus "co-ordination should first be limited to the establishment of minimum conditions"[42]: so there is no objective of making all laws the same, but rather ensuring that they are based on a minimum level of regulation in all Member States that would permit the movement of approvals to be passported in time between Member States. The directive is concerned to achieve "closer alignment" of national regulatory rules,[43] through a "first step" which led to the Prospectus Directive and the Transparency Directive. One of the principal misalignments between different national systems of securities regulations are the "safeguards" for investor protection in those different codes. CARD is intended to eliminate them by "coordinating the [various national] rules and regulations" without necessarily making them completely uniform.[44]

The detailed policies: passporting and investor protection in CARD

35–23   There are two underlying policies in CARD beyond the co-ordination of laws. First, mutual recognition in all Member States of any authorised listing of securities in the issuer's home Member State.[45] This is the "passport" granted to such securities which enables a security admitted to listing in Member State *x* to be admitted to listing as a result in Member State *y*. Secondly, "to ensure that sufficient information is provided for investors".[46] The provision of information is to be achieved by making accounts available, principally by means of making annual reports and other information available to investors, with some exceptions in relation to debentures.

35–24   There were three results which were expected to flow from the implementation of CARD. First, the improvement of investor protection. This was intended principally to arise from issuers being required to make information available to investors. Secondly, an increase in investor confidence, principally by virtue of requiring issuers of listed securities to bear continuing obligations to provide identified classes of information to the investing public and so reassuring investors about the efficacy of the information available to them. Thirdly, ensuring that securities markets function correctly. As for the more general viability of the mooted pan-European market in securities, CARD provides that its expectation "by making [investor] protection more equivalent" is that "coordination of that policy at community level is likely to make for greater

---

[40] CARD, recital 5.
[41] CARD, recital 5.
[42] CARD, recital 6.
[43] CARD, recital 7.
[44] CARD, recitals 9 to 11.
[45] CARD, recital 13.
[46] CARD, recital 21.

inter-penetration" of securities markets.[47] That is, by generating a greater equivalence between national securities regulations it is hoped that issuers and investors will be prepared to act across borders within the EU.

The detailed provisions of CARD still in effect in relation to admission of securities to official listing are discussed in detail in Chapter 37.[48]

E. The Prospectus Directive

The general purpose behind the Prospectus Directive 2003

The Prospectus Directive is concerned with the approval of a prospectus by the competent authority in any given Member State prior to the admission of securities to listing and to the admission of securities to trading on a regulated market. The Prospectus Directive creates the core principles on which the UK Prospectus Rules are based. The Prospectus Directive was implemented in the United Kingdom by amendment to the FSMA 2000, which was done by means of a statutory instrument known as the "Prospectus Regulations 2005",[49] and by the creation of the Prospectus Rules. The Prospectus Rules also implemented the Commission technical regulations in relation to this Directive. The detail of prospectus regulation under these various instruments is considered in Chapter 36.

35–25

In short the Prospectus Directive furthers the over-arching policy objective of creating a single internal market for the EU.[50] The directive's particular objective is to co-ordinate earlier directives and to replace those earlier directives so as to achieve the single passport for securities issues.[51] The rules relating to the requirement for and publication of prospectuses are concerned with the minimum contents of the prospectus which is to be published when securities are to be offered to the public or are to be admitted to trading on a regulated market (such as the London Stock Exchange), to facilitate the mutual recognition of prospectuses so that issues of securities can be offered to the investing public across the EU, and thus to facilitate the creation of a viable Europe-wide securities market with (as the bureaucratic metaphor has it) "deep, liquid pools of capital". Each of these facets is considered in outline below.

35–26

The single passport regime within the Prospectus Directive

The Prospectus Directive[52] was as an "instrument essential to the achievement of the internal market" as part of the Risk Capital Action Plan. This move towards the internal market is to be effected in part by the provision of a single passport to each issue of securities so that its authorisation by the competent authority in one

35–27

---

[47] CARD, recital 32.
[48] See para.11–03.
[49] SI 2005/1433.
[50] PD, recital (4).
[51] PD, recital (1).
[52] 2003/71/EC.

Member State shall be recognised in all other Member States.[53] The "country of origin" principle, has the effect that, in relation to an offer of securities which is to be made across borders within the EU, the regulator from the issuer's home Member State is the one best placed to regulate that issue.[54]

The definition of the "public offer of securities"

35–28   Among the problems identified by the Lamfalussy Report which are addressed by the Prospectus Directive is the lack of a common definition of the term "public offer of securities" across the EU.[55] The directive also encompasses a wider scope of "securities" than hitherto, including cash-settled securities (such as equity derivatives) generally, covered warrants and non-equity securities. The requirement that the securities are intended to be admitted to trading on a regulated market may cover issues of securities which are not intended to be offered to the public. Thus, even a private placement of shares will fall within the requirements of the directive if those shares are to be admitted to trading on a regulated market. This is a significant broadening of the principles contained in the previous listing regime because it is not concerned solely with issues offered to the public generally but rather it is concerned to protect the integrity of all regulated markets whether or not the securities are not offered to the public initially. There are exempt categories of issue—such as issues which are not to be admitted to a regulated market and which are made to fewer than 100 people or which are comprised of high denomination securities –as discussed in Chapter 36

The publication requirements under the Prospectus Directive

35–29   A prospectus must be approved and published before an offer is made to the public or before a request is made to admit securities to trading on a regulated market. These requirements are considered in Chapter 36.

Enhancement of investor protection under the Prospectus Directive

35–30   The provision of sufficient and suitable information for investors is a key plank of investor protection under the Prospectus Directive. The issuer bears an "ongoing disclosure obligation" to make "reliable information" available to the investing public throughout the life of the security.[56] The bulk of the Prospectus Directive is therefore concerned to sculpt the best means for the preparation and publication of suitable prospectuses. To achieve this end the directive borrows from the IOSCO standards in an effort to give effect to "best practices" in EC securities markets.[57] The procedures for the authorisation of a prospectus, and the time limits within which those procedures are to be performed, are set out in the

---

[53] Prospectus Directive ("PD"), recital 4.
[54] PD, recital 14.
[55] PD, recital 5.
[56] PD, recital 27.
[57] PD, recital 22.

directive. Differences of detail between national laws are permitted provided that they do not discriminate between issuers. It is anticipated, however, that such "differences should be eliminated by harmonising the rules ... to achieve an adequate degree of equivalence of the safeguards [for investor protection by means of] provision of information".[58]

The policy underpinning the Commission's technical regulation on prospectuses

The Prospectus Directive a provides a list of principles which are to guide the preparation of the Commission's technical regulation, namely: **35–31**

> " the need to ensure confidence in financial markets among small investors ...;
> the need to provide investors with a wide range of competing investment opportunities and a level of disclosure and protection tailored to their circumstances;
> the need to ensure that independent regulatory authorities enforce the rules consistently, especially as regards the fight against white collar crime;
> the need for a high level of transparency ...;
> the need to encourage innovation in financial markets if they are to be dynamic and efficient;
> the need to ensure systemic stability of the financial system by close and reactive monitoring of financial innovation;
> the importance of reducing the cost of, and increasing access to, capital;
> the need to balance, on a long-term basis, the costs and benefits to market participants ... of any implementing measures;
> the need to foster the international competitiveness of the Community's financial markets without prejudice to a much-needed extension of international cooperation;
> the need to achieve a level playing field for all market participants by establishing Community legislation every time it is appropriate;
> the need to respect differences in national financial markets where these do not unduly impinge on the coherence of the single market;
> the need to ensure coherence with other Community legislation in this area, as imbalances in information and a lack of transparency may jeopardise the operation of the markets and above all harm consumers and small investors."[59]

This statement of principle is a development peculiar to the more recent generation of financial legislation in the EU. Four features are worthy of note. First, there are prudential objectives to maintain the financial system and to ensure investor protection. Secondly, there are commercial objectives to make access to capital cheaper and easier by evening out some of the key differences between financial regulation in various Member States. Thirdly, to dilute the earlier objective of harmonising regulation across the EU and instead to move towards it gradually by first recognising valid differences between securities markets in various Member States and then, in effect, by removing the obstacles to future harmonisation. Fourthly, a genuinely European identity is observable in the determination to ensure the competitiveness of the Community's financial markets and to respect the Community's role within the larger context of international regulatory initiatives.

---

[58] PD, recital 30.
[59] PD, recital 41.

The continuing importance of domestic law

35–32   Sanctions for breach of these regulations are to be provided by means of municipal substantive law and regulation, rather than by some European mechanism.[60] The directive requires that each Member State must create a right to compensation, which is contained in s.90 of the FSMA 2000 in the UK, as considered in Chapter 39. Similarly, it is a requirement that there be appeal from any decision of a national, regulatory authority within national law, and that there be a right of "judicial review" from such decisions.[61] Thus, it is clear that it is a question for national law as to what exactly happens once there has been a breach of any regulatory principle, let alone in relation to any claim for compensation any loss suffered by reference to the municipal law of that Member State.

F.   The Transparency Obligations Directive

The general principles underpinning the Transparency Obligations Directive

35–33   The Transparency Obligations Directive was implemented in the UK by Part 43 of the Companies Act 2006 and by means of the introduction of new "Disclosure and Transparency Rules" to the *FCA Handbook*, as discussed in Chapter 36 of this book.[62] The Transparency Obligations Directive is concerned primarily with the provision of sufficient information to investors in the securities markets. It is expected that markets will become "transparent" when sufficient information is made available to the public so that nothing is opaque or obscure. As the Directive provides[63]:

> "This Directive establishes requirements in relation to the disclosure of periodic and ongoing information about issuers whose securities are already admitted to trading on a regulated market situated or operating within a Member State."

The Transparency Obligations Directive is concerned with the disclosure of information in relation to securities which have already been issued and therefore with obligations to maintain levels of information affecting the securities after issue. Much of the Directive, as is discussed below, is concerned with the provision of appropriate forms of financial information and with information on an on-going basis about the voting control of the issuing entity.

Obligations to publish information under the Transparency Obligations Directive

35–34   The Transparency Obligations Directive imposes obligations on issuers of securities and on other "persons responsible" to publish a variety of types of

---

[60] PD, recital 43.
[61] PD, recital 44.
[62] Transparency Obligations Directive, art.31(1).
[63] Transparency Obligations Directive, art.1.

information so that prospective investors in those securities will be able to make informed decisions based on this statutorily-defined minimum amount of information. That information falls broadly into two types: financial information and information about shareholdings in the issuer. Issuers are obliged to publish annual financial reports and half-yearly financial reports (the latter containing a condensed set of financial statements, an interim management report and similar statements) so that there is more timely and more reliable information available to the investing public, and so that the information given constitutes a true and fair view of the state of the issuer.[64] The Member States are then obliged to ensure that those responsible people are suitably liable within the private law of their municipal legal systems. Secondly, information relating to changes in major shareholdings in the issuer are to be included in the material which must be made known to the public[65]; in particular changes in voteholder control which cross a series of statutorily defined thresholds. A detailed discussion of these provisions is contained in Chapter 36.

Implementation of the policies underpinning the Transparency Obligations Directive in Member States: "gold-plating"

The means by which the competent authorities of Member States give effect to this Directive can be "subject to requirements more stringent than those laid down" in the Directive.[66] However, it is important to note that it is only when acting as the "home Member State" that the competent authority may impose more stringent requirements; by contrast if that competent authority is dealing with an issue of securities which has already been authorised by the competent authority of another Member State (so that that competent authority is the "host Member State" rather than a home Member State) then the competent authority of the host Member State may not impose more stringent requirements on those securities which have been authorised elsewhere.[67]

35–35

G. MiFID and trading on regulated markets

The effect of the Markets in Financial Instruments Directive ("MiFID") is to level out the competition between forums for trading in securities between recognised exchanges, multilateral trading platforms and the activities of "systematic internalisers".[68] As part of the drift towards this broadening of securities markets across the European Union, the regulation of securities markets is now focused on any securities which are traded on "regulated markets" and not simply on listed securities. A list of regulated markets in each jurisdiction is maintained by each competent authority. Consequently, a prospectus is now required whenever securities are to be traded on a regulated market, even if there is no security being

35–36

---

[64] Transparency Obligations Directive, art.4.
[65] Transparency Obligations Directive, art.9.
[66] Transparency Obligations Directive, art.4(1).
[67] Transparency Obligations Directive, art.4(2).
[68] See para.7–23.

offered to the public: which would previously have been the requirement for the publication of regulated documentation to accompany the securities issue.

5.   LISTED SECURITIES

A.   The Official List

35–37   The most significant market for securities is the market for listed securities, that is securities which are listed on the "Official List" which is maintained by the Financial Conduct Authority ("FCA"), when acting in its capacity as the UK Listing Authority ("UKLA"). These securities are referred to as "listed securities". By definition, securities which are listed on the Official List as securities belonging to public companies, although not all public companies have their securities entered on the Official List. The regulations which govern the process of seeking admission to listing and maintaining listing are governed by the Listing Rules created by the FCA. The penalties for breach of the listing rules are set out in s.91 FSMA 2000.[69] This cadre of regulation is considered in Chapters 37 and 38. This section contains only an outline of the main principles.

B.   The Listing Principles

35–38   The Listing Rules are governed by a set of over-arching principles known as the "Listing Principles". These are principles which govern the manner in which issuers and their professional advisors are required to act when complying with the Listing Rules and when dealing with the competent authority. Those Listing Principles imposed on companies whose securities are listed are: the enablement of directors to understand their obligations; the maintenance of adequate procedures, systems and controls; the conduct of activities with integrity; the communication of information so as to avoid the creation or continuation of a false market in listed equity securities; the equal treatment of all shareholders; and the conduct of dealing with the FCA in an open and co-operative manner. The Listing Rules are then to be interpreted in the light of those general principles.

C.   The Model Code

35–39   A key part of securities regulation is the prevention of market abuse: principally the prevention of the abuse of inside information relating to securities. The Model Code is concerned with corporate governance within listed companies as it relates to the misuse of inside information. As such it is that part of the Listing Rules which seeks to prevent market abuse, as considered in the next section. Briefly put, during prohibited periods in relation to a company's securities, any insider (such as a person discharging management responsibilities or an employee in an applicable role) who wishes to deal in that company's securities must seek clearance under the procedure identified in the Rules. The aim is not only to

---

[69] See para.38–42.

prevent actual abuse but also to prevent the suspicion of abuse, so as to preserve confidence in the market for those securities.

D. Corporate governance

The Listing Rules provide that the annual financial report of a listed company must include a statement as to the extent of that company's compliance with the UK Code on Corporate Governance.[70] Also to be included with this statement is a further statement as to whether or not the listed company has complied with the UK Code on Corporate Governance throughout the accounting period or whether there are any provisions in relation to which there has not been compliance.[71]

35–40

E. Admission to listing

The procedure for admission to listing is considered in Chapter 38. The procedure for admission to listing requires that an applicant comply with the application procedure set out in the Listing Rules. The general conditions in the Listing Rules divide between conditions relating to the applicant itself, conditions relating to the nature of the securities which are to be issued, and conditions as to the documentation which is to be provided. There are requirements that the applicant issuer must be duly authorised, have appropriate accounts prepared, have published the prescribed financial information, have appropriate management, have appropriate working capital, and so forth. There are also requirements as to the nature of the securities themselves, which relate severally to the admission of the securities to trading on a recognised investment exchange, the need for the securities to be validly issued and freely transferable, the market capitalisation of the securities, that a sufficient number of securities are to be issued, and the preparation of an appropriate prospectus. Applicants must also have a sponsor who is, in effect, an expert in matters such as admission to listing, who will be required to ensure that the application and its supporting materials are appropriate and suitably prepared.

35–41

F. Powers of punishment held by the FCA

The FCA has four separate powers under FSMA 2000 to prohibit or suspend or otherwise control securities transactions: first, a power to discontinue or to suspend listing further to s.77 of the FSMA 2000[72]; second, a power suspend or prohibit an offer of transferable securities to the public under s.87K of the FSMA 2000[73]; third, a power to suspend or prohibit admission to trading on a regulated market under s.87L of the FSMA 2000[74]; and, fourth, a power to suspend trading

35–42

---

[70] Listing Rules, 9.8.6(5)R. See para.37–23 for a discussion of these corporate governance norms.
[71] See para.6–07.
[72] See para.15–04.
[73] See para.15–09.
[74] See para.15–11.

in a financial instrument on grounds of breach of the disclosure rules under s.96C of the FSMA 2000.[75] All of these powers are considered in Chapter 38.

6.   GENERAL OBLIGATIONS UNDER SECURITIES REGULATION

A.   Continuing obligations

35–43   There are a number of continuing obligations in the FCA securities regulations. First, under s.87A of the FSMA 2000 a duty of disclosure in a prospectus so as to enable an investor to make an informed assessment about the securities.[76] Secondly, under the transparency obligations are duties to make public financial information and information about voting control of companies. Thirdly, the Listing Rules contain a number of continuing obligations, such as requirements: that listed securities must continue to be admitted to trading on a regulated market[77]; that the securities must also remain in public hands as to 25 per cent of their number[78]; that the company must comply with the Disclosure and Transparency Rules—specifically relating to the publication of inside information—while its securities are listed[79]; and that the company is required to comply with the Model Code on corporate governance in the Listing Rules on a continuing basis.[80] Fourthly, the company is required to treat each of its shareholders equally, in accordance with the Listing Principles. Fifthly, by means of the regulation of market abuse, requiring notification to a RIS "as soon as possible"[81] of any inside information which "directly concerns the issuer",[82] These continuing obligations are each considered in greater detail in the chapters to follow.

B.   Market abuse

35–44   Market abuse regulation was considered in Chapter 12. The regulation of the use of inside information is a key feature of securities regulation. The need to maintain the integrity of securities markets and to ensure fairness between contracting parties in securities transactions are key goals of regulators and legislators alike. The sources of regulation of market abuse of securities markets in the UK are manifold. Such regulation can be found in: the criminal law in relation to insider dealing and manipulation of markets; the power to impose civil penalties granted to the FCA; the Model Code in the Listing Rules and the

---

[75]   See para.15–13.

[76]   See para.12–45. In relation to listing particulars there is a similar duty of disclosure in s.80 FSMA 2000.

[77]   Listing Rules, 2.2.3R.

[78]   Listing Rules, 6.1.19R.

[79]   Listing Rules, 9.2.6R.

[80]   Listing Rules, 9.2.8R.

[81]   This will be satisfied if the issuer acted as soon as was possible in the circumstance of factors which were only gradually coming to light: Disclosure and Transparency Rules, Ch.2, para.2.2.2R. A short delay in publication of the information will be acceptable if it is "necessary to clarify the situation": Disclosure and Transparency Rules, Ch.2, para.2.2.9G.

[82]   Disclosure and Transparency Rules, Ch.2, para.2.2.1R.

Disclosure and Transparency Rules; the regulation of takeovers and mergers when price sensitive information surrounding a possible bid abounds; and the control of market abuse in the Code on Market Conduct contained in the Market Abuse Rulebook ("MAR1"). The old Financial Services Authority created MAR 1 further to s.119 of the FSMA 2000 originally. Section 118 of the FSMA 2000 sets out the categories of behaviour which constitute market abuse,[83] and then MAR1 provides detail as to the FCA's attitude to those various categories. The three categories of market abuse which arise under MAR1 are as follows: first, when a person is "dealing on the basis of inside information which is not trading information"[84]; secondly, when an insider discloses information to another person; and, thirdly, when a person fails to observe proper market conduct when dealing with price sensitive information which is not in the public domain.

C. Liability to pay compensation for untrue or misleading statements or omissions in a prospectus

Liability to pay compensation under s.90 FSMA 2000

Further to s.90 of FSMA 2000, any person responsible for a prospectus is liable to pay compensation to a person who has acquired securities to which the prospectus applies; and who suffered loss in respect of them as a result of any untrue or misleading statement in the prospectus or as a result of the omission from the prospectus which should have been included under the duty of disclosure under the Prospectus Rules. This head of liability does not prejudice any action under the general law.[85] The recent cases on liability for the tort of misrepresentation in relation to issues of securities have begun to accept the possibility of a general liability to any buyer in the market after issue,[86] something which is likely to be exacerbated by the obligations of disclosure which are contained in the Prospectus Rules.[87] The heads of liability for losses resulting as part of mis-selling securities are discussed in detail in Chapter 39. A number of defences are then provided in Sch.10 to FSMA 2000 relating to the defendant's belief in the truth of the statement, or relying on a statement by an expert or a statement in an official publication, or relating to an attempt to publish a correction.

35–45

Penalties

There are a variety of types of penalty for breaches of securities regulation. In relation to listed securities, the penalties associated with cancellation and suspension of listing are discussed in Chapter 38 of this book. Censures of sponsors may be issued in relation to listed securities; a company may be publicly or privately censured further to s.87M and s.91 of FSMA 2000. The principal

35–46

---

[83] FSMA 2000 s.118, (1)(a)–(c).

[84] MAR, 1.3.2(1)E.

[85] Financial Services and Markets Act 2000, s.90(6).

[86] e.g. *Possfund Custodian Trustee Ltd v Diamond* [1996] 2 All E.R. 774.

[87] See para.39–17 et seq.

provision governing penalties for breach of FCA securities regulation is s.91 of FSMA 2000 as discussed in Chapter 38, and may open the company up to a fine and may also open any director of the company who was knowingly concerned up to a breach up to a fine.

7. OFFENCES CONNECTED TO ISSUES OF SECURITIES

35–47   The criminal law relating to securities is principally concerned with market abuse in relation to the criminal offences relating to insider dealing under Part V of the Criminal Justice Act 1993[88] and the offences relating to market manipulation under s.397 of FSMA 2000.[89] Under the criminal law there are also offences relevant to securities transactions under various provisions of the Theft Acts and the Fraud Act 2006; as well as the offences which are created under FSMA 2000 of relevance to securities transactions, dealing severally with the restriction on financial promotion, the publication of prospectuses and so forth.[90] These offences were considered in Part IV of this book.

8. PROTECTING UK SECURITIES MARKETS FROM NON-EU REGULATION: INVESTMENT EXCHANGES AND CLEARANCE HOUSES ACT 2006

A.   The mischief at which the legislation was directed

35–48   The Investment Exchanges and Clearance Houses Act 2006 ("IECHA 06") was passed in the heat of concerns about mooted takeovers of the company which operates the London Stock Exchange. The principal concern was that the London Stock Exchange might be acquired by a company owning an exchange operating in the US which would be subject to US securities regulation, including the Sarbanes-Oxley Act, with the anticipated effect that the London Stock Exchange and shares traded on that exchange would similarly be subject to that US regulation. The principal concern was that the US rules would impose excessive requirements on users of the London Stock Exchange which are required by neither UK securities law nor by EC securities law. The purpose of the IECHA 06 was therefore to enable any excessive provisions of US regulation to be displaced by the FCA, so that no regulations beyond the requirements of the EC securities directives and the requirements of the *FCA Handbook* would be imposed either on the exchange or on shares admitted to trading on that exchange.

---

[88] See para.25–03.
[89] See para.25–60.
[90] See para.26–01.

B. The powers of the FCA in relation to excessive regulatory provisions

IECHA 06 introduces new provisions to the FSMA 2000.[91] Thus, s.300A(1) of the FSMA 2000 provides for the scope of this power in that[92]:

35–49

> "This section applies where a recognised body proposes to make any regulatory provision in connection with its business as an investment exchange or the provision by it of clearing services."

The term "recognised body" is not defined in the legislation. The power which the FCA (as "that Authority") has as a result is as follows:

> "If it appears to the Authority—
> (a)   that the proposed provision will impose a requirement on persons affected (directly or indirectly) by it, and
> (b)   that the requirement is excessive,
> (c)   the Authority may direct that the proposed provision must not be made."[93]

Therefore, the FCA has the power to prevent the implementation or creation of regulations which would impose requirements on regulated persons which are deemed by it to be "excessive": that term is defined in the next section. The FCA is required to consider the effect of that proposed regulation, allowing time to receive representations, and publish a notice of its decision.[94]

C. Identifying an "excessive" proposed regulation

The term "excessive" in this context is defined as follows[95]:

35–50

> "A requirement is excessive if—
> (a)   it is not required under Community law or any enactment or rule of law in the United Kingdom, and
> (b)   either—
>   (i)it is not justified as pursuing a reasonable regulatory objective, or
>   (ii)it is disproportionate to the end to be achieved."

In considering whether or not a provision is excessive, the FCA is required to consider all of the circumstances, and not simply the terms of the regulatory provisions.[96] Among the matters to be taken into account are[97]; the effect of existing legal and other requirements (such as accounting standards); "the global character of financial services and markets and the international mobility of activity"[98]; the desirability of facilitating innovation in financial market practice

---

[91] These provisions apply from December 20, 2006: Investment Exchanges and Clearance Houses Act 2006, s.1.
[92] Financial Services and Markets Act 2000, s.300A(1).
[93] Financial Services and Markets Act 2000, s.300A(2).
[94] Financial Services and Markets Act 2000, s.300D.
[95] Financial Services and Markets Act 2000, s.300A(3).
[96] Financial Services and Markets Act 2000, s.300A(4).
[97] Financial Services and Markets Act 2000, s.300A(4).
[98] Financial Services and Markets Act 2000, s.300A(4)(b).

and in the nature of financial instruments; and the impact of the proposed provision on market confidence, including (it is suggested) the confidence of market participants as to the extent of the regulation of their markets if there are multiple regulators involved in overseeing the London stock market indirectly and if it may be unclear what those market participants' obligations will be.

35–51   Thus an excessive regulatory provision has the following features. First, it imposes either direct or indirect requirements on a person, whether on the London Stock Exchange, on an authorised investment firm, on a sponsor (that is, a functionary who brings securities to listing), on an issuer of securities which are intended to be or which are admitted to trading on a regulated market, or on any other person subject to that regulation. Secondly, if those requirements are not required by EC securities law or by FCA regulation or by substantive law (whether English law, Scots law or Northern Irish law). Thirdly, the proposed regulatory requirement must not be pursuing a reasonable regulatory objective: it is suggested that this should be interpreted to mean that the proposed regulation is not pursuing an objective which is required either by EC securities regulation or by UK securities law (such as the *Principles for Businesses* rulebook, or the UKLA Listing Principles, or some objective contained in the EC securities directives). Alternatively, under this third head, the regulatory objective may be disapplied if is disproportionate for the objective which is to be proposed: thus, for example, an objective connected to ensuring the provision of properly audited accounts under the Listing Rules would not justify the introduction of the panoply of regulation associated with s.404 of the US Sarbanes-Oxley Act, where the latter would be a disproportionate requirement associated with the achievement of the former objective which would be satisfied by compliance with EC directives on the proper preparation of accounts.

D.   The private law effect of the disapplication of a regulation

35–52   The effect of the FCA having a power to disapply regulatory provisions before they come into effect is that that regulatory provision will have no effect under UK securities law at all even if the regulatory body which is seeking to impose it does purport to give effect to it subsequently. Thus, for example, there can be no question under English law of a transaction being unlawful simply because a regulator outside the EU purported to impose an excessive regulatory requirement in relation to such securities transactions.

E.   The duty to notify a proposal to make regulatory provisions

35–53   There is a duty on a "recognised body" to notify the FCA of any proposal to make a regulatory provision in writing "without delay".[99] The FCA may, further its powers under s.293 of the FSMA 2000, specify to which proposed provisions its

---

[99] Financial Services and Markets Act 2000, s.300B(1).

scrutiny relates. The regulatory provision may not be made by the regulator before notice is given nor within 30 days of communication to the FCA.[100]

F. The actual ambit of s.300A compared to the mischief at which it was aimed

The IECHA 06 was aimed at the mischief associated with a takeover of the London Stock Exchange and the feared introduction of regulatory provisions beyond the requirements of EU financial services law or beyond UK securities law. However, as drafted s.300A et seq of FSMA 2000 apply beyond the ownership and indirect control of the London Stock Exchange. The regulations captured under the FCA's powers under IECHA 06 govern any "rule, guidance, arrangements, policy or practice"[101] of *any* "recognised body"—where that last term is not defined. Thus, with the definition of the term "recognised body" not being defined in s.300A, nor in the interpretation provision s.300E, the FCA would appear to be able to recognise a large number of bodies dealing with any aspect of securities or other financial services activity in the UK which are connected to "its business"[102] as an investment exchange or as a clearance house.

35–54

9.   Dealings in Uncertificated Securities

A.   The Uncertificated Securities Regulations 2001

The Uncertificated Securities Regulations 2001[103] govern dealings with securities which exist in dematerialised form (that is, securities which are no longer issued in the form of a paper certificate). Modern securities practice has moved away from the issue of paper certificates to evidence title to securities and instead has adopted a paperless system of electronic registration of ownership of those securities.[104] This movement away from tangible certificates is termed "dematerialisation". It is a requirement of the admission of securities to listing that those securities are eligible for electronic settlement.[105]

35–55

The regulations provide for a mechanism for the approval of an operator of the uncertificated securities system.[106] The purpose of the regulations is to "enable title to units of a security to be evidenced otherwise than by a certificate and transferred otherwise than by a written instrument".[107] The regulations require that the company's articles of association permit an uncertificated form for that company's securities, in that a special procedure is required if the articles do not permit such a form. If the articles do not permit uncertificated securities, then the

35–56

---

[100] Financial Services and Markets Act 2000, s.300C.
[101] Financial Services and Markets Act 2000, s.300E.
[102] Financial Services and Markets Act 2000, s.300A(1).
[103] SI 2001/3755.
[104] There is little discussion of these regulations in the literature. The reader is referred to the comprehensive discussion of these regulations by J. Tuckley, in *Palmer's Company Law*.
[105] Listing Rules, 6.1.23R.
[106] In Pt 2 of the Uncertificated Securities Regulations 2001, reg.2.
[107] Uncertificated Securities Regulations 2001, reg.2.

directors may resolve to issue securities and to transfer securities by means of an uncertificated system,[108] at which point the regulations provide that the articles cease to have effect.[109] Notice of that directors' resolution, if not given to the members in advance, must be given within 60 days of the resolution.[110] The members of the company may by ordinary resolution decide that the directors' resolution shall have no effect or shall cease to have effect, as appropriate.[111] The members may change the articles of association in the ordinary way.[112]

35–57   Registers of holders of securities must be maintained by the operator of the system and by the issuer.[113] There is also a separate register of public sector securities.[114] In general terms, entry of ownership on an appropriate register is prima facie evidence of the ownership of those securities by the person recorded as the owner.[115] Once a transfer has taken place, the operator is required to register that change in ownership on its register[116]; unless the transfer has been prohibited by a court order, or is void under some legislation, or would constitute a transfer to a deceased person.[117] The operator is only entitled to register a uncertificated securities other than under the procedure in the regulations if there has been a court order requiring the recognition of the ownership of some other person.[118] The operator must notify the participating issuer of the transfer of securities. Rectification of the issuer's register may not take effect without rectification of the operator's register.[119] If a person suffers loss as a result of a forged dematerialisation instruction, then that person may apply to the court for an order that the operator compensate her for her loss.[120]

B.   CREST

35–58   Dealings in uncertificated securities take place mainly on CREST.[121] CREST is an electronic system for the holding and transfer of securities, which also enables payment to be made simultaneously with transfer. The CREST system is governed by the "CREST Rules", the CREST Manual and the Security Application Form.[122] CREST is not the only possible system for conducting such transactions but it is the system which is used most commonly in the UK. Admission to CREST is dependent on the securities qualifying under the

---

[108] Uncertificated Securities Regulations 2001, reg.15(2).
[109] Uncertificated Securities Regulations 2001, reg.15(3).
[110] Uncertificated Securities Regulations 2001, reg.15(4).
[111] Uncertificated Securities Regulations 2001, reg.15(6).
[112] Companies Act 2006 s.21 et seq.
[113] Uncertificated Securities Regulations 2001, reg.20.
[114] Uncertificated Securities Regulations 2001, reg.21.
[115] Uncertificated Securities Regulations 2001, reg.24.
[116] Uncertificated Securities Regulations 2001, reg.27(1).
[117] Uncertificated Securities Regulations 2001, reg.27(2).
[118] Uncertificated Securities Regulations 2001, reg.27(5).
[119] Uncertificated Securities Regulations 2001, reg.25.
[120] Uncertificated Securities Regulations 2001, reg.36.
[121] See J. Tuckley, "Settlement Arrangements—CREST", in Maule (ed.), *A Practitioner's Guide to the AIM Rules* (City & Financial Publishing, 2006), p.225, which sets out an excellent summary of the appropriate regulations.
[122] Available at *http://www.crestco.co.uk*. See also the *CPSS-IOSCO Disclosure Framework*, 2005.

Uncertificated Securities Regulations 2001, as considered above. The shares must be fungible, they must be freely transferable and their issue must not be subject to any condition. Admission to CREST is made formally by completion of a Security Application Form.

10.   PRIVATE COMPANIES MAY NOT OFFER SECURITIES TO THE PUBLIC

A private company—that is, a company which is not a public company[123]— which is limited by shares or limited by guarantee may not "offer to the public any securities of the company" nor "allot or agree to allot any securities of the company with a view to their being offered to the public".[124] It is a cornerstone of securities law that offers of securities to the public may only be made by public companies which are expressly subject to the securities regulations. An "offer to the public" is defined by s.756 of CA 2006 so as to include an offer made to a section of the public. Offers which are not to be regarded as being offers to the public are offers which, after consideration of all the appropriate circumstances, are "not calculated to result, directly or indirectly, in securities ... becoming available to persons other than those receiving the offer" or are "otherwise ... a private concern of the person receiving [the offer] and the person making it".[125]

35–59

11.   SHORT-SELLING

The phenomenon of short-selling arises when speculators take a position that they will sell more securities to their counterparties than they actually own at the time of making the transaction. The "bet" which the speculator is making is that the market price of those securities will fall before the time when the speculator will be required to deliver them up to their counterparties. (Alternatively, the transaction can be entirely cash-settled, in the sense that the parties simply settle in cash what they would have realised if they had actually transferred securities between one another.) The effect of short-selling is that off-exchange (and thus beyond the sight of the regulators) downward pressure is put on the securities of those entities, often on the basis of very short-term concerns. In the wake of the financial crisis, this practice was controlled by regulation so as to control the amount of volatility in financial markets. Those EU regulations are now contained in the EU Short Selling Regulation ("SSR").[126] The EU short-selling regulations have been implemented into UK finance law by means of the FCA Financial Stability and Market Confidence Sourcebook ("FINMAR").

35–60

---

[123] Companies Act 2006, s.4(1).
[124] Companies Act 2006, s.755(1).
[125] Companies Act 2006, s.756(3).
[126] Regulation (EU) No.236/2012.

CHAPTER 36

PROSPECTUSES AND TRANSPARENCY OBLIGATIONS

CORE PRINCIPLES

Under s.85 FSMA 2000, a prospectus in prescribed form must be authorised and published in relation to any issues of securities which are either to be offered to the public or in relation to which admission to trading on a regulated market is sought; other issues of securities do not require such a prospectus. The Financial Conduct Authority ("FCA") regulates prospectuses through the Prospectus Rules.

The definition of an "offer to the public" in s.102B FSMA 2000 is very broad indeed: it relates to an offer to any person of any securities with enough information to allow her to make a decision whether or not to buy those securities. At first blush, therefore, most issues of securities will be caught. There are, however, specified circumstances in which a prospectus will not be required, even if it would otherwise be an offer to the public: these are in the form of statutory exceptions to the need for a prospectus. The exempt types of issues are set out in s.86 and Sch.11A of FSMA 2000.

The required contents of a prospectus in particular circumstances are described in detail by the Prospectus Rules, but all prospectuses are governed by a general duty of disclosure. This duty of disclosure is set out in s.87A FSMA 2000 and requires that all prospectuses contain all of the information necessary to enable an investor to make an informed assessment as to whether or not to buy securities. Importantly, this is not a test which stipulates exactly what must go in a prospectus but rather it is a principle which places the burden on the issuer of the securities to identify how much information and what type of information is required to be included. This provision provides a lodestar for the interpretation of the remainder of the prospectus regulations. It is in the Prospectus Rules that the detailed material about the contents of prospectuses is set out, in great detail, but even then the onus is placed on the issuer and its advisors as to precisely how the information is presented and expressed.

Once securities are in issue there are requirements in prescribed cases for the issuing company to make information public about the people who have voting control as shareholders over it, and about the people who control those shareholders; and also to make public identified types of financial information about the company's performance. These requirements are referred to as "transparency obligations". These obligations are provided for by Part 43 of the Companies Act 2006, as required by the EC Transparency Obligations Directive. The FCA regulates transparency obligations through the Disclosure and Transparency Rules.

1. INTRODUCTION

Information is key to securities markets. Both professional and lay investors rely on information about companies in which they may seek to invest—especially information relating to their prospects, their businesses, market sentiment about their markets, and so forth—and therefore securities regulation focuses in large part on the regulation of information. The principal means by which securities law has always sought to regulate the issue of securities is by requiring that suitable amounts of information are given to investors in the form of a *prospectus*. Prospectuses have long been a feature of dealings in shares and other securities. Even the old 19th century common law dealt with statements in prospectuses. The case law has since been replaced by formal regulation by the Financial Conduct Authority ("FCA") as to the contents of prospectuses and the need to keep the investor community appraised of updated information relating to that prospectus. Consequently, what is meant by the term "prospectus" today is prescribed in detail in the regulations and differs from earlier understandings of the term. There is no central definition of what constitutes a "prospectus" today: instead it should be understood as a document (or documents) which provide investors with all of the information necessary for them to decide whether or not to acquire the securities described in that document,[1] which must therefore comply with the prospectus regulations as to its form and contents.[2]

36–01

Latterly, regulatory concerns turned to investors' need to know not only about the information contained in a prospectus but also about matters such as the ownership of the company issuing the securities and its financial condition. The issuer of the securities must now make public this sort of information which is referred to as the issuer's transparency obligations, which are also considered in this chapter. Transparency obligations require, amongst other things, that the ultimate control and ownership of the company is made known to the investing public and that financial information of the prescribed kind is also made public.

36–02

Also of great importance in relation to information is the criminal law prohibiting *insider dealing* and *market abuse*, as considered in Chapters 14 and 12 respectively. The insider dealing code demonstrates how significant the law considers it to be to prevent inside information being misused by some investors to gain an unfair advantage over other participants in the market by criminalising the misuse of inside information and market manipulation. The FCA is also empowered to regulate the treatment of inside information by means of the Market Abuse Rulebook ("MAR1"). The importance of ensuring free flows of

36–03

---

[1] Financial Services and Markets Act 2000, s.87A.
[2] As is required in effect by Financial Services and Markets Act 2000, s.85.

information in securities markets was considered as part of that discussion. Those principles will not be rehearsed here, but their presence should be borne in mind when considering the way in which securities law deals with information.

36–04 This chapter will therefore focus, first, on the legislative requirements for a prospectus; secondly, on the *Prospectus Rules* dealing with the preparation and authorisation of prospectuses; and, thirdly, on transparency obligations.[3] The liability for losses caused by any defect in a prospectus or a failure to comply with transparency obligations are considered in Chapter 37. We begin, however, with an overview of prospectus regulation which, it is hoped, will make the later discussion easier to comprehend.[4]

2. PROSPECTUSES

A. The fundamental principles of the regulation of prospectuses

The prospectus as the principal means of providing information to investors

36–05 Securities law is concerned with the provision of enough of the right sorts of information to the investing public to enable potential investors to make informed decisions about their investments. It does not seek to protect investors against the possibility of loss; nor does it seek to protect investors against their own folly. Instead having sufficient information to make an informed decision places the onus for making investment decisions onto the investor. The principal means by which information is provided to investors is by a prospectus; or on certain occasions when offering securities only to expert, professional investors by means of a document known as "listing particulars" (although in this chapter we will concentrate on the more important regime dealing with prospectuses). The Prospectus Directive of 2003[5] is the securities directive which set out the high-level principles governing the regulation of prospectuses. The regime which it created applies to offers of transferable securities to the public and to applications for admission of securities to trading on a regulated market.

The statutory requirement for a prospectus in the UK

36–06 The significance of the prospectus in modern securities law can be summarised in the following manner. It is a criminal offence[6] under s.85 of the Financial Services and Markets Act 2000 ("FSMA 2000") either to offer transferable

---

[3] This discussion is based on elements of A. Hudson, *Securities Law* (London: Sweet & Maxwell, 2008), Ch.12 "Prospectuses", which have been rewritten for this chapter of this book. A more detailed discussion of the FCA Prospectus Rules can be found in that book.

[4] This is a technique of "cognitive reinforcement" which I use as a teacher: begin with the core principles and then layer on the detail. It is not intended to be repetitive, but rather to make explanation clearer by tunneling slowly from overarching principles into detailed rules.

[5] 2003/71/EC.

[6] Financial Services and Markets Act 2000, s.85(3).

securities for sale to the public in the United Kingdom[7] or to request the admission of securities to trading on a regulated market[8] without a prospectus in relation to that issue having first been approved by the competent authority (which is the FCA) and then having been published.[9] These offences are considered in detail below. To put the matter the other way around: a prospectus is required for an issue of securities which are to be offered to the public in the UK, and that prospectus must be approved by the FCA before any such offer is made, unless the offer is exempted from this requirement by the terms of the statute.[10] The prospectus must be "published" in the sense of being made available to the public. Importantly, there will have been an "offer of transferable securities to the public" if there is "a communication to any person which presents sufficient information" to enable the recipient of that communication to decide whether or not to buy those securities.[11] Therefore, the concept of an "offer" is very broad indeed in that it encompasses an offer to only one person and does not require that the offer is made to a number of people.[12]

The new regime of prospectus regulation under the Prospectus Regulations 2005

In 2005 the UK Prospectus Regulations[13] implemented the EC Prospectus **36–07** Directive by means of amending existing sections of Part 6 of FSMA 2000 and also by introducing new sections to that Part 6. The UK Prospectus Regulations 2005 ("the Prospectus Regulations 2005") repealed the Public Offers of Securities Regulations 1995[14] (which had previously dealt with unlisted securities) and also repealed the Financial Services and Markets Act 2000 (Official Listing of Securities) Order 2001[15] (which had dealt with offers of listed securities before 2005).[16] The Prospectus Regulations 2005 completely changed the manner in which prospectus material is to be prepared and the legal principles governing prospectuses, as was required by the EC Prospectus Directive. Before the Prospectus Regulations 2005 were introduced, it had been important to know whether securities were to be listed on the Official List or were to be unlisted so that one could identify which regulatory code would deal with those securities. For the purposes of prospectus regulation today, as a result of the Prospectus Regulations 2005, it is now important to know whether securities are to be

---

[7] Financial Services and Markets Act 2000, s.85(1).

[8] Financial Services and Markets Act 2000, s.85(2).

[9] Financial Services and Markets Act 2000, s.85, as amended by the Prospectus Regulations 2005 (SI 2005/1433) in the manner discussed in the text.

[10] This is the effect of Financial Services and Markets Act 2000, s.85(1).

[11] Financial Services and Markets Act 2000, s.102B.

[12] Financial Services and Markets Act 2000, s.102B.

[13] SI 2005/1433.

[14] SI 1995/1537

[15] SI 2001/2958. Also revoked are the Financial Services and Markets Act 2000 (Official Listing of Securities) Regulations 2001 (SI 2001/2956).

[16] At the time of writing many practitioner and student texts on finance law and company law still discuss these statutory instruments and the codes which they created even though they have been repealed. It is a testament to the complexity of securities law that these fundamental changes in principle have escaped the attention of so many authors and editors.

offered to the public, or whether they are to be the subject of a request for admission to trading on a regulated market; or alternatively whether the offer falls outside either of these categories, or is an exempt offer under the prospectus regulations. These categories of offers of securities will be considered below.

36–08   After 2005, it is only important to know whether securities are listed or unlisted so that one can know whether or not the Listing Rules—as considered in Chapters 37 and 38—will apply to those securities. In the wake of the Prospectus Regulations 2005, the FCA was empowered to create further securities regulations in the form of the "Prospectus Rules" which govern the preparation, authorisation and dissemination of prospectuses, which are considered next.

B.   The principles of the Prospectus Rules

The genesis of the Prospectus Rules

36–09   The detailed regulation of prospectuses generally is set out in the FCA Prospectus Rules ("the Prospectus Rules"), which form part of the *FCA Handbook* and which are one of the key parts of securities regulation in the UK. The Prospectus Rules were created originally by the old Financial Services Authority under powers granted to it by s.84 of FSMA 2000; they are now maintained by the FCA. The bulk of the Prospectus Rules is made up of the provisions of the Commission's technical regulation which fleshes out the detail of the high-level principles in the Prospectus Directive 2003, in line with the Lamfalussy methodology for securities regulation, as amended in the wake of the Larosière Report to account for the defects in the regulatory scheme which were brought to light by the financial crisis 2007–09 (as considered in Chapter 7). Rather, than paraphrase the Commissions' technical regulations, those technical regulations are simply copied into the Prospectus Rules with a small EU flag icon to identify their derivation.

The objectives of the Prospectus Rules

36–10   The objectives of the Prospectus Rules are to provide for categories of exempt securities, the format of a prospectus, the minimum information to be included in a prospectus, the procedure for applying for approval of a prospectus, the methodology for the publication of a prospectus, the validity of a prospectus, and the persons responsible for a prospectus. These topics are considered in detail in this chapter. The bulk of the discussion in this chapter, after the analysis of the policy underpinning the Prospectus Directive and the key provisions of FSMA 2000 in this context, are concerned with a discussion of the Prospectus Rules.

The applicability of the Prospectus Rules beyond listed securities

36–11   For the regulations relating to prospectuses to apply, the securities in question do not have to be admitted to the Official List nor do they have to be the subject of an application for admission to the Official List. It is sufficient for a prospectus to be required, and thus for the regulations dealing with prospectuses to apply, that those securities are the subject of a request for admission to trading on a regulated market or that they are the subject of an offer to the public.[17] A list of regulated markets for the purposes of securities regulation is maintained by the FCA. That prospectuses are required in relation to any admission to trading on a regulated market has broadened the scope of prospectus regulation considerably from its previous focus on listed securities. For example, whereas previously when an offer was made to a restricted number of investors, so as to fall within one of the regulatory exemptions, there was no obligation to prepare a prospectus in the form required by the regulations. The effect of requiring prospectuses to be prepared and published in an approved form in relation to any securities which are the subject of an application for admission to trading on a regulated market is that the prospectus regulations will now apply even to such offers which would previously have been exempted from the need for a prospectus.

The amount of professional work which is bound up with the preparation of a prospectus—involving lawyers, accountants, investment bankers, and others—is enormous and the costs are therefore commensurately high. The prospectus regulations, as we shall see in this chapter, are both detailed and yet also governed by high-level principles of disclosure, integrity and so forth, with extensive obligations to pay compensation for any loss suffered as a result of an untrue or misleading statement in the prospectus.[18] Consequently, the widening of the ambit of prospectus regulation across the EU in 2005 (with the implementation of the Prospectus Directive) has increased the costs associated with various kinds of securities issues which were previously exempt from this sort of regulatory scrutiny.

36–12

What is a prospectus?

A prospectus, broadly defined, is a document which makes prescribed forms of information about securities and about their issuer available to the investing public. That prospectus will therefore constitute a series of representations on which purchasers of those securities will rely when making the decision whether or not to acquire them. The prospectus is therefore the root of any contract for the acquisition of securities, and consequently the approach of securities regulation in this context has been to prescribe the minimum contents of a prospectus for certain types of issuer and for certain types of security, and to demand the continued accuracy of that prospectus during its lifetime so that the investing public is provided with sufficient, appropriate material with which to make informed investment decisions. This chapter, then, considers both the requirements for a prospectus, the circumstances in which a prospectus will not be required, the continuing obligations associated with prospectuses and the required contents of such a prospectus.[19]

36–13

---

[17] Financial Services and Markets Act 2000, s.85.
[18] Financial Services and Markets Act 2000, s.90.
[19] The old definition of "prospectus" in the Companies Act 1985 s.744 required the offer to be "for subscription or purchase". In *Government Stock and Other Securities Investment Co Ltd v Christopher* [1956] 1 W.L.R. 237 Wynn-Parry J. interpreted that definition as being inapplicable to a

That this chapter only considers offers of transferable securities to the public or requests for admission of securities to trading on a regulated market

36–14 The regulations considered here relate only to an offer of transferable securities to the public[20] or a request for admission of securities to trading on a regulated market.[21] The exemptions from this code are considered below. It is important to note that an offer which is not made to the public or which does not involve a request for admission of securities to trading on a regulated market will not fall within these regulations. Transfers and issues of such securities will therefore be governed by the provisions of contract and company law in this regard,[22] and the general law liabilities which are considered in Chapter 39 of this book.

C. The contractual role of the prospectus under the general law

36–15 This chapter is primarily concerned with the detail of the prospectus regulations. It should not be forgotten, however, that a prospectus is a document which forms the representations on which initial subscribers for securities and purchasers in the after-market can be expected to rely when making their investment decisions. Therefore, these representations found contracts for the purchase of securities and may be actionable under contract law. Consequently, the Prospectus Rules provide, inter alia, that the people responsible for the preparation of the prospectus must ensure that the prospectus contains all of the necessary information which a reasonable investment advisor would require so as to be able to make an informed decision as to the purchase of the securities described therein.[23] The prospectus constitutes a contractual document above all else. The underlying purpose of the prospectus regulations, therefore, is to do two things. First, to provide for the terms on which a purchaser may rely if there is any suggested breach of contract or tort, and, secondly, to ensure the integrity of securities markets of the European Union further to the EC Prospectus Directive.

---

circular by a take-over bidder to the target company's shareholders offering shares in the bidder (yet to be allotted) in exchange for shares in the target company. It was not an offer for the "purchase" of shares (as they were by then unissued *Re VGM Holdings Ltd* [1942] Ch. 235) nor was it an offer for "subscription" (as that was taken to connote taking shares for cash (on which see *Arnison v Smith* (1889) 41 Ch.D. 348, and *Chicago Ry Terminal Elevator Co v IRC* (1986) 75 L.T. 157 and *Brown v IRC* (1900) 84 L.T. 71; but compare *Akierhelm v De Mare* [1959] A.C. 789 (PC), and *Broken Hill Proprietary Co Ltd v Bell Resources Ltd* (1984) 8 A.C.L.R. 609.

[20] Financial Services and Markets Act 2000, s.85(1).
[21] Financial Services and Markets Act 2000, s.85(2).
[22] See A. Hudson, *Securities Law*, Pt 9 generally.
[23] Financial Services and Markets Act 2000, s.87A.

3.   THE EXTENT OF THE REQUIREMENT FOR A PROSPECTUS

A.   Introduction

There are two contexts in which a prospectus is required both to have been approved by the FCA and to have been made available to the public by s.85 of the FSMA 2000: that is, before any offer of a transferable security to the public, and before a request is made for a transferable security to be admitted to listing on a regulated market. In criminal law terms, a failure to comply with either of these requirements constitutes a criminal offence[24]; in private law terms, a failure to comply with either of these requirements is "actionable" on behalf of any person who suffers loss as a result that contravention either under s.90 of the FSMA 2000 (as discussed in Chapter 39) or under the general law (in the manner discussed in Chapter 39).[25] Each of these provisions within s.85 is considered in turn in the paragraphs to follow.

36–16

B.   Offers of transferable securities require the publication of an approved prospectus: s.85(1) FSMA 2000

It is a criminal offence to fail to have a prospectus approved and to publish it in the following circumstances set out by s.85 of FSMA 2000. The first offence deals with the making of offers to the public without a prospectus relating to that offer having been approved first, under s.85(1) of FSMA 2000:

36–17

> "It is unlawful for transferable securities to which this subsection applies to be offered to the public in the United Kingdom unless an approved prospectus has been made available to the public before the offer is made."

Thus, a prospectus must be approved and "made available" to the public before transferable securities are offered to that public. The term "transferable securities" in this context[26] "means anything which is a transferable security for the purposes of MiFID,[27] other than money-market instruments for the purposes of that directive which have a maturity of less than 12 months".[28] The breadth of an offer to the public is set out in s.102B of the FSMA 2000 considered below. However, Sch.11A FSMA 2000 provides for a variety of categories of exempt instruments which would otherwise be transferable securities but which are excluded from the ambit of "transferable securities" for the purposes of s.85(1) FSMA 2000. The definition of these various terms is considered in detail below.

---

[24] Financial Services and Markets Act 2000, s.85(3).
[25] Financial Services and Markets Act 2000, s.85(4).
[26] Financial Services and Markets Act 2000, s.102A(1), referring to all provisions in Pt VI of that Act.
[27] The Markets in Financial Instruments Directive ("MiFID") which took effect in the UK from November 1, 2007.
[28] Financial Services and Markets Act 2000, s.102A(3).

C. Requests for admission to trading on a regulated market require a prospectus

36–18   Section 85(2) of FSMA 2000 sets out a second criminal offence, which may also give rise to a civil liability to compensate for loss, in the following terms:

> "It is unlawful to request the admission of transferable securities to which this subsection applies to trading on a regulated market situated or operating in the United Kingdom unless an approved prospectus has been made available to the public before the request is made."

This second offence, then, relates to the admission to trading on any regulated market, not necessarily the Official List (considered in Chapter 37) and not necessarily in conjunction with an offer falling under s.85(1). Notably, it is not a requirement that securities have already been admitted to trading on that regulated market: rather, it is sufficient that a mere "request" for their admission to trading has been made. The term "transferable securities" in this context refers to all transferable securities except for units in an open-ended investment scheme, non-equity transferable securities issued by a public body in an EEA state, shares in the capital bank of an EEA state, securities guaranteed by a public body in an EEA state, non-equity transferable securities issued in a repeated manner by a credit institution,[29] and non-fungible shares of capital intended to provide a right in immoveable property which cannot be sold without giving up that right.[30] These exemptions are considered in greater detail below.

D.   The meaning of an "offer to the public"

36–19   The requirement that an offer must have been made to the public does not require that the offer is made to an appreciable section of the public at large nor that it is made to more than a "fluctuating class of private individuals".[31] Section 102B of the FSMA 2000 draws the concept of an "offer of transferable securities to the public" very broadly indeed. Section 102B(1) provides:

> "For the purposes of [Part 6 of FSMA 2000] there is an offer of transferable securities to the public if there is a communication to any person which presents sufficient information on—
> (a)   the transferable securities to be offered, and
> (b)   the terms on which they are offered,
> to enable an investor to decide to buy or subscribe for the securities in question."

The communication need be received by only "any person", in the singular, and not a given number of investors large enough to constitute the public. Therefore, the concept of an "offer" is very broad indeed in that it encompasses an offer to only one person and does not require that the offer is made to a number of people. The communication will be an "offer" is there is sufficient information about the securities and the terms of the offer to enable the offeree to make up her mind whether or not to buy them. So, the mere suggestion: "are you interested in some shares?" would not be an "offer" in this sense; whereas, the statement: "are you

---

[29]   Which are not subordinate, convertible or exchangeable.

[30]   Financial Services and Markets Act 2000, Sch.11A.

[31]   An expression used in charities law to define "the public": *Dingle v Turner* [1972] A.C. 601.

interested in subscribing for ordinary shares in A Plc carrying ordinary voting rights at a price of 100p each?" would constitute an "offer" if it is made to "any person" whatsoever. Interestingly, the Irish regulations provide expressly that an invitation to treat will constitute an offer in this context. It is suggested that this would only be an appropriate reading of s.102B in the UK if that invitation to treat was a communication which also contained sufficient information as to the "terms on which the [securities] are offered".[32] If those requirements were satisfied, however, then it is suggested that even a communication which might be interpreted as being merely an invitation to treat under English contract law should be considered to be an "offer" in this context.

There is perhaps one question of interpretation left. Does the expression "to enable an investor to decide to buy or subscribe for the securities in question" mean either that the investor must have enough information to satisfy the obligation under s.87A of the FSMA 2000 (considered below) to provide all the information necessary for an investor to make an informed decision, or that the investor must simply have had a modicum of information on which someone could possibly have decided whether or not to buy the securities? It is suggested that the latter interpretation is the only one which could sensibly fit within the purpose of s.85 and the Prospectus Directive because the legislative intent is to catch as many offers of securities as possible *while also* ensuring that a sufficiency of information is given to investors: to adopt the first interpretation would be to permit offerors to avoid the regulations by providing less information than the regulations would otherwise require. **36–20**

First, then, there must be an offer. While this definition does not specify that the offeror must have an intention to effect legal relations with the recipient of that offer, it is suggested that that must be inferred from the context or else there would not be a contractually valid offer nor a meaningful invitation to treat under English contract law. The question of invitations to treat was considered immediately above. What is significant, it is suggested, is what sort of circular information might be said to constitute an invitation to treat as opposed to an offer in the strict sense. The key distinction between a binding offer and a mere invitation to treat is that an offer must be specific to the intended counterparty and not be an overly general statement. The offeror must intend to make an offer which, if accepted, would bind her to the agreement.[33] As suggested immediately above, the Irish Prospectus Regulations 2005, for example, make it plain that an "offer" includes "an invitation to treat"; and it is suggested that that interpretation should be placed on s.102B of the FSMA 2000 in the UK. In relation to the offer of securities to the public, no offer can be made which breaches the terms of the financial promotion code considered in Chapter 10. **36–21**

Secondly, it is required that a "communication" was made, that that communication "presented sufficient information" as to the securities themselves and the terms on which those securities are offered. The communication can be made, it would seem, in any form and by any means. There is no formality

---

[32] Invitations to treat were considered in para.17–15.
[33] *Storer v Manchester C.C.* [1974] 1 W.L.R. 1403.

required to constitute a communication for these purposes.[34] The communication can be made directly by the offeror or it can be made through an intermediary.[35] However, a communication for the purposes of this section will not have been effected if it is connected with trading on a regulated market, or a multilateral trading facility,[36] or on a market which has been prescribed as a regulated market under FSMA 2000.[37] Therefore, there need not be a binding contract in place for there to have been a communication made. Instead, it is sufficient that an offer has been made which was intended to effect legal relations. If such an offer is made to a person in the UK then it is taken to be an offer of transferable securities in the UK.[38]

36–22   Therefore, the liability to comply with prospectus regulation is very broadly drawn. Indeed, that was the policy underpinning the Prospectus Directive. The aim was to bring all offers to the public, even very small offers, theoretically within the scope of prospectus regulation. However, having thrown the net very widely indeed, the Directive then excluded a number of different types of offer, as discussed below.[39]

E. The definition of "securities" and "transferable securities"

36–23   For the purposes of the Prospectus Directive 2003, the term "securities" is defined so as to constitute[40]:

> "shares in companies and other securities equivalent to shares in companies,
>   bonds and other forms of securitised debt which are negotiable on the capital market [sic] and
>   any other securities normally dealt in giving the right to acquire any such transferable securities by subscription or exchange or giving rise to a cash settlement excluding instruments of payment."

However, the Prospectus Directive provides that national legislation may supplement this definition.[41] The listing rules refer generally to "transferable securities", as considered in the next chapter. The definition of "transferable security" in the Glossary to the *FCA Handbook* is "anything which is a transferable security for the purposes of MiFID, other than money-market instruments for the purposes of that directive which have a maturity of less than 12 months". The indicative definition[42] of "transferable security" in MiFID is[43]:

---

[34] Financial Services and Markets Act 2000, s.102B(3).
[35] Financial Services and Markets Act 2000, s.102B(4).
[36] Financial Services and Markets Act 2000, s.102B(6).
[37] Financial Services and Markets Act 2000, s.102B(5).
[38] Financial Services and Markets Act 2000, s.102B(2).
[39] See para.36–28.
[40] Prospectus Directive art.2(1)(a), as supplemented by the definition in art.1(4) of Directive 93/22/EEC.
[41] Prospectus Directive art.2(1)(a).
[42] "Indicative" in the sense that we are told only what is included with the concept "transferable securities" rather than being given a comprehensive definition of the term.
[43] MiFID art.4(18).

"'Transferable securities' means those classes of securities which are negotiable on the capital market, with the exception of instruments of payment, such as:

(a)   shares in companies and other securities equivalent to shares in companies, partnership or other entities, and depositary receipts in respect of shares;

(b)   bonds or other forms of securitised debt, including depositary receipts in respect of such securities;

(c)   any other securities giving the right to acquire or sell any such transferable securities or giving rise to a cash settlement determined by reference to transferable securities, currencies, interest rates or yields, commodities or other indices or measures."

Each of these three categories of security is considered in turn.

The first class of security is straightforward. Shares have always been understood as being securities. What is more difficult is knowing what is "equivalent" to a share in a company. An option to acquire shares physically, as opposed merely to receiving a cash settled amount as though one had owned shares, could be said to be equivalent to a share in relation to the profit which it might generate, although it would not be equivalent to a share in that it carries no voting rights in the company nor any right to a dividend from the issuing company. Under English law, rights in ordinary partnerships do not equate to shares in companies; matters may be considered to be different in relation to limited liability partnerships. **36–24**

The second class of securities is similar. Bonds have always been understood as being securities. What is more difficult is knowing what is "equivalent" to a bond. A bond ordinarily attracts a right to be paid a rate of interest and the capital price of the bond on sale. Securitised debt is transferable and it may be structured so that the interest paid on the underlying debt is payable to the holder of the security as opposed to the original lender. In this sense, the similarities between these two types of instrument are more evident than in relation to shares. **36–25**

The third class of securities encompasses securitised derivatives, whether they are cash settled or physically settled (i.e. whether the rightholder is entitled only to a cash flow equivalent to holding the underlying asset, or is entitled to demand delivery of the underlying asset).[44] However, such transactions are frequently transacted on an over-the-counter basis which does not make them transferable, except to the extent that the buyer of the derivative may contract to sell its right to receive an asset or payment to a third party: although the seller of that derivative may not be obliged by the contract to obey instructions from that third party. The transferability of the transaction to a third party so that that third party may give directions to the seller of the derivative would be expressive of its status as a "security", as opposed to a private, bilateral contract. This definition is somewhat obscure then because it is not clear *from the terms of the legislation itself* what will cause such a transaction to become a security, although it is suggested that its transferability and ability to be traded as a result would be dispositive of that question where the instrument had those qualities. **36–26**

---

[44] See A. Hudson, *The Law on Financial Derivatives*, Ch.2 on this distinction.

F.   Private law liability further to s.85 FSMA 2000

36–27   Breach of the duties implied by s.85 of FSMA 2000 (as considered above) creates an action to recover compensation for loss suffered as a result of a breach of s.85. The nature of the private law liability which might arise further to s.85 FSMA 2000 is expressed[45] in s.85(4) FSMA 2000 in the following terms:

> "A contravention of subsection (1) or (2) is actionable, at the suit of a person who suffers loss as a result of the contravention, subject to the defences and other incidents applying to actions for breach of statutory duty."

A person who commits a breach of statutory duty which causes another person loss will be liable in tort for damages.[46] The tort of "breach of statutory duty simpliciter"[47] will render the defendant liable for damages.[48] The source of the claim is the loss suffered "as a result of" the contravention of s.85: that is, a loss which is caused by the breach of s.85.

G.   Exemptions and exclusions from the prospectus regulations

Matters which are excluded from being offers of transferable securities under s.85

36–28   Schedule 11A to the FSMA 2000 provides for three categories of securities which are excluded from the ambit of the term "transferable securities" for the purposes of the offence committed under s.85(1) of FSMA 2000. The first category deals primarily with government and similar securities. Thus, the term "transferable securities" in the context of the prospectus rules does not refer to: units in a collective investment scheme; non-equity, transferable securities issued by the government or local authorities in an EEA State, or by the European Central Bank, or the central bank of an EEA State; shares in the share capital of the central bank of an EEA State; transferable securities which are irrevocably and unconditionally guaranteed by the government or a local or regional authority of an EEA State.[49] Also excluded from the definition of "transferable securities" in this context are non-equity transferable securities which are "issued in a continuous or repeated manner by a credit institution"[50] on the condition that[51] they are not subordinated, convertible or exchangeable, that they do not give a right to subscribe to or acquire other types of securities and are not linked to a

---

[45] The suggested weakness in the drafting was considered in the preceding footnote.

[46] *Groves v Lord Wimborne* [1898] 2 Q.B. 402; *X (minors) v Bedfordshire County Council* [1995] 2 A.C. 633; *O'Rourke v Camden LBC* [1998] A.C. 188. See para.25–53.

[47] *X (minors) v Bedfordshire County Council* [1995] 2 A.C. 633. See generally *Clerk & Lindsell on Torts*, 19th edn (London: Sweet & Maxwell, 2006), para.9–06 et seq.

[48] *Cutler v Wandsworth Stadium Ltd* [1949] A.C. 398. See para.25–54.

[49] Financial Services and Markets Act 2000, s.85(5)(a), as supplied by Financial Services and Markets Act 2000, Sch.11A.

[50] Financial Services and Markets Act 2000, s.85(5)(a), as supplied by Financial Services and Markets Act 2000, Sch.11A, para.5(1).

[51] Financial Services and Markets Act 2000, s.85(5)(a), as supplied by Financial Services and Markets Act 2000, Sch.11A, para.5(2).

derivative instrument; that they "materialise reception of repayable deposits"[52]; and that they are covered by a deposit guarantee under the EC deposit guarantee directive.[53] The final exclusion in the first Part of Sch.11A relates to non-fungible shares of capital intended to provide a right in immoveable property which cannot be sold without giving up that right.[54]

The second category relates to securities in not-for-profit organisations. Part 2 of Sch.11A then contains a further set of entities which may issue securities without falling within the prospectus rules. Broadly-speaking, these entities are not-for-profit entities which would not have shareholders with the result that the underlying policy concerns of the prospectus rules as to investor protection would not ordinary apply to these entities. Consequently, the term "transferable securities" within the prospectus rules does not apply to securities issued by a charity,[55] a housing association, an industrial and provident society,[56] or a "non-profit making association or body" recognised by an EEA State.[57]

36–29

The third category then divides between two further types of security which do not constitute "transferable securities" for the purposes of the prospectus rules. First, non-equity transferable securities which are "issued in a continuous or repeated manner by a credit institution" if the total consideration for the offer is less than 50 million and they are not subordinated, convertible or exchangeable, that they do not give a right to subscribe for nor to acquire other types of securities and are not linked to a derivative instrument; that they "materialise reception of repayable deposits"; and that they are covered by a deposit guarantee under the EC deposit guarantee directive.[58] Secondly, an offer where the total consideration for the offer is less than 2.5 million.[59]

36–30

Exemptions from the requirement for a prospectus

The exemptions from liability for failure to make available an approved prospectus in relation to the offences in s.85 are provided in s.86 of FSMA 2000.[60] There is no contravention of s.85 in any of these circumstances. The first exemption relates[61] to an offer which is only made to or directed at people (whether financial institutions, public bodies or recognised individuals) who are registered by the FCA as being qualified investors. The second exemption relates to offers made to fewer than one hundred people, because such a small group

36–31

---

[52] Financial Services and Markets Act 2000, Sch.11A, para.5(2)(c).
[53] 94/19/EC.
[54] Financial Services and Markets Act 2000, Sch.11A, para.6.
[55] The Charities Act 2011 has extended the range of charitable purposes under English law: see A.S. Hudson, *Equity & Trusts* (Routledge, 2012), Ch.25, "Charities".
[56] See Ch.54 of this book.
[57] Financial Services and Markets Act 2000, Sch.11A, para.7.
[58] Financial Services and Markets Act 2000, Sch.11A, para.8.
[59] Financial Services and Markets Act 2000, Sch.11A, para.9(1).
[60] These provisions are expanded on in broadly similar terms in Prospectus Rules, para.1.2.2R "exempt securities—offers of securities to the public" and Prospectus Rules, para.1.2.3R "exempt securities—admission to trading on a regulated market".
[61] Financial Services and Markets Act 2000, s.86(1).

would not be "the public".[62] The third exemption relates to large issues beyond the reach of ordinary, retail investors in which the minimum consideration is at least 50,000. The fourth exemption relates to large denomination issues where the securities being offered are denominated in amounts of at least 50,000. The fifth exemption relates to small issues where the total consideration for the transferable securities being offered cannot exceed 100,000. The sixth possible exemption relates to situations in which a non-qualified investor engages a qualified investor to act as his agent and where that agent has discretion as to his investment decisions,[63] because the expertise of the qualified investor will shield the issuer from liability to comply with the prospectus requirement in s.85 of FSMA 2000.

Further exempt categories under the Prospectus Rules

36–32   The FCA is given a power, further to s.85(5)(b) of FSMA 2000, to create regulations under the Prospectus Rules to exempt further categories of offers of securities. In relation to offers of securities to the public, they include shares issued in substitution for shares of the same class[64]; transferable securities offered in connection with a takeover[65] or with a merger[66]; shares which are to be offered or allotted free of charge to existing shareholders and dividends which are to be paid in the form of shares[67]; or transferable securities offered or allotted to existing or former directors or employees by their employer where those transferable securities have already been admitted to listing.[68] Securities which are to be admitted to trading on a regulated market may be exempt under this head where they are shares representing less than 10 per cent of the shares of the same class already admitted to trading on the same regulated market over a period of twelve months[69]; or securities of the type mentioned above in relation to offers of securities to the public.

H.   Transactions where the issuer elects to have a prospectus

36–33   In relation to offers of securities which are exempted from the requirement to have a prospectus, it is possible for an issuer to elect to have a prospectus further to s.87 of FSMA 2000. If a person so elects to have a prospectus then that person is bound by the Prospectus Rules[70] but not by the UKLA Listing Rules[71] (because the Listing Rules would only apply if the securities were to be listed, and if they were to be listed then a prospectus would be required in any event).[72] An issuer

---

[62] Financial Services and Markets Act 2000, s.86(3).
[63] Financial Services and Markets Act 2000, s.86(2).
[64] Prospectus Rules, para.1.2.2(1)R.
[65] Prospectus Rules, para.1.2.2(2)R.
[66] Prospectus Rules, para.1.2.2(3)R.
[67] Prospectus Rules, para.1.2.2(4)R.
[68] Prospectus Rules, para 1.2.2(5)R.
[69] Prospectus Rules, para.1.2.3(1)R.
[70] Financial Services and Markets Act 2000, s.87(2).
[71] Financial Services and Markets Act 2000, s.87(3).
[72] Listing Rules, para.2.2.10(2)(a)R.

might decide that there is a marketing advantage to be had by complying with the Prospectus Rules, such as the promotion of investor confidence in the high quality, transparency and probity of the issuer demonstrated by its compliance with these stringent regulations if that issuer is not well known to the market. The kinds of transferable securities which are most commonly at issue here are[73] non-equity transferable securities issued by a public body in an EEA state, securities guaranteed by a public body in an EEA state, non-equity transferable securities issued in a repeated manner by a credit institution,[74] transferable securities included in an offer of less than 2.5 million.[75]

4.   THE APPROVAL OF A PROSPECTUS: CONTENTS AND PROCEDURE

A.   The general duty of disclosure of information in prospectuses

The duty of disclosure in s.87A FSMA 2000

There is a general duty of disclosure of information in the sense that there is a **36–34** duty to make full disclosure of the necessary information in a prospectus before that prospectus can be approved for the purposes of s.85 of FSMA 2000 by the FCA. Therefore, the general duty of disclosure suggested in this discussion is to be inferred from the fact that without such disclosure the criteria for the FCA to approve the prospectus will not have been satisfied, and so there cannot be an offer of transferable securities to the public[76] nor a request for admission of securities to trading on a regulated market.[77]

This general duty of disclosure is set out in s.87A of FSMA 2000. The effect of **36–35** this duty of disclosure is that prospectuses must contain all the information which investors would require to make an informed assessment of the securities. The duty of disclosure is rooted in the requirement that the prospectus must contain the "necessary information" before it can be approved by the FCA. Section 87A(1) of FSMA 2000 provides as follows:

> "The competent authority may not approve a prospectus unless it is satisfied that—
> (a)   the United Kingdom is the home State in relation to the issuer of the transferable securities to which it relates,
> (b)   the prospectus contains the necessary information, and
> (c)   all of the other requirements imposed by or in accordance with this Part or the prospectus directive have been complied with (so far as those requirements apply to a prospectus for the transferable securities in question)."

Therefore it is s.87A(1)(b) which contains the requirement that the "necessary information" be contained in the prospectus. The requirements that the UK is the home state, briefly put, means that the issue must have been presented for authorisation in the UK first.

---

[73] Financial Services and Markets Act 2000, s.87(4).

[74] Which are not subordinate, convertible or exchangeable.

[75] Financial Services and Markets Act 2000, Sch.11A.

[76] Financial Services and Markets Act 2000, s.85(1).

[77] Financial Services and Markets Act 2000, s.85(2).

36–36   The definition of "necessary information" is contained in s.87A(2) of FSMA 2000 in the following terms:

> "The necessary information is the information necessary to enable investors to make an informed assessment of—
> (a)   the assets and liabilities, financial position, profits and losses, and prospects of the issuer of the transferable securities and of any guarantor; and
> (b)   the rights attaching to the transferable securities."

There are therefore four significant elements to this general duty of disclosure, which are considered below; first we consider who is responsible for the prospectus.

Persons responsible

36–37   The Prospectus Rules sets out the people who are responsible for the preparation of the prospectus, further to s.84(1)(d) FSMA 2000, over-and-above any liability under the law of tort. Paragraph 5.5.3R of the Prospectus Rules provides that the following categories of people are responsible for the contents of the prospectus: the issuer (i.e. the entity issuing the securities); directors and anyone else who authorises themselves to be named as being responsible for the prospectus; each person who accepts responsibility for the prospectus; and any other persons who have authorised the contents of the prospectus. However, para 5.5.6R of the Prospectus Rules provides that a person is not responsible for a prospectus if it is published without his knowledge or consent; and provided that that person gives reasonable public notice that it was published without his knowledge or consent as soon as practicable when they became aware of its publication. Among the professional advisors—solicitors, accountants, public relations consultants, investment bankers and so forth—there will have been a large number of people who will have worked on the prospectus. Consequently, para.5.5.3(2)(c)R provides that responsibility for the prospectus will extend to each person who accepts, and is stated in the prospectus as accepting, responsibility for the prospectus.

The "informed assessment" criterion

36–38   Secondly, the test for what type of information should be contained in the prospectus is an "informed assessment" test. This is not a requirement of "reasonableness", nor is it a test based on the information which a professional advisor would require. That there is no reference to a professional advisor in s.87A FSMA 2000 means that those preparing the prospectus cannot assume the presence of a professional advisor and so cannot assume that they can omit information which a professional advisor is bound to know. Instead, because s.87A(2) refers only to "investors" making an informed assessment it is necessary for the prospectus to contain all of the information which might be required for those investors to make an informed assessment, including information and warnings as to risks and so forth which it would be expected that professional advisors would appreciate. Therefore, the prospectus must couch its information in language which makes those risks evident even to a layman; it must avoid communicating only in jargon which retail investors may not understand, unless those terms are defined or explained. There may also be similar difficulties relating to the use of prospectuses by investors in the after-market. The liability to such people in tort is considered in detail in Chapter 39 of this book. However, it is suggested that the prospectus must also cater for the sorts of technical information (accounting, legal terminology and so forth), which a professional investor and its advisors would also expect to find or which such a professional investor would also require so as to make a decision about the securities, even if that is the sort of information which an inexpert investor might not think to consider.

The keynote of this duty of disclosure in s.87A is the need to ensure the investor **36–39** can make an "informed assessment". Those preparing the prospectus must consider what level of information is required in writing in the prospectus so that the investor can be sufficiently well informed so as to make an assessment of the investment prospects offered by the securities. This requirement is, however, not concerned with the presentation or discussion of absolutely all of the information which may possibly affect the issuer or its market. A prospectus has never been intended to be a textbook on management theory or economics which eventually hones in on the securities issue in question. Rather, the investor must decide whether or not she wishes to take a risk by investing in this security rather than taking a risk by investing in another security. After all, all investment involves risk.[78] What is required of a prospectus is that it contains all of the information which is necessary to enable the investor to decide in an appropriately informed manner about the securities in question. This question can only really be understood by approaching it from the opposite direction from that which is taken in s.87A(2): the question is how much information must be provided so that the investor knows all that it is necessary to know when deciding whether or not to buy the securities.

Consequently, the issuer and its advisors are involved in an art as well as a **36–40** science in terms of casting the net of information contained in the prospectus as widely as they need to cast it, but also judging at what point the informational coverage can stop. The question then is as to the information which an *informed* investor would *need* to find in a prospectus. This is, it is suggested, different from asking what sort of information a *reasonable* investor would *expect* to find in a prospectus. The statute does not ask us to imagine a reasonable investor. A reasonable investor would not require information of the sort that one may find in "an idiot's guide to investing", relating for example to the effect which macroeconomic data like movements in interest rates or the commencement of an unexpected land war in Europe might have on a company's prospects. However, we might want to *read in* a standard of reasonableness to the preparation of prospectuses or else the business of producing them would become untenable with the weight of background information which some particularly naïve retail investors may be thought to require. However, it should be noted that such a standard of reasonableness is not contained in s.87A explicitly.

---

[78] *Royal Brunei Airlines v Tan* [1995] 2 A.C. 378, per Lord Nicholls.

36–41   In this regard, s.87A(4) provides that:

> "The necessary information must be must be prepared having regard to the particular nature of the transferable securities and their issuer."

This provision tells us that the information must be relative to the nature of the securities in question and to the nature of the issuer. It also requires the prospectus to present information about the securities themselves, as opposed to generic information, and about the issuer particularly such that an unusual issue would require more information, or a little known start-up company issuing securities would require more information, and so forth, than would a well-known company in a well-known market. Well-known companies in well-known markets (such as high street retailers or clearing banks) making issues of plain vanilla securities (such as ordinary shares of the same class as those already in issue) would not require a large amount of specialist information beyond that normally found in prospectuses. Thus, the provision of information can start at a level relative to the issuer's particular market and particular corporate structure and financial condition. However, a technology company developing new products in new markets and which is little known in the markets in which a general offer to the public is being made would require a much larger amount of background information as to the company's organisation, products, markets and so forth to be made available to investors. It is when there are matters which may not be obvious to all investors—as to the issuer's market, or as to the manner in which the issuer's accounts were prepared, or as to the issuer's group structure, or some such—that the issuer is required to begin to provide information which goes further than might ordinarily be required.

The relevant information to be provided

36–42   Thirdly, the relevant information which must be provided is not *all* information which may possibly relate to the issuer. Rather, the information which is required is that information which enables an investor to make an informed assessment of four things: the assets and liabilities of the issuer, the financial position of the issuer, the profits and losses of the issuer, and the prospects of the issuer. The prospectus is likely to range across other issues which are likely to be of significance to an investor, but the types of information which are identified in s.87A of FSMA 2000 are limited to these four. A discussion of the issuer's prospects, for example, will require a greater range of types of information than simply accounting information. As is considered below, the nature of the information which is required may also be dependent on the likely pool of investors, where more expert investors may require less information (for example) as to the basic risk profile of ordinary securities than retail investors.

Information as to the rights attaching to the securities

36–43   Fourthly, the prospectus must provide information as to the rights which will attach to the securities which are to be issued. In relation to debt securities or convertible securities, this may be more complex than in relation to the voting and other rights attaching to ordinary shares.

The requirement for comprehensible and easily analysable presentation of the necessary information

The manner in which the necessary information is to be set out is described in s.87A(3) of FSMA 2000 in the following way: **36–44**

> "The necessary information must be presented in a form which is comprehensible and easy to analyse."

The obligation to make the information comprehensible and easy to analyse is a result of requiring disclosure of information which will satisfy ordinary investors. The dictionary definition of "comprehensible" is that the matter "may be understood".[79] If something may be understood by someone, then it might be comprehensible even if it cannot be understood by everyone. What is important, it is suggested, in relation to prospectuses is that an ordinary investor would be able to understand what assertion is being made by the statement in the prospectus on a reasonable basis. That is, no ambiguity must be permitted which would conceal the true meaning of a statement in a prospectus which is otherwise encouraging investors to acquire securities; and there must also be sufficient disclosure of the basic information.

The significance of the general duty of disclosure in s.87A FSMA 2000

Section 87A therefore provides an underpinning standard which is to be observed by those creating a prospectus by reference to which any more specific provision can be interpreted and any matter beyond the scope of those detailed rules can be considered. As was considered in Chapter 8, the significance of high-level principles in these contexts is that they both contain flexible rules in themselves—requiring professional advisors to be acclimatised to regulatory practice in relation to different types of securities issues—and also serve as a means of interpreting detailed regulation.   **36–45**

B. The requirement for a supplementary prospectus: s.87G FSMA 2000

Even after the preparation of a prospectus is complete there may be events which take place which affect the prospects or condition of the issuer significantly, and therefore a supplementary prospectus may be required to be published which deals with those intervening events. Section 87G of the FSMA 2000 provides that a supplementary prospectus is required to be published in the following circumstances[80]:   **36–46**

---

[79] *Shorter Oxford English Dictionary.*
[80] Financial Services and Markets Act 2000, s.87G(2).

"if, during the relevant period, there arises or is noted a significant new factor, material mistake or inaccuracy relating to the information included in a prospectus [or in a supplementary prospectus][81] approved by the competent authority."

The "relevant period" is the time between the regulatory approval of the prospectus and the start of trading in the securities. This obligation arises in relation to prospectuses which have already been approved. If the prospectus had not been approved when such a matter came to the parties' attention then, it is suggested, the obligation under s.87A of FSMA 2000 to provide all necessary information would require that the prospectus was amended and that this information was added to it before approval could take place. The requirement of "significance" is defined by s.87G(4) to be something which is significant in relation to the categories of "necessary information" in s.87A(2).

C. Criteria for the approval of a prospectus by the FCA

36–47   An application for approval of the prospectus by the FCA acting as the UK competent authority must be made on submission to the FCA of a copy of Form A and of the prospectus.[82] The FCA may impose conditions before it will approve a prospectus. Such conditions must be given to the issuer by notice in writing.[83] Section 87C of the FSMA 2000 provides the timetable by reference to which the FCA must give its decision in relation to an application for the approval of a prospectus. In relation to applications by a new issuer[84] the FCA must notify the applicant of its decision within 20 days from the first "working day" after the date on which the application was received.[85] In relation to applications which are not made by a new issuer, the FCA must notify the applicant of its decision within 10 days from the first "working day" after the date on which the application was received.[86] During whichever of those periods is applicable, the FCA may, by notice in writing, require the applicant to provide specified documents or information, or documents or information of a specified description,[87] provided that those documents or that information are reasonably required in the discharge of its duties as competent authority.[88] The FCA may also require any authentication or verification to be provided by the applicant in relation to that documentation or information.[89] In relation to supplementary prospectuses, the FCA must give its decisions within seven days of the application being received.[90] In any of these cases, failure to comply with this timetable does not

---

[81]   Financial Services and Markets Act 2000, s.87G(7).
[82]   Prospectus Rules, para.3.1.1R.
[83]   Financial Services and Markets Act 2000, s.87J.
[84]   A "new issuer" is a person who does not have transferable securities admitted to trading on any regulated market and which has not previously offered transferable securities to the public: Financial Services and Markets Act 2000, s.87C(11).
[85]   Financial Services and Markets Act 2000, s.87C, especially s.87(3)(b).
[86]   Financial Services and Markets Act 2000, s.87C, especially s.87(3)(a).
[87]   Financial Services and Markets Act 2000, s.87C(4) and (5).
[88]   Financial Services and Markets Act 2000, s.87C(6).
[89]   Financial Services and Markets Act 2000, s.87C(8).
[90]   Financial Services and Markets Act 2000, s.87C(9).

constitute an acceptance of the application.[91] Approval or disapproval of a prospectus must be given in writing to the issuer.[92] In either event, the notice of the decision must give the FCA's reasons for that decision[93] and inform the applicant of its right of appeal to the Markets Tribunal under the 2000 Act.[94]

D.   The required contents of a prospectus

The central principle as to the contents of a prospectus

The required contents of a prospectus can be best understood as operating on the basis of the general obligation to make disclosure under s.87A of FSMA 2000, as was considered in detail above. Thus, the prospectus must provide all of the "necessary information" to enable an investor to be able to make "an informed assessment" as to those securities. Bearing that underlying principle in mind, we shall now consider some of the key requirements of detail in the Prospectus Rules.

36–48

The form of a prospectus

A prospectus may be in the form of a single document or of separate documents.[95] A prospectus in a single document must be divided between a registration document, a securities note and a summary.[96] A prospectus in the form of separate documents must have a registration document which contains the information relating to the issuer and a securities note which contains the information about the transferable securities which are to be offered to the public or to admitted to trading.[97] Beyond these structural issues, the PD Regulation[98] requires that, for a prospectus in a single document, there must be a clear and detailed table of contents, a summary (in the form discussed in the next section), the risk factors linked both to the issuer and to the security covered by the issue, and the other items set out in the schedules and building blocks in the PD Regulation.[99] A prospectus in separate documents must also contain a clear and detailed table of contents, the risk factors linked both to the issuer and to the security covered by the issue, and the other items set out in the schedules and building blocks in the Commission's PD Regulation.[100]

36–49

---

[91] Financial Services and Markets Act 2000, s.87C(10).

[92] Financial Services and Markets Act 2000, s.87D(1), and (2) and (4) respectively.

[93] Financial Services and Markets Act 2000, s.87D(3).

[94] Financial Services and Markets Act 2000, s.87D(5).

[95] Prospectus Rules, para.2.2.1R; PD art.5.3.

[96] Prospectus Rules, para.2.2.2(1)R.

[97] Prospectus Rules, para.2.2.2(2)R.

[98] This regulation is the document prepared by the Commission to supply technical information beyond the framework principles of the Prospectus Directive.

[99] Prospectus Rules, para.2.2.10: PD Regulation, art.25.1.

[100] Prospectus Rules, para.2.2.10: PD Regulation, art.25.2.

The manner in which detailed contents of a prospectus are identified in the regulations

36–50   The detailed required contents of prospectuses depend on the type of securities which are in issue. The minimum information to be included in a prospectus is considered in arts 3 to 23 of the Commission's Prospectus Directive Regulation.[101] Appendix 3 to the Prospectus Rules then contains a large amount of material divided between schedules of required minimum information, and building blocks containing additional information required for different types of issue.

36–51   Broadly-speaking, the issuer will be required to prepare a base prospectus, which is subject to the foregoing principles and in that sense might be considered to be in broadly a common form, before the various specific requirements of different types of security are also included in the prospectus. Where a base prospectus is prepared, then, that base prospectus must contain the following information in the following order: a clear and detailed table of contents, a summary, the risk factors linked both to the issuer and to the security covered by the issue, and the other items set out in the schedules and building blocks in the PD Regulation.[102] The requirements in the "building blocks" for certain types of issues are described in the Commission's PD Regulation only in outline form, in that they indicate the type of information which is required and which the issuer and its advisers must formulate that information in a form sufficient to comply with those requirements. Those building blocks are reproduced in the Prospectus Rules.

36–52   The lists of information which must be provided are far too long to be reproduced here, but can be viewed on the FCA's website.[103] To give you a taste of the contents, dear reader, we can consider the headings which are required in relation to one particular type of securities issue (from the many set out in the regulations) which is a "share registration document". In the regulations it is provided that the "minimum requirements" for a prospectus in relation to such a security are (in the order in which they appear in the technical regulation) information as to[104]: persons responsible for the information in the document; information about the statutory auditors; selected historical financial information about the issuer; prominent disclosure of risk factors specific to the issuer or its industry in a separately headed section within the document; information about the issuer's history and investments; a business overview of the issuer's principal activities and principal markets; the issuer's organisational structure; the issuer's property, plant and equipment; the issuer's financial condition and operating results; the issuer's capital resources in the long and short term; the issuer's research and development profile; trend information in relation to the issuer's prospects; profit forecasts and estimates; the management structure of the issuer; remuneration and practices of senior management, and board practices; the number of employees and information as to employee shareholding; the identity of major shareholders

---

[101]   Prospectus Rules, para.2.3.1.
[102]   Prospectus Rules, para.2.2.10: PD Regulation, art.26.1.
[103]   http://www.fca.gov.uk
[104]   As set out in PD Regulation, Annex V.

in the issuer and their voting rights; information as to related party transactions; financial information relating to the issuer's assets and liabilities, financial position, and profits and losses; share capital; any material contracts other than those entered into in the ordinary course of business; and the issuer's constitutional documents. Further provisions relating to other equity securities, debt securities, asset-backed securities, derivative securities, and so on are set out in the PD Regulation in similar form. Thus, those preparing the prospectus are given a large number of "headings" under which they must provide information which complies with the general duty of disclosure in s.87A, as discussed above.

E. The requirement for a summary with a prospectus

Section 87A(5) of FSMA 2000 provides that a prospectus must include a summary, except where the prospectus rules provide to the contrary. That summary must be prepared in accordance with the following principle:

36–53

> "The summary must, briefly and in non-technical language, convey the essential characteristics of, and risks associated with, the issuer, any guarantor and the transferable securities to which the prospectus relates."[105]

Thus, beyond the requirement of identifying all "necessary information" in s.87A, the issuer must also identify the "essential characteristics" of the issuer, of any person providing a guarantee and of the securities themselves. The summary must also summarise the risks: this is an important part of ensuring that an investor is educated as to the principal downsides associated with the investment and thus to giving that investor a clear picture with which to make an informed assessment of any potential investment in the securities.

F. The authorisation of omission of information in a prospectus by the FCA

The FCA may authorise omission of information otherwise required to be included in a prospectus further to s.87B of the FSMA 2000 if its disclosure would be contrary to the public interest; or would be seriously detrimental to the issuer (provided that its omission would be unlikely to mislead the public); or where the information is only of minor importance. Such an authorisation must be made in writing by the applicant.[106]

36–54

If the prospectus does not include the final offer price nor the amount of the transferable securities to be offered to the public then the issuer must notify the UKLA in writing of that information "as soon as that element is finalised".[107] The prospectus must disclose the criteria or conditions which will inform the decision of that final price if it is not included in the prospectus.[108] Investors have a right to withdraw from an agreement to buy or to subscribe for transferable securities

36–55

---

[105] Financial Services and Markets Act 2000, s.87G(6).
[106] Prospectus Rules, para.2.5.3R.
[107] Financial Services and Markets Act 2000, s.87A(7).
[108] Prospectus Rules, para.2.3.2R.

which were offered to the public if the offer price was not included in the prospectus.[109] A price will be treated as having been provided if the criteria or conditions for calculating that price are provided in the prospectus.[110] The right to withdraw lasts for two working days from the investor's acceptance.[111]

G.   The general obligation to obey the Prospectus Rules

36–56   There is a general obligation imposed on all persons to whom any individual rule is specified as being applicable to obey that rule.[112] Further to s.91(1A) of FSMA 2000, any contravention of the listing rules opens an issuer or any persons offering securities for sale to the public or seeking their admission to a regulated market up to a penalty from the FCA if there has been either a contravention of Part 6 of FSMA 2000 generally, or a contravention of the prospectus rules, or a contravention of the transparency rules. Penalties may also be imposed on directors of the perpetrator if the FCA considers it to be appropriate.[113] In place of financial penalties, the FCA may instead issue a statement of censure.[114]

H.   Passporting applications and prospectuses between member states

Transfers of applications between the competent authorities of EEA states

36–57   The EC Prospectus Directive permits passporting of successful applications and thus permits issuers to move between Member States. This latter option is of particular significance to groups of companies with offices in different Member States which may have an option as to which group company should be the issuer of the securities. Therefore, the FCA may transfer an application for the approval of a prospectus or of a supplementary prospectus to the competent authority of another EEA state,[115] provided that it has the agreement of that transferee authority.[116] Any transfer must be notified to the applicant within three days of the first working day after receipt of the application.[117] Once the application has been transferred then the FCA ceases to have responsibility for the application.[118] Under s.100A of FSMA 2000 the FCA has the power to give a notice of a regulatory infringement to the issuer's home state, where that home state is not the UK.

---

[109] Financial Services and Markets Act 2000, s.87Q(1).
[110] Financial Services and Markets Act 2000, s.87Q(3).
[111] Financial Services and Markets Act 2000, s.87Q(2).
[112] Prospectus Rules, para.1.1.3R.
[113] Financial Services and Markets Act 2000, s.91(2).
[114] Financial Services and Markets Act 2000, s.91(3).
[115] Financial Services and Markets Act 2000, s.87E(1).
[116] Financial Services and Markets Act 2000, s.87E(2).
[117] Financial Services and Markets Act 2000, s.87E(3).
[118] Financial Services and Markets Act 2000, s.87E(4).

Alternatively, an application may be transferred by the competent authority of another Member State to the FCA provided that the FCA agrees to accept that application.[119] Once the FCA accepts the application, the United Kingdom will be treated as the home State in relation to the issuer of the transferable securities to which the prospectus relates, and the timetable considered in the preceding section will be treated as applying to the issuer as if the application had been made to the FCA from outset[120] as from the date that that transfer is accepted.[121]

36–58

Certification of "passported" prospectuses

A prospectus which has been approved in one EEA state may be transferred to another Member State in reliance on the approval of the first, or "home", State without requiring separate approval in the second, or "host", State. This is one of the basic objectives of the Prospectus Directive. However, a prospectus accepted from another EEA state is only an approved prospectus for the purposes of avoiding the commission of an offence under s.85 of FSMA 2000 if the prospectus is accompanied by a certificate of approval; a copy of the prospectus as approved; and (if requested by the FCA) a translation of the summary of the prospectus.[122] A certificate of approval, to be valid for this purpose, unless it states that the prospectus has been drawn up in accordance with the Prospectus Directive; that it has been approved, in accordance with that Directive, by the competent authority providing the certificate[123]; and unless it gives reasons for any authorisation to omit information.[124]

36–59

5.   The Contexts in which Listing Particulars are Required

Listing particulars were required for the admission of securities to listing generally before the introduction of the Prospectus Regulations on July 1, 2005. Listing particulars are now required only in relation to offers of securities which are being made to a specified category of, effectively, expert investors, further to Chapter 4 of the Listing Rules. Due to their reduced significance they will receive no further specific coverage in this book.[125]

36–60

---

[119] Financial Services and Markets Act 2000, s.87F(1).
[120] Financial Services and Markets Act 2000, s.87F(1).
[121] Financial Services and Markets Act 2000, s.87F(2).
[122] Financial Services and Markets Act 2000, s.87H(1).
[123] Financial Services and Markets Act 2000, s.87H(2).
[124] Financial Services and Markets Act 2000, s.87H(3).
[125] See A.S. Hudson, *Securities Law*, Ch.13 for a detailed account of the applicable statutory rules and regulations.

6.   TRANSPARENCY OBLIGATIONS

A.   Introduction

36–61   This section is concerned with the obligations imposed in relation to offers of securities to the public further to the Transparency Obligations Directive.[126] The purpose of the rules considered in this section is to maintain a flow of information to the investing public once securities have been admitted to trading on a regulated market. Principally the regulations are concerned with "voting information" in relation to shareholdings and comparable instruments so that investors can know who has ultimate control of a company in which they are considering investing. In this way it is expected that the transparency of the issuer will be maintained.

36–62   The Transparency Obligations Directive[127] was implemented in the UK by means of Pt 43 of the Companies Act 2006 ("CA 2006"). Part 43 of CA 2006 interpolates new provisions into Pt 6 of FSMA 2000 alongside the prospectus rules considered above. Implementation of the directive is thus achieved by means of additions to Pt 6 of FSMA 2000 and, in time, by the introduction of "Disclosure and Transparency Rules" ("DTR") as part of the *FCA Handbook* to give effect to the more detailed provisions both of the directive and of the Commission's technical regulation relating to the directive. The Transparency Obligations Directive imposes obligations on issuers of securities and others to maintain the availability of relevant information to investors after those securities have been offered to the public for the first time. Therefore, whereas the prospectus provisions, considered in the previous section, are concerned with the provision of information before an offer is made to the public, the transparency obligations provisions considered in this chapter are concerned to maintain information once those securities have been offered to the public.

36–63   Briefly put, transparency obligations impose continuing obligations on the issuers of securities traded on regulated markets to provide certain types of information to investors about those securities once those securities have been issued. Obligations are also imposed on the professional advisors and directors of those issuers, and on shareholders. Thus, what is meant by the term "transparency" is the publication of all the information which is required by those regulations so that potential investors will be able to make informed decisions about whether or not to invest in those securities. Thus, it is anticipated that the affairs of the issuing entity will become *transparent* to the investing community. Breach of these provisions which causes loss creates a liability to compensate that loss further to s.90A of the FSMA 2000, as considered in Chapter 39.[128]

---

[126] 2004/109/EC.
[127] This directive has been referred to as the "Transparency Directive" for some time in the literature but the Companies Act 2006 refers to this directive as the "Transparency Obligations Directive".
[128] See para.39–47.

B. The scope of the transparency regulations

Section 89A of FSMA 2000 grants the FCA powers to make rules dealing with transparency obligations. Those rules are contained in the Disclosure and Transparency Rules, which constitute a separate rulebook within the *FCA Handbook*. We are concerned in this section of this chapter with the transparency rules only. The Disclosure and Transparency Rules relate to dealings on "regulated markets" generally, rather than simply admission to listing on the Official List.[129] The term "regulated market" is defined as being[130]:

> "... a multilateral system operated and/or managed by a market operator, which brings together or facilitates the bringing together of multiple third party buying and selling interests in financial instruments—in the system and in accordance with non discretionary rules—in a way that results in a contract in accordance with the provisions of Title II [of the Directive]."

The transparency rules extend to cover not only people who hold shares but also "persons who hold comparable instruments".[131] The term "comparable instruments" is qualified by s.89F(1)(c) of FSMA 2000 which refers to an "article 13 instrument". The term "article 13 instrument" refers to art.13 of the Transparency Obligations Directive. There is a code in the directive relating to people who hold financial instruments which, although not vote-carrying shares, grant rights equivalent to such shares which is set out principally in new ss.89B through 89E of FSMA 2000, as considered in detail below. Article 13(1) of the Transparency Obligations Directive defines such an instrument to be one which provides a person with:

> "an entitlement to acquire, on such holder's own initiative alone, under a formal agreement, shares to which voting rights are attached, already issued, of an issuer whose shares are admitted to trading on a regulated market"

These instruments are further defined by Commission technical regulation in similar terms. This category of instrument seems to cover bonds which are convertible into voting shares and physically-settled options to acquire shares.[132] It is not clear whether an option which is automatically exercisable, however, would be an option exercisable on "such holder's own initiative", unless that initiative includes the creation of such a contract in the first place.

C. A summary of the information required by the transparency regulations

The purpose of transparency regulation is to ensure that minimum levels of information are provided to the marketplace so that investors can make informed decisions about whether or not to invest in a given security. The bulk of the

36–64

36–65

---

[129] Disclosure and Transparency Rules, 1.1.1R (as to the disclosure rules)
[130] Transparency Obligations Directive, art.4(14), as implemented by Companies Act 2006, Sch.15, para.11.
[131] Financial Services and Markets Act 2000, s.89A(3)(b).
[132] On the legal treatment of derivatives like options, see Ch.43, and see also A.S. Hudson, *The Law on Financial Derivatives*, para.2–30 et seq. in particular.

transparency regulations relate to the issuer, but other people may be required to provide information under those regulations. First, the issuer must provide the following types of information to the FCA: "voteholder information" at the date of the Directive coming into effect, and subsequent changes in that information; annual and half-yearly accounts, and interim management statements as described in the Directive; information relating to the rights attaching to any and all securities; information relating to any new loans or related security interests connected to them; information as to voting rights held by the issuer in the issuer itself; information as to any proposed amendments to the issuer's constitution. Secondly, investors must provide "voteholder information" to the issuer. Thirdly, the FCA may demand information from the following types of person: the issuer; a voteholder, or a person who controls or is controlled by a voteholder; an auditor of an issuer or a voteholder; or a director of an issuer or a voteholder. Each of these categories is considered in turn below.

D. Issuer's disclosure obligations in relation to voteholder information

36–66   Section 89B(1) of FSMA 2000 empowers the FCA to make regulations which require that "voteholder information" is to be made known to the issuer and to the public. "Voteholder information" means "information relating to the proportion of voting rights held by a person in respect of the shares".[133] There is an obligation on the issuer further to Disclosure and Transparency Rulebook at DTR, para.5.6 at the end of each calendar month during which there have been dealings in the securities to disclose "to the public" the total number of voting rights and capital in respect of each class of issued shares and also the total number of voting rights attaching to shares of the issuer which are held in treasury.[134]

36–67   The purpose of many of the transparency rules, and of ss.89B through 89E of FSMA 2000, is to treat all voting rights under common control as constituting a single block of voting rights. As defined in s.89F(4) FSMA 2000 "voting rights" are rights attaching to a share which permit the shareholder to vote at company meetings (provided that the shares at issue have been admitted to trading on a regulated market). Thus the transparency obligations provisions are concerned to enable investors to know who holds and who ultimately controls such rights, as well as to make transparent financial and other information about the company.

36–68   "Shares" in this context refers to shares carrying rights to vote at a general meeting of the company and which are admitted to trading on a regulated market.[135] The principal focus of the new s.89B of FSMA 2000 is to provide authorisation for FCA Disclosure and Transparency Rules to make provision for significant changes in the shareholding of any given person. A person whose proportionate holding of voting rights in the issuer's share capital crosses one of the statutorily identified thresholds of the total shareholding in a company, is

---

[133] Financial Services and Markets Act 2000, s.89B(3).
[134] DTR, 5.6.1R.
[135] DTR, 5.1.1R.

required to make a notification of that fact in the manner considered below. Thus, "transparency" in its securities law sense involves, in part, the notification of the identity of those people who control given proportions of the voting control of companies both to the issuing company itself and to the FCA. As will emerge from the discussion to follow, the regulations will deal with voting rights which a person controls (for example by means of contract, trust, agency or otherwise) and not simply with direct, absolute ownership of shares.

The concept of "control" is clearly significant in this context. The term "control" is defined by s.89J(2) of FSMA 2000 so as to include the following categories of person: people who hold a majority of voting rights in other persons, who have the right to alter the composition of another person's board of directors, who control the voting rights in another person perhaps by virtue of some shareholders' agreement, who either have a legal right to exercise a dominant influence over another person, or who "actually exercise" a dominant influence over that other person. **36–69**

E.   Shareholders' obligations to make notification of voteholder information

The extended definitions of "shareholder" and "holder of voting rights"

Notification obligations extend beyond the owners of shares to people who, more specifically, hold shares with voting rights or who are able to control the use of voting rights in relation to shares.[136] By making transparent the underlying voting control in a company, the FCA regulations will enhance the transparency of that company's affairs. Thus, Pt 43 of the Companies Act 2006 is concerned with control of voting rights as opposed to ownership of shares per se.[137] **36–70**

A person holds voting rights in a company in the following three circumstances.[138] First, if they are a shareholder in the issuer. Under s.89F(1) of FSMA 2000 and art.2.1e of the Transparency Obligations Directive, a "shareholder" is: **36–71**

> "any natural person or legal entity governed by private or public law, who holds, directly or indirectly ... (i) shares of the issuer in its own name and on its own account ... (ii) shares of the issuer in its own name, but on behalf of another natural person or legal entity ... (iii) [or] depositary receipts".

Secondly, if that person is entitled to deal with those voting rights under an agreement where parties are acting in concert in relation to the use of those shares, or where the shares are "lent"[139] or held as collateral,[140] or where the shares are held on trust (whether subject to a life interest, or on discretionary trust or on bare trust), or where the rights in the shares are controlled by some other undertaking, or where control is exercised by an agent as a proxy. Thirdly, under

---

[136] Financial Services and Markets Act 2000, s.89F.
[137] Financial Services and Markets Act 2000, s.89F(1)(a).
[138] Financial Services and Markets Act 2000, s.89F(1)(b).
[139] See para.44–01.
[140] See para.42–01.

a financial instrument which entitles the instrument holder to acquire voting rights in the issuer. As a fourth category, it is possible under the regulations that two or more people may be regarded as holding voting rights in respect of shares at the same time,[141] although it is not explained exactly on what basis those people are to be treated as owning the same voting rights simultaneously under s.89F(3) of FSMA 2000.

When notification must be made

36–72   Article 30 of the Transparency Obligations Directive requires that "a shareholder shall notify the issuer … of the proportion of voting rights and capital it holds … unless it has already made a notification before that date". There is a cross-reference from this provision to arts 9, 10 and 13 of the directive which relates to "information about major shareholdings". Thus, the obligation to make notifications falls only on shareholders identified in arts 9, 10 and 13 as holding major shareholdings carrying voting rights.

36–73   Article 9 requires notification on crossing thresholds of 5 per cent, 10 per cent, 15 per cent, 20 per cent, 25 per cent, 30 per cent, 50 per cent and 75 per cent of the total number of shares in an issuer which are "admitted to trading on a regulated market and to which voting rights are attached".[142] Notification is also required in relation to "events changing the breakdown of voting rights", such as the issue of new shares or the cancellation of shares. Market makers are not required to make such notifications when they cross the 5 per cent threshold, provided it is authorised so to act under MiFID[143] and neither "intervenes in the management of the issuer concerned nor exerts any influence on the issuer to buy back such shares or back the share price".[144]

36–74   Article 10 deals with a number of different situations in which there could be control exercised over shares by virtue of parties acting in concert under an agreement as to the use of those shares, or where the shares are "lent" or held as collateral, or where the shares are held on trust (whether subject to a life interest, or on discretionary trust or on bare trust), or where the rights in the shares are controlled by some other undertaking, or where control is exercised by an agent as a proxy. Article 9 is extended so as to apply to any of these situations. Article 13 extends the notification provisions of art.9 to situations in which the persons obliged to make notification of their shareholding actually hold "financial instruments", such as a physically-settled call option, which entitle them to acquire shares carrying voting rights.[145] This instrument must be in the form of a formal agreement. The purpose of these provisions, then, is to anticipate the variety of situations in which there might be indirect control of shares and not simply direct ownership of this shares. The aim of the directive is thus to ensure

---

[141] Financial Services and Markets Act 2000, s.89F(3).

[142] As implemented by Financial Services and Markets Act 2000, s.89B(4). See also DTR, 5.1.2R in relation to significant changes in shareholdings.

[143] The EC "Markets in Financial Instruments Directive", 2004/39/EC.

[144] Transparency Obligations Directive, art.9(5).

[145] These principles are implemented by the Disclosure and Transparency Rules, at 5.3.

genuine transparency as to control of the issuing company and not simply a statement of the ostensible, common law ownership of shares.

F.   Further categories of information to be provided by issuers

The issuer of securities will be obliged by the Disclosure and Transparency Rules to make notification of three types of information. The obligation to make notification of the information provided in the transparency rules may be an obligation to make that information public or an obligation to make notification to the FCA as competent authority only, or to do both (whereby the obligation formally to notify the FCA specifically imposes an obligation over and above one to make information generally known).[146] These principles apply to equity securities and to debt securities.[147]

36–75

The three categories of information are: periodic accounting information; information relating to the rights attached to the securities in question; and information about new loan issues and any connected guarantee or security.[148] These categories are all provided for under s.89C of FSMA 2000. The first category of information relating to periodic accounting information under s.89C(2) focuses primarily on matters set out in art.4 of the Transparency Obligations Directive (where art.4 deals with annual financial reports); and under s.89C(4) which focuses primarily on matters in arts 5 and 6 of the Transparency Obligations Directive (where art.5 deals with half-yearly financial reports and art.6 with interim management standards).[149] The second category of information is "information relating to the rights attached to the shares or other securities".[150] The third category of information is information about new loan issues and any connected guarantee or security.[151] Notification of voteholder information and of proposed amendments to the issuer's constitution have been separated out into ss.89D and 89E respectively.[152]

36–76

Under s.89C(4) of FSMA 2000, then, there is an obligation on the issuer to notify the FCA of the accounting information and "voteholder information", as

36–77

---

[146] Financial Services and Markets Act 2000, s.89C(1).

[147] Financial Services and Markets Act 2000, s.89C(3).

[148] Financial Services and Markets Act 2000, s.89C(2).

[149] Periodic financial reporting is dealt with in the *FCA Handbook* in DTR 4.

[150] Financial Services and Markets Act 2000, s.89C(2)(b). The expression "information relating to the issuer's capital" is potentially extraordinarily broad. At its absolute broadest, the expenditure of any money or the disposal of any asset at all would have some trifling effect on the issuer's capital. In this context, it could be interpreted so as to be limited only to matters which have an effect the issuer's share capital—such as the acquisition or disposal of shares in the issuer, as well as decisions to issue new shares or redeem existing shares. It could be interpreted so that any change in the company's shareholding which would cross the thresholds identified in s.89B(3)(a) would be the only information which would be notifiable. Alternatively, it could be limited so that only information which was notifiable *to* the issuer or to the FCA would be notifiable *by* the FCA, beyond more general obligations in the listing rules and elsewhere on the issuer to make notification to the FCA as competent authority of matters affecting the issuer and the value of its shares.

[151] Financial Services and Markets Act 2000, s.89C(2)(c).

[152] Consequently, whereas five matters were dealt with under s.89C(2) previously, there are now only three.

considered above. There must also be notification of the total voting rights in respect of shares in the issuer and in any particular class of shares in the issuer.[153] Some changes may require notification: a change which requires notification is a "notifiable change" and relates to some alteration across a threshold identified in the transparency rules, either by means of an increase or a decrease, in the proportionate holding of the total number of shares carrying voting rights in the issuer.[154] If the issuer proposes to amend its constitution then that proposed amendment must be notified to the FCA by the issuer.[155]

G. The FCA's powers to call for information

36–78   The FCA, acting as competent authority, is entitled to demand information from a variety of people in connection with issues of securities, provided always that that information is specified clearly and that it is reasonably required by the FCA in connection with its functions as competent authority in relation to s.89A through 89G (considered immediately above).[156] These principles are encapsulated in the *Disclosure and Transparency Rulebook* at DTR 1A.3. Section 89H of the FSMA 2000 empowers the FCA to require further information from the issuer of securities and others to maintain the "transparency" of the issue.

H. Powers exercisable in the event of an infringement of transparency obligations

36–79   The penalties for breach of any of the requirements of the preceding provisions are limited to the public censure of the issuer of the securities or to the power to suspend or prohibit trading in securities, as is considered in Chapter 38. Appeal from either of these penalties may be referred by the respondent to Tribunal created by FSMA 2000 to hear such matters under that Act generally.

---

[153] Financial Services and Markets Act 2000, s.89D(2).
[154] Financial Services and Markets Act 2000, s.89D(3).
[155] Financial Services and Markets Act 2000, s.89E.
[156] Financial Services and Markets Act 2000, s.89H; Companies Act 2006, s.1267.

CHAPTER 37

OFFICIAL LISTING OF SECURITIES 1: PRINCIPLES OF LISTING

CORE PRINCIPLES

The Financial Conduct Authority, acting as the UK Listing Authority ("UKLA"), maintains the Official List of publicly issued securities which is the principal market for securities in public companies the UK. This responsibility was required to be allocated to a competent authority under the EC Consolidated Admission and Reporting Directive 2001: the EU has thus replicated the Official List system across the Union. While the Official List is maintained by UKLA; those securities are traded separately in the UK on the Main Market of the London Stock Exchange under the Exchange's own rules: generally admission to one is sought in tandem with admission to the other. The mechanics of admission to the list and maintenance of listing are considered in the next chapter. The purpose of this chapter is to identify the core regulatory principles which underpin listing.

The attraction of having securities listed is precisely the burdens involved in acquiring a listing. If a company has gone through the listing process with its burdensome regulatory requirements, then the investing public will probably be reassured about the reliability of an investment in that company and consequently that company widens the market for its securities and probably can reduce their cost of funding in general terms. Other companies take the view that the burdens of acquiring and maintaining listing are too onerous or too expensive, and so do not bother.

The FCA Listing Rules are interpreted in accordance with the six listing principles, as are set out below in this chapter.

1. INTRODUCTION

37–01   The Official List of securities is the principal market for the securities of public limited companies which is open to the public. Securities on this list include shares, bonds, convertible bonds, warrants, securitised derivatives, and other securities as set out in this chapter. These securities are also admitted to trading on the London Stock Exchange's "Main Market" in the UK because it is a requirement of listing that securities be available on such a market. This chapter considers the interpretative principles which underpin the regulation of the Official List maintained by the Financial Conduct Authority ("FCA"),[1] whereas the next chapter considers the regulations governing admission to listing and the maintenance of listing. The remainder of this Part 10 has considered the regulations governing prospectuses, transparency obligations, liabilities for losses caused by securities issues, and acquisitions of companies, but this chapter and Chapter 38 focus specifically on so-called "listed securities".

37–02   The statutory regime governing the official listing of securities is contained in Part 6 of FSMA 2000, comprising ss.72–103. The Official List in the UK is the list maintained by the "competent authority" under the EC securities directives for the purposes of Part 6.[2] The FCA is acting specifically as the competent authority and consequently as the UK Listing Authority ("UKLA") in this context. It is responsible for the maintenance of the Official List in the UK and also has the responsibility for the creation of listing rules. The Official List is regulated by means of the FCA-maintained *Listing Rules* (referred to in this chapter as "the Listing Rules").

37–03   The regulations considered in this Part 10 focus on the scope of the FCA securities regulations dealing with "offers of securities to the public", on the FCA's obligations in relation to those regulations, and on the Listing Principles which govern the interpretation of those regulations. The next chapter focuses on the admission of securities to the Official List and to trading on regulated markets, on the mechanics of maintaining a listing, and on the regulation of inside information in this context.

37–04   While this chapter is focused on the fundamental principles of the Listing Rules it is important to bear in mind the general context within which these regulations are operating. The provisions considered in this Part 10 relate to offers of securities made to the public, or exceptionally situations in which an issuer of other securities has elected to be bound by those regulations.[3] Securities may only be offered to the public once a prospectus has been approved by the FCA (as considered in Chapter 36); once the UKLA has admitted those securities to the

---

[1] The Financial Services Authority ceased to exist on April Fool's Day 2013, and was renamed the Financial Conduct Authority ("FCA") by the Financial Services Act 2012, s.6. The bulk of the former authority's responsibilities passed to the FCA, including listing securities.

[2] Financial Services and Markets Act 2000, s.72: which came into effect on June 18, 2001: Financial Services and Markets Act 2000 (Commencement No.3) Order 2001 (SI 2001/1820).

[3] Financial Services and Markets Act 2000, s.87.

Official List (as is considered in the next chapter); and in compliance with the control on advertisements contained in the financial promotion rules (considered in Chapter 11).

2. THE LISTING RULES WITHIN SECURITIES REGULATION MORE GENERALLY

As was discussed in detail in Chapter 35[4] there are several tiers of law and of regulation in this area: the relevant EC securities directives and technical regulations; Part 6 of FSMA 2000, as amended; the secondary legislation introduction under FSMA 2000; the FCA securities regulations and the guidance notes included in those regulations. The Listing Rules contain the rules relating to the admission of securities to the Official List maintained by UKLA.

37–05

This chapter focuses on securities which are in compliance with the prospectus regulations and which are then subjected to a further regulatory regime if the issuer of those securities wishes to have them listed on the Official List (which also involves admission to trading on the Main Market of the London Stock Exchange). This is the principal market for the securities of typically the largest entities in the UK and which therefore carries with it access to the largest pool of investment capital in the UK. Listing also has the marketing benefit of having complied with the stringent listing rules while bearing the burden of having to comply with this further set of regulations. UKLA regulates the listing process and the maintenance of a listing by means of the Listing Rules. Section 96 of the FSMA 2000 gives the FCA the power in its listing rules to provide for the obligations of issuers of listed securities and for the consequences of breach of those obligations.[5]

37–06

3. THE LISTING RULES

A. Introduction

This section considers the core principles which underpin the Listing Rules and by reference to which those rules are interpreted. The next chapter considers how applications are made for listing, the sort of prospectus which must be made available to the investing public, the continuing transparency obligations which bind an issuer of securities, penalties for breach of these regulations, and so forth. Before coming to those detailed matters, however, it is important to know how the Listing Rules are structured, what are their fundamental principles, and how those principles percolate down through the detailed rules. The framework principles which guide the interpretation of the Listing Rules are the "Listing Principles".

37–07

Before the FSMA 2000 was enacted, the listing of securities was governed by the Stock Exchange rules on listing known as the "Yellow Book". The last complete

37–08

---

⁴ See para.35–09.
⁵ Financial Services and Markets Act 2000, s.96.

re-writing of the Yellow Book took place in May 2000. In the wake of the implementation of the FSMA 2000 on December 1, 2001, the first version of the old Financial Service Authority's own *securities regulations* were issued in 2002 and the Yellow Book was repealed. The old Financial Service Authority, acting as UKLA, assumed authority for the listing rules at this time from the Stock Exchange. The current version of the listing rules (no longer bound as a "yellow book") were those originally published in their entirety in June 2005 and updated in 2007. It is to this version of the listing rules that this discussion will refer.[6]

The Financial Services Authority ceased to exist on April Fool's Day 2013, and was renamed the Financial Conduct Authority ("FCA") by the Financial Services Act 2012, s.6. The bulk of the former authority's responsibilities passed to the FCA. Therefore references in this chapter are to the FCA.

B. The power of UKLA to modify or dispense with its rules

37–09   UKLA has the power[7] to modify or dispense with individual listing rules where it considers it to be appropriate to do so on an application from a company. Under the present regime UKLA may dispense with any of its rules on application by a company.[8] The FCA's power to waive its rules is always subject to FSMA 2000 and to the EC securities directives.[9] The precise form of the waiver which UKLA may grant is either a "modification" or a "dispensation" such that an issuer may have particular obligations merely modified or alternatively may have particular modifications dispensed with altogether.[10] There is nothing in the listing rules which stipulates precisely who must make the application, although it is envisaged in the rules that either the issuer or a sponsor may make an application.[11] Where it is the issuer or a sponsor who has made an application or been granted a waiver, there is a continuing obligation imposed on that person to inform UKLA "immediately" of any "matter which is material to the relevance or appropriateness of the dispensation or modification".[12]

37–10   One of the common reasons for seeking a modification or dispensation is that the issuing company is in "severe financial difficulty". In the event that that is the reason for seeking the modification or dispensation, the issuing company is

---

[6] Guidance notes for the operation of the listing rules are now interspersed throughout the listing rules, as opposed to being collected in a separate manual. Consequently, it is important to understand the hierarchy of provisions in the listing rules. The listing rules comprise "rules" (denoted with an "R" in the margin) which are rules properly so-called and "guidance notes" (denoted with a "G" in the margin and displayed in a different font) which give a gloss to the detailed rules indicating UKLA's practice in relation to the application of that rule. The listing rules generally are available on-line, at the time of writing, at the FSA's web-site *http://www.fsa.gov.uk/* The reader is then advised to follow the links (which change from time-to-time, thus making a full internet reference here possibly unhelpful for the future) to the appropriate part of the *Handbook* containing the UKLA material.

[7] Listing Rules, 1.2.2R.
[8] Listing Rules, 1.2.2R.
[9] Listing Rules, 1.2.1R.
[10] Listing Rules, 1.2.1R.
[11] Listing Rules, 1.2.1(3)R.
[12] Listing Rules, 1.2.1(3)R.

expected to comply with s.10.8 of the Listing Rules[13] which deals, inter alia, with dispensations generally for companies in severe financial difficulty from requirements of providing information to the public, or from the need to seek shareholder approval for its actions in an extraordinary general meeting, in either event due to pressures of time which make such actions impossible in the circumstances.

4. THE SIX REGULATORY PRINCIPLES GOVERNING UKLA

Section 73 of FSMA 2000 provides that the FCA must itself observe six regulatory principles when acting as UKLA and when "determining the general policy and principles by reference to which it performs particular functions" under Part 6 of the FSMA 2000.[14] These six regulatory principles considered above are similar in tone and content to the general obligations imposed on the FCA by the FSMA 2000, as considered in Chapter 8. That much is evident in the first two of these principles. The first of the six principles provides that there is a duty of economic efficiency borne by UKLA itself in relation to the use of its own resources.[15] Secondly, UKLA must ensure that a burden or restriction which is imposed on a person should be proportionate to the benefits which are expected to accrue from it.[16]

37–11

Thirdly, when exercising its powers in relation to the admission of securities to listing, UKLA must consider "the desirability of facilitating innovation".[17] It is generally considered among practitioners to be a key feature of the future good health of London as a financial centre that regulation allows financial institutions to be innovative with their financial products: the derivatives and securitisation markets are examples of this. As securities markets develop, so too will the practices and types of security which will be traded. The underlying policy within the EU is to create deep, liquid pools of capital.[18] In general terms, the FCA has obligations under FSMA 2000 to protect and to enhance competition within the UK financial system, with the result that the FCA is not only a regulator charged to protect investors and to monitor market participants but it also has an active role to enhance the UK's financial sector.

37–12

Fourthly, in relation to UKLA's own role within the economic efficiency of the securities markets which it regulates, UKLA must have regard to "the international character of capital markets and the desirability of maintaining the competitive position of the United Kingdom".[19] It is a large part of the strategic vision of the City of London that it should attract financial services business to London and not simply provide capital for companies resident in the UK. Consequently, in exercising its regulatory function, UKLA must be aware of this

37–13

---

[13] Listing Rules, 1.2.4G.
[14] Financial Services and Markets Act 2000, s.73(2).
[15] Financial Services and Markets Act 2000, s.73(1)(a).
[16] Financial Services and Markets Act 2000, s.73(1)(b).
[17] Financial Services and Markets Act 2000, s.73(1)(c); as supplied by Financial Services and Markets Act 2000, (Market Abuse) Regulations 2005 (SI 2005/381), reg.4, Sch.1, para.1(1), (2).
[18] See para.7–41.
[19] Financial Services and Markets Act 2000, s.73(1)(d).

international context when imposing its powers and also when drafting listing rules. In terms of competition, overly stringent regulations may be off-putting to international business; whereas an overly permissive regime may lose some of the investor confidence in London's markets which is based in part on the gold-plating of the UK's securities regulations. Similarly, a protectionist attitude by UKLA would be off-putting to potential issuers of securities which are ordinarily resident in other jurisdictions, whereas otherwise the presence of a sophisticated marketplace with investors seeking opportunities to invest in international companies would otherwise be attractive to those potential issuers. This is the balancing act which UKLA must bear in mind when exercising its powers.

37–14 Fifthly, and related perhaps to the previous principle, UKLA must consider "the need to minimise the adverse effects on competition of anything done in the discharge of those functions".[20] Sixthly, UKLA must have regard to:

> "the desirability of facilitating competition in relation to listed securities and in relation to listed securities and in relation to financial instruments which have otherwise been admitted to trading on a regulated market or for which a request for admission to trading on such a market has been made."[21]

The obligations on UKLA are therefore economic as well as regulatory.

5. THE LISTING PRINCIPLES

A. The Listing Principles—imposing general obligations on the issuer

37–15 The Listing Rules are to be interpreted in according with six, framework "Listing Principles" which apply to issuers of securities which are offered to the public in accordance with the Listing Rules. They comprise a set of "high level" principles by reference to which those issuers are required to act from the time of first seeking a listing of securities right through the life of any listing. In line with the modern nature of financial regulation in the UK, detailed rules are to be interpreted and applied in the light of high-level principles. In this sense, the Listing Principles in relation to issues of listed securities are similar to those principles imposed on authorised firms by the *Handbook* in its "Principles for Businesses" rulebook, as considered in Chapter 8.

37–16 Chapter 7 of the Listing Rules introduced these "Listing Principles" to the old Financial Services Authority regime for the first time in 2005 as part of the reform of those regulations. Responsibility for those regulations now lies with the FCA. The general purpose behind the creation of these Listing Principles is to acknowledge the important role which listed companies themselves have to play in ensuring the proper regulation of the securities markets in that the proper

---

[20] Financial Services and Markets Act 2000, s.73(1)(e).
[21] Financial Services and Markets Act 2000, s.73(1)(f); as supplied by Financial Services and Markets Act 2000, (Market Abuse) Regulations 2005 (SI 2005/381), reg.4, Sch.1, para.1(1), (3).

conduct of issuers and the proper provision of information is essential to the integrity of the securities markets. To this effect, the listing rules provide that[22]:

> "The purpose of the Listing Principles is to ensure that listed companies pay due regard to the fundamental role they play in maintaining market confidence and ensuring fair and orderly markets."

Further, the listing rules provide that[23]:

> "The Listing Principles are designed to assist listed companies in identifying their obligations and responsibilities under the listing rules and the disclosure rules and transparency rules."

So, the Listing Principles are educative as well as instructive. Whereas the UKLA *Guidance Manual* of 2002 rehearsed principles culled from the unamended version of s.73 of FSMA 2000[24] (which placed an emphasis on the regulatory goals of UKLA), the Listing Principles set out in Chapter 7 of the 2007 Listing Rules are concerned with the responsibilities of issuers and their managers to act suitably in their dealings with the FCA in its role as UKLA. The six Listing Principles operate as follows.

B.   The detailed Listing Principles

The first principle requires that a "listed company must take reasonable steps to enable its directors to understand their responsibilities and obligations as directors", thus throwing a light on the significant role of a company's management in complying with the issuer's listing obligations. The "issuer" legally-speaking is the company which issues the securities, but it is that company's officers who are actually responsible for that organisation complying with its obligations. In ordinary company law, it is convenient to think of the company as being a distinct legal person because this simplifies the business of companies and it reduces the risks borne by shareholders[25]; but in relation to securities law there can be no avoiding the fact that it is the human agents of a company, principally its directors, who control its actions and therefore it is those same human agents who must be trained to understand what securities law requires of the entity. In this sense, securities law cannot be content with the economically useful fiction of the separate personality of companies: rather, we must recognise that it is the human agents who control the activities of the company. This may require the training of directors and other employees, and it may require the creation of adequate internal systems to ensure compliance with the listing rules. This feeds into the second principle.

37–17

---

[22] Listing Rules, 7.1.2G.

[23] Listing Rules, 7.1.3G.

[24] It was the amended version which was discussed in detail in the previous section. As considered below, sections of Pt 6 of FSMA 2000 were amended in 2005 by SI 2005/381 and SI 2005/1433.

[25] The business of companies is simplified by not needing to have each contract signed by each director and so on: rather the company can act on its own. The risks of shareholders are reduced in relation to a limited company by the company itself taking on all the legal risk of dealing with third parties, instead of imposing any of that risk on the shareholders personally.

37–18   The second listing principle requires that a "listed company must take reasonable steps to establish and maintain adequate procedures, systems and controls to enable it to comply with its obligations". The concern for securities regulation is that adequate information is made available to the investing public and that companies remain transparent. Consequently, it is important that the internal procedure and the culture of a listed company ensures the full disclosure of all material which it is necessary for a listed company to disclose under the listing rules. Therefore, there need to be procedures for making information available—such that the necessary employees of the company know what is expected of them—and there is also a need that there are controls within a company to ensure that no-one in a position of authority is able to prevent the publication of such information, and so on. Let us take an example from the US. One of the things which must be made available to investors is financial information which gives a true and fair view of the state of the listed company. In both Enron and in WorldCom in the US there was a group of very senior executives who were able to control and thus to falsify the company's financial information so that the company was restating long-term liabilities as being current profits. A company's controls must not only allocate responsibility for identifying and publishing requisite information, but adequate controls must ensure that that information is not blocked, altered or otherwise interfered with.

37–19   What is difficult here is knowing what is meant in the abstract by the "reasonable steps" which a listed company is required to take in ensuring that it has appropriate internal controls and so forth. The regulations do not give detailed instruction on such points, but instead require listed companies, their agents and professional advisors to take a reasoned view on what is "reasonable" in any context. The minimum would seem to require the use of external advisors, the dilution of the power of senior executives in sensitive areas with the use of non-executive directors, the creation of a culture in which "whistleblowers" are taken seriously, and ensuring adequate training for directors and other advisors in sensitive departments as to the sorts of action and publication which are required.

37–20   The third principle for listed companies mirrors the central principle of "integrity" governing regulated financial institutions in the *Principles for Businesses* rulebook[26] in that it requires that a "listed company must act with integrity towards holders and potential holders of its listed equity securities". Whereas the now-repealed 2002 Listing Rules focused on the need for sponsors to introduce elements both of professionalism and integrity to an application for admission to listing, the 2007 Listing Rules have broadened those requirements of integrity out to issuing companies as well as their sponsors (as discussed at para.38–19), whilst also continuing to rely on sponsors for the professionalism and the integrity expected of "authorised persons" regulated by the FCA. The word "integrity" means "freedom from moral corruption . . . [s]oundness of moral principle; the character of uncorrupted virtue; uprightness, honesty, sincerity." In relation to issuers of securities this clearly requires compliance in the utmost good faith with requirements as to the provision of all information necessary to make an informed decision about whether or not to acquire securities (as required

---

[26] See para.8–29.

by the Prospectus Rules) and to provide information as to shareholders and voting control on an on-going basis (as required by the Transparency Rules).

The fourth principle then sets out the need for a listed company to "communicate information to holders and potential holders of its listed equity securities in such a way as to avoid the creation or continuation of a false market in such listed equity securities". The term "false market" is not defined in the listing rules. It is suggested that one useful interpretation of this term would be to think of the listed company as being obliged to disclose any information which an investor or her professional advisors would ordinarily require to make an informed decision about whether or not to invest in those securities. Failure to disclose such material, it is suggested, would cause an investor to make investment decisions otherwise than on a correct basis: in that sense it would be a "false" market.

37–21

The fifth principle provides that a "listed company must ensure that it treats all holders of the same class of its listed equity securities that are in the same position equally in respect of the rights attaching to such listed equity securities". Thus, equity must be preserved between the holders of shares (equity securities) in relation to voting and other rights. The sixth principle stipulates that a "listed company must deal with the [FCA] in an open and co-operative manner". This principle appears to operate in parallel with the third listing principle relating to acting with "integrity". The ramification of failing to be open and co-operative will be that the listed company will be in breach of its obligations under the listing rules and that it will be open to the liabilities considered in Chapter 38 below.

37–22

6.   CORPORATE GOVERNANCE

The approach to corporate governance which is taken in the Listing Rules is, in essence, that listed companies must either "comply or explain". That is, a listed company must publish a statement to the effect that it is either in compliance with the UK Corporate Governance Code[27] (which used to be referred to as the Combined Code on Corporate Governance until September 2012) as to its management practices, or else it must provide an explanation as to why it is not in compliance with those principles. Therefore, the Listing Rules provide that the annual financial report must include:

37–23

> "a statement of how the listed company has applied the principles set out in Section 1 of the Combined Code, in a manner that would enable shareholders to evaluate how the principles have been applied".[28]

Also to be included with this statement is a further statement as to whether or not the listed company has complied with the Combined Code throughout the accounting period or whether there are any provisions in relation to which there

---

[27] The code is outlined in para.35–23 et seq, or see A.S. Hudson, *Understanding Company Law* (Routledge, 2012), 169 et seq. See: *http://www.frc.org.uk/Our-Work/Publications/Corporate-Governance/UK-Corporate-Governance-Code-September-2012.aspx*

[28] Listing Rules, 9.8.6(5)R.

has not been compliance.[29] It is a requirement that an auditor review the accuracy of this disclosure statement.[30] The Combined Code falls into four parts, with provisions relating to: directors, remuneration, accountability and audit, and relations with shareholders. It is important to bear in mind, however, as Parker J. held in *Re Astec (BSR) Plc*,[31] that corporate governance codes do not in themselves create legal rights and obligations.

37–24 Clearly one of the principal arenas for corporate governance is in relation to the management of the company by its directors. If the directors' means of conducting business are inadequate, or if their personal qualifications or knowledge as individuals are inadequate, then that will evidently have a deleterious effect on the management of the company. Contrariwise, effective management will be to the benefit of a company. The main principles relating to the board of directors are that 'every company should be headed by an effective board, which is collectively responsible for the success of the company'.[32]

37–25 A balance is sought to be struck in the Combined Code between controlling excessive executive pay and setting pay at high enough levels to be attractive to the highest calibre of potential employees and board members.[33] The aim is to 'attract, retain and motivate directors of the quality required to run the company successfully' and yet not to pay 'more than is necessary'.[34] In part remuneration should reward performance. One of the principal issues on the agenda in the EU has been the excessive remuneration of the directors of banks and of individual traders within banks, something which is said to have encouraged excessive risk-taking and to have failed to punish failure.

37–26 A third dimension of corporate governance which is particularly important is the manner in which the board of directors makes itself accountable for the performance of the company to its shareholders. This is done in three ways: by financial reporting throughout the financial year, by the maintenance of internal controls to monitor the company's performance in terms of the position of shareholders, and by the effective audit of the company. In relation to financial institutions, however, this does not emphasise the need to obey regulatory rules and the instructions of regulators. Instead, company law classically focuses on the bifurcation between ownership of the company through the shareholders and management of the company through the directors. Financial regulation—in particular securities regulation—creates an entirely different dimension of reporting obligation. From the perspective of securities law, as is discussed in Chapter 9 in relation to the FCA SYSC rulebook,[35] there is a need for the development of internal controls which are sufficiently sound 'to safeguard shareholders' investment and the company's assets'.[36] The board is expected to

---

[29] Listing Rules, 9.8.6(6)R.
[30] Listing Rules, 9.8.6(10)R
[31] [1998] 2 B.C.L.C. 556, 590.
[32] Combined Code, A.1.
[33] Combined Code, B.1, Main Principle. See generally the Directors' Remuneration Report Regulations 2002 in relation to directors of listed companies.
[34] Combined Code, B.1, Main Principle.
[35] para.9–41.
[36] Combined Code, C.2, Main Principle.

conduct an annual review of these internal controls and to report to the shareholders as to the result of that review.[37]

---

[37] Combined Code, C.2.1.

CHAPTER 38

OFFICIAL LISTING OF SECURITIES 2: ADMISSION AND MAINTENANCE OF LISTING

CORE PRINCIPLES

The Financial Conduct Authority ("FCA"), acting as the UK Listing Authority ("UKLA"), maintains the Official List of publicly issued securities which is the principal market for securities in the UK, further to the EC Consolidated Admission and Reporting Directive 2001. The Official List is maintained by the FCA as a separate activity from the shares being traded in the UK on the Main Market of the London Stock Exchange under the Exchange's own rules, but generally admission to one is sought in tandem with admission to the other.

Admission to listing requires authorisation from the UKLA, which in turn requires the issuer of securities to have a sponsor who attests to the propriety of the securities, their issuer, and their compliance with the relevant regulations. Maintenance of listing is dependent upon the performance of a number of continuing obligations, primarily to do with the publication through a recognised information service of significant information which would affect the price or perception of the securities in the market. Breach of any of the listing rules opens the issuer up to the discontinuance of their securities' listing, or to censure by the UKLA.

The attraction of having securities listed is precisely the burdens involved in acquiring a listing. If a company has gone through the listing process with its burdensome regulatory requirements, then the investing public will probably be reassured about the reliability of an investment in that company and so that company widens the market for its securities and probably can reduce its cost of funding in general terms. Other companies take the view that the burdens of acquiring and maintaining listing are too onerous or too expensive, and so do not bother.

1. INTRODUCTION

38–01   This chapter is concerned with admission to listing on the Official List, maintenance of listing by means of observance of continuing obligations, and discontinuance of listing. If you like, we shall be considering the birth, life and death of a listing. The previous chapter explained how listing operates and how it is regulated. In this chapter we shall observe that a prospectus is necessary for admission to listing and that transparency obligations are a part of the maintenance of a listing: those two areas have, however, already been given their own detailed treatment in Chapter 36. More specifically we shall consider how an application for listing is made, the role of the sponsor in bringing a listing and how applications are accepted or declined by the Financial Conduct Authority ("FCA"), acting in its role as the UK Listing Authority ("UKLA"). Each Member

State of the EU is required to have a "competent authority": in the UK, that competent authority is the UKLA, a role which is performed by the FCA just as it was performed in its previous incarnation by the Financial Services Authority.[1] Thereafter, we consider the obligations which face a listed company on an ongoing basis and how a listing can be discontinued, either by regulatory application or on an application by the listed company itself.

2. ADMISSION TO LISTING

A. Sources of law on admission to listing

This section considers the process of seeking admission of securities to listing. There are three principal sources of regulation in this area: the EC Consolidated Admission and Reporting Directive 2001 ("CARD"), which is the core EC directive relating to the admission of securities to listing; the Financial Services and Markets Act 2000 ("FSMA 2000"); and the UKLA Listing Rules, part of the *FCA Handbook*. CARD was implemented into UK securities law most recently by the amended Part 6 of FSMA 2000 and the 2007 version of the Listing Rules (together with the Prospectus Rules, and the Disclosure and Transparency Rules constituting the UK securities regulations) created by the UKLA further to FSMA 2000. The principal focus of this discussion will be on the Listing Rules.

38–02

B. The Consolidated Admission and Reporting Directive 2001

CARD was discussed above in Chapter 35. It has been amended by the Prospectus Directive and the Transparency Obligations Directive. This discussion will focus on the provisions of the UKLA Listing Rules, which implement the requirements of those directives and which quotes the directive directly on occasion. The detailed provisions of CARD are considered in tandem with the appropriate provisions of the Listing Rules in this chapter when appropriate.

38–03

C. Provision of information

General obligations as to the accuracy of information

The core of the regulation of the securities markets is the provision of information by the issuing company to the investing public, overseen by UKLA. Consequently it is important that the issuer is compelled to make full and frank disclosure of all material facts in such a way that they will be publicly available. Under the listing rules, the issuer is under a duty in general terms to "take reasonable care to ensure that any information it notifies to a [regulatory information service[2]] or makes available through the UKLA is not misleading,

38–04

---

[1] The evolution of the regulatory bodies in the UK was discussed in Ch.8.

[2] If information cannot be made through a recognised information service then it must be made in not less than two national newspapers, two newswire services in the UK and a recognised information service as soon as one opens: Listing Rules, Ch.1, para.1.3.4R.

false or deceptive".[3] Furthermore the issuer must not only ensure that all information is not misleading and so forth, but must also ensure that it does not "omit anything likely to affect the import of the information".[4] The continuing obligations in relation to the provision of information are considered below.[5]

Powers in the UKLA to require information

38–05   In relation to an application for admission to listing the UKLA may request any information which the UKLA may "reasonably require to decide whether to grant an application for admission".[6] The UKLA may also require that the issuer provide any information which the UKLA considers "appropriate to protect investors or ensure the smooth operation of the market".[7] Finally, the UKLA may request any further information which it requires to verify whether or not the listing rules are being complied with or whether the listing rules have been complied with at some point in the past.[8]

D.   Conditions as to the nature of the issuer itself

The preconditions for making an application for listing

38–06   The procedure for admission to listing requires that an applicant comply with the listing rules. An application for listing must be made in accordance with s.75 of FSMA 2000 to the effect that[9]:

> "Admission to the official list may be granted only on an application made to the competent authority in such manner as may be required by listing rules."

That is, the application must be made to the UKLA as the UK's competent authority (referred to as UK Listing Authority ("UKLA") in this chapter) in such a manner as the listing rules generally may require.[10] As is considered below,[11] the Listing Rules impose general conditions on all listed securities.

General conditions for admission to listing

38–07   The conditions to be fulfilled by the applicant before the applicant's securities will be admitted to listing are numerous. These conditions operate in effect as conditions precedent to the authorisation of admission to listing. It is in Chapters 2 and 6 of the Listing Rules that the principles dealing with the pre-requisites for admission to listing are set out. Briefly put, the company is required to be duly

---

[3] Listing Rules, Ch.1, para.1.3.3R.
[4] Listing Rules, Ch.1, para.1.3.3R.
[5] See para.38–05.
[6] Listing Rules, Ch.1, 1.3.1(1)R.
[7] Listing Rules, Ch.1, 1.3.1(2)R. See also CARD, art.16.1.
[8] Listing Rules, Ch.1, 1.3.1(3)R.
[9] Financial Services and Markets Act 2000, s.75(1).
[10] Financial Services and Markets Act 2000, s.75(1).
[11] See para.38–07.

incorporated,[12] and the securities must have been duly authorised for listing under the company's constitution,[13] the shares must be freely transferable,[14] and the shares must be admitted to trading on an RIE's market for listed securities.[15] The issuer's securities must have a minimum capitalisation.[16] Significantly, as considered in Chapter 36, an approved prospectus must have been published in respect of those securities.[17]

The second tranche of information relates to the company's financial condition. The company must have published and filed audited accounts for at least three previous years,[18] the company must have an independent business and the company's business activities must have been continuous for the previous three years,[19] and it must have a minimum working capital identified in the rules.[20] The securities themselves must be 25 per cent in public hands after the issue within the EU and EEA,[21] and they must be capable of electronic settlement.[22]

38–08

Special conditions on a particular listing application

The Listing Rules empower UKLA to impose special conditions on any application for listing. CARD provides that any special conditions should be used "solely in the interests of protecting investors" and so may relate, for example, to the provision of particular information necessary to keep the investing public informed about the issuer's business activities.[23] An inappropriate dispensation or modification of these rules on grounds of unreasonableness or procedural impropriety would be subject in general terms to an application for judicial review. Admission to listing may not be permitted unless and until those general conditions and any special conditions have been complied with.[24] The admission procedure is set out in the Listing Rules, with the provisions as to the need for a prospectus being set out primarily in the Prospectus Rules. The requirements of the listing rules, especially as to the form of any prospectus, vary according to the nature and circumstances of the listing application. Those requirements will also differ depending on the method by which the securities are brought to listing.

38–09

---

[12] Listing Rules, 2.2.1R.
[13] Listing Rules, 2.2.2R.
[14] Listing Rules, 2.2.4R.
[15] Listing Rules, 2.2.3R where "RIE" is a recognised, regulated investment exchange.
[16] Listing Rules, 2.2.7R.
[17] Listing Rules, 2.2.10R.
[18] Listing Rules, 6.1.3R.
[19] Listing Rules, 6.1.4R.
[20] Listing Rules, 6.1.16R.
[21] Listing Rules, 6.1.19R.
[22] Listing Rules, 6.1.23R.
[23] CARD, art.12.
[24] Financial Services and Markets Act 2000, s.75(4); and Listing Rules, Ch.2, para.2.1.2G.

That the issuer must have consented to the listing

38–10   It is a pre-requisite that the entity which is issuing the securities must have consented to the application for listing.[25] This rule also means that no individual holder of securities may unilaterally seek a listing of the securities. Also prohibited is an application for listing in respect of securities to be issued by a private company or an old public company.[26]

Requirements as to the company's management

38–11   The Listing Principles (considered in the previous chapter) require that a listed company ensure that its directors understand their responsibilities and obligations as directors.[27] The focus in the Listing Rules in this context is on the directors specifically and on their ability to act properly as directors, rather than on the "management" of the company in general terms. Where there might be any conflict of interest, the applicant is required to demonstrate that appropriate mechanisms are in place to cope with such a situation: a matter which would now fall within the company's obligations under the first Listing Principle that directors understand their obligations to promote the success of the company[28] and under the second Listing Principle to maintain "adequate procedures, systems and controls"[29] to comply with the requirements of the listing rules.[30] Therefore, the focus of the listing rules is on the professionalism of the individual directors rather than on continuity of management. Directors bear obligations under the Companies Act 2006 to exercise reasonable care, skill and diligence,[31] to avoid conflicts of interest,[32] and to promote the success of the company in good faith.[33] It is suggested that all of these obligations should be interpreted as being broadly sympathetic one with another where the Companies Act 2006 establishes the fundamental duties of directors[34] and the listing rules then finesse the application of those duties (incumbent on the directors personally and on the company which employs them) in the context of public offers of securities.

Requirements as to working capital

38–12   The final significant requirement in relation to issues of equity securities to primary listing in Chapter 6 of the Listing Rules is that the issuer must have "sufficient working capital"[35] and must make a statement to that effect. The

---

[25] Financial Services and Markets Act 2000, s.75(2).

[26] Financial Services and Markets Act 2000, s.75(3).

[27] See para.39–17.

[28] Companies Act 2006, s.172.

[29] See para.39–18.

[30] See para.39–18.

[31] Companies Act 2006, s.174.

[32] Companies Act 2006, s 175.

[33] Companies Act 2006, s.172.

[34] On directors duties, see A.S. Hudson, *Understanding Company Law* (Routledge, 2012).

[35] Listing Rules, Ch.6, paras.6.1.16R. Note the exceptions in favour of banking, insurance or other companies providing financial services, in *Listing Rules*, Ch.6, para.6.1.18G.

issuer is required to satisfy itself after "due and careful enquiry" that it (and its subsidiaries, where appropriate) have sufficient working capital for the group's requirements for a twelve month period after the publication of the prospectus.[36] There are two stated exceptions to this requirement. The first applies where the applicant already has securities listed and instead provides proposals as to how working capital will be obtained in the future to make good any shortfall in working capital at the time.[37] The second applies where the applicant's business is that of banking or insurance.[38]

Requirement for a prospectus

Section 85 of FSMA 2000 requires that a prospectus be prepared and approved before admission of securities to the Official List in that it provides that it is unlawful to seek admission to listing without a prospectus: therefore, no securities can be admitted to listing until such a prospectus has been approved by FCA. This requirement is considered in detail in Chapter 36.[39] Contravention of the requirement to publish a prospectus only once it has been approved by the competent authority is actionable by anyone suffering loss[40] and failure to make an approved prospectus available to the public before an offer or before seeking admission to a regulated market will constitute criminal offences.[41] In Chapter 2 of the Listing Rules a prospectus in relation to those securities must have been approved by UKLA and published before listing may be authorised.[42] If the UK is not the home state for the issue, then the application for listing may be denied if the applicant has failed to comply with the requirements for listing in another EEA State.[43]

38–13

E. Conditions to be satisfied in relation to the securities themselves

There are further requirements which must be met by the securities themselves, in addition to the conditions which must be met by the issuer itself as to its corporate capacity and management (as considered in the preceding section).[44] The first requirement is that for securities to be listed they must be admitted to trading on a recognised investment exchange's market for listed securities.[45]

38–14

The second requirement is that the securities must be validly issued according to the law of the place of the applicant's incorporation, they must accord with the entity's memorandum and articles of association, and any necessary statutory or

38–15

---

[36] Listing Rules, Ch.6, paras.6.1.16R. It is also required that the sponsor accede to this statement and the information contained in it.
[37] Listing Rules, Ch.6, paras.6.1.17G.
[38] Listing Rules, Ch.6, paras.6.1.18(1)G.
[39] See para.38–01.
[40] cf. Financial Services and Markets Act 2000, s.90 and s.85(4).
[41] Financial Services and Markets Act 2000, s.85(1).
[42] Listing Rules, Ch.2, paras.2.2.10(2)(a)R.
[43] Listing Rules, Ch.2, 2.1.3G.
[44] See para.38–13.
[45] Listing Rules, Ch.2, para.2.2.3R.

regulatory consents must have been obtained.[46] Furthermore, the securities must be "freely transferable".[47] It is also a requirement of the admission of securities to listing that those securities are eligible for electronic settlement.[48] Exceptionally, UKLA may dispense with the requirement of free transferability (further to its guidance notes) in relation to public companies in circumstances in which the issuer has the power to disapprove the transfer of its shares if it is considered that that power would not disturb the market in those shares.[49]

38–16   The third set of requirements relate to the total market capitalisation of that class of securities. Except where securities of the same class are already listed, the expected aggregate market value of all securities to be listed must be at least £700,000 for shares and £200,000 for debt securities.[50] These requirements do not apply to tap issues[51] nor to small issues where there are already sufficient securities of that class in circulation.[52] However, "the UK Listing Authority may admit securities of lower value if satisfied that there will be an adequate market for the securities."[53] Whether or not there is an adequate market for the securities will depend on the circumstances of the particular issue. The application for admission must be for all securities of the same class issued or proposed to be issued.[54]

F.   The application procedure for admission to the Official List

38–17   The Listing Rules contain a detailed application procedure for companies to gain admission to listing in Chapter 3, setting out all of the documents which must be lodged with the UKLA before, in accordance with its guidance notes, the UKLA will consider the application. There are different, detailed rules for different types of security.[55] UKLA guidance provides that it will consider applications only once all the documentation has been delivered, and that UKLA will consider any and all information which it considers appropriate, possibly going beyond the documentation which has been lodged with it in accordance with Chapter 3 of the Listing Rules.[56] This may result in UKLA conducting enquiries, verifying the accuracy of the documentation, and requesting any further information which it requires. UKLA may then impose any further conditions on the application which it considers appropriate.[57] In the ordinary case of events, the specified documents must be lodged by the issuer at least two business days prior to UKLA hearing the

---

[46]   Listing Rules, Ch.2, para.2.2.2R. See CARD arts 45 and 53.

[47]   Listing Rules, Ch.2, para.2.2.4(1)R. Special provision is made for partly paid securities and for permission to be granted (by the competent authority) to disapprove the transfer of shares. See CARD, arts 46, 54, and 60.

[48]   Listing Rules, 6.1.23R.

[49]   Listing Rules, Ch.2, para.2.2.6G.

[50]   Listing Rules, Ch.2, para.2.2.7(1)R.

[51]   Listing Rules, Ch.2, para.2.2.7(2)R.

[52]   Listing Rules, Ch.2, para.2.2.7(3)R.

[53]   Listing Rules, Ch.2, para 2.2.8G. See CARD, arts 43 and 58.

[54]   Listing Rules, Ch.2, para.2.2.9R.

[55]   See A. Hudson, *Securities Law*, Pt 4 generally.

[56]   All of the material considered in this paragraph is set out at Listing Rules, Ch.3, para.3.2.6G.

[57]   Listing Rules, Ch.3, para.3.2.6(5)G.

listing application (hence them being known as "the 48 hour documents"),[58] including the application for listing in prescribed form, any declaration required from a sponsor, and a copy of the prospectus, and any other document required by the regulations in that context.[59] Other documentation may include a copy of any circular which has been published in connection with the application[60]; any approved supplementary prospectus[61]; a copy of the board resolution of the issuer allotting the securities[62]; any accounts or interim financial statements; and so on. The application processes for block listing[63] relate to applicants who issue securities "on a regular basis" and "in circumstances which do not require the production of a prospectus or listing particulars".[64]

G. Announcement of admission to listing

Admission to listing only becomes effective once UKLA's decision has been disseminated by a RIS or posted on a designated UKLA noticeboard.[65]

38–18

H. The role of sponsors in listing applications

The requirement for a sponsor

Sponsors are usually regulated investment firms which are required, in effect, to vet the suitability of an issue of securities, and to warrant that suitability to the UKLA. It is a requirement of seeking admission to the Official List that each listed company has a sponsor[66]: the sponsor in turn will be required to have sufficient professional expertise in securities issues to be authorised to act as such by the UKLA. The sponsor's primary role is to assist the issuer to bring an issue of securities before the market. However, the sponsor has an equally significant secondary role, as expressed in the listing rules, in supplying information to UKLA and also requiring the sponsor to certify and to ensure that the listing rules have been complied with by the issuer during the application process and thereafter.

38–19

UKLA maintains a list of approved sponsors on its website.[67] To be included on the list of approved sponsors, the sponsor must be authorised under the Financial Services and Markets Act 2000[68] or must be a person regulated by a professional body recognised by that Act.[69] To be appointed as a sponsor, a person must be

38–20

---

[58] Listing Rules, Ch.3, para.3.3.2R.
[59] Listing Rules, Ch.3, para.3.3.2R.
[60] Listing Rules, Ch.3, para.3.3.2(3).
[61] Listing Rules, Ch.3, para.3.3.2(4).
[62] Listing Rules, Ch.3, para.3.3.2(5).
[63] Listing Rules, Ch.3, para.3.5.1R.
[64] Listing Rules, Ch.3, para.3.5.2G.
[65] Listing Rules, Ch.3, para.3.2.7G.
[66] Listing Rules, Ch.8, para.8.2.1R.
[67] Listing Rules, Ch.8, para.8.6.1G.
[68] Listing Rules, Ch.8, para.8.6.2R.
[69] Listing Rules, Ch.8, para.8.6.5R.

competent to perform designated services, including being able to assure the UKLA that the listed company's obligations have been fulfilled,[70] and being able to guide the applicant as to its responsibilities under the Listing Rules and other regulations.[71] A sponsor must have a "sufficient number of suitably experienced employees" to discharge its responsibilities[72]; and thus experience of a suitable range of types of issue. While the sponsor may appear at first blush to be the applicant's agent in seeking admission to listing, it is the UKLA which must be satisfied as to the sponsor's abilities and competence.[73]

Principles governing the activity of sponsors

38–21 There are four principles governing the activities of sponsors. First, the sponsor must exercise due care and skill in advising the listed company as to its obligations under the securities regulations.[74] Secondly, the sponsor must take reasonable steps to ensure that the directors of the listed company understand the nature and extent of their obligations under the listing rules.[75] Thirdly, the sponsor must deal with the UKLA in an open and co-operative manner, dealing promptly with all of the UKLA's enquiries and disclosing any "material information" of which it has knowledge to the UKLA in a "timely manner".[76] Broadly, this mirrors the obligation placed on listed companies by the Listing Principles in Chapter 7 of the Listing Rules.[77] Fourthly, the sponsor is required to be independent of the listed company[78] and to complete a form attesting to its independence in relation to each admission for listing in which it participates.[79] The definition of independence here requires that the sponsor not own more than 30 per cent of the equity of the listed company nor have a "significant interest" in the listed company's debt securities.[80]

The obligations imposed on sponsors as to the suitability of the issue

38–22 The listing rules require the appointment of a sponsor[81] in relation to new applications for admission to listing where the issuer has no equity securities then in issue.[82] In relation to such an issue the sponsor is required to form the "reasonable opinion", after making due and careful inquiry, that the applicant has satisfied all of the requirements of the Listing Rules and of the Prospectus Rules, that the directors of the applicant have put in place adequate procedures to enable the applicant to comply with the listing rules, and that the directors of the

---

[70] Listing Rules, Ch.8, para.8.3.1(1)R.
[71] Listing Rules, Ch.8, para.8.3.1(2)R.
[72] Listing Rules, Ch.8, para.8.3.10R.
[73] Listing Rules, Ch.8, para.8.3.2G.
[74] Listing Rules, Ch.8, para.8.3.3R.
[75] Listing Rules, Ch.8, para.8.3.4R.
[76] Listing Rules, Ch.8, para.8.3.5R.
[77] See para.39–15.
[78] Listing Rules, Ch.8, para.8.3.6R.
[79] Listing Rules, Ch.8, para.8.7.12R.
[80] Listing Rules, Ch.8, para.8.3.6R.
[81] See generally Listing Rules, s.8.4.
[82] Listing Rules, Ch.8, para.8.4.1R.

applicant have also put in place procedures on the basis of which they are able to make "proper judgments on an ongoing basis" as to the applicant's financial position and prospects.[83] A sponsor must also ensure that no shares are placed with connected clients of the sponsor or with any financial intermediary involved in the issue except for the purposes of market-making for on-sale to clients[84]; that the results of any marketing or any allotment are notified to a recognised information service[85]; and that a notification is made to a recognised information service if any of the listed company's advisors or intermediaries acquires more than 3 per cent of a class of equity shares.[86]

A sponsor is also required in two further situations: in relation to further issues of equity securities which are already listed[87]; and when a listed company is seeking to refinance its own shares up to 25 per cent of the issued share capital[88] such that it is required to produce a Class 1 Circular.[89] In each of these circumstances, the sponsor must have formed the reasonable opinion after a due and careful enquiry that the applicant satisfies all of the requirements of the Listing Rules and of the Prospectus Rules and that the directors can attest to the working capital requirements for listing, before the application may be presented to the UKLA.[90]

38–23

I. Deciding on a listing application

UKLA must reach a decision on an application for listing within six months of the application or a longer period if further information is required.[91] In the event that such a decision to admit the securities to listing is not reached within that time period, the application is deemed to have been refused.[92] In the event of a decision to refuse admission to listing, the competent authority is required to give the applicant a warning notice[93] and a decision notice.[94] A decision to admit securities to listing is to be accompanied by a written notice from the competent authority.[95] UKLA may refuse an application if it does not comply with the listing rules,[96] or if any special condition imposed on the issue has not been complied with[97]; alternatively, if UKLA considers "that granting it would be detrimental to

38–24

---

[83] Listing Rules, Ch.8, para.8.4.2R.
[84] Listing Rules, Ch.8, para.8.4.5(1)R.
[85] Listing Rules, Ch.8, para.8.4.5(2)R.
[86] Listing Rules, Ch.8, para.8.4.5(3)R.
[87] Listing Rules, Ch.8, para.8.4.7R.
[88] See Listing Rules, Ch.10.
[89] See para.38–39, et seq.
[90] Listing Rules, Ch.8, para.8.4.12R.
[91] Financial Services and Markets Act 2000, s.76(1).
[92] Financial Services and Markets Act 2000, s.76(2).
[93] Financial Services and Markets Act 2000, s.76(4).
[94] Financial Services and Markets Act 2000, s.76(5).
[95] Financial Services and Markets Act 2000, s.76(3).
[96] Listing Rules, Ch.2, para.2.1.2(1)G.
[97] Listing Rules, Ch.2, para.2.1.2(2)G.

the interests of investors"[98]; or thirdly, if the securities are already in issue and "if the issuer has failed to comply with any obligations to which he is subject as a result of that listing".[99]

J.   Sanctions

38–25   Further to ss.77 and 78 of FSMA 2000, the competent authority may, in accordance with the listing rules, discontinue or suspend the listing of any securities if satisfied that there are "special circumstances which preclude normal dealings with them".[100] The rules on discontinuance are considered below.[101]

K.   Financial promotion

38–26   The regulation of financial promotion and advertisement of instruments such as securities was considered in detail in Chapter 11.

3.   MAINTENANCE OF LISTING

A.   Introduction

38–27   This section focuses on the continuing obligations which are imposed on a listed company and its agents once securities have been admitted to the Official List. Failure to comply with these obligations under the securities regulations generally will constitute a breach of those regulations. Therefore, maintenance of a listing requires the observance of these continuing obligations.

B.   General continuing obligations in the Listing Rules

Rules which must be complied with on a continuing basis

38–28   The Listing Rules create a number of rules which can be understood as continuing obligations. The securities which are listed must continue to be admitted to trading on a regulated market.[102] The securities must also remain in public hands as to 25 per cent of their number.[103] The company must comply with the Disclosure and Transparency Rules—specifically relating to the publication of inside information—while its securities are listed.[104] The company is required to comply with the Model Code on a continuing basis, as is considered below.[105]

---

[98] Financial Services and Markets Act 2000, s.75(5). Also Listing Rules, Ch.2, para.2.1.3(1)G.
[99] Financial Services and Markets Act 2000, s.75(6).
[100] Financial Services and Markets Act 2000, s.77(1) and (2): which came into effect on June 18, 2001: Financial Services and Markets Act 2000 (Commencement No.3) Order 2001 (SI 2001/1820).
[101] See para.38–44.
[102] Listing Rules, 2.2.3R.
[103] Listing Rules, 6.1.19R
[104] Listing Rules, 9.2.6R.
[105] Listing Rules, 9.2.8R.

Continuing obligations to keep the UKLA informed of administrative matters

The company is required to keep the UKLA informed of two kinds of administrative information. The company must provide the UKLA with contact details of a person who is to be the first point of contact between the UKLA and the company.[106] The company must also provide the UKLA with two copies of any mooted amendment to its constitution.[107]   **38–29**

Continuing obligations as to the equal treatment of shareholders

The company is required to treat each of its shareholders equally, in accordance with the fifth Listing Principle. The Listing Rules formerly required that information must be provided to all shareholders equally.[108] Those rules have now been revoked, although the fifth Listing Principle remains. It is suggested that the revocation of these rules should not be interpreted as a general permission to discriminate unreasonably between different classes of shareholders, nor between different individual shareholders. The position of existing shareholders is also required to be protected by reference to the right of pre-emption of existing shareholders in s.561 of the Companies Act 2006, which means that new shares must be offered to existing shareholders first. The City Code on Mergers and Takeovers also requires the equal treatment of shareholders in takeover situations.   **38–30**

Continuing obligations relating to financial information

Listed companies must publish a preliminary statement of their annual results as soon as such a statement has been approved, in any event within 120 days of the end of the period to which it relates.[109] This information must be published through a recognised information service once those matters have been agreed with the company's auditors, together with any decision as to the payment of a dividend.[110] However, the UKLA may authorise the omission of any of this information if its disclosure would be either "contrary to the public interest or seriously detrimental to the listed company".[111] This power to condone omission of information is nevertheless subject to a proviso that the omission would not be "likely to mislead the public with regard to facts and circumstances, knowledge of which is essential for the assessment of the shares".[112]   **38–31**

As to its annual report and accounts, a listed company must publish these documents as soon as possible after they have been approved,[113] and in any event   **38–32**

---

[106] Listing Rules, 9.2.11R.
[107] Listing Rules, 9.2.14R.
[108] Listing Rules, 9.3.1R.
[109] Listing Rules, Ch.9, para.9.7.1R.
[110] Listing Rules, Ch.9, para.9.7.2R.
[111] Listing Rules, Ch.9, para.9.7.3R.
[112] Listing Rules, Ch.9, para.9.7.3R.
[113] Listing Rules, Ch.9, para.9.8.1(1)R.

with six months after the end of the accounting period.[114] These accounts must have been prepared in accordance with the listed company's "national law" (which it is suggested relates to the law of the state of its incorporation, although that term is not defined for this purpose) and in accordance with applicable international accounting standards such as the EC's IAS Directive.[115] In the event that the accounts do not give a true and fair view of the "state of affairs, profit or loss and cash flows" of the company then more detailed, additional information must be provided to expand upon these items.[116] A list of information, if applicable to the company in the given accounting period, which is to be provided is then listed in the listing rules, together with information which is to be provided by way of a report to shareholders.[117] This material is then applied, mutatis mutandis, to half-yearly reports which listed companies are also obliged to produce.[118] The half-yearly report is required only to contain information which is primarily financial information (as to net turnover, finance income, operating profit or loss, finance costs, a balance sheet, a cash flow statement, and so forth)[119] together with an explanatory statement which will provide significant information sufficient to enable investors to make an informed assessment of the "trend of the group's activities and profit or loss".[120]

Continuing obligations relating to treatment of shares

38–33   There are a number of mini-codes of obligations within the listing rules dealing with a listed company's dealings with its shares, requiring, in effect, notification of certain information to UKLA and compliance with UKLA's listing rules. A listed company is required to comply with proper procedures as to the notification of shareholders of meetings at which they may vote and to make proxy votes and so forth available[121]; and to comply with regulations as to notifications through a recognised information service relating to changes to capital or voting rights attaching to capital, changes to major interests in shares and board changes.[122] Similarly, documents such as employee share schemes and long-term incentive plans, and discounted option arrangements must be cleared with UKLA.[123] In relation to rights issues, the company must (in the ordinary course of events) ensure that the placing relates to at least 25 per cent of the maximum number of securities offered[124]; in relation to open offers, a listed company must ensure that it has the approval of the recognised investment exchange on which the securities are traded[125]; in relation to vendor consideration placings, that all vendors have an equal opportunity to participate in the

---

[114] Listing Rules, Ch.9, para.9.8.1(2)R.
[115] Listing Rules, Ch.9, para.9.8.2(1)R.
[116] Listing Rules, Ch.9, para.9.8.2(4)R. See CARD, art.67.
[117] Listing Rules, Ch.9, paras 9.8.4, 9.8.5 and 9.8.6 generally.
[118] Listing Rules, Ch.9, s.9.9 generally.
[119] Listing Rules, Ch.9, para.9.9.8.
[120] Listing Rules, Ch.9, para.9.9.8(6).
[121] Listing Rules, Ch.9, s.9.3 generally.
[122] Listing Rules, Ch.9, s.9.6 generally.
[123] Listing Rules, Ch.9, s.9.4 generally.
[124] Listing Rules, Ch.9, para.9.5.1R.
[125] Listing Rules, Ch.9, para.9.5.7R.

placing[126] and that the discount is not set at more than 10 per cent[127]; in relation to offers for sale or subscription, that letters of allotment are issued simultaneously and numbered serially, or that there is equal treatment of rightholders if the securities are held in uncertificated form[128]; and in relation to reconstructions or refinancings, that the circular complies with Chapter 13 of the Listing Rules.[129]

C. Continuing obligations in relation to market abuse and inside information

The range of continuing obligations in relation to market abuse

When a company seeks admission to the Official List, then it is bound by the Disclosure and Transparency Rules[130] which prevent market abuse in the manner considered in Chapter 10. Put simply, if a listed company or its officers participate in market abuse then they will be in breach of the requirement of integrity in the *Principles for Businesses* rulebook, as well as being open to civil and criminal penalties described in Chapter 14 *Insider dealing*. In the same vein, the Listing Rules contain a Model Code for the prevention of the misuse of inside information. This section outlines the two contexts in which the UKLA regulates market abuse in the *FCA Handbook* in the Model Code and in the Code of Market Conduct. The avoidance of involvement in market abuse in relation to a listed company's own securities constitutes a form of continuing obligation, without the creation of explicit obligations, outside the Model Code.

38–34

The continuing obligations in the Disclosure and Transparency Rules

One of the most significant continuing obligations in relation to the Listing Rules relates to the obligation to disclose inside information. This principle derives from the Market Abuse Directive, as implemented by the Disclosure and Transparency Rules. In general terms, the Disclosure and Transparency Rules oblige an issuer to notify a recognised information service "as soon as possible"[131] of any inside information which "directly concerns the issuer",[132] unless the issuer (on its own initiative) considers the prevention of disclosure to be necessary to protect its own "legitimate interests".[133] This requirement of disclosure is in common with the fifth Listing Principle, discussed in Chapter

38–35

---

[126] Listing Rules, Ch.9, para.9.5.9R.

[127] Listing Rules, Ch.9, para.9.5.10R.

[128] Listing Rules, Ch.9, para.9.5.11R.

[129] Listing Rules, Ch.9, para.9.5.12R.

[130] Listing Rules, 9.2.5G and 9.2.6R.

[131] This will be satisfied if the issuer acted as soon as was possible in the circumstance of factors which were only gradually coming to light: Disclosure and Transparency Rules, Ch.2, para.2.2.2R. A short delay in publication of the information will be acceptable if it is "necessary to clarify the situation": Disclosure and Transparency Rules, Ch.2, para.2.2.9G.

[132] Disclosure and Transparency Rules, Ch.2, para.2.2.1R.

[133] Disclosure and Transparency Rules, Ch.2, para.2.5.1R. See Market Abuse Directive ("MAD"), art.6(1).

39.[134] The obligation is then to make disclosure of any inside information so that the entire market has equal access to the same information. The definition of inside information set out in s.118C of FSMA 2000 was considered in Chapter 12 *Market Abuse*.[135] Section 119 of FSMA 2000 requires the FCA to create a code to specify what sorts of behaviour may constitute market abuse.[136] This code is known as the Code on Market Conduct: or more commonly by the acronym "MAR 1". It is contained in Chapter 1 of the FCA Market Abuse Rulebook.[137] This was also discussed in Chapter 12 *Market Abuse*.[138]

D. The Model Code

The purpose of the Model Code

38–36   The Model Code is part of the Listing Rules. It relates to the control of the misuse of price sensitive information by those with managerial responsibilities in a listed company and by employee insiders in a listed company by dealing in that company's securities during prohibited periods without first obtaining clearance in accordance with the procedure set out in the Model Code. The provisions of the Model Code create obligations for the listed company in framing appropriate internal procedures to deal with these issues. The purpose of the Model Code is set out in its "Introduction" in Annex 1 to Chapter 9 of the Listing Rules:

> "This code imposes restrictions on dealing in the securities of a listed company beyond those imposed by law. Its purpose is to ensure that persons discharging managerial responsibilities and employee insiders do not abuse, and do not place themselves under suspicion of abusing, inside information that they may be thought to have, especially in periods leading up to an announcement of the company's results."

The underlying focus of this code is on the integrity of the securities market in the UK generally. The integrity of the market in this context does not rest solely on the prevention of actual misuse of information but also on the "suspicion" that information may have been misused. Furthermore, it is not required that the agents of this misuse actually had access to that information but rather the code's focus is on suspicion that the information which may be used was information which those people might be "thought to have", whether they did in fact have it or not. The principal focus of the code on its surface is to deal with the possibility of the "misuse" of information either by those "discharging managerial responsibilities" or "employee insiders". For ease of reference in this chapter such people will be referred to collectively as "managers and insiders".

---

[134] See para.39–15.
[135] See para.12–37.
[136] Financial Services and Markets Act 2000 s.119.
[137] Published under the Financial Services Authority, Market Conduct Sourcebook Instrument 2001 (MAR 1).
[138] See para.12–08.

The general prohibition in the Model Code

38–37 The Model Code contains a central restriction to the effect that no manager or insider may deal in the securities of a listed company within an identified "restricted period" unless that person has clearance so to deal.[139] The central restriction appears in the following form:

> "3. A restricted person must not deal in any securities of the company without obtaining clearance to deal in advance in accordance with paragraph 4 of this code."

The Model Code imposes a general prohibition on "a person discharging managerial responsibilities or employee insider"[140] dealing on the basis of unpublished, price-sensitive information at any time without clearance.[141] An "employee insider" is defined as being:

> "an employee of the company, its parent undertaking or any member of its group whose name is required to be placed on the insider list in accordance with DTR 2.8.1R".[142]

A "dealing in securities" include acquiring, disposing, entering into a contract for securities of the company, and derivatives relating to the securities of that company.[143] Dealings are prohibited when they fall within "any close period" (that is, the 60 day period before the preliminary announcement of the company's financial statements) or "any period when there exists any matter which constitutes inside information in relation to the company",[144] perhaps during the lead-up to an announcement of a merger or before an exceptional announcement involving profit forecasts via a recognised information service. A restricted person must obtain clearance to deal with a listed company's securities before dealing. Clearance must be obtained from the person who is designated in the code as being appropriate to give clearance to a person holding the applicant's position in the company.

E The obligation on listed companies to make prescribed communications

The obligation to communicate information

38 38 This section considers the legal principles which govern the content of communications by listed companies, the need for corporate communications in certain situations under the Listing Rules, and the requirement to distribute circulars under the Listing Rules. The fourth of the Listing Principles provides that:

---

[139] Listing Rules, Ch.9, Annex 1, para.3.
[140] Listing Rules, Ch.9, Annex 1, para.1(1)(f).
[141] Listing Rules, Ch.9, Annex 1, para.1.3.
[142] Listing Rules, Ch.9, Annex 1, para.1.1(d). On the composition of insider lists see Disclosure and Transparency Rules, Ch.2, s.2.8 generally.
[143] Listing Rules, Ch.9, Annex 1, para.1(c).
[144] Listing Rules, Ch.9, Annex 1, para.1(e).

"A listed company must communicate information to holders and potential holders of its listed equity securities in such a way as to avoid the creation or continuation of a false market in such listed equity securities."

There are a number of matters about which a listed company must make disclosure either at the time of making an issue of securities or on a continuing basis thereafter. The keynote here is the avoidance of the creation of a "false market" in the equity securities at issue.

The requirement for circulars

38–39 Circulars are required to be circulated to holders of equity securities by Chapter 13 the Listing Rules in a number of circumstances. A circular may incorporate by reference any information in a prospectus or any other document which has been published and filed with the FCA.[145] Circulars may not be circulated until they have been approved.[146]

38–40 All circulars are required to have the following contents.[147] Circulars which contain the following forms of information do not require approval unless there is some unusual feature about them.[148] A circular must contain a clear and adequate explanation of the subject matter of the circular explaining its essential characteristics, its benefits and its risks. The circular must state why the recipient is being sent the circular and asked to vote. The circular also explain how the recipient may respond to the circular, by voting or otherwise. If voting is required, the circular must contain the board's recommendation as to how that vote should be exercised. Other information is required depending on the purpose of the circular.

38–41 Circulars are required in a number of circumstances, many of which are those set out in s.13.8 of the Listing Rules. Circulars are required in relation to votes connected with the authority to allot shares, disapplying pre-emption rights in relation to the allotment of shares, increasing authorised share capital, reducing the company's capital, in relation to a capitalisation or bonus issue, in relation to a scrip dividend, giving notice of meetings, making amendments to the company's constitution, in relation to an employees' share scheme, in relation to discounted option arrangements, and in relation to reminders of conversion rights over convertible securities. Other circumstances in which circulars of particular sorts are required include Class 1 transactions relating to corporate acquisitions or disposals or to takeovers generally.

F. Penalties for breach of the listing rules

38–42 There are two potential penalties for breach of the listing rules as provided in s.91 of FSMA 2000. The first arises when there has been any contravention of the listing rules such that the issuer, or any of its managers or any person connected

---

[145] Listing Rules, 13.1.3R.
[146] Listing Rules, 13.2.1R.
[147] Listing Rules, 13.3.1R.
[148] Listing Rules, 13.2.2R; or alternatively if only a name change is involved.

to a manager, is subject to such penalty as the FCA thinks fit. Liability for a second form of penalty arises under s.91(1A) of FSMA 2000 when there has been a contravention of Part 6 of FSMA 2000 or of the Prospectus Rules: the penalty is such as the FCA considers appropriate.

G. Statutory duties of disclosure in prospectuses and under transparency obligations

There is a duty to have a prospectus prepared, approved and published before transferable securities are offered to the public or are subject to a request for admission to trading on a regulated market.[149] Section 87A of FSMA 2000 places a duty of disclosure in a prospectus on those people responsible for its production and publication to enable an investor to make an informed assessment of the investment opportunity presented by the securities described in that prospectus. Prospectus obligations relate to the information which is to be provided before securities are offered to the public or admitted to trading on a regulated market. Transparency obligations, considered in Chapter 38, relate to the obligations imposed on the issuer of securities and on investors to notify the FCA ultimately about "voting information" in relation to the control of the company issuing the securities. The aim of transparency obligations is to make the control of the company transparent to the investing public.

38–43

4. DISCONTINUANCE OF LISTING

A. The scope of the UKLA's powers

The UKLA has powers to cancel or to suspend listing. This may occur either as a punishment or because the company has, for whatever reason, decided that it wishes to terminate its listing. There are two forms of discontinuance of listing and of trading on a regulated market: temporary suspension, and outright cancellation. Each is considered in turn.

38–44

The UKLA has four separate powers under FSMA 2000 to prohibit or suspend or otherwise control securities transactions: first, a power to discontinue or to suspend listing further to s.77 of FSMA 2000[150]; second, a power to suspend or prohibit an offer of transferable securities to the public under s.87K of FSMA 2000[151]; third, a power to suspend or prohibit admission to trading on a regulated market under s.87L of FSMA 2000[152]; and, fourth, a power to suspend trading in a financial instrument on grounds of breach of the disclosure rules under s.96C of FSMA 2000.[153] Guidance on the operation of those provisions is then given in the listing rules and the disclosure rules. In art.18(1) of CARD it is provided that UKLA "may decide to suspend the listing of a security where the smooth

38–45

---

[149] Financial Services and Markets Act 2000, s.85.
[150] See para.38–46.
[151] See para.38–47.
[152] See para.38–48.
[153] See para.38–52.

operation of the market is, or may be, temporarily jeopardised or where protection of investors so requires"[154]: language which is adopted in the listing rules.[155]

B.   The various powers of discontinuance

38–46   The UKLA is empowered by s.77(1) of FSMA 2000 to discontinue the listing of securities when it is "satisfied that there are special circumstances which preclude normal regular dealings" in the securities. Under s.77(2) of FSMA 2000 to suspend securities from listing in general terms. The procedure for either discontinuance or suspension of listing is set out in s.78 of FSMA 2000 and in the FCA "Decision Making Manual ('DEC')",[156] requiring that a written notice in the appropriate form be given to the company once a decision to discontinue listing has been taken. The notice must give reasons for the discontinuance. UKLA must invite representations from the issuer in relation to the notice to discontinue or suspend,[157] and inform the issuer of a right of referral to the Tribunal, informing the issuer of the procedure for such a referral.[158] A procedure for appeal is thus created.

C.   The various powers of suspension

38–47   FCA has a power to suspend or to prohibit an offer of securities under s.87K of FSMA 2000. This provision applies if there has been an offer of "transferable securities to the public".[159] Section 87K(2) requires that[160] FCA must have "reasonable grounds for suspecting that an applicable provision has been infringed". The FCA therefore has two alternative powers: either to suspend the offer once it has been made or alternatively to prohibit the advertisement of the offer. Moreover, under s.87K(3) of FSMA 2000 the FCA is granted a power to order the withdrawal of an offer of securities once a person has made an offer of transferable securities to the public in the UK[161] if it has reasonable grounds for suspecting that it is "likely" that an "applicable provision" will be infringed.[162] Similarly the competent authority may order the withdrawal of such an offer if it finds that an "applicable provision" has already been infringed.[163] The term "applicable provision" is a reference to any provision of Part 6 of FSMA 2000, or any provision of the prospectus rules, or any other provision implementing the

---

[154]   CARD, art.18(1).

[155]   Listing Rules, Ch.5, para.5.1.1(1)R.

[156]   Listing Rules, Ch.5, para.5.5.1G.

[157]   The period for receipt of representations may be extended by the competent authority: Financial Services and Markets Act 2000, s.78(4).

[158]   Financial Services and Markets Act 2000, s.78(7).

[159]   Financial Services and Markets Act 2000, s.87K(1). See Financial Services and Markets Act 2000, s.102B for a definition of this expression.

[160]   Financial Services and Markets Act 2000, s.87K(2).

[161]   As established by Financial Services and Markets Act 2000, s.87K(1).

[162]   Financial Services and Markets Act 2000, s.87K(3).

[163]   Financial Services and Markets Act 2000, s.87K(4).

Prospectus Directive.[164] The statute does not give any guidance as to what is meant by "reasonable grounds" for suspicion in this context.

D. Powers to interfere with trading in an instrument

The FCA has a power to prohibit admission to trading on a regulated market under s.87L of FSMA 2000 once an applicant has sought admission for securities to trading on a regulated market.[165] The basis for the use of this power is therefore a finding of reasonable grounds for suspecting that an applicable provision has been infringed. A similar power exists over the operator of a market in circumstances in which those transferable securities have already been admitted to trading on the regulated market in question.[166] The FCA has powers of suspension if as competent authority it has "reasonable grounds for suspecting that an applicable provision has been infringed and the securities have been admitted to trading on the regulated market in question".[167]

38–48

The FCA has the power to "suspend trading in a financial instrument" in accordance with the Disclosure and Transparency Rules under s.96C of FSMA 2000.[168] The issuer of that financial instrument is then able to refer that suspension to the Markets Tribunal.[169] Section 96C(3) imports the procedure for imposing suspension in s.78 of FSMA 2000 into this context.[170] The Disclosure and Transparency Rules provide that the FCA may require the suspension of trading of a financial instrument "if there are reasonable grounds to suspect non-compliance with the disclosure rules".[171] Suspension is likely in circumstances in which an issuer fails to make a RIS announcement when required to do so by the disclosure rules or in circumstances in which there has been a leak of inside information.[172] When suspending financial instruments, the FCA may impose whatever conditions it considers to be appropriate.[173] The suspension of a company's financial instruments does not release persons discharging managerial responsibilities within that company from being bound by the disclosure rules.[174]

38–49

---

[164] Financial Services and Markets Act 2000, s.87K(5).
[165] Financial Services and Markets Act 2000, s.87L(1).
[166] Financial Services and Markets Act 2000, s.87L(3).
[167] Financial Services and Markets Act 2000, s.87L(3).
[168] Financial Services and Markets Act 2000, s.96C(1).
[169] Financial Services and Markets Act 2000, s.96C(2).
[170] See para.
[171] Disclosure and Transparency Rules, Ch.1, para.1.4.1R.
[172] Disclosure and Transparency Rules, Ch.1, para.1.4.4G. The term "inside information" is discussed at para.10–15.
[173] Disclosure and Transparency Rules, Ch.1, para.1.4.3R.
[174] Disclosure and Transparency Rules, Ch.1, para.1.4.2R.

E. Suspension of listing under the Listing Rules

38–50   The Listing Rules provide that the UKLA may suspend the listing of any securities in one of two circumstances: first, "if the smooth operation of the market is, or may be, temporarily jeopardised"[175] or, secondly, if "it is necessary to protect investors".[176] The focus of these powers is, therefore, on market integrity and on investor protection respectively. The continuing obligations of the issuer of those securities continue in existence even when the listing of those securities has been suspended.[177] UKLA may then impose any conditions which it considers to be appropriate before that suspension may be lifted.[178]

F. Suspension at the issuer's request

38–51   The issuer may request suspension of the listing of its own securities.[179] Suspension will only be granted if the UKLA is satisfied that "the circumstances justify the suspension".[180] Therefore, the listing rules specify the information which must be provided along with a request for suspension or for cancellation.[181] Among the items of information to be provided are a clear explanation of the background and the reasons for requesting suspension or cancellation,[182] the time at which suspension is desired to take place,[183] any applicable supporting evidence,[184] any conditions which are proposed to be attached to the suspension or cancellation, and the text of any announcement which the issuer proposes to make.[185] Notably, however, the UKLA will not suspend the listing of securities so as to fix the price of those securities at a particular level.[186]

G. Cancellation of listing under the listing rules

38–52   The Listing Rules provide that UKLA may cancel the listing of securities, adopting the words of CARD, "if it is satisfied that there are special circumstances which preclude normal regular dealings in them".[187] There clearly arises an issue as to whether or not "normal regular dealings" are possible in any particular set of circumstances, as was considered above.[188] The UKLA may cancel the listing of securities in three circumstances, according to the guidance

---

[175] Listing Rules, Ch.5, para.5.1.1(1)R.
[176] Listing Rules, Ch.5, para.5.1.1(1)R.
[177] Listing Rules, Ch.5, para.5.1.1(2)R.
[178] Listing Rules, Ch.5, para.5.1.1(3)R.
[179] Listing Rules, Ch.5, para.5.1.4G.
[180] Listing Rules, Ch.5, para.5.1.4G.
[181] Listing Rules, Ch.5, para.5.3.1R.
[182] Listing Rules, Ch.5, para.5.3.1(3)R.
[183] Listing Rules, Ch.5, para.5.3.1(5)R.
[184] Listing Rules, Ch.5, para.5.3.1(6)R.
[185] Listing Rules, Ch.5, para.5.3.1(11)R and Listing Rules, Ch.5, para.5.3.1(12)R.
[186] Listing Rules, Ch.5, para.5.1.3G.
[187] CARD, art.18(2); Listing Rules, Ch.5, para.5.2.1R.
[188] See para.38–46.

notes in the Listing Rules. First, if the securities are no longer admitted to trading in compliance with the listing rules.[189] Secondly, listing may be cancelled if the listing of the securities has been suspended for more than six months.[190] Thirdly, if a listed company fails to comply with its continuing obligations,[191] for example if the number of shares which are publicly available falls below 25 per cent of the company's share capital.[192] Outwith the listing process, s.96C of FSMA 2000 provides that the "competent authority may, in accordance with disclosure rules [sic], suspend trading in a financial instrument".[193] The issuer of the financial instrument at issue may then refer the matter to the Tribunal.[194]

H.   Censure and publication of censure

Further to s.87M of FSMA 2000, UKLA may publish a statement of censure if an issuer of transferable securities, or a person offering transferable securities to the public, or a person requesting the admission of transferable securities to trading on a regulated market, has in either case failed to comply with its obligations under any provision of the securities regulations stemming from Part 6 of FSMA 2000.[195] Before such a statement of censure is published, UKLA must deliver a warning notice to the object of the censure statement setting out the proposed terms of that statement.[196] If that person makes any representations in relation to the statement of censure, then UKLA must give that person a decision notice.[197] Anyone in receipt of a decision notice in this context may refer the matter to the Tribunal under the 2000 Act.[198] An applicant's sponsor may also be the subject of censure.[199]

38–53

5.   THE ALTERNATIVE INVESTMENT MARKET

A.   The role of AIM and its regulation

The Alternative Investment Market ("AIM") is a market for smaller companies seeking to grow but which do not want to comply with the expensive and extensive regulatory requirements of the Official List, considered above. This market was launched in June 1995 as the UK's second tier stock market. AIM is operated and regulated by the London Stock Exchange Plc (referred to in the rulebooks as "the Exchange"). Significantly, from the perspective of a company seeking admission to AIM, there are no pre-requisites as to the company's prior track record, nor any requirements as to its minimum worth, nor as to its

38–54

---

[189] Listing Rules, Ch.5, para.5.2.2(1)G.
[190] Listing Rules, Ch.5, para.5.2.2(3)G.
[191] Listing Rules, Ch.5, para.5.2.1R: see CARD, art.18(2).
[192] Listing Rules, Ch.5, para.5.2.2(2)G.
[193] Financial Services and Markets Act 2000, s.96C(1).
[194] Financial Services and Markets Act 2000, s.96C(2).
[195] Financial Services and Markets Act 2000, s.87M(1).
[196] Financial Services and Markets Act 2000, s.87M(2).
[197] Financial Services and Markets Act 2000, s.87M(3).
[198] Financial Services and Markets Act 2000, s.87N(1).
[199] See para.38–19.

shareholders. The intention, then, is to appeal to small companies and new companies, especially in the technology industries, in that they can acquire access to this capital market with a comparatively light regulatory touch. Indeed, the principal selling point of AIM when compared to the Main Market on the London Stock Exchange is that its regulations are cheap and not burdensome by comparison.

A detailed discussion of the regulation of AIM is set out in Alastair Hudson *Securities Law*.[200]

38–55   The principal means of regulating "AIM companies"[201] is to use experienced corporate financiers to advise companies seeking admission to AIM and who can vouch for the suitability of each company for admission on the basis of its own due diligence. These experienced professionals are referred to as "Nominated Advisors", although they are known colloquially as "Nomads". While the Exchange retains overall regulatory control for AIM, the role of the Nomad is essential to the proper functioning of AIM.

38–56   Securities which are quoted on AIM are not "listed securities" admitted to the Official List; nor is AIM a regulated market for the purposes of s.85(2) of the FSMA 2000, such that compliance with the Prospectus Directive as implemented by Part 6 of FSMA 2000 is not required, nor is a failure to comply with those rules a criminal offence when an application is made for admission to trading on AIM.

38–57   The AIM regulations ("the AIM rules")[202], after a consultation conducted from October 2006 2, into early 2007.[203] There are three AIM rulebooks. The first is the "AIM Rules for Companies" which deals with admission to AIM, the duties of disclosure of AIM companies, the requirements for professional advisors, and sanctions. The second rulebook is the "AIM Rules for Nominated Advisors" which sets out the rules governing the eligibility, obligations and disciplining of Nomads. The third rulebook is the "AIM Disciplinary Procedures and Appeals Handbook" which sets out the procedures relating to disciplinary matters and appeals. There is a fourth rulebook of relevance to those dealing on AIM which is the "Rules of the London Stock Exchange" which sets out the rules for trading securities quoted on AIM.[204]

38–58   AIM's regulations have been described as being loosely based on the Prospectus Directive 2003,[205] with omissions made from that regulatory code in contexts in which it is not considered useful nor meaningful for such a rigorous regulatory code to be applied to smaller companies, such as those ordinarily quoted on AIM.

---

[200] Alastair Hudson, *Securities Law*, (Sweet & Maxwell, 2008), Ch.19.

[201] The expression "AIM companies" is the one used in the London Stock Exchange literature to refer to a company whose securities are traded on AIM. That is the sense in which that term is used in this chapter.

[202] References here are to the AIM rules published in February 2007.

[203] There is little literature on the AIM rules. The extremely useful H. Maule (ed.), *A Practitioner's Guide to The AIM Rules* (City & Financial Publishing, 2006) is now a little out-of-date as a result of these rule changes.

[204] The text of all of the AIM rulebooks can be found at *http://www.londonstockexchange.com/aim*.

[205] See, for example, M. Graham, "AIM", in II. Maule (ed.), *A Practitioner's Guide to The AIM Rules* (City & Financial Publishing, 2006), 4.

The result, while there may be superficial similarity to the skeleton of the FSA's Prospectus Rules, is a very much slighter set of rules which are much less prescriptive and exacting than the regulations relating to listing, prospectuses, and transparency obligations.

B. The role of Nomads under the AIM rules

The principal obligation of a Nomad is set out in rule 14 of the AIM Rules for Nominated Advisors:

    38–59

> "The nominated advisor to an AIM company is responsible to the Exchange for assessing the appropriateness of an applicant for AIM, or an existing AIM company when appointed as its nominated advisor."

The Nomad also bears a continuing obligation to notify "AIM Regulation" at the Exchange if it later comes to believe that a company is no longer appropriate for admission to AIM.[206] A Nomad bears a general duty of "skill and care at all times".[207] The bulk of the obligations which Nomads are stated to owe by the AIM Rules for Nominated Advisors are framed so that they are owed to the Exchange specifically, rather than to the company which is relying on the Nomad's advice. So, a Nomad is required to give a "nominated advisor's declaration" to the Exchange, in the form contained in Sch.2 to the AIM Rules for Nominated Advisors to certify that it has made due and careful enquiry into the affairs and constitution of the company for which it is acting, that the securities are appropriate for admission, and that all necessary professional advice has been taken. This declaration consequently imposes burdens of representation onto the Nomad on which the Exchange will rely when making decisions to admit or not to admit securities to trading on AIM. All of the following obligations are owed to the Exchange.

A Nomad is "responsible to the Exchange for advising and guiding an AIM company on its responsibilities under the AIM rules".[208] This obligation relates not only to the admission of a company but also to that company's compliance with its continuing obligations under the AIM rules. It is expected that a Nomad will be able to advise any AIM company for which it is responsible 'at all times'. Two qualified employees are expected to the responsible for each AIM company.[209]

    38–60

Schedule 3 to the AIM Rules for Nominated Advisors sets out the principal obligations of the Nomad in relation to each AIM company on whose behalf it acts.[210] The first responsibility requires that the Nomad has a "sound understanding of the applicant and its business".[211] The second responsibility relates to the appropriateness of each individual director and of the board of

    38–61

---

[206] AIM Rules for Nominated Advisors, r.14.
[207] AIM Rules for Nominated Advisors, r.16.
[208] AIM Rules for Nominated Advisors, r.17.
[209] AIM Rules for Nominated Advisors, r.17.
[210] AIM Rules for Nominated Advisors, r.18.
[211] AIM Rules for Nominated Advisors, Sch.3, AR1.

directors as a whole for admission to AIM.[212] The third responsibility relates to the supervision of due diligence undertaken as to the legal issues connected to the application, and as to the financial information relating to working capital and financial reporting systems.[213] The fourth responsibility relates to the requirement that the Nomad should itself be 'actively involved' in the preparation of the admission document, as well as overseeing its preparation.[214] Finally, the Nomad must ensure that the company has in place adequate "systems, procedures and controls" so that it will be able to comply with the AIM Rules for Companies.[215]

38–62 There are also "Ongoing Responsibilities" incumbent on the NOMAD which relate to the company's continuing appropriateness for trading on AIM. The first ongoing responsibility imposed on a Nomad is that it should "maintain regular contact with an AIM company for which it acts".[216] Therefore, a Nomad cannot simply abandon a company once it has been admitted: rather it must maintain a watching brief. The second ongoing responsibility is for the Nomad to "undertake a prior review of relevant notifications" made by an AIM company to ensure that that company complies with the AIM Rules for Companies rulebook.[217] The Nomad must ensure, so far as "reasonably possible" that the information provided by the company is appropriate to comply with the rulebook. The third ongoing responsibility is to monitor the trading in the securities of any AIM company for which it acts to watch for large price movements and to consider whether or not an announcement needs to be made as a result.[218] The fourth ongoing responsibility is for the Nomad to advise the company on any proposed changes to the board of directors.[219] A Nomad's "Engagement Responsibilities" impose obligations when a Nomad begins to act for a company which has already been admitted to AIM. The first engagement responsibility mirrors the first admission responsibility in that the Nomad is required to gain a sound understanding of the company and its business.[220] The second responsibility requires a survey of the suitability of each director of the company and of the efficacy of the purposes of compliance with the rulebook of the board of directors as a whole.[221] The third responsibility requires that the Nomad must ensure that the company has in place adequate "systems, procedures and controls" so that it will be able to comply with the AIM Rules for Companies.[222]

---

[212] AIM Rules for Nominated Advisors, Sch.3, AR2.
[213] AIM Rules for Nominated Advisors, Sch.3, AR3.
[214] AIM Rules for Nominated Advisors, Sch.3, AR4.
[215] AIM Rules for Nominated Advisors, Sch.3, AR5.
[216] AIM Rules for Nominated Advisors, Sch.3, OR1.
[217] AIM Rules for Nominated Advisors, Sch.3, OR2.
[218] AIM Rules for Nominated Advisors, Sch.3, OR3.
[219] AIM Rules for Nominated Advisors, Sch.3, OR4.
[220] AIM Rules for Nominated Advisors, Sch.3, ER1.
[221] AIM Rules for Nominated Advisors, Sch.3, ER2.
[222] AIM Rules for Nominated Advisors, Sch.3, ER3.

C. Admission to AIM

The AIM rules require that an "admission document" must be produced by an **38–63** applicant, and that that admission document must disclose the information specified in Schedule 2 to the AIM Rules for Companies. The admission document must then be available publicly and free of charge for at least one month from the admission of the applicant's securities to AIM. Importantly, this admission document does not have to comply with anything like the detail required of prospectuses under the full Prospectus Rules, as considered below in this section; and furthermore the admission document need only be available for one month from the admission of the securities to trading and not thereafter. At least ten business days before the anticipated date for admission to trading on AIM an ordinary applicant must provide the Exchange with the information listed in Sch.1 to the AIM Rules for Companies, which comprises mainly bare details about the company, its business and country of incorporation, information as to the securities which are to be traded, the anticipated market capitalisation of the securities on admission, information as to the members of its board of directors, information as to significant shareholders, and so forth.

An applicant must produce an admission document which complies with the **38–64** requirements of Sch.2 of the AIM Rules for Companies. The admission document must comply with Annex I through III of the Prospectus Rules, as was discussed in Chapter 38. Annex 1 relates to selected financial information, and information about: substantial assets, operating and financial review, capital resources, research and development, patents and licences, profit forecasts and estimates, the composition of senior management, remuneration and benefits, the audit and remuneration committees, and other miscellaneous items. Annex II deals with the "pro forma financial information building block" and that must be satisfied in full. Annex III of the Prospectus Rules provides for the "minimum disclosure requirements for the share securities note", although again only some elements of this Annex need be satisfied for the purposes of the AIM rules, in particular information relating to: working capital, capitalisation and indebtedness, the interest of natural and legal person involved in the issue, the terms and conditions of the offer, the arrangements for admission to trading and dealing, and statements by the directors to the effect that they have made due and careful enquiry of all of the matters required by the rules. Consequently, the admission document serves as a form of truncated prospectus in this context

D. Disclosure of corporate transactions

An AIM company is required to disclose "substantial transactions", in accordance **38–65** with Sch.3 of the rules,[223] and "related party transactions", in accordance with Sch.4 of the rules.[224] The company is also required to make disclosure of reverse take-overs which would result in fundamental change in its business, board or

---

[223] AIM Rules for Companies, r.12.
[224] AIM Rules for Companies, r.13.

voting control.[225] Similarly the company is required to make disclosure of any disposals which result in a fundamental change in the business.[226]

E. Financial reporting and other information

38–66 An AIM company is required to issue notification of a variety of information identified in rule 17 of the AIM Rules for Companies relating to deals by directors, relevant changes to significant shareholders, changes in the composition of the board of directors, a material change in any financial information given in the admission document, and so forth. More specifically, the company is required to publish half-yearly reports,[227] and annual accounts.[228] An AIM company is also required to maintain a web-site which is free-to-view with information about the company's directors, its constitutional documents, its securities and so forth.[229] This does not amount necessarily to the publication and maintenance of the admission document on a website, however.

6. REFORM OF THE LISTING RULES

38–67 In September 2009, the FCA announced that it intended to introduce a two-tier approach to listing securities. Before the announcement it should be understood that there were already two tiers of regulation in the UK for listed securities: first, those securities admitted to the Official List (which have been the principal focus of this chapter) and, secondly, those securities which are admitted to AIM. The intention of these (at the time of writing) draft proposals is that there be a difference for admission to the Official List between "premium" and "standard" listing whereby issuers can elect to be subject to a less onerous set of requirements. In effect, the less onerous regime will not require as much accounting information and information about internal management of the issuing entity. The intention behind this proposal is to make London seem a more attractive forum for listing securities due to a reduced set of regulatory requirements for entities opting for the less stringent regulatory approval process. This development is somewhat surprising given the genesis of the global financial crisis in "light touch" regulation. Some commentators have been quoted in the financial press as suggesting that a lighter regulatory regime will improve clarity by making it clear to investors which structure the issuer has chosen. However, the opposite appears to be true. By having two rulebooks existing side-by-side, it will be even more difficult for investors (especially non-expert investors) to differentiate between the level of disclosure required of issuers and consequently their assessment of the risks associated with securities will be harmed. This restriction on transparency is, it is suggested, a retrograde step.

---

[225] AIM Rules for Companies, r.14.
[226] AIM Rules for Companies, r.15.
[227] AIM Rules for Companies, r.17.
[228] AIM Rules for Companies, r.18.
[229] AIM Rules for Companies, r.26.

CHAPTER 39

LIABILITY FOR SECURITIES ISSUES

| B. | Excluded general law liability under transparency obligations | **39–48** |

CORE PRINCIPLES

Offers of securities lead to the creation of a contract and the prospectus (considered in Chapter 38) therefore constitutes a series of representations relating to the securities which are being sold. Consequently a large number of liabilities may arise under contract law and under tort law in relation to the sale of those securities if those representations turn out to have been false. The seller may be liable in contract law under the Misrepresentation Act 1967, or under tort law on the basis of the tort of negligent misrepresentation (that is, the principle in *Hedley Byrne v Heller* specifically) or of the tort of fraudulent misrepresentation. These principles were considered in Chapters 25 and 24 respectively, but in relation to negligence specifically it will become apparent in this chapter that the presence of the FCA Prospectus Rules means that makers of representations may not necessarily be able to hide behind a claim that their statements were intended to be made only to a limited class of buyers (so as to avoid liability to the marketplace at large). The first part of this chapter therefore focuses on how those general concepts apply specifically to securities transactions.

The Financial Services and Markets Act 2000 also provides for a right to compensation in s.90, over and above the common law, if the claimant has suffered loss as a result of any false or misleading statement in the prospectus or any omission from the prospectus. This right to compensation, it is suggested, tallies closely with the duty of disclosure in s.87A of the FSMA 2000 to provide all necessary information in the prospectus. Section 90A provides a broad comparator in relation to transparency obligations.

1. INTRODUCTION

39–01 This chapter considers the liabilities which may arise in relation to offers of securities.[1] Offers of securities are offers to enter into a contract. That contract may be entered into between the issuer of securities and a subscriber for those securities, or it may be entered into between an owner of securities and a purchaser in the after-market. Typically, in relation to both kinds of securities, it will be the issuer of the securities which will have made a number of representations as to the quality and nature of those securities in any prospectus that was published in advance of their issue. If the issuer is a party to the contract, then liability may lie in contract or in tort for fraudulent or negligent misrepresentation. If the issuer is not a party to the contract, then liability may lie in tort for misrepresentation. The people who are liable for the preparation of the

---

[1] This chapter is based on elements of Alastair Hudson, *Securities Law*, 1st edn (London: Sweet & Maxwell, 2008), which contains a much more detailed discussion of the contents of this chapter in pp.533–741.

prospectus and for other statements about the securities extend beyond the issuer itself into a range of other agents, advisors and experts, as considered below.[2]

Liability of this sort arises under the general law and further to s.90 of the Financial Services and Markets Act 2000 ("FSMA 2000"). This chapter begins by considering the general law of misrepresentation as it applies to securities issues before turning to the heads of statutory liability under FSMA 2000 because that is the most convenient way of explaining the issues which have arisen and how developments in securities regulation will effect the older case law principles.

39–02

2.   LIABILITY UNDER THE GENERAL LAW

A.   The approach of the old cases to issues of securities

The old cases dealing with issues of shares were clear that the people preparing a prospectus must state everything with "strict and scrupulous accuracy",[3] must include every fact which investors could require to know and must not mask information in ambiguity. The approach to the preparation of prospectuses was set out by Kindersley V.C. in *New Brunswick, etc., Co v Muggeridge*[4] in the following way:

39–03

> "Those who issue a prospectus, holding out to the public the great advantages which will accrue to persons who will take shares in a proposed undertaking, and inviting them to take shares on the faith of the representations therein contained, are bound to state everything with strict and scrupulous accuracy, and not only to abstain from stating as fact that which is not so, but to omit no one fact within their knowledge, the existence of which might in any degree affect the nature, or extent, or quality, of the privileges and advantages which the prospectus holds out as inducements to take shares."

This approach—that a prospectus must be prepared with "strict and scrupulous accuracy"—in the case law was approved in many subsequent cases. So, in *Central Railway of Venezuela v Kisch*,[5] Lord Chelmsford held that no misstatement nor concealment of any material facts or circumstances ought to be permitted. In his Lordship's opinion the public, who were invited by a prospectus to join in any new venture, ought to be given the same opportunity as the promoters themselves to judge everything which had a material bearing on the true character of the company's proposed undertakings. Consequently, it was held that the utmost candour ought to characterise the public statements of the promoters of a company.

It is interesting to note that the Prospectus Rules (overseen by the Financial Conduct Authority ("FCA"))[6] take a broadly similar approach to the obligations of those preparing the prospectus to include all necessary information. It is

39–04

---

[2] See para.37–36.

[3] *New Brunswick, etc., Co v Muggeridge* (1860) 1 Dr. & Sm. 363, 383, per Kindersley V.C.

[4] (1860) 1 Dr. & Sm. 363, 383.

[5] (1867) L.R. 5 H.L. 99, 123.

[6] The Prospectus Rules were discussed in detail in Ch.38. They were created originally by the Financial Services Authority to implement the EU Prospectus Directive. The regulatory baton has now passed to the Financial Conduct Authority ("FCA").

mandatory to produce a prospectus when making an offer of securities to the public or when seeking admission of securities to listing on a regulated market, in that it is an offence not to made such a prospectus available beforehand.[7] The Listing Principles contained in Chapter 7 of the listing rules require that those preparing prospectuses to act with "integrity" not only in the preparation of prescribed documentation but also in all of their dealings with the Financial Conduct Authority. Those preparing the prospectus must ensure that it contains all "necessary information" for an investor to make an informed decision when investing in securities.[8] A listed company is also required to have adequate procedures to identify any further information which should be made available to the investing public through a recognised information service.[9] Consequently, securities regulation now imposes positive, continuing obligations on companies as to the full disclosure of relevant information and are not limited to "strict and scrupulous accuracy" as to the things which the issuer chooses to mention in the preparation of the initial prospectus.

B.   Liability for a false prospectus at common law

39–05   Liability for a false prospectus at common law will arise in a number of different contexts, as considered in this chapter. The first question is whether or not the persons responsible for the contents of the prospectus acted fraudulently. If so, liability for damages for fraudulent misrepresentation in contract law may arise.[10] Alternatively, liability may lie for damages in tort for deceit.[11] If dishonesty was involved, then criminal liability may lie for theft or for fraud in the ways considered in Chapter 16.[12] If there was no fraud, then liability may lie for damages in contract for negligent misrepresentation: primarily under the doctrine set out in the leading case of *Caparo v Dickman*[13] and the head of liability established in *Hedley Byrne v Heller*.[14] This head of liability was considered in Chapter 25. The cases on negligence which relate specifically to securities transactions are considered below.[15] A range of other remedies may also lie in equity: primarily the remedy of rescission to unpick the sale of securities,[16] as was considered in Chapter 20.

---

[7] Financial Services and Markets Act 2000, s.85.
[8] Financial Services and Markets Act 2000, s.87A.
[9] Listing Rules, Ch.7, s.7.2.
[10] See para.18–18.
[11] See para.24–01.
[12] See para.16–01.
[13] See para.25–01.
[14] See para.25–01.
[15] See para.37–07.
[16] See para.20–28.

C.   Fraudulent misrepresentation

The tort of deceit (or, fraudulent misrepresentation) was considered in detail in Chapter 24.[17] In short, a defendant will be liable to compensate losses suffered by a claimant in reliance on a false representation made by the defendant in circumstances in which the defendant knew that representation to be untrue, or was reckless as to its truth or falsity, and intended that the claimant would rely on that statement. If the representation was not deceitful in this fashion, then liability may arise under the tort of negligence, as considered in the next section of this chapter.

39-06

3.   TORT OF NEGLIGENT MISREPRESENTATION

A.   The central principle of the tort of negligence: *Caparo v Dickman*

In order to recover damages based on the tort of negligent misrepresentation, the plaintiff must establish that the defendant owed her a duty of care not to cause loss or damage of the kind caused by breach of that duty. The leading decision of the House of Lords in *Caparo Industries Plc v Dickman*[18] was considered in Chapter 25.[19] The principal liability in this context is related to the making of a negligent misstatement in a prospectus on which a purchaser of securities relies and so suffers loss. The principle underpinning liability in tort for negligent misrepresentation is contained in the decision in *Hedley Byrne v Heller*.[20] That principle was summarised for the purposes of negligent misrepresentations made in prospectuses by Lightman J. in *Possfund v Diamond*[21] in the following terms:

39-07

> "In 1963 the House of Lords in *Hedley Byrne v Heller & Partners Ltd*[22] established that at common law a cause of action exists enabling the recovery of damages in respect of a negligent misrepresentation occasioning damage and loss where the necessary proximity exists between the representor and representee. It is clearly established (and indeed common ground on these applications) that in a case such as the present, where the defendants have put a document into more or less general circulation and there is no special relationship alleged between the plaintiffs and the defendants, foreseeability by the defendants that the plaintiffs would rely on the prospectus for the purposes of deciding whether to make after-market purchases is not sufficient to impose upon the defendant a duty of care in such a situation requires a closer relationship between representor and representee, and its imposition must be fair, just and reasonable."

There are three criteria for the imposition of a duty of care in any given situation: foreseeability of damage, proximity of relationship and reasonableness.[23]

---

[17] See para.24–01.
[18] [1990] 2 A.C. 605.
[19] See para.25–34.
[20] [1963] 2 All E.R. 575; [1964] A.C. 465.
[21] *Possfund Custodian Trustee Ltd v Diamond* [1996] 2 All E.R. 774; [1996] 1 W.L.R. 1351; [1996] 2 B.C.L.C. 665, per Lightman J.
[22] [1963] 2 All E.R. 575; [1964] A.C. 465.
[23] See *Smith v Bush* [1990] 1 A.C. 861 (H.L.) at 865 per Lord Griffiths, and also *Caparo Industries Plc v Dickman* [1990] 2 A.C. 605.

39–08   The position was expressed in the following terms by Lord Oliver in *Caparo Industries Plc v Dickman*[24]:

> "What can be deduced from the *Hedley Byrne*[25] case, therefore, is that the necessary relationship between the maker of a statement or giver of advice (the adviser) and the recipient who acts in reliance on it (the advisee) may typically be held to exist where (1) the advice is required for a purpose, whether particularly specified or generally described, which is made known, either actually or inferentially, to the adviser at the time when the advice is given, (2) the adviser knows, either actually or inferentially, that his advice will be communicated to the advisee, either specifically or as a member of an ascertainable class, in order that it should be used by the advisee for that purpose, (3) it is known, either actually or inferentially, that the advice so communicated is likely to be acted upon by the advisee for that purpose without independent inquiry and (4) it is so acted on by the advisee to his detriment. That is not, of course, to suggest that these conditions are either conclusive or exclusive, but merely that the actual decision in the case does not warrant any broader propositions."[26]

What this formulation does not take into account is a regulatory requirement under the Prospectus Rules[27] that the statement in question was included in the prospectus and that there would be continuing obligations under those same regulations to ensure the continued accuracy of that statement. In such a circumstance, it is suggested, that the issuer must have known that the statement would be relied upon by investors in the after-market as well as initial subscribers for the securities. The principles established in the cases considered in this section were decided before the modern regulatory environment emerged, but should nevertheless now be read in the light of those regulations.

B.   Liability for negligent misrepresentations in accounts prior to a takeover: *Caparo Industries v Dickman*

The appeal in Caparo Industries v Dickman

39–09   The *Caparo Industries Plc v Dickman* appeal related to a claim brought by a claimant which had acquired shares in a target company, Fidelity Plc, as part of a takeover. The claimant contended that it had relied on Fidelity's accounts for the accounting year 1983–84, which had been audited by the accountants Touche Ross and which showed a pre-tax profit of £1.3 million. After acquiring a controlling shareholding in the target company, the claimant discovered that the company's financial position ought to have demonstrated a loss of £0.4 million. Consequently, the claimant sought to establish a breach of a duty of care in negligence on the part of the accountants when acting as the auditors of the company. The claimant argued that, as a person intending to acquire a controlling shareholding in the company, the accountants owed it a duty of care when auditing the company's accounts. Lord Bridge held that:

---

[24] [1990] 2 A.C. 605.
[25] [1964] A.C. 465.
[26] [1991] 2 A.C. 605 at 638. See also Lord Bridge at 620–621 and Lord Jauncey at 659–660 (esp. at 660E "the fundamental question of the purpose").
[27] See para.36–34.

"If a duty of care were owed so widely, it is difficult to see any reason why it should not equally extend to all who rely on the accounts in relating to other dealings with a company as lenders or merchants extending credit to the company".[28]

Therefore, it was held that on policy grounds a general duty of care ought not to be imposed on auditors in such situations.[29]

The claim brought in *Caparo v Dickman* asserted a very wide duty of care in relation to those contemplating takeover the of companies. An assertion which was considered by the House of Lords simply to extend too far. What emerges from Lord Bridge's speech, however, is a range of issues beyond this narrow focus on the context of takeovers and the wider policy considerations. Lord Bridge also held that the salient feature of cases following *Hedley Byrne v Heller*,[30] relating to the liability of those making misstatements in tort to those relying on those statements and suffering loss as a result, was that the defendant "knew" either that the advice or statement made would be communicated to the claimant directly or indirectly, and further that the defendant "knew" that the claimant was very likely to rely on that advice or statement. Significantly, then, the *Hedley Byrne* line of cases had referred to situations in which the claimant was a person within the contemplation of the person responsible for the statement. **39–10**

The effect of the change in principle in Caparo Industries v Dickman

In applying the principle in *Anns v Merton LBC* (which pre-dated *Caparo v Dickman*) Woolf J. held at first instance in *JEB Fasteners Ltd v Marks, Bloom & Co*[31] that where accounts had been prepared in a situation in which a takeover of the company was a possible and foreseeable means of obtaining finance, then the accountants owed a duty of care to the claimant who subsequently did take the company over and who did suffer loss as a result of having relied, inter alia, on misstatements in those accounts. As a result of the decision in *Caparo Industries Plc v Dickman*, such an approach became untenable. So in *McNaughton Papers Group v Hicks Anderson*,[32] accounts were prepared specifically for the target company, MK, and therefore were not considered to be statements on which the claimant (who was seeking to take over MK) could rely as having created a duty of care once the claimant had taken over the target company in reliance on misstatements made in those accounts. The rationale for this decision was that the purpose for which the statements were made (here, as part of accounts prepared for the benefit of MK alone) precluded any other person from relying on them to found a duty of care. **39–11**

In slightly different circumstances in *Morgan Crucible Co Plc v Hill Samuel Bank Ltd*,[33] the directors and financial advisors of the target company had made **39–12**

---

[28] [1990] 2 A.C. 605.
[29] Approving *Al Saudi Banque v Clark Pixley* [1990] Ch. 313.
[30] [1964] A.C. 465.
[31] [1981] 3 All E.R. 289.
[32] [1991] 1 All E.R. 134.
[33] [1991] 1 All E.R. 148.

express representations in the course of a contested takeover forecasting a 38 per cent increase in pre-tax profits at a time when an identified bidder for the company had emerged. The purpose behind these and other representations had been to induce the bidder to make a higher bid. The bidder relied on those statements. The Court of Appeal held that there was therefore a relationship of sufficient proximity between the bidder and those who had been responsible for the statements to found a duty of care in negligence. The decision in *Caparo Industries Plc v Dickman* was distinguished on these facts on the basis that in *Caparo* no identified bidder had emerged at the time when the statements had been made, whereas in *Morgan Crucible Co Plc v Hill Samuel Bank Ltd* an identified bidder had emerged and the statements had been made to induce a reaction from that particular bidder.

39–13 As outlined immediately above, in *James McNaughton Papers Group Ltd v Hicks Anderson & Co (a firm)*[34] it was held that accountants acting for a target company in takeover negotiations owed no duty of care to the bidder in respect of alleged inaccuracies in draft accounts provided to the target company for use in the negotiations. Neill L.J., delivering the judgement of the Court of Appeal, identified six matters which were likely to be of importance in reaching a decision as to whether or not a duty exists: first, the purpose for which the statement was made; secondly, the purpose for which the statement was communicated; thirdly, the relationship between the adviser, the advisee and any relevant third party; fourthly, the size of any class to which the advisee belongs; fifthly, the state of knowledge of the adviser; and, sixthly, the nature, reasonableness and extent of the reliance of the advisee.[35]

C. The application of the *Caparo* doctrine to prospectuses put into wide circulation

39–14 It is important, for present purposes, to consider how the *Caparo* principle—relating on its facts specifically to takeover cases—would apply in situations in which the statements made in prospectuses are likely to be put into wide circulation either among a class of investors or made available to the public generally. Beyond the narrow context of takeovers, there is a problem with applying the logic of the preceding cases to cases involving the acquisition of shares on a regulated market in ordinary circumstances precisely because the preparation and publication of a prospectus is obligatory in relation to public offers of securities and in relation to the admission of securities to trading on a regulated market because it is intended to be a statement made to the investing public on which that public can rely when acquiring securities.[36] Therefore, in the context of prospectuses prepared under the prospectus rules it is not a question of a private document being prepared necessarily for the benefit of a limited class of people but rather it is a public document required by statute to be prepared for the

---

[34] [1991] 1 All E.R. 135.
[35] But cf. *Morgan Crucible Co Plc v Hill Samuel Bank Ltd* [1991] 1 All E.R. 148.
[36] Financial Services and Markets Act 2000, s.85. See para.36–01.

benefit of the public at large and concomitantly for the proper regulation of the securities markets. In this context, Lord Bridge held that:

"The situation is entirely different where a statement is put into more or less general circulation and may foreseeably be relied on by strangers to the maker of the statement for any one of a variety of different purposes which the maker of the statement has no specific reason to anticipate."[37]

Therefore, his lordship's view was that statements put into general circulation would be less likely to attract liability in tort because the maker of that statement could not ordinarily know the purposes to which his statement would be put to use by the claimant. However, in relation to a prospectus it is well known to what use its readers will put that document: they will use it to decide whether or not to invest in the securities to which it relates. From the facts of *Caparo Industries Plc v Dickman*, however, it emerges that an auditor's role is primarily to verify for the company that the accounts constitute a true and fair view of the financial position of the company and an auditor cannot also be said to be liable for the reliance which a person, even if a current shareholder, might choose to place on that auditor's report in deciding whether or not to acquire a controlling stake in the company.

The distinction between these cases reflects the debate which arises in relation to liability for misstatements in prospectuses. On the one hand those responsible for the prospectus may seek to restrict their liability for statements made in the prospectus by means of contractual exclusion clauses or by providing that their statements are intended only for a limited audience, whereas on the other hand it could be said that the public at large could be expected to have sight of those statements and therefore expect that they ought properly to be able to hold their authors to account in the event that they are proved to have been made negligently. This latter argument has particular force when the offer is an offer of securities to the public.

39–15

Two points arise. First, it could be said that such statements made in prospectuses governed by the prospectus rules are known by the persons responsible for preparing them to be statements which are to be relied upon by investors generally and therefore that it does no violence to Lord Bridge's dicta in *Caparo Industries Plc v Dickman*, quoted above, to suggest that the entire investing public is within the contemplation of the person responsible for the contents of the prospectus. Indeed, the purpose of the prospectus rules could be said, in part, to be to bring the general public within the contemplation of those preparing prospectuses in relation to shares to be offered for sale to that public. Secondly, and following on from that first point, it may be that if an offer of securities were to be made to a restricted class of investors, then it would be in line with the *Caparo* principle to find that the general investing public were not within the contemplation of the person responsible for the contents of the prospectus. As a result, people not within the contemplation of any person responsible for the prospectus ought not to be able to bring a claim in tort in the event that they rely

39–16

---

[37] [1990] 2 A.C. 605; [1990] 1 All E.R. 568, 576. Approving *Scott Group v Macfarlane* [1978] 1 N.Z.L.R. 553, 566, per Richmond P.

on the prospectus otherwise than as a member of the identified class when acquiring those securities subsequently. However, this latter context pre-supposes, it is suggested, that the offer of securities involved is outwith the prospectus rules and the listing rules because otherwise minimum contents are required in a prospectus (as considered in Chapter 36 of this book) and that prospectus is required to be made available to the public further to s.85 of FSMA 2000.

D.   Whether the duty of care extends to purchasers not within the contemplation of the issuer

The issue

39–17 The most difficult question to have arisen on the cases dealing with negligent misrepresentations in prospectuses is the following. Suppose an issuer is seeking to issue securities to a narrow range of investors only, for example by means of a placement where shares are intended only for a limited number of potential investors. The prospectus may be prepared with only those intended placees in mind. However, those securities will latterly be traded in the after-market: that is, they will be sold to people subsequently who were not among the placees. Therefore, the question arises whether or not those people responsible for the prospectus owe a duty of care to the purchasers in the after-market or whether they only owe a duty of care to the placees. The people responsible for the prospectus would like to limit their liability to placees only and would protest that it was only the placees who would be in their contemplation when preparing the prospectus. However, in the context of modern securities regulation which requires the publication of a prospectus which complies with the prospectus rules and the general duty of disclosure in s.87A of FSMA 2000 discussed in Chapter 36,[38] the alternative approach is that issuers of securities which are to be offered to the public or which are to be admitted to trading on a regulated market (even if not offered to the public) will necessarily be communicating to the general investor community by virtue of publishing that prospectus and maintaining the currency of its contents. The narrow approach has the support of *Al-Nakib Investments (Jersey) Ltd v Longcroft*[39]; whereas the alternative approach has the support of Lightman J. in *Possfund v Diamond*[40]: both cases are considered in turn below.

The narrow conception of the obligation: Al-Nakib Investments (Jersey) Ltd v Longcroft

39–18 In *Al-Nakib Investments (Jersey) Ltd v Longcroft*,[41] C Plc incorporated a subsidiary, M Ltd, for the purpose of developing a product. It resolved to float M

---

[38] See para.36–34.
[39] [1990] 3 All E.R. 321.
[40] *Possfund Custodian Trustee Ltd v Diamond* [1996] 2 All E.R. 774; [1996] 1 W.L.R. 1351.
[41] *Al-Nakib Investments (Jersey) Ltd v Longcroft* [1990] 3 All E.R. 321.

Ltd on the now-disbanded Unlisted Securities Market ("USM")[42] and issued a prospectus inviting the shareholders of C Plc to subscribe for shares in both C Plc and M Ltd by way of a rights issue. The plaintiff subscribed for shares in M Ltd and some months later made purchases of shares in C Plc and in M Ltd through purchases on the open market. The plaintiff sued C Plc and its directors alleging that the prospectus and two interim reports issued by M Ltd contained misrepresentations as to the identity of the person who would be manufacturing the company's products. Moreover, they argued that the defendants owed the plaintiff a duty of care in issuing the prospectus and interim reports based on the reasonable foreseeability of loss being consequent on the plaintiff's acquisition of those shares. The defendants successfully applied to have the allegations struck out, in so far as they related to the purchases in the after-market, on the basis that they disclosed no reasonable cause of action. As to the prospectus, it was held by Mervyn Davies J. that it had been issued for a particular purpose, namely to encourage subscription for shares by a limited class of subscribers and that any duty of care in relation to its issue was directed to that specific purpose only. It had not been directed at purchases in the after-market and therefore any misrepresentation therein could not found a claim based on the tort of negligence.[43]

In this regard, Mervyn Davies J. relied, inter alia, on dicta of Lord Jauncey in *Caparo Industries Plc v Dickman*[44] to the effect that reliance might not be placed on the accounts by the claimant in that case if they had been prepared for certain, limited purposes.[45] Mervyn Davies J. sought to rely on that point to the effect that a prospectus prepared for limited purposes ought similarly to be incapable of founding a general liability in tort for any member outwith the contemplated class of readers who may rely on it. Furthermore, and perhaps crucially in the modern context, his lordship found that the fact that these shares were to be listed on the USM, and thus subsequently to be made available for sale to the public, did not in itself create any duty of care in favour of those who did subsequently buy those securities in the after-market.

39–19

The broader conception of the principle: Possfund Custodian Trustee Ltd v Diamond

By contrast in *Possfund Custodian Trustee Ltd v Diamond*[46] there had been a placement of shares on the Unlisted Securities Market and subsequent purchases of those shares after the placement in the after-market. The prospectus prepared in relation to the initial placement greatly understated the issuer's liabilities, being a company specialising in insuring second hand vehicles, to pay extra premiums to syndicates at Lloyds. The company subsequently went into

39–20

---

[42] The forerunner of the present Alternative Investment Market (AIM).

[43] Reliance was placed on *Peek v Gurney* (1873) L.R. 6 H.L. 377 in which similar conclusion was reached.

[44] [1990] 2 A.C. 605; [1990] 1 All E.R. 568, 607.

[45] His lordship also placed reliance on dicta of Lord Griffiths in *Smith v Eric S. Bush* [1989] 2 All E.R. 514, 536, to similar effect.

[46] [1996] 2 All E.R. 774.

receivership due, in no small measure, to the burden of paying those extra premiums. Purchasers of those shares in the after-market contended that they had relied on those statements made in the prospectus, that it had been reasonable for them to rely on the prospectus in that way in making their purchases, and that those responsible for the prospectus had breached a duty of care owed to purchasers of the shares. In *Possfund Custodian Trustee Ltd v Diamond*[47] claims were brought in the tort of deceit and in the tort of negligent misrepresentation. Lightman J. held that, historically both at common law and in statute, the purpose of a prospectus had been[48]:

> "... to provide the necessary information to enable an investor to make an informed decision whether to accept the offer thereby made to take shares on the proposed allotment, but not a decision whether to make after-market purchases."

The statutory attitude had not appeared to have changed. The question before the court was, therefore, whether changed market conditions—in which it was alleged that prospectuses were now commonly relied upon by the investor public in the after-market—could justify a change in the attitude of the common law such that the prospectus could be recognised to have an effect on decisions whether or not to make purchases in the after-market.

39–21   The principal issue was then one of the proximity of the investor public to the maker of the statement in the prospectus. It was held that where the maker of the statement intends that the prospectus will be relied upon by the public in making investment decisions, then it is reasonable to assume that there is sufficient proximity between those parties. Developing that point more precisely, Lightman J. went on to find that even if intention is not in itself a factor sufficient to generate the necessary proximity to found a claim in negligence, it must nevertheless be an important factor in establishing that necessary proximity.[49] As a result Lightman J. was prepared to find that where a prospectus is prepared with the intention of inducing the investor public to acquire securities, then a duty of care does arise between those responsible for the contents of the prospectus and that investing public. This issue is considered in greater detail in relation to the section on "proximity" in Chapter 25.[50]

39–22   It is suggested that this approach accords with the principles underpinning the Financial Services and Markets Act 2000 and the listing rules that where offers of securities are made to the public, then those obligations identified by the Prospectus Rules as being responsible for the contents of the prospectus[51] ought to be held liable at common law to account to any investor for any loss suffered as a result of some statement in or omission from that prospectus. The argument made in *Possfund v Diamond* was that market practice relating to the publication of prospectuses constituted a different context from *Peek v Gurney*, decided in

---

[47] [1996] 2 All E.R. 774, [1996] 1 W.L.R. 1351; [1996] 2 B.C.L.C. 665.
[48] [1996] 2 All E.R. 774, 787
[49] Relying on *Morgan Crucible Co Plc v Hill Samuel Bank Ltd* [1991] All E.R. 148, 160, per Slade L.J.
[50] See para.25–13.
[51] See para.37–36.

1873.[52] It was held in *Possfund v Diamond*—before the stringency of the current Prospectus Rules was introduced—that the public availability of the prospectus meant that those responsible for the prospectus must necessarily have had any investor who would refer to that information within their contemplation, even when preparing a prospectus merely for a placement.[53] Lightman J. held that:

> "it does seem to me to be at least arguable that a duty of care is assumed and owed to those investors who (as intended) rely on the contents of the prospectus in making such purchases".[54]

The decision in *Possfund Custodian Trustee Ltd v Diamond* is a recognition that prospectuses are intended to be relied upon by the public at large and that there was "nothing in the authorities or textbooks which precludes the finding of such a duty".[55] Therefore, while the cases might seem to be capable of a slightly uneasy reconciliation (that is, on the basis that *Al-Nakib* was a placement to limited placees, whereas *Possfund* concerned a more general offer); in truth a reconciliation of these cases is not possible. Lightman J. expressed his view in *Possfund* that the decision in *Al-Nakib Investments (Jersey) Ltd v Longcroft* was one which ought to be overturned by a higher court.[56] His Lordship's intention was clearly for the common law to strike out in a new direction. It is suggested that this approach is to be preferred.

E.   Reliance on the misrepresentation

It must be shown that the people making the misrepresentation intended that the claimant relied on the representation, and also that there was sufficient proximity between the statement made and the loss that resulted.[57] When establishing an intention, that intention must be objectively established.[58] It is suggested that if the information was information of a sort which was expected to be provided further to the prospectus rules or the duty of disclosure in s.87A of FSMA 2000, then it would be reasonable for an inexpert investor to rely on that information precisely because its provision was required by the prospectus rules because it was the sort of information which an issuer must supply and on which an investor can therefore reasonably rely.

39–23

---

[52] (1873) L.R. 6 HL 377; [1861–73] All E.R. Rep. 116.
[53] *Possfund Custodian Trustee Ltd v Diamond* [1996] 2 All E.R. 774; [1996] 1 W.L.R. 1351; [1996] 2 B.C.L.C. 665, per Lightman J.
[54] See above.
[55] [1996] 2 All E.R. 774, 788.
[56] [1996] 2 All E.R. 774, 789.
[57] *Possfund Custodian Trustee Ltd v Diamond* [1996] 2 All E.R. 774; [1996] 1 W.L.R. 1351; [1996] 2 B.C.L.C. 665, per Lightman J.
[58] See above.

F.   No fiduciary duty

39–24   Australian authority has suggested that there will not be a *fiduciary* duty to ensure, in issuing new shares to the shareholders of another company as part of a takeover, that a proper valuation of the target company's shares is reflected in circulars sent to shareholders.[59]

4.   MISREPRESENTATION ON THE DECIDED CASES

A.   Introduction

39–25   This section considers the various types of misrepresentations made in prospectuses which have been held to found liability for damages in tort. Many of these cases were decided in the 19th century when the promotion of new companies generated a large number of fraudulent schemes. When giving judgment in *Henderson v Lacon*[60] Page-Wood V.C. described the principles in these cases as being a "golden legacy". These cases, taken together, have defined the perimeter of situations in which misstatements in prospectuses will and will not attract private law liability. What is particularly significant is the treatment of ambiguous and half-true statements which were intended to entice investors to buy shares while seeking to avoid making any literally untrue statements. The approach of the courts has been to establish an approach in the old cases which would not permit any statement which effectively sought to create a false market in the securities by seeking to give an incorrect impression of the investment opportunity when considered as a whole.

B.   Whether or not statements create a misleading impression

39–26   A statement included in a prospectus will be deemed to be untrue if it is misleading in the form it is made and in the context in which it is included.[61] So, one cannot escape liability by making statements which appear to be literally true but which give a misleading impression of the facts. It has been held[62] that:

> "[i]t is not that the omission of material facts is an independent ground for rescission, but the omission must be of such a nature as to make the statement actually made misleading".[63]

Grandiloquent statements which are substantially true are not misrepresentations.[64] So, saying that "we believe this company offers a great hope for the future of this country" is a grandiloquent statement which may not be a misrepresentation; whereas, saying "this company will be the most successful widget manufacturer in the UK by the end of the financial year" would be

---

[59] *Pilmer v Duke Group Ltd (in liquidation)* [2001] 2 B.C.L.C. 773.
[60] (1867) L.R. 5 Eq. 249, 262.
[61] *R. v Kylsant* [1932] 1 K.B. 442.
[62] *McKeown v Boudard Peveril Gear Co Ltd* (1896) 74 L.T. 712, 713, per Rigby L.J.
[63] *Coles v White City (Manchester) Greyhound Assn. Ltd* (1929) 48 T.L.R. 230, CA.
[64] *City of Edinburgh Brewery Co v Gibson's Trustees* 1869 7 M. 886.

misleading if the people making that statement knew that the company was unable to pay its debts and was therefore insolvent. The question is whether or not the statement is misleading.

Clearly, statements in financial accounts which misstate the condition of the company will be misleading statements. On the decided cases, making an incorrect statement that more than one-half of the first issue of shares had already been subscribed for[65] will be a misleading statement. Similarly stating that the surplus assets as shown in the last balance sheet amounted to upwards of £10,000 when they did not was a misleading statement.[66] These matters were clearly significant in relation to the financial standing of the company and would have encouraged potential investors to believe that the business was sound, when the true position was different. Statements as to the company's assets or the condition of its accounts would be material representations.[67]

39–27

Misleading statements have been held to be actionable misrepresentations on the following bases: that a particular mine was in full operation and making large daily returns[68]; that patented articles were a commercial success and beyond the experimental stage[69]; that the company was the sole manufacturer of asbestos in France and had a practical monopoly[70]; that the company's process was a commercial success[71]; and that the vendors in nitrate grounds had obtained a supply of water brought to them in pipes such that the company would have the right of using a certain part of the water.[72] All of these statements were incorrect and therefore constituted misleading statements in their respective documentation. A statement that something will be done in the future is not a statement of an existing fact so much as a contract or promise. It may, however, imply the existence of facts which are non-existent, or it may be a material term in the contract,[73] and a representation of belief, expectation or intention may be a representation of fact, for "the state of a man's mind is as much a matter of fact as the state of his digestion".[74]

39–28

C. Statements about new businesses

When dealing with start-up companies before their incorporation, it is common for enthusiastic statements to be made to encourage investors to participate in the new business. In relation to start-up companies, the statements made in the prospectus as to the condition and financial position of the company will be more

39–29

---

[65] *Ross Estates Investment Co* (1868) L.R. 3 Ch. 682; *Kent v Freehold Land Co* (1868) L.R. 3 Ch. 493; *Henderson v Lacon* (1867) L.R. 5 Eq. 249. As to the meaning of "subscribed", see below.
[66] *Re London and Staffordshire Fire Insurance Co* (1883) 24 Ch.D. 149.
[67] *Re London and Staffordshire Fire Insurance Co* (1883) 24 Ch.D. 149.
[68] *Reese River, etc., Co v Smith* (1869) L.R. 4 H.L. 64.
[69] *Greenwood v Leather Shod Wheel Co* [1900] 1 Ch. 421.
[70] *Hyde v New Asbestos Co* (1891) 8 T.L.R. 121.
[71] *Stirling v Passburg Grains, etc., Ltd* (1891) 8 T.L.R. 71.
[72] *Lagunas Nitrate Co v Lagunas Nitrate Syndicate* [1899] 2 Ch. 392, 397, 429.
[73] *Karberg's Case* [1892] 32 Ch. 1; *Beattie v Ebury* (1874) L.R. 7 Ch. 777, 804; *Alderson v Maddison* (1883) 3 App. Cas. 467; *Bellairs v Tucker* (1884) 13 Q.B.D. 562.
[74] *Eddington v Fitzmaurice* (1885) 29 Ch.D. 459, 483, per Bowen L.J.

important than otherwise because there is no trading record on which investors can rely. Therefore, it is suggested, it will be easier for investors to demonstrate that they were acting in reliance on such statements. Where a company was formed to buy a mine, and extracts from the report of an expert were set out which gave a misleading impression of that report and induced the belief that the mine was similar to a rich adjacent mine, it was held that a subscriber was entitled to relief.[75] Similarly, it would be a misrepresentation in a prospectus to state that the company had a contract in place for the purchase of a property when, in fact, that arrangement was only in negotiation.[76] It is not a misrepresentation if the prospectus states that the capital is £x and the memorandum and articles contain the usual powers to increase or reduce the capital.[77] It has been held that a representation in a prospectus to the effect that the members of the company were comprised of "a large number of gentlemen in the trade and others", when only a dozen out of a total membership of 55 were in fact in the trade, was not a material misrepresentation.[78]

D. Reports referred to in a prospectus

39–30   If the company takes it upon itself both to assume the authenticity of the reports referred to in the prospectus and to represent as fact the matters stated in those reports, then it must take the consequences should the reports prove to be false.[79] So, in *Re Pacaya Rubber and Produce Co Ltd*[80] the prospectus contained extracts from a report of a Peruvian expert as to the condition of a rubber estate which the company sought to acquire. It was held that these extracts from the report contained in the prospectus formed the basis of the contract. On the basis that the company had not distanced itself from the report nor suggested that it did not vouch for the accuracy of the report, the company was taken to have contracted on the basis of the contents of the report. Therefore, the contracts of allotment could be rescinded because those reports were incorrect and misleading.

E. Ambiguity will not prevent a statement being misleading

39–31   When publishing a prospectus, the issuer cannot avoid liability for misstatements by couching that document in ambiguous language. Rather, an ambiguous statement in a prospectus will be deemed to have asserted anything which it could have been reasonably interpreted to have asserted.[81] Otherwise, a false market

---

[75] *Re Mount Morgan, etc., Ltd* (1887) 56 L.T. 622. There are a number of cases in which the benefits which the promoters stood to take from the company were concealed, thus constituting actionable misstatements: *Re London and Staffordshire Fire Insurance Co* (1883) 25 Ch.D. 149; *Lodwick v Earl of Perth* (1884) 1 T.L.R. 76; *Capel & Co v Sim's, etc., Co* (1888) 58 L.T. 807; *Re Liberian Government Concessions, etc., Co* (1892) 9 T.L.R. 136.

[76] *Ross Estates Investment Co* (1868) L.R. 3 Ch. 682.

[77] *City of Edinburgh Brewery Co Ltd v Gibson's Trustees* (1869) 7 M. 886.

[78] (1869) 7 M. 886.

[79] *Reese River, etc., Co v Smith* (1869) L.R. 4 H.L. 64.

[80] [1914] 1 Ch. 542. See also *Mair v Rio Grande Rubber Estates Ltd* (1913) S.C. (H.L.) 74.

[81] *R. v Kylsant* [1932] 1 K.B. 442; *Hallows v Fernie* (1868) L.R. 3 Ch. 467, 476; *Arkwright v Newbold* (1881) 17 Ch.D. 301, 322; *Smith v Chadwick* (1884) 9 App. Cas. 187.

could be created in the securities by dint of the ambiguity. It is not sufficient for those responsible for a prospectus to say that the facts can be verified by investors by inspection of documents at the company's officers.[82] Rather, it is the person making that statement in the prospectus who bears the risk of the investor relying on it without doing more. To suggest that the investors bear the risk of the falsity of such statements was considered by Lord Watson to be "one of the most audacious pleas that ever was put forward in answer to a charge" of misrepresentation.[83]

F. Remedies at common law

Introduction

The remedies at common law for the various actions considered in this chapter were discussed in detail in Chapter 20. The reader is referred to that discussion.

39–32

The measure of damages in tort for a fraudulent misrepresentation

Where shares are acquired in reliance upon a fraudulent misrepresentation, the measure of damages is that appropriate to claims in tort. The plaintiff is entitled to be placed in the position which he would have occupied if the misrepresentation had not been made.[84] The decision of the House of Lords in *Smith New Court Securities Ltd v Scrimgeour Vickers (Asset Management) Ltd*,[85] which was considered in Chapter 24, held that the damages recoverable would be the difference between the contract price and the amount actually realised by the plaintiff on disposal of the shares.[86] The defendant is bound to make reparation for all damage which was caused directly by the transaction by reference to the full price paid by the claimant for the securities less the market value of those securities.[87]

39–33

Misrepresentation in contract law

The general law on misrepresentation founding a contract was considered in detail in Chapter 18 *Validity of Contracts*. What is different about contractual misrepresentation in the securities law context is that issuers are obliged to make certain kinds of statement in prospectuses, and therefore there is no possibility of excluding liability on the basis that matters were omitted instead of being stated. Whereas contract law would ordinarily not consider a withholding of information

39–34

---

[82] *Redgrove v Hurd* (1881) 20 Ch.D. 1, 14, per Lord Jessel M.R.; *Smith v Chadwick* (1884) 9 App. Cas. 187. See also *Venezuela Co v Kisch* (1867) L.R. 2 H.L. 99; *Aaron's Reefs v Twiss* [1896] A.C. 273.

[83] *Aaron's Reefs v Twiss* [1896] A.C. 273.

[84] *Smith New Court Securities Ltd v Scrimgeour Vickers (Asset Management) Ltd* [1994] 4 All E.R. 225; the correct measure is the difference between what the purchaser paid and the price which, absent the misrepresentation, the shares would have fetched on the open market.

[85] [1996] 4 All E.R. 769.

[86] [1996] 4 All E.R. 769, 780, per Lord Browne-Wilkinson.

[87] [1996] 4 All E.R. 769, 778/9, per Lord Browne-Wilkinson.

to constitute a misrepresentation,[88] in the context of a prospectus the general duty of disclosure in s.87A of FSMA 2000 would mean that a representor should be taken to have misrepresented any information which is not disclosed in a prospectus if it should have been disclosed further to s.87A or under the prospectus rules more generally.[89] In particular in circumstances in which the omission was intended to conceal facts from potential investors then it is suggested that that should constitute a misrepresentation in any event.[90]

5. COMPENSATION UNDER S.90 OF FSMA 2000

A. Introduction

39–35   This section is concerned with the availability of compensation for loss occasioned by some defect in a prospectus as provided by s.90 of FSMA 2000. This provision expressly preserves any action under the general law.[91] Those actions under the general law were considered immediately above. Section 90 itself is sufficiently vague that it is suggested that the case law principles will still be important as an aid to the interpretation of that provision. First, we shall consider the people who are defined in the Prospectus Rules as being legally responsible for the preparation of the prospectus.

B. Persons responsible for the contents of the prospectus

39–36   The definition of the persons responsible for the contents of a prospectus or of a supplementary prospectus are set out in Chapter 5 of the Prospectus Rules.[92] The persons responsible for a prospectus are subject to the general duty of disclosure in s.87A of FSMA 2000. In relation to equity securities, the persons responsible for the prospectus are[93]: the issuer; directors and those authorising themselves to be named as responsible for the prospectus; any other person who accepts responsibility for the prospectus; in relation to an offer, each person who is a director of a body corporate making an offer of securities; in relation to applications for admission to trading, each person who is a director of a body corporate making an offer of securities; and other persons who have authorised the contents of the prospectus. In relation to securities which are not equity securities, the persons responsible for the prospectus are[94]: the issuer; anyone who accepts and is stated in the prospectus as accepting responsibility for the prospectus; any other person who is the offeror of the securities; any person who requests an admission to trading of transferable securities; any guarantor for the issue in relation to information about that guarantee; and any other person who has authorised the contents of the prospectus. That someone has given advice in a

---

[88] See, for example, *Percival v Wright* [1902] 2 Ch. 421.
[89] See generally the obligations considered in Ch. 38 *Prospectuses*.
[90] See *Chitty on Contracts*, para.6–015; *Percival v Wright* [1902] 2 Ch. 421.
[91] Financial Services and Markets Act 2000, s.90(6).
[92] Prospectus Rules, Ch.5.
[93] Prospectus Rules, para.5.5.3R.
[94] Prospectus Rules, para.5.5.4R.

professional capacity about the contents of a prospectus does not make that person responsible for the contents of the prospectus in itself[95]; unless they consent to being so named or they authorise those contents of the prospectus which are the subject of the action, and even then they are liable only to the extent that they have agreed to be so liable.[96]

C. Compensation under s.90(1) of FSMA 2000 for loss due to a defect in a prospectus

The basis of the right to compensation under s.90 FSMA 2000

Section 90 of FSMA 2000 creates a means of acquiring compensation for defects in a prospectus which is not stated as being subject to all of the requirements of proximity, causation and foreseeability which arise in the common law, particularly on the case law decided before the creation of the Prospectus Rules. However, as set out above, this case law can now be read as being more expansive than hitherto. Nevertheless, s.90 constitutes an important development in the potential liability of those responsible for the preparation of a prospectus. Section 90(1) of FSMA 2000 provides that: **39–37**

> "Any person responsible for listing particulars is liable to pay compensation to a person who has:
> (a) acquired securities to which the particulars [or the prospectus] apply; and
> (b) suffered loss in respect of them as a result of
>   (i) any untrue or misleading statement in the [prospectus];
>   (ii) or the omission from the [prospectus] of any matter required to be included by [the duties of disclosure in] section [*87A or 87B*]".[97]

It is unclear whether any statement under para.(b)(i) of s.90(1) must be both untrue and also misleading, or whether liability attaches to a statement on grounds that it is either untrue or that it is misleading. It is suggested that because the word "or" is used in relation to them, and because the requirements of a statement being "untrue" are not necessarily the same as the requirements of it being "misleading", then they should be treated as being alternative heads of liability and therefore the word "or" should be considered to be disjunctive.[98] If so, there are three heads of liability resulting from this provision.

The first head of liability relates to untrue statements. It is not a requirement of the statutory language that there have been fraud or any other intention to deceive; rather, the statement made must have been untrue. Equally, the concept of "untrue" statements would seem to include statements which are "incorrect"   **39–38**

---

[95] Prospectus Rules, para.5.5.9R.
[96] Prospectus Rules, para.5.5.8R.
[97] Financial Services and Markets Act 2000 s.90(1). Words in square brackets added by the author to reflect Financial Services and Markets Act 2000 s.90(11)(a) and the fact that this discussion focuses on prospectuses, and not the limited regime relating to listing particulars for offers only to expert investors.
[98] The word "or" can be conjunctive: for example, "he is happy being called Francis or Frank" suggests that the word "or" joins those two concepts. The word "or" is disjunctive in circumstances such as "he turned left or he turned right" when it suggests either one thing or alternatively another.

and does not require that they be untrue as a result of some lie or deceit. It is enough that the loss arose "as a result of" the untrue statement; there is no explicit requirement of causation or foreseeability on the model ordinarily required for damages in tort at common law.

39–39 The second head of liability relates to misleading statements made in a prospectus. The element of causation in the statute is satisfied if the loss is "a result of" the misleading statement. It is not a requirement of the statutory language that there have been fraud or any other intention to deceive; rather, the statement made must have misled the claimant. As above, it is duty of the person responsible for the prospectus to ensure that all statements made in the prospectus or any omissions made from the prospectus are not likely to be misleading. The effect of this provision is therefore to place an implied obligation on those responsible for the contents of a prospectus not to make any misleading statements in that prospectus, whether advertently or inadvertently.

39–40 The third head of liability relates to the omission of material which would otherwise be required by the duty of disclosure in s.87A of FSMA 2000, as was discussed in Chapter 36.[99] The duty of disclosure is rooted in the requirement that the prospectus must contain the "necessary information" before it can be approved by the FCA.

D.   Defences to liability under s.90

39–41 Schedule 10 to the FSMA 2000 then sets out the exemptions from liability for compensation under s.90. There are five possible defences to a claim under s.90 that a statement was incorrect or misleading and so caused a loss. The first defence applies when the defendant believed in the truth of the statement that was made in the prospectus.[100] The second defence applies when the statement was made by an expert which is included in a prospectus or a supplementary prospectus with that expert's consent and is stated in that document to be included as such.[101] The third defence requires the publication, or the taking of reasonable steps to secure publication, of a correction.[102] The fourth defence requires the taking of all reasonable steps to secure the publication of a correction of a statement made by an expert.[103] The fifth defence applies when the statement was made by an official person or contained in a public, official document, provided that the statement was accurately and fairly reproduced.[104] The sixth defence applies if the court is satisfied that the investor acquired the securities with knowledge that the statement was incorrect, and therefore that the investor was not misled by it.[105]

---

[99] See para.36–34.
[100] Financial Services and Markets Act 2000, Sch.10. para.1.
[101] Financial Services and Markets Act 2000, Sch.10, para.2(1).
[102] Financial Services and Markets Act 2000, Sch.10, para.3.
[103] Financial Services and Markets Act 2000, Sch.10, para.2(3), and para.4.
[104] Financial Services and Markets Act 2000, Sch.10, para.5.
[105] Financial Services and Markets Act 2000, Sch.10, para.6.

E.   The persons who can bring a claim under s.90 FSMA 2000

The category of potential claimants under s.90 includes any person who has **39–42** acquired or who has contracted to acquire securities or any interest in some of the securities to which the defective prospectus relates.[106] Further that person must have suffered a loss in respect of the securities; and the loss must have been suffered as a result of the relevant untrue or misleading statement or omission.

F.   Interpretation of s.90 of FSMA 2000 in the light of the decided cases

The foregoing sections of this chapter have considered the interpretation of s.90 **39–43** on its own words. What is evident about the principles underpinning the common law from the 19th century was that they required the utmost good faith in the preparation of prospectuses because the prospectus was the only document on which the investor could rely when deciding whether or not to invest in an undertaking. As is considered below, this requirement of the utmost good faith went further than sanctioning the careful drafting of prospectuses so as to put a positive spin on every statement and so as to mask any unattractive information. The common law would not permit ambiguity and half-truth to save the draftsmen from liability. In the light of the Prospectus Rules it is suggested that s.90 should be interpreted as requiring an equally stringent standard of disclosure, or else it will always remain in the shadows behind the common law actions.

Section 90 ought to offer a greater means of establishing liability for **39–44** compensation than the common law because the common law contains requirements as to causation and the burden of proof. In consequence, the range of causes of action available to a person who has acted in reliance upon misstatements in a prospectus is much wider now than then it was. Interestingly, while it was once thought that the "golden legacy" cases constituted an overly stringent code for preparing prospectuses, it is nothing compared to the formalism of modern securities regulation.[107]

The current policy underpinning the regulation of the preparation of prospectuses **39–45** is predicated on the need to provide as much information in an accurate fashion as investors could reasonably require in making their investment decisions. This was effectively the approach of the cases which comprised the so-called "golden legacy" in the case law,[108] although without the giant architecture of positive obligations created by FCA regulation in the form of continuing obligations, conduct of business rules and so forth. The golden legacy itself, in relation to the obligations of those who issued prospectuses, was described by Kindersley V.C. in *New Brunswick, etc., Co v Muggeridge*[109] as requiring that those responsible for the prospectus "are bound to state everything with strict and scrupulous

---

[106] Financial Services and Markets Act 2000, s.90(7).
[107] See para.36–50.
[108] When giving judgment in *Henderson v Lacon* (1867) L.R. 5 Eq. 249, 262, Page-Wood V.C. described these common law principles as being a "golden legacy".
[109] (1860) 1 Dr. & Sm. 363, 383.

accuracy, and not only to abstain from stating as fact that which is not so, but to omit no one fact within their knowledge, the existence of which might in any degree affect the nature, or extent, or quality, of the privileges and advantages which the prospectus holds out as inducements to take shares."

39–46 What is missing, to a modern mind, in this conceptualisation of the responsibilities of those who prepared the prospectus is an understanding of there being any continuing obligations in relation to changes in the company's performance after the prospectus was published and the suitability of the process by which the securities were marketed. Otherwise, in the light of the Prospectus Directive and of the Prospectus Rules of 2005[110] this conceptualisation of the golden legacy seems unremarkable. The key focus of securities regulation at the time of writing is in the public availability of information. As a result, where securities regulations—principally the prospectus rules—apply, then the issuers and people responsible for that prospectus know that that prospectus will be published. Indeed, its publication is a requirement of s.85 FSMA 2000 whether securities are to be offered to the public or admitted to trading on a regulated market. Therefore, those "people responsible" for the prospectus know that any potential investor—whether a subscriber, or a placee, or a purchaser in the after-market—will consult and rely on the statements made in that prospectus. Consequently, all potential investors must be within the issuer's contemplation when the prospectus is prepared. This issue is considered in detail in my book *Securities Law*.[111]

6. MISLEADING STATEMENTS IN DISCHARGE OF TRANSPARENCY OBLIGATIONS

A. The purpose of s.90A FSMA 2000

39–47 Section 90A of FSMA 2000 provides for compensation to be paid in relation to untrue or misleading statements contained in, or in relation to omissions from, the annual financial reports, the half-yearly financial reports, or interim management statements which are required to be published by arts 4, 5 and 6 of the Transparency Obligations Directive, as was discussed in Chapter 38. Thus s.90A in effect extends the effect of s.90 to the new dimension which is added to securities regulation by the Transparency Obligations Directive. Section 90A(2), introduced to the bill in its final stages, makes clear that the Act relates only to securities traded on regulated markets. Section 90A of FSMA 2000 provides that the issuer of securities will be liable to "pay compensation" to any person who has both:

"(a)   acquired such[112] securities issued by it, and
(b)   suffered loss in respect of them as a result of—

---

[110] SI 2005/1433.
[111] A.S. Hudson, *Securities Law*, Ch.23.
[112] The reference to "such securities" seems to be a reference to the particular securities which have been issued and in relation to which the loss must have been suffered.

(i)   any untrue or misleading statement in a publication to which this section applies, or

(ii)   the omission from any such publication of any matter required to be included in it."[113]

There is one important caveat to the issuer's liability, however. As provided in s.90A(4):

"The issuer is so liable only if a person discharging managerial responsibilities within the issuer in relation to the publication—

(a)   knew the statement to be untrue or misleading or was reckless as to whether it was untrue or misleading, or

(b)   knew the omission to be dishonest concealment of a material fact."[114]

Therefore, the basis of liability is predicated, first, on the making of an untrue or misleading statement and, secondly, also the requisite knowledge of someone discharging managerial responsibilities within the issuer.

B.   Excluded general law liability under transparency obligations

It is provided in s.90A(6) of FSMA 2000 that the defendant issuer is not to be liable for "any other liability than that provided for" by the preceding provisions of s.90A of FSMA 2000.[115] It is provided further in s.90A(7) that:

39–48

"[a]ny reference to . . . a person being subject to a liability includes a reference to another person being entitled as against him to be granted any civil remedy or to rescind or repudiate an agreement."

Nevertheless, s.90A(8) provides that s.90A "does not affect . . . (b) liability for a civil penalty; [or] (c) liability for a criminal offence." The meaning of these provisions when read together is unclear. At first blush, it is not clear is whether it is all obligations, including obligations at common law or in equity relating to loss, which are to be excluded; or whether it is only obligations under FSMA 2000 which are to be excluded. However, s.90A(7) suggests that it is all civil remedies which are to be excluded, seemingly unless they are "civil penalties" (such as those relating to market abuse) which are saved by s.90A(8). What is unclear then, is which civil actions may be saved and which excluded by s.90A of FSMA 2000.

---

[113] Financial Services and Markets Act 2000, s.90A(3).

[114] Financial Services and Markets Act 2000, s.90A(4).

[115] Financial Services and Markets Act 2000, s.90A(6).

PART XI

FINANCIAL DERIVATIVES & REFINANCING

This Part XI is referred as "refinancing" in that it relates to the techniques of financial derivatives and securitisations which repackage existing assets or which enable the holders of assets to repackage the financial effect for them of those assets; alternatively, they can be used for straightforward speculation so that the owner of the product can acquire a cash flow as though she had invested in an underlying asset. So, for example, a loan requiring a borrower to pay a floating rate of interest can be swapped for a fixed rate of interest which the borrower would rather pay: thus the cost of the loan to the borrower can be changed. More generally, refinancing permits one type of product, such as a share, to be mimicked so that by means of another derivative called an "option" an investor can contract to be paid the return it would have made as if it had actually acquired those shares: thus, the investor's cash stake can be converted into the return it would have made if it had actually bought shares but without the need actually to buy shares. The products in this Part XI enable speculation to be taken on different markets and products or for protection to be bought by way of "hedging" against those products. They are an entirely new collection of financial techniques which create a form of Alice in Wonderland effect in financial markets by altering their risk profile and speculation on them. The specific financial techniques discussed in this Part XI build on the foundational legal concepts considered in Pts IV through VII of this book.

CHAPTER 40

FINANCIAL DERIVATIVES PRODUCTS AND REGULATION

CORE PRINCIPLES

Derivatives Products

Financial derivatives are financial products which derive their value from an underlying product. The financial derivatives considered in this chapter are primarily derivatives which are traded off-exchange, which are known as "over-the-counter" derivatives. The principal forms of financial derivative are: swaps (including interest rate swaps and currency swaps), options (including equity options and debt options) and futures (including forwards). Swaps enable the buyer to swap an obligation for another obligation: for example, swapping an obligation to pay a floating rate of interest on a debt for a fixed rate of interest. Options entitle the buyer to buy or to sell (as appropriate) a specified amount of an underlying product (such as a share or a bond) if she so chooses: i.e. the buyer will only exercise that right if it would be profitable for her to do so. By contrast a future, or forward, obliges the buyer to buy or sell at the contractually specified price whether or not that would be profitable for her.

Derivatives can be used either to protect their users from risk ("hedging") or can be used for speculation so as simply to earn profit. The most controversial form of financial derivative is the "credit derivative". Credit derivatives enable their buyers either to speculate on the credit worth of other entities or to protect themselves against any exposure to those entities (as though buying insurance). One form of credit derivative, the credit default swap, enabled a very large amount of speculation to build up with the result that the investment banks which sold those credit default swaps were obliged to pay out an enormous amount to speculators, thus contributing to the harm wrought by the global financial crisis of 2007–09.

Regulation of derivatives

In the wake of the financial crisis, the call for the regulation of derivatives grew louder. For the first time derivatives are to be subject to regulation as a distinct market in the EU. In essence, over-the-counter derivatives of specified types will have to be cleared through a clearing house: this means that the rights and obligations of professional derivatives dealers will be set off against one another through the clearing house so that each dealer owes or is owed only net amounts of their activity in the market. Furthermore, information about derivatives transactions will have to be lodged with approved information providers, so that in future regulators will have more information about the state of the market. There will still be some derivatives products falling outside the regulatory net; derivatives business will still be conducted geographically outside the EU and so beyond the reach of these regulations; and future product innovation is likely to test the definitions provisions of the regulations in any event. In the USA, the Dodd-Frank Act is crawling painfully slowly into effect with a view to subjecting derivatives to regulation in that jurisdiction for the first time.

Later chapters in this Part XI deal with the documentation of financial derivatives, taking security in relation to financial derivatives by way of "collateralisation", and terminating derivatives contracts.

1. INTRODUCTION

This group of chapters in Part XI of this book deals with financial derivatives. In this chapter we shall consider the nature of the key financial derivatives products, the plans for the systematic regulation of derivatives for the first time, how we manage the principal risks associated with derivatives, and how those products are understood by lawyers. This chapter is concerned to describe the principal forms of financial derivative. It begins with a consideration of options, then forwards, and then swaps, before outlining credit derivatives and hedging strategies. In Chapter 41 we shall consider the key issues in the documentation of derivatives, a centrally important area of financial law practice. In Chapter 42 we shall consider *Collateralisation* which is the key technique in taking security in derivatives practice and which remains one of the most complex areas of derivatives law practice. In Chapter 43 we shall consider how derivatives are terminated in practice, and the large amount of case law which has been generated by the termination or invalidity of derivatives contracts.

40–01

For a more detailed discussion of financial derivatives you should consult Alastair Hudson, *The Law on Financial Derivatives*.[1]

2. THE FUNDAMENTALS OF FINANCIAL DERIVATIVES

A. What is a "derivative"?

Briefly put, a *derivative* is a product which derives its value from another product.[2] Financial derivatives divide between exchange-traded futures and options,[3] those off-exchange derivatives which re-package existing obligations by providing inter alia for an alternative rate of interest to be payable,[4] and privately negotiated, off-exchange derivatives which provide for cash flows to be paid or assets to be transferred between counterparties dependent on the movement of

40–02

---

[1] A.S. Hudson, *The Law on Financial Derivatives*, 5th edn (London: Sweet & Maxwell, 2012)). I have also written or edited the following books on derivatives: A.S. Hudson, *Swaps, Restitution and Trusts* (London: Sweet & Maxwell, 1999); A.S. Hudson (ed.), *Modern Financial Techniques, Derivatives and Law* (London: Kluwer, 1999); and A.S. Hudson (ed.), *Credit Derivatives: law, regulation and accounting issues* (London: Sweet & Maxwell, 1999). Other books dealing with financial derivatives include: S. Henderson and Price, *Understanding Swaps* (London: Sweet & Maxwell, 1992); E. Swann, *The Regulation of Derivatives* (Cavendish, 1995); James, *The Law of Derivatives* (London: LLP, 1999); Firth, *Derivatives Law* (London: Sweet & Maxwell, looseleaf).

[2] This word "product" is used a lot in the financial literature. It derives, I would suggest, from the notion that a derivative is a financial instrument which has to be created and structured, and so it is a "product" which has been "produced". More interestingly, I would suggest further, the use of the word "product" makes banking activity sound more like wholesome manufacturing in which something tangible and valuable is being made.

[3] Which are not the focus of this part of this book.

[4] The examples considered in this chapter include interest rate swaps which change the rate of interest in fact paid by the borrower on existing bank debt and also embedded swaps in bond issues which permit the bond issuer to pay a different rate of interest to its swap counterparty than that specified in the bond documentation as being payable to its investors.

underlying market rates.[5] In this chapter we shall be focusing on Over-the-Counter ("OTC") derivatives: that is, derivatives which are traded off-exchange, as opposed to derivatives which are traded on an organised exchange. These products are referred to as "financial derivatives" generally in this chapter.

40–03 The term "derivative" is not capable of a precise definition: instead it is taken in the marketplace to cover a range of financial products which derive their value from other financial products, and which are understood by financial theory as being built loosely on "option theory". The standard forms of financial derivative are the option, the forward and the swap. Each of these products derives its value from underlying products. For example, an option to buy a share at some point in the future is a financial product whose value is derived from the value of the underlying share. Similarly, a swap on an interest rate is a product derived from the value of the underlying loan with a rate of interest which the borrower may wish to swap for a preferable rate of interest. Hence the term "derivative" encapsulates this notion of derived value.[6]

B.   That there is nothing new under the sun

40–04 It is difficult to know with any precision when the first derivative contract was created. It is clear, however, that derivatives in various forms have been in existence for some considerable time. The ancient Greeks used to trade olive oil futures, that is contracts fixing the price of olive oil at some time in the future; and in Holland the sale price of tulips was fixed in similar fashion as long ago as the 17th century.[7] Both of these futures contracts fixed a price in the future at which the right-holder agreed to buy a given quantity of either olive oil or tulips. There are tales of even more ancient Babylonian kings selling instruments which permitted the holder of the instrument to call on the king to deliver up one mercenary soldier and two slaves for each instrument held on payment of the price specified in the instrument. This particular contract for the acquisition of soldier is similar to something which will be described in this chapter as being a "physically-settled call option"[8] in that it permits the buyer of the option to call for delivery of an identified form of asset in consideration for the payment of the contractually specified price. Each of these transactions is similar to modern derivatives. Significantly, all of these contracts in themselves, whether the Greek olive oil future, or the Dutch tulip future, or the Babylonian mercenary instrument, are capable of being traded. That is, each of these contracts is capable of being sold, pledged or otherwise transferred to third parties. The essence of these contracts as derivatives contracts is that they are transferable and thus bear

---

[5] That is, both cash-settled and physically-settled transactions which are considered in detail in what follows.

[6] Often, the definition of what will constitute a derivative is purely taken to be whichever types of business financial institutions have grouped together in their derivatives departments: such a definition may nevertheless encompass the otherwise distinct areas of debt, equity, foreign exchange and ordinary lending activities.

[7] James, *The Law of Derivatives* (London: LLP, 1999), 1.

[8] Below at para.36–17.

their own independent value which is in turn derived in some way from the asset—whether olive oil, tulips or mercenaries—which underpins the contract.

What is important to learn from these fragments of historical trivia is that the ideas which underpin the modern financial derivatives markets are well-established.[9] They are all based on the essential characteristics, from a lawyer's perspective, that a right-holder be entitled to receive some payment or asset on the exercise of its rights under a contract which itself has a distinct value. This is a very important point. The ideas which underpin derivatives have been used by merchants and even warrior kings for many centuries. Those same ideas are built on structures which have been known to lawyers for nearly as long. There is nothing new under the sun: these ideas have been known to lawyers and to merchants for centuries. What is new is the use of these techniques to manipulate financial instruments and the use of complex mathematical models to predict, estimate and price these derivatives products. So, while derivatives are exciting, occasionally hugely profitable and mathematically incredibly complex, from a lawyer's perspective there is nothing which is beyond analysis by our current legal concepts. This Part XI of this book is concerned to analyse derivatives products and their documentation through a lawyer's eyes. This is how we construct a law of finance: by understanding how core legal concepts and the principles appropriate to the context of finance law deal with financial practice..

40–05

C. The commercial purposes of financial derivatives

The commercial objectives in using financial derivatives

Financial derivatives have two principal, commercial rationales: first, to acquire protection against some existing obligation ("hedging"); and, secondly, to speculate on the future movement of the prices of securities or of financial indices, such as interest rates or a share index ("speculation").

40–06

Hedging

The first rationale, *hedging*, may be concerned with the management of the risk associated with some pre-existing obligation (such as the interest rate to be paid on a loan) or with a perceived risk in the movement of components of an investment strategy. Hedging is dependent upon being able to find a derivative whose value will move upwards to balance out the loss on an existing investment if it should move downwards. So, if Xeno Plc makes higher profits when interest rates are low, then shares in Xeno Plc will become less valuable when interest rates rise. So, if one held a large number of shares in Xeno Plc, hedging the risk of losing money on Xeno Plc shares would require buying derivatives the value of which will increase in value when interest rates rise. The financial engineer's role is to estimate the likely future movement of interest rates and the type of

40–07

---

[9] See also Khang, *Barings Bankruptcy and Financial Derivatives* (Cavendish, 1998), p.31 in relation to future contracts being created in Japan in the late 17th century.

derivative and the quantity of that derivative which is needed to balance out that risk of loss. In this way, the risk of losing money on Xeno Plc is "hedged".

40–08　Dealing with the perceived risk on a complex, portfolio investment strategy (where the investor holds a lot of different types of investments in a lot of different types of market) is more complex. In the example of Xeno Plc above it is easy to match a loss in one product: it is a far more sophisticated business to attempt to do that with a large number of investments in different markets simultaneously. The investor would have to identify the sensitivities of the various investments in that investment strategy, and acquire derivatives which would generate a profit if the various components of that investment strategy should generate a loss. The derivatives package would need to identify the risks of loss associated with each element of the investment portfolio. Clearly, whenever there are major movements in markets, it will be necessary to recalibrate the hedging strategy across the entire portfolio. The most difficult portfolio hedging is that carried out by financial institutions themselves: at the end of every business day, a financial institution will need to calculate its exposures across all of its products in all markets through all branches, and having done that it will need to identify the range of hedging instruments that will be necessary to offset all of those risks. The management of risk is considered in greater detail in Chapter 42 *Collateralisation* in transactions between financial institutions.

40–09　So hedging is, in effect, an attempt to manage the risk associated with that obligation by creating an entitlement to receive some cash flow which will counter-act the loss which might result from the original investment. Similarly, derivatives can be used to manage (or control) a risk. For example, if a customer has a loan with a floating interest rate, the risk is that interest rates increase and so the cost of that loan increases. Controlling the interest rate on a loan can be achieved, for example, by acquiring an interest rate swap—as considered below[10]—which entitles the customer to pay only a fixed rate of interest even though the terms of the loan were that the customer should pay the rising floating rate of interest. An interest rate swap will allow the customer to change the effective interest rate paid on that loan.

Speculation

40–10　The second rationale enables the parties to *speculate* on the performance of some identified, underlying marketplace—but the investor does not necessarily need to invest directly in that marketplace because derivatives replicate the performance of a real market in a virtual form. A derivative is used for speculation by supposing that some notional investment were made in that market and that the return generated by that fictional investment on that market were in fact payable by one party to the other. Thus cash settled options,[11] when they pay a profit, pay out an amount *equivalent to the profit which would have been made* as if the buyer had actually invested in the underlying instrument.

---

[10] See para.36–26.
[11] See para.36–17.

Speculation is the easiest market activity to understand. Derivatives enable investors to speculate on the movement of real financial markets but without the need to participate directly in those markets. It is a little like gambling on horse racing: placing a bet means that a gambler can take the profit of her horse winning but without needing actually to ride the horse. So, a derivative product can enable an investor to mimic the result of trading on an underlying financial market by entering into an off-market transaction with a financial institution. For example, a speculator who buys a "call option"[12] to buy shares quoted on the FTSE-100 share index can obtain the effect of speculating on the FTSE-100 without actually having to buy shares in companies in the FTSE-100. If the shares on the FTSE-100 increase in value, then the speculator is paid an amount of cash (in this example) equal to the profit she would have made if she had invested in that market by means of actually buying those shares. One advantage of the derivative is therefore administrative convenience: for example, there is no need to accord with exchange market rules when dealing off-exchange using a derivative. Further, the entry costs to speculation on a derivative are smaller than the cost of speculating on an exchange or other underlying market: in part because there are no registration or other costs involved, nor is the transaction subject to public scrutiny. That the transaction is not subject to public scrutiny raises a regulatory and economic problem because it is not possible for regulators to know how much speculation is going on in their jurisdiction because a lot of it is going on clandestinely on derivatives trading floors, possibly in different jurisdictions. Thus, volatility can be introduced into share prices in a way that is known about among derivatives traders and their colleagues, but which is not entirely transparent everyone else in the market. This has led to the introduction of regulations in the EU, considered below, which require that information is lodged with approved information providers about the derivatives business that a firm conducts: those regulations are not yet in force at the time of writing.

40–11

The most common assumption surrounding the use of derivatives is that they are only used with speculative intent.[13] The core of the English local authority swaps cases[14] was the commercial intentions of the local authorities to improve their debt exposure while generating some collateral income. The approach taken by Lord Templeman in *Hazell v Hammersmith & Fulham*[15] was that the contracts were used by the authorities with "no other interest than seeking to profit from interest rate fluctuations".[16] One issue which has arisen out of this understanding that derivatives are primarily speculative is whether they constituted contracts for differences which were void under the old Gaming Act 1845. This issue was examined by Hobhouse J. in *Morgan Grenfell v Welwyn & Hatfield DC*[17]. It was

40–12

---

[12] See para.36–17.

[13] *Hazell v Hammersmith & Fulham LBC* [1991] 1 All E.R. 545, 549, per Lord Templeman.

[14] That is, the cases dealing with the two hundred writs seeking restitution of moneys paid under void swaps contracts served in the wake of the decision of the House of Lords in *Hazell v Hammersmith & Fulham LBC* [1991] 1 All E.R. 545: those decisions being considered in detail in Chs 7 and 9 of this book. See generally A. Hudson, "The law of finance", in Birks and Rose (eds), *Lessons from the swap cases* (Oxford: Mansfield Press, 1999), p.45.

[15] [1992] 2 A.C. 1.

[16] [1991] 1 All E.R. 545, 549.

[17] [1995] 1 All E.R. 1.

held that interest rate swaps were not void gaming contracts on the basis that they were used for a commercial purpose in connection with (the now-repealed) s.63 of the Financial Services Act 1986.[18] However, his lordship was not able to reach this conclusion before finding that they have:

> "at least potentially a speculative character deriving from the fact that the obligations of [parties] are to be ascertained by reference to a fluctuating market rate which may be higher or lower than the fixed rate at any time".[19]

This identification of a speculative intention may render the derivative unenforceable against certain entities in relation to certain products where, for example, building societies or local authorities are only permitted to use derivatives for hedging and debt management purposes: therefore, a derivatives lawyer must always take care when dealing with any new product in relation to any new market, or new jurisdiction or new customer, to ensure that that product will be valid under the applicable laws.[20]

40–13 Derivatives enable the contracting parties to assume a trading position on the anticipated movements of financial markets in the future. By acquiring an option to buy a share at a given time in the future for a given price, the buyer is able to speculate on the level of those markets in the future. Similarly, the seller is speculating that the price to be paid for the security under the option is greater than the price of acquiring that security in the market. The basic technique of acquiring some ability to acquire an asset at a speculative price other than the spot price[21] in the market is common to all derivatives when they are being used for speculative purposes. At each time a payment is required to be made under a transaction there is a risk that that payment will be greater or less than the price payable in the open market.

40–14 A range of derivatives enables a speculator to benefit from fluctuations in financial markets quickly so as to capture short-term market movements: this is known as "arbitrage". There might be a small window of opportunity between news hitting the market and the market reacting when, for example, the market price of a share only changes several minutes or hours after a piece of information has become public knowledge. If a speculator has a range of options entitling her to buy those shares at a good price then she can enforce her options, buy the shares in at the price set out in those options, and then sell the shares at the new market price resulting from that news. This simple example shows how the use of derivatives can establish an entire trading strategy in advance of market movements so that the speculator can stand ready to take instant profits from a market movement. In this way, the speculator is also able to arbitrage a difference in movements between different markets by, for example, taking out derivatives in advance which pay a profit depending on the difference in the performance of

---

[18] See A.S. Hudson, *The Law on Financial Derivatives*, Ch.6; *Validity of financial derivatives contracts*.

[19] [1995] 1 All E.R. 7.

[20] See A.S. Hudson, *The Law on Financial Derivatives*, Ch.6; *Validity of financial derivatives contracts*; e.g. in relation to contracts with UK building societies and other similar entities.

[21] The "spot price" is the price at which a standard unit of an asset, security or currency is trading at any given time on the real-time market.

two different markets: thus, the speculator is able to play different markets against each other. Derivatives of this sort are comparatively cheap to put in place—requiring payment of a small "premium" up-front—and, if structured in the manner considered below, will not require the speculator to make any further payment if the market does not move in that way that she had hoped. As part of a portfolio management structure, the derivative facilitates the creation of complex speculative or hedging strategies. Alternatively, the derivative will be embedded in another financial instrument, such as publicly issued debt, to attract a different interest rate.

As we will consider below, many derivatives are "cash-settled", which means that the investor does not acquire the underlying product that is linked to the derivative. Instead, the investor is paid an amount of money equivalent to the profit she would have made as if she had invested in that underlying product. Therefore, cash-settled derivatives offer "virtual speculation": that is, a means of speculating on financial markets without the need to engage physically in those markets. By entering into a transaction with a market counterparty it is possible for that party to obtain the same return (for example) on a share's performance as if it had entered the market and actually bought that share but, significantly, without ever owning that share at all because the amounts payable under most derivatives are calculated by reference to some notional amount of money rather than some existing financial instrument. Thus the seller of a cash-settled call option[22] is effectively promising the buyer: "I will pay you the amount of money which you would have received *as if* you had actually invested on that particular market". Therefore, the investor can also remove the incidental costs associated with dealing on that market, of possibly needing to be registered as a dealer on that market, of needing to take delivery of an asset, and of being seen to be investing in a particular market when secrecy might be preferable. This is particularly important where the party and the relevant market are in different jurisdictions when the costs of dealing in another jurisdiction—and of acquiring premises or personnel or regulatory permissions—would be all be the greater. **40–15**

We shall begin by considering the most straightforward form of derivative—the option—and having done that we shall consider some of the key issues with the structure of derivatives, using the option as an example. **40–16**

3. OPTIONS

A. The nature of an option: a right without an obligation

An option gives the owner of the option a right, but not an obligation, to buy or to sell the property identified in the option contract. An option entitling the holder to sell property is referred to as a "put option": the option holder is entitled to sell a given quantity of the asset specified in the contract at a given price at a given time specified in the contract. An option entitling the holder to buy property is **40–17**

---

[22] See para.36–17.

referred to as a "call option": the option holder is entitled to buy a given quantity of the asset specified in the contract for a given price at a given time specified in the contract.

If the price of the underlying asset on the open market is more attractive than the price at which the option can be exercised on the terms of the option contract, then the holder of the option will decide not to exercise it. Because it is merely an option, there is no obligation to exercise the option at an unattractive price, unlike a forward (considered below) which requires the buyer to complete the transaction whether or not it is profitable.

Call options may be exercised so that the option holder becomes the owner of the underlying assets (known as "physical settlement"), which will be important if the option holder wants to own the underlying assets instead of simply being paid an amount of money as if she had owned them. Alternatively, a call option or a put option is more usually settled in financial markets purely in cash without any actual assets being transferred: this is referred to as "cash settlement". Cash settlement is common because investors in options usually only want the equivalent cash profit they would have made as if they had been the owner of the actual underlying asset. In effect, this enables investors to invest "virtually" on financial markets without having to invest physically: this is particularly useful if one wants to invest in a market in another jurisdiction in which one does not have an office nor authorisation to trade. Cash settlement operates by calculating how much profit the option holder would have made by buying or selling (as appropriate) the number of assets identified in the option contract on the dates identified in the contract.

There are a number of different ways of settling an option. Options may be exercised on one particular date (known as a "European option") or over a period of time between specified dates (known as an "American option") or on some dates but not others during a period of time (known as an "Asian option"). Clearly, if the option buyer can exercise her rights over a period of time then this is riskier for the seller because it is more likely that at some point during that time period the option will be "in-the-money" for the buyer, and will thus require the seller to pay out. Now, let us consider a simple example of an option.

B.   An example of a simple option transaction

40–18   An example of an option would work as follows. Suppose that Alpha wanted to speculate that the price of *x* shares would increase in value from £2.00 on the open market to £2.20. We must assume that Alpha has analysed the markets and decided that that is the most likely movement in the value of those shares. Alpha would buy a call option on *x* shares. The option contract would identify the number of *x* shares which Alpha would be able to buy and the time period during which that option may be exercised, and the time at which that option will expire. Suppose then that Alpha wanted to be able to buy *x* shares for £2.00 from its counterparty, whatever their market value, and that Alpha could find an investment bank which was prepared to sell Alpha an option with the right to buy *x* shares for £2.00. (The investment bank may agree to do this if it simply took a different view on the future movement of *x* shares.) If Alpha's projection for the value of x shares is correct, then Alpha will make a profit of 20 pence per share. Here's why. A call option entirely Alpha to buy a share for £2.00 *derives* its value from the underlying market value of the share on the open market: i.e. if the market cost of the share is £2.20 then the option is worth 20 pence because that is the profit that can be generated by exercising the option to buy the share for £2.00 and then selling it on the open market for £2.20.

It is common, however, for such options to be cash settled. In this example, cash **40–19** settlement would involve a payment of 20 pence being made to Alpha for every unit of the underlying asset identified in the option contract, instead of Alpha needing to take delivery of the number of shares specified in the option and then having to find a buyer for them in the marketplace. Cash settlement means that the investment bank selling the option calculates that Alpha would have made 20 pence profit on each option and therefore simply pays that "cash settlement amount" to Alpha in whatever currency is specified in the option contract. This is because a speculator only wants the cash profit which would have been made *as if* the shares had actually been bought but the speculator does not want the trouble and expense of actually having to buy shares physically on the market.

The payment flows work in the following manner. At the outset of the transaction **40–20** the buyer, Alpha, is required to pay a "premium", that is a small lump sum up-front to the financial institution selling the option. The level of that premium will differ depending on the seller's view on the risk that the transaction will show a profit for the buyer. If the buyer chooses to exercise its option, then the buyer is notionally required to pay an exercise amount to the seller (that is, the price fixed for the underlying securities in the option contract) and the seller is required to pay a settlement amount to the buyer (that is, the actual market value of those underlying securities). These gross amounts will never actually be paid. Instead, in practice, the parties will set off those reciprocal amounts so that the seller only pays the net surplus of the actual market value less the price specified in the contract. So, if the market value is £2.20 and the option exercise price is £2.00 per share, then the seller will simply pay over the 20 pence net surplus, as opposed to Alpha paying £2.00 per option unit and the investment bank paying £2.20 per option unit. If the buyer chooses not to exercise the option for some reason then it loses its premium but nothing more than that.

The risk that Alpha runs, of course, is that its projection for the value of x shares is wrong and the market value of those shares does not increase. So, if the market cost of that share fell to £1.90, then the option would be worthless unless and until the market cost of the share rose above £2.00. If the expiry date on the option contract came and if the market value of x shares had not risen beyond £2.00 by that time, then the option would simply lapse without being exercised.

What is important, but frequently not specified in the standard form of contract, is the point in time at which the option is deemed to be exercised. For example, in an American equity call option, if the price of the underlying share seems likely to keep on rising then it would be bad for the buyer if the option were deemed to have been exercised on Day 1 when Alpha's shares were worth (say) £2.01 when the market value of the share (and therefore the cash settlement amount) is likely to increase further by Day 15 to (say) £2.20. Therefore, a mechanism would need to be established for identifying the precise point in time at which the option is deemed to have been exercised: whether it was to be exercised at £2.01 (when it first crossed the £2.00 barrier) or £2.20 (where the price ended up). Identifying in the contract whether this is to be left to the calculation agent to decide or left to the buyer would be important to identify. The mechanism for exercise is considered further below.[23]

40–21   Options can be used across all markets. Indeed options have existed for centuries in land law where the seller of land grants another person an option to buy that land for a given price. Thus the buyer of an option may be acquiring a right to acquire or to sell shares, bonds, foreign exchange, commodities, and so on. The attractiveness of the option is that the buyer's risk is the amount of the premium; but if the speculation goes awry, then there is no obligation to make any further payment under an option.

C.   The manner in which the option is to be exercised: automatic or non-automatic

40–22   The parties are also required to decide whether the option is to exercise automatically or whether there is a need for notice to be given by one or other party that the option is to be exercised. This issue is considered in detail in the next chapter in relation to documentation.[24] The benefit of automatic exercise is that the parties do not need to know that the market value of the underlying share has moved: instead, the contract will provide that the option is to be exercised if it is "in the money" on the exercise date. Thus a non-expert buyer can rely on the option having been exercised without the need for them to take any action or to give notice to the seller. The downside to automatic exercise is that an expert buyer may consider that the market value of the shares underlying the option may continue to increase, and so automatic exercise may bite at an inappropriate moment. Furthermore, automatic exercise may cause a transaction to terminate when the parties might prefer for it to continue in existence for other commercial reasons.

40–23   There are particular procedures which must be followed in some markets. The central issue in relation to the physical settlement of bond options is to ensure that the market practices associated with the settlement of bonds fits with the performance obligations in the option confirmation. Where bonds are held under a global note, the delivery obligation will refer to the practice of the custodian and registrar to the transfer of title in the securities. In the case of bearer bonds not held under a global note, physical delivery and maintenance with a custodian will be necessary.[25] The ISDA form of bond option confirmation makes reference to transfer being made through the appropriate clearance system within a given period.

---

[23] See the section following immediately below.
[24] See para.39–01.
[25] On the issues surrounding custodians see Ch.42, *Collateralisation*.

4. FORWARDS

The forward is similar, in finance theory, to the option; but there are important differences (not least from a lawyer's perspective).[26] There are some forward contracts traded on organised exchanges and others which are the preserve of the over-the-counter markets. Typically, a forward contract traded on an exchange is known as a "future" or as a "futures contract". The forward is a promise to supply a particular commodity, security or other asset at a set price on a set date in the future (often in a set place). Significantly, the buyer of a forward is obliged to pay the purchase price for the underlying asset whether or not the forward contract is "in-the-money". This is the principal difference between a forward and an option because under an option there is no such obligation to make payment if the option is not "in-the-money". In the commodity markets it is usual to buy wheat, for example, at a pre-determined price in a given amount to be delivered at a pre-determined time in a given place. So, a bread manufacturer will want to secure its wheat supply ahead of time by entering into a contract whereby it knows how much it will be paying for its wheat and that it will have a given quantity of wheat delivered to it on a given date. However, in the time it takes for the contract to mature (which might include the time necessary for the wheat to grow, be harvested and shipped) the price of wheat can fluctuate wildly. If the harvest is bad (perhaps due to a bad summer) then the price of wheat will be high: therefore, having fixed the price of its wheat in advance will be beneficial for the bread manufacturer because the price it will have agreed in its futures contract is probably lower than the eventual market price. Contrariwise, the bread manufacturer may have made a bad deal if the wheat harvest is plentiful and the market price of wheat is therefore very low because it will be committed to paying the price agreed in its futures contract. The futures contract itself, that is the right to receive the wheat at a price at a time in the agreed place, can be sold to others at a greater or lower price than that paid for it originally. This means that speculators can trade in futures contracts and speculate on the current and future market price of commodities like wheat and other market indices. The same is true, to a greater or lesser extent, of forward contracts entered into between private parties.

40–24

A forward conveys the right to purchase or sell a specified quantity of an asset at a fixed price on a fixed date in the future. In exchange-traded futures contracts, which are a standardised form of forward contract, the quantity of the underlying asset to be delivered per contract is fixed, as is the underlying financial instrument or index, the minimum price movement for the contract and the life of the contract. In a forward agreement, these elements are at large for negotiation between the parties.

40–25

---

[26] Forward sale agreements were at issue in *Socimer International Bank Ltd v Standard Bank London Ltd* [2008] EWCA Civ 116; [2008] Bus. L.R. 1304.

5. SWAPS

What is a swap?

The evolution of swaps

40–26   The evolution of swaps was one of the principal theoretical developments in the structure of financial products. The mathematics underpinning swaps are very complex and the financial theory on which the pricing of swaps is based is similarly sophisticated. The basic idea is, however, straightforward. If I have an obligation to pay money that I think is too onerous then I can swap that obligation for one which I consider to be acceptable. The bank which sells me the swap effectively assumes my onerous obligation for me, and in return I pay to that bank the obligation which I would prefer to pay in exchange. This technique has become a powerful tool both for effectively refinancing obligations and for taking complex speculative positions across a range of markets. These uses of the swap are considered below. An interest rate swap was described by Woolf L.J. in *Hazell v Hammersmith & Fulham LBC* in the following terms[27]:

> "[An interest rate swap is] an agreement between two parties by which each agrees to pay the other on a specified date or dates an amount calculated by reference to the interest which would have accrued over a given period on the same notional principal sum assuming different rates of interest are payable in each case. For example, one rate may be fixed at 10% and the other rate may be equivalent to the six-month London Inter-Bank Offered Rate (LIBOR). If the LIBOR rate over the period of the swap is higher than the 10% then the party agreeing to receive "interest" in accordance with LIBOR will receive more than the party entitled to receive the 10%. Normally neither party will in fact pay the sums which it has agreed to pay over the period of the swap but instead will make a settlement on a "net payment basis" under which the party owing the greater amount on any day simply pays the difference between the two amounts due to the other."

This definition was cited with approval by Lord Templeman in the House of Lords in *Hazell v Hammersmith & Fulham LBC*[28] The many variations which are possible on this basic theme are outlined below. First, we shall consider a worked example of a very simple interest rate swap.

Sample transaction: an interest rate swap used to manage interest payments on a loan

40–27   To illustrate how an interest rate swap works, let us take the example of a large corporate customer borrowing money—the simplest example of a modern swap, and let us assume that interest rates are rising at the time. In a time of rising interest rates, having a loan with a floating rate of interest is unattractive because as market rates rise so does the rate payable on the loan. So, if a customer has an obligation which it does not want—such as a floating interest rate obligation during a time of rising interest rates—then a swap enables that customer to exchange that obligation with a financial institution for an obligation which it

---

[27] [1990] 2 Q.B. 697, 739; [1990] 3 All E.R. 33, 63.
[28] *Hazell v Hammersmith & Fulham LBC* [1991] 1 All E.R. 545, 550.

does want, such as a fixed rate of interest. So, as set out in the worked example below, if Alpha owes payments of floating rates of interest on a loan with its bank, then it might be able to put a swap in place whereby it can change its floating rate obligations for fixed rate obligations which it hopes will remain below the level of the market's floating rate of interest. In this context, then, an interest rate swap is simply a means of changing the rate of interest which a borrower is paying for a preferable rate of interest.

Let us suppose that Alpha Plc has taken out a loan from Lend Bank of £10 million, on which it is required to pay floating rate interest payments of "LIBOR+100 basis points"[29] (an example of a floating rate of interest) over ten years. The cash flow movements under the loan would work as follows.[30] At first, Lend Bank will pay £10 million to Alpha Plc.

40–28

| **Alpha Plc** | ← | GB£10million | **Lend Bank** |

The second payment flow would be payments of interest made by Alpha every six months for ten years and a repayment of the capital amount at the end of the ten-year period (under this particular example of a loan contract).

| **Alpha Plc** | LIBOR + 100bp | → | **Lend Bank** |

(Where "bp" stands for "basis points".)

If interest rates are rising, then the level of "LIBOR" will rise too. Consequently, Alpha Plc would prefer to have a fixed rate of interest. We must assume that Lend Bank will not renegotiate the terms of the loan, or even that Lend Bank would prefer to put an interest rate swap in place rather than renegotiate the loan contract.[31]

Let us suppose that Alpha Plc approaches Profit Bank seeking an interest rate swap. Suppose that the parties agree on a fixed rate of interest at 9 per cent. Alpha Plc would benefit from a fixed rate of interest because it would be able to fix its future cash outflows for strategic planning purposes at a maximum of 9 per cent on this loan; and it will also be based upon Alpha Plc having an expectation that LIBOR will rise, such that "LIBOR +100bp" will be more than 9 per cent for most of the ten year period of the loan. The payment flows under the interest rate swap would function as follows.

40–29

The payment dates would be the same as Alpha Plc owes on its loan contract with Lend Bank: that means, there will be twenty payment dates in total, being semi-annual payment days over the life of the 10-year loan. Interest rate swaps usually last for a number of years. The interest rates would be calculated by

---

[29] "LIBOR" stands for the "London Inter-Bank Offered Rate", which is a rate of interest paid between banks in London which is ordinarily more stable than other commercial interest rates in London and usually lower than other commercial interest rates. "Basis points" are each one hundredth of a whole percentage point of interest: e.g. where 50bp = one half of one per cent.

[30] Lending was discussed in detail in Ch.33.

[31] Perhaps because an interest rate swap is something on which Lend Bank expects it will make a profit.

reference to the loan capital of £10 million. Ultimately the objective is that Alpha Plc will be able to make its loan payments to Lend Bank in a timely manner. So under the interest rate swap, Profit Bank will owe LIBOR+100bp calculated on £10 million to Alpha Plc; and simultaneously Alpha Plc will owe 9 per cent calculated on £10 million to Profit Bank. The parties will actually set off the amounts which each owes to the other so that there is only a single net amount paid between Alpha and Profit Bank in fact on each payment date: so, if LIBOR+100bp is higher than 9 per cent on a payment day, then Profit Bank will be obliged to pay the surplus of LIBOR+100bp over 9 per cent on that payment date, and so on. This process of setting off the amounts that are owed by each party is known as "payment netting".[32] The gross amounts that are owed are as follows:

Because the parties only make one net payment, the actual payment flow would be more like this, depending on which party is required to make the payment.

Profit Bank ◄——— single net payment ———► **Alpha Plc**

It should be remembered that the rates will probably have moved again before the next payment date. Therefore, while Profit Bank may, for example, be required to make a net payment on this first payment date, it may be that Profit Bank simply has a different expectation of interest rates than Alpha Plc. Alpha Plc may have different commercial objectives, such as wanting to control its interest rate costs prior to making a new issue of shares, or preparing for a takeover, or to ensure it can remain in profit by controlling its interest rate cost, or whatever other motivation it may have. In relation to Alpha Plc's loan with Lend Bank, if LIBOR+100bp is higher than 9 per cent then effectively Profit Bank is paying Alpha Plc the difference between the rate of 9 per cent which it is content to pay by way of interest and the level of LIBOR+100bp: so, Alpha Plc will simply pay that money on to Lend Bank and so have reduced its effective interest cost. The effect of the entire transaction would look like this:

---

[32] See para.19–13.

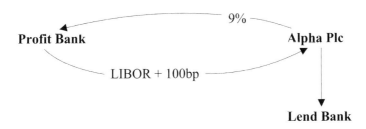

It is worthwhile spending a moment to consider how Profit Bank makes a profit from this transaction. As considered above, it may be that Profit Bank simply has a different expectation of the future movement of interest rates and so expects to make a profit over the ten year life of the transaction. Profit Bank will also charge a fee which is priced into the transaction (by adjusting the rate paid by Alpha Plc) for putting the interest rate swap in place. Equally importantly, however, Profit Bank will be able to acquire sterling at a lower rate than 9 per cent or LIBOR+100bp. The secret to banks trading on foreign exchange markets and money markets is that banks can acquire money at a much lower rate of interest than anyone else (because in effect they are buying their money wholesale while everyone else buys it on a retail basis), and therefore part of Profit Bank's profit may be bound up in its ability to acquire that money at a lower cost of funding. Profit Bank may also be able to hedge this transaction at a low cost which means that its relationship with Alpha Plc—which may be an important client, or even a new client—will prove to be profitable in the long run, even if this particular transaction becomes a loss leader.[33]

B.   Elements in ordinary interest rate swap business

Net payments calculated by reference to a notional amount

The example given above is untypical of much interest rate swap business because it dealt with a real underlying loan. The amounts which are to be paid between the parties are usually in the form of interest rates calculated by reference to a notional amount of money, as opposed to by reference to a real debt. This makes it possible to use swaps for speculation as considered next.

40–30

---

[33] Perhaps the least useful definition of a "swap" is provided by Rix L.J. in *Haugesund Kommune v Depfa ACS Bank (No.2)* [2011] EWCA Civ 33, [2012] Bus. L.R. 230, at [8]: "As Lord Goff there stated [in *Westdeutsche Landesbank v Islington* [1996] A.C. 669, 680], the practical effect of the transaction is to achieve a form of borrowing by the bank's counterparty. In the same way, the effect is to achieve a form of lending by the bank." This is not true. There is no need for any kind of lending between the parties to create a swap (even though, for ease of explanation, a loan was supposed in the example given in the text above). Instead the parties exchange periodic payments (usually at fixed and floating rates of interest) by reference to an actual or a notional amount of money, or by reference to some other market rate (such as Libor) or index. In *Westdeutsche Landesbank* itself there had been an off-balance sheet loan as part of the transaction but that is not in any way definitive of a swap.

Interest rate swaps used for speculation

40–31   At root, then, a swap is an exchange of cash flows between two parties. Speculation is achieved by betting, in effect, that one rate will generate a surplus over the other. An ordinary swap transaction has one fixed interest rate payable by one party and a floating interest rate paid by its counterparty. It is possible, however, for a swap to involve two floating rate payments. Therefore, speculation can be achieved at the simplest level by taking a position on whether a market index will outperform a rate of interest or not. The interest rate swap can be applied in a number of speculative contexts. A speculator, Alpha, can contract with a financial institution, Profit Bank, so that Alpha will receive the return it would have received on paying a floating rate of interest against the performance of a specified market. For example, if Alpha believed that a UK interest rate paid between banks (such as a rate of interest calculated by reference to movements in LIBOR[34]) would outperform a particular index of shares, then Alpha could agree to pay a rate based on LIBOR, calculated by reference to a notional amount of capital, to Profit Bank, and Profit Bank would owe Alpha an amount equal to that same notional amount of money if invested in that index of shares. In effect, the parties will have recreated the effect of investing that notional amount of money on that given share index, without the parties actually having to acquire any such shares. The higher of the two amounts—adjusted LIBOR or the return on that share index—would be paid by the appropriate party to the other party on a series of identified payment dates. This sort of speculative swap transaction is similar to the cash settled call option considered above in that the successful party receives a cash flow equal to a notional investment in the appropriate market. Indeed the financier Das describes swaps as being "portfolios of forward and option contracts".[35] However, we lawyers do not need to delve into that sort of finance theory here.

Different types of swap used for speculation

40–32   This section considers, briefly, some of the basic techniques for using swaps for speculation. Interest rate swaps are really just exchanges of cash flows and therefore speculation can be carried on by means of taking a position on the movement of one cash flow against the movement of another cash flow: such as the return on LIBOR versus the return on that share index. This is the basis of an *equity swap*. The equity swap uses the idea of the swap to enable two parties to benefit from the different rates of appreciation between two indicators. Typically these products can cover the full range of equity products. It is possible to match the movement in the price of a particular equity, of a given equity index or of a non-equity market indicator. So, the parties may contract so that they owe floating rates to each other: one paying an amount calculated by reference to

---

[34] "LIBOR" stands for the "London Inter-Bank Offered Rate", which is a rate of interest paid between banks in London which is ordinarily more stable than other commercial interest rates in London and usually lower than other commercial interest rates.

[35] Das, *Swaps and Derivative Financing*, 2nd edn (Irwin, 1994), p.119. See Hudson, *The Law on Financial Derivatives*, Ch.4, for a disucssion of some of the structuring possibilities.

LIBOR and the other paying the return on a share index (either one that exists in the world or one which the parties create artificially between themselves). Thus, the return on any stock or index can be swapped for a fixed amount of interest or even the return on another stock or index.

The more complex equity products offer a basket of currencies and stocks in emerging markets as the floating rate payment in return for a fixed rate payment or a payment linked to an established market indicator such as LIBOR. Such structures can replicate the effect of a portfolio of investments across many different markets. Thus, one of the parties (usually the seller of the swap) will act as calculation agent in creating and calculating a bespoke index. The credit implications of these products are clearly complex. Added to the risk of counterparty failure, is the risk of trading on a given exchange or against a market indicator. The further risk that is posed is the complexity of the products themselves. In dealing with the so-called exotic markets, there are risks of failure of the market, large movements in the value of the underlying stock, and political risk. Swaps can be used to acquire a cash flow whereby one party pays an amount calculated by reference to the cost of acquiring a commodity or a given amount of electricity, and in return the counterparty pays an amount calculated by reference to the interest paid on a notional amount of money: the result is that the customer acquires the excess of the cost of electricity or of that commodity above the identified rate of interest, and so guards against increases in electricity or commodity prices.[36]   **40–33**

Swaps are used in high volumes in relation to currencies on foreign exchange markets, in which parties either want to exchange amounts in one currency for another currency, or in which parties want to speculate on the different interest rate payable on one currency against the interest rate payable on another currency by entering into a swap. In the case of a *currency swap*, then, rather than a straightforward swap on interest rates like an interest rate swap, the two parties agree to pay each other the interest rate which would be paid on the money markets on the two different currencies. The floating interest rate that is used is the interest rate attaching to a given currency in the money markets. It is of course possible to have two floating interest rates matched against one another or two currency prices matched against one another where one party takes a view on the likely performance of one floating indicator against another.   **40–34**

Many currency swaps used in foreign exchange markets require physical delivery of the currency, as opposed simply to payment of an amount as if an investment had been made in that currency. The obligation owed is to execute an obligation to provide a physical amount of currency calculated by reference to market movements. In circumstances where physical amounts of currency are exchanged, the documentary regime is sometimes different for a foreign exchange transaction from that for an interest rate swap. Whereas the documentation published by ISDA most often used for interest rate swaps, the IFXCO Master Agreement is more usually the standard document for transactions which involve the physical movement of cash amounts.[37] The differences are in   **40–35**

---

[36] See, for example, *Enron Australia Finance Pty Ltd v TXU Electricity Ltd* [2003] N.S.W.S.C. 1169.
[37] See para.36–11 et seq.

the specificity of the terms in the IFXCO contract to do with events of failure, termination and execution on foreign exchange markets.

40–36   An *embedded swap* (usually referred to as an "embeddo" in market jargon) refers to an interest rate swap which is embedded in an underlying financial instrument. The most common example is a swap used to alter the interest rate on a bond issue.[38] Suppose a bond issuer is seeking to raise capital in a market in which it does not have a sufficiently strong market presence to acquire a sufficiently low rate of interest which would have been available to it otherwise: an example would be a German company which is little known in the UK seeking to raise sterling funds by way of a bond issue. Investors in the UK may require a high rate of interest on that bond before agreeing to invest in the German company's bonds because of the risk of not knowing much about the company. By embedding a swap into the bond transaction, the German company ("the issuer") is able to swap the rate of interest payable on the bond for a rate of interest more acceptable to it, such as the rate it would usually pay in Germany in euros. The issuer will pay a rate related to its preferred German interest rate, and in return it will receive the rate of interest which it is obliged to pay to its UK bond investors. Thus, the seller of the interest rate swap will effectively undertake to pay to the issuer the rate of interest which it is required to pay on the bond, whereas the issuer will owe a floating rate of interest to the seller of the swap. It is important in this context that the documentation for the swap matches the payment conventions, dates and so forth for payment under the bond documentation, and also that the events of default for each product also match.

That an interest rate swap compels payment

40–37   Whereas an interest rate swap may have a similar effect to a cash settled call option when it is in-the-money, in that the successful speculator receives an amount of money equal to the profit it would have earned if it had invested directly in that market, there is a significant difference: under a swap transaction, both parties are compelled to account to the other party[39] whether or not the transaction is in-the-money. Therefore, a swap is more akin to a forward than to an option, although financial theory tends to talk of "options". So, one must make a payment even if the swap causes one a loss. This is the vortex that the Hammersmith and Fulham local authority became caught in, thus triggering the two hundred and more cases which are discussed in Chapter 43 under the moniker "the local authority swaps cases".[40] The local authority read the market movements wrongly on a series of occasions and entered into many hundreds of separate transactions in an attempt to make good its early losses. Ordinary companies can be caught in this loop, the risks of suffering financial loss are the same for every organisation in the derivatives markets.

---

[38] See para.34–01 et seq.

[39] It is said that they must account to one another because amounts are paid on a net basis, not on a gross basis.

[40] *Hazell v Hammersmith & Fulham* [1992] 2 A.C. 1.

The effect of the pricing and structure of swaps

This section is a little more complex than the example given above. Our aim is to start to think about how the pricing of interest rate swaps could affect their legal analysis.[41] An interest rate swap which, for example, lasts for ten years with twenty payment dates is usually priced on the basis that it is made up of a series of forwards under which each party is required to pay an amount calculated by reference to a rate of interest. Effectively, the party paying the fixed rate of interest has twenty forwards over ten years; the party paying the floating rate of interest has twenty forwards over ten years. The financial engineers price each forward in turn according to market expectations of the level of those interest rates at the date each payment is to be made.[42] Then the financial engineers effectively "add up" those different segments and adjust the pricing according to the capital market cost of the entire transaction to the selling bank,[43] the credit risk associated with the counterparty and the availability of any means of taking security, the expected volatility in the markets on which the swap is based, and so forth.

40–38

Now, if the swap is thought of as being one single executory contract which is only completed when the last payment is made, then if one of the parties went into insolvency the transaction would have to be accounted for as a single contract which is not yet complete. By contrast, if we follow the segmental approach set out above which considers a swap as being made up of twenty separate payment obligations (akin to forwards) which are to be made by each party over ten years (i.e. forty distinct payment obligations in total) then if one party goes into insolvency the following analysis could be followed: any payments which have been made by the time of the insolvency are treated as having been completed; any payments which are outstanding but unpaid must be resolved in the insolvency proceedings; whereas any payments which are to be made in the future can be treated as not having yet arisen to be payable and can therefore be cancelled. The advantage of this segmental analysis is that it reduces markedly the amount which remains to be resolved in the insolvency by focusing in on the few payments which remain outstanding; whereas the executory contract analysis would take the entire amount to be paid between the parties over the ten years as requiring resolution in the insolvency and thus increases the parties' potential losses in that insolvency. This brief discussion demonstrates how structuring a transaction either as a single executory contract or as a number of small forward contracts can have a significant impact on the profitability of the transaction. By using techniques like this and by understanding how legal analyses can be manipulated or restructured, a lawyer can and does contribute to

40–39

---

[41] This discussion is based on the more complex discussion in A.S. Hudson, *The Law on Financial Derivatives*, Ch.4.

[42] See for example, the concept of the "decomposition" of the swap in Satyajit Das, *Swaps and Derivative Financing*, p.113 et seq.

[43] Given that the use of swaps is often to arbitrage the funding possibilities between different financial markets, the comparative costs of transacting in different markets is an important factor in pricing these products: Das, *Swaps and Derivative Financing*, p.126.

the structuring of financial products. This analysis of structuring swaps is set out in greater detail in Chapter 4 of my book *The Law on Financial Derivatives*.

6. CONTRACTS FOR DIFFERENCES

40–40 The development of the swap was the pivotal event in the creation of the financial derivatives markets because it developed a means of speculating on underlying market movements in a cash-settled format: that is, the parties created a right to pay or receive a cash return on the performance of a notional amount of money as though that notional amount of money had been invested in a given market. In statutory parlance the term "swap" is not used; instead cash-settled financial derivatives in general are referred to as "contracts for differences". The expression "contracts for differences" is the blanket term given by statute to financial derivatives which are valued by reference to movements in some underlying rate, price or index. Contracts for differences are defined in the Financial Services and Markets Act 2000 (Regulated Activities) Order 2001 (the "RAO") as including:

"(a)   a contract for differences; or
(b)   any other contract the purpose or pretended purpose of which is to secure a profit or avoid a loss by reference to fluctuations in—
    (i)   the value or price of property of any description; or
    (ii)   an index or other factor designated for that purpose in the contract."[44]

The definition is therefore somewhat circular (in that it defines itself in part by reference to itself). This definition is provided in the RAO for the purposes of defining those types of investment which may only be dealt in by way of business by people who are authorised so to do by the Financial Conduct Authority. As will emerge in that discussion, the term "contract for differences" covers most of the derivatives, particularly the cash-settled derivatives, considered in this book, as opposed to the statutory definitions of "option" or "future". The concept of a contract for differences does have a longer pedigree in the case law, however.

40–41 In the 19th century case *Universal Stock Exchange v Strachan*[45] the House of Lords held that contracts for differences, in which participants speculated on the performance of any underlying price, were void as gaming contracts.[46] In the Court of Appeal in *City Index v Leslie*[47] it was held by Leggatt L.J. that spread bets did constitute contracts for differences and by Lord Donaldson MR and Cowan L.J. that they fell within the second paragraph of the definition of contracts for differences that they were contracts "the pretended purpose of which is to secure a profit or avoid a loss". It was held further that a contract to "secure a profit or avoid a loss" is not limited to a hedging transaction but may also include such a contract used for speculative purposes.[48] Contracts for differences will also include cash-settled foreign exchange transactions in which the parties'

---

[44] See para.15–25.
[45] [1896] A.C. 166, HL.
[46] See para.18–22 et seq.
[47] [1992] Q.B. 98; [1991] 3 All E.R. 180.
[48] [1992] Q.B. 98; [1991] 3 All E.R. 180.

intention is only to deliver the profit between the movement of two amounts of foreign exchange as opposed to taking physical delivery of the gross foreign exchange amount.[49] In circumstances in which a contract has a floating redemption amount, it has been held that that would constitute a contract for differences because the parties' intention was to secure a profit or avoid a loss by providing a right to redeem which is calculated by reference to movements in some underlying index.[50]

7.   CREDIT DERIVATIVES

A.   Introduction

Credit derivatives are a sophisticated extension to the armoury of the financial engineer in that they enable speculators to speculate on the credit worth of entities, as opposed to speculating directly on their share price or on interest rate movements, and they also provide protection against identified entities failing to make a payment on their bonds and so forth. Let us begin by analysing credit derivatives from the perspective of someone who has invested in a bond but who is concerned that the issuer of the bond will not make all of its interest payments to its investors.[51] A credit derivative enables an investor to receive a return calculated by reference to the credit performance of a specified entity ("the reference entity"). To make a long story short, if the issuer (referred to as the "reference entity") owes a payment of *10* on its bonds but only actually pays *8*, then the credit derivative will pay the investor who is the buyer of the credit derivative *2* (which is the loss on what the investor would otherwise have been entitled to receive on the bond), effectively compensating the buyer of the credit derivative for that loss of *2*. It is common for speculators to use credit derivatives too. So, instead of the buyer of the credit derivative being an investor in the bond with the risk of an actual loss, the speculator may be simply taking a speculative position on whether or not it considers the reference entity is likely to default on its payments. Much of the complication with credit derivatives revolves around defining what will constitute a default sufficient to trigger payment under the derivative and also the regulatory problem of deciding how to classify an entirely novel product which does not fit into the traditional categories of equity, debt or interest rate markets.

40–42

One of the systemic risks associated with credit derivatives is that the derivative requires payment in the event that the reference entity fails to make payment even though a speculator who is entitled to be paid had no risk of loss resulting from the failure to make payment. So, more pressure is built into the system because the sellers of the credit derivatives are required to make payments over and above the losses which are caused in the system among actual investors.

40–43

---

[49] *Larrussa-Chigi v Credit Suisse First Boston* [1998] C.L.C. 277.
[50] *Morgan Stanley v Puglisi* [1998] C.L.C. 481.
[51] See para.34–01 in relation to the nature of bonds.

B. The credit event triggering payment under a credit derivative

40–44   A credit derivative will cause a payment to be made to the buyer on the happening of an event connected to the credit performance of the reference entity: "the credit event". The precise phrasing and structuring of the credit event is therefore central to the operation of the derivative transaction. The documentation may identify any one of a number of credit events, but generally they fall into two kinds. The first form of credit event may therefore relate to a specified level of performance of the reference entity in relation to "specified underlying obligations", such as a bond issue. The precise framing of the credit event would therefore be an issue to be decided between the seller and buyer of the credit derivative. Credit derivative documentation usually requires payment to be made to the buyer when there has been a material breach of the reference obligation by the reference entity. Therefore, in broad terms, when the issuer of a bond commits a material breach of that bond, that is the point at which the buyer of protection under the credit derivative becomes entitled to receive payment.

40–45   The more technical the credit event, the more the seller's expertise will be relied upon: that is, if the credit event is not simply a publicly acknowledged default on a bond or a downgrading by a credit rating agency, then it may be that the credit event results from a more complex analysis of the credit worth of the reference entity, of its gearing, leverage and so forth. These more complex credit events require precise conceptualisation in the documentation if the calculation agent is not to have completely free rein in deciding whether or not payment is required under the credit derivative.

40–46   These calculations are usually defined as being carried out by reference to "publicly available information" which has been published by a RIS or by a ratings agency or by the issuer of the bond itself. It is more difficult to know how to deal with other information, such as articles in newspapers or in academic journals—such material may or may not be considered to be authoritative information at one end of the spectrum or to be mere journalistic speculation at the other end. So in *Deutsche Bank AG v ANZ Banking Group Ltd*[52] in relation to a credit default swap where the International Financing Review published an article which made explicit reference to the reference entity and the reference obligation—here a loan by a bank to the City of Moscow—and the fact that the borrower had defaulted under that loan obligation. The claimant therefore contended that this article was sufficient to constitute publicly available information on which payment could be sought, thus triggering a right to payment under the credit default swap in question. Langley J. considered the argument that the article might have been "self-serving information" placed in the Review by the party which stood to receive payment under the credit default swap with the aim of triggering payment to it under that agreement. The court's view was that, even if the article were self-serving information, it would not take

---

[52] *Deutsche Bank AG v ANZ Banking Group Ltd* Unreported May 24, 1999 (2000 W.L. 1151384), per Langley J.

that factor into account because the agreement did not contain any provision which excluded such information from the category of "publicly available information".[53]

The second type of credit event is more generic in nature and form: the majority of such credit events being effectively the same as those used in the ISDA master agreement, as considered in detail in the next chapter. They commonly include the insolvency of the reference entity, a downgrade in the credit worth of the reference entity or some identified party, the acceleration of, or other default in, some other specified transaction, and so on. The most significant form of credit event in this context is the insolvency of the reference entity. The definition of insolvency would seek to extend beyond actual insolvency to events which are expected to indicate the impending insolvency of the reference entity: the presentation of a bankruptcy petition, a vote taken by the entity in a general meeting to wind the entity up, or where the company is unable to meet its public debt or ordinary bank debt obligations.[54]

40–47

C.   The principal structures of credit derivatives

There are two basic means of structuring a credit derivative: the total return swap and the credit option. As outlined above, their common purpose is to identify a "reference entity" whose credit worth or ability to make payment under an identified financial instrument ("the reference obligation") fails and to require the seller of the credit derivative to make a payment to the buyer of that credit derivative equal to any failure of the reference entity to make any payment on its reference obligations.

40–48

Total return swaps and credit default swaps

The first type of credit derivative is a credit default swap ("CDS") known as a "total return swap". The complexity of this structure is due to the market's desire to use swaps in this new context.

40–49

---

[53] See above.

[54] The last category as to the inability to meet debt obligations contains the same issues as to sufficient financial knowledge about the reference entity on the part of the contracting parties. As with a credit downgrade clause, the parties require access to information about the reference entity which will enable it them to isolate the occurrence of such an incident.

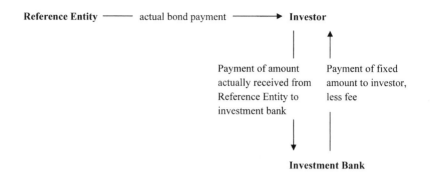

Reference Entity ——— actual bond payment ———→ **Investor**

Payment of amount actually received from Reference Entity to investment bank

Payment of fixed amount to investor, less fee

Investment Bank

Here there is a swap arrangement between the Investor and the Investment Bank. The supposition here is that the Investor actually has acquired bonds in the Reference Entity. The transaction begins with a reference to the amount of coupon (that is, bond interest) which is actually paid under the bond. If the Reference Entity performs its obligations properly then that full coupon payment is paid to the Investor; the Investor is then obliged to pay that amount onwards to the Investment Bank. In return the Investment Bank is required to pay to the Investor the amount which the Reference Entity should have paid to the Investor, less a fee. So, if the Reference Entity makes its interest payment in full, then the Investor notionally pays that amount to the Investment Bank and in turn notionally receives that same amount back from the Investment Bank: in practice, the two amounts will set off, less the fee which the Investment Bank charges. However, if the Reference Entity *fails* to make payment in full, then the Investment Bank will receive less than it pays out to the Investor; but the Investor still receives the entire amount which it should have been paid by the Reference Entity by means of the Investment Bank paying it the fixed amount which it was entitled to receive from the Reference Entity. The Investment Bank does this by paying the difference between what the Investor actually received from the Reference Entity and the amount which it was entitled to receive. Consequently, in effect the Investor has acquired insurance against the Reference Entity failing to make payment in full.

40–50 To use this structure for speculation, the Investor need not actually own bonds issued by Reference Entity but rather can simply take a bet on whether or not it considers the Reference Entity is likely to default on its bond payments. The Investor would therefore contract to pay a comparatively small amount to the Investment Bank and in return to receive a payment equal to any shortfall on the payments actually made by the Reference Entity: the Investor would therefore be betting that the Reference Entity would fail to make all of its bond interest payments. Consequently, the Investor would simply be profiting from its position on the Reference Entity's credit worth. The Investment Bank is taking the risk that the Reference Entity fails to make payment, and presumably is also take a position that it believes the Reference Entity will make all of its bond interest payments.

In *Nomura International Plc v Credit Suisse First Boston International*[55] the **40–51**
parties had created a credit default swap whereby a credit event occurred on the
entry into administration of Railtrack Plc, which was the reference entity. The
claimant was prima facie entitled to force the defendant to buy its Railtrack Plc
bonds from it for a price which was fixed in the contract: that price was fixed at
a level which was much higher than their market value. The defendant sought to
renege on its obligation to buy those bonds for the fixed price. Langley J. held
that the parties' contractual purpose had been to provide the claimant with a right
to receive a payment from the defendant in the event of a reduction in the credit
worth of Railtrack Plc without that right being capable of disturbance by any
other factor. Therefore, on the facts of this case the claimant's rights to force the
defendant to buy the bonds were enforceable.[56]

Credit options

The second typical type of structure is a form of cash settled option under which **40–52**
a fixed payment by the seller on the happening of a credit event. This payment is
made on each date when the reference entity is obliged to make payment under
the bond. The fixed payment is made in the form of an option premium. The cash
settled amount which the seller pays to the investor is equal to any shortfall in
what the investor should have received from the reference entity under the bond.
There is a further payment structure is predicated on any deterioration in the
reference entity's credit worth, such that the seller pays an amount to the investor
calculated by reference to the market value of the specified, underlying
instrument.

D.   Collateralised debt obligations ("CDOs")

CDOs are considered in detail in Chapter 44.   **40–53**

8.   THE REGULATION OF DERIVATIVES

A.   Underlying policy objectives

The Larosière Report, considered in Chapter 7, transformed the EU policy **40–54**
approach to financial services regulation in the wake of the financial crisis.
Over-the-counter derivatives, along with hedge funds and credit rating agencies,
remain the *bêtes noire* of EU policy.[57] Of particular concern to EU policymakers
has been the rapid, unchecked and largely unregulated growth of global
derivatives markets which the EU identifies as having grown from a value in
1998 of less than US$100 trillion to a peak figure at the end of 2007 of nearly
US$700 trillion.[58] The opacity of these markets, their complexity and their role in

---

[55] [2002] EWHC 160 (Comm); [2003] 2 All E.R. (Comm) 56.
[56] See para.3–37A for a further discussion of this decision.
[57] The Larosière Report, 17.
[58] The Larosière Report, 17 18.

amplifying the crisis in the US housing market made them a target for systematic regulation for the first time. That they were to be subjected to "systematic regulation for the first time" means that while financial institutions were regulated in general terms in their interaction with customers (something which might encompass derivatives activity), the derivatives markets as distinct markets had never been regulated. This meant that the derivatives markets which were conducted over-the-counter between private parties were carried on beyond the regulatory gaze. When the financial crisis struck, it was impossible for regulatory authorities to know what the conditions of those markets were. Therefore, two policy ideas have been identified by the EU as being significant: requiring that information about derivatives transactions are provided to information agencies, and that set-off between all professional parties to derivatives transactions is to be conducted through clearing houses so that the genuine, net amount owed between market participants is reduced to smaller sums than hitherto. This would protect core commodities markets (including agricultural produce) as well as the more abstract speculative, cash-settled markets. Off-exchange, over-the-counter ("OTC") derivatives are considered by the Impact Assessment accompanying the regulation to have "contributed to the spreading of the crisis beyond its point of origin ... and to magnifying it into a full-blown global financial crisis that almost brought the financial system, and with it the global economy, to its knees".[59] Again, opacity and a lack of information for regulators are presented as being key issues – hence the need for clearing and information gathering.

B.   The European Market Infrastructure Regulation ("EMIR") on OTC derivatives clearing and trade repository regulation

The outline of EMIR

40–55   The European Market Infrastructure Regulation ("EMIR")[60] was passed into law by the EU in 2012.[61] However, at the time of writing there remained several technical regulations to be effected and finalised so that EMIR can come fully into force, and so that the process of implementing it into the finance laws of member states can be identified.[62] It is the European Securities and Markets Authority ("ESMA") which will be responsible for overseeing the application of the final form of the regulation and its attendant technical regulations. The principal aims of EMIR were twofold: require the clearing of identified types of derivatives transactions through "central counterparties" ("CCP's") akin to clearing houses (as discussed in Chapter 22), and to require information to be supplied to trade repositories ("TR's") about derivatives transactions.

40–56   The CCP's and the TR's are both private sector bodies which will be authorised to act as such. Consequently, the much-vaunted regulation of derivatives is in

---

[59] Impact Assessment, p.13.
[60] 648/2012/EU.
[61] The regulation was adopted in August 16, 2012, but it was not until September 27, 2012 that the precise formulation of the technical rules was finalised, after much lobbying from the business sector.
[62] The date for implementation into UK finance law has not yet been identified: but it is likely not to be before August 2013, according to Bank of England sources.

truth merely oversight by the EU of the private sector bodies which will actually carry out the functions of clearing transactions and gathering information. EMIR had been the subject of an intense lobbying campaign on behalf of the finance industry to reduce the obligations which would be placed on derivatives market participants. The final version of EMIR reduced the amount of reporting of collateral that would be required from market participants, it reduced obligations to take insurance, and it reduced the amount of capital which clearing houses would be required to put into a fund against default among its members.

The policy behind the proposal

The policy underpinning the regulation is ultimately predicated on the Larosière Report, as considered above, and the initiative set out by the Commission in the document "Driving economic recovery", published on March 4, 2009. As the Commissioner for the Internal Market and Services, Michel Barnier, said:[63]

40–57

> "No financial market can afford to remain a Wild West territory. OTC derivatives have a big impact on the real economy: from mortgages to food prices. The absence of any regulatory framework for OTC derivatives contributed to the financial crisis and the tremendous consequences we are all suffering from. Today, we are proposing rules which will bring more transparency and responsibility to derivatives markets so we know who is doing what, and who owes what to whom. As well as taking action so that single failures do not to stabilise the whole financial system, as was the case with Lehman's collapse."

The extravagant rhetoric of treating derivatives markets as being peopled by cowboys is balanced by a more genuine focus on the impact of derivatives markets on the real economy and the lives of ordinary people (for example, through the impact on food prices).

C.   The provisions of EMIR

The scope of EMIR

There are two principal obligations imposed on professional counterparties when dealing in financial derivatives in the first part of the regulation: an obligation to clear derivatives with a central clearing counterparty and an obligation to report transactions to a trade repository. The regulation applies both to financial institutions (including banks, investment firms, insurance companies, collective investments schemes, and pension funds, but not central banks), and to non-financial counterparties in certain circumstances identified in the following section.

40–58

Clearing

The central principle in relation to the obligation to clear derivatives transactions is this: all counterparties in all relevant derivatives transactions are required to clear their OTC derivative contracts through a central clearing counterparty

40–59

---

[63] IP/10/1125.

("CCP") from the date that the clearing obligations come into effect, unless those transactions fall into one of the exempt categories of transaction. The types of transaction which fall inside and outside the clearing requirements are the following, as set out in art.4(1). The various categories of transaction, between various forms of counterparty, are set out in the regulation as follows.

40–60   Any OTC derivatives transaction between "two financial counterparties" will always require clearing. The term financial counterparty includes any investment firm authorised further to MiFID (or COBS in the UK), any authorised bank, any authorised insurance company, any occupational pension fund, or any hedge fund regulated under AIFM.

40–61   Any OTC derivatives transaction between a financial counterparty and a "non-financial counterparty"[64] will always require clearing if it meets the conditions in art.10(1)(b): that is, if the size of its derivatives dealings crosses the regulatory threshold requiring clearing. The threshold is a measurement of the rolling average position over a period of 30 days, as opposed to a simple aggregate volume of transactions. A non-financial counterparty ceases to be obliged to clear in this fashion if its dealings fall below that threshold. There are two further caveats in art.10(3). First, the non-financial counterparty is obliged to take into account all OTC derivatives transactions entered into by companies in its corporate group. Secondly, importantly, the only transactions which are to be brought into account are those which "which are not objectively measurable as reducing risks directly relating to the commercial activity or treasury financing activity of the non-financial counterparty or of that group". Therefore, hedging transactions do not need to be brought into account. However, if the objective of the regulation as a whole is to reduce risk and to increase the information available to regulators then it is illogical to exclude such an important part of the market: the intention is, nevertheless, to limit the clearing activity to speculative activity. Moreover, what the financial crisis made clear is that financial institutions often take eccentric positions in relation to the measurement and valuation of their derivatives exposures—therefore, something which was claimed to be a hedging transaction might in truth be an open speculative position if rates move in an unexpected direction.

40–62   Any OTC derivatives transaction between "two non-financial counterparties" will require clearing only on the same basis as a transaction between a financial counterparty and a non-financial counterparty further to art.10(1)(b).

40–63   Any OTC derivatives transaction between either into between either a financial counterparty or a non-financial counterparty compliant with the threshold provisions in art.10(1)(b), and a person from outside the EU, will require clearing.

---

[64] Where that means a person which is not a financial counterparty.

Any OTC derivatives transaction between two entities from outside the EU will require clearing only if it would fall within the clearing obligations just set out, and if the transaction has a "direct, substantial and foreseeable effect within the Union".[65] **40–64**

No intra-group transaction between corporate bodies in the same corporate group will fall within the clearing obligation.[66] **40–65**

Authorisation to as a CCP

The role of the CCP is important in this process. The entire regulatory scheme depends upon private sector bodies in the form of the CCP's conducting the clearing activities. The CCP's are therefore to be regulated by ESMA and by national regulators. The authorisation of CCP's is performed by the regulatory "competent authority" of each member state, with that regulator notifying ESMA of each authorisation as it is made.[67] Applications are made further to art.14, with a time limit of 30 days on the competent authority which receives the application to decide whether or not the application is complete. The applicant must supply any information requested by the competent authority in question, further to art.17. The competent authority can only grant authorisation, under art.17(4), when it is satisfied that all of the regulatory requirements are met. Notably, this provision suggests that the competent authority can grant authorisation to act as a CCP. Assuming authorisation is given, the competent authority has the power to withdraw that authorisation if the CCP has not used its authorisation within 12 months, if the CCP gave false statements in its application, if the CCP is no longer in compliance with the terms of its authorisation, or if the CCP "has seriously and systematically infringed any of the requirements laid down in [EMIR]".[68] **40–66**

The operation of a CCP

Importantly, there is a concentration of market risk in the operation of the CCP and in the solvency of the CCP itself. That is, instead of being concerned about the solvency of their counterparties, market participants must now be concerned about the solvency of the CCP itself. This structure requires the CCP to collect and to make payments as a third party standing between the counterparties, and therefore those counterparties are now both directly involved in a separate transaction with the CCP itself. Notably the CCP's will be private sector bodies carrying on a commercial activity of clearing derivatives transactions and so the principal regulatory weapon is the removal the licence to conduct that business. This is not a system in which public bodies will be conducting that clearing on an arm's length, completely disinterested basis. **40–67**

---

[65] What is less clear, however, is what will happen in relation to subsidiaries of EU financial institutions which are situated outside the EU and conducting their business outside the EU.
[66] EMIR, art.4(2).
[67] EMIR, art.5(1).
[68] EMIR, art.20(1).

40–68   Once a CCP has been authorised to act as such, it is obliged to accept clearing on a non-discriminatory basis regardless of where the transactions are created.[69] Clearly, it is an essential part of the system that all participants wishing to create a derivative transactions are able to clear them so that they will be in compliance with the regulation. Similarly, access to a trading venue must be possible.[70] The internal organisation of a CCP must be conducted in compliance with art.26 et seq. of EMIR as to the clarity and robustness of its internal structure and management processes, its corporate governance procedures relating to its senior management and its board, and so forth. Each CCP is required to have a risk committee, including representatives drawn from its clearing members, its clients, and independent board members, with the general aim of assessing risk management by the CCP.[71] The competent authority can insist on attending these meetings. The CCP is required to act in accordance with the conduct of business rules set out in art.36 et seq. of EMIR, including a requirement that it acts "fairly and professionally in accordance with the best interests of the clearing members and clients and sound risk management".[72]

Identifying the derivatives covered by EMIR

40–69   ESMA is empowered by art.5 of EMIR to create technical regulations which identify those categories of derivative which must be cleared. Therefore EMIR itself does not make those categories clear. Instead, it identifies the factors which ESMA must take into account when deciding. The ESMA is required to base its decision in relation to each species of derivative transaction on four criteria. First, the need to reduce systemic risk generally. Second, on "the degree of standardisation of the contractual terms and operational processes" of the type of derivative at issue. In relation to clearing, it must be possible to clear like transactions with like transactions at some level, or else the clearing process will simply be about setting off amounts on a profit and loss basis across the parties' entire derivatives businesses. Therefore, the more standardisation there is, the easier it will be to clear transactions off against one another. In a perfect world, clearing would take effect across identical units, as on an exchange. In relation to over-the-counter derivatives, however, there would need to be some level of standardisation to justify clearing. The result will be that the more esoteric types of derivative will not be cleared in this way; and more troublingly, there will be an incentive for swaps dealers to tend towards the use of deliberately obscure products so as to elude the regulatory net. Third, on the volume and liquidity of the relevant type of derivative. Fourth, on the availability of "fair, reliable and generally accepted pricing information" relating to that class of derivatives. Again, with the result that more obscure types of derivative will tend to avoid the regulatory net. ESMA is then required by art.6 to maintain a public register of those types of derivatives that fall within the regulatory net on its website.

---

[69] EMIR, art.7(1).

[70] EMIR, art.8.

[71] EMIR, art.28.

[72] Article 34. This is another example of poor drafting. There is the uncomfortable grouping of the human components of clearing members and clients with the interests of the abstract concept of sound risk management. Again, this provisions seems more eager to achieve rhetoric than sense.

Transactions not cleared through a CCP

In relation to transactions which fall within the regulation but which are not **40–70** cleared through a CCP, the parties are required to "ensure that appropriate procedures and arrangements are in place to measure, monitor and mitigate operational and credit risk".[73] This means ensuring an electronic settlement of the transaction by means of a "timely confirmation" and "robust, resilient and auditable processes in order to reconcile portfolios".[74] Self-evidently these provisions are open to criticism in that they make little literal sense: the draftspeople are clearly particularly keen on achieving alliteration ahead of achieving common sense or coherence.[75] What makes an agreement "robust and resilient" as opposed to being "legally effective" is difficult to know: it tells us nothing about the contents of that contract nor about the goals which it must achieve. Similarly, why parties have to "measure, monitor and mitigate" anything as opposed simply to keeping accurate records which are provided to regulators and ensuring that their transactions are subject to effective contracts is unclear. Exactly what is being "mitigated" by reference to what else is not clear. The method of drafting this form of legislation is overly concerned with rhetorical effect, to the detriment of creating clear principles.

The authorisation and supervision of CCP's

As outlined above, CCP's are to be regulated by the competent authority of the **40–71** state in which they are established.[76] Such an authorisation is effective, however, across the entire EU.[77] CCP's are required to be capitalised in accordance with the regulations[78] to provide a buffer against the insolvency risk associated with CCP's in these clearing structures. The ultimate sanction here is that authorisation may be withdrawn from a CCP where it has not acted for 12 months, or where it obtained its authorisation through false statements or some other irregularity, or where it failed to remain in compliance with any terms placed on its authorisation, or where it has "seriously and systematically infringed" the general requirements of the Regulation, as outlined above. However, regulatory oversight is not left at questions of authorisation and the maintenance of that authorisation. Rather, the competent authority of the relevant member state is responsible for the supervision and oversight of CCP's within their jurisdiction, and shall have the investigative powers necessary for the carrying out of their functions. Notably, however, there is no statement of principle as to how those competent authorities should conduct themselves. Therefore, the precise supervision of CCP's is a matter for regulators to identify on the hoof. A part of the regulatory process is that competent authorities from the various jurisdictions should co-operate with one another. The competent authorities are required to exchange

---

[73] EMIR, art.11(1).
[74] EMIR, art.11(1).
[75] Readers may have noted that I was deliberately alliterating in this part of the text.
[76] EMIR, art.22(1).
[77] EMIR, art.22(2).
[78] At present this is at Euro 5 million in permanent and separate capital.

information with ESMA so that that body can effectively assemble a picture of these markets across the EU as a whole.

Prudential requirements for a CCP

40–72 Given the risks which are now relocated to the CCPs themselves, it is important to ensure the prudential regulation of the CCPs. Therefore, the Regulation contains provision for the prudential maintenance and supervision of CCPs in art.40 of EMIR to the effect that:

> "A CCP shall measure and assess its liquidity and credit exposures to each clearing member and, where relevant, to another CCP with whom it has concluded an interoperable arrangement, on a near to real-time basis. A CCP shall have access in a timely manner and on a non discriminatory basis to the relevant pricing sources to effectively measure its exposures."

Thus, CCPs are required both to assess its risks to each clearing member individually and to maintain sufficient liquidity. It is a requirement, furthermore, that CCP's must be able to access pricing mechanisms so as to identify these exposures from time-to-time as necessary. In essence, this is a competence requirement for a CCP as well as a requirement of its operations.

40–73 As part of the process of "limiting" its credit exposures to clearing members, a CCP must "impose, call and collect margins" under art.41. Article 45 identifies the "default waterfall" (i.e. the order in which its obligations are to be met and losses covered) which requires a CCP first to use margin which has been posted with it before turning to other resources to cover its losses.

40–74 Not satisfied with meeting exposures as though on calm seas, however, the CCP's must also plan ahead and have contingencies in place for market shocks in the form of a "default fund", as required by art.42. So, each CCP is required to "develop scenarios of extreme but plausible market conditions, which include the most volatile periods that have been experienced by the markets" and the default fund must "at all times" be able "to withstand the failure of the two clearing members to which it has the largest exposures and shall enable the CCP to withstand sudden sales of financial resources and rapid reductions in market liquidity.[79] The CCP is required to maintain default procedures, to act promptly in the event of a default so as to "contain losses and liquidity pressures", and to notify the competent authority.

D. Reporting transactions

Reporting to a trade repository

40–75 There is a second obligation imposed on parties entering into derivatives transactions which fall within this regulation: that is a reporting obligation under

---

[79] EMIR, art.42. The CCP is required to maintain a "default fund" by art.42. However that provision reads, at present, "[a] CCP shall maintain a default fund to cover losses arising from *the* default"—where it is not made clear what "the default" is.

art.9 of EMIR. Parties to OTC derivatives contracts are obliged to report to a "trade repository" ("TR") within one working day the details of any OTC derivatives contract which they have created, or which they have modified, or which they have terminated.[80] The definition of a trade repository in art.2 is as follows: "'trade repository' means an entity that centrally collects and maintains the records of OTC derivatives'. The reporting function may be delegated, although the regulation imposes no qualifications on the type of person who may act as a delegate.[81] Records of transactions must be kept for five years.[82] Where reporting cannot be made to a TR, it must be made to ESMA instead.[83]

The regulation of trade repositories

A trade repository must register itself with ESMA.[84] ESMA may reject an application for registration as a trade repository, in accordance with art.57 et seq of EMIR. ESMA is then responsible for monitoring trade repositories and has the power to access documents, to demand information, "to carry out on-site inspections with or without announcement" and "to require records of telephone and data traffic".

40–76

9.   THE INTEREST RATE SWAP MIS-SELLING CASES

In the wake of the financial crisis there were several claims brought by the owners of small businesses which had been allegedly mis-sold interest rate swaps and similar derivatives products. At the time of writing, those cases have not yet gone to trial, and the litigation process appears to be particularly drawn out.[85] In essence, the claimants have found that derivatives which were marketed to them as a means of controlling their interest rate and similar risks have incurred tremendous losses for them as a result of market movements in the wake of the financial crisis. Some of the claims relate specifically to mismatches between the terms of those businesses' borrowing and the terms of the derivatives: including differences in the duration of those products and differences between the notional amount of the swap and the amount of the buyer's underlying loan. In some cases it has been alleged that the buyer was obliged to enter into the swap as a condition precedent to being granted the loan that it was seeking. There is a common complaint that the fees and break costs associated with these derivatives were not explained to the customers. In essence, the banks are alleged to have breached their regulatory obligations under COBS (discussed in Chapter 10) and,

40–77

---

[80] EMIR, art.9(1). It is acceptable for other persons to report these matters to the trade repository so long as there is no duplication of reporting. Many participants argued in the consultation process that too much transparency would harmful to liquidity: i.e. people would not want to deal if their transactions had to be reported: Impact Assessment, p.107.

[81] EMIR, art.9(1).

[82] EMIR, art.9(2).

[83] EMIR, art.9(3).

[84] EMIR, art.55.

[85] The suggestion made by several complainants who have contacted me directly for advice is that the banks are deliberately seeking to slow the litigation down so as to increase the claimant's costs and to force them into settling or dropping their claims.

as argued in Chapter 3, that should found a claim at common law on the basis that COBS constitutes the manner in which a reasonable bank should act when dealing with an inexpert customer.

40–78 The first decided case dealing with these factual issues on an interlocutory basis was *Graisley Properties Ltd v Barclays Bank Plc*.[86] The allegations in that instance were brought by fifteen claimants against Barclays in the wake of the Libor-rigging scandal (which are discussed in Chapter 45 in detail). The claimants alleged, inter alia, that by rigging Libor, Barclays had affected the amount that was payable by the claimants under the interest rate swaps which had in any event been mis-sold to them. These proceedings were an attempt by Barclays to have the claims dismissed on a summary basis: in essence, an interlocutory proceeding claiming that the fifteen claimants had no prospect of success at trial. Flaux J. held that Barclays' petition for summary judgment was "wholly without merit".[87] Moreover, his lordship considered that

> "any senior manager who had given the matter a moment's thought would surely have appreciated that customers who were dealing with the bank would assume and would be entitled to assume that LIBOR was being set in accordance with the BBA definition as an independent benchmark and was not being manipulated by Barclays or any other bank for its own personal interest or gain".[88]

Therefore, it was held that there was a case to answer which justified this matter proceeding to full trial.

40–79 These claims are expected to turn on questions of negligence in the mis-selling of interest rate swaps, as considered in Chapter 25 generally, and questions of fraud, as considered in Chapter 26. The principal claim will be for negligent misstatements made in describing, or failing to describe, those products (as outlined above). Of significance here is the failure to make plain fees and other charges, and to warn customers adequately about the risks associated with complex derivatives. Among the advertent negligence claims will be the creation of unnecessarily complex products as part of ordinary small business loans, involving a misstatement as to their future performance. Where the banks can be shown to have advocated, cajoled or required their inexpert customers to enter into those transactions then that heightens the sense further to *Hedley Byrne v Heller* that the banks were in a position in which their customers would repose confidence in them, that their customers would rely on their statements, and that those statements were negligently made so as to cause loss to the customers when the markets fell. The precise statements would be important. The banks will allege that they did not know the financial crisis would come; but if their

---

[86] [2012] EWHC 3093 (Comm), heard before Flaux J. on October 31, 2012. This case is often referred to as *Guardian Care Homes v Barclays* in the press. See also now: *Graisley Properties Ltd v Barclays Bank Plc* [2013] EWHC 67 (Comm).

[87] [2012] EWHC 3093 (Comm), heard before Flaux J. on October 31, 2012. This case is often referred to as *Guardian Care Homes v Barclays* in the press. See also now: *Graisley Properties Ltd v Barclays Bank Plc* [2013] EWHC 67 (Comm). at [21].

[88] [2012] EWHC 3093 (Comm), heard before Flaux J. on October 31, 2012. This case is often referred to as *Guardian Care Homes v Barclays* in the press. See also now: *Graisley Properties Ltd v Barclays Bank Plc*[2013] EWHC 67 (Comm).at [22].

salespeople contended that derivatives would *never* constitute a risk then that would tend to obviate the purported unforeseeability of the crash. However, in the wake of the Libor scandal it is more difficult for the banks to contend that they played no part in fixing the rates at which those interest rate swaps would require payment: that the traders in London were probably unaware of specific customers acquiring derivatives in provincial English branch offices, does not take away from the fact that they must have been aware that some customers would necessarily lose if they altered the true Libor rate. This is the avenue down which a claim based on fraud would also proceed. In relation to claims that the banks required their customers to enter into derivatives (especially if those salespeople stood to take some benefit of their own, by way of bonus from the transaction), that would seem to raise an argument based on undue influence (as considered in Chapter 26) to have the entire transaction set aside *in toto*.

CHAPTER 41

DOCUMENTATION OF FINANCIAL DERIVATIVES

CORE PRINCIPLES

Financial derivatives are typically documented by means of the International Swaps and Derivatives Association ("ISDA") standard form master agreement architecture. Any individual transaction contracted between two parties will be created by means of telephone conversation between traders or occasionally in writing between a bank and a corporate client, and it will be documented by means of a "Confirmation". Two financial institutions may well have between many thousands of derivatives of various types outstanding between them. All of these many transactions are grouped together as a "single agreement" under the umbrella of a "Master Agreement". The master agreement provides the terms which govern the basis on which the parties enter into all their derivatives contracts. Of particular importance are the "events of default" and "termination events" which provide grounds for all of the outstanding derivatives to be terminated and settled. The master agreement is on market standard terms, but the parties can amend or expand on those standard terms by means of the

"Schedule" to the Master Agreement. The Master Agreement and Confirmations may be supplemented by a "Credit Support Annex" or "Credit Support Deed" (which provide for collateralisation, considered in the next chapter) or by a guarantee or other credit support document (as discussed in Chapter 22). All of these documents are intended to constitute a single agreement. The ISDA master agreement is the model for the discussion of master agreements in the abstract in Chapter 19.

1. INTRODUCTION

A. The scope of this chapter

41–01   This chapter considers the most significant principles in the documentation of derivatives. There is a much fuller analysis of the standard market documentation and of the issues which arise from it in my book *The Law on Financial Derivatives*.[1] The documentation architecture for derivatives is built on the International Swaps and Derivatives Association ("ISDA") standard market documentation—and that is the documentation which will be discussed here for the most part. It is open to parties to over-the-counter derivatives to create their own documentation which is different from the ISDA standard, and in many contexts (principally to do with reducing the cost of putting ISDA documentation in place) that is what parties do. Nevertheless, it is thought that the ISDA Master Agreement is used to document 90 per cent of all of the financial derivatives contracts in the world,[2] in a market which was estimated by the Bank for International Settlements ("BIS") to be worth a gross amount of US$ 19.5 trillion in June 2011, down from US$25.3 trillion in June 2009.[3] The notional amount outstanding, according to BIS, was US$707.5 trillion in June 2011.

This chapter will consider the generic provisions which are included in the ISDA standard documentation and will thus cover the most common provisions found even in the bespoke[4] documentation. The provisions which deal with the termination of derivatives contracts specifically are analysed in Chapter 43 below.

41–02   There are three tiers of derivatives documentation in the ISDA documentation architecture. First, a *confirmation*, one of which documents each individual transaction and therefore there may be many hundreds of such contracts in existence between these parties. Secondly, the *master agreement* which sets out the more general terms on which the parties agree to conduct all of their

---

[1] Alastair Hudson, *The Law on Financial Derivatives*, 5th edn (London: Sweet & Maxwell, 2012), Chs 2 and 3.

[2] Briggs J. accepted ISDA's estimate of this usage of their agreement in *Lomas v JFB Firth Rixson Inc* [2010] EWHC 3372 (Ch); [2011] 2 B.C.L.C. 120.

[3] *http://www.bis.org/statistics/otcder/dt1920a.pdf*

[4] "Bespoke" documentation, like a bespoke suit, is documentation which has been drafted solely for one transaction, as opposed to being standard form documentation which is used in all transactions. Commonly it is corporate clients or small hedge funds which do not want to use market standard documentation because it is long and complex and because they do not want either to spend a large amount of money having lawyers consider it or to be lashed into documentation which they fear has been drafted for the benefit of the investment banks.

derivatives business. The ISDA master agreement is in standard form in a pre-printed set of terms. It is the *schedule* to the master agreement in which the parties amend or particularise provisions in the standard form contract: this is the part of the documentation which occupies the bulk of a derivatives lawyer's drafting time. Thirdly, any *credit support* documentation which provides for the collateralisation or the guarantee of payments to be made in relation to specified transactions.[5]

B.   Standardisation of documentation

The aim of the parties in the use of standard contracts, such as the ISDA documentation considered in detail in this chapter, is to "commoditize" the risks which are created by providing for common, cross-border solutions to issues which arise in all derivatives products. By "commoditize", in this context, is meant a process of rendering all of the risks of the products the same by using standard market documentation which provides for identical definitions of, and solutions to, those issues. However, this can have the result that parties too frequently do not consider in detail their own particular needs but rather rely on the standard market documentation in its unamended form to capture all of the provisions which they might require. **41–03**

It is important to bear in mind that well-drafted derivatives documentation will require the parties to be sensitive to the needs and risks associated with their own transactions and also to be conscious of the particular risks which each bears in relation to any particular transaction. This point cannot be over-emphasised: standard contracts will only cater for standard situations; there is still a need for documentation to be reviewed and re-calibrated for novel products, new clients, and new situations. What is missing from the master agreement, necessarily, is the full range of risk management tools at the lawyer's disposal such as the guarantee, pledge and trust which the parties themselves will need to shape for their own purposes. It is precisely that lack which led the ISDA to adopt a rigid, standard master agreement structure with a schedule designed to be adapted and negotiated so that the parties are required to match their own needs to the challenges which the law offers them. **41–04**

C.   The central role of the "single agreement" approach

The philosophy behind ISDA documentation is that all of the confirmations entered into between two parties together with their master agreement, schedule and credit support documentation are to construed as constituting one single contract, and not that each transaction is a separate contract. Without such an express provision there would be no reason to consider that, for example, all of the parties' interest rate swaps were to be considered to constitute a single agreement together with each individual equity option and so on. The reason for introducing this artificial link between the transactions is so that on termination **41–05**

---

[5] See para.22–77 et seq.

of the relationship between the parties it is possible to set off all of the amounts owed between the parties across all of their various types of derivatives transactions and to come to one final, net sum which will meet all of their exposures one to another, even if one of the parties has gone into insolvency.[6] This is a problem which is particularly acute when dealing across jurisdictions.[7]

41–06 The market's greatest concern is always for the insolvency of a counterparty which would mean, under most systems of insolvency law, that an unsecured creditor would be precluded from recovering an amounts owing to it from the insolvent party while leaving it liable to make all outstanding payments to the insolvent party. The English insolvency law position in this regard was considered in Chapter 22.[8] Therefore, it is important from the perspective of the solvent party that the parties be able to reduce their exposures to a net amount across all of their transactions. The provision for the single agreement approach of the ISDA documentation consequently assuages this fear and also expresses the pre-occupation of those who created this standard documentation with the spectre of the insolvency of non-market counterparties. The House of Lords has upheld the validity of insolvency set-off provisions in relation to bilateral contracts where there are mutual debts owed,[9] but it has refused to uphold agreements whereby more than two parties have agreed to set off any amounts owed between them on a periodical basis by means of a clearing house if one of the parties went into insolvency.[10] The former cases applied statutory rules requiring such a set-off in the context of mutual debts,[11] whereas the latter case refused to permit set-off on the basis of public policy because it would have contravened the statutory pari passu principle.[12] That position was resolved by the Settlement Finality Regulations 1999, which are considered in the next chapter.

41–07 In a subtly different context, in *Inland Revenue Commissioners v Scottish Provident Institution*,[13] it was held that a collateral agreement was a separate contract from the two options which it was created to secure, and so it was held that it was not a "single agreement". In that case, two parties had created two options which cancelled one another out as part of a complex tax avoidance transaction which created an artificial tax loss. The court refused to hold that the various elements of the transaction (an ISDA Master Agreement and a collateral

---

[6] *Stein v Blake* [1996] 1 A.C. 243; *Morris v Rayner Enterprises Inc* Unreported October 30, 1997; *Re Bank of Credit and Commerce International SA (No.8)* [1997] 4 All E.R. 568.

[7] *In Re Bank of Credit and Commerce International S.A. (No.11)* [1997] 2 W.L.R. 172.

[8] See para.22–91 et seq.

[9] *Stein v Blake* [1996] 1 A.C. 243; *Re BCCI (No.8)* [1998] A.C. 214.

[10] *British Eagle v Air France* [1975] 2 All E.R. 390. Significantly, as Lord Cross explained in that case, there was no charge nor any other proprietary right created in favour of any creditor under the clearing house arrangement in that case. Consequently, the parties had no explicit protection against insolvency and the creditors were therefore reduced to arguing that the insolvent party should have been considered to have held a fund of assets, probably in the form of book debts, on charge for the creditors. In the absence of any such explicit right, the majority of the House of Lords refused to uphold the enforceability of any set-off in this insolvency.

[11] Insolvency Rules 1986, r.4.90.

[12] See para.22–91.

[13] [2003] S.T.C. 1035.

agreement) did in fact constitute a single agreement, even though that is what the ISDA master agreement explicitly provided. This suggests that, while the ISDA master agreement provides that these documents will form a single agreement, there would not otherwise be thought to be any legal, analytical connection between distinct transactions as a single agreement. This reminds all lawyers that the court will look to the substance of the transaction and not necessarily to the form which is suggested by the documentation. In *BNP Paribas v Wockhardt EU Operations (Swiss) AG*.[14] In that case, two banks entered into an ISDA Master Agreement and Schedule, and Confirmations, in relation to foreign exchange forward agreements.[15] Wockhardt failed to make payments in relation to these transactions. Consequently, BNP gave notice (as required by the Master Agreement) that it was commencing the Early Termination procedure under that Master Agreement which required a set-off of the outstanding amounts owed between the parties.[16] BNP then sought summary judgment for payment of this amount. BNP contended that it had calculated that amount in a "commercially reasonable manner".[17] Among the issues which arose on those facts was whether or not the "single agreement" provision in the master agreement was valid, or whether it should be ignored on the basis that it was only an artificial link between those transactions. Clarke J. held that the parties had freedom of contract and so could choose to link these transactions together as a single agreement if they wished. Therefore, in this context (outside insolvency or revenue law) the single agreement approach was upheld.

2. THE CONFIRMATION

A. The role of the confirmation

The confirmation is, as its name suggests, a confirmation of the trade which the two parties' traders have already entered into, usually, by telephone. The confirmation is expressed to be subject to the terms of the master agreement, as discussed below. The legal questions which arise from this confirmation process received a more detailed consideration in Chapter 17 *Formation of contracts*.[18] There is frequently a division here between the theory by which all transactions are reduced into writing and the market practice that very many transactions are never documented at all, typically because the transactions are speculative transactions which have expired before the respective parties' lawyers have been able to agree on a form of words acceptable to both parties. A practice then

41–08

---

[14] [2009] EWHC 3116 (Comm).

[15] All of these strands of documentation are explained in Alastair Hudson, *The Law of Finance*, (London: Sweet & Maxwell, 2009), p.1117.

[16] On which see para.3–94.

[17] Failure to satisfy a court that a calculation of a person's losses and costs had been conducted in a commercially reasonable manner had previously led to a refusal by Moore-Bick J. to grant an order that such payment be made in *Peregine Fixed Income v Robinson*: [2000] Lloyd's Rep. Bank 304. In so doing, Moore-Bick J. was relying (somewhat unfortunately) on the seminal public law case of *Associated Provincial Picture Houses v Wednesbury Corp* [1948] 1 K.B. 223 on "reasonableness" in public administration. Unfortunately, this case was not referred to in *BNP v Wockhardt*.

[18] See para.17–03.

develops of not even seeking with any degree of seriousness to document transactions because the process of negotiation would be expected in all cases to take longer than the transaction would be intended to last. In relation to larger, more structured transactions, such as swaps embedded in bond issues,[19] all of the documentation including the confirmation would need to be complete before the transaction commenced and therefore the confirmation might in truth be the contract itself rather than a mere confirmation of such a contract. Therefore, larger transactions are more likely to have been properly documented.

41–09   The typical mechanics of the creation of a complex financial transaction were considered in Chapter 17.[20] The tendency not to put any documentation in place in a very large number of derivatives transactions, particularly the high volume types of business between large financial institutions, constitutes a large source of regulatory risk because these transactions have no agreement between the parties as to any of the standard contractual terms which are not discussed between the traders. In many transactions it will be these detailed legal issues—such as the governing law of the contract, or its tax treatment, or set-off on insolvency and so on—which may constitute a ground for invalidity if it remains undecided.

41–10   The confirmation stands for all the terms of the contract until a master agreement is put into place. The role of the master agreement is to deal with eventualities affecting the range of dealings between the parties, such as insolvency, events of default, the mechanics for the termination of the parties' outstanding transactions, and so on. The standard terms of a confirmation do not deal with these sorts of issues. It is common for a master agreement to be put into place months after the first transaction between parties, by which time many further transactions might have been transacted.[21] Therefore, while the confirmation must evidence all the terms of the transaction between the parties until a master agreement is put in place, a confirmation will not ordinarily contain all of the terms which the parties require between them. Nor will the confirmation deal with the credit risk between the parties—that is something which must be dealt with by means of a credit support agreement, as considered in Chapter 42 *Collateralisation*.

B.   The contents of a typical confirmation

41–11   This section simply outlines the types of provisions which would be expected to appear in a Confirmation. We shall consider the order of provisions usually found in an ISDA standard form of confirmation for dealing in bond, debt or equity derivatives. The first provision will set out the parties to the transaction. It is important to record the transaction between the correct subsidiaries, special purpose vehicles or affiliates of a large financial institution which may have many hundreds of vehicles for conducting securities and other business. The tax or regulatory effect of recording the wrong party may cause complications. The second provision records the purpose of the Confirmation as evidencing the terms and conditions of the transaction between the parties, but not usually the

---

[19] See para.40–36.
[20] See para.17–03.
[21] As such giving rise to a need for a mechanism for set-off on insolvency and so forth.

commercial purpose for which the transaction was effected.[22] The third provision then sets out the linkage between the Confirmation and a Master Agreement as a single agreement,[23] the way in which the Master Agreement supplements the terms of the Confirmation as to events of default and so forth, and which document will have priority in which eventuality.

Then come the economic terms of the transaction which will have been agreed between the parties. In this list of general terms, there is first the trade date of the transaction. Secondly, assuming the transaction is an option, there is the "option style" which specifies whether the transaction is "European", "American", or "Asian" in style which governs the manner in which and the dates on which the option can be exercised.[24] Clearly the confirmation will then need to specify the dates on which such an option can and cannot be exercised: this is set out under the "procedure for exercise" heading. Thirdly, the confirmation will need to identify the "Option Type" and whether it is a put or a call option. Fourthly, the confirmation will identify which party is the seller of the option and which party is the buyer of the option. Fifthly, the confirmation will specify on which index or on which particular security the option is based. If the transaction is based on a one-off index created specially for that transaction or a basket of instruments then the confirmation would need to specify which one and who is responsible for calculating and publishing it (if appropriate). It is unusual to attach the formulae for calculating this sort of bespoke basket to the confirmation, but it is suggested that that would be good practice for the reasons considered below.[25] Sixth, the confirmation will provide the number of units which the option may acquire: "units" in this context refers to the number of individual units of the underlying instrument (share, bond, or whatever) on which the option is based. This amount may be an absolute amount or a maximum which may be acquired as the parties may provide. Seventh, the "strike price" identifies the price for which a call option permits the buyer to buy units, or for which a put option permits the buyer of the option to sell its units. Eighth, the premium is the fixed sum which the buyer must pay up-front to establish the option. An option confirmation should specify that the payment of the premium is a condition precedent to the validity of the option. Ninth, the premium payment date establishes the date on which the buyer is required to pay its premium. Tenth, the exchange on which the underlying product is traded (if it is indeed traded on an exchange).

41–12

An important provision thereafter is the identification of the "Calculation Agent", as considered later in this chapter. The calculation agent identifies whether or not the option is "in-the-money"—meaning that it is in profit and that the option will be exercised—and if so by how much. Clearly, the role of the calculation agent is very important in relation to establishing whether or not a profit has been made, and of what size. Usually, the calculation agent will be the seller of the option, particularly if the buyer is not an expert in this particular market. The most common term in this area is usually that the calculation agent will be the seller "whose determinations and calculations shall be binding in the absence of

41–13

---

[22] See para.39–26.
[23] *ISDA Master Agreement* s.1(c).
[24] See para.40–17.
[25] See para.39–26.

manifest error". However, if the option is being sold between two financial institutions, and if it relates to a complex underlying product which is not traded on an exchange, there may be some concern about leaving control of the calculations to one party, in which case the parties may provide that their traders are to agree on all calculations. In the event of a dispute it is usually provided that an independent market maker be appointed to reach the calculations, or else that a number of market makers to be appointed and that the average of their calculations will be binding in the absence of manifest error. If the transaction contains advanced features or sophisticated modelling then it may be something which the seller does not want to pass on to third party market makers, in which case that means of resolving disputes will not be used.

41–14 The "Procedure for Exercise" provisions identify over which period the option may be exercised and, importantly, the "Expiration Date" for the option after which time the buyer may not exercise any of the rights contained in it. These provisions will be subject to the appropriate conventions for identifying what will be and what will not be a business day for the index or exchange or other market in question.

41–15 The confirmation will then identify the choice between cash settlement and physical settlement: that is, whether the parties will simply account for the profits of an in-the-money option in cash, or whether the parties will actually transfer the number of units in the underlying instrument to settle the transaction, or whether the buyer is to have the choice to exercise the option either by cash settlement or by physical settlement. If the option is to be cash settled, the option will have to identify how the cash settlement amount is to be calculated, by reference to the "Strike Price Differential" which is the excess of the market price of the underlying instrument in relation to the strike price identified in the option itself. If physical settlement is selected then the option will have to identify the date and mechanism for transferring physical ownership of the underlying instrument.

41–16 There is then a range of other possible provisions depending on the nature of the underlying instrument and the market on which it is traded. The possibility of market disruption is considered in detail below.[26] Also important in the Confirmation are the governing law of the contract and the jurisdiction in which disputes will be resolved,[27] and the details of the accounts to which payments are to be made. These provisions will be adapted *mutatis mutandis* for other types of derivatives.

C. Failure of the basis of the contract through the Confirmation, and identifying the purpose of the transaction

Frustration of contract

41–17 One key issue which arises in relation to Confirmations of individual transactions is how to deal with some disruption caused to the free flow of business which

---

[26] See para.39–27.
[27] Both of which are considered in detail in Ch.6, *Conflict of Laws*.

causes the pricing of that derivative to be thrown out of kilter or to reach levels which the parties had not anticipated. The legal issues which arise here are typically how to understand the parties' intentions as to the possibility of acquiring a price for that derivative and whether or not the disruption caused to the market is sufficient so as to constitute a frustration of that contract. This section considers how provisions frequently included in the Confirmation dealing with market disruption, unexpected losses and exceptional events may invoke the doctrine of frustration of contract. This includes events such as a temporary disruption in the market on which the underlying asset is traded such that the derivative cannot be valued effectively due to extraordinary events whereby one or other of the parties themselves are unable to perform their obligations under any one or more of the transactions contracted under the master agreement. In any event, the key issue will be whether the derivative can nevertheless be performed, perhaps by the calculation agent estimating the price which the derivative should have reached but for the market disruption event, or whether that transaction should be considered to have been frustrated by virtue of that same event.

The importance of stating the purpose of the contract in the Confirmation

The law relating to frustration of contract was considered in Chapter 19.[28] Briefly **41–18** put, a contract will be treated as having been frustrated if the subject matter of the contract becomes "for business purposes something else"[29] from the bargain which the parties intended, that is something other than that for which the parties can have been intended to have contracted.[30] It is a frequent shortcoming of derivatives contracts that they do not identify precisely the purpose for which the contract was created, and so it is difficult to identify what, for business purposes, the objectives of the transaction were. The sorts of statement which might usefully be included would differentiate between a transaction being intended for pure speculation (in which case the parties might be said to take the risk of abnormal market movements) or to act as a hedge for a particular risk (in which case the parties' commercial purpose could be said to be to take risks which were only intended to match or approximate to the risk which is being hedged, such that the parties were not intending to expose themselves to abnormal market risks). If the intention was to hedge a risk, and the parties had the forethought to include a term in the Confirmation expressing their intentions in relation to that transaction, then an abnormal market movement might not be something which the calculation agent would be permitted to price into the transaction so as to oblige the buyer of the derivative into paying out more than had been anticipated.

---

[28] See para.19–76.
[29] *Asfar & Co v Blundell* [1896] 1 Q.B. 123, 128. See also *Bank Line Ltd v Arthur Capel & Co* [1919] A.C. 435.
[30] See above, where a shipment of dates were waterlogged such that there were no longer of suitable quality; *The Badgary* [1985] 1 Lloyd's Rep. 395. cf. *Horn v Minister of Food* [1948] 2 All E.R. 1036.

Market disruption or an extraordinary event

41–19   A market disruption event relates, for example, to an exchange on which a share is traded ceasing to operate for a long or a short period of time: this would clearly have an impact on a call option to buy shares because the price of the underlying share would be affected by that market disruption. There is also a question as to how to deal with the situation in which there is an extraordinary event leading, perhaps, to the merger or nationalisation or liquidation of any relevant entity, or constituting some material adverse change in the ability of the contract to function normally. Thus, one of the most common concerns in relation to the drafting of a Confirmation is that the underlying market will suffer such a serious disruption that the assumptions underpinning the derivative, and the pricing of that derivative, will undergo such a change that the contract will cease to reflect the parties' commercial intentions. Therefore, it is necessary to provide for a mechanism for the re-calibration of the derivative transaction when the underlying market alters significantly.

41–20   The most straightforward example of this sort of activity relates to equity derivatives in which the derivative is priced according to the performance of units traded on a stock exchange. In relation to a stock exchange such a market disruption might be defined in the Confirmation as occurring if trading in a given percentage of the shares on the exchange is suspended, or if some concerted attempt to manipulate the price of a share or shares has had an effect on a given proportion of the market, or if a sufficient number of companies quoted on the exchange go into insolvency, or if trading on the exchange as a whole is suspended for a given period of time.[31] In relation to the publication of a share index, as opposed to shares traded on an exchange, this could relate to a cessation of the publication of the index or a material alteration in the manner in which the level of that index is calculated. In the equity and commodity markets it is a pre-requisite that there be a functioning market before there will be an index against which the derivative can be priced.

41–21   Market disruption will only affect cash-settled derivatives if it stops the index or other payment-device from being calculated; otherwise it should usually be possible for the calculation agent to arrive at some reasonable substitute valuation, provided that the documentation gives that calculation agent sufficient powers and guidelines with which to do so. By contrast, in relation to physically-settled derivatives, which require that an amount of the commodity or share be delivered to the buyer, there is clearly risk of the commodity or share being in short supply if the relevant market has failed or has ceased trading temporarily. In such cases, there will be a need to provide for default interest in relation to late payment or delivery,[32] or to provide for an alternative means of

---

[31] On some stock exchanges a movement in a particular share will account for a significant proportion of the volume of the exchange. For example, there might be a particular company which is so important to the economy encompassing that exchange that it accounts for a significant percentage of the size of the equity transacted on that exchange or of the size of a particular index. If that company were to become insolvent, for example, the effect the index would be very large indeed and arguably contrary to the expectations of both of the parties on entering into the agreement.

[32] See para.43–10.

making reparation to the other party for any loss suffered. Such reparation will usually be in the form of cash settlement according to the calculation agent's deliberations, as provided for in the confirmation.

The occurrence of frustration of contract

The legal question is then whether or not there will have been frustration so that the contract can be taken to have been avoided. The test is whether or not the contract is rendered "as a matter of business a totally different thing",[33] or whether or not matters have become impossible so that the subject matter of the contract has become "for business purposes something else",[34] so that it is something other than that for which the parties can have been intended to have contracted.[35] Such an analysis may be made easier by the inclusion of some maximum volatility clause or similar provision in the documentation, as considered in the next section, which would specify the purpose of the transaction, or the point in time at which the parties would consider its purpose to have been frustrated. In the absence of such a contractual provision it will be a matter of degree whether or not the performance of the contract is to be considered to be too onerous in the circumstances.[36]

41–22

In relation to frustration of contract, it may not be as simple as the contract becoming absolutely impossible to perform. The guiding principle remains whether or not the contract is rendered "as a matter of business a totally different thing" from what the contract was supposed to be.[37] For example, there might be a question as to the effect of the change in the trading on the index resulting from the failure of a significant part of the index. Arguably, the position of the parties would be that the true intention of the contract, to create a synthetic security payments which mirror the normal movements of that index, had been frustrated by the index itself being all but destroyed by the violent, and unexpected movements of one of the components within it. Clearly that will be a question of degree.

41–23

Maximum volatility provisions, the role of calculation agents and stating the purpose of the transaction

The key legal difficulty with establishing frustration of contract is the absence of clear evidence as to what the parties' intentions were. There are, of course, the recordings of the discussions between the traders. Over the course of a long negotiation, however, identifying a single, clear intention may be difficult. What would be clearer, however, would be a straightforward contractual statement of

41–24

---

[33] *Bank Line Ltd v Arthur Capel & Co* [1919] A.C. 435, 460.

[34] *Asfar & Co v Blundell* [1896] 1 Q.B. 123, 128.

[35] *Asfar & Co v Blundell*, where a shipment of dates were waterlogged such that there were no longer of suitable quality; *The Badgary* [1985] 1 Lloyd's Rep. 395. cf. *Horn v Minister of Food* [1948] 2 All E.R. 1036.

[36] cf. *Multiservice Bookbinding v Marden* [1979] Ch. 84 where it was held that such a shift will be immaterial if agreed by commercial parties who were properly advised.

[37] *Bank Line Ltd v Arthur Capel & Co* [1919] A.C. 435, 460.

the parties' intentions, in the manner that old-fashioned contracts used to open with a recital "whereas the parties intend . . ." such-and-such, and thus gave a clear signal as to the underlying purpose of the contract. The parties would be well-advised to include in their documentation some provision as to the maximum amount of volatility which they expected from the indices. On this basis they could cap either party's duty to pay or right to be paid and so protect themselves against unanticipated movements in the underlying market.[38] A structured derivative product used for hedging purposes or to swap the effective rate of interest payable on a bond issue are, it is suggested, less prepared to take open-ended risk exposure to market movements than straightforward speculative contracts. Of course, it is a feature of the use of financial instruments to manage risks—as opposed to insurance, or to taking security in the way discussed in Chapter 22—that the instrument which is used to manage risk will also create risks of its own.[39]

41–25 Linked to this question of identifying the maximum volatility anticipated in a contract is the broader question of identifying the purpose of the contract in the round. So, where a transaction is entered into to hedge a particular exposure, it would make sense to state that contractual purpose in the confirmation so that it becomes easier for the parties to identify when some extraordinary event has occurred or some event in general terms which ought to lead to the contract being frustrated and therefore set aside, as considered in detail in Chapter 17.

41–26 As an illustration of the need for such statements of commercial intention in contracts, consider the following case. In *Nomura International Plc v Credit Suisse First Boston International*[10] the parties had created a credit default swap whereby a credit event occurred on the entry into administration of Railtrack Plc. The claimant was prima facie entitled to deliver exchangeable bonds to the defendant on the occurrence of this event so as, in effect, to recoup its loss on its exposure to Railtrack Plc. The parties had agreed that the delivery obligation was "not contingent" and issues arose as to the meaning of this term. Langley J. held that an obligation would only be contingent if it was beyond the control of the claimant as seller of the bonds. The contract was "not contingent" if the only purported contingency was the claimant's decision whether or not to exercise its rights to sell the bonds. Rather it was held that a contingency would have to be something beyond the claimant's control. Langley J. identified the parties' contractual purpose as having been to secure for the claimant a right to receive a payment in the event of a reduction in the credit worth of Railtrack Plc without that right being capable of disturbance by some extraneous factor. Therefore, on the facts of this case the claimant's rights to deliver the bonds were enforceable.

---

[38] In any event it is suggested that it is important that market participants include some statement of the purpose of their transaction in their documentation so that they acquire insulation against unexpected market disruption or other events. At the time of contracting such provisions typically seem unnecessary because, by definition, no one expects the unexpected to take place. However, that is precisely the role of the lawyer, to protect the client against the risk of future events whether seen or unseen at the time of creating the contract.

[39] See para.1–47 et seq.

[40] [2002] EWHC 160 (Comm); [2003] 2 All E.R. (Comm) 56.

However, it has been suggested by one commentator that this decision is wrong on the basis that the precise definition of the term "not contingent" in the ISDA Credit Derivatives Definitions 1999 refers not to the claimant's rights as holder of the bond but rather to the issuer's obligations, and that the court seemed to have overlooked the precise structure of that provision.[41] Despite these reservations, the court's interpretation of the meaning of "contingency" in this context is entirely reasonable in the context of ordinary understandings of that term in English commercial law.[42] It has been suggested further, however, that this interpretation did not reflect the parties' actual commercial intentions in this context and that the defendant should have been able to resist delivery and its concomitant obligation to make payment.[43] This argument cannot hold water. Indeed it takes us to the heart of the issue, which is considered on numerous occasions in this Part XI of this book, to the effect that parties to derivatives contracts do not tend to include in their documentation a clear statement as to what their commercial intentions actually are. If they did so, the courts would be much more likely to identify and enforce those intentions instead of having to summon them up out of thin air as is the case at present. Instead derivatives market participants tend to assume that their common intentions are well-understood and that any outside agency, such as a court, which fails to apply enforce those intentions are interlopers who fail to understand the niceties of that market. As mentioned above, a well-drafted, traditional contract would have begun with a recital to the effect that "Whereas the parties intend [to do such-and-such], the following provisions are created ...", thus leaving the parties' commercial intentions in plain sight.

41–27

When dealing with complex derivatives—such as equity swaps where the parties have created an artificial basket of currencies and securities on which the buyer of the swap wishes to speculate—there is clearly a complex mathematical formula underpinning the calculation as to whether the currencies or securities underlying that derivative are in-the-money or not. Yet the Confirmation rarely includes a statement of that formula or of any other considerations which the calculation agent will rely on when establishing whether or not the transaction is in-the-money. Clearly, if the parties fall into a dispute as to whether or not the calculation agent has acted properly, or has made a mistake in the calculation, or if the transaction has ended up not reflecting the parties' original intentions (such as if one of the key shares in the basket ceases to be traded), then there will be a question as to whether or not the purpose of the transaction has been frustrated or whether it is simply a question of breach of contract by the calculation agent. It would be advisable to include a contractual statement of the parties' expectations of any calculations required to be carried out during the performance of any transaction in the Confirmation in general terms. In relation particularly to complex derivatives, a copy of the formula used to calculate the level of the index or basket on which the value of the derivative is based should be included as an

41–28

---

[41] See Henderson, *Derivatives* (LexisNexis, 2002), p.722 on this issue.
[42] His lordship made passing reference to the following authority, deciding it was of little assistance on the facts: *Winter (Executors of Sir Arthur Monro Sutherland) v IRC* [1963] A.C. 235; [1961] 3 All E.R. 855.
[43] Henderson, *Derivatives*, p.277.

appendix to the Confirmation. The traders or the financial engineers for the respective parties will have discussed the manner in which that basket should function, but it is rare for the lawyers to include such a statement in the Confirmation. Instead lawyers tend to rely on the standard ISDA wording for Confirmations, even if the transaction has a number of mathematically unusual features. The lawyer needs to anticipate mathematically unusual features of the transaction and not simply its legally unusual features. Failing to include a statement of the transaction's formula leaves the calculation agent entirely at liberty when making its calculations and it also leaves the parties with no contractual guidance as to what the underlying purpose of the contract was in the event of a dispute.

D.   Failure to deliver or to make payment

41–29   The Confirmation will also deal with the effect of a failure to deliver in relation to a physically-settled transaction or with the effect of a failure to pay in relation to a cash-settled transaction. Typically, in relation to a failure to deliver, the Confirmation will need to anticipate what measure of loss is foreseeable as a result: for example, whether delivery was required on a particular date because the buyer had obligations of its own to deliver that same property to a third party which would cause the buyer to suffer penalties for late delivery.[44] In relation to late payment in a cash settled transaction, the question is limited to the imposition of default interest on top of the amount which was payable. The position relating to late payment in relation to the Master Agreement and the Confirmation is considered in Chapter 43.[45]

E.   Mistake

The different types of mistake

41–30   Two particular forms of mistake arise with reference to the confirmation of a financial derivatives transaction. Either the mistake is made by some organisation with responsibility for the operation of the underlying market or the mistake is one made by the parties in relation to their own contract. Each is considered in turn. The law on mistakes and their effect on a contract was considered in Chapter 18.[46] Importantly, it emerged there that there might be common mistakes as to the facts surrounding a contract, or a mistake just by one party, or a misapprehension as the result of a misrepresentation, or a misunderstanding as to the proper interpretation of the contract, or an unspoken disagreement as to the

---

[44] See s.2(e), *ISDA Master Agreement,* which provides that "... [the defaulting party] will compensate the other party on demand if and to the extent provided for in the relevant Confirmation ...".

[45] See para.43–10.

[46] See para.18–03.

underlying purpose of the transaction, and so on. In truth, a wide range of different legal doctrines are important in resolving what might be considered to be a "mistake" in the broadest sense.

Market publication error

It is normal for confirmations to provide for mistakes made in the published level of an index or market. Such mistakes may be corrected, with the result that an in-the-money derivative may subsequently be considered to have been out-of-the-money, and so on. Generally, confirmations will provide that a correction must be published within 30 days of the mistake for the amount paid mistakenly to be adjusted or repaid (as appropriate). Otherwise, the general law on mistake would apply. If the mistake was made by a third party who published the index in question, then that would be a common mistake between the parties such that the transaction would be capable of rescission. A mistake by one of the parties is considered next.

41–31

Party error

The primary issue with reference to mistake is that of an error made between the parties when conducting the transaction ab initio. The position is no different with reference to a derivatives transaction from any other contract. This position was considered in Chapter 18.[47]

41–32

3.   THE MASTER AGREEMENT

A.   The role of the master agreement

The three elements of the ISDA documentation architecture—confirmation, master agreement and its schedule, and credit support document—are intended to constitute a "single agreement". The ISDA Master Agreement is in a standard form—being available from ISDA in a pre-printed form. If the parties want to amend those provisions or to select one or other of the elective provisions it includes, then they do this by making those selections in the Schedule to the Master Agreement which includes a "Part 5" and then a blank page to which the parties can add as many dozens of extra provisions as they wish. While the confirmation deals with only one transaction, the terms of the Master Agreement are intended to cover every derivative entered into between the parties. As considered in this section, the Master Agreement provides for the basis on which the parties can terminate all of their transactions, what happens if one of them goes into insolvency, the tax treatment of their derivatives and so on. If each confirmation is akin to a single game of football, then the Master Agreement constitutes the rules of the sport of football in total.

41–33

The market has moved towards an increasing "commoditisation" of derivatives products: now that "vanilla" swaps have become commoditised products, that is

41–34

---

[47] See para.18–03.

to say they conform to basic structural similarities and have few exotic features, there is often no need to create sophisticated documentation for each transaction outwith the standard model. (Indeed, such standard derivatives products will be subject to mandatory clearing through central counterparties as a result, as considered in the previous chapter.) Even with the development of more complex products, there are legal issues which have been rendered generic to these particular kinds of products with the publication of books of individual terms and definitions by ISDA for each family of products. By standardising the documentation between the parties for all derivatives transactions, the risks associated with these legal issues can be managed more efficiently across the entire derivatives market. The most recent version of the ISDA Master Agreement is that agreed in 2002, being its third edition.

41–35 The purpose of the Master Agreement, in truth, is to provide a series of escape hatches through which financial institutions can escape derivatives contracts with third parties. This, I would suggest, is a genuine account of how the ISDA Master Agreement evolved from its original form in 1987—when banks were purportedly able to enforce payment obligations on its counterparties but were obliged to pay none themselves, in some circumstances—through to the 2002 edition which developed greater equality between the parties on its face. The Master Agreement is primarily—but not exclusively—concerned to provide the parties with pretexts for terminating all of the derivatives outstanding between them and to provide mechanisms for calculating how the outstanding transactions should be cancelled out. Thinking of the Master Agreement from this perspective will make sense of the account given of it here. In this section we consider the structure of the Master Agreement; in Chapter 42 we consider *Collateralisation* and how security is taken in derivatives transactions; and in Chapter 43 we consider the important termination provisions in the Master Agreement in detail. Most of these types of provision were considered in general terms in Chapter 19.

B.   Provisions of the master agreement

Interpretation

41–36 As was considered above, the Master Agreement is intended to be interpreted as constituting a single agreement with all of the confirmations and any credit support documentation. The interpretation provision at the beginning of the master agreement suggests that provisions in the master agreement are to take priority in the event of any discrepancy between the terms of the master agreement and of either the confirmation or the credit support agreement.[48] Occasionally, one party to a master agreement will seek to argue that some external aid to interpretation should be used in relation to a master agreement or that a particular market practice should be read into the agreement (always, surprisingly enough, in a way that benefits their argument entirely). However, in the important case of *Lomas v JFB Firth Rixson*[49] this sort of argument was

---

[48] ISDA Master Agreement s.1(b).
[49] [2010] EWHC 3372 (Ch), [2011] 2 B.C.L.C. 120.

dismissed by the very strong judgment of Briggs J. It had been argued on behalf of the administrators of the insolvent investment bank Lehman Brothers that terms should be read into an ISDA Master Agreement so as to infer a requirement of "reasonableness" in the calculation of the amounts payable on the termination of derivatives transactions and so forth. Briggs J. held that there was no reason to read such a standard of reasonableness into the parties' extensive documentation, nor was there anything on the facts of that case to justify such inferences in the parties' contract. Rather, Briggs J. held that:

> "The ISDA Master Agreement is one of the most widely used forms of agreement in the world. It is probably the most important standard market agreement used in the financial world. English law is one of the two systems of law most commonly chosen for the interpretation of the Master Agreement, the other being New York law. It is axiomatic that it should, as far as possible, be interpreted in a way that serves the objectives of clarity, certainty and predictability, so that the very large number of parties using it should know where they stand…"[50]

In essence the parties were to be held to the precise terms of their bargain without any further terms being read in nor particular principles of construction being applied so as to turn the interpretation away from an ordinary reading of the words which the parties had used. That leaves little room for error when the documentation is being drafted and negotiated—and is part of the reason why those negotiations can take many years.

Late payment

The master agreement provides that the parties are obliged to make all payments required of them by the calculation agent under the terms of any transaction or any confirmation.[51] By specifying that all payments calculated by reference to the confirmation are to be paid as a contractual obligation under the master agreement, each payment is susceptible to payment netting under the master agreement, and to set-off on insolvency, and importantly it may trigger an event of default leading to termination of the parties' dealings, as considered below. Failure to pay under a cash-settled transaction may cause termination of the master agreement; whereas late payment may only trigger an obligation to pay default interest (under the wording of some master agreements).[52] With reference to physically-settled transactions, it is important that the confirmation should deal with the mechanism for calculating damages for late payment, as well as setting out the scope of issues which are entitled to be taken into account in calculating the parties' loss under the relevant transactions.

41–37

Condition precedent

The ISDA Master Agreement specifies that it is a condition precedent of the formation of the contract under either the master agreement or the payment of

41–38

---

[50] Referring to *Scandinavian Trading Tanker Co, v Flota Petrolera Ecuatoriana* [1983] Q.B. 529 ("the Scaptrade") per Robert Goff L.J. at 540.
[51] ISDA Master Agreement, s.2(a)(i).
[52] ISDA Master Agreement, s.2(a)(i).

any obligation under a Confirmation that no event of default, actual or potential, has occurred and is continuing at the time any such payment is made.[53] This provision enables the parties to avoid the contract ab initio in the event that there is any hidden defect in the capacity or credit worth of the counterparty.[54] This express, contractual form of condition precedent is therefore set out as a mechanism which enables either party to rescind or terminate the contract where it later transpires that the requirements were not satisfied, as considered below.[55] A stream of litigation relating to the precise interpretation of the condition precedent provision in s.2 of the ISDA Master Agreement has arisen. This litigation is considered at the end of this chapter.

Force majeure

41–39 In the 2002 version of the ISDA Master Agreement there was included for the first time (in its standard version) a force majeure provision. In the abstract, such a provision might take two forms. First, force majeure might cover inhuman forces such as earthquakes, hurricanes and other "acts of god". Alternatively, force majeure might extend to include human activity such as coups d'etat—in effect, political risk—and more random events—loosely dubbed "terrorism" and relating generally to the destruction of property or kidnapping. In effect the purpose is the same. Should such an event take place, the 2002 version of the ISDA Master Agreement defines this as constituting a termination event. Its inclusion as a termination event (rather than as an event of default) is significant because it gives the parties the opportunity to search for a means of continuing with their transaction regardless of the occurrence without calling an automatic termination to their dealings.[56]

Payment netting

41–40 Payment netting entitles the parties to a Master Agreement to set off amounts owed reciprocally between them. It is possible in theory for the parties to elect to set off across all of their derivatives transactions of whatever type; but in practice no bank's systems would be able to set off across currencies, let alone between different types of derivative (i.e. between interest rate swaps, equity options, bond options, credit default swaps, and so on) because each of these types of business is usually booked through a different operations systems from the others. Therefore it is practicality rather than legal concepts which control the extent of payment netting in practice. There is an express provision in the ISDA Master Agreement for the netting of payments which are either to be made in the same currency or in respect of the same derivatives transaction.[57] The standard ISDA

---

[53] ISDA Master Agreement, s.2(a)(iii).

[54] ISDA Master Agreement, s.2(a)(iii).

[55] However, this provision in the ISDA Master Agreement was ignored by all of the courts in the local authority swaps cases: see, for example, *Westdeutsche Landesbank v Islington LBC* [1996] A.C. 669, [1996] 2 All E.R. 961, HL.

[56] ISDA Master Agreement s.5(b)(ii).

[57] ISDA Master Agreement, s.2(c).

provision is for payment netting to be effected within a single transaction.[58] However, that provision is frequently altered to provide for payment netting to be made across different transactions contracted in the same currency, where payment is to be made on the same date.[59]

Withholding tax

The parties will generally contract to make all payments without deduction of tax. That means that any tax required to be withheld by a party as a result of any withholding tax will have to be paid by that party but also means that the counterparty is still entitled to receive the full amount owed to it. Therefore, in situations where any withholding tax will be liable from the inception of any transaction, the parties may choose to gross up the amounts to be paid; that is, so that the payer is required to pay a larger amount such that the payee will receive the amount it had anticipated but after deduction of tax by the payer.[60] If a withholding tax is introduced at a later date after entering into the transaction, then this may constitute a termination event which brings the parties' transactions to an end.

41–41

Representations and the effect of their unenforceability

It is usual in a master agreement to have the parties make representations as to their competence to enter into each and every transaction and as to the formal validity of their entry into the contract through their agents, whether employees or fiduciaries. It is therefore necessary, as considered in Chapter 18, to consider the capacity of one's counterparty to enter into a contract, particularly when it is a novel form of complex derivative because if that counterparty does not have the legal capacity to enter into that contract then that contract will be void ab initio.[61] The purpose of the representation made in the Master Agreement is that if the representation is false in any way then the agreement's termination provisions are triggered.

41–42

However, if the party had no capacity to enter into the Master Agreement then it also had no capacity to agree to be bound by the orderly termination provisions in that agreement either: therefore, the parties will be forced to fall back on the general law for the recovery of such moneys as discussed in Chapter 20 of this book. The risks associated with the party having no capacity or the agent having no authority to bind the party are very great. All of the parties' attempts to control the risks between them by means of their documentation will be ineffective. It was found in *Westdeutsche Landesbank Girozentrale v London Borough of*

41–43

---

[58] ISDA Master Agreement, s.2(c).
[59] Which approach is taken is generally a matter which depends upon the operations systems capabilities of each party. Were it possible, set-off could be effected across all transactions payable on the same payment date across currencies. The restriction is practical rather than theoretical.
[60] ISDA Master Agreement, s.2(d).
[61] *Westdeutsche Landesbank v Islington* [1996] A.C. 669.

Islington[62] expressly that no term in the contract could be efficacious if the contract itself had been held to be void.[63] As Leggatt L.J. put it:

> "The parties believed that they were making an interest rate swap contract. They were not, because such a contract was *ultra vires* the local authority. So that they made no contract at all."[64]

Therefore, the termination provisions based on the representation, the credit support language and all of the other provisions would be ineffective because the entire contract was beyond the powers of the defendant.

41–44   There is a further question as to the authority of the signatory to enter into the contract on behalf of the party to the contract.[65] The detail of the law of agency and of the authority of agents—such as employees and fund managers—is considered in detail in Chapter 18 *Validity of contracts*.[66] The representation which is usually sought is that the signatory, as listed on any signatory register authorised by the board of directors within the terms of the company's memorandum and articles of association, does have the authority to bind its principal to the agreement.

Regulatory observance and illegality

41–45   The parties typically represent that nothing in the creation or performance of the agreement will constitute an illegality in any of the jurisdictions in which performance, or any action taken in connection with the transaction, will be carried out,[67] and that there is no litigation outstanding which would call into question the validity of the contract.[68] The parties also represent that any necessary regulatory approvals have been acquired. They also represent that all of the obligations which they assume as part of the agreement are legally binding upon them.[69] The logical point must be made again that if the obligations assumed by the party have no legal validity under their governing law such that the contract is deemed to be void ab initio, then any such representation or any contractual rights purportedly founded on it would be similarly ineffective.[70]

4.   CREDIT PROTECTION AND COLLATERALISATION

41–46   Credit protection and collateralisation are discussed in detail in the next chapter, Chapter 42 *Collateralisation*.

---

[62] [1996] A.C. 669.

[63] *Westdeutsche Landesbank v Islington* [1994] 4 All E.R. 890, 967, per Leggatt L.J. See also A. Hudson, "Proprietary rights in financial transactions" (1997: 2) *Amicus Curiae*, 27.

[64] See above.

[65] *ISDA Master Agreement,* s.3(a).

[66] See para.18–27

[67] ISDA Master Agreement, s.5(b)(i).

[68] ISDA Master Agreement, s.3(a).

[69] ISDA Master Agreement, s.3(a).

[70] *Westdeutsche Landesbank v Islington* [1994] 4 All E.R. 890, 967, per Leggatt L.J.

5.   Termination of the Master Agreement

The termination procedure is considered in detail in Chapter 43.   **41–47**

6.   The Schedule to the Master Agreement

A.   The schedule to the master agreement in standard form

The role of the Schedule in recasting the standard terms

The Schedule to the Master Agreement is the arena in which the counterparties   **41–48**
seek to control their legal risk. This is the portion of the documentation which is
negotiated between the parties to amend the standard provisions of the pro forma
master agreement. The usual method of negotiating these documents is an
exchange between the parties of their own standard form schedules which seek to
gain them what they perceive to be the maximum advantage. The major
categories of legal risk dealt with in the schedule are: credit risk; alteration in
corporate structure; insolvency; default under the terms of the transaction; and
tax. Each of these various categories is considered in the substantive sections of
this chapter. The Schedule has some portions which the parties are (as suggested
by the hard copy agreement) required to fill in by hand (or, today, insert
electronically), and other places where the parties select whether or not they want
particular provisions of the standard form Master Agreement to apply to their
transactions, and yet other places where the parties can include as many new
provisions as they wish. There is nothing compulsory about the ISDA Master
Agreement—it is after all a voluntary contract advocated by a trade association—
and therefore the parties may choose which transactions they want to affirm and
those which they do not.

The inter-relationship between the Schedule and the Master Agreement's termination provisions

Among the most significant matters for the parties to decide in the Master   **41–49**
Agreement is which of the standard termination provisions are to apply between
them and also which of their affiliated entities can be caught within those entities
whose defaults will trigger the termination of the Master Agreement. The
termination provisions are considered in Chapter 43.

The parties

In relation to the parties to a master agreement there are two central questions: **41–50**
which counterparty company should be made a party to the contract and which
counterparty group companies should be referred to in the contract for credit
control purposes? The first stage in the documentation is to identify the relevant
parties to the transaction. Derivatives business is frequently conducted through
special purpose vehicles. In the case of financial institutions this is often to

ring-fence derivatives business for regulatory purposes: either to centre transactions on a company which is overseen by a specific regulator or which is beyond the jurisdiction of that regulator.

41–51 From a credit perspective there may be a difference between the entity which conducts the derivatives business and the most creditworthy company in counterparty's group, usually trading entities as opposed to special purpose vehicles. There is the further credit consideration that a default by another entity in the counterparty's group may indicate a likelihood that the counterparty itself will go into default under the derivative transaction in the future. Therefore, as is considered in Chapter 43, when constructing the credit protection machinery in the Master Agreement, the ISDA code requires the parties to identify not only which entities will be parties to the Master Agreement but also which other group companies or affiliated entities should be drawn into the agreement such that their defaults on other transactions will constitute a default under the ISDA Master Agreement. This process known as *cross default* where a default in one transaction infects another transaction, or a default by one company infects the credit worth of another company to which it is linked.[71] The selection of the appropriate counterparty affiliates and group companies to be incorporated into the credit provisions in the Master Agreement is therefore a centrally important credit decision. Thus, the standard ISDA master agreement approach works by isolating each "Specified Entity" (to use the jargon) which is to be incorporated into the contract for the purpose of establishing the counterparties' credit worth. The definition of entities which are included for credit support purposes creates the total set of companies whose default in the types of transaction referred to, will initiate a default. So, if a Specified Entity of Xavier Bank commits a default under a specified type of transaction with a third party (perhaps it fails to make an interest payment on a syndicated loan), then that will trigger an event of default under the derivatives master agreement which Xavier Bank has with its counterparty. The Master Agreement therefore aggregates all the possible defaults of a range of entities—both the parties and any Specified Entities—across their derivatives business between each other, their derivatives business with third parties, and in relation to their general borrowings. The idea, as considered in Chapter 43, is that it should be possible for a party who is not in default to terminate the Master Agreement and all outstanding transactions under that agreement if the counterparty or any Specified Entity commits an event of default under any of the types of transaction—derivatives, ordinary debt, or whatever—which are specified in the Master Agreement.

Conflict of laws questions

41–52 There is a very significant cross-border element to derivatives transactions which raises questions of private international law (also known as "conflict of laws")—as was discussed in Chapter 6—as to the governing law of a transaction, as to which system of law should govern any private law dispute arising in connection with that agreement, and the jurisdiction in which any litigation or

---

[71] See para.19–49.

arbitration is to take place. Thus a choice of governing law and of jurisdiction is made in the Schedule to the Master Agreement, and will be binding under private international law. That will be decisive of contract law questions but not necessarily of other private law questions, particularly when the parties are acting through branches in different jurisdictions or complying with regulation in different jurisdictions. Therefore, the Schedule also requires the parties to identify the branches through which either party will act.

Calculation agent

The role of the calculation agent is very important in derivatives transactions. In relation to Confirmations, it is the calculation agent who identifies whether or not a transaction is in-the-money and how much is required to be paid by whom to whom. The more complex the transaction, the more significant the role of the calculation agent in measuring the level of indices (particularly if the transaction requires that the parties create their own index or basket of instruments) or the performance of sophisticated products. In relation to Master Agreements, the calculation agent's role is most significant in relation to the calculation of the termination amounts which are necessary to terminate the outstanding transactions by reducing them to single, net figures. Clearly, calculating the value of all outstanding transactions and the amounts owed by each party one to another under those transactions, and then converting them into a single currency (as specified in the Master Agreement) is an important and complex mathematical task. Therefore, selecting which party is to act as calculation agent is important; as is identifying how the parties will deal with the situation in which the findings of the calculation agent are disputed. This office was considered in para.19–43 in general terms. **41–53**

Credit support documents

The Schedule also provides details as to the credit support documents on which the parties are reliant, for example, in relation to the agreement's termination procedures. **41–54**

Set-off on insolvency

The Schedule will also be the place in which the parties will include a provision which ensures that they can set off amounts owed under all of the Confirmations which are outstanding and which are bound into a single agreement with the Master Agreement. The law on set-off on insolvency was considered in Chapter 22.[72] **41–55**

---

[72] See para.22–91.

B. Issues as the precise drafting of the master agreement

The condition precedent conundrum

41–56 A significant difficulty with the drafting of the ISDA Master Agreement has arisen in recent cases. (In truth, the ISDA documentation in its standard form has a number of defects.) There is a logical inconsistency in that the parties expect to set off amounts owed between them, but that set-off only applies if the amounts are "payable". And yet, s.2(a)(iii) provides that no amounts are payable if there is an event of default in existence. So, if a party has failed to make a payment, then that constitutes an event of default, which means that there is no amount "payable" which means that set-off cannot apply. Therefore, the non-defaulting party cannot set off amounts it owes against amounts owed to it. It fell to the courts to unravel this problem. The ISDA provisions are as follows, before the text to follow examines the case law. The form of s.2 which was used in the master agreement in *Lomas v JFB Firth Rixson Inc*[73] and in *AWB (Geneva) SA v North America Steamships Ltd*[74] was in the following standard form:

> "(a) General Conditions
> (i) Each party will make each payment or delivery specified in each Confirmation to be made by it, subject to the other provisions of this Agreement.
> (ii) Payments under this Agreement will be made on the due date for value on that date in the place of the account specified in the relevant Confirmation or otherwise pursuant to this Agreement, …
> (iii) Each obligation of each party under Section 2(a)(i) is subject to (1) the condition precedent that no Event of Default or Potential Event of Default with respect to the other party has occurred and is continuing, (2) the condition precedent that no Early Termination Date in respect of the relevant transaction has occurred or been effectively designated and (3) each other applicable condition precedent specified in this Agreement.
> (c) *Netting.* If on any date amounts would otherwise be payable:—
> (i) in the same currency; and
> (ii) in respect of the same Transaction,
> by each party to the other, then, on such date, each party's obligation to make payment of any such amount will be automatically satisfied and discharged and, if the aggregate amount that would otherwise have been payable by one party exceeds the aggregate amount that would otherwise have been payable by the other party, replaced by an obligation upon the party by whom the larger aggregate amount would have been payable to pay to the other party the excess of the larger aggregate amount over the smaller aggregate amount."

The first problem of interpretation arose in *Marine Trade SA v Pioneer Freight Futures Co Ltd BVI*[75] in which Flaux J. considered forward freight agreements executed under a 1992 ISDA Master Agreement. The first problem of interpretation was in effect whether the s.2(a)(iii) condition precedent effects a once-and-for-all termination of the obligation to make payment or merely a suspensory termination of the obligation to make payment. It was held by Flaux J. that because the defendant had been in breach, then the claimant was relieved

---

[73] [2010] EWHC 3372 (Ch); [2011] 2 B.C.L.C. 120, at [11].
[74] [2007] EWCA Civ 739; [2007] B.P.I.R. 1023.
[75] *Marine Trade SA v Pioneer Freight Futures Co Ltd BVI* [2009] EWHC 2656 (Comm); [2009] All E.R. (D) 30 (Nov).

of its obligation to make payment to the defendant on a literal reading of s.2(a)(iii).[76] This had the effect that under s.2(c) "credit only had to be given, by way of netting, for an amount that was payable, and not for an amount that, because of an unfulfilled condition precedent under Section 2(a)(iii), was not payable".[77] It was held further that the claimant bore the burden of proving that the defendant had committed an event of default.[78]

Flaux J. advanced this analysis again in the later case of *Pioneer Freight Futures v COSCO Bulk Carriers*.[79] However, Gloster J. refused to follow either judgment in *Pioneer Freight Futures v TMT Asia*,[80] as is considered below, on the basis that it was against the overall purpose of the ISDA Master Agreement when interpreted as a whole.   **41–57**

Suspensory or permanent interruption?

The nature of the condition precedent was also considered by Briggs J in *Lomas v JFB Firth Rixson Inc.*[81] This case was an application brought by the administrators of the insolvent bank Lehman Brothers which, inter alia, revolved around whether or not the condition precedent in s.2(a)(iii) meant that payment did not have to be made under outstanding derivatives. Lehman Brothers had gone into Chapter 11 protection under the US bankruptcy code, which it was accepted by the parties fell within the event of default in s.5(a)(vii) of their master agreement as a bankruptcy event. An event of default had consequently taken place. Therefore, it was argued on behalf of the defendant that it was not obliged to make payment under any outstanding derivatives transaction on the basis that s.2(a)(iii) constituted a continuing obligation which was a condition precedent to each obligation to make payment under any such transaction. It was argued on behalf of the claimant administrator that the condition precedent under s.2(a)(iii) should be deemed only to operate for a "reasonable period", even though such a concept of reasonableness does not appear in the provision itself. Briggs J. considered that the terms of s.2(a)(iii) "leave significant matters unsaid about the condition precedent to any payment obligation, namely that no event of default or potential event of default with respect to the other party has occurred and is continuing".[82]   **41–58**

---

[76] The decision in *Deutsche Morgan Grenfell Group Plc v IRC* [2007] 1 A.C. 588 [2007] 1 All E.R. 449 was applied by Flaux J.

[77] This is how Briggs J. summarised the argument of Flaux J. in *Lomas v AFB Firth Rixson* [2010] EWHC 3372 (Ch), [2011] 2 B.C.L.C. 120, [61] which Flaux J. in turn accepted as an accurate summary in *Pioneer Freight Futures v COSCO Bulk Carriers* [2011] EWHC 1692 (Comm).

[78] [2009] EWHC 2656 (Comm), [30]. It is suggested that this decision is unfortunate in the context of the ISDA Master Agreement as a whole because, for example, in the event of the defendant's insolvency it would be unable to set its payment obligations off against the amounts owed to it by the claimant on this analysis. Or, to put the point more accurately, the defendant would not be entitled on these facts to obtain the net surplus of US$ 5 million which the claimant owed to it so as to maximise the amount available to its creditors.

[79] [2011] EWHC 1692 (Comm).

[80] [2011] EWHC 1888 (Comm).

[81] [2010] EWHC 3372 (Ch); [2011] 2 B.C.L.C. 120, at [11].

[82] [2010] EWHC 3372 (Ch); [2011] 2 B.C.L.C. 120, at [58].

41–59   Two arguments were raised: first, that if there was an event of default in existence then no obligation to make payment ever arose (a "once and for all" interpretation); alternatively, that the obligation to make payment was only suspended while the event of default was in existence but that the obligation to pay awoke again if the event of default was cured (a "suspensory" interpretation). Briggs J. considered the approach taken by the New South Wales Supreme Court in *Enron Australia v TXU Electricity* that the suspensory approach was preferable,[83] and upheld the suspensory approach. It was held that "the once and for all construction would produce a pointlessly draconian outcome, in the event of a minor and momentary default"[84] and furthermore that it would include a Potential Event of Default which might not mature into a full event of default in any event.[85]

41–60   The issue which flows from the finding by Briggs J. that the better interpretation is a suspensory approach means that the obligation to pay may be reignited at a later date. The question arises as to the length of time for which the suspense of that obligation to pay may last: either "until the end of the Transaction" or indefinitely. The argument (advanced on behalf of ISDA) that the obligations should be "indefinite" was based in part on s.9(c) which provided that "the obligations of the parties under this Agreement will survive the termination of any Transaction".[86] Briggs J. held that the obligation could be suspended only until the end of the Transaction because the "indefinite" analysis was unworkably open-ended in that it gave rise to "indefinite contingent liabilities" and thus was not what the parties could have intended.[87] A third interpretation of s.2(a)(iii) was advanced by the administrators of Lehman Brothers: it was argued that that provision "serves a specific limited purpose, namely to protect the Non-defaulting Party from making payments to the Defaulting Party while exposed to that party's credit risk in the future".[88] There is some attraction in this argument. However, Briggs J. rejected it on the basis that there are derivatives, such as hedging transactions, in relation to which there are reasons for the condition precedent other than the protection of the non-defaulting party.

---

[83] [2003] NSWSC 1169, at [12].

[84] [2010] EWHC 3372 (Ch); [2011] 2 B.C.L.C. 120, at [73].

[85] It should be noted, however, that a Potential Event of Default is defined in s.14 of the ISDA Master Agreement as being "any event which … would constitute an Event of Default", and so the distinction between the level of culpability in the two situations is more apparent than real because the former must constitute the latter.

[86] This is a good example of the confusion in the ISDA Master Agreement as to whether this provision is intended to operate across all transactions or only in relation to a specific transaction. Indeed it is a somewhat counter-intuitive provision because on the one hand the termination procedure seeks to terminate all outstanding transactions by novating them into a new contract in satisfaction of all earlier obligations and yet s.9(c) provides that those obligations may persist even after termination. A better reading of the provision would be that it is the other obligations (as to making representations and so forth) under the agreement which persist.

[87] [2010] EWHC 3372 (Ch); [2011] 2 B.C.L.C. 120, at [78].

[88] [2010] EWHC 3372 (Ch); [2011] 2 B.C.L.C. 120 at [81].

Taking the trade association's word for it: a purposive approach

The question which fell to be decided in *Pioneer Freight Futures v TMT Asia*[89] **41-61** was this: if a party is in breach of the condition precedent in s.2(a)(iii) (e.g. because there is an event of default in existence) should the payment that it owes or is owed be treated as not being "payable", and in consequence should that payment be treated as not being available for set-off under s.2(c)?[90] Gloster J. took a view which was based on the interpretation of the master agreement as a whole,[91] which relied on the dicta of Lord Mance in *In re Sigma Finance Corporation*,[92] to the effect that in interpreting a commercial contract one should not fixate on the literal meaning of a particular provision where that would lead one away from the overall purpose of the entire agreement. Gloster J. considered that because the overall purpose of the ISDA Master Agreement was to achieve payment netting and set-off then s.2 should be interpreted as requiring that all amounts should be brought into account in the set-off, including the amounts which would have been payable but for the event of default which triggered the condition precedent in s.2(a)(iii).

Interestingly, what Gloster J. was doing was reaching outside the wording of the **41-62** contract (which was clearly ambiguous) and looking beyond any contractual intention of the parties themselves, and instead trying to uncover an unspoken and unwritten intention which the trade association which oversaw the writing of the master agreement claims is the true meaning of that master agreement. In truth, the master agreement can necessarily be adapted by the parties to suit their needs and therefore it is the parties' intentions and not ISDA's intentions which should take precedence. When ISDA had failed so clearly to generate a watertight agreement, it is odd to rely on them for the proper analysis of their work. Moreover, under the doctrine of precedent we might have thought that Gloster J. would have been bound by the earlier decision of Flaux J. (unless, like Briggs J. she managed to produce a pretext for distinguishing her case from it): but instead her ladyship treated it as just another interpretation of a contractual provision which she could choose to take or leave depending on her analysis of the case before her.

---

[89] [2011] EWHC 1888 (Comm).

[90] A further issue arises here as to why any payments should be payable on a gross basis at all, as opposed to all payments under the master agreement being terminated at the same time – the better reading, it is suggested is that the entirety of payments under the master agreement should be treated as being either payable or not payable en masse, without any division between some payments and other payments. This point is considered in the text below.

[91] The ISDA Master Agreement at issue was the 1992 form.

[92] [2009] UKSC 2, [2010] 1 All E.R. 571, relying inter alia in turn on *Charter Reinsurance Co Ltd (In Liquidation) v Fagan* [1997] A.C. 313.

CHAPTER 42

COLLATERALISATION

CORE PRINCIPLES

Collateralisation is a blanket term for different sets of techniques for taking security in derivatives transactions (and also in relation to some stock-lending and repo transactions). These techniques are predicated on the models discussed in Chapter 22. Collateralisation, in essence, relates to the provision of assets by one contracting party to its counterparty equal to the exposure which that counterparty has to derivative transactions with the party providing those assets. For example, if Alpha owes £x to Beta on a net basis across the hundred transactions outstanding between Alpha and Beta, then Alpha will be required to make assets worth £x available to Beta until those transactions have been performed satisfactorily. When the exposure between the parties changes then Alpha will be entitled either to recover assets or to post further assets, as appropriate.

Collateralisation may take the form of "personal collateral" whereby assets ("collateral") are transferred outright by one party to the other, subject to a contractual obligation on the recipient to return those assets once the underlying transactions have been performed. This form of structure is documented normally by means of the ISDA Credit Support Annex. Alternatively, collateralisation may be "proprietary collateral" whereby the secured party acquires proprietary rights in the collateral but must hold those assets either on trust, or subject to a charge or a pledge or a mortgage in favour of the counterparty who provided the collateral initially. This form of structure is documented normally by means of the ISDA Credit Support Deed. In this second structure, the party providing collateral runs a lesser risk that its counterparty will not return collateral; whereas in the former structure the party providing collateral bears the risk that its counterparty will breach its merely contractual obligation to return collateral of like kind.

The collateral structures used in standard form in the marketplace have a number of drawbacks—for example, describing the rights acquired by the parties as being "mortgage, charge and pledge" where such a combination of rights is doctrinally impossible because those three property law models are different. The practical application of collateralisation is bedevilled by practitioners who do not think clearly about what it is that they are trying to achieve from the techniques which were set out in Chapter 22, and who instead are content to follow the herd's use of doctrinally suspect contractual structures. Collateralisation has been adopted as part of English law by means of implementing the EC Collateral Directive and by UK statutory instrument.

1. INTRODUCTION

42–01   The derivatives markets have developed a particular collection of techniques when seeking to take security in relation to their transactions known as *collateralisation*.[1] It is important to understand from the outset that there is no single activity which constitutes collateralisation: instead, collateralisation is a collective term for a range of different ways of taking security when used in

---

[1] This chapter draws on elements of Alastair Hudson, *The Law on Financial Derivatives*, 5th edn (London: Sweet & Maxwell, 2012), Ch.12 "Collateralisation".

derivatives and other complex financial markets. These techniques build on the basic blocks for taking security which were discussed in detail in Chapter 22 *Taking security*. Collateralisation is nothing new to a lawyer familiar with the legal techniques for taking security. There is no compulsion to use collateralisation: rather, the markets have developed ways of using collateralisation ideas to their advantage beyond simply taking security. In essence, all collateralisation requires the parties to derivatives transactions to identify their exposures to each other under their various transactions, and to "put aside" securities or money equal to their net exposure in the event that one or other of them should default on their obligations. The manner in which these assets are "put aside" is a question which we will consider below. By putting assets aside by way of collateral, the parties might be thought to be incurring greater expense. However, as will emerge below, by measuring their exposures to derivatives and covering them with collateral structures, financial institutions are able to reduce their obligations to post capital for their regulators. Having to put regulatory capital aside to satisfy regulators (so as to offset a proportion of the amounts owed in an institution's derivatives business) is expensive for a financial institution. Thus, in the era of financialisation,[2] the impulse of financial institutions is to use yet more financial techniques, like collateralisation, to reduce their regulatory capital costs and to deal with risk, as opposed simply to using guarantees, trusts and so forth.

This chapter considers, first, the commercial issues underpinning collateral **42–02** structures[3]; secondly, the EC Collateral Directive[4] and the UK collateral regulations[5]; thirdly, the International Swaps and Derivatives Association's ("ISDA") *personal* collateral structure (the ISDA Credit Support Annex)[6]; fourthly, ISDA's *proprietary* collateral structure (the Credit Support Deed)[7]; and fifthly legal issues which arise from these structures. The principal focus of this chapter, however, is on the ISDA documentation and the structures that are used in practice. The legislation has been cast in an effort to mirror that market practice which is, as will emerge, probably unfortunate.

2. THE FOUNDATIONS OF COLLATERALISATION

A. Collateralisation in a nutshell

As was highlighted above, collateralisation requires the parties to derivatives (and **42–03** some other) transactions to identify their exposures to each other under their various transactions. That is, at frequent intervals the parties have to identify the open market value of all of their outstanding derivatives transactions (known as

---

[2] See para.1–71.
[3] See para.42–06.
[4] See para.42–15.
[5] See para.42–21.
[6] See para.42–33.
[7] See para.42–51.

"marking-to-market"[8]) which are covered by the collateral agreement. The parties then identify the net exposure: that is, the excess which one party owes to the other at that date once all of the outstanding amounts have been set off on the derivatives transactions between them. Having identified that one party ("the debtor") owes a net amount to its counterparty ("the secured party"), the debtor is required to "put aside"[9] an amount of assets in the form of securities or money ("the collateral") equal to that net exposure. There are questions as to how one values the outstanding transactions and how one selects and values the type of asset which is to be provided as the collateral. The process of "putting aside" the collateral shall occupy us first. I have used a deliberately neutral expression at this stage because the way in which the collateral may be provided will differ significantly from case to case. Putting aside the assets may involve either the secured party taking an outright transfer of those assets, or alternatively of the secured party holding those assets so that the debtor retains a proprietary right in them. The mechanism which is used will depend on the parties' contractual negotiations and perceptions of the credit risk involved. First, we shall distinguish between these two types of collateral.

B.   The two principal forms of collateral

42–04   There are, broadly-speaking, two types of collateralisation, which we will refer to in this chapter as "personal collateral" and "proprietary collateral". They are my own terminology and not market usages. They reflect a lawyer's understanding of these transactions. The term "personal collateral" refers to the situation in which a secured party receives an outright transfer of assets from its counterparty with only a *personal* obligation to re-transfer assets of a like kind or of an equivalent value to that counterparty if the counterparty performs its obligations under the derivatives transaction.[10] This form of collateral is dubbed "personal collateral" because the secured party owes only personal, contractual obligations to re-transfer property to the counterparty,[11] as opposed to any proprietary obligations (such as holding assets on trust[12] or subject to a charge or subject to a possessory obligation such as a pledge[13]). By contrast, "proprietary collateral" refers to the situation in which a counterparty transfers assets to the secured party such that the secured party owes obligations to the counterparty to preserve those very assets which were transferred to it by holding them on trust,[14] or subject to a fixed charge[15] or a mortgage,[16] or subject to a possessory obligation such as a

---

[8] The problem with "marking to market", as emerged in 2008, is that no value can be obtained if there is no properly functioning market able to publish a price; or alternatively the market value on Tuesday may be a fraction of what the market value had been on Monday if there is a market crash.

[9] This is not a market jargon term: it is a general term I am using here for ease of reference at the start.

[10] See para.41–01 et seq.

[11] See para.42–33 et seq.

[12] See para.21–01 et seq.

[13] See para.22–64 et seq.

[14] See para.21–01 et seq.

[15] See para.22–47 et seq.

[16] See para.22–30 et seq.

pledge,[17] or subject to some retention of title in favour of the counterparty.[18] Thus, if the secured party were to go into insolvency or if it were to fail to perform its obligations to retransfer those assets under the derivative contract, then the counterparty would have proprietary rights in the collateral assets so as to secure its position.

There is therefore a simple distinction to be made in any collateral structure: either the counterparty posting collateral assets has purely personal rights against the secured party in contract law, or the counterparty has proprietary rights against segregated assets held by the secured party. This was a core distinction made in Chapter 22 in relation to taking security generally. Similarly, the secured party will either take absolute title in the collateral assets under a personal collateral structure, or else it will be obliged to hold the collateral assets to the account of its counterparty (unless and until the counterparty fails to perform its obligations under the derivative contract) under a proprietary collateral structure. The mechanics of these various structures are considered in detail below. There are a number of commercial complexities as to which form of structure is used, how it is priced and so forth (as considered in the next section of this chapter); nevertheless, the legal questions resolve themselves to this simple distinction between having purely personal or proprietary rights in the collateral assets. What is important to note at this stage is that the structures on those menus are simply stylised methods of taking security which are already well-known to all commercial lawyers.

42–05

3.   COMMERCIAL ISSUES WITH COLLATERAL STRUCTURES

A.   The requirement for collateral

The first issue is the commercial decision whether or not collateral is required at all. It is now usual to take collateral in derivatives markets between financial institutions because the existence of a collateral arrangement can be used to offset regulatory capital requirements and because the volatility in the marketplace since the collapses in Asian economies and the Russian banking moratorium in the 1990s made banks nervous of one another's credit worth. In the wake of the 2007–09 global financial crisis the requirement for collateral is not going to ease. Before these market events it was more common to take collateral only from parties of lower credit worth. In the early days of collateralisation, it was common to use trusts to hold collateral property taken from the counterparty and to hold those assets to one side on trust until the counterparties' obligations under the outstanding derivatives transactions were performed.

42–06

Collateralisation has since developed into a means of holding a running account between the parties so that their net exposure between one another can be offset. The secret of collateral is that by simple arithmetic, the huge notional exposures which institutions have to one another under their derivatives transactions can be reduced to a much smaller, single net amount. By generating a purely net amount

42–07

---

[17] See para.22–64 et seq.
[18] See para.22–20.

across as many of those transactions for which the calculation of such a net exposure is feasible for the parties' operations systems, it is possible to reduce the parties' total exposure for regulatory capital purposes either to a single net sum (if their operations systems allow) or to a series of smaller net sums for each type of derivatives business conducted.[19] Some banks' operations systems will only set off in relation to the same currency, or the same type of derivative, or the same geographic location, or any combination of those three. The limitations on this mathematical exercise are consequently purely practical, as opposed to being legal limitations.

B. The type of asset taken as collateral

42–08   The second issue is then as to the type of asset that is required to be provided as collateral. (Market usage in this context is to refer to whatever property is taken to secure a transaction as being itself "collateral".) Collateral is usually provided in cash or in securities. The parties will often not wish to provide cash, of whatever currency, because that is considered to be an expensive form of security. The securities are usually taken in the form of bonds, not equities. The choice in relation to bonds is then between high-quality, sovereign debt with governmental support, and the less attractive, high-quality corporate bonds. The amount of collateral which is required to be posted will depend on the form of the collateral itself. The more volatile the value of non-cash collateral, the greater the risk of the collateral itself decreasing in value. It is usually the case that bonds are taken at a discount to their market value to allow for this potential for a change in their value or a change in applicable foreign exchange markets. Deciding what level of collateral to take is a credit decision for the parties involved. During the credit crunch, lower value assets were taken as collateral on occasion.

42–09   The property which is defined as constituting "financial collateral" under the Collateral Regulations is in turn defined to cover "either cash or financial instruments".[20] The financial instruments which are taken to fall within this definition are[21] "shares in companies" or "securities equivalent to shares in companies"; bonds or other instruments acknowledging indebtedness "if these are tradeable on the capital market"; and any other securities, including instruments such as physically-settled options, forwards and warrants "which are normally dealt in" and "which give the right to acquire any such shares, bonds, instruments or other securities",[22] equivalent cash-settled instruments; and units in a collective investment scheme,[23] eligible debt securities within the meaning of the Uncertificated Securities Regulations 2001, money market instruments; and "claims relating to or rights in or in respect of any of the financial instruments included in this definition and any rights, privileges or benefits attached to or

---

[19] Collateral Directive 2002, considered at para.42–15.
[20] Financial Collateral Arrangements (No.2) Regulations 2003, art.3.
[21] Financial Collateral Arrangements (No.2) Regulations 2003, art.3.
[22] The right to acquire can take place by subscription, purchase or exchange or which give rise to a cash settlement (excluding instruments of payment).
[23] See A.S. Hudson, *The Law and Regulation of Finance*, para.52–01.

arising from any such financial instruments".[24] This puts into statutory language the general market practice for arrangements which fall within the protections offered by the Collateral Regulations.

Bonds, and indeed nearly all securities, are typically issued in "dematerialised" form—that is, they are issued under a global note and title in them is evidenced by an entry in an electronic register. The problem with global notes used in bond issues being taken as collateral is that it is difficult to identify with sufficient certainty the property which is being subjected to a proprietary collateral structure because no rightholder has ownership of any distinct asset. Without sufficient certainty of subject matter, proprietary collateral structures will be void. This issue was considered in detail in Chapter 22,[25] and bonds were considered in Chapter 34.

42–10

There are also questions in a cross-border derivatives market as to the enforceability of security rights created in a collateral arrangement governed by English law over property held in a jurisdiction other than England and Wales. Security will need to be recognised on enforcement by the jurisdiction in which the relevant asset is located and its appropriate system of law.[26] This issue was considered in Chapter 6 in relation to conflict of laws.[27]

42–11

C. Measurement of exposure and of the level of collateral

The third question is linked to the second question: it is one of measurement. The parties need to measure both the derivatives obligations which are to be secured and they also need to value the assets which are to be put up as collateral. The process of measuring the value of the outstanding derivatives is known as "marking-to-market", which takes a measurement of the anticipated gain or loss on even long-term instruments such as interest rate swaps and identifies their present market value and/or the cost of replacing the existing transactions. That value will fluctuate according to market movements and yield curve[28] adjustments. Given the many possible approaches to the construction of a mark-to-market model, the calculation agent occupies a powerful role in assessing the exposure existing between the parties.[29] The role of the calculation agent was considered in the previous chapter.[30] The weakness of mark-to-market models is that if there is no market functioning properly at the time of the calculation, then no value for the parties' exposure or for the collateral can be obtained.

42–12

---

[24] Financial Collateral Arrangements (No.2) Regulations 2003, art.3.

[25] See para.21–13.

[26] On the distinction between jurisdiction and system of law see para.6–02.

[27] See para.6–01.

[28] The yield curve is the graph which represents current market expectations of future movements in the value of the instruments in question.

[29] The mechanism for calculation under the ISDA arrangements is considered below at para.

[30] See para.41–61.

D. Formalities and regulatory requirements

42–13   The fourth question then concerns the formal and regulatory requirements that govern the manner in which that property is to be provided. If property is to be transferred, there will be formalities to be performed with the different types of securities at issue, possibly held in different jurisdictions. The EU collateral directive also contains a range of formalities, such as the need for the arrangement to be put into writing, which are considered below.[31]

E. Title in the collateral assets

42–14   The fifth question concerns the rights that the secured party has in respect of that property particularly whether or not the seller is entitled to take absolute possession of the collateral property; also what further action a party can take if the property does not equal the size of the exposure to its counterparty if something does go wrong; and furthermore what rights attach to the seller in respect of the property while it is being held under the collateral arrangement. In current market practice, financial institutions insist that collateral is lodged directly with them rather than with a third party as custodian.

4.   THE EC COLLATERAL DIRECTIVE 2002

A.   The enforceability of collateral arrangements

The Directive in outline

42–15   The Collateral Directive 2002[32] deals with the enforceability of collateral arrangements in the EU, provided that they are "evidenced in writing or in a legally equivalent manner"[33] and takes effect over such arrangements "once [financial collateral] has been provided".[34] Such collateral arrangements must take effect between parties which can be one of any of the following categories of person: public authorities, central banks, credit institutions, investment firms, financial institutions, insurance undertakings, collective investment schemes or management companies.[35] The directive deals with cash collateral and securities collateral of two kinds: *title transfer collateral arrangements* and *security financial collateral arrangements*. The Directive was implemented by the UK Collateral Regulations,[36] considered in the next section.[37] For all its ambiguities, the Directive is somewhat clearer than the UK regulations have contrived to be.

---

[31] See para.42–15.
[32] 2002/47/EC ("Collateral Directive 2002").
[33] Collateral Directive 2002, art.1(5).
[34] Collateral Directive 2002, art.1(5).
[35] Collateral Directive 2002, art.1(2).
[36] Financial Collateral Arrangements (No.2) Regulations 2003 (SI 2003/3226).
[37] See para.42–21.

"Title transfer" arrangements

The term "a title transfer financial collateral arrangement", as used in the   **42 16**
Collateral Directive, is defined to mean:

> "an arrangement, including repurchase agreements, under which a collateral provider transfers full ownership of financial collateral to a collateral taker for the purpose of securing or otherwise covering the performance of relevant financial obligations".[38]

This form of arrangement is considered below in relation to the ISDA Credit Support Annex in which parties transfer title absolutely in the collateral property by means of personal collateral structures.

"Security financial collateral" arrangements

The term a "security financial collateral arrangement", as used in the Collateral   **42–17**
Directive, is defined to mean "an arrangement under which a collateral provider provides financial collateral by way of security in favour of, or to, a collateral taker, and where the full ownership of the financial collateral remains with the collateral provider when the security right is established".[39] The reference here to "full ownership" is problematic. Taken literally, this term would not include a trust nor would it include a mortgage because in those instances there are two distinct forms of proprietary right over the same property—legal title and equitable interests in relation to the trust, the separate rights of mortgagor and of mortgagee in relation to the mortgage—such that the collateral provider would not retain *full* ownership. Rather, this literal interpretation would seem to include retention of title clauses. If the credit provider retains "full ownership" then the only other form of security which the secured party could acquire would be by way of a charge under which the chargee acquires no title in the charged property until the chargor fails to perform the underlying obligation and the charge then entitles the chargee to seize the charged property. Alternatively, if "full ownership" were taken to mean "full beneficial ownership", then it would include a bare trust in favour of the secured party because the secured party would be an absolutely entitled beneficiary. That would not, however, cover a trust in which both the secured party and the party posting collateral were beneficiaries under the same trust with their rights being contingent on the performance by each of the performance of their obligations in relation to the underlying transaction. In relation to a charge or mortgage, "full ownership" would only possibly be satisfied if there was no other charge or mortgage in effect over that property.

The Directive ensures that collateral arrangements will be legally effective, and   **42–18**
top-up arrangements to add collateral to the fund will be enforceable in all member states when mark-to-market measurements suggest that such additions are necessary to meet the agreed collateral exposure levels between the parties.[40]

---

[38] Collateral Directive 2002, art.2.
[39] Collateral Directive 2002, art.2.
[40] See para.42–06.

B.   Certainty of subject matter in collateral arrangements

42–19   The Collateral Directive 2002 addresses the issue of certainty of subject matter, albeit in two different provisions. First, it is provided that the "evidencing of the provision of financial collateral must allow for the identification of the financial collateral to which it applies".[41] In this regard, book entries recording a credit, in relation to securities or to cash collateral, are sufficient to identify the collateral. More specifically, it is sufficient if "book entry securities collateral has been credited to, *or forms a credit in*, the relevant account and that the cash collateral has been credited to, *or forms a credit in*, a designated account".[42] The italicised portions of this provision (in which that emphasis was added) suggest that the securities or the cash do not need to be held in an account segregated from all other securities or cash. Consequently, this provision appears to be broader than the principle in English trusts law as to certainty of subject matter. The traditional approach under trusts law required that any property which is to be subject to a trust must be segregated from all other property. The recent Lehman Brothers cases have opened up the possibility that a trust could be inferred over the entirety of a pool of property so that there are property rights identifiable as part of that pool without the need for the specific property which is to be subjected to that trust being segregated from other property.[43] This issue was considered in detail at paras 22–13 et seq.

C.   Enforceability of set-off and netting

42–20   The laws of each member state are required to ensure that parties to a transaction are able to set off the collateral property against amounts owed under the relevant transactions, or to be able to set off cash collateral, "by sale or appropriation" of that collateral property.[44] It is suggested, however, that the parties may wish to turn the assets to account more generally than by necessarily selling them: as such "appropriation", which is undefined for this purpose even though it has a number of meanings in English law,[45] would be the preferable mechanism often in practice in that it gives the secured party greater flexibility in the use of the collateral property. The proviso governing this power to set off is that the parties must have provided for such a set-off if it has been "agreed by the parties in the security financial collateral agreement"—including, it is suggested, an executed ISDA Credit Support Annex or Credit Support Deed—and that the parties have

---

[41]   Collateral Directive 2002, art.1(5).

[42]   Collateral Directive 2002, art.1(5). Emphasis added.

[43]   e.g. *Re Lehman Brothers International (Europe)(in administration) v CRC Credit Fund Ltd* [2012] UKSC 6, [2012] Bus. L.R. 667.

[44]   Collateral Directive 2002, art.4.

[45]   In English equity, "appropriation" refers inter alia to the recourse of a secured party to assets which were set aside to secure an obligation (*Ex p. Waring* (1815) 19 Ves. 345) or the taking of an identified asset to satisfy a legacy (c.g. *Re Lepine* [1892] 1 Ch. 210). At common law it is inter alia a reference to goods being set aside to satisfy delivery obligations under a contract for the sale of goods (Sale of Goods Act 1979, s.18): as to the difficulty of achieving a satisfactory definition of the term "appropriation" at common law see *Benjamin's Sale of Goods*, 6th edn (London: Sweet & Maxwell, 2002) para.5–069.

agreed on the valuation of the collateral in that same agreement.[46] Close-out netting, that is set-off on insolvency, under English law is considered in detail in Chapter 22.[47]

5. FINANCIAL COLLATERAL ARRANGEMENTS (NO.2) REGULATIONS 2003

A. The scope of the Collateral Regulations

The legislation which implements the Collateral Directive is the Financial Collateral Arrangements (No.2) Regulations 2003 (referred to in this chapter as the "Collateral Regulations").[48] The purpose of these regulations, it is suggested, is not to explain how collateralisation operates "from the ground up", but rather is concerned to resolve some long-standing issues which had concerned derivatives lawyers as to the enforceability of collateral agreements, particularly in relation to the reliability of the security under English insolvency law. This section begins by defining the types of collateral structure which fall within these regulations— because falling outside the scope of the regulations would mean that a collateral arrangement would not have the benefit of the protections provided here—and then considers the effect of those protections themselves.

42–21

B. The collateral structures as defined under the Collateral Regulations

The Collateral Regulations provide their own definitions of *personal collateral* and *proprietary collateral* structures, as they are defined in this chapter. The personal collateral structures are referred to in the Collateral Regulations as "title transfer financial collateral arrangements"; the proprietary collateral structures are referred to in the Collateral Regulations as "security financial collateral arrangements".

42–22

Title transfer arrangements

Title transfer financial collateral arrangements are defined as being:

42–23

> "...an agreement or arrangement, including a repurchase agreement, evidenced in writing, where—
> (a)   the purpose of the agreement or arrangement is to secure or otherwise cover the relevant financial obligations owed to the collateral-taker;
> (b)   the collateral-provider transfers legal and beneficial ownership in financial collateral to a collateral-taker on terms that when the relevant financial obligations are discharged the collateral-taker must transfer legal and beneficial ownership of equivalent financial collateral to the collateral-provider; and
> (c)   the collateral-provider and the collateral-taker are both non-natural persons."[49]"

---

[46] Collateral Directive 2002, art.4(2).
[47] See para.22–91.
[48] Financial Collateral Arrangements (No.2) Regulations 2003 (SI 2003/3226).
[49] Financial Collateral Arrangements (No.2) Regulations 2003, art.3.

Therefore, title transfer arrangements only apply between companies. These arrangements cover not only derivatives but also "repos".[50] Such arrangements must be made in writing—which is a problem in relation to the problem of undocumented dealings between the parties to derivatives transactions if they want to attract the protection of these regulations.[51] The principal provision in para.(b) is that absolute title is transferred to the secured party so that that party can deal with the property unencumbered by any proprietary obligations.

Security arrangements

42–24   Security financial collateral arrangements are defined as being:

> "... an agreement or arrangement, evidenced in writing, where—
>
> (a)   the purpose of the agreement or arrangement is to secure the relevant financial obligations owed to the collateral-taker;
>
> (b)   the collateral-provider creates or there arises a security interest in financial collateral to secure those obligations;
>
> (c)   the financial collateral is delivered, transferred, held, registered or otherwise designated so as to be in the possession or under the control of the collateral-taker or a person acting on its behalf; any right of the collateral-provider to substitute equivalent financial collateral or withdraw excess financial collateral shall not prevent the financial collateral being in the possession or under the control of the collateral-taker; and
>
> (d)   the collateral-provider and the collateral-taker are both non-natural persons[52]"

Therefore, security financial collateral arrangements only apply between companies. These arrangements are not expressed as covering "repos". Such arrangements must be "evidenced in writing"—which means that the arrangement itself must not have been created by means of a written instrument, but only that the making of the arrangement (even orally) can be demonstrated by means of writing: there is nothing in the provision to suggest that the writing must be contemporaneous with the creation of the arrangement. The principal provisions are in paras (b) and (c). Paragraph (c) does not require that there is a specific mechanism for creating the security: whether by means of a specific type of structure (whether trust, charge, mortgage, pledge, lien or whatever), nor that there need be any proprietary rights transferred. Instead it provides that there must be a "designation" that the delivery, transfer, holding, registration or other dealing with the collateral property is that it is "in the possession or under the control" of the secured party. Therefore, the secured party need not acquire proprietary rights nor does the debtor need to retain any proprietary rights in the collateral property. Therefore, this aspect of the definition would be satisfied by a transfer of title structure because the collateral property in that instance is both in the possession and under the control of the secured party when absolute title is transferred. The question as to the difference between the two types of structure will only be satisfied by understanding the nature of the security interest which is

---

[50]   See Hudson, *The Law and Regulation of Finance*, para.50–14 on repos.

[51]   Nevertheless, the definition of a financial collateral arrangement, the collective term for both structures, in the Collateral Regulations includes arrangements in writing and arrangements which have not been reduced into writing: Financial Collateral Arrangements (No.2) Regulations 2003, art.3.

[52]   Financial Collateral Arrangements (No.2) Regulations 2003, art.3.

required to fall under this definition: it is that provision which carves out the difference from the title transfer arrangement. It has been held in *Gray v G-T-P Group Ltd, Re F2G Realisations Ltd*[53] that for a person to have "control" over collateral property then that person must have a legal right to compel or control the use of that property and not simply occupy a role which de facto means that the person is consulted in practice about the use of that property. So, it was held insufficient to constitute "control" that the person would be consulted prior to any money being taken out of an account and that instead that person would be required to have a legal right to prevent dealings with the account before they would be deemed to have control over it

In para.(b) a security interest is created. The term "security interest" is defined in the Collateral Regulations so as to mean: **42–25**

> "... any legal or equitable interest or any right in security, other than a title transfer financial collateral arrangement, created or otherwise arising by way of security including—
> (a)   a pledge;
> (b)   a mortgage;
> (c)   a fixed charge;
> (d)   a charge created as a floating charge where the financial collateral charged is delivered, transferred, held, registered or otherwise designated so as to be in the possession or under the control of the collateral-taker or a person acting on its behalf; any right of the collateral-provider to substitute equivalent financial collateral or withdraw excess financial collateral shall not prevent the financial collateral being in the possession or under the control of the collateral-taker; or
> (e)   a lien."[54]

Therefore, as discussed in Chapter 22, this list includes pledges, mortgages, fixed charges, floating charges, and liens. There is a problem as to the "pledge" in this context because the instrument which is defined by ISDA as being a "pledge" is one in which property is transferred outright under the Credit Support Annex, considered below.[55] A pledge, as ordinarily understood,[56] would involve the owner of property—in the circumstances of a derivatives contract, the party required to post collateral—parting with possession of the property by delivering it to the secured party without giving that secured party the right to deal with that property as though its absolute owner.[57] The secured party is prevented from dealing with the property as its absolute owner until such time as its proprietary rights crystallise.

Oddly missing from this list is a trust. Given what is said in Chapter 43 about the failure of ISDA master agreements in some termination of arrangements—and the failure of the credit support arrangements too—it is likely that a trust is the only arrangement which could stand outside the contract and so survive the failure of the credit support. It is suggested that such an equitable interest under a trust ought to have been included in this list.   **42–26**

---

[53] [2010] EWHC 1772 (Ch).
[54] Financial Collateral Arrangements (No.2) Regulations 2003, art.3.
[55] See para.42–33.
[56] The most common example of a pledge would be an arrangement with a pawnbroker.
[57] *The Odessa* [1916] 1 A.C. 145.

C.   Legislative carve-outs in the Collateral Regulations

42–27   A "carve-out" in legislation is an exception created for a particular context to an otherwise generally applicable rule. There are particular concerns in the marketplace about the need to register charges if they are created against a company and about the difficulty of enforcing charges in some insolvency situations. The concern in the marketplace about the need to register charges created under proprietary collateral arrangements was assuaged by art.4(4) of the Collateral Regulations which provided (in its original form) that:

> "Section 395 of the Companies Act 1985[58] (certain charges void if not registered) shall not apply (if it would otherwise do so) in relation to a security financial collateral arrangement or any charge created or otherwise arising under a security financial collateral arrangement".

There are also legislative carve-outs in relation to the enforcement of charges in cases of insolvency. Thus, there are exceptions in relation to financial collateral arrangements to restrictions on the enforcement of charges in insolvency proceedings:

> "The following provisions of Schedule B1 to the Insolvency Act 1986 (administration) shall not apply to any security interest created or otherwise arising under a financial collateral arrangement—
> (a)   paragraph 43(2) (restriction on enforcement of security or repossession of goods) including that provision as applied by paragraph 44 (interim moratorium); and
> (b)   paragraphs 70 and 71 (power of administrator to deal with charged property)."[59]

Similarly, the Collateral Regulations exclude the application of principles which would otherwise avoid property arrangements akin to collateral transactions[60]:

> "In relation to winding-up proceedings of a collateral-taker or collateral-provider, section 127 of the Insolvency Act 1986 (avoidance of property dispositions, etc) shall not apply (if it would otherwise do so)—
> (a)   to any property or security interest subject to a disposition or created or otherwise arising under a financial collateral arrangement; or
> (b)   to prevent a close-out netting provision taking effect in accordance with its terms."

Importantly, there is express provision in the Collateral Regulations that a close-out netting provision will be effective in relation to a financial collateral arrangement.[61] There is nothing in this provision which requires that there are mutual debts between the parties, as is required by r.4.90 of the Insolvency Rules 1986.[62] Instead, it is suggested, for there to be a financial collateral arrangement there must be some provision of cash or securities "to cover the relevant financial obligations" owed to the secured party by the debtor, as outlined above. Therefore, it is suggested there will necessarily be mutual debts. What is less clear is what would be the position if only one party owed payment obligations to

---

[58]   Now replaced by Companies Act 2006, s.860 et seq, discussed at para.22–54.
[59]   Financial Collateral Arrangements (No.2) Regulations 2003, art.8(1).
[60]   Financial Collateral Arrangements (No.2) Regulations 2003, art.10.
[61]   Financial Collateral Arrangements (No.2) Regulations 2003, art.12.
[62]   As discussed at para.22–91 et seq.

the other—due to the use only of options which would only be settled by one party to the other, or swaps on which payments were only owed one way—such that there are no "mutual" debts owed because only one party owes anything. It is suggested that in relation to a swap, there are mutual fixed and floating amounts owed, even if payment netting provides for only one-way payment in practice; in relation to an option, the requirement that the buyer of the option must pay a premium upfront as well as the seller being obliged to make payment of the cash settlement amount means that there are also "mutual" amounts owed if the option is conceived of in the round.

D. Personal collateral

To ensure that the nature of a financial collateral arrangement is clear art.16 of the Collateral Regulations sets out the right of use under a security financial collateral arrangement, such that[63]:   **42–28**

> "(1)   If a security financial collateral arrangement provides for the collateral-taker [the secured party] to use and dispose of any financial collateral provided under the arrangement, as if it were the owner of it, the collateral-taker may do so in accordance with the terms of the arrangement."

Thus a provision entitling the secured party to absolute title to the property has its contractual effect of transferring unencumbered use of and title to the property to the secured party:

> "(2)   If a collateral-taker exercises such a right of use, it is obliged to replace the original financial collateral by transferring equivalent financial collateral on or before the due date for the performance of the relevant financial obligations covered by the arrangement or, if the arrangement so provides, it may set off the value of the equivalent financial collateral against or apply it in discharge of the relevant financial obligations in accordance with the terms of the arrangement."

Thus the duty to transfer collateral property back to the debtor is a duty to transfer property of like kind and value, not an obligation to return the exact property which was originally provided by the debtor to meet its net exposure.

> "(3)   The equivalent financial collateral which is transferred in discharge of an obligation as described in paragraph (2), shall be subject to the same terms of the security financial collateral arrangement as the original financial collateral was subject to and shall be treated as having been provided under the security financial collateral arrangement at the same time as the original financial collateral was first provided."

This odd provision introduces a fiction to the effect that the collateral property which is transferred when the net exposure is reduced (such that a duty arises for the secured party to transfer an amount of collateral property equivalent in value to that reduction) is to be treated as though it was the original property. This cannot be sufficient to impose any obligation equivalent to a fixed charge nor to a trust because the original property is not required to be held for the benefit of the

---

[63] Financial Collateral Arrangements (No.2) Regulations 2003, art.16.

debtor. Consequently, the utility of this fiction is obscure. It cannot be sufficient to create a proprietary right in the form of a fixed charge or a trust, so it is has no obvious purpose other than pretence.

> "(4) If a collateral-taker has an outstanding obligation to replace the original financial collateral with equivalent financial collateral when an enforcement event occurs, that obligation may be the subject of a close-out netting provision."

This provision ensures the enforceability of a close-out netting provision in the event of the insolvency of either party, as was discussed Chapter 22.[64]

E. Enforceability of mortgage under Collateral Regulations without the need for a court order for foreclosure

42–29   Under the Collateral Regulations, there is a specific carve-out to the effect that if a legal or an equitable *mortgage* is taken over property, then there is no need to apply to the court to enforce that mortgage for an order for foreclosure.[65] This provision does not apply to charges nor to pledges. This is a problem in the ISDA Credit Support Deed, considered below,[66] because that provision does not make it plain whether the right in that agreement should be considered to be a mortgage or a charge or a pledge. Therefore, it is not clear whether or not this provision applies to the rights created under the ISDA Credit Support Deed. Whether there is now a requirement for a court order, and the manner in which the collateral can be realised, is considered in the next section in the light of the decision of the Privy Council in *Cukurova Finance International Ltd v Alfa Telecom Turkey Ltd*.

F. Realisation of the collateral

42–30   Valuation of the collateral must take place in a "a commercially reasonable manner" before it is realised.[67] The parties are thus left, to all intents and purposes, to their own devices. Under reg.17 there is a right of appropriation of property, without needing to seek a court order inter alia to terminate the equity of redemption, whether the right is in the form of a mortgage, a charge or an ordinary personal collateral agreement. Regulation 17 provides as follows:

> "Where a legal or equitable mortgage is the security interest created or arising under a security financial collateral arrangement on terms that include a power for the collateral-taker to appropriate the collateral, the collateral-taker may exercise that power in accordance with the terms of the security financial collateral arrangement, without any order for foreclosure from the courts."

---

[64] See para.22–91.

[65] Financial Collateral Arrangements (No.2) Regulations 2003, art.17: "Where a legal or equitable mortgage is the security interest created or arising under a security financial collateral arrangement on terms that include a power for the collateral-taker to appropriate the collateral, the collateral-taker may exercise that power in accordance with the terms of the security financial collateral arrangement, without any order for foreclosure from the courts."

[66] See para.42–51.

[67] Financial Collateral Arrangements (No.2) Regulations 2003, art.18.

The question has arisen in a case in the British Virgin Islands, which was appealed to be Privy Council, as to the manner in which this "appropriation" should take place. The decision of the Privy Council in *Cukurova Finance International Ltd v Alfa Telecom Turkey Ltd*[68] held that it was not necessary under the regulations to take "full ownership" of the rights (as under Art.2.1(b) and (c) of the Collateral Directive) before being able to exercise the collateral rights. As Lord Walker held in relation to the process of appropriation in this context:[69]

> "... appropriation is to be a self-help remedy available to a collateral-taker so long as the SFCA provides for it, and also contains provisions for valuation. If the power of appropriation is exercised the collateral-taker takes the collateral as his own property, at its value under the agreed mechanism, subject (if that value exceeds the secured debt) to a liability to pay the excess to the collateral-provider, and with a claim for the balance of the debt if the value is less than the secured debt. In these respects (as well as in not needing an application to the court) appropriation differs from the traditional (but now obsolescent) English remedy of foreclosure."

On the facts of that case, complex loan arrangements were accompanied by charges which granted the lender the "right ... to appropriate" property by way of credit protection in the form of a financial collateral arrangement. The question arose as to whether or not English law required a registration formality or a court order (as in an old foreclosure action) to "appropriate" property or whether it was simply a form of "self-help" remedy (to use Lord Walker's term) which did not require a court order. The court at first instance in the British Virgin Islands had considered that the court order was required on the basis that "full ownership" was required by the Directive which underpinned the UK regulations and on the basis that:[70]

> "It strikes me as unacceptable that in the world of global commerce, a collateral-provider or lender could appropriate a security by just determining to do so which really amounts to an inner thought process, which is not required to be translated into any overt action. Such a state of affairs would not be commercially reasonable, acceptable or commercially effective especially when one recalls that under the Regulations a collateral-taker is not required to give notice."

The Privy Council, in a judgment delivered by Lord Walker, held that "the judge [at first instance] did rather overstate the importance of giving 'appropriation' an autonomous Community meaning"[71] (under the Collateral Directive) and that instead member states were expected to transpose what was after all only a Directive into their national law by reference to existence concepts of their national laws.[72] Lord Walker preferred a pragmatic approach to the interpretation of the Regulations. His Lordship acknowledged that "Commercial practicalities require that there should be an overt act evincing the intention to exercise a power of appropriation, communicated to the collateral-provider",[73] such that appropriation would not need to be a covert act which the counterparty

---

[68] [2009] UKPC 19, [2009] 3 All E.R. 849.
[69] [2009] UKPC 19, [2009] 3 All E.R. 849 at [13].
[70] Cited at [2009] UKPC 19, [2009] 3 All E.R. 849 at [28].
[71] [2009] UKPC 19, [2009] 3 All E.R. 849 at [32].
[72] [2009] UKPC 19, [2009] 3 All E.R. 849 at [32].
[73] [2009] UKPC 19, [2009] 3 All E.R. 849 at [35].

might not realise had happened; and indeed art.4.4(a) of the Directive required prior notice before appropriation which would render that point nugatory.

6. ISDA Collateralisation Documentation

A. The two principal types of collateralisation in the ISDA architecture

42–31 The ISDA credit support documentation falls into two types: the first, "the Credit Support Annex", is intended not to create a registrable charge and thus effects only "personal collateral"[74]; whereas the second, "the Credit Support Deed", purports to create a "security interest" which may take the form of a charge and so effects "proprietary collateral".[75] In the derivatives markets there is a reluctance to use proprietary structures in case they create a charge which requires registration and perhaps maintenance as a result.

42–32 The ISDA documentation architecture provides that all of the documentation between the parties—the Confirmations, the Master Agreement and Schedule, and any Credit Support Document—taken together constitute a "single agreement".[76] It has nevertheless been held by the English High Court that a collateral agreement should be treated for tax purposes as being separate from the two option contracts which it secured, and therefore not a single agreement with those other documents.[77] The forms of ISDA document considered in this discussion are what ISDA refers to as the "bilateral forms" governed by English law[78] under which both parties owe "two way" collateral obligations to each other.[79]

B. Personal collateralisation—the ISDA Credit Support Annex

The structure of personal collateral arrangements

42–33 Personal collateralisation refers to the structure in which no proprietary rights in the form of a trust, mortgage or charge are created over any collateral property: rather, whichever party owes the net exposure across all of the parties' relevant[80]

---

[74] The issue with charges is that they may require to be registered in many circumstances so as to be valid and participants in financial markets do not want the expense or risk of failure associated with maintaining such registrations. This question was considered in the preceding chapter: see para.22–54.

[75] Whether or not it does create such a charge is doubted in the discussion below.

[76] See para.41–05.

[77] *Inland Revenue Commissioners v Scottish Provident Institution* [2003] S.T.C. 1035.

[78] Whereas previous editions of this book have included references to the New York law version and to the Credit Support Deed.

[79] These two-way, "bilateral" obligations are used instead of the "one way" obligations which were contained in the 1987 version of the ISDA Master Agreement under which only one party would owe obligations to deliver collateral to their counterparty.

[80] By "relevant" here is meant whichever derivatives transactions are intended to be covered by the collateral agreement at issue.

outstanding transactions ("the debtor") is obliged to transfer collateral property equal in value to the net exposure to the other party ("the secured party") to cover that net exposure. The aim of the ISDA Credit Support Annex ("the Annex") is that the secured party, who is owed the net exposure from the debtor across their derivatives transactions, is entitled to take an outright transfer of assets from that counterparty equal to the value of the net exposure. The term "outright transfer" means that the secured party becomes absolute owner of those assets.[81] This is important: the debtor must give (that is, transfer outright) collateral equal to the value of the net exposure to the secured party. The secured party can therefore use those collateral assets as their absolute owner; it can sell them, use them as security for something else, or whatever. Once there has been proper performance of the underlying derivative transactions (that is, once the debtor has paid what she owed and thus reduced the net exposure to zero[82]) the debtor is entitled to recover an amount of collateral property of the same kind and of the same value from the secured party. That is, once the surplus owed between the parties falls in part or falls to zero when the underlying derivatives obligations have been properly performed, then the debtor is entitled to recover the amount of that reduction in the exposure between the parties from the secured party. The personal collateral structure is therefore a form of running account between the parties which matches in value the net exposure between them.

A worked example of a personal collateral arrangement

A worked example may help to illustrate how this structure functions. Suppose **42–34** that Alpha and Beta are conducting a large amount of interest rate swaps business between them, and that there is a net exposure across all of that interest rate swap business such that Beta owes £50,000 to Alpha at the first valuation date specified in the credit support annex. Alpha may therefore demand delivery from Beta of collateral of the kind specified in the credit support annex in a net[83] amount equal to £50,000. Alpha then becomes the absolute owner of those assets and is able to use, sell or otherwise deal with them as their absolute owner. Meanwhile, Alpha and Beta will be performing their interest rate swaps business in the ordinary way and making payments as required under those swaps contracts irrespective of the collateral arrangements in place between them. If, subsequently, Alpha's net exposure to Beta falls to £40,000 (because Beta has performed its interest rate swap obligations to that extent), then Beta may demand a transfer from Alpha of assets of the kind specified in the credit support annex to the value of £10,000 (being the amount by which the net exposure has fallen). These assets which are transferred from Alpha to Beta are not required to be made up of the very assets which Beta transferred to Alpha at the outset, because Alpha took an outright transfer of those assets and was entitled to transfer them away. Consequently, we can say that Alpha owes merely personal obligations in contract to Beta (to effect

---

[81] ISDA Credit Support Annex, para.2 and 3.
[82] As was outlined above, when the net exposure falls by any amount above a threshold identified in the collateral agreement, then the debtor is entitled to a repayment of collateral equal to that reduction.
[83] That is, taking into account any haircuts (i.e. discounts on the value of bonds) and established by reference to a mark-to-market method.

a transfer of assets back on demand) but that Alpha owes no proprietary obligations to Beta (because Alpha was entitled to take the collateral assets as their absolute owner). Beta's risk, therefore, is that Alpha might go into insolvency or be otherwise unable to perform any duties of transfer of collateral assets to Beta. Alpha's risk was that Beta would not perform its obligations under the interest rate swap contracts: that risk was assuaged when Beta transferred an amount of collateral to Alpha equal to the net exposure between the parties at that time.

42–35   The jargon in which the ISDA Credit Support Annex explains these transactions is considered in the next section. In the discussion to follow, the same structure as was discussed above is described in the technical language used by the ISDA draftspeople.

The ISDA terminology for this structure

42–36   Under the terms of the ISDA Credit Support Annex the terminology works in the following fashion, where all capitalised terms are defined terms in the ISDA Credit Support Annex. At the commencement of the Credit Support Annex, when there is a net exposure ("the Credit Support Amount") between the parties under their relevant derivatives transactions on any given Valuation Date,[84] the party which owes the surplus on that net basis ("the Transferor") is obliged to effect an outright transfer[85] of collateral ("Eligible Credit Support") to its counterparty ("the Transferee") of the Delivery Amount.[86] From that time, the parties maintain an account between themselves of the Credit Support Amount from time-to-time and the amount of Eligible Credit Support held on account at that time: such that the size of the obligation to maintain the Credit Support Amount varies at each Valuation Date.[87] All obligations under the Annex are to be made "in good faith and in a commercially reasonable manner".[88]

42–37   Two important further points arise. First, the obligation to make a transfer only arises once the Transferee makes a demand for such a transfer.[89] There is no obligation to make a transfer simply because an amount is due under the collateral agreement, unless and until a demand has been made to transfer those collateral assets. Secondly, the transfer is to be made to the Transferee (or, the "secured party", as discussed in this chapter) personally, as opposed to being made to some third party trustee to hold on trust for the Transferee.[90] As considered below,[91] the Transferee is then entitled to treat the collateral assets as though the Transferee is absolutely entitled to them.[92] This is the feature which

---

[84]   ISDA Credit Support Annex, para.2(a).
[85]   ISDA Credit Support Annex, para.3.
[86]   ISDA Credit Support Annex, para.2(a).
[87]   ISDA Credit Support Annex, para.2(a), below.
[88]   ISDA Credit Support Annex, para.9(b).
[89]   ISDA Credit Support Annex, para.2(a).
[90]   ISDA Credit Support Annex, para.2(a).
[91]   See para.42–41.
[92]   ISDA Credit Support Annex, para.5(a).

makes the ISDA Credit Support Annex a purely personal obligation, as opposed to a proprietary obligation, because "all right, title and interest in" the collateral assets are vested in the Transferee.[93]

The periodic Valuation Dates are identified in the schedule to the ISDA Credit Support Annex.[94] On each Valuation Date the party who is appointed to be the Valuation Agent is required to calculate the net exposure over the relevant derivative transactions so as to carry out the calculations at the Valuation Time identified in the schedule to the annex, and then to notify the parties at the Notification Time as identified further in the schedule to the annex.[95] The precise mechanism by which the Valuation Agent is obliged to carry out these calculations is not specified in the transaction. Rather it is left to the Valuation Agent to carry out a valuation of the exposure owed by each party to the other on all derivatives intended to be covered by the Credit Support Annex. Instead there is a rough equation provided in the Annex which provides that the Transferor is obliged to transfer.

42–38

> "the amount [of Eligible Credit Support] by which:
> (i)   'the Credit Support Amount'
>   exceeds
> (ii)   the Value as of that Valuation Date of the Transferor's Credit Support Balance (adjusted to include any prior Delivery Amount and to exclude any prior Return Amount, the transfer of which, in either case, has not yet been completed and for which the relevant Settlement Day falls on or after such Valuation Date)".[96]

The Credit Support Amount is thus the exposure which the Transferor is obliged to match with Eligible Credit Support on each delivery date. The reference to "the Transferor's Credit Support Balance" in this equation is the amount in the Transferor's account at the Valuation Date: if the new amount of collateral required at that time is greater than the balance, then the Transferor must add more assets to the account; contrariwise, if the new amount of collateral required is less than that held in the account, then the Transferor is entitled to receive a repayment (a Return Amount) from that account, as considered below.

The "Eligible Credit Support" which is to be transferred is a collective term for the types of asset which the parties are prepared to accept as part of their collateral arrangements.[97] The forms of Eligible Credit Support are selected by the parties in the schedule to the Credit Support Annex from a pro forma list including cash (in whatever currency), government bonds, corporate bonds and other securities.[98]

42–39

So, if on a Valuation Date, there is a reduction in the amount of collateral which is needed to meet the net exposure between the parties at that time, then the Transferor is entitled to a Return Amount.[99] The Transferor will, however, only

42–40

---

[93] ISDA Credit Support Annex, para.5(a).
[94] ISDA Credit Support Annex, para.3(b).
[95] ISDA Credit Support Annex, para.3(b).
[96] ISDA Credit Support Annex, para.2(a).
[97] ISDA Credit Support Annex, para.9 "Eligible credit support".
[98] ISDA Credit Support Annex, para.11(b)(ii).
[99] ISDA Credit Support Annex, para.2(b).

be entitled to such a re-transfer if the amount to be retransferred is sufficiently large (as identified in the schedule to the Credit Support Annex) to merit the effort of such a re-transfer: this threshold amount is defined as the Transferor Equivalent Credit Support.[100]

The way in which this structure is said to provide security

42–41 It is useful to think of derivatives transactions secured by collateral as being comprised of two layers. On the underneath is the underlying derivative contracts (whether option, forward or swap) which the parties are obliged to perform under the terms of their confirmations and master agreement as though no credit support agreement existed. On the upper layer is the credit support agreement which provides the obligation to post collateral whenever there is a net exposure between the parties on their underlying derivative contracts: the obligation to post collateral exists separately from any obligation to make payment in relation to the underlying derivative contracts. The two layers therefore operate in parallel but never meet, except that a breach of the collateral agreement will ordinarily constitute an event of default under the master agreement. The method by which this structure affords security is by means of the secured party, who is owed the surplus, receiving a transfer of assets equal in value to the amount of its net exposure to the debtor before any payment is owed under the underlying transaction, although the payment and delivery obligations on the underlying derivative transaction must still be made. The secured party thus receives payments equal to its net exposure in advance and is obliged to return a value equivalent to the collateral property subsequently if the debtor performs its obligations in relation to the underlying derivatives contracts properly. Failure to perform under the credit support agreement would constitute an event of default under the master agreement and thus would start the appropriate termination procedures under that master agreement.

42–42 Many of the issues surrounding personal transactions were considered at the outset of this chapter in relation to the commercial issues surrounding collateralisation; in this section reference will be made specifically to the ISDA Credit Support Annex. In outline, the party supplying collateral property transfers that property outright to the counterparty. The counterparty's obligations are obligations to transfer property of like kind and like value back to the supplier on satisfaction of the underlying obligations. Therefore, this is a purely personal, contractual obligation which creates no rights in property by way of trust, charge or mortgage when returning value to the supplier.

Credit support obligations

42–43 The purpose of the Credit Support Annex is to enable whichever party has a net exposure to its counterparty to demand a transfer to it of an amount of collateral property equal to that net exposure in each valuation period.[101] If the amount of

---

[100] ISDA Credit Support Annex, para.11(b)(i).
[101] ISDA Credit Support Annex, para.2.

collateral property posted with either party exceeds the net exposure from time-to-time, then the debtor is entitled to recoup assets of the same kind as the collateral property equal in value to the surplus of posted collateral over the then level of the net exposure. Thus, the parties maintain accounts with one another containing collateral property equal in value to the net exposure between the parties from time-to-time. Consequently, the parties have no rights to any specific property but rather have only personal rights to demand collateral property or to demand a return of property equal to a reduction in the exposure. The securing effect of this structure is to secure what is effectively a prepayment of the net exposure, such that any failure to deliver constitutes an event of default under the master agreement, as opposed to establishing any rights in property or any rights by way of guarantee.

Transfers

All transfers are to be made "in accordance with the instructions of the Transferee **42–44** or Transferor, as applicable": thus Delivery Amounts and Return Amounts must be made to the accounts ordered by the recipient, or by means of a book entry in the appropriate form so as to effect a transfer to the recipient where appropriate, or by re-registration with the depositary in relation to securities issued under a global note.[102] Transfer must take effect before the Settlement Time[103] on the Settlement Day once a demand for transfer has been received: in relation to cash the Settlement Day is the next local business day, whereas in relation to securities the next local business day after settlement of trades in such securities may be effected.[104]

Calculations and dispute resolution

All calculations are to be made by the Valuation Agent by reference to the **42–45** Valuation Time. The Valuation Agent will ordinarily be the person "making the demand" and so the Valuation Agent is ordinarily the recipient of the transferred property: unless the parties specify some other person to act as Valuation Agent.[105] Valuation Time means the close of business on the appropriate date in the market for the property at issue.[106]

Either party may dispute "reasonably" any calculation made by the Valuation **42–46** Agent or the valuation given for any Eligible Credit Support.[107] If the dispute is made otherwise than reasonably, for example so as to delay any obligation to make a transfer but not on the basis of a genuine error in any valuation, then it is to be assumed (because the Annex is silent on this point) that the dispute resolution procedure need not be activated and that the party obliged to make a transfer is obliged to make that same transfer in the same amount in good time:

---

[102] ISDA Credit Support Annex, para.3(a).
[103] As defined by the parties.
[104] ISDA Credit Support Annex, para.3(a).
[105] ISDA Credit Support Annex, para.11(c)(i).
[106] ISDA Credit Support Annex, para.11(c)(iii).
[107] ISDA Credit Support Annex, para.4(a).

the parties are well-advised to make this clear in their Annex. The dispute resolution procedure requires the Disputing Party to give notice to the other party before the close of business on the date on which the transfer is to have been made.[108] To the extent that there is no dispute between the parties, the transferor is obliged to effect that transfer to the extent of the "undisputed amount".[109] As to the amount that is in dispute the parties are required to consult with a view to resolving their differences,[110] but if the issue remains outstanding then the parties should take up to four quotations for that valuation by means of Market Quotation[111] (as considered in relation to the master agreement).[112] Failure to make a transfer which is in dispute between the parties will not constitute an event of default under the Annex or under the master agreement.[113] As considered above, it must be assumed (although the Annex is silent on this point) that an unreasonable dispute will not prevent a failure to pay or deliver from being defined as being an event of default.

Title in transferred property

42–47   Significantly there is an outright "transfer of title" from the Transferor to the Transferee.[114] It is provided that:

> "Each party agrees that all right, title and interest in and to any Eligible Credit Support, Equivalent Credit Support, Equivalent Distributions or Interest Amount which it transfers to the other party under the terms of this Annex shall vest in the recipient free and clear of any liens, claims, charges or encumbrances or any other interest of the transferring party or of any third person (other than a lien routinely imposed on all securities in a relevant clearance system)."[115]

All assets transferred under the Annex thus become absolutely the property of the Transferee.[116] The ISDA Credit Support Annex therefore creates a purely personal obligation to transfer a Return Amount to the Transferor in the future if the net exposure between the parties falls.[117] The Return Amount is in the form of assets which are also in the form of Eligible Credit Support but those assets are not the very same assets which were originally transferred to it but are instead "Equivalent Credit Support", which must be "Eligible Credit Support of the same type, nominal value, description and amount as that Eligible Credit Support".[118] Thus the obligation is a personal obligation to make repayment by way of a Return Amount comprising assets of like kind and value, whereas if the obligation were an obligation to effect a re-transfer of the original assets posted as collateral by the Transferor then the obligation would be a proprietary obligation.

---

[108]   ISDA Credit Support Annex, para.4(a)(1).
[109]   ISDA Credit Support Annex, para.4(a)(2).
[110]   ISDA Credit Support Annex, para.4(a)(3).
[111]   ISDA Credit Support Annex, para.4(a)(4).
[112]   See para.43–32.
[113]   ISDA Credit Support Annex, para.4(b).
[114]   ISDA Credit Support Annex, para.5(a).
[115]   ISDA Credit Support Annex, para.5(a).
[116]   ISDA Credit Support Annex, para.5(a).
[117]   ISDA Credit Support Annex, para.2.
[118]   ISDA Credit Support Annex, para.10.

That it is not a proprietary obligation but rather a purely personal obligation is further evidenced by the provision that "all right, title and interest in" the collateral assets are vested in the Transferee.[119] The effect of this structure is that the Transferor is taking the risk that, once the collateral assets have been posted under the Credit Support Annex, the Transferee will go into insolvency (or become otherwise incapable of performing its obligations under the Annex) because there is no property held to its account.

Representation as to title in collateral property

Each party represents that there are no prior claims to the collateral property which the party delivers to the other party.[120] As a matter of property law this does not mean that there will not be any prior claims at law or in equity to that collateral property, simply that if there if that party does not have good title to that property then that party will have committed a breach of its obligations under the credit support agreement.

42–48

Default

The default provision in para.6 of the Annex is ambiguously drafted. If there is an event of default caused under the master agreement generally, and any amount remains unpaid or undelivered under the credit support agreement, that amount unpaid under the credit support agreement is an Unpaid Amount which falls to be taken into account in the termination of the master agreement or any terminated transactions under that master agreement. What is unclear here is how this avoids double-counting: if the collateral structure requires the pre-payment of the net exposure between the parties then set-off between the terminated transactions would identify that net exposure in the same amount as the net exposure payable under the credit support agreement. It is suggested that this would be a double payment. An alternative analysis of para.6, which does not repay close attention to the words of the provision, would be that an event of default under the Annex requires payment of that Unpaid Amount under the Annex. The only sensible structure in this context would be to waive the secured party's obligations to make any re-transfer of a Return Amount.

42–49

If a payment or delivery is not made by the time it is supposed to be made under the terms of the Annex, then Default Interest is payable.[121] The amount of interest payable is an amount calculated by reference to the amount which should have been paid at that time at the Default Rate.[122]

42–50

---

[119] ISDA Credit Support Annex, para.5(a).
[120] ISDA Credit Support Annex, para.7.
[121] ISDA Credit Support Annex, para.9(a).
[122] ISDA Credit Support Annex, para.9(a). This term is, oddly, not defined in the Annex. It therefore falls to the parties to define it.

C. Proprietary collateralisation—the ISDA Credit Support Deed

Taking a right secured over property

42–51 Typically a commercial lawyer would be more comfortable with a form of security which permits recourse to some identified property in the event that the counterparty fails to perform its obligations, as opposed to having some purely contractual right from that counterparty. It is proprietary collateralisation which provides this form of protection, unlike the personal collateralisation considered in the preceding section. Proprietary collateralisation is embodied by the ISDA Credit Support Deed ("the Deed") whereby the contracting parties seek to take proprietary rights in the collateral property advanced. What remains at issue, however, is the precise form of the property right which is acquired by the secured party. The Deed is intended to form a single agreement with an ISDA Master Agreement, as discussed in Chapter 41. The ordinary form of this Deed anticipates that both parties will provide such collateral property as is required to off-set any surplus which they owe to their counterparty across all of the relevant derivatives transactions outstanding between them.

The problem in identifying the nature of the property right in the standard contractual language

42–52 The nature of the proprietary right in this context is, however, very problematic. Paragraph 2(b) of the deed provides that[123]:

> "Each party as the Chargor, as security for the performance of the Obligations: (i) mortgages, charges and pledges and agrees to mortgage, charge and pledge, with full title guarantee, in favour of the Secured Party by way of first fixed legal mortgage all Posted Collateral (other than Posted Collateral in the form of cash), (ii) to the fullest extent permitted by law, charges and agrees to charge, with full title guarantee, in favour of the Secured Party by way of first fixed charge all Posted Collateral in the form of cash; and (iii) assigns and agrees to assign, with full title guarantee, the Assigned Rights to the Secured Party absolutely."

The principal point to make on the basis of para.2(b) is this: it is impossible to know from this provision what the nature of the secured party's right is. In subpara.(i) the provision that the relevant party "mortgages, charges and pledges" is simply doctrinally impossible. As was considered in Chapter 22, a mortgage grants a property right (but not absolute title) in the mortgaged property subject to an equity of redemption, whereas a charge effects no transfer of title but rather suggests an appropriation of property contingent on the satisfaction of underlying payment obligations and contingent on a judicial order permitting possession of the property, whereas a pledge connotes a mere possessory right, or in the ISDA sense of that term[124] connotes a transfer of absolute title. Clearly, a person has one or other of these rights but it is not possible to have all three simultaneously. Matters are further complicated in (ii) where a charge is described and then in

---

[123] ISDA Credit Support Deed, para.2(b).
[124] It was discussed in Ch.11 that the ISDA sense of the term "pledge" is not the manner in which this term is ordinarily understood by commercial lawyers.

(iii) where an "assignment", which ordinarily would mean a transfer of absolute title, is described: a chargee does not take a full transfer of title of the charged property. Therefore, any person intending to use the Credit Support Deed should amend this provision to make it plain exactly which form of right is intended: whether mortgage, charge, transfer of absolute title or mere pledge. As drafted and without more, the right in para.2(b) is so poorly described that it possibly creates no single right at all. At best it would be for a court to decide what form of right is created under the governing law of the contract: it is therefore suggested that the parties to a Deed should specify more precisely the nature of the right which is intended to be created between them.

The objective underlying this provision would seem to be that the secured party becomes a chargee of the collateral property such that there is no other charge in existence over that property (whether at all or in such a way as to be able to claim a priority over the rights of the chargee). This is not a mortgage nor is it a pledge. The issue raised is as to whether or not the charge granted would require registration under the Companies Act 2006.[125] If, alternatively, the parties' intention is that the chargee have a proprietary right in the collateral property, then a legal[126] mortgage or even a trust would be more appropriate.

42–53

The release of the security

The security will be released in accordance with the following provision[127]:

42–54

> "Upon the transfer by the Secured Party to the Chargor of Posted Collateral, the security interest granted under this Deed on that Posted Collateral will be released immediately, and the Assigned Rights relating to that Posted Collateral will be re-assigned to the Chargor, in each case without any further action by either party. The Chargor agrees, in relation to any securities comprised in Posted Collateral released by the Secured Party under this Deed, that it will accept securities of the same type, nominal value, description and amount as those securities."

This provision suggests that the charge is released by means of an outright transfer of the collateral property to the secured party. The result would be that absolute title is passed to the secured party: a result which could not obtain if a mortgage were intended, as considered in the previous section. The second sentence of this provision ostensibly obliges the chargee merely to return property of like kind to the charged property. Therefore, this is not really a charge relationship at all; rather, the secured party receives an outright transfer of the property and is able to turn that property to its own account with a purely personal obligation subsequently merely to transfer property of like kind back to the chargor. Ordinarily a fixed charge would entitle the chargee to take possession of the property only if the chargor's payment obligations were not performed. It is unclear, therefore, how there could be said to be a charge in existence here at all when in truth there has been an outright transfer of property.

---

[125] See para.22–54.
[126] That is, a legal mortgage as opposed to an equitable mortgage.
[127] ISDA Credit Support Deed, para.2(c).

The preservation of the security

42–55   The Deed provides that there will be "preservation of security" such that the "security constituted by this Deed shall be a continuing security".[128] The term "continuing security" is not defined in the documentation. It should be taken to mean that the security is not intended to cease while there are transactions outstanding between the parties. This term is problematic for two reasons. First, the identity of the collateral property will change from time-to-time because the agreement necessarily anticipates that new collateral property will be posted or removed from the fund as the exposure between the parties waxes and wanes: thus, there cannot be a continuing security in the form of a fixed charge over all of the property if some of the property can be redeemed during the life of the transaction. Secondly, the term "continuing security" is not a term of art, even though we can guess at what is intended. It would suggest, given that the identity of the collateral will change over time, that the charge could only be a floating charge: it could be "continuing" in the sense that that right is not intended to terminate until all outstanding derivatives transactions are resolved. This issue develops with the following provision of the Deed.

42–56   We are told that this continuing security "shall not be satisfied by any intermediate payment or satisfaction of the whole or any part of the Obligations but shall secure the ultimate balance of the Obligations".[129] The "Obligations" referred to are "all present and future obligations of that party under the Agreement and this Deed and any additional obligations specified [by the parties in the schedule to the Deed]".[130] Thus the obligations which are to be secured do not include the *past* obligations of the parties, and this raises issues as to the provision that no "intermediate payment" can discharge the charging obligation. Consequently, we are left with the definition of the "ultimate balance" for which the security must be preserved. This term "ultimate balance" is not defined. It could be taken to refer to satisfaction of all of the outstanding transactions in existence between the parties under the master agreement: however, in relation to many market counterparties there may never be a time at which there are no obligations at issue between the parties. Therefore, if the parties did structure their deed as a mortgage, this might be held to be void as a mortgage on the basis that there would not redemption of the mortgage over the collateral property and thus that there would be no valid equity of redemption.[131]

Custody of the collateral property

42–57   Paragraph 6 of the credit support deed deals with the obligations of a secured party in relation to the collateral property. The main obligation is to "exercise reasonable care to assure the safe custody of all Posted Collateral to the extent required by the applicable law".[132] This obligation is made up of two conflicting

---

[128] ISDA Credit Support Deed, para.2(d).
[129] ISDA Credit Support Deed, para.2(d).
[130] ISDA Credit Support Deed, para.12.
[131] See Hudson, *The Law and Regulation of Finance*, para.49–08.
[132] ISDA Credit Support Deed, para.6(a).

parts. First, the secured party must take reasonable care to ensure the property's safe custody; secondly, it is required to do so only to the extent required by the applicable law (in the case of this deed, English law) when that applicable law has no general *requirement* that any particular thing be done or not done. To ensure safe custody might involve placement in a segregated account operated by the secured party or it might involve deposit of the property with a third party custodian as trustee: but there is no single thing required by the general law, instead we must look to the Deed for the precise nature of that obligation. Under the terms of the Deed, the secured party is entitled either to retain the property itself or to appoint a custodian.[133] The second obligation is then defined by the deed to be that the secured party or its custodian (if one is used) "shall . . . open and/or maintain one or more segregated accounts . . . in which to hold Posted Collateral".[134] Significantly, then, the secured party and the custodian (as appropriate)

> "shall each hold, record and/or identify in the relevant Segregated Accounts all Posted Collateral (other than Posted Collateral in the form of cash) held in relation to the Chargor, and, except as provided otherwise herein, such Collateral *shall at all times be and remain the property of the Chargor* [emphasis added] and segregated from the property of the Secured Party or the relevant Custodian, as the case may be, and shall at no time constitute the property of, or be commingled with the property of, the Secured Party or such Custodian".[135]

The italicised portion of this provision ensures that the collateral property is owned by the chargor throughout the transaction. Given that the property has been paid into an account in the name of the secured party or the custodian, this property must be owned at common law by that secured party or custodian and in turn the chargor can only have equitable ownership of that property. Therefore, the effect of this provision is most likely to create a trust over the collateral property. This would be made more evident if the provision simply read that "the Posted Collateral shall be held on trust by the [secured party] or the custodian (as appropriate) for the Chargor". As drafted the trust is required to be inferred from the circumstances, which is unfortunate if a trust is intended or doubly unfortunate if a trust is not intended.

As considered above, this provision appears, prima facie, to establish a trust over **42–58** the collateral property. And yet, as discussed above, para.2(b) provided that the parties agreed to mortgage, charge and pledge the collateral property. If the effect of para.6(c) is intended to be to impose an equitable charge over the collateral property as opposed to a trust, then that intention should be made plain in the drafting. More confusingly yet, para.2(c) provides that the obligation to post collateral property is discharged by delivery of collateral property of like kind (where para.2(c) provides that the "Chargor agrees [and thus binds itself] . . . that it will accept securities of the same type") as opposed only to being capable of discharge by transfer back of the very property which was originally supplied by the chargor. Holding this collateral property in segregated accounts could be analysed as creating a beneficial interest under a trust in specific property, rather

---

[133] ISDA Credit Support Deed, para.6(b)(i).
[134] ISDA Credit Support Deed, para.6(c).
[135] ISDA Credit Support Deed, para.6(c).

than merely a right to receive and transfer back of property of a like kind. There is therefore, across paras 2 and 6, the possibility that the secured party bears on the one hand purely personal rights and on the other hand proprietary rights of indeterminate kind. In either event the deed provides that the secured party has no right to use the property.[136]

42–59 Thus the drafting of the Credit Support Deed is potentially self-contradictory because it contains mention of so many proprietary concepts and permits analysis of further forms. It is advised that users of these structures prepare their own documentation, based perhaps on the ISDA standard, which makes plain which type of proprietary right the secured party is intended to receive.

42–60 It is suggested that the only structure which will meet both objectives in this context is the trust. To avoid the need to register a charge, a trust should be used. To ensure that the secured party is required to segregate the collateral property from all other property, a trust whereby the secured party holds the collateral property on trust for the benefit of the chargor would be advisable. The additional advantages of the trust structure are that any distributions attaching to the underlying property will also form part of the trust fund in turn[137] and the secured party as trustee will owe fiduciary obligations to the chargor.[138] The issues in relation to trust structures, as to certainty of subject matter, were considered in Chapter 22.[139]

Rights of enforcement

42 61 The secured party, in spite of the fiduciary obligations which she may owe in relation to the collateral property, may take a beneficial interest in some or all of the collateral property in any one of three occasions: a Relevant Event (being an event of default within the terms of the deed), an Early Termination Date pursuant to an event of default or termination event under the master agreement, or a Specified Condition which is stipulated specifically by the parties in the schedule to the deed. The three forms of Relevant Event stipulated in the Deed[140]: first, an event of default under the master agreement; secondly, a failure to make any transfer of collateral property under the Deed; or thirdly, failure to perform any other obligation which continues for 30 days after notice of that failure has been given to the defaulting party. In the event of any of these three occasions, the secured party is able to deal with the collateral property as though its absolute owner. In relation to property other than money, the secured party is empowered to sell the property and to use the proceeds to set off against its exposure to the counterparty. In relation to money, the secured party is able to use that money to set off against its exposure to the counterparty, including making any necessary

---

[136] ISDA Credit Support Deed, para.6(d). This raises the question why the secured party may return property other than the original property to the chargor.

[137] Otherwise under the deed, the secured party has no obligation to collect distributions in relation to the collateral property (ISDA Credit Support Deed, para.6(e)) although any distributions collected must be transferred to the chargor (ISDA Credit Support Deed, para.6(f)).

[138] See G.W. Thomas and A.S. Hudson, *The Law of Trusts*, p.307 et seq.

[139] See para.21–13.

[140] ISDA Credit Support Deed, para.7.

currency conversions. The secured party is purportedly granted a power of attorney on behalf of the chargor in relation to any rights of the chargor to deal with the collateral property.[141] A purchaser of the collateral property in good faith is stipulated to take good title in the property.[142] However, whether or not the purchaser can take good title may depend on the validity of the chargor's title, although in equity a bona fide purchaser for value without notice of any other person's rights will take good title in the purchased property.[143]

D. Insolvency and collateral

An issue arises in relation to insolvency of one of the parties to a derivatives transaction as to whether the collateral agreement may be enforced. If the collateral structure were effected in the form of a trust then the trust would take effect regardless of the insolvency of the party acting as trustee of it.[144] Otherwise in relation to personal collateral arrangements and other collateral arrangements which do not automatically accord effective proprietary rights on the secured party, the Settlement Finality Regulations 1999[145] preserve the effect of such arrangements even on the insolvency of one of the parties.[146] These regulations are considered in detail in Chapter 22.[147] Further to the EU Collateral Derivative[148] "close-out netting provisions shall be effective notwithstanding the commencement or continuation of winding-up proceedings or reorganisation measures in respect of the collateral provider and/or the collateral taker".[149] The forms of "collateral" which fall within the Settlement Financial Regulations are described in reg.1 of the 1999 Regulations as follows:

42–62

> "'collateral security' means any realisable assets provided under a charge or a repurchase or similar agreement, or otherwise (including [credit claims and] money provided under a charge)—
> (a)   for the purpose of securing rights and obligations potentially arising in connection with a ... system ('collateral security in connection with participation in a ... system'); or
> (b)   to a central bank for the purpose of securing rights and obligations in connection with its operations in carrying out its functions as a central bank ('collateral security in connection with the functions of a central bank')"

Therefore, collateral arrangements encompass as a "repo" and other arrangements.

---

[141] ISDA Credit Support Deed, para.8(b).
[142] ISDA Credit Support Deed, para.8(c).
[143] *Westdeutsche Landesbank v Islington* [1996] A.C. 669.
[144] *Re Kayford* [1975] 1 WLR 279.
[145] The Financial Markets and Insolvency (Settlement Finality) Regulations 1999 (SI 2979/1999).
[146] para.13–57.
[147] See para.22–129 et seq.
[148] 2002/47/EC.
[149] Art.8.

E.   A flawed system

42–63   The standard market collateral structures are clearly not fit for purpose. As this chapter has demonstrated, there are a number of issues which remain outstanding, principally an inability to select clearly between the various different models which can be used to take security which were discussed in Chapter 22.

CHAPTER 43

TERMINATION OF FINANCIAL DERIVATIVES

CORE PRINCIPLES

Termination of the master agreement is the purpose of the master agreement: it exists as a means of providing escape hatches for the parties to derivatives contracts so that each is able to release itself from its contractual obligations in the event that there is any difficulty with its counterparty's ability to perform its obligations. In that sense it complies with the general forms of master agreement which were considered in Chapter 19.

The "events of default" under the master agreement entitle the parties to terminate the master agreement as of right, subject to formalities as to giving notice contained in the standard terms of the agreement. The events of default in the standard form agreement include: failure to make payment or delivery; failure of any representation made by the parties; breach of any condition of the

[1269]

contract; misrepresentation; failure of credit support; cross default and cross acceleration; and "bankruptcy" and related insolvency-related events;

The "termination events" under the master agreement do not permit the parties to terminate the master agreement immediately but rather provide a mechanism by which the parties must seek to resolve the termination event. Only if that process is unsuccessful will termination of the master agreement, or of transactions affected by that termination event, be permitted. The standard form termination events include: illegality of the transactions; the introduction of a new tax treatment of the transactions; and a corporate restructuring which leads to the resultant entity being of a lower credit worth.

The termination procedure involves the identification ultimately of a single net figure in the identified termination currency which sets off all of the outstanding transactions between the parties. This requires a valuation of those outstanding transactions. Valuation is achieved by establishing either the replacement value of those transactions, or by acquiring market quotations from market makers in those products for replacement transactions, or by establishing the parties' loss: the valuation mechanism must be selected in the schedule to the master agreement. These termination procedures have been the subject of a number of cases in England and Wales, as discussed in detail below.

1.   TERMINATION OF THE MASTER AGREEMENT

A.   The legal mechanism for termination of derivatives transactions

The termination procedure in outline

43–01   The ISDA master agreement has a two-tier system of termination.[1] The agreement differentiates between events which arise out of some default or failure connected to one of the parties, and events which arise as a result of circumstances beyond the control of the parties. The first category is dubbed "Events of Default" in the ISDA Master Agreement and the latter category is dubbed "Termination Events". That nomenclature will be retained here.

43–02   The termination procedure operates, in outline, in the following way. An *event of default* is a serious default which was considered by the drafters of the ISDA agreement to be so grievous as to require a rapid termination of the Master Agreement after compliance with a notice formality. Where there is an event of default, it is incumbent on the non-defaulting party to give notice to the defaulting party (in many circumstances) specifying the event of default. That event of default will generally trigger the procedure for the termination of the Master Agreement without more, as considered below.[2] By contrast, a *termination event* is something which is not the fault of either party—usually relating to a change in the law or the action of a regulator—and which might possibly be something which can be manoeuvred around. Therefore, where there is a termination event it is expected that the parties will attempt to find some way

---

[1] ISDA, *Multicurrency Master Agreement 2002* (ISDA, 2002), at ss.5 and 6.
[2] See para.40–28.

of affirming their transaction by transferring it to other subsidiary entities, or by transferring it to other offices, or something of that sort, as indicated in the agreement. It is only where such efforts to affirm the transaction fail within the specified grace periods that the final termination procedure is activated. Where an event occurs which is both an event of default and also predicated on a termination event (such as a supervening illegality[3]), the event is treated as being a termination event such that the parties will seek to negotiate their way around the problem.[4]

In either case the final termination procedure requires that the parties select a date **43–03** on which all applicable,[5] outstanding transactions[6] will be deemed to be terminated.[7] At such time the calculation agent[8] calculates the amount payable in relation to each outstanding transaction on that date either to acquire replacement transactions or to compensate the parties' loss (as selected by the parties in their master agreement). Those various amounts are then set-off so that the calculation agent identifies a single amount which constitutes the net balance owed between the parties in satisfaction of all of their outstanding transactions. The Court of Appeal in *Socimer International Bank Ltd v Standard Bank London Ltd*[9] held that a calculation agent will be bound "as a matter of necessary implication, by concepts of honesty good faith, and genuineness, and the need for the absence of arbitrariness, capriciousness, perversity and irrationality".[10] Those principles should apply to the calculation agent in these circumstances, even though in practice it is likely that the calculation agent will be the non-defaulting party.

The availability of the general law relating to termination of contracts

It should be noted that there is nothing in this termination procedure which in any **43–04** way prevents the parties from relying on the general law relating to the

---

[3] That is, where some aspect of the transaction has become illegal or legally unenforceable since the creation of the agreement.

[4] See para.40–28, s.5(c); *Nuova Safim SpA v The Sakura Bank Ltd* [1999] C.L.C. 1830; [1999] 2 All E.R. (Comm) 526.

[5] In relation to the "applicable" outstanding transactions, there remains a question as to whether the parties wish to terminate all or only some of the transactions between them. In s.14, the definition of "Terminated Transactions" suggests that some only of the transactions may be terminated by referring only to the notice of termination whereas s.6(a) suggests that "all outstanding Transactions" will be terminated when there has been an event of default. By not making this explicit, the document is possessed of an unfortunate level of uncertainty. However, the general expectation in using this document is that the non-defaulting party would be entitled to specify which transactions are to be terminated and which not. In relation to insolvency of the defaulting party, however, it would not be possible for the non-defaulting party to "cherry-pick" which transaction it wishes to enforce and which to repudiate: para.13–20.

[6] It may be that all outstanding transactions are set-off in this way or else it may be that only an identified group of transactions are set-off, for example if it is only interest rate swaps which have become unlawful for one or other of the parties in a given jurisdiction.

[7] Hence the importance in Ch.40 of identifying in relation to complex transactions whether they constitute single agreements or bundles of independent, separate transactions some of which are not outstanding at the time of termination.

[8] For a discussion of this term, see para.41–32.

[9] [2008] EWCA Civ 116; [2008] Bus. L.R. 1304.

[10] [2008] EWCA Civ 116; [2008] Bus. L.R. 1304 at [66], per Rix L.J.

termination of contracts or the recovery of property or compensation, as was discussed in Chapter 20. At the end of this chapter is a brief survey of the local authority swaps cases which serve as a stark warning of what will happen if the contract fails for some reason, such as the lack of capacity of the parties. If the contract fails, then the parties will be entirely reliant on the general law to identify their rights on termination of the contract.

B.   Automatic termination or termination by notice?

43–05   The use of either of the event of default or the termination event mechanisms for identifying an early termination date might be obviated by the agreement of the parties if they opt for automatic termination of their contractual relations in one of two ways: either by electing for "Automatic Early Termination" in the Schedule to their ISDA Master Agreement itself, as considered below;[11] or by choosing to alter the standard ISDA procedure by providing expressly in their agreement for mandatory automatic termination to apply to all events of default, as in *Anthracite Rated Investments (Jersey) Ltd v Lehman Brothers Finance S.A. in liquidation*.[12] (It should be recalled that the ISDA Master Agreement provisions are a pre-printed standard form contract which the parties are entirely at liberty to alter, amend or otherwise lacerate. Therefore, the entire termination architecture can be replaced with another scheme if the parties so desire. And, on occasion, parties do desire just that.) The question whether termination should take place automatically or only on giving notice is a central issue relating to the construction of a master agreement's termination procedures. The pro forma ISDA Master Agreement operates on the basis that the various termination procedures only become operational once the non-defaulting party has given notice to its counterparty that an event of default or a termination event has arisen. The onus is also on the non-defaulting party to specify the breach and so forth. This requirement to give notice has been found to be a condition precedent to the operation of the termination provisions in the master agreement.[13] As a result the ordinary availability of damages for breach of contract is displaced by the remedy provided for in the master agreement by means of the termination provisions.[14]

43–06   The question remains whether termination by notice is preferable to termination being activated automatically without the need to give notice. There may be transactions conducted with counterparties which are not known sufficiently well to the non-defaulting party so that the non-defaulting party would not know that such a termination event had come into existence. One example would be the obligation in the master agreement that the counterparty has to maintain authorisations with its regulator, another would be an obligation to maintain a given level of credit worth where there is no published credit rating. In either case the non-defaulting party might have no means of knowing whether or not

---

[11]   para.3–07.

[12]   [2011] EWHC 1822 (Ch); [2011] All E.R. (D) 171 (Jul), where the parties used mandatory termination on the occurrence of any events so defined in their agreement.

[13]   *Nuova Safim SPA v The Sakura Bank Ltd* [1999] C.L.C. 1830.

[14]   [1999] C.L.C. 1830; on termination see para.40–28 et seq.

authorisations had been maintained nor whether information which had significance in relation to the counterparty's credit worth had come to light until the counterparty was already on the brink of insolvency.[15] The master agreement is typically constructed so that either party is able to terminate all outstanding transactions as soon as one of a range of events occurs which would indicate a *future* inability of the counterparty to perform its obligations under the master agreement. Therefore, the requirement that the non-defaulting party give notice to the defaulting party appears to be generative of problems in itself.

43–07

The solution to this problem is to provide that termination of the master agreement will take place automatically on the occurrence of one of the events of default or of the termination events.[16] This would remove the obligation on the non-defaulting party to give notice before the termination procedures would be activated. A suitable provision would provide that termination took place at the time of the event and not at the time when it was discovered subsequently. Therefore, the non-defaulting party would be able to rely retrospectively on the automatic termination of those transactions which had been outstanding at that time. If there were a collateral structure in place,[17] then the non-defaulting party would be able to have recourse to that structure.

43–08

The weakness of automatic termination is that it gives the non-defaulting party no opportunity to decide whether or not it would wish the transaction to be terminated. It may be that, even though an event of default of some sort had occurred, the defaulting party is continuing to make payment under the transaction and that transaction was profitable for the non-defaulting party at that time. In such a circumstance, the non-defaulting party would not want the defaulting party to be able to rely on the automatic early termination provision, activate the termination procedures in the master agreement, and so end its obligation to keep making payment to the non-defaulting party. Therefore, a preferable provision in that instance would give the non-defaulting party the option whether or not to terminate or to affirm the transactions. This would raise issues in cases of insolvency relating to the unacceptability of allowing a solvent party to cherry-pick[18] which transactions it would prefer to affirm and which it would prefer to repudiate. It is suggested that such a provision would not be acceptable in relation to insolvency set-off and as such ought to be excluded.

---

[15] This would not be true for events of default such as failure to pay because the non-defaulting party would know whether or not it had received a payment which is was expecting to receive. However, where payment was delayed that party might not know that the counterparty was unable to pay rather than simply delayed in paying: in short, to misconstrue strategy for lethargy.

[16] As accepted, below, in *Peregrine Fixed Income Ltd v Robinson* [2000] C.L.C. 1328; [2000] Lloyd's Rep. Bank 304.

[17] See para.42–01 et seq.

[18] "Cherry-picking" refers to the process of choosing to affirm profitable transactions while simultaneously repudiating unprofitable transactions.

2. "EVENTS OF DEFAULT"

A. The order of the discussion to follow

43–09   Each of the standard events of default in an ISDA-style master agreement is outlined below. If any one of these events of default has taken place, the non-defaulting party is required to give notice of that fact to the defaulting party so as to initiate the termination procedure. The shortcoming with this approach is that it requires the non-defaulting party to know that an event of default has occurred and that therefore a notice must be served: the termination procedure cannot begin until that notice is served. Thus, as was discussed above, there is a need to decide whether or not automatic termination would be preferable. There is an issue as to whether or not the provisions in s.5(a) of the master agreement constitute a fraud on the insolvency legislation by providing, in effect, that an insolvent person's assets are being reduced by the amount which is set off by the calculation agent in calculation the early termination amount contrary to the "anti-deprivation rule" in insolvency law. It was held in *Belmont Park Investments Pty Ltd v BNY Corporate Trustee Services Ltd*[19] and in *Lomas v JFB Firth Rixson Inc*[20] that the ISDA Master Agreement provisions will not constitute a "fraud on the bankruptcy laws" in the ordinary course of events. In *AWB (Geneva) SA v North America Steamships Ltd*[21] it was held as a matter of policy that the ISDA Master Agreement should not be rendered invalid.

B. Failure to perform a payment or delivery obligation

43–10   The most fundamental event of default is that of a failure to pay by either party. Clearly payment on a timely basis is the essence of the contractual intention of the parties. Generally the term will contain a grace period (subject to the payment of interest as indicated above) to cover for any administrative error or other event which might legitimately be said to have interfered with proper payment, as considered below.[22] There are two potential remedies provided for in the master agreement. Where payment is in fact made but where it is made late, the defaulting party is required to pay default interest. The rate of default interest specified in the ISDA Master Agreement is one per cent per annum over the cost of funding that amount of money calculated on a compound basis.[23] Where payment is late because the payer intends to renege on its payment obligation or where the party will be permanently unable to pay then that will constitute an event of default once there has been no payment within three local business

---

[19] *Belmont Park Investments Pty Ltd v BNY Corporate Trustee Services Ltd* [2011] UKSC 38, [2011] 3 W.L.R. 521.
[20] [2011] 2 B.C.L.C. 120.
[21] [2007] EWCA Civ 739; [2007] B.P.I.R. 1023. cf. *Anthony Gibbs & Sons v La Société Industrielle et Commerciale des Métaux* (1890) 25 Q.B.D. 399 in which it was held that a party was not excused from its contractual obligations under English law by insolvency under French law. See Fletcher, *Insolvency in Private International Law*, 2nd edn (OUP, 2007), at para.2.85.
[22] ISDA Master Agreement s.5(a)(i).
[23] ISDA Master Agreement, s.14, "default interest".

days.[24] The difficulty with charging default interest is whether or not it constitutes a penalty clause, such that it should be void.[25] In *BNP Paribas v Wockhardt*,[26] in relation to a derivatives transaction, Wockhardt failed to make payments on time and therefore BNP gave notice under the master agreement that it was commencing the Early Termination procedure. The issue was whether or not the early termination amount calculated by reference to the termination provisions in the master agreement constituted a penalty clause. It was held that the parties' freedom of contract should be upheld by the court and that that included enforcing a penalty clause which was voluntarily included in their contract. Consequently, Clarke J. held that the amounts which were to be paid on a net basis between the parties were in truth payments of amounts which Wockhardt already owed to BNP under their pre-existing transactions, and as such were not in the nature of penalties for late payment in any event.

Where there is no provision for default interest there would need to be some provision to identify those forms of loss which would be sufficiently proximate to satisfy common law tests of foreseeability.[27] It should be remembered that penalty damages clauses will typically not be enforceable, although a liquidated damages clause will be enforceable; the distinction between the two is that the former must require payment of an unconscionable amount of money.[28] In *Nuova Safim SpA v The Sakura Bank Ltd*[29] a company owned entirely by the Italian state was dissolved by official decree. The counterparty successfully served notices in the form required by the master agreement detailing the failure to make payment as being an event of default. The agreement was consequently held to have been terminated in accordance with the terms of the master agreement.[30] However, on those facts under s.5(c) of the master agreement, because the failure to pay was also bound up with an illegality under s.5(b)(i), the failure fell to be determined under the termination events procedure rather than as an event of default. Thus the possibility of the parties negotiating a way around the problem overrode the possibility of automatic termination under the event of default procedure.

43–11

In relation to physically-settled derivatives the buyer may be content to wait until the underlying asset is delivered and to receive payments of default interest in consideration for that late delivery provided that delivery will be made at some reasonable time in the future. However, if there were some back-to-back arrangement planned for the underlying asset under which the buyer is obliged to

43–12

---

[24] ISDA Master Agreement, s.5(a)(i).

[25] Colman J. set out the approach for distinguishing between valid clauses and void penalty clauses in *Lordsvale Finance Plc v Bank of Zambia* [1996] Q.B. 752, at 762: it was "a matter of construction to be resolved by asking whether at the time the contract was entered into the predominant contractual function of the provision was to deter a party from breaking the contract [and so be void] or to compensate the innocent party for breach" and so be valid. This process can also be understood in the following way: "[t]hat the contractual function is deterrent rather than compensatory can be deduced by comparing the amount that would be payable on breach with the loss that might be sustained if breach occurred".

[26] [2009] EWHC 3116, [24].

[27] See para.25–01.

[28] *Dunlop Pneumatic Tyre Co Ltd v New Garage & Motor Co Ltd* [1915] A.C. 79.

[29] [1999] C.L.C. 1830; [1999] 2 All E.R. (Comm) 526.

[30] See above.

make delivery of that security to one of its own clients, perhaps imposing damages on the buyer for late delivery, then the buyer would not be content to accept late delivery with a payment of interest. Instead, the buyer would require compensation for any loss of bargain or for any penalty interest which would be imposed on it as a result of the seller's late delivery. As was considered in Chapter 41, the right to receive compensation would need to be identified in the Confirmation.[31]

C. Breach of contract

43–13   As was discussed in Chapter 20 in relation to the *Termination of Contracts*, where there is a breach of a term of a contract which is identified as being a condition of that contract then that will found a right to damages and to rescission.[32] It is also provided in the ISDA Master Agreement that when there is a breach of a condition of the contract, that will constitute an event of default. There is therefore a need for the parties to consider which provisions they intend to classify as being conditions, as opposed to being mere warranties, of their contract. In Chapter 41 we considered the representations which the parties make as being conditions of the contract.[33] Other provisions which could be highlighted as being conditions in this way include performance under credit support arrangements, maintenance of credit worth, and delivery of specified information as to credit worth or regulatory status. In relation to a breach of contract in this context, the standard form of the ISDA Master Agreement requires that the non-defaulting party give notice to the defaulting party of any such breach and a grace period of thirty days follows the giving of that notice.[34]

D. Failure of credit support

43–14   The provision of credit support, as considered in Chapter 42, is vital to derivatives business. Consequently, if the credit support should fail to be effective then that will constitute an event of default under the master agreement. Given that the purpose of the master agreement is to enable the parties to extricate themselves from dealings with a counterparty who, for example, cannot maintain valid credit support, it is necessary that this constitutes an event of default. So, on the insolvency of Lehman Brothers in September 2008, it ceased to be able to provide credit support under ISDA master agreements and therefore an event of default was triggered.[35]

---

[31] See para.41–23.

[32] See para.20–28.

[33] See para.41–50.

[34] ISDA Master Agreement, s.5(a)(ii).

[35] *Lehman Brothers Commodity Services Inc v Credit Agricole Corporate and Investment Bank* [2011] EWHC 1390 (Comm).

E.   Misrepresentation

The general law relating to misrepresentation—whether negligent or fraudulent— **43–15** will apply to the parties.[36] There is also an express provision in the ISDA master agreement to the effect that any representation made in the confirmation or in a credit support agreement or in the master agreement (such as the capacity of the parties or the absence of litigation) which turns out to be false will ground an event of default and so enable the master agreement to be terminated.[37] By specifying which representations are to be treated as being breached, the parties can avoid the question as to whether or not those representations were material to the master agreement. The common law would be limited to representations which induced the parties into creating the agreement or which were fundamental to that contract. The representations relate to matters such as capacity, authority and so on, as were considered in Chapter 41.[38] These might not be considered to be fundamental without an express provision in the agreement to the effect that they are considered by the parties to be fundamental to the contract.

F.   Cross default

The purpose and nature of cross default provisions

The concept of *cross default* was considered in Chapter 19.[39] Cross default is a **43–16** process whereby there will be a breach of contract A if one of the parties to that contract has committed a breach of contract B; or if a different entity has committed a breach of some other transaction which is of a type identified in contract A. The purpose of cross default is to enable a party to terminate a derivatives master agreement with X Plc if either X Plc has committed a breach of another derivatives master agreement, or if an identified affiliate of X Plc has committed a breach of another master agreement, or if one of X Plc's credit support providers has committed a breach of another master agreement, or if any of these entities has committed a breach of any of the types of non-derivatives transaction which are identified in the master agreement. The schedule to the derivatives master agreement therefore requires that the parties identify which of their affiliated entities (whether subsidiaries, parents, or entities under common control) should be treated as falling within the ambit of the master agreement for the purposes of cross default (a "Specified Entity"), and also to identify any other type of transaction a default in which will fall within the ambit of the cross default provisions of the master agreement (a "Specified Transaction"). It will clearly be a matter for negotiation between the parties as to what sorts of affiliated entities and what sorts of transactions they will agree to include in the schedule to this agreement; it will also be a matter for the credit departments of the parties to decide what sorts of entities and transactions they will be prepared to accept being included and, more importantly, which they will be prepared to

---

[36] See para.24–01 and 25–01.
[37] See para.24–01 and 25–01 at s.5(a)(iv).
[38] See para.41–50.
[39] See para.19–49.

accept being excluded from the agreement. If you are dealing with a company from the Xavier banking group and the next payment under your swap agreement is due in six months, then you want to be able to extricate yourself from the transaction as soon as you learn that another entity in the Xavier banking group has failed to make its payment under a different swap agreement: you do not want to have to wait six months until the same failure to pay happens to you. Therefore, a cross-default provision enables you to terminate your own swap agreement while both parties are solvent on the basis that trouble is clearly brewing for Xavier group when another of its companies has breached its derivatives agreement. Waiting until the entire group goes into insolvency (as Lehman Brothers showed) means that you will recover very little of what is owed to you, or you will be obliged to make payments to Xavier without receiving anything you are owed in return.

Cross acceleration

43–17   Another, subtly different form of cross default which is specified in the ISDA Master Agreement[40] is a "Default under [a] Specified Transaction", which is in truth a form of cross acceleration clause as described in Chapter 19. The effect of this provision is that there is an event of default under the master agreement if an identified Specified Entity of one of the counterparties is obliged to make a payment under any type of debt specified in the master agreement ("Specified Indebtedness") earlier than it was otherwise contractually required. As was discussed in Chapter 32 in relation to lending, when a borrower commits a default under a loan contract, the lender is ordinarily entitled to demand immediate repayment of the loan: this is referred to as being an "acceleration" of that borrower's obligations because they become payable sooner than would otherwise have been the case because of the borrower's default. The term "specified indebtedness"[41] in the ISDA master agreement encompasses any of these sorts of accelerations in respect of whatever sorts of obligations over borrowed money as the counterparties agree to include in their master agreement. This may potentially include bond issues, ordinary bank debt and so on. It may also include any situation in which a party is acting as a guarantor for another person in respect of that other person's debt obligations.[42] Thus, if any one of the Specified Entities is required to make payment early under any of these types of indebtedness, then that will constitute an event of default under the master agreement. Consequently, default under a derivatives transaction or under a loan contract could include one day's lateness in meeting a payment obligation or it might involve the total repudiation of a debt or other transaction by the counterparty's affiliate. So, in Abu Dhabi Commercial Bank v Saad Trading[43] there were defaults under a syndicated loan and other credit agreements by a party to a derivatives contract which included cross default language: it was held that the defaults under the loan and credit agreements would constitute events of

---

[40]   ISDA Master Agreement, s.5(a)(vi).
[41]   ISDA Master Agreement, s.14.
[42]   ISDA Master Agreement, s.14.
[43]   [2010] All E.R. (D) 294 (Jul).

default under an ISDA master agreement and therefore that the master agreement termination procedure could be commenced.

These events of default are subject to a threshold condition: that is, a de minimis provision which excuses defaults of a trifling value. Therefore, the parties will not be able to terminate their master agreement in relation to small defaults or small early payments of debt. In their Schedule, the parties agree to the threshold level which the default must cross before it constitutes an event of default under the master agreement. There is also a requirement, born out of practicality, that there are no mismatches between any default language under the ISDA Master Agreement and under whatever other contractual provisions govern the Specified Indebtedness.

43–18

Cross default on other derivatives

The other form of cross default in the ISDA Master Agreement relates to default under other derivatives transactions by any Specified Entity, as was outlined above. The scope of the derivatives to be covered by this provision will be specified by the parties in the schedule to the master agreement. Thus, a default under one derivatives transaction will constitute an event of default under another master agreement. There are three specific defaults envisaged in the ISDA Master Agreement.[44] First, any "liquidation" or "acceleration" of any "obligations" under a specified type of derivative transaction, or any early termination of such a transaction with the result, significantly, that other outstanding transactions linked under that documentation are terminated. A relevant default under that other derivatives transaction may be committed by the counterparty itself, by any party providing credit support under the master agreement, or any entity specified in the schedule as being a relevant party for the ambit of this event of default.[45] The definition of "specified transaction" in this context in the standard documentation is defined so as to include[46] a large range of derivatives transactions (listed exhaustively and ranging from "rate swap transactions" to transactions relating to "measures of economic risk or value"). The effect of this provision, therefore, is to provide that a default under another derivatives transaction by any entity specified in the schedule will constitute a default under the master agreement at issue, and so permit the non-defaulting party to terminate that master agreement. Thus the non-defaulting party is able to terminate its own master agreement even before their counterparty has committed a default under that other master agreement.

43–19

G.   Credit downgrade clause

The parties may decide to include a provision that if the counterparty's credit worth deteriorates, that would constitute either an event of default or a termination event under the master agreement. This is not part of the standard

43–20

---

[44] ISDA Master Agreement, s.5(a)(v).
[45] ISDA Master Agreement, s.5(a)(v).
[46] ISDA Master Agreement, s.11.

documentation language. The issues as to the availability of credit downgrade and credit evaluation clauses were considered in relation to *credit derivatives*.[47] The difficulty is whether the parties are prepared to wait for an official downgrading from a credit ratings agency, or whether the parties instead choose to provide for the means by which they themselves will calculate whether or not the counterparty has had its credit worth deteriorate: the latter option would be difficult to negotiate into contractual language, whereas at least the former has the merit of objectivity. In relation to the standard provision in the ISDA master agreement for credit downgrade on a merger of one of the parties, it is provided simply that there will be a termination event if the "creditworthiness of the resulting ... entity is materially weaker" than that of the original contracting party.[48] This would be one way of providing for such a credit downgrade but it leaves open all of the issues of calculation of that credit worth.

H.   Corporate restructuring

43–21   An event of default will take place in circumstances in which there is some alteration of the corporate structure of one of the parties to a transaction, whether in the form of a takeover, merger or substantial restructuring. The concern is that the resultant entity will not assume the obligations of the predecessor. There may also be concerns about non-corporate entities which alter their capital markedly—such as trusts or partnerships which do not alter in structure but which distribute a large amount of their capital among their beneficiaries or partners respectively. Clearly, in this instance the credit worth of the resultant entity will tend to be different from the entity which entered into the master agreement originally.

I.   "Bankruptcy"

43–22   The longest single provision in the ISDA Master Agreement is the event of default relating to "bankruptcy", which encompasses a range of activities ranging from outright insolvency through to the commencement of proceedings seeking an order for many outcomes under insolvency law.[49] Clearly, insolvency would make it impossible to perform future obligations under the master agreement.[50] The ISDA master agreement from its earliest inception was concerned to achieve two things: to allow a non-defaulting party to terminate the master agreement if there was any appreciable risk of its counterparty going into insolvency and to prevent the insolvency of any single market participant from causing systemic risk by standardising the rights and obligations of all market participants in the over-the-counter market as far as possible. The ISDA definition of "bankruptcy" includes: actual bankruptcy, liquidation or insolvency; orders for receivership or the vesting of title in a trustee in bankruptcy; service of a creditor's petition for

---

[47] See para.40–44.
[48] ISDA Master Agreement, s.5(b)(iv).
[49] See generally the discussion of close-out netting in para.22–91.
[50] ISDA Master Agreement, s.5(a)(vii).

winding up which is not dismissed within 30 days; where the entity itself admits its inability to pay under any specified type of transaction; or when it is unable to meet its financial obligations generally or when it repudiates its obligations under the master agreement generally. When the entity is not a company, however, it will be important to encompass their equivalent to insolvency, such as a de-capitalisation of a fund, or the winding up of an unincorporated association, or the termination of a trust. The eighth category of "bankruptcy" in the ISDA master agreement is a reference to any event which "has an analogous effect" to any of the foregoing seven categories. So, in *Merrill Lynch v Winterthur Swiss Insurance*[51] it was held by Gloster J. the "sauveguarde" proceedings under French insolvency law would have an analogous effect to the other bankruptcy events because it was a procedure which was used to seek relief so as to protect creditor's rights.

3. NO-FAULT "TERMINATION EVENTS"

A. The nature of termination events

The no-fault "termination events" are a range of events which are beyond the control of the parties—relating typically to a change in the law or in some regulatory practice—which affects the validity or pricing of transactions falling under the master agreement. The expectation is that these are eventualities which the parties could find a way of avoiding through negotiation and which therefore do not trigger the termination procedure automatically in the way that the events of default (considered immediately above) do. Instead, the parties have a period of time in which they can seek to resolve the problem caused by the termination event, and it is only if that proves impossible that the termination procedure is commenced.

43–23

B. Illegality

Among the representations[52] ordinarily given by the parties in a master agreement is that there is no illegality in existence at the time of creating the master agreement which would make any of the parties' derivatives transactions illegal in any of the places where they are to be performed by virtue, inter alia, of a "change in [an] applicable law". This provision is a Termination Event so that the parties can attempt to negotiate a way out of the illegality, whether by booking the transaction through offices in different jurisdictions or through some other means. Where the illegality cannot be avoided, it will be open to the non-affected party to terminate the agreement.[53] As was considered in Chapter 6,

43–24

---

[51] *Merrill Lynch International Bank Ltd v Winterthur Swiss Insurance Company* [2007] EWHC 893 (Comm), [2008] B.I.P.R. 129.
[52] See para.41–50.
[53] ISDA Master Agreement, s.5(b)(i).

as a question of the English conflict of laws, a contract will not be enforceable where it is illegal under its applicable law[54] or where the contract is illegal in the place of its performance.[55]

43–25   In relation specifically to derivatives in *Nuova Safim SpA v The Sakura Bank Ltd*[56] an Italian state-owned company was put into liquidation and legislation prohibited it from trading. It was held that this constituted an "illegality" within the terms of the master agreement being "a change . . . in [an] applicable law". Notice was validly given under the terms of the master agreement. The terms of the applicable Treasury decree prohibited the transfer of the agreement to any other entity. Thomas J. therefore affirmed the validity of this termination event based on illegality and ordered that the master agreement had been properly terminated.

C.   Tax provisions

43–26   The master agreement will ordinarily contain provisions in which the parties represent to one another the tax effect of their transactions so that there is no interference with the pricing of their transactions. Among the termination events, therefore, are provisions as to a change in the applicable tax laws (including a change in regulatory practice or case law), or the introduction of a withholding tax, or a different tax treatment resulting from a merger between the counterparty and another entity. In any of these cases, the idea is that the parties should seek to restructure their dealings so as to avoid the tax impact of these changes, and only if that is impossible to terminate the master agreement.

D.   The effect of restructurings

43–27   If one of the parties were to merge with or to take over or otherwise to substantially restructure itself, then a number of problems might result. The first problem is that the restructuring might lead to a different tax treatment for the parties' transactions. The second problem is that the resultant entity after the restructuring may not be bound by the legal obligations created in the master agreement. The third problem is that the credit worth of the resultant entity might be weaker than the credit worth of the original contracting party. All of these issues will constitute separate termination events, requiring the parties to seek to resolve the problem or, failing a resolution, to terminate the master agreement according to the termination procedure.

---

[54]   art.8, Rome Convention.
[55]   *Ralli Bros v Cia Naviera Sota y Aznar* [1920] 2 K.B. 287, especially at 304, per Scrutton L.J.
[56]   [1999] C.L.C. 1830; [1999] 2 All E.R. (Comm) 526.

4. The Termination Procedure

A. "Early termination"

The jargon terminology describing termination of the transactions in an ISDA Master Agreement refers to "Early Termination" whereby, once an event of default has been proved or a termination event has arisen, the parties identify an early termination date on which the calculation agent identifies the value of the outstanding transactions between the parties and reduces all of the outstanding balances between them to a single, net amount in a currency identified in the Master Agreement which one party is to pay to the other in resolution of all outstanding transactions between them. This section considers this procedure and the case law which has arisen in relation to the termination provisions.

43–28

The standard-form ISDA Master Agreement identifies the manner in which it shall be terminated as a result of a termination event or an event of default.[57] The usual mechanism is to provide for notice of termination to be provided by the non-defaulting party. This might be obviated by the agreement of the parties where they opt for automatic termination of their contractual relations. In relation to events of default the position varies from event to event, as considered in the discussion of the various events of default above. In relation to late payment the non-defaulting party is required to give notice after which the defaulting party has three local business days to make payment.[58] The position in relation to any other material breach of the contract is the same but with a grace period of thirty days after notice has been given.[59] In any event, after any applicable grace period has passed and the event of default is still continuing, then the non-defaulting party is required to give twenty days' notice of the activation of the termination procedure. As mentioned above, the procedure then operates on the basis of the selection of an "Early Termination Date"[60] at which time all outstanding transactions are valued and a single, net figure is identified by the calculation agent to satisfy all outstanding transactions under the master agreement.[61] No further payments or deliveries are required to be made under any transaction outstanding at that time.

43–29

B. Payments on early termination: "market quotation", "loss" and "replacement value"

The process of calculating the early termination amount

There are two key issues when deciding the early termination amount. First, the detailed question of establishing the termination value of each outstanding transaction. This is a mathematical or financial-theoretical question. Secondly,

43–30

---

[57] ISDA Master Agreement s.6.
[58] ISDA Master Agreement, s.6.
[59] ISDA Master Agreement, s.6.
[60] ISDA Master Agreement, s.6(c).
[61] ISDA Master Agreement, s.6(d).

and the focus of this section, there is a legal question as to the identification of the criterion on the basis of which those calculations are to be established. There are two possible approaches this legal question: identifying the cost of acquiring replacement transactions from market-makers, or instead compensating the non-defaulting party for the loss which results from the termination of that transaction. In the terminology used in the old 1992 ISDA Master Agreement that is, a choice respectively between "market quotation" and "loss". In the terminology used more generally after the introduction of the 2002 ISDA Master Agreement that is a choice respectively between "market quotation" and "replacement value".[62] It is the definition of these provisions which has featured in litigation under English law. The parties then select their preferred approach in the schedule to the master agreement.

43–31 It has been accepted under New York law that they will not constitute extortionate or unconscionable payments if they are not in excess of the damage suffered by the non-defaulting party by way of loss[63]; under English law, the problem has been as to what forms of loss or expense may be brought into account when calculating the early termination amount. They must not be "penalty clauses" under English law, as discussed in Chapter 19.[64] The effect of the English cases was a change in the standard Master Agreement terminology mentioned above.

"Market quotation"

43–32 "Market quotation" involves the calculation of the early termination amounts by reference to quotations obtained from a given number of market participants who are market makers in the appropriate product. Roughly speaking, "market quotation" is the amount which the market would pay on the date of termination for another product which would "have the effect of preserving for such party the economic equivalent of any payment or delivery".[65] Importantly this requires the market-maker to consider the precise commercial effect of the terminated transaction and to isolate the cost of replicating that in a replacement transaction. The provision assumes that the mean quotation will be taken, usually from five market makers or exceptionally from fewer market makers, depending on the product at issue.[66] This underlines once again the importance of including in derivatives contracts some statement as to the purpose of the transaction for its purchaser so that any particularly important feature of the product, which may affect its pricing, can be taken into account by those market makers. Importantly market quotation includes a valuation of all outstanding, contingently-owed obligations and not simply obligations which have matured at the early termination date. In consequence, this provision assumes that the outstanding transactions are executory transactions which remain unperformed until all

---

[62] ISDA Master Agreement, s.6(e) and s.14.

[63] *Drexel Financial Products v Midland Bank Ltd* 1992 US Dist LEXIS 21273 (SDNY)

[64] See para.19–39.

[65] ISDA Master Agreement, s.14 "market quotation".

[66] Market quotation may be an awkward measure in markets in which few institutions are sufficiently expert or in which the derivative being used by the parties has confidential components which the seller would not want to have revealed to its competitors who would ordinarily make up the reference market makers in this context.

payments have been made. By contrast, the definition of "loss" refers only to amounts lost by the early termination date.

The extent of the definition of "market quotation" has been considered in **43–33** *Peregrine Fixed Income Ltd v Robinson*.[67] Peregrine was a seller of derivatives which went into liquidation at a time when it had outstanding swap transactions with Robinson, a Thai company which operated department stores in Thailand which had also gone into liquidation. The parties' transactions fell to be subjected to the early termination procedure. The question arose as to the parties' selection of market quotation as their method of early termination. When market quotations as to the cost of replacement transactions were taken, the quotations took into account, amongst other things, Robinson's impending liquidation. Necessarily Robinson's credit worth affected the price at which the reference market makers were prepared to offer replacement transactions. Robinson contended that, further to the definition of "market quotation",[68] the parties were entitled to rely on the alternative method of "loss"[69] in circumstances in which the use of the market quotation method would not generate a "commercially reasonable result" when calculating the final "settlement amount" under the termination procedure.[70] It was held by Moore-Bick J. that to take into account the deterioration in Robinson's credit worth was not commercially reasonable, in part because there was no credit support document in place in relation to this transaction. In deciding whether or not a party is acting in a commercially reasonable manner as calculation agent in this sense, in the absence of straightforward bad faith, his lordship expressed the view that the test to be used was the test of reasonableness used in judicial review of public bodies in *Associated Provincial Picture Houses Ltd v Wednesbury Corporation*.[71] This is quite remarkable given that that test related to the finding of reasonableness in relation to public bodies in administrative law, as opposed to finding commercial reasonableness in derivatives transactions. Further, it was held that a party is not entitled to include within the measurement the cost of funding the payment of the early termination amount itself.[72]

However, the definition of "market quotation" provides that the quotations should **43–34** be reached on any basis "that would have the effect of preserving the economic equivalent of any payment or delivery"[73] In a situation in which a credit support arrangement were in place, it could be argued that the credit worth of the counterparty would be something which would be taken into account. Indeed it

[67] [2000] C.L.C. 1328, [2000] Lloyd's Rep. Bank 304.
[68] ISDA Master Agreement, s.14, "market quotation".
[69] See para.40–38.
[70] ISDA Master Agreement, s.14, "settlement amount"; [2000] C.L.C. 1328, [2000] Lloyd's Rep. Bank 304, at [17].
[71] [1948] 1 K.B. 223. This is surprising given that the *Wednesbury* doctrine relates only to actions against public bodies for irrationality and not to situations in which one party to a commercial contract is seeking to make a profit at the expense of the other party to that contract. For example, how should the post-*Wednesbury* public law idea of "legitimate expectations" be adapted to fit into commercial situations, other than by private law estoppel. It is suggested that these public law doctrines ought to have no part to play in private law without more careful scrutiny.
[72] [2000] C.L.C. 1328; [2000] Lloyd's Rep. Bank 304, at 32.
[73] ISDA Master Agreement s.14, "market quotation".

would be advisable to amend the definition of "market quotation" and of "settlement amount" in the master agreement because it is likely that a default by a counterparty leading to early termination will necessarily be bound up with a deterioration in its credit worth.

43–35 A theoretical question must arise as to what a court should do if the quotations which are received are simply unreasonable. The question of how to conduct the market quotation process in this regard was considered in the Australian case of *Enron Australia Finance Pty (in liquidation) v Integral Energy Australia*[74] in relation to instruments contracted on the illiquid Australian electricity derivatives market. In that case four market quotations were sought, in relation to which one price was about one quarter of the value of the other three quotations. The court held that if three experts quoted higher replacement costs at levels at which it subsequently emerged that the contracting parties would never have actually contracted, then those quotations may be ignored. Instead the court in that case accepted the quotation of the single expert who provided a price taking into account only the mid-price of the average bid/offer prices in these illiquid instruments and so reached a price at which these parties might in fact have done business. The Australian court was keen to recognise that the parties had altered the standard master agreement provisions to take account of the specific Australian experience of contracting in the Australian electricity derivatives market rather than relying on general derivatives market practice in the rest of the world. This demonstrates that the quotations for replacement values of derivatives may not necessarily be found to be decisive by the courts. Indeed, the experience of the ISDA termination provisions before English and Australian courts, as discussed in this chapter, is that the courts have generally been unimpressed by the effects of purportedly standard practice in the over-the-counter derivatives markets. An understanding of the general law of contract under the governing law of the contract will therefore always be essential even in the closed contractual universe of derivatives market practice and jargon, particularly when dealing with a party who is not a market counterparty or with a novel form of product.

43–36 Demonstrating the existence of a market and the features of the market in relation to which a calculation is to be effected will be important. So in *Dampskibsselskabet "Norden" AS v Andre & Cie SA*[75] issues arose in relation to a forward freight agreement. The defendant published a press release which suggested that it was unable to meet its financial obligations when due because it no longer had access to credit, and so the claimant contended that the defendant was therefore in breach of its continuing contractual representations that it was still of good standing. Issues arose more specifically as to whether the claimant was entitled to damages as though the contract had been properly performed or whether it was entitled only to damages for the cost of effecting a replacement transaction. The question therefore arose whether or not there was a market in existence in which a replacement transaction could in any event have been acquired. It was found as a fact by Toulson J. that a market for such a transaction did exist and therefore

---

[74] [2002] NSWSC 819.
[75] [2003] EWHC 84 (Comm); [2003] 1 Lloyd's Rep. 287.

that an estimate of the claimant's loss could be identified as the cost of effecting such a replacement. In *Flame SA v Primera Maritime*[76] the issue arose as to whether or not there can even be a proper calculation in circumstances in which there is no market—for example, in the situation after the collapse of Lehman Brothers in September 2008 when banks would not deal with one another and as such it was almost impossible to acquire a meaningful market price for some assets. It was contended that the ISDA termination procedure could not operate when no price can be found for the assets in question, and in particular when those prices were entirely extraordinary.[77] This case proceeded on a purely interlocutory basis but, on the basis that the calculation agent appeared to have identified prices in good faith, it was held that the ISDA termination procedure would operate normally. It was held that no alternative mechanism for calculating the amounts payable nor any alternative amount had been provided to the court, and therefore that the termination should proceed. In essence, what one can draw from this case is reassurance that the ISDA termination procedure will be applied in the ordinary course of events, even if market prices are volatile. Alternatively, one could take the view that the operation of the termination procedure can be entirely random because the prices acquired here would be entirely guesswork and would probably be entirely different once the crisis had passed.

In exceptional circumstances an English court will look behind the parties' documentation and consider their underlying commercial intentions either in the interpretation of that documentation or by amending that documentation to achieve a just result.[78] So, in *Boom Time Holdings Ltd v Goldman Sachs*[79] the Court of Appeal held that where a calculation agent effected calculations in relation to a barrier call option in relation to shares in P Ltd, under a contract which did not take into account the possibility of P Ltd issuing bonus shares, an alteration in the knock-out price and the rebate amount was necessary to give effect to the genuine intentions of the parties and so achieve "economic equivalence" between the parties' expectations and their contractual documentation. Thus the courts will rectify commercial contracts where the circumstances demand it.

43–37

"Loss"

The alternative method of calculating the early termination amount under the 1992 version of the master agreement was that of "loss" which, broadly put, required proof of the loss suffered by the non-defaulting party. This term was replaced in the 2002 version of the ISDA Master Agreement by the term "replacement value" which is considered below.[80] However, the following

43–38

---

[76] [2009] EWHC 1973 (Comm), Judge Chambers QC.

[77] As was argued in the previous chapter, this is another reason for the parties including a provision in their agreement which explains their purpose in creating the agreement and their contractual expectations as to the limits within which prices will move.

[78] See para.17–01 on this issue as to the difficulties in the creation of accurate contracts on trading floors.

[79] Unreported February 25, 1997, per Colman J.; reversed on appeal, [1998] EWCA Civ 169.

[80] See para.40–47.

discussion of "loss" is retained because it remains a feature of many currently existing master agreements and because it has been the focus of specific litigation.

43–39 The definition of "loss" refers to "an amount which the [the non-defaulting party] reasonably determines in good faith to be its total losses and costs in connection with" the master agreement and terminated transactions.[81] The factors falling within that definition include "any loss of bargain, cost of funding, or at the election of such party . . . loss or cost incurred as a result of its terminating, liquidating, obtaining or re-establishing any hedge or related trading position".[82] Interestingly the term "Loss" in this context does not include the parties' legal expenses.[83] Importantly, these matters "include" the things which the parties can take into account and, consequently, do not constitute a comprehensive list of the losses which might be included.[84] This method of "loss" is often easier to police than "market quotation" although it does have problems of evidence in terms of loss and also in taking into account the full range of issues which can be included in the scope of loss. The cost of unwinding hedging transactions is one matter which the non-defaulting party would usually seek to include in its calculations. Significantly, in decided cases where the contract was held to have been void, the courts have held that the cost of unwinding a hedge is not a loss which falls to be taken into account when seeking to identify the total loss which can be claimed by any one of the parties.[85] Therefore, once again, it is important to ensure that the means of calculating such a hedging cost, and indeed any other anticipated loss, is specified in the contract.

43–40 The question of what constitutes "loss" has been considered by the English High Court in *Australia and New Zealand Banking Group v Societe Generale*.[86] Australia and New Zealand Banking Group ("ANZ") entered into derivatives with Societe Generale ("SG") in relation to Russian interest rates. SG had entered into hedging transactions with a third party which was subject to Russian banking law. The transaction between ANZ and SG was terminated early on the happening of a special event of default, akin to a form of market disruption provision, included in their agreement which related to the suspension of trading in the Russian banking market. There was a moratorium on payments in the Russian banking system which called that event of default into effect. That moratorium also prevented payments being made to SG under its hedging transaction. SG sought to bring the loss of that hedge into account as part of its "loss" under the master agreement.

43–41 At first instance,[87] Aikens J. held that the hedging transaction was unconnected to the main derivatives transaction. In part, his lordship's concern was that such a hedge may be open to abuse in that ANZ would have had no control over the

---

[81] ISDA Master Agreement, s.14, "loss".
[82] ISDA Master Agreement, s.14, "loss".
[83] ISDA Master Agreement, s.14, "loss".
[84] ISDA Master Agreement, s.14, "loss".
[85] *Kleinwort Benson v Birmingham C.C.* [1996] 3 W.L.R. 1139.
[86] [2000] 1 All E.R. (Comm) 682 (CA).
[87] *Australia and New Zealand Banking Group v Societe Generale* Unreported, September 21, 1999, Aikens J.

amount which SG would be able to claim was lost to it by way of loss of that hedge. Indeed, SG's contention was that its sizeable gain under the derivatives transaction with ANZ was turned into a loss when the hedge was included. Therefore, the hedging cost was excluded from the calculation of loss. That decision was upheld by the Court of Appeal on appeal.[88]

On appeal SG sought to rely on two further procedural points. In seeking a new trial, SG contended that the Russian banking moratorium itself constituted an event of default under the master agreement such that the amounts to be brought into account for the calculation of "Loss" were different from those agreed at first instance. They sought to distinguish between "clean" payments which assumed the proper functioning of the Russian banking system and the more (allegedly) realistic "dirty" payments which would reflect the diminished value of the payments given the Russian banking crisis which had precipitated the moratorium. A second "new point" raised by SG on appeal was that the definition of "loss" begins with the word "including" to qualify the exclusivity which one might otherwise assume in the list of issues which are to be taken into account when calculating "loss". On this basis SG contended that it should be entitled to bring into account the loss of its hedge, the "dirty" payments, and so forth.

43–42

The Court of Appeal, in the person of Mance L.J., nevertheless refused both of these points of appeal on the basis that it was "inherently unlikely" that ANZ would have entered into a "futures contract" [sic] on the basis that it share the risk of a "simple collapse" in SG's hedge. In effect, the two points on appeal were capable of being disposed of using the analysis which Aikens J. had used at first instance. Therefore, to bring the cost of such a hedge within the transaction it would have been important that SG included expressly some provision as to its hedging strategy.

43–43

The Court of Appeal's decision in *Australia and New Zealand v Societe Generale* is in similar terms to the decision of the Court of Appeal in *Kleinwort Benson v Birmingham C.C.*[89] was not referred to by the Court of Appeal. It would be essential for the inclusion of the cost of losing or unwinding a hedge within the terms of the documentation as something the parties intended to include within their definition of "loss".[90] The ISDA master agreement did expressly include mention of the "loss or cost incurred as a result of its terminating, liquidating, obtaining or re-establishing any hedge or related trading position" as something which is included in the ISDA definition of "loss" for precisely these purposes.[91] The courts are maintaining a common lawyer's notion of foreseeability here and not applying the literal terms of the ISDA master agreement. The decision of the court at first instance in *Australia and New Zealand v Societe Generale* was that it was the Russian banking moratorium which caused the loss by preventing payment and not the loss of the hedge itself; it is suggested that the dividing line between those things is very narrow indeed.

43–44

---

[88] *Australia and New Zealand Banking Group v Societe Generale* [2000] 1 All E.R. (Comm) 682 (CA); [2000] C.L.C. 833; [2000] Lloyd's Rep. Bank 304, at [16].
[89] [1996] 3 W.L.R. 1139; [1996] 4 All E.R. 733.
[90] A. Hudson, *The Law on Financial Derivatives*, para.2–117.
[91] ISDA Master Agreement (ISDA, 1992), s.14, "loss".

43–45   The decision of the Court of Appeal in *Kleinwort Benson v Birmingham City Council*[92] took a similar approach to recovering the cost of hedging. In that case, the bank contended that the defence of passing on should be available to it on the basis that it had entered into interest rate swap agreements with third parties to "hedge" its risk under the agreement with the respondent local authority. It was this hedge that was said to constitute the passing on; but the local authority was objecting that its right to recover its payments should not be offset by the bank's cost of hedging. The Court of Appeal held that the hedging agreement was not a part of the main agreement with the local authority and therefore amounts paid under it would not attract the defence of passing on. Thus, even though hedging is a necessary part of the derivatives process, the English courts have tended to refuse to take the cost of hedging into account when calculating "loss" in relation to termination of a master agreement or in relation to defences (such as passing on) under the general law.

43–46   In Scotland it has been held that the cost of funding and closing-out a hedge is something which could possibly be taken into account when calculating losses.[93] This approach is based on evidence of market practice which suggested that both parties would have hedged their transaction and therefore that the inclusion of the costs of these hedging positions ought properly to be taken into account.[94] This market-sensitive approach is clearly at odds with the approach in England.[95] However, the apparent willingness of the Scots court to admit such a calculation was tempered by a requirement that the nature and size of the hedge be something which was within the reasonable contemplation of the counterparty. That much is similar to the English approach.[96]

"Replacement value"

43–47   The "replacement value" of the terminated transactions is arrived at by the determining party calculating in good faith

> "the amount of the costs ... or gains ... of the Determining Party that would be incurred or realised to replace, or to provide the economic equivalent of the remaining payments, deliveries or option rights in respect of that Terminated Transaction or group of Terminated Transactions".[97]

Adopting the language of the court in *Peregrine Fixed Income Ltd v Robinson*,[98] these calculations are to be performed "using commercially reasonable procedures".[99] While this provision includes some of the factors, such as yields, which may be taken into account in making these calculations, there is no comprehensive list of the formulae (indeed regrettably one would not find that

---

[92] [1994] 4 All E.R. 890.

[93] *Bank of Scotland v Dunedin Property Investment Co Ltd (No.1)*, *The Times*, May 16, 1997.

[94] See above.

[95] *Australia and New Zealand Banking Group v Societe Generale* [2000] 1 All E.R. (Comm) 682 (CA), [2000] C.L.C. 833, [2000] Lloyd's Rep. Bank. 304, at [16].

[96] See above.

[97] ISDA Master Agreement s.14, "replacement value".

[98] [2000] C.L.C. 1328; [2000] Lloyd's Rep. Bank 304.

[99] ISDA Master Agreement, s.14, "replacement value".

the standard agreement would contain that) but it is suggested that contracting parties ought to include more detail either in confirmations or otherwise as to the basis on which it would expect such calculations to be made in relation to specific groups of transactions. That matters such as the cost of funding the termination and any loss of hedging are intended to included, are contained in the definition. As considered in the foregoing two paragraphs, such express provisions have been ignored by the English courts when deciding that it would not be commercially reasonable to include the cost of a hedge within the losses calculated by either party as having been suffered by it. It is suggested therefore that the parties to master agreements ought to include specific mention of any hedging strategies they might use in relation to their derivatives transactions so that there is no doubt that they were within the parties' contemplation.

5.   LIMITS ON THE EXTENT OF THE EFFICACY OF THE ISDA DOCUMENTATION ARCHITECTURE

The local authority swaps cases offer a very significant warning about the ramifications of using standard form contracts when dealing with non-typical market participants (such as local authorities) without taking better security against the risk that those non-typical market participants did not have the capacity to enter into those contracts. If a person does have the capacity to enter into a contract then that person cannot create a valid contract: and if there is no valid contract then there are no terms on which the people involved can rely to terminate their arrangement in the way that they may wish. Instead, they are thrown back on the tender mercies of the general law. In the local authority swaps cases the result of being thrown back on the general law was that the standard market contracts were held to be of no effect in the context (and so the courts did not even bother to read them), the banks did not receive the remedies which the derivatives markets wanted, and the banks were left without any effective security against losses which could have been much greater if the defendants had not been public bodies with deep pockets. The lesson to be drawn from these cases is that it is not possible to contract away the general law with standard contracts if transactional lawyers do not pause and consider the basic issues with their clients' business and the simple risks associated with taking security which that business raises.   **43–48**

In the local authority swaps cases (decided under English law) it was held to be beyond the powers of UK local authorities to enter into interest rate swap contracts (although the legislation dealing with local authorities has since been altered).[100] In those cases it was held that the termination provisions set out in the master agreements signed between the banks and the local authorities were of no relevance to the courts' analysis of those cases because the creation of those contracts was beyond the powers of the parties. So in the Court of Appeal in *Westdeutsche Landesbank v Islington* it was held that the parties had simply failed to make a contract on the grounds that it was void ab initio being outwith the capacity of the local authority. Legatt L.J. held that: **43–49**

---

[100] *Hazell v Hammersmith & Fulham* [1992] 2 A.C. 1; [1991] 2 W.L.R. 372; [1991] 1 All E.R. 545.

"There can have been no consideration under a contract void ab initio. So it is fallacious to speak of the failure of consideration having been partial. What is meant is that the parties did, in the belief that the contract was enforceable, part of what they would have been required to do if it had been. As it was, they were not performing the contract even in part: they were making payments that had no legal justification, instead of affording each other mutual consideration for an enforceable contract."[101]

Similarly, Hobhouse J. held at first instance that "[i]n the case of ultra vires transactions . . . there is not and never has been a contract".[102] The ramification of that finding was that the court applied the general law of restitution of payments and did not enforce the terms of master agreement, the confirmation nor any credit support document. In this light, the ISDA philosophy of combining all of the transactions into one contract was shown to be at its most dangerous because when one part of the contract was found to have been void ab initio such that the entire contract was unenforceable.

43–50 When a contract is found to be void for whatever reason, the claimant will be entitled to recover any moneys paid to its counterparty under a personal claim for money had and received at common law.[103] However, such a personal claim will be of no practical worth if the defendant has gone into insolvency, or if the defendant's assets are held in a jurisdiction in which such a judgment for money had and received cannot be enforced. The claimant will not be entitled to a proprietary claim over moneys paid under a contract where the parties intentions were that absolute title in moneys passed under the transaction are to become the absolute property of their recipient, which is the usual practice in financial transactions.[104] If the contract is void then no credit support documentation will be effective if it forms part of the single agreement with the master agreement. Therefore, the claimant has no effective remedy other than a personal claim for money had and received. A preferable arrangement would have been to have had a free-standing trust structure such that either party would have been entitled to be vested with full equitable title in any collateral posted in that structure. There was nothing to suggest that the parties did not have the capacity to create a trust. The trust structure would mean that the beneficiary under such a trust would have been entitled to be treated as a secured creditor in any insolvency or other failure to pay.[105] These issues are considered in greater detail in my book, *Swaps, Restitution and Trusts* (London: Sweet & Maxwell, 1999).

---

[101] [1994] 1 W.L.R. 938, 953; [1994] 4 All E.R. 890, 969.
[102] [1994] 4 All E.R. 890, 924, Hobhouse J.
[103] *Westdeutsche Landesbank v Islington* [1996] A.C. 669.
[104] [1996] A.C. 669.
[105] *Re Goldcorp* [1995] 1 A.C. 74.

CHAPTER 44

SECURITISATION

CORE PRINCIPLES

Securitisation transactions enable institutions with large income streams to turn that income into capital. So, if a credit card company or a mortgage provider wants to realise an immediate capital sum instead of waiting to receive thousands of small income streams from its customers, then a securitisation structure turns those income streams into securities which are issued to investors.

The structure of a securitisation is complex. A significant by-product of a securitisation is that the income-producing assets are transferred off the selling institution's balance sheet by transferring all of those assets to a special purpose vehicle (either a trust or a company), with a trustee holding those assets on trust for the investors. The investors in turn acquire bonds from the special purpose vehicle: i.e. the investors transfer capital to the special purpose vehicle (and thus indirectly to the originator of the transaction) and in return the investors acquire an income stream in the form of interest on those bonds.

The credit profile of the transaction can be enhanced by including a credit default swap in the structure whereby the investors are entitled to receive any shortfall in the pay-out from the underlying bonds by an increase in the amounts owed to it under the swap. A credit default swap (as considered in Chapter 40) involves a swaps dealer which, for a fee, agrees to pay out the difference between what a bond investor should have received under the bonds and what she actually received: it is in effect a form of insurance against non-payment under a bond.

Complex collateralised debt obligations ("CDOs") group a large number of underlying receivables into one security which is then marketed to investors. The combination of receivables is organised into tranches with receivables of different credit qualities being grouped separately. Different qualities of investor typically acquire different forms of right in the event of the failure of CDO. CDO transactions failed in large numbers during the banking crisis of 2008.

1. INTRODUCTION

A. What is "securitisation"?

44–01 Literally, the process of "securitisation" means translating a financial instrument or a group of financial instruments into a security.[1] Securities were discussed in Part X of this book. The collective term "security" includes shares, bonds and so forth. A security is a bundle of rights (whether to receive a stream of income like a bond, or to receive a dividend and to vote at company meetings like a share, or something of that sort) which can itself be traded and thus transferred in return for a market value. Securitisation is the process of taking rights (such as a right to receive a stream of income) and translating that bundle of rights into a security which can be traded on the open market.

44–02 Our working definition of a simple "securitisation" will be as follows[2]:

> "Securitisation is the process by which a range of cash receivables or similar assets are grouped together and offered to investors in the form of a security in return for a capital payment from the investors."

That is a reasonable definition of a simple form of securitisation, but perhaps a worked example would be helpful. Suppose a bank has lent money to 10,000 ordinary homeowners by way of 10,000 different mortgages all of which were contracted on the same standard terms,[3] all of which are due to last for the same 25 year period of time before redemption, and all of which attract interest payments on a monthly basis from borrowers at the same rate of interest. The bank's profits will therefore be earned in monthly increments by means of the interest payments made on a monthly basis over 25 years before the loan capital is repaid. The downside in this arrangement is that the bank has to wait 25 years to accrue all of its profits and to receive the return of its capital. The bank may decide that it would prefer to get most of its profits up-front, rather than wait for 25 years, by selling off the 10,000 mortgages to someone else who is prepared to earn those income profits slowly over 25 years and who is also prepared to pay a

---

[1] The following books usefully consider securitisation in some detail: P. Jeffrey (ed.), *A Practitioner's Guide to Securitisation* (City & Financial Publishing, 2006); P Wood, *Project Finance, Securitisations, Subordinated Debt*, 2nd edn (London: Sweet & Maxwell, 2007), pp.111–174.

[2] This is my own attempted, general definition. The definition of "securitisation" in *Barron's Dictionary* is a "process of distributing risk by aggregating debt instruments in a pool, then issuing new securities back by the pool".

[3] It makes it easier (for the purposes of this example at least) to bundle the contracts together if they are effected on the same or broadly similar terms.

large capital sum for the privilege.[4] "Securitisation" is the description of this process of taking the 10,000 separate mortgages and bundling them up together into a single security (hence the term "securitisation") which can be sold off for a single capital amount to a buyer or buyers.

The sale price for this security would be at a discount to the actual total of future profits from the 25 mortgages for three reasons. First, because it cannot be known exactly what those future profits will be (because we cannot know what market interest rates will actually be in the future). Secondly, because the only incentive for the buyer of this security would be to earn a profit through 25 years over the capital amount paid for the security up-front: no buyer will pay the total expected return from the 10,000 mortgages in cash today, and then wait 25 years to get its money back. Instead, the buyer will expect a discount so that it can earn a profit over 25 years. Thirdly, because it is likely that a given number of borrowers will default on their payment obligations under the mortgages. This is expressed by finance theorists as "the time value of money": that means that there is a benefit to having a capital sum up-front as opposed to waiting for a stream of income payments which means that the capital sum paid by the purchaser will have to be less than the anticipated aggregate of the mortgage interest payments. Because the securitised assets are sold as securities, a number of buyers can be acquired, as with an issue of shares. The holders of those securities will find that there are times when market interest rates are such that the return on the mortgages is better than market interest rates and times when the return on the mortgages is worse than the return on market rates: consequently, the value of the securities will change from time to time when compared to market rates and so a market in those securities will be available.

44–03

Securitisations are also referred to by some market participants as "asset-backed securities", where "asset-backed" means there are underlying receivables or assets (in this example, the mortgages) which provide income for the structure. More precisely, the particular example set out here would be known as a "mortgage-backed security" by some people, because it is "backed" by mortgages.

44–04

Securitisations can take effect over various forms of assets or receivables. Mortgages were used here merely as an example. This process of selling off debts is a very old one indeed: it used to be known as "debt factoring". What is different is the complexity of selling off very large numbers of assets at once and doing it by way of the securities markets. This is part of the process of financialisation whereby financial instruments, financial markets and financial theory with its complex pricing models are being used to reorganise the market in products like mortgages. The nature of the securitisation market is considered below.[5]

44–05

---

[4] Clearly, the capital sum paid upfront would be less than the aggregate of those monthly interest payments over 25 years, or else there would be no profit for the investors.

[5] See para.41–07.

B. Securitisation and the global financial crisis of 2007–09

44–06 Securitisation became very newsworthy in 2007–08 with the so-called "credit crunch". As discussed above, however, securitisation seemed like a sensible twist on an old-fashioned idea: if you are owed a debt, that debt could be sold to someone else at a discount and you can realise some of the cash value of that debt without waiting for your debtor to pay. Financial institutions who were owed large numbers of debts at once used the same idea, with the financial twist that the debts were pooled and turned into securities.

44–07 The step change[6] in securitisation business seems to have come when market practice changed from only securitising assets, which were already in existence, to a practice in which market participants realised that there was a large amount of money to be made from securitisation and therefore that it was attractive to create mortgages solely for the purpose of being able to securitize them. This problem is a problem of a pressure to "originate" new assets to be securitized. By origination is meant the process of changing sales policy so that the mortgage company relaxes its policy on what level of risk it is prepared to take. As is explained in Chapter 45, this is the story of the now-legendary "sub prime"[7] mortgage market in the USA in which mortgage companies began to sell mortgages to people who could not be expected to be able to repay their loans. Loans were made at the market value of the mortgaged property and sometimes for even more than the market value of the mortgaged property. The expectation was that the housing market in the USA would continue to rise and so that all of the property taken as security for the mortgages would increase in value too, so that the loans would eventually be less than the market value of the security even if the borrowers could not make repayment. Furthermore, the attractions of securitisation meant that having more assets—for example in the form of sub-prime mortgages—which could be bundled up and traded at a profit was also attractive to the investment banks who bought them as well as to the mortgage companies who sold the original mortgages.

44–08 Let us take the example of an old-fashioned mortgage lender—as Northern Rock used to be[8]—which operates as a building society recently transformed into a bank and which uses the money it receives from its borrowers to lend out to new customers. This is a conservative business model for a financial institution. There is comparatively little borrowing compared to the levels of leverage in other financial institutions; perhaps there is some issuing of shares once the building society takes the decision like so many building societies in the UK to convert from a building society into a bank. Such an institution will nevertheless remain fairly small compared to the competition from large investment and retail banks if it relies for a large amount of its capital on turning its mortgage interest income round into new lending capital to find new depositors and new customers. With the advent of securitisation, this mortgage lender is able to access a lot more

---

[6] A "step change" is a significant shift in the practice before that change.

[7] Where "sub prime" refers, somewhat euphemistically to borrowers who credit worth is less than the highest quality.

[8] See Ch.32 for a discussion of the Northern Rock failure.

investment capital by securitising its existing mortgages and then finding new customers. But once all of the mortgages have been securitised and a large amount of capital has flowed into its accounts, it will be difficult to maintain its rate of growth because there is nothing else to securitise, nothing else to sell. So, a mortgage lender like this which is eager to continue growing its business needs to find new customers to whom to sell new mortgages: the easiest customer base for it to access is made up of those people who want mortgages but cannot get them because their personal credit worth is too low. Knowing that securitisation is a profitable means of accessing market capital, the urge to find new business is increased. So, the mortgage lender begins to accept customers with a weaker credit profile than previously and accepts them even in jurisdictions in which the institution has never previously done business. Therefore, new business is originated solely for the purpose of securitising it and thus acquiring new capital.[9] Some of that new capital is ploughed into acquiring parts of other institution's securitisations. The securitisations are credit rated and the many thousands of individual loans are packed into a single box, a single security. These securitisations were generally rated at AAA, the highest possible rating.

Before the crisis of 2007–09 began in earnest, something simple went wrong. The poor credit risks to whom many mortgages were sold in the USA (known as "sub prime") were unable to meet their mortgage repayments when the US economy weakened. Then the housing market began to fall and the mortgage lenders could not recover their loans by selling the houses. It became evident that the securitisations which had been bought up with such enthusiasm by their investors were not as valuable as had previously been thought because so many of their constituent parts—the individual mortgage contracts—were not earning any income. Some contracts had been sold fraudulently, others had been sold optimistically or negligently. Other species of securitisations like CDOs ("collateralised debt obligations") also began to suffer enormous losses for their investors (often because they involved mortgage debt within their bundles of securities), causing many investment banks to restate the profits which they thought they were going to make as enormous write-downs and enormous losses—reaching into many billions of US dollars for those banks.[10] Banks then began to stop lending money to one another because they were unsure what level of loss each bank might face on mortgages and on the linked credit default swaps. Banks also began to stop lending as much to ordinary retail customers too. The reason for this cessation of lending business was a seizing up of liquidity: the banks had invested a lot in securitisations and then started to make large losses on them, with the result that they could not borrow as much money as they needed to write new business, and so on in a chain reaction whereby there was less and less money available in the system. This shortage of money to borrow in the system is referred to in the jargon as "liquidity drying up". Securitisation started this. Securitisations though, as was said before, are very old-fashioned ideas about selling debts to make short-term capital gains. There is nothing inherently problematic about them, unless and until they are used over-enthusiastically and they cause a drought in market liquidity. When I was young, somebody pointed

44–09

---

[9] This "originate to securitise" model, as considered below, is more common with CDO structures.

[10] See para.41–23 below relating to CDOs.

out to me that anything can kill you in the wrong circumstances: you can drown in nothing more dangerous than water, plasticine can kill you if you use it to block your airways, and too much good living will kill you eventually. So, even the most old-fashioned ideas, like debt factoring, can kill you too if you use them unwisely. The question is knowing when and how you are to use it wisely.

C.   The structure of a basic securitisation transaction

The basic structure

44–10   This section presents a basic securitisation structure.[11] In an ordinary bond transaction, the investors lend money to the issuer and then receive coupon payments during the life of the bond before receiving repayment of capital at the end of the loan. Things are different with a securitisation. The capital which the investors put up in a securitisation is not repaid by an issuer of the security because the investors are buying the underlying assets outright. Instead, the investors' risk is centred entirely on the assets which are being securitised because those assets are ordinarily moved into a "special purpose vehicle" (or, "SPV"). The opening steps of the transaction look like this:

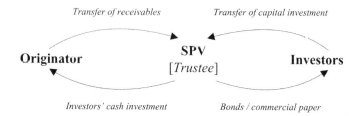

The originator seeks to transfer assets away from its own balance sheet by selling those assets, in a roundabout way, to investors who pay capital sums for them. The person who would be known as the issuer in a bond transaction is known as an "originator" in a securitisation transaction. It is the originator (under advice from many professionals) which initiates the transaction. This means that the originator is the person who owns the assets at the start of the transaction. At the outset, money is raised from investors and the assets are transferred outright to the special purpose vehicle (the "SPV"). The transfer of the assets to the SPV is intended to shift the risk of having to make payments to the investors away from the originator. The investors are issued with bonds: that is, the investors pay their capital amount to the trustee of the SPV and in return acquire a right to receive income from the "receivables". Instead, the investors recover their investment from the assets held by the SPV. Furthermore, because the assets are transferred outright to the SPV, the investors have the security of knowing, as considered below, that they can receive what they are entitled to from the SPV. Thus, the originator receives cash from the investors, in an amount constituting a

---

[11] A very clear discussion of securitisation structures is set out by P. Jeffrey, "Introduction", in P. Jeffrey (ed.), *A Practitioner's Guide to Securitisation* (City & Financial Publishing, 2006), p.3 et seq. which assisted the presentation of this discussion greatly.

discount of the market value of the assets. The assets are referred to as "receivables" because the assets are income-generating, and therefore constitute a package of receivables.

The nature of the SPV

The SPV is either a trust or a company, but with a trustee ultimately holding the assets on trust for the investors as beneficiaries (as with an ordinary bond transaction). Let us suppose it is a trust in the first place. If so, a trustee is appointed over the assets held in the SPV. The rights of beneficiaries in the assets held on trust are passed to the investors once their investments have been received. This has the result that the beneficiaries acquire equitable proprietary rights in the SPV—assuming there is no commercial or tax law reason why the investors would prefer to avoid such rights—and importantly the investors also acquire rights based on the law of breach of trust against the trustee. (The law of trusts was considered in Chapter 21 in detail, in particular the extensive rights of beneficiaries and the duties of trustees.) Thus, the investors have private law rights both against the trustee who holds the assets and in the assets themselves. The structure can also retain a proprietary right for the originator until the entire investment capital taken from the investors has been paid to it, at which point the originator's beneficial interest would cease to exist.

44–11

If the SPV were organised as a company, then the investors would not acquire equitable proprietary rights in the receivables because those receivables would be owned by the SPV company. The investors' rights would be purely personal rights against the company to be paid the cash flow to which it is entitled under the bonds which is issued in its favour. It is common in using a SPV company to have the shares held by some person other than the originator to keep those receivables off the originator's balance sheet: the originator is not their owner because those receivables have been transferred to the SPV. Sometimes it is a charitable trust or company which holds the shares, although it is difficult to see how this squares with the requirement that a charity's activities be entirely charitable.[12] Provided that the cash flows operate unimpeded, it should make little difference whether a trust or a company is used for this purpose. The principal difference is that the investors acquire more extensive private law rights against a trustee if they are beneficiaries than they do against a company with whom they have a bond contract.

44–12

There are many possible permutations of this sort of structure. Frequently, the structure requires that the SPV is a company, but the arrangement *also* requires a trustee who holds the money received from the investors and the assets received from the originator, and thereby acts as an honest broker or custodian in relation to all of the property involved in the transaction. (The use of a trustee in this way is standard practice in bond issues (as discussed in Chapter 34) to ensure that the issuer of the bonds performs its obligations properly and to watch out for any events of default under the bond agreement.) The company is therefore simply a shell to hold assets, while the trustee operates as a manager of the pooled

44–13

---

[12] See A. Hudson, *Equity & Trusts*, s.25.3.1.

investment capital and the receivables. It is also common for the SPV to be organised in an "offshore" jurisdiction where legislation dealing with trustees often recognises no need for a beneficial interest for beneficiaries but nevertheless will recognise the obligations of a trustee in relation to the holding of property, and where regulatory oversight and tax liabilities are nearly non-existent.[13] These details will differ from transaction to transaction.

Issues with the relationship of the investors and the SPV

44–14   Assuming that the SPV is a trust, the investors thus acquire rights in the receivables which are held on trust in the SPV by the trustee. The investors acquire more rights than just beneficial rights under trust, however. The investors are issued with bonds or commercial paper which expresses their participation rights in the income generated by the receivables held in the SPV. As bondholders—discussed in Chapter 34—the investors are entitled to an income stream on the bond derived from the underlying assets which are held on trust in the SPV. So, if the underlying assets were mortgages with ordinary homeowners, the monthly interest payments from the mortgages would be accrued by the trustee and held on trust in the SPV, and then the investors' rights as bondholders would entitle them to receive a proportion of the total income stream from the mortgage, depending on how many bonds they hold. These bonds therefore supplement the trust rights of the investors: the trust rights provide security, whereas the rights expressed by the bonds constitute contractual rights to receive income. As discussed below,[14] this structure usually has some further feature built into it so as to increase the ostensible credit worth of the structure—usually in the form of some collateral provided by the originator or some other right in the debt of the originator itself. The further detail of these structures is considered in greater detail below.

That the originator divests itself of all rights in the receivables

44–15   As has been set out above, the originator is intended to divest itself of all of the property rights it held in the receivables. This has two purposes First, the investors must know that all of the rights to the receivables have been transferred to the SPV, that there is no encumbrance with the income stream passing through into the bonds as intended, and that the originator cannot recover title in those assets.[15] Secondly, the outright transfer of the assets to the SPV, in such a way that the originator has no proprietary right in them nor any contingent right to them, means that the assets are put beyond the reach of originator in the event that the originator should subsequently go into insolvency. Thirdly, and similarly

---

[13] See generally G. Thomas and A. Hudson, *The Law of Trusts*, 2nd edn (OUP), for a survey of the "offshore" trusts jurisdictions; and A. Hudson, "Asset Protection Trusts" in D. Hayton (ed), *The International Trust* 3rd edn (Jordans, 2011), Ch.6 for an analysis of the laws of offshore jurisdictions in this context.

[14] See para.41–23.

[15] Although it is common that any excess profits earned on the receivables are passed back to the originator—and to that extent the originator retains some contractual right to the receivables' cash flow.

to the avoidance of insolvency, the originator is able to remove the assets from its balance sheet for accounting, tax and other regulatory purposes.

Assignment of the receivables

One problem which may arise in relation to the securitisation of receivables, and thereby in relation to the need to assignment the receivables outright to the SPV, is the contract governing the receivables precluding any transfer of that agreement. There are a number of cases which have held that even if a contract is defined as not being transferable, any cash flow which might come from that contract could itself be settled on trust.[16] Otherwise, it has been held that there cannot be an assignment at common law of a contract which is defined in its own terms as not being assignable,[17] or where assignment is made contrary to a provision requiring consent to be acquired.[18]

44–16

Credit enhancement

Ordinarily, the risk which the investors take is that the bonds which are issued to them will generate exactly the same return as they expect to receive under the receivables. This is a question of putting the documentation together so that there are no mismatches between the amounts to which the asset holder is entitled under the receivables, and the amount which is to be paid out under the bonds. Nevertheless, there may be concerns as to the credit worth of the assets and the structure itself.

44–17

There are various ways in which the credit worth of this structure can be enhanced so as to provide greater security to the investors. On occasion a guarantee is provided in relation to the SPV's obligations. Alternatively, the originator may make a subordinated loan to the SPV so that the SPV has cash in-hand in the event that there is any shortfall in what is owed to the investors. As considered immediately above, a trust structure offers different private law rights to an investor from a company. Those rights are both different and ordinarily more extensive. However, that assumes that the obligations of the trustee are not limited by the trust instrument so that the rights to breach of trust proceedings are not excluded,[19] and that there were sufficient assets held on trust to meet the obligations to the investors from the outset. Otherwise, the investors have rights only under the bonds to receive a cash flow as per the terms of the securitisation document. As is considered below, there is one further means of increasing the credit enhancement for the investors: that is by using a credit derivative. Thus, if (as in this example) there are actually receivables then a credit default swap could

44–18

---

[16] *Don King Productions Inc v Warren* [1998] 2 All E.R. 608, Lightman J.; affirmed [2000] Ch. 291, CA; *Re Celtic Extraction Ltd (In Liquidation), Re Bluestone Chemicals Ltd (In Liquidation)* [1999] 4 All E.R. 684; *Swift v Dairywise Farms* [2000] 1 All E.R. 320. See also the older cases of *Re Turcan* [1888] 4 Ch.D. 5; *Gregg v Bromley* [1912] 3 K.B. 474.

[17] *Linden Gardens Trust Ltd v Lenesta Sludge Ltd* [1993] 3 All E.R. 417, HL. The terms of such contracts are typically read literally: *The Argo Fund v Sressar Steel Ltd* [2004] EWHC 128.

[18] *Barbados Trust Co Ltd v Bank of Zambia* [2007] EWCA Civ 148. Such consent is not to be unreasonably withheld: *Henry v Chartsearch Ltd, The Times*, September 16, 1998.

[19] See para.26–01.

be put in place. Credit default swaps were considered in detail in Chapter 40.[20] Using a credit default swap, the investors would pay the swaps dealer the amount actually received from the securitisation trustee and then the investors would be paid (directly or indirectly) the amount they are entitled to receive under the securitisation documentation by means of the swaps dealer making its fixed rate payment under that swap equal to that amount on each payment date: if there were a shortfall, then the investors would only pay the reduced amount they received to the swaps dealer but would receive from the swaps dealer the full amount to which they were entitled, as with any credit default swap. Another means of securing such a transaction would be to post collateral either as part of a credit default swap transaction or without it.

The range of documentation

44–19   Securitisations, as with all complex financial products, require a large amount of documentation—in effect, one document at least for each component in the structure. Thus in an ordinary securitisation there is a need for documentation for the bond issue to the investors; documentation relating to the transfer of the assets to the SPV or its trustee; a trust document or constitutional documents for the SPV itself; documentation between the originator and the SPV (and its managers if appropriate) as to the operation of the SPV; documentation in relation to any credit enhancement. The bond documentation and offer circular are required to set out the terms of the bond that is being offered. If the bond is in relation to different tranches of instrument—as with a CDO, below—then the terms associated with each component of the instrument need to be identified. With securitisations that have many tranches, it is common to require representations from the originator as to the terms and nature of each underlying asset. It is important that the terms, default terms, payment dates, payment conventions and so forth relating to the bond documentation match the equivalent terms in all of the other documents relating to the securitisation. The transfer documentation from the originator to the SPV must set out, as considered above, the complete relinquishing of all rights in the receivables by the originator, warranties as to the terms and condition of the assets, provisions to the effect that any assets which should come to stand for the original receivables must be governed by the main documentation in the same way as the original receivables. The documentation as to the operation of the SPV must deal with the interest rates which are to be paid, the management of any surplus income not needed to pay the investors (which generally will pass back to the originator), the fees to which the SPV's managers are entitled, the liability of the parties in the event of default, and so forth. Credit enhancement was considered above and is considered in greater detail below in relation to CDOs.

Talking in different languages

44–20   It is worth taking a moment to consider how we are describing this transaction. Let us return to our original example of 10,000 mortgages being securitised under

---

[20] See para.40–49.

the structure just discussed. To a financier, a securitisation involves 10,000 monthly cash inflows being valued over 25 years with an actuary's calculations as to what proportion of these mortgages are likely to go into default at what stage being used to re-calibrate the amount that is expected to be received. The bonds issued to investors then constitute further cash flows. And further financial theory is required to value the volatility and the value of those bonds against other markets, and perhaps to provide security against failure in the way considered below. To a financier this structure is entirely made up of cash flows which carry risk of failure to pay or of falling behind other market rates. However, to a lawyer this transaction is made up of property rights and contractual obligations to pay money. So, proprietary rights securing rights to receive repayment of a loan (the mortgages) are transferred outright to a trustee to hold them on trust so as to generate income which is to be paid to investors subject to the terms of the bond agreement which in turn entitle the investors to receive payment; in turn, the investors have acquired those bond rights by paying a purchase price for them to the originator (directly or through an agent) which caused the originator to transfer the mortgages in the first place. The deal is the same, but the concepts which lawyers use are different from the concepts which financiers use; the same with accountants, with risk managers, and so on. Each species of professional talks in their own language, translating the financier's concepts into the language of their own field of expertise.

D.   What are the different types of securitisation?

There are, it is suggested, three principal types of securitisation: first, a securitisation to raise funding participation; secondly, a risk transfer, credit default securitisation; and, thirdly, a collateralised debt obligation ("CDO").[21] The first type was set out above; the other two are considered in the discussion to follow.

44–21

2.   A SECURITISATION USED TO TRANSFER RISK

A securitisation can also be used simply to transfer risk without seeking to raise investment capital from a large pool of investors. One of the attractions for an originator in creating ordinary securitisations was said above to be to move the receivables away from the originator and into the legal ownership of a trustee.[22] The originator thus divested itself of any property rights in the receivables and consequently of any liability in respect of them. If the originator wanted only to distance itself from the risks associated with the receivables but did not want to lose all proprietary control over them, then it would be conceivably possible that the receivables could be settled on trust (perhaps retaining some contingent rights for the originator) and a credit derivative used to generate a cash flow which

44–22

---

[21] This accords broadly with the division used by P. Jeffrey, "Introduction", in P. Jeffrey (ed.), *A Practitioner's Guide to Securitisation*, p.3 et seq.
[22] A trustee owns the legal title in the trust property: G. Thomas and A. Hudson, *The Law of Trusts*, Ch.1.

would offset any loss on the receivables. It is common to use a credit default swap (or total return swap) for this purpose. Credit default swaps were discussed in detail in Chapter 40.[23] In essence, a credit default swap involves a person with an interest[24] in the cash flow from an asset—which could include a mortgage, or more usually a bond—agreeing to a swap whereby that person pays the return it actually receives from the asset to a swaps dealer (that is, a floating amount) and in return the swaps dealer pays the amount which that person is entitled to under the terms of the asset (that is, a fixed amount). Thus, the credit default swap ensures that the originator receives the full amount it is entitled to under the asset either directly under the asset, or else from the swaps dealer who will be paying the difference between the full amount owed under the asset and the amount actually received in the event of a shortfall. Credit derivatives of this sort are a distant cousin of insurance contracts which effectively make good any loss which the buyer of the derivative suffers on an underlying asset. The transaction would look like this:

Originator   →   **SPV**   *Credit default swap*   **Swaps dealer**
Transfer of receivables   *[Trustee]*   →

In many circumstances this structure would be organised so that the credit default swap is owed between the SPV and the swaps dealer, but so that the income stream under the swap is passed from the SPV to the originator. The fixed and floating rate amounts typical of a swap are paid between the SPV and the swaps dealer. The SPV either receives payment in full from the SPV or the swaps dealer makes up any shortfall, effectively, through the credit default swap, as outlined above.

3. COLLATERALISED DEBT OBLIGATIONS ("CDOS")

A. What is a CDO?

44–23   A CDO is a "collateralised debt obligation" and is a vehicle for raising investment capital sold by investment banks which bundle together packages of different debt instruments. The investors are able to acquire a speculative position on assets of the type bundled into the CDO. The investors acquire bonds from a SPV which holds the receivables, just as with the ordinary securitisation considered above. There is a credit derivative included in the structure however which either provides protection against the receivables failing or acquires a speculative exposure to receivables of that type without the need actually to acquire them. There are different instruments bundled into a single CDO which are often of different qualities or different maturities and so are organised into layers, where each layer contains receivables of the same type. This structure is explained below.

---

[23] See para.40–49.

[24] That is, an interest either in the sense of being a rightholder in relation to that asset or of simply having a speculative interest in its performance as effected through a credit default swap.

B.   The layers of instruments in a CDO

As was outlined above, once securitisations had been used for some time for lenders to package assets together into a security, there grew an interest in originating securitisation products which could be sold to investors without the need for pre-existing receivables which could be packaged. The receivables in this context are usually debt instruments. So, while some new mortgages were sold to fuel new securitisations, there were also other packages of investments which were put together to be sold off to investors as a unit. A collateralised debt obligation ("CDO") is a package of such investments organised into different layers (or, "tranches"[25]). An analogy will explain this more clearly.

44–24

When I was a boy growing up in the 1970s[26] there was a type of ice cream which was thought to be the height of sophistication. It was called Neapolitan ice cream. I have no idea whether or not the people of Naples actually spent their evenings eating it, but that they probably did was the received notion in suburban north London. Like the storeys in a three-storey building, or the layers in a wedding cake, Neapolitan ice cream came in a rectangular brick and was formed of three brightly-coloured, horizontal layers: there was one layer of vanilla ice cream, one layer of strawberry[27] ice cream, and one layer of chocolate ice cream. One might have a preference for a particular flavour of ice cream and so eat only that layer, or else one might relish eating all three layers. Collateralised debt obligations are similar in structure to Neapolitan ice cream. CDOs are organised in tranches with different types and qualities of investment in each layer. The different tranches may have different maturity dates, or credit values, or be made up of different types of asset, or they may be different in other ways. Investors in CDOs can therefore invest in a way which gives them priority rights in particular layers of high-quality investment tranches, or investors may invest generally in the entire package without discriminating between the layers: this is comparable to choosing to eat only one flavour of the Neapolitan ice cream or choosing to eat all three stripes in your slice off that ice cream block. Each layer receives a different rate of return, depending on the risk associated with investing in that particular layer. Investors who invested in other layers received a lower rate of return but they were entitled to be repaid first if the CDO failed. Significantly, however, before the financial crisis the investment banks which constructed these CDO's managed to use sufficient financial alchemy to convince the ratings agencies (independent organisations which rated the credit risk associated with companies and securities issues, albeit for a fee often from the person who was being rated) to give the CDO's the highest possible rating: in essence expressing an opinion that the CDO's would not fail.

44–25

That some investors acquired priority rights to the high-quality investments in the package was part of the documentation of some CDO products which failed during the 2008 financial crisis. The pricing of some CDOs prior to the credit

44–26

---

[25] "Tranche" is the French word for "slice" but it is commonly used by Anglo-American lawyers and bankers.
[26] Be gentle with me, dear reader, for autumn is undoubtedly creeping into the garden of my life.
[27] It might have been raspberry—I cannot recall.

crunch worked on the basis that it would be credit rated at AAA even if some components of those transactions taken separately were not of that quality. In the event, when some CDOs unravelled in the lead-up to the 2008 financial crisis, some investors did have preferential rights to better classes of debt obligations when some event of default arose in relation to the entire package. That some investors were prepared to invest in CDOs even though their participation was subordinate to the rights of other investors indicates the popularity and perceived profitability that these products have had in the professional investment community. This in turn indicates something else about the CDO. The CDO contains high-quality, medium-quality and other qualities of instrument all packaged together in one. This is a little like packaging three films together in a DVD three-pack: often there is an excellent film or two in there, but the other one or two are usually undesirable films which can be sold more easily if bundled together with the excellent films, and they can also be sold for more money than could be raised for the best film if the best film was being sold on its own. Thus, the attraction and shine of the good quality merchandise can raise the attractiveness of a package which may contain some less attractive goods. So it is with many CDOs.

C.   The structure of a CDO

44–27   The financial institution—whether an investment bank or a fund manager—ordinarily acquires the instruments which are to be marketed to the investors by using the investment capital which is raised from the investors. The bones of the securitisation structure are used here too. The financial institution is effectively the originator of this structure, albeit that it is not necessarily selling its own receivables, but instead they will often be arm's length investments. The financial institution therefore transfers outright the instruments to the SPV so that the financial institution retains no property rights in those instruments. The property in the SPV is held on trust by a trustee. The financial institution is thus able to transfer away the risk of holding these instruments on its own balance sheet by transferring them outright to the SPV, and the financial institution is also able to create a portfolio of debt instruments where some instruments will be of high credit quality (and therefore of comparatively low yield) and others of lower credit quality (but therefore of higher yield, albeit with a higher risk of failure). Nevertheless, in putting the CDO together, it is important to bear in mind that the credit rating agencies must be convinced for marketing purposes that the entire package is of high credit quality; unless a CDO is deliberately being put together to attract expert investors to a lower credit worth but high-yielding investment. The structure looks like this:

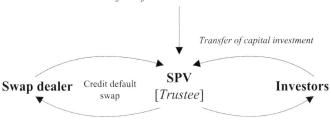

Financial Institution

Transfer of instruments into SPV

Transfer of capital investment

Swap dealer — Credit default swap — **SPV** *[Trustee]* — **Investors**

Bonds / commercial paper

Some of the features of this diagram require explanation: namely the role of the investors and the role of the credit default swap. There are two means of earning a speculative return in this context. The first is to buy instruments in the open market and then to settle them in trust on the SPV. The money to pay for the instruments is acquired from the capital raised from the investors. Again, the investors have a similar right to investors in an ordinary securitisation in that they receive bonds or commercial paper in return for their investments which pay out the return that is earned on the underlying instruments. There is a difference, however, from an ordinary securitisation in that the instruments are held in different tranches. The risk of default on the underlying instruments can then be managed by means of a credit default swap, as discussed above in relation to securitisations used to transfer risk. The credit default swap obliges the swaps dealer effectively to "insure" the investors' income stream by making good any shortfall in the amount received on the underlying investments. Alternatively, taking a speculative investment on the underlying instruments could be achieved by using the credit default swap, instead of buying the instruments in the open market at all. A credit default swap provides a speculative return from the credit worth of the underlying investment or investments. Thus, without actually buying the instruments, the investors could speculate on the credit associated with those instruments as with a credit derivative, as discussed in Chapter 40.[28]

Lord Collins held in *UBS AG v HSH Nordbank AG* that a CDO can be understood as follows:[29] **44–28**

> "A CDO is a financial structure at the centre of which a special purpose vehicle (SPV) issues tranches of debt securities, the performance of which is linked to a portfolio of assets. The SPV may either hold the underlying assets (a 'cash CDO') or take exposure to assets such as corporate bonds or asset-backed securities via a credit default swap with a financial counterparty (a 'synthetic CDO'). The performance of CDOs is linked or 'referenced' to the pool of underlying bonds or securities, the 'Reference Pool'.
>
> "In the case of a synthetic CDO the issuer may (as in the present case) invest the proceeds of issue of the CDOs in a portfolio of high quality, typically AAA-rated assets (collateral); those collateral assets are used to generate income to make coupon (interest) payments on the CDOs and, in the case of a default of any of the reference pool to which the SPV is exposed, to pay the financial counterparty the loss due under the credit default swap. On each occasion on which one of the assets in the reference pool defaults or is subject to some other 'credit

---

[28] See para.40–49.
[29] [2009] EWCA Civ 585; [2010] 1 All E.R. (Comm) 727, [10]–[11].

event' (such as a downgrading of its credit rating), then a payment becomes due from the SPV to the financial institution under the credit default swap. At the same time, the principal and interest due from the SPV to the CDO noteholder is correspondingly reduced. The usual practice is for CDO notes to be issued in different classes, whereby the losses are allocated sequentially commencing with the most 'junior' tranche of notes until the original principal amount of such class of notes are written down to zero, and then losses are allocated to the next 'higher' tranche of notes, until the entire capital structure is exhausted or the maturity date of the CDO notes occurs. As a consequence junior notes suffer as a result of earlier reference pool defaults/other credit events and the less risky 'senior' tranches suffer loss only after the underlying classes of CDO notes have been reduced to zero principal value."

The complex layering of these structures both enables low value assets to be bundled into a composite product which is nevertheless of high credit worth and enables different parts of the structure to be marketed to different classes of investor. A large amount of litigation has begun in England relating to these products—at the time of writing, those cases have only reached the interlocutory stage of asking questions as to jurisdiction. For example, the nature of a CDO product was also considered in detail in *Cassa di Risparmio della Repubblica di San Marino SpA v Barclays Bank Ltd*[30] in which allegations of fraud and negligent misrepresentation were made against Barclays in relation to their structuring of CDO products, which were rated AAA by ratings agencies, but which turned out to be worth considerably less. The allegations of fraud were not made out on the facts.

D. The role of credit rating agencies in securitisation transactions

44–29   The role of credit rating agencies was discussed in Chapter 34.[31] The ratings agencies have assigned ratings to securitisation products, including CDOs. A large number of the CDO products were assigned a AAA rating on the basis that they comprised some assets which were AAA among the other assets which turned out to be "sub-prime", on the basis that the CDOs were structured in such a way that their accounting treatment suggested that they were high quality assets, and on the basis that the credit enhancement which was attached to them appeared to make them valuable: what was problematic, however, was that they included sub-prime assets on which the ultimate human beings required to pay money to the originator under the original contract were simply not able to pay. A fertile source of litigation in the future is therefore likely to be on the liability of those ratings agencies for making statements to the effect that those assets were of a higher credit quality than ultimate turned out to be the case. This issue was considered in Chapter 25.[32]

---

[30] [2011] EWHC 484 (Comm).
[31] See para.34–13.
[32] See para.25–51.

PART XII

CRISIS, REGULATION AND FINANCE LAW

CHAPTER 45

THE FINANCIAL CRISIS AND ITS AFTERMATH

CORE PRINCIPLES

This chapter considers the financial crisis of 2007–09 and its aftermath. It begins with a brief summary of the causes of the financial crisis—but from the perspective of a lawyer, rather than an economist. The principal events of the crisis are laid out, before presenting a series of case studies relating to the causes of the crisis and its aftermath so as to highlight legal and regulatory issues already considered in this book.

It is only possible in this chapter to consider some of the financial institutions which played a leading part in the crisis (particularly Citigroup and Goldman Sachs) and in the scandalous aftermath to the crisis (particularly Barclays). Other institutions are considered in greater detail in the longer version of this chapter which is presented online at *http://www.alastairhudson.com*, complete with hyperlinks to all of the principal reports into the crisis and into banking regulation held online.

1. INTRODUCTION

A. The purpose of this chapter

45–01   This chapter presents an overview of the financial crisis of 2007–09 and its aftermath.[1] It presents that overview through a lawyer's eyes, identifying fraud, negligence, corporate governance and regulatory failures, and not simply economic issues. Too much of the discussion about finance and law is dominated by one particular ideology shared among economists of a particular stripe.[2] A discussion of finance law needs to see the world through the eyes of law and legal theory. This chapter begins with a brief history of the events of the crisis, while identifying some of the legal issues which that crisis raised. Then it considers the scandals and failures which have come to light in the wake of the financial crisis: again with an eye to their legal context. These discussions identify the key government and other reports which have been published into the causes and effects of the crisis, and some of the other literature surrounding those issues. The final section then considers in outline the regulatory responses to the crisis, which have been analysed in detail in other chapters in this book. In essence, this chapter is a central repository for considering the events of the financial crisis, and event which has changed so much of the regulation which has already been considered in this book, and the many scandals which have come to light in its aftermath. As Warren Buffett so presciently put it: it is when the tide goes out that we will see who has been swimming naked. Now that the crisis has come and stripped the finance industry back to its bones, the world has learned far more about the finance industry than it could ever have wanted to know.

---

[1] An extended version of this chapter is available on *http://www.alastairhudson.com* in the "finance law" area.

[2] For a variety of approaches to the idea that the dominant ideology of free market economics has been proved to have had its foundations built on ideological sand, see: S. Keen, *Debunking Economics* (London: Zed Books, 2011). Important among UK policymakers is A. Turner, *Economics After The Crisis* (MIT Press, 2012).

B.   A capsule summary of the financial crisis

The reader may want a brief, capsule summary of the financial crisis.[3] So here 45–02
goes. The fraudulent mis-selling of domestic mortgages to risky, "sub-prime"
borrowers[4] by mortgage companies in the USA created a huge number of
mortgages with borrowers who could not pay them back. Many of those
mortgages had been created so that they could be packaged into securitisation
issues (especially CDOs)[5] which were being sold among investment banks and
large scale investors around the world. The sub-prime borrowers began to default
on their payments as the economy contracted and the fraudulent terms in their
contracts bit. So, the risky sub-prime mortgages infected the global securitisation
markets with the result that a huge bubble of mis-pricing of CDOs (and the
derivatives which were sold alongside them) exploded, nearly bankrupting a large
number of systemically important financial institutions. The CDOs had been the
invention of maths graduates ("quantitative analysts") in investment banks who
failed to account for a failure in the US real estate market when they created their
mathematical models.[6] The supposedly independent credit ratings agencies gave
these CDOs their highest credit ratings, which reassured investors, even though
many of those products were downgraded to the lowest possible rating only a few
months later. When the crisis hit, banks stopped lending money to one another
(something known as "the credit crunch") with the result that many banks which
had become dependent on short-term financing for their long-term obligations
could not access funding anymore. This credit crunch began in earnest in August
2007 and then reached its nadir in September 2008 with the collapse of US
investment bank, Lehman Brothers. The result was the near collapse of the entire
financial system.[7] Many financial institutions needed to be taken into public
ownership, or bailed out by governmental loans, or forced into mergers with other
financial institutions, because they were otherwise insolvent. In the aftermath of
the crisis, those financial institutions have resisted changes to financial regulation
at the same time as a number of scandals and other problems have come to light.
This chapter will unpick the key themes after presenting a potted history of the
key events of the crisis and its aftermath.

---

[3] An excellent overview is provided by the BBC three-part documentary *The Love of Money* (BBC,
2009); first broadcast on September 24, 2009 (*http://www.bbc.co.uk/programmes/b00mqmjs*). For an
excellent, easy-to-read summary of the principal issues in the financial crisis, see T Ciro, *The Global
Financial Crisis: Triggers, Responses and Aftermath* (Ashgate, 2012). For popular accounts of the
crisis and the issues which it has raised, see also: P. Mason, *Meltdown* (Verso, 2009); C. Ferguson,
Inside Job (Oxford: Oneworld, 2012) which is the companion book to the excellent, Oscar-winning
documentary "Inside Job" (2011), narrated by Matt Damon. See C. Kindleberger and R. Aliber,
Manias, Panics and Crashes, 6th edn (Palgrave Macmillan, 2011) looking at crashes through a longer
lens.
[4] The term "sub-prime" is a euphemism used to describe a borrower whose credit worth is less than
perfect (i.e. less than "prime").
[5] These securitisation were discussed in detail in Ch.47.
[6] The threats posed by automated trading systems and the algorithims which control them are
discussed in S. Patterson, *Dark Pools* (Random House, 2012); E. Perez, *The Speed Traders* (McGraw
Hill, 2011); D. Duffie, *Dark Markets* (Princeton University Press, 2012).
[7] The IMF estimated initially that the total, global cost of the crisis at August 2009 would be US$11.9
trillion (£7.1 trillion) (accessible via *http://www.imf.org*). That estimate was revised downwards
eventually to US$ 2.3. trillion in April 2010 by the IMF.

2. SOURCES AND CAUSES OF THE FINANCIAL CRISIS

A. The roots of the crisis in the fraudulent mis-selling of mortgages

45–03   The financial crisis began with fraud; it grew into an international, financial panic through collateralised debt obligation and credit default swap markets only later. Probably the best investigative account of the roots of the financial crisis is Michael W Hudson's *The Monster*[8] which identifies the roots of the mis-selling of sub-prime mortgages in a series of unscrupulous financial institutions which were feted by politicians, poorly overseen by regulators, and in which immoral sales staff were allowed to commit criminal offences by senior management who were interested only in fast profit growth. The entirety of these institutions appear to have been at fault: from senior executives, through middle-management, to supervisors on sales floors, to individual salespeople. Michael W. Hudson, focuses on Ameriquest Mortgage: one of the most aggressive sub-prime mortgage lenders in America. Ameriquest was controlled by one Roland Arnall. His personal determination to keep his sales-force selling ever larger volumes of mortgages every month, no matter how that was done, was central to the organisation operating as it did. Obsequious subordinates did their master's bidding by encouraging their salespeople into hideous acts. Hudson's account begins with the account of Mark Glover, who worked at Ameriquest Mortgage, who:[9]

> "looked up from his cubicle and saw a coworker do something odd. The guy stood at his desk on the twenty-third floor … He placed two sheets of paper against the window. Then he used the light streaming through the window to trace something from one piece of paper to another. Somebody's signature."

This sort of fraud was endemic at many mortgage companies. It was common to have customers sign lots of paperwork, having told them that their interest rates would be *x*, and then to discard much of that paperwork and re-staple the signature page to another contract altogether with an interest rate of *y*, or to leave only pages requiring payments of *y*, or simply to bamboozle the customer so that they did not realise that soon after the mortgage began their rate would jump to *y* from the low rate which had first attracted their interest. The "monster" referred to in the title of Hudson's book was a lever-arch file of sales techniques and information which was used to train salespeople so that they could mis-sell mortgages to subprime borrowers successfully. This illustrates the importance, as considered below, of regulators ensuring that financial institutions are training staff appropriately.

45–04   The reason why companies like Ameriquest and Long Beach (owned by the soon-to-be-bankrupt Washington Mutual) were prepared to mistreat customers like this (even though the likelihood of future delinquencies in payments was

---

[8] Michael W Hudson, *The Monster—how a gang of predatory lenders and Wall Street bankers fleeced America—and spawned a global crisis* (New York: Times Books, 2010).
[9] Michael W Hudson, *The Monster—how a gang of predatory lenders and Wall Street bankers fleeced America—and spawned a global crisis* (New York: Times Books, 2010), 1.

self-evident) was that Wall Street had come to desire those mortgage contracts. As was discussed in Chapter 44 *Securitisations*, complex securitisations and CDOs were constructed which comprised mortgage contracts of this sort which could be marketed to investors. Therefore, mortgage companies sought to originate new mortgages solely so that they could be sold on to securitisation programmes operated by Wall Street investment banks. Because sub-prime borrowers had to pay higher rates of interest on their mortgages, the CDOs with sub-prime mortgages in them promised a better return for investors than other products (assuming the borrowers kept up their repayments). But when the borrowers began to default on their mortgages, then the CDOs did not pay out. The smarter investment banks (like Goldman Sachs) began to notice the rates of delinquencies in 2006 and so reversed their strategies (as considered below). Other investment banks like Citigroup and Lehman Brothers increased their exposures to a growing marketplace which nearly everyone had predicted would continue to grow in perpetuity. As McDonald describes it, most Wall Street traders were unaware that the mortgage lenders in California, Florida and elsewhere were living high on the bubble that they were helping to create.[10] There was a complete disconnection between the mortgage companies out in the field and the buttoned-up Wall Street analysts who were assuming that because it said "30-year mortgage" on the label that there was a wholesome 30-year mortgage inside.

B.   The macro-economic context of the crisis

There was a large amount of "cheap money" in the USA in the lead-up to the crisis. China in particular invested massively in the USA so as to prevent inflation at home while its own economy was booming. Consequently, interest rates in the USA were low and so people borrowed money rather than saving it. Indeed, personal savings rates in the USA fell from 7 per cent of disposable income in 1990 to "below zero" in 2005 and 2006.[11] Thus Americans literally spent more money than they owned. At the same time sub-prime mortgage lending in the USA rose from US$180 billion in 2001 to US$625 billion in 2005 as sub-prime borrowers were sold the dream of owning their own homes. However, this fuelled inflation in the USA which led to a need to raise interest rates, which in turn meant that interest rates on mortgages began to rise, which in turn meant that sub-prime borrowers were unable to meet their mortgage repayments. (Many sub-prime borrowers also saw their interest rates rise, as mentioned above, because their contracts were created fraudulently.) In that sense, the roots of the crisis are well known.

45–05

There was also an effect on global investment markets. In particular, there was a boom in "asset-backed securities" like collateralised debt obligations based on sub-prime mortgages. In USA the issuance of asset-backed securities effectively quadrupled from US$337 billion in 2000 to US$1,250 billion in 2006; and

45–06

---

[10] L. McDonald, with P Robinson, *A Colossal Failure of Common Sense* (New York: Random House, 2009).

[11] Larosière Report, para.8.

mortgage-backed securities rose from US$100 billion in 2000 to US$773 billion in 2006. That is an increase in CDO-related markets of approximately US$1.5 trillion in five years before the collapse began. It is an axiomatic example of a bubble. It created an enormous amount of risk. In essence, if the underlying sub-prime mortgage contracts failed, then that would cause the CDO's which had been built on them to fail as a result, and then the credit default swap ("CDS") markets would implode too. What was remarkable was where much of that risk was held. CDO's were supposed to be held off-balance sheet by sensible investment banks, but many financial institutions had taken them onto their balance sheets, as is discussed below.

C. The first failures in the credit crunch

45–07 The financial crisis seemed to unfurl in slow motion in 2007. In essence, the fears about the US real estate markets began to make financial institutions fearful of one another. There was less money in the marketplace than before and banks would only lend to one another at higher rates of interest than previously, or they would not lend at all. This was known as "the credit crunch" because access to credit became very difficult. In market jargon, this lack of available funding is known as liquidity drying up. A general nervousness became more focused with institutional failures later than summer. BNP, a French bank, closed two of its investment funds in August 2007, citing technical problems at first, but this was the first of several losses. Then, in that same month, Northern Rock experienced the first run on a British bank in living memory.[12] Television pictures of large numbers of ordinary customers queuing to remove their deposits and close their accounts were on the evening news for several days. Notably, even ordinary members of the public had realised that something was wrong in August 2007, even though the CEO of Citigroup had said in July 2007 that his institution was still active in that market: as he put it "while the music is still playing, you have got to get up and dance".[13] On September 13, 2007, it was reported that Northern Rock had applied for and had received emergency financial support from the Bank of England. Northern Rock had once been a staid British building society which had lent out a conservative multiple of the amount it received on deposit from its customers. However, under its new CEO, Mr Applegarth, Northern Rock expanded its activities by funding itself in the short-term money markets (a poor idea because it was funding long-term activities with this funding, which would be unsustainable in an illiquid market) and by structuring its activities through offshore trusts and onshore charities (presumably for tax purposes). When the credit crunch hit, Northern Rock could not access the funding it needed to keep its business moving because there was no liquid capital available to it. The British government had to try to find a buyer for Northern Rock, but there were no takers, with the result that a Labour government was obliged to nationalise a bank after nearly 15 years of trying to lose its socialist image.

---

[12] The previous bank run had been in 1866 in relation to Overend, Gurney & Co. See Treasury Select Committee, Fifth Report 2007-08, *The Run on the Rock* (January 26, 2008), 8; G Elliott, *The Mystery of Overend & Gurney: A Financial Scandal in Victorian London* (London, 2006).
[13] See para.45–13.

The Treasury Select Committee, under the chairmanship of John McFall MP, published a report into the failure of Northern Rock after having conducted a number of hearings.[14] That report identified the bank's problems as having been caused by a "reckless business model" and found that they were the fault of the bank's directors. It was also found that the FSA "systematically failed in its regulatory duty to ensure that Northern Rock would not pose a systemic risk". **45–08**

D. Citigroup poor internal controls and risk management

Introduction

While the investment banks were happy to bank the profits from their CDO activities, many of them began to allow those CDOs to remain on their balance sheets instead of using special purpose vehicles to dispose of those risks. Given that CDO products were so profitable and so highly rated, these banks were very relaxed about allowing them to remain on their own balance sheets and about selling credit default swaps which entitled investors to be paid if those CDOs failed to pay out. **45–09**

Citigroup: too big to fail, too big to manage

One institution stands out from the crowd, not least in the report of the Financial Crisis Inquiry Commission in the USA, for its very size and its consequent inability to manage its own risks. Citicorp merged with the Travelers Group in 1999 to form the genuinely colossal "Citigroup". This was something which was in breach of US competition law at the time; and yet the law was changed ex post facto so as to permit that merger. From the outset, the new "Citigroup" had made a simple statement: we are more powerful than the law. Citigroup had been embroiled in several regulatory issues in the early 21st century. Most serious were the regulatory responses to Citigroup's involvement in the frauds at Enron, the energy company and derivatives trading house, which had collapsed in 2001 as a result of false accounting by senior executives.[15] As a consequence, Citigroup paid fines of US$120 million in 2003 to the SEC and agreed to reform its risk management practices radically. In March 2005, the Federal Reserve "had seen enough"[16] and so Citigroup was "banned" from further growth through mergers and acquisitions until it could demonstrate that its management and legal systems were suitable. **45–10**

At the time the crisis struck, Citigroup was comprised of more than 2,000 subsidiary companies. For a bank of that size to operate at all, huge amounts of power had to be delegated to middle and lower management. The transactions which caused Citigroup to publish losses of US$ 60 billion in 2008 were hidden away in a small department created in 2003 to deal in CDO's which was off senior management's radar. Citigroup was simply too big to manage at the time **45–11**

---

[14] Treasury Select Committee, Fifth Report 2007–08, *The Run on the Rock* (January 26, 2008).
[15] B. McLean and P. Elkind, *The Smartest Guys in the Room* (Portfolio, 2003).
[16] FCIC Report, p.137.

and its risk management protocols were clearly inadequate. Given its central place in the US economy (operating everything from the Citibank retail banking franchise through to commercial banking for the largest corporations in the USA) the Bush administration felt it had no option but to pile public money into Citigroup to save it from insolvency. In effect, Citigroup was taken into public ownership. Its many, many failings were effectively absolved by the socialisation of its losses when the US taxpayer became owner of one-third of Citigroup's share capital.

The development of CDO risk in Citigroup and US$60 billion in losses

45–12   When Citigroup created a small department in 2003 to deal with CDO business, it also hit upon a different way of funding this business: it used short-term commercial paper as opposed to the long-term debt used by most other market participants. To encourage investors to participate in these issues, the issuer had to bridge the problem of liquidity which is inherent in commercial paper[17] by including "liquidity puts" in its agreements: these liquidity puts meant that Citigroup was obliged to buy up any securities which were not acquired by investors under CDO programmes. In time, the commercial paper market dried up when sub-prime mortgage borrowers began to default. This meant that Citigroup was obliged to take these worthless securities back onto its balance sheet under the liquidity puts. As this liquidity problem was growing, Citigroup's losses began to mount. In his evidence to the US Financial Crisis Inquiry Commission ("FCIC"), CEO of Citigroup at the time, Chuck Prince, said that he would not have done anything differently, even with the advantage of hindsight.[18] Prince's explanation for that remarkable statement was that Citigroup was besieged with other problems at the time, so that he could not have given more than 1 per cent of his attention to this issue. Moreover, because these securities had been rated AAA by the credit rating agencies, Prince considered that there was no reason for him to suppose that they would have created the problems which later they did.

45–13   The most strikingly daft thing that was ever said by a CEO of a bank, perhaps, was Prince's response to a question from a *Financial Times* journalist in July 2007 about Citigroup's exposure to the CDO and mortgage-backed securities market, which had already begun to show signs of collapse. It is worth bearing in mind that that was about a year after Goldman Sachs had reversed its own investment policy, and only days before ordinary citizens in the UK began their run on Northern Rock. Prince was quoted as saying, in light of these concerns about liquidity among banks generally:[19]

> "When the music stops, in terms of liquidity, things will be complicated. But as long as the music is playing, you've got to get up and dance. We're still dancing."

---

[17] This means that because these contracts are short-term in nature, it is necessary to keep trading in them regularly to maintain funding for long-term business like CDOs.

[18] Financial Crisis Inquiry Commission, *The Financial Crisis Inquiry Report* (New York: Public Affairs, 2011). 137 et seq.

[19] *Financial Times,* July 9, 2007: "Citigroup chief stays bullish on buy-outs": http://on.ft.com/usHc3q [Accessed March 14, 2013]

In other words, while the market is still trading you have to keep trading too; even though everyone else was extricating themselves from those markets. In spite of Prince's bacchanalian optimism, Citigroup's losses in these markets reached US$700 million only a month later.[20] At the time, those losses were said by Citigroup's spokespeople to be unproblematic, given their earnings of US$20 billion in the previous year.[21] However, within twelve months those losses had risen to a colossal US$60 billion. Citigroup continued to underestimate its potential losses.

Citigroup is the principal target which many commentators have in mind when they describe a bank as being too big to fail (because of its important Citibank retail network in the USA and the size of its other financial operations), and also as being too big to manage. We are told that there were regulators "living" on Citigroup premises both before and throughout the crisis because of the low opinion which they had of that institution.[22] It is interesting to note that in books such as Sorkin's *Too Big to Fail*, Citigroup is generally quoted as being referred to derisively by its competitors and its regulators, as though it is a clumsy behemoth without the necessary skill to cope in modern financial markets. For example, after the US government had invested US$25 billion through TARP and another US$20 billion in November 2008, Sorkin tells us that Treasury officials had nicknamed Citigroup "the Death Star", presumably a reference to its size, its capacity to destroy the US economy and its atmosphere of grey bureaucracy.[23] In the original *Star Wars* movie[24] it had indeed been a tiny threat in the form of a single craft which had found a small weakness and used that to destroy the entire Death Star. Citigroup fell because of one glitch in the products sold by one small department to which no-one had previously paid much attention. This demonstrates that financial institutions which are too big to regulate are simply too big to be allowed to continue in that state.[25] Without proper systems and controls throughout the institution, huge universal banks simply contain too many risks within them. The ability of such large institutions like Washington Mutual (which went insolvent during the crisis) and JP Morgan Chase (which incurred a

45–14

---

[20] *Financial Times*, August 11, 2007: "Citigroup faces the $700m music".

[21] *Financial Times*, August 11, 2007: "Citigroup faces the $700m music", quoted in that article.

[22] See generally R. Suskind, *Confidence Men* (Harper, 2011), 207 et seq, and N. Schreiber, *The Escape Artists* (Simon & Schuster, 2011), 174 et seq. In relation to Sheila Bair's own account, as Chair of the FDIC (Federal Deposit Insurance Corporation, a key regulator of Citigroup), see her memoir *Bull by the Horns* (New York: Free Press, 2012), in which she expresses her view that members of Citigroup senior management had been "indifferent to [their] culpability" and that the bank had ceased to be a commercial bank (dealing with retail customers) because it had been "hijacked" by an investment bank culture (at p.122). She clashed regularly with the Federal Reserve and Treasury because she wished, in effect, to see the universal banks broken up.

[23] Sorkin, *Too Big To Fail* (New York: Allen Lane, 2010), p.530.

[24] Somewhat eccentrically, of course, the six *Star Wars* films began with the fourth in the series, *Star Wars IV: A New Hope*, in 1977.

[25] See the Treasury Select Committee Report, *Banking Crisis: Regulation and Supervision* (Fourteenth Report, July 21, 2009) which identified the inappropriate size of banks which were simply too big to regulate. Some banks are simply too big, and others are too complex and inter-connected in the entire financial system such that it is impossible to deal with them in a vacuum. Each type creates systemic regulatory problems.

US$6.2 billion loss after the crisis through poor internal controls) to implode through risks of this sort has been demonstrated time and again.

E. The role of credit ratings agencies

45–15   Three organisations—Moody's, Standard & Poors, and Fitch—are the key credit ratings agencies which provide analyses and ratings of individual corporations and individual issues of securities (including bonds and CDOs), and the performance of countries. The investment market relies on these analyses when making their investment decisions. What the financial crisis revealed was that investors were too reliant on these ratings because they undertook too little analysis of their own. Most of the CDO issues in the lead-up to the financial crisis were rated at AAA (or Aaa),[26] the highest possible ratings. As the crisis loomed larger, many of those AAA ratings fell to "junk" status which was the lowest possible rating.[27] The credit rating agencies were a focus of the US Senate Permanent Subcommittee on Investigations[28] and of the US Financial Crisis Inquiry Commission:[29] both of these official US inquiries were very critical of them indeed, as was the EU Larosiere Report. What all of these reports indicate is the following. The credit rating agencies were notionally independent but their services were paid for by the issuers of the CDOs and other securitisation products. Therefore, when the credit ratings agencies accorded AAA ratings they were reassuring market investors about the goods sold to them by the organisations which had paid their fees. Second, the ratings agencies were put under enormous pressure by the issuers of these securities. It was common for ratings paperwork to be submitted to the agencies as close as possible to the deadline for producing the rating so that the analysts were forced to work very quickly indeed. They were also put under competitive pressure by issuers who threatened to take their business elsewhere. As profit-making corporations, the ratings agencies were concerned with their own profit growth. Third, a very large number of ratings turned out to be wrong, and that happened on many occasions in a matter of a few months between the rating and a securities issue clearly losing all or most of its worth.

---

[26] S&P uses the ranking system in capitals and Moody's uses the mixture of capitals and lower case letters.

[27] This extraordinary fall in the perceived value of these securities was considered in Ch.25 in relation to *Camerata Property Inc v Credit Suisse Securities (Europe) Ltd* [2011] EWHC 479 (Comm); [2011] 2 B.C.L.C. 54, at para.25–45.

[28] US Senate Permanent Subcommittee on Investigations, "Wall Street and the Financial Crisis: Anatomy of a Financial Collapse", April 13, 2011. Accessible through *http://www.hsgac.senate.gov/subcommittees/investigations/reports*. [Accessed March 14, 2013]

[29] Financial Crisis Inquiry Commission, *The Financial Crisis Inquiry Report* (New York: Public Affairs, 2011).

F. Panic!

The real shock, however, came in September 2008 with the collapse of Lehman **45–16**
Brothers. The condition and position of Lehman Brothers is discussed in detail
below.[30] The events of the weekend of its insolvency are detailed in many
documentaries[31] and books, but particularly by Andrew Ross Sorkin in *Too Big
To Fail*.[32] The story revolves around the CEO of Lehman Brothers, Dick Fuld,
and his determination to make Lehman Brothers the greatest investment bank on
Wall Street through a series of enormous bets on the US real estate market,
CDO's and credit default swaps. As is discussed below, Lehman Brothers
over-valued its assets and when the credit crunch hit it was unable to find funding
to meet the losses which flowed from the downturns in those markets. Ultimately,
over Lehman Brothers' final weekend as a viable concern, US Treasury Secretary
Hank Paulson and President of the Federal Reserve Bank of New York (and later
Treasury Secretary under President Barack Obama) Tim Geithner, and a host of
other officials, allowed Lehman Brothers to fail. There was no government
bail-out of Lehman Brothers. None of the accounts give a single, straight answer
as to "why". The common thread could be that Lehman Brothers was known to
be involved with the sort of shenanigans which are discussed below (including a
lot of "optimistic" accounting, huge exposures to markets in free-fall, and poor
executive management) and as such there was no genuine desire on the part of
any of its competitors to buy out that bank without government support.[33] CEO
Dick Fuld was excluded from the weekend of meetings that were held at the
Federal Reserve's offices seeking either to put together a private sector rescue or
a private sector purchase of Lehman Brothers. No buyer emerged. Instead, other
banks agreed to merge with one another (including Bank of America and the very
troubled Merrill Lynch). Chancellor of the Exchequer Alastair Darling in the UK
(together with the regulatory authorities) refused to sanction Barclays acquiring
Lehman Brothers.[34] Therefore, Lehman Brothers was simply allowed to collapse
and its holding company filed for insolvency on September 15, 2008.[35]

That a bank of that age and size could go bankrupt caused panic both in the **45–17**
already febrile stock markets of the world and in the inter-bank lending markets.
The result was an intense panic. The financial community realised that any bank
could fail and that there might not be a safety net if they did.[36] There was also the

---

[30] See para.5/–43.

[31] See *The Fall of Lehman Brothers* (BBC, 2009). First broadcast on September 9, 2009.
http://topdocumentaryfilms.com/fall-lehman-brothers/

[32] Andrew Ross Sorkin, *Too Big To Fail* (New York: Allen Lane, 2010).

[33] Later, Barclays acquired large amounts of the profitable parts of Lehman Brothers post-insolvency.

[34] It is not clear on what legal basis that permission was refused: Alistair Darling, *Back from the Brink*
(London: Atlantic Books, 2011), p.123, suggests that there was disagreement on the Barclays board of
directors as to whether or not the acquisition of Lehman Brothers would have been a good thing, and
from Darling's own perspective that the terms of the proposal were too unclear for any view to be
expressed. No other explanation is offered.

[35] See the first person account of Hank Paulson (including his admission that he was so worried that
he was regularly physically sick during the crisis): *On the Brink* (New York: Grand Central, 2010).

[36] The concept of "moral hazard"—that banks might not behave properly if they know that they will
be bailed out by government—was briefly satisfied by Lehman Brothers being allowed to fail, and
then spoiled by almost every other bank being bailed out to a greater or lesser extent later.

knowledge that Lehman had left enormous holes of tens of billions of dollars in financial markets as it fell and that in consequence other banks might have hidden exposures to Lehman Brothers which could cause them to fail next. Consequently, no bank dared to deal normally with one another because it was not clear whether or not the collapse of Lehman Brothers would cause other banks to fail on the systemic risk principle discussed in para.1–54.

45–18   Despite having allowed Lehman Brothers to fail, only days later the US government stood behind the enormously important quasi-public US mortgage houses Freddie Mac and Fannie Mae, and behind the insurance company American International Group ("AIG"). The enormous AIG was the surprise package in all of this confusion. AIG had begun a disastrous financial products group which insured securitisations through credit default swaps (as discussed in Chapter 43) and insurance contracts. When the market began to collapse under the weight of failed CDOs, it also began to suffer as a result of the credit default swaps which were payable once the bond payments which should have been made under the CDO contracts were not made (because the underlying mortgage borrowers were defaulting on their payments). Many speculators had taken the position that the real estate market would fail and that the CDOs that were dependent on them would also fail. Therefore, when AIG was required to make payment under the credit default swaps it had sold and when it was required to pay out under related insurance policies, this generated an enormous loss for the company. AIG had been clumsy in a world it had not understood.[37] One department had made a healthy profit while the market was booming, but once the market began to collapse then AIG was on the verge of insolvency, and a staggering range of insurance policies around the world would go unpaid. Consequently, the US government bailed out AIG to the tune of US$85 billion while the ashes of Lehman Brothers were still smouldering.

G.   The immediate aftermath

The governmental response: nationalising the banks

45–19   The most remarkable effect of the banking crisis, which would have been improbable before September 2008, was that governments nationalised banks, or they recapitalised banks with public money, or they cajoled banks into mergers with one another. This was an idea not meaningfully considered in the UK since the manifesto of the Labour Party in 1983, a document that was described as "the longest suicide note in history". Consequently, the notion that a Labour government should be required to pursue that policy in 2007 was all the more difficult for it precisely because it had tried to throw off that radical heritage for so long. The idea that banks could be taken into state hands began in 2007 with the movement towards the nationalisation of Northern Rock and the enactment of the Banking (Special Provisions) Act 2008, which gave the UK government the power to acquire banks, as was discussed in Chapter 29. What is important to

---

[37] See Sorkin, *Too Big To Fail* (New York: Allen Lane, 2010), especially p.394 et seq., and the Financial Crisis Inquiry Report, generally relating to AIG.

note from a legal perspective is that crisis management of this sort is not governed by law in the sense that the law does not instruct politicians, economists, bankers, civil servants and others what they should do; rather, those people address the crisis in whatever way seems appropriate at the time but at various points during that crisis they will require legal powers to take whatever actions they need so that they can force other people to comply with them. Thus, during the crisis it was necessary to force failed banks into temporary public ownership or, as in the USA, to pass legislation rapidly so as to enable the Bush administration to lend in the aggregate nearly US$750 billion to Wall Street institutions to keep them solvent and the financial system operating.

The US Troubled Asset Relief Program ("TARP")

In September 2008, Hank Paulson (the US Treasury Secretary under the outgoing Bush administration) concocted a plan to spend US$750 billion initially to rescue US banks and to prop up the financial system: this was known as the "Troubled Assets Relief Program", or "TARP".[38] The haphazard and hurried creation of this programme is set out in detail by Sorkin.[39] The proposal in its original form was voted down by the House of Representatives, causing a worldwide panic and frenzied selling on stock markets because this initiative had been trumpeted as the means of saving the financial system. It was passed at the second attempt. For such a huge investment of public money, it was remarkably light on detail. On reading how officials in Paulson's office had drafted the legislation with very few checks and balances on two sheets of paper, it is clear how crisis management on this scale resembles a high-wire act in a circus more than thoughtful governance. Again, a law was necessary to grant Paulson and the Bush administration the power to lend remarkable amounts of money out to the failed financial institutions. Thus law performed its role here of enabling and empowering officials to act as they consider necessary during crises.

45–20

In a later memoir, Barofsky (the former Special Inspector General for TARP) roundly condemned the operation of TARP as a means of handing colossal amounts of money to Wall Street financial institutions with very little accountability as to how that money was spent; while ordinary Americans saw their businesses going into insolvency and their homes being repossessed.[40] The litany of bankers' bonuses which were funded with this money, stretching from millions of dollars for senior employees right the way down to a bonus of US$7,700 for a kitchen assistant at AIG,[41] was an affront the credulity of a nation.[42] The intention, in the public eye at least, had been to rebuild the banks' balance sheets so that they could start trading again: that much of that money was

45–21

---

[38] I assume that the acronym "tarp" is also supposed to lend the programme the reassuring sense of being a "tarpaulin" sheltering the US economy from the rain.

[39] A. R. Sorkin, *Too Big to Fail* (Allen Lane, 2009), Ch.18 et seq.

[40] N. Barofsky, *Bailout* (New York: Free Press, 2012).

[41] N. Barofsky, *Bailout* (New York: Free Press, 2012), 182.

[42] The tortured logic is that if bankers are not paid high bonuses then they will go to work elsewhere. However, given that most bankers (*qua* bankers) have few transferable skills outside banking, and given that the entire banking market had almost collapsed, it was difficult to see where exactly these disappointed bankers would have found alternative employment at the time.

paid out in bonuses was something of a surprise. That no-one had thought to prevent such unconscionable uses of public money by an expression condition to that effect in the contracts which passed over the money is nothing short of scandalous.

57–22   A few days later in the UK, the Labour government provided £37 billion to acquire preference shares in UK banks, to make them loans, and so forth (although multiples of this amount of public money was made available over time).[43] These policies were given statutory form in the Banking (Special Provisions) Act 2008 and the Banking Act 2009, which redrew the State's powers to nationalise banks, to administer insolvent banks and so on, as discussed in Chapter 29. The aim of the Labour administration was to recapitalise banks: that is, the government bought shares in the banks by giving them billions of dollars in return for preference shares which entitled the government to receive a fixed dividend from those banks; and in return the banks undertook to begin lending to small- and medium-sized businesses so as to ease the upcoming economic recession. This approach mimicked the approach of the Swedish government in the 1990s during the Nordic banking crisis and also the approach of the Japanese government in the 1990s.[44] Consequently, the British people became the part-owners of many of their banks through their government. Much of this inexpensive money (lent at very low rates of interest indeed) was used to pay bonuses to banks and too little of it was used to make loans to ordinary businesses.

Political leadership

57–23   Politicians during this period were unsurprisingly caught in the headlights of a tremendous crisis which they could only resolve by taking unprecedented and previously unthinkable forms of action. Nevertheless, where there should have been political leadership there was often either thinly-disguised panic, dithering or, in the US, a vacuum. US President George W Bush had only a few months remaining of his eight-year presidency: a presidency which had allowed this bubble to grow and grow, encouraging the sort of home ownership expansion which was at the roots of the problem. Bush had publicly positioned himself next to Kenneth Lay, CEO of the disgraced Enron corporation, and next to every sub-prime lender in the USA, even making Roland Arnall (the CEO of Ameriquest, a key, abusive subprime lender) his ambassador to the Netherlands. Deeply unpopular in the USA and either thought of as a figure of fun or as a war criminal overseas, Bush struck a marginalised, peripheral figure during this crisis. The financial crisis was the final word on his presidency. Whereas the role of politicians faced by an economic crisis of this proportion is to sound as positive as possible, President Bush was quoted as making a disturbing statement on September 25, 2008 at a much-publicised White House crisis meeting to consider the banking collapse, only shortly after a stock market panic caused by the House of Representatives voting down his administration's mooted rescue package. With reference to the financial system, he is reported to have said: "We got a big

---

[43] G. Brown, *Beyond the Crash* (London: Simon & Schuster, 2010).
[44] On the Japanese banking crisis see the excellent G. Tett, *Saving the Sun* (Random House, 2004).

problem . . . This sucker could go down".[45] As ever, attempting to describe events in a folksy idiom, President Bush had somewhat ingenuously hit the nail on the head, even though it was unusual for an incumbent president to do anything other than try to calm the markets down. As the satirical newspaper *The Onion* described this presidential statement: "Bush calls for panic".[46]

The EU response

As was discussed in detail in Chapter 7, the EU response to the crisis was twofold. First, the Larosière Report was commissioned and recommended the development of a single regulatory rulebook for the EU by using directly applicable Regulations in place of Directives. Second, the EU turned its back on the Anglo-American finance model (with its risk, derivatives, and shadow banking sectors) and sought a new model based on Larosière's demand for proper regulatory supervision and real teeth for regulators. As President Sarkozy of France put it: *"le laissez faire: c'est fini"*,[47] which signalled an end to the previous policy of light-touch regulation of financial markets. Unfortunately, the eurozone currency area fell into profound crisis at the same time. The struggling economies of Greece, Ireland,[48] Portugal and Cyprus, together with real pressure on Spain and Italy, meant that it was unclear whether or not the euro currency would fall apart. The pressure on the eurozone and the euro lasted from 2009 up to the time of writing with the contentious bail-out of banks in Cyprus in March 2013.

45–24

3.   PRINCIPAL EVENTS AND PARTICIPANTS IN THE CRISIS, AND THEIR LEGAL EFFECTS

A.   Introduction

This section continues the analysis of the development of the financial crisis by examining the nature, condition and policies of some of the key participants in that crisis so as to illustrate the challenges to law and to financial regulation posed by key financial institutions. Of particular significance here are Citigroup, Lehman Brothers and Goldman Sachs, all of which took significant positions in relation to crumbling CDO market and which caused the crisis in their own ways. In the section to follow, we consider key participants in the aftermath of the crisis, in particular Barclays, which have become embroiled in significant banking scandals which also pose a challenge to orderly bank regulation and to finance law.

45–25

---

[45] *The Times*, September 26, 2008.

[46] *http://www.theonion.com/articles/bush-calls-for-panic,2578/*

[47] Speaking in Toulon on September 25, 2008. See for example: *http://www.liberation.fr/politiques/010133587-le-laisser-faire-c-est-fini.*

[48] On the Irish crisis, see the excellent F. O'Toole, *Ship of Fools* (London: Faber, 2009).

B. Lehman Brothers

Introduction

45–26 The collapse of Lehman Brothers has been well-documented. The bank's business model and risk management practices were clearly inadequate. Lehman Brothers was exposed to the US real estate market, the CDO market and the CDS market: it simply could not find enough investment capital or loan capital to cover its losses. Its assets were over-valued and it was required to write them down. The management culture at Lehman Brothers was clearly inadequate in the long-term. Television documentaries have revealed that its CEO would call on his employees via internal video presentations to rip out the beating hearts of their competitors. What has already emerged in this book is its culture for flagrant disregard of regulatory obligations such as the protection of client assets under the CASS rulebook.[49] The many breaches of client money regulations by Lehman Brothers were considered in Chapters 9 and 22.[50] However, as troubling as anything about Lehman Brothers, is the revelation that it was in the practice of massaging the quality of its balance sheet. Immediately before the assessment of its assets and liabilities in each quarter leading up to the crash, Lehman Brothers did this by transferring US$50 billion in bad assets temporarily to third parties through its "Repo 105" account, before being obliged to reacquire those assets (after payment of a fee) a few days later.[51] (This is considered below.) The impression that is left is that Lehman Brothers, within its many lawful activities, contained an arrogant core which ignored both the letter and the spirit of the law to maintain an outward appearance of constant profit growth.

The repo 105 trick: a symptom of a sick bank

45–27 This subsection considers a single practice detailed in the very full report prepared by A.R. Valukas for the US Bankruptcy Court into Lehman Brothers Holdings Inc.[52] That report detailed many of the shortcomings in the Lehman Brothers organisation. This was an organisation which was prepared to breach the letter and the spirit of the law to reach its short-term goals. The Repo 105 transaction was a means for Lehman Brothers to conceal US$50 billion in bad assets just before its balance sheet was prepared. The balance sheet is a single snapshot of the bank's assets and liabilities. The repo transaction involved finding a counterparty which was willing, for a fee, to take those US$50 billion in bad assets off Lehman's balance sheet and onto its own balance sheet for a few days, subject to an obligation that Lehman would repurchase those assets at an identified time in the future. Through this device, Lehman Brothers reduced its liabilities by US$50 billion at the time that its accounts were prepared

---

[49] See para.9–58 et seq.
[50] See, for example, para.9–58 et seq.
[51] This practice is revealed in the report of A.R. Valukas prepared for the US Bankruptcy Court into Lehman Brothers Holdings Inc, dated March 11, 2010.
[52] A.R. Valukas, "Report prepared for the US Bankruptcy Court into Lehman Brothers Holdings Inc", March 11, 2010.

disingenuously on the basis that those assets formed no part of its balance sheet at the time of making that valuation. It is suggested that a bank which is prepared to act in this way is not acting with integrity. Its internal culture is clearly geared up to deceive its regulators, its shareholders, the financial market and the investment community as a whole. It is difficult to see how any sensible system of jurisprudence could see this sort of deceit as anything other than a criminal act.

A colossal failure of common sense

In a passionate memoir of his time on the bond trading desks at Lehman Brothers, McDonald presents a tale of "lions led by donkeys" in which senior management at Lehman Brothers failed to communicate with the trading floors (CEO Dick Fuld generally rode his private lift to the 32nd floor and thus avoided contact with everyone else in the bank) and failed to notice the instability of the bank's enormous exposures to the US real estate market.[53] The failure of Lehman Brothers is presented as a ruination of a great bank (with highly-motivated, knowledgeable and professional employees) by an ultimately incompetent cadre of senior executives.

45–28

C.   Goldman Sachs

The public image of Goldman Sachs

One of the most high-profile financial institutions during, and especially in the wake of, the financial crisis was Goldman Sachs. Principally this was because Goldman Sachs appeared to continue to make money throughout the crisis and appeared to have been smart enough to have managed its risks better than almost all of its Wall Street competitors.[54] However, to suggest that Goldman Sachs escaped the crisis unscathed would be a gross exaggeration. In common with Morgan Stanley, Goldman Sachs had to reclassify itself as a bank holding company (as opposed to an investment bank) for regulatory purposes so that it could access Federal Reserve money to recapitalise itself. However, what began to cling to the name Goldman Sachs in the wake of the crisis was a sense that it was unscrupulous in making money. Indeed, the most extraordinary sentence written during the entirety of the financial crisis was by Matt Taibbi in *Rolling Stone* magazine, describing Goldman Sachs[55]:

45–29

> "The world's most powerful investment bank is a great vampire squid wrapped around the face of humanity, relentlessly jamming its blood funnel into anything that smells like money."

---

[53] L. McDonald, *A Colossal Failure of Common Sense* (New York: Random House, 2009). See also J. Tibman, *The Murder of Lehman Brothers* (New York: Brick Tower Press, 2009). For a history of Lehman Brothers, including its earlier near collapses, from 1844 until its insolvency see P Chapman, *The Last of the Imperious Rich* (New York: Portfolio Penguin, 2010).
[54] W. Cohan, *Money and Power* (New York: Allen Lane, 2010).
[55] Reproduced in M Taibbi, *Griftopia* (New York: Spiegel & Grau, 2011), Ch.7 "The Great American Bubble Machine", p.206 et seq.

Taibbi's general points were twofold. First, that Goldman Sachs was very powerful politically, with many of its former employees holding particularly sensitive official positions.[56] During the crisis many of its alumni were in positions of power: Treasury Secretary during the financial crisis, Hank Paulson, had been CEO of Goldman Sachs; President Clinton's Treasury Secretary Robert Rubin had been at Goldman Sachs for 26 years; Joshua Bolten, chief of staff to President George W Bush during the crisis, had been at Goldman Sachs; as had the CEO of Merrill Lynch, John Thain. Many of the junior advisors in the process of establishing the Troubled Asset Relief Program which bailed out US banks were former investment bankers, many of them at Goldman Sachs.

45–30 Secondly, Taibbi presented a thesis that Goldman Sachs had been culpably involved in many important financial crises in the preceding hundred years. Goldman Sachs was blamed in large part for the Great Crash of 1929 in New York for its role in "leveraged" investment transactions.[57] Taibbi's article then drew a straight line through Goldman Sachs's involvement in several other market collapses (including the tech stocks collapse in the 1990s), the CDO boom, and the boom in oil prices in which Goldman Sachs had played a significant part as one of the world's largest commodities traders. Ultimately, Taibbi sought to affix blame to Goldman Sachs (one of the beneficiaries of the US government's nearly US$1 trillion bail-out) for bailing out Wall Street but not ordinary citizens.

The transformation from a partnership to a corporation

45–31 One of the principal changes which affected Goldman Sachs was that it ceased to be an ordinary partnership and transformed itself into a corporation (registered in Delaware) in 1998. This, it is suggested, led to a great change in the corporate culture at Goldman Sachs. When Goldman Sachs had been a partnership each of its partners had been personally responsible for the losses and defaults of the firm, just as they owned all of the assets and profits of the firm personally under the terms of the partnership agreement. Consequently, in the event that there was any concern about the legality of a course of action on the trading floors or elsewhere, then each of the partners in the business units concerned would insist on the irregularity, issue or illegality being resolved immediately. The firm's approach to risk management was also very responsive. It is possible that Goldman Sachs's success in avoiding the bulk of the risks associated with the collapse in the mortgage-based securities markets from 2006 onwards (by selling all of its exposure and taking positions which would profit from such a fall) was due to its history as a partnership and its concomitant need to control risk. However, the post-incorporation Goldman Sachs became an even leaner, hungrier profit-making machine without partners. For some, this was a reason to leave the firm.[58] Consequently, Goldman Sachs executives were entitled to salaries and bonuses from the company, as opposed to owning the firm's profits, losses and property. There is a significant ethical difference between a partnership, where

---

[56] To declare an interest, I am myself a former employee of Goldman Sachs from the 1990's.

[57] See, for example, J.K. Galbraith, *The Great Crash 1929* (1954; Penguin, 1992), 85–90.

[58] G. Smith, *Why I left Goldman Sachs* (New York: Grand Central, 2012).

the partners are personally responsible for every default of the partnership (and the defaults of other partners), and a company in which the directors personally face little direct accountability because the losses are ultimately borne by the company and the shareholders, given that they only have a vested interest through their shareholdings and their bonuses. As is considered next, Goldman Sachs became embroiled in ethically questionable trading practices.

The CDO shorts

Goldman Sachs and Deutsche Bank had been two of the most significant marketers of CDO's involving sub-prime mortgages from later discredited lenders such as New Century and Long Beach in the USA. In 2006–07, however, Goldman Sachs ("GS") reversed its position as delinquencies in the underlying mortgages began to increase. GS sought to build a series of positions so that it would benefit from a fall in the market. In many circumstances, GS simply took out a "naked" credit default swap (i.e. one that was not hedging any particular position and as such was purely speculative) as a bet that the market would fall. GS had been US$6 billion "long" on the mortgage-backed CDO market in the summer of 2006 (meaning that it had an exposure to the market in that total amount); whereas by early December 2006, GS had "passed home" as it turned its "long" position into a net "short" position (whereby it would benefit if the market fell), with the result that its first short positions started to accrue benefits in early 2007. Or, put more simply, in about six months GS transformed a US$6 billion exposure to CDO's, into a bet that would profit if the CDO market collapsed. The principal issue which arose in relation to GS, and which made it into the national press, was the revelation that while GS had been selling mortgage-backed CDO's to its clients (i.e. securities which took positions on the performance of the US real estate mortgage and related markets) GS itself had been taking the exact opposite position on those same transactions: therefore, GS had been speculating that those CDO's would fall in value while selling them to its clients.[59]

45–32

These CDO transactions were the subject of a case study in the US Senate Permanent Subcommittee on Investigations report into the financial crisis, titled "Wall Street and the Financial Crisis".[60] In relation to one particular transaction, known as "Timberwolf", the Senate Subcommittee Report found that GS took 100 per cent of the opposite side of the transaction to its clients. This meant that GS was taking the exact opposite bet from its clients on the same transactions. In market parlance, they were "short" those CDOs. This raised concerns, first, that GS had a conflict of interest in seeing the CDOs fall in value and, second, that Goldman Sachs may have made deliberate misrepresentations to the clients which had bought those CDOs.

45–33

---

[59] For a discussion of short trading strategies in relation to this market, see G. Zuckerman, *The Greatest Trade Ever* (New York: Broadway Books, 2009).
[60] US Senate Permanent Subcommittee on Investigations, "Wall Street and the Financial Crisis: Anatomy of a Financial Collapse", April 13, 2011. Accessible through *http://www.hsgac.senate.gov/ subcommittees/investigations/reports*. [Accessed March 14, 2013]

45–34　The Senate hearings involved the revelation of a series of distasteful emails between traders[61] as to the manner in which they were treating their clients. There were three CDO issues of particular importance: "Hudson 1", "Anderson" and Timberwolf". It was Timberwolf which attracted the most press attention. As one GS employee put it in an email to a fellow employee: "that was one shitty deal",[62] by which he meant that the deal would result in large losses for the buyers but profits for GS. The Senate Subcommittee found in its report that, in the case of Timberwolf, "Goldman sold the securities to its clients even as it knew the securities were falling in value".[63] The question which is asked in legal terms is therefore whether or not GS made any fraudulent misrepresentations as to the condition of those CDOs. In relation to the Anderson CDO, it was found that GS personnel had tried to dispel client concerns about the quality and condition of the underlying New Century mortgages included in the CDO, and the fact that GS had itself taken 40 per cent in the short position on that CDO (to the effect that it was betting that the CDO would fail) was not disclosed to clients. In relation to a fourth CDO, Abacus, GS created the CDO so that a hedge fund, Paulson & Co, could take the short position while other clients were sold the long position on it. The Senate Subcommittee found that GS "marketed Abacus securities to its clients, knowing the CDO was designed to lose value".[64] Three clients lost US$1 billion from Abacus, while Paulson & Co took a profit of approximately the same amount.[65] In relation to Hudson 1, the GS documentation recorded that GS's own position was "aligned with that of investors", even though it was taking the opposite position as to US$2 billion. Moreover, it was found by the Senate Subcommittee that GS took "months" to liquidate the positions of customers who were "long" this transaction.[66] Goldman was fined US$550 million by the SEC in relation to the Abacus transactions. The question for finance law, as discussed in Chapter 25, remains: at what point is this sort of behaviour to be considered to be fraud, or does this sort of behaviour constitute lawful, if sharp, practice?

---

[61] Is there any other kind?

[62] US Senate Permanent Subcommittee on Investigations, "Wall Street and the Financial Crisis: Anatomy of a Financial Collapse", p.394, in an email from GS Mortgage Department "head" Daniel Sparks: "boy that timeberwof [sic] was one shitty deal". It was the view of one GS trader that the day Timberwolf was first sold was "a day that will live in infamy": "Wall Street and the Financial Crisis: Anatomy of a Financial Collapse", p.395. Timberwolf lost 80% of its value.

[63] "Wall Street and the Financial Crisis: Anatomy of a Financial Collapse", p.18.

[64] "Wall Street and the Financial Crisis: Anatomy of a Financial Collapse", p.18.

[65] The examination of trader GS Fabrice Tourre was a feature of press coverage of this deal.

[66] "Wall Street and the Financial Crisis: Anatomy of a Financial Collapse", p.392. Morgan Stanley, for example, lost nearly US$960 million on Hudson: *ibid*.

4.   AFTER THE TIDE WENT OUT: THE SCANDALOUS AFTERMATH OF THE CRISIS

A.   Introduction

The well-known investor Warren Buffet, the Sage of Omaha, famously said: "After all, you only find out who is swimming naked when the tide goes out".[67] He meant that in the context of the financial markets, once a crisis strikes and the initial chaos subsides then you can see what people had really been doing beforehand because those things will come to light when that market falls. So, for example, when the markets collapsed and investors sought to withdraw their money in a hurry, the fraudulent investment schemes which had been operated by Bernard Madoff collapsed and his criminal activities were laid bare to view, to the astonishment of the whole of New York City. When the tide withdrew, it became clear that Madoff had been operating a Ponzi scheme: this a fraudulent scheme to raise money from investors while pretending to invest their money, and simply paying them back a small part of their capital as a purported profit on those investments.[68] Madoff's enterprise was estimated as being somewhere between US\$13 billion and US\$60 billion.[69] In the period before the crisis, lots of institutions had been mispricing their assets and their risks, and floating on the high tide of a growing market: but when that market fell, then the weaknesses in their practices became clear. So, it was only when the crisis began that senior management at Citigroup realised how exposed their bank had been to securitisation markets for the first time. The several banking scandals in the UK only came to light once the crisis had lit a fire under financial regulators across the world for the first time. We learned a lot more about the financial sector as a result of the financial crisis: albeit things which anyone who had worked in banking should have suspected, but which policymakers chose to believe could never happen.

45–35

The purpose of this section is to consider the lessons which should be drawn from the things we have learned. To this end, some of the more significant events are highlighted here. No particular fault is attached to any of the entities considered here which is greater than other financial institutions. However, these entities have been the subject of published reports and therefore the detail of their faults are in the public domain at the time of writing. Moreover, there are some institutions like Barclays and Citigroup which simply seem to crop up more often than others in this context.

45–36

---

[67] Berkshire Hathaway Annual Report, Chairman's letter, 2001: *http://www.berkshirehathaway.com/ 2001ar/2001letter.html.*

[68] Ibid.

[69] What the Madoff affair reveals is that regulators have often been reluctant to believe the worst, even when the evidence has been plain. Large numbers of people and philanthropic organisations were ruined by Madoff. The trial judge described his deeds as "extraordinarily evil".

B. Barclays

Introduction

45–37 This section focuses on Barclays precisely because it has been involved in so many of the principal banking scandals which have come to light in the wake of the financial crisis. It was the most "complained about" bank in the UK in 2011 and 2012.[70] Barclays had also been particularly high-profile during the crisis: its senior executives appearing regularly on the television to trumpet the fact that the bank had not required a government bail-out (even though it depended on a sector which had been bailed out by several governments and even though it sought a huge capital injection from the sovereign wealth fund of Abu Dhabi). It was Barclays, under the stewardship of its high-profile Chief Executive Bob Diamond,[71] which bought up large portions of Lehman Brothers after its insolvency and which sought to reinvent itself as a global investment banking behemoth.

A potted history of Barclays Bank

45–38 The historical trajectory of Barclays is a metaphor for the entire banking sector. It is genuinely fascinating as a history of the emergence of a sort of financialised capitalism in the early 21st century which was very different from other models of capitalism.[72] Barclays Bank emerged from a firm founded by East Anglian Quakers in 1690. Consequently, it can claim to be the oldest surviving bank of any size in London—older even than the Bank of England. The business morality of the Quakers (which is also the ethical foundation of chocolate manufacturers Cadbury and Fry, and Quaker's Oats) is well-known.[73] One of the more celebrated senior partners of Barclays was John Henton Tritton, who joined the firm in 1782, who was described by a contemporary in the following terms:[74]

> "He was the most deliberate and exact man I ever knew. ... He followed up the details of every part of our concern with minute particularity which kept all the clerks up to the mark, silently overlooking their work and making all his observations in a low tone of voice, so that the same quiet habit of transacting the business prevailed throughout the House. Extreme caution, inflexible integrity and firmness were his characteristics as a man of business ..."

---

[70] *http://www.which.co.uk/news/2013/01/barclays-most-complained-about-company-in-2012-309245/* [Accessed March 14, 2013]

[71] In all seriousness, if one wrote a fictional account of a banking system in which the over-confident Chief Executive of a bank with a pearly white smile was called "Diamond", in which the head of the central bank was called "King", and in which the Chief Executive of a competing, loss-making investment bank was called "Prince", then derision for your ham-fisted satire would be the only result. The head of Barclays investment banking division at the time of writing is "Rich Ricci" (try saying it out-loud).

[72] The process of "financialisation" was discussed at para.1–71 et seq.

[73] See, for example, D. Cadbury, *Chocolate Wars* (Harper Press, 2010) for a recent history of Quaker business practices; and more specifically Quakers and Business Group, *Good Business: Ethics at Work* (2000) on practical business ethics in the Quaker tradition.

[74] The words are those of Robert Barclay II, as quoted by David Kynaston, *The City of London, Volume 1: A World of Its Own* (London: Chatto & Windus, 1994), 15.

How different things would have been if prudence and inflexible integrity remained the cornerstone of universal banking in the 21st century. The probity in the earliest incarnations of their banking house are self-evident; whereas by 2012, Barclays would have become associated in the public mind with fraud and sharp practice.[75]

Interestingly, Barclays grew to be one of the four principal UK banks over time as a result of the aggregation of a large number of small, regional banks, albeit with a significant presence on Lombard Street in the City of London. It was a very decentralised bank historically, including many regional offices which ran almost as separate banks, and also a number of international offices.[76] Like all early banks, Barclays was a partnership, which means that the partners were personally responsible for all of the losses and defaults of the firm, and also that they owned the firm. Consequently, the firm's ethos reflected the morality of its partners. In this case, the Quakers had a very high standard of moral probity, as well as an active work ethic. The Barclays partners were serial acquirers of banks and their customers. So, while the Quaker heritage is one of moral rectitude, there was always an eccentric determination to grow by acquiring smaller banks. Even in the 20th century, the directors of the bank were drawn almost exclusively from members of the founding families and their descendants, and from the alumni of particular public schools, universities and regiments.[77] Barclays was always a cultural outlier, but that image was greatly tarnished in the 21st century.

45–39

The Libor scandal

Perhaps the most significant scandal, and probably the most newsworthy in 2012–13, was the news that employees at Barclays had been involved in fraudulently affecting the quotation of the London Inter-bank Offered Rate ("Libor") which is the most significant benchmark rate against which financial instruments from complex derivatives to domestic mortgages are ultimately priced. This involved 14 Barclays employees in London. In essence, nominated employees from each institution would collect data from within their institutions as to the rates at which banks were trading with one another, and then pass that information to the British Bankers Association ("BBA") which would then publish a price for Libor for that day. It was simple then for traders inside Barclays to put pressure on those people who were nominated to collect the data ("the submitters") to quote a higher or lower rate so that Libor would be quoted more profitably for Barclays. It has emerged that Barclays alumni at other banks were also involved in this fraud.

45–40

The Financial Services Authority ("FSA") imposed a fine on Barclays Bank Plc of £59.5 million further to s.206 of the FSMA 2000, under a Final Notice dated June 27, 2012. The FSA found that Barclays had breached Principle 5 of the PRIN rulebook (that a firm must observe proper standards of market conduct)

45–41

---

[75] During the 1980s, Barclays had been associated with investment in apartheid South Africa.

[76] Indeed, the famous spread-eagle logo actually belonged to Gosling's Bank before it was taken over by Barclays. Barclays had also taken over banks with wholesome grasshopper and "three squirrels" logos.

[77] M. Vander Weyer, *Falling Eagle* (London: Weidenfeld and Nicholson, 2000).

and that it had been derivatives traders in particular who had sought the misquotation of Libor. The motivation behind these misquotations which the FSA set out in the Final Notice was that Barclays was concerned about its reputation in the marketplace during the financial crisis ("between September 2007 and May 2009") and in particular the rate at which it was able to obtain funding. This meant that Barclays wanted it to appear that it could attract funding at a lower rate than in fact it could (because that would make it appear to be of a higher credit worth). Therefore, Barclays sought to lower its quotations for Libor purposes. Barclays also breached Principle 3 (by failing to have appropriate systems in place) and Principle 2 (by failing to conduct its business with sufficient skill, care and diligence).

45–42   The FSA fines were in parallel with the work of the US Commodities and Futures Trading Commission ("CFTC") into Barclays misdemeanours.[78] The CFTC imposed a "civil monetary penalty" on Barclays of US$200 million. The CFTC Order (of June 27, 2012) published extracts from emails between Barclays traders and the submitters which showed the contentment of the submitters to conspire in this fraud ("Done … for you big boy" and "We always try and do our best to help out") and the traders' gratitude ("Dude. I owe you big time! Come over one day after work and I'm opening a bottle of Bollinger"; "When I retire and write a book about this business your name will be written in golden letters"; and simply "superstar").[79] Among the more remarkable features of these exchanges are the relaxed attitude to writing on email systems on which internal supervisors or external regulators could have read about the fraud; the idiocy of assuming that one might write a book about these crimes; and the awful use of the word "dude". Some of the emails reproduced by the CFTC suggested that traders were often seeking to raise the level of Libor so as to make profit and suggested that those traders were using this misquotation of Libor to make money (and not simply to massage Barclays' public relations position). For example: "I have a huge 1m fixing today and it would really help to have a low 1m tx a lot" and "we have to get kicked out of the fixings tomorrow".[80] The FSA Final Notice only deals with these issues later. The FSA found that "between January 2005 and May 2009 at least 173 requests for US dollar Libor submissions were made to Barclays Submitters"; with 58 requests made in relation to Euribor and 26 in relation to Yen Libor. That is a remarkable, systematic culture of fraud within one bank over nearly five years. The CFTC found that Barclays tried to fix the Libor levels on "numerous occasions and sometimes on a daily basis". Therefore, this was not simply about public relations (which supposes the involvement of very senior management in the bank) but also about ordinary profit on individual transactions (which might be limited to more junior traders).[81]

---

[78] See: *http://www.cftc.gov/ucm/groups/public/@lrenforcementactions/documents/legalpleading/ enfbarclaysorder062712.pdf*. [Accessed March 14, 2013]

[79] See, for example, *http://www.telegraph.co.uk/finance/newsbysector/banksandfinance/9359392/ Key-emails-how-Barclays-manipulated-Libor.html*. [Accessed March 14, 2013]

[80] This last indicates that Barclays wanted to be excluded from the ratings ("fixings") by being higher or lower than the group used to fix the rate so as to earn a profit.

[81] Barclays has also been fined £290 million by the US Federal Energy Regulatory Commission for allegedly attempting to manipulate electricity prices in California between 2006 and 2008.

When Bob Diamond was questioned about these revelations by the Treasury **45–43** Select Committee in the UK on July 4, 2012, his line of defence (repeated on several occasions) was that this had happened a long time ago (as long ago as three years previously!), that it had related to a part of the bank with which he was unfamiliar (even though he had been CEO of the Barclays investment bank), and that Barclays had co-operated with the regulators when all of this had come out (as though that made up for committing all these breaches in the first place). Three years may seem a long time in investment banking, but in point of fact it is not a long time. Under the SYSC rulebook, there are obligations on the CEO personally to acquaint himself with the bank and to ensure that there are systems and controls in place to prevent market abuse and other regulatory breaches.[82] Unfortunately, the select committee members did not question him about these regulatory obligations nor did they penetrate his well-coached responses to their questions. Clearly, not only did Diamond have personal regulatory obligations in relation to the internal systems of his own institution but moreover any decent system of regulation must impose such direct, personal legal obligations on senior management. It is only if senior management is made personally liable for such defaults, and thus for constructing systems which will prevent the possibility of such defaults occurring in practice, that genuine change will occur.

This news precipitated the formation of the Parliamentary Commission on **45–44** Banking Standards in the UK because the self-evident fraud at the heart of such important banks shocked the regulatory and political establishment to its core. The financial crisis and the system's other shortcomings were no longer just a matter of economic theory, but rather this was a matter of simple fraud. Barclays received a 30 per cent discount on its FSA fine because it admitted its wrongdoing and co-operated with the regulator from the outset. However, this did also mean that Barclays became perceived as the bank most closely associated with Libor scandal. Other banks have been fined by the FSA, including UBS.[83]

The Wheatley Review (chaired by the future Chair of the FCA) looked into the **45–45** Libor scandal and made proposals for changes in the law: those proposals were considered in Chapter 29 in relation to the Financial Services (Banking Reform) Bill 2013 and in Chapter 14 in relation to the new offences of misreporting a benchmark rate.[84]

Failure to segregate client assets

A Final Notice from the FSA (dated January 27, 2011) shows that Barclays Bank **45–46** was in breach of the FSA Client Asset rulebook ("CASS") which required that clients' money were segregated from the bank's own money. Barclays was fined £1.12 million as a result. Consequently, Barclays was in serious breach of its fiduciary duties to its customers. There is no integrity in a bank which breaches its fiduciary duties and which cannot operate accounts properly. Again, this

---

[82] See para.9–41 et seq.
[83] UBS was fined £160,000 further to a Final Notice dated December 19, 2012.
[84] *http://cdn.hm-treasury.gov.uk/wheatley_review_libor_finalreport_280912.pdf.* [Accessed March 14, 2013]

demonstrates a bank which was not able to operate basic accounting systems properly, and one which did not protect its clients' assets.

45–47 Of course, Barclays was not the only bank caught engaging in this activity. JP Morgan was also fined £33.3 million by the FSA for breaches of its CASS obligations on June 3, 2010: this was the second largest fine of all time. As was discussed in detail in Chapter 9, Lehman Brothers breached its CASS obligations with breath-taking frequency.[85] What emerged in those cases was that Lehman Brothers was mixing client money with its own money—in one strand to the litigation it was operating a regional "hub" which all assets in a pool and then applied them for clients or for the bank itself as was necessary[86]—and yet a senior management team (dubbed "Rascals") had been created to consider this problem years before the bank went into insolvency, with no effect. This demonstrates a bank which was not simply negligent in the use of client money and consistently acting in breach of trust in relation to client money, but also a bank which had a knowing and flagrant disregard for the regulations which bound it. At this point, one has to ask why no-one has been imprisoned for these flagrant breaches, and why there is no branch of the criminal law to deal with these issues.

Failure to operate basic banking systems in line with regulatory requirements

45–48 Perhaps the least we would expect from a bank is that it will maintain accurate record systems. After all, a bank account is merely the bank's record of the amount of money which it owes to any customer in credit. Consequently, it is problematic to note that several retail banks have demonstrated themselves to be incapable of operating basic records systems in different contexts.

45–49 Most egregiously, Barclays was subject to a Final Notice from the FSA (dated August 19, 2009) which shows that Barclays misreported approximately 57.5 *million* transactions to the FSA in 2006 alone, this total coming from different business sectors.[87] The FSA imposed a penalty of £2.45 million on Barclays as a result. Remarkably, Barclays had conducted an internal review of its systems in 2006 and had found only 17 misreports: an error of something over 57 million missing reports. It was by chance that the FSA turned up this misreporting while investigating something else entirely. The FSA found that Barclays failed "to take reasonable care to organise and control its affairs responsibly and effectively, with adequate risk management systems" and that Barclays failed "to conduct its business with due skill, care and diligence in failing to respond sufficiently to opportunities to review the adequacy of its transaction reporting systems". In some ways, this is worse than fraud by rogue traders. This goes to the heart of the bank's competence to act as a bank. Moreover, it is impossible for the regulator to

---

[85] The several cases which have addressed whether or not their clients had effective proprietary rights in the Lehman Brothers' insolvency were considered at para.9 59 et seq and in relation to trusts law at para.22–19 et seq. See especially *Re Lehman Brothers International (Europe) (in administration) v CRC Credit Fund Ltd* [2012] UKSC 6, [2012] Bus. L.R. 667.

[86] *Re Lehman Brothers International (Europe) (In Administration)* [2010] EWHC 2914 (Ch).

[87] That is, the total was not constituted of one simple computing error.

combat financial crime, to oversee the stability of the financial system and so forth if banks like Barclays misreport their transactions.[88]

As was considered in Chapter 9, the "SYSC" rulebook requires that board directors and "senior managers" take "appropriate practical responsibility for their firms' arrangements" in relation to that firm's regulatory responsibilities. The CEO is specifically identified as being responsible for these structures. Under SYSC, "[a] firm must take reasonable care to establish and maintain such systems and controls as are appropriate to its business" and to maintain "robust arrangements" including "a clear organisational structure with well defined, transparent and consistent lines of responsibility, effective processes to identify, manage, monitor and report the risks it is or might be exposed to" as well as appropriate internal control mechanisms.[89] The firm's "senior personnel" must ensure that the firm "complies with its obligations under the regulatory system" and those personnel must "assess and periodically review the effectiveness of those policies". Barclays failed to assess their systems effectively because they identified 17 misreported transactions and missed something in the region of 57,499,983 more; they failed to observe their obligations under CASS; and they allowed the Libor fraud to take place.

45–50

Mis-selling to retail customers

Barclays has not only committed misdemeanours at the investment banking level but rather also in relation to retail customers. Barclays was fined £7.7 million on January 18, 2011 by the FSA for breaching its obligations under the Conduct of Business Sourcebook when selling funds to retail customers. It failed to establish the level of expertise of those customers and their "risk appetite", as required by the regulations.[90] These regulations are the absolute core of consumer protection regulation in the UK (implementing EU MiFID rules). Importantly, Barclays was found to have trained its staff inadequately and to have provided customers with inadequate literature. This question of training staff appropriately is very significant for the regulation of financial regulation. The creation of a banking profession with mandatory training and examinations would be a significant part of restoring faith in banking and in ensuring that in practice individual employees do not become the agents of corporate mis-selling. The most important example of mis-selling is the payment protection insurance ("PPI") scandal.[91] Barclays has been fined, along with other banks, by the FSA for mis-selling payment protection insurance.

45–51

---

[88] One is also tempted to ask: what does this say about Barclays' attitude to regulatory observance? Were their accounts and accounting procedures reliable at this time?
[89] SYSC, 4.1.1.R.
[90] See para.10–01 et seq.
[91] Considered below at para.45–63.

Mis-selling CDOs

45–52   In the decided case of *Cassa di Risparmio della Repubblica di San Marino SpA v Barclays Bank Ltd*[92] (2011), there were allegations that a very complex AAA-rated CDO product was really "junk", and therefore that the buyer (a tiny San Marino bank) had been misled into buying that product. Those allegations would have stood a much greater chance of success if they had been put on the basis of negligence. However, the presence of an exclusion of liability clause in the contract meant that the San Marino bank was only allowed to allege fraud (which is very difficult to prove in practice) because that was all that was not covered by the exclusion of liability clause. Fraud could not be demonstrated on those facts to the satisfaction of Hamblen J., although (as was considered in Chapter 25) there were many aspects of that case in which the behaviour of employees at Barclays was questionable at best. When putting together a CDO which fell nearly to junk status a few months after being sold, it is questionable whether or not that constitutes an action in the best interests of the customer or best execution.

C.   JP Morgan Chase

45–53   A particularly important banking scandal was exposed by a report by the US Senate Permanent Subcommittee on Investigations, chaired by Senator Levin, titled "JP Morgan Chase Whale Trades: A Case History of Derivatives Risks and Abuses",[93] There had been press reports about a series of trades made on credit derivatives markets on behalf of JP Morgan by "the London Whale" through their offices in London—hence the reference to "Whale Trades". A "whale" in market parlance usually refers to an investor with a very large amount of money, typically one who makes large losses and therefore is an easy target for clever traders.[94] Within the bank, the Chief Investment Office ("CIO") was established in 2005, and in turn the CIO created the Synthetic Credit Portfolio ("SCP") in 2008 to make investments in the credit derivatives area. In 2011, JP Morgan made profits of approximately US$400 million from this activity on an outlay of US$1 billion. In the following year, so as to reduce its regulatory capital as a whole, JP Morgan senior management instructed its CIO to reduce regulatory capital in the SCP. However, the CIO decided to acquire *more* credit derivatives which it expected would offset any need for a reduction in regulatory capital (as opposed to disposing of risk-weighted assets so as to reduce capital). This simply increased the amount of risk which JP Morgan was taking on. In the first quarter of 2012, there was a "sustained trading spree"[95] by CIO traders which increased the size of the SCP from US$51 billion to US$157 billion, so that by the end of

---

[92] [2011] EWHC 484 (Comm).
[93] *http://www.hsgac.senate.gov/subcommittees/investigations/hearings/chase-whale-trades-a-case history-of-derivatives-risks and-abuses* [Accessed March 14, 2013].
[94] This is the sense in which the term "whale" is used, for example, in the movie *Boiler Room* (discussed in detail at the beginning of Ch.11) to denote rich investors who are easy targets for salesman trying to offload securities.
[95] Levin JPM Report, 10.

March 2012 the SCP contained over 100 credit derivative instruments. By the end of March 2012, the SCP had generated losses of US$719 million. This caused the head of the CIO, Ina Drew, to tell the traders to "put phones down".[96] However, the SCP continued to lose money, such that the losses reached US$ 6.2 billion by the end of the year. Nevertheless, the CIO changed its accounting practices (as the Report relates it) so as to conceal the extent of those losses.

While JP Morgan chose to present these positions as being hedges (whereby the credit derivatives would make a profit if the markets deteriorated and thus would balance out losses elsewhere), there was in fact no documentation within JP Morgan suggesting that there were actual risks which had been identified and which were to be balanced out by these credit derivatives.[97] This trading strategy was defined by the Senate Subcommittee as being a classic form of proprietary trading whereby the bank was simply speculating with its own money on these credit markets. Senior management within the CIO, specifically Ina Drew, later claimed not to have understood, nor to have been properly informed, about the risks which were being assumed in the SCP because junior traders did not pass that information up the chain to her. This clearly calls into question the efficacy of those internal systems if that was the case. It suggests a remarkable lack of oversight if a hedging operation was allowed to operate as a proprietary trading operation and if losses of US$6.2 billion could be built up in just a few weeks of trading.

45–54

However, perhaps the most serious aspect of the entire affair was the manner in which JP Morgan treated its regulators at this time. The Senate Subcommittee describes JP Morgan as having "dodged" their regulators by omitting mention of the SCP in routine reports to its regulators and by failing to warn them of increases in the size of the position. The principal regulator of JP Morgan's holding company was the Official Controller of the Currency ("OCC"). The Senate Subcommittee found as a fact that JP Morgan used deposits (which were protected by federal regulation) to fund these positions, and that JP Morgan did not supply correct information to the OCC about this trading position when it was asked and required to do so by the OCC. As the Levin JPM Report puts it, JP Morgan provided almost no information about the SCP to the OCC before media reports began to circulate in April 2012. Indeed, JP Morgan admitted that no explicit reference had been made to the SCP until January 2012 in a general VaR report, after the SCP had already lost US$100 million. Information was either not provided or incorrect information was provided, as found by the Senate Subcommittee. The full story was not made known to the OCC until May 2012, when JP Morgan was about to reveal that it had suffered US$2 billion of losses (an amount which was to rise to 6.2 billion).

45–55

In outline, some of the principal legal issues appear to be the following. First, internal corporate governance systems at JP Morgan failed to identify the large amount of risk which was building up in the SCP area. Second, and more seriously, JP Morgan failed to make full and accurate reports of the bank's positions to its regulators in relation to the SCP. It is suggested that failures to

45–56

---

[96] Levin JPM Report, 10.
[97] Levin JPM Report, 10.

make proper reports to regulators (whether intentionally or inadvertently through negligence) should result in criminal offences in the future (where those offences differentiate between intentional actions, reckless actions and negligent actions). Third, CEO Jamie Dimon and the CFO Braunstein sought determinedly to play down the effect on the bank of these transactions—dismissing the affair as a "tempest in a teacup" as late as April 2012, and claiming that the affair had been disclosed to the OCC when it had not—while the Senate Committee questions the amount of information which was available to senior management when those statements were made. The question arises whether or not this was a legally actionable attempt to mislead financial markets under criminal or civil law. Fourth, the Senate Committee found that there was a "bank culture in which risk limit breaches were routinely disregarded".[98] What was initially dismissed as merely a "tempest in a teacup" may continue to have ramifications for that bank for some time to come.

D.   The utility role of banks

The banks' role as a utility in modern society

45–57   Banks are no longer private sector institutions which provide a limited number of deposit-taking and lending functions solely in relation to the wealthy, bourgeois members of society. In the 21st century, approximately 90 per cent of the adult population has a bank account, with about 1.5 million adults[99] living in households with no access to a bank account at all.[100] This marks a great shift from the 1970s, when approximately only half of the adult population had a bank account. Banks now operate a utility service in the form of the banking payments system without which ordinary life would become impossible. The advent of electronic payment processing and of internet shopping have revolutionised economic life. Salaries, pensions and benefits are now routinely paid electronically into bank accounts. Small businesses and large all require credit services, just as their customers require credit cards and other payment systems to deal with those businesses. Consequently, the role of the banks is no longer that of a private sector service provider which extends voluntary services to a select clientele. Instead, they are part of the warp and weft of ordinary life and they need to be regulated as such. The providers of gas, electricity and water are treated very differently from other service providers because their services are essential to their end-users. The quality of their service and the manner in which they are able to withdraw or deny their services are greatly circumscribed. As a result, they are subjected to positive obligations in the standard of their service. This attitude must be brought to bear on banks, which are no longer simply entitled to earn whatever profit they agree on a privately contracted basis with

---

[98] Levin JPM Report, 13.

[99] This number includes a large number of single parent households and single pensioner households.

[100] The "unbanked" are those with no access to a bank account in their household. HM Treasury, "Statistical Release: households without access to bank accounts 2008–09", December 2010, *http://www.hm-treasury.gov.uk/d/stats_briefing_101210.pdf.*

their customers, but which are instead the providers of essential services without which economic life cannot function and the cost of whose services can therefore be controlled.

E.   Rogue traders

Introduction

Rogue traders are the epitome of an investment banking culture in which it is **45–58** difficult for management to control the actions of their junior employees. The importance of regulation governing internal controls within banks, and indeed the law on vicarious liability and the criminal law on fraud, is precisely that banks must nevertheless create systems which control these problems. The most famous rogue trader of all is Nick Leeson, the Singapore derivatives trader who bankrupted Barings Bank single-handedly by concealing his mounting losses in a fictitious account with a fictitious client. Senior management at Barings in London failed to get to the bottom of what this Watford Grammar School boy was up to so many miles from home in Singapore, and instead they kept booking his "profits". Ultimately, as always happens, the deceit could not carry on for sufficiently long. What was important about Leeson was that he set a template for most rogue traders in the future. Leeson was in a branch office away from central control, he was able to control the employees immediately around him, he was in an age bracket falling between late twenties and mid-thirties, and he had an excellent knowledge of how the bank's operations systems worked (so that he knew how to book and conceal false trades in the system).

John Gapper's book *How to be a Rogue Trader*[101] quotes the following advice **45–59** from risk consultant Nick Gibson to his bank clients when UBS trader, Kweku Adoboli, was arrested in London:

> "Do you employ a likeable twenty-eight-year-old male index derivatives trader who has been promoted to the trading floor [from the back office]? Does he have a good understanding of your back- and middle-office systems, including where the weaknesses are? … If so, go and take a closer look at what he's doing."

The principal rogue traders have all fitted this pattern. Leeson had been able to run up a loss of £830 million in a matter of weeks at a bank which had been in existence for 233 years. Joseph Jett had worked in the dull-as-ditchwater mortgage desk at Kidder Peabody before developing a trading technique (which he would not explain to anyone) which booked profits of US$264 million: except that the technique was simply the practice of hiding losses (of US$74 million in total) by entering false transactions into the computer system which were to mature in the future but which the system mistakenly valued as having shown an

---

[101] J. Gapper, *How to be a Rogue Trader* (Penguin, 2012).

immediate profit.[102] Jerome Kerviel lost 4.9 billion on Societe Generale's Delta One equity derivatives trading desk. What was interesting about Kerviel was that he had been promoted from the back office operations area to the trading desk, and he had seemed to conduct his activities almost as a game rather than as a real attempt to make money for himself.[103]

45–60   In each of these circumstances, the rogue traders were able to use the bank's systems to conceal losses, instead of those same systems making it impossible to hide anything. If the rogue knows how the systems are constructed and where odd amounts can be explained away or go unnoticed (for example, by programming a false trade having the opposite effect to the losing trades, or by entering the trades so that they are due to be completed only in the future) then it is possible to hide losses.

45–61   Of course, the definition of rogue traders as encompassing only these young men begs the question whether or not institutional rogue traders, or large scale group errors such as the JP Morgan "London Whales" should also be thought of as being rogue traders. The common feature between both categories is that they act beyond the reach of their agency (that is, they are necessarily acting beyond the terms of their authority to bind their employer institution), and they necessarily use fraud to conceal their actions from their employer (by falsifying records) and possibly also from regulators (as with the JP Morgan's failures to report all of the facts to the OCC, as considered above).

45–62   The criminal liabilities of most rogue traders are most obviously related to the Fraud Act 2006 in which they arguably use a false representation to make a gain or reduce a loss, or more significantly abuse a position so as to expose another person to a risk of loss. The difficulty with the false representation offence (or with theft offences before the 2006 Act) is that the rogue traders are not always seeking to take a profit for themselves directly. The gain for the rogue traders themselves comes from the bonus which they stand to receive at the end of the year: as with Joseph Jett's US$9.3 million bonus in 1993, for example. That would be enough to make out the false representation or even the theft offence, as considered in Chapter 16. However, otherwise, the profit which they are seeking to make is for the firm; or the losses which they are ultimately seeking to hide (as with Leeson) will hit the firm. The UBS trader, Kweku Adoboli, was charged with fraud in the form of abuse of position and false accounting after having established a huge trading position at UBS and used his knowledge of the back office (where he had previously worked before being promoted to trade in derivatives) to conceal his activities. He was convicted of two charges of fraud by way of abuse of position; but the jury did not find him guilty of false accounting, which presumes that they did not find that he had acted for his own personal

---

[102] The CEO at Kidder Peabody, Jack Welch, later explained in his memoir (*Straight from the Gut* (Headline, 2003)) that he wished in retrospect that he had inquired more closely into how a trader who had made a bonus of $5,000 in 1991 could have made sufficient profits to take home a bonus of $9.3 million in 1993.

[103] See the somewhat self-serving J Kerviel, *L'engrenage: memoires d'un trader* (Flammarion, 2010).

financial interest. That offence, under s.4 of the Fraud Act 2006,[104] required that he occupied a position where he was expected to safeguard the financial position of another, which he dishonestly abused, and which either caused a loss for another or exposed another to a risk of loss. It is this offence, considered in detail in Chapter 14, which clearly encompasses the actions of a rogue trader.

F. The payment protection insurance scandal

Approximately 34 million payment protection insurance policies were sold in the UK from 2001 onwards. It has emerged that many of those policies were mis-sold to customers who did not need them. They constituted an enormous source of profit, however, for the high street banks and building societies which sold them. It is important to get a sense of the scale of the losses, and therefore of the prior mis-selling, that is involved here. In essence, large financial institutions were using their retail customers as a source of core profit, just as they use bank charges to earn huge profits from their customers (as discussed in Chapter 18).[105] The following table sets out the amounts which some of the leading banks and building societies in the UK have set aside to settle PPI mis-selling claims by the beginning of March 2013.[106]

45–63

Capital requirement in £

Lloyds Group	£6.7 billion
HSBC	£1.5 billion
Santander	£538 million
Nationwide	£173 million
Royal Bank of Scotland	£2.2 billion
Barclays	£2.6 billion
Cooperative Bank	£244 million
Total	*£14.1 billion*

The FSA tells us that between January 2011 and January 2013, a total of £8.9 billion was refunded to customers who had been mis-sold PPI policies.[107] The PPI mis-selling scandal constituted a systemic, industry-wide activity of bleeding ordinary, retail customers for profit. It demonstrates that regulatory breaches take effect in ordinary call centres and high street branches, as well as on investment bank trading floors. What is needed is a banking profession and a professional body to impose a code of ethics on all participants in financial markets so as to

---

[104] See para.16–14.
[105] See para.18–88 et seq.
[106] Source: *The Guardian*, March 4, 2013 and March 22, 2013.
[107] *http://fsa.gov.uk/consumerinformation/product_news/insurance.*

protect ordinary customer from this sort of treatment in the future. A "welfare principle" will be essential to the protection of the real economy from a finance industry which has become so detached from an ordinary standard of good conscience in its dealings with its customers

5. OFFICIAL REPORTS IN RESPONSE TO THE CRISIS

A.   Introduction

45–64   This short section sets out potted summaries of some of the key reports in the UK relating to the financial crisis. The intention is to collect in one place summaries of some of the more significant reports into the financial crisis that have been published in the UK. Reference has been made to these reports at various stages throughout this book. Their analyses of the causes of the financial crisis—in particular the extensive, valuable work done by the Treasury Select Committee— have provided a large amount of testimony and evidence which must continue to form the basis for the examination of the best form of regulation of financial markets in the UK.

B.   The Treasury Select Committee

45–65   The House of Commons Treasury Select Committee in the UK, under the chairmanship of John McFall MP,[108] published a series of 14 reports into various aspects of the financial crisis.[109] Many of those reports have been considered in the course of this book already. Of particular significance for the issues considered in this chapter are the reports into the failure of Northern Rock;[110] corporate governance in financial institutions;[111] dealing with failed banks and bank insolvency;[112] and the future of regulatory supervision in the wake of the crisis.[113] The detailed findings of those reports are not re-considered here because they have been considered elsewhere. However, they constitute an exceptional library for the continued study of the failings of financial markets and of finance law and regulation.

---

[108] Latterly, Baron McFall of Alcuith: *http://johnmcfall.com/*.

[109] Those reports can be found at *http://www.publications.parliament.uk/pa/cm200809/cmselect/cmtreasy/*

[110] Treasury Select Committee, Fifth Report 2007–08, *The Run on the Rock* (January 26, 2008).

[111] Treasury Select Committee, Ninth Report 2008–09, *Banking Crisis: reforming corporate governance* (May 15, 2009).

[112] Treasury Select Committee, Seventh Report 2008 09, *Banking Crisis: dealing with the failure of UK banks* (May 1, 2009), which examined the circumstances which led to the failure or failings in the principal UK banks. These issues were considered in Ch.29 in relation to the Banking Act 2009, as well as earlier in this chapter.

[113] Treasury Select Committee, Fourteenth Report 2008–09, *Banking crisis: regulation and supervision* (July 31, 2009).

C. Turner Review—a regulatory perspective on the financial crisis

The report of Adair Turner, who became the Chairman of the Financial Services **45–66**
Authority,[114] considered the regulatory context in which the FSA had acted, the
history of the crisis, and the regulatory response to it. Among the regulatory
failures which are examined are the failure to identify the threat posed by
Lehman Brothers, and also the risks posed by Icelandic banks like Landsbanki
whose unstable business model left it far too highly leveraged and thus exposed
to any downturn in financial markets. The way in which Icelandic banks had
sought savers in the UK, and the fact that those savers had no protection under
UK finance law if their moneys were held in Iceland, was simply not anticipated
and prevented. Among the changes which Turner advocated were avoiding
pro-cyclical regulation (that is, storing up capital in the good times in case of a
future crash), and identifying limits for banks' leverage (i.e. limiting their
borrowing unless there is capital to off-set it).

The report is a jargon-heavy economist's review of the crisis and has very little **45–67**
focus on the regulatory detail. Of particular significance for regulatory theory,
however, was the identification of the shortcomings in the FSA's "light-touch"
approach to regulation.[115] While the FSA had never used the term "light-touch"
itself, Turner acknowledges that the FSA had believed that markets were
self-correcting, that the principal duty to oversee the good health of the firm lay
with the management of that firm (especially the board of directors), and that
consumer protection was best achieved by leaving those markets unfettered and
as transparent as possible. This is a clear dereliction of duty, and it is somewhat
ironic given the discussion among legal academics before the FSMA 2000 was
brought into force that the FSA was likely to be an unaccountable, draconian
regulator which would stifle market innovation.[116] In retrospect, a sort of
regulatory Alsatia over UK financial markets might have been a blessing.

More particularly, Turner identifies that the FSA became focused on micro- **45–68**
prudential management (albeit without creating sufficiently strenuous stress-
tests) and conduct of business regulation, as opposed to considering the systemic
risks to the entire financial system. The Financial Services Act 2012 regime—as
considered in detail in Chapters 8 and 9—was a conscious reversal of that
regulatory policy and structure.

In response to the financial crisis, the FSA undertook its Supervision **45–69**
Enhancement Programme ("SEP"), which was considered in Chapter 9. This new
regulatory attitude (as opposed to a wholesale change in regulatory rules) has
already resulted in numerous prosecutions for insider dealing and for market
abuse, and a slew of regulatory enforcement notices in relation to the banking
scandals already considered in this chapter (as well as many others too numerous
to mention here). As Turner observes entirely correctly, the problem was never a

---

[114] FSA, "The Turner Review—A Regulatory Response to the Global Banking Crisis", March 2009.
[115] FSA, "The Turner Review—A Regulatory Response to the Global Banking Crisis", March 2009,
p.86 et seq.
[116] See Hudson, *The Law and Regulation of Finance*, 2nd edn (Sweet & Maxwell, 2013), para.57–19
et seq.

shortage of regulations. The FSA Handbook was a vast tome which was kept online and rarely seen in hard copy for a good reason: it was so large and it kept changing in response to market conditions and new regulatory policy. Regulated entities were subject in theory to a large number of regulatory rules. The problem was that there was insufficient regulatory will to enforce them closely; and there was also an ideological assumption that the markets would correct themselves such that there was no need for the regulators to pursue those firms too closely. This meant that Northern Rock was simply not stress-tested sufficiently stringently because the regulators had not considered the possibility that the market might collapse. The same was true of other banks such as RBS, HBOS and so forth.

45–70   There had been signs that all was not well. Turner identifies the tripling in repo contracts which took place in the run-up to the crisis: an indication that too many institutions were funding themselves with short-term, illiquid instruments which would dry up in the event of a market collapse. He also identifies the way in which too many institutions kept CDOs on their balance sheets. Moreover, the use of Value at Risk ("VaR") models focused bank's attention on too recent a timeframe in examining historical data. However, Turner's analysis fails to notice the presence of fraud and basic short-sightedness at the roots of these failures. Taking a short timeframe on VaR data, for example, not only meant that the models were too limited, but it also prevented quantitative analysts from thinking "outside the box" about future risks which might attend the entirely new products (like CDOs) which would not have been present in their historic data. Those models did not consider the possibility that fraud might have infected the quality of the underlying mortgages in mortgage-backed securitisations. It was not simply a problem of mathematics; it was also a problem of common sense. Otherwise Turner identifies problems that we have already considered in this chapter: the shortcomings in the efficient markets theory, the errors in the idea that VaR mathematical models will effectively anticipate risk, and that securitised credit will necessarily ensure financial stability. From the perspective of a lawyer, however, there is too little consideration of the human foibles which caused this crisis, and there is too little focus on the human cost of the crisis (and how that can be addressed through a refreshed regulatory approach).

D.   Walker Review—corporate governance in banks

45–71   The review conducted by Walker, *A review of corporate governance in UK banks and other financial industry entities* ("the Walker Review")[117] considered the vexed question of the corporate governance of banks. The remit which was given to Sir David Walker did focus primarily on the boards of directors of those institutions. As the UK Treasury Select Committee report into the failure of Northern Rock had found, the responsibility for the failure of that bank lay with its management, although its regulators had also failed to anticipate that

---

[117] Sir David Walker, *A review of corporate governance in UK banks and other financial industry entities*, July 16, 2009.

failure.[118] Therefore, Walker continued the process of focusing on the responsibilities of the board of directors and the proper way in which corporate governance within banks should proceed. There were five key themes to emerge from the report. First, that the Combined Code on Corporate Governance (referred to as the UK Corporate Governance Code[119] since September 2012), including the "comply or explain" approach under the Listing Rules,[120] remained fit for purpose: that finding was in spite of the several governance failures already considered in this chapter. Second, the principal failings among boards of directors were due to their attitude as opposed to being due to their organisation. Third, there is a need to enhance the amount of board oversight of risk management issues within financial institutions, as opposed to delegating that function in effect to risk management departments within the bank. This does not explain whether it is a few extra hours a week by directors on that issue, or the appointment of identified members of the board with exclusive responsibility for risk management, which is required. A part of the difficulty of management from the board of directors of a universal bank is that those directors are almost invisible to many officers and traders within the bank at lower levels, and that those executives are more likely to become embroiled in headline issues concerning the bank (developing new markets, key clients, public relations work) than the day-to-day business of overseeing low-level risk management or the maintenance of ordinary activities. Fourth, there is a need for directors and institutional investors to have a closer dialogue. This approach, unfortunately, supposes that shareholder activism will control the worst excesses of individuals within banks, as opposed to greater regulatory or senior management involvement. Fifth, the observation that remuneration policies within banks need to be addressed, as was considered in Chapter 29.[121]

The field of corporate governance is a subset of company law in that corporate **45–72** governance norms are primarily a non-binding set of principles governing the way in which public companies ought to be organized.[122] As a part of company law it necessary focuses on the (non-legal) responsibilities of directors and the organisation of sub-committees of the board of directors to oversee matters such as remuneration and the audit process. This is in stark contrast to the manner which financial institutions—in particular universal banks—operate in practice. There are many layers of management below the board level which are very important in a universal bank. There are important in the sense that it is commonly middle management which has its hands on the levers of the bank's operations systems and so forth, so that if a money launderer wanted access to the bank's systems then a contact in middle management or the operations area would be far more valuable than a member of the board of directors. Rogue traders are ordinarily to be found among the junior traders and certainly not on

---

[118] Treasury Select Committee, Fifth Report 2007-08, *The Run on the Rock* (January 26, 2008).
[119] The code is outlined in para.39–23 et seq, or see A.S. Hudson, *Understanding Company Law* (Routledge, 2012), 169 et seq. See: *http://www.frc.org.uk/Our-Work/Publications/Corporate-Governance/UK-Corporate-Governance-Code-September-2012.aspx*
[120] See para.39–23.
[121] para.29–32.
[122] See A.S. Hudson, *Understanding Company Law* (Routledge, 2012), 169 et seq; A.S. Hudson, "Directors' Duties" in *Charlesworth's Company Law* (Sweet & Maxwell, 2012), 402 et seq.

the board of directors. Therefore, to focus a review into corporate governance on the board of directors is to miss the point in large part. Moreover, the FCA Handbook already has principles in the SYSC rulebook relating to the need for internal systems which govern the entirety of the institution's activities, among junior traders as well as among those in senior management with a key to the executive washroom. The harm happens lower down the organisation, as in Citigroup and as with all of the rogue traders considered above: therefore, the focus of regulatory reform in this area needs to be on the implementation of firm-wide systems and controls, and on the personal responsibility of all members of senior management for the effectiveness of those systems and controls. There is no doubt that an institution needs to be strictly managed from the top, but to focus entirely on the governance of the board of directors is to miss the dangers that lurk beneath.

F.   Parliamentary Commission on Banking Standards

45–73   The Parliamentary Commission on Banking Standards[123] was established in the summer of 2012 in response to revelations about the Libor scandal.[124] The Commission's remit was as follows:

> "The Commission is appointed by both Houses of Parliament to consider and report on:
> *   professional standards and culture of the UK banking sector, taking account of regulatory and competition investigations into the LIBOR rate-setting process;
> *   lessons to be learned about corporate governance, transparency and conflicts of interest, and their implications for regulation and for Government policy;
> and to make recommendations for legislative and other action."

At the time of writing, the Commission has not published its findings. The Commission's work, broadly speaking, fell into three parts. First, pre-legislative scrutiny of the Financial Services (Banking Reform) Bill proposals for the separation of banks between retail banking and investment banking activities, as considered in detail in Chapter 29.[125] Second, examinations of regulators and senior bank executives in the style of the Treasury Select Committee, albeit with questioning by counsel. Third, more detailed investigations of matters such as the ethics of banks (in particular a sub-panel under the chairmanship of Lord McFall into the PPI mis-selling scandal[126]). The sub-panels of the Commission have been able to gather evidence about the consumer experience of banking, the effect of management policies on ordinary bank employees, and the broader context of bank ethics. What the Commission has achieved is placing in the public arena a large amount of testimony about the internal workings of banks which could previously only be accessed through anecdote or somewhat scattered first-person accounts of banking. An assessment of the Commission's final report will be made available online at *http://www.alastairhudson.com* in time.

---

[123] The Commission's webpages, including transcripts of the evidence which they took, can be accessed at: *http://www.parliament.uk/bankingstandards*.

[124] See para.45–40 above.

[125] See para.29–110 et seq.

[126] See above, para.45–63.

6. CONCLUSION

A. The most significant, single reform: create personal liability for bank directors

The most far-reaching, single reform which could be made to financial regulation, which would have a direct effect on every trading floor and in every branch office, would be to make bank directors and other nominated members of senior management outside the board ("nominated officers") personally legally liable for all of the losses and defaults of the institution as though they were partners under a traditional English law partnership. In this way, a substantive law liability will transform the internal governance of financial institutions.

57–74

In my personal experience, financial institutions which are organised as partnerships are far more responsive to the need to control risks and are far more likely to seek actively to comply with the spirit of financial regulation than financial institutions which are organised as large companies. In a classic English law partnership the individual partners face personal responsibility for any losses suffered by the firm and liability for any wrong or criminal act committed by the partnership. If members of the board of directors and senior managers occupying identified offices (and performing specified functions within the institution) were personally liable for any default made by any officer of that bank (whether in tort, contract, criminal law or equity), then the type of system which would be created would be completely different from the sort of loose systems which are typically created in corporate entities where no individual is likely to face direct personally liability. It would be impossible for a senior manager at JP Morgan to blame underlings for a loss of US$6.2 billion because no information was passed up the chain; it would be impossible for the executives at Citigroup to throw up their hands and say that they did not know that there was a loss of US$60 billion fermenting in the belly of their institutions; and it would be impossible for the CEO of Barclays Bank to say that he did not know well the corner of the bank in which criminal activity appears to have taken place.

45–75

The benefit of these policy suggestions would be that the directors of financial institutions would be required to take positive steps to ensure that the institution is not taking inappropriate risks or that there are no traders who are indulging in practices which breach conduct of business rules, on pain of being personally liable for any loss or liability caused thereby. In my personal experience, where a large trading floor contains many hundreds of traders, it is very difficult to watch over all of them every minute of every day, but a well-run institution will nevertheless put systems in place—typically having at least one person on each trading desk (aside from any executive or senior trader) whose role is solely to ensure regulatory compliance, appropriate booking of trades with the middle office, and so forth—to oversee all of those traders' activities. By making the directors personally responsible for any loss or liability caused by any trader, the observation of all traders will be much closer and therefore the institution will

45–76

develop a conscious ethic and culture of active regulatory compliance, instead of merely the intermittent lodging of reports or capital to achieve the minimum necessary to satisfy the regulator.

B.   Transforming the financial system

45–77   This book began with a definition of finance as being "the wherewithal to act", a means of enabling actions to take place. The financial crisis demonstrated that the financial system might not create the wherewithal to act, but that instead it might destroy economic activity. The financial system has no tangible existence, instead it has tangible effects: that means, money and securities are all held electronically and so have no tangible existence, but they nevertheless allow aeroplanes to be made, food to be bought, and corn to be delivered. The purpose of this financial system was to create the wherewithal to act, but a large proportion of it has been shown in this chapter to be concerned with speculative profit that has no other practical use, and to become bound up with fraud and a loss of ethics. In short, we have forgotten what banking and finance is meant to be for. In Chapter 1, we considered a short story written by Borges in which a world was called into existence because scientists wrote about it and imagined every tiny detail of it.[127] Just as Borges described the creation of a planet out of thin air simply because human minds could conceive of it, we created the financial system out of mere words and ideas. In place of coins made of precious metals, we created financial instruments, securities, electronic money, payment cards and even banknotes which claim to be intrinsically worth the number printed on their face. All of this financial system came into existence simply because human minds could imagine it. Now it runs much of our lives. But we have all now realised, after the events of recent years, that the system we had built was dangerous in some contexts and that it was capable of operating unethically. However, we can re-imagine that financial system. We can make it again, and make it better. We can create a financial system which befits the civilised, democratic societies of the 21st century.

---

[127]   See para.1–09: JL Borges, "Tlon, Uqbar, Orbis Tertius", *Fictions* (1944).

CHAPTER 46

REFORM PROPOSALS

CORE PRINCIPLES

This chapter presents a series of proposals for the reform of financial regulation and the financial system in the UK. It builds on the previous chapter which considered in outline the financial crisis of 2007–09. The single most significant reform which could be made is to make the directors of regulated financial institutions and other nominated officers among senior management personally liable for any losses or defaults of the institution as though they were partners in a traditional English law partnership. This would have the most profound impact on the effectiveness of the internal systems and procedures of financial institutions. Goldman Sachs was organised on this model until a few years ago.

Another important change would be the creation of a professional body for "bankers" and a requirement for independent professional training for identified roles within retail and investment banking and other financial services activity, and in particular the creation of a code of professional ethics.

Other suggested regulatory changes relate to the treatment of ordinary customers and the regulation of derivatives: including a requirement that all commodities traders must take a binding undertaking to acquire the underlying commodity, and that no credit derivative can be acquired without an equivalent to an "insurable interest" in the underlying asset. Several changes are suggested to the substantive law, including a closer proximity between conduct of business regulation and contract law (so that the former become implied terms in the latter), and the outlawing of exclusion clauses in contexts in which liability could not be excluded for the same activity under financial regulation.

1.   INTRODUCTION

A.   Rethinking financial regulation

46–01   This chapter sets a series of proposals for the further reform of finance law and regulation in the UK. It builds on the many suggestions for reform made throughout this book and focuses on further suggestions which have not been discussed in relation to the reform of banking regulation in Chapter 28 and so forth.[1] These reforms relate to the substantive law as well as to financial regulation because a synthesis of these two sources of law is essential if the law of finance is going to develop in such a way that it can contribute to the stability of the financial system, to the viability of the UK economy, and to the protection of ordinary consumers of financial services. (This chapter was written before the Parliamentary Commission on Banking Standards was due to report in June 2013.)

46–02   Questions about financial regulation are commonly treated as though they are purely economic questions, when in truth they are moral questions, political questions, legal questions and even questions about national security in an age of "cyber attacks". The dominant economic analyses of financial regulation as being part of a free market have failed to accommodate the other conceptualisations of

---

[1] The principal focus is on the reform of the regulatory and legal system in the UK: the requirement for international regulatory co-operation, the need for conduct of business regulation ensuring consumer protection, the appropriateness of high-level regulatory principles, and so forth, are all taken as read as they have been set out in earlier chapters. The ideas in this chapter go beyond those issues. They suggest a manifesto rather than a textbook chapter; although, it is suggested, any good textbook should challenge its reader either to disagree or at the very least to look under the rocks and think about what is slithering under there.

financial markets.[2] Typically, the argument against financial regulation is taken to be a "yes/no" question of either preventing banks from making profits by regulating them or allowing banks the freedom to make profits by not regulating them. The events considered in the previous chapter demonstrate that the finance industry requires regulation. The real questions are *how* we regulate financial markets and what we allow them to do, as opposed to *whether* we regulate financial markets. In the incontrovertible presence of the tremendous harm caused by financial institutions to the social, political and economic life of those countries impacted directly by the financial crisis of 2007–09, there are different questions which fall to be answered beyond the confines of the dominant free-market ideology in mainstream economics.

B. The welfare principle

The welfare principle in its essence

At root, it is suggested, the central principle governing financial regulation should be that all regulation is based on a "welfare principle". The welfare principle provides that: the welfare of society and the real economy is paramount. The reference to the "real economy" here is a reference to economic activity beyond the financial sector. It is the real economy which relies upon the utility services which financial institutions like the high street banks provide.

46–03

The corollary to the welfare principle is that public money should never be used to rescue a financial institution from its self-inflicted losses. Instead, regulators should be empowered to separate the "good assets" held in a ring-fenced subsidiary (containing all of the utility operations, assets and liabilities of that institution) from whatever has forced that institution into insolvency or "failure" (under the Banking Act 2009).[3] So, ordinary bank accounts, domestic mortgages, business loans and so forth should be continued within a state-organised entity until that part of the bank can regularise itself. The utility operation must therefore continue as before, entirely distinct from the other operations of that institution (as considered below),[4] and any private law arrangement purporting to bind the utility operations into the performance of the other operations of that institution should be rendered void *ab initio*. Investors in such a financial institution – whether shareholders or bondholders – must bear the entirety of the loss bound up with their investment: thus removing moral hazard from the investment community. Shareholders in the utility operations of the financial institution must be entirely distinct from the other operations in that the utility operations must be contained in a separate corporate entity (in the form of a

46–04

---

[2] e.g. S. Keen, *Debunking Economics* (London: Zed Books, 2011).

[3] The retail banking operations of a financial institution will generally be the "good assets" whereas the investment banking activities will generally contain any "bad assets". The exception to this principle is where the retail bank was mis-selling mortgages to borrowers who could not repay their debts or insurance to customers in breach of their regulatory and substantive law obligations: in such a situation, those mis-sold contracts are bad assets which will create losses (as with the PPI mis-selling scandal considered at para 45-63).

[4] See para 46–13.

public holding company) which is quoted separately on the Stock Exchange and separately subject to the Listing Rules from the other entities and operations which make up its collective operations. In essence, those entities must be held on separate corporate groups. It must be unlawful for the state to intervene to rescue the non-utility activities of any financial institution. Risk must be privatised in the investors in a financial institution; only the utility services of financial institutions can be socialised; whereas at present profit is privatised in financial institutions and risk has been socialised.

The welfare principle in operation

46–05   In financial regulation, the welfare of the customer is paramount.[5] And by extension, therefore, the good health of the economy more broadly which is served by that financial system is of central importance. If one begins every analysis of financial regulatory policy from the position that the questions are all questions of economics then one will necessarily come to a particular answer: that is, an answer based ideologically on the perceived need to protect both the banks' profitability and freedom to conduct their business as they see fit without overmuch regulatory intrusion. By contrast, if one begins an analysis from the perspective that the principal goal of financial regulation is to protect the ordinary customer, then bank profitability and freedom to contract as they wish are no longer the foremost goals. Instead, conduct of business regulation and the control of financial institutions' activities would take priority. If one thinks the policy through from the perspective of the customer and the real economy,[6] then there are many aspects of banking practice which one might wish to control or even outlaw.

46–06   That the welfare of the customer is paramount means that customers must be treated suitably by financial institutions in accordance with their level of expertise as customers, that the risks associated with their transactions must be explained to them, and that any contract created in contravention of that principle must be rendered void *ab initio*. The improvements to conduct of business regulation which this involves are considered below.

46–07   That the welfare of the customer is paramount also means that customers are to be protected from the worst excesses of the financial system, and even from the mundane excesses of banking practice. The proposed "ring-fence" for banks in the UK (in the Financial Services (Banking Reform) Bill 2013 at the time of writing) is both conceptually imprecise and inadequate for the purpose of protecting the customer and the real economy from future shocks, not least because the precise manner in which each bank will construct its "ring-fence" is (currently) entirely a matter for it under the 2013 Bill. The EU system for ring-fencing retail banks remains similarly imprecise at the time of writing.

---

[5] A.S. Hudson, "Financial Regulation and the Welfare State", in A. Hudson (ed.), *Modern Financial Techniques, Derivatives and Law* (Kluwer Law International, 2000), 235.
[6] That is, that aspect of the economy which relates to employment, the prosperity of ordinary citizens and small businesses, and so forth.

Ensuring the welfare principle is applied will require detailed changes in the **46–08** operation of financial markets. This is true at the retail end of the spectrum. Among the worst excesses of the banks during the financial crisis and thereafter were the excesses and failures of its personnel: management, investment bank traders, and call centre operations. The mis-selling of financial instruments was made possible by poor management practices and poor training of sales staff who had the wrong incentives dangled in front of them, as became clear during the sitting of the UK Parliamentary Commission on Banking Standards. There needs to be a profession to govern the training and ethics of bank employees at many levels. This is true at the inter-bank end of the spectrum. The belated regulation of derivatives and similarly complex financial instruments has nevertheless placed responsibility for collating information about those markets into the hands of private-sector bodies—in the form of central counterparties and trade repositories—as opposed to independent regulatory bodies.[7] Moreover, a large number of such transactions will escape even that oversight. A better alternative would have been a more proactive attempt to control the use of derivatives by statutorily-created regulators and to empower regulators to rule (subject to appeal through the courts) that individual transactions which transgress private law or regulatory norms are void *ab initio*. Similarly, the shadow banking system as whole, and all buyers of financial instruments as well as sellers of financial instruments, must be brought within the regulatory net.[8] Nothing can be permitted to be conducted in the dark, as was the case with the credit default swap market before the crash.

In turn, the regulators must be subject to genuine democratic oversight and a **46–09** more responsive system of appeals that can create a proper jurisprudence for our regulatory norms, instead of leaving them at the whim of the regulatory authorities. At present, the lines of accountability are tenuous at best.

A wall, not a ring-fence

Instead of envisaging the UK as an economy with the City of London and the **46–10** financial sector as its principal drivers, we should think of the UK as being a modern, democratic society with citizens and businesses that deserve to live useful, happy lives, which also hosts a casino enterprise in the City of London. This "casino" comprises all of the speculative and other financial market activity which financial institutions conduct, except for the utility banking and financial services activities which are an essential part of ordinary life. The appropriate metaphor is to think of that casino as being contained within a high wall so that it cannot harm any of the ordinary activities that are carried on beyond that wall in ordinary society. In essence, consumer protection from the excesses of the financial sector is paramount, and must taken priority over the principle of freedom of contract. The idea of a "ring-fence" is simply not enough.[9] What the financial crisis demonstrated is that the City of London is capable of bringing contagion to dull banking activities on the high street and to parts of the economy

---

[7] See para 40-56 *et seq.*
[8] The welfare idea is considered in further detail at the end of this chapter at para.46–50.
[9] See the discussion of the banking regulation reforms in Ch.28 as to the "ring-fence".

which have no direct connection to the City of London. In an age with the risk of contagion, it is necessary to contain that contagion behind a high wall.

46–11 Many conclusions flow from this idea of a wall. Financial regulation must be astute to preserve a clear, rigid and constant division between speculative and non-speculative activities, as considered below. It is the role of a regulator to assume the worst and thus to prevent the worst from affecting the rest of society, no matter what the activities of financial institutions. This necessitates changes in our private law so that unconscionable or unsuitable or dangerous transactions are simply rendered void *ab initio*. Whatever the potential confusion in financial markets if a contract is held to be void, it is more important that ordinary society is protected from the effects of such contracts: the contagion must be kept behind the wall.

46–12 In essence, we must think of the UK as hosting a very successful casino activity in the City of London in which innovative quantitative analysts and motivated traders develop inter-bank activities as part of a global market; but none of that activity must be allowed to affect pension funds, retail banks and other institutions providing utility functions, public services, or the real economy.

Distinguishing between "utility" and "casino" activities

46–13 There is an important distinction to be made between the "utility" functions of financial institutions and their "casino" functions. The utility functions include deposit-taking, the operation of bank accounts, the provision of overdrafts, credit and ordinary loans, the provision of mortgages, and the payments systems which are now an essential part of economic life. These utility functions were considered in previous chapters. At root, the identification of a utility function is a recognition that while banks are private corporate entities, they nevertheless play a role in society which puts them on a plane of importance with water, electricity, gas and the transport network. By contrast, the casino function is concerned with speculative investment activities which are used by large corporations (which are sufficiently well-advised to fend for themselves if they choose to participate in those markets), and with straightforward profit-seeking by hedge funds, investment banks, and other entities created for the sole purpose of trading professionally in financial risk. In essence, we have forgotten the role that banking, insurance and related services are intended to serve in our society. A clear distinction between the utility and casino functions is necessary to ensure that the welfare principle is observed.

46–14 The difficult middle territory, clearly, for this welfare principle is occupied by the capital markets which are used by large corporate entities to raise share capital, bond capital, and so forth; and, as a separate matter, to manage their financial risk. It is suggested that capital markets should be considered to be part of the utility function of financial markets because they connect investors who have been provided with all the necessary information (as dictated by securities regulation) to make informed decisions as to whether or not they should invest. What is important, as part of the welfare principle, is that short term investment is outlawed in relation to large corporations with employees and customers in the real economy; short-selling should be prevented because it is morally objectionable, and investors should only be permitted to enter into physically-settled transactions (where they agree to acquire a company's securities) on-exchange and not cash-settled transactions (where they simply speculate on that company's future performance) in relation to specified groups of companies and public entities off-exchange. As for risk management activities, they should only be permitted where the selling institution can demonstrate precisely the risk which will be covered by risk management instrument, they should be subject to a maximum volatility clause such that the selling financial institution may not take payment beyond a maximum amount specified in the contract, and such that they shall be void *ab initio* in all other circumstances.

A paradigm shift

If financial regulation is considered first and foremost to be subject to the welfare **46–15** principle so that regulation constitutes state protection of private citizens, small businesses and other entities of particular significance to the real economy (as opposed to being considered primarily as an economic question), then the answers which are generated in the debate about the appropriate mechanism for financial regulation are different from the answers which are generated by economics. Instead of focusing on economic efficiency and the need for banks to be free to make profits in a free market, the principal focus shifts to the need to protect economically important actors from the excesses, abuses and mistakes of all financial institutions, thus permitting many more practices to be prohibited to prevent the possibility of a repeat of the scandals of recent years, ranging from another systemic financial crisis at one end of the spectrum right down to mis-selling insurance products or unnecessarily complex interest rate swaps to private customers or small businesses at the other end. What became self-evident in the autumn of 2008, even to those who had refused to acknowledge the problem before, is that this current form of capitalism (which is predicated on complex financial markets as a means of creating growth and managing risk through purported mathematical wizardry) is inherently unstable (based as it is on volatile financial markets to turn a profit) and dangerous for people, public bodies and businesses who play no direct part in those markets. If the nation state has a purpose at all, then it is to enhance the security of its citizens.

2. INTERNAL SYSTEMS AND CONTROLS

A. Introduction

The discussion in the preceding chapter and in Chapter 9 demonstrated both that **46–16** the *FCA Handbook* and the *PRA Handbook* contain regulations which require the preparation and maintenance of appropriate internal systems and that many banks simply do not observe these regulations (and that their senior executives do not appreciate that they personally are subject to those regulations). The entire financial crisis demonstrated that a lack of effective internal controls has allowed many colossal risks to arise within institutions (such as Citigroup and JP Morgan

Chase). Moreover, a misplaced focus in the Walker Review solely on corporate governance at the level of the board of directors is insufficient to cope with rogue trader and similar problems. The crises are often created deep underground, and not in the sunlight of the boardroom.

B. The personal legal liability of all bank directors and "nominated officers"

46–17   The most far-reaching single reform which could be made to banking regulation, which would have a direct effect on every trading floor and in every branch office, would be to make bank directors and other nominated members of senior management outside the board ("nominated officers") personally legally liable for all of the losses and defaults of the institution as though they were partners under a traditional English law partnership. In this way, a substantive law liability will transform the internal governance of financial institutions.

46–18   In my personal experience, financial institutions which are organised as partnerships are far more responsive to the need to control risks and are far more likely to seek actively to comply with the spirit of financial regulation than financial institutions which are organised as companies. In a classic English law partnership, the individual partners face personal responsibility for any losses suffered by the firm and liability for any wrong or criminal act committed by the partnership. If members of the board of directors and senior managers occupying identified offices (and performing specified functions within the institution) were personally liable for any default made by any officer of that bank (whether in tort, contract, criminal law or equity), then the type of system which would be created would be completely different from the sort of loose systems which are typically created in corporate entities where no individual is likely to face direct personally liability. It would be impossible for a senior manager at JP Morgan to blame underlings for a loss of US$6.2. billion because no information was passed up the chain; it would be impossible for the executives at Citigroup to throw up their hands and say that they did not know that there was a loss of US$60 billion fermenting in the belly of their institutions; and it would be impossible for the CEO of Barclays Bank to say that he did not know well the corner of the bank in which criminal activity appears to have taken place.

46–19   Therefore, the legal liabilities of directors of banks, directors of regulated financial institutions and the equivalent fiduciary officers of unregulated financial actors (such as hedge funds) when falling under the jurisdiction of English law, should mimic those of ordinary partners. For ease of reference, all of the fiduciary officers in any sort of financial institution will be referred to here as "directors", as they are at present. Individual directors should face personal liability both in damages for any losses suffered by any person dealing with the institution or by the institution (and thus its shareholders) directly, and those individual directors shall also be personally liable for any fraud, negligence, criminal offence or other wrong committed by any employee or other agent of that institution, whether or not acting within the terms of her agency but where acting on behalf of the institution. All such liabilities should operate jointly and severally on all of the directors, so that there is no opiate on the conscience of any single director by dint of saying that the wrong was committed in another department of the institution.

The benefit of these policy suggestions would be that the directors of financial institutions would be required to take positive steps to ensure that the institution is not taking inappropriate risks or that there are no traders who are indulging in practices which breach conduct of business rules, on pain of being personally liable for any loss or liability caused thereby. In my personal experience, where a large trading floor contains many hundreds of traders, it is very difficult to watch over all of them every minute of every day, but a well-run institution will nevertheless put systems in place—typically having at least one person on each trading desk (aside from any executive or senior trader) whose role is solely to ensure regulatory compliance, appropriate booking of trades with the middle office, and so forth—to oversee all of those traders' activities. By making the directors personally responsible for any loss or liability caused by any trader, the observation of all traders will be much closer and therefore the institution will develop a conscious ethic and culture of active regulatory compliance, instead of merely the intermittent lodging of reports or capital to achieve the minimum necessary to satisfy the regulator.

46–20

In corporate institutions there is otherwise no incentive for managers and senior traders to avoid sharp practice or corners being cut. It is not unknown for compliance departments in financial institutions in London to be located in offices more than a mile away from the building in which the traders sit, so that regulatory compliance is conducted at arm's length. The compliance officers are strangers on the trading floor and their presence is often actively resented. There are many in-house counsel, documentation specialists and compliance officers who know only too well what it is like to receive the sharp end of a senior trader's tongue for suggesting that a practice is being conducted inappropriately and who know only too well what it is like to be told that they are "simply making trouble" when identifying a technical legal problem with a transaction. These sort of badly-run banks are not only treating their lawyers in this fashion but are generally also dismissive of risk management and long-term investment strategies because their traders' goals are to maximise their individual bonuses and not to look to the long-term good health of the institution nor its customers. Poorly run financial institutions cannot anticipate that exposure to some markets runs the risk of bankrupting the entire firm, and so the risk of failure is all the higher.

46–21

C.   The personal responsibility of nominated officers

Universal banks are so big that imposing liability on a few sacrificial objects at the top will not ensure that there is proper performance on the trading floor. In banks that size, it is possible never to meet a bank director after years and years of successful service. Therefore, it would make sense within banks to have "nominated officers" from among senior- or middle-management (as appropriate) to be responsible for any of a list of "outward-facing" activities, ranging from

46–22

regulatory reporting, to settling Libor, to selling specified forms of financial instrument (mainly corporate instruments).

46–23   There should be a "New Deal" in relation to the regulation of internal systems in retail banks which would involve the following. First, a rigorous examination of actual transactions and sales techniques in banks. Second, the introduction of much stiffer penalties for breach of the regulations – in particular the imposition of personal liability on nominated officers within banks. For example, individual branches where there is more than one substantial infringement of BCOBS should be closed for add-on sales while those sales staff are re-trained by outsiders for a two month period, and a compulsory letter circulated to all customers of that branch and notices put up in the branch to that effect. Changing bank culture in retail branches is about punishing them visibly for breaches of the regulations. Too much regulatory focus at present is at the corporate level. There is too little in the high-street branches; the regulation of retail banking needs to be pro-active. A more pro-active regulatory culture should actually reassure ordinary banking customers that a real change is afoot and so help to mend fences with their bankers.

3.   CODIFYING THE POWERS OF REGULATORS

A.   Introduction

46–24   The responsibilities and the objectives of the regulatory authorities in the UK were set out in Chapters 8 and 9. What was clear was that they were broadly stated and very difficult to assess. Whether or not the FPC has achieved "stability" is something that is difficult to assess, for example, until things have gone demonstrably wrong. Therefore, those responsibilities are not useful as a means of holding those regulators to account. However, a greater problem than that, it is suggested, is that the full extent of the *powers* of the regulators are not clear. One of the key lessons from the financial crisis of 2007–09 was that the regulators had not had legal powers beforehand which were sufficient to cope with the phenomenon of a failed bank: hence the passage of the Banking Act 2009. The FSMA 2000 does create powers in particular circumstances (for example to conduct investigations, or to commence prosecutions in relation to market abuse) but there are many aspects of micro-prudential regulation, for example, in which it is unclear whether or not the regulators have the legal power to prevent a merger, or whether it can seek to set aside a transaction on grounds that it breaches conduct of business regulation, and so on. Instead, the regulators require a constant flow of information which means in practice, as the JP Morgan "London Whale" affair shows, that the regulator is dependent on the goodwill of the regulated person disclosing all useful information in all circumstances. What is suggested is that the powers of the regulators need to be codified more clearly, including general powers to intervene in the event of any occurrence which affects the stability of the financial system in the UK, or the solvency of an entity with a significant presence in the UK (whether a seller or a buyer of regulated financial instruments), or the performance of any given financial market with an effect in the UK. At present, too much depends upon regulatory practice and not enough is made clear in terms of legal powers, as became briefly clear when Northern Rock failed. As a central matter, any breach of a regulatory "rule" (denoted with an "R" in the rulebooks) should constitute an offence, with different rules being graded as to the severity of both the punishment and the conception of the offence which is understood. Any professional involved in such a breach should automatically be taken to have committed a breach under the code of professional ethics for bankers set out below.

B. Codifying the powers of regulators in relation to undesirable transactions

The powers of regulators are generally too obscure. While it is true that HM Treasury and the Bank of England's subsidiary entities do possess the seemingly unrestrained powers of overseer, recipient of information, investigator, prosecutor, judge and jury in relation to many regulated activities, nevertheless the sanctions which are available to them are narrow. They have the power to withdraw an authorisation where there is sufficient cause; they have the power to impose "civil penalties", and they have the power to mount prosecutions in relation to market abuse offences, but they are oddly lacking in explicit powers in the event of inappropriate market activity. In relation to solvent market participants, the regulator needs the power avoid transactions which contravene the regulations, especially conduct of business regulation. That power can be appealed beyond the Market Tribunal, but it is an important element of consumer protection. In spite of the financial services legislation which will shake up the regulatory structure, there are still too many contexts in which the Bank of England will have too few *legal powers* to force banks to do, or to refrain from doing, anything. The Banking Act 2009 merely deals with failed banks, but it does not create *legal powers* to prevent unsuitable banking transactions (whether huge deals or inadvisable takeovers). At present, it is merely the perception that HM Treasury or the Bank of England might withhold some important permission in the future which prevents banks from doing what they might otherwise have done. Therefore, the regulators require statutory powers to vet mooted mergers of financial institutions (whether centred here or merely conducting operations here), as well as a power to order the separation of banks which are too large to manage properly or which demonstrate inadequate internal systems and controls. **46–25**

The Bank of England (acting through its regulatory subsidiaries) needs legal powers to prevent undesirable action before a full-blown crisis develops, including the following: powers to prevent bank takeovers and mergers, on grounds of financial instability or alternatively because the resultant entity will be too large; explicit (and thus codified) powers explaining when it has the power to prevent any regulated person or unregulated person from doing anything, and the **46–26** procedure for exercising these powers;[10] and formal requirements for due diligence and cooling off periods in relation to bank takeovers and mergers,[11] and other specified types of transaction.

C.   Codification of accountability procedures

46–27   As well as the codification of powers, there also needs to be a codification of the means by which the regulator will be rendered accountable. The current arrangement of the preparation of minutes held within the committee structure of the Bank of England is not the same as transparent accountability. Operational independence for the Bank over economically vital functions is only satisfactory in a democracy if it is clear how the Bank and other agencies are to be held properly to account for their actions. Not simply explaining themselves to a select committee (however highly-motivated it is) without a clear system for hearings, censure and control of any excesses by people who are democratically accountable themselves. Therefore, codification would require the formal explanation of the full extent of the regulators' powers and the means by which they can be held to account in all situations.

4.   THE CREATION OF A BANKING PROFESSION

46–28   Banking is an activity in which the word "professional" is bandied about commonly: it refers usually to dress (sober), to attitude (compliant with the firm's mission statement, in step with the herd, and obedient to the chain of command), and to communications (obscurantist and jargon-heavy). It generally does not refer to an explicit form of ethics nor to any body of knowledge which exists *outside the institution*. Instead, banks are institutions which seek to control dress, behaviour, attendance and thought processes, but which do not ordinary permit any connection between the individual employee and some larger set of knowledge or ethical principles which should govern the individual employee's activities. The ramifications of this sort of sclerotic culture are plain to see. Whistleblowers are not encouraged in banks, even when they are senior compliance officers identifying problems in a Mexican subsidiary; objectively ethical behaviour is not encouraged on sales floors where supervisors encourage the systematic mis-selling of PPI policies or interest rate swaps to retail customers; and risk-taking is performed by traders hungry for personal gain and assumed by their employers as a result. The ramifications are plain to see from

---

[10] Too often in the accounts of banking collapses through the 20th century, there are references to "the Governor's eyebrows" contracting in disapproval as a means of forcing banks into line. In the modern age, there needs to be a clear, statutory code of powers for the regulator, and a clear code governing the regulator's means of formal accountability.

[11] The merger of Lloyds TSB Bank with HBOS during the financial crisis was conducted in 36 hours in lawyers' offices, with each party's employees being herded into specific conference rooms and the regulators in another. There was no opportunity for proper due diligence in that time. Much that was not known about HBOS came to light only latterly, something which ought to have been possible for Lloyds to find out for itself. At the very least, a mechanism for reversing out of the transaction would have excused those overly-rapid, repent-at-your-leisure negotiations.

the case studies presented in the previous chapter. In truth, banking is not a profession properly so-called because it has no single professional institution, no enforceable code of ethics, nor any body of knowledge which its members are required to absorb through an accredited form of education.

What is needed, without delay, is the establishment of a professional body for financial services activity in the UK: a Chartered Banking Institute. That Institute should be responsible for drafting a code of Professional Ethics, in common with the regulatory institutions. Generic types of regulated activity should be identified within financial institutions for which professional accreditation from the new professional body will be required. Areas such as compliance, legal, trading, retail client-facing activity, corporate client-facing activity, and so forth should all require formal education and qualification. An all-encompassing qualification of "chartered banker" which covers all of these types of activity should be created for individuals who want to proceed to the management grade. Separate from the profit-driven, ideological enthusiasms of the business school model, this qualification should educate students as to the basics of banking practice with an emphasis on professional ethics, regulatory obligations (including legal and accounting standards) and any other activities which are considered appropriate. The qualification will help to rehabilitate the reputation of the finance profession in the UK.[12]

46–29

The *Commission on the Future of Banking*[13] identified this idea as a key part of the future for banking. By educating bankers in a code of ethics and educating them as part of a body of knowledge, each individual banker will be aware from the outset of their personal responsibilities.

46–30

The following would be the outline for such a profession. First, make banking a profession in relation to specified "reserved occupations" within banks, including any employees dealing with third parties[14] in the following fields: corporate finance; risk management; credit control and treasury; operations and payment systems; legal, documentation and compliance; trading in securities, derivatives, foreign exchange, repo and stock-lending; and any financial advisor or intermediary. All reserved occupations should be subject to the same education about the same code of ethics which spans the entire profession, although the "elective" components of any person's qualification should enable them to focus on a narrow range of fields in which they wish to work: but their authorisation to act for their bank will be limited to those electives. The Institute should then create a professional qualification for reserved occupations. This Institute would create a professional body (like the Law Society does with solicitors in England and Wales) with a formal complaints procedure and tribunal. The operation of proper internal controls in banking institutions should be linked to these

46–31

---

[12] There will, of course be difficulties in identifying precisely which roles within banks will require professional qualification (e.g. do we want to include counter staff?). Similarly, a professional body would have to be created and a curriculum agreed upon. However, there are currently record numbers of students in university Business Schools and the idea of a professional qualification will attract students to it (because of a perception of job security following it) and a broad enough curriculum will.

[13] *The Future of Banking Commission*, *http://www.which.co.uk/banking*.

[14] That is, "client-facing" employees.

professional ethics and a component of the education which relates to learning about the internal controls and systems requirements of financial institutions, including whistle-blowing.

46–32 The effect on banking culture will be on creating a generation of self-reflective banking professionals who are tied to their professional ethics and not simply to their employers' profits. This will establish the UK as a world centre for ethical banking practice, and repair its reputation.

5. REFORMS TO THE SUBSTANTIVE LAW

A. Introduction

46–33 This book has made several suggestions for the reform of the substantive law relating to financial transactions. Some of the key points are highlighted here.

B. Synthesising substantive law and regulation

46–34 As considered in detail in Chapter 3 and throughout this book, there are contexts in which the courts are already beginning to use regulatory principles to decide whether or not case law tests are satisfied on any given set of facts.[15] The point is a simple one. Suppose you are a judge, you are deciding a case involving a complex financial instrument and it relates to a question of the substantive law; perhaps the defendant is alleged to have dishonestly assisted in a breach of fiduciary duty (a common claim in recent years). You are required to decide, for example, whether or not the defendant has been dishonest. The applicable test is whether or not the defendant has failed to act as an honest person would have acted in the same circumstances.[16] Financial regulation stipulates clearly the manner in which business was to be conducted between financial institutions and their customers. It is therefore open to the court to consult the terms of those regulations as a statement of suitable behaviour for a finance professional in those circumstances. The question as to what an honest or a reasonable bank employee should have done in any given circumstances, and what the bank should have known about in the light of their responsibility to maintain appropriate internal systems and controls, is objectively defined in the appropriate regulations.

---

[15] See for example *Investors Compensation Scheme v West Bromwich Building Society* (1999) Lloyd's Rep PN 496; *Loosemore v Financial Concepts* (2001) 1 Lloyd's Rep 235; *Seymour v Christine Ockwell* (2005) PNLR 39.
[16] *Royal Brunei Airlines v Tan* [1995] 2 AC 378; *Barlow Clowes International Ltd v Eurotrust International Ltd* [2006] 1 WLR 1476.

C.   Reforms to contract law

The regulatory context of contract law

There follows a compilation of eight proposals for the reform of contract law in relation to financial transactions. It should be recalled that the conduct of business regulation considered in Chapter 10 was said to affect the practical process of creating contracts which are governed by financial regulation. Particularly significant in that discussion was the identification of several positive obligations on banks which run counter to the traditional common law approach that contracting parties should only be subject to the terms which they choose to put in their agreements. The clear exception to that common law principle is where the performance of the contract would be illegal: in essence, what is being suggested here is that contravention of financial regulation should be considered to be unlawful in relation to the creation, performance and interpretation of contracts.

46–35

(1)   Outlaw exclusion of liability clauses for banks

A big part of imposing liability on banks is their use of exclusion of liability clauses. As was considered in Chapter 24,[17] for example in relation to *Cassa di Risparmio della Repubblica di San Marino SpA v Barclays Bank Ltd*,[18] an exclusion of liability clause will prevent an action being brought for an action which is both in breach of regulations and negligent – therefore, the claimant is limited to claiming fraud. Such clauses are banned under Conduct of Business regulation by the FCA, but ordinary contract law still enforces them. There is currently no direct, statutory ability to enforce Conduct of Business regulations through the courts; so customers must rely on ordinary contract law. A legislative change should be made to prevent ordinary contract law from enforcing these clauses where financial regulation does not permit it.[19]

46–36

(2)   Clearer statutory rights of action for consumers

Given that litigation in this area is complex and that ordinary private law makes liability unlikely (e.g. because of exclusion of liability clauses), there should be a statutory right of action for customers where the bank is fraudulent, or negligent, or fails to comply with its regulatory obligations. This last ground would be make a real difference: if a bank fails to comply with its obligations, then there should be a presumption that it is liable in damages; as opposed to placing the burden of proof on the customer. This would also require an adjustment of the burden of proof so that the onus is on the bank to demonstrate proper treatment of its

46–37

---

[17] Para.24–39.

[18] *Cassa di Risparmio della Repubblica di San Marino SpA v Barclays Bank Ltd* [2011] EWHC 484 (Comm).

[19] What is also needed is for breach of regulations to sound in damages through the courts, instead of the limited powers of Financial Services Compensation Scheme – the courts do not need to provide a slow remedy if the law is made simpler.

customers; as opposed to the clients bearing the burden of proving liability. Thus, s.150 of the FSMA 2000 should be expanded in this area to found a clear liability without the benefit of exclusion of liability clauses.[20] There should be a legal presumption that a contract is void under the general law if the conduct of business regulations (e.g. BCOBS and MCOBS) have not been observed. For example, mis-selling due to failing to follow regulatory procedures would lead to the contract being presumptively void automatically.

(3)   Conduct of business litigation

46–38   As was considered in Chapter 31, the Banking Conduct of Business Sourcebook (BCOBS) governing retail banking (and something similar for mortgage selling (MCOBS) and insurance) was introduced so as to regularise the voluntary Banking Codes which pre-dated it. There is now a need to ask whether or not these codes are obeyed in practice; whether they are something which bank employees are trained in appropriately (anecdotally, among acquaintances working in retail banking, it does appear as though many high street bank branches do not really bother with BCOBS training at all); and whether or not they should be replaced by something more stringent in the light of PPI and interest rate swap mis-selling scandals. Mandatory training through the proposed Chartered Banking Institute (as considered below) should be used to meet lapses in the observance of BCOBS.

(4)   Unfair contract terms legislation

46–39   The Court of Appeal in *Office of Fair Trading v Abbey National*, relating to unfair contract terms legislation and consumer products, took the view that no customer could be expected to read the detail of bankers' leaflets and other literature (especially in the light of the finding in Chapter 31 that many banks do not give customers their full terms and conditions in any event). The question is what we expect customers to figure out for themselves, and what we oblige the banks to explain to them succinctly. There should be cooling-off periods for financial products sold in person so that the customer has an opportunity to review the literature calmly without a salesperson being present. The law should be amended so as to ban financial products which do not pass the test (as administered by the Office of Fair Trading) for being sufficiently comprehensible for ordinary customers. Financial products to be sold to retail customers could be pre-vetted by the FCA and kite-marked, but without removing the obligation on the bank to explain the risks associated with that product properly. All of this taken together could lead to a re-writing of Conduct of Business regulation in the UK, and it should become a part of qualifying as a "banker" entitled to deal directly with the public.

---

[20] See para.9–20.

(5)   Re-write financial promotion legislation

Financial promotion legislation should be made more stringent. The lesson from **46–40** the PPI mis-selling scandal is that banks cannot be trusted to treat their retail customers fairly. The regulations currently allow a lot of cold-calling by banks with which the customers has had only slight contact; and a lot can be done online or by email. What is the difference between mainland selling by banks and boiler rooms offshore in the light of the PPI scandal? The banks should be prevented from indulging in predatory selling, and criminal offences introduced for instances of recklessly misleading bank customers into buying grossly unsuitable products (as with the interest rate swaps that were mis-sold to SMEs).

(6)   Recording selling to consumers, and limitation on contractual terms

Just as investment bank traders have their calls recorded, and just as many call **46–41** centres record some calls, meetings in person on bank premises between salespeople and clients should be recorded so that the customers' lawyers have something specific to work on when the bank denies mis-selling. This would also keep salespeople "honest" when talking to customers. Those recordings must be made available to customers on request. It must be a regulatory offence to destroy those recordings (sounding in a fine and a presumption that the customer's claim for mis-selling was correct). Financial products which are contracted off bank premises should be voidable at the instance of the customer, unless a good reason for contracting business that way can be demonstrated.

(7)   Limitation on changing terms of contracts

Banks, of course, change the terms of their contracts constantly. It is very difficult **46–42** to see why the unilateral change of contractual terms is permitted. As considered in Chapter 31, banks should be capable of being bound to the original contract to which they agreed, or else they should compensate customers when they seek to change the terms. The same principle should apply to bank accounts, mortgages, insurance contracts, and so forth.

(8)   Compulsory provision of full terms in writing

As considered in Chapter 31, all retail financial transactions (bank accounts, **46–43** mortgages, insurance, etc.) must have the full terms of that agreement provided in writing to the customer.[21] Otherwise, how can that possibly allow the customer to know what the terms are covering their contract? It also makes it impossible for their lawyers or the CAB, or whoever, to bring a meaningful complaint after the event, because the terms at the time of creating the contract are unknown.

---

[21] Often call centres simply refuse to do this (often on the basis that "the terms change all the time, so we can't give them out in writing"), as was discussed in Chapter 31.

D. Responses to the PPI mis-selling scandal

46-44 The systematic mis-selling of PPI on such a massive scale is proof that banks' selling practices on the high street are generally unacceptable. The responses to PPI should divide into three categories: criminal sanctions; civil sanctions and liabilities; and structural changes.

Criminal liability of banks

46-45 The Fraud Act 2006 already applies to banks.[22] However, it should be amended so that the "abuse of position" offence includes "undue influence" and "duress" in the following circumstances: where a bank is selling a product to a customer, at the bank's own instigation, which has negligible or no manifest advantage to the customer, and which causes the customer loss (including lost fees paid to the bank). We should also criminalise "recklessness" in selling financial instruments to the public and SMEs by making it a criminal offence to sell a product to a customer in the following circumstances: without having performed the regulatory Banking Conduct of Business Sourcebook "know your client" checks; without investigating whether or not the customer wants or needs or will benefit from this product; and by misrepresenting the nature, effect or desirability of that product. The sanctions for the bank's misbehaviour should include fines, and withdrawal of authorisation to sell that type of financial product for 12 months minimum, and until the Financial Conduct Authority and Serious Fraud Office are both convinced that internal systems, training and products have been reorganised.

Civil liabilities of banks

46-46 There should be mandatory tape recording of all sales discussions between salespeople and customers so that there is evidence of risks having been explained to customers. A failure to record and failure to comply with regulations would lead automatically to a voidable contract.

Personal liability of bank employees

46-47 Salespeople will already be liable personally under the Fraud Act 2006. However, directors of the separated retail bank at board level should be personally liable for

---

[22] As discussed in Chapter 14. The Fraud Act 2006 provides for a number of criminal offences relating to fraud by false representation, fraud by failure to disclose information, and fraud by abuse of position. The offence of fraud by way of false representation requires that the false representation be made dishonestly with the intention that the representor make a gain for herself with the other person being exposed to the risk of loss. The offence of fraud by way of a failure to disclose information involves a dishonest failure to disclose information which the defendant was under a legal duty to disclose, and that the defendant intended to make a gain or to cause or risk loss to another person as a result. The offence of fraud by way of abuse of position applies to people who occupy a position which requires her to safeguard the financial interests of another person, and who dishonestly abuse that position with an intention to make a gain or to cause or risk loss to another person as a result.

failure of internal systems, including trading and the internal oversight of salespeople. The sanction should be a presumption that they are not a fit and proper person to serve on the board of directors of a bank, or disqualification from acting as a bank director.

E. Coping with sales staff scandals

Many of the biggest scandals in recent years have involved ordinary bank employees acting as sales staff: mortgage mis-selling to subprime customers in the USA, the PPI mis-selling scandal, and the interest rate swap mis-selling scandal involving SMEs. Therefore, thought needs to be given to this area of banking practice, and not simply to investment banking traders. The best way of fixing the lapses in ordinary sales practices are fourfold. First, create a state bank with standards that outstrip the standards of the private sector competition, thus setting a new benchmark. The private sector institutions ape one another's products and practices so closely that they are almost effectively operating a cartel, so there is no harm in copying their products. Using a state bank would actually be a better use of public money than quantitative easing, which is simply throwing money at bank capital and at bond traders. (Even if a state bank makes some bad loans, that could not be more inaccurate than throwing cash into the financial system through repeated quantitative easing programmes. By March 2013, the British government had committed £375 billion to quantitative easing since 2009; whereas the US government had committed US$2.3 trillion since 2008.[23]) Second, make directors and nominated senior managers in banks personally responsible for the performance and defaults of their divisions by creating civil liabilities to that effect, as well as regulatory responsibilities.[24] Third, de-couple remuneration from performance among sales staff, so that there are no more bonuses above a maximum level of total remuneration. It would be preferable to have sales staff paid good fixed salaries instead; to fix minimum salary levels in relation to the amount of the average wage; to ensure job security for sales staff, so that there is no threat of the sack to encourage sales performance; and outlaw the sort of "motivational whiteboard" practices (such as producing league tables of top sales staff, including shaming sub-par sellers and withholding bonuses) which are used to compel sales staff to sell useless financial instruments at any cost. Fourth, there must be mandatory training for all bank

46–48

---

[23] *http://www.bbc.co.uk/news/business-15198789* [Accessed March 7, 2013]. This also puts into focus the amount that is being committed to returning financial markets to stability and the top-end of the economy to profitability, while "austerity" programmes in public services and so forth were still being rolled out across both economies. Quantitative easing is referred to by some people as "helicopter finance" in that it resembles throwing cash out of a helicopter and hoping that some of it will land somewhere useful. Very little money has been lent out into the real economy by the retail banks when compared to the need for capital and funding in the economy generally. Many banks have simply been using this "free" money (in that the interest rates on it are almost negligible) to fund their own balance sheets and their speculative activities.

[24] All bonuses ("non-fixed remuneration") to be payable over three years but never payable immediately; no liabilities to be capable of exclusion by contract; and reinforce the regulatory obligation that board directors (especially the CEO) are personally responsible for creating robust internal systems with civil law obligations to that effect, as under the FCA SYSC rulebook at present.

sales-staff, in line with the ethics of the new banking profession. There should also be enhanced whistleblower legislation for bank staff: e.g. protection of employment status after whistle-blowing; anonymity when a complaint first made; with a nominated officer in the FCA responsible for receiving whistle blows.

F.   A Standing Commission on Banking

46–49   The breadth and nature of bank defaults in relation to its retail business necessitates the creation of a Standing Commission on Banking, which would be separate from the banking industry and the regulatory architecture that would be established by statute to continue the sort of fact-finding that has been conducted by the Parliamentary Commission on Banking Standards. The Commission should continue to investigate both banking practice and standards, and also the activities of the new regulators.

G.   Facilitate class actions

46–50   Proving malfeasance by a bank often requires a number of similar claims to corroborate one another, and banks are particularly good at delaying litigation such that there needs to be a team of lawyers bringing the claim. Therefore class actions become necessary.

H.   Fiduciary liabilities

46–51   Ordinarily, a bank will not owe fiduciary obligations to its customers. This legal principle was formed in the 19th century when banks only operated normal bank accounts. Banks are only fiduciaries if they occupy a specific role in relation to a particular customer; e.g. where they sell their services as a trustee. However, a bank is not a trustee of money or other assets held in a bank account: instead, the relationship is a purely contractual relationship which can be excluded by contractual agreement. It is suggested that the contexts in which a bank may be treated as a fiduciary should be extended by statute to include the following: when selling any investment product to a retail customer; when selling any speculative investment product to any client who is not a "market professional" under COBS, except for levying a reasonable and well disclosed fee; when selling any product in which the bank itself stands to make profit from the transaction which has not been disclosed to the customer; when selling any product as a market maker which has not been disclosed to the customer; when acting as a calculation agent in speculative transactions; in relation to the "client best interests" principle under MiFID/COBS; in relation to the "best execution" principle under MiFID/COBS; in the exercise of any positive obligation imposed on a financial institution by the COBS rulebook; and when exercising any power in relation to a mortgage in which the borrower is in arrears and the mortgagee is seeking not to sell the property and terminate the mortgage contract.

I.   Reforms to the banker-customer relationship

As part of identifying banking standards in relation to retail banking, it is **46–52** important to re-balance the relationship between banker and retail customer. The following suggestions would have a wide-ranging effect on consumer protection and on the standards of banks when dealing with retail customers. First, enhance the financial promotion (i.e. advertisement) regulations so that banks are prevented from using "pushy" selling of financial services, prevented from cold-calling their own customers with additional financial services, and prevented from insisting that customers meet with an independent financial advisor whenever they visit the branch. There should be changes made to the UCTA regime so that all "unfair" contract terms are struck down in agreements, without the complexity in the current legislation which allowed banks to escape liability because those terms constituted part of the principal bargain between the parties. There should be mandatory "health warnings" on all investment and insurance products which are sold "in-bank" by banks to their customers without the customer having genuinely initiated the inquiry about the product. We have health warnings on packets of cigarettes; why not on bank leaflets?

To maximise consumer protection, the regulations should create special **46–53** categories of "vulnerable customer" who should not be sold products without genuinely independent advice or who have longer cooling off periods. Categories would include: those over retirement age (especially being sold investment products for their savings); those categorised as having learning difficulties; those under the age of 21. Similarly, there should be cooling off periods for banking products sold as "add-ons" to ordinary bank accounts so that the customer can cancel them. Financial regulation should enhance mortgage protection.[25]

As a general point, financial regulation should make any contracts which breach **46–54** these principles legally ineffective. These contracts should be rendered voidable at the instance of the customer. What we have learned from the PPI mis-selling scandal and everything else discussed in Chapter 45 is that banks set out programmatically to gouge profit from their retail customers. Therefore, the law needs to be re-aligned so as to protect the customer first, and the bank second.

6. Reforms to Financial Regulation

A.   The coverage of financial regulation

Historically, too much bank regulation has been focused on regulating the sellers **46–55** of financial instruments, whereas what needs to happen is that the entirety of financial markets are regulated (both buyer and seller, and the systemic risk context of each market). No aspect of a bank's business should be unregulated, and no buyer should be beyond the reach of regulatory inspection. The regulation of financial derivatives for the first time means that there is some regulation of

---

[25] For example, by reinforcing the principle in *Palk v Mortgage Securities* which prevented the sale of a mortgaged property where the contract was "unconscionable".

that market: had it been regulated earlier than that, then it might have been possible to identify the boom in CDS markets. There are still a series of important markets which are only lightly regulated: foreign exchange markets and money markets, and a large amount of "repo" and stock-lending activity (all of which have an impact on market liquidity); the process for generating Libor and many other market indices and benchmarks; the activity of acting as calculation agent or market maker, or operating a MTF or acting as a systemic internaliser must all be capable of being regulated; and the "buy side" of all investment transactions. The lodestar must be to regulate entire markets (i.e. buyers as well as sellers should be regulated, measuring total exposures, and setting aside unsuitable transactions) and not simply the authorisation of sellers of financial products as at present.

46–56   There are many other significant markets which are unregulated. Hedge funds will only be very lightly regulated under the AIFM Directive (i.e. submission of limited amounts of information), by the provision of information under the upcoming EC legislation. There are still large gaps and many "dark pools" in the "shadow banking" market. Where markets operate internationally without any regulation or with only regulation which is less effective than EU regulation, then any EU regulator should consider itself empowered to assume the right to regulate the effect of that unregulated activity directly or indirectly in its own jurisdiction.

B.   Problems with the concept of regulatory compliance

46–57   Whereas usually we talk about "obedience" to law, we talk about mere "compliance" with regulation. The word "com-pliance" suggests "working with" as opposed to "obeying". Banks expect to be consulted about the regulations which will be imposed on them and they lobby lawmakers intensively (as with the passage of Dodd–Frank in the USA, and every piece of legislation in the EU and in the UK). We do not consult burglars about the law on theft. Compliance departments in banks expect to negotiate with regulators about the treatment of financial instruments. Their role is to do the minimum necessary while still being in formal compliance with the rules. In effect, regulation specialists in magic-circle law firms advise banks on the least they need to tell regulators while being compliant with their regulatory obligations.

C.   Reforms to the regulation of derivatives

Persistent problems with derivatives

46–58   Even though derivatives have been subjected to EU regulation for the first time, that regulatory regime is limited to clearing transactions and to delivering information to trade repositories: in either case, private sector bodies are being trusted to oversee the operation of the derivatives market. There must be more intrusive regulation by public sector bodies. There are other issues, over and above the shortcomings identified in Chapters 40 to 44 above, than those that are identified here.

Hedging strategies

The Senate Permanent Subcommittee on Investigations, chaired by Senator Levin, made several significant proposals in relation to the regulation and use of complex derivatives in its report into the JP Morgan Chase "London Whale" losses, as discussed in the previous chapter.[26] The proposals which were made were, in terms, as follows. First, where a derivatives trading strategy is contended to be a hedge (whether because that is required by regulation, or because that is necessary to reduce regulatory capital costs) then the financial institution must be able to document precisely the open positions which are being hedged and the manner in which the hedging strategy is expected to match those risks. Second, require financial institutions to provide information to regulators about derivatives positions which are held on its own balance sheet, including regular reports on movements in those positions.

46–59

Commodity derivatives to require ownership of the underlying asset

There is a very real concern that commodity trading is affecting access to basic foodstuffs and raw materials. The Arab Spring began in Tunisia in the wake of rioting over food prices. Many countries in the world have too little access to fresh water. The price of oil restricts the ability of many countries in the world to develop or maintain their economies. To the extent that commodity price speculation contributes to the artificial increase in the price of raw materials, foodstuffs and so forth, then it should be prohibited. A significant reform to commodities law would be a requirement that commodity traders must take ownership of the underlying asset once they acquire that contract. Consequently, speculation on the future price of commodities (e.g. through derivatives) would be outlawed unless the speculator agreed to take delivery of the underlying commodity.

46–60

Requiring an interest in the underlying asset in credit derivatives

Credit derivatives are often described colloquially as being "insurance contracts", which in law they are not. However, they do provide insurance-like recourse for those who suffer a loss when a payment is not made on an underlying asset; but they also generate a speculative gain or loss for people who are speculating on the performance of that underlying asset. In insurance law, to prevent speculation or fraud, it is unlawful to take out insurance over property in which you have no insurable interest. Therefore, to prevent the sort of damaging speculation which hit CDO and real estate markets during the financial crisis, and which hit sovereign debt markets (particularly in the eurozone), it should be unlawful to take out a credit default swap or any credit derivative over an entity or asset in

46–61

---

[26] See para 45-53.

which you do not have something equivalent to an "insurable interest" in the underlying asset. Therefore, a credit default swap will be void if there is no underlying asset in which the claimant can demonstrate they have some right which is covered by the derivative, as with the insurable interest under a contract of insurance.

D. A welfare state approach

Protect what's important

46–62 My personal view is that constructing an architecture for financial regulation should begin with the protection of those parts of our society and of our economy which we want to protect from the vagaries of financial markets as a first step, and then start to think about how we organise the retail banking and inter-bank banking sectors afterwards. I have argued for such an approach for some time now. The following summarises my view of this first part of the debate[27]:

> "The principal question must be: which part of the economy are we seeking to protect by regulation? The answer to that question must be that the thing which is to be protected is any part of the economy which will have a direct impact on individual citizens. In the organisation of the modern economy, it is important to ensure that insurance companies, building societies and pension funds—which are vital in the provision of services to private citizens on which their security and long-term prosperity depend—are sufficiently and efficiently protected from the thousand natural shocks that finance is heir to."

So, my suggestion is that we begin by asking "whom and what do we want to protect?" and then prioritising them. I would suggest that this first tier is a matter for the welfare state.

> "At the domestic level, banking services and financial provision are, regrettably, coming to replace [the] welfare state … State provided pension services ought not to wither away, similarly healthcare and other services should be provided by means of a welfare state. The welfare state ensures that all citizens have access to comparable services. Rather than leave citizens exposed to unequal financial markets, it is better to ensure parity between State-provided pensions and other services within the private sector. The most important regulatory goal in this context is to ensure that entities which provide pensions and other insurance services (on which ordinary citizens rely for their core wealth and well-being) are prevented from involving themselves in markets or investment strategies which put those services at unacceptable risk. The role of the welfare state, and a welfare-orientated system of financial regulation, is to remove risk, providing security between the cradle and the grave."[28]

Regulation must follow function and it must follow a need to protect the disadvantaged, the weak and the poor as a priority. Therefore, this first tier of regulation is concerned with the welfare state. Those services and entitlements which have been lost to the welfare state—such as a large part of the pensions pot—must be regulated so as to give pensioners an equivalent protection to those taking their pensions from the public sector. That same quality of regulation must extend to the financial activities in which pension funds participate on the

---

[27] A. Hudson, "Financial Regulation and the Welfare State", in A. Hudson (ed.), *Modern Financial Techniques, Derivatives and Law* (Kluwer Law International, 2000), 235 at 236.

[28] A. Hudson, "Financial Regulation and the Welfare State", 235 at 236.

financial markets. The same is true of regulation of any financial activity which impinges on the family home—such as mortgage regulation and markets which deal with domestic mortgages and property held in the rented sector.

As to which regulator is responsible for which entity—whether the Bank of England or the FCA—it matters little in one sense. The badge on the letterhead matters much less than the assiduity of the human beings retained by whichever body is the regulator in exercising genuine and active oversight over the affairs of the regulated entities.

46–63

Protect the domestic user of financial services

The second focus of regulation—once the poorest and the weakest in society have been carried above the torrent—should be to look to the protection of "retail" consumers of financial services: particularly those "inadvertent" participants in financial market who are forced to take a position on financial markets because that is the only way they can acquire a pension or can insure themselves against the effect of illness or through life assurance for their dependants. Regulation for the investor in this context should provide for prudent growth in the long-term and, helpfully, reliably deep pools of investment capital for steady economic growth. There is a second context of this sort of regulation, however, which requires the protection of citizens' assets—such as their mortgaged homes—as opposed simply to their cash investments in financial products. The third context for this sort of regulation is the preservation of the broader economy from the worst of the process of financialisation with its tendency to soak up spare capital and leach it away from the "real" economy towards financial speculation and so forth.

46–64

Principles-based, close scrutiny of financial institutions

The current trend for *principles-based regulation* is to be encouraged. It can only be expected that the pace of innovation in financial markets will continue. The development of financial derivatives and techniques akin to securitisation indicate that almost any financial instrument can be repackaged so as to resemble another and that almost any market or moving indicator can be a source of speculative activity. To regulate such markets effectively, it is essential that the rulebooks set out core principles which can weather change as well as detailed rules: as discussed in para.3–32. What principles-based regulation must not mean is a "light touch" in regulation which means that banks are in effect left to their own devices. Instead, what is needed is a close supervision of regulated persons to stress-test their business models and to intervene more aggressively generally. This should be done under an umbrella of general principles to make clear what are the ultimate goals of regulation, together with detailed rules as to a large number of prudential matters and the general conduct of business.

46–65

7. CONCLUSION

46–66   This book began with a definition of finance as being "the wherewithal to act", a means of enabling actions to take place. The financial crisis demonstrated that the financial system might not create the wherewithal to act, but that instead it might destroy economic activity. The financial system has no tangible existence, instead it has tangible effects: that means, money and securities are all held electronically and so have no tangible existence, but they nevertheless allow aeroplanes to be made, food to be bought, and corn to be delivered. The purpose of this financial system was to create the wherewithal to act, but a large proportion of it has been shown in Chapter 45 to be concerned with speculative profit that has no other practical use, and to become bound up with fraud and a loss of ethics. In short, we have forgotten what banking and finance is meant to be for. In Chapter 1, we considered a short story written by Borges in which a world was called into existence because scientists wrote about it and imagined every tiny detail of it.[29] Just as Borges described the creation of a planet out of thin air simply because human minds could conceive of it, we created the financial system out of mere words and ideas. In place of coins made of precious metals, we created financial instruments, securities, electronic money, payment cards and even banknotes which claim to be intrinsically worth the number printed on their face. All of this financial system came into existence simply because human minds could imagine it. Now it runs much of our lives. Nevertheless, we have all now realised, after the financial crisis 2007–09 and its ongoing aftermath, that the system we had built was dangerous and that its actors were capable of acting unethically. But let us not lose heart. We can re-imagine that financial system. We can make it again, and we can make it better. We can create a financial system which befits the civilised, democratic societies of the 21st century.

---

[29] See para 1-09: JL Borges, "Tlon, Uqbar, Orbis Tertius", *Fictions* (1944).

GLOSSARY

Terms which are identified in bold are defined elsewhere in the glossary.

Bond Bonds are discussed in Chapter 34. A bond is a security which represents a loan made by the investor to the company or other entity which issued the bond. The investor lends an amount of money to the issuer of the bond and acquires a proportionate number of bonds from the entire bond issue. As with any loan, the issuer is required to pay interest to the lender and also to repay the capital amount of the loan at the end of the term. That a bond is a security means that the bond can itself be traded on the bond markets.

Call option See the definition of this term given in relation to **option** below.

Charge A charge is defined in Chapter 22.

Collective investment scheme Collective investment schemes are created by the UCITS Directive. Under English law they comprise **unit trusts** and **open-ended investment companies** ("oeic"). Investors (or, "participants") in a collective investment scheme acquire units in that scheme in proportion to the size of their investment. The scheme constitutes a pool of investment capital from a range of investors which seeks to generate profits for the investors which are then shared out among them in proportion to the number of units they hold. The investor can redeem her units—and thus cash in her profits—whenever she chooses. Collective investment schemes are regulated by the **FCA**.

Constructive trust A constructive trust is a form of **trust**, as defined below under "trust".

Credit crunch 2007/08 The credit crunch of 2007/08 was an early stage of the financial crisis 2007–09. It is discussed in Chapter 45. The "credit crunch" specifically was a lack of liquidity which caused banks to stop lending money to one another because there was insufficient confidence and thus insufficient money available in the financial system.

Credit default swaps are discussed in Chapter 43. In short a credit default swap is a mean of acquiring insurance against the failure of a bond issuer, or other person, to make payment under that bond; or it can be a means of speculating that such a person will default on its obligations.

Credit derivatives are discussed in Chapter 43.

Collateralisation Collateralisation is discussed in detail in Chapter 42. Collateralisation is the process by which security is taken in derivatives transactions by paying amounts equal the exposure between the parties owed between contracting parties, or in which the parties provide property subject to proprietary rights.

[1377]

Collateralised debt obligation ("CDO") Discussed in Chapter 44. A collateralised debt obligation ("CDO") is a package of different bonds or other obligations which constitute a form of **securitisation** sold to investors and which is secured by **collateralisation**.

Financial Conduct Authority ("FCA") The FCA is the renamed form of the FSA which was created by the Financial Services Act 2012 and which has regulatory responsibility for all conduct of business and related matters. The FCA is a subsidiary entity of the Bank of England: for all that it has purported operational independence, it is ultimately answerable to Governor and the Court of the Bank of England.

Financial crisis 2007-09 The financial crisis of 2007–09 is discussed in detail in Chapter 45. It has been described as the most significant disruption to financial markets since the Great Crash of 1929. The crisis hit a peak in September 2008 in the wake of the bankruptcy of the investment bank Lehman Brothers, but there were failures in a number of other banks, financial institutions and insurance companies which required unprecedented amounts of support from governments around the world with public money. The effects of that crisis were continuing to be felt in 2013 in the real economies of countries in the Western hemisphere in particular, especially in the USA and in Europe. The crisis began with a failure in the US sub-prime housing market (caused in part by fraudulent lending practices) and was amplified out into the global financial system by failures in **CDO**'s and in **credit default swaps** which were dependent on sub-prime mortgages. The losses caused to the largest banks were colossal. In the wake of the crisis proper there were a range of other scandals and examples of bad practice which were revealed.

Financial derivative The three classic forms of financial derivative are: **swaps, options** and **forwards**. These products are considered in detail in Chapters 40 through 42 of this book. A derivative is so called because it derives its value from the market value an underlying financial product such as a share or a bond.

Financial institution The term "financial institution" is used in this book as a catch-all term for any professional entity engaged in selling financial services or conducting investments as its business or as part of its business. This may encompass banks, building societies, professional fund managers, credit institutions as defined for EC regulation, hedge funds and so forth.

Financial instrument A financial instrument is, literally, a document which creates financial transactions. The term is often used, however, in financial market parlance to denote any financial product.

Floating charge A floating charge is a form of **charge** which takes effect over a floating pool of property (the precise components of which may change from time-to-time) but that charge is expressed to take effect over assets up to a given value. When the charge crystallises—at the time specified in the agreement giving rise to the charge—then the chargee may take rights in property only from that moment. This concept is considered in Chapter 22.

FCA Handbook The *FCA Handbook* is the term given to the entire collection of regulatory rulebooks and guidance notes generated by the Financial Conduct Authority in furtherance of its statutory powers from April 2013 onwards.

FCA financial regulations This term is used in this book to refer to all of the FCA regulations dealing with financial services activity which is not "prudential" regulation administered by the **PRA**. This includes the general principles set out in the Principles for Businesses rulebook, and regulations dealing with conduct of business, financial promotion and market abuse. These regulations underlie all of the more specific rulebooks considered in this book.

FCA securities regulations The FCA *securities regulations* are those regulations within the FCA Handbook which deal specifically with securities transactions: the Listing Rules, the Prospectus Rules, and the Transparency Rules. These regulations are predicated on the general FCA regulations.

Financial Services Authority The Financial Services Authority ("FSA") was the principal regulator for financial services activity in the UK from 1997 until 2013. It was widely considered to have failed in the financial crisis 2007–09. It was renamed the "**Financial Conduct Authority**" by the Financial Services Act 2012, s.6, albeit that the FCA has sought to proclaim a new beginning very different from the FSA.

FSA Handbook The *FSA Handbook* was the term given to the entire collection of regulatory rulebooks generated by the FSA in furtherance of its statutory powers before April 2013.

FSA 2012 Financial Services Act 2012

FSMA 2000 Financial Services and Markets Act 2000

Hedging Hedging is the process of using one financial product to off-set any potential loss which may be caused by another financial product.

In-the-money A transaction is "in-the-money" if it is profitable. This jargon is used particularly in relation to derivatives in this book.

Interest rate swap An interest rate swap is a derivatives transaction which allows the buyer to exchange a fixed or floating rate which it is required to pay for a floating or fixed rate which it would prefer to pay by agreement with the seller of the swap. Swaps are discussed in Chapter 40.

Lamfalussy Process The Lamfalussy Process refers to the report of the EU Committee of Wise Men, chaired by the central banker Baron Lamfalussy, which reformed the manner in which EC securities regulation was implemented. Discussed in Chapter 7.

Larosiere Report The Larosiere Report is considered in Chapters 7 and 45. It was the EU's scathing, fact-finding response to the financial crisis 2007–09 and marked a change in EU legislative policy in relation to financial services: significantly, it altered the approach suggested by the Lamfalussy Process by requiring that legislation is effected by means of regulations and that a single rulebook is created for the entire EU.

Letter of credit A letter of credit is a documentary credit which entitles a shipper of goods to payment from a paying bank on delivery up of documentary evidence of delivery of those goods.

Leverage Leverage is the means by which a company is able to raise amounts of money, usually by borrowing, greatly in excess of any liquid assets which could pay back that money if it fell due immediately. Leverage is an expression of the amount by which that debt exceeds the borrower's liquid assets. A "highly leveraged" entity is one which has a large amount of debt compared to its other assets and is consequently thought to be a poor credit risk.

Liquidity The term "liquidity" in economics refers to the level of availability of money in financial markets. A liquid market is a market in which there is a large amount of money available; an illiquid market has insufficient money available. A liquid market is generally a good thing: it refers to there being plenty of money available for people to borrow so as to make investments or to expand their businesses or whatever.

Limited liability partnership (LLP) A limited liability partnership ("LLP") has separate legal personality and the liabilities of the partners are limited (similar to the limited liability of shareholders in companies).

Listing Rules The Listing Rules are securities regulations created by the **FCA** under its general powers granted to it by **FSMA 2000** and by the appropriate **EC Securities Regulations**. The Listing Rules govern the means by which securities can be admitted to the Official List maintained by the **FCA** in its role as the UK Listing Authority ("UKLA"), and so offered to the public with the benefits of entry on the Official List. The listing process is considered in Chapter 37.

Loan Loans are discussed in Chapter 32. A loan is a transaction which takes place entirely at common law whereby the lender transfers absolute title in the loan moneys to the borrower, subject to a contractual obligation to pay periodical amounts of interest to the lender and a further contractual obligation to repay an amount equal to the loan at a future time identified in the loan contract. Loans will be qualified by "covenants" which are contractual terms imposing obligations on the borrower; in particular "events of default" which trigger the termination of the contract.

Market maker The term "market maker" is defined in Downes and Goodman, *Barron's Dictionary of Finance and Investment Terms*, 7th edn (Barron's Educational Series, 2006) to mean: "A dealer firm that maintains a firm bid and offer price in a given security by standing ready to buy or sell at publicly quoted prices." Therefore, a market maker is someone who publishes prices at which they will buy and sell securities (thus making a market in those securities). There is a tension between that person's personal interest in making a profit from such transactions, and any other legal duties which it might owe to the buyers who will also be its customers and may rely on its advice.

Oeic Open-ended investment company.

Option An option gives the owner of the option a right, but not an obligation, to acquire or to sell property identified in the option contract for an identified price at an identified time in the future. An option entitling the holder to sell property is referred to as a "put option": the option holder is entitled to sell a given quantity of the asset specified in the contract at a given price at a given time specified in the contract. An option entitling the holder to buy property is referred to as a "call option" : the option holder is entitled to buy a given quantity of the asset specified in the contract for a given price at a given time specified in the contract. If the price of the underlying asset on the open market is more attractive than the price at which the option can be exercised on the terms of the contract, then the holder of the option will decide not to exercise it. Because it is merely an option, there is no obligation to exercise the option at an unattractive price. Options are discussed in Chapter 40.

Over-the-counter "OTC" transactions are transactions which are not conducted on an exchange nor subject to the rules of an exchange, but rather are negotiated and contracted privately between the parties. OTC transactions are difficult to regulate because they are conducted off-exchange and so are difficult to observe, and the terms of any transaction could conceivably include anything whereas transactions conducted on an exchange are both visible (because all trades have to be cleared through the exchange) and conducted on standard terms required by the rules of the exchange.

Put option See the definition of this term given in relation to **option** above.

RIS An RIS is a "recognised information service" which is empowered to disseminate officially information to the market place, particularly in relation to securities which have been offered to the public.

Securitisation Securitisation is the process by which a range of cash receivables or similar assets are grouped together and sold in the form of a single security for a capital amount. The assets are held by a special purpose vehicle and that vehicle issues bonds to investors. Discussed in Chapter 44.

Security A "security" is a share, bond, or similar financial instrument which can be transferred between buyer and seller, as defined in Chapter 35.

Shadow banking The pejorative term given to the informal system for providing liquidity to the banking system (such as repo markets and unregulated derivatives) and to unregulated financial institutions like hedge funds which operate beyond the mainstream geographically-limited financial markets. The reference to "shadow" is generally a reference to unregulated and thus largely invisible entities (from the regulators' perspective) which use these shadow banking markets, as in someone who lurks in the shadows. The threat, after the financial crisis 2007–09, is the lack of information which regulators and others can amass about the activities of shadow entities so as to supervise markets appropriately and to measure systemic risk.

Speculation "Speculation" describes the activity of acquiring financial products or investments solely to generate a profit and not for any other purpose (such as to invest in a business, or to protect some other position (as with "hedging"). Speculation thus opens the investor up to the risk of loss as well as to the possibility of profit.

Swap See "interest rate swap" above. Discussed in Chapter 40.

Syndicated lending Discussed in Chapter 33, syndicated lending is lending of a very large amount by a group (or, syndicate) of banks where usually each bank enters into a separate loan arrangement with the borrower but on terms negotiated by the syndicate agent on behalf of the syndicate: consequently, the precise duties and rights of the parties will depend upon the precise drafting of the contract.

Systemic risk Discussed at para.1–54, systemic risk is the risk that the entire financial system or a significant financial market will fail. Typically, systemic risk is understood as beginning with the insolvency of a major market player such that the inability of that person to make payment under its obligations would introduce such pressure into the system that other market participants would fail (because they had not been paid by the first insolvent person) and this second tranche of failures would increase the pressure in the system and cause yet more market participants to go into insolvency too. "Systemic risk" therefore refers to the "domino effect" of one insolvency leading to another insolvency and so on throughout the system, until the financial system in general collapsed or seized up. The **credit crunch of 2007/08** created a sort of sclerosis in the banking system which was feared by some to constitute systemic collapse: instead it appeared to stop at a sort of systemic seizure.

Taking security "Taking security" is discussed in Chapter 22 and is the way in which contracting parties seek to protect themselves against loss.

Trader The term "trader" is used in this book to refer to any individual employed by a **financial institution** working on a trading floor conducting investment and trading activity for that financial institution and/or its clients. Usually this business is conducted by telephone, although transactions are usually intended to confirmed by letter, fax, or electronic communication. The trading floor may be organised in the offices of that financial institution or it may be a trading floor on a physical exchange like LIFFE.

Trust A trust arises in any circumstance in which the conscience of the legal owner of property is impacted by knowledge of some factor which is said to affect that conscience. Under a trust, the "trustee" holds the "legal title" in the trust property, and in turn is said to hold the property on trust for the "beneficiary" (or beneficiaries). The beneficiary holds the "equitable interest" in the trust property. This means that more than one person can have ownership of the trust property simultaneously: but the trustee owes "fiduciary duties" to the beneficiary as to the treatment of the trust property. There are three types of trust:

(i)   Express trusts are created intentionally by the "settlor" who owns the absolute title in property before a trust is declared over that property, from which time the trustee acquires the legal title and the beneficiary acquires the equitable interest in the trust property. Express trusts can be declared by means of an instrument containing all of the terms of the trust, or can be declared orally (unless the law relating to the specific type of property prohibits oral declaration, as with land), or the declaration of an express trust may be inferred by the court from the circumstances.

(ii) Constructive trusts are created by operation of law in any situation in which the defendant is deemed to have acted unconscionably in relation to that property: for example by stealing that property from the claimant, or by defrauding the claimant so as to acquire that property, or by receipt of a bribe, or by profiting as a fiduciary from a conflict of interest without authorisation, or otherwise acting unconscionably.

(iii) Resulting trusts arise by implication when a transfer of property or a declaration of trust fails, such that the equitable interest in the property jumps back to the claimant; or where more than one person contributes to the purchase price of property such that each contributor acquires a proportionate share of the equitable interest in that property.

The beneficiary acquires a proprietary right in the trust property (as qualified by any terms in any instrument creating an express trust), and the beneficiary also acquires rights against the trustees for breach of trust and against any third persons who may participate in any breach of trust.

United Kingdom Listing Authority ("UKLA") The **FCA** is the UKLA— that is, the authority responsible for the maintenance and enforcement of the listing rules relating to offers of securities to the public which are entered on the Official List, as discussed in Chapters 37 and 38.

INDEX